Ancient double-entry bookkeeping. Lucas Pacioli.s treatise (A. D. 1494– the earliest known writer on bookkeeping) reproduced and translated with reproductions, notes and abstracts from Manzoni, Pietra, Mainardi, Ympyn, Stevin and Dafforne

John B. 1872- Geijsbeek, Luca Pacioli, Domenico Manzoni, Angelo Pietra, Matteo Mainardi, Jan Ympyn Christoffels, Simon Stevin, Richard Dafforne

Ancient Double-Entry Bookkeeping

Lucas Pacioli's Treatise (A. D. 1494—the earliest known writer on bookkeeping) reproduced and translated with reproductions, notes and abstracts from Manzoni, Pietra, Mainardi, Ympyn, Stevin and Dafforne

By

John B. Geijsbeek, LL.B., M.C.S., C.P.A.

1914

Published by

John B. Geijsbeek

Denver, Colorado

Dedicated to My Wife

Marie Lillie Schmidt,

whose initials I have always loved to connect with

My Little Sweetheart,

without whose patience, kindness, help,
and indulgence, my contributions to the
educational field of the professional
accountant would not have been possible.

TABLE OF CONTENTS

INTRODUCTION

By Page Lawrence, C P A

Nearly all historians, when tracing the growth of an art or science from mere empiricism to the establishment of recognized principles, are confronted with an apparent insurmountable gap or complete silence during the period known in history as the Dark Ages

Archaeological and historical researches have convinced this civilization that in Ancient Babylon, Greece and Rome there was a high state of civilization—both industrial and social

Today we may study Aristotle's politics with great profit in our attempts to understand the political and economic conditions confronting this generation An acquaintance with the Greek philosophers is essential in understanding our present philosophical thought

It would seem that, since we find so much help in consulting these ancient writers in an attempt to solve the political problems of today which are presented by this complex civilization, in a large measure at least our mentors must have been confronted with the same economic and industrial difficulties that we are attempting to solve now as accountants

One is convinced that the ancient writers on political economy and commerce were closely allied with the scribes or accountants who recorded the business transactions of those days. This allegiance seems to have been lost after the Roman supremacy (and the consequent growth and spread of commerce), and it is only within recent years that the modern economist and accountant has acknowledged that a truer understanding of modern commerce can be had with cooperation and that the two sciences (economics and accounting) are finding so much in common that each is dependent upon the other for a full understanding of modern business conditions

Mr John P Young, Editor of the San Francisco Chronicle, ably presented accounting in antiquity before the convention of the American Association of Public Accountants at San Francisco (Year Book 1911, page 153). He showed that Rome in Cicero's time was dependent upon the independent verification of accounts and statements thereof by one skilled in accountancy The familiarity with which he mentions the accountant would seem to indicate that his place in the Roman social organization was well established

However, after the recorded utterances of Cicero the historian finds in the pages of history no further mention of those individuals acknowledged to be skilled in accounts, which we are pleased to call accountants, until the writings of Pacioli in 1494 and Stevin in 1604

It seems especially appropriate that one so greatly interested as the author in that work dear to the hearts of all progressive accountants, and who has done so much to place the education of the accountant on equal footing with that of law or medicine, should be the first of modern times to translate this first recorded book of the principles of debit and credit into the English language

It is a significant fact that the rules and principles elucidated by Pacioli are contained in a book given over to mathematics One cannot help but believe that the derivation of double-entry bookkeeping is an explanation of the algebraic equation used with such skill by the ancient Greek mathematicians, applied practically to the scientific recording of business transactions for, just as in algebra, the equation once established cannot be changed but by the addition of positive or negative quantities

This work will give an added assurance that the apparently empirical rules of commerce are based upon an ancient scientific and mathematical foundation, to those who have attempted to instill into the commercial mind the idea that accountancy is a science, the prime requisite of a mastery of which is a thorough education in the theory of economics and allied sciences supplemented by practical experimentation in the application of formulae to practical business situations

The accountant has to correct constantly, or at least modify, the attitude of the business man toward matters which are his dearest heirlooms handed down from the days of the Ancient Guild system, i e, that the only way to learn how to do business is to do it along the rule-of-thumb method communicated from father to son by word of mouth

Accountants, who remember the dearth of accountancy literature in this country up to a few short years ago, are dumbfounded at the mass of accountancy publications which are constantly flooding the market at this time While I believe that the profession of accountancy as a whole recognizes the inestimable value of these publications, one cannot help but think in perusing their pages that they are largely influenced by the empirical methods of general business, rather than based on scientific principles In other words, on "how" but never "why"

We are wont to look in vain through mazes of descriptions, forms and precedence of some particular business enterprise for a principle of accountancy which can be applied to the specific difficulty we have in hand It should be the aim of some of the brilliant members of the profession of accountancy to take the great mass of historical records which have been published in the last few years of how this or that business should be kept and, with the aid of recognized authorities on economics, codify, with quotation of their source, the scattered and ill defined principles of accountancy for the benefit of accountancy education, and to this end no better examples of axiomatic principles can be had than in the books of Pacioli, Pietra and Stevin

The author, recognizing from his experience as an educator in accountancy (coming as he did from Holland some twenty years ago without knowledge of American commercial practices or language) the lack of clearly expressed principles in accountancy, commenced researches which have finally culminated in this published translation in English of the first known writings on the subject of double entry bookkeeping

At every turn in the preachment of the scientific principles of his profession to the commercial mind, in his successful efforts for the passage of the Certified Public Accounts law in Colorado, then in his work as secretary of the first examining board in that state, in his labors as Dean of the School of Commerce, Accounts and Finance of The University of Denver, and as an instructor on practical and theoretical accountancy subjects and, finally as Chairman of the Educational Committee of The American Association of Public Accountants, the author has ever been confronted with the dearth of practical exemplification, historical or otherwise, of the true foundation of what in modern times might be called the Art of Accountancy

To weld together into a well balanced whole the two plans of accountancy education, as embraced in the curriculi of universities and colleges offering training to the embryo accountant, has long been the goal of his educational endeavors, i e, to leaven the purely academic training by instructors or professors whose own knowledge of accountancy is in the main pedagogical, with the practical knowledge as imparted by the practicing accountant and the business man (The author, in the American Association of Public Accountants Year Books for 1911-12-13 and 14, has gone into this subject extensively, showing that educational institutions of the country have chosen either the one or the other of the two methods of teaching—the academic training in pure theory, treated in much the same manner as economic subjects are presented and without the same degree of accuracy, or the practical lecturing upon accountancy subjects by practicing accountants and business men, supplemented by the best text books obtainable—and urging the while the necessity for the development together of the two accountancy educational plans, as is done in Great Britain)

While it is true that to men of little or no practical experience in accountancy must be given the credit for producing some of the finest examples of purely theoretical accounting which the literature of accountancy has today, the first mentioned criticism that this pedagogical instruction does not teach the actual application of the theory to modern business, again applies On the other hand, with the practical accountant as the instructor or the writer of text books, too little cannot be said of the difficulty he has in imparting to students and laymen the principles which seem exceedingly clear to him And it was through this research, this labor to combine in accountancy education theory with practice and practice with theory, that this book was born It is apparent in reading the ancient works of Pacioli, of Stevin and Pietra, in their exhaustive explanations and their lengthy and precise instructions that in their endeavors to systematize the recording of the transactions of commerce of their time, they encountered many of the same sort of, if not the identical, problems with which we are confronted today The modern translations of their works, with the author's own views presented as notes, it is believed will shed some light into the darkness which has so long shrouded the actual foundation of the practice and the theory of the profession of public accountancy

DENVER, COLORADO, August, 1914

PREFACE

As no technical books worth while can be prepared without diligent and persistent research, it naturally follows that no such works can be produced unless there is material furnished to build upon, and the cheapest and easiest foundation is usually the writings of men who have excelled in the same line of endeavor In other words, a library of books is absolutely essential to the advancement of thought on technical and professional subjects

While studying to Americanize my knowledge of accountancy twenty years ago, I came to the conclusion that there were then on that subject few modern books and still fewer ancient ones This conviction was constantly strengthened by conversation with my fellow-workers, and it remained unchanged until a few years ago

When my duties came to include the teaching of accountancy and the direction of the thought of my students, the choice of books for their reading became a serious problem It was then my privilege to start the collection of a considerable library of works on accountancy and its allied subjects.

However, I could learn of but few books of ancient date, and they were so scarce, difficult to get, and high priced, that most of them remain yet to be acquired Among those which I did get is an original copy of the oldest published work on bookkeeping The price for copies of this book ranges from $50 to $250, and it is thus not within the means of ordinary students and is even beyond the inclination of acquisition of many of the most wealthy libraries It became my desire to have it reproduced, together with a free translation of its most important parts

This desire increased when my research showed me that the first man to follow the teachings of this Italian book and to translate it into another language, was a fellow-countryman of mine, a Hollander named Jan Ympyn Christoffels He translated it into the Holland, French, and English languages, and to this day we follow his lead, (as outlined in the title of his book), of calling double-entry bookkeeping by the use of day book, journal, and ledger, the Italian method of bookkeeping

The Hollanders of ancient New Amsterdam (now New York) have left their unmistakable imprint on our American political and social life, by the introduction into this country of many things which originated in their mother-country and which were unknown even in England prior to their use in America To this day many of these things remain unused in England, which is one reason why we are so different from the English. Among these things may be mentioned *

The recording of deeds and mortgages in a public office, the equal distribution of property among the children of a person dying intestate, the office of a district attorney in each county, the practice of giving a prisoner the free services of a lawyer for his defense, the township system, by which each town has local self-government, the practice of making prisoners work, the turning of prisons into work houses, the system of university education, free public school system, the red, white and blue striped flag, the principles contained in our Declaration of Independence, the granting of religious freedom, the cultivation of roses, the present banking system, the use of reading and spelling books for children, the telescope, the microscope, the thermometer, the discovery of capillary circulation of the blood, the pendulum clock, measuring degrees of latitude and longitude, the compass, the wind-mill with movable cap, the glass hothouse, the use of underclothing, the bedstead, the brick, the game of golf

It has seemed to me fitting that another Hollander should present to his American professional brethren, and put within the reach of every student of accounting, for research and study, a reproduction of that prized Italian book, which, as we shall see, has influenced us to such an extent that the principles it enunciates as of use in its day, remain the foundation of our present methods of bookkeeping

It was not my aim to give a complete literal translation, because much of the text is reiteration and pertains to subject-matter purely local and now entirely obsolete, which would necessitate lengthy explanations of ancient methods of no present value or use Therefore, numerous foreign terms and ancient names have been left untranslated Furthermore, as the book was written in contemporary Italian, or, in other words, in the local dialect of Venice, which is neither Italian nor Latin, it is extremely difficult to get local talent sufficiently trained in this work to translate it all literally

The old style of writing is unattractive and tiresome to follow While it is customary and proper in translations to follow the original style as much as possible, and to change it no more than is necessary to make it readily understood and easily read in modern language, it was found extremely difficult to do that in this instance, and furthermore, it would have served no practical purpose And then, who is there at the present time but a scholar of some eminence and a linguist of no mean accomplishment, who will presume to say what is correct and what is incorrect? Such authorities never agree among themselves, and it would be useless to attempt to please them all Therefore, we are extending the translations, not so much for academic purposes as for the practical use of less pedantic people, upon the theory that they who wish to obtain knowledge of any science must first learn its history and then trace its gradual growth There is hardly another science about which there is as much doubt and darkness as bookkeeping, and therefore we merely present this translation as a contribution to the history of bookkeeping

*William Elliott Griffis in "The Ladies' Home Journal"

Criticism has been made of the title of this book, "Ancient Double-Entry Bookkeeping," in the use of the word "Ancient" as applied to the year 1493 A. D. The long obscurity of the "Dark Ages," during which there was no light whatever upon this important subject, has, in our belief, made the treatise of Pacioli ancient, and, further the abrupt "leap through the dark" from this ancient work to the works of modern times, we believe justifies the title

The reader is further referred to the German translation of Pacioli's book by E L Jager which appeared in 1876, and the Russian translation by E G Waldenberg which was printed in St. Petersburg in 1893

Pacioli's book was first photographed and plates made from these photographs Proof sheets from these plates were then sent to Rome, Italy, and there transcribed on a typewriter in modern letters, to facilitate translating The typewritten transcript was then translated into English, which was then compared with an existing German translation by Dr Jager Discrepancies were carefully noted by reference to the original book, and the best possible corrections made This method brought to the surface obvious and glaring short-comings in the German translation, and it also demonstrated our own inability to comprehend and properly translate some of the old terms and words, which even the Italy of today has long forgotten With it all then, we are free to admit that in numerous places our English translation is defective. However, we are not imposing on those who are better scholars than we, because we give the original Italian side by side with our English version, and any one so disposed can easily check it and correct our copy to suit his fancy

The only object of our endeavors is to give something where there was nothing to those who heretofore could not avail themselves of the contents of this old and pioneer work on a subject now universally recognized as being the foundation of all our modern industrial and commercial problems.

We ask your indulgence for errors and omissions, and for the price of this book, as the work had to be done hastily and cheaply, for the financial success of this enterprise is exceedingly problematical, owing to the excessive cost of preparation and reproduction, and the very small possible circulation The work therefore should be viewed largely as a labor of love, a voluntary philanthropic contribution to the profession of accountancy

Acknowledgment is due and most gladly given to my wife, a Certified Public Accountant of the State of Colorado, who aided with the German translation, to Mr Robert Ferrari, LL D Roma, Italy, who aided with the Italian translation, to Mr Henry Rand Hatfield, PH.D, University of California, who criticized the work, and to Mr Page Lawrence, C P A., who wrote the introduction—truly a veritable combination (trust) of formidable minds in restraint of duplication (competition) of this work, a combination of love and harmony, for without friends and without consideration for our neighbor there is neither peace nor accomplishment

The book, therefore, is the result of a faithful compliance with the motto of the Boers of South Africa "*Eendracht maakt macht,*" which translated does not mean, as commonly stated, "In union there is strength," but rather that "United, harmonious, loving cooperation to the same lawful end tends toward power that brings just results"

J B. Geijsbeck Molenaar

DENVER, August, 1914

PARTIAL BIBLIOGRAPHY

1494 to 1636

Sixteen of the most influential books out of a possible total of 50 works

I. ITALIAN

Summa de Arithmetica, Geometria,
Proportioni et Proportionalita

Part 1, Section 9, Treatise 11,
Particularis de Computis et Scripturis

Frater Lucas de Burgo Sancti Sepulchri, Ordinis Minorum
et sacre theologie magistei, in arte arithmetice et geometrie — Venice 1494

Geijsbeek-Lawrence Library, Denver
Harvard University Library, Cambridge, Mass

La Scuola perfetta dei mercanti

Fra Paciolo di Borgo Santo Sepolcro — Toscana 1504

Summa de Arithmetica

(see full title above, this being practically a duplicate edition of 1494, but contains less contractions and abbreviations) — Venice 1523

Edinburgh, Chartered Accountants' Library
Library, University of California

Quaderno doppio col suo giornale secondo il costume di Venetia

Domenico Manzoni — Venice 1534
Also 1554-1564-1565-1573-1574

Edinburgh, Chartered Accountants' Library (1554 edition)

Indrizzo de gli economi

Don Angelo Pietra de Genoa — Mantua 1586

Geijsbeek-Lawrence Library, Denver

La Scrittura Mercantile fatta e riordinata

(Reprinted in 1700 under the title of 'L'Economo overo La Scrittura tutelare, Scrittura Mercantile ")

Matteo Mainardi — Bologna 1632

Geijsbeek-Lawrence Library, Denver

II GERMAN

Ein Teutsch vertendig Buchhalten fur Herren oder Gesellschafter inhalt Wellischem process

Johann Gotlieb — Nuremberg 1531

Royal Library, Munich, Germany

Zwifach Buchhalten

Wolffgang Schweicker — Nuremberg 1549

Kheil Library, Prag
Edinburgh, Chartered Accountants' Library

Buchhalten nach arth und weise der Italianer

Passchier Goessens from Brussels — Hamburg 1594

State Library Stuttgart, Germany

III DUTCH

Nieuwe Instructie Ende Bewijs der Looffelijcker Consten des Rekenboeckse ende Rekeninghe te houdene nae die Italiaensche maniere
Jan Ympyn Christoffels

Antwerp (Dutch) 1543
Antwerp (French) 1543
Antwerp (English) 1543

City Library at Antwerp (Dutch)

Library of the Nicolai Gymnasium at Reval, Russia (English).

Fideicommiss-Bibliothek at Maihingen-Wallerstein, Germany (French)

Verrechning van Domeine (including chapters on) Coopmans Bouckhouding op re Italiaensche wyse and Vorstelicke Bouckhouding op de Italiaensche wyse

Simon Stevin

Amsterdam 1604

Geijsbeek-Lawrence Library Denver

Hypomnemata Mathematica

Simon Stevin

Leijden 1608

IV ENGLISH

A briefe instruction and maner to keepe bookes of accompts after the order of Debitor and Creditor, and as well for proper accompts partible, etc newely augmented and set forth by John Mellis, Scholemaister (purporting to be a reprint of a book by Hugh Oldcastle, London, 1543)

John Mellis

London 1588

Library of Institute of Chartered Accountants in England and Wales (London)

The Merchants' Mirrour or Directions for the Perfect Ordering and Keeping of his Accounts Framed by Way of Debitor and Creditor after the (so-termed) Italian Manner

Richard Dafforne.

London 1636
Also 1651-1660-1684

Geijsbeek-Lawrence Library, Denver
Harvard University Library, Cambridge, Mass
Library of Congress, Washington, D C

HISTORICAL REFERENCES

Schatzkammer Italienischen Buchhaltens
Christophorus Achatius Hagern — Hamburg 1654
State Library Stuttgart, Germany

Beitrage zur Geschichte der Erfindungen
Johann Beckmann — Leipzig 1786
Library of Congress, Washington, D C
State Library Stuttgart, Germany

Origin and Progress of Bookkeeping
B F Foster — London 1852
Library of Institute of Chartered Accountants in England and Wales (London)

Die Berechtigung der einfachen Buchhaltung gegenuber der doppelten
Ernst Ludwig Jager — Stuttgart 1868
Library, University of California

Beitrage zur Geschichte der Doppelbuchhaltung
Ernst Ludwig Jager — Stuttgart 1874
Library University of Chicago
Library, University of California

Lucas Paccioli und Simon Stevin
Ernst Ludwig Jager — Stuttgart 1876
Library, University of Chicago

Luca Pacciolo, considerato come ragionere, lezione tenuto alla r scuolo di commerzio
Guido Brandaglia de Arezzo — Venice 1882
Elenco Cronologico della opera di computisteria e ragioneira venute alla ence in Italia — Rome 1886
Library of Congress, Washington, D C

Ueber einige altere Bearbeitugen der Buchhaltung—Tractates Von Luca Pacioli
Carl Peter Kheil — Prag 1896
Geijsbeek-Lawrence Library, Denver

The History of Accounting and Accountants
Richard Brown Editor — Edinburgh 1905

HISTORICAL

Printing from blocks of wood in which the letters were carved, was known long before the Christian era, but this was cumbersome and slow and hence but few books were published in that manner. Printing from loose metal type which could be set up in the way known to us to-day did not begin to be a success until after A D 1462, when the German city of Maintz or Mentz (where the first well-known printer, Gutenberg, and his students lived) was sacked by Adolph of Nassau, and those who were printers were scattered far and wide through other cities

Even during the first part of the sixteenth century, one-fourth of all the books printed came from one city only, i e, Venice in Italy Therefore a book produced from loose type in 1494 in Venice, must have been among the very first printed, and its subject must have been at that time of such prime importance as to make it worthy of being among the first to be published The oldest treatise which has come down to us either printed or written on the subject of bookkeeping, is included as a part of a rather large printed volume on arithmetic and geometry This volume was published in November, 1494, in Venice, Italy It has been used considerably by later writers on the subject of arithmetic and geometry, and is mentioned in numerous works of bibliographers, both ancient and modern The title is Summa de Arithmetica Geometria Proportioni e Proportionalita " Bookkeeping is treated in Part One, Section 9, Treatise 11, under the chapter title of "Particularis Computis et Scripturis," which translated would mean "Particulars of Reckonings and Their Recording"

The exact name of the author cannot be established definitely from this work, as his full name does not appear on the title page nor anywhere else The author calls himself in this book Frater Lucas de Burgo Sancti Sepulchri, which translated into English may be called Brother Lucas of the City of the Holy Sepulchre The City of the Holy Sepulchre, or Sancti Sepulchri, is a city in the northern part of Italy near Venice On page 67-2, line 5, of Frater Lucas' book "Summa de Arithmetica," he states that about A D 1470 he dedicated a certain book to his students named Bartolo, Francesco, and Paulo, the three sons of a prominent merchant of Venice named (Antonio de) Rompiasi From other writings and other evidence, bibliographers have come to the conclusion through their researches that the real name of this "Frater Lucas" was Lucas Pacioli

The copyright of the book published in 1494 expired in 1504, and about that time a reprint of the chapter on bookkeeping appeared in Toscana, under the title of "La Scuola perfetta dei Mercanti " A copy of this reprint was not in the possession of the writer, but it would appear that there the name of the author was given as Fra Paciolo di Borgo Santo Sepolcro In other writings he is known as Patiolus, which is supposed to be the Latin for Pacioli.

In 1509, shortly before he died, he wrote a book called "Divina Proportione," in which he gives a foreword and reproduces several letters he has written In these he signs himself as Lucas Patiolus This book was written in Latin On page 33-b of this book, in section 6, treatise No 1, chapter No 1, the author refers to his book published in 1494 in the following words *"in opera nostra grande dicta summa de arithmetica etc impressa in Venetia nel 1494 et al Magnanimo Duca d'Urbino dicata"* We underscored the word "nostra," which means "our "

Lucas Pacioli, as we will call him hereafter, believing that to be his proper name, was born about 1445 in the little city of Sancti Sepulchri in the Province of Arezzo, of Tuscany, west south-west of the City of Urbino He was a great lecturer, mathematician, writer, scholar, teacher, and traveler, a well-known and famous man, who was the first to translate into Latin the works of Euclid Successively he was professor of mathematics at Perugia, Rome, Naples, Pisa and Venice, and was chosen for the first occupant of a professor's chair founded by Louis Sforza He was in Milan with Leonardo da Vinci at the Court of Louis the Moor until the invasion of the French It is not improbable that Leonardo da Vinci helped Pacioli in the writing of this work as there are indications of two distinct styles of writing He belonged to the Order of Friars Minor of St Francis It is apparent that he took the cloth late in life, for protection and standing needed in his many traveling tours, during the unrest then existing in Italy He wrote his treatise on bookkeeping when he was about 50 years old, and died near the end of the year 1509, at the age of 65

It is but natural that bookkeeping should be always in its greatest perfection in those countries where commerce has reached its highest stage It is well known that during the twelfth, thirteenth, fourteenth and fifteenth centuries Venice was a powerful republic, from which all European commerce radiated, until in 1498 the East Indian ocean route was discovered, from which time on the commercial power of Venice waned It is safe to assume that the book here reproduced faithfully depicts the conditions existing at the time of its writing and the prevailing system of recording the transactions of commerce All the world's commerce, practically speaking, was concentrated in this small territory, therefore its system of bookkeeping must have been the most perfect known in the world at that time The existence of a well advanced system of bookkeeping in the centers of commerce must have caused considerable confusion and correspondence with the places where such a system did not exist, in order to equalize and settle accounts between the merchants residing in these various places.

It is therefore probable that a great need existed for taking advantage of the facilities which the new inventions in printing permitted, to present to the commercial world outside of these centers a systematic treatise of the most important part of commerce, namely, the recording of its transactions and results Pacioli does not claim that he invented double-entry bookkeeping, but on the other hand mentions in his book the existence of ancient customs and numerous methods named after the places where they were used Thus he calls the method of bookkeeping he describes, the method of Venice, as distinguished from those in use in other cities, the names of which appear in the translation we have made of his book

While Pacioli gives in his book on arithmetic and geometry copious illustrations, as will be seen from the sample page of that portion of the book herein reproduced, he did not give examples and illustrations of the day book, the journal and ledger, which he describes His book therefore has never become as popular as those of later writers who give these examples Pacioli, however, was very lengthy and careful in his minute and detailed description of the various methods employed The reading of his book will be a revelation to those who have an idea that the present high state of development of American commerce should have produced methods of bookkeeping unknown at such an early period as when Pacioli wrote They will find that there then existed the little safeguards which are not described or explained in present books of instruction on bookkeeping, but which we accountants are always wont to preach about to those bookkeepers who come under our observation, and which we do not pass by simply as mere suggestions but upon which we insist emphatically with a "You *must* do this" Pacioli especially describes these little things with great emphasis, and in a style cunning in the extreme, fully punctuated with adages to bring the truth home so no one could forget it He, however, on the other hand, does not spend any time in explaining the modus operandi of bookkeeping, which we learn only by practice (as he puts it), as he doubtless appreciated that he was not writing his treatise to teach bookkeeping to those who did not know anything about it, but only describing the advantage of the particular method in use in Venice in order to convert merchants to a change from their system to the best system then known

Writers who have followed after Pacioli have practically all given full illustrations of the journal and ledger, but have rather neglected to explain the "whys" and "wherefores" of the little and valuable details upon which Pacioli has laid so much stress, taking them as matters of fact rather than as fundamental principles As we all know, it is the little things which throw the safeguards about a proper system of bookkeeping

It is not the writer's aim to go into detail as to the history of bookkeeping Any one desiring to study this subject in its entirety, is referred to the most remarkable records and researches of Jager, Kheil, and Row Fogo as edited by Brown, the title of whose books are fully described in the bibliography hereto appended

Jager and Kheil were prominent German scholars, who must have devoted an enormous amount of time to their researches as to the origin and growth of bookkeeping Jager was somewhat hasty and inaccurate, Kheil is somewhat brief, and therefore difficult to understand by those who have not read other books on the subject Both of these books are written in German

Happily we Americans have the aid of the recent book written in Scotland by Brown and his associates The treatise they present is exhaustive, brief, to the point, and exceedingly accurate, fully illustrated, and is of immense value to every student of the subject of accountancy

The writer does not wish to duplicate the work of any of these three, but by the present volume he desires to emphasize the fact that Pacioli's work is the real foundation of all books published in Germany, Holland, France, and England within the first hundred years after it was written We will do nothing more than describe the effect of Pacioli's book on Manzoni and Pietra which appeared in Italian, Gotlieb, Schweicker, and Goessens, which appeared in German, Ympyn and Stevin in Dutch, Ympyn in French, and Ympyn, Oldcastle, Mellis, and Dafforne in English, as these books undoubtedly have been the basis for subsequent works in these various languages, most of which are at present available for comparison and study The titles of other contemporary books can be found in the bibliography of Mr Brown's work, for he gives an exhaustive list of over 150 books written on this subject between Pacioli's time and the beginning of the nineteenth century Of these, 50 were written prior to the publication of Dafforne's "The Merchants' Mirrour" in 1636, which is really the first popular English work Most of these 50 were written in Italian, Dutch, or German, with the honors about evenly divided

As we have said, Lucas Pacioli's book appeared in Venice in 1494, with a ten-year copyright At the expiration of that period, or in 1504, the same printers published an exact duplicate of this book, under a different title Twenty-one years after the last date, or in 1525, there appeared in Venice a very unsatisfactory and incomplete work on bookkeeping by Giovanni Antonio Tagliente, of which the historians do not say much

Forty years after Pacioli's book of 1494, or in the year 1534, Domenico Manzoni published in Venice his book on bookkeeping, which proved very popular, as during a period of 40 years it went through six or seven editions, which may be termed a tremendous success, considering the conditions of those times

Manzoni dedicated his book to Alouisius Vallaressus, a rich brother of a friend of his named Petrus It seems apparent from his preface that he commenced the book years before it was published, when all three (the author, his friend, and the latter's rich brother) were going to school in Venice In the title he mentions "the method of Venice," but he does not tell anywhere how or where he gained his knowledge and does not give Lucas Pacioli any mention or credit

Manzoni wrote in dialect, or what is called "patois" He says in his preface that he is not a scholar and cannot use flowery language but only the speech of his mother, which he learned by word of mouth He states too that he is a poor man In those days only the very rich and the clergy could attend schools The poor were usually artisans, learning their trade from their parents

Manzoni's book may be termed a revised reprint of Pacioli Page after page is identical and word for word and the remainder is merely shorn of the religious expressions, adages, and peculiar repetitions which Pacioli so freely indulged in. Much of value and many of the details given in Pacioli's book are here omitted

This book is divided into two parts, one for the text and the other for examples of journal and ledger While the text covers but 12 of the 36 chapters of Pacioli, the two parts combined may be said to reproduce about 18 chapters of Pacioli At the beginning of the writer's translation of Pacioli's book herein, a comparative index is given, which illustrates just how much of Pacioli's book Manzoni copied and what he left out The only new idea in his book as compared with that of Pacioli, is the consecutive numbering of the journal entries In some respects, however, Manzoni is clearer than Pacioli, as for instance, he gives definite rules for the making of journal entries, tabulates six things or matters of information always contained in every journal entry, describes the form of journal better by mentioning five "standing" or "down" lines, explains the use of more than one day book, and gives a chapter to the apparent transposition of the terms "A" (our "To") and "Per" (our "By") in the ledger from its customary use in the journal

Manzoni gives full illustrations of the journal and ledger, with its entries, which Pacioli, for reasons stated, did not deem necessary The addition of these illustrations of course has made the book more popular and Manzoni, while a plagiarist in other respects, must be given the credit of having really been the first to do this The writer regrets that Manzoni's book is not accessible to him for on that account only one reproduction can here be given, namely, the last page of the journal, which is taken from Brown's history of accounting

In 1586, nearly 100 years after Pacioli wrote, we find that Don Angelo Pietra published a work on bookkeeping fully illustrated with numerous examples The book was printed in Mantua by Franz Osanna Pietra was a monk, born in Genoa, stationed at the Monastery of Monte Cassino, Neapel, Province of Caserta, near Sora He was the auditor, storekeeper, and cellarer of that monastery He belonged to the Order of St Benedict, and dedicated his book to Lastancius Facius, the abbot of the Benedictine monastery at Mantua Pietra's style is very clear and concise, and his book contains some 60 short but pithy chapters As will be seen from the comparative index heretofore mentioned, and given farther on in this book, Pietra had for his guide the books of both Pacioli and Manzoni, for he covered matters which Pacioli did, and also the items which we have just seen Manzoni mentioned in his book but which we do not find in Pacioli Especially is this true in the enumeration of the items which always must appear in a journal entry Pietra uses Manzoni's six items in the same order, but adds thereto two others He also gives the definite rules for making journal entries mentions the transposition of "A" and "Per,' the five standing lines in the journal, and enumerates several day books He gives further some 30 additional items which neither Manzoni nor Pacioli mentions Jäger does not speak very highly of Pietra, but it seems to the writer that Pietra was an ingenious man, fully as well educated as Pacioli, and a good deal more experienced in the necessities required of a bookkeeper He recommends several innovations, prominent among which is double entry bookkeeping for those who are not in business for profit but are capitalists or associations not organized for the making of profits, which we might call eleemosynary corporations For this purpose he describes three different ledgers, one for merchants, one for bankers, and one for capitalists and those similarly situated He calls the ledger for the capitalist "economic ledger."

Unlike Pacioli and Manzoni, Pietra does not begin with an inventory, but with a proprietorship account He is exceedingly careful in the taking of his inventory, and gives in his book a large folded insert containing a tabular inventory. He gives a tabulation of entries for the ledger which do not have to go through the journal (such as closing entries) He advocates the vouchering of disbursements He minutely explains that expense accounts can show two balances, and that they can show a profit as well as a balance to be carried forward in the nature of an inventory. The detail of some 30 items which he mentions in his book and which neither Manzoni nor Pacioli describes, we give farther on, by the side of the reproduction of some of the pages of Pietra's book

In 1632 there appeared in Bologna a work on bookkeeping written by Matteo Mainardi This book is of a far later date than the ones heretofore mentioned, but it is somewhat remarkable in that it attempts to describe, besides the system for the merchants, one for the keeping of executor's and trustee's accounts In many respects this book compares favorably with that of Pietra, and Mainardi undoubtedly had all the three books just described at his command In the reproductions herein, we are giving only the title, the preface, and two pages of the journal, the last for the purpose of indicating the method then in use of showing journal entries with more than one debit or more than one credit, and to indicate further that bookkeeping made far greater progress in Holland than in Italy, as will be apparent from the discussion of Simon Stevin's book published in 1604

We will now pass to the German authors We have mentioned before that Venice and other places in the northern part of Italy were the centers of commerce from which the distribution of merchandise was made to the inland The nearest commercial city of the inland known in those days was Nuremberg, and it is therefore but natural that we should find there the first work on bookkeeping published in the German language The author was Johann Gottlieb, and the book was published in Nuremberg in 1531, three years before Manzoni, the second Italian writer, published his book The author states frankly that he has translated his work from the "Welsh," meaning by this term "Italian" His book is considered a brief and very poor copy of Pacioli

Gotlieb's book, however, is not the first that we know of in Germany Henricus Grammateus, who called himself in German Heinrich Schreiber, lived for a long while in Vienna and there wrote in 1518 a book called "Rechenbüchlin, Kunstlich, behend und gewiss auf alle, Kauffmanschafft gerichtet" containing mostly a text on arithmetic, but devoting some pages to the description of a very poor system of bookkeeping, which by a stretch of the imagination may be identified as possibly covering double-entry bookkeeping This work was printed in Erfurt in 1523, and in Frankfurt in 1572

After Gotlieb's book we find one published in 1549 at Nuremberg entitled "Zwifach Buchhalten," by Wolfgang Schweicker This work can not be called excellent, nor is it as exhaustive or as good as that of either Pacioli or Manzoni, but there is no doubt that he had both of these books at his command, and especially followed Manzoni The three German books thus far mentioned were undoubtedly not good enough to have become standards, and they have exerted little influence on the methods of bookkeeping used since then in Germany

The first writer who was able to leave an impression which is lasting to this day was Passchier Goessens, a Dutchman from Brussels. He wrote, in 1594, at Hamburg where he was then living, a book on bookkeeping Goessens states very plainly in his preface where he had learned the art and the title indicates that he followed the Italian system He obtained his information from some of the earlier Dutch writings, which we will soon mention German bookkeepers therefore, have benefited more by the knowledge which the Dutch imparted to them than by that which their own countrymen brought direct from Italy

Next in importance and period of time, we come to the influence of the Dutch writers on the German, French, and English subsequent authors on the subject of bookkeeping The Dutch for centuries controlled the supremacy of the seas, as they were great ship-builders and navigators They were excellent, careful and honest tradesmen, and their trade was sought far and wide Yet the Italian cities, through their ancient relation with the eastern nations, had become the world's leaders in commerce and the Dutch people were therefore forced to trade with these Italian republics until the discovery in 1498 of an all-ocean route to the eastern countries Thereafter the center of commerce was shifted from Venice and its surrounding republics to Holland As the Dutch were such travelers on water, they naturally sent their young men by water to the trade centers, for education and training, and in this way the knowledge of commerce also shifted from Venice to the Dutch countries

Jan Ympyn Christoffels was one of the Dutch merchants who visited Venice and the northern part of Italy and he remained there for twelve years He returned evidently wise in the knowledge of the keeping of books according to the Italian manner and wrote a book on that subject He did not, however, live to see his book published, but his widow Anna Swinters published his manuscripts in the Dutch and French languages during the year 1543 Of the Dutch edition there seems to be but one copy in existence, which is in the City Library at Antwerp The French work, however, can be purchased The discovery by Hugo Balg of an English copy of this book in a Russian library was reported by the German scholar Kheil, although it was so mutilated that the name of the author does not remain, and the exact date of its publication is not known However, from the similarity of the contents Kheil established the authorship of this book The widow of Jan Ympyn Christoffels (better known as Jan Ympyn), says very distinctly in the preface of the Dutch book that it was written by her husband and that she merely published it, which statement would indicate that the English book was written prior to 1543. The illustrations in the book bear date of 1536 and 1537

Ympyn claims to have obtained his knowledge in Italy, and says he used Italian books for the foundation of his work He gives credit, however, indirectly to a person who has never been known as an author on bookkeeping, and historians rather indicate that this person was merely an excellent bookkeeper from whom he gained considerable knowledge He mentions, however, very distinctly the book of Lucas Pacioli, although he calls him Brother Lucas de Bargo We find Lucas Pacioli's name thus quoted in a large number of books subsequently published, from which we may infer that Ympyn's work was well known and used by a good many writers, because from no other source could they have obtained this faulty version of Pacioli's name

The next important writer in the Dutch language was Simon Stevin, who wrote in Latin a book on mathematics, which was published in Leyden in 1608, in which he includes several chapters on bookkeeping These were a reproduction of a book published in the Dutch language on "bookkeeping for merchants and for princely governments," which appeared in Amsterdam in 1604, and was rewritten in The Hague in 1607 in the form of a letter addressed to Maximilhaen de Bethune, Duke of Seulley This Duke was superintendent of finance of France and had numerous other imposing titles He had been very successful in rehabilitating the finances of France, and Stevin, knowing him through Prince Maurits of Orange, was very anxious to acquaint him with the system which he had installed and which had proven so successful This manuscript of 1607 was published in book form by Stevin's son Hendrick "in the second year of the Dutch Peace" of Munster (1648), which ended the eighty year war with Spain, this would make the date of publication 1650 Hendrick Stevin dedicated the book to the sister of the deceased Prince Maurits, expressing the hope that she may continue with the system of municipal bookkeeping which had made her brother's stewardship of the affairs of government so successful Stevin's book becomes very important to Americans, because he materially influenced the views of his friend Richard Dafforne, who through his book "The Merchants' Mirrour," published in 1636, became practically the English guide and pioneer writer of texts on bookkeeping

Simon Stevin, who was born in Bruges near Antwerp in 1548, and died in The Hague in 1620, was a traveler, author, mathematician, engineer, and inventor, a highly educated man who thought bookkeeping important enough to induce Prince Maurits of Orange, the then governor of the Dutch countries, to install double-entry bookkeeping throughout his territory, thus practically putting municipal accounting on the double-entry system, the very thing we are today after more than three hundred years sighing for. Stevin wrote part of the text of his book in the form of a dialogue, consisting of questions and answers, which he says actually occurred in the arguments he had while teaching Prince Maurits the art of bookkeeping

Simon Stevin served his apprenticeship in a mercantile office in Antwerp, where he learned bookkeeping After that he held important public offices such as quarter-master-general, surveyor of taxes of Bruges and, under Prince Maurits was minister of finances and chief inspector of public works There he displayed such inventive ingenuity in engineering that he may be said to have been the founder of modern engineering His discoveries were in dynamics and hydrostatics, and among his many other inventions may be mentioned an important improvement to the canal locks He was the first to bring into practical use decimal fractions His works on engineering and fortifications have remained standards until the last decade or two

Stevin was a prolific writer on many varied subjects Among other things, he wrote about the art of war on land as well as on sea, about the construction of buildings, residences, and fortifications, the improvement of cities and agricultural lands, about water mills, canals, the art of singing, the art of oratory, rhetoric, mathematics, geometry, and about the weighing of metals and alloys through the difference in weight above water and under water

The writer would consider Stevin to be one of the first men of whom we have a record as performing duties equal to those of a modern accountant We have seen that his regular work was that of superintendent of finance (secretary of the treasury) and chief engineer of fortifications and public buildings of Holland, besides being tutor and adviser to Prince Maurits of Orange In addition to all of this, he was continually called in to settle disputes between partners, audited numerous mercantile books and drew therefrom financial statements, made up partnership books to obtain their settlements, installed systems in all departments of government, in mercantile houses, royal households, municipalities, for construction of specific fortifications and public buildings, traveled to England, France, Germany, Italy, Denmark and Belgium, in order to appear before courts to give testimony in the settlement of financial affairs, and performed numerous other duties of an accountant which we may infer from his remarks throughout his book

Jager, Kheil, and Row Fogo through Brown ridicule to a considerable extent the old writers on bookkeeping, instead of describing the worthy things about them and marveling at their accuracy and ingenuity Especially do they harangue about Stevin's Latin, but overlook entirely the many worthy suggestions from Stevin's inventive genius

In Brown's book on the history of accounting Stevin's treatise on mercantile bookkeeping is highly spoken of but Stevin is ridiculed for his endeavor to put municipal accounting on the double-entry system We feel this to be an injustice to Stevin, for the reason that while his descriptions on municipal accounting may at first blush appear to be faulty, we learn from the descriptions and illustrations he gives of mercantile bookkeeping that he was exceedingly brief but accurate, and that therefore in the text we should take much for granted

Stevin did not fully illustrate municipal accounting, for three reasons first of all the officials who were to use the system he installed received regular orders with forms attached from headquarters, therefore his book was not a full exposition of all these orders with their forms, but was merely a review of the entire system Secondly, (as he states) he was writing an argument in favor of his system to those officials who were forced to use it and might hesitate to support it loyally This he did in an authoritative manner, by quoting continually the friendly and close association he had with the Prince, which of course he could not make use of in his official orders Thus he put power and dignity behind his orders Thirdly, he fully illustrated mercantile accounting and insisted on the employment only of clerks who were well versed in the art of bookkeeping according to the Italian method After illustrating mercantile accounting thoroughly, he then simply describes the difference between the two systems, which (he reiterates) is his only aim He gives eight pages of journal and forty pages of ledger on municipal accounting, although they contain only opening and not closing entries The latter he explains fully in his text by stating deviations from the system used by merchants

Yet apparently Stevin's treatise on municipal accounting is judged only by the absence of illustrations, but no credit is given him for the ingenious devices he mentions and which we now call internal checks Brown evidently had not read much of the text, nor his son's subsequent book and notes, which as we have seen heretofore were published in 1650, at which time his son states that while some defects were found in the previous treatise, the system had survived until that day and had been improved upon, he describing such improvements in addition to reproducing his father's works

Stevin was very ingenious in prescribing methods for what we now are wont to call "internal checks" For instance, in order to check the pay roll of the soldiers and other public officials, he demanded that the pay roll be sent direct to the auditors (and he calls them *auditeurs*, the French for auditors), and then insisted that the cook at the mess-house where all the soldiers and officials were being fed, should report independently to the auditors the number of meals served

Another internal check which he suggested in order to stop the making of errors and the stealing in the collection of taxes and rents, was to make the sub-treasurer's report to the general treasurer each month of not only the cash receipts and disbursements but the persons remaining delinquent in their payments After the reported delinquents remained so for three months, he suggested the sending of the sheriff by the general treasurer (not the sub-treasurers) to sell the property of the delinquent tax-payer or to collect from him a bond He explains that thus you can force the tax-payer to demand a receipt from the sub-treasurer when paying, and display it to the sheriff, and thus get evidence against the sub-treasurer of stealing

Towards the end of this book we are reproducing Stevin's journal and ledger, and appended thereto we have given some further remarks describing the superiorities of Stevin's work, which will prove interesting reading Stevin undoubtedly followed Ympyn, who in turn as we have seen, obtained his knowledge from Pacioli

Up to this date then, we have, besides general mercantile books, records of specific systems of bookkeeping for merchants, branch stores, traveling salesmen, partnerships, household accounts, bankers, capitalists, monasteries, executors, and municipalities, as we will see from the specialties enumerated by these writers

We next will make a survey of how the knowledge of bookkeeping came to England, whence it probably came to America

We find that a school teacher by the name of John Mellis wrote in London in 1588 a book on bookkeeping, which in his preface he states to be a reprint of a book by Hugh Oldcastle, which Mellis says appeared in London in 1543 under the title of "A profitable treatyce called the Instrument or Boke to learne to knowe the good order of the kepying of the famouse reconynge called in Latyn Dare and Habere and in Englyshe Debitor and Creditor" No copy exists as far as is known of this book of Oldcastle, and it is not therefore an absolute certainty that it ever existed It might have been a manuscript only, and again, the date may not be reliable It may also be that the book was written by some one else, and given to John Mellis by Hugh Oldcastle It may therefore have been Jan Ympyn's book in English, especially as the dates are so close together However this may be, Mellis's book is nothing more than a translation of Pacioli's book, and Mellis states that he had traveled and studied in the Dutch country Brown in his history of accounting openly says that every English writer on accounting in the early days gained his knowledge from the Dutch, because Holland was the training school for English merchants, and he gives numerous instances to support his statement

Any one doubting that Mellis's book is a translation of Pacioli should compare Mellis's description of the checking of the ledger, as quoted by Brown, with our translation of this same subject in Pacioli's book That Mellis is undoubtedly a copy of Pacioli, appears from an error he made in referring in one of his chapters to a chapter previously mentioned, naming it chapter 15, the same as Pacioli stated in his chapter 16, but as Mellis left out chapter 5 of Pacioli, containing a short introduction and also chapter 7 about the certification of books by notaries, Mellis's chapter 14 is the same as Pacioli's 16, and Mellis's chapter 13 is the same as Pacioli's 15, yet Mellis makes reference to chapter 15 the same as Pacioli, instead of using chapter 13 The discovery of this error is mentioned in Brown's history of accounting

Next in importance, and the last book we will mention in our survey, is "The Merchants Mirrour," by Richard Dafforne Dafforne says that in Germany, Italy and Holland, there had existed a great many able writers on bookkeeping, and he gives a large list of authors He attributes the existence of these books to the demand, stating that there would not be a supply unless there was a demand He very much deplores the fact that such a demand did not exist in England, nevertheless he contributes his book, which is undoubtedly a very able treatise He even speaks of his acquaintance with Simon Stevin, and he writes his book on the same order as Stevin, namely, in dialogue style or questions and answers Dafforne's book was published in London for the first time in 1636, and appeared afterwards in 1651, 1660, and 1684 Later English writers have followed Dafforne and Mellis Therefore, directly and indirectly, Pacioli through the Dutch, has laid the foundation of our present accounting literature and our present knowledge of bookkeeping

We are reproducing most of the text of Dafforne's book and a few pages from the daybook journal and ledger Anyone doubting that Dafforne followed Simon Stevin and other Dutch writers on bookkeeping will be convinced by reading his text Numerous quotations are made from these and other Dutch authors throughout the text and even in the title page In one place an abstract from the bible is rendered in the Dutch language Further Dafforne states that he received his knowledge and ideas in Holland and that part of the illustrations and text was written in Holland The mentioning of so many Dutch customs and Dutch names in the ledger accounts shows that he himself succumbed to what he feared "They being then at Rome, will do as there is done"

While we have described thus far the oldest text books in existence on the subject of bookkeeping, the records of books of account predate these considerably, and for further information on this subject we can do no better than refer you to Brown's history of accounting, where not only detail is given but where also convincing illustrations are reproduced However, the purpose of presenting to the reader a correct idea of what was done in this line, we might state that the books of the steward of the city of Genoa in 1340 were kept on the double-entry principle The oldest mercantile ledger at Venice is dated 1460, and is that of the firm of Donado Soranzo & Brothers This ledger has a profit & loss and a capital account Specimens of this ledger are reproduced in Brown's history of accounting on pages 99 to 106, and will greatly help the reader to understand Pacioli's instructions, in respect to the year, the Roman figures in the money column, and the Arabic figures for the smallest coin or Picioli, etc

DISCURSION IN THEORY

We find in the translations of the old treatises on bookkeeping the terms debit, credit, inventory, journal, cash, capital, balance, per (modern by), a (modern to), assets, liabilities, etc, and a definition of each of these with their use in the olden times should prove of interest

Our word debit is put in Italian as "*debito*", which comes from the old Latin *debita* and *debeo*, which in business and from the standpoint of the proprietor means "owe" or "he owes to the proprietor," that which was loaned or given him by the proprietor (The old authors do not use it in ledger accounts)

Our word credit is put in Italian as "*credito*," coming from the old Latin word "*credo*," which means "trust or believe," as in business our creditors were "believers" in the integrity of the proprietor, and therefore loaned or gave him something Therefore, from the proprietor's point of view the word should be translated as the creditor "is owed by the proprietor," that which was loaned or given to the proprietor (The old authors do not use it in ledger accounts)

Inventory in Italian, "*inventario*,' comes from the Latin "*invenio*," which means to find out or discover

Journal in Italian "*giornal* ' comes from the Latin "*diurnalis*" which means daily happenings or diurnal

Ledger comes from the Dutch "*Legger*" meaning "to lie down" and was originated probably from the necessity that the ledger, which was called the big book, became so large and cumbersome that it remained, or was lying, always in one place

Cash in Italian, "*cassa*," comes from case or box, which is the same as the Italian *borscia* from the Latin *bursa* or purse

Capital, which is mentioned in Italian as "*Cavidale*," comes from the old Latin "*capitalis*," which means "chief" or 'head," and also from the Latin "*capitali*," which means property Thus capital would mean "the property of the chief," i e, proprietorship

As to the word "balance," the following will indicate its meaning A clear distinction is made by the old writers between (1) the difference in an account between the debit amounts and the credit amounts, (2) the reason for entering this difference in the account, and (3) the status of the account after equalizing both sides by the making of an entry and closing the account We term all three balances and balancing, while two are distinctly opposite In Italian they call the difference or the remainder, "*resto*," and say they have entered this remainder in order to close (*saldo*), and then they state that the account is in balance (*bilancio*)

As to the terms "By" and "To, ' Manzoni says, as does Pacioli, that in the journal entries the word "Per" denotes the debtor and always precedes it, and that "A" denotes the creditor

Manzoni then goes on to point out that the prevailing system (which Pacioli describes) in his time was to use "Per" only (and not "A") as far as it relates to the ledger He calls it a misuse which experts do not condone, and in his examples of ledger entries he uses in the debit of the debtor's account "A" because the name following it must of necessity be the name of the creditor and, as "A" denotes the creditor, so it must here precede the name of the creditor, as well as in the journal, in spite of the fact that it is written on the debit side of the ledger Likewise he puts on the credit side ' Per" in front of the name of the debtor Stevin, as explained, follows Pacioli

Until the very recent present day we used in the ledger "To" on the debit side as a prefix to the name of the creditor and "By" on the credit side as a prefix to the name of the debtor

It is difficult to say whether we can translate the Italian "*Per*" into our "By" and the Italian "*A*" into our "To," as these two expressions or words can be translated in many different ways according to the noun or verb following or preceding it, together with the consideration of the tense and case used

If, however, we take a literal translation of the Italian ledger heading used for our debit, or "*dee dare*," we come to "shall give " Putting this into a sentence read from a ledger we have as at the present time, 'John Doe debit to Richard Roe" and in the old Italian, "John Doe *dee dare* (shall give) A (To) Richard Roe," and as to the credit, we have in our present day "Richard Roe credit by John Doe," and in the old Italian, "Richard Doe *dee havere* (shall have or receive) Per (by the hand of) John Doe "

Our version, therefore, is that today we follow Manzoni rather than Pacioli and Stevin in this respect

As to the journal, the old necessity for being particular in designating and separating the debtor from the creditor by Per and A and the much commented upon little diagonal lines (//), has been obviated through the use of two columns in the journal—one for the debit amount, the other for the credit amount—and by the use of two lines of writing and by careful indentation Thus, while we do not use the old expressions (Per and A) in the journal, we are more careful and systematic in separating debits from credits than the old authors were

It would be interesting to learn when and where and under what circumstances and conditions the double column in the journal originated From the fact that a trial balance, with total debits and total credits instead of differences between debits and credits, is called a French trial balance, we might infer that that system originated in France because a French trial balance is based upon the system that all entries are journalized and the total debits and the total credits of the journal are added to the total debits and credits of the previous trial balance in order to arrive at the totals which the present trial balance should show Such a trial balance makes an absolute necessity for the having of two columns in the journal

Stevin explains debit and credit as follows

"Genomen dat ymant met naem Pieter, my schuldich vvesende, doet daer op betaling van 100 L Enick 't gelt in een casse leggende, al of ict heur te bevvaren gave, segh dat die casse my 't selve gelt schuldich is, vvaer deur ick haer al oft een mensch vvaer, debiteur make, en Pieter crediteur, om dat hy syn schult vermindert, stellende int Iornael 't begin der partie aldus, 'Casse debet per Pieter' "

The above translated would be about as follows

"Suppose that some one by the name of Peter owed me some money, on account of which he paid me £100, and I put the money in a cash drawer just as if I give it the money for safe keeping I then say that that cash drawer owes me that money, for which reason (just as it it were a human being) I made it a debtor and Peter of course becomes a creditor because he reduces his debit to me This I put in the Journal thus 'Cash Debit Per Peter' "

From the above translation of the previous Dutch quotation it would seem that the journal entry shown is rather a hasty conclusion The entry, in order to follow his explanations, should have been a double entry somewhat as follows Cash Debit to Myself—Proprietor Credit—for the money I gave the cash drawer for safe keeping To be followed by Myself Debit to Peter Credit—he gave me money which I may have to return to him if he does not owe it to me

As most of the entries, if made in this form would have both a debit and a credit to the proprietor for the same amount, these are simply omitted

If we eliminate on both sides, according to algebraic formulae, the word "myself," we then have abbreviated the two entries to a real algebraic term, namely, "Cash Debit to Peter" Thus we have condensed two entries of thought to one entry written down, very much the same as in algebra $a = b$, $b = c$, hence $a = c$ In many of the old Dutch books Stevin's idea of a twofold double entry is mentioned, and is brought down to the present day, which accounts for the existence of a clear idea on this principle in Holland and in modern Dutch books on bookkeeping (see N Brenkman, 1880, Theory of Double-Entry Bookkeeping)

It must be admitted that if we today would abolish the use of the words debit and credit in the ledger and substitute therefor the ancient terms of "shall give" and "shall have" or "shall receive," the personification of accounts in the proper way would not be difficult and, with it bookkeeping would become more intelligent to the proprietor, the layman, and the student

Elsewhere we have seen that Stevin insists upon testing when a journal entry in debit and credit must be made by asking the question, "When does proprietorship begin" or "When does proprietorship end," from which it is apparent that proprietorship *must* enter in the consideration of each entry and, if it is not there, it is simply eliminated by the rules of algebra This, of course, would at once lead to the personification of the capital and profit or loss accounts into "the proprietor" as differentiated from "the business," and would then immediately show the fallacy of the statement that capital and surplus are liabilities, as well as of the absurd theory that assets must equal liabilities

The following translation of the dialogue between Simon Stevin and the Prince Maurits of Orange on this subject fully illustrates that Stevin then understood his subject far better than do some modern text writers and theorists, and it makes certain recent so-called "discoveries" appear mere mental vagaries, as far as the credit for discovery is concerned It merely illustrates that they are today as deep thinkers as Stevin was 300 years ago

The Prince	I must ask another question The entries stand in my ledger as debits and credits Which of these two stand to my advantage and which to my disadvantage?
Stevin	Debits in the ledger are your advantage, for the more Peter owes you the more your capital is, and likewise much pepper in the warehouse, which stands as a debit, will make much money in the cash drawer However, credits are the reverse
The Prince	Are there no exceptions to this?
Stevin	I cannot recall any
The Prince	Yet capital as a debit does not seem to me as an advantage, and capital as a credit being a disadvantage to me appears entirely wrong
Stevin	I forgot that You are right I meant to say that capital is an exception
The Prince	Further, expense is a debit and it, together with the debit in the profit and loss, are both disadvantages
Stevin	Because these two are a part of the capital account they are included in the exception
The Prince	The credits in the cloves account in the ledger are in excess of the debits by £74-4-7 This is an advantage to me because it represents a profit, yet it is in the credit
Stevin	The reply to this would be that if the account were closed (which you can do when you please, but usually at the end of the year), the excess in the credits would be transferred to the profit and loss account and your question would not arise
The Prince	Yet it remains that with accounts like the cloves account, where they show a profit or a loss, it is not so frequently true that at all times debit is an advantage and credit a disadvantage

Stevin That appears to be true and in that respect it is somewhat similar to your exception, but it shows all the more positively that in all accounts of capital, or those pertaining to capital debit is always a disadvantage and credit an advantage

The Prince Why has capital more exceptions than all the others?

Stevin Because capital debit means as much as though the proprietor said, "I am debit to all the other accounts" It follows that the more a proprietor is debtor in this manner the more it is to his disadvantage, and the more he is creditor the more it is to his advantage, for which reason capital must be the reverse of other accounts, and it is not therefore really an exception

The Prince If capital stands for the name of the proprietor, why is the proprietor's name not used instead of the word capital inasmuch as through the use of that word so many things become so difficult to understand?

Stevin Merchants often form partnerships with many who together put in one principal sum of money For this reason we need one designation indicating them all at once as proprietors, and for this the word capital is used with good reasons

Furthermore, at that time the words assets and liabilities were not known in bookkeeping Happy days they must have been These terms ought not to be known or used now What we now term liabilities, and some of which some of us are almost tempted to call "near liabilities" very much the same as we define "near silk," never are and never will be liabilities, for at the time the financial statement is prepared these amounts are not supposed to be due, hence the proprietor cannot possibly be liable for them at that time At most he is "trusted" for them by his creditors, as the old authors expressed it correctly Neither are assets at any time, in a going, solvent business real assets The words assets comes from "*assez*" which means "enough" The question of whether the proprietor has enough to cover his liabilities does not come up until his ability to meet his obligations is questioned or until he is called upon to render a statement to the court wherein he is brought for this purpose to answer the question whether he has enough (*assez*—assets) to cover that for which he is liable (liabilities) or past due credits or trustings by the creditors Those who doubt this should study from the reported court cases the difference between mercantile insolvency and legal insolvency

In analyzing a financial statement I believe these assets and liabilities may be interpreted to mean something like this The proprietor, in order to be permitted to continue to do business on credit, makes here a showing to those interested by which he agrees that his books show that the personifications of cash, real property, personal property, merchandise, as well as the persons owing him, are obligated to him and "shall give" him the amounts stated on the left hand side of the statement or the amounts appearing to the debit of these accounts in the ledger and to the credit of his own account, and that thereby the proprietor will be able to meet whatever obligations he contracts with those with whom he has dealings He further states in this report that persons interested should take notice that the books show that the following persons "shall have" or "shall receive" from him the items when they become due and payable and standing on the right hand side of the statement, or the amounts appearing to the credit of these accounts in the ledger and to the debit of his own account That these items are to be deducted from the items of cash, real property, personal property, etc , before those interested in the statement can judge as to whether they shall trust (*credito*—credit) him further Thus it becomes at once apparent that capital, together with surplus and losses and gains, represent the ownership of the things owned less those owed, leaving a net ownership, and net ownership can never be a liability (i e, a thing to be liable for) If surplus ever can be a liability then a minus-surplus or a deficit must of necessity become an asset, which is an absurdity

The statement of affairs described by Stevin and elsewhere reproduced, may be considered to be merely a statement of the closing entries as they would be made in the respective individual ledger accounts in order to make both the debits and the credits even and equal For whatever each debit account shows more in the debit than in the credit, as Stevin explained, it is given by the owner to that account for safe keeping as if it were a person—hence this person or this account owes the proprietor, therefore, the proprietor trusts these personified accounts and becomes the creditor With the credit accounts it is the reverse, hence Stevin's statement of affairs is the capital account itemized with a preponderance of credits to represent net capital The English follow this method of rendering a financial statement to this day Why Americans reverse the process is difficult to perceive

From the foregoing it will further be seen that thus with the aid of ancient terms we can read intelligently and explain the abbreviated forms used in bookkeeping so that it becomes at once apparent why accounts like the cash account, which to the uninitiated looks like proprietorship, can be shown on the debit side of the ledger and why capital account, which always represents ownership, appears on the credit side This at first thought may seem contradictory, but the reason for this apparent inconsistency lies in the elimination (through bookkeeping) of equal terms (as per rules of algebra) brought about by the theoretical making of double entries (two entries, each with a common debit and credit) and thus abbreviating it beyond the interpretation of ordinary language Thus we may go on and with equal ease prove as the German scholar Jager has done, that double-entry bookkeeping is much older than single-entry bookkeeping, the latter being a still further shortening of methods of classification by the use of the terms debit and credit Stevin very clearly suggests this in his explanation of the rules of partnership

It is to be regretted that in the transfer of the expositions of the theory from the Dutch language (as so plainly exemplified by the scholar Simon Stevin) to the English (by the flowery schoolmaster Richard Dafforne) should have been so badly done that all records of the scientific part of the art and theory have been so completely obscured as to suggest even in the present day an argument on theories so well known in those olden days

LUCAS PACIOLI REPRODUCED

The following eight pages, from 18 to 26, and the succeeding 32 left-hand pages, numbers 28 to 80, represent photographic reproductions of the oldest extant book on double-entry bookkeeping, published in Venice, Italy, in 1494 The reproductions are of the same size as the original, and fully illustrate the make-up of the book, which is one of the oldest books ever printed from loose metal type in Roman letters, as explained at the opening of the historical chapter The ink used was vegetable dye ink, and is today as black and as fresh as India ink, after 420 years of use and exposure It is printed on hand-made rag paper, unsized, which after so many years of exposure to air and light is still so far superior to the very best modern paper that a comparison cannot be made

On page 18 appears the title of this book, "Summa de Arithmetica, Geometria, Proportioni et Proportionalita," (Review on Arithmetic, Geometry, and Proportions) Below the title is a brief synopsis of the contents of the book Part 1, Section 9, Treatise 11 of this ancient book treats of double-entry bookkeeping and begins on page 199-a of the original, or page 32 of this volume, under the title of 'Particularis de computis et Scripturis" (Particulars of Reckonings and Their Recording) This can be found in the seventh line of page 32 The picture directly under the title, on page 32, is said by some to be that of the author of this book, but there is nothing in this or any other book which substantiates this assertion

Page 19, which immediately follows the title page of the original, contains a dedicatory letter by the author, whose name appears on the second line The lower half of this page is occupied on the right by an epigram of praise to Pacioli by a friend of his and on the left by an epigram by the author to the reader

The first of the four last lines of this page contain, a list of the letters to be used by the printer, merely as a guide for those who are not familiar with this style of printed letters Thereafter, on the last line, the year (1494), then the date (November 20th), and then the place (Venetia or Venice), all of these pertaining to the record of publication

Page 20 is another dedicatory letter to the Duke of Urbino The author's name appears here in the third line

On page 22, in the third line of the center paragraph, the author's name is given again, this time in the genetive case, hence Fratris Luce instead of Frater Lucas

Pages 24 and 25 are reproduced in order to show the marginal notes there given, indicating the abbreviations used in the book, and their interpretation Page 25 is also given for the reference the author makes in line 7 to three of his pupils, Bartolo, Francesco, and Paulo, the three sons of a prominent merchant of Venice named (Antonio de) Rompiasi The dash over the "o" in the original indicates that an "m" follows the "o"

Page 23 is given to reproduce the type of numerous marginal illustrations the author gives on nearly every page of his chapters on geometry and arithmetic, considering the many illustrations here used it seems very strange that he should not have given some in his chapter on bookkeeping

Page 26 is given to show that our modern so-called "efficiency engineers" have nothing the best of this monk of over 400 years ago, as to "organization charts" This chart illustrates the intricacies of proportions

Pages 28 and 30 contain the index of the chapter on double-entry bookkeeping No translation is given of these pages, because they are merely repetitions of the headings of each chapter, and therefore their translation appears at those places In their stead, a comparative index is given of four of the earliest writers on bookkeeping, in order to illustrate how closely they have followed each other

On pages 32 to 80 (left-hand only) are the reproductions of the original chapter on double-entry bookkeeping Opposite each reproduction is given the translation in modern English subject to the qualifications mentioned in the preface

Sũma de Arithmetica Geometria Proportioni & Proportionalita.

Continentia de tutta lopera.

De numeri e misure in tutti modi occurrenti.

Proportioni e ꝑportiõalita anotitia del. 5° de Euclide.e de tutti li altri soi libri.

Chiavi ouero euidentie numero.13.ꝑ le q̃ntita continue ꝑportiõali del.6°e.7° de Euclide extratte

Tutte le pti delalgorismo: cioe relevare. ptir. multiplicar.sũmare.e sotrare cõ tutte sue ꝓue i sani e rotti.e radici e progressioni.

De la regola mercantesca ditta del.3.e soi fõdamenti con casi exemplari per cõm°.8.G.guadagni: perdite: transportationi: e investite.

Partir.multiplicar.summar.e sotrar de le proportioni e de tutte sorti radici.

De le.3.regole de' catayn ditta positiõe e sua origie.

Evidentie generali ouer conclusioni n°66.absoluere ogni caso.che per regole.ordinarie nõ si podesse.

Tutte sorte binomii e recisi e altre linee irratiõali del decimo de Euclide.

Tutte regole de algebra ditte de la cosa e lor fabriche e fondamenti.

Compagnie i tutti modi.e lor partire.

Socide de bestiami. e lor partire

Fitti: pesciõi: cottimi: livelli: logagioni: egodimenti.

Baratti i tutti modi semplici: composti: e col tempo.

Cambi reali.secchi.fittitii.e di minuti ouer comuni.

Meriti semplici e a capo danno e altri termini.

Resti.saldi.sconti.de tempo e denari e la recare a un di piu partite.

Ori.argẽti.e loro affinare. ecarattare.

Molti casi e ragioni straordinarie varie e diuerse a tutte occurentie commo nella sequente tauola appare ordinatamente de tutte.

Ordine a saper tener ogni cõto e scripture e del quaderno in vinegia.

Tariffa de tutte usanze e costumi mercanteschi in tutto el mondo.

Pratica e theorica de geometria e de li.5.corpi regulari e altri dependenti.

E molte altre cose ō grandissimi piaceri e frutto cõmo difusamente per la sequente tauola appare.

Magnifico Patritio veneto Bergomi pretori designato. D. Marco sanuto viro in omni discipli-
narum genere peritissimo Frater lucas de burgo sancti sepulcri ordinis minorum ⁊ inter. Sa. Theo.
professores minimus. S. P. D.

NOn me preterit Magnifice senator omnes: quos aliquod virtutis speciīē oblectet tibi q̄
plurimum debere: tum nobilitate: quā preclaram a maioribus tibi traditam: indies magis
illustras: tū humanitate: eruditōe: ⁊ eloquētia: quibus pauci nō dico tue ciuitatis homies:
s; totius italie te equauerint. Ego vero humanitate allectus: eruditionē admiratus: operā
⁊ diligentiam tuam de amicis bene merendis expertus: maxime tibi me debere cōfiteor. S; quom ani
mo repeto qua cura ⁊ studio laboraueris: vt nostrum hoc volumē perpetuis impressorum monumen-
tis traderetur non satis mihi ipsi sufficere videor: vt aliqua ex parte quātulacūq; tibi satisfaçerem Alij
pleriq; multi si quippiā in aliqua doctrina profecerint: libros: quibus ad id perueniūtur maxime latere
cupiunt. Tu cōsumatissimus astrologus: in Arithmetica eminētissimus: in Geometria excellētissimus
nostra: vt ederentur nobis solititius curasti. Profecto illud existimo: ingenii tui foecunditatem nō for
midasse: si hec in manus hominū peruenirent: propterea nō tibi plurima superfutura: que alios fuge-
rent: uerissimūq; esse illud Plynianum ex te didici. Ita certe recondunt qui pauca aliqua nouere inuidē
tes alijs. Opus itaq; ipsum te hortante ⁊ impellente impressum: qd̄ Illustrissimo Urbini Duci dicaui
mus ad te recognoscendum mitto: cui si canes nostri oblatrauerit qd̄ soles tuis clientibus egregiū pa
trocinium: mihi prestes: obsecro. Nam certus sum non defuturos qui has nostras vigilias multo stu
dio multoq; labore desudatas: reprehēsuri sint: Opus certe variū: copiosū: iocūdū: vndiq; mathemati-
cis theorematibus scatens ⁊ qd̄ nō mediocrē fructum sit allaturum hijs qui Euclidi Astrologie ⁊ ne
gotiationi operam sunt daturi. Sed vide queso quid nobis obtigerit: dum tibi satisfacere conor ma-
ius mihi obligationis vinculum inecto: non satis fuerat: q̄ te auctore noster liber in lucem prodiret.
tutelam etiam tuam deposcimus. Uerum quod nos efficere non possumus deum optimum maximu;
vna cum serafico nostro sancto Francisco adiuuantibus cōfratribus nostris frequenter orabimus: vt
tibi pares gratias ingenio doctrine virtuti ⁊ nobilitati tue referant. Uale Ad uota

Fa. Pompilij epigrāma ad lectorem.

Que fuerant medijs carie consumpta latebris
Restituit lucas lector amice tibi
Moenia si lapides quot habēt erecta subauras:
Aut ubi phoebeos temperet annus equos:
Et que ceruleas ducat te stella per undas:
Et que decliuo corpore signa cadant:
Linea: quid corpus: quid circus et angulus ois:
Que sit apelles picta tabella manu:
Ultima que terris regio. quas fluctibus urbes
Extremus gelidis abluat oceeanus.
Tempore seu certo concordem emittere uocem
Nature mores discere seu cupies.
Demere seu numeros numeris siue adderetētas
Solicitum medio seu iuuat esse foro:
Hunc eme: quicquid erit liber hic cōducet agēti:
Quod non dant plures: hic feret unus opem.

Clarissimi uiri Domini Giorgij Sūmarippa ve
ronēsis patricij Epigramma ad auctorem.

Chi douesse lodar tua nobeltate:
La pratica: Teorica e Doctrina
Per lopra non humana: ma diuina
Hoggi impressa in uenetia alma citate
Luca burgense mio excellente frate
Conuerria hauer studiato in medicina:
Astronomia: e in liberal foccina
De larti tutte: e in le Mechanicate.
Ma essēdo cussi ben dillucidata
Da tua excellença in ogni loco e parte
E a Guido Ubaldo Illustre intitulata
Sera da tutto il mondo si bramata
Che ogni poema ogni eloquença et arte
Di comendarla rimarra excusata.
Pur uedendo tu a grata
Pongo sto grandi sale in tua uiuanda
Per farla saporita A cui la manda:

Tabula. a.b.c.d.e.f.g.h.i.k.l.m.n.o.p.q.r.s.t.u.x.y.ç.⁊.ɔ.ꝝ. AA. Omnes sunt quater-
ni preter ꝝ qui est quinternus. Et AA qui est septernus.

Registrum Geometrie: quere in ultima carta totius operis.

M°. cccc°. lxxxxiiij°. xx°. Nouembris. venetijs

¶ Ad Illustrissimũ Principẽ Gui. Ubaldũ Urbini Ducẽ Montis feretri: ac Durantis Comitẽ: Grecis latinisq3 litteris Ornatissimũ: 7 Mathematice disciplie cultorẽ feruẽtissimũ: Fratris Luce de Burgo sancti Sepulchri: Ordinis minorũ: 7 sacre Theologie Magistri. In artẽ arithmetice: 7 Geometrie. Prefatio.

La quãtita Magnanimo duca e si nobile 7 excellẽte cosa che molti phylosophi p q̃sto lhano giudicata ala substãtia para: e comessa coeterna. Perochebano cognosciuto p verũ modo alcuna cosa in rerũ natura senza lei nõ potere existere. Per la qual cosa de lei itẽdo (cõ laiuto de colui che li nostri sensi reggi) tractarne: nõche p altri priscbi e antichi phylosophi nõne sia copiosamẽte tractato: e i theorica e pratica. Ma p che lor dicti gia ali tẽpi nostri sono molto obscuri: e da molti male apresi. e ale pratiche vulgari male applicati: diche in loro opationi molto variano. e cõ grãdi elaborosi affanni mettano in opa: si de nũeri cõmo de misure: vnde di lei parlãdo nõ itẽdo se nõ quãto che ala pratica e opare sia mestiero: mescolãdoci secõdo iluoghi oportuni ancora la theorica: e causa de tale opare: si de numeri cõmo de geometria. Ma pria acio meglio q̃llo che sequita se habia apphendere: essa quãtita diuideremo secõdo el nr̃o pposito: e diuidẽdola aciascun suo mẽbro assegnaremo sua ppria e vera diffinitiõe e descriptiõe. E aloza poi sequira q̃llo che Arist. dici in secũdo poster. Tũc eni maxime scit aliq̃d cũ habet suũ q̃d est 7c.

Diffinitiones 7 diuisio discrete 7 continue quantitatis: articulus primus prime distinctionis.

Dico adõca. La quãtita essere imediate bimembre: cioe cõtinua e discreta. La continua e quella lechui parti senno copulate e gionte a certo termine comune: cõme sõno legni: ferro: e saxa 7c. La discreta ouveramẽte nũero: e quella lecui parti nõ sonno giõte ad alcuno termine cõe: cõmo e. 1. 2. 3. 7c. Diche prima dela discreta: cioe del nũero: e poi dela continua cioe geometria: quãto alo intento aspecta chiaramente tractaremo.

Diffinitio numeri propinquissima. articulus secundus.

Numero e (secõdo ciascuno phylosophãte) vna multitudine de vnita cõposta: et essa vnita nõ e numero. ma ben principio de ciascun numero: ede q̃lla mediãte laquale ogni cosa e ditta essere vna. E secõdo el seuerin Boetio in sua musica: e la vnita ciascũ nũero i potẽtia: 7 passi3 i sua arithmetica Regina e fondamẽto dogni numero lapella. Laqual piu magnificãda in le cose naturali disse in q̃llo che fa de vnitate 7 vno. Omne q̃d est: ideo est: q2 vnũ nũero est. Ene ancora el nũero in ifiniti mẽbri diuiso: p quel che esso Aristo. dice: cioe. Si q̃d ifinitum est: nũerus est. E p la terza petitiõe del septio de Euclide: la sua serie in ifinito potere pcedere: et quocũq3 nũero dato: dari põt maior vnitatẽ addẽdo. Ma noi pigliaremo quelle parti anoi piu note e accomodate. E pero dico cõ glialtri alcuno essere primo: ede quello che solo dala vnita e nũerato: e nõ ha altro nũero: che itegralmẽte apõto lo parta. Altro e ditto cõposto: ede q̃llo che da altro nũero e mesurato: ouero nũerato. Exẽplũ primi Cõmo. 3. 7. 11. 13. e. 17. 7c. Exẽplũ secũdi. Cõmo. 4. chel doi lo mesura e nũera: e. 8. chel. 2. e. 4. E l. 12. 14. 18. e simili: tuti sõno ditti nũeri cõposti: nõ solo che cõstino ex digito 7 articulo (secondo sacro busco in suo algorismo) ma pche itegralmẽte p altri nũeri si possano mesurare e ptire secõdo el sẽso de Euclide in septio anche. 20. 30. 40. che sõno meri articuli: p esso sõno ditti cõpositi. Alcuni sono nũeri cõtra se primi: 7 sono q̃lli (cõmo e detto) che p sola vnita sono mesurati e nũerati: cõme sõno. 11. 13. 17. 19. che luno a laltro e laltro a luno e pmo: nec reliquũ p alterũ itegraliter diuidi põt vt p3 ituẽti. De q̃li alcuno po essere cõposto e laltro primo e luno laltro po esser primo: cõmo p la. 24. del. 7° si dimostra. Exẽplu3

WHAT WAS PACIOLI'S REAL NAME?

In the historical chapter, we have stated that the name of the author of the first book on bookkeeping was not definitely known This is quite apparent from the different versions of the spelling of the name, which we find in the various books, and it becomes rather amusing to read how the various authors mentioning this name take delight in stating that the other fellow is wrong and they are right Yet no two of them apparently give it alike

Brown in his history of accounting especially ridicules Ympyn's version, and with it all Brown himself spells it Paciolo, with an "o" at the end, whereas all the authorities he quotes spell it with an "i" at the end, and he gives no explanation as to why he prefers the "o" Below we give a tabulation of the various spellings of these names by the various authors, each one being preceded by the authority from which we have taken the name We have adhered to the spelling of Lucas Pacioli throughout, because we believe that to be the proper spelling, from the two best researchers who have written about him, namely, the two Germans Jager and Kheil, and further, because we believe that the "li" in the old Italian was Latinized into "lus," and the "c" is the old Italian for the Latin "t" in most all cases where the Latin "t" is preceded and followed by a vowel Furthermore, we have the author's own version of his own name, as we have seen elsewhere, in the only book that is published with his name in full, namely "Divina Proportione," which was written in Latin and where he gives the Latin of his own name While "*Luca*" is the Italian for the Latin "*Lucas*," we follow the author's own spelling in his Italian as well as Latin books, namely "Lucas"

AUTHORITY	SPELLING OF NAME
Summa de Arithmetica (author's original)	Frater Lucas de Burgo Sancti Sepulchri

(The above name appears first on the second line of page 19 of this book, which is the second page of the original, also on the third line, page 20 of this book, which is page 3 of the original, and in the third line of the second paragraph, page 22 of this book, being page 4 of the original—here, however, it is given in the genitive, hence Fratris Luce instead of Frater Lucas)

AUTHORITY	SPELLING OF NAME
La Scuola perfetta dei Mercanti (second edition of Summa de Arithmetica by same printers)	Fra Paciolo di Borgo Santo Sepolcro
Divina Proportione (author's original)	Lucas Patiolus (the Latin of the Italian Pacioli)
Contemporary writers	Lucas Pacciolus
Jan Ympyn Christoffels (in his French book)	Frere Lucas de Bargo Sancty Sepulcry
Guido Brandaglia	Luca Pacciolo
Ernst Ludwig Jager	Lucas Paccioli
Carl Peter Kheil	Fra Luca Pacioli di Borgo Sansepolcro
Beckmann's History	Lucas von Borgo
Anderson's History	Lucas von Borgo
Clitofonte Bellini (Trattato Elementare Teorico—Pratico di Ragionesia Generale)	Luca Paciolo
V Vianello (Luca Paciolo nella Storia della Ragionesia)	Luca Paciolo
Pawell Ciompa (Grundrisse einer Oekonometrie)	Luca Paciolo
L Gomberg (Grundriss der Verrechnungswissenschaft)	Luca Paciolo
V Gitti (De Computio—modern)	Fra Luca Pacciolo
Moritz Cantor (Geschichte der Mathematik)	Paciuolo
Sigismund Gunther (Geschichte der Mathematik)	Paciolo
Catholic Encyclopedia	Lucas Pacioli
Richard Brown	Fra Luca Paciolo Da Borgo San Sepolchro
John B Geijsbeek	Lucas Pacioli

tria. Proportioni e Proportionalita possi intendere. Certo nullo sia che tal laude se attribuesca. Lascio hormai ognaltra cosa che longo seria el dire: ma solo tutte le cose create sta nostro specchio. che niuna si trouera che sotto numero. peso e mesura non sia constituita commo e ditto da salamone: nel secondo de la sapientia. Hanc deniqꝫ preoculis summus opifex in celestium terrestriumqꝫ rerum dispositione semper habuit. Dum orbium motus: cursusqꝫ syderum ⁊ planetarum omnium ordinatissime dispone ret. Hec quando ethera firmabat sursum. Et appendebat fundamenta terre ⁊ librabat fontes aqua- rum. Et mari terminum suum circundabat legemqꝫ ponens aquis ne transirent fines suos: cum eo erat cuncta componens ⁊c. Non sia chi temerariamente giudicando dica quel che fin qua de le Mathe- matici discorso habiamo i persuasioni a. V. D. S. sia facto. Ala qual (siando di loro e de ognaltra excel- lente) non acadeua per connumeratione de lutilita segue in ogni doctrina e pratica per esse persuader li e infiammarla a seguirle e abraciarle. Ma solo a suasione aperimento de la nobilita e vtilita grandissima (commo sopra dicemmo) de li Reuerenti di. V. D. S. quali in simili exercitandose lor vi ta sustengano. Commo per tutte degne terre a. V. D. D. subiecte si fa chi al trafico. E altri laudabili exercinj sonno dati. Di quali la degna. V. Cita de Vrbino principalmente e piena. Lascio de la cita de Vgobio essential membro de. V. D. D. La quale de ogni trafico reluce. Lascio Fosambrone. Cagli e Macerata altre. V. degne cita. Castel durante. Santagnolo e Mercatello. E molti altri luocghi al. V. D. D. sottoposti ne li quali non me curo stendermi per che da se sia manifesto. Chi con poco e chi con asai sua vita exercitando sempre insu le famose fiere per aqua e per terra. Ora a vinegia. Ora a Roma. O a fiorença se retrouano. Per le qual cose non dubito la presente opera summamente esserli grata: con cio sia che in lei a tutte occurrentie (commo habian deducto) li sia suffragatorie seruente. Non altro e per lo presente a. V. D. S. da exponere se non che in tutti versi vie e modi lo infimo de quella figlio- lo e seruo frate Luca dal Borgo san sepolcro de lordine de li minori humile de sacra Theologia pro fessore deuotamente alei se recomanda. La qual lo omnipotente dio secondo ogni suo bon desiderio li piacci aacrescere e conseruare con tutti de la casa sua excelsa: e di quella beniuoli e aderenti. Vale.

Ad illustrissimum Principem Gui. Vbaldum Vrbini Ducem Montis feretri: ac durantis Comitem. Grecis latinisqꝫ litteris Ornatissimum: ⁊ Mathematice discipline cultorē feruentissimum: Fratris Luce de Burgo sancti Sepulchri: Ordinis minorum: ⁊ sacre Theologie Magistri: In arte Arithmetice: ⁊ Geometrie. Epistola.

Cum animaduerterem Illustrissime Princeps imensas dulcedines: ac maximas vtilitates quas ex his scientijs assequimur: que greci mathe- mata nostri disciplinas possunt appellare: si recte pratice ⁊ Theorice animo demandentur. Constitui nouum hoc volumē pro ingenij nostri tenuitate componere maxime in eorum visum ac voluptatem edere qui virtutum ȝelo affecti essent. In quo (vt ex subscripto indice facile perspi ci potest) varias diuersasqꝫ Arithmetice Geometrie Proportionis et Proportionalitatis partes plurimum necessarias: tum in praxi: tum in Theorica collegimus: firmissimisqꝫ rationibus ⁊ canonibus perfectissi mis subiecimus: ex antiquis ⁊ recentibus philosophis cuiuscunqꝫ pra- xis indubitata fundamenta. Quamobrem non immerito libri titulus. Summa Arithmetice Geometrie Proportionum ⁊ Proportionalitatum dicatur. Vbi ante omnia studuimus exactam in huiuscemodi facultatibus praxim tradere quemadmodū ex ordinatissima eius serie haud difficulter intueri licet. Verum quia temporibus nostris verba propria matheseos ob rari tatem bonorum preceptorum apud latinos ferme interiere: cupiens ego visui esse hijs qui vestre ditiōi parent (non ignarus stilo elegantiori. Eloquio Ciceroniano te salientem eloquentie vndas adiri opor tere) quid qꝫ vnusquisqꝫ non hec caperet: si latine per scripta essent: potius vernaculo sermone descri psimus. Litterature vtraqꝫ peritis pariter. Et imperitis hec commodum et iocunditatem afferent: si in eis se exercuerint vacent quibuslibet facultatibus et artibus: ob per tractata que cōmunia vnicuiqꝫ vi dentur ⁊ optime applicari posse. Et primo quis non dico doctus: sed multo minus qꝫ mediocriter eruditus est: qui non perspicue videat quantum habeant quantumqꝫ necessaria sint. Astrologie cuius principes hac tempestate vigent auunculus tuus princeps Ottauianus: vna cum Reuerendissimo fori simpronij Episcopo Paulo mindeburgensi quos in omnibus semper admiror ⁊ veneror; quorumqꝫ exactis iudicijs hoc ipsum opus non immerito caritate subiecimus: vt que bene scripta sint approbent

no al.q.sia la linea.q k.catetto del triangolo.q b d.nelquale menato la linea.f r. equedistan/te ala k.sira.f r.equale a la linea.i k.perche equedistante e la linea.f i.ala linea.k c.b k.e sia.r k.iguale al.f i.e il triangolo.q i f.e.f r b.sonno simili. Onde se traremo.r k.cioe.i f.del.k b. rimarranno.b r.3.e perche egli e cosi.b r.al.r f.cosi.f i.al.i q. Onde multiplicando.r f.per.f i.e diuidendo per.b r.vienne.5.per lo catetto.q i. Onde tutta.q f.e.20.che e laltezza de la pira/mide.q a b c d.

SE innuna spera si piglia vn ponto dalquale.4.rette linee si menino infra loro iguali e vadino ala superficie de la spera e quelle linee nõ sieno in vna superficie piana quel ponto sia il centro de la spera. Verbi gratia sia la spera.a b.e in q̃lla sia il ponto.ç.dalquale sieno menate.4.linee infra loro iguali.ç b.ç g.ç d.ç e.e nõ sienno li ponti.b.g.d.e.innuna superficie piana dico il ponto.ç.essere centro de la ditta spera e questo euidentemente appare e po nõna bisogno de dimonstratione.

QUando sira menato dal ponto del capo dogni piramide colonnale al cẽtro d̃la basa sua perpendiculare sopra la sua basa: alora le linee rette che sonno menate dal ponto del capo suo al cerchio contenente la superficie de la sua basa sonno i fra loro iguali. E la multiplicatiõe duna di quelle linee che sonno menate dal ca/po loro al cerchio contenente la sua basa: ne la mita del cerchio contenente la ditta basa. E la/rea de la superficie de ditta piramide colonnale: verbi gratia: sia la piramide colonnale.a b g d.delaquale la sua somita sia.a.e la sua basa sia il circulo.b g d.del quale sia il centro e. E la li/nea.a e.ortogonalmente sia ritta sopra il piano del cerchio.b g d.e dal ponto.a.ala linea cir/cunferentiale contenente il circulo.b g d.de la basa de la data piramide di colonna se meni molte linee.a b.a g.a d.dico certamẽte le rette.a b.a g.a d.infral loro essere iguali. La p̃ua me/nise dal centro.e.le rette.e b.e g.e d.che sonno tutte iguali infra loro. E perche.a e.e perpen/diculare sopra il piano del circulo.b g d.sienno gliangoli.a e b.a e g.a e d retti. Onde li triã/goli sonno ortogonii.a e b.a e g.a e d.e hano le base iguali che sonno.e b.e g.e d.e il lato.a e.e commune. Onde li lati subtendenti a gliangoli retti che sonno.a b.a g.a d.sonno infra loro iguali. E per questo e manifesto che tutte le rette linee che si possono menare dal.a.ala linea circunferente.b g d.essere iguali a la linea.a b.

ANcora dico che multiplicato.a b.nela mita de la linea circunferente.b g d. fara larea de la superficie de la piramide: cioe larea difuora de la superficie.a b g d.la quale superficie e dal circulo de la basa.b g d.infino ala sua summita. E se nõ fos/se cosi. Alora sia la multiplicatiõe de la linea.a b.de la mita del circulo.b g d.ma/giore o minore quella che facia larea de la superficie dico che quella quantita che se mul/tiplica per.a b.a fare larea de la superficie sua minore ouer magiore de la mita de la linea cir/cũferente.b g d. E sia la quantita.i ç.e il doppio del.i ç.e piu chel cerchio.b g d. Adonca fa/ro sopra il cerchio.b g d.vna figura retti linea hauente e lati e gliangoli iguali contenente quello: e sienno li lati insiemi agionti meno che lo doppio del.i ç.che sia la figura.l k t. E me/nero la linea.a b.laquale e perpendiculare sopra la linea.b k.in questo modo. Menero la li/nea.e t.sienno li quadrati de le linee.e b.e b t.iguali al quadrato de la linea.e t.e commune a tutti sia il quadrato de la perpendiculare.a e.siranno li quadrati de le linee.e b.e b a. Igua/li al quadrato de la linea.e t.e communamente sagionga il quadrato de la perpendiculare.a e.sienno li quadrati de le linee.a e.e b.b t.cioe li quadrati de le linee.a b.e.b t.iguali al qua/drato.a t.onde langolo.a b t.e retto Perpendiculare e adonca la linea.a b.sopra la linea.t k. Similmente si mostra la linea.a g.essere perpendiculare sopra.k l.e.a d sopra la linea.t l. E perche le rette.a b.a g.a d.sonno infra loro iguali virtu de la multiplicatione duna di quel/le commo del.a b.ne la mita de lati del triangolo.t k l.lembado ouer area de la superficie de la piramide.a t k l.magiore de la superficie de la piramide.a b g d.conciosia cosa che la con/tenga quella: cioe quello che infral cerchio.b g d.e il ponto.a e la mita de lati del triangolo .t k l.e minore che la quantita.i ç. Adonca gia fo la multiplicatione de la linea.a b.quello ch̃ e meno de la linea.i ç.e magiore de la superficie de la piramida di colonna che e impossibi/le. Adonca non ne possibile che la multiplicatione de la linea.a b.ne la linea che sia magio/re de la mita del cerchio.b g d.sia lembado ouer continentia de la superficie.a b g d. Anco/ra porro la linea.i ç.miore de la mita de la circũferentia del circulo.b g d.e se possibile e ch̃ d̃l dutto.a b.i.i ç.ne puẽga larea de la supficie d̃la piramide.a b g d. A multiplicare adõca d̃ la .½.d̃ la circũferẽtia d̃l circulo.b g d.fara la supfic.dũa miore piramide d̃ la piramide.a b g d.

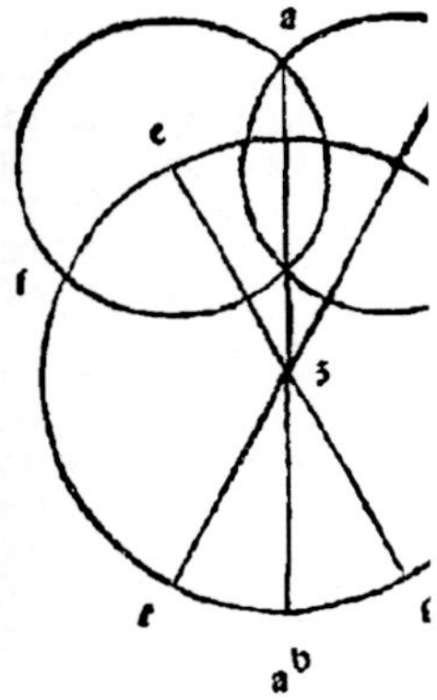

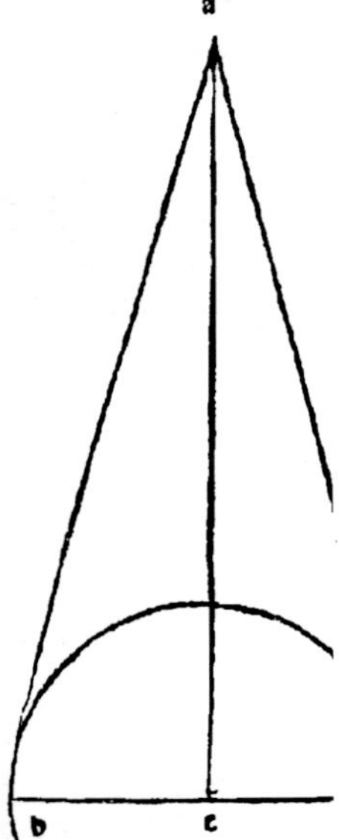

rum: e partendo soldi per.20.neuē ₰.Per che la lira vbiq3 si tene soldi.20.Le ₰.poi a farne oro: si partano per la valuta de quel oro occurrente: secondo li luoghi.E quello ch avança de li δ partendoli in.12.sonno δ.E cio che avança de li ß.partiti in.20.sono ß.E cio che auāça de le ₰.partite in la valuta de loro occurrente sonno.₰.Et sic in ceteris discurrendo: verbi gratia. Poniamo che tu habi arecdure ale magiori valute ouer magiori monete questa q̄tita de picioli: cioe picioli numero.96598.Dico che prima facci commo festi di sopra in li pesi ordinamente reducendo prima ala immediata moneta sequente: quale e el soldo in questo modo. Partendo la ditta summa de picioli per.12.neuen.8049.e sono soldi e avança.10 che son.10.picioli.E poi a farne ₰.partirai questi soldi venuti per.20.neuene.402.E queste sono ₰.de valuta: e avança.9.che son.9.soldi.E poi per farne oro. Partirai le ₰. per la valuta del ditto oro a ₰.E virratte loro.E quello che avançara sira ₰.Commo se volesse far duc.li quali in questo hauemo posto valere ₰.7.luno.Le ditte ₰.venute partirai per.7.ne uen.57.E son duc.e avança.3.che son ₰.Si che de primo ad vltimum reducendo li ditti picioli ala magior moneta siranno duc.57.₰.3.ß.9.δ.10.E cosi regerate in tutte valute menori: reducendole ale magiori: vt in ista.

Tertium notandum. Eadem via procedens.

Quello che habiamo detto deli pesi e moneta: ancora se habia a intedere de le q̄tita che vadano a numero: e anche a mesura o sia colma: longa: e rasa secōdo loro ingordita: si commo de sopra dicemmo. Meglio: e pegio.e longo e corto: e ingordo diuersamente se atendano: secondo le quantita: vt supra declarauimus. Si che hauendo tu octaui de braccio de panno numero.46595. de panni a volerli redure a canne: la qual communiter se tien braccia.4.Prima partirai ditti octaui per.2. e virratte quarte: per che sempre in ogni quātita.2.octaui fanno.¼.e lo remanēte sira octauo. E poi le quarte partirai per.4.e virratte braccia per che.4.fanno braccio.1.E lauanço sirá quarte.E poi li bracci partirai per.4.e virratte cāne: e lauanço siran braccia. Si commo hauesse li octaui preditti partili in.2.neuen.23297.E son quarti. E avança.1.che e.1.octauo. E poi parti.23297.per.4.e virranne.5824.E sonno braccia e auāça.1.che e.1ª.quarta. E poi parti li braccia per.4.neuen.1456.e sonno canne: e avança nulla che son: nullo braccio. Siche de primo adultimum la ditta reductione fa canne.1456.braccia o quarte.1.octaui.1. E tu i tutte altre simili per te farai 7c.

Quartum notandum de caratteribus praticis hoc in opere vsitatis.

Mestiero e ancora da notare quello importino li caratteri per noi in questopera vsitati acio le loro abbreuiature sien intese per chi legera hauenga che molti per le proposte questioni per se stessi le aprendino. Non dimanco piu sonno quelli di poca pratica (per li quali principalmente questo libro si fa) che non sonno quelli che intendano. E impero qui sequente tutti li caratteri: e abreuiature che per noi cōmunamente in questo libro se vsaranno: dechiararemo: si in larte menore ouer mercatoria: commo in arte magiore: ouer algebra Le quali piu per li pesi: e monete: e mesure: che p altro sonno trouati: excepto in algebra che per força (differentie causa) fo bisogno trouare. Per che non si potte a tutte quantita metter nome. Ideo 7c.

Duc. ducati.
₰. Lire. lira. libra. libre.
ß. Soldo. soldi.
δ. Denaro. denari.
p̄. Piciolo. picioli. pegga.
G. Oncia. once.
qʳ. quarti. qº. qª qᵉ.
Oct. octauo. octaui.
Cha. cāna. cāne.
b. Bracio. braci.
m̄. Mina. mine. meno. mesetaria.
m̄ª. Marca. m̄ᶜ. marchi.
k. Caratto. caratti.
gª. grane. grani.
gº. Grossi. grossoni.
bl. Bolognino. bolognin bolçone.
vª. Uia.
rª. Regula. resta. rº.
Mca. multiplica.
Mcare. multiplicare.
Mcato. multiplicato.
Drā. differentia.
Drē. differentie.

Questi caratteri e abreuiature commo vedi. Alcuni sonno che piu de vna cosa representano. Peroche ale volte peso.e ale volte valuta di monete. Si commo questo ₰.che dici lira a valuta de moneta che sintende soldi.20.E libra a peso che sintende once.12.e cosi questa p̄.che dici.piu. picioli. pegge .piedi. Per la q̄l cosa tu nelli luoghi doue le trouerai per tuo ingēgno chiaro cognoscerai quale de luno de questi te representara: secondo el suon de la materia che li se contira. Onde fra le valute .p̄. denota picioli. Fra mesure piedi Fra quantita de panni pegga . In operatione de algebra piu: e cosi de ciascuna de laltre: secondo li lochi e le materie te representarāno luna de le cose ditte qui al suo incontro siche tu per te vsarai lo ingēgno tuo: el qual bisogna sia supplemento a quello chio mancasse. Quia suppletio fit loco defectus. Per che non e possibile mai ponere tutto quello che alarte se ricerca: si commo e manifesto a quelli che di componere volumi se delettano. Iuxta illud. Dicite pierides non omnia possumus omnes: e cosi farai dele sequenti che son per algebra.

Idem notādum de caratteribus algebraticis.

Per loperare de larte magiore: ditta dal vulgo la regola de la cosa ouer algebra e amucabala seruaremo noi in questo le qui da lato abreuiature ouer caratteri:

i mi

℞. p^a. n^o. nũo.
℞. 2^a. co. cosa.
℞. 3^a. ce. censo.
℞. 4^a. cu. cubo.
℞. 5^a. ce. ce. censo decenso.
℞. 6^a. p^o. r^o. primo relato.
℞. 7^a. ce. cu. censo decubo e anche cubo decenso.
℞. 8^a. 2°. r^o. secundo relato.
℞. 9^a. ce. ce. ce. censodecenso de censo.
℞. 10^a. cu. cu. cubo decubo.
℞. 11^a. ce. p^o. r^o. censo de primo relato.
℞. 12^a. 3°. r^o. terço relato.
℞. 13^a. cu ce. ce. cubodecenso decenso. Quoi dir econuerso.
℞. 14^a. 4°. r^o. quarto relato.
℞. 15^a. ce. 2°. r^o. censo de secundo relato.
℞. 16^a. cu. p^o. r^o. cubo de primo relato
℞. 17^a. ce. ce. ce. ce. censodecēso decenso decenso.
℞. 18^a. 5°. r^o. quinto relato.
℞. 19^a. cu. ce. cu. cubo decenso de cubo. Ouer cēso cubo cubo.
℞. 20^a. 6°. r^o. sexto relato.
℞. 21^a. ce. ce. p^o. r^o. censo decēso de primo relato.
℞. 22^a. cu. 2° r^o. cubo de scdo r^o.
℞. 23^a. ce. 3. r^o. censo de terço r^o.
℞. 24^a. 7° r^o. septimo relato.
℞. 25^a. cu. ce. ce. ce. cubo decēso decenso decēso. Ouer censo de cubo decenso decēso. Ouer censo decenso decenso de cubo.
Que oia idem important.
℞. 26^a. 8°. r^o. octauo relato.
℞. 27^a. ce. 4°. r^o. censo de quarto relato.
℞. 28^a. cu. cu. cu. cubo decubo decubo.
℞. 29^a. ce. ce. 2°. r^o. censo decēso de secundo relato.
℞ 30^a. r^o. nono relato.
Finis.

℞. Radici.
℞ ℞. Radici de radici.
℞ v. Radici vniuersale. Ouer radici legata. Ouoi dire radici vnita.
℞ cu. Radici cuba.
q^a. quantita.

si commo ancora nelli altri nostri quatro volumi de simili disciplinc per noi cõpilati haue-mo vsati: cioe in quello che ali gioueni de perosca in titulai nel. 1476. Nel quale non con tanta copiosita se tratto. E anche in quello che a çara nel. 1481. de casi piu sutili e forti com ponẽmo. E anche in quello che nel. 1470. derigãmo ali nostri releuati discipuli ser Bart^o. e francesco e paulo fratelli de rõpiasi da la çudeca: degni mercatanti in vinegia: figliuoli gia de ser Antonio. Sotto la cui ombra paterna e fraterna i lor propria casa me releuai. E a si mili scientie sotto la disciplina de miser Domeneco bragadino li in vinegia da la excelsa si gnoria lectore de ogni sciētia publico deputato. Qual fo imediate successore: al perspicacis simo e ℞do doctore: e di san Marco canonico maestro paulo da la pergola suo preceptore. E ora a lui: al presente el Magnifico et eximio doctore miser Antonio cornaro nostro condiscipulo: sotto la doctrina del ditto bragadino. E questo quando erauamo al secolo. Ma da poi che labito indegnamante del seraphyco san francescho ex voto pigliãmo: p di uersi paesi ce conuenuto andare peregrinando. E al presente q̃ i perosca per publico e mo lumento a satisfation cõmuna: a simili faculta el retrouiamo. E sempre p ordine de li nostri Reuerēdi prelati: maxime del reuerendissimo. p. nostro generale presente maestro Francesco sãsone da brescia: correndo glianni del nostro segniore Jesu Christo. 1487. lanno. 4°. del pontificato del sanctissimo in christo. p. innocētio octauo.

ORa tornando al proposito de li caratteri questi. sono maxie in algebra. E ben che in infinitum si possa procedere non dimeno quãto al proposito nostro in questo: li trenta gradi ascendenti per viaz et modum algebre et almucabala. Hoc est restaurationis z oppositionis sonnõ bastanti. E se pur tu piu ne vorrai per te stesso gradatiz porrai formarne. E questi sonno li gradi quasi modernamẽte cosi nomati ben che in tutte le cose li nomi sieno a placito. E se cõdo qualche similitudine materiale iposti si cõmino di sopra nella distinctione. 2^a. nel trattato. 3°. al articulo. 9°. de chiarammo. E cosi ancora sonno a placito tutti li caratteri quali noi qui habiamo posti p che tante terre tante vsançe. Juxta illud tot capita tot sensus. Et velle suũ cuiqz ẽ: questo dico acio tu imperito non credeste necessitassero. De li quali poi in algebra trattãdo formaremo loro libretti si commo in questo al suo luogo vederai. E quelle figure denançe poste che començano. ℞. prima. ℞. 2^a. ℞. 3^a. zc. fin. ℞. 30^a. sono denominationi dela pratica de algebra secondo li arabi primi inuentori de si facte pratiche operatiue. Ma del numero i genere apresso li greci foron secondo ysidoro etymologiarum: e molti altri Pictagora el primo e da poi lui Nicomaco: dal qual el piu de la sua arithmetica Boe. prese. E a presso li latini foron prima Apuleo e poi Boe. e de la geometria forono li egyptij ab in vndatione nili vt ipse ibidem inducit. Jdco ipsum lege qui optime de huiusmodi materia i plerisqz locis tractat quem pluries memini me legisse vade z tu fac similiter z proderit tibi zc.

Distinctio sexta de proportionibus z proportionalitatibus. Tra. primus. ar. primus.

OGnuno che di numeri alcuna cosa ha scripto sempre ancora insiemi cõ q̃lli de mesure al quãto ha tractato: e i cõpagnia desse del cõmun lor vestimẽto ditto pportione. E q̃sto sia manifesto se bẽ si leggi di molti phy lor libri: de mathematiche facilta cõpilati. Cõmo de Euclide megarense: La cui opa sempre tutti li antichi gimnasij: cioe de stoyci: academici: peripatetici: platonici zc. anc di degna disciplina mathematica illustrati. Nella q̃le lui de arithmetica: cioe de numeri trattando: ancora de geometria: cioe de misure largamẽte disse: e con quelle a giõse (cõmo e ditto) el lor cõmun velo ditto pportiõe. Unde diuise ditta opa i. 15. libri partiali. De li q̃li. 10. sono de geometria: cioe p^o. 2°. 3°. 4°. 6°. 11°. 12. 13°. 14°. 15°. E quatro sonno de arithmetica pncipalmẽte: cioe. 7°. 8°. 9°. 10°. e vno (a tutti q̃sti cõe: cioe el q̃nto) so de la pportiõe. La q̃l (cõmo se dira) cosi se aspecta al nũo: cõmo ala mesura. Del seuerino Boetio ãcora se ben si guarda i la sua arithmetica: trouerasse le forçe de geometria: e anche particulare mẽtiõe de le pportiõi. De thebit ancora degno pho (del q̃l molto Boetio exponẽdo Euclide fa mẽtione: maxime nel q̃nto) p sue ope diffusamẽte d luna e di laltra isiemi cõ le pportioni tratto. De Ameto figliuolo de Joseph (del qual el campano exponẽdo el quĩto de Euclide fa

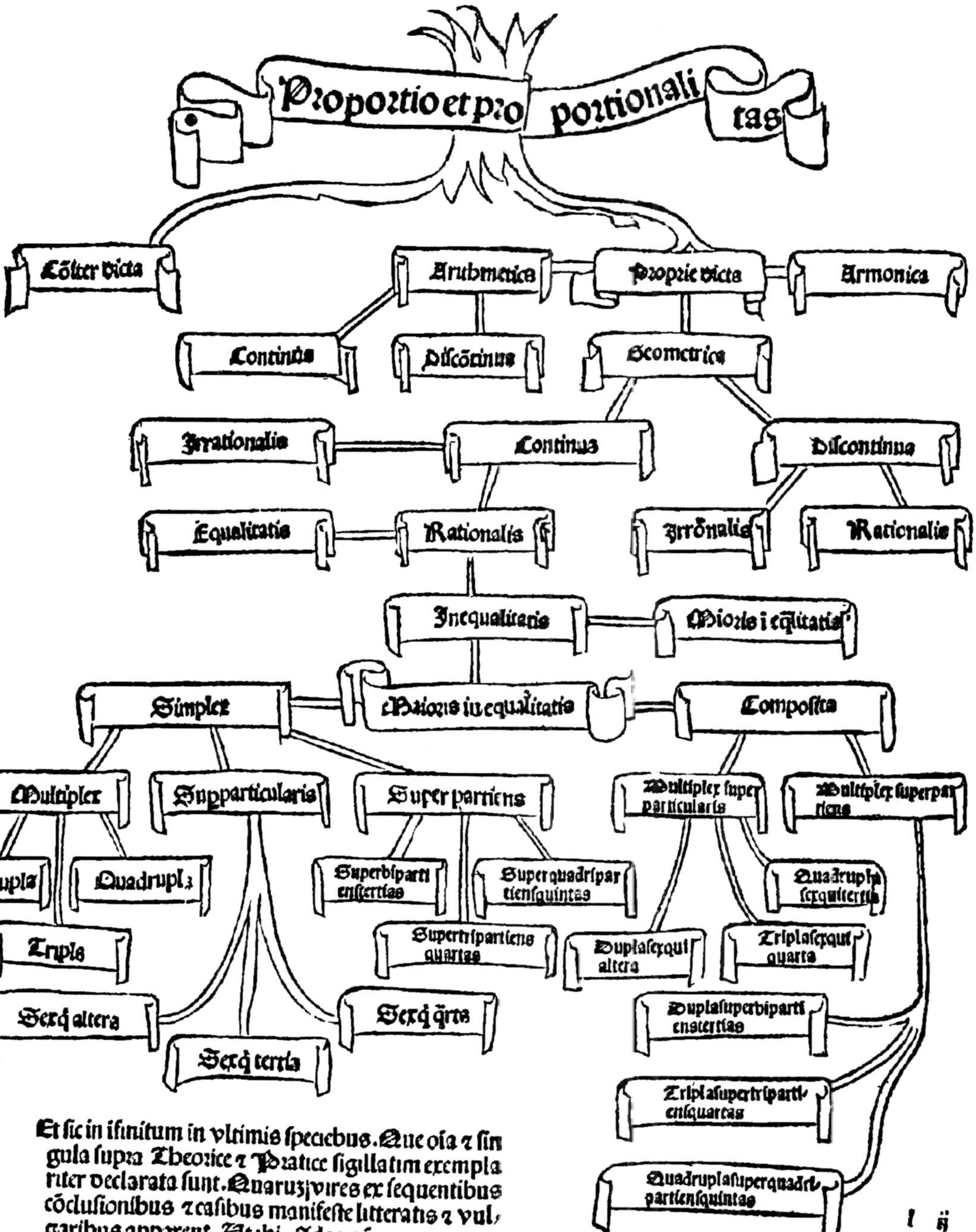

Et sic in ifinitum in vltimis speciebus. Que oia ꝛ singula supra Theorice ꝛ Pratice sigillatim exemplariter declarata sunt. Quaruz vires ex sequentibus cōclusionibus ꝛ casibus manifeste litteratis ꝛ vulgaribus apparent. Ut ibi. Ideo ꝛc.

l ij

PECULIAR SAYINGS OF PACIOLI

Chapter 1 "Where there is no order there is confusion"

2 "Every action is determined by the end in view"

3 "Defining diligently and truthfully so that truth will always guide you"

4 "More bridges are necessary for a good merchant than a lawyer can make"

"The merchant is like a rooster, which of all the animals is the most alert, and in winter and summer keeps his night vigils and never rests"

"Also it is said that the head of the merchant has a hundred eyes and still they are not sufficient for all he has to say or do"

"The law helps those that are awake—not those that sleep"

"Dante says

'My son it behooves that you quit your laziness
God promised the crown to the watchful ones
He who lies on feathers or under cover will never amount to anything Such a one leaves on this earth the same trace as the smoke in the air or foam on the water' "

"Work should not seem to you strange for Mars never granted a victory to those that spent their time resting"

A sage said to the lazy man to take the ant as an example

Apostle Paul says that no one will be worthy of the crown except he who shall fight valiantly for it

Remember God and your neighbor

Attend religious meditation every morning, for through this you will never lose your way

By being charitable you will not lose your riches

The Saviour in the book of St Matthew admonishes, "Seek you Christians first the Kingdom of God and then the other temporal and spiritual things you will easily obtain"

18 and 31 Who does nothing makes no mistakes, who makes no mistakes learns nothing

22 Officials do not bother about details

23 Accounts are nothing else than the expressions in writing of the arrangement of his affairs which the merchant keeps in his mind

If you are in business and do not know all about it, your money will go like flies, that is, you will lose it

29 Books should be closed each year, especially in partnership because frequent accounting makes for long friendship

33 If the losses are in excess of the gains—from which state of affairs may God keep every one who really lives as a good Christian

35 If you do not put the place and date on a letter you will be made fun of, because we say the letter which does not bear the date was written during the night, and the letter which does not bear the place we say that it was written in the other world and not in this one

Uno mette pegno.10.contra.15.vnaltro mette 20.contra.27.dimandase chi che uantagio e quanto p c. Fa cosi prima uedi quanto meritaria.20.de sconstro a rata.che.10.a.15.e dise.10.a.15.che hara.20.uirra hauer.30 donca uedi che non ha debito scontro habiando.27 or uedi che li manca che li mãchera da.27.a.30. che son 3.uedi che pte son de suo capital che e. o.che son li.$\frac{1}{10}$ e tãto ebbe di dãno n l so capitale respecto a laltro.donca arguesci che laltro habia uãtagio li.$\frac{1}{10}$ del suo capitale cb uol dir.15.per.c°.che si troua anche a questo modo dicendo colui mettendo.10.tiraria 15.se mettesse.100 che tiraraue opera tiraria 150.qual salua.Poi p laltro dirai se.20 uol.27.che uora.100.che uirra a uolere.135.cb uedi che manco che.150 del p°.si che ebbe suãtagio A sapere qto p c°.abbati.135.de.150.resta.15.e tãto ebbe dãno i tutto per hauer messo.100.cioe haue damno tal parte qual son.15.de.100.che son li $\frac{3}{20}$.ut supra la tro auanço p u che lui 15 in tutto che son li $\frac{3}{20}$ pur de 100.suo capitale:siche auantagio.15.p c°.fatta per che sempr tal parte quale pde luno qlla medesima pte uene a uãçare laltro e cosi i baratti.

Tauola del Quadernõ.

COMPARATIVE INDEX OF THE EARLIEST WRITERS

The following is a schedule showing comparatively the contents of the chapters of Pacioli, Manzoni, Pietra and Ympyn, so that the reader may have a quick perception of the extent to which Manzoni, Pietra and Ympyn have followed Pacioli. Only the most important items are given. Carefully note the coincidence that even the order in which the chapter is given practically remains unchanged from that of Pacioli.

CONTENTS OF CHAPTERS	CHAPTER NUMBERS			
	Pacioli	Manzoni	Pietra	Ympyn
The things a merchant needs and description of system of keeping a journal and a ledger	1	Vol I/1	1	1
Description of an inventory, movables, immovables accounts receivable, accounts payable	2	Vol I/2	6-8	2
Sample of an inventory in full detail by lots	3	Vol I/3	9	-
Useful instruction to a merchant	4	Vol I/4	10	
Introduction to second part of the treatise covering "Disposition"	5	-		3
Description etc., of the day book	6	Vol I/5	16	4
The marking of the books and the use of the cross on them	6		21	
Authentication of books by notaries	7	Vol I/7	16	
Sample entry for the day book	8			5-6
Nine methods of purchasing goods, as many for selling	9	Vol I/11	26-28	7
Description of the journal	10	Vol I/8	20-24	8
The two terms "Per" and "A" and the two little lines //	11	Vol I/10	2	9
The term "Cash"	12	Vol I/9	49	9
The term "Capital"	12	Vol I/9	30-33	9
Samples of journal entries	12	Vol I/12		9
One kind of money in amount column	12	Vol I/12	30	9
Line under each entry and through money column, diagonal line through day book entry when journalized, or check off at beginning or end of entry	12	Vol I/12	30	9
The Ledger	13	Vol II/1	30	10
The Index	13	Vol I/11	36	10
Four lines for money, one for ledger pages, two for dates	13	Vol II/1		10
Posting from journal to ledger	14	Vol II/5	39	11
Two diagonal lines, one on left and one on right, when entry is posted	14	Vol II/6		
Posting figures one above other, divided by a little line	14	Vol II/7	38	11
The place for the date	15	Vol I/11		12
Year in Roman figures	15	Vol II/2	14	12
Change in year between entries	15	Vol I/11		12
In personal account more detail required	15	Vol II/4		
Spacing of ledger to save transfer	15	Vol I/12	36	12
Index	15	Vol I/11	36	10
Further instruction about merchandise entries in the ledger	16	Vol I/12	36	

CONTENTS OF CHAPTERS	CHAPTER NUMBERS			
	Pacioli	Manzoni	Pietra	Ympyn
About the entries in accounts with public officials and banks	17			
Transactions with the market master, and sales for cash or on time with brokers' commissions	18			
Transfer of money through an order on another firm or a bank	19			-
Trades and exchanges, and their book entries	20			17
Joint venture accounts and trades	21		51	18
General expenses, commissions, and salaries, income and expenses, profit and loss	22		35	27
Branch stores or houses	23			15-23
The bank or private draft and their duplicate receipt	24		-	20
A separate book for income and expenses	25	-	43	
A separate ledger and journal when traveling with goods	26		-	-
Profit and loss	27	-	43	16
Why these entries do not go through the journal	27		42	16
Transfer of an account to another page in the ledger (difference only), not entered in journal	28	Vol II/9	40	
The change in the year between entries in the ledger	29			-
The preparation of a statement of account for customers	30	Vol II/12	60	14
Correction of an error in posting	31	Vol II/11	41	13
Balancing of the ledger and transfer to a new ledger	32	-	52	25
Checking with dots	32		52	26
Checking with other marks	32	Vol II/10		
What to do with new entries during period of closing ledger	33			
The balancing of all accounts	34		52	25
Profit and loss account	34		35	25
Final closing of the profit and loss into capital	34		52-56	25
The trial balance and balance account	34		52-56	25
Letters and documents—how preserved and filed, mercantile letters give date and place at top, non-mercantile at bottom	35	-		
Resume of entire treatise	36	Vol I/13	56	28
Balancing entries marked Ro (*resto*)	36	Vol II/9	11	

Distinctio. nona. Tractatus. xi°. ꝑticularis de cōputis ꝛ scripturis.

De quelle cose che sōno necessarie al uero mercatante: e de lordine a sape bē tenere vn q̄derno cō suo giornale i vinegia e anche p ognaltro luogo. Capitolo primo.

I reuerenti subditi de. V. D. S. Magnanimo. D. acio a pieno de tutto lordine mercantesco habino el bisogno: deliberai (oltra le cose dinançe i q̄sta nr̄a opa ditte) ancora particular tractato grandemēte necessario cōpillare. E in q̄sto solo lo iserto: p che a ogni loro occurrēça el p̄sente libro li possa seruire. Si del modo a conti e scripture: cōmo de ragioni. E per esso intendo darli norma sufficiente e bastante in tenere ordinatamente tutti lor conti e libri. Pero che. (cōmo si sā) tre cose maxime sōno oportune: a chi uole con debita diligētia mercantare. De le q̄li la potissima e la pecunia numerata e ogni altra faculta sustantiale. Iuxta illud phy vnū aliquid necessariorū ē substantia. Sēça el cui suffragio mal si po el manegio traficante exercitare. Auēga che molti gia nudi cō bona fede cōmençando: de grā facēde habio fatto. E mediante lo credito fedelmēte seruato i magne richeççe siēno peruenuti. Che asai p ytalia discurrēdo nabiamo cognosciuti. E piu gia nele grā republiche non si poteua dire: che la fede del bon mercatante. E a quella si fermaua lor giuramento dicēdo. A la fe de real mercatante. E cio nō deuesse admiratione: cōciosia che i la fede catolicamēte ognuno si salui: e sença lei sia ipossibile piacere a dio. La secōda cosa che si recerca al debito trafico: sie che sia buon ragioneri: e ꝓmpto cōputista. E p questo cōsequire. (disopra cōmo se ueduto) dal pricipio al fine: hauemo īducto regole e canoni a ciascuna opatione requisiti. In modo che da se: ogni diligēte lectore. tutto potra īprendere. E chi di questa pte non fosse bene armato: la sequēte in uano li serebbe. La. 3ª. e vltima cosa oportuna sie che cō bello ordie tutte sue facēde debitamēte disponga: acio con breuita: possa de ciascūa hauer notitia: quanto alor debito e anche credito: che circa altro non satēde el trafico. E q̄sta pte fra laltre e alor utilissima: che i lor facēde altramēte regerse seria ipossibile sēça debito ordine de scripture. E sēça alcū reposo la lor mēte sempre staria in gran trauagli. E po acio con laltre q̄sta possino hauere. el p̄sēte tractato ordiai. Nel q̄le se da el mō a tutte sorti de scripture: a ca°. p ca°. ꝓcededo. E bē che nō si possa cusi apōto tutto el bisogno scriuere. Nō dimeno p q̄l che se dira. El pegrino igegno q̄lūcaltro laplicara. E seruaremo i esso el mō de vinegia: q̄le certamēte fra glialtri e molto da cōmēdare. E mediante q̄llo i ogni altro se porra guidare. E q̄sto diuideremo i. 2. pti pncipali. Luna chiamaremo iuētario. E laltra dispōne. E pª de luna: e poi de laltra successiuamēte se dira sc̄do lordie i la p̄posta tauola contenuto. Per la q̄l facilmente el lectore porra le occurentie trouare secondo el numero de suoi capitoli e carti.

Chi cō lo debito ordie che saspecta uol sap bē tenere vn q̄derno cō lo suo giornale a q̄l che qui se dira con diligētia stia atēto. E acio bē sintēda el ꝓcesso idurremo i cāpo vno che mo dinouo comēçi a traficare cōmo p ordie deba procedere nel tenere soi conti e scripture: acioche sucītamēte ogni cosa possi ritrouare posta al suo luogo p che nō asettando le cose debitamēte a li suoi luochi uerebbe i grandissimi trauagli e cōfusiōi de tutte sue facēde. Iuxta cōe dictū vbi nō ē ordo ibi est cōfusio. E pero a pfecto documēto dogni mercatante de tutto nr̄o ꝓcesso faremo cōmo di sopra e ditto. 2. pti pncipali. Le q̄li aptamēte q̄ sequēte chiariremo: acio fructo salutifero sabia iprēdere. E prima dimostrando ch̄ cosa sia iuētario e cōmo sabia fare. De la pª pte pncipale de q̄sto tractato detta iuētario. E che cosa sia iuētario: e cōme fra mercatanti sabia fare. ca°. 2 Cōuiense adonca pª mēte ꝓsupponere e imaginare che ogni opante e mosso dal fine. E p poter q̄llo debitamēte cōseqre fa ogni suo sforço nel suo ꝓcesso. vnde el fine de q̄lūche traficante e de cōsequire licito e cōpetēte guadagno p sua substētatiōe. E po sempre con lo nome de meser domenedio: debiano cōmençare loro facende. E i nel pn°. dogni lor scripture: el suo sancto

COMPLETE TRANSLATION OF PACIOLI

SECTION NINE—TREATISE XI

PARTICULARS OF RECKONINGS AND THEIR RECORDING

CHAPTER 1

THINGS THAT ARE NECESSARY TO THE GOOD MERCHANT AND THE METHOD OF KEEPING A LEDGER WITH ITS JOURNAL, IN VENICE AND ELSEWHERE

In order that the subjects of His Illustrious Highness, the most honorable and magnanimous Duke of Urbino (D U D S.—*Docis Urbini Domini Serenissimi*), may have all the rules that a good merchant needs, I decided to compile, in addition to the subjects already treated in this work, a special treatise which is much needed I have compiled it for this purpose only, i e, that they (the subjects) may whenever necessary find in it everything with regard to accounts and their keeping And thereby I wish to give them enough rules to enable them to keep all their accounts and books in an orderly way For, as we know, there are three things needed by any one who wishes to carry on business carefully The most important of these is cash or any equivalent, according to that saying, *Unum aliquid necessarium est substantia* Without this, business can hardly be carried on

It has happened that many without capital of their own but whose credit was good, carried on big transactions and by means of their credit, which they faithfully kept, became very wealthy. We became acquainted with many of these throughout Italy In the great republics nothing was considered superior to the word of the good merchant, and oaths were taken on the word of a good merchant On this confidence rested the faith they had in the trustworthiness of an upright merchant And this is not strange, because according to the Christian religion, we are saved by faith, and without it it is impossible to please God

The second thing necessary in business is to be a good bookkeeper and ready mathematician To become such we have given above (in the foregoing sections of the book) the rules and canons necessary to each transaction, so that any diligent reader can understand it all by himself If one has not understood this first part well, it will be useless for him to read the following

The third and last thing is to arrange all the transactions in such a systematic way that one may understand each one of them at a glance, i e, by the debit (*debito*—owed to) and credit (*credito*—owed by) method This is very essential to merchants, because, without making the entries systematically it would be impossible to conduct their business, for they would have no rest and their minds would always be troubled For this purpose I have written this treatise, in which, step by step, the method is given of making all sorts of entries Although one cannot write out every essential detail for all cases, nevertheless a careful mind will be able, from what is given, to make the application to any particular case

This treatise will adopt the system used in Venice, which is certainly to be recommended above all the others, for by means of this, one can find his way in any other We shall divide this treatise in two principal parts The one we shall call the Inventory, and the other, Disposition (arrangement) We shall talk first of the one and then of the other, according to the order contained in the accompanying Table of Contents, from which the reader may take what he needs in his special case

He who wants to know how to keep a ledger and its journal in due order must pay strict attention to what I shall say. To understand the procedure well, we will take the case of one who is just starting in business, and tell how he must proceed in keeping his accounts and books so that at a glance he may find each thing in its place For, if he does not put each thing in its own place, he will find himself in great trouble and confusion as to all his affairs, according to the familiar saying, *Ubi non est ordo, ibi est confusio* (Where there is no order, there is confusion) In order to give a perfect model to every merchant, we will divide the whole system, as we have said, in two principal parts, and we will arrange these so clearly that one can get good results from them First, we will describe what the inventory is and how to make it

CHAPTER 2

FIRST PART OF THIS TREATISE, WHICH IS CALLED INVENTORY—WHAT INVENTORY IS, AND HOW TO MAKE IT

First, we must assume that every action is determined by the end in view, and in order to pursue this end properly, we must use every effort The purpose of every merchant is to make a lawful and reasonable profit so as to keep up his business Therefore, the merchants should begin their business with the name of God at the beginning of every book and have His holy

NOTE—The words in parentheses are the author's, as also the punctuation and paragraphing, as the original is extremely deficient in these The words in italics are copied exact from the original

nome haurra mēte ꝛc. E p̄o p°. cōuen che facia suo diligente iuētario: i q̄sto modo che sem pre p°. scriua in vn foglio o uero libro da p̄te. Cioche se ritroua hauer al mōdo: de mobile e destabile. Cōmençando semp̄ da le cose che sōno in piu p̄gio e piu labili al perdere. Cōmo sō li d. cōtanti. Gioe. Argenti ꝛc. Per che le stabili. Cōmo sōno. Casi. Terreni. Lacune valle. Peschiere e simili nō si possano smarire: cōmo le cose mobili. E successiuamente poi de mano i mano. scriuase laltre. Ponendo sēpre p° el di: e milesimo el luogo. el nome suo nel ditto iuētario. e tutto ditto iuētario si deue tenere in vn medesimo giorno. p che altramēte darebe trauaglio nel mānegio futuro. E p̄o a tuo exēplo: porre q̄ vn p̄ n°. cōmo se debia fare. Per lo q̄l tu p̄te porrai i ogni luogo el p̄posito sequire ꝛc. v3.

Forma exēplare cō tutte sue solennita in lo inuentario requisite. ca°. 3

Al nome de dio 1493. a di. 8. nouembre in vinegia.

Questo se quēte si e lo iuētario de mi. N. da vine°. de la cōtrada de scō apostolo. El q̄le ordenatamēte io de mia mano ho scripto o vero fatto scriuere dal tale ꝛc. de tutti li miei beni: Mobili: e Stabili. Debiti e Crediti che al mōdo mi ritrouo: fin q̄sto p̄sēte giorno sopra ditto. p°. p̄tita. Jn p°. mi trouo de cōtāti fra oro e moneta: duc. tanti ꝛc. Di q̄li tāti sōno doro venitiani. E tāti doro ongari. E tāti. fio. larghi fra papali: senesi: e fiorētini ꝛc. Lauāço mōete dargēto e rame de piu sorti: cioe. Trōi. Marcelli. Carlini de re. E de papa. E grossi fiorētini. Testoni milanesi ꝛc. 2a Jtē mi trouo i çoie ligate e desligate. Peççi n°. tāti ꝛc. De li q̄li tanti sōno balassi i tauola ligati: i oro ancili pesano. ℥. e caratti grani ꝛc. luno o uero i sūma. Qui poi dire a tuo mō ꝛc. E tanti sōno safili pur a tauola i formagli da dōna. Pesano ꝛc. E tāti sōno rubi coculegni desligadi pesano ꝛc. Laltri sōno diamāti greççi a tauola: e pōndi ꝛc. Narrādo le sorti e pesi a tua uoglia. 3a Jtē mi trouo veste de piu sorte. tāte de la tale e tante de la tale ꝛc. Narrādo suoi cōditiōi. Colori. fodre e fogie ꝛc. 4a. Jtē mi trouo argēti lauorati de p̄ sorti. Cōmo tacce bacili. Rāmi. Cosileri. Pironi ꝛc. E q̄ narra tutto le sorti a vna p vna ꝛc. E pesa ciascuna sorta da p se sotilmēte. E tiē cōto de peççi e de pesi ꝛc. E de le leghe. O veneciana. O ragusea ꝛc. E anche stāpo. o uero segno che hauessero farne mentiōe ꝛc. 5a. Jtē mi trouo i massaria d̄ panni lini: cioe Lēçoli. Touagli. Camise. Façu. li ꝛc. Capi n°. tāti ꝛc. lēçuoli de. 3. teli. O di. 2 ½. ꝛc. tele padouane o altre ꝛc. nuoui o vsati lōghi tanti br. ꝛc. E camise tante ꝛc. touagle de rele ꝛc. fazuoli grandi n°. tanti ꝛc. E piccoli tanti ꝛc. noui vsati ꝛc. a tuo mō narra°. le sorti. 6a. Jteȝ mi trouo letti d̄ piūa. n°. tanti ꝛc. cō soi cauecali de piu° noua o vero vsata ꝛc. federa noua ꝛc. q̄li pesano i tutto. o vero vno p vno. lb. tante ꝛc. Segnate del mio seg°. o dalt°. cōmo si costuma ꝛc. 7a Jtē mi trouo de mercantie i casa ouer i magaçeni. ꝛc. de piu sorti. p°. Colli tanti de çēçari. michini pesano lb. tan°. ꝛc. Segnati del tal seg°. ꝛc. E cosi andarai narran°. a sorta p sor° ditte mercantie cō tutti cōtrasegni sia possibile. e cō q̄ta. piu chiareçça si possa. de peso n°. e misura ꝛc. 8a Jtē mi trouo colli tanti de çēçari bellidi ꝛc. E carchi tāti de pip ꝛc. pip lōgo. o uer pip tōdo scōdo che sira ꝛc. E fardi tanti di canelle ꝛc. pesa°. ꝛc. E colli tanti garo°. ꝛc. pesa°. ꝛc. cō fusti poluere e capelleti. o vero sēça ꝛc. E peççi tāti. de vergini ꝛc. pesa°. ꝛc. e peçi tanti san°. rossi o bianchi pesa°. ꝛc. E cosi andarai mettēdo p ordie v°. sotto laltro ꝛc. 9a Jtē mi tr°. pelami da fodre: cioe agnelle bia°. e albertōi puglisi o marchiani ꝛc. n°. tanti de la tal sor°. ꝛc. e volpe mar°. n°. tante cōçe ꝛc. e n°. tante crude ꝛc. E camoçe cōnçe e crude ꝛc. n°. tante ꝛc. 10a Jtē mi trouo pelle fi°. fo°. arme°. dossi. vari. çebelini ꝛc. n°. tanti de la tal sorte. E n°. tanti de la tale ꝛc. Cosi destiguēdo a v° a v°. diligētemēte con tutta verita. acio el uero te habia a guidare ꝛc. Auendo sēp auertēça a le cose che uāno a n°. E a q̄lle che uāno a peso. E a q̄lle ch vāno a misura. p̄o ch di q̄ste. 3. sor°. si costūa fare el trafico p tutto. e alcune si mercatio a. M°. Altre a. c°. altre a lb. altre a. ℥. altre a n°. cioe a cōto cōmo pellami ꝛc. altre a peççi. cōmo çioie: e perle fine ꝛc. Si che di tutte fa ben nota a cosa per cosa ꝛc. E queste te bastino a tua guida. Laltre per te poi sequirai sempre ꝛc. 11a. Jtem mi trouo destabile p°am. vna casa a tanti solari ꝛc. a tante camere. Corte. Poçço Orto ꝛc. posta in la contra de sancto apostolo. sora canale ꝛc. apresso el tale: e tale ꝛc. Nominando li cōfini: e referēdoti ali instri se ui sōno āntichi piu veri ꝛc. E cosi se piu hauesse de le case i diuersi luoghi. nolarle a simili ꝛc. 12a. Jtē mi trouo terreni lauoratiui cāpi o uero staiore. o o uero panora ꝛc. Nominādoli scōdo luso del paese doue te troui. o uero doue sōno situati ꝛc. n°. tāti ꝛc. Jntēdēdo el cāpo o uero staiora de tauole tāte o cāne o ptiche o beuolche ꝛc. Posti in la tal villa de padouana o altrōde ꝛc. Apresso li beni del tale ꝛc. Chiamādo li cōfini ꝛc. E instrumēti. o uero p̄tita de catasti p li q̄li paghi le fationi i cōmuno ꝛc. Quali li lauora el tale ꝛc. rēdano lāno de fitto cōmūo: stara tāti e. d. tāti ꝛc. E cosi p̄te ua narādo tu tuoi possessiō ꝛc. Bestiami. soci°. 13a Jtē mi tro° ha° ala came°. d̄ ip̄sti°. ouer alt°. mōte i v°

name in their minds To begin with, the merchant must make his inventory (*inventario*) in this way· He must always put down on a sheet of paper or in a separate book whatever he has in this world, personal property or real estate, beginning with the things that are most valuable and most likely to be lost, such as cash, jewels, silver, etc , for the real estate, such as houses, lands, lakes, meadows, ponds, etc., cannot be lost as personal property Then all the other things must be put down one after another In the said inventory give always first the day, the year, the place and your name This whole inventory must be completed in one day, otherwise there will be trouble in the future in the management of the business

As an example for you, I will give you, now, an idea as to how the inventory is to be made, so that you may use it as a guide in any particular case

CHAPTER 3

EXAMPLE OF AN INVENTORY WITH ALL ITS FORMAL REQUIREMENTS

In the name of God, November 8th, 1493, Venice

The following is the inventory of myself, N N , of Venice, Street of the Holy Apostles

I have written down systematically, or had written by Mr So-and-So, this inventory of all my property, personal and real, what is owed to me (*debiti*), and what is owed by me (*crediti*), of which I on this said day find myself possessed in this world

First Item· First I find myself possessed in cash, in gold and coin of so many ducats, of which so many are Venetian, and so many gold Hungarian, of so many large florins made up of Papal, Siennese and Florentine, etc The rest consists of many different kinds of silver and copper coins, i e , *troni, marcelli*, papal and royal *carlini* and Florentine *grossi*, and Milanese *testoni*, etc

Second Item I also possess, in set and unset jewels, so-and-so many pieces, among which are many *balassi* set in gold rings weighing so-and-so-many ounces, carats, grains, etc , per piece or in bulk, etc , which you can express in any manner you wish There are so-and-so-many sapphires set on clamps for women, they weigh so much And there are so-and-so-many rubies, unset, weighing so much The rest consists of unpolished pointed diamonds etc Here you may give such descriptions and weight as you desire

Third Item· I have clothes of many kinds, so many of such kind, and so many of such-and-such kind, etc , describing their condition, colors, linings, styles, etc

Fourth Item I have several kinds of silverware, as cups, basins, rammi, cosileri, piromi, etc Here describe all the different kinds one by one, etc , and weigh each kind diligently Keep an account of pieces and weights, and of the alloy, whether the Venetian or the one used at Ragusa, etc Also mention the stamp or mark that they might have

Fifth Item I have so much *massaria dei lini*—that is, bed sheets, table cloths, shirts, handkerchiefs, etc , so many of each Of the bed sheets, so many are made three-piece sheets, and so many are three and one-half, etc , mentioning whether the linen is Padua linen or some other kind, new or used, length so many *braccia*, etc , so many shirts, etc , table cloths of so many threads so many big handkerchiefs and so many small, mentioning whether new or used, giving the different kind in your own way

Sixth Item I have so many feather beds and their respective pillows, mentioning whether the feathers are new or used, whether the pillow-cases are new or used, etc , which altogether or one by one weigh so much, marked with my mark or with some other mark, as the custom is

Seventh Item I have at home or in the store so much goods of different kinds First, so many cases of ginger *michino*, weighing so many pounds, marked with such-and-such mark, and so on, describing each kind of said goods with all their marks that you might possibly give and with all the possible accuracy as to weight, number, measurement, etc

Eighth Item· I have so many cases of ginger *belledi*, etc , and so many sacks of pepper, long pepper or round pepper, depending on what it is, so many packages of cinnamon, etc , that weigh so much , so many packages of cloves, etc , that weigh so much, with *fusti polvere* and *cappelletti* or without, etc , and so many pieces of *verzini* weighing so much, and so much sandalwood, red or white, weighing so much, and so on, entering one item after another

Ninth Item I have so many skins for coverings, that is, so many white kids and so many *albertoni* or *marchiani*, etc , so many of such-and-such kind, etc so many fox skins, so many tanned and so many raw, so many chamois skins tanned, and so many raw

Tenth Item I have so many fine skins, *fore armenti, dossi varii, zebelini*, etc , so many of such-and-such kind, and so many of such-and-such kind—defining diligently and truthfully each time so that truth will always guide you, etc , distinguishing the things that ought to be entered by pieces from those that ought to be entered by weight, and those that ought to be entered by measurement, because in these three ways business is conducted everywhere , certain things are reckoned by the bushel, others by the hundreds, others by the pound, others by the ounce, others by number, others by a *conto* (by single numbers) as leather goods or skins, others by the piece, as precious stones and fine pearls, etc , so you will make a notation of each thing These examples will serve as a guide for all the rest, etc

Eleventh Item I have in real estate first, a house with so many stories, so many rooms, court yard, wells, garden, etc , situated in St Apostle Street over the Canal, etc , adjoining such-and-such parties, etc giving the names of the boundary line properties, making reference to the oldest and most reliable deeds, if there are any, and so, if you have more houses in different localities, you will enter them in a similar way

ducati tanti de caucdale nel sestier de canareggio &c. O vero pte i vno sestieri e pte i vnaltro. Narrando anchora i nome de chi sonno scripti. E chiamando el libro de quello officio. El numero de le carti doue e la tua partita. El nome del scriuano che tien ditto libro: acio cõ piu tua facilita qn̄do vai a scotere li possi trouar. Pero che in tali officij bisogna hauere molti scontri alcuolte per la gran multitudine che ci interuiene &c. E nota el millesimo che respõdano a tẽpo p tẽpo acio sappia quãdo vengano li so pro: e quãto per cẽto respõdino &c. 14

Item mi trouo debitori numero tanti &c. luno e ß tale del tale &c. che me deue dare ducati tanti &c. Laltro e el tale del tale &c. E cosi narrali a vno a vno con boni contra segni, e cognomi e luoghi e quanto te debano dare e p che. E cosi se ui son scripti de mã o instrumẽti de nodari fra voi fãne mẽtione &c. In sũma debo scotere ducati tãti &c. De boni d. Se sirã persone da bene &c. altramẽti dirai de tristi d. &c. 15.

Item mi trouo essere debito i tutto ducati tanti &c. tanti a al tale e tanti al tale &c. Nominãdo li toi creditori a uno a vno. E se ui sono chiarezze fra uoi o de scripti o de instrumenti nominarli. E chi. E commo. el di el luogo per molti casi poteriano occorrere in iudicio e for de iudicio &c.

Utilissima exortatione: e salutiferi documẽti al bõ mercatãte ptinẽti ca°.4

E Cosi discorso cõ diligẽza tutte le cose che te retroui imobile e stabile: cõme e detto a una per una: se fosser ben diecimillia di che conditioni e faculta si sia e banchi e imprestiti &c. tutte al buono ordine cõuiensse nominarle in ditto cuẽtario co tutti cõtrasegni nomi: e cõgnomi qn̄to sia piu possibile. Per ch al mercatante nõ possano mai le cose essere troppo chiare. Per linfiniti casi che nel trafico possano occorrere: commo ala giornata sa chi in esso se exercita. E pero bẽ dici el prouerbio che bisogna piu ponti a fare vn bõ mercatãte. che a fare vn doctore de leggi. Chi e colui che possa nũerare li ponti: e casi che ale mani uengono ali mercatanti. Ora p mare. Ora p terra. Ora a tempi de pace e dabondantia. Ora a tempi de guerre e caresti e. Ora a tempi de sanita e morbi. Ne quali tẽpi e occurrẽce li conuiene saper prendere soi partiti. Si p li mercanti cõmo p le fieri che ora i una patria e cita si fãno. E ora in laltra &c. E pero ben se figura e asimiglia el mercatante al gallo. Quale e fra glialtri el piu uigilante animale che sia e diuerno e di state fa le sue noturne uigilie che mai per alcũ tempo resta. Auenga che de filomena se dica: cioe del rosignuolo che tutta la notte canti. non dimeno questo si po de state al caldo tempo uerificare: ma non dinuerno: cõmo la experiencia e impronto adimostrarlo. E ancho ria sumigliata la sua testa a vna che habia cẽto ochi che anchora nõ li sõno bastãti: ne in dir ne i fare. Le qual cose solo le dica chi le proua. Marrinolo. Venitiani Florẽtini. Genouesi. Napolitani Milanesi Ancõitãi Bressiani Bergamaschi. Aqlani. Senesi Luchesi Perusini. Urbiani Forosimproniani Cagliesi. E Ugubini Castellani Borghesi e Fulignati cõ Pisãi Bolognesi. e Feraresi Mãtouai Verõesi Uigẽti. e Padouãi. Trani Lecia. Bari cõ Betonta. Leql tpu'ra laltre i ytalia del trafico tengano el principato. Maxime la excelsa cita de venetia cõ fiorẽza. Norma e regola dogni partito chal bisogno aprender sabia. Si che bẽ dicão le leggi municipali vz. uigilantibus ⁊ non dormientibus Iura subueniunt: cioe a chi ueggbia e no a chi dorme le leggi souengão. E cosi neli diuini officij si canta da la sancta chiesia. che idio ali vigilanti a promesso la corona. E pero questo fo el documẽto di virgilio dato a Dante cõmo a suo figliuolo Quando nel cãto 24°. de lo iferno li dici exortandolo a la fatiga per laqle al monte de le uirtu se peruiene. Or mai conuien figliuolo che tu te spo'rti. Disse el maestro mio che pur in piuma In fama nõ si uiene ne sotto coltre. Sotto la qual chi sua uita cõsuma. Cotal uestigio disse in terra lascia. Qual fume i aere e i aqua la schiuma &c. E vnaltro vulgar poeta al medesimo ci cõforta dicẽdo. Non te para strania la fatiga ch marte nõ concesse mai bataglia. A quelli che possando se nutrica &c. Lo exemplo anchora del sapiẽte molto fo acio conueniẽte. Dicẽdo al pigro che si specchiasse nella formicha. E paulo apostolo dici che niũ sira degno di corona saluo che chi hara legittimamete combattuto &c. Questi recordi li o uoluti adure per tua utilita: acio non te para graue la cotidiana solicitudine in tue facende maxime in tenere la pẽna in carta e tutte scriuere a di per di: quel che te occorre: cõmo se dira nel seqn̄te. Ma sẽp sopra tutto p' idio el primo te sia auanti gliochi e mai nõ manchi daludire la messa la matina. Recordãdote che p lei mai si pde camio. Ne p la carita si scema richezze cõmo p qsto sctõ uerso se dici. Nec caritas opes. nec missa minuit iter &c. E a qsto ci exorta el saluator i sa matheo qn̄do dici. Primũ qrite regnũ dei ⁊ hec oia adiciẽtur uobis. Cercate xpiani pmamẽte el reame d li cieli e poi laltre cose tẽporali e spũali facil

Twelfth Item I have so many pieces of land under cultivation (fields or staiore or panora) etc, entering them by the name according to the usage of the country where you are, saying where they are situated, etc, as, for instance, a field of so many *tavole*, or *canne*, or *pertiche*, or *bevolche*, etc, situated in such-and-such town in the Province of Padua or somewhere else, adjoining the land of so-and-so, giving all the boundary lines and referring to deeds or the description from the recorder's office, for which land you pay taxes in such-and-such municipality, which are worked by so-and-so with a yearly income of so much, and so on, you will enter all your possessions, etc cattle, etc

Thirteenth Item I have in deposit with the Camera de l'Impresti (a bank), or with another bank in Venice, so many ducats, or with the parish of Canareggio, etc, or part in one parish and part in another, giving the names under which they have been deposited, mentioning the book of the bank, the number of the page where your account is, and the name of the clerk who keeps said book, so that you can easily find your account when you go to get money, because in such offices they must keep very many accounts on account of the big crowd that sometimes goes there, and you must also see that dates are put down precisely so that you know when everything falls due and what the per cent is

Fourteenth Item I have so many debtors (*debitori*) one is so-and-so, who owes me (*me dee dare*—shall give me) so many ducats, and so on, giving the names of each one, putting down all annotations as to the names, their family names, and how much they owe you (*te debbono dore*—shall have to give you) and why, also whether there are any written papers or notarial instruments In total I have so many ducats to collect, you will say, of good money, if the money is due from good people, otherwise you will say of bad money

Fifteenth Item I am debtor in total to the extent of so many ducats, etc I owe so many to so-and-so Here mention your creditors (*creditori*) one by one, writing down whether there are any documents or writings or instruments, if possible, mention the persons present when the debt was incurred, the reason, the time and the place, for any case that might arise in court or out of court

CHAPTER 4

VERY USEFUL ADMONITION AND GOOD ADVICE TO THE GOOD MERCHANT

And so, as we have said you shall enter diligently every thing that you have, whether personal property or real estate, one by one, even if there were ten thousand items, putting down the condition and nature, whether deposited or loaned etc You will have to mention each thing in proper order in the said Inventory with all marks, names, surnames—as far as possible—for things are never too clear to a merchant on account of the different things that may happen in business, as anybody in business knows Right is the proverb which says More bridges are necessary to make a good merchant than a lawyer can make Who is the person that can count all the things that can happen to a merchant—on the sea, on land, in times of peace and abundance and times of war and famine, in times of health or pestilence? In these crises he must know what to do, in the marketplaces and in the fairs which are held now in one place and now in another For this reason it is right to say that the merchant is like a rooster, which of all the animals (*animale*) is the most alert and in winter and summer keeps his night vigils and never rests And they say of the nightingale that it sings throughout the whole night, however, this may be in the summer during the hot weather, but not during the winter, as experience shows Also it is said that the head of the merchant has a hundred eyes, and still they are not sufficient for all he has to say or to do These things are told by people who have had experience in them, such as the Venetians, Florentines, Genoans Neapolitans Milanese, people of Ancona, Brescia, Bragama Aquila, Sienna, Lucca, Perugia, Urbino, Forosempronio, Cagli, Ugubio, Castello, Brogo, Fuligno, Pisa, Bologna, Ferrara, Mantua, Verona, Vincenza, Padua, Trani, Lecce, Bitonto which are among the first cities of Italy and have the first place in commerce—especially the cities of Venice and Florence, which adopt rules that respond to any need And well say the municipal laws *Vigilantibus et non dormientibus jura subveniunt*—which means, The law helps those that are awake, not those that sleep So in the divine functions of the Holy Church they sing that God promised the crown to the watchful ones, and this was the instruction that Virgil gave to Dante as to his son, in Canto 24 of the Inferno, where he exhorts him to the work by which one can reach the hill of virtue Now, my son, it behooves that you quit your laziness, said my master, for he who lies on feathers or under covers will never amount to anything Whoever spends his life in this way, he said, will leave on this earth the same trace as the smoke in the air or foam on the water, etc, and another Italian poet admonishes us in the same way, saying Work should not seem to you strange, for Mars never granted a victory to those that spent their time resting And it is also very good to quote that sage who said to the lazy man to take the ant as an example, and the Apostle Paul says that no one will be worthy of the crown except he who shall fight valiantly for it

I wanted to bring in these reminders for your own good so that the daily care about your business would not seem heavy to you, especially the writing down everything and putting down every day everything that happens to you, as we shall unfold in the next chapters But above all, remember God and your neighbor, never forget to attend to religious meditation every morning for through this you will never lose your way, and by being charitable, you will not lose your riches, as the poet says *Nec caritas, nec Missa minuit iter*, etc And to this our Savior exhorts us in the book of St Matthew, when he says *Primum quaerite regulum dei, et haec omnia adiicietur vobis*, which means Seek you, Christians, first the kingdom of God and then the other temporal and spiritual things

mente conseguirete. Pero chel padre vostro celestiale sa molto bene vostro bisogno ⁊c. E q̃sto voglio te sia bastāte a tuo amaestramēto de lo inventario ⁊c e altri boni documenti al ben fare ⁊c

De la .2ª. parte pricipale del presente tractato ditta disponē: cōme la sabia a intendere e in che cōsiste: circa al trafico: e de li .3. libri pricipali del corpo mecātesco. c°.5

SEquita ora la secōda parte principale del presente tractato laqual dicēmo essere la dispositione di laquale alquāto piu longo cōuiē chio sia che i la pcedēte a ben chiarirla. E pero di lei faremo doi pti. Luna ditta corpo o vero monte de tutto el trafico Laltra ditta corpo o vero monte de botega. E prima dirēmo del cor po generale de tutto el manegio le sue exigētie. Al quale dico prima imediate doppo suo inventario bisognare .3. libri p piu sua destreça e cōmodita. Luno ditto memoriale. E laltro detto Giornale. Laltro detto. Quaderno. Auēga che molti p le poche lor facende facino solo cō li doi secōdi: cioe giornale e quaderno E pero prima diremo di luno cioe memoriale. E poi susequētemēte de li altri doi de lor modi: versi e vie cōmo debisno essere tenuti. E prima daremo sua diffinitione.

Del primo libro ditto memoriale o vero squartafoglio o vachetta q̃l che senten da e commo in esso se habia a scriuere: e p chi. ca° 6

VNde memoriale o vero secondo alcuni vachetta o sq̃rtafoglio e vn libro nel q̃le tutte le facēde sue el mercatāte piccole e grādi che a mā li vēgano. a giorno p giorno e ora p ora iscriue Nel q̃le difusamēte ogni cosa di uēdere e cōprare (e altri manegi) scriuēdo se dichiara nō lasando vn iota El chi. El che. El quādo. El doue: cō tutte sue chiareçe: e mētioni: cōmo a pieno di sopra in lo inventario te dissi: sença piu oltra te le replichi. E i questo tal libro molti costumano ponere loro inuētario. Ma p che el puene a molte mani e ochi nō laudo de li mobili e stabili soi a pieno porre E questo li bro sol si fa p la furia de le facēde che si fesse. nel quale deue scriuere el Patrone. li Fattori Garçoni: le dōne (se sāno) in absēça lū de laltro. Pero chel grā mercatāte nō terra sempre fermi li garçoni ne factori Ma ora li manda in qua: ora li manda in la: i modo che alcuolte lui cō loro sōno fora. Chi a fiere chi a mercati ⁊c E solo le dōne o altri garçoni restano a casa che forse a pena sāno scriuere. E pure loro p non reuiare li aventori conuengano vendere e scotere pagare: e cōprare secōdo lordine che dal principale li sia iposto. E loro secōdo loro potere ogni cosa debono scriuere i ditto memoriale nominādo semplicimēte le monete e pesi che sāno: e trar fore a tutte sorte de monette che vendano e cōprano o uero pagano e scotano po che in questo tale non fa caso a che moneta si caui fore. cōmo nel giornale e quaderno ch disotto se dira ⁊c. El quadernieri assetta tutto poi lui quādo deli pone i giornale. Siche tornando poi lo principale vede tutte sue facende e rasettale se li pare altramēte ⁊c. E pero e necessario ditto libro a chi fa asai facēde. Per che serebe fatiga belleguiare: e per ordine ogni cosa la prima volta mettere i li libri auctentici e con diligentia tenuti. E i questo e in tutti altri prima ponere el segno di fora i sula copta: acio nel succcesso de le facēde siādo pieno d scriptura o uero fornito certo tēpo p la qual cosa tu porrai vnaltro libro prendere. o uero de necessita te cōuerra quādo questo fosse pieno. Ma ale volte molti costumano i diuerse pti: bē che nō sia pieno anoualmēte far saldi e anche li libri nuoui cōmo desotto itēderai. E i ditto secondo libro per debito ordine bisogna renouare segnale diferente dal primo: acio de tempo in tēpo si possa cō presteçça trouare loro facēde. Per tal vie ancora milesimo. E pero bene si costuma fra li veri catolici segnare li primi loro libri de quel glorioso segno dal q̃l fuggi ogni nostro spiritual nemico: e la caterua tutta infernal meritamente trema del segno: cioe de la sancta croci dal quale ancora neli teneri anni a iparar de legere lalfabeto cōmençasti. E poi li seguēti libri segnarai per ordine dalfabeto: cioe de. A. E poi li terçi del. B ⁊c. discorrendo per ordine d lalfabeto. E chiāmāse poi libri croci cioe Memorial croci. Gioanal croci cioe Quaderno croci cioe Alfabeto o vero extratto croci: cioe. ⁊c. E poi ali scōi libri se dici Memorial. A. Giornal. A. Quaderno. A. ⁊c. E de tutti questi libri. el numero de lor carti si conuen segnare per molti respecti e cautele che alo operante fanno de bisogno. Aueuga che molti dichino nel giornale e memoriale non bisognare: p che le cose se guidano ifilcate a di p di: vna sotto laltra che sia bastante a lor ritrouare. Questi tali dichono el vero se le facende de vna giornata non passassero vna carta. Ma noi vedemo che molti grossi traficanti non che una carta ma doi e tre nēpirano in vn giorno de le qual poi (chi volesse far male) ne potrebbe tagliare e cauare una. La qual fraude nō si potrebe poi per uia d li giorni cognoscere ne discernere. Per che li di son quilli che sença dubio

you will easily obtain, because your Heavenly Father knows very well your needs, etc

And this I hope will be sufficient as an instruction for you to make the Inventory, etc, and to do other things well

CHAPTER 5

SECOND PRINCIPAL PART OF THIS TREATISE NAMED DISPOSITION (ARRANGEMENT)—WHAT IS UNDERSTOOD BY IT—WHAT IT CONSISTS OF IN BUSINESS, AND THE THREE PRINCIPAL BOOKS OF THE MERCHANT

Comes now the second principal part of this treatise, which is called disposition, and of this I have to talk more at length than of the first part, in order to make it very clear I will divide it in two parts We shall call the one, *Corpo overo monte de sutto el trafico,* the other, *Corpor overo monte de botega* (Commerce in general, and Your store in particular)

First, we shall speak of commerce in general and its requirements Immediately after the Inventory, you need three books to make the work proper and easy One is called Memorandum (*Memoriale*), the second Journal (*Giornale*), and the third Ledger (*Quaderno*) Many, on account of their small business, use only the last two, that is, the journal and the ledger

We shall speak about the first—that is, of the memorandum book, and thereafter of the other two, about their makeup, and how they should be kept First of all, we will give the definition of the memorandum book

CHAPTER 6

OF THE FIRST BOOK, WHICH IS CALLED MEMORANDUM BOOK (*MEMORIALE*), OR SCRAP BOOK (*SQUARTA LOGLIO*), OR BLOTTER (*VACHETTA*) WHAT IS UNDERSTOOD BY IT AND HOW ENTRIES SHOULD BE MADE IN IT AND BY WHOM

The memorandum book, or, according to others, scrap book or blotter, is a book in which the merchant shall put down all his transactions, small or big, as they take place, day by day, hour by hour In this book he will put down in detail everything that he sells or buys, and every other transaction without leaving out a jot, who, what, when, where, mentioning everything to make it fully as clear as I have already said in talking about the Inventory, so that there is no necessity of saying it over again in detail Many are accustomed to enter their inventory in this book, but it is not wise to let people see and know what you possess It is not wise to enter all your personal property and real property in this book This book is kept on account of volume of business, and in it entries should be made in the absence of the owner by his servants, or his women if there are any, for a big merchant never keeps his assistants idle, they are now here, now there, and at times both he and they are out, some at the market place and some attending a fair, leaving perhaps at home only the servants or the women who, perhaps, can barely write These latter, in order not to send customers away, must sell, collect or buy, according to the orders left by the boss or owner, and they, as well as they can, must enter every transaction in this memorandum book, naming simply the money and weights which they know, they should note the various kinds of money that they may collect or take in or that they may give in exchange As far as this book is concerned, it is not as important to transfer to standards the various kinds of coin handled as it is with the journal and ledger, as we will see hereafter

The bookkeeper will put everything in order before he transcribes a transaction in the journal In this way, when the owner comes back he will see all the transactions, and he may put them in a better order if he thinks necessary Therefore, this book is very necessary to those who have a big business It would be too much trouble to put down in a beautiful and orderly way every transaction immediately after it take place, in books which are authentic and kept neat with care You must make a mark on the cover of this book, as well as on all the others so that you can distinguish them when, in the process of the business, the book is filled or has served for a certain period of time and you take another book You must take another book when the first one has been used entirely, yet many are accustomed in different localities to balance annually these books although they are not full, and they do likewise with the other books not yet mentioned, as you will see hereafter

On the second book you should put another mark different from the first, so that at any time you can trace your transaction easily For this purpose we use the date Among true Christians there is the good custom to mark their first books with that glorious sign from which every enemy of the spiritual flees and before which all the infernal spirits justly tremble—that is the holy cross, by which in our tender years we begin to learn to read The books that follow, you may mark in alphabetical order, calling A the second, and B the third, etc So that we call the first books with the Cross, or Memorandum with Cross, and the second Memorandum A, Journal A, Ledger A The pages of each of these books ought to be marked for several reasons known to the merchant, although many say that this is not necessary for the Journal and Memorandum books The transactions are entered day by day, one under the other, in such way that it may be easy to trace them This would be all right if all the transactions of one day would not take more than one page, but as we have seen, for many of the bigger merchants, not one, but several pages have to be used in one day If some one would wish to do something crooked, he could tear out one of the pages and this fraud could not be discovered, as far as the dates are concerned, for the days would

possano successiuamente sequire: e non dimanco el mancamento sira fatto. Si che per q̄sto
e altri asai respecti sempre e buono numerare e signare in tutti li libri mercanteschi E di ca
sa e di botega tutte le carti 7c.

Del mō cōmo i molti luoghi se habio auctēticare tutti li libri mercāteschi e p chi e dachi. ca°.7

Questi tali libri cōmegōsi secondo lusançe bone de diuersi paesi: neli quali luo-
ghi miso retrouato portarli e apresentarli a certo officio de mercatāti cōmo son
no consoli nela cita de perosa e a loro narrare cōmo questi sono li toi libri i liqli
tu intendi scriuere o uero far scriuere de mā del tale.7c.ogni tua facenda ordina-
tamēte. E dire a che monete tu li uoli tenere: cioe a.₰ de piccoli: o uero a.ß. de grossi: o uero
a duc.e.₰ 7c. O vero a fio e.ß.d̄.o vo a.G tari grani.d̄.7c. Le q̄l cose sēpre el real mercatāte
nel pricipio dogni suo libro deue pōere nella p^a carta. E q̄do mano se mutasse nella scriptu
ra daltri che nel pricipio se dicesse: conuiense p via del ditto officio chiarirlo. El scriuā poi d̄
tutto cio fa mētiōe i registri de ditto officio cōmo i tal di tu presentasti tali e tali libri segna
ti del tal segno 7c. E chiamato lū cosi e laltro cosi 7c Di q̄li el tale a tante carti el tale tāte 7c
li quali disse douere essere tenuti p mā sua o del tale 7c Ma i vno (ditto memoriale. O vo
uachetta. o secondo alcuni ditto squartafacio). ciascuno di suoi famiiari de casa a la gior
nata poteua scriuere per le ragioni sopra asegnate. E alora ditto scriuā de sua propria mano
in nome de lofficio scriuara el medesimo nella prima carta de li toi libri: e fara fede ogni tut
to 7c. E bolleralli del segno del ditto officio i fede autentica per tutti li iudicij che acadesse p
durli. E questa tal usança merita sumamēte essere cōmēdata 7c. E cosi li luoghi che la obser
uano. Pero che molti tēgano li loro libri dopii e uno ne mostrano al conpratore e laltro al
uenditore. e che pegio e secondo quello giurano e spgiurano 7c. che malissiō fāno. E po p
tal uia dofficio degno andando: nō possano cosi de facili dir buscia ne fraudare el primo 7c

Li quali poi con diligença segnati e ordinatamente disposti tu te neuai cō lo nome d̄ dio
a casa a gomēcare a scriuere tue facēde. E prima nel giornale ponere per ordine tutte le p̄te
de lo inuentario nel modo che seque te intenderai. Ma prima intendi cōme nel memoriale
se costuma dire 7c.

Cōmo se debino dittare le partite i ditto memoriale cō exēpli ca° 8

Gia e ditto se bene ai amente cōmo i ditto memoriale o uero uachetta o vero sq̄r
tafacio secondo altri che ognuno di tuoi li po scriuere. E pero del dittare tal p̄te
i esso nō si po dare piena doctrina Pero che chi intēdera: e chi non di toi di ca-
sa. Ma el cōmū costume e questo cioe. Metiamo che tu habi cōprato alquante
peççe de pāno (vt pura. 20. biāchi bresiani) p duc 12 luna basta che semplicemēte ponga la
p̄tita cosi dicēdo cioe. In questo di habiamo o uero io o cōprato da s. felipo de rufōi da bres
sa pāni n°. 20. blāchi bresiāi posti i su lauolta di s. stefāo taglia pietra 7c Lōga lūa d̄ le peççe
di cōuēto br̄.tāti 7c. Per duc tanti luna 7c segnate del tal n° 7c nominado se sōno atre lici
o uero a la piana bassi o alti fini o mecāi bergamaschi o uigētini o verōesi padoani fiorētini
o mātoāi 7c. E similiter nominar se ci fosse sensale e narrar sel mercato fo a cōtāti tutto o vo
parte cōtāti e p̄te termene e dir quāto tēpo O uero notar se fosse p̄te d̄ cōtāti e parte robbe
E specificare che robbe.o de numero peso e misura E a che pregio el M°.o elc°: o uero ß
o uero a rasō de conto 7c. O uero se fossero tutti a tēpo e narrare che termie O de galie d̄
barutto.o de galie de fiādra o de retorni de naui 7c. E specificare la muta de ditte galie O
de naui 7c. o se fosse termine de fiere o altre solenita: commo per lasensa proxima futura
7c.o uero p la pasqua denadal 7c.o uero de resurecti.o uero carleuale 7c. Piu e māco si dō
che uoi cōcludeste el mercato. E finaliter i ditto memoriale nō si conuerria lassare ponto alcu
no E se possibile fosse dir quāte parolle uesinterposero p che (cōmo nel inuentario sopra so
detto) al mercante le chiareççe mai forō troppo 7c

De li.9 modi p li quali cōmunamēte si costuma fra li mercāti cōprare e de le mercātie qua li al piu d̄ le uolte de necessita a tempo si comprano ca° 9

Poi che al comprare siamo nota che quello che tu compri po acadere communa
mente i.9 modi cioe a denari contanti.o uero a termine o vero alincontro dar
robba. Qual cto cōmunamente edito baratto.o uero a p̄te d̄ e parte termie o
vero a parte cōtāti e parte robbe.o uero a p̄te robbe.e p̄te termine.o vero p asse
gnatione de ditta o uero parte i ditta e p̄te termie a te o uero p̄te ditta e parte robba In li
q̄li.9.modi el piu de le uolte se costuma comprare. E se per altro uerso facesse inuestita: i q̄l

follow properly one after the other, and yet the fraud may have been committed Therefore, for this and other reasons, it is always good to number and mark each single page in all the books of the merchants, the books kept in the house or kept in the store

CHAPTER 7

OF THE MANNER IN WHICH IN MANY PLACES MERCANTILE BOOKS ARE AUTHENTICATED, WHY AND BY WHOM

All these books, according to the good customs of several countries where I have been, should be taken and shown to a certain mercantile officer such as the Consuls in the City of Perosa employ, and to him you should state that those are the books in which you intend to write down, or somebody else write down for you, all your transactions in an orderly way, and also state in what kind of money the transactions therein should be entered—that is, whether in *lire di Picioli*, or in *lire di Grossi*, or in *ducats* and *lire*, etc, or in *florins* and *denari*, or in ounces, *tari*, *grani*, *denari*, etc The good merchant should put down these things always on the first page of his book, and if afterwards the handwriting should be done by somebody else than the one stated at the beginning of the book, this should be recorded at the office of the said officer The clerk should mention all this in the records of the said officer—that is, on such and such a day you presented such and such books, marked with such and such mark, which books are named, one so-and-so, the other so-and-so, etc, of which books one has so many pages, another so many, etc, which books you said would be kept by you or by so-and-so, but that it may be that in said Memorandum Book or Scrap Book or Blotter, some person of your family might enter said transaction, as explained before. In this case, the said clerk shall write down on the first page of your books, in his own handwriting, the name of the said officer, and will attest to the truth of everything and shall attach the seal of that office to make the books authentic for any case in court when they might be produced

This custom ought to be commended exceedingly, also the places where the custom is followed Many keep their books in duplicate They show one to the buyer and one to the seller, and this is very bad, because in this way they commit perjury By presenting books to the said officer one cannot easily lie or defraud These books, after they have been carefully marked and authenticated, shall be kept in the name of God in your own place, and you are then ready to start your business But first you shall enter in an orderly way in your Journal all the different items of the Inventory in the way that I will tell you later But first you must understand how entries should be made in this Memorandum Book

CHAPTER 8

HOW ENTRIES SHOULD BE MADE IN THE SAID MEMORANDUM BOOK, AND EXAMPLES OF THE SAME.

We have said already, if you will remember, that any one in your family can make entries in the said Memorandum Book, or Scrap Book or Blotter Therefore, it cannot be fully stated how the entries should be made, because some members of your family will understand and some will not But the common custom is this Let us say, for instance, that you bought several pieces of cloth—for instance, 20 white *bresciani*, at 12 ducats apiece. It will be enough simply to make the entry in this way On this day we have or I have bought from Mr Filippo d'Rufoni of Brescia, 20 pieces of white *bresciani* These goods are at Mr Stefano Tagliapietra's place, one piece is so long, according to the agreement, and paid for at so many ducats, etc, marked with such and such number, etc You mention whether the cloth is *a trelici*, or *a la piana*, wide or narrow, fine or medium, whether the Bergamo kind, or Vincenza, or Verona, or Padua, or Florence, or Mantua Also you have to state here whether the transaction was made through a broker and whether it was made in cash entirely or part only in cash and part on time, stating the time, or whether it was part in cash and part in trade In this case you must specify the things that were given in exchange, number, weight, measurement, and the price of the bushel or of the piece, or of the pound, etc, or whether the transaction was all by payment on time, stating the time when the payment should be made, whether on *Galia de Barutto*, or on *Galia de Fiandra*, or on the return day of a ship, or on the date of some fair, or other festivity, as for instance, on the next harvest day or on next Easter, or on next Christmas, or on Resurrection day or Carnival day, etc, according to what was understood in the transaction Finally, I must say that in this memorandum book nothing should be omitted If it were possible, it should be noted what many others had said during the transaction because, as we have said about the Inventory, the merchant never can be too plain

CHAPTER 9

OF NINE WAYS IN WHICH THE MERCHANT USUALLY BUYS, AND THE GOODS WHICH IT IS MORE OR LESS NECESSARY TO BUY ON TIME

Since we are talking about buying, you must know that usually you can make your purchase in nine ways—that is either in cash or on time, or by exchanging something, which is usually called a trade, or partly in cash and partly on time, or partly in cash and partly by trading and partly on time, or by draft (*assegnatione de ditta*), or partly by draft and partly on time, or partly by draft and partly by trading In these nine ways it is customary to make purchases If you would make your purchases in some other way

modo proprio fa che tu e gli altri per te nel memoriale la narri aponto con verita e farai bene 7c. E cosi quando tu facesse le tue compre a tempo Commo se costuma ale volte torsi de guati O vero biade vini sali E curami dabecari. E seghi. che si obliga el uenditore al compratore de dar tutto el guato che per quel tempo hara E cosi el becaio te uende e promette tutti li cori pelle. sego che per quello anno in sua becaria fara 7c La tal sorta per tanto la 3 7c. E la tale per tanto 7c. E cosi de li seghi de manzo castroni 7c E le pelle motonine nere per tanto el c°. acoto. E tanto le montonine bianche 7c E cosi de liguati O biade specificar tanto el M° E tanto lo staro o el moggio. o la corba dele biade commo in sul chiusi de perosia si costuma. E de guati al Borgo sãsepolcro nostro Mercatello Santagnolo. Cita de castello. Furli 7c. Siche de ponto in ponto far mentione de tutto a pieno in ditto memoriale. o per te: o per altri che si scriua E narra la cosa semplicemente. commo la nasceua 7c E dipoi el bon quadernieri i capo de 4. o 5. o vero 8 giorni Piu e manco che stesse del ditto memoriale metarle in giornale a di per di tutte comme le sonno nascute. Ma solo in questo differente che non bisogna che in ditto giornale se distenda con tante filastocch de parolle commo se fatto in ditto memoriale Pero che basta alui vna uolta hauere la cosa ben digesta in ditto memoriale. Al qual poi el giornale sempre sa a referire Pero che quelli che costumano tenere 3 libri (a modo ditto) mai debano ponere cosa in giornale che prima non labino in ditto memoriale 7c. E questo basti quanto alordine de ditto memoriale. O per te o per altri cosi sia tenuto 7c. E nota che per quanti modi tu da altri poi comprare. cosi tu per tanti poi vendere. E per consequente altri po comprare da te Nel qual vendere non mi stedo altra mente. Pero che tu per te habiando questa forma de comparare. porrai asetarlo 7c

Del 2° libro principale mercantesco. ditto giornale. quel che sia e comme se debia disponere ordinaramente. Capitolo 10

L 2° libro ordinario mercantesco. e ditto giornale. Nel quale (comme e ditto) deue essere el medesimo segno che in lo memoriale: E carti segnate 7c Commo di sopra del memorial e ditto. Per le dite cagioni E sempre nel principio de caduna carta se deue mettere el Milesimo e di E dipoi de mano in mano ponere prima le partite tutte del tuo enuentario Nel qual giornale (per essere tuo libro secreto) porrai a pieno narrare e dire tutto quello che di mobile e stabile te ritroui. Referendote sempre al ditto foglio che per te. o per altri fosse scritto. el quale in qualche cassa. o scatola o filza. o mazo. o tasca: che cosi se usa el seruarai Commo te diro de le lettere E scripture menute. ma le partite del ditto giornale si conuengono formare e dittare per altro modo piu ligiadro. non superfluo. ne anche tropo diminuto. commo qui seguente de alquante partite te daro exemplo. Ma prima e da notare el bisogno di doi termini che in ditto giornale si costuma vsare. nela cita maxime excelsa de Vinegia. Di qualli immediate diremo.

De li 2. termini nel ditto giornale vsitati maxime i Venegia. Luno ditto Per. e laltro ditto. A e quello che per loro se habia a denotare. Capitolo. 11

Oi sonno (commo e ditto) li termini vsitati i ditto giornale. Luno e ditto. Per E laltro e ditto A Liquali hano loro significati ciascuno separato. Per lo. Per. sempre se dinota el debitore o vno o piu che se sieno. E per lo. A. se dinota lo creditore. o vno o piu che se sieno. E mai si mette partita ordinaria i giornale (che al libro grãde sabia aporre) che nõ se dinoti p°. p liditti doi termini. Deli quali sepre nel principio de ciascuna partita si mette el Per. Pero che p°. si deue specificare el debitore. e di poi immediate el suo creditore diuiso lũ dalaltro p doi vergolette cosi //. Commo nelo ex° disotto te sira noto 7c. Del modo a sap ponere e dittare le partite i lo giornale del dare e de lauere cõ molti exẽpli. E deli doi altri termini nel quaderno vsitati luno detto Cassa. e laltro Cauedale E quello che per essi se habia intendere. Capitolo. 12

A Dõca cõ lo nome de dio comẽzarai aponere nel tuo giornale. La p° partita del tuo inuẽtario. cioe la qtita deli d cõtati che te ritroui E p sape ponere ditto inuentario al libro e giornale bisogna ch tu imagini doi altri termini. luno ditto Cassa e laltro ditto Cauedale Per la cassa sintede la tua p° ouero borscia Per lo cauedale se intende tutto el tuo mõte e corpo de faculta pnte E lqle cauedale. i tutti li principii de qderni: e giornali mercãtesch sẽpre deue essere posto creditore. E la ditta cassa sepre deuessi posta debitrice. e mai p nullo tpo nel mancgio mercantesco. la cassa po esere creditrice ma solo debitrice ouero para. Pero ch qn nel bilacio del libro si trouasse creditrici denotarebe errore nel lib° cõmo di sotto a suo loco te daro sũmaria recordanza. Ora nel giornale ditta partita de contanti si deue mettere e dittare in questo modo. v3. P

you must state in your memorandum book with precision the way that you have made the purchase, or have somebody else do it for you, and you will do well

You buy on time usually when you buy *guati* or oats, wines, salt, remnants from a butcher shop, and fats In these cases, the seller promises to the buyer to give all the *guati* that he will have in that season The butcher will sell you and promises to give you all the hearts, skins, fat, etc, that he will have during that year This kind for so much a pound, that kind for so much a pound, etc, and similarly for the fat of beef, of mutton, etc, the black skins of mutton at so much apiece, and the white mutton skins, etc, and so with the oats, or *guati*, you must specify the price for each bushel or other measure and the kind of oats as is the custom at Chiusi de Perugia In buying *guati* you must see whether they are of our city San Sepolcro or Mercatello, or Sant' Angelo, or Citta de Costello, or Forli, etc

In this memorandum book, whether kept by you or by others, you must mention every single point You state the things in a simple way as they happened, and then the skillful bookkeeper, after four or five days, or eight days, may enter all these transactions from the said memorandum book into the Journal, day by day, with this difference, though, that it is not necessary for him to put down in the Journal all the long lines of words that were used in the memorandum book, because it is sufficient to put them down in an abridged way, and besides, references should always be made from one book to the other Those that are used to keeping these three books in the way we have said never must enter one thing in Journal if they have not first entered it in the memorandum book This will be enough as to the arrangement of the said memorandum book, whether it is kept by you or others Remember that there are as many ways to buy as to sell, therefore, I need not explain the ways of selling, because you knowing of the ways of buying can understand the selling

CHAPTER 10

THE SECOND IMPORTANT MERCANTILE BOOK WHICH IS CALLED JOURNAL, WHAT IT IS, AND HOW IT SHOULD BE KEPT IN AN ORDERLY WAY

The second common mercantile book is called the Journal (*Giornale*) which as we have said, must have the same mark that is on the memorandum book and the pages marked as we have said in talking of the memorandum book

Always at the beginning of each page you must put down the date, and then, one after another, enter all the different items of your inventory

In this Journal, which is your private book, you may fully state all that you own in personal or real property, always making reference to the inventory papers which you or others may have written and which are kept in some box or chest, or *filza*, or *mazzo* or pouch, as is customary and as is usually done with letters and other instruments of writing

The different items entered in the said Journal ought to be entered there in a neater and more systematic way, not too many or too few words, as I will show in the few following examples But first of all you must know that there are two words or expressions (*termini*) necessary in the keeping of a Journal used according to the custom of the great City of Venice, and of these I will now speak

CHAPTER 11

THE TWO EXPRESSIONS USED IN THE JOURNAL ESPECIALLY IN VENICE, THE ONE CALLED "PER," AND THE OTHER "A," AND WHAT IS UNDERSTOOD BY THEM

As we have said, there are two expressions (*termini*) used in the said Journal, the one is called "per," and the other is called "a," each of which has a meaning of its own "Per" indicates the debtor (*debitore*) one or more as the case may be, and "a," creditor (*creditore*), one or more as the case may be Never is any item entered in the Journal which also is to be entered in the Ledger, without preceding it by one of the two expressions At the beginning of each entry, we always provide "per," because, first, the debtor must be given, and immediately after the creditor the one separated from the other by two little slanting parallels (*virgoleite*), thus, //, as the example below will show

CHAPTER 12

HOW THE ENTRY SHOULD BE MADE INTO THE JOURNAL BY MEANS OF THE DEBIT AND THE CREDIT WITH MANY EXAMPLES THE TWO OTHER EXPRESSIONS USED IN THE LEDGER, THE ONE CALLED "CASH," AND THE OTHER "CAPITAL," AND WHAT SHOULD BE UNDERSTOOD BY THEM

With the name of God you shall begin to enter into your Journal the first item of your Inventory, that is, the quantity of cash that you possess, and in order to know how to enter this Inventory into the Ledger and Journal, you must make use of the two other expressions (*termini*) the one called "cash" (*cassa*) and the other "capital" (*cavedale*) By cash is understood your property or pocketbook (*borscia* from *bursa*, or bag), by capital is understood the entire amount of what you now possess

This capital must always be placed as creditor (*creditore*) in all the principal mercantile Ledgers and Journals and the cash always debtor Never at any time in the management of your business may cash be creditor, but only debtor unless it balances For if, in balancing your book, you find that cash is in the credit, it would denote a mistake in the book, as I will remind you hereafter at its proper place Now this entry ought to be made in the Journal, and ought to be arranged in this way

Debitore 1
Creditore 2

Linea del Dedare

Poi p la 2ª ptita dirai cosi

Forma d metter i giornale. M.cccc°.Lxxxxiii.a di.8.nouẽbre i venegia. pª

Per cassa de cõtanti. A cauedal de mi tale 7c.p cõtanti mi trouo i qlla al pñte.fra oro e monete.arzẽto e ramo d diuersi cogni.cõe ape i lo foglio delo iuẽtario posto i cassa.7c. i tutto duc.tãti doro.E monete duc tanti val i tutto al modo nro venitiano.a oro.cioe a grossi.24 per duc.e picioli.32.per grosso a ₰.a oro. 2ª. ₰ ß g p̃

Per gioie ligate e disligate de piu sorti: A cauedal ditto. per balassi tanti. ligati 7c. pesano 7c.E saffili tanti 7c.e rubini e diamãti 7c.Cõe ape al sopraditto iuẽtario.Quali metto ua lere a comũ corso. li balassi tanto. 7c. E cosi dirai de ciascuna sorta.suo ꝑgio cõuno. montano in tutto ducati tanti 7c. vagliano. ₰ ß g p̃

E hauẽdo tu nominato vnauolta el di.E ancora el debitore.e ancora.el creditore.nõ tramezandose altra ptita poi dire. A di ditto.Per ditto.E al ditto 7c.per piu breuita. 3ª.

Per argenti lauorati: Al ditto che sintẽde pur el cauedal p piu sorte argẽti cal pñte mi trouo cioe Bacili tanti 7c.E rami tanti 7c.E tazze tante 7c.E piron tanti 7c.E cosilier tãte 7c. pesano in tutto tanto 7c.val ₰ ß g p̃

Destinguẽdo.bene di põto p qste prime ptite ogni cosa cõe festi in lo inuẽtario. Ponẽdoli tu p te vn comun ꝑgio.E fallo grasso.piu presto che magro.cioe Se ti pare che vaglino. 20.e tu di.24.7c.Acio che meglio te habia reuscire el guadagno.E cosi de mano in mano porrai tutte laltre cose con suoi pesi nº.e valute.7c. 4ª.

Per panni de lana de dosso: Al ditto p veste tante di tal colore 7c.E a tal foggia 7c. Foderate 7c.vsate o vero noue 7c.a mio dosso.o vero de la mia dona.o uero de figlioli 7c.Metto valere a comune stima.luna p laltra in tutto duc tanti 7c.E p mantelli tãti de tal colore 7c.Cõe dicesti dle veste e cosi dirai de tutti ditti pãni p tutto. 5ª. ₰ ß g p̃

Per pãni lini: Al ditto p lenzoli tanti 7c.E tutto narra comme sta in lo inuentario. montano E vagliano.7c. 6ª. ₰ g a

Per letti de piuma: Al ditto 7c.p piume tãte 7c.E qui narra commo sta in lo inuentario. montano o vagliano. 7ª. ₰ g p̃

Per zenzer mechini: Al ditto.p colli tanti 7c.narra cõmo i inuẽtario.si contene.montano e vagliano a comune stima 7c.duc.tanti 7c. ₰ ß g p̃

E cosi poi tu p te stesso seqrai di porre tutte laltre ptite de qlaltre robbe.deciascuna faciẽdo sua ptita.sepata.cõmo q d zẽzer se ditto.Ponẽdoli ꝑgio de comũ corso.commo disopra e ditto.E lor nᵒ.segni.e pesi.commo de ponto stãno i ditto foglio diuẽtario.Chiamãdo dentro la ptita.ch moneta ch tu voli.E nel trar fora.conuẽ poi ch sieno a vna sorta.Perch non staria bene.a cauar fora a diuerse sorte 7c. E tutte ditte ptite d giornale sererai a 1ª.a vna tirando la riga.de qto dura tua scriptura.narratiua.fin al termine che si tra fora.El medesimo modo seruarai ale ptite del memoriale 7c.E fo che tu del memoriale mettarai i giornale.cosi a vna a vna.andarai depẽnando i lo memoriale.con vna sola.riga.a trauerso cosi./. ch denotara qlla tale ptita.eẽr posta i lo giornale 7c.E se tu non volesti trauersare la prª.cõ vna linea e tu lãciarai.la pª.lrã del pricipio dela ptita.o vero lultia.commo al capo di qsta.e fatto. O vero farate tu da te qlch altº.segno.tale ch tu itẽda.p qllo ditta ptita eẽr stata messa i giornale 7c.E auẽga ch tu da te possi usare molti varij e diuersi termini e segni.nõ dimeno te debi sẽpre studiare de vsare li comuni.che p li altri traficãti i tal paese si costuma di fare. Acio non para tu sia discrepante dal usitato modo mercãtesco 7c.

Del 3º.e vltimº.libº pricipale mercãtesco.detto el qderno cõmo deba eẽr fatto e dl suo alfabeto commo se debia ordinare.vgnolo e dopio. Capº 13. E poste che tu harai ordinatamẽte tutte le tuoi ptite al giornale.poi bisogna che di qllo.le caui E porile in lo 3º.libro ditto qderno grãde.El ql communamẽte si costuma fare de doi tãte carti chel giornale.In lo qle conuerra eẽr vno Alfabeto.overo Repertorio ovoi dir Trouarello fo alcuni. ala fiorẽtina se dici lo stratto.Nel ql porrai tutti debitori.e creditori. Per le lrẽ che comenzano con lo nº.dele sue carti.cioe quelli che comenzã p.a.i.a.7c. E del dopio alfabeto.E questo similmẽte commo sopra dicẽmo conuiẽ ch sia segnato del medemo segno chl giornale e memoriale.Postoui el nº.dele sue carti.E disopra i margine.da luna bãda e laltra.el millesimo E in la prima.sua carta.dentro porrai debitrice la cassa.si commo ella e la pª. nel giornale. cosi deue eẽre pª.nel qderno.E tutta qlla faciata.si costuma lasarla stare per ditta cassa.E in dar ne i hauere non si pone altro.E qsto p che la cassa se manegia piu che ptita chesia.a ora p ora.i metter e cauar dinari.E po li se lassa el cãpo largo.E qsto qderno cõuiẽ che sia rigato.de tãte righe.qte che sorte monete vorrai trar fore.Se trarai. ₰ ß d p. Farai.4.righe. e dinãzi ale ₰.farane vnaltra.p metarui el nº.dele carti de le ptite che isieme de dare. E ha-

EXAMPLE OF MAKING AN ENTRY IN THE JOURNAL

FIRST November 8, MCCCCLXXXXIII in Venice

Debit 1 — Credit 2 — Line of the debit. Per cash // A—Capital of myself so and so, etc In cash I have at present, in gold and coin, silver and copper of different coinage as it appears in the first sheet of the Inventory in cash, etc, in total so many gold ducats and so many silver ducats All this is our Venetian money, that is counting 24 *grossi* per ducat and 32 *picioli* per *grosso* in gold is worth L... (*Lire*), S (*Soldi*), G (*Grossi*), P (*Picioli*)

For the second item you shall say this way

SECOND Per mounted and unmounted precious stones of several kinds // A capital ditto for so many mounted *belassi*, etc, weighing, etc, and so many sapphires, etc, and rubies and diamonds, etc, as the said Inventory shows to which, according to current prices I give these values *Belassi* worth, etc, and so you shall state a price for each kind in total that are worth so many ducats Their value is L , S , G , P

After you have once named the day, the debtor and the creditor, you may say for brevity—if you don't make any other entry in between On the day ditto, per ditto, // a ditto

THIRD Per silver // A ditto—by which capital is understood—for several kinds of silver which at present I possess—that is, wash basins so many, so many coppers, so many cups, so many *pironi*, and so many *cosilier*, etc, weighing in total so much. Their value is L , S , G P

You shall give all the details in entering these items for everything as you have them in the Inventory, giving to each thing a customary price Make the prices rather higher than lower, for instance, if it seems to you that they are worth 20, you put down 24, so that you can make a larger profit, and so you will enter everything, putting down for each thing its weight, number, value, etc

FOURTH Per woolen clothes // A ditto, for so many clothes of such and such color, etc, of such and such style, etc, lined, etc, new or used, etc, for myself or for my wife or for my children, I give the total value, according to the current price, so many ducats And for cloaks, so many of such and such color, etc, and so on, for all the other clothes L , S , G , P

FIFTH Per linen // A ditto, for so many bed sheets, etc, and put down their number and value as the Inventory shows L , S , G , P

SIXTH. Per feather beds // A ditto, etc, for so many feathers—and here put down all that the Inventory shows, number and value L , S , G , P

SEVENTH Per ginger // A ditto, for so many packages, etc, giving all the details that are contained in the Inventory, number value, according to common prices, etc, so many ducats L , S , G , P

In this way you can continue to enter all the other items, making a separate entry for each different lot, and as we have said before, giving the current prices, number, marks, weights, as the Inventory shows Indicate only one kind of money, to which you reduce the estimated values In the column for the amounts, only one kind of money should appear, as it would not be proper to have appear in this column different kinds of money

You shall close each entry in the Journal by drawing a line from the end of the last word of your descriptive narrative (explanation) up to the column of the figures You shall do the same in the memorandum book, and as you transfer an entry into the Journal from the memorandum book, you shall draw a single diagonal line (*una sola riga a traverso*) through it in this way /, this will show that this item has been entered (*posta*) in the Journal

If you should not draw this line through the entry, you shall check off (*lanciarai*) the first letter of the beginning of the entry, or the last letter, as we have done at the beginning of this, or otherwise you shall use some other sign by which you will understand that the said item has been transferred into the Journal Although you may use many various and divers expressions or marks, nevertheless you must try to use the common ones which are used by the other merchants so that it will not look as if you would deviate from the usual mercantile custom

CHAPTER 13

THIRD AND LAST PRINCIPAL MERCANTILE BOOK CALLED THE LEDGER HOW IT IS TO BE KEPT ITS ALPHABET (INDEX), AND HOW THIS CAN BE KEPT SINGLE AND DOUBLE

After you have made all your entries in the Journal in an orderly way, you must transfer them to the third book, called Ledger (*Quaderno Grande*, i e, big book) This Ledger contains usually twice as many pages as the Journal In it there must be an alphabet or repertory or *"trovarello"* (finding key) according to some, the Florentines call it *"Stratto"* In this index you shall write down all the debtors and creditors in the order of their initial letter, together with the number of their respective pages You shall put the names that begin with A in the A page, etc

This Ledger, as we have said before, must bear the same sign or mark that is on the Journal and memorandum book, its pages should be numbered, and at the top at the right margin as well as at the left margin you shall put down the date On the first page you shall enter cash as debtor As in the Journal, so in the Ledger, cash should be entered on the first page It is customary to reserve the whole of the first page to cash, and not to enter anything else either under the debit (*in dare*) or the credit (*in havere*) This because the cash entries are more numerous than all others on account of almost continuously paying out and receiving money, therefore, it needs much space This Ledger must be ruled, and should have as many lines as there are kinds of money that you want to enter If you enter *lire, soldi, denari* and *picioli*, you shall draw four lines, and in front of *lire* you shall draw another line in order to put in the number of the pages of the Ledger debit and credit entries

uere se icatenano. E dinãçe farai.2.righe.p potere mettere.li di ō mano i mano. commo ne li altri q̃derni hai visto che piu non mistẽdo i q̃sto ₇c.p poter trouar p̃sto lep̃tite ₇c. E pur sira segnato croci commo li altri.

Del modo a portar le p̃tite de giornale in quaderno.e pche de una in giornale sene facia doi in quaderno: e del modo a depennare le p̃tite in giornale e de li doi numeri dele carti del quaderno che in le sue margine si pone e pche. Cap° 14.

PEr laqual cosa.sappi che di tutte le p̃tite che tu harai poste in logiornale.al quaderno grãde.te ne cõuẽ sẽpre fare doi.cioe vna in dare e laltra in hauere pche li si chiama debitore p lo. Per. E lo creditore p lo. A. cõmo disopra dicẽmo ch ō luno e de laltro.si deue da pse fare 1ª.p̃tita: q̃lla del debitore.ponere ala man sinistra. E q̃lla del creditore.ala man dextra. E in q̃lla del debitore.chiamare lacarta. doue sia q̃lla del suo creditore. E cosi in q̃lla del creditore.chiamare la carta di q̃lla doue sia. El suo debitore. E in q̃sto modo sẽpre uẽgano incatenate tutte le p̃tite del ditto q̃derno grãde. nel q̃l mai si deue mettere cosa in dare che q̃lla ancora non si ponga in hauere E cosi mai si deue mettere cosa in hauere che ancora.q̃lla medesima cõ suo amõtare nõ si metta in dare. E di qua nasci poi.albilancio che del lib°.si fa.nel suo saldo tãto cõuiẽ che sia el dare.q̃to lauere. Cioe sũmate tutte le p̃tite che sirãno poste in dare se fossero bene. 10000. da p̃te in su vn foglio. E di poi sũmate similmẽte tutte q̃lle che in hauere si trouano. tanto debbe fare luna summa q̃to laltra.altramẽte demostrarebbe eẽre errore nel ditto q̃derno.cõe nel modo del far suo bilancio se dira apieno ₇c. E cosi cõe duna de giornale ne fai.2.al q̃derno.cosi a q̃lla p̃tita che del giornale leui farai doi righe a trauerso fo che vai leuando.cioe se p².tu la metti i dare. Pria farai 1ª.riga atrauerso.verso al prin°.dela p̃tita.che dimora eẽr posta in dare al q̃derno. E se la metti in hauere.o prima.o poi cõe acade ale uolte fare al q̃dernieri q̃do li acade scriuere i luogo.ch li in q̃lla carta li nandera.2.o.3. p nõ ui hauere a tornare.sene spaça di metterle li alora. E po fo che mette cosi deue depennare p hauerla messa in hauere.farai laltra depẽnatura.verso man dextra.dal canto doue finesci la p̃tita che ō notara eẽr messa i hauere.leq̃l linee staranno cõe disopra in q̃sto uedi figurato a lap̃tita. P².dela cassa. luna ditta linea.de dare.e lalt².de hauere. E cosi dalato i margine dinançe al principio bisogna che põghi.2.nu¹.luno sotto laltro.q̃l di sopra che denoti la p̃tita.del debitore.a q̃te carti che la sia posta in lo q̃derno E q̃llo de sotto che denoti le carti de ditto q̃derno.doue sia posto el creditore.cõe vedi li ala p̃tita dela cassa disopra i q̃sto.che sta cosi.¹⁄₂. sẽça tramezo. E ancora alcuni costumano cosi cõ tramezo. ½. a guisa de rotti.che nõ fa caso. Ma e piu bello sẽça tramezo. Acio achi vede nõ paressero speççati. O vero rotti ₇c. E vol dire q̃llo.1°.di sopra che la cassa. E nella p².carta del q̃derno. El cauedale. E nella 2ª carta de ditto q̃derno.i hauere. e q̃lla in dare ₇c. E nota che sẽpre q̃to piu p̃sso tu porrai mettere elcreditore al suo debitore. sera piu liçadro.auẽga che posto doue siuoglia tanto mõti. Ma p rispetto del milesimo.che ale uolte se iterpõe fra 1ª.p̃ti².e lalt² respõde male. E cõ fatiga.nõ poca.se ritrouano lor t̃pi cõe sa chi.p̃ua ch ogni cosa cosi apieno nõ si po dire. Ma bisõ².ch ãcora tu alq̃to cõ tuo naturale ingegno ta iuti. E po sẽpre studia dasettar ditto creditore immediate a p̃sso el suo debitore in la medema faciata.o vero ila imediate seq̃nte.nõ interponẽdoui fra luno e laltro.altra p̃tita. Peroche nel.p̃prio giorno che nasci el debitore in q̃llo medemo nasci el creditore E p q̃sto rispetto sẽpre se deue acostar luno a lalt° ₇c.

Del modo a sape dittare le p̃tite de lacassa e cauedale nel quaderno in dare e hauere: e dl milesimo che disopra nel principio dela carta a lanti co si mette in esso: e dela sua mutatione e del cõptir lispacij dele carti fo le p̃tite piccole e grãdi fo elbisogno dele facẽde. Cap°. 15.

OR q̃ste cose discorse.a tuo amaestramẽto.ormai diramo la p² p̃tita de la cassa i dare e poi q̃lla del cauedal in hauere in lo libro grãde. Ma cõe e ditto p². desopra nel quaderno porrai el milesimo alabacco antico. cioe per alfabeto cosi. M cccc. Lxxxxiiij. ₇c. El di nõ se costuma mettarlo disopra in loquaderno cõe in lo giornale.pche 1°.p̃tita in quaderno.hara diuersi di. E po nõ si porra seruar ordine deli di.disopra cõe apieno nel seq̃nte cap°.se dira. Ma dẽtro dela p̃tita cõe intẽderai la p² uolta E poi cosi dalato in lo spacio che disopra dicẽmo dinançe ala p̃tita.q̃do tal p̃tita nascesse daltro milesimo che disopra nel principio dela carta fosse scritto che sole auenire achi de anno in anno nõ riporta e salda suoi libri siche tal milesimo si porra difuora.nendo in margine ripetto a põto a q̃lla p̃tita li nata cõe uedi posto qui disotto. q̃sto solo auene in lib° grande che in li altri nõ po auenire. Dõca diraai cosi.traẽdola fore pure alabacco ãtico p piu bellezza

P ii

Before these lines you shall draw two more lines wherein to mark the dates as you go on, as you have seen in the other books, so that you may find each item quickly This book shall also bear the sign of the cross as the others

CHAPTER 14

HOW THE ENTRIES SHOULD BE TRANSFERRED FROM THE JOURNAL INTO THE LEDGER AND WHY, FOR EACH ENTRY OF THE JOURNAL, YOU HAVE TO MAKE TWO IN THE LEDGER, HOW ENTRIES IN THE JOURNAL SHOULD BE CANCELLED THE TWO NUMBERS OF THE PAGES OF THE LEDGER WHICH ARE PLACED IN THE MARGIN OF EACH ENTRY AND WHY

For each one of all the entries that you have made in the Journal you will have to make two in the Ledger. That is, one in the debit (*in dare*) and one in the credit (*in havere*) In the Journal the debtor is indicated by per, the creditor by a, as we have said. In the Ledger you must have an entry for each of them The debitor entry must be at the left, the creditor one at the right, and in the debitor entry you must indicate the number of the page of the respective creditor In this way all the entries of the Ledger are chained together and you must never make a credit entry without making the same entry with its respective amount in the debit Upon this depends the obtaining of a trial balance (*bilancio*) of the Ledger

There can not be a closing (*saldo*) because there must be as much in credit as there is in debit In other words, you shall add together all the debit entries, even if there are ten thousand, on a separate sheet, and then add together in the same way all the credit entries, the totals of the one should be the same as the totals of the other, otherwise it would show that some mistake has been made in the Ledger We will speak at length about this when we talk about the way of making the trial balance (*bilancio*) And since for one entry of the Journal you make two in the Ledger, you shall draw two diagonal lines as you make the transfer—that is, if you first transfer the debit entry, you shall first draw a diagonal line (*riga a traverso*) at the beginning of the entry in the Journal which shows that the entry has been posted (*posta*) to the debit into the Ledger If you transfer the credit entry, either at this time or later, as it often happens that the bookkeeper can make two or three entries on the same page in order to prevent his coming back to write on that same page—in which case he should draw a line at the right side where the entry terminates This will show that the entry has been transferred to the credit of the Ledger These two lines, you may see in the preceding diagram, drawn in the margin by the first cash entry, the one is called debit line, and the other credit line At the side, in the marginal part, you shall write down two numbers before the beginning of the entry, the one under the other. The upper indicates at what page of the Ledger the debit entry is, and the lower indicates the page of the Ledger where the credit is, as you will see at the cash entry in the above example, like this $\substack{1\\2}$, without a line between them Some are accustomed to draw a line in between, like this, $\frac{1}{2}$ This does not matter, but it looks nicer without the line between, so that the figures will not appear to the reader as if they were fractions. The upper figure, 1, means cash was entered in the first page of the Ledger, and capital was entered in the second page of the said Ledger, the cash on the debit, and the capital on the credit side You should know that the closer to the debtor you can place the creditor, the nicer it will look It is just the same, however, no matter where it is, but it may look bad on account of the date which at times must be put between entries, and it makes it difficult then to find the dates We can not tell you everything fully, but you with your natural ingenuity must guide yourself Therefore you always try to put the said creditor immediately after its debtor on the same line or on the line immediately following without entering anything else in between, for whenever there is a debit item there must exist at the same time a credit item. For this reason, get the one as near as possible to the other

CHAPTER 15

THE WAY IN WHICH THE CASH AND CAPITAL ENTRIES SHOULD BE POSTED IN THE LEDGER IN THE DEBIT AND THE CREDIT THE DATE WHICH AT THE TOP OF THE PAGE IS WRITTEN DOWN ACCORDING TO THE ANCIENT USE CHANGING OF THE SAME HOW TO DIVIDE THE SPACE ON THE PAGES FOR SMALL AND LARGE ACCOUNTS AS THE BUSINESS REQUIRES

After having told you these things for your instruction, we write now the first entry of the cash in the debit column, and then the first entry of the capital in the credit column, in the Ledger But, as we have said, you shall write down in the Ledger the year in the old way by using the alphabet, thus MCCCCLXXXXIII, etc It is not customary to put the day at the top in the Ledger as in the Journal, because one account in the Ledger may have several dates, and therefore you can not keep the dates in order by putting them at the top, but you shall put the days in the body of the entry, as you will understand hereafter

We put the day to one side, in the space of which I have spoken, just before the entry If an item refers to a transaction which happened in a different year than that written at the top of the page, which happens when one does not balance and transfer his books at the end of each year, then this year shall be put on the side, in the margin near the entry of the item to which it refers This only happens in the Ledger, and can not happen in the other books In making this entry for the year, use the antique letters, which are neater,

non dimeno a qual che tu te caui non fa caso &c. Donca dirai cosi.

yhs. M cccc Lxxxxiij.

Cassa de cõtanti die dare a di. 8. nouẽbre. per cauedal per contanti de piu sorte fra oro e monete me trouo hauere in quella in questo presente di in tutto ca. 2. ₰. xm. ß g p̃

E qui nõ bisogna che troppo te stẽda. p hauer bẽ gia steso in giornale. Ma sempre studia dir breue. La prima nel comẽçare se dici alquanto: ale sequẽti in la medema sol se dici. e a di ditto &c. per lo tale. car. ₰ ß g p̃

La qual cosi posta che harai. depẽnarai in giornale in dare comme sopra te dissi. E poi i hauer per lo cauedal dirai cosi vz.

yhs M. cccc°. Lxxxxiii

Cauedal de mi tale &c. die hauere a di. 8. nouembre. per cassa per contanti me trouo in quella fin al di presente in ori e monete de piu sorte in tutto. car. 1. ₰. xm. ß o g o p̃ o

E cosi ancora i q̃sta basta succintamẽte dire per la cagion sopra ditta. Laltre poi che q̃ sotto ala medema p̃tita se hauerãno a porre fin che la sia piena bastara a dire. E a di tanti &c. per tal cosa &c. Cõe uedi acẽnato qui da canto. e anco in fin di q̃sto harai exemplo. cosi sequirai con breuita in tutte maxime in quelle partite che a te solo aspettano. cioe che non hai a rendere conto adalcuno. Ma in q̃lle che tu hauerai a rendere cõto adaltri al q̃to piu ti cõuerra dire. auenga che sempre se recorre. per le chiareçe al giornale &c. E poi darai laltra depẽnatura. a q̃lla del giornale in hauere. cõe sopra ti dissi in 12°. cap°. E in la margine dauanti. ala p̃tita porrai li doi numeri cõe dissi pur in ditto loco dele carti doue sõno. El debitore el creditore. cioe q̃llo del debitore de sopra. E q̃llo del creditore de sotto cõe facẽmo di sopra. ala p̃tita de la cassa. E poi subito porrai in lo tuo alfabeto. cioe repetorio. q̃sto debitore e creditore. ognuno ala sua l̃ra cõe sai che disopra dissi. Cioe la cassa. al la l̃ra. C. dicẽdo detro in q̃sto modo. cioe. Cassa de cõtanti. k 1. E ancora el cauedal porrai al. C dicendo Cauedal de mi p̃prio. k. 2. E cosi p̃ tuo ingegno ãdarai asettando. tutte le p̃tite. e li nõi de li debitori persõe e robbe &c. E cosi de creditori. porrai nel ditto repertorio. a le sue lettere acio poi con facilita possi subito retrouarli in ditto quaderno grande & cetera.

E nota che hauendo tu p̃duto el tuo q̃derno p̃ alcun caso de robaria o incẽdio di foco. o naufragiũ &c. E hauẽdo tu luno de li altri doi libri. Cioe memoriale. o vero giornale. cõ esso porrai sempre refare vnaltro q̃derno. cõ le medesime p̃tite a di p̃ di. E ponerle al numero de le medesime che i q̃l p̃so si retrouauano. Maxime hauẽdo tu el giornale. doue q̃do ne leuasti le p̃tite. E põesti al lib°. tu i margie ponesti. li doi nu°. dli debitori e creditori luño soura laltro che chiamauano le carti. del q̃derno doue erano situati. e di põto atante carti li porrai fare ritornar cõ tuo ingegno &c. E q̃sto basti q̃to a vna p̃tita posta &c. Poi la sa p̃tita che fo dele çoie al q̃derno ponẽdola a suo cõdecẽte luogo dittarai cosi. E pri°. sempre sença piu te replichi. porrai disopra nel principio dela carta. el milesimo se nõ vi fosse posto p̃ altra p̃tita. p°. poche ale uolte in vna medema facia el quaderno ci asettara. 2. o. 3. p̃tite so che cognoscera lo spatio eẽr bastãte al manegio di q̃lla. p̃che forse uedara q̃lla tale p̃tita hauersi chiare fiade adoperar. E p̃ q̃sto li dara vn luoco piu angusto. che a quelle che spesso li acade. adopare: ala giornata cõe di sopra. al cap°. 13°. de la cassa e cauedal fo detto q̃l si costumaua lasarli tutta la faciata del lib°. p̃che spessissime fiade p̃ eẽre grãdi le facẽde si conuẽgano manegiare. E q̃sto sol si fa p̃ nõ hauer tãto spesso a far reporto inãçe &c. ora al p̃posito trouato li el loco cõe se dici. dirai cosi in dare cioe verso man sinistra cosi sempre sa aporre el debito.

Zoie de piu sorte. dienno dare a di. 8. nouẽbre. p̃ cauedale p̃ peçi n° tanti &c pesano tanto &c. de quali tanti sonno balassi legati &c. E tanti safili &c. E tãti rubini cocul(e)gni &c. E tanti diamanti cregi &c. lequali in tutto. o vero a sorta per sorta metto valere a comun p̃gio. de cõtanti duc̃. tanti &c. val car. 2 ₰ 40 ß o. g o. p̃ o.

E cosi depennerai. la p̃tita in giornale nel dare tirando la linea comme de sopra al. 12°. cap°. te dissi. E poi andarai al cauedal E porrai q̃sta medema con mãco parolle per le ragion gia disopra adutte in questo capitolo e porrala in hauere sotto quella p°. che gia li hai posto dela cassa. E dirai cosi. vz.

a di o detto. per çoie de piu sorte commo li apare &c. car. 3. ₰. 40. ß o. g o. p̃ o.

E cosi posta farai laltra depẽnatura. al giornale i hauer̃. cõe te mõstrai disopra al. 12°. ca°. E porrai i margine li numeri d̃le carti doue tal p̃tite al quaderno ponesti cõmo dicemmo vno sopra laltro. comme qui denançe apare che metto habi posta la p̃tita in dar a carti. 3. E q̃lla del cauedal sta pure alogo suo a carti. 2. p̃ fin tanto che lla non e piena. che dipoi innãçe

although it does not matter very much

Thus, you shall put it this way

JESUS MCCCCLXXXXIII

Cash is debtor (*dee dare*—shall give) on November 8, "per" capital On this day I have in moneys of different kinds, gold and other coins, page 2 L Xm, S G , P ...

Here you do not need to be very lengthy if you have already given the description in the Journal Try to be very brief.

At the beginning of the page we say more, but in the entries following it is enough to say on ditto, "per" such and such, page, etc, L... , S... ... G ... , P

After you have made the entry in this way, you shall cancel in the Journal as I have explained to you Then in the credit side you shall write down this way

JESUS ... . MCCCCLXXXXIII

Capital of myself, so and so, is creditor (*dee havere*—shall have) on November 8, "per" cash On this day I have in cash, in gold and other kinds of money, page 1

This entry is also sufficient, express yourself briefly for the reason above said If there are other items to be entered in the same account, it will be enough to say, on ditto, "per" such and such, etc, as has just been shown. At the end of this treatise, I will give you an example, and thus you will go on expressing yourself briefly especially in those things which are private—that is, of which you do not have to give an account to any one But as to other things for which you have to give an account to other people, it will be better for you to be more explicit, although for explanations we always rely on the Journal Then you will cancel, by drawing a line, the credit entry in the Journal as I have said above in Chapter 12 In the margin, just opposite the entry, you shall write down the two numbers of the pages where the debit and credit entries are That is, you should put the number of the debit page above, and the number of the credit page below as we have done above in the cash entry Then you shall at once enter in the alphabet or repertory (index) this debtor and this creditor, each one under its own letter as I have told you before That is, cash at the letter C, by saying in this way· Cash, page 1 And capital also at the letter C, saying Capital belonging to me, page 2 And so on, you shall enter (in this repertory) all the creditors under their respective letters, so that you may find them easily in the Ledger mentioned

Take notice, that if by any chance you should lose this Ledger through robbery, or fire, or shipwreck, etc if you have either of the other two books, that is, the memorandum book or Journal, you can, by means of this book always make up another Ledger with the same entries, day by day, and enter them on the same pages on which they were in the last book, especially so, if you have the Journal in which, when you transferred the different entries into the Ledger, you wrote down at the margin the two numbers of the debit entry page and the credit entry page, the one above the other, which two numbers indicated the pages of the ledger where the two entries had been entered In this way you can duplicate your Ledger This is enough said for the posting of one entry

For the second entries, which pertains to precious stones, you shall enter in the Ledger as follows

FIRST, without my telling it to you over again, you shall write down at the top of the page the date, if there has been no date written before because of another account, for at times on the same page two or three accounts are made Sometimes you won't give much space to one special account because you know that you will not have to use that account over again Therefore you will give to this account a smaller space than the space you give to other accounts which you had to use more, as we have said above in Chapter 13, when talking about cash and capital, to which we give the whole page, as we have to use these two accounts very often because of the many transactions This is done in order to lessen transfers

Now then, after you have found the proper place (in the ledger), you shall write down on the left—because the debtor must always be at the left Precious stones of many kinds debit (*dienno dare*—shall give), on November 8, per capital, for so many pieces etc, weighing so much, so many are counted *balassi*, etc, and so many sapphires, etc, and so many rubies, etc, and so many unpolished diamonds in bulk (or divide the different kinds), for a value of so many ducats, page 2 L40, S0, G0, P0

You shall cancel this item in the Journal on the debit side by drawing a line as I have told you in Chapter 12 And then you will go to capital and you shall enter this entry with fewer words, for the reasons above expressed in this chapter, writing it down on the credit side under the first entry that you have already made, and you shall express yourself this way

On the day, or ditto, for precious stones of several kinds, as it appears at page 3 L40, S0, G0, P0

After which you shall draw another line on the credit side of the Journal, as I have shown in Chapter 12, you shall put down in the margin the two numbers of the pages of the Ledger in which you have made these entries, one above the other, as I have told you We shall say, for instance, that you have entered the debit entry at page 3, the capital entry will still appear at page 2, as long as that page is not filled

a tutte laltre la porrarai. cõme disotto ne reporti intẽderai apieno. E q̃sto p q̃sta. e a sue simi
lie na bastãte 7c. E posta che larai al ditto q̃derno. E asettata in giornale. e tu subito lapor
rai al reptorio o vero alfabeto. cõe disopra ĩ q̃sto cap° fo detto. Cioe ala sua lr̃a. G. o vero.
Z. fo p che lr̃a la pferirai. cõe idiuersi paesi acade. che qui ĩ uinegia molto si costuma pone
re el. Z. doue noi in toscana ponemo el g. siche acordarala tu a tuo Judicio 7c.

Cõe se debino dittare le ptite delemercantie che per inuentario o altro modo lhomo se ri
troua nel quaderno in dare e in hauere. Cap°. 16°.

P E altre. 4. ptite poi su sequẽti del tuo mobile. cioe argẽti. pãni. lini. letti de piuma
E veste de dosso 7c. Poi p te stesso facilmẽte mettarai del iuẽtario in giornale de
põto cõe li le ponesti. denotate. p che cõe dicẽmo disopra cap°. 6° q̃sto tal inuenta
rio nõ si caua del memoriale. p la ragiõe li asegnata E p suo dittare in giornale
E ancora nel grã lib° ĩ dare e hauere. e di porre ala fabeto. lasciaro or mai seq̃re al tuo pegri
no ingegno del q̃l molto me cõfido E solo la. 7ª. ptita de çẽçer mechini che ti troui asettare
nõ igiornale. E ancora al q̃derno laq̃l te fia bastãte e sufficiẽte amaestramẽto a tutte le altre
che di mercãtia alcun . . . e ritrouasse hauẽdo sẽpre tu da te ĩnãçe gli occhi lor n°. pesi. e misure e
valute ĩ tutti li modi che tal mercãtie se costumasse vẽdere. e cõprare fra mercãti ĩ rialto o fo
ra. fo li paesi. dele q̃li cose q̃ apieno nõ e possibile ponere exẽpli ma cõ facilita. da q̃sti pochi
q̃ cõpẽdiosamẽte posti porrai di q̃lũcaltri ĩprẽdere a tua sufficiẽça p che se noi volẽmo dar
te exẽplo del modo verso e via. di mercare a trani. lecia. bari. E betõta. cioe a lor nomi d pesi lo
ro. E misure loro 7c. E cosi dela marca. E anche dela nr̃a toscana. troppo serebbe grãde el
volume. che cõ breuita itendo concludere E p q̃lla. 7°. de çẽçer nel giornale. dirẽ cosi. vz.
Per çençeri mechini ĩ mõte a refuso. o ĩ colli dirai cõe a te pare 7c. Al ditto che sintẽde caue
dal. p che li disopra imediate larai p ordine de ditte iuẽtario cõe dicẽmo disopra cap°. 12°.
in la ptita sa de le çoie. p colli tanti pesano. 7c. E p. lb. tante q̃ndo fossero arefusso ĩ mõte 7c.
q̃li me retrouo hauere in lemani al di p̃nte metto di comũ corso valere el c°. o vero la lb. 7c.
duc. tanti 7c. mõtano in tutto netti duc. tanti 7c. val lb s g p̃

E cosi posta ch larai nel giornale. E tu al memoriale. o vero inuẽtario. la dipẽna. e lãca al
modo ditto sopª. al. 12°. cap° 7c. E cosi obseruarai p tutte laltr°. 7c. Di q̃sta cõe fo detto e de q̃lũ
che altra che ĩ giornale si metta. sẽpre al gran lib°. si fanno doppie. cioe 1ª. ĩ dare. e laltra ĩ ha
uere cõe disopra dicẽmo cap. 14°. La qual poi nel quaderno in dare. ponendola dittarala ĩ
q̃sto modo. Posto pª. sẽpre el millesimo se nõ ui fosse in capo de la carta. sẽça mettarui el gior
no disopra po che cõe dicẽmo disopra cap. 15°. El di nõ si costuma porre sopra nel princ° de
la carta del quaderno p rispetto che in q̃lla medesima facia potrebono eẽre piu ptite d diuer
si debitori e creditori lequali bẽche le nascano sotto vn millesimo. Ma siranno in diuersi me
si e çorni. cõe discorrẽdo p tutto poi aprendere. E q̃ndo bene ancora in ditta facia del libro
grande nõ vi fosse altro che 1ª. sola ptita di cassa. o daltro ancora el çorno posto disopra nel
quaderno nõ si porrebbe seruare p che in ditta ptita. ocorira di mettere casi ocorsi in diuersi
mesi E di e p q̃sto e che li antichi disopra nel quaderno nõ hano ĩ libri mercãteschi vsitato
mettere el giorno p che non hano ueduto verso ne via ne modo che con uerita si possa aset
tarcilo 7c. La qual partita in dare cosi porrai dicẽdo 7c.

Zençeri me chini. in monte o uero colli 7c dien dare a di 8. nouembre per cauedal. per colli
tanti 7c pesano. lb. tante 7c. quali mi trouo hauere in casa o uero magaçen al presente qual
de comun corso stimo valere el cento 7c. duc. tanti 7c. E per tutti monta duc. g p̃. 7c. val
carti. 2. lb s g° p̃

E cosi depennarai la partita del çornale in dare. cioe a man senestra cõme piu uolte to dit
to E poi in hauere asettarala in q̃sto modo al cauedal comme te monstrai ponere quella
dele çoie sopra a cap°. 15° cosi vz.

a di o detto per çençeri mechini in monte o vero colli 7c. car. 3 lb s g° p̃.

E cosi posta che lharai depennarai la partita del giornale in hauere cioe verso mande
stra cõe dinançe vedi fatto. E poni li numeri dele carti dinãçe alei in margine vno sopra lal
tro. Cioe el. 3. disopra el 2 disotto p che tu hai messo el debitore a carti. 3 nel quaderno. el cre
ditore e a 2 Cioe el capital e subito poi la metti in alfabeto. o vero reptorio ala sua lr̃a. Cioe
al Z. se p Z. la cõpiti o vero al G. p la rasõ ditta in lo p̃cedẽte ca°. a q̃lla ptita sa dele çoie 7c.

Del modo a tenere conto con li officii publici: e perche: e de la camera delimpresti in ve
netia che se gouerna per via de sestieri. Cap° 17°

p iu

This example will guide you in other cases

After you have made the entries in the Ledger and marked it in the Journal, you shall put it at once in the index as I have told you above in this chapter—that is, under the letter G or Z, according as to how *Gioie* (stone) is pronounced. In Venice the custom is to pronounce it with Z, in Tuscany, with G Guide yourself according to your own understanding

CHAPTER 16

HOW THE ENTRIES RELATIVE TO THE MERCHANDISE OF WHICH ONE IS POSSESSED ACCORDING TO HIS INVENTORY, OR OTHERWISE, SHOULD BE MADE IN THE LEDGER BOTH IN THE DEBIT AND THE CREDIT

You will be able to transfer easily by yourself from the Inventory to the Journal the four items of your personal goods—that is, silver, linen, feather beds, clothes, etc, exactly as you write them in the Inventory, as we explained in Chapter 6 This Inventory was not contained in the memorandum book, for the reasons therein expressed

And as to how to make these entries in the Journal and the Ledger, and as to how to record them in the Index, I will leave to your ability, on which I count very much

We shall proceed to enter in the Journal, as well as in the Ledger, the seventh item (of the Inventory), which pertains to Ginger This must be a sufficient instruction for you by which to make any other entry relative to your merchandise You should always have in mind their number, weights, measurements and values according to the different ways in which it is customary to make purchases or sales among merchants in the Rialto, or elsewhere It is not possible to give here full examples for all these operations, but from those few that we give here you will be able to understand how to go ahead in any other case For if we wanted to give you an example of all the ways in which merchants do business in Trani, Lecce, Bari and Bitonto—that is, to give you the names of their weights, measurements, etc, and also to tell you about the ways that they use them in Marca and in our Tuscany, this would make our treatise very long, which, on the contrary, I intend to make short

As to this seventh item to be entered in the Journal, we shall proceed thus Per Ginger in bulk or package—you shall express yourself as you like— // a ditto—by which capital is understood, because you have already mentioned it in the entry immediately preceding, when you entered your second item from the inventory, that is, precious stones—as we said in Chapter 12—I possess on this day so many packages weighing so much, or I possess so many pounds, if in bulk, according to the current prices, of a value by the hundred or by the pound, of so many ducats, in total I give them the value of so many ducats

L... ,S... ,G ,P ...

After you have entered it in the Journal in this way, you shall cancel it in the memorandum book or inventory, as we have said in Chapter 12, and you shall do the same for the other items Of this entry, as we have said, as well as of any entry made in the Journal, you shall make two different entries in the Ledger, that is, one in the debit and the other in the credit —See Chapter 14 In making the entry in the Ledger in the debit, you shall proceed in this way First you shall put the year, in case there is none, at the top of the page, without there putting down the day, for, as we have said in Chapter 15, it is not customary to put down the day at the beginning of the page of the Ledger because on that same page several entries may be made under the debit and credit which, while belonging to the same year, refer to transactions made in different months and days Even if on that page of the Ledger there was only one cash entry or other entry, the day put at the top of the page could not be very well kept because, under the said entry, it would be necessary to write down transactions which happened in different months and days For this reason the ancient people never put the day at the top of the pages in mercantile ledgers, as they saw that there was no justification for it, etc

You shall make this entry in the debit (in the Ledger) in the following manner Ginger in bulk, or so many packages, debit (*dee dare*—shall give) on November 8 per capital, for so many pieces, weighing so many pounds, which I on this day have in my store, or at home in my house, and which according to current prices are worth so many ducats and in total so many *ducats, grossi, picioli*, etc , Page 2

L ,S ,G ,P ...

Then you shall cancel this entry on the debit side of the Journal—that is, at the left, as I have told you often, and then you shall enter it on the credit side under Capital, as I have shown you in entering the precious stones item in Chapter 15, that is

On ditto per Ginger in bulk or packages, etc , Page 3 L ,S ,G ,P

After you have entered it in this way, you shall cancel the entry on the credit side of the Journal—that is, at the right—as I have shown you before, and you shall also write down at the margin the numbers of the respective pages of the Ledger one above the other—that is, three above and two below, as you have made the debit entry at Page 3 and the credit entry at Page 2, and you shall thereafter enter it in the alphabet or repertory under its respective letter, which may be Z or G, for the reasons given in the preceding chapter

CHAPTER 17

HOW TO KEEP ACCOUNTS WITH PUBLIC OFFICES, AND WHY THE CAMERA DE L'IMPRESTI (MUNICIPAL LOAN BANK) IN VENICE, WHICH IS MANAGED BY *SESTIERI* (DISTRICTS)

Hora de laltre nō te ne do. altra norma. cioe di q̄lla de pellami. da fodre cōçe e cru
de. e fine 7c̄. dele quali a 1ª. p 1ª. formarai la ptita in giornale e quaderno p ordie
depēnando. e segnando in tutti li lochi che non tescordi. perche al mercante bi-
sogna altro ceruello. che de beccaria 7c̄. Quella dela camera di presti o dal-
tro mōte cōe in firença. el mōte dele dote i genoa li lochi o uero altri officii che si fossero cō
liquali tu hauesse a fare. per alcuna cagione fa che sempre con loro tu habia buono scōtro.
de dare e de hauere in tutti li modi con qualche chiareçça se possibile e de man deli scriuani
di q̄lli luochi q̄l tiē sotto bona custodia al modo che dele scritture e lettere te diro. pche a q̄
sti tali officii spesso se sogliano mutare scriuani. liq̄li ognuno a sua fantasia uole guidare lili
bri delo officio. biasimādo sempre li scriuan passati. che non teneuan bon ordine 7c̄. E sem-
pre ognuno psuade el suo ordine megliore deli altri. imodo che ale volte incrociano le ptite.
de tali officii. che non sene tien 1ª. cō laltra. E guai chi cōtali a afare. E po fa che sia a casa. E
col capo aborega. cō q̄sti tali. E certamēte forsi el fāno a bon fine nō dimeno mostrāo igno
rāça. E cosi tirrai cōto. cō li gabellari. e datiari de robbe che tu uēdi e cōpri. caui e metti nele
terre 7c̄. Cōe si costuma fare in vinegia. che si tiene p li piu dela terra. cōto lōgo cō lo officio
dela messetaria. chi a. 2. p. c°. E chi a 1ª. p c°. E chi a. 4. p c°. 7c̄. Chiamando el libro. del sen-
saro. che vi si interpone e notare al tuo libro. E anche la mare. in su ch fa. cioe el lib° doue da
in nota li mercati al ditto officio che cosi lo chiamano in venetia po che ciascuno sensaro a
vn suo libro. o uero luogo in qualche libro al ditto officio doue lui va a dare in nota li mercati
che fa si cōterrieri. cōe forestieri altramēte caçano in pena. saltramēte facessaro. E sonno pri
uati. E bene q̄lla excelsa. S. li castiga e loro. e scriuani ch mal si portasero cōe de molti me ri
cordo. gia neli tpi passati eēre puniti stranamēte. E po santamente fanno a constituire vno
elq̄le a solo q̄sta cura. in reuedere tutti li officii. cioe se li loro lib¹. sōno bñ. o uero male tenuti 7c̄.

Comme se debia tener conto con lo officio dela messetaria in venetia e del dittare le sue partite in memoriale. giornale e quaderno. e ancora deli impresti. Cap°. 18.

Si che q̄do vorai cō tali offitii tener conto. la camera de impresti. farai debitrici
de tutta la sorte de caueddali a tanto el c°. 7c. Noiando li sestieri doue son posti. E
similmente se piu a la giornata. ne cōprasse che molti se ne vendano p te o p altri
cōe sa chi realto vsa. Nota bñ inche sōno scritti e luoghi. 7c̄. E cosi nel scorere li
loro p. sēpre farala creditrici. a di p di. E sestier p sestieri 7c̄. E cosi cō lo offitio dela messetaria
El cōto tirrai i q̄sto modo cioe q̄do tu comprarai alcuna mercantia p meçço d̄ sēsari. alora
de tutto lo amōtare. a rasone de. 2. o de. 3. o de. 4. 7c̄. p c°. farane creditore el ditto officio dela
messetaria. E debitrici q̄lla tale mercantia. p la q̄l cagione tu paghi 7c̄. E po conuene che l cō
pratore sempre ritēga al uēditore nel pagamēto. de contanti. o vero p altro modo che labia
a satisfare non fa caso. pche l ditto officio. non vol andar cercando altro senon la rata che li
aspetta. auenga che li sensari reportino el mercato in nota. cōmo. e ch. e cho. le stato fatto. per
chiareççe euidēte de contracti q̄do fra loro. nascesse differença alcuna cōe acade. El comun
puerbio dici. chi non fa non falla e chi non falla non impara 7c̄. delequali dēe uolendose le pti
chiarire hano regresso al mercato notato. p lo sensaro. al quale p li decreti publici li si psta
fede cōe a publico instrumento de notaro. E p la forma di q̄llo. el piu dele volte. El degno
offitio de consoli de mercanti. formano le loro iuridiche sentençe 7c̄. Dico adonca compran-
do tu alcuna robba. tu dic sape. q̄llo che la paga de m̄. E p la mita retieni. al uenditore. Cioe
se la robba paga. 4. p c°. a q̄llo officio p decreto publico del dominio. E tu a lui retieni. 2. p c°.
E tanto manco li conta. E hara el suo douere. E tu poi del tutto resti obligato al ditto offi-
tio. E del tutto larai a far creditore al tuo libro contādo cō lui E q̄lla tal mercantia farai dbi
trici. cōe dicēmo 7c̄. pche el ditto offitio non uol cercare. chi vende. ma chi compra. E po poi
a tal compratori li e concesso di cauare tanto di q̄lla mercantia. p q̄to a pagato la m̄. fora d̄
la terra. in loro bolette. ala tauola. de luscita. o per mare o p terra che la uogliono cauare ala
giornata. E po conuēgano li mercanti tenere ben conto con lo ditto officio. acio sempre sa-
pino q̄to possino cauare pche non si lassano cauar. per piu che si comprino se di nouo non
paghino la m̄. de contanti 7c̄ delequali compre q̄ sequente ti pongo exēplo e cosi del ditto
officio. comme se habino a dittare in giornale. E anche in libro grande. E diro cosi. Pri
ma. in memoriale. semplicemente. Io o vero noi in questo di posto di sopra o comprato da s
zuan antonio da mesina çucari palermini cassi n°. tante pani n°. tanti. pesano in tutto. netti.
de panelle cassi. corde. e paglie tante per duc. tāti. el c°. montano duc. tāti 7c. abatto per la
sua parte dela m̄ a ragion de tanto per c°. duc. g. p̄. tanti 7c. sensaro s zuan de gagliardi. vale
netti ducati. g. p̄. tanti 7c. pagammo contanti.

I shall not give you any more rules for the other items—that is, leather goods for coverings, tanned or raw, etc, for each of which you shall make entries in the Journal and Ledger, carefully writing down everything and checking off, etc, without forgetting anything, because the merchant must have a much better understanding of things than a butcher.

If you have accounts with the Camera de L'Imprestı, or with other banks, as in Florence, or with the Monte de La Dote, in Genoa, as well as similar offices or bureaux with which you have business, see that you keep these accounts very clearly and obtain good written evidence as to debits and credits in the handwriting of the clerks in those institutions This advice you will carefully follow, for reasons to be explained in chapter on documents and letters Because in these offices they often change their clerks, and as each one of these clerks likes to keep the books in his own way, he is always blaming the previous clerks, saying that they did not keep the books in good order, and they are always trying to make you believe that their way is better than all the others, so that at times they mix up the accounts in the books of these offices in such way that they do not correspond with anything Woe to you if you have anything to do with these people Therefore, be very careful when dealing with them, and be observant at home and keep your head in the store Maybe they mean well, nevertheless they may show ignorance In this way you shall keep accounts with the *Gabellari* and *Datiarii* (revenue officers) as to the things that you might sell or buy, things that you grow, things that you plant, etc, as it is the custom in Venice where people are used to keeping an account through the office of the *Messetaria* (market master or exchange), some at 2%, some at 1%, some at 4% You should mention the book of the broker through whom the transaction was made, and also mention the special mark that the broker has in this book—that is, the book in which he makes a record of the market transaction at said office which they call "*Chiamans*" in Venice For each broker has a book in the said office, or a place in some book in the said office, in which he has to make a record of all the transactions which he has with the citizens of the town or with outsiders If the broker should not do that he would be fined and dismissed

And justly the glorious republic of Venice punishes them and their clerks who should misbehave I know of many who in the past years have been heavily punished, and right they are in having one officer whose only duty is to oversee all these officers and their books whether they are well kept or not, etc

CHAPTER 18

HOW YOU SHOULD KEEP YOUR ACCOUNTS WITH THE OFFICE OF THE *MESSETARIA* IN VENICE HOW TO MAKE ENTRIES PERTAINING THERETO IN THE MEMORANDUM BOOK, JOURNAL AND LEDGER, AND ABOUT LOANS

When you want to do business with the said offices, you shall always charge to the Camera de L'Imprestı (municipal loan bank) so many per cent on all your funds or capital, naming the district where one resides Likewise, for the amount of the daily sales for many are the sales made for you or for others, as those people know who are familiar with the Rialto Be careful to put down the name of the party that buys and his place of business, etc When you withdraw said funds, you shall always credit the said bank, day by day and district by district

In doing business with the office of the *Messetaria* (exchange), you shall keep the account in this way When you buy any merchandise through brokers, you shall credit the said office of the *Messetari* with the 2% or 3% or 4% of the whole amount, and shall charge it to that specific merchandise, for you are thus paying for it, etc Therefore the buyer, when he makes his payments to the seller, should always retain that percentage, no matter whether the payments are made in cash or otherwise, as the said office does not concern itself about anything except the rate (%) to which it is entitled The brokers make a report of the transaction, how and what for and with whom made, in order to have things clear in case any question should arise, which may happen

A common proverb says Who does nothing, makes no mistakes, who makes no mistakes learns nothing, etc.

If any question should arise and the parties wish to settle it, they would go and examine the records of the transaction made by the broker, to which records, according to the public decrees, as full faith is given as to a public notarial document, and according to these records very often the office of the Consuls of the merchants issues its judgment.

I say, then, when you buy anything, you must always know what is due to the *Messetaria,* and you withhold half of this from what you pay to the seller, that is, if the particular thing that you buy is subject to a 4% payment to that office, as per public decrees of the Republic, you withhold 2% of what you give to the seller You give him that much less in order that he receives what is due him You then will become a debtor for the whole amount which is due the said office, and you shall credit the said office with it in your Ledger when you keep an account with that office and charge it to the goods that you have bought, as we have said, because that office does not interest itself in the party who sells out, but in the party who buys In accordance with this, the buyer will be allowed to take out of the official warehouses merchandise in proportion to the brokerage paid and according to their books kept at the shipping counter, whether it came by land or sea Therefore, the merchants should keep a careful account with the said office so that they know how much merchandise they can take out They are not allowed to take out more than they have bought unless they have paid the extra brokerage

Of these purchases, I will give you here an example and how the transaction with the said office must be recorded in the Journal and in the Ledger First, you shall express yourself in the memorandum book in the following manner

I (or we), on this day above mentioned, have bought of Mr Zuan Antonio, of Messina, so many boxes of Palermo sugar and so many loaves of the net weight—that is, without the boxes, wrappers, ropes and straw—so many pounds at so many ducats per hundred, I deduct for what is due to the *Messetaria* at the rate of so much per cent, so many *ducats, grossi, picioli,* etc. The broker was Mr Zuan de Gaiardi, net value, so many *ducats, grossi, picioli,* paid in cash.

La medesima in giornale dira cosi   a contanti.

Per çucari de palermo. A cassa contanti a ser çuan de antonio da mesina. per cassi n°. tante pani n°. tanti. pesano netti. de cassi. panelle. corde e paglie lb. tante. a duc. tanti el c°. montano duc. tanti &c. abatto. p la sua parte de la m̃ a rason de tanti per c°. &c. duc. tanti &c. restano netti. duc. tanti &c. sensar ser çuan de gaiardi.   lb s g p

La medesima in quaderno dira cosi

Zucari de palermo diẽ dare. adi tale. p cassa contanti a ser çuan dantonio de mesina. per panni numero tanti pesano netti. lb. tante per duc. tanti el cento. montano netti in tutto a carti 1ª.

E farai creditrice la cassa di quel tanto &c.   lb s g p

E sempre farai lofficio de la m̃. creditore del doppio che tu retenesti al suo creditore. cioe p la sua e p la tua pte. &c. E sẽpre subito notato la robba imediate i vn altro. ptita sotto farai creditore ditto officio per ditto çucaro cõe harai disotto. E debitrici ditta robba. Per exemplo duna pagata a contanti. Or prendine vna pte a cõtanti e parte a tẽpo p°. i memoriale cosi dirai.

A contanti e tempo. a di tanti &c.

Io o comprato a di detto da ser çuan dantonio. da mesina. çucari de palermo pani n°. tanti. pesano netti. lb. tante per duc. tanti el c°. montano duc. tanti abatto per sua parte de m̃. a rasõ de tanti per c°. duc. tanti &c. de quali al presente. li no contati duc. tãti p parte e del resto mi fa tẽpo fin tutto agosto pxi° che uien &c. sensar ser çuan de gaiardi val   duc.   g p

E sappi che de q̃lle cose che se scriue mercato per lo sensaro a lofficio non bisogna far scritto de man. perche el mercato basta. ma pure a cautela ale uolte si fa &c.

In giornale la medema dira cosi. prima quel tal de tutto creditore. E poi debitore de q̃lla parte de d. che lui haue.

yhs.   1493. a di tanti del tal mese &c.

Per çucari palermini: A ser çuan dantonio de mesina per pani numero tanti pesano netti in tutto lb. tante. a duc. tanti el c°. montano duc. tanti &c abatto per la sua pte de messetaria a rason de tanti per c°. duc. tanti &c. resta netto duc. tanti &c de quali al presente li ne debo contar tanti &c. E del resto. mi fa termine fin tutto agosto proximo che vien. sensaro ser çuan de gaiardi. val.   lb s g p

Fanne creditore subito lofficio de la m̃ de la sua rata

Per li ditti: a lofficio de la m̃ per la montar soura ditto. cioe de duc. tãti &c a rasõ de tãti p c°. p la mia parte e q̃lla del debitore i tutto monta duc g. p tanti val.   lb s g p

La parte de contanti. debitor lui. E creditore la cassa. cosi

Per ser çuan dãtonio. de misina: A cassa cõtati a lui p pte de li soura ditti çucari fo la forma dl mercato. duc tãti &c. ape del receuere scritto de sua mano val.   lb s g p

La medema in quaderno dira cosi.

Zucari de palermo. dien dare a di tal di nouembre. per ser çuan dantonio da mesina per pani n°. tãti pesano netti lb tante &c. p duc. tanti el c° mõtano netti de m̃. K. 4.   lb s g p

Quando uolesse farne partita nuoua. Ma uolendo sequitare la preposta bastaua dire a di. tanti &c. per ser çuan dant°. da mesina p pani n° tãti pesano lb tãte &c. mõta. K. 4.   lb s g p

La medema in hauere dira cosi

Ser çuan dãtonio de mesina die hauere a di tanti de nouembre. per çucari de palermo pani n°. tanti pesan netti lb tante per duc tanti el c°. montano. netti de m̃ duc tanti de quali al presente li ne debio dar contanti duc. tanti &c. del auanço. mi fa tẽpo per tutto agosto pxio futuro. sensar ser çuan de gagliardi val   K 4.   lb s g p

In dare la medema. Per la parte deli contanti dira cosi.

Ser çuan al incontro. die dare a di. tale &c. p cassa. cõtati a lui p pte de çucari hebi da lui son i patti duc. tanti &c. ape p suo scritto de man in libreto val.   K 1ª.   lb s g p

La medema. a la m̃. e anche per la precedente i quaderno cosi

Offõ. de la m̃. die hauer a di tal p çucari de palermo cõprai da ser çuan danto°. de mesina p la montare de duc. tãti. a tãti p c°. sensar ser çuan de gaiardi monta   K. &c   lb s g p

Comino se debia ordinare el pagamento che hauesse a fare per ditta e banco ò scritta ne li tuoi libri principali: Cap°. 19.

E Cosi p tal cõpre. q̃sta ti basta a guidarte. o sia a tutti cõtanti. o a pte cõtanti. E p tempo. o cõtati e ditta o tutti in banco. o cõtanti e banco o cõtãti. E robbe. o robba e ditta. o tutta ditta o robbe. e tẽpo. o robba e banco. o banco e tẽpo o bãco e ditta. o banco. cõtanti. ditta e robbe &c. poche i tutti q̃sti modi. se costuma cõprare. le q̃li tu per te. al sẽso de la pcedẽte metteraile i memoriale. E driçarale i giornale. e quaderno.

p iiij

The same should be entered in the Journal in the following manner

Per Palermo sugar // A cash Cash paid to Mr Zuan Antonio of Messina for so many boxes and so many loaves, of the net weight—that is, without the boxes, wrappers, ropes and straw—so many pounds, at so many ducats per hundred, it amounts to so many ducats, I deduct what is due to the *Messetaria* at so much per cent, so many ducats, etc, net residue, so many ducats, etc The broker was Mr Zuan de Gaiardi. L , S , G , P

In the Ledger you shall make the entries as follows

Palermo sugar debit (*dee dare* or shall give) cash Cash paid to Mr Zuan Antonio of Messina for so many boxes and so many loaves, weighing, net, so many pounds at so many ducats per hundred, which amounts to—Page 1 L , S , G P

And you shall credit cash with the same amount, and shall always credit the *Messetaria* with twice the amount which you withhold from the price paid to the seller—that is, for the commission due by the seller and by you

Immediately after, you shall make another entry crediting the said office with the said sugar and charging the said merchandise This will do for a purchase by cash Now we shall consider one made partly in cash and partly on time

First, in the memorandum book you shall say as follows By cash and on time on such and such day, I have bought on the said date of Mr Zuan Antonio of Messina so many loaves of Palermo sugar, weighing net so many pounds, at so many ducats per hundred, making a total of so many ducats This is in part payment, for the rest I shall have time to pay until the whole month of August next, etc The broker was Mr. Zuan Gaiardi D , G P

You must understand that you do not need to have a written paper containing the terms of the transaction, for the broker shall record that in the said Office This record is enough for you, but as a precaution, sometimes people require a contract

You will make the entry in the Journal as follows First you shall credit Mr So-and-So for the total amount, and then charge him for the money that he has received

JESUS 1493

On such and such a day of such and such month, etc, per Palermo sugar // A Mr Zuan Antonio, of Messina, for so many loaves, weighing net so many pounds at so many ducats per hundred, making a total of so many ducats, deducting for his share of the brokerage at so much per cent, so many ducats, leaving a net balance of so many ducats of which now I have to pay so many, and as to the rest I have time until the end of next August The broker was Mr Zuan de Gaiardi, value L , S , G , P

Immediately after, credit the office of the *Messetaria* with the commission due to it Per ditto // A Office of the *Messetaria* For the amount above mentioned—that is, so many ducats at the rate of so much per cent for my share and for the share of the debtor (seller), in all amounting to so many *ducats, grossi, picioli* value L S , G P

For the cash payment, you shall charge him and credit cash in the following manner

Per Mr Zuan Antonio of Messina // A cash By cash paid him for part payment of said sugar according to the terms of the transaction, so many ducats, as it appears from his receipt written in his own handwriting. Value L , S , G , P

In the Ledger you shall write down as follows

Palermo sugar debit (*dee dare*—shall give) on such and such a day of November, per Zuan Antonio of Messina, for so many loaves, weighing net so many pounds, etc at so many ducats per hundred, making a total, net of the brokerage, Page 4 L , S , G , P

These items shall be entered in the credit column as follows

Mr Zuan Antonio of Messina credit (*dee havere*—shall have), per Palermo sugar so many loaves weighing net so many pounds, at so many ducats per hundred, amounting, net of the brokerage, so many ducats, of which I must now pay so many ducats, and for the rest I have time until the end of next August Broker, Mr Zuan de Gaiardi, Page 4, value L , S , G , P

For the cash payment you shall put in the debit column

Mr Zuan, debit (*dee dare*—shall give) on such and such a day, etc, per cash to him paid for part payment on sugar—I received from him according to our agreement—so many ducats, as it is shown by his own handwriting in his book, page 1 L , S , G , P

The account of the *Messetaria* in the Ledger shall be as follows

Office of the *Messetaria*, credit (*dee havere*—shall have), on such and such day, per Palermo sugar bought from Mr Zuan Antonio, of Messina, for the amount of so many ducats at so many ducats per hundred Broker, Mr Zuan de Gaiardi, Page, etc L , S G , P

CHAPTER 19

HOW WE SHOULD MAKE THE ENTRIES IN OUR PRINCIPAL BOOKS OF THE PAYMENTS THAT WE HAVE TO MAKE EITHER BY DRAFT OR THROUGH THE BANK

And as to the purchases, this should be sufficient to guide you, whether the payment of the purchase should be made all in cash or part in cash and part on time, or part in cash or part by bill of exchange or draft (*ditta*), or all through the bank, or part in cash and part through the bank, or part through the bank and part on time, or part through the bank and part by bill of exchange, or part through the bank, part in cash, part by bill of exchange and part by merchandise, etc

For in all these ways it is customary to make purchases, and in each case you shall make entries, first in the Day Book, then in the Journal, then in the Ledger, taking as a guide the foregoing example

Mā q̄do hai a far pagamēto a p̄te bāco e ditta. Fa ch p°. cōsegni la ditta. e poi p re°. scriui i banco. p piu figurta vnde ancora q̄sta cautella s'usa p molti e bene. q̄do ben pagassero ḋ contanti. de far per resto in bancho. E p cōpito pagamēto ꝛc̄. E pagandolo p̄te. banco p̄te. robba. parte ditta e parte cōtanti. de tutte q̄ste faralo debitore. E q̄lle tal cose farale creditrici ognuna al suo luogo ꝛc̄. E se per altri modi te acadesse cōprare. per simili te gouerna. ꝛc̄

E hauēdo inteso el corso ḋl cōprare p tanti uersi p̄nderai el vēdere tuo ad altri. facēdoli debitori. e creditrici le tue robbe. E debitrici la cassa. se ti da contanti. e ḋbitrici le ditte se te le cōsegna in pagamēto. E creditore. el banco. se tel da. E cosi di tutto p ordine cōe disopra e ditto ḋl cōprare. E lui de tutto q̄llo ti da in pagamēto faralo creditore ꝛc̄. e q̄sto ti basti a q̄sta materia a tua instructiōe ꝛc̄. Dele p̄tite famose e p̄ticulari nel maneggio traficāte cōe sono baratti cōpagnie ꝛc̄. cōe le se habbino a settare e ordinare neli libri mercātesch e p°. ḋ li baratti sēplici cōposti e col tēpo cō apti exēpli ḋ tutti i memoriale. giornale e q̄der°. Ca. 20.

Equa. douer dar modo cōe se habino asettar alcūe p̄tite famose p̄ticulari ch ne li maneggii traficāti si sogliano el piu dele volte solēnizare. E metterle dap se acio di q̄lle distinte dal altre. se ne possa cognoscere el p e dāno che di q̄lle seq̄sse cōe sono li baratti e le cōpag°. viaggi recomādati. viaggi i sua mano cōmissiōe hauute p altri banchi de scritta. o vero ditta. Cābi reali. Ducicōto de botega ꝛc̄. delcq̄li q̄ seq̄ēte succitamēte a tua bastança. te daro notitia. cōe le debi guidare. e reggere neli tuoi libri ordinatamēte acio nō te abagli in tue facēde E p°. mostraremo cōe se debia asettare 1°. baratto. Sono li baratti cōmunamēte de. 3. sorte cōe disopra in le ractiō fo detto. Distictio. 9ª. T. 3°. carti 161. fin in 167. apieno si chi li recorri a itenderli. Dico adōca che in tutti uersi che te acadesse scriuere i lib° el baratto. sēpre puramēte. p°. in lo memoriale debi narrarlo ad li9 in der°. dela p̄tita cō tutti suo modi e condiriōi chel sira stato fatto e cōcluso. o começani o fra voi soli. E q̄do sarai cosi narrato. E tu poi ala fine riduralo i su li cōtanti. E so che q̄lle tal robbe veder ai ualere. a cōtanti p tāto tirarai fora la p̄ti°. a che moneta si voglia i memoriale che non fa caso poche poi el q̄dernieri la redura tutta a 1ª sorta al auttētico. cioe q̄do la mettara al giornale. E al q̄derno grāde ꝛc̄. E q̄sto si fa p che cauādo tu fori le valute dele robbe a q̄l che ti stanno a baratto. nō potresti neli tuoi cōti. e scripture cognoscere sēça grādissima difficulta. tuo vtile. o vero p̄dita sequita. La q̄li sēpre cōuiēsi redure a cōtanti p volerle ben cognoscere. ꝛc̄. E se di tali mercātie hauute p baratti: volessi da p̄te p̄ticularmēte tenerne cōto. p poder veder il suo retratto. separamēte da lalt°. robbe che di tal sorta hauesse p°. in casa. o che da poi cōprasse p cognoscere qual sia stata megliore i cepta. lo poi fare. E ācora accumulare tutte mercātie insiemi. cōe se hauesse. p° çençeri da te. E hora q̄sti receuesti del baratto li quali voler metter con li altri. nel çornal dirai cosi. cioe.

Per çēçeri bellidi i mōte. o vero in colli: A çucari de la tal sorta ꝛc̄. p colli tanti pesano 8 tāte haui dal tal a baratto de çucari fatto i q̄sta forma. cioe che mi li misi el c°. de çucari duc. 24. ꝛc̄. cō q̄sto che mi desse el ⅓. de contanti ꝛc̄. E mettese el c°. di çēçeri duc. tanti. p li quali çençeri. li cōti çucari. pani. n°. tanti. pesan 8 tante che a contanti el c°. val duc. 20. E p li ditti çençari nebbe 8 tante ꝛc̄. pani n°. tanti ꝛc̄. vagliano ciascuno. 8 6 g p̄

E p che ale volte nō saprai a pōto lo n°. deli pani che p ditti çēçeri intrasse nō fa caso p che poi nela p̄tita seq̄nte. si suplesci q̄l che li mancasse e q̄l che li fosse piu i q̄lla dela cassa. māca ra nō dimeno. al incōtro de çucari sēpre harai el douere a ponto. p che tutte dua. vāno a çucari i modo che la p̄tita de çucari non p̄de el n°. de pani. ne ḋl peso. p che nō e sēpre possibile dogni frascheta. da p se tener cōto. ꝛc̄. Ora di q̄lla p̄te de cōtanti che vi sono cosi. farane debitrici la cassa. E pure el simile creditori ditti çucari. dicendo cosi cioe.

Per cassa: A li ditti ꝛc̄. Per contanti hebi nel ditto baratto. dal ditto ꝛc̄. per pani n°. tanti ꝛc̄. pesano 8 tante val. 8 ß g p̄

E simili p̄tite subito q̄lli mettano i mediate nel giornale a p̄sso q̄lla del baratto. nel q̄l hauesti li conti ꝛc̄. si che a q̄sto modo dittaresti. non volendone tener separato conto. Ma se separato lo uoi tener nel giornale dirai cosi. cioe.

Per çençeri bellidi. per conto di baratto sebbero dal tale ꝛc̄. A çucari ꝛc̄. narrando tutto. poi a ponto commo disopra. E in lo quaderno. poi harano loro partita. distincta ꝛc̄. E questo uo glio che ti basti. per tutti li altri baratti che so per te sença piu mi stenda. li sapa rai guidare ꝛc̄.

De laltra partita famosa ditta Compagnie: comme se debino ordinare. e dettare in tutti li modi occurenti in ciascuno libro. Cap°. 21.

But when you make a payment part through the bank and part by bill of exchange, deliver first the bill of exchange and then settle through the bank, which is safer Many observe this precaution on good grounds, whenever they have to make payments part in cash to settle this balance through the bank, etc If you make payments part through the bank, part by trading something or part by a bill of exchange and part in cash, you shall charge the seller for all these things and you shall credit each of the said things, each thing in its own place

Now that you know how to go ahead whenever you make purchases, you will also know what you have to do when you sell In this case, you shall charge the different buyers and shall credit the different goods that you sell and shall charge cash if you get money for the same, and you shall charge bills of exchange if you get a bill of exchange in payment, and credit the latter when the bank pays the exchange

Therefore, referring again to the purchase, you shall credit the purchaser with all that he gives you in payment, etc

This will be enough for your instruction on this subject

CHAPTER 20

ENTRIES FOR THE WELL-KNOWN AND PECULIAR MERCANTILE CUSTOMS OF TRADING AND PARTNERSHIP, ETC HOW THEY SHOULD BE ENTERED IN THE MERCANTILE BOOKS FIRST SIMPLE TRADINGS, THEN COMPLEX TRADINGS AND EXAMPLES OF ENTRIES FOR THEM IN THE MEMORANDUM BOOK, JOURNAL AND LEDGER

Now we shall speak of how certain well-known and peculiar entries should be made which are of the highest importance in commerce, and which usually are kept separate from the others so that they can show their respective profits and losses (*pro e danno*) They cover tradings, partnerships, suggested business trips, trips on your own ventures, commissions from others, drafts (*ditta*) or bills of exchange (*bancha descritta*) actual trades, store accounts, etc I will tell you briefly about these accounts, how you should make the entries in your books so that you don't get mixed up in your affairs

First, we shall show how to enter a trade (*barato*) Trades are usually of three kinds, as we said in Section 9 of Treatise III, Pages 161 to 167, where it is stated fully and you can refer to it

I say therefore, that no matter how you make a record of the trade in your books, you shall first enter it in the memorandum book, stating in detail all about it, its terms and conditions and whether it was made through a broker After you have so described it, you then at the end shall put a money value on it, and you shall put down such price in accordance with the current value which the things that you have traded have, reckoning in any kind of money in the memorandum book Afterwards the bookkeeper, when he transfers the entry to the Journal and Ledger, will reduce that money to the standard money that you have adopted

This is done because, without entering the value of the things that you have traded, you could not, from your books and accounts, learn, except with great difficulty, what your profit or loss is The merchandise must always be reduced to actual money value in order to take care of it (in the books)

You may keep a separate account of the goods received in trade, if you wish to do that, in order to know how much you make out of them separate from those of the same kind that you might already have at home, or separate from those that you might get after that, in order to know which was the best transaction. You also may keep only one account of all the goods—for instance, if you have already some ginger, and you get some more ginger through a trade In this case you shall make the entries in the Journal as follows

Per Ginger in bulk or in packages // A sugar, such and such kind, so many packages weighing so many pounds Received from a trade for sugar in this manner I valued the sugar 24 ducats per hundred, of which I should receive one-third in cash, and I valued the ginger at so many ducats per hundred The said sugar is in so many loaves weighing so many pounds, worth 20 ducats per hundred, and for the said ginger I received so many pounds of sugar and so many loaves, and their value is L..., S..., G..., P...

And if you do not know exactly how many loaves of sugar you have received for the said ginger, it does not matter, because you may correct the mistake in the following entry, whether the mistake was made plus or minus, or correct it through the cash entry On the contrary, you know exactly the weight and money value, and you lose nothing in either by not knowing the number of loaves It is not always possible to keep an account of all small details

Now you will debit cash for whatever cash you received, and you shall credit sugar in the following manner

Per Cash // A ditto In the said trade I received cash from so and so for so many loaves of sugar weighing so many pounds, value L , S..., G P

You shall record in the Journal direct all these different items soon after the trade is made, and should take the name of the merchandise if you do not want to keep a separate account, but if you want to keep them in a separate account, you will write this way in the Journal

Per ginger *bellidi* received by trade from so and so, etc // A sugar, etc , stating everything as shown above In the Ledger then they will have separate accounts

This will be sufficient for you for all kinds of trades

CHAPTER 21

THE OTHER WELL-KNOWN ENTRY CALLED PARTNERSHIP HOW IT SHOULD BE WRITTEN IN EACH BOOK IN THE PROPER MANNER

L'Altra partita famosa e la cōpa. ch cō alcūo facesse p ragiōe di q̄lūche cosa si fa cesse o di panni o de sete o de spetiarie o de gottōi e de tētoria o de cābi 7c. Queste tali simili sēpre uogliāo sua ptita sepata i tutti li.3.libri detti. Nel p°.cioe memoriale posto che tu harai el di di sopra narrarala sēplicamēte tutta con modi e cōditiōi ch lauete fatta alegan°.scripto ouer altro istr̄o ch fra noi fosse e noiando el tpō q̄to la fintēde:e di che faculta si fa eli fattori e garçoni che sauesse a tenere 7c.e quello che mette ciascū perse o de robba o de d.7c.o debitori o creditori e di tutto a vno a vno farane creditori li cōp' ognū di q̄l tanto che mette da pse e debitrici la cassa d la dc̄a cōpa.se da perse la tiei ch meg°.se reggi el trafico tēnēdola sepata dala cassa tua priculare q̄°.tu fosse q̄l ch talcōa. guidasse p la q̄l te cōuē fare libri.dapse cō q̄llordie mō evia ch di sop e dcō:d tutto el tuo maneggio p mē briga:nō dimēo potresti tutta tenerla nelli medēi toi libri. uericādo noue ptite cōmo al p̄ñte dicemo ch si chiamāo famose p eēr sepate da tutte lalt'.d le q̄li q te do el mō succito cōmo labi adittare i tuo mēoriale e di poi i giornale e q̄derno 7c. Ma tenēdo di lei lib'.sepati nō ti do alt°.documēto senō ch liguidi si cōmo d tutto el tuo trafico e dcō. Dirolla cosi ime'. In q̄sto di hiamo fcō cōpa.cō li tali e tali alarte d la lana 7c.cō pacti e cōditioni 7c.cōmo ape p scripto o istr̄o 7c.p āni tāti 7c.onde el tal dette cōtāti tāti 7c. Lalt° balle tāte lana frāca.pesa netta ℔.tāte 7c.messa cōto duc.tāti el m°.7c.ela lt° aseg°.tāti veri debitori.cioe el tal de duc.tāti.el tal de tanti 7c.e cosi io sborsai d p̄sēte duc.tāti 7c.e so i sūma tutto el cor.duc.tāti 7c. Poi in tuo giornale dirai i q̄sto modo asettādo tutte cose a suo luogo imagina v°.cassa d compagnia.e vn cauedal di cō'.e cosi a tutte le ptite ch tu metterai dirai sēpre p cōto d cpa.acio labi acognoscere dalt'.toi ptite priculari 7c.e pa.pmo festi da la cassa comēçarai e poi successiuamente asettarai laltre. Per cassa de compagnia.al tale de ragion de compagnia acio se hauesse altri conti con teco non si impacino 7c.per contanti misei q̄sto di p la sua rata.2°.li n̄ri pacti cōmo apare p scripto ouer istr̄o 7c.val ℔. ß. g°. p̄. Poi similmēte dirai de le robbe che hano messe cosi. Per lana franca.de la cōpa.al tale p balle tante pesano nette i tutto ℔.tante so cōta dacordo con tutti ducati tanti el m°.secondo la for'. del cōtratto ouer scripto fra noi 7c.mōta i tutto duc.7c.val ℔. ß. g°. p̄. E cosi andarai ponēdo tutte.p li debitori cōsegnati dirai cosi. Per lo tale de ragiō de cōpa. Al tale q̄l secōdo n̄ri pacti ci cōsegno p vero debitore de duc.tanti val ℔. ß. g°. p̄. Or mai che alq̄to sei itrodutto nō mi curo stēderme piu si cōmo in lo pncī°.di q̄sto trattato feci che troppo seria auolerte ogni cosa di nuouo replicare. E po del modo de metterle al q̄derno grande nō ne dico perche lo te fia facile cognoscēdo gia tu in lo giornale q̄l ua debitore e q̄l creditore.siche asettarale tu i dare e hauere in quel modo che di sopra i questo te isegnai a ca°.15°.e depēnarale i giornale cōmo dissi di sopra al ca°.12°.ponēdo sēpre denançe i margine li nūeri del debitore e creditore:a q̄te carti li harai posti al libro.e cosi cōmo tu li metti al libro grande:cosi li asetta i alfabeto cōmo di sopra piu fiade hauemo mostro 7c.

De lordine de le ptite de ciascuna spesa:cōmo de casa ordinarie:straordinarie:e di mercantie:salarij de garçoni e factori cōmo sabino a scriuere:e dittare nelli libri. ca°.22.

Oltra tutte le cose ditte te couiene hauere i tutti toi libri q̄ste ptite.cioe spesi d mercātia spesi de casa ordiarie spese straordiarie vna de itrata e vscita e vna de pro e dāno o uoi dire auançi e disauāçi o utile e dāno o guadagno e pdita che tāto uale le q̄li ptite sōno sūmamēte necessarie i ogni corpo mercātesco p potere sempre cognoscere suo capitale.e ala fine nel saldo cōmo getta el trafico 7c.le q̄li q seq̄nte abastança chiariremo cōmo se debino guidare nelli libri. Unde q̄lla de spese mercātesche si tene p rispecto che nō sēpre ogni peluço si po mettere subito i la ptita de la robba che tu uendi o cōpri cōmo acade che da poi piu di p q̄lla ti cōuerra pagare fachini e pesadori e ligadori e barca.e bastagi.e simili a chi vn soldo.a chi.2.7c.de le q̄li volēdone fare pticular ptita serebbe lōgo e nō meritano la spesa poche de minimis nō curat p̄tor 7c. E ācora acade che tu adoprarai q̄lli medesimi bastagi.fachini.barca.e legatori i vn pōto p piu diuerse cose cōmo itteruene.ch i ū pōto scarcādo o carcādo diuerse sorte mercāne li afatigarai e tu li paghi p tutte a vn tratto che nō potresti a ogni mercātia carattare la sua spesa. E po nasci q̄sta ptita chiamata spese de mercātia la q̄l sēpre sta acesa i dare cōmo tutte laltre spesi fāno. Salarii ancora de factori e garçoni de botega si mettano i q̄ste e alcuni ne fa ptita aso posta p sapere i ditti che spēdano lāno 7c.e poi i q̄sta la saldano:che p niū mō nō possano essere creditrici:e q̄do cosi le trouassi seria errore nel libro. E pero i memoriale el dirai cosi.

In questo di habian pagato abastasi barcaroli ligadori.pesadori 7c.ch carcaro e scarcaro 7c.le tali e tali cose 7c.duc.tanti 7c.

The other well-known entry is the buying of anything in partnership (*compra* or *compagnie*—may also mean joint venture but not corporation) with other people, such as silks, spices, cotton, dyes, or money exchanges, etc These accounts must all be entered in all three books separately from your own In the first, that is, the memorandum book, after writing down the date at the top, you shall state in a simple way all the purchases with terms and conditions, referring to papers or other instruments that you might have made, stating for how long it was made and what were its objects, mentioning the employes and apprentices that you should keep, etc, and the share, and how much each of you puts in the business, whether in goods or cash, etc, who are the debtors and who are the creditors You should credit the partners (*compratori*) for the amount which each of them contributes, and you shall debit cash with the same if you keep the account with your own But it is better for the business if you keep this cash account separate from your private one when you are the one at the head of the business, in which case you should have a separate set of books in the same order and way we have shown previously This will facilitate things for you However, you might keep all these accounts in your own personal books opening new accounts which, as we have said, are referred to as well-known accounts because they are kept separate from all the others, and I will show here how to enter them in your Day Book and then in the Journal and Ledger—but if you keep separate books, I will not give you any further instruction, because what I have said so far will be sufficient for you—you shall do as follows On this day we have made a contract with so and so, and so and so, jointly, to buy (*facto compra*) wool, etc, under terms and conditions, etc, as appears from such and such paper or such and such instrument, for so many years, etc So and so put in as his share, so much in cash, the other put so many bales of French wool, weighing net so many pounds, etc, estimated at so many ducats per, etc The third, so and so, put in so many credits, namely, one for so many ducats, etc

Then, in the Journal, putting everything in its own place, you shall imagine that you have a partnership's cash (*cassa de compagnia*) and a partnership's capital (*cavedale de compagnia*), so that in each entry you make, you shall always name the accounts of the partnership so that you can distinguish them from your own entries First, you make the cash entry, and then follow it systematically by the other entries

Per Partnership cash // A such and such partner's account—so that if you have other accounts, you will not get confused—so and so put in on this day as his share according to our agreement as appears from the contract, etc, value L , S , G , P

Then you shall mention the other things that they have contributed

Per French wool // A partner's account, for so many bales weighing in total, net, so many pounds, as examined by all of us, at so many ducats per bushel, according to the terms of the contract we have made, etc, worth in total so many ducats; value L , S , G , P

And so on for the other different items, and as to the due bills which have been put in the Company, you shall state this way

Per Mr So and So Partnership's account // A so and so, according to our agreement, which so and so transferred to the Partnership as a good due bill of so many ducats L , S , G P

Now that I have given you a kind of introduction to these new entries, I won't go any further, as it would be a very tiresome thing to repeat all I have said.

And I will not say anything as to the way in which to make these entries in the Ledger, as I know it will be easy for you to know what should be entered as debit and what as credit from the Journal You shall enter them accordingly as I have told you at Chapter 15, and shall cancel these entries in the Journal as I told you at Chapter 12, always writing in the margin just opposite them the number of the debit and credit pages of the Ledger and as you enter them in the Ledger you shall also enter them in the index, as I have told you repeatedly before

CHAPTER 22

REGARDING THE ENTRIES OF EVERY KIND OF EXPENSE, AS FOR INSTANCE HOUSEHOLD EXPENSES, ORDINARY OR EXTRAORDINARY, MERCANTILE EXPENSES, WAGES OF CLERKS AND APPRENTICES HOW THEY SHOULD BE ENTERED IN THE BOOKS

Besides the entries so far mentioned, you shall open these accounts in your books that is, mercantile expenses, ordinary household expenses, extraordinary expenses, and account for what is cashed in (*entrata*) and what is paid out (*uscita*), one for profits and loss (*pro e danno*—favor and damages) or (*avanzi e desavanzi*—increase and deficit), or (*utile e danno*—profit and damage) or (*guadagno e perdita*—gain and loss), which accounts are very necessary at any time so that the merchant can always know what is his capital and at the end when he figures up the closing (*saldo*) how his business is going

I will show here clearly enough how these accounts should be kept in the books The account named "small business expenses" is kept because we can not enter every little thing in the account of the merchandise that you sell or buy For instance, it may happen that after a few days for these goods that you sell or buy, you will have to pay the porter, the weigher, the packer, the shipper and the driver, and others, paying to this one one penny, to the other one two pennies, etc, if you want to keep a separate account for each of these different transactions, it would be too long and too expensive As the proverb says

De minimis non curat Praetor (Officials do not bother with details) And it may be that you will have to employ those same people—drivers, porters, shippers and packers—for different things, as, for instance, you may need them for loading the several merchandises in a seaport, and you will employ them and will have to pay them for all these services at one time, and you could not charge the several kinds of merchandise with its proportion of these expenses Therefore you open this account which is called "small business expenses," which is always used in the debit as are all the other expenses You enter in this account the salaries of your store employes, although some keep a separate account of the salaries that they pay so that they know how much they pay for salaries every year, etc This should also always appear as a debit If the account should be in credit, this would show that there is a mistake Therefore you shall say as follows in the memorandum book

On this day we have paid to drivers, shippers, packers, weighers, etc, who loaded and unloaded such and such goods, so many ducats, etc,

Poi in lo giornale cōuerra dir cosi. Per spese de mercãtie: A cassa contati: per barche e
bastagi corde e ligatori de le tal cose in tutto duc. tãti ⁊c. val ₰. ß. g°. p̄. In lo q̃derno
dirai cosi. Spesi d̄ mercãtia diē dare adi tãti p̄ cassa ⁊c. val ₰. ₰. ß. g°. p̄. Quella d̄
le spesi di casa ordinarie nō si po far sença. E itendanse spesi di casa ordinarie: cōmo formē
ti: vini: legne: ogli: sale: carne: scarpe: çopelli facture de veste: giupponi: calçe: e sartori ⁊c. be
ueraggi: bēuestite: mancie: ouer bonemani ⁊c. barbieri: fornaro: aquaruoli: lauature de pan
ni ⁊c. masarie de cocina vasi. bichieri. e uetri: tutti secchi. mastelli. botti ⁊c. bēuēga che mol
ti de simili masarie vsino tener conto separato per poter presto trouar suo cōto e fãno p̄tita
noua. cōmo ãcora tu poi fare nō che di q̃ste ma di qualũche altra ti parra. ma io te amaestro
di quelle che'l trafico nō po far sença ⁊c. e tal p̄tita di spesi di casa dittarala si cōmo e ditto
de quella de la mercãtia. e secōdo che tu vai facēdo spese grosse adi p̄ di metti in li libri com
mo del formento e vini legne ⁊c. de le quali ancora molti costumano fare p̄tita daperse per
poter poi ala fine de lanno o a tēpo p̄ tp̄o facilmente sapere quãto de tali cōsumano ⁊c. ma
per le spesi piccole cōmo sono amenuto cōprar carne e pesci: barbieri e traghetti si uol torre
o vno ouer doi duc. a vn tratto e tenerli da parte in vno sachetto e di quelli andar spēdēdo
a menuto. Perche nō seria possibili a vna a vna di tali tener conto. E cosi dicano per li con
tanti in giornale. Per spesi di casa. A cassa q̃li trassi per spendere amenuto in vno sachet
to duc. tanti ⁊c. val. ₰. ß. g°. p̄. E poi se ti pare ancora con queste spesi de casa meter
ui le spesi straordinarie che non fa caso. cōmo quãdo spendesse per andare a solaçço: e p̄ tra
rere alarco o balestro e altri giochi o perdite che ti cascassero e p̄desse robbe o denari o ch̄ te
fossero tolte o perdesse in mare o per fuochi ⁊c. che tutti simili sintendano spese straordina
rie. Le quali ancora se le voli tenere da parte similmente lo poi fare e molti lusano per sa
per netto ala fin delanno quanto hano speso de straordinario per le quali anco sintende do
ni e presenti che tu facesse adalcuno per alcuna cagione ⁊c. d̄ le quali spese non mi curo piu
oltra stenderme peroche so certo che tu per te meglio ormai hauendo amente le cose dette
dinance asettarai che prima non haresti facto siche queste lasciando diremo del modo da
settare le partite de vna botega si nel tuo quaderno. e libri ordinarii: cōmo se tu la volesse te
ner tu da te cōmo laresti a tenere che fia bella cosa a sapere e bē notale.

De lordine e mō a sap̄ tener vn cōto de botega ī tua mão o adaltri recōmãdata e cōmo
se debino nelli libri autentici del patrone e anche in quelli de botega separatamente scriuere
e dittare. capi. 23.

Dico adonca quãdo hauesse vna botega la q̃l tenesse fornita ala giornata for de
casa tua e fore del tuo corpo di casa. alora p̄ bono ordine terrai q̃sto mō: cioe de
tutte le robbe che tu ui metterai adi p̄ di farala debitrici ali toi libri. e credetrici
q̃lle tal robbe che vi metti. a vna p̄ vna e fa tua imagiatiōe ch̄ q̃sta bote.ª sia vna p̄
sona. tua debitrici di q̃l tãto che li dai e p̄ lei spēdi i tutti li modi. E cosi p̄ lauerso de tutto q̃l
lo ch̄ne caui e receui farala creditrici cōmo se fosse vn d̄bitore ch̄ti pagasse a p̄te a p̄te. E poi
ogni uolta che tu voli con lei cōtare tu porrai vedere cōmo ella te butta. o bene o male ⁊c. E
cosi poi saprai q̃llo arai afare e i ch̄ mō larai a gouernare ⁊c. E molti sōno ch̄ ali soi libri fã
no debitore el p̄ncipale che li atēde a ditta botega. benche q̃sto nō si possa debitamente sēça
volũta di q̃l tale. poch̄ mai si deue mettere ne ãcora de ragiō si puo porre vn debitore alli.b°
sēça sua saputa ne ãch̄ creditore cō cōditiōi alcũe sēça sua uolũta. che q̃l cose facēdole tu sere
sti mãco che da bene. E li toi libri serieno reputati falsi. e cosi d̄ le masarie ch̄ i. q̃lla metesse e
ordegni necessarii al a ditta botega secōdo sua occurēça: cōmo se fosse speciaria ti conuerra
fornirla d̄ uasi. caldieri. ramini. da lauorare ⁊c. di q̃li tutti farala debitrici o colui che li attē
de cōmo ditto. e p̄ bello iuētario li le asegna scripto d̄ sua mão o dalui d̄ sua uolũta ⁊c. acio
de tutto sia bē chiaro. e q̃sto voglio sia bastãte q̄ñdo la botega hauesse consegnata a vnaltro
ch̄ p̄ te la facesse o fosse tuo cōmesso ⁊c. Ma se la d̄ca botega vorrai tener a tuoi mãi q̃sto or
die sarai e stara bene: e metiamo ch̄ cōpri e trafichi tutto p̄ la ditta botega e nō haui altro
maneggio alora formarai li libri commo e ditto. E di cio che vendi e compri farai credito
ri chi te da le robbe per tanto tempo se compri a tempo e creditrici la cassa se compri a con
tanti e debitrici la botega. E quando tu vendesse a menuto cioe che non aruasse a. 4. o. 6. du
cati ⁊c. alora tutti ditti denari reporrai in vna cassetta. ouer salua denaro dōde i capo d̄. 8. o
10. giorni line cauarai. e alora farãe debitrici la cassa e credetrici la bo.ª di q̃l tãto. e i la p̄tita
dirai p̄ piu robbe uēdute de le q̃li gia hauerai tenuto el cōto e molte altre cose in le q̃li nō mi.

then in the Journal you shall say as follows·

Per small business expenses // A cash Cash paid for boats, ropes, etc, for such and such goods in total, so many ducats, value L , S , G , P

In the Ledger, you shall state as follows

Small business expenses (*dee dare*—shall give) debit per cash on this day, etc, value, page, etc L , S. , G , P

We can not do without the account of ordinary household expenses By these expenses we mean expenses for grains, wine, wood, oil, salt, meat, shoes, hats, stockings, cloths, tips, expenses for tailors, barbers, bakers, cleaners, etc, kitchen utensils, vases, glasses, casks, etc

Many keep different accounts for all these different things, so that they can see at a glance how each account stands, and you may do so and open all these different accounts, and any accounts that you like, but I am talking to you about what the merchant can not do without And you shall keep this account in the way I have told you to keep the small business expense account, and make each entry day by day as you have such expenses, as for grain, wine, wool, etc Many open special accounts for these different things so that at the end of the year or at any time they may know how much they are paying out, but for the small accounts, as meat, fish, boat fares, etc, you shall set aside in a little bag one or two ducats and make small payments out of this amount It will be impossible to keep an account of all these small things

In the Journal you shall state so

Per household expenses // A cash Cash set aside in a little bag for small expenses, so many ducats, value· L S , G , P

If you wish, you can include in the household expenses the extraordinary expenses, as those that you make for amusements or that you lose in some game, or for things or money that you might lose, or that might be stolen or lost in a wreck or through fire, etc, for all are classified as extraordinary expenses If you want to keep a separate account for them, you may do so, as many do, in order to know at the end of the year how much you have expended for extraordinary expenses, under which title you should include also gifts and presents that you might make to any one for any reason Of these expenses, I will not speak any longer, because I am sure that you, keeping in mind what we have said so far will know how to manage yourself And leaving this subject, I will tell you of the way to open your store accounts in the Ledger and in the other books as if you wanted to conduct a store for your own account I shall tell you that you must pay good attention for it is a very nice thing for you to know

CHAPTER 23

IN WHAT MANNER THE ACCOUNTS OF A STORE SHOULD BE KEPT WHETHER THE STORE IS UNDER YOUR CARE OR UNDER THE CARE OF OTHER PEOPLE HOW THE ACCOUNTS SHOULD BE ENTERED IN THE AUTHENTIC BOOKS OF THE OWNER SEPARATE FROM THOSE OF THE STORE ITSELF

I say then that if you should have a store outside of your house (branch store) and not in the same building with your house, but which you have fully equipped, then for the sake of order you should keep the accounts in this way You should charge it in your books with all the different things that you put into it, day by day, and should credit all the different merchandise that you put in it also each one by itself, and you must imagine that this store is just like a person who should be your debtor for all the things that you may give (*dai*) it or spend for it for any reason And so on the contrary you shall credit it with all that you take out of it and receive from it (*cavi e recevi*) as if it were a debtor who would pay you gradually Thus at any time that you so desire, you may see how the store is running—that is, at a profit or at a loss—so you will know what you will have to do and how you will have to manage it There are many who in their books charge everything to the manager of the store This, however, can not be done properly without the consent of that person, because you can never enter in your books as a debtor any person without his knowing it, nor put him as a creditor under certain conditions without his consent If you should do these things, it would not be right and your books would be considered wrong

As to all the fixtures which you might put in said store necessary to the running of it according to the circumstances—if you had for instance a drug-store, you would have to furnish it with vases, boiling pots, copper utensils, with which to work—you shall charge your store with all this furniture So all of these things you shall charge, and he who is at the head of the store shall make a proper inventory of all these things in his own handwriting or in the handwriting of somebody else, at his pleasure, so that everything should be clear And this will be sufficient for a store whose management you may have turned over to somebody or to some of your employes But if you want to run the store yourself, you shall do as I will tell you and it will be all right Let us suppose that you buy and do all of your business through the said store and do not have to take care of any other business, then you shall keep the books as I have said before, whether you buy or sell You shall credit all those that sell goods to you on time, if you buy on time, or credit cash if you buy for cash, and charge the store, and if you should sell at retail, as when the sale should not amount to four or six ducats, and so on, then you shall keep all these moneys in a small drawer or box from which you shall take it after eight or ten days, and then you shall charge this amount to cash and shall credit the store, and you shall make this entry as follows·

Per various merchandise sold—for which you shall have kept an account—and so on I shall not talk at length about this because

uoglio troppo distendere. p che so cómo disopra diffusamẽte habiã dcõ ormai saprai per te intenderle cõciosia che cõti non sono altro che vn debito ordine d: la fantasia che si fa el mer-catante per el qual uniforme seruato puene ala notitia de tutte sue facẽde e cognosci facil-mẽte p qllo se le sue cose uano bene o male. p che el prouerbio dici chi fa mercãtia e nõ la co-gnosca li soi denari douẽtan mosca 7c. e secõdo le occurrençe li fa remedio. E pero piu e mã-co li sipo sempre agiongere in numero e i multitudine de ptite. E po de qsto tacõteta.

Cómo se habino a lettare nel giornale e quaderno le partite de li bãchi de scritta: eqli se i-tedino e doue ne stato de cãbi: tu cõ loro stando mercatãte: e tu cõ altri qdo fosse bãchieri: e de le quietãçe che p li cãbi se fãno. e p che lene facia doi de medesimo tenore ca. 24

HOra per li banchi de scripta d quali se ne trouã oggi di in vinetia i bruggia ãuersa e barçelõa e certi altri luoghi famosi e trafichãti ti cõuiẽ sap cõ loro saper scõtrare cõ grãdissima diligẽtia. E pero e da notar che cõ lo bancho te poi cõmunamẽ-te impaciare da te ponẽdoui denari per piu tua sigureçça. o uero p modo de di-posito a la giornata poter con quelli far tuoi pagamenti chiari a piero gioãni e martino per che la ditta del bancho e comme publico istrumẽto de notaro p che son per li dominij alci-gurati onde ponedoui tu da te. d. farai debitore ditto bancho nominando patroni o uero cõpagni del bacho e creditrici la tua cassa cosi dicẽdo i giornale Per bancho de li pama-ni. A cassa per cõtanti li misi cõ tali.o o altri che per me fosse in questo di de mio conto fra oro e moneta 7c. i tutto ducati 7c. Val. ß. f. g. p. E farate fare dal banchieri doi uersi i suo foglio p piu cautela. E cosi giongẽdogline tu ala giornata farai el simile: cauandone tu lui te fara scriuere a te el receuere: e cosi le cose si uengano sempre a mãtener chiare: Uero e che alcuolte tal scritte nõ si costumano p che cómo e ditto li libri del bancho sempre sono publi-chi e autentichi: ma pur e buono la cautela p che cómo disopra so ditto al mercante le cose mai forõ troppo chiare. Ma se tu uolesse tal ptita tenerla con li patroni: o uero cõpagni del bancho ancora so poi fare che tanto uale po che noiando tu el bãcho a modo disopra sintẽ-de li patrõi e cõp°. de quello: per li patrõni diresti cosi. Per miser Girolimo lipamani dal bancho e cõpagni qdo fossero piu. A cassa ut supra sequita tutto. E sempre farai neli tuoi li-bri mentione de le chiareçe: patti: e cõditioni che fra uoi nascessero cómo de scripti de mã: e del luogo doue li reponi i filça: scatola tascha: o cassa acio possi facilmẽte retrouarle: po che cõ bona diligẽça simili scripture si debono seruare. ad ppetuam rei memoriã: p li pericoli oc-corrano 7c. E p che alcuolte cõ lo bãchieri porresti hauer in piu facẽde e maneggi i mercã-tia p te o per altri cómo cõmesso 7c. po sempre cũ lui ti cõuiẽ tener cõti diuersi p non itriga-re lance cõ ronchoni che nascieria grã confussione: e dire i le tue ptite p cõto de la tal cosa: o p cõto del tal o p ragiõ de mercantia o p ragion de contanti depositati i tuo nome o daltri cómo e detto: le quali cose so p tuo igegno ormai reggerai 7c. E similmẽte te reggerai saltri te aconciasse d. a te p che cõto si uolesse: faralo debitore al tuo libro p ql tal cõto: cioe d pagamẽ-to noiando p pte o p resto 7c. e ql tale farai creditore p lo medesimo cõto e stara bene E qn-do tu de dcõ bancho cauasse. d. i cõtãti o p paga mẽti che adaltri facesse p pte o resto o uero p remetter a daltri i altri paesi 7c. alora farai el cõtrario de ql che fiuora e dcõ: cioe se caui cõtanti farai debitrici la tua cassa: e creditore el bancho o uer patrõi di quel tanto che ne ca-uasti. E se tu li scriuesse adaltri farai debitore ql tale e creditore detto bancho o patrõi di ql tanto noiando el p che dicẽdo i giornale p li cõtanti cosi. Per cassa al bancho o uer mi-ser girolimo li pamani p contanti i tal di. o i qsto di ne trassi a mio bisogno 7c. i tutto. duc. tãti 7c. ual. ß. f. g. p. E se adaltri li scriuesse dipura a martio di rsti cosi. Per mart° del ta-le. Al ditto ut supra per duc. tãti 7c. li scrissi p pte o p resto o abõ cõto o p ipresto 7c. i qsto di. ual. ß. f. g. p. E cosi leuãdo ditte ptite dl giornale sẽpre a suo luogo i qderno asettarale: e i alfabeto cõ modi disopra dati e depẽnandole cómo to mostro in memoriale e giornale. p. e mancho per te stesso giõgnẽdoli parolle. po che non e possibile q de tutto a pieno narrare si che conuiẽ dal tuo cãto sia uigilante 7c. El medesimo mõ te cõuerra obseruare p remette-re li cãbi altroue. cóme lon°: brugia: ro°: liõ 7c. e per ritrar daltro 7c. nominando le termi-ni 7c. o ala uista o aladata o al suo piacere: cómo se costuma facẽdo mẽtiõe de p°. 2°. e. 3°. 7c. acio non nasca errore fra te el tuo respondente e de le monete che tu trai e rimetti e le lor ualute e puisiõi e spese dãni e interessi che cõ li protesti poderebono nascere 7c. si che di tutto si uol far mẽtiõe el p che e cóme. E cóme o messo che tu habi afare con bãcho: cosi uersa uice prẽdi se fosse tu el banchieri mutatis mutandis che quando paghi fa debitore quel tale e la tua cassa creditrici e sel tuo creditore sença cauare. d. adaltri li scriuesse dirai nel tuo giorna

I have given you sufficient explanation previously and you know how to go ahead by this time For accounts are nothing else than the expression in writing of the arrangement of his affairs, which the merchant keeps in his mind, and if he follow this system always he will know all about his business and will know exactly whether his business goes well or not Therefore the proverb If you are in business and do not know all about it, your money will go like flies—That is, you will lose it And according to the circumstances you can remedy what is to be remedied, for instance, if necessary, you might open other accounts And this will be sufficient for you

CHAPTER 24

HOW YOU SHOULD KEEP IN THE JOURNAL AND LEDGER THE ACCOUNTS WITH THE BANK WHAT IS UNDERSTOOD BY THEM BILLS OF EXCHANGE—WHETHER YOU DEAL WITH A BANK OR YOURSELF ARE A BANKER RECEIPTS FOR DRAFTS—WHAT IS UNDERSTOOD BY THEM AND WHY THEY ARE MADE OUT IN DUPLICATE

In respect to banks, which you can find nowadays in Venice, in Bruges, in Antwerp, Barcelona, and other places well known to the commercial world, you must keep your accounts with them with the greatest diligence.

You can generally establish connections with a bank. For instance, you may leave your money with the bank as a place of greater safety, or you may keep your money in the bank as a deposit in order to make therefrom your daily payments to Peter, John and Martin, for a bank draft is like a public notarial instrument, because they are controlled by the state

If you put money in the bank, then you shall charge the bank or the owner or partners of the bank and shall credit your cash and make the entries in the Journal as follows

For Bank of Lipamani // A cash Cash deposited with so and so by me, or others, for my account, on this day counting gold and other money, etc, in all so many ducats, value
L...... , S ..., G ...... , P ...

And you will have the banker give you some kind of a written record for your surety, if you make other deposits you shall do the same In case you should withdraw money, the banker shall have you write a receipt, in this way, things will be kept always clear

It is true that at times this kind of receipt is not given, because, as we said, the books of the bank are always public and authentic, but it is better to require this writing, because, as I have told you, things can't be too clear for the merchant

If you want to keep this account in the name of the owners or partners of the bank, you may do so, as it is the same thing, because, if you open the account under the name of the bank, by the bank you mean the owners or the partners If you keep it under the name of the owners, you shall say this way

Per Mr Girolimo Lipamani, banker, and associates—if there are many— // A cash—and here you write as above In your books you shall always mention all agreements, terms, conditions that there might be, also instruments of writing and places where you keep them, whether file box, pouch or trunk, so that you may easily find them, as these papers should be diligently kept for an everlasting memorial of the transaction (*ad perpetuam memoriam*) on account of dangers

As you may have several different business relations with the bankers for yourself, or for others, you must keep various accounts with them so that you won't mix one thing with another, and avoid confusion, and in your entries you shall say On account of such and such thing, or on account of so and so, or on account of goods, or on account of cash deposited in your name or in the name of others, as we have said You will know yourself how to make these entries In the same way you will proceed in case others should turn money over to you for some account, you shall charge that account in your book—that is, you shall charge the bank, stating whether it was in part payment or in full, etc, and you shall credit the person that gave you the money This will be all right

When you should withdraw money from a bank either to pay somebody else as part payment or payment in full, or to make a remittance to parties in other countries, you shall do in this case just the opposite of what we just said—that is, if you withdraw money you shall charge your cash and credit the bank or owners of the bank for the amount withdrawn, and if you should give an order on the bank for somebody else, you shall charge this party and credit the bank or owners of the bank for that much, stating the reasons. You shall enter the cash item in your Journal as follows

Per cash // A bank, or Mr Girolimo Lipamani, for cash which on this day or on such and such day I withdrew for my need, in all so many ducats, value L... , S ..., G , P

And if you should issue an order in favor of Mr Martino, for instance, you shall say thus

Per Martino on such and such a day // A ditto for ditto for cash, etc, for so many ducats, for which I gave an order, in part payment or in full payment, or for a loan, etc, on this day, value
L......... , S..... ... , G , P ...

Every time you transfer these entries from the Journal into the Ledger, you shall also record them in the index and cancel them, as I have shown you, adding more or less words according to the facts in the case

You must do the same in case you want to send drafts elsewhere, as to London, Bruges, Rome Lyons, etc. You shall mention in the letter the terms, conditions, etc, whether these drafts are at sight or at a certain date or at pleasure of the payor, as it is customary, mentioning also whether it is a first, second, third draft, etc, so that no misunderstanding can occur between you and your correspondent, mentioning also the kind of money in which you draw or transmit, their value, the commission, the costs and interest that might follow a protest—in a word, everything must be mentioned, why and how

I have told you how you have to proceed in dealing with a bank If on the contrary you are the banker you have to do in the opposite way (*mutatis mutandis*), when you pay you charge the man to whom you pay and credit cash If one of your creditors, without withdrawing money, should issue a draft to somebody else, you shall say in the journal

le per quel tale tuo creditore a quel tale achi lui li acõcia.e cosi vieni a far cõmutatione da vno creditore a unaltro e tu rimani pure debitore e uieni in q̃sto atto essere persona meççana e cõmuna.cõmo testimonio e factore de le parti a tuo inchiostro carta fitto fatiga e tempo si che di qua si caua la honesta ꝓuisiõe nel cambio essere sẽpre licita q̃do mai nõ ui corrisse picolo de uiaggio altre remesse in mano de terçe ꝑsone ⁊c.cõmo nelli cambi reali in q̃sto a suo luogho estato apieno detto ⁊c.Ma siando bãchieri ricordare nelli saldi cõ toi creditori far te tornare fogli poliçe o altri scripti che di tua mano hauesse de le q̃li quando ne fai sẽpre fanne nel tuo libro mentiõe acio te recordi a fartele tornare e straçarli:acio nõ uenisse a tẽpo cõ q̃lli altri a domandarte e fatte fare sẽpre bone quietançe cõmo costumano fare chi attẽde al cãbio:ꝑo che lusança e che se tu vieni.verbi grã da gineuera con vna di cãbio q̃ in vi°.a miß giouãni fresco baldi da fio°.e cõpa°.ch alauista o data:o a tuo piacere te douesse pagare metiamo duc. 100.p altre tanti che dila hauesse nele man de chi li scriue cõ segnati:alora el ditto miß giouãni e cõp°.acceptãdo la lr̃a:e sborsciãdote ditti.d̃.te fara scriuere d̃ tua mano doi q̃tançe de vn medesimo tenore:e se tu nõ sapesse scriuere le far vn terço ꝑte o x̃po notaro: nõ sa cõ tentara duna ꝑ che luna cõuiẽ che rimandi a q̃l banchieri a gineuera:che li scriue che a te ꝑ suo cõto paghi li ditti duc.100.i farli fede cõmo cortesemẽte a fatto q̃l tanto che li scrisse i cui fede in una sua li mãda laquietãça di tua mano:e laltra tene i filça apresso di se: acio q̃do cõtasse cõ lui non potesse negarlilo:e di la ancora tu tornãdo nõ potesse.lamẽtarte di lui ne de miß giouãni ꝑo che se tu lo fesse el te mostraria detta quietança di tua mano e remaresti confuso:si che tutte q̃ste cose sonno cautele che si conuengano de necessita fare ꝑ la poca fede si troua oggi di del quale atto ne nascano doi ꝑtite i lo q̃derno loro.vna in q̃l di meß giouãni facẽdo d̃bitore q̃l che li scriue ꝑ vigore de la dicãbio:e laltra i q̃llo del respõdẽte a gineuera facẽdo creditore miß giouãni di quelli duc.100.per virtu de ditta tua quietãça receuuta.e questo e el debito modo e ordine de cambiatori ꝑ tutto el mõdo: acio le lor cose vadino cõ chiareçe:si che dal tuo lato alquãto affatigandote porai ogni cosa con summa diligença asettare.⁊c.

De unaltra partita che ale uolte se costuma nel q̃derno tenere detta entrata e uscita e ale uolte senefa libro particulare:e per che. ca.25.

Sonno alcuni che ne lor libri usano tenere vna ꝑtita detta entrata e vscita i la q̃l põgano cose straordinarie o altre cõmo ala.fantasia pare. Altri ne tirra una d̃ spese straordinarie e i simili mettano cõmo i q̃lla dintrata i sita ꝑsẽti che li fosser fatti.v.grã.e cosi scdo che riceuano e dãno e tẽgano cõto i dare e hauere e poi a la fine cõ laltre le saldãno i ꝓ e dãno e cauedale cõmo itenderai nel bilancio ⁊c.Ma i uero q̃lla detta di sopra spese di casa ꝑ tutte e bastãte se nõ chi uolesse per sua curiosita tener conto da ꝑ se fin a vn põtale de strẽga che lo poria fare ma ach fine:ꝑo si d̃ba a le cose cõ breuita asettarse.Altri luoghi costuma de litrata e uscita tener vn libro a sua posta:e poi quello saldano a tẽpo del bilãcio nel vltimo autẽtico isiemi cõ le altre facẽde:la q̃l cosa non e dabiasmare auẽga sia de piu fatiga.

Cõmo se habino asettare neli libri le ꝑtite de li uiaggi i sua mano:e quelle de li viagdi recomandati:e cõmmo di necessita de tali nascono doi quaderni ca.26.

I uiaggi si costumano fare i doi modi:cioe i sua mano e recomandato.vnde nascano diuersi modi i tener lor cõti ꝑo che sẽpre si prosupõgano libri doppi:o sia i tua mano o sia recõmandato.Perche lũ q̃derno resta i casa e laltro ti cõuẽ fare i uiaggio.vnde sel ditto viagio sia i tua mano ꝑ bõ ordie de cioche tu porti forma tuo iuẽtario q̃dernetto:giornaletto ⁊c.tutto cõmo di sopra se detto:e uẽdẽdo cõprãdo baratãdo ⁊c.de tutto fa debitori e creditori ꝑsone:robbe: cassa:cauedal:de uiaggio:e ꝓ e danno de uiaggio ⁊c.e q̃sto e lo piu schietto e dica ch si uoglia altri.Auẽga ch porresti tener cõto cõ la casa dala q̃l tu togli la faculta che al ditto uiaggio porti facẽdola nel libretto del tuo uiaggio creditrici:e le robbe debitrici a una ꝑ v°:e cosi formaresti tua cassa.tuo cauedale ⁊c. ordenatamẽte cõmo nel tuo famoso.E tornãdo a saluamẽto rẽdaresti ala casa altre robbe ali contro.o uero.d̃.e cõ lei saldaresti cõto e lutile o dãno seq̃ro asettaresti a suo luogho nel quaderno grãde.si che aq̃sto modo ancora le tue facẽde uerebono chiare.Ma sel viaggio recõmãdasse adaltri:alora faresti de tutto nel tuo libro debitore q̃l tale achi lareco mãdi dicẽdo per uiaggio recomãdato al tale ⁊c.e cõ lui terresti conto cõme se fosse vn tuo auẽtore de tutte robbe:e d̃.a ꝑtita per partita ⁊c.E lui dal cãto suo formara suo q̃dernetto:e i q̃llo te conuerra fare creditore de tutto.E retornãdo saldara conteco.E sel tuo cõmesso fosse i le bãde

as follows Per that special creditor of yours // A the man to whom the money was assigned In this way you just make the transfer from one creditor to another and you still remain as debtor and act as a go-between, as witness or agent of the two parties For ink paper, rent, trouble and time you get a commission, which is always lawful, even though through a draft there is no risk of travel, or the risk when money should be transferred to third parties, etc, as in actual exchanges, of which we have spoken in its place If you are a banker, whenever you close an account with your creditors always remember to get back all the papers, documents or other writings in your own handwriting that they might have When you issue any such paper always mention it in your books so that when the time comes you will remember to ask for them and to destroy them so that nobody else should appear with these papers and ask money for the second time You must always require good receipts as those do who are accustomed to this kind of business For the custom is this If you, for instance, come from Geneva to Venice with a draft on Messrs Giovanni Frescobaldi & Co, of Florence, which draft might be at sight or on a certain date or at your pleasure, and the amount were for a hundred ducats, that is, for as many ducats as you have paid to the drawer of the draft, then the said Messrs Giovanni & Co, when they honor the draft and give you the cash will require you to give two receipts written in your own handwriting, and if you should not know how to write, a third party or a notary public will make them out He will not be satisfied with one because he has to send one to the banker at Geneva, who wrote him to pay the hundred ducats to you for his account just to show that he honored his request, and for this purpose he will send to the other banker a letter enclosing your receipt written in your handwriting The other receipt he will keep for himself on file so that in balancing with the other banker, the banker could not deny the transaction, and if you should go to Geneva you could not complain of him or of Mr Giovanni for if you should complain he would show you your receipt written by yourself and you would not play a beautiful part in it All these precautions ought to be taken by necessity on account of the bad faith of the present times Out of these transactions two entries ought to be made in the Ledger, one entry in the account with Mr Giovanni, in which you shall charge the drawer of the draft, (*letter de cambio*) the other entry in the account of your correspondent at Geneva, crediting Mr Giovanni with that hundred ducats paid through a draft This is the method that the bankers of all the world keep so that their transaction may appear clear, therefore you will have to take some trouble on your part and try to enter everything in its own place with great care

CHAPTER 25

ANOTHER ACCOUNT WHICH IS USUALLY KEPT IN THE LEDGER, CALLED INCOME AND EXPENSES, FOR WHICH OFTEN A SEPARATE BOOK IS USED, AND WHY

There are some who, in their books, are accustomed to keep an account called Income and Expenses (*Entrata e uscita*), in which they enter extraordinary things, or any other thing that they deem proper, others keep an account called extraordinary expenses and in it they record gifts, which they receive or give They keep it as a credit and debit account, and then at the end of the year they ascertain the remainder (*resto*) which is either a profit or a loss and transfer it to capital as you will understand when we talk about the balance But really the account we have called "household expenses" is sufficient for all this unless someone should like to keep a separate account for his own curiosity, but it would be of no great value because things should be arranged as briefly as possible In other places it is customary to keep the income and expense account in a separate book which is balanced when they balance the authenticated books and all other affairs This custom is not to be criticized but it requires more work

CHAPTER 26

HOW ENTRIES SHOULD BE MADE IN MERCANTILE BOOKS RELATIVE TO TRIPS WHICH YOU CONDUCT YOURSELF OR YOU ENTRUST TO OTHER PEOPLE AND THE TWO LEDGERS RESULTING THEREFROM

Trips are made usually in two ways, either personally or through somebody else, therefore two are the ways to keep their accounts and the book always ought to be in duplicate whether the trip is made by you personally or it is in charge of somebody else One ledger is kept at home and the other one is taken along and kept on the trip If you conduct the trip yourself, for the sake of order and system, you must take a new inventory also a small Ledger and small Journal among the things you take with you and follow the instruction above given If you sell or buy or exchange, you must charge and credit according to the facts, persons, goods, cash, traveling capital, traveling profit and loss, etc This is the best way, no matter what other people may say You might keep an account with the mercantile house which furnishes you with the goods which you take on the trip In this case you shall credit the said house in your little Ledger and charge the different goods one by one In this way you would open your mercantile house accounts, capital account, etc, as in your main books, and coming back safe and sound you would return to the mercantile house either other goods in exchange for those that you took or money, and you would close the accounts with the entering in your big Ledger the respective profit or loss item In this way your business will be clear If, however you entrust the trip to some other party, then you should charge this party with all the goods that you entrust with him, saying Per trip entrusted to so and so, etc, and you should keep an account with him, as if he were one of your customers, for all goods and moneys, keeping separate accounts, etc, and he on his part will set up a little Ledger in which he makes you creditor for everything When he comes back he will balance with you, and if your traveling salesman were in fetters (sentence remains unfinished in the original)

De 1ª. ptita famosa ditta ꝓ e dãno o vero auanço e desauanço. cõe la sabbia a tenere nel q̃derno. e pche ella nõ si metta nel çornale comme le altre ptite Cap°. 27

SEqta doppo ogni altª pti°. 1ª. chiamata de ꝓ e dãno o voi dire vtile e dãno seqto o vero auanço e desauãço fo alcũo paese ilaqle tutte lalt°. del tuo q̃der° sẽp se hano a saldare cõe nel bilãcio se dira. E q̃sta nõ bisogna si metta i giornale. ma basta solo nel q̃der° pch̃ la nasci i q̃llo d̃le cose auãçate o vero mãcate i dare e hẽre p laqle dirai ꝓ e danno die dare. E ꝓ e dãno die hẽre. cioe q̃do dalcũa robba hauesse pduto. lacui pti°. piu nel tuo q̃derno restasse i dare ch̃ i hẽre. alora aiutarai el suo hẽre p pegiarla al dare acio se saldi. de q̃l tanto che li mancasse. dicẽdo. e die hẽre p ꝓ e dãno q̃l q̃ metto p saldo de q̃sta. p danno seqto 7c. e segnarai le carti d̃l ꝓ e danno nel trar fuora la ptiª. E al ꝓ e dãno andarai i dare. dicẽdo ꝓ e dãno die dare a di 7c. p la tal robba. p danno seqto tanto 7c. posto i q̃lla alchie hẽre p suo saldo ape a carti 7c. E se la fosse piu i hẽre ditta robba ch̃ i dare. alora faresti p lo aduerso.. E cosi andarai facẽdo a 1ª. p 1ª. de tutte robbe finite. o male o bñ ch̃ sieno andate acio sẽpre el tuo q̃derno se ritroui paro de pti°. cioe ch̃ tante sene troui i dare q̃te i hẽre. pch̃ cosi se deue ritrouare a star bñ çõe se dira nel bilancio. E cosi succinta mẽte vedarai se guadagni o ꝑo pdi e q̃to. E q̃sta ptita. poi ancora lei si cõuerra saldare i q̃lla del cauedale. laqle e vltĩa de tutti li q̃derni. e p cõseq̃nte receptaculo d̃ tutte le alt°. cõe itẽderai 7c. Comme se debino reportare innançe le ptite d̃l quaderno. q̃n fossero piene e in che luoco sabia portare el resto. a cio nõ sia p̃sa malitia nel quaderno. Cap°. 28.

ANcora e danotare q̃do 1ª. ptita e piena. o i dare o i hẽre che nõ ui si ripo metter piu bisogna portarla innãçe imediate a tutte lalt°. nõ lasciãdo spacio nel q̃derno fra el ditto reporto. e lalt°. pti°. ch̃ se reputaria fraude nel lib°. E deuese reportare i q̃sto modo. cõe disop°. dicẽmo d̃ saldarle i ꝓ e dãno. cosi nelli reporti. ilor medesime cõuiẽse obsuare i dare e i hẽre sẽça metterle in çornale pch̃ li reporti nõ bisogna poner li i çornale bẽch̃ si potrebbe achi volesse e verria a respõdere ancor bñ. ma nõ fa bisog°. pch̃ se hẽria q̃lla fatica. piu sẽça frutto. siche bisogna aiutar la minor q̃tª. cioe se le. piu in dare ch̃ i hẽre ditta ptiª. di q̃l tanto aiuta el suo hẽre 7c. E p ex°. chiaro tene mettaro q̃ 1ª. e mettiamo che Martino habia fatto cõ teco cõto lõgo de piu pti°. i modo. che la sua posta sia. da reportare e sia nel tuo q̃der°. a carti. 30. e lultiª. ptiª. de tutto el q̃der°. sia a carti. 60. i q̃ma. e ala medesima façata sia luogo da poterui ancora locare q̃lla de Mart°. E siate d̃bito el ditto ₰. 80 ß 15. g. 15. p̃. 24. deliq̃li in tutto te habia dato. ₰ 72. ß 9. g. 3. p̃. 17. dico che batta el suo hẽre d̃l suo dare. cioe. 72. 9. 3. 17. resta. ₰ 8 ß 6 g. 5 p̃ 7. E de tanto lo deui portar debitore auanti. E de q̃llo medesimo deui aiutare la ptita in hẽre. e dirai cosi. a di. 7c p lui medẽo q̃l porto auanti in q̃sto al dia dare p resto q̃l põgo q̃ p saldo. ₰ 8 ß 6 g 5 p̃ 7. val a carti. 60. ₰ ß g. p̃ E d̃pẽnerai la ptiª in dare e in hẽre cõ 1ª. linea diametraliter. E fatto q̃sto andarai a carti. 60. in dare porrai ditto resto ponẽdo sẽpre disop°. pª. se nõ ci fosse el M° cõe dinançe fo ditto. E dirai cosi Martino die dare a di 7c. p lui medemo p resto tratto da drieto in q̃sto posto al die hẽre p saldo d̃ q̃lla. val a carti. 30. ₰ 8 ß 6 g 5 p̃ 7. E q̃sto medesi° modo obsuarai in tutte pti° che hauesse a reportare auanti incatenandole al modo ditto e sẽça interuallo alcũo. po ch̃ sẽpre le pti°. si vogliano ponere cõe nascano d̃ luogo. sito. di. e milesi° acio niũ te possi caluniare. 7c. Del modo a sapere mutare el milesimo nel quaderno fra le partite che ala çornata acascano quando ogni anno non si saldasi li libri. Capitolo. 29.

POrria esser alcuolte che nele tue ptite in quaderno, tu hauessi a mutar milesi° E nõ, hauesse saldato. alora ditto milesi°. deui ponere in margine aripetto ditta ptita ch̃ cosi e nata. cõe fo detto sopra in cap. 15°. E tutte laltre che la seqteranno se intẽderanno al ditto mile°. Ma sẽpre e buono desaldare ognanno. maxime chi e in cõpª. pche el ꝓuerbio dici ragion spessa amista lõga. E cosi farai a tutte simili.

Comme se debia leuare vn conto al debitore che lo domandasse. e ancora al suo patrõe siando fatore e commesso de tutta la amministratione de le robbe Capitolo. 30.

BIsogna oltra li dati documẽti. sape leuare vn cõto al tuo debitore ch̃ te lo domãdasse. El q̃le nõ si po de ragion negare. p̃stim q̃do cõ teco hauesse tenuto conto lõgo. de piu anni e mesi 7c. alora farate da prin° ch̃ insiemi haueste a fare. o da altro termine ch̃ lui el volesse q̃do fra voi fossero stati altri saldi da q̃l tp̃o ch̃ lo vole per vna volta volentieri li le leua. E de tutto farai vna partita in vn foglio che ui capa. E q̃do in 1ª. facia non capisse saldarai tutto quello che li hauerai posto e porterai el resto dalaltro lato del foglio in dare. overo hauere commo nel capitolo 28°. fo detto. E va continuando. E a lultimo. redullo in resto netto duna sola partita in dare. o hauer secondo che la nascera. E questi tali conti si uogliano leuare con grandissima diligentia.

CHAPTER 27

ANOTHER WELL-KNOWN ACCOUNT NAMED PROFIT AND LOSS, OR PROFIT AND DEFICIT HOW IT SHOULD BE KEPT IN THE LEDGER AND WHY IT IS NOT KEPT IN THE JOURNAL AS THE OTHER ACCOUNTS.

After the other accounts, there must follow one which is named variously, according to different localities, Favor and Damage (*Pro a Danno*), or Profit and Damage (*Utile a Danno*), or Increase and Deficit (*Avanzi e Desavanzi*) Into this other accounts in the Ledger have their remainders, as we will show when we speak of the trial balance You should not put these entries in the Journal, but only in the Ledger, as they originate from overs or shorts in the debits and credits, and not from actual transactions You shall open the account this way

Profit and Loss debit (*dee dare*—shall give), and Profit and Loss credit (*dee havere*—shall have)

That is, if you had sustained a loss in a special line of merchandise and in this account in your Ledger would show less in the credit than the debit, then you will add the difference (*saldo*) to the credit so as to make it balance, and you shall enter as follows

Credit (*dee havere*—shall have), per Profit and Loss, so much, which I enter here in order to balance on account of loss sustained—and so on, and you will mark the page of the Profit and Loss account where you write down the entry Then you go to the Profit and Loss account and in the debit column you shall enter as follows

Profit and Loss debit (*dee dare*—shall give), on this day, to such and such loss sustained, so much—which has been entered in the credit of said merchandise account in order to balance it at page so and so If the account of this special merchandise would show a profit instead of loss—that is, more in the credit than in the debit—then you will proceed in the opposite way The same you shall do one by one for all accounts with merchandise or different things, whether they show good or bad results, so that your Ledger always shows the accounts in balance—that is, as much in the debit as in the credit This is the condition the Ledger will be in if it is correct, as I will explain to you when I am talking of the balance In this way you will see at a glance whether you are gaining or losing, and how much. And this account must then be transferred for its closing (*saldo*) into the capital account, which is always the last in all the ledgers and is consequently the receptacle of all other accounts, as you will understand

CHAPTER 28

HOW FULL ACCOUNTS IN THE LEDGER SHOULD BE CARRIED FORWARD AND THE PLACE TO WHICH THEY MUST BE TRANSFERRED SO THAT NO CROOKEDNESS CAN BE PRACTICED IN THE LEDGER

You should know that when an account has been filled out, either in the debit or in the credit, and you cannot make any more entries in the space reserved for such an account, you must at once carry this account forward to a page after all your other accounts, so that there is no space left in the Ledger between this transferred account and the last of the other accounts Otherwise it would be considered a fraud It must be carried forward in the manner which we have given above when writing about the balancing of profit and loss In making the transfers, you should make entries on the debit and credit sides only, without making any entry in the Journal Transfers are not made in the Journal, still, if you so desired, you might do that and it would be all right, but it is not necessary, because it would be that much more trouble without any necessity All that need be done is to increase the smaller quantity—that is, if the account shows more in the debit than in the credit, you ought to add the difference to the credit I will give you, now, an example of one of these transfers

Let us suppose that Martino has had a long account with you of several transactions, so that his account should be transferred from ledger page 30 Suppose further that the last account of your book is at page 60, and is at the top of said page, so that on the same page there is space enough to transfer the Martino account Suppose that there is on debit side, L 80, S 15, G 15, P 24, and the credit shows that he has given you, L 72, S 9, G 3, P 17 Deducting the credit from the debit, there is a remainder (*resta*) of L 8, S 6, G 5, P 7 This is the amount that you should bring forward to the debit side of the new page, and on the old page you must add the same amount in the credit column to make it balance, saying as follows

On such and such day, etc, per himself, I bring forward (*porta avanti*) this amount to the debit side as a remainder (*resta*), and the same amount I enter here per closing (*saldo*), that is L 8, S 6, G 5, P 7 see at page 60
L , S _, G , P

And you shall cancel the account both on the debit and credit side with a diagonal line After that, you will go to page 60 and shall enter in the debit column the said remainder, always writing down at the top of the page the year, if none already has been mentioned, as has been said above You shall enter there as follows

Martino debit on such and such day per himself, as per remainder (*resta*) taken from the page of his old account and therein entered per closing (*saldo*), see page 30 L 8, S 6, G 5, P 7

This is the way for you to proceed with all occounts that you should transfer Place them, as I have told you, without leaving any space in between The accounts should be opened in the order in which they originate in such place and at such time, so that nobody can speak evil of you

CHAPTER 29

HOW TO CHANGE THE YEAR IN THE LEDGER BETWEEN TWO SUCCESSIVE ENTRIES IN CASE THE BOOKS ARE NOT CLOSED EVERY YEAR

It might be that you must change the year in your ledger accounts before you balance it. In this case, you should write the year in the margin before the first entry of the new year, as has been previously said at Chapter 15, all the following entries should be understood as having occurred during that year

But it is always good to close the books each year, especially if you are in partnership with others The proverb says Frequent accounting makes for long friendship Thus you will do in similar cases

CHAPTER 30

HOW AN ABSTRACT OR STATEMENT OF AN ACCOUNT SHOULD BE MADE TO A DEBTOR WHO MIGHT REQUEST IT, OR FOR YOUR EMPLOYER IN CASE YOU ARE MANAGER OR COMMISSIONER OF THE ADMINISTRATION OF HIS PROPERTY

In addition, you must know how to make an abstract or a statement of an account if your debtor requests it. This is a favor that cannot be refused, especially if your debtor has had an account with you for years or months, etc In this case you should go away back to the time when you began to have transactions with him, or back to the time from which he desires to have his statement, in case you have had previous settlements And you should do this willingly You should copy all his account on a sheet of paper large enough to contain it all If it should not be large enough, you will draw a balance at the end of the page and shall carry the latter, in debit or credit, forward to the other side of the sheet, as I told you at Chapter 28 And so on, until the end of the account, and at the end you must reduce the whole account to the net remainder in a single entry in debit or credit, according to the facts These statements must be made out very carefully

E q̃sto modo obsuarai neli fatti tuoi ꝓprij.e tuoi auctori. Ma se tu aministrasse ꝑ altri. ꝑ usa
de acomãde.o de cõmisiõi alora similmẽte cosi lo leuarai al patrõe cõe ho pōto lhauarai dolto
al libro facẽdote creditore de tp̃o i tp̃o dele tuoi ꝓuisiõi fo vñ patti. E poi i fine ꝑ resto ner
to.del retratto.farate suo debitore o vero creditore q̃do del tuo lihauesse messo e lui poi lo re
uedara.pōtãdolo.cõ lisuoi. E trouãdolo star bene.te uorra meglio. E piu te fidara.ꝑ chebi
sogna che de tutto q̃llo te a dato o mandato che del receuere a lĩe di tua mano li ne asegni
aministrationi ordinatamẽte. E po nota bene. E ꝑ lauerso farai tu leuarlo a tuoi fattori o
vero cõmessi similiter. Ma p°.che fora se dieno li conti si uogliano ben pontare cõ tutte lo
ro ꝑtte i q̃derno i giornale e memoriale. E con tutti luoghi che lauesse scritte acio nõ nascesse
se errore fra le ꝑti. Del modo e ordine a sape retrattare o vero istornare 1ª. o piu ꝑtte
che ꝑ errore hauesse poste i alt° luogo ch douessero ãdare cõe auene ꝑ smẽoragie. Cap° 31.

E Ancora necessario al bon quadernieri sapere retrattare. o voi dire storna-
re ala fiorentina vna partita che per errore hauesse posta in altro luogo che el
la douesse andare. comme se lauesse messa in dare. E douiala ponere in hauere
Et econtra. E quando douia porla aconto de Martino. E lui la misse a conto
de giouani et ecõtra. Pero che ale volte non si po tanto essere attento che non si falli comme el
prouerbio sona. Cioe chi non fa non falla. E chi non falla non impara. E pero in retrat-
tarla tirrai q̃sto modo. Cioe q̃do hauesse messa la ꝑtita poniamo a dare e douia andare in
hauere ꝑ retrala porraine 1ª.alt°.alicontro dessa i hauere de q̃l tanto de ponto. E dirai in q̃
sto modo a di.7c.ꝑ altretanto posto dincontro al die dare. E douia metterla q̃ i hauere val
a carti 7c. E tra fora q̃lle medesime.℔.ß.g. p̃ che ponesti ꝑ erro. E denançe a ditta ꝑtita farai
1ª.croci.o altro segno. acio leuando tu elcõto laueghi alassare. E subito posta q̃sta ꝑ retrat
to.ch e q̃to se nulla hauesse scritto del deuere. E tu poi la reponi i ditto hauere cõe douia an
dare e stara bñ. Comme se debbia fare elbilancio del libro e del modo a reportare vn
libro in laltro.cioe el q̃derno vecchio nel quaderno nuouo e del modo a pontarlo con lo suo
giornale e memoriale e altri scontri dẽtro e difuore del ditto quaderno. Cap°. 32.

Q Ueste cose finora bẽ notate bisogna hora dar modo al reporto de vn libro in lal
tro q̃do uolesse mutar libro ꝑ cagione che fosse pieno o vero ꝑ ordine annuale
de milesimo cõe el piu si costuma fare ꝑ luochi famosi che ogni anno. maxime
anni milesimi nuoui li gran mercatanti sẽpre lo obsuano. E q̃sto atto insiemi con li
seq̃nti. E detto elbilancio del libro. La q̃l cosa voler seq̃re.bisogna grandissima diligẽtia e ꝑ
ordine tirrai q̃sto modo.cioe P°.farai de hauere vn cõpagno.che mal porresti ꝑ te solo far
lo. E alui darai in mano el giornale ꝑ piu tua cautella. E tu tirrai el q̃derno grande e dirai
alui gomẽçando dala p°.ꝑtita del giornale che chiami le carti del tuo q̃derno. doue q̃lla
sia posta. p° i dare e poi i hauere. E cosi tu lubbidirai. E trouerai sẽpre doue te manda. E q̃l
te dira la ꝑtita de ch o de chi la sira. E q̃to sia elsuo tratto fore. E cosi tu vedarai i q̃l tal luo
go doue te manda se hauerai q̃l ch.o q̃l chi. E q̃l tanto apoāto tratto fore. E trouãdola
stare aponto cõe i giornale lançarala.cioe pontarala. overo farali q̃lche segno alibito i su le
℔.o altroue che non te abagliasse. E q̃l tal segno o vero lançata che cosi in altri luochi si co
stuma dir.dirai che faça.elcõpagno nel giornale.ala medesima ꝑti°. E guarda che mai tu sẽ
ça lui ne lui sença te pōtasse.overo lãçasse ꝑtita alcũa ꝑche porrebe nascere grãdi errori.ꝑo
che la ꝑtita pōtata che sia vol dire star bñ col debito modo. E q̃sto ancora se obsua i leuar
de conti a debitori nançe che li le daghi in mano hauerlo scõtrato e pontato cõ li luochi dl
q̃derno e del giornale o daltri luochi che auesse notate ditte ꝑtite cõe sopra al.30.ca° fo dt
to. E fatto q̃sto ꝑ ordine a tutto el q̃derno e giornale. E trouando tu aponto cõe lui i dare e
hauere le ꝑtite siran giuste e ben poste. Nota ch lui nel giornale ꝑ bona memoria fara doi
lançate o vero pōti a 1ª.sola ꝑtita. E tu nel q̃derno usei solo a farne 1°.ꝑ ꝑti°. si cõe duna ꝑti°
de giornale in q̃derno sene fa doi cosi si fa doi ponti. E ꝑo nel pontare del bilancio i giorna-
le ach e buono far doi pōti lũo sotto lalt°.ale ℔ o uero doi lãçate 1ª. sotto lalt°.ch dinora dit
ta ꝑti°. star bñ i dare e hẽre al q̃der° Alcũi nel giornale ꝑ lo dare pōtano dauãti al.p. E ꝑ lo
hauere dreto ale ℔. cõe se sia lũo e lalt° sta bñ. Nõ dimeno si porria far ãcora cõ 1ª.pōtatu
ra sola i giornale.cioe solo ꝑ lo dare.ꝑche tu poi per testesso porresti pontare lhauere a qual
partita che hai in dare nel quaderno sempre te manda per che subito tu hai quiui el numero
dele carti doue sta lhauere quando bene quel del giornale non te mandasse siche scontran-
dote tu con lui solo indare per te stesso porresti sequire lo hauere ma piu commodo te fia cõ
lo compagno a modo ditto. Ma se fornito el giornale de pōtare a te auançase in quaderno
ꝑtita alcũa che non uenisse pōtata in dare o in hauere denotaria nel quaderno esser errore.
cioe che q̃lla seraue posta superflua in q̃l dare o vero hauere el qual errore tu subito retratta-

The following is the way you have to proceed in adjusting your own business with the business of your employer But if you should act for others as an agent or commissioner, then you will make out a statement for your employer just as it appears in the ledger, crediting yourself from time to time with your commissions according to your agreements Then at the end you shall charge yourself with the net remainder, or you shall credit yourself if you had to put in any money of your own Your employer will then go through this statement, compare it with his own book, and if he finds it correct, he will like you better and trust you more For this reason, of all the things that he gave or sent you, you should with your own handwriting keep an orderly account when you receive them Observe this carefully

On the contrary, if you are the employer, you may have your managers or commissioners make out these statements for you But before these statements are delivered they ought to be compared carefully with each entry in the Ledger, Journal and Memorandum Book, or with any other paper relative thereto, so that no mistake could be made between the parties

CHAPTER 31.

HOW TO TAKE OUT ONE OR MORE ENTRIES WHICH BY MISTAKE YOU MIGHT HAVE ENTERED IN A DIFFERENT PLACE FROM THE RIGHT ONE, WHICH MAY HAPPEN THROUGH ABSENTMINDEDNESS

The good bookkeeper should also know how to take out—or as they call it in Florence "*stornare*"—an entry which by mistake you might have written down in the wrong place as, for instance, if you had entered it as a debit instead of a credit entry, or when you have to enter it in the account of Mr Martino and you put it in the account of Mr Giovanni

For at times you cannot be so diligent that you are unable to make mistakes The proverb says He who does nothing, makes no mistakes he who makes no mistakes, learns nothing

And you shall correct this entry as follows If you had placed this entry in the debit column while you should have put it in the credit column, in order to correct this, you shall make another entry opposite this one in the credit for the same amount And you shall say thus On such and such day for the amount which has been entered opposite here under the debit and should have been put in the credit, see page, etc , and you shall write down in the column of figures L.... S.... G.... P.... which you wrote down by mistake in the other column In front of these two entries you shall mark a cross or any other mark so that when you make out an abstract or statement of the account you should leave these entries out After you have made this correction it is just as if you had written nothing in the debit column You then make the entry in the credit column as it should have been and everything will be as it should have been

CHAPTER 32

HOW THE BALANCE OF THE LEDGER IS MADE AND HOW THE ACCOUNTS OF AN OLD LEDGER ARE TRANSFERRED TO A NEW ONE

After all we have said you must know now how to carry forward the accounts from one Ledger to another if you want to have a new Ledger for the reason that the old one is all filled up or because another year begins, as is customary in the best known places, especially at Milan where the big merchants renew every year their Ledgers

This operation, together with the operations of which we will speak, is called the balancing (*bilancio*) of the Ledger, and if you want to do this well you shall do it with great diligence and order That is, first you shall get a helper as you could hardly do it alone You give him the Journal for greater precaution and you shall keep the Ledger Then you tell him, beginning with the first entry in the Journal, to call the numbers of the pages of your Ledger where that entry has been made, first in debit and then in credit. Accordingly in turn you shall obey him and shall always find the page in the Ledger that he calls and you shall ask him what kind of an entry it is, that is, for what and for whom, and you shall look at the pages to which he refers to see if you find that item and that account If the amount is the same, call it out If you find it there the same as in the journal, check it (*lanzarala*—mark it with a lance Λ or V) or dot it (*pontarala*), or any proper mark over the lire mark, or in some other place, so that you can readily see it You ask your helper to make a similar mark or check—as we are used to call it in some places—in the Journal at the same entry Care must be taken that no entry will be dotted (*pontata*) either by you without him, or by him without you as great mistakes might be made otherwise, for once the entry is dotted it means that it is correct The same is done in making out statements of accounts for your debtors before you deliver them They should have been compared with the Ledger and Journal, or with any other writing in which the entries of the transaction have been recorded, as we have said at Chapter 30

After you have proceeded in this way through all the accounts of the Ledger and Journal and found that the two books correspond in debit and credit, it will mean that all the accounts are correct and the entries entered correctly Take care that your helper shall mark each entry in the Journal with two dots or little lances, in the ledger you mark down only one for each entry because you know that for each entry in the Journal there are two made in the Ledger, therefore, the two dots or lances

In making this balance it is good if you mark in the Journal two dots or lances under the lire, one under the other This will mean that the entry is correct in debit and credit in the Ledger Some use these marks in the Journal They put a mark before the per for the debit and after the lire for the credit Any way both customs are good, however, one single mark in the Journal might be enough, that is, only the debit mark, because you can then mark yourself the credit side on the page of the Ledger where that entry is as this page is mentioned in the debit entry in your ledger It will then not be necessary for your helper to call to you this credit page So that by comparing only the debit side with him you could yourself check the credit side But it would be more convenient for you if you proceed with your helper in the manner above said

After you have finished checking off the Journal, if you find in the Ledger some account or entry which has not been checked off in debit or credit, this would indicate that there has been some mistake in the Ledger that is, that that entry is superfluous whether in the debit or credit, and you shall correct this error

rai daẽdo lamedesima q̃ª alincontro. cioe se la sira de piu in dare. E tu altre tanto porrai in
havere. Et ecõtra. laq̃lcosa cõe sabia aditare disopra te fo detto al cap°. p̃cedẽte. E cosi ha
rai medicato tutto. El medesimo seria q̃do lui havesse in giornale ptita supflua. che a te nel
quaderno mãcasse in dare o in havere che pur fallo nel quaderno denotarebbe. El quale si
deue repare al modo contrario del supfluo. Cioe che tu alora ditta ptita subito lapongbi ĩ
dare e in havere in quaderno. facendo mẽtione dela varieta del çorno. pche lanascera mol-
to piu tarda in quaderno che nõ douia. Dele quali varieta. sẽpre elbõ quadernsero deue far
ne mẽtione pche lenaschino p levar il suspetto del lib°. amodo el bon notaro neli suoi instru
mẽti. nequali non po ne giongnere nẽ sminuire sença pticulare mẽtione de tal augumẽto. o
vero decremento. cosi sẽpre tal respetto cõuiẽ che sia nel bon quadernieri. acio la rialita mer
cantesca. debitamẽte se venga amantenẽre. Ma se la ditta ptita. solo mancasse dal dare o dẽ
lhavere. alora basta la ponghi 1ª. sola volta. da q̃l tal lato doue la mancasse. con ditte mentio
ni. Cioe cõe p errore lai fatto ꝛc. E cosi harai tutte gustate tue ptite. lequali trouandole a soi
scontri cõe e discorso denota eltuo quaderno eẽr giusto e ben tenuto. Unde nota che nel dit
to quaderno sirãno a levolte molte ptite non pontate con lo scontro del giornale p chenon
si hano aritrouare inesso. E q̃ste sirãnno li resti posti al die dare o in havere p saldi dele p-
tite nel portarle havanti cõe dicẽmo in lo cap°. 28. alora da te stesso di q̃lli tali resti trouerai
ĩ. ditto q̃derno suoi scontri. cioe in dare. E in havere regẽdote p lo n°. de le carti che ila ditta
ptita notate sirãno. E trouãdo scontro a suoi luoghi giudica similmẽte elq̃derno star bñ ꝛc.
E q̃llo che finora se detto del scõtro del quaderno con lo giornale. el simile intẽdi p°. douersi
fare del memoriale o vero squartafoglio cõ logiornale a di p di. q̃do vsassi tener memoria
le a modo che in principio di q̃sto trattato de lui te dixi. e cosi cõ tutti altri libri tenesse. Ma
lultimo conuen essere elquaderno. elo penultimo el giornale. Jdeo ꝛc.

Del modo e ordine ascriuere lefacende che occuressero nel tempo che si fa elbilancio. cioe
che si saldano li libri. e comme neli libri vechi non si debia scriuere ne innouare cosa alcuna
in ditto tempo e lacagione perche. Cap°. 33.

Tutte q̃ste cose ordinatamente fatte e obseruate. guarda non innouasse piu ptiᵉ
in alcũ libro antiano al quaderno. cioe immemoriale. E giornale. perche el saldo
tutto de tutti li libri sẽpre si deue intendere fatto in 1°. medesimo çorno Ma se fa
cende te acadesse in q̃l meçço che fai el tuo saldo o vero bilancio. porrale in libri
nuoui nequali intẽdi fare reporto. cioe in lomemoriale o vero giornale. ma nõ in quaderno
p fin tanto che non li hai portati li resti del p° quaderno. E se ancora non havesse ordinati
libri nuoui porrai le facẽde con li suoi çorni da pte in 1°. sfoglio p fin siran fatti ditti libri. E
alora li leporrai. signati che siran tutti de nuouo segno. Cioe se q̃lli che saldi sirã segnati. cro
ci q̃sti segna de. A. ꝛc. Cõme se debiano saldare tutte le ptite del q̃derno vecbio. e ĩ chi
e pche: e de la sũma sũmarũ del dare e delauere vltio scontro del bilãcio. Cap°. 34.

Fatto che harai q̃sto cõ dilegẽtia. E tu date saldarai tutto eltuo q̃derno aptita p
pti°. ĩ q̃sto modo. che p°. comẽçarai dalacassa debitori. robbe e auentori. E quelle
portarai in libro. A. cioe in quaderno nuouo che non bisogna cõe fo detto diso
pra liresti ponere ingiornale. summarai tutte lor ptite in dare e havere aiutãdo
sẽpre lamenore cõe te diti. sopra del portare auãti. che q̃sto atto de 1° quaderno in laltro. E
de põto simile aq̃llo e fra loro non e altra differentia senon che in q̃llo elresto si porta auan
ti nel medesimo quaderno. E in q̃sto de 1° libro in laltro. E doue in q̃llo chiamani le carti d
q̃l libro pprio in q̃sto sichiama lecarti del libro seq̃ẽte in modo che nel reporto de vn libro
in laltro. solo 1ª. uolta p ciascũo quaderno se mette laptita. E q̃sta ꝓrogatiua a lultima ptita
sempre deli quaderni che nullaltra mai po havere cõe nel pcesso deto hai notato. E deuesse
tal riporto cosi ditare. cioe mettiamo che tu habia. Martino debitore p resto nello tuo qua
derno. croci. a carti. 60. de. ₰ 12. ß 15. g 10. p̃ 26. E habilo a portare in quaderno. A. a carti. 8:
in dare te conuen nel libro croci aiutare lhavere. doue dirai cosi desotto a tutte laltre partite
E a di ꝛc. ponẽdo sempre el medesimo di. che fai elbilancio. p lui medemo porto in quader
no. A. aldie dare per resto qual q̃ põgo per saldo de questa val acarti. 8. ₰ 12. ß 15. g 10. p̃ 26
E depennarai la ditta partita in dare e havere diametraliter cõe nel reporto te insegnai po-
nẽdo lasũma de tutta laptita sotto nel cãpo de ditta ptita in dare e in hẽre. cioe tãto da lũo
lato q̃to da lalt°. acio pa a locbio subito star bñ e iq̃le cõe se recerca al bõ saldo. ponẽdo nel
trar fora. el numero dele carti del quaderno. A. doue tal resto porti. E poi in lo quaderno.
A. in dare dirai cosi prima ponendo sopra incima de la carta. el suo milesimo. El giorno ne
la partita per lacasone detta sopra in lo cap. 15°. cioe Martino deltale ꝛc. die dare a di. ꝛc p

by making an entry for the same amount in the opposite side—that is, if the superfluous entry was in the debit, you make an entry on the credit side, or *vice versa* And how you should proceed to correct the error I have told you in the preceding chapter The same would be done in case your helper finds some entry which your ledger did not show whether in the debit or credit column, which also would indicate an error in the ledger and should be corrected in a different way That is, you should make that entry or open that account in the debit or credit, mentioning the different dates, as the entry would be made later than it should have been A good bookkeeper should always mention why such differences arise, so that the books are above suspicion, thus the notary public in his instruments need not mention what has been added or omitted Thus the good bookkeeper must act so that the mercantile reputation be kept up

But if the said entry should have been entered on only one side, debit or credit, then it would be sufficient for you to put it where it is missing, mentioning how it happened through mistake etc So you will go on through all your accounts and, if they agree, you know that your Ledger is right and well kept

You must know that there may be found in the Ledger some entries which are not in the Journal and cannot be found in the Journal These are the difference between the debit and credit placed there to close (*per saldi*) the different accounts when they are carried forward, as we have said in Chapter 28 Of these balances or remainders, you will find their correlative entries in the Ledger, whether in debit or credit, on the page indicated in these accounts When you find each correlative entry in its proper place, you may conclude that your Ledger is in proper order

What we have said so far about comparing the Ledger with the Journal, should be observed also in comparing the memorandum book or scrap book with the Journal, day by day, if you use the memorandum book, in the manner I spoke about at the beginning of this treatise If you have other books, you should do the same The last book to be compared should be the Ledger, the next to the last the Journal

CHAPTER 33

HOW THE TRANSACTIONS WHICH MIGHT OCCUR WHILE YOU BALANCE YOUR BOOKS SHOULD BE RECORDED, AND HOW IN THE OLD BOOKS NO ENTRY SHOULD BE MADE OR CHANGED DURING THAT TIME, AND REASONS WHY

After you have regularly done and observed all these things, see that no new entry is made in any book which comes before the Ledger—that is, in the memorandum book and Journal—because the equalizing or closing (*el saldo*) of all the books should be understood to take place on the same day But if, while you are balancing you books, some transactions should occur, you shall enter them in the new books to which you intend to carry forward the old ones—that is, in the memorandum book or Journal, but not in the Ledger, until you have carried forward all the different accounts of the old Ledger If you have not yet a new set of books, then you will record these transactions and their respective explanations on a separate sheet of paper until the books are ready When the new books are ready, you enter them in these books which shall bear new marks—that is, if the old ones that you are balancing now were marked with a cross, then you should mark these new ones with the capital letter A

CHAPTER 34

HOW ALL THE ACCOUNTS OF THE OLD LEDGER SHOULD BE CLOSED AND WHY ABOUT THE GRAND TOTALS OF THE DEBITS AND CREDITS, WHICH IS THE PREPARATION OF THE TRIAL BALANCE

After you have done this carefully, you shall close your Ledger accounts in this way You should commence first with cash account, then the different debtors, then the merchandise, and then your customers Transfer the remainders in Ledger A, that is, in the new Ledger You should not, as I have said above, transfer the remainders in the new Journal

You shall add all the different entries in debit and in credit, always adding to the smaller side the difference, as I have told you above when explaining the carrying forward of the remainder These two accounts are practically the same thing, the only difference is that in the first case the remainder was carried forward to another page of the same Ledger while in this instance it is carried forward from one Ledger to another While in the first instance you would mark down the new page of the same Ledger, in this case you mark down the page of the new Ledger, making the transfer from one ledger to another, any account should appear only once in each ledger This is a peculiarity of the last entry of the accounts of the Ledgers

In making the transfer, you should proceed as follows Let us suppose that the account of Mr Martino has a debit remainder (*resto*) in your "Cross" Ledger at page 60 of L 12, S 15, G 10 P 26, and you want to transfer it to Ledger A at page 8 in debit, in the "Cross" Ledger you have to add to the credit column and you shall put the following at the end of all the other entries On such and such day—putting down always the same day in which you do the balancing (*bilancio*)—per himself as posted to Ledger A to the debit, per remainder (*resto*), which amount I add here in order to close (*saldo*)—value, see page 8 L 12, S 15, G 10, P 26

And then you shall cancel the account in the debit and credit diagonally, as I have told you in talking about the bringing forward of the accounts Then put down the total of all the entries, in the debit as well as in the credit, so that the eye can see at a glance that it is all even You shall also write down at the new page in Ledger A, in the debit column, as follows First you put down at the top of the page the year, and you put the day in front of the place where you make the entry for the reason mentioned in Chapter 15, then you say, Mr Martino so and so, debit (*dee dare*—shall give) on such and such day

lui medemo p resto tratto del libro.croci.posto al dic hauere per saldo de.qlla.val a car. 60. ß 12.ß 15.g° 10.p 26.E cosi andarai saldado tutte le ptite nel lib°.croci.ch tu intedi portare i qderno. A. de cassa cauedal.robbe mobili. e stabil.debitori.creditori.officii.sensarie. pesadori de comun 7c. con liquali se vsa ale uolte andare aconto longo 7c. Ma quelle partite che non volesse portare in ditto quaderno. A. che porriéno eére qlle che solo a te saptégano. E nõ se obligato a segnarne cõto ad alcu? cõe son spesi de mercãtia.spesi de casa intrata isita.e tutte spese straordinarie.fitti.pesciõi.feudi. o liuelli 7c.qste simili conuégonse saldare in lo medesimo libro.croci nla ptita del p e danno o vero auãçi e desauanç o voi dire vtile e dãno.i qsto modo che loro dare portarai i dare :ch raro si possano hauere i credito qlle de le spesi dicédo.nel saldo aiutando cõe piu volte e ditto sempre lamenore quantita in dare o i hauere p p e dãno i qsto a carti tãte 7c. E cosi tutte le hauerai saldate i qsta del p e danno doue subito poi sũmando suo dare e hauere porai cognescere tuo guadag°.e pdita p ch fira i tal bilancio fatto la parita.cioe ch le cose ch se douiã diffalcare firan diffalcate qlle che se douiano agiongnere firã pportionatamẽte a suci luochi agiõte. E se de qsta ptita.fira p el dare ch lauere tu hauera pdutto ql tanto i tuo trafico dache lo goméçasti. E se fia piu lo hauere alora dirai che ql tanto habia i ditto tpo guadagnato 7c. E veduto ch harai p qsta lutile.e danno tuo seqto.alora qsta saldarai i la ptita del cauedale.doue nel pricipio del tuo manegio ponesti lo inẽtario de tutta la tua faculta. E saldarala i qsto modo che sel dãno se qto fira piu che dio ne guardi ciascuno che realmẽte fo buon xpiano se adopa alora aiutarai lohauere amodo vsato dicẽdo e a di 7c.p cauedal i qstop danno seqto a carti 7c.val 7c. E depẽnerai laptita diametraliter i dare e hauere.vt su°.ponẽdo pure la sũma nel cãpo i dare e hauere che deue hattere para. E poi ala ptita del cauedale i dare dirai.cauedale die dar a di 7c.p p e danno. p danno seqto posto in quella al die hauere p saldo suo val a carti 7c. ß f.g° p.7c. E cosi sene fosse seqto vtile.ch serebbe qdo qlla del p e danno se retrouasse piu i hauere che i dare alora sugiõgiaresti al dare p saldo ql tanto chiamãdo elcauedale ale carti suoi 7c.e alui la porresti i hauere isiemi cõ laltre robbe mobili e stabili.e di nuouo i qsto cauedal qle cõuiẽ eẽre sẽpre lulti°.ptita õ tutti liqderni porrai sẽpre cognoscere tutta tua faculta.giõgnẽdo li debiti e crediti che in lib°. A. portasti 7c E qsta del cauedal del qderno. croci saldarai ancora. E portarala cõe laltre nel qderno. A. in resto e sũma o voi a ptita p ptita che lo poi anche fare.ma si costuma farla in sũma pche 1ª.volta tutto tuo inẽtario ape. E recordate chiamaĩ sue carti.7c. E assetarai poi tutte lepture õl qderno. A.ne lalfabeto ognuna al suo luogo cõe disopra te dissi cap? 5°. Acio sẽpre possi cõ facilita trouare le tue facẽde secondo loro occurençe e cosi fia saldo tutto el primo quaderno con suo giornale e memoriale. E acio fia piu chiaro de ditto saldo.farai questo altro scontro Cioe summarai in vn foglio tutto el dare del quaderno.croci. E ponlo a man sinistra. E summarai tutto suo hauere E põlo aman dextra. E poi queste vltime summe resummarai. E farane de tutte quelle del dar vna sũma che si chiamara sũma sũmarũ. E cosi farai vna sũma õ tutte qlle dalauer che si chiamara ancora lei vna sũmasũmarũ. Ma lap°.fira sũma summarũ.del dare e la fasi chiama summasũmarũ de lo hauere. Or se qste doi sũme summarũ firã pare.cioe che tanto sia luna qto laltra.vz qlla del dare e qlla delo hauere.arguirai el tuo qderno eẽre bẽ gu dato tenuto e saldato p la cagiõe ch di sopra nel cap? 14.fo detto. Ma se luna õ ditte summe summarũ auançasse laltra denotarebbe errore nel tuo quaderno.el qual poi con diligẽtia ti cõuerra trouarlo cõ la industria õlo itelletto che dio te ha dato.e cõ lartefitio dele ragioni che harai bene inparato.laqual pte cõe nel pricipio del pñte dicẽmo e summamẽte necessaria albon mercatante altramente non siando bon ragioneri neli soi fatti andara a tastõi cõe ciecho. E poralline seqre molto dãno.adonca cõ ogni studio e cura sforçarati sopra tutto eẽre buon ragioneri chel modo a tua cõmodita in qsta sublima opa a pieno a tua bastança.te lo dato con tutte sue regole a tutti suo luoghi debitamente poste.si cõe tutto facilmẽte per la tauola nel principio di qsta opera posta porai trouare. E ancora p le cose dette q sequente cõme disopra nel cap°.12° te pmisi a piu tuo recordo faro 1°.epilogo.cioe sumaria recolta cẽtiale de tutto el pñte trattato.che molto sença dubio te fia vtile. E p me recordarati laltissimo pgare che a sue laude e gloria. Jo possa de bene i meglio opãdo pcedere 7c.

Del modo e ordine asap tener le scripture menute cõe sõno scritti de mano lettere familiari police pcessi snie e altri istrumẽti e del registro de le lr̃e.ipoztãti. Ca? 35

S Equita el modo e ordine de saper tener le scripture e chiareçe menute comme sonno scritti de mano de pagamenti facti quietançe de cambi.de robbe date.letere familiari.quali cose sonno fra mercanti de grãdissima stima.e molta impor

per himself as per remainder (*resto*) carried from "Cross" Ledger, which has been added in the credit column in order to close (*saldo*), see page 60, value L 12, S 15, G 10, P 26

Thus you will proceed with all the accounts of the Cross Ledger which you want to transfer to Ledger A cash account, capital account, merchandise, personal property, real property, debtors, creditors, public officers, brokers, public weighmen, etc, with whom we have sometimes very long accounts But as to those accounts which you should not care to transfer to Ledger A, as, for instance, your own personal accounts of which you are not obliged to give an account to another, as, for instance, small mercantile expenses, household expenses, income and expenses and all extraordinary expenses—rentals, *pescioni, feudi* or *livelli*, etc All these accounts should be closed (*saldore*) in the Cross Ledger into the favor and damage account, or increase and deficit, or profit and damage account, as it is sometimes called You shall enter them in the debit column, as it is rare that these expense accounts should show anything in the credit side As I often have told you, add the difference to the column, either debit or credit, which shows a smaller total, saying Per profit and loss in this account, see page, etc By doing so, you shall have closed (*saldore*) all these different accounts in the profit and loss account through which then, by adding all the debit and all the credit entries, you will be able to know what is your gain or loss, for with this balance all entries are equalized, the things that had to be deducted were deducted, and the things that had to be added were added proportionately in their respective places If this account shows more in the debit than in the credit, that means that you have lost that much in your business since you began If the credit is more than the debit, that means that in the same period of time you have gained

After you know by the closing (*saldorai*) of this account what your profit or loss is, then you shall close this account into the capital account in which, at the beginning of your management of your business, you entered the inventory of all your worldly goods You shall close the account in this way If the losses are in excess—from which state of affairs may God keep every one who really lives as a good Christian—then you have to add to the credit in the usual manner, saying On such and such day, Per capital on account of losses in this account, see page so and so, value, etc Then you shall cancel the account with a diagonal line in debit and credit, and put in the total amount of all the debit entries, as well as of the credit entries, which should be equal And then in the capital account you shall write in the debit column Capital debit (*dee dare*—shall give) on such and such day, per profit and loss account on account of losses as marked down in the credit column of said account in order to close (*per saldo*), value, etc

L—, S , G , P

If instead there should be a profit, which will happen when the profit and loss account would show more in the credit than in the debit, then you should add the difference to the debit side to make the equalization, referring to the capital account and respective page You should credit the same amount to the capital account, making the entry on the credit side where all the other goods of yours have been entered, personal or real Therefore, from the capital account, which always must be the last account in the entire Ledger, you may always learn what your fortune is, by adding together all the debits and all the credits, which you have transferred in Ledger A.

Then this capital account should be closed and carried forward with the other accounts to Ledger A, either in total or entry by entry You can do either way, but it is customary to transfer only the total amount, so that the entire value of your inventory (*inventario*) is shown at a glance Don't forget to number the pages, after which you will enter all the different accounts in the alphabet of Ledger A, each at its own place, as I have said at Chapter 5, so that you may find very easily the account you want In this way the entire first Ledger, and with it the Journal and memorandum book, are closed and closed up

In order that it may be clearer that the books were correct before the said closing, you shall summarize on a sheet of paper all the debit totals that appear in the Cross Ledger and place them at the left, then you shall write down all the credit totals at the right Of all these debit totals you make one sum total which is called grand total (*summa summarum*), and likewise you shall make a sum total of all the credit totals, which is also called grand total (*summa summarum*) The first is the grand total of the debits, and the second is the grand total of the credits Now, if these two grand totals are equal—that is, if one is just as much as the other—that is, if those of the debit and those of the credit are alike—then you shall conclude that your Ledger was very well kept and closed, for the reason that I gave you in Chapter 14 But if one of the grand totals is bigger than the other, that would indicate a mistake in your Ledger, which mistake you will have to look for diligently with the industry and the intelligence God gave you and with the help of what you have learned This part of the work, as we said at the beginning is highly necessary to the good merchant, for, if you are not a good bookkeeper in your business, you will go on groping like a blind man and may meet great losses

Therefore, take good care and make all efforts to be a good bookkeeper, such as I have shown you fully in this sublime work how to become one I have given you all the rules and indicated the places where everything can be found, in the table of contents which I have placed at the beginning of this work

Of all the things thus far treated, as I promised you in Chapter 12, I will now give you a summary of the most essential things for your own recollection, which no doubt will be very useful to you

And remember to pray God for me so that to His praise and glory I may always go on doing good

CHAPTER 35

HOW AND IN WHAT ORDER PAPERS SHOULD BE KEPT, SUCH AS MANUSCRIPTS, FAMILY LETTERS POLICIES, PROCESSES, JUDGMENTS AND OTHER INSTRUMENTS OF WRITING AND THE RECORD BOOK OF IMPORTANT LETTERS

Here follow the manner and rules for keeping documents and manuscripts, such as papers relative to payments made, receipts for drafts, or gifts of merchandise, confidential letters, which things are very important for merchants

tança e de gran pericolo in perderle e smarrirle. E prima. dele lettere familiari quali spesso fra te e li toi auentori possano acadere. queste sempre stendi e serba in vn banchetto ala fin del mese. E finito el mese legale in vn maço. e ripolle daparte segnando ognuna defore el di che la receui el di che li respondi. E cosi si fa amese p mese. E poi ala fin de lanno de tutti qsti maçi farai vn maço grande e luoga e segna suo M°. E qn̄do voi alcuna lr̄a a ql ricorri. hauerai i tuo studio ouero scrittoio vna tasca. nela ql reporrai lr̄e ch̄ li amici te desidero ch tu cō lettori mandasse alora. se dici che lamandi a roma. mettila in tasca di roma. e se a firença in qlla de firença 7c. E poi nel spaciare del fante pigliale con le tuoi al tuo respōdente in quel tal luogo le manda pche el seruire sempre e buono e anche suola dar suo beueragio per eser seruito 7c. atorno esso cinta cōpera cōe si fa i piu taschette. cioe in tante q̄te sonno le terre e luoghi in le quali fai le toe facēde cōe diciamo. Roma. Firēçe. Napoli. Milano. Zenoa. Lion. Londra Bruga 7c. E sopra ditte taschette p ordine scriuerai il suo nome. cioe a luna dirai Roma. ala altra. Firēça 7c. in le quali poi reporrai le lr̄e che p qlli luoghi te fossero mandate da qualche aico che lamandasse. E fatta che li harai resposta e mandata pur e in ditta lr̄a de fora. cōe festi del suo receuere. e p chi. Cosi similiter porrai mentione de la resposta. E pche lo mandasti con lo suo giorno. El qual di mai in alcu°. tua facenda fa che mācha. o piccola o grāde ch la sia maxime in lr̄e in le qli sempre ti deue porre il millesimo el di e luogo. el nome tuo el qual nome si costuma mettarlo da pede aman dextra de la lr̄a in vn cātone el M°. cō lo di e luogo fra mercatanti se usa ponerlo disopra nel principio de la lr̄a. Ma p°. a modo bon xp̄iano harai sempre amēte de ponere el glorioso nome de nr̄a salute. cioe el dolci nome de Ihū. ouero in suo scābio la figura de la scā croci. nel cui nome sēp tutte le nr̄e opatiōni debano eēr principiate E farai cosi. croci. 1494. a di. 17. aprile i vinegia. E poi seq̄ta tuo dire. cioe carissimo 7c. ma li studiāti e altre genti cōe sonno religiosi 7c. che non traficano. vsano nel luogo doue la lettera e fatta poner di sotto con lo di e M°. E li mercāti costumano disopra a modo ditto alr°. mente non vi ponendo el di serebe confusione. E di te seria fatto beffe pche se dici la lr̄a che non ha el di notato che le fatta de notte. E qlla che non a notato el luogo se dici che le fatta i lalt°. mōdo e non in q̄sto. e oltra le beffe che pegio e ne seque scandalo vt dixi. Expedita che harai sua resposta poscia al deputato luogo la poni cōe hai inteso. E q̄sto che ditto habiamo de vna sola itēdilo p tutte. Unde e ancora danotare che q̄do le lr̄e che tu mā di fossero de īportança. qlle tale se vogliano p° registrarle in vn libro da parte solo a q̄sto dputato. nel ql registro si deue ponere la lr̄a de verbo ad verbū sella sia d̄ grande īportāça cōe sonno lr̄e de cambio. o de robe mandate o d̄. 7c. o vero registrare solo la substança. cōe memoriale dicēdo i q̄sto di 7c. habiamo scritto al tale 7c. cōe p lo tale 7c. li mandamo le tal cose 7c. so p 1c. sua de di tanti 7c. ci cōmise e richiese 7c. la qual ponēmo in tasca 7c. E di fuore sigilata che harai la tua che mādi e fatto la sopra scritta suso. p molti ponerui el suo segno di fuore. acio si cognosca che sia de mercanti. a iquali molto se deue hauere riguardo. pche son qlli cōe i pricipio di q̄sto trattato dicēmo che mantēgano le repub. E a q̄sto fine de reuerentia el simile li R^mi. Cardinali. pongano defore el loro distito nome. acio niūn se possi scusare de non sape de chi la fossi. E molto piu aptamēte el sancto padre fa le sue patētemēte apte cōe sōno bolle breuilegi 7c. Auēga che alcune cose piu intrinseche. pōga sotto el sigillo dl pescatore 7c. Le qli lr̄e poi a mese p mese o vero anno p anno recorrai i maçi. ouero filçe e da pte le poni ordinaramēte i vno armaro. o tularetto. securo. E cōe nascano ala çornata cosi la setta. acio possi piu p̄sto a tue occurēçe retrouarle d̄ laqlcosa. nō curo piu dire pch so aba stança mai inteso 7c. Scritti de mano nō pagati de tuoi debitori cōme te acēnai disopra nel cap°. 17. seruarai in vn altro luogo piu secreto cōe son cassi e scatole priuate 7c. E le q̄tāçe similiter. serua in luogo securo p ogni respetto. Ma q̄do tu pagasse tu ad altri el riceuere farallo scriuere i 1° libretto de pagamēti cōe in pricipio te dixi. acio nō si possa cosi facilmēte smarire e pdere. E cosi obseruarai de le polliçe che īportano. cōe sōno notole de sensaria d̄ mercati. o de pesadori o bolette d̄ robbe messe o tratte de dogane da mare o da terra e setēçe o cartuline de cōsoli o altri officii o altri istrumenti de notari i pgamena qli se debano reporre i vn luogo da pte. E cosi copie scritture e pcessi delite de pcuratori. E auocati. E similmēte e buono hauere vn lib° separato pli recordi. che si chiami recordāçe nel ql ala çornata farai le tue memorie dele cose che dubitasse nō recordarte. che te ponē tornar dāno. nel ql ogni di al manco la sera nançe vadi adormire darai ochio. se cosa fosse daspedire o dafare che non fusse expedita 7c. ala qll spaçata darai de pēna. E cosi q̄ farai memoria de cose che al vicino e amico p vno o doi di p̄stasse cōe sonno vasa de botegga caldare e altri ordegni 7c. E queste

and, if they are lost, may cause great danger

First, we shall talk of confidential letters which you may write to or receive from your customers You should always keep these in a little desk until the end of the month. At the end of the month tie them together in a bunch and put them away and write on the outside of each the date of receipt and the date of reply, and do this month by month, then, at the end of the year, of all these papers make one big bundle and write on it the year, and put it away Any time you need a letter, go to these bundles

Keep in your desk pouches in which to place the letters that your friends may give you to be sent away with your own letters If the letter should be sent to Rome, put it in the Rome pouch, and if to Florence, put it in the Florence pouch, etc And then when you send your messenger, put these letters with yours and send them to your correspondent in that particular town To be of service is always a good thing, and it is customary also to give a gratuity for that good service

You should have several little compartments or little bags, as many as there are places or cities in which you do business, as, for instance, Rome, Florence, Naples, Milan, Genoa, Lyon, London, Bruges and on each little bag you shall write its proper name—that is, you will write on one "Rome," on another "Florence,' etc, and in these bags you shall put the letters that somebody might send you to be forwarded to those places

When you have answered a letter and sent the answer away, you shall mention on the outside of the said letter the answer, by whom you sent it and the day, just as you did when you received the letter

As to the day, you shall never forget to mark it in any of your transactions, whether small or large, and especially in writing letters in which these things must be mentioned, namely the year, the day, the place, and your name It is customary to put the name at the end of the right side in a corner It is customary among merchants to write the year and the day and the place at the top at the beginning of the letter But first, like a good Christian, you shall always remember to write down the glorious name of our Savior—that is, the name of Jesus or in its place the sign of the Holy Cross, in whose name our transactions must always be made, and you shall do as follows Cross 1494 On this 17th day of April in Venice.

And then go on with what you want to say—that is, "My very dear," etc But the students and other people, like the monks or priests, etc, who are not in business, are used to writing the day and year at the end after writing the letter The merchants are accustomed to put at the top as we have said If you should do otherwise and not write the day, there will be confusion and you will be made fun of because we say the letter which does not bear the day was written during the night, and the letter which does not bear the place we say that it was written in the other world, not in this one and besides the fun made of you, there would be vexations, which is worse, as I have said

After you have sent your answer away, you put your letter in its proper place, and what we have said of one letter will apply to all the other letters It must be observed that when the letters you send away are of importance, you should first make a record of them in a book which is kept for this special purpose In this book the letter should be copied, word for word, if it is of great importance—as, for instance, the letters of exchange, or letters of goods sent, etc, otherwise only a record of the substantial part should be made similarly as we do in the memorandum book, saying On this day, etc, we have written to so and so, etc, and we send him the following things, etc, as per his letter of such and such date he requested or gave commission for, etc, which letter we have placed in such and such pouch

After you have sealed the letter on the outside and addressed it, it is the custom of many to mark on the outside your special mark so that they may know that it is correspondence of a merchant, because great attention is given to merchants, for they are the ones, as we said at the beginning of this treatise, who support our republics

For this purpose, the Most Reverend Cardinals do likewise by writing their name on the outside of their correspondence so that nobody could claim as an excuse that he did not know from whom it was The correspondence of the Holy Father remains open so that its contents may be known, like bulls, privileges, etc, although for things which are more personal or confidential the seal representing the Fisherman (*Pescatore*—St Peter) is used to seal them

All these letters, then, month by month year by year, you shall put together in a bundle and you will keep them in an orderly way in a chest, wardrobe or cupboard As you receive them during the day, put them aside in the same order, so that if necessary you might find them more easily, and I won t talk any longer about this, as I know that you have understood it

You shall keep in a more secret place, as private boxes and chests, all manuscripts of your debtors who have not paid you, as I said in Chapter 17 Likewise keep the receipts in a safe place for any emergency But when you should pay others, have the other party write the receipt in a receipt book, as I told you at the beginning, so that a receipt cannot be easily lost or go astray

You shall do the same as to important writing, as, for instance, memoranda of the brokers, or of merchants, or of weighmen, or relative to goods placed in or taken out of the custom house, either land or sea custom houses, and judgments or decrees of the consuls or of other public officials, or all kinds of notarial instruments written on parchments which ought to be kept in a place apart The same should be said of the copies of instruments and papers of attorneys or counselors at law relative to lawsuits

It is also wise to have a separate book for memoranda, which we call memoranda book, in which day by day you shall keep a record of the things that you might be afraid of forgetting and, if you forget them, may prove to be dangerous to you Every day, the last thing in the evening, just before going to bed, you shall glance over this book to see whether everything which should have been done has been done, etc, and you shall cancel with your pen the things that have been done, and in this book you shall make a record of the things that you have lent to your neighbor or friend for one or two days, as, for instance, store vases, caldrons, or any other thing

simili documēti con gli altri utilissimi sopra dati reporrai ₢c. piu e māco conçando e sminu
endo so luoghi e tpi a te per tuo ingegno parera. pero chi non e possibile apieno de tutto a
ponto per ponto i mercātia dare norma. e notitia poch cōme altre uolte se ditto vol piu pōti
a fare 1° mercatāte che un dottore de leggi. Ideo ₢c. Cose ch finora sono dette. se bn̄ la prēde
rai son certo i tutte tue facēde bn̄ te reggiarai. mediāte el tuo peregrino ingegno ₢c.

Summario de regole E modi sopra il tenere vno libro di mercanti. Cap°. 36.

Tutti li creditori si debono mettere al libro dala tua mano destra. E li debitori dala tua
mano sinistra. Tutte le ptite che se metteno al lib° hano a eēre doppie: cioe se tu fai vno cre
ditore al si fare 1°. debitore. Ciascūa ptita cosi ī dare cōe i hēre dbbe cōtenere ī se. 3. cose cioe
il giorno del pagamēto. La sōma del pagamēto. E la cagiōe del pagamēto. Lultimo
nome dela ptita del debito debbe eēre il prio della ptita del credito. In qllo medesimo
giorno che e scritta la ptita del debito. i qllo medesimo giorno debbe eēre qlla del credito.
Lo bilancio del lib° sintēde 1° foglio piegato p lo lōgo sul qle dala mano destra si copiāo
li creditori del lib°. e dala sinistra li debitori. E vedese se la sūma del dare e qnto qlla de laue
re. E allora il lib°. sta bene. El bilancio del libro debbe eēre pari. cioe che tanto debbe eēr
la sūma non dico de creditori. ne debitori. Ma dico la sūma del credito qnto la sūma del de
bito. E nō eēndo saria errore nel libro. El conto di cassa conuiene che sēpre sia debitrice.
overamēte pari. E se altrimēte fusse saria errore nel libro. Non si debbe e non si puo fare
1°. debitore al libro sença licēça e uolūta di qllo tale che a eēre debitore e se pure si facesse ql
la scrittura seria falsa. Ne similmēte non si puo porre neppati ne conditioni a. 1° credito sē
ça licēça e volonta del creditore. E se pure si facesse qlla scrittura saria falsa. El lib°. conuie
ne che sia tutto tratto fuori a 1ª. medesima mōeta. Ma dētro poi bn̄ noīare qllo ch accades
se o duc. o ₤. o fiorini. o scudi doro. o qllo che fussi. Ma nel trarre fuori conuiene che sia tut
to a 1ª. medesima moneta cōe pricipiasti il lib° cosi conuiene seguire. La ptita del debito.
o del credito che si fa i conto de cassa si puo abreuiare chi vuole. cioe sença dire la cagione so
lamēte dire da tale di tale. o a tale di tale. pche la cagione si uiene a dichiarar nella ptita op
posita. Hauēdo a fare 1°. cōto nuouo si debbe scriuere ī carta noua sença tornare adietro an
cora ch a drietro vi trouassi spacio da metterla. Non si die scriuere idrietro. Ma sēpre auā
ti per ordine cōe vanno li giorni del tpo che mai non ritornano indrieto E se pure si facesse
saria da reputare qllo libro falso. Se 1ª. partita fosse al libro messa per errore che non do
uessi eēre cōe aduiene ale volte per ismemoragine e tu la uolessi istornare farai cosi segna
qlla tale partita in margine duna croci o duna. H. E dipoi scriui 1ª. ptita al incontro. cioe a
lo opposito di qlla nel medesimo conto. cioe se la partita errata fusse creditrice poniamo di
₤ 50 ß 10 ð 6. E tu la farai debitrice. E dirai. e de dare. ₤ 50. ß 10 ð 6 sonno per la partita di
ptro segnata croci che si storna perche era errata e non haueua a eēre. E qsta partita segna
la. croci cōe e laltra e ð fatta. Quando lo spacio duno cōto fusse pieno. in modo ch nō ui
potesse mettere piu ptite. E tu volessi tirare qllo conto innançi. Fa cosi guarda qllo ch e il re
sto del ditto conto. cioe se li resta hauere o a dare Ora poniamo che qllo conto resti hauere
₤ 28 ß 4 ð 2. Dico che tu debbi fare 1°. verso soletto dala parte opposita sença mettere gior
no. e dirai cosi. E de dare ₤ 28 ß 4 ð 2 per resto di qsto conto posto hauere in qsto a car. e ð
fatto E lo detto verso si debe segnare in margine dauanti cosi. cioe R°. che significa resto
cioe chel detto uerso non ne debitrice ancor che sia dala banda del debitore. Ma uiene a es
sere trasportato qllo credito per la via del debito. Ora ti cōuiene uolgere carta e andare tā
tō auanti che truoui 1ª. carta nuoua. E qui fare creditore il detto conto. E nominarlo e fa
re ptita nuoua sēça metterui il giorno. E dirai cosi tale di tale ð tali de hēre. ₤ 18 ß 4. ð 2. sō
no per resto duno suo conto leuato in qsto a ca. E qsta partita si debbi segnare in margine
cosi. cioe R°. che significa resto E e fatta. E cosi comme io to mostro quando il conto resta
a hauere cosi ancora hai a fare quando restassi a dare. cioe quello cai messo dala banda del
credito metter dala banda del debito.

QUando el lib° fusse tutto pieno o uecchio e tu uolessi ridullo a 1° alr° li°. nuouo
fa cosi p°. ti cōuiene vedere che se il tuo lib°. vecchio e segnato ī su la couerta poni
amo p caso. A bisogna ch ī sul lib° nuouo doue lo voi ridurre sia segnato in su
la couerta. B pche li lib°. de mercanti vāno p ordie luno doppo lalt°. so le lre
delo. a b c ₢c. E dipoi leuare il bilancio del lib° vecchio che sia giusto e pari cōe debba essere
e da qllo bilancio copiare tutti li creditori e debitori ī sul lib°. nuouo tutti p ordine cōe elli
stāno ī sul bilācio. E fare tutti li debitori e creditori ciascūo da pse. e lascia a ciasc° tāto spatio

These rules, and the other very useful rules of which I have spoken before, you shall follow and, according to the localities and times, you shall be more or less particular, adding or omitting as it seems best to you, because it is impossible to give rules for every little thing in the mercantile business, as we have already said The proverb says that we need more bridges to make a merchant than a doctor of laws can make

If you understand well all the things that I have spoken of so far, I am sure you with your intelligence will carry on your business well.

CHAPTER 36

SUMMARY OF THE RULES AND WAYS FOR KEEPING A LEDGER

All the creditors must appear in the Ledger at the right hand side, and all the debtors at the left

All entries made in the ledger have to be double entries—that is, if you make one creditor, you must make some one debtor

Each debit (shall give—*dee dare*) and credit (shall have—*dee havere*) entry must contain three things, namely the day, the amount and the reason for the entry

The last name in the entry of the debit (in the Ledger) must be the first name in the entry of the credit On the same day that you make the debit entry, you should make the credit entry

By a trial balance (*bilancio*) of the Ledger we mean a sheet of paper folded lengthwise in the middle, on which we write down all the creditors of the Ledger at the right side and the debtors at the left side We see whether the total of the debits is equal to that of the credits, and if so, the Ledger is in order

The trial balance of the Ledger should be equal—that is the total of the credits—I do not say creditors—should be equal to the total of the debits—I do not say debtors If they were not equal there would be a mistake in the Ledger

The cash account should always be a debtor or equal If it were different, there would be a mistake in the ledger

You must not and cannot make any one debtor in your book without permission or consent of the person that has to appear as debtor, if you should, that account would be considered false Likewise you cannot add terms or conditions to a credit without permission and consent of the creditor If you should, that statement would be untrue

The values in the Ledger must be reckoned in one kind of money In the explanation of the entries, you may name all sorts of money, either *ducats*, or *lire*, or *Florence*, or gold *scudi*, or anything else, but in writing the amount in the column, you should always use the same kind of money throughout—that is, the money that you reckon by at the beginning should be the same all through the Ledger

The debit or credit entries of the cash account may be shortened, if you desire, by not giving the reason for the entry, you may simply say from so and so, for so and so, because the reason for the entry is stated in the opposite entry

If a new account should be opened, you must use a new page and must not go back even if there was room enough to place the new account You should not write backward, but always forward—that is, go forward as the days go, which never come back If you do otherwise, the book would be untrue

If you should make an entry in the Ledger by mistake which should not have been made, as it happens at times through absentmindedness, and if you wanted to correct it, you shall do as follows Mark with a cross or with an "H" that special entry, and then make an entry on the opposite side under the same account That is, if the erroneous entry was on the credit side—say, for instance, for L 50, S 10, D 6—you make an entry in the debit side, saying Debit (*dee dare*) L 50, S 10, D 6, for the opposite entry cross marked which is hereby corrected, because it was put in through a mistake and should not have been made Then mark with a cross this new entry This is all

When the spaces given to any particular account are all filled so that no more entries can be made and you want to carry forward that account, do in this way Figure out the remainder of the said account—that is, whether it is debit or credit remainder Now let us say that there is a credit remainder of L 20, S 4, D 2 You should write on the opposite side, without mentioning any date, as follows Debit L 28, S 4 D 2, per remainder (*per resto*) of this account carried forward in the credit at page so and so And it is done The said entry is to be marked in the margin so, namely *Ro*, which means "*resto*" (remainder), but this does not mean that it is a true debit entry although it is on the debit side It is rather the credit which is transferred through the debit side Now you must turn the pages and keep on turning them until you find a new page where you shall credit that account by naming the account and making a new entry without putting down any day And you shall say in the following manner So and so is credit (*dee havere*) L 28, S 4, D 2, per remainder (*per resto*) of account transferred from page so and so, and you should mark this entry in the margin by *Ro*, which means "*resto*" remainder, and that is done

In the same way as I have shown you, you shall proceed if the account has a debit remainder—that is, what you enter on the credit side you should transfer to the debit side

When the ledger is all filled up, or old, and you want to transfer it into a new one, you proceed in the following manner First you must see whether your old book bears a mark on its cover—for instance, an A In this case you must mark the new Ledger in which you want to transfer the old one by B, because the books of the merchants go by order, one after the other, according to the letters of the alphabet Then you have to take the trial balance of the old book and see that it is equal From the trial balance sheet you must copy in the new Ledger all the creditors and debtors all in order just as they appear in the trial balance sheet, but make a separate account for each amount,

q̃to tu arbitri hẽre a trauagliare cõ seco. E i ciascũa ptita del debitore hai a dire p tãti resta adare al lib°. uechio segnato A. a car. e i ciascũa ptita del creditore hai a dire p tanti resta a hauere al lib° vechio segnato. A a car E cosi e riducto al libro nuouo. Ora p cancellar il libro uechio ti cõuiene a ciascũo coto acceso ispegnerlo cõ lo bilancio sopra dicto. cioe se vno cõto del libro uechio sara creditore che louedrai p lo bilancio faralo debitore e dirai p tanti resta hauere a q̃sto cõto posto debbi hauere al lib°. nouo segnato. B a car. E cosi harai ispẽto tutto il lib° uechio e acceso al lib° nuouo E cosi cõmo io to mostro duno creditore cosi hai afare duno debitore. Saluo che doue al creditore si fa debitore posto debbi hauere E tu hai a fare creditore posto debbi dare z e fatto.

Casi che aptiene amettere al libro de mercanti.

Tutti li d. cõtanti che tu ti trouassi che fussino tuoi ꝑprii. cioe che hauessi guadagnati i diuersi tp̃i pel passato o che ti fussino stati lassati da tuoi parẽti morti. o donati da qlche principe farai creditore te medẽmo. E debitore cassa. Tutte le gioie e mercantie che fussino tue ꝑprie che tu hauessi guadagnate. o ch ti fussino state lassate p testamẽto. o che ti fussino state donate. E q̃ste tale cose si vogliono stimare da p se luna da lalt° q̃llo che vagliano a d. cõtanti. E tante q̃te cose elle sono tante ptite fare al lib°. e fare ciascuna debitrice e dire p tãte mi trouo stimare q̃sto di tanti d. zc. Posto medesimo creditore i q̃lto a car. E farai creditore il tuo cõto cioe te medesimo di ciascũa ptita. Ma nota che q̃lle ptite sintẽde ch nõ sieno mãco di dieci duc. luna po che le cose minute di poco valore non simettano al libro.

Tutte le cose stabile che tu ti trouassi che fussino tue ꝑprie cõe sono case possessiõi botteghe hai afare debitore detta casa e stimare q̃llo che la uale a tua discretiõe a d. cõtanti. E fane creditore te medẽmo al tuo sopra detto cõto. E dipoi fare debitore la possessiõe da pse e stimarla cõe e ditto e fane creditore te medemo al tuo sopradetto cõto. e cõe nelle regole to ditto tutte le ptite vogliono hẽre i loro tre cose cioe il giorno e la q^a dela pecũia e la cagiõe.

Cõpre che tu facessi di mercantie o di che cosa si fusse p li d. cõtãti debbi fare debitore q̃lla tale mercantia o q̃lla tale cosa e creditore la cassa. E se tu dicessi. io la cõprai a d. cõtãti. cõe e ditto Ma vno banco gli pago p me o veramẽte vno mio amico gli pago p me. Rispondoti che a ogni modo hai afare debitore q̃lla tale mercantia cõe di sopra o ditto. Ma doue io ti dissi farai creditore la cassa tu hai afare creditor q̃l banco o q̃llo tuo amico ch p te glia pagati.

Cõpre che tu facessi di mercantie. o diche cosa si sia a termine dalcuno tpo debi fare debitore q̃lla tale mercantia e creditore colui da cui tu lai cõpata p q̃llo tpo. Cõpre che tu facessi di mercantia. o diche cosa si sia a pte d. e pte tpo debbi fare debitore q̃lla tale mercantia E creditore colui da cui tu lai cõpata p q̃llo tpo cõ q̃sti patti che li habbi hauere diciamo il terço di d. cõtãti E lo resto fra sei mesi ꝓximi futuri. E doppo q̃sto fare unaltra ptita. cioe debitore colui da cui tu lai cõpata di q̃lla q^a di d. cõtanti che mõta q̃lla terça parte che fu di patto di cõtanti E creditore la cassa o q̃llo bancho che gli pagasse pte. Tutte le uẽdite che tu facessi di mercantie o daltre cose hai a fare tutto cõme di sopra saluo chai a mettere p lo opposito. cioe che doue di sopra ti dissi che sẽpre facessi debitore la mercantia. q̃ nelle uẽdite hai a fare sẽpre creditore la mercantia E debitore cassa se e uenduta a d. cõtanti o debitore q̃l banco che te li hauesse ꝓmessi E se e venduta a termine hai a fare debitore colui acui tu lhai uenduta p q̃llo termine e se fusse uenduta a pte d. e pte tpo hai a fare cõe di sopra ti mostrai nelle cõpre q̃lle due ptite. Se tu vẽdessi una mercãtia abaratto diciamo Io ho vẽduto libbre mille di lana dinghilterra abaratto di peuere cioe a libre dumilia di peuere domando comme sa a cõtare q̃sto scrittura al lib° fa. cosi stima q̃llo che vale il pipe a tua discretiõe a d. cõtãti. Or poniamo che tu lo stimi duc. dodici il cento adõq̃ le dumilia libbre vagliono duc. 240 cõtãti e po farai creditore la lana d. duc. 240. p q̃to lai venduta E q̃sto modo obserua sẽpre i leptite tutte dli baratti de qli sene hauto S. duamilia di peuere stimato. 240. duc. posto detto peuere debbi dare i q̃sto a car E fane debitore il peuere. Danari cõtanti che tu pstassi a q̃lche suo amico hai a fare debitore lamico achi tu gli hai p̃stati e creditore cassa. Se tu riceuessi d. cõtanti in pstança da q̃lche amico hai afare debitore cassa e creditore lamico.

Se tu hauessi p̃so otto o dieci. o vẽti duc p assicurare naue o galee o altra cosa debbi fare creditore sicurta di nauilij e chiarire che e cõe e q̃ndo e doue e q̃to p cẽto. E debitore cõto di cassa. Mercantie che ti fussino mandate da altri co cõmissione diuẽderle o barattarle dele quali tu hauessi hauere la tua ꝓuisiõe Dico che tu debbi fare debitore al libro q̃lla tale mercantia attenere al tale di tale p lo porto. o p gabella o p nolo o p mettere i magaçino E creditore cõto di cassa Tutte le spese di mercantie di d. cõtanti che tu farai. o p nolo. o p gabelle. o vetture o senserie o portature fa creditore la cassa. E debitore quella tale mercantia per laq̃le tu gli hai ispesi.

and leave to each account all the space that you think you may need And in each debit account you shall say: Per so much as per debit remainder (*resta a dare*) in the old book marked A, at page so and so. And in each credit account you shall say Per so much as per credit remainder (*resta a havere*) in the old book marked A, at page so and so. In this way you transfer the old Ledger into the new one Now, in order to cancel the old book, you must cancel each account by making it balance, of which we have spoken—that is, if an account of the old Ledger shows a credit remainder as the trial balance would show you, you shall debit this account for the same amount, saying, so much remains in the credit of this account, carried forward in the credit in the new Ledger marked B, at page so and so In this way you shall have closed the old Ledger and opened the new one for, as I have shown you how to do for a creditor, the same you shall do for a debtor, with this difference, that while you debit an account, which may show a credit remainder, you shall credit the account which may show a debit remainder This is all

THINGS WHICH SHOULD BE ENTERED IN THE BOOKS OF THE MERCHANTS

Of all the cash that you might have, if it is your own—that is, that you might have earned at different times in the past, or which might have been bequeathed to you by your dead relatives or given you as a gift from some Prince, you shall make yourself creditor (*creditore te medesima*), and make cash debitor As to all jewelry or goods which might be your own—that is, that you may have got through business or that might have been left you through a will or given to you as a present, you must value them in cash and make as many accounts as there are things and make each debitor by saying For so many, etc, of which I find myself possessed on this day so many *denari*, posted credit entry at such and such page, and then you make creditor your account (*tuo conto*), that is yourself (*medesimo*), with the amount of each of these entries But remember these entries should not be for less than ten ducats each, as small things of little value are not entered in the Ledger

Of all the real property that you might own, as houses, lands, stores, you make the cash debitor and estimate their value at your discretion in cash, and you make creditor yourself or your personal account (*tuo sopradette conto*). Then you make debitor an account of that special property by giving the value, as I have said above, and make yourself creditor because, as I have told you, all entries must have three things· The date, the value in cash, and the reason

If you should buy merchandise or anything else for cash, you should make a debtor of that special merchandise or thing and like creditor cash, and if you should say, I bought that merchandise for cash, but a bank will furnish the cash, or a friend of mine will do so, I will answer you that any way, you must make a debitor of that special merchandise, but where I told you to credit cash, you should, instead, credit that special bank, or that special friend who furnished the money

If you should buy merchandise or anything else, partly for cash and partly on time, you shall make that special merchandise debitor, and make a creditor of the party from whom you bought it on time and under the conditions that you might have agreed upon, as, for instance, one-third in cash and the rest in six months After this you will have to make another entry—that is, make a debitor of the party from whom you bought it for the amount of the cash that you have given him for that one-third and make creditor cash or the bank which might have paid that much for you

If you should sell any merchandise or anything else, you should proceed as above with the exception that you should proceed in the opposite way—that is, where I told you that when you bought you should make the merchandise debitor, when you sell you will have to make your merchandise a creditor and charge the cash account if it is sold for cash, or charge the bank that might have promised the payment And if you make a sale on time, you will have to charge the party to whom you sold it on time, and if you make the sale partly for cash and partly on time, you shall proceed as I have shown you in explaining about the buying

If you should give merchandise in exchange, for instance, let us say I have sold 1,000 pounds of English wool in exchange for pepper—that is, for 2,000 pounds of pepper—I ask, how shall we make this entry in the Ledger? You shall do as follows Estimate what the value of the pepper is, at your discretion, in cash Now let us say that you estimated 12 ducats per hundred, the 2,000 pounds would be worth 240 ducats Therefore, you shall make the wool a creditor with 240 ducats, for which amount you have sold it This is the manner that you should follow in all the trade entries If you have received 2,000 pounds of pepper valued at 240 ducats, you shall make the pepper a debitor and say Said pepper debtor on this day, see page, etc, etc

If you should loan cash to some of your friends, you shall charge the friend to whom you have given it and credit cash If you should borrow cash from some friend, you will have to debit cash and credit your friend.

If you have received 8 or 10 or 20 ducats in order to insure a ship or a galley, or anything else you should credit the account "ship insurance," and explain all about it—how, when and where, and how much per cent, and shall charge the cash account

If anybody should send you any goods with instructions to sell them or exchange them on commission, I say that you have to charge in the Ledger that special merchandise belonging to so and so with the freight, or duty, or for storage, and credit the cash account You shall credit the cash for all cash that you have to pay on account of goods for instance, cash paid for transportation or duty, or brokerage, etc, and charge the account of that special goods for that which you have paid in money

Casi che acade mettere ale recordançe del mercante.

Tutte le masseritie di casa o di bottega che tu ti truovi. Ma vogliono essere per ordine. cioe tutte le cose di ferro da perse con spatio da potere agiongnere se bisognasse. E cosi da segnare in margine quelle che fussino perdutte o vendute o donate o guaste. Ma non si intende masseritie minute di poco valore. E fare ricordo di tutte le cose dottone da perse comme e detto. E simile tutte le cose distagno. E simile tutte le cose di legno. E cosi tutte le cose di rame. E cosi tutte le cose dariento e doro ⁊c. Sempre con spatio di qualche carta da potere arrogere se bisognasse. e cosi dadare notitia di quello che mancasse. Tutte le malleverie o obbrighi o promesse che promettessi per qualche amico. e chiarire bene che e comme. Tutte le mercantie o altre cose che ti fosseno lassate i guardia o a serbo o i prestança da qualche amico. e cosi tutte le cose che tu prestassi a altri tuoi amici. Tutti li mercati condicionati cioe compre o vendite comme per exemplo uno contrato cioe che tu mi mandi con le prossime galee che torneranno dingbliterra tanti cantara di lane delumistri a caso che le sieno buone e recipienti. Io ti daro tanto del cantaro o del cento o veramente ti mandaro al incontro tanti cantara di cottoni. Tutte le case o possessioni o botteghe o gioie che tu affitassi a tanti duc. o a tante lire lanno. E quando tu riscoterai il fitto alora quelli dinari sanno a mettere al libro comme di sopra ti dissi. Prestando qualche gioia o vasellamenti dariento o doro a qualche tuo amico per otto o quindici giorni di queste tale cose non si mettono al libro. ma sene fa ricordo ale ricordançe. perche fra pochi giorni lai bariavere. E cosi per contra se a te fossi prestato simili cose non li debbi mettere al libro. Ma farne memoria ale ricordançe perche presto lai a rendere.

Comme si scrivono lire e soldi e danari e picioli e altre abreviature.

Lire	soldi	danari	picioli	libbre	once	danarpesi	grani	carati	ducati	fiorini larghi.
₤	ß	δ	p̄	libbre	℥	d̄p̄	g°.	ꝃ	duc.	fio. lar̄

Comme si debbe dettare le partite de debitori.

Mcccc°. Lxxxxiii°.

Lodovico di piero forestani de dare a di xiiii. novembre. 1493. ₤. 44. ß. 1. δ. 8. porto contanti in prestança. posto cassa avere. a car. 2 — ₤ 44 ß 1 δ 8.

E a di 18. detto ₤. 18. ß. 11. δ. 6. promettemo per lui a martino di piero foraboschi a suo piacere posto havere i questo. a c. 2. — ₤ 18 ß 11 δ 6.

Cassa i mano di simone dalesso bombeni de dare a di. 14. novembre 1493. ₤. 62. ß. 13. δ. 2. da francesco dantonio cavalcanti in questo a c. 2 — ₤ 62 ß 13 δ 6.

Martino di piero fora boschi de dare a di. 20. novembre. 1493. ₤. 18. ß. 11. δ. 6. porto lui medesimo contanti posto cassa a car. 2. — ₤ 18 ß 11 δ 6.

Francesco dantonio cavalcanti de dare a di. 12. di novembre. 1493. ₤. 20. ß. 4. δ. 2. ci promisse a nostro piacere per lodovico di piero forestani a c. 2. — ₤ 20 ß 4 δ 2.

Comme si debbe dittare le partite di creditori.

Mcccc°. Lxxxxiii.

Lodovico di piero forestani de havere a di. 22. novembre 1493. ₤. 20. ß. 4. δ. 2. sono per parte di pagamento. E per lui celia promissi a nostro piacere francescho dantonio. cavalcanti posto dare a c. 2. — ₤ 20 ß 4 δ 2.

Cassa in meno di simone dalesso bombeni de havere a di. 14. novembre. 1493. ₤. 44. ß 1. δ. 8. a lodovico di piero forestani in questo. a car. 2. — ₤ 44 ß 1 δ 8.

E a di. 22. novembre. 1493 ₤. 18. ß. 11. δ. 6. a martino di piero foraboschi. a ca. 2. — ₤ 18 ß 11 δ 6.

Martino di piero fora boschi di havere a di. 18. novembre. 1493. ₤. 18. ß. 11. δ. 6. gli promettemo a suo piacere per lodovico di piero forestani posto debbi havere i questo a c. 2. — ₤ 18 ß 11 δ 6

Francescho dantonio cavalcanti de havere a di. 14. novembre. 1493. ₤. 62. ß. 13. δ. 6. recco lui medesimo contanti posto cassa dare a. car. 2. — ₤ 62 ß 13 δ 6.

THINGS THAT SHOULD BE RECORDED IN A RECORD BOOK (*RECORDANZE*) OF THE MERCHANT

All the house and store goods that you may find yourself possessed of—these should be put down in order—that is, all the things made of iron by itself, leaving space enough to make additions if necessary, also leaving room to mark in the margin the things that might be lost or sold or given as presents or spoiled But I don't mean small things of little value

Make a record of all the brass things separately, as I have said, and then a record of the tin things, and then the wooden things, and copper things, and then the silver things and gold things, always leaving enough space between each class so that you may add something if necessary, and to put down a memorandum of any object that might be missing

All sureties or obligations or promises of payment that you might make for some friend, explaining clearly everything

All goods or other things that might be left with you in custody, or that you might borrow from some friend, as well as all the things that other friends of yours might borrow from you

All conditional transactions—that is, purchases and sales, as, for instance a contract that you shall send me by the next ship coming from England, so many *cantara* of *woll di li mistri*, on condition that it is good, and when I receive it I will pay you so much per *cantara* or by the hundred, or otherwise, I will send you in exchange so many *cantara* of cotton

All houses, lands, stores or jewels that you might rent at so many ducats and so many lire per year And when you collect the rent, then that money should be entered in the Ledger, as I have told you

If you should lend some jewels, silver or gold vase to some friend, say, for instance, for eight or fifteen days, things like this should not be entered in the Ledger, but should be recorded in this record book because in a few days, you will get them back. In the same way, if somebody should lend you something like the things mentioned, you should not make any entry in the Ledger, but put down a little memorandum in the record book, because in a short time you will have to give it back

How *Lire, Soldi, Denari* and *Picioli*, etc, should be written down as abbreviations

Lire, Soldi, Denari, Picioli, Libbre, Once, Danarpesi, Grani, Carati, Ducati, Florin larghi

(See other side for their abbreviations)

HOW THE DEBIT (LEDGER) ENTRIES ARE MADE

MCCCCLXXXXIII Lodovico, son of Piero Forestani, shall give on the 14th day of November, 1493, L 44, S 1, D 8, for cash loaned, posted cash shall have at page 2 — L 44, S 1, D 8

And on the 18th ditto, L 18, S 11, D 6, which we promised to pay for him to Martino, son of Piero Foraboschi at his pleasure, posted said shall have at page 2 — L 18, S 11, D 6

Cash in hands of Simone, son of Alessio Bombeni, shall give on Nov 14, 1493, for L 62, S 13, D 2, for Francesco, son of Antonio Cavalcanti, page 2 — L 62, S 13, D 6

Martino, son of Piero Foraboschi, shall give on Nov 20, 1493, for L 18, S 11, D 6, taken by him in cash, posted Cash at page 2 — L 18, S 11, D 6

Francesco, son of Antonio Cavalcanti, shall give, on Nov 12, 1493, L 20, S 4, D 2, which he promised to pay to us at our pleasure for Lodovico, son of Pietro Forestani, page 2 — L 20, S 4, D 2

HOW THE CREDIT (LEDGER) ENTRIES ARE MADE

MCCCCLXXXXIII Lodovico, son of Piero Forestani, shall have, on Nov 22, 1493, for L 20, S 4, D 2, for part payment And for him Francesco, son of Antonio Cavalcanti, promised to pay it to us at our pleasure, posted shall give at page 2. — L 20, S 4, D 2

Cash in hands of Simone, son of Alessio Bombeni, shall have, on Nov 14, 1493, for L 44 S 1, D 8, from Lodovico Pietro Forestani L 44 S 1, D 8, and on Nov 22, 1493, L 18, S 11, D 6, to Martino, son of Piero Forbaschi, page 2 — L 18 S 11, D 6

Martino, son of Piero Foraboschi, shall have on Nov 18, 1493, for L 18, S 11, D 6 which we promised to pay him at his pleasure for Lodovico, son of Pietro Forestani, posted shall give entry at p 8 — L 18 S 11, D 6

Francesco, son of Antonio Cavalcanti shall have on Nov 14 1493, for L 62, S 13, D 6, which he brought himself in cash posted cash shall give at page 2 — L 62, S 13, D 6

294 4/3 4/0	Per	Pro & danno // A doni uarij, per danno feguido, tratto in resto, per faldo di quello ꝺ 1 — ual ℒ	Di faldar la partida de li doni, ponendo il resto di quelli in pro & danno. — ℓ 2 ß — p
295 4/3 4/1	Per	Pro & danno // A Spese de uiuer di casa, per piu spese fatte, come in esse appar, per saldo di quelle, ꝺ 154 g 20 p 14 — — — — ual ℒ	Di faldar le spese di vestir in ditto pro & danno, 15 ℓ 9 ß 8 p 14
296 3/4 4/4	Per	Fitti della possession da Moian // A Pro & danno per fitto di quella per l'anno presente, finira de Luio 1541, per saldo de quelli ꝺ 45 g — ual ℒ	Di faldar li fitti della possession, in pro & danno. 4 ℓ 10 ß — p
297 4/3 4/3	Per	Pro & danno // A Spese diuerse per piu spese fatte l'anno presente, come in esse appar, per saldo suo ꝺ 399 g 12 p — — — — ual ℒ	Di faldar le spese diuerse, in ditto pro & danno, 33 ℓ 19 ß — p
298 4/4 4/0	Per	Pro & danno // A Spese de salariadi in monte, per piu spese fatte l'anno presente, come in esse appar, per saldo di quelle ꝺ 48 g 12 p — — ual ℒ	Di faldar le spese de falariadi, in ditto pro & danno, 4 ℓ 17 ß — p
299 4/4 0/4	Per	Pro de zecca in monte // A Pro & danno, per utilita seguida, come in quello appar, per saldo suo, ꝺ 150 g — p — — — ual ℒ	Di faldar in pro de zeccha, in lo ditto pro & danno. 15 ℓ — ß — p
300 4/3 4/3	Per	Pro et danno // A Cauedal de mi Aluise Vallaresso, per utilita seguda de l'anno 1540, tratto in resto, per saldo di quello, ꝺ 900 g 22 p 17 — ual ℒ	Di faldar poi il pro & danno nel tuo cauedal, per vltima conclusione. 90 ℓ 1 ß 10 p 17

Fine del presente Giornale, tenuto per mi Aluise Valaresso, per conto d'ogni traffico, & negotio à me occorso, da di primo Marzo 1540, fin adi ultimo Febraro del ditto millesimo, nel qual ordinatamente de giorno in giorno, ho scritto di mia mano, ne in esso piu intendo scriuere, per hauer quello concluso & saldato in 12 partide, lequal ho reportate nel libro nouo segnato

A

MANZONI'S JOURNAL REPRODUCED

On the opposite page is given an enlarged reproduction of the last page of Domenico Manzoni's journal As stated before, the writer has not an original copy of Manzoni's book at hand, therefore only this page can be given which was enlarged from a reproduction appearing on page 121 of Brown's History of Accounting

As we have seen in the historical chapter, Manzoni wrote forty years after Pacioli, but he was the first author to give illustrations of the journal and ledger, although in the text he practically copied Pacioli verbatim Therefore, in Manzoni's book we have the first expressions in examples and illustrations of the writings of Pacioli

The page here reproduced is the last page of the journal and contains the journal entries covering the closing of the profit and loss account (*Pro et danno*)

We will note that the date is in the middle at the top of the page, that the name of the debtor account is separated from the name of the creditor account by two slanting lines, thus //, that each entry is separated by a line in the explanation column only (not in the money column), that immediately to the left of each entry we find two figures, separated by a short horizontal line or dash, these are the pages of the ledger to which the debit and credit are posted, the top figure representing the debit and the lower one the credit Immediately before these two figures, we find two slanting lines or dashes, they are the checking marks We will see that Pietra uses a dot in this place and that Pacioli prefers a dot but mentions a check mark or any other mark They are not the two slanting lines which are drawn through an entry when it has been posted These two we find represented in the two little diagonal dashes at the beginning and end, as well as on the under and upper side, of the lines separating the journal entries The writer believes from the descriptions he has read and illustrations he has seen, that these dashes are the beginning and end of the much described "diagonal lines" and illustrates his idea by the two lines he added to the reproduction in the last journal entry The omission of these lines like that of the standing lines in the money column, is probably due to lack of printing facilities You will recall that Pacioli mentions these lines to be made at the beginning of the entry and at the end of the entry, just before the *lire* sign

The numbers from 294 to 300 in the left-hand margin, are the consecutive numbers of the journal entries, which Manzoni alone and no other writer herein referred to mentions

On the right we find the four signs of the various denominations, *lire, soldi, denari,* and *piccoli* A dash is provided wherever a cypher should appear in the money column

The two lines of printing above the money in the money columns are merely directions which Manzoni as textwriter gave to his reader They are not a part of the journal entry You will note that he prints them in different type The difference in coin between the uniform one used in bookkeeping and the one used locally is also apparent, as the local coin is given as a part of the explanation to the journal entry The "p" to the left of the journal entry and to the right of the figures in the margin stands for "per" (our by), and immediately after the slanting dashes "//" in front of the name of the credit account is used 'A" (our to)

Elsewhere we have stated that except as to numbering the journal entries Manzoni mentioned nothing that Pacioli did not describe While he copies whole chapters word for word, in some of them, however, he was clearer, more brief and more systematic than Pacioli We give one of the chapters as an example

ABSTRACT FROM DOMENICO MANZONI'S BOOK

CAP XIII

Regole breuissime del giornal & quaderno

Nota che la Regola del Giornale & Quaderno, in se contiene sei cose, cio e
Dare, Havere, Qualita, Quantita, Tempo & Ordine
Dare, significa douer dare, cio e il debitore, o uno o piu che siano
Havere, uvol dir douer havere, cio e il creditore o uno o piu che siano
Qualita sono quelle cose che tu maneggi, & siano di che sorte si vogliono
Quantita, e il numero, peso over misure, o piccioli, o grandi che si siano
Tempo, si e il giorno, ilmese & lanno, sotto il quale tu fai la partida
Ordine, e quello, che nella presente opera con facilita insegnamo
Le due prime, sono affermative, e principali in ogni cosa.
La cosa debitrice, sempre va posta avanti a la creditrice
Davanti a la cosa debitrice, vi si pone uno per a questo modo P
Davanti a la cosa creditrice, vi si pone uno A cosi A
Il P in tal luogo significa la cosa debitrice
E lo A in tal luogo significa la cosa creditrice
Il giornale, si divide il debitore dal creditore, con due linette a questo modo
lequali dinotano che de una partida dalgiornale, sempre se ne convien
far due nel quaderno
Il giorno, si nota nel giornal di sopra da la partida
Et nel quaderno, si nota, dentro dalla partida
Il numero de le carte del quaderno, nel giornale, si mette avanti la partida
Et nel quaderno, il medesimo si mette dopo la partida
Li nomi de le partide vive in l'alfabeto, vi si poneno a man destra
Et quelli de le cose morte, si notano a man sinistra
Per le cose vive, qui s intende ogni creaturi animata
E per le morte, s intende robbe, over ogni altra cosa

TRANSLATION OF THE ABOVE ABSTRACT FROM DOMENICO MANZONI'S BOOK

CHAPTER XIII

Very Short Rules for the Journal and the Ledger
(In verse form)

You should note that the rules for the Journal and the Ledger contain six things, namely:
Give, Have, Quality, Quantity, Time and Order
Give (Debit), means as much as "shall give", that is, the debtor be it one or more
Have (Credit), means as much as 'shall have", this is, the creditor be it one or more
Quality by this we understand the things you handle of whichever nature they may be.
Quantity, by this we understand the number, the weight or the measure, be it big or little
Time, means the day, the month and the year in which the transaction is made
Order, means that which we can easily learn from the present book
The first two are most important and refer particularly to all things
The things made debtor should be placed before the creditor

In front of that which is made debtor is placed ' Per ', in this way "P"

Before the creditor we place an "A" in this way "A"

The "P" signifies that in this spot the things were made debtor

And the "A" signifies that in this spot the things were made creditor

In the Journal one must divide the debtor from the creditor by means of two small lines in this way //, which denotes that from one entry in the Journal two entries should be made in the Ledger

In the Journal, The day should be given above the entries

In the Ledger, The same is carried into the body of the entry

In the Journal, the number of the Ledger pages is placed in front of the entry

And in the Ledger we place the same after the entry

The name of the living account is written in the Index to the right

And those of the dead things are written to the left

With "living things ' is understood every creature with a soul (ogni creatura animata)

And with "dead things" is understood merchandise and everything else

In Chapter eleven Manzoni also gives eight rules for journalizing The four principal things pertaining to buying, selling, receiving, paying, exchanging, loaning and gifts are

1 The one who gives
2 The one who receives
3 The thing which is given
4 The thing which is received

It should be noted that here are four conditions to each transaction While Manzoni does not explain their use, as we will see later on, Stevin gives us the proper interpretation for this, somewhat as follows

One transaction will always need a double-entry. If Peter pays £100 we must consider

1 The one who gives, i e, Peter
2 The one who receives, i e, proprietor
3 The thing which is given, i e, cash by Peter
4 The thing which is received, i e, cash from the proprietor

Hence proprietor debit to Peter and cash debit to proprietor, which combined by eliminating the quantities of similar name and value, or by cancelling (as in algebra a=b, b=c, hence a=c) makes cash debit to Peter

Manzoni then follows with these eight rules

1 Debit merchandise for purchase
2 Credit merchandise for sales
3 Debit cash for cash sales
4 Credit cash for cash purchase
5 Debit buyer for sales on credit
6 Credit seller for purchase on credit
7 Debit persons who promise to pay
8 Credit persons to whom we promise to pay

In order to give the reader some idea of the scope of Manzoni s work, we give here a translation of the Index to his book

PART I JOURNAL

Chapter
1 Those things which the merchant needs and the system of keeping a Ledger and its Journal
2 The inventory, what it is and how merchants make it up
3 Form and example of inventory.
4 Last urging and good instruction for the merchant in connection with the inventory
5 A certain book, which majority of people use and which is called Memorial, Strazze or Vachetta, what it is, how we must write it up and for whom
6 Some special little books, which it is customary to use, what they are and how they are written up (Separate day books for petty expenses, household expenses, salaries, repairs, rents, separate classes of merchandise)
7 The manner in which in some places the books are authenticated by law

Chapter

8 The first book, which is called Journal, what it is and how it is started and kept (Mentioning the five customary standing lines of a journal.)

9 The two terms which are used in the Journal and the Ledger, the one named "Cash," the other "Capital," and what they mean

10 Two other terms which are used in the Journal and which are mixed quite often, and what they mean ("Per" and "A"—Debits separated from Credits by //.)

11 The principles underlying the use and arrangement of the Ledger (Author claims this is very difficult to understand; "Per" and "A" used to separate debit from credit, but does not say how to make debits and credits except that he gives in connection with the various methods of buying and selling, eight rules for Journal entry.)

12 The manner and system by which each entry in the Journal must be written under the proper terms (Samples of Journal entries, with application of rules from Chapter 11.)

13 Short rules for the Journal and Ledger, and the six things each entry must contain

14 Explanation of old abbreviations and what is meant by "*Lire de grossi*." The kind of money used by merchants in bookkeeping and which really does not exist. Common people use Lire=20 soldi, 1 soldi=12 Piccioli

(In Ducats.)

1 ducat = 24 grossi
1 grosso = 32 Piccioli in gold
1 Picciolo in gold = 1-15/16 Piccioli in money by common people

(In Lire de grossi.)

1 lira = 10 ducats   1 soldo = 12 grossi.
1 lira = 20 soldi   1 grosso = 32 Piccioli
1 grosso in gold = 5 grossi common money

15 Explanation needed in order to understand the examples of journal and ledger entries

PART II. LEDGER.

1 The second and last principal mercantile book, called Ledger, what it is, how it is opened and kept

2 The manner in which the old year is written in this book and about the kind of money used in posting (Year and usually also the money is written in Roman figures, Arabic too easy to change 0 to 6 or 9. Do not repeat date, but put a line. Leave no open spaces for others to fill in.)

3 The reason for having two entries in the Ledger for each single entry in the Journal

4 The manner in which we use both terms for each entry in the Ledger ("A" on debit of Ledger, "Per" on credit of Ledger, unlike the Journal, where "A" denotes credit and "Per" debit.)

5 The manner and system to be used in transferring entries from the Journal to the Ledger (Crosses Journal entry off with one diagonal line, at the time he enters the Ledger page, but does not say where to put this line.)

6 The manner of marking entries in the Journal which have been posted to the Ledger

7 The two numbers of the Ledger pages which are written in the margin of the Journal, when the entry is posted from the Journal to the Ledger, the one above the other and separated by a line

8 Another number, which we write at the beginning of each entry, through which each entry can easily be located again (Numbers each Journal entry consecutively.)

9 The manner in which the entries are carried to another place in the Ledger when one page is filled (Cancel blank space on either side to lowest place of writing. Balance not entered in the Journal. Carries balance only, with an abbreviation which means "Carried forward.")

10 The manner and system which should be followed in the checking of the books in order to detect errors (Gives Ledger to assistant and keeps Journal, thus reversing method of Pacioli. He does not use a dot but "another mark than that used first." (See chapter 6 above and two lines before each entry in the reproduction.)

11 The manner in which a correction in the Ledger is made when we have posted an entry to the wrong page in the Ledger (Never cross the wrong entry out or erase it, for you cannot prove what was there, and hence it will be construed as deceit. If an entry is posted to debit that should be credit, put another on the credit to offset it, for same amount, then proceed correctly. Mark erroneous and corrective entries with an X or H (*havere*), some make correction in one entry by using double the amount.)

12 How to prepare an account for a debtor or a creditor when he asks for a statement of his account

PIETRA'S JOURNAL AND LEDGER REPRODUCED

As stated in the historical chapter, in 1586, or nearly 100 years after Pacioli wrote, Don Angelo Pietra published a work on bookkeeping, which was fully illustrated with numerous examples Undoubtedly Pietra had both Pacioli and Manzoni before him when writing his book, because he describes matters which Manzoni omitted but Pacioli gave, and also some which Manzoni mentioned and Pacioli did not This will be explained fully elsewhere

Pietra was a monk who endeavored to give a system to be used for monasteries, but which he claimed was expedient for those who do not trade, or in other words, for corporations not for profit, and for capitalists The first page is a reproduction of the title page, in which the reader will find the author's name just above, and the date of publication just below, the picture

The next page gives a chart of the various methods of buying and of selling, of each of which Pacioli says there are nine Pietra sets them up here in a far more systematic manner, showing fifteen in all

We show next the first four lines of the title page to the journal, which are the dedication of the journal "In the Name of the most holy and undivided Trinity, Father, Son, and Holy Ghost" Also note the cross in the sixth line which is the sign used for the first journal and the first ledger when beginning a new business Such journal and ledger as we have seen in Pacioli, is called the "cross journal" and the "cross ledger"

Next we give a page of the journal From this page, we note

(1) That the first page of the journal carries the opening of "In the Name of God"

(2) That thereafter comes the date in the middle of the page The date is not again given until it is changed and then only the day of the month is given, omitting the year and the name of the month, "*a di detto*," meaning "on the ___ day of the aforesaid month"

(3) That each journal entry is divided by a line, not clear across the page, but from page column to money column

(4) That as in Manzoni's journal, no standing division lines in money columns are given (probably due to lack of printing facilities)

(5) That the money consideration of each entry is not only mentioned in the money column but also in the explanation of the journal entry

(6) That the name of the debit account is given first and the credit last, that they are divided by two small slanting strokes followed by the preposition "a" like this //a

(7) That the name of the debit account is not preceded by "P" or by "Per" as Pacioli and Manzoni require

(8) That the pages of the ledger to which the entries are transferred or posted are divided by a horizontal line or dash between the figures, the debit being always on top and the credit below

(9) That each entry has a brief but full explanation of the transaction represented by the entry

(10) That each entry is carefully checked with a dot (not a check mark as we use and Pacioli described or a dash as Manzoni showed) on the left of the ledger pages in the journal These dots also appear in front of each ledger entry

(11) That Pietra shows no combination journal entry or entries with more than one debit or credit

(12) That he does not show the diagonal cancellation lines in the journal as an evidence of posting to the ledger

(13) That he does not give any other value sign than the "Lire," omitting the *soldi, denari,* and *piccioli* signs

(14) That he very carefully provides a dash in the money column in the place of the cyphers

The illustrations of the journal are followed by those of the ledger The title page contains the name of the ledger, in the fifth line "*Libro maestro*" (master book or principal book) The ledger has the same dedication as the journal

Folio one of Pietra's ledger is the equivalent of an opening balance account, giving the name of the old and new account, the page in the old ledger and the page in the new ledger, it being posted from the closing balance account in the old ledger and not from the journal The assets are on the credit side and the liabilities on the debit side of the ledger The account shows a deficit of L 1706 - 10 - 3 The assets are divided in two first, the accounts receivable and their total, then the merchandise and other specific accounts

This page corresponds to the English form of a balance sheet It is the proprietor's half of the opening inventory journal entry placed direct in the ledger instead of in the journal and as such this represents a proprietor's account upon the theory that the proprietor is credited for furnishing or loaning to the personification of the asset accounts and charged with the negative assets or liabilities As our modern capital account represents a net difference between assets and liabilities (leaving surplus out of consideration), it cannot be said that Pietra employed a modern capital account, although the result is the same

Page 59 of this ledger also represents an account with the proprietor or owner, and is really a continuation of the account on page one The first entry on the debit is the balance and deficit of L 1706 - 10 - 3, properly transferred from page one without the aid of a journal entry The following five entries are entries corrective of the net capital, because they refer to transactions of previous years and are of little importance for our study except that they show that the principle of surplus adjustments then existed

The seventh entry on the debit, of L 4 - 17 10, refers to the same ledger page as this selfsame account bears (namely, 59) We find, therefore, the credit end of the entry on the credit side of this page. This entry does not come from the journal, but is merely a "cross' or "wash" entry in the nature of a memorandum for the purpose of recording an omitted transaction Note how carefully both entries are marked with a little circle (o) to set them off from the others, much the same as we use a cross (X) nowadays for the same purpose and as Pacioli and Manzoni also mention

The last entry on the debit side (L 3744 - 0 - 3) is made also without the aid of the journal Its counterpart is on page 61 of the ledger It represesents the net worth or capital invested at the end of the year, and balances on page 61 with the difference between assets and liabilities, and is merely a methodical closing entry in order that all accounts may be closed at the transfer of all open accounts to the new ledger

On the credit side we find the first five entries to be surplus adjustment entries The sixth one is the cross entry already explained and the last one, L 5448 - 10 - 5, is the net profit balance transferred from ledger page 60 without the use of the journal Here then we have an account named "Monastery,' the proprietor for which these books are kept It stands charged with a capital deficit, credited with the annual profits and closed with a debit balance representing present net worth, identical with our present day Capital account The deficit in the opening entry, as would appear from the text, seems to be due to the low values given to the fixed assets in order to avoid heavier taxation by the church authorities The account shows no definite ledger heading, although the first word on the left page "*Monastero*" (monastery) is the name of the proprietor and is not repeated in each entry The same method Pacioli and Manzoni describe and therefore we have not approached closer to the definite ledger heading

Page 60 represents what we call today an 'Income and Expenses" account, sometimes misnamed but being similar to a "Profit or Loss" account It is not so named here The debit side is called "*Spesa Generale* ' (General Expenses),—the credit side "*Entrata Generale*" (General Income)

It should be remembered that these books were not kept for a mercantile establishment, which operates with the object of a profit in view, but only for a monastery, an eleemosynary corporation, an institution or corporation not for profit, hence it could not use the words profit or loss

The balance on the debit of L 5448 - 10 - 5 is the excess of general income over general expenses, and is transferred to page 59, which we have explained is the proprietor's account or equivalent to our present capital account

Page 61 contains the last page of the ledger of Pietra's book It is similar to page one, except that debits and credits are reversed Here then we have the closing "Balance account," called ' *Esito*," which means final or exit It accurately represents our modern balance sheet, but is placed in the ledger as a permanent record and used as a medium to close all accounts in the ledger It usually was and quite often now is the custom to start a new ledger each year, hence all accounts should be closed when the ledger is laid away Pacioli nor Manzoni describe this account They transfer the open balances of the asset and liability accounts direct to the new ledger

You will note that the closing entry of L 3744 - 0 - 3 on the credit is taken from page 59 the monastery or capital account You will also note that it is on the credit side of the account, and a total of the liabilities is drawn before the final balance This is not done anywhere else in the ledger, showing that this account is different and represents two purposes one, that of a final trial balance (after Profit and Loss accounts are closed) and thus becomes a statement of assets and liabilities, and, further, that net worth or capital is not considered a liability, but an item distinct from liabilities, for the purpose of closing the capital account in the ledger, and transferring it in the new ledger

Page 21 of the ledger is given to show how carefully all blank spaces are cancelled by slanting lines, how accounts are kept in two kinds of money with the aid of a double column that no reference is made to the pages in the journal from which the entries were posted, for the reason stated in the text that the date was a close enough reference that the journal entries are not numbered, as was done by Manzoni Pages given immediately before the amounts refer to the ledger page on which the other side of the double-entry appears, note that on the debit the preposition "a" is used for our "to" and on the credit 'per" for our "by " following Manzoni in this respect, but entirely opposed to Pacioli's teachings, opening and closing entries do not carry these prepositions, because they do not constitute true debits and credits as those transferred from the journal, printers then, as now, make errors in figures, as the fourth figure from the bottom of the debit side should be 250 instead of 205, as per addition and the opening entry on page one, the explanation in the journal is repeated in the ledger and more than one line is used for an entry if needed, a single line is drawn under the figures only and then the total put in, the word "*somma*" (total) is used in front of the figures instead of the double line we now rule under the total no totals or lines are drawn when the account contains only one item, every entry is carefully checked with a dot in the left margin, the name of the account is engrossed at the beginning of the first line on the left and thus approaches the definite ledger heading of the present day, the date belonging to each entry is not set out in a definite column, although the text mentions this, "*dee dare*" (should give or debit) and "*dee havere* ' (should have or credit) is only stated once at the beginning of each account and not in every entry, as we would infer from Pacioli the custom was

In order to give the reader a clear understanding of what is contained in Pietra's book and to show how much more polished, complete and advanced it is than the book of either Paciolo or Manzoni, and to indicate the many new features he introduces, we are giving here a brief description of each chapter in the nature of an index

1 Day book or scrap book and similar books are necessary in order to get journal and ledger in good form

2 Explains debit and credit as to "A" and "Per"—our "To" and "By," and the two little lines // which separate debits from credits

3 Makes a distinction between bookkeeping for bankers merchants, and capitalists

4 Describes the three ledgers for these three methods

5 Says some more about the ledger for capitalist and calls it the "Economic Ledger" Author uses this kind of ledger in his book of samples which he adapts to the business of a monastery

6 The first part of the inventory covering immovable assets

7 The second part of the inventory covering merchandise or goods for use in the house (not fixtures—they belong to movables)

8 The third part of the inventory of movable assets

9 Gives tabulated detailed inventory of the movable assets of a monastery

10 About qualifications of bookkeeper, namely, bright and of good character, good handwriting, also knowledge, ambition, and loyalty, and gives reasons for each of these

11 Necessity for use of but one particular coin in the Ledger as the money used in Italy is of so many different varieties Here is used
1 Scuto = 4 Lire = 80 Soldi in gold

12 Describes the measures and weights used by the author

13 Put a value on those things which are harvested and manufactured, but this should be lower than current prices so that the proceeds will not fall below this value in case of sale What has been used should be charged to the proper department at the end of the year

14 About the figures to be used The Roman figures are difficult to change, but because fraudulent changes are more to be feared by bankers and merchants, he used the easier and more commonly used Arabic figures Changes can be easily prevented by putting the money sign for lire directly in front and separating the divisions of the lire by little dashes, thus L 18 - 8 - 2—very much the same as done at present in England

15 About the fiscal year It can begin when one chooses, but must be twelve months long and must keep the same figures for the same year, namely, from June 1, 1586, to May 31st, 1586, not 1587

16 Day books or memoranda books are necessary because the journal and ledger, due to their legal authentication, can be used only by the one bookkeeper appointed therefor and whose signature appears therein Furthermore transactions must be written down at the time and the place where they occur, and that may not be where the books are kept Therefore, there are several memoranda books concurrently used, the first one of which is marked with a cross and those which follow with a letter in the order of the alphabet

17 There should be at least three of these day books or memorials used—one for the cash receipts and disbursements and the deposits in the bank, one for the petty cash disbursements and one for all other entries from which the journal is written up, the latter to be in greater detail than the others
Other day books can be kept with the sales and purchases, rents taxes, etc A book is needed for the library and information pertaining to contracts, leases, employes, due dates, etc Receipts for money loaned should be kept in bound book form so that they may not be lost or stolen Each department head should keep such a book with its transactions, such as the shoe maker, gardener tailor, etc

18 Describes a blotter or tickler which contains a sheet for each month, and a line for each day in which the duties of the storekeeper and butler are written, one for each day in the year

19 Gives such a book in full detail

20 About the journal and how to keep it Journal is basis of the ledger and therefore it is essential that it is kept correctly

21 The beginning of the journal, in the name of God The value of prayer to success and the use of the little cross (†) as explained elsewhere

22 Entries should be made in the journal from day to day and hour to hour but some times this is not possible, especially in a monastery, where the memoranda or day books of the various departments are delivered only once a month

23 About the manner and order in which the entries are made in the journal A list of days on which entries are to be made is prepared by days from all the memoranda or day books, the cash entries always first

24 Gives an example of this list

25 Eight things always needed to make a proper journal entry Debit—Credit—Time—Value—Quality—Quantity—Price—Arrangement,
The first two being the most important

26 The greatest difficulty is to find what to debit and what to credit All entries can be reduced to three principles

27 List of above three principles

1 (Receipt, sales, payment of an account due, borrowing
(Disbursement, purchase, payment of a debt, loaning

2 (Purchasing on credit or for cash
(Selling on credit or for cash
(Exchanging with money or without

3 (Assignment of a debt to settle with a creditor, or vice versa, called drafts.

28 About the six other things needed for a proper journal entry

29 How the journal is arranged (See reproduction of journal page and explanatory notes appended, omits the consecutive numbering of Journal entry as so many do, because the date is a sufficient guide to locate the entry in the journal)

30 About the ledger and its formation

Explains the opening account on page 1 of the ledger, and states it is the reverse of the closing account Here he mentions debit as *debito* and credit as *credito,* although he usually states debit as "*dee dare*" and credit as "*dee havere* " Capital account is the key and the seal of the ledger

31 Explains the use of the two ledger accounts—"Opening' and "Monastery " "Opening" is what the merchant calls 'Capital" and practically he claims the same for "Monastery '

32 Explains what entries may be made in the capital account Corrections of errors and profits or losses belonging to previous years What we call surplus adjustments

33 Gives a table of such capital account entries

34 About the arrangement of accounts in the ledger, the capital account to be at the end of the book

35 List of accounts in the ledger

36 The ordinary index

37 The special index

38 Posting figures in the journal (one above the other)

39 How the entry is written in the ledger (' A" on debit side of ledger, "Per" on credit side of ledger)

40 Transfer to a new page is made by drawing the difference between the two sides and transferring this to the new page

41 How to correct errors in the entries

42 Entries which are written direct in the ledger without having been put in the journal

43 About the income and expense account and the method of buying and selling The author here states that merchants use this account for their profits or losses.

44 The vouchering by a signature of the principal disbursements

45 About the difference in bookkeeping for land rented and that cultivated for one's own account

46 Three principal reasons why the income should be divided over the same accounts in which the expenses and salaries are separated, namely to each departmental sub-division

47 When the best time is to enter the rentals from lands In the fall when the harvest is made, as at the end of the fiscal year is a busy enough time

48 About personal accounts and the carrying of accounts with two different money values

49 About the cash account in the ledger, and its peculiar uses

50 About the acquisition and alienation of lands, for which separate accounts are provided

51 About the accounts with partners or joint ventures

52 When and how to check with dots

53 A short method of checking with dots

54 How to take a trial balance, which also constitutes the balance sheet Divides the same in four 1, expenses, 2, income, 3, assets, 4, liabilities

55 How to find trial balance errors in a checked ledger

56 How to refute a wrong opinion about the trial balance Explains the fact that while debits and credits must equal, that such does not mean that the assets equal the liabilities

57 How to compute the income and expense account This he considers the most difficult, as some accounts will have three closing entries,—one for profit on sales, one for merchandise used by other departments of the business, and one for merchandise remaining on hand. Furthermore, measures and weights should also be brought in balance.

58 The manner in which the closing balance account is made up Accounts are only ruled at the end of the year by a line under the figures or amounts, then entering the total, which must be the same on both sides If an account is closed during the year, only a line is drawn, but the total is put inside the column and not under the line

59 About other methods of closing the ledger and their shortcomings Here the author describes several methods used at that time of closing a ledger and prefers his own because it gives finally in one account the status of the capital, whereas the other methods do not do so

60 How an account is rendered to the church authorities at the end of the fiscal year

In the comparative index we have given the items which are discussed by all the four authors there mentioned There are, however, a number of items which some of the authors use and others do not From among these, the following are taken as the most important

Pietra discusses the following in his book, but Pacioli and Manzoni do not

Chapter	
3	distinction in bookkeeping for bankers, merchants, and capitalists
4	describes three ledgers for these three businesses
5	describes more in detail the ledger for capitalists—called "Economic Ledger"
7	inventory of merchandise in stores
10	qualifications of bookkeepers
12	description of measures and weights used in book
13	put value on things harvested and used, and those not sold but used in other departments
15	describes fiscal year—use same numerals, although calendar year changes
17	separate daybooks for the following subjects cash—bank—petty cash—library—contracts—leases—salaries—due dates—loans—and one for each department
18 & 19	daily tickler for bookkeeper and storekeeper s duties
22	journal written up once a month in a monastery, because all daybooks are in use
23	the order in which transfers from daybook to journal are made—a list of this prepared before-hand—cash entries always first
25 & 28	eight things always needed in any journal entry
26 & 27	rules for journalizing
29	arrangement of journal with five standing lines, but omits numbers of journal entries
31	divides capital into two accounts—opening capital at beginning of year—closing capital at end of year
32	interim entries in capital account or surplus adjustments
33	table of such capital entries
34	capital account always at end of the ledger
37	special index
39	apparent transposition of 'A" and "Per" in ledger from its use in journal
42	list of entries which do not go through journal
43	vouchering of disbursements
45	book for lands rented and cultivated for own account
46	income divided in same accounts as expenses
47	when to enter rentals—in fall or end of fiscal year
48	personal accounts and accounts with two different values of moneys
50	acquisition and alienation of lands
53	a short method of checking the ledger

Pietra mentions the following in his book, as does Manzoni, but Pacioli does not, proving by this that Pietra had apparently available both Manzoni and Pacioli

more than one memoriale
five standing or ' down" lines in journal
definite rules for journal entries
six things always needed in each journal entry
about transposition of "A' and "Per" in ledger from its use in the journal
(Pietra does not explain definitely although his examples give it)
numbering of journal entries

Pietra's Chapter 33 explains all entries which may appear in the capital account and illustrates them with the following tabulation

1 During the year
2 At the end of the year

1 During the year

A Profits

a omitted credits

a collected	Cash to capital
b uncollected	Debtor to capital

b judgments obtained

a collected	Cash to capital
b uncollected	Debtor to capital

B Losses

a omitted debts

a paid	Capital to cash
b to be paid	Capital to creditor

b judgments lost

a paid	Capital to cash
b to be paid	Capital to creditor

2 At the end of the year

A Extraordinary Accounts

a balances of accounts

a what is due	Capital to creditor
b what is owed	Creditor to capital

b balance sheet adjustment

a what is owed	several kinds and without
b what is due	connection with the books

B Ordinary Accounts

a excess in expenses	Capital to income
b excess in income	Expenses to capital

Pietra's Chapter 42 explains about the many entries which are made in the ledger, without going through the journal, and classifies them as follows

Refers to entries which we transfer from the old ledger into the new, partly daily, partly at the end of the year

1 the introduction

2 the opening of capital account when it is transferred from the closing capital account and not from a new inventory

3 balances transferred from one account to another

4 contra entries to correct errors

5 profit or loss due to inventory adjustments

6 the balance of the income and expense account

7 all closing entries at the end of the year

8 the closing of the closing capital account

INDRIZZO
DEGLI ECONOMI.
O SIA ORDINATISSIMA
INSTRVTTIONE DA REGOLATAMENTE FORMARE QVALVNQVE SCRITTVRA IN VN LIBRO DOPPIO;

AGGIVNTOVI L'ESSEMPLARE DI VN LIBRO NOBILE, CO'L SVO GIORNALE, AD VSO DELLA CONGREGATION CASSINESE, DELL'ORDINE DI S. BENEDETTO.

CON DVE TAVOLE, L'VNA DE'CAPITOLI, ET L'ALTRA DELLE COSE PIV DEGNE, A PIENO INTENDIMENTO DI CIASCVNO

Opera nuoua, non meno vtile che necessaria, a Religiosi, che viuono delle proprie Rendite, & ad ogni Padre di Famiglia, che si diletti del Libro Doppio

Composta da Don Angelo Pietra Genouese Monaco, & indegno seruo di Giesu Christo.

IN MANTOVA, Per Francesco Osanna. Con licenza de' Superiori. MDLXXXVI

Tauola Analitica delle ſopraſcritte quindici partite. *Cap. 27.*

Tutte le partite ſi riducono a queſte tre Operationi.

1	Imborſo	Vendere	Ingroſſa Caſſa / Creſce l'entrata	1	Adi 1. Settembre.
		Scodere	Ingroſſa Caſſa / Mancano crediti	2	
		Impreſtito	Ingroſſa Caſſa / Si fa debito	3	
	Sborſo	Comprare	Creſce la ſpeſa / Minuiſce la Caſſa	4	
		Pagar debito	Mancano i debiti / Minuiſce la Caſſa	5	
		Impreſtare	Si fa credito / Minuiſce la Caſſa	6	
2	Côprare	A credenza	Creſce la ſpeſa / Si fa debito	7	Adi 2. Settembre.
		In pagamẽto	Creſce la ſpeſa / Si ſcode credito	8	
	Vendere	A credenza	Si fa credito / Creſce l'entrata.	9	
		In pagamento	Si paga debito / Creſce l'entrata	10	
	Barattare	Col prezzo	Creſce la ſpeſa / Creſce l'Entrata	11	
		Senza prezzo	Creſce la ſpeſa / Creſce l'entrata	12	
3	Ceſſione	Partita di Banco	Paga debito / Scode credito	13	Adi 3. Settembre.
		Sequeſtro patiente	Rinuoua debito.	14	
		Sequeſtro agente	Rinuoua credito	15	

Delle

AL NOME DELLA SANTISSIMA ET INDIVIDVA TRINITA'

PADRE, FIGLIO, E SPIRITO SANTO.

GIORNALE DEL LIBRO MAESTRO, SEGNATO ✠ DEL MONASTERO, DEL GLORIOSO PRECVRSOR DI CHRISTO. SAN GIO. BATTISTA D'ORIANA, DELL'ANNO. 1586.

Cominciato adì primo Giugno. Scritto da me Don Gabriello da Parma, Celleraro del detto Monaſtero, di ordine del molto Reuerendo Padre Don Romano Seneſe Abate, della Congregation Caſsineſe, dell'ordine del noſtro Santiſsimo Padre Benedetto.

AL NOME DI DIO,

Adì primo di Giugno 1586

Per 4/31	Cartoleria / a Cassa. lire venti ß 10. spese in questo libro doppio, col suo Giornale & Alfabeto, con altre due vacchette, e squarciafogli ———— £	—20—10—
7/32	Mutationi / a Cassa, lire cinquantacinque ß 10 date, cioe £ 22 al P.D.Benedetto da Bologna Decano, mutato questo capitolo a Modona, per sua mutatione di vn anno, e buona mano e £ 33—10 date a Don Gio. Pietro da Salò, mutato a Praglia, per sua mutatione di vn'anno, spese fatte, e buona mano, come per loro riceuere appare distintamente nel libro di essi ———— £	—55—10—
7/35	Dette / a D Mauro da Piacenza Concelleraro, lire dicisette ß 12. conte a D. Valentiniano da Napoli mutato a Roma, per sua mutatione e buona mano, di mesi noue, ch'ei dimorò in questo Monastero, come per suo riceuere ———— £	—17—12—
	Adì 2 detto.	
32/53	Cassa / a Federico barbarossa malghese, lire trecento quaranta otto ß 12. contemi per mano di Marco Sollitario formaggiaro, a buõ cõto del suo debito £	—348—12—
35/32	D. Mauro Concelleraro / a Cassa. lire cento trenta, contegli per spendere, come al mio libretto appare distintamente ———— £	—130—
38/32	F Thomaso di Val camonica spenditore // a Cassa lire nonantasette ß 14. 8 contegli per spendere a minuto ———— £	—97—14—8—
58/35	Cornelio Landino seruidore // a D.Mauro Concelleraro, lire uenti, da lui hauute a buon conto del suo credito ———— £	—20—
32/51	Cassa / ad Alessandro del Sole Affittuale, lire quattrocento ottantasette ß 10. da lui hauute a buon conto del suo debito ———— £	—487—10—
37/32	P.D Placido Mantouano Rettore di Badia / a Cassa, lire cento quaranta, contegli da spendere, come al mio libretto ———— £	—140—
39/32	F.Mansueto Bresciano custode al Priorato // a Cassa, lire settantacinque, contegli da spendere intorno alle possessioni ———— £	—75—
40/32	P.Vigilantio Comasco Oblato, custode a Santi Martiri / a Cassa. lire cẽtouenti, mandategli da spendere, per mano di Fabritio Gallo nostro fattore ———— £	—120—
13/35	Limosine / a D. Mauro, lire otto, date d'ordine del Reuerendo P Abate, ad alcuni hebrei fatti christiani ———— £	—8—
58/39	Berengario Serpentino camparo // a F. Mansueto, lire sette ß 10. da lui hauute a buon conto del suo salario ———— £	—7—10—
	Adì 3 detto.	
48/51	m.Sigismondo Tranquillo // a Gordiano Lampridio affittuale, lire dugento ottanta, contegli a nostro nome in pagamento ———— £	—280—
16/37	Badia // al P D.Placido, lire vndeci ß 18 per dodici rastelladori, & 24. forche di legno, compre per rastellare & custodire il fieno, come al suo libro ———— £	—11—18—
19/40	S. Martiri // a F.Vigilantio, lire sette ß 15. 6. per diece pale compre per lo frumento, come al suo libro appare ———— £	—7—15—6—

AL NOME DELLA SANTISSIMA ET INDIVIDVA TRINITA'

PADRE, FIGLIO, E SPIRITO SANTO.

LIBRO MAESTRO SEGNATO ✠, DEL MONASTERO, DEL GLORIOSO PRECVRSOR DI CHRISTO, SAN GIO. BATTISTA D'ORIANA, DELL'ANNO. 1586.

Cominciato al primo Giugno. Scritto da me Don Cesario da Cremona, monaco del detto Monastero; di ordine del molto Reuerendo Padre Don Romano Senese Abate, E del P. D. Gabriello Parmiggiano Decano, e Celleraro del detto Monastero, della Congregation Casi- nese, dell'ordine del nostro Santissimo Padre Benedetto.

INTROITO del presente libro ✠ dee dare adi primo Giugno, per gl'infrascritti Creditori del Monastero, qui tirati dall'Esito del libro dell'anno passato, segnato Z carte 486 & a quello da i cõti loro come appresso cioe

	.Alienationi dal libro Z.	car. 429	Tirato in questo libro	car. 15	£ 2750
Ven	.Congregatione nostra Casinese	430	Δ 96 — 4 7 — 6	car. 42	£ 386 - 10
R D.	.Clemente Aleni	431		car. 43	£ 57 16 - 6
m	Ottauio Fortunato in Vinegia	436	Δ 1200. a 5 per 100	car. 45	£ 4800
m	.Quintiliano Poeta in Vinegia	436	Δ 600 a 4 per 100	car. 45	£ 2400
m	.Pompilio Desiderato in Vinegia	436	Δ 600. a 4 per 100.	car. 45	£ 2400
m.	Bartholo Saladino in Vinegia	437	Δ 500. a 4 per 100.	car. 46	£ 2000
m.	.Zacheo Verace in Milano	437	Δ 600. a 4 per 100.	car. 46	£ 2400
	.Mario Palmerino	438		car. 48	£ 547 - 16 8
	.Ramondo Pipino	438		car. 48	£ 493 10
m.	.Sabino Pistoia	438		car. 48	£ 643 - 18
	.Quintilio Purpurato	439		car. 48	£ 370 - 17 - 6
	Sigismondo Tranquillo	446		car. 48	£ 280
m.	.Torquato Rinieri	446		car 49	£ 325
	.Enea Saiano	448		car. 49	£ 195 16
	.Illiano dalla Scala	449		car. 49	£ 485 - 10 8
m.	.Liberio de' Mauri	449		car. 49	£ 893 - 15 5
	.Horatio Lauréato	450		car. 49	£ 289 - 16 - 2
m.	.Seneca Valoroso affittuale	451		car. 52	£ 785 - 18 4
	.Agolante de' Mori ferraro	463		car. 57	£ 127 12
	.Agrippa Tibullo marangone	464		car. 57	£ 68 - 7 - 8
	.Pompeio Belcolore ciroico	473		car. 57	£ 18 10
	.Eugenio da Pistoia barbero	474		car. 57	£ 12
	.Dante Congiurato barbero	474		car. 57	£ 10 - 6
	.Gerbino Rustico fornaro	476		car. 57	£ 37 - 12 - 10
	.Delfino Commodo camparo	477		car. 58	£ 78 12
	.Berengario Serpentino camparo	477		car. 58	£ 18 17 8
	.Annibale Germano seruidore	480		car. 58	£ 130
	.Cornelio Landiuo seruidore	480		car. 58	£ 30 - 15
	.Agapito Pagani seruidore	481		car. 58	£ 12 - 17 - 9
				.Somma	£ 23052 - 16 - 2

.DEe hauere adi primo Giugno, per gl' infraſcritti Debitori del Monaſtero, qui tirati dall Eſito del lib. dell'anno paſſato ſegnato Z. car. 436. & a quello da i conti loro come appreſſo. cioè

R D.	.Lorẽzo de' Simoni dal libro Z. carte	431	Tirato in queſto libro	car. 45	₤ 12 — 6 —
m.	.Carlo Bianchino conto di tempo	450		car. 45	₤ 2750 —
m.	Emanuelle Claudiano cõ to di tẽpo	451		car. 55	₤ 1850 —
	.Altolfo Corrado	455		car. 47	₤ 657 — 18 —
	.Maggio de' Popoli	455		car 47	₤ 600 —
	.Coſtante Dragone	455		car 47	₤ 150 —
	.Tiberio Stellato	456		car. 47	₤ 235 16 - 10
	.Ottauiano Giordano	456		car. 47	₤ 258 —
	.Aleſſandro del Sole affittuale	457		car. 51	₤ 1370 —
	.Gordiano Lampridio affittuale	458		car. 51	₤ 1645 10 —
	.Federico Barbaroſſa malgheſe	459		car. 53	₤ 2248 10 —
	.Marino Orlando molinaro	461		car. 54	₤ 485 — 12 —
	.Ricardo Salomone molinaro	462	ſtara 30 Frumento	car. 54	₤ 372 —
	.Caſsiano Amirante molinaro	463	ſtara 70. Miſture	car. 55	₤ 348 —
	.Deodato Falcone maſſaro	465		car. 56	₤ 597 — 10 —
	.Demetrio Conteſtabile maſſaro	466		car. 56	₤ 642 - 14 —
	.Valerio Leoni maſſaro	467		car. 56	₤ 378 — 18 - 8
	.Fabritio Gallo fattore	476		car. 57	₤ 25 — 15 —
	.Celeſtino Roſſo ſeruidore	480		car. 58	₤ 16 14 - 7 —
m.	.Zerbonio Quaranta gia affittuale	481		car. 58	₤ 947 - 16 —
m.	.Marco T. Villanuoua gia affittuale	482		car. 58	₤ 358 - 17 —
	.Fauſto Giouiale gia noſtro maſſaro	482		car. 58	₤ 588 — 18 6
	.Innocentio Maiorano già fattore	483		car. 58	₤ 75 - 8 —
	.Leontio Manfredi gia noſtro mol.	483		car 58	₤ 18 — 7 - 6 —
				Somma	₤ 16634 - 12 — 1

Reſtanti di queſto anno.

.Ordinaria	323	Sale Peſi 70.	car. 2	₤ 70 —
.Caſciaria	324	Formaggio Peſi 50.	car. 3	₤ 225 —
.Magazino d'Oglio	325	Oglio Peſi 30	car. 3	₤ 120 —
.Forno di Farina	327	Farina Stara 45	car. 4	₤ 90 —
.Veſtieria	332	Raſcie pezze cinque	car. 6	₤ 130 —
.Calzoleria	333	Cordoani, & ſuole	car. 7	₤ 80 —
.Barbaria	342	Sapone Peſi 10.	car. 9	₤ 30 —
.Cantina di uino in Camerone	364	car. 20. di uino per uſo	car. 24	₤ 100 —
.Cantina detta	364	car. 20. da uendere a ₤ 15	car. 24	₤ 300 —
.Cantina di uino diuerſa	365	car 18. per uſo	car. 25	₤ 90 —
.Cantina di uino in Monaſtero	366	car. 20. per uſo	car. 25	₤ 100 —
.Granaro di frumento in Camerone	367	ſtara 25. per uſo	car. 26	₤ 50 —
.Granaro detto	367	ſtara 155. da uendere a ₤ 3. 18	car. 26	₤ 600 —
.Granaro di Frumento diuerſo	368	ſtara 45. per vſo	car. 26	₤ 90 —
.Granaro di Frumẽto in Monaſtero	369	ſtara 20. per uſo	car. 27	₤ 40 —
.Granaro detto	369	ſtara 285. da uendere a ₤ 3. 18	car. 27	₤ 800 —
.Granaro di frumentata	370	ſtara 80 per uſo	car. 27	₤ 120 —
.Granaro di Vena, e Spelta	380	ſtara 60. per vſo	car. 30	₤ 60 —
.Magazino di Lino	381	Peſi 30. da uendere a ₤ 8. 6. 8.	car. 21	₤ 250 —
.Caſſa del P. Celleraro	412	In contanti	car. 32	₤ 1258 — 10 — 5
.D. Mauro Concelleraro	418	In contanti	car. 34	₤ 75 — 12 8
.F. Thomaſo ſpenditore	422	In contanti	car 38	₤ 32 10 6
			Somma	₤ 21346 — 5 — 9
.Monaſtero NOSTRO.	484			1706 10 — 5
			Somma	₤ 23052 — 16 — 2

DEe hauere adi 23.Luglio per Granaro del Monastero, per lo prezzo commune a 2 di stara 196 frumento hauutegli quest'anno, come al libro de'Granari appare distintamente ——— car. 27 £ – 392 ———
.Et più per Granaro di frumentata, hauuragli questo anno, ragionata a β 30 prezzo commune ——— car. 27 £ – 123 ———
.Et adi 26.Ottobre / per Cantina del Monastero, per carra 18. uino, hauutogli come sopra, ragionato a £ 5. prezzo commune —— car. 25 £ – 90 ———
.Et più / per Granaro di Miglio, stara 46. ragionato a β 30. —— car. 28 £ – 69 ———
.Et più / per Granaro di Melega, stara 48. ragionata a β 20. —— car. 29 £ – 48 ———
.Et adi 11. Maggio, per F. Vigilantio, hauuti da Piò 8. di prato affittato a £ 5.4. a Simone Guarnaccia ——— car. 40 £ – 41 – 12 ———

.Somma £ – 763 – 12 ———

DEe hauere adi 23. Luglio / per Aquila Gradito affittuale ex parte r. per lo prezzo commune a £ 2, di stara 250. frumento ne dee questa raccolta, per lo fitto del primo anno ——— car. 52 £ – 500 ———
.Et più / per Aquila detto, per stara 40. di Vena, ne dee come sopra, ragionata a β 20. prezzo commune ——— car. 52 £ – 40 ———
.Et adi 26. Ottobre / per Aquila detto, per carra 18. uino ne dee come sopra, ragionato al prezzo commune ——— car. 52 £ – 90 ———

.Somma £ – 630 ———

DEe hauere adi 23. Luglio / per Seuero Biondo massaro, & affittuale, per stara 70. frumento ne dee per lo fitto di questo 4. anno —— car. 52 £ – 140 ———
.Et adi 26. Ottobre / per Seuero detto per car 10. di uino ne dee come sopra, ragionato a £ 5. prezzo commune ——— car. 52 £ – 50 ———
.Et adi 11. Nouembre / per Seuero detto, per lo fitto in denari di questo quarto anno finito a S. Martino, da pagarci come al suo côto car. 52 £ – 400 ———

.Somma £ – 590 ———

DEe hauere adi 27 Luglio / per Granaro di Faua, hauutagli questo anno in nostra parte, ragionata a β 30. prezzo commune ——— car. 29 £ – 52 ———
.Et più / per Granaro di Legumi, stara 8. hauuti, & ragionati ut s. car. 29 £ – 12 ———
.Et adi 26. Ottobre, per Cantina del Monastero, per carra 12. uino hauutogli come sopra, ragionato al prezzo commune di £ 5. —— car. 25 £ – 60 ———

.Somma £ – 124 – 10 ———

DEe hauere adi 14. Aprile / per Cassa, uenduto a Gentile Massimino, a £ 10. il peso, per mano del P. D. Placido Rettore in Badia ——— car. 34 pesi 102. 12. 6 £ 1025 ———
.Et per saldo di questo conto, calato per quanto si e stimato di più, in le due partite côtroscritte-car. 21 Pesi – 2. 12. 6 ———

.Somma pesi 105 —— £ 1025 ———

1586.

.PIETRA SALDA di la dal Fondico uecchio, Massaria nostra, dee dare adi ultimo Maggio / a Valerio Leoni massaro, per carrezzi, & opere da lui hauute quest'anno, come al suo libro saldato d'accordo distinctamente appare —— car. 56 ₤ — 31 — 17

.Et piu / all'Entrata generale di quest'anno, tiratogli per saldo di questo conto —— car 60 ₤ — 731 — 15

.Somma ₤ — 763 — 12

.DEUS DEDIT appresso la Città, Massaria nostra, dee dare adi ultimo Maggio / all'Entrata generale di quest'anno, tiratogli per saldo - car. 60 ₤ — 630

.ISOLANA in uia nuoua, Massaria nostra, dee dare a di ultimo Maggio / all'Entrata generale di quest'anno, tiratogli per saldo —— car. 60 ₤ — 590

S. IGNATIO in Riua, Ronco nostro, dee dare adi ultimo Maggio / all'Entrata generale di quest'anno, tiratogli per saldo —— car. 60 ₤ — 114 — 10

.MAGAZINO di Lino, dee dare adi pr. Giugno / all'Introito di questo, per resto qui tirato da car. 363. libro Z car. 1 pesi 30 — ₤ — 205

.Et adi 16. Giugno / a Badia, hauutogli questo anno, stimato in circa al prezzo, & quantità —— car. 16 pesi 75 — ₤ — 625

.Et adi 14. Aprile / a Badia, per saldo di questo conto spettante à essa Corte —— car. 17 pesi 0 — ₤ — 150

Somma pesi 105 — ₤ 1025

1586.

.MONASTERO nostro del glorioso Precursore, e degno Martire di
Christo S Gio: Battista d Oriana, quale nostro Sig. per sua diuina bō
tà si degni diffendere, e prosperare, dee dare adi primo Giugno / al-
l'Introito generale di quest'anno, tiratogli da car. 484. del libro Z.
del l'anno passato ———— car. 1 ₤ 1706 — 10 — 5 —

5. .Et adi 7. Ottobre / a Cassa, conti a Delio Pescatore, in pagamento di
quanto restaua ad hauere, per pesce da lui hauuto questa quaresima
passata, come per sua lista in filza ———— car. 32 ₤ — 95 — 15 — 6 —

6 .Et più / a Prisciano Volpe, p resto di panno, rascia, e tele da lui hauu
te gli anni passati, come per sua lista in filza appare distintamēte, che
per iscordo non si scrissero ———— car. 50 ₤ — 47 — 8 ———

7 .Et più / a Cassa, conti a m. Bartholomeo Calcinato, in uirtù di vna sen
tenza della Ruota, per acqua godutagli da nostri di Badia gli anni
passati, della sua rata parte, come appare ne gli atti di m. Andrea Lo
douici notaro diffusamente ———— car. 32 ₤ — 135 ————

8 .Et più / a Santo Squarcialupo, per tanti gli douemo pagare fra otto
mesi, in uirtù di una sentenza della Ruota, vscita ne gli atti del detto
notaro, per ristoro di tempesta patita l'anno 1582. che esso era Affit
tuale a S. Remigio, con le spese ———— car. 50 ₤ — 135 — 10 — 2 —

9 .Et adi ultimo Maggio / a F. Thomaso spenditore, per saldo di suo con
to qui tirato, per suario occorsogli questo anno ———— car. 39 ₤ — 0 — 18 — 1 —

10 O .Et più / per Suario occorso quest'anno nel bilancio, come si uede car. 59 ₤ — 4 — 17 — 10 —

.Et più / all'Esito generale di quest'anno, tiratogli per saldo di questo
conto ———— car. 61 ₤ 3744 — 0 — 3 —

.Somma ₤ 5870 — 0 — 3 —

1 .DEe hauere adi primo Ottobre / per Cassa, contone dal R.P. F. Pietro Martire da Turino di S. Domenico, p tāti hauuti da un penitēte, in sodisfattione di vno debito suo, che noi si haueuamo scordato-car. 32 £ —127—13—8—

2 .Et più / per Riginaldo Campione, per la Boschetta del Vallone, datta gli l'anno passato da tagliare, e da pagarne a S. Michele prossimo passato, che non si scrisse per iscordo ———————— car. 47 £ —50————

3 .Et più / per Cassa, contone da Domino Turchino già nostro Affittuale, in virtù di una Sentēza di Ruota, per lo danno da lui hauuto in arbori tagliati, e non piantati in quel tempo, come ne gli atti di m. Vincēzo Rosso notaro appare distintamente———————— car. 32 £ —146————

4 .Et più / per Nastagio Calandra, per tanti ne dee in uirtù di una sentenza del Mag Podestà. per l'interresse patito in uno paro di caualli da carrozza uendutine per sani ———————— car. 47 £ —90————

10 .Et adi ultimo Maggio / per D. Mauro secondo Celleraro, per saldo del suo conto, nel quale e seguito suario questo anno ———— car. 36 £ —2—18—4—

11 O .Et più / per Cōtroscrittione della consimile partita per contro, posta per essempio, essendo il bilancio uero, e reale ———————— car. 59 £ —4—17—10—

12 .Et più / per la Spesa generale, per saldo di quel conto qui tirato, per quanto s'e speso meno questo anno dell'Entrata hauuta———car. 60 £ 5448—10—5—

.Somma £ 5870—0—3—

1586.

SPESA generale di queſt'anno, finito adi ultimo Maggio, dee dare, per ſaldo degli infraſcritti conti, qui tirati, & eſtinti dalle loro pertite, come in eſsi conti diſtintamente appare cioè

.Ordinaria in danari	car.	4	₤	3372	13	11
.Caſciaria formaggio peſi 202.	car.	3	₤	690	14	4
.Magazino d'Oglio peſi 168	car.	3	₤	719	11	
.Foreſteria	car.	3	₤	205	16	5
.Forno, di Farina ſtara 438	car.	4	₤	876		
.Vino conſumato, carra 53	car.	4	₤	265		
.Infermeria	car.	4	₤	402	17	5
.Spetieria	car.	5	₤	262	17	
.Straordinaria	car.	5	₤	361	13	7
.Veſtieria	car.	6	₤	1892	5	8
.Calzoleria	car.	7	₤	419	12	6
.Mutationi	car.	7	₤	276	7	6
.Viaggi	car.	8	₤	298	6	1
.Taſſe, & Annate	car.	8	₤	3337	4	
.Datij, e Grauezze	car.	8	₤	616	13	
.Speſe Capitolari	car.	8	₤	100	16	
.Cartoleria	car.	9	₤	156	6	3
.Libraria	car.	9	₤	229	16	6
.Porti di lettere	car.	9	₤	87	13	6
.Barbaria	car.	9	₤	115	9	8
.Maſſeritie	car.	10	₤	496	0	10
.Vtenſigli	car.	10	₤	582	17	5
.Stalla	car.	11	₤	1028	4	8
.Fabrica	car.	11	₤	1131	9	6
.Reparationi	car.	11	₤	210	9	10
.Liti, e Scritture	car.	12	₤	411	10	3
.Salariati	car.	12	₤	1095	18	8
.Limoſine	car.	13	₤	680	6	6
.Sagriſtia	car.	14	₤	900	19	4
.Acquiſti fatti	car.	15	₤	437	8	6
	Somma		₤	21660	19	10
.Speſo meno dell'Entrata di queſt'anno, che ſi tira al Monaſt. nro.	car.	59	₤	5448	10	5
	.Somma		₤	27109	10	3

1586. 60

ENTRATA generale di quest'anno finito adi ultimo Maggio, dee hauere, per saldo degl'infrascritti Conti qui tirati, & estinti dalle loro parti te, come in essi conti distintamente appare cioè

.Badia di S.Fulgentio in Cameroo e		car. 17	£	4427	19	10
.Priorato di S.Remigio, Corte nostr		car 18	£	1805	9	5
.S Mauro Massaria, e Corte nostra		car. 19	£	1621	3	
.S.Martiri, Massaria, e Corte nostra		car. 19	£	179	14	1
.Romea, Massaria nostra		car. 20	£	1010	18	
.Acqua chiara, Massaria nostra		car. 20	£	2925	11	
.S.Dionigi, Massaria nostra		car. 20	£	747	10	
.Honorata, Massaria nostra		car. 20	£	1988		
.Pietra Salda, Massaria nostra		car. 21	£	731	15	
.Deusdedit, Massaria nostra		car. 21	£	636		
.Isolana, Massaria nostra		car. 21	£	590		
.S.Ignatio, Ronco nostro		car. 21	£	124	10	
.Malgheria nostra		car. 22	£	483	12	
.Socida di Bestiami		car. 22	£	52		
.Razza di Caualli		car. 22	£	68		
.Terratici diuersi		car. 22	£	227	10	
.Selue, e Boschi		car. 22	£	345		
.Molina		car. 23	£	1187	15	
.Censi, e Liuelli		car. 23	£	126	19	11
.Fitti di Case, e Botteghe		car. 24	£	980	4	
.Horto del Monastero		car. 24	£	221	18	
Aumenti dal commun prezzo.						
.Cantina di uino in Camerone, in carra 50. uenduto		car 24	£	444		
.Cantina diuersa, in carra 10. uenduto		car. 25	£	84	3	4
.Cantina del Monastero, in carra 16. uenduto		car. 25	£	128	12	
.Granaro in Camerone, in stara 937 Frumento uenduto		car. 26	£	1825	16	
.Granaro diuerso	stara 478	car. 26	£	1074	15	
.Granaro del Monastero	stara 250	car 27	£	888	16	
.Granaro di Frumentata	stara 220	car. 27	£	320	10	
.Granaro di Segala	stara 618	car. 28	£	900		
.Granaro di Migho	stara 362	car. 28	£	171	10	
.Granaro di Panigo	stara 175	car. 28	£	157	10	
.Granaro di Faua	stara 198	car. 29	£	319	10	
.Granaro di Legumi	stara 15	car. 29	£	22	8	8
.Granaro di Melega	stara 230	car. 29	£	172	10	
.Granaro d'Orgio	stara 30	car. 30	£	24		
		.Somma	£	27109	10	3

1586.

ESITO generale di quest'anno, finito adi ultimo Maggio, dee dare, per li infrascritti crediti del Monastero, qui tirati dai conti loro, cioe

	.Quilico Fedele, e fratelli	car.	50	£	473	18	
m.	.Gordiano Lampridio affittuale	car.	51	£	354	14	7
	.Eutitio Lanciano fornasaro	car.	48	£	824	10	
	.Henrico Lanfranco malghese	car.	54	£	2008	12	6
	.Oberro Basilisco molinaro	car.	55	£	109	10	
	.Et piu Frumento stara 10.	car.	55	£	20		
	.Demetrio Contestabile massaro	car.	56	£	414	18	
	.Valerio Leoni massaro	car.	56	£	276	12	8
	.Vittorio, e Cortese Palladini massari	car.	56	£	153	15	6
	.Rinaldo Sansone massaro	car.	56	£	191	6	
	.Temistio Solimano massaro	car.	56	£	67	13	
	.Dante Congiurato barbero	car.	57	£	3	10	
	Inessigibili, & a lungo tempo						
m.	.Marco Tullio Villanuoua gia affittuale	car.	58	£	318	17	
	.Fausto Giouiale gia massaro	car.	58	£	588	18	6
	.Innocentio Maiorano gia fattore	car.	5[illegible]	£	75	8	
	.Leontio Manfredi gia molinaro	car.	58	£	18	7	6
		Somma		£	5940	11	3

Restanti di questo anno

.Casciaria formaggio, per uso	pesi 50 a £ 2	car.	3	£	100		
.Cantina di Camerone, per uso	carra 12 a £ 5	car.	24	£	60		
.Cantina diuersa, per uso	carra 20 a £ 5	car.	25	£	100		
.Cantina del Monastero, per uso	carra 16 a £ 5	car.	25	£	80		
.Granaro di Camerone, per uso	stara 10 a £ 2	car.	26	£	20		
.Da uendere	stara 50 a £ 4. 10	car.	26	£	225		
.Granaro diuerso, per uso	stara 10 a £ 2	car.	26	£	20		
.Granaro del Monastero, per uso	stara 82 a £ 2	car.	27	£	164		
.Da uendere	stara 250 a £ 4. 10	car.	27	£	1125		
.Granaro di Vena, e Spelta	stara 50 a £ 1	car.	30	£	50		
.Cassa in contanti		car.	34	£	596	19	6
		Somma		£	8481	1	9

IL FINE.

1580 61

ESITO generale di quest'anno finito adi ultimo Maggio, dee hauere per gli infrascritti debiti del Monastero, qui tirati dai conti loro, cioè

m.	.Bartholo Saladino in Vinegia, a Censo Δ 500	car. 46	£	2000	
m.	.Aquila Gradito affittuale, conto di tempo	car. 52	£	2500	
R.D.	Clemente Aleni nostro Curato	car. 43	£	37—16—6	
	.Fabritio Gallo nostro fattore	car. 57	£	24—5	
	.Delfino Commodo camparo	car. 58	£	60	
	.Annibale Germano seruidore	car. 58	£	115	
		Somma	£	4737—1—6	
	.Monastero nostro resta in credito, come si uede	car. 59	£	3744—0—8	
		.Somma	£	8481—2—2	

IL FINE.

MAINARDI'S JOURNAL REPRODUCED

In 1632 there appeared in Bologna a work on bookkeeping, written by Matteo Mainardi This book is of far later date than the ones heretofore mentioned, but as explained in the historical chapter it is remarkable in that it attempts to describe, besides the system for the merchants, one for the keeping of executors' and trustees' accounts It follows Pietra and Manzoni closely in a good many instances

The illustrations have small value for us except to indicate the little progress that was made in Italy with the shifting of the center of trade from Italy to Holland, as Simon Stevin's book hereinafter reproduced, which was published in 1604 in Holland was far in advance of this of Mainardi's We reproduce the title page of the second edition of this book, and a page which explains the purpose of the book as far as trustees' and executors accounts are concerned The two pages of the journal we give in order to show that each page is provided with the address to the Deity, that the dot is used for checking, and that we here find so-called combination journal entries, by which we mean entries in which are combined more than one credit or more than one debit in one entry We do not, however, find the use of the word "sundries," as in Stevin s work and as we use it to this day It will be noted that in such entries the debits are always named first and itemized before the credits are enumerated, and that the division between debits and credits is made with two horizontal lines or dashes, one below the last debit and one above the first credit We also note the absence of the money signs, except the principal or the lire sign

IL CAMBIO REALE PER OGNI PIAZZA.

Formalmente Ragguagliato

DA

MATTEO MAINARDI.

Con diuersi altri Quesiti vtili, curiosi, e necessarij alla Mercatura.

In questa nuoua Impressione aggiontoui il modo, che hoggidì si pratica.

IN BOLOGNA, M. D. CC.

Per il Longhi. *Con licenza de' Superiori.*

M. DC. XXXIV.

A Laude, e gloria della Santiſsima, & Indiuidua Trinità Padre, Figliuolo, e Spirito Santo; della Glorioſiſsima Vergine Maria, delli Santi Apoſtoli Pietro, e Paolo, e delli Santi N. N. noſtri Protettori, come ancora di tutta la Corte Celeſtiale. Amen.

Queſto preſente Libro chiamato Giornale, di forma N. di carte N. coperto di N. di carte num. N. e ſegnato N. è di Rutiglio figliuolo del già Sig. Leonido Fongarelli pupillo, d'età d'anni N. & erede (ò ab inteſtato, ò teſtamentario) del ſudetto Sig Leonido, paſſato à miglior vita li 16. Gennaro del preſente anno, ſotto la tutela di N. ſopra del quale, per mano di N. ſarà notato regolatamente, e formalmente, ogni qualità di beni ſtabili, e mobili, beſtiami, debitori, e creditori del d. già Sig. Leonido, e per conſeguenza hora ſpettante al medeſimo Sig. Rutiglio ſuo figliuolo, & erede, come ſopra; e ſuſſeguentemente tutte l'entrate, e ſpeſe, che frà l'anno ſeguiteranno in queſta eredità, le quali partite tutte ſaranno leuate da queſto Libro, e portate per mano del ſudetto N. ſopra vn altro Libro chiamato Libro Maeſtro di forma, carta, coperta, e ſegno come queſto, di carte num. N. à ſuoi appartati luoghi, conforme è lo ſtile Mercantile, che però eſſo Pupillo (e per eſſo il Sig. N. ſuo Commiſſario Teſtamentario) intende, che li ſia data piena, & indubitata fede in giudicio, e fuori.

In fede di che &c.

Io N. Commiſſario Teſt. &c. affermo quanto di ſopra.
Io N. Scriuano accetto, e giuro quanto di ſopra.

A GIOR-

Laus Deo, & B. Virg. Rosarij M. DC. XXXIII.

Adì 31. Decembre Sabbato.

---

10 *Alli Mammi, &c. al banco lir. quattrocentotrè, sol tredici, den quattro quat li portò il nostro Caneuaro contanti, retratti fino à questo giorno sudetto, di Fassi diecimilla da cauazzatura venduti à minuto, à bolognini sette la carica, e numero settemilla di vite, à bolognini trentadue il cento, come si vede per vna taglia.* L. 403. 13. 4

11 *A credito Fassi da cauazzatura in casa num. 10000.* L. 291. 13. 4

11 *A credito Fassi di vite in casa num. 7000.* L. 112.

---

9 *A spese di fuoco lir. vintisei, sol. trè, den. due quat. per num. ottocentoquindici Fassi da cauazzatura, e num. quattrocent'ottantadue di vite serbati per casa.* L. 26. 3. 2

11 *A credito Fassi da cauazzatura num 815.* L 20. 7. 6.

11 *A credito Fassi di vite num 482.* L. 5. 15. 8.

---

7 *A Luca Barbini nostro lauoratore alla Possessione di Pondi lir. centodiciasette quat. cioè lir. cento per li patti in denari contanti, e lir. diciasette per corbe quattro d'Orzo hauuto più mesi sono dal nostro Fattore, à lir. quattro, sol. cinque la corba, d'accordo.* L. 117. —

7 *A credito alla Possessione di Pondi.* L 100.

9 *A credito Orzo à Montorio cor. 4.* L. 17.

---

7 *A Domenico Manganello nostro Suozzo alla Possessione di Bella lir. centoquarant'vna, sol. cinque quat. cioè lir. centouinti per li patti, che deue pagare in denari lir. vent'vna, sol. 5. per corbe 5. d'orzo hauuto dal Fattore, d'accordo.* L. 141. 5. —

8 *A credito alla Possessione di Bello.* L 120.

9 *A credito à Orzo in granaro di Montorio corbe 5.* L. 21. 5.

---

7 *A Liuio Carboni, e fratelli nostri mezzaiuoli à Montorio lir. centosessantatrè, sol. due, den. sei quat. cioè lir. centoquaranta per li patti, che paga in denari, e lir. ventitrè, sol. due, den. sei per corbe cinque, e meza d'Orzo hauuto, d'accordo.* L. 163. 2. 6

8 *A credito la Possessione di Montorio.* L. 140.

9 *A credito Orzo à Montorio corbe cinque, e meza.* L. 23. 2. 6.

---

7 *A Angelo Susa nostro Suozzo à Romanello lir centoquarantatrè, sol. due, den. sei quat. cioè lir. centouenti per li patti che paga in danari, e lir. vintitrè, sol. dieci, den sei per corbe cinque, e meza d'Orzo hauuto, d'accordo, più di sono.* L. 143. 2. 6

8 *A credito la Possessione di Romanello.* L. 120.

9 *A credito Orzo in granaro di Montorio corbe cinque, e meza.* L. 23. 2. 6.

A Mi-

Laus Deo, & B. Virg. Rosarij M. DC. XXXIII.

Adì 31. Decembre Sabbato.

14 *A Michele Landinelli nostro bracente à Romanello lir. vintinoue, cioè lir. vinti per la pigione della casa, e lir noue quat. per corbe due, quar. due d orzo, hauuto più giorni sono dal Fattore, d'accordo.* L. 29. —

7 *A credito Luogo di Romanello.* L. 20.

9 *A credito Orzo in granaro cor. 2. quar. 2.* L. 9.

---

13 *A spese d'Elemosine lir. centononanta, sol. otto, quat. dispensate il Natale passato à diuersi Luoghi Pij, & à poueri della nostra Parochia, per l'anima del Sig. Leonido,*

10 *per noi dalli Mannini, &c.* L. 190. 8. —

A credito alli Mannini, &c. al banco.

---

12 *A Canape grezzo in Villa lir. cinquecentosessantanoue, sol. quattordici quat. per valuta di lib. duemillaottocentoquarant'otto, e meza di Canape, battuta dalli nostri lauoratori, della sua parte, apprezzata senza pregiuditio lir. vinti il cento.* L. 569. 14. —

A credito Luca Barbini per lib 537. e meza. L. 107. 10.

7 *A credito Domenico Manganelli per lib. 711.* L. 142. 4.

7 *A credito Liuio Carboni per lib. 837. e meza.* L. 167. 10.

7 *A credito Angelo Susa, per lib. 612. e meza.* L. 122. 10.

7 *A credito Michele Landinelli lib. 150.* L. 30.

14

---

7 *A spese di reparationi, e fabriche lir. centotrentanoue, sol. sei, den. otto quat. pagati per mandato questo giorno sudetto à M. N. nostro Capelletto, e sono, cioè lir. cinquanta per la sua annua prouisione di coprire, e riuedere tutte le nostre case di Villa, e di Città, e il resto per spese, che dà conto hauere fatto in risarcire le case di Villa, come di tutto ne appare lista in filza di più somma, per mandato dalli Mannini, &c. al banco.* L. 139. 6. 8

10 *A credito li Mannini, &c. al banco.*

---

7 *Alla Possessione di Pondi lir. settantasette, sol. otto, den 8. quat si fanno buoni à M. Sabadino Pazaglia di Mal'albergo, e sono per sei nauate di stramo, mandatoci li mesi passati, compresoui le condotte, così d'accordo insieme.* L. 77. 8. 8

8 *Alla Possessione di Bello lir. settantasette, sol. otto, den. otto quat. buoni al sudetto, come sopra, per sei nauate di stramo da letto, come sopra detto.* L. 77. 8. 8

8 *Alla Possessione di Montorio lir. centocinque, sol. tredici per otto nauate di stramo da letto mandatoli il sudetto, come sopra.* L. 105. 13. —

8 *Alla Possessione di Romanello lir centocinque, sol. tredici quat. buoni al sudetto per altre otto nauate di stramo da letto hauute, come sopra.* L. 105. 13. —

14 *A credito Sabadino Pazaglia lir. 366. 3. 4.*

A Sa-

Nieuwe Instructie

Ende bewijs der looffelijcker Consten des Rekenboecks/ ende Rekeninghe te houdene nae die Italiaensche maniere/ allen Cooplieden/ Rentmeesteren/ Tollenaren/ Assijsmeesteren/ zeer nut ende profytelijck: Informerende eenen yeghelijcken/ hoe hy zekere ende perfecte Rekeninghe houden sal met dobbel boecken nae der manieren voorsz. Waer duer elck by hem seluen lichtelijck in allen sinen saken eñ affairẽ groote experientie crighen sal.

¶ Ghetranslateert met grooter diligentien/ wt die Italiaensche tale in onser spraken duer Jan ympyn Christoffels (saligher memorien) Coopman van Antwerpen: Ende nu ter liefden eñ profyte des ghemeynen weluaerts eerst wtghegeuen int Jaer M.CCCCC.XLIII.

¶ Cum Gratia & Preuilegio/ vier Jaren lanck duerende/ zoot blijct by der Copien van die Keyserlijcke Maiesteyt verleent.

NOTES ON YMPYN

We are reproducing herewith the title page of Ympyn's book, which we have taken from Kheil's book, where a thorough comparative study is made between Ympyn and Pacioli. Ympyn, as we have seen was the first Dutch writer who practically translated Pacioli into Dutch, French and English, and from him continental Europe has derived its subsequent texts on bookkeeping. The original of this book was not available to the writer, but we have taken from Kheil's book the most important subject-matters which we review in the following lines.

Ympyn, as stated heretofore copied Pacioli practically verbatim. We find, however, here and there a few deviations which we think it important to mention at this place.

Pacioli speaks about the two divisions of his book, one covering inventory and the other "disposition." He is somewhat vague in explaining this latter term. Ympyn says that "disposition" is "the establishment, systematizing and execution of the current and customary as well as the extraordinary affairs of a business.

Ympyn suggests that the index should be bound in parchment and placed either at the beginning or the end of the ledger, but in such a manner that it can be taken out if necessary. He uses the Italian terms "Per" and "A" untranslated. In front of corrective ledger entries he uses a cross and does not mention any other distinguishing marks. The term "cash" is personified to cashier instead of pocket book, as used by Pacioli. He enlarges on the terms "Cash" and "Capital" more than Pacioli does. For branch stores the sales are entered into a sales journal, and totaled once a week for transfer to the ledger. Ympyn is more extensive in his explanations than Pacioli about *barrato* or trade, also about the draft and its use. We should remember, however, that Pacioli describes these more fully in the parts of his book not covered by the subject of bookkeeping.

Ympyn recommends a separate book for household expenses, and a petty expense book for the small expenses of the business. The totals are transferred from these books to the journal once a month. He mentions a special cash book for special kinds of species or for foreign money which is handled by the firm very much as some banks today use a separate account with bank notes of large denominations. He advocates the use of separate books for statistics, or memoranda, in the nature of diaries, and suggests a shipping book. As to accounts, he mentions interest, building rents, ground rents, expenses, household expenses, merchandise expenses, building repair, garden expenses, salaries, loans, expenses of childbirths and an account for marriage gifts.

Like Pacioli and Manzoni, Ympyn uses a profit and loss account, very much the same as we do today. He also draws off a balance to prove the correctness of the ledger. Ympyn, however, puts the balance at the end of the ledger as an account, although he does not explain it as such in his text, in this he does not follow Pacioli. He balances the profit and loss account to capital account without passing it through the journal.

Ympyn specifically mentions that merchandise must be inventoried at cost and he uses a merchandise inventory account, to which all accounts showing an inventory of merchandise or goods on hand are closed and then this account in turn is closed to the balance account. He does not journalize these entries. However, we find that he does journalize his profit and loss items, as does Manzoni, but which Pacioli does not do.

Assets in the balance account are put on the credit side and liabilities on the debit side. He uses no opening balance account in the new ledger, but evidently posts from the old balance account in the old ledger in reverse order to the new ledger, because the closing balance account in the old ledger gives the folios to which the items are posted in the new ledger. We have seen that Pacioli says that you can transfer the capital account either as a balance in one item, or itemized, the latter having the advantage of then representing a summary of the inventory, and each new ledger then starts with an inventory.

The journal, profit and loss, capital, and balance accounts illustrated by Ympyn are printed in Kheil's German review of Ympyn, but we regret that he did not reproduce them actually, as with the modern printing much of the form and arrangement is lost.

Ympyn permits no erasures. He wishes a line drawn through the wrong amount or words the same as Pacioli does, in order to be able to prove of what the error consisted. He insists that explanations to the journal entries must be so clear that anybody can understand the transactions they record, that books kept in the Italian manner as described by him, with a journal and a ledger "make everything as clear as daylight and will prevent swindles and defalcations, as occur now so frequently and almost daily."

He adds the freight to the merchandise and posts it to the merchandise account. He deprecates trading on long credit, and announces it as bad because "the wolf does not eat any days and the due date comes nearer not only by day but as well by night."

The two diagonal lines of which Pacioli speaks are used in the journal when the posting is finished and in the ledger when the account is closed or transferred to the new ledger. Capital account Ympyn credits with the assets and debits with the liabilities, which agrees with the idea of the personifying of accounts and results in a net credit in this account, which net credit is the same as we use in the capital account to this day. Ympyn uses no ledger headings and shows but one column in the journal. He uses Roman figures in all money columns, both ledger and journal.

STEVIN'S JOURNAL AND LEDGER REPRODUCED

The following pages, Nos 119 to 136, represent reproductions of the journal and ledger and other interesting forms as given in the book of Simon Stevin, which appeared in the Dutch language in Amsterdam in 1604, was rewritten in The Hague in 1607, republished in Latin in 1608, and republished by Stevin's son Hendrick in 1650 As we have seen, Stevin was a tutor and adviser of Prince Maurits of Orange, then Governor of some of the Dutch provinces Stevin first taught the Prince bookkeeping and then induced him to install a double-entry system of bookkeeping throughout his domains and government establishments

Stevin apologizes for the use of terms in foreign languages, such as debit credit, debitor, creditor, balance, journal, finance, etc, but says they are necessary because if he used Dutch terms the bookkeepers would not understand what he was writing about, and as bookkeepers only are supposed to profit by the regulations promulgated and ordered by Maurits, the Prince of Orange, for the double-entry municipal accounting system, he insists that he must use the foreign terms

The objection of the Prince that government clerks would not understand Italian or double-entry bookkeeping, he overcomes by advising that he could hire and should hire clerks who did know it for they undoubtedly would be better men

The objections to the necessity of double-entry bookkeeping for municipalities and governments he reasons away by stating that a merchant has some direct personal supervision over his bookkeepers and cashiers, but the government must direct them through other persons As this is not as safe as the merchant's personal supervision, it follows that if a merchant needs double-entry bookkeeping and finds it profitable, the government needs it that much more

Stevin does not give rules for the making of journal entries, but he explains a difficulty which the Prince evidently met, when the latter asks "If Peter pays me $100, there are two debits and two credits I am his debtor and my cash is also a debtor, he is my creditor and his cash is also a creditor Which two of these four must I select for my books?' Stevin answers "Take always my creditor and my debtor because Peter keeps books with his creditor and his debtor"

Stevin urges upon the Prince that governmental treasurers invariably become rich, and when they die leave such a muddled state of affairs and records that there is nothing left but to forgive and forget, but that such is not the case with bookkeepers and cashiers of mercantile establishments, they invariably die poor A merchant, he says, knows what his bookkeeper or his cashier or treasurer should have, but this is not so with a Prince, who has to take the cashier's word for it

The Prince then asks if bookkeeping ever had been worthy of such consideration that books were published on it Stevin replied that numerous writers had taken up the subject, and that while doubtless the double-entry system was originated in olden times, yet in Italy where it is said to have been executed first, it is considered an art of which no other is so honorable and worthy

The Prince (apparently floored by Stevin's lucid arguments) thereupon agrees to take up the study with the view of installing double-entry bookkeeping in the governmental departments as soon as Stevin and he were through with their studies of algebra

Stevin has a firm place in the heart of the writer, because he mentions in his book that one of his forbears was a treasurer of the city of Flissingen, thus supplying the missing data for the genealogy of his family

Comparison of the journal and the ledger with the reproductions of the Italian writers heretofore given, will at once show that in printing as well as in arrangement the Dutch were far superior to the Italian A comparison with Pietra and Mainardi will make this very plain The examples must be pronounced as being excellent for their time The journal entries are differently grouped than has been done by any previous writers, very much more systematic, and in many instances only totals from other records are used

It will be noted that all religious terms at the top of pages or at the beginning of books, customarily used in the Italian method, have been omitted The slightest reference to the Deity is absent in these books, due to the fight for religious freedom which then waged in Holland Stevin was a great supporter of the Protestant party, so much so that Brown relates that when in 1645 a proposal was made to erect a statue at Bruges to his memory, a Catholic agitation was aroused in the House of Representatives to defeat the project Even a clerical editor expunged his name from a Dutch dictionary of biography, where it had appeared in earlier editions However that may be, the writer having been born in Holland and there having kept numerous sets of books, can vouch that twenty years ago the majority of books which came under his supervision were opened and closed in the name of the Diety

Stevin's omission of the use of religious terms was followed in England, whereas Europe to this day follows Ympyn and others which is corroborating evidence that Stevin through Dafforne has influenced English and American bookkeeping more than has Mellis, who followed Pacioli in the use of religious terms.

Through a peculiar coincidence the use of the terms "pepper" and "ginger" appear as frequently in his illustrations and examples, as they do in those of the Italian and other previous writers

Stevin personifies the impersonal or economic accounts when he states that cash account is an account with the cashier and follows this idea throughout his work in connection with other accounts He mentions the three methods of buying and selling theretofore described by the Italians, namely, on account, for cash, and in trade, and the combinations that can be made with these three Like his predecessors, he states that in the beginning of every book two entries are necessary, which should cover merchandise, and cash on hand, as also the debts owing and accounts owning, and like Pacioli and Ympyn he explains fully that sometimes a business can be started on credit but he doubts the advisability

Stevin is the first to use the system of controlling accounts, and as shown in the first page herewith reproduced, in the second line after the table, the same name for these accounts is retained today He uses the word "*contrerole*," which comes from the French '*controler*," which in turn comes from the two Latin words "*contra*" and "*rotulus*" (our roll) and "*rota*" (our wheel) The definition of the word "control" is "to check by a duplicate register" or "verify an account" The total of his controlling account was obtained from the detailed monthly reports from the sub-treasurers or cashiers of the various places and departments, and were posted to these controlling accounts through the medium of journal entries From these accounts tables were compiled showing the delinquencies for each year of each sub-treasury or of each place He describes that an endless variety of these tables may be made in order to show the true status of the various operations at various places He also states that if no tables are desired, then there should be a separate account for each column in these tables, and especially for each year The table reproduced shows how particular and careful he was on this subject

The ledger shows both the page of the journal and the page upon which the other part of the double-entry appears in the ledger. This is one of the first writers who enters the journal pages in the ledger The pages of the journal are, however, put in the margin, on the left of the date in the ledger and not directly to the left of the amount, as we are accustomed to do at the present time The explanations in the ledger will appear to you to be shorter and clearer and more to the point as to relevancy than was customary in the Italian method It should also be noted that the term "per" is used on both sides of the ledger Stevin says that many bookkeepers use "a" on the debit side where he uses 'per" He suggests that his method is more reasonable as can be learned by translating the entry in an ordinary sentence, thus, which is better language? "Peter is debit to me 'for' ('per') pepper sold to him," or 'Peter is debtor to me to' ('a') pepper sold to him ' He then states that it is not a matter of importance, that his readers can do as they like, but he wishes them to follow the better sentence

In the journal he does not use the expression "per" before the debitor, nor "a" before the creditor, nor does he divide them with the two slanting lines // as do Pacioli, Manzoni, Pietra and Ympyn Stevin simply used "debit per' between the names of the debtor and creditor thus coming closer to our present form of journal entry

It is difficult to state what the two diagonal lines (//) between the debits and credits mean

In the chapter entitled "Discursion in Theory" there has been set forth in detail Stevin's theory of a double entry with two debits and two credits thus carrying the transaction through the proprietor's account but eliminating the same by algebraic formula.

The late Joseph Hardcastle, C P A, of New York, in 1903, in his "Accounts of Executors and Trustees," chapter on "The Personalistic Theory," very plainly sets forth the same idea elucidated by Stevin He even goes so far as to state that Pacioli (he spells it with an "i") and Manzoni used the slanting lines between debits and credits to indicate the omission of the word "proprietor" twice

Stevin explains that Roman figures in the ledger are not needed because they are never used in the journal, which is a book of more importance, and if they are not put in the book of more importance why should we put them in the book of less importance? He explains (as does Pacioli) that the ledger is not important because if the ledger is lost it can be written up entirely from the journal, whereas the reverse is not true, because the detail which the journal contains is lacking in the ledger He further states that in the Italian books Roman figures are not used in the day book

It will be noticed that each page of the ledger has a consecutive number (not as we number by giving two pages, the debit and the credit, one and the same number) Stevin explains that this is better because then all your debit pages will be uneven and the credit pages will be even numbers, which will aid in checking if an error is made in putting the little dividing line between figures representing the pages of the debit and the credit in the journal, as is customary in the Italian method The fact that but one column is used in the journal, makes this little dividing line between the figures of the debit postings and those of the credit postings very important Stevin further explains in this connection that it is still more confusing with a combination journal entry, where there are a number of debits and but one credit, or vice versa, when the word "sundries" is used. This because the debit of a combination journal entry comes first, and thereafter a number of credits, yet the total of the journal entry (which is the amount for the debit entry), stands at the last and therefore the debit is posted last, as will be seen from the illustration reproduced

Stevin is the first of the writers mentioned in this book to use combination journal entries with the word "sundries" We have seen that Mainardi has combination journal entries or journal entries with more than one debit and more than one credit, but he does not use the word "sundries"

In the ledger it will be noted that the first entries, or the opening balances on some of the accounts, bear the date of "0 January" The use of the cipher at the beginning of the year, he says is absolutely necessary, because the books are opened on neither December 31st nor January 1st It is a period in between these two He explains this with the illustration that the first rung is not the beginning of the ladder

The date in the ledger is repeated before each entry, instead of following the Italian method of using the words "*a di detto*," which mean "the ... day of the above month," because he says the date to which "ditto" refers may be several pages back and therefore hard to read at first sight

Unlike Pacioli, Pietra and Ympyn, Stevin uses definite headings for his ledger accounts, and is the first one to use the terms "debit" and "credit" instead of "*dee dare*" and "*dee havere*" He puts the year on top of the page, and he balances his ledger accounts by making a sub-total Closing entries do not go through the journal Profit and loss account is written up at the end of the year, and also at the close of particular transactions, and while Stevin does not give a trial balance, in his descriptions he speaks very particularly of the same, and describes how to prepare it While in his illustration he credits a legacy to the profit and loss account, in his text he admonishes the reader to put it to the capital account, giving his specific reasons for it Cash entries are journalized in daily totals He maintains a separate cash book in which the receipts are put on the debit and the disbursements on the credit, the same as they would be found in the ledger if it were a ledger account He also explains that this looks as if it were double work but it is not, as it is not the bookkeeper's work to keep a cash book, but the cashier's He further argues that because the bookkeeper is sometimes also the cashier, that fact should not alter the rule He has a separate cash book for petty expenses, in which to enter small items which are posted to the ledger only once a month, in order to lessen the number of entries.

About the reconcilement of differences between bookkeepers, cashiers, treasurers and others, he claims that these variations are due to the different closing periods of accounts and reports by the various officials and requires that they be preserved by writing their full detail in the journal and making a reference of the same on the ledger account affected Stevin says that as the head bookkeepers through these reconcilements would discover entries which belonged to a period previous to the date of their discovery and their entry in the journal, that the current date on which the entry is made in the journal should be used in that book, but that in the explanation the original date should be used (we now use "as of date" so and so) But he warns his readers that when posting these entries to the ledger, the original date and not the journal entry date should be used He advises that trial balances be taken in February, May, August, and November, which are customary mercantile due dates, which in turn will lead to a settlement of many accounts and will make this work easy and light Furthermore, it will give data and statistics upon which the merchants can base their buying, selling, and credit budgets for the future He advises that the Italian method of bookkeeping is so adapted to expansion that whereas before but one bookkeeper could be employed, under the double-entry system any number of bookkeepers can be used, for, if the work becomes too much for one man the system should be revised so as to provide for controlling accounts This means to post in totals only, so that one sub-division can be given to a bookkeeper to be controlled by one head bookkeeper, who deals in totals only

As to the cash book, it is used because it obviates the making of numerous journal entries every day, thus shortening the work greatly He fully illustrates this, and transfers the totals of the cash book to the ledger by journal entries, preferably monthly

Stevin provides a double column in the ledger account for merchandise In one of these he puts the weights and measures, and insists that they be balanced also He says that in his illustrations he made them come out even, although he admits that that very seldom happens The result, however, would be the same, for the balance to be carried to the new ledger or to be used in "the statement of affairs" would be based upon the weight, and whatever is over or short, as far as weight and measure is concerned, would automatically adjust itself in the profit and loss

He objects to the name of "*memorial*" as used in the Latin countries for the day book, stating that "*memorial*" is a book of memoranda (things to be remembered), whereas the day book is used to write in roughly the daily transactions preparatory to journalizing them This he calls a blotter. He draws a line between each journal entry from one side of the book to the other side of the book, through all the standing lines and columns He explains that this line is necessary, because some entries cover several pages (How we accountants wish some bookkeepers would make journal entries with explanations pages long!)

Stevin says it is customary to ascertain once a year what the profit or the loss of the business has been This is what he calls "balancing" or "making a statement of balance" or "ascertaining of capital" For this purpose, he advises to "add together cash and merchandise on hand and actual accounts receivable, deduct therefrom the accounts payable, the difference is net capital provided the accounts receivable are all good The difference between the net capital of last year and this year is the profit or loss for the year " According to Stevin, the making of a statement of affairs was not done concurrently with the closing of the books, the latter being done only when a new ledger is opened or where the merchant retires from business or dies

To prove his profit and loss arrived at through the making of a statement of affairs as above explained, he makes up a profit and loss account, which he calls "proof statement" Therefore, his profit or loss is ascertained first from the balance sheet, and in order to prove whether that is correct, he builds a profit and loss account How few modern bookkeepers and young accountants understand this principle today!

It will be seen from the reproduction of his financial statement and profit and loss account, that the profit and loss statement is just as it would appear in the ledger account if these entries were really posted to a ledger account as we do today The balance sheet therefore represents an unposted journal entry, whereas the profit and loss account shows the result of a posted journal entry In this Stevin is of course inconsistent

Stevin makes the statement of affairs a mathematical problem rather than the result of debits and credits He adds and subtracts, but does not reason where "proprietorship begins and ends," as he does with all other journal entries Hence, the entries comprising the closing of the ledger and the profit and loss account should not be in the journal (he reasons), as the making of such entries is only done when proprietorship is affected They are merely the bringing together to a conclusion of net proprietorship or net capital

He further explains that the ledger must always be in balance because of the mathematical rule of "equal amounts added to equal amounts must give equal totals"

In closing the ledger, Stevin transfers the balance of the various accounts direct to other accounts in the ledger without the aid of journal entries, and calls it often "by *slote*" the Dutch, and sometimes "*per solde*" the Italian for "in order to close" He puts his assets and liabilities into the capital account, and his profit and losses in the profit and loss account He finally closes all accounts by closing the profit and loss account into the capital account As the difference between present assets and liabilities or net proprietorship must be equal to the capital at the beginning of the year, plus or minus the current profits or losses, the entering of the present assets and liabilities in his capital account is an unnecessary duplication, except it be to effect a closing of all ledger accounts and using the capital account for this purpose as a clearing account

Stevin explains this method by saying that other writers, and especially the Dutch writer Bertholomi de Rentergem, have in the rear of their ledgers a "balance account," (as Pietra and Ympyn) into which they close their ledger accounts This, Stevin says, is built from a journal entry made in the old journal This entry is also posted in reverse order in the new ledger from the journal entry in the old journal This method Stevin does not like. He says these writers when opening their first journal and ledger, in the beginning of a new business, start with an inventory (see Pacioli and others), but in subsequent ledgers he says they do not do this, and there they call it a balance account Why not be consistent, he pleads, and open each subsequent journal and ledger with an inventory? He dislikes the balance account method evidently so very much that he wants to get away from it as far as he can, and thus he dumps it all into the capital account, because, he adds, "the result is exactly the same"

Stevin gives an exhaustive chapter about the settlement of partnership affairs He states that if all the partners are active and were conducting a portion of the business in various cities on the principle of branch stores, each partner should keep a separate set of books, very much the same as the method he explains for consignments or traveling agents, and at headquarters or at one of the branches there should be a joint bookkeeper, whose duty it is to deal in totals, so that each partner may know where he stands in relation to the others If only one partner is active, this partner should keep the books

He learned in one instance, as very likely modern accountants will learn from time to time, that a good merchant, no matter how illiterate he is or how ignorant he may be about bookkeeping, usually can tell very accurately whether the accountant's financial statement and bookkeeping results are correct Stevin was called in to adjust the affairs between a number of partners, of a large partnership The five active partners were residents of the cities of Venice, Augsburg, Cologne, Antwerp, and London, where they conducted branch establishments of the firm One of these partners had not kept any books Stevin was finally induced by this partner to visit him and to write up a full set of books of all the transactions of the partnership which he could find, and thus ascertain the financial settlement between the partners This he did, after considerable labor The particular partner who had kept no books, however, objected to the settlement, because it was £300 less than he figured was coming to him To prove this, he stated that they had no assets or liabilities of any kind, having liquidated the business, therefore he said "If I deduct my disbursements from my receipts, and add to the balance what is due me from the others, the total must be my portion of the profit" Stevin agreed with him that this was right, and the set of books was discarded and a settlement made upon the argument of the partner who was ignorant as far as bookkeeping was concerned From this experience Stevin determined upon the following rule when called in to make a partnership settlement, he would demand three things first, the amount each partner has received more in cash than he paid, or what he paid more than he received, second, the difference between presently existing accounts receivable and accounts payable, to which he added the cash and merchandise on hand, third, what the agreement was between the partners as to divisions of profits and losses He illustrates the application of this rule by the following example

A paid more than he received by	£2,000
B received more than he paid by	4,000
C paid more than he received by	3,000

The net assets, or the difference between accounts receivable and payable, added to the cash and merchandise on hand, amounted to £7,000

Each partner was to receive one-third of the profits or stand one-third of the losses He then puts up the following account

Partnership Debit		Partnership Credit	
Due A	£ 2,000	Due from B	£ 4,000
Due C	3,000	Net assets	7,000
Total due A and C	£ 5,000		£11,000
Net profit	6,000		
Total	£11,000		

As of above profit one-third is due to each of the partners, each partner's account would stand as follows

Due A as per above	£2,000	
Plus one-third of the profits	2,000	
		£4,000
Due C as per above	£3,000	
Plus one-third of the profits	2,000	
		5,000
		9,000
Due from B as per above	£4,000	
Less one-third of the profits	2,000	
		2,000
Net assets		£7,000

Those of us who have read the numerous involved court cases on partnership settlement, certainly must admire Stevin's ingenuity

Consignment accounts which Pacioli calls traveling accounts, are more thoroughly described in this work Stevin thinks it wrong to debit consignment account and credit merchandise, when the goods are shipped on consignment because the test when to make an entry is "the beginning and the end of proprietorship " He says it would be foolish to debit a clerk and credit merchandise when a clerk takes goods from a cellar or warehouse to the store or from one part of the store to another And he feels that consignment is a transaction of a similar nature, with only a greater distance between the places of storage He states if we want to keep track of these consignment transactions it should be by way of memoranda but not in the regular books Like Pacioli, he wants the traveling man or consignee to keep books on the double-entry system and report sales at convenient times these reports to be entered in a separate journal and ledger until there is "a beginning and an end of proprietorship ' It is important to note that Stevin very seldom uses the word 'capital," but substitutes the word "proprietorship" throughout.

All the way through, Stevin uses as a test for the making of a journal entry "the beginning and end of proprietorship " Thus when goods arrive in the warehouse, that is the beginning of proprietorship, and that account is not touched again, as far as the journal and ledger are concerned, until the goods have left proprietorship through consumption So, if a barrel of beer were received from the brewer, it would go into the warehouse account or the merchandise account, and there remain until finally the butler on one of the war vessels would distribute it to the sailors, when it would be charged out to them In the interim, however, the warehouse has sent it to a small ship, which brings it to the ocean, there it is transferred onto a transport, and probably is transferred on the ocean two or three times from one steward's warehouse on one ship to another steward's warehouse on another, until it finally reaches the war vessel upon which it is consumed While he urges the necessity of following this barrel of beer from place to place, he states that this should be done only in memorandum accounts and not in the general ledger

Equally insistent he is on the reissue of tools used in the construction of fortifications, canals and buildings, or on the farms and in the field He says that tools are first purchased, issued to one particular piece of work and then returned to the warehouse and used in other places and transferred from place to place until finally worn out All of this he feels should be carefully recorded but not in the general ledger

As to the wages, he very carefully explains that a wages or pay roll account avails one nothing The wages he says should be carefully distributed to each department for which they are incurred, exactly the same as we have seen Pietra does He first distributes his wages, as he distributes all his supplies, to definite departments Thus he says we can arrive at true costs This method he uses also in checking up the supply house and the cook, for he instructs the cook, as we have seen to give a record of the daily meals served in order to check the pay roll, and he checks the cook by instructing the warehouse men to figure out the cost of the meals per man Thus he says, if the cost per meal is considerably higher than the average, and the pay roll agrees with the meals served, then the warehouse man has either made an error or stolen some goods

In this connection, he provides a perpetual inventory, in which each kind of merchandise has two columns, one for the receipts or ' ins" and one for the disbursements or the "outs " He balances each column when new goods arrive, then counts what is left, and adjusts his books to the actual count

Gifts of merchandise, he states, must be valued, for three reasons first, in order to be able to ascertain actual expenses and consumption of merchandise for each department, second, the proprietor should know at all times for how much he is obligated to others, third, in order to know exactly the actual capital invested

In municipal accounting, he urges that the ledger of any year be held open until at least the end of the next year, to prevent heavy transcribing, very much the same as is done now with some tax rolls

Stevin in instructing his bookkeepers in the municipal department, tells them to use the words "debit" and 'credit" in the explanation of each journal entry, thus making it a little plainer to the uninitiated in the terms of bookkeeping From the illustrations it will be noted that he does not do so in mercantile bookkeeping, but only uses the term "debit '

What the writer has said in praise of Stevin should not be interpreted as meaning that he considers Stevin's system perfect or even as perfect as we have today, for in many respects, it is not But the writer believes that Stevin has left his unmistakable stamp on modern American methods It would be interesting to study the earliest American financial books and ledgers in order to establish that through the Dutch settlers of New Amsterdam (now New York) Stevin's ideas were brought to America, rather than by way of England through Dafforne, who we will see further on in the book, failed to translate to the English language many of Stevin's ideas

VERRECHTING
VAN
DOMEINE
Mette CONTREROLLE en ander behouſten vandien.

't Welck is

Verclaring van ghemeene Regel, waer deur verböet worden alle abuyſen mette ſwaricheden uytte ſelve ſpruytende, diemen tot noch toe uyt geen Rekencamers van Domeine en Finance heeft connen weren

Weſende Oeffeninghen des Doorluchtichſten Hoogſtgheboren Vorſt en Heere MAVRITS by Gods Ghenade Prince van Orange, &c. Ho Loff Memorie.

Beſchreven deur SIMON STEVIN van Brugghe, in ſijn leven des Hooghghemelten Heere PRINCEN Superintendent vande Finance, &c En uyt ſijn naghelaten Hantſchriften by een ghestelt deur ſijn Soon HENDRICK STEVIN Ambachtsheere van Alphen.

TOT LEYDEN,
Ter Druckerye van IVSTVS LIVIVS,
In't tweede Iaer des Vredes.

STAET VAN MY DIERICK

Roose gemaeckt op den laetsten December 1600.

Staet of capitael debet.		Staet of capitael credit.	
Per Aernout Iacobs fol. 14	51. 8 0	*Per noten fol* 7 - 173 ℔ 5 *onc tot* 7 ß 't *pont, comt* - -	60 13. 2
Rest debet hier gestelt by slote van desen - - -	3140. 9 1.	*Per Peper fol* 7 - 120 ℔ *tot* 40 g 't *pont, comt* - - - -	20. 0. 0
Somme	3191. 17.1	*Per Omaer de SVVarte fol* 9 -	513 12 0.
		Per Adriaen de VVinter fol 11 -	150. 6 0.
		Per Pieter de VVitte fol. 11 - -	448 0 0
		Per Iacques de Somer fol. 13 -	54 18 6.
		Per casse fol. 19 - - -	1944 7 5.
		Somme	3191 17 1.

Sulcx dat Debiteurs, met gereet gelt en vvaren, hier meer bedragen dan Crediteurs voor vveerde des capitaels op den laetsten van December 1600 - 3140.9.1.

Maer op den laetsten December 1599, of 't begin des jaers 1600 dat een selve is, vvas het capitael van 2153 £ 3 ß 8 g, vvant treckende den debet 514 £ 6 ß, vanden credit 2667 £ 9 ß 8 g, blijft als vooren - - - - - - 2153 3 8.

VVelcke getrocken vande 3140 £ 9 ß 1 g, blijft voor 't gene datter op dit jaer verovert is, ende in dese staet gesocht vviert - - - 987. 5. 5.

STAET PROEF.

Maer om nu te sien of het boveschreven vast gaet, so dient dit tot een proef. Ick vergaer al de resten der posten van vermeerderende of verminderende capitael, 't vvelck syn de resten der posten die inde voorgaende staetmaking niet en quamen,

men, als totte wesentliche staet niet behoorende. Ende want de selve syn partyen van winst en verlies voorgevallen inden tijt deser bouckhouding, dats sedert 0 Ianuarius 1600, welcke by aldienmen het bouck slote (gelijck int volgende 10 Hoofstück gedaen sal worden) op rekening van winst en verlies souden commen, soo moet dan daer deur oock verovering bevonden worden van 987 ℔ 5 ß 5 ₰. Tot desen einde begin ick het Schultbouck te overloopen van vooren aen, ende ontmoet my eerst de poste der nagelen fol 5, waer op ick winst bevinde van 75. 4. 7 daer na ontmoeten my noten en ander goeden, als hier na volght. Doch staet noch te gedencken, dat overschietende goeden hier berekent worden ten selven prijse als inden voorgaenden staet, om dat wy nemen haer weerde soo te wesen, wildemen in d'een en d'ander nemen den prijs verandert te zijn, men soudet oock meugen doen.

VVinst en verlies debet.		VVinst en verlies credit.	
Per oncosten van coomschap fol 16 -	57 7 0	*Per winst op nagelen fol 5 - -*	75 4. 7.
Per oncosten vanden huyse fol 16 -	107 10 0	*Per winst op noten fol 7 - -*	109 7 2.
		Per winst op peper fol 7 - -	18 19. 0.
Somme	164 17 0	*Per winst op gimber fol 9 - -*	41 8 4.
Rest credit als prouffijt overeencommende met de voorgaende rekeuing hier gestelt per solde - -	987 5 5.	*Per rekening van winst en verlies (wiens poste te gedencken is dat ten tyde deser werking in debet alleenelick hadde twee partyen, te weten van 100 ℔ en 12 ℔, maer in credit drie partien als 4 ℔ 3 4 en 15 ℔ met 1000 ℔) fol 19 - - -*	907. 3 4
Somme	1152 2 5	*Somme*	1152 2 5.

Nu dan het prouffijt deur dese wyse oock bevonden sijnde van 987 ℔ 5 ß 5 ₰, als te vooren int slot des staets, soo mach dit tot proef des wercx verstrecken.

MERCKT

				ℒ	ß	₰
			't Iaer 1600.			
	0	Ianua	Verscheyden partien debet per Capitael van my Dierick Roose 1667 ℔ 9 ß 8 ₰, deur dat ick ten voornoemden dage staet van goet makende, my bevonden hebbe toe te behooren de navolgende partien van gelt, vvaren en schulden. Ende eerst			
4			Casse in gereden gelde - - - -	880	0	0
4			Nagelen 4 balen vvegende nº 3 - 87 - tar 1 2 5 - 90¾ tar 1 4 4 - 86½ tar 1 2 7 - 91¼ tar 1 0 355 tar 4 8 Net 350 ℔ 8 onc. tot 10 ß 't pont, comt	175	5	0
6			Noten 4 balen vvegende nº 9 79 tar 1 4 7 - 82 tar 1 4 6 84 tar 1 2 8 - 80 tar 1 6 325 tar 5 0. Net 320 ℔ tot 9 ß 't pont, comt	144	0	0
6			Peper 3 balen vvegende nº 9 - 250 tar 2 0. 10 - 160 tar 2 0 11 - 254 tar 2 0 764 tar 6 0 Net 758 ℔ tot 30 ₰ 't pont, comt	94	15	0
8			Gimber 5 balen vvegende nº 4 - 166 tar 2 0 5 - 260 tar 2 0 6 - 258 tar 2 0 7 - 264 tar 2 0 8 - 256 tar 2 0. 1304 tar 10 0. Net 1294 ℔ tot 32 ₰ 't pont, comt	172	10	8
			Het navolgende syn Debiteurs getrocken uyt de voorschreven staet.			
8	-	- -	Omaer de Svvarte verschynende 6 Meye 1600. - -	200	0	0
10	-	- -	Adriaen de VVinter verschynende 8 Iunius 1600. -	350	6	0
10	-	- -	Pieter de VVitte verschynende 20 Iunius 1600 - - -	360	8	0
12	-	- -	Iacques de Somer verschynende 1 Martius 1600 - -	290	5	0
3			Somme	2667	9	8
2	0	Ianua.	Capitael van my Dierick Roose debet per verscheyden Crediteuren, an de vvelcke ik my ten voornoemdē dage deur de voorschreven staetmaking bevinde schuldich te syne als volght:			
13	-	- -	Ioos Noirot verschynende den 7 Maerte 1600 - -	100	0	0
15	-	- -	David Roels verschynende den 2 Meye 1600, - -	150	0	0
15	-	-	Aernout Iacobs verschynende den 10 April 1600. - -	264	6	0
			Somme	514	6	0

D 3 Cateosten

			't Iaer 1600.	£	ß	d
16 / 5	28	Februa	Oncosten van coomschap debet per casse, deur betaelt in dese maent van Februarius blyckende by 't memoriael van dien	3	0	0
16 / 5	28	Februa.	Oncosten vanden huyse debet per casse, deur betaelt in dese maent van Februarius blyckende by 't memoriael van dien	3	4	0
12 / 5	7	Maerte	Iacques de Somer debet per nagelen, deur dat ick an hem vercocht heb 2 balen te betalen binnen 2 maenden, vvegende nº 3 - 87 - tar 1 2 5 - 90¼ tar 1.4 } Net 174 ℔ 14 onc tot 12 ß 't pont 177¼ tar 2 6	104	18	6
6 / 15	28	Maerte.	Noten debet per Davit Roels, deur dat ick van hem gecocht heb 3 balen te betalen binnen 3 maenden, vvegende nº 4 - 79 tar 1 0 5 - 80 tar 1 0 6 - 82 tar 1 0 } Net 238 ℔ tot 8 ß 't pont, comt - 241 tar 3 0	95	4	0
16 / 5	31	Maerte	Oncosten van Coomschap debet per casse, deur betaelt in dese maent van Maerte blyckende by 't memoriael van dien	4	-	0
16 / 5	31	Maerte	Oncosten vandē huyse debet per casse, deur betaelt in dese maent van Maerte blyckende by 't memoriael van dien - -	6	6	0
4 / 5	6	April	Casse debet per nagelen, deur dat ick contant vercocht heb 2 balen an Iosep Sanders vvegende nº 4 86½ tar e 2 7 92¼ tar 1 0 } Net 175 ℔ 10 onc tot 13 ß 't pont 177¾ tar 2 2	114	3	1
8 / 5	10	April.	Gimber debet per casse, deur dat ick contant gecocht heb 3 balen van Louys Ianß, vvegende nº 14 - 264 tar 2.0 15 - 270 tar 2.0 16 - 266 tar 2 0 } Net 794 ℔ tot 30 d 't pont - 800 tar 6.0	99	5	0
16 / 5	30	April	Oncosten van coomschap debet per casse, deur betaelt in dese maent April blyckende by 't memoriael van dien - -	3	10	0
16 / 5	30	April	Oncosten van den huyse debet per casse, deur betaelt in dese maent van April blyckende by 't memoriael van dien -	6	0	0
14 / 9	12	Meye	Davit Roels debet per Omaer de Svvarte, deur dat ick Davit geassigneert heb van Omaer t ontfangen in volle betalingh van dies ick Davit schuldich ben, vervallende den 2 Maerte 1600, en in minderingh van dies my Omaer schuldich is, vervallende 6 Meye 1600	150	0	0

Verschuy

't Iaer 1600.

				£	ß	d
	30	Meye	*Verscheyden partien debet per Aernout Iacobs, van hem gecocht de navolgende partien te betalen binnen een maent, en eerst:*			
4	-	- -	Nagelen 2 balen vvegende nº 11 - 90 tar 1 0 12 - 88 tar 1. 0 178 tar 2 0. } Net 176 lb tot 10 ß 't pont -	83	0	0
6	-	- -	Noten 2 balen vvegende nº 13 - 86 tar 1 8 14 88 tar 1 8 174 tar 3 0 } Net 171 lb tot 8 ß 't pont -	68	8	0
15			Somme	151	8	0
10	30	Meye.	*Pieter de VVitte debet per verscheyden partien, an hem vercocht te betalen binnen 5 vveken, en eerst*			
9	-	- -	Gimber 8 balen vvegende nº 4 - 266 tar 2 0 5 - 250 tar 2 0 6 258 tar 2 0 7 - 264 tar 2 0 8 - 256 tar 2 0 14 - 264 tar 2 0 15 - 270 tar 2 0 16, 266 tar 2 0 2105 tar 16 0 } Net 2088 lb tot 36. ß 't pont -	313	4	0
7	-	- -	Noten 7 balen vvegende nº 4 79 tar 1 0 5 - 80 tar 1 0 6 - 82 tar 1.0 9 - 79 tar 1.4 7 82 tar 1 4. 3 - 84 tar 1 2 8 - 80 tar 1 6 566 tar 8 0 } Net 558 lb tot 12 ß 't pont -	331	16	0
			Somme	648	0	0
4/9	31	Meye	*Casse debet per Omaer de Svvarte, van hem ontfaen in mindering van 't verschenen den 6 Meye 1600*	30	0	0
12/5	31	Meye	*Ioos Noirot debet per casse, an hem betaelt in mindering van 't verschenen den 7 Maerte 1600*	50	0	0
14/5	31	Meye.	*Aernout Iacobs debet per casse, an hem betaelt in minderingh van 't verschenen den 10 April 1600 - - -*	200	0	0
16/5	31	Meye	*Oncosten van coomschap debet per casse, deur betaelt in dese maent van Meye blyckende by 't memoriael van dien - - -*	4	5	0
16/5	31	Meye	*Oncosten vanden huyse debet per casse, deur betaelt in dese maent van Meye blyckende by 't memoriael van dien - -*	7	0	0
4/13	20	Iunius.	*Casse debet per Iacques de Somer, van hem ontfaen in minderingh van 't verschenen den 1 Maerte 1600*	100	0	0

Aernout

't Iaer 1600.

				£	ß	§
14 / 5	28	Iunius	Aernout Iacobs debet per casse, an hem betaelt in voldoeningh van 't verschenen den 10 April 1600 - - -	64	6	0
16 / 5	30	Iunius	Oncosten van Coomschap debet per casse deur het uit in dese maent van Iunius blyckende by 't memoriael van dien - -	2	10	0
16 / 5	30	Iunius	Oncosten vanden huyse debet per casse, deur betaelt in dese maent van Iunius blyckende by 't memoriael van dien - -	5	0	0
8	4	Iulius	Omaer de Swarte debet per verscheyden partien an hem vercocht te betalen binnen 2 maenden, die gelevert zyn in handen van Andries Corssyn Facteur. En dat deur last vanden voorschreven Omaer, blyckende by syn missive vanden 16 Iunius 1600 En ten eersten			
7	-	-	Peper 3 balen weegende nº 9 - 250 tar 2 0 10 - 260 tar 2 0 11 - 254 tar 2 0. 764 tar 6 0 } Net 758 ℔ tot 36 § t pont.	113	14	0
7		- -	Noten 2 balen weegende nº 13 - 86 tar 1 8 14 - 88 tar 1 8 147 tar 3 0 } Net 171 ℔ tot 10 ß 't pont -	85	10	0
5	-	- -	Nagelen 2 balen weegende nº 11 - 90 tar 1 0 12 - 88 tar 1 0 178 tar 2 0 } Net 176 ℔ tot 13 ß t pont -	114	8	0
			Somme	313	12	0
4	8	Iulius	Casse debet per verscheyden persoonen, van hemlien ontfaen gereet gelt als volght			
11	-	- -	Adriaen de Winter in mindering van verschenen 8 Iunius 1600	200	0	0
11	-	- -	Pieter de Witte in volle betaling vant verschenen 20 Iulius 1600	360	8	0
11	-	- -	Pieter de Witte in mindering van 't verschenen den 5 Iulius 1600	200	0	0
13	-	- -	Iacques de Somer in volle betaling vant verschenen 1 Maert 1600	90	5	0
13	-	- -	Iacques de Somer in mindering vant verschenen 7 Meye 1600	50	0	0
			Somme	900	13	0
	16	Iulius	Verscheyden persoonen debet per casse, an hemlien betaelt gereet gelt als volght			5
12	-	- -	Ioos Norrot in volle betaling van 't verschenen 7 Maerte 1600	50	0	0
14	-	- -	David Roels opt verschenen den 28 Iunius 1600	60	0	0
14	-	- -	Aernout Iacobs opt verschenen den 30 Iunius 1600 -	100	0	0
5			Somme	210	0	0
14 / 5	20	Iulius	David Roels debet per casse, an hem betaelt in voldoeningh van 't verschenen den 28 Iunius 1600	35	4	0
6 / 19	28	Iulius.	Noten debet per casse, deur dat ick gecocht heb 3 balen gereet gelt weegende net 240 ℔ tot 7 ß 't pont - - -	84	0	0

Peper

't Iaer 1600.

				£	ß	g
	4	Aug	Peper debet per noten, deur dat ick gemangelt heb tegen Andries Claesz als volcht			
6	-	- -	Peper 120 lb tot 40 g 't pont by Andries Claesz an my gelevert, comt - - - -	20	0	0
7	-	- -	Noten 66 lb 11 oncen tot 6 ß 't pont, die ick an Andries Claesz gelevert heb, comt - - -	20	0	0
18 / 19	18	Aug	Rekening van vvinst en verlies debet per casse, deur dat ick met Catrine myn dienstmaecht ten huyvvelicke gegeven hebbe -	100	0	0
	21	Aug	Verscheyden partien debet per Aernout Iacobsz deur dat ick van hem geleent hebbe 1000 £ op intrest tegen 12 ten hondert t'siaers, en dit voor een maent, vvaer af de verscheyden partien dusdanich zyn			
18	-	- -	Casse deur dat ick van hem ontfaen hebbe de boveschreven hoofsomme van - - - -	1000	0	0
18 / 15	-	- -	Rekening van vvinst en verlies deur dien den intrest der boveschreven hoofsomme op een maent bedraecht - - -	12	0	0
			Somme	1012	0	0
12	10	Sept	Iacques de Somer debet per verscheyden partien, deur dat ick hem gegeven heb 500 £ op intrest tegen 10 ten hondert t'siaers, en dit voor een maent, vvaer af de verscheyden partien dusdanich zyn			
19	-	- -	Casse deur dat ick hem gelt hebbe de boveschreven hoofsomme van	500	0	0
19	-	- -	Rekening van vvinst en verlies, deur dien den intrest der boveschreven hoofsomme op een maent bedraecht - - -	4	3	4
			Somme	504	3	4
10	18	Sept	Adriaen de VVinter debet per verscheyden partien 180 £, deur dat hy van my ontfaen heeft op vvissel 100 £ sterlinx tot 33 ß het pont, bedragende 165 £, om die vveerom te betalen an Omaer de Svvarte binnen Lonnen op tvvee maenden na sicht, het pont sterlinx gerekent op 36 ß, vvaer af de verscheyden partien dusdanich zyn			
19	-	- -	Casse deur dat hy van my ontfaen heeft de boveschreven somme van	65	0	0
19	-	- -	Rekening van vvinst en verlies, deur dien de vvissel van 3 ß te pande op de 100 £ sterlinx bedraecht - - -	15	0	0
			Somme	180	0	0
14 / 19	23	Sept	Aernout Iacobsz debet per casse, an hem betaelt datter verschenen vvas den 21 September 1600 - - -	1012	0	0
18 / 19	21	Sept	Casse debet per rekening van vvinst en verlies, deur geerft te hebben het goet mijns Ooms - -	1000	0	0
18 / 13	12	Octob	Casse debet per Iacques de Somer, van hem ontfaen datter verschenen vvas den 10 October 1600 - - -	504	1	4

E Omaer

			't Iaer 1600.	£	ß	d
8 / 11	14	*Decem*	*Omaer de Svvarte tot Lonnen debet per Adriaen de VVinter, deur dat hy voor my ontfaen heeft op vviſſel vanden ſelven Adriaen, blyckende by ſyn ſchryven - - -*	180	0	0
16 / 19	31	*Decem*	*Oncoſten van coomſchap debet per caſſe, deur betaelt inde maenden van Iulius, Auguſtus, September, October, November, en December blyckende by 't memoriael van dien - - -*	40	0	0
16 / 19	31	*Decem*	*Oncoſten vanden huyſe debet per caſſe deur betaelt inde maenden van Iulius, Auguſtus, September, October, November, en December, blyckende by 't memoriael van dien - - -*	80	0	0

Merckt dat deſe tvvee laetſte partien van oncoſten ſouden na 't gemeen gebruyck verdeelt behooren te vvorden ten einde van yder maent, ſoo veel op elcke viel. Doch alſoot vergeten vvas, ick en hebt niet vvillen verſchryven, te meer dattet inde daet ſomvvylen ſoo toegaet.

2

			Capitael debet. 't Iaer 1600.	£	ß	g
1	0	Ianua.	Per verscheyden partien - - -	513	6	0
	31	Decem	Per noten fol 7, deur datter inde slaetmaking bevonden zyn 171 ℔ 5 oncen, nu weerdich 7 ß 't pont, comt - - -	60	13	8
	31	Decem	Per peper fol 7, deur datter inde slaetmaking bevonden zyn 120 ℔, nu weerdich 40 g 't pont, comt - -	20	0	0
	31	Decem	Per Omaer de Swarte verschynende den 4 September en 14 Decem ber 1600 fol 9 - - - -	513	12	2
	31	Decem	Per Adriaen de Winter verschynende den 8 Iunius 1600 fol 11	150	6	0
	31	Decem	Per Pieter de Witte verschynende den 5 Iulius 1600 fol. 11 -	448	0	0
	31	Decem	Per Iacques de Somer verschynende den 7 Meye 1600 fol 13 -	54	18	6
	31	Decem	Per casse fol 19 - - - -	1941	7	5
			Somme	3706	3	

4

Fol.			Casse debet 't Iaer 1600.	£	ß	g
1	0	Ianua.	Per capitael fol 3 - - -	880	0	0
2	6	April	Per nagelen fol 5 - - - - -	114	3	1
3	31	Meye	Per Omaer de Swarte fol. 9 - - - -	30	0	0
3	20	Iunius	Per Iacques de Somer fol 13 - - -	200	0	0
4	8	Iulius.	Per verscheyden partien - - -	500	13	0
			Somme	2124	16	1

			Nagelen debet. 't Iaer 1600.	℔	onc.			
1	0	Ianua.	Per capitael fol. 3 - - -	350	8	175	5	0
3	30	Meye.	Per Aernout Iacobs fol. 15 - - -	176	0	83	0	0
			Somme	526	8	258	5	0
	31	Decem.	Per rekening van winst en verlies fol 19 hier gestelt by slote van desen, wesende prouffyt op nagelen - -			75	4	7
			Somme	526	8	333	9	7

Fol			Noten debet. 't Iaer 1600.	℔	onc.	£	ß	g
1	0	Ianua	Per capitael fol 3 - -	320	0	144	0	0
2	28	Maerte	Per David Roels fol 15 - - -	238	0	95	4	0
3	30	Meye	Per Aernout Iacobs fol 15 - -	171	0	68	8	0
4	28	Iulius	Per casse fol 19 - - -	240	0	84	0	0
			Somme	969	0	391	12	0
	31	Decem	Per rekening van winst en verlies fol. 19, hier gestelt by slote van desen, wesende prouffyt op noten -			109	7	2
			Somme	569	0	500	19	2

			Capitael credit. 't Iaer 1600.	£	ß	d
						3
2	0	Ienna	Per verscheyden partien - - -	1667	9	8
	31	Decem.	Per Aernout Iacobs verschynende den 30 Iunius 1600 fol. 14 -	31	8	0
	31	Decem	Per rekening van winst en verlies fol. 18 - -	987	5	5
			Somme	3706		1

Fol.			Casse credit. 't Iaer 1600.	£	ß	d
						5
2	28	Februa	Per oncosten van coomschap fol 16 - - -	3	0	0
2	28	Februa	Per oncosten vanden huyse fol 16 - - -	3	4	0
2	31	Maerte	Per oncosten van coomschap fol 16 - - -	4	2	0
2	31	Maerte	Per oncosten vanden huyse fol 16 - - -	1	6	0
2	20	April	Per gimber fol 8 - - - - -	99	5	0
2	30	April.	Per oncosten van coomschap fol 16 - - -	3	10	0
2	30	April	Per oncosten vanden huyse fol 16 - - - -	6	0	0
3	31	Meye	Per Ioos Nerret fol. 12 - - - - -	50	0	0
3	31	Meye	Per Aernout Iacobs fol 14 - - -	200	0	0
3	31	Meye.	Per oncosten van coomschap fol 16 - - -	4	5	0
3	31	Meye	Per oncosten vanden huyse fol 16 - -	7	0	0
4	28	Iunius	Per Aernout Iacobs fol 14 - -	64	6	0
4	30	Iunius	Per oncosten van coomschap fol 16 - -	2	10	0
4	30	Iunius	Per oncosten vanden huyse fol 16 - - -	5	0	0
4	16	Iulius	Per verscheyden partien - - -	210	0	0
4	20	Iulius.	Per David Roels fol 14 - -	35	4	0
			Somme	703	12	0
			Per slot van desen, en overgedragen in debet fol 18 - -	1421	4	1
			Somme	2124	16	1

			Nagelen credit. 't Iaer 1600.	lb	onc	£	ß	d
2	7	Maerte	Per Iacques de Somer fol 12 - -	174	14	10	18	6
2	6	April	Per casse fol 4 - - -	178	10	114	3	1
4	4	Iulius	Per Omaer de Swarte fol 8 - - -	176	0	114	6	0
			Somme	526	8	333	9	7

			Noten credit 't Iaer 1600	lb	onc	£	ß	d
								7
3	30	Meye.	Per Pieter de Witte fol 10 - -	558	0	334	16	0
4	4	Iulius.	Per Omaer de Swarte fol 8 - -	171	0	85	10	0
5	4	Aug	Per peper fol 6 - - -	66	11	20	0	0
			Somme	795	11	440	6	0
	31	Decem.	Per capitael fol. 2 deur datter inde slaetmaking bevonden zyn 173 lb 5 oncen noten, nu weerdich 7 ß 't pont, comt - - -	173	5	60	13	2
			Somme	969	0	500	19	2

			Peperdebet. t Iaer 1600.					
1	0	Ianua	Peper capitael fol 3	758	0	94	15	0
5	4	Aug	Per noten fol 7 -	120	0	20	0	0
			Somme	878	0	114	15	0
	31	Decem.	Per rekening van vvinst en verlies fol 19, hier gestelt by slote van desen, vvesende prouffyt op peper - -			18	19	0
			Somme	878	0	133	14	0

			Gimber debet. 't Iaer 1600.	℔	one	£	ß	₰
1	0	Ianua.	Per capitael fol 3 - -	1294	0	172	10	8
3	10	April	Per cassa fol 5 - - -	794	0	99	5	0
			Somme	2088	0	271	15	8
	31	Decem	Per rekening van vvinst en verlies fol 19 hier gestelt by slote van desen vvesende prouffyt op gimber -			41	8	4
			Somme	2088	0	313	4	0

			Omaer de svvarte debet. t Iaer 1600			
1	0	Ianua	Per capitael verschynende 6 Meye 1690 fol 3 - -	200	0	0
4	4	Iulius.	Per verscheyden partien verschynende 4 Sept. 1600 - -	313	12	0
6	14	Decem.	Per Adriaen de VVinter op vvissel fol 11 - -	180	0	0
			Somme	693	12	0

10

			Adriaen de VVinter debet. 't Iaer 1600.	£	ß	₰
1	0	Ianua	Per capitael verschynende 8 Iunius 1600 fol 3 - -	350	6	0
5	18	Sept	Per verscheyden partien verschynende 2 maenden na sicht des vvissel briefs - - - -	180	0	0
			Somme	530	6	0

			Peper credit. 't Iaer 1600					
4	4	Iulius	Per Omaer de Svvarte fol 8 - -	758	0	113	14	0
	31	Decem	Per capitael fol 2 deur datter inde staetmaking bevonden zyn 120 ℔ peper, nu vveerdich 40 g' pont, comt - - -	120	0	20	0	0
			Somme	878	0	133	14	0

9

Fol			Gimber credit. 't Iaer 1600.	℔	onc.	£	ß	g
3	30	Meye.	Per Pieter de VVitte fol 10 -	2088	0	313	4	0

			Omaer de Svvarte credit. 't Iaer 1600.			
2	12	Meye.	Per David Roels opt verschenen 6 Meye 1600 fol. 14 -	150	0	0
3	31	Meye	Per casse opt verschenen 6 Meye 1600 fol 4 -	30	0	0
			Somme	180	0	0
	31	Decem.	Per capitael fol. 2 hier gestelt by slote van desen - - -	513	12	
			Somme	693	12	0

11

Fol			Adriaen de VVinter credit. t Iaer 1600.	£	ß	g
	8	Iulius	Per casse opt verschenen 8 Iunius 1600 fol 4 - -	200	0	0
4 6	14	Decem	Per Omaer de Svvarte opt verschenen hier neven fol 8 -	180	0	0
			Somme	380	0	0
	31	Decem	Per capitael fol 2 hier gestelt by slote van desen - -	150	6	0
			Somme	530	6	0

			Pieter de VVitte debit. 't Iaer 1600.			
1	0	*Ianua.*	*Per capitael verschynende 20 Iunius 1600 fol 3* - -	360	8	0
3	30	*Meye*	*Per verscheyden partien verschynende 5 Iulius 1600* -	648	0	0
			Somme	1008	8	0

12

			Iacques de Somer debet. t Iaer 1600.	£	ß	g
1	0	*Ianua*	*Per capitael verschynende 1 Maerte 1600 fol. 3* - -	290	5	0
2	7	*Maerte*	*Per nagelen verschynende 7 Meye 1600 fol 5* - -	104	18	6
5	10	*Sept.*	*Per verscheyden partien te betalen 10 Octob 1600* - -	504	3	4
			Somme	899	6	10

			Ioos Noirot debet 't Iaer 1600			
3	31	*Meye.*	*Per casse opt verschenen 7 Maerte 1600 fol 5* - -	50	0	0
4	16	*Iulius*	*Per casse opt verschenen 7 Maerte 1600 fol 5* - -	50	0	0
			Somme	100	0	0

14

			Davit Roels debit t Iaer 1600.	£	ß	g
2	12	*Meye*	*Per Omaer de Swarte opt verschenen 2 Meye 1600 fol. 9* -	150	0	0
4	16	*Iulius*	*Per casse opt verschenen 28 Iunius 1600 fol 5* - -	60	0	0
4	20	*Iulius.*	*Per casse opt verschenen 28 Iunius 1600 fol 5* - -	35	4	0
			Somme	215	4	9

			Aernout Iacobs credit. Iaer 1600.			
3	31	*Meye*	*Per casse opt verschenen 10 April 1600 fol 5* - -	200	0	0
4	28	*Iunius*	*Per casse opt verschenen 10 April 1600 fol 5* - -	64	6	0
4	16	*Iulius*	*Per casse op 't verschenen 30 Iunius 1600 fol 5* - -	100	0	0
5	23	*Sept*	*Per casse op 't verschenen 21 Sept 1600 fol 19* - -	1012	0	0
			Somme	1376	6	0
	31	*Decem.*	*Per capitael fol 3 hier gestelt by slute van desen* - -	51	8	0
			Somme	1427	14	0

			Pieter de VVitte credit. 't Iaer 1600.			
4	8	Iulius.	Per casse opt verschenen 10 Iunius 1600 fol 4 - -	360	8	0
4	8	Iulius.	Per casse opt verschenen 5 Iulius 1600 fol 4 - -	200	0	0
			Somme	560	8	0
	31	Decem	Per capitael fol 2 hier gestelt by slote van desen -	448	0	0
			Somme	1008	8	0

			Iacques de Somer credit. 't Iaer 1600.	£	ß	₰
3	20	Iunius	Per casse opt verschenen 1 Maerte 1600 fol. 4 - -	100	0	0
4	8	Iulius	Per casse opt verschenen 1 Maerte 1600 fol. 4 - -	90	5	0
4	8	Iulius	Per casse opt verschenen 7 Meye 1600 fol 4 - -	50	0	0
5	12	Octob	Per casse opt verschenen 10 Octobris 1600 fol 18 - -	504	3	4
			Somme	844	8	4
	31	Decem.	Per capitael fol 2 hier gestelt by slote van desen - -	54	18	6
			Somme	899	6	10

			Ioos Noirot credit. 't Iaer 1600.			
1	0	Ianua	Per capitael verschynende 7 Maerte 1600 fol 2 -	100	0	0

			Davit Roels credit. 't Iaer 1600.	£	ß	₰
1	0	Ianua.	Per capitael verschynende 2 Meye 1600 fol 2 - -	150	0	0
2	28	Maerte	Per noten verschynende 18 Iunius 1600 fol 6 -	95	4	0
			Somme	245	4	0

			Aernout Iacobs credit. 't Iaer 1600			
1	0	Ianua	Per capitael verschynende 10 April 1600 fol 2 -	264	6	0
3	30	Meye	Per verscheyden partien verschynende 30 Iunius 1600 -	151	8	0
5	21	Aug	Per verscheyden partien verschynende 21 Sept 1600 -	1012	0	0
			Somme	1427	14	0

16

			Oncosten van Coomschap debet 't Iaer 1600	£	ß	δ
6	28	Februa	Per casse fol 5	3	0	0
2	31	Maerte	Per casse fol 5	4	2	0
2	30	April	Per casse fol 5	3	10	0
3	31	Meye	Per casse fol 5	4	5	0
4	30	Iunius	Per casse fol 5	2	10	0
6	31	Decem.	Per casse fol 19	40	0	0
			Somme	57	7	0

			Oncosten vanden huyse debet. 't Iaer 1600.			
2	28	Februa.	Per casse fol 5	3	4	0
2	31	Maerte	Per casse fol 5	6	6	0
2	30	April.	Per casse fol. 5	6	0	0
3	31	Meye	Per casse fol 5	7	0	0
4	30	Iunius	Per casse fol 5	5	0	0
6	31	Decem.	Per casse fol 19	80	0	0
			Somme	107	10	0

18

			Casse debet. t Iaer 1600.	£	ß	δ
	20	Iulius	Per slot van casse fol 5, 't welck daer in credit gebrocht was	1421	4	1
5	21	Aug	Per Aernout Iacobsen fol 15	1000	0	0
5	24	Sept	Per rekening van winst en verlies fol 19	1000	0	0
5	12	Octob.	Per Iacques de Somer fol. 13	504	3	4
			Somme	3925	7	5

			Rekening van wwinst en verlies debet 1600			
5	18	Aug	Per casse fol 19	100	0	0
5	21	Aug	Per Aernout Iacobsen fol. 15	12	0	0
	31	Decem	Per oncosten van coomschap fol 17	57	7	0
	31	Decem	Per oncosten vanden huyse fol 17	107	10	0
			Somme	276	17	0
	31	Decem	Per capitael fol 3 hier gestelt by slots van desen	987	5	5
			Somme	1264	2	5

17

		Oncosten van Coomschap credit 't Iaer 1600	£	ß	§
31	Decem	Per rekening van vvinst en verlies fol 18 hier gestelt by slote van desen - - -	,7	7	‘

		Oncosten vanden huyse credit. t Iaer 1600.			
31	Decem.	Per rekening van vvinst en verlies fol 18 hier gestelt by slote van desen - - -	107	10	0

19

Fol			Casse credit. 't Iaer 1600.	£	ß	§
4	28	Iulius	Per noten fol. 6 - - -	84	0	0
5	18	Aug	Per rekening van vvinst en verlies fol. 18 - - -	100	0	0
5	10	Sept	Per Iacques de Somer fol 12 - - -	500	0	0
5	18	Sept	Per Adriaen de VVinter fol 10 - - -	165	0	0
5	23	Sept.	Per Aernout Iacobs fol 14 - - -	1012	0	0
6	31	Decem	Per Oncosten van coomschap fol 16 - - -	40	0	0
6	31	Decem	Per Oncosten vanden huyse fol 16 -	80	0	0
			Somme	1981	0	0
	31	Decem	Per capitael fol 2, hier gestelt by slote van desen - -	1944	7	5
			Somme	3925	7	5

			Rekening van vvinst en verlies credit. 1600.			
5	10	Sept	Per Iacques de Somer fol 12 - - -	4	3	4
5	18	Sept	Per Adriaen de VVinter fol 10 - - -	15	0	0
5	24	Sept	Per casse fol 18 - - - -	1000	0	0
	31	Decem.	Per vvinst op nagelen fol 4 - - -	75	4	7
	31	Decem.	Per vvinst op noten fol 6 - - -	109	7	2
	31	Decem	Per vvinst op peper fol 6 - -	18	19	0
	31	Decem	Per vvinst op gember fol 8 - - -	41	8	4
			Somme	1264	2	5

Reſtanten van Hoghenhuyſe.

	1611	1612	1613	1614	1615
1611	800-0-0				
1612	500-0-0	900-0-0			
1613	370-0-0		600-0-0		
1614	150-0-0		330-0-0	930-0-0	
1615	70-0-0	0-0-0	300-0-0	700-0-0	590-0-0

Den ſin der voorſchreven tafel is duſdanich: Ghenomen d'eerſte vijf jaren van 'velen, dattet houden der contrerolle gheduert heeft, te weſen van 1611. 1612 1613. 1614. 1615. Hier af ſijn vijf colommen, voor elck jaers beſonder contrerolle een Noch ſijn op den cant gheſtelt derghelijcke vijf jaren, haer anwijſingh doende op elck der reſten daer nevens ſtaende, waer af't ghebruyck duſdanich is.

Ghenomen datmen na het jaer 1615 wil weten de ſommen der Reſtanten dieder ſijn ten eynde van yder jaer, der jaren 1611. 1612. 1613. 1614. 1615. Om dat te vinden, ick ſie dat nevens het jaer 1615 op den cant ſtaen 70-0-0 onder het jaer 1611, Daer na 0-0-0. onder 1612, voorts 300 onder 1613. En ſo voorts 700-0-0. onder 1614. en 590-0-0 onder 1615. Angaende voorſchreven 0-0-0. ſtaende nevens het jaer 1615, en dat onder 1612, ſulcx beteyckent het jaer 1612 heel voldaen te weſen, ſonder daer na van dat jaers rekening eenighe Reſtanten meerte connen vallen.

O 2 Het

RICHARD DAFFORNE PARTLY REPRODUCED

In the Library of Congress and in the Library of Harvard College, we find a book by Gerard Malynes, printed in London in 1656, under the title of "*Consuetudo Vel Lex Mercatoira,*" or "The Ancient Law Merchant" This book is a voluminous work, written in the English language, one-half of which contains a digest of the law merchant as then existing, the other half of the volume is occupied by a reprint of Richard Dafforne's book on bookkeeping, "The Merchants' Mirrour" It also contains an introduction to merchants' accounts, by John Collins, together with a treatise by Abraham Liset of Ghent, called "Amphithalami or the Accomptants Closet"

We have seen that Richard Dafforne was really the first writer in the English language whose work went through several editions and therefore may be considered as having been more popular than that of his predecessors Ympyn, Oldcastle, Mellis, and Peele Dafforne resided for a good many years in Holland, where he obtained his knowledge of bookkeeping He was a teacher in the Dutch and English languages and in bookkeeping Part of his treatise called "The Merchants' Mirrour' was written in Amsterdam before he moved to London The preface to his book indicates his familiarity with the then existing books on bookkeeping as he names quite a number Most of the authors of these books he discredits, but he seems to think highly of Simon Stevin, whom he copied in a number of instances Simon Stevin, however, was a great scholar, whereas Dafforne evidently was but a shallow teacher, for while he quotes freely from Stevin on the most important points, yet he omits to bring home the force of the question as Stevin does Thus through Dafforne's faulty transfer of the bookkeeping ideas of the Dutch authors into the English language, we have lost the very essence and foundation of the theory of bookkeeping Any one reading Stevin first and then Dafforne, will have no trouble in arriving at this conclusion It is like the reading of a letter from an experienced old man, followed by the treatment of the same subject by a high school student

In the following pages we are giving a partial reproduction of Dafforne's book, consisting of the title page, the introduction, about half of the text, and a few pages of the journal and ledger, together with the entire trial balance We are omitting part of the text, because it is simply a repetition of previously mentioned methods, applied to numerous mercantile transactions All of the text in which he attempts to give some theory or explanations, we have reproduced It will at once be seen that Dafforne was great at explaining HOW a thing should be done, but incapable of expressing clearly WHY a thing should be done He has attempted this in one or two places, and failed signally We are reproducing so much of his book, because, as explained before, we believe that in Pacioli, Manzoni, Ympyn, Stevin, and Dafforne we have the gradual steps of the transfer of bookkeeping knowledge, within a little over one hundred years, from the Italian through the Dutch into the English, unless, indeed, the Dutch transferred their knowledge to America, direct through the settlers of New Amsterdam (now New York)

At the time of Dafforne's writing, English mercantile customs and bookkeeping methods certainly were in a bad way, judging by Dafforne's own words and complaints There is an entire absence in the journal and ledger of references to the Deity, although the text is full of them Dafforne even quotes in the language in which it was written a Dutch dissertation on "God, the Giver of all good, all knowledge, and all wisdom"

He explains that a merchant in Amsterdam uses a cash book and a bank book, because his ledger and journal are always behind in posting, otherwise "the ledger might cause the avoidance of the use of these two books" He urges the use of a petty expense book, the totals of which are posted once a month or quarterly, in order to avoid numerous small entries

What Pacioli calls the memorandum book he calls a waste book, because he says everything is transferred from it into the journal, and when this is done it is useless to preserve it In Holland they do not preserve it The inventory and the trial balance are not written in this waste book, because they contain information of a private nature Blotting or erasures in the journal are improper He puts his slanting lines (//) in the left-hand margin of the waste book, in order to indicate the transfer to another book, and he evidently prefers this method to the diagonal line drawn through the entries, because, as he says, "it obscures the writing and the figures' Checking of the journal and ledger he calls "re-pointing," using the translation of the old Italian expression of "lancing" or 'pointing" as explained elsewhere under Pacioli Dafforne, however, does not say how he does it

He does not use the expressions "debit" or "credit" throughout his books, but names them debitor and creditor He charges the one and discharges the other He insists that nothing can be entered in the ledger unless it is first entered in the journal This includes the forwarding of balances from a full page to a new page also the closing entries for profit or loss, and the balancing of the accounts

Inventory he says consists of stock or estate or capital of the owner, which consists of "increasing improperly" and "decreasing improperly" of the stock or estate He attempts to explain what the word "improperly" means by quoting from Stevin, but he missed entirely what Stevin meant, as he applies it wrongly

He uses the word "stock" wherever Stevin uses the word "capital" As the word "stock" comes evidently from stick or stem, it really has the same origin as the word "capital," as through all the definitions and derivations of the word "stock" the thought of "main" or "principal" seems to appear From this we might state that capital stock is really tautology, for the two words mean the same thing

In explaining the first journal entry "cash debitor to stock," he personifies the cash account, because it "represents (to me) a man" He indicates the meaning of debitor by stating that by reason of giving the cash to the man, he is obliged to "render it back," or, as we have seen in Italian, "shall give" He indicates the meaning of creditor by mentioning the words "upon confidence," or, as we have seen in Italian "trusting." In spite of his quoting so freely from Stevin, and coming so near to what Stevin says, Dafforne has failed entirely to transfer to posterity the idea of the real reason for a double entry or two debits and two credits The nearest he comes to it is by stating that cash, merchandise, and all we possess are but "members of that whole body (*stocke*), therefore by the joint meeting of all those members the body (*stocke*) is made compleat" Thus it goes through the entire book, always HOW but never WHY, the very opposite of Stevin

Merchandise of large size and quantities is always kept in a separate account, designated by the name of the merchandise it deals in If, however, the merchandise consists of small articles of which but a few are handled the account is called a general merchandise account He credits a legacy in one place to stock or capital account, and in several other places direct to the profit and loss account Debitors he calls those "of whom we are to have," or in other words, as written in the Italian, those who "shall give" Creditors he calls "debt-demanders" and as far as inventory items are concerned, he says that *stocke* is debitor to these debt-demanders

He says that through a personal or private ledger you can keep a secret of a person's present worth or estate He is very emphatic in denouncing the use of the cash account for this purpose, as he states three Dutchmen do in their treatise, namely, Waninghen, Buingha, and Carpenter Here he again barely rubs elbows with Stevin's ideas of proprietorship He flays the three Dutchmen for promulgating ideas as "book deforming" instead of "book reforming," and he calls their ideas "indefendable errour," "forged imagineries," "forrain bred defects" He further says "If we were as exact discussors as we are imitators, we had not been so besotted as to entertain those forrain defects, having better at home" It should be noted that elsewhere he praises Stevin, and nowhere does he flay him like the above three Dutchmen, yet had Dafforne been less of a discussor and more of an imitator, he would have presented Stevin's exact theories without fault, and thus preserved them for us in the English language as Stevin did for his Dutch countrymen

He gives 15 rules each for journalizing debits and credits, but he personifies everything to debitor and creditor In the ledger he uses a double column, one for money, the other for quantities and weights. Cash discounts he deducts from cost of merchandise, whereas rebates are credited to profit and loss Thus he disagrees, as he says, with Passchier Goossens, Johannes Buingha, J Carpenter, and Henry Waninghen Dafforne succeeded here through his faulty reasoning, in mixing up things to such an extent that many minds today are still mixed up on this subject Waninghen and Carpenter want to carry trades of merchandise through the cash account Rightly he objects to this, for cash he says should have no entry unless money is really paid or received

He does not call in his text the difference between the debits and the credits "the balance," as we do today He says deduct the lesser from the greater, and make a journal entry for "the difference" In his ledger accounts, however, he does not call it, like the Italians do, "difference" but he calls it "balance to close" He uses the word "equalizing" where we now use "balancing" the same as we translated Pacioli's word "*saldo*" into "equalizing" or "closing" The closing of the ledger he calls "ballancing of the leager," or "leagers-conclusion" Like Stevin he claims that the ledger needs to be balanced when new books are started, or when the merchant ceases to trade or the owner dies Balancing he says, consists of three things the equalizing of all open accounts, the entering of the difference and transferring of the same to the new account or to the balance account He does not like the word "balancing," and prefers to call it "estate reckoning," the same as Stevin does and in this connection he refers to Stevin by saying that Stevin carries his closing balances into his opening capital account, which he calls contradictory, and merely a mistake on Stevin's part The balancing is divided into a trial balance and a true balance, the trial balance consists of debits and credits of the open ledger accounts before profit and loss entries are made He published in Amsterdam a "three-fold-mony-ballance" which we have reproduced further on The true balance he says consists of the "remainders" of the ledger accounts after profit and loss entries have been made

It should be noted that he says "remainders," as does Pacioli, and not "balances," as we use today The remainders of the accounts he puts in the true balance on the same side as they are in the ledger, namely if cash is debit in the ledger it should be debit in the true balance, for he says, balance is a debitor in the place of cash He gives a detailed explanation of how to close accounts kept in foreign money, and to take care of the profit or loss in the exchange at the time of closing While he exhibits a balance account and makes journal entries in order to close all accounts in this balance account, he is very particular in explaining that such a procedure is not needed if you desire to use the balance book in the nature of private information In that case, he says, post direct from the old account in the old ledger to the new account in the new ledger

The illustrations given of the journal will show that all entries are numbered, that he uses "debitor to" instead of "debit per," as Stevin uses Neither does he use the slanting lines (//) so customary in the Italian method, for a division between the debit and the credit, although but one column is given The ledger page references in the journal are written in the form of a fraction, as Pacioli mentions Ledger headings, while not as used at this day, are more pronounced than the Italian method, and are almost identical to Stevin's ideas.

In the ledger accounts herewith reproduced, "to" is used on the debit side and "by" on the credit The journal page is also given as well as the ledger folio of the relative entry in the other part of the ledger Both sides of the ledger bear the same number of the page, and they are called folio He does not use the word "sundries," in the journal nor in the ledger, nor does he use a sub-total in balancing his ledger accounts, as Stevin does, but uses in front of the total the Italian word "*summe*" Nowhere in his work does he use the term "assets and liabilities" He uses dots instead of check marks

THE

MERCHANTS MIRROUR.

OR,

DIRECTIONS

For the perfect Ordering and Keeping of his

ACCOUNTS.

Framed by way of DEBITOR and CREDITOR, after the (so termed) *Italian Manner*: Containing 250 Rare Questions, With their Answers, in forme of a DIALOGUE.

AS LIKEWISE

A VVASTE-BOOK, with a complete JOURNAL and LEAGER thereunto appertaining; Unto the which I have annexed two other *Waste-Books* for exercise of the *Studious*. and at the end of each is entred the brief Contents of the *Leagers* Accounts, arising from thence.

AND ALSO

A MONETH-BOOK, very requisite for Merchants, and commodious for all other *SCIENCE-LOVERS* of this Famous Art.

The Third Edition, Corrected and Amended.

Compiled by RICHARD DAFFORNE of *Northampton*, *Accountant*, and *Teacher* of the same, after an Exquisite Method, in the *English* and *Dutch* Language.

J. Vanden V.

Soo eenigh licht-berispend-Man,
Myn werk veracht, off soeckt t'onteeren,
Die maecket beeter, Soo hy kan:
'Khebb groote lust noch meer te Leeren.

H. L. S.

Oordeelt iemant voor het Leezen;
Niet goet kan syn Oordel weezen.

Leerende, leere ick.

The Contents are immediately prefixed before the Book.

LONDON,
Printed by *R. H.* and *J. G.* for *Nicholas Bourn*, at the South-entrance of the Royall Exchange, 1660.

TO THE RIGHT HONOURABLE

AND

RIGHT WORSHIPFULL

THE

GOVERNOURS,

AND

FELLOWSHIP

OF
- *Merchants Adventurers of England.*
- *English Merchants for the Discovery of New Trades*
- *Merchants of East land.*
- *Merchants of England, trading into the Levant Seas.*
- *Merchants of London, trading into the East-Indies.*
- *Adventurers of the City of London, for a Trade upon the Coasts and In-lands of divers parts of America*

RICHARD DAFFORNE so wisheth your Understandings Illumination, in your Terrestriall Talents Administration, that with comfort you may hear the joyfull Sentence of your twice commended service, *Mat* 25. Ver. 21, 23.

Well done thou good, and faithfull servant true,
Thou hast been faithfull over things a few,
Ile make thee Ruler over many things,
Possesse the joy of thy Lord, King of Kings.

RIGHT HONOURABLE, *&c.*

AFter many yeers residence at Amsterdam in Holland, I (upon the often Importunate Letters of some Merchants, my very good Friends) resolved to pitch the Tent of my abode in *London*, which being effected *in Anno* 1630. I then (after some rest) set my course unto severall Stationers Shops; there gazing about me (as one reviving from a Trance) to view what the Laborious Artist had acted and divulged in Print (as other Nations) for the Assistance of Merchandizing, wherewith (BLESSED BE THE GREAT ALL) this Renowned City is throughly Enterlaced, and Adorned.

But as a Shipper anchoring upon an unknown Ile, presently perceiveth those

a 2 parts

parts not to be inhabited, by the *Non-tillage,* or the like; even so (contrary to my expectation) I perceiving the number of Writers to be few, feared that love to this Art was likewise small: SEEING THAT GOOD ACCEPTANCE ENGENDERETH GOOD PERFORMANCE. The truth of this I can *averre* with many Instances in severall Authors; as *Forestain*, *John Impen*, *Cloot*, *Mennher*, *Savonne*, *Nicholas Peterson*, *Rentergem*, *Marten Vanden Dyck*, *Hoorbeck*, *van Damme*, *Wencelaus*, *Coutereels*, *Simon Stevin*, *John Willemson*, *Waninghen*, *Passchia*, *Goossen*, and divers others, whose Books are extant. By which may evidently be conjectured, that in those times, and in their parts where they then published their Works, were found many *Science-lovers* that affected this Art; by whose allurements those worthy Writers were induced to set Pen to Paper, endeavouring with their best gifts to satisfie the desire of those Art-desirers.

The Merchants of the Low-countries (of whom I can speak in part) being generally enamoured of this Art, because of its Utility, allure their Teachers to industry, by applauding their Vigilancy, encouraging them (with the presence of their Children and Servants in the Schooles) daily to publish new Questions; or at least to revive the profitable Labours of ancient Authors, making them fit for our times.

But we, alas, the small love (pardon my truth speaking) that a great part of our Merchants bear to this Science, daunteth the Pen of Industry in our Teachers, making them with a suspective fear to doubt (& not altogether groundless) that the profit will not countervail their pains; by which means *Teachers*, *Merchants*, and therefore *Youth*, are linked in *Arts enemies shackles*.

What may be the cause of this Ignorance? Are our *Teachers* so insufficient? Or both *dame Nature*, with her *Coadjute* or industry bestowed her Benevolence more sparingly upon our Nation than upon others? The last cannot be: for we can learn it exquisitly abroad of other Nations (as multitudes can witness) why not at home? I answer, as before, because at home (for want of love to this Art) many *Merchants* are insufficient *Presidents* to their Servants, who by their *Documents* can be but *Equivalent Imitators*. Want of love to this *Art*, is the cause why *James Peele*, and others that have written in English upon this subject, are knowne by *Name onely*, and not by *Imitation*. Yea, even the memory of their *Names* dieth, being there is no cause to commit their painfull Labours to the *Name-reviving* Press. How then shall our Youth attain unto this Art, but by frequenting abroad amongst other *nations*? And

They being then at Rome,
VVill do as there is done.

This stupidity cannot be imputed to our *Teachers*: for if at home (as other people do) we did by *Love* allure, and with *Reward* induce each other to Art by a competent Dispensation amongst our selves, of that money which we bestow abroad amongst *Aliens*, then would our *Teachers* be vigilant, our *Land* adorned with this Knowledge, and our *Youth* should not need to be transported into other Countries for *Arts documents*.

Against the foresaid Ignorance I have emboldened *my self* to prepare this

this *Antidote*, being by *Nature* obliged to offer up part of the *Widowes Mite* of my knowledg unto the *Land* of my *Breaths first drawing*.

Divers are the humours of men: therefore there is but small Probability to please all: yet to endeavour a generall satisfaction is unblameable.

My intent is not to prescribe these *Principles* as fully sufficient, though for their *Number* approveable: for time at present doth not yield permission to impart what my Affections desired, and *Will* determined to divulge, but these are *Allurements onely*, to stir up the *better experienced* to amend what I (through want of Art) have not so compleatly handled as I desire, and it deserves, being an *Art* (saith *Simon Stevin* in his Princely Book-keeping, *fol.* 7, & 12.) worthy to be numbred amongst the *Liberall* Sciences. But I already hear Objections against the *First*, & *Second* Waste books; that therein are exercised some accounts, which are altogether needlesse here in *England*: as is the *Banck-Account*. I grant it to be an Account not usefull in our Kingdome; but that the knowledge thereof should be un-usefull to this Arts-Learners, I deny. True it is, that by *Birth* we are *Circumferenced with the Ocean*; but the *Great-All* hath not so strictly limited us within the bounds thereof, that we are abridged from the *Conversation* and *Entercourse of Merchandizing* with forrain Nations, as well by their frequenting of our *Borders*, as we Commercing with them in the Body of their *Countries*. And when our Merchants (Old or Young) trade with them in their places, *must not they learn to be acquainted with their phrases* used among them concerning *Commerce?* Of which BANCK is none of the least in severall places of Europe, unto which our English Merchants have their Concourse. And must the advertisement of the *Course* thereof (before we come to the Actuall exercise) be a *Blemish*, and accounted as a *needlesse thing* in my Book? *Right Worshipfuls* behold the Rancor of black Envy, that endeavoureth to have us ignorant of Martiall affairs, untill we come to the point of Battail. The like Objection is alleaged against my entring of an Account of *Time* and *Ready-mony*. What if we have them not in use amongst our selves? Let us cast up our accounts with other *Nations*, and (to our cost) they will teach us how to frame an account of *Time* and *Ready mony*, if our *Factor*, or *Correspondent* be in disburse for us any quantity of mony, and for Time worth the reckoning, as experience hath shewed me in many passiges. And what then? Must not we seek the aid of some experienced to assist us? because we regarded not the documents of them (at home) that endeavoured to inform us of the *Manner* and *Matter*. What *Amercement* doth not this *Disdain-worthy* wilfull Ignorance merit?

Again, the keeping of an account of Time and Ready-mony (say they) may be avoided with an *account Currant*, or a *General account*, upon which is entred matters *Bought*, *Sold*, *Drawn*, *Remitted*, *Given*, or *Taken* upon Deposito, and the like: of which manner I am no way ignorant. But let us come to the Period, or Foot of that *General account*, and there the Conclusion sheweth, that I am DEBITOR to another, or the *Contrary*: how shall I find *Ready-money* that at present I am to *receive* or *pay* upon that account?

a 3

OPINION OF BOOK-KEEPINGS
ANTIQUITY.

A Good Friend of mine (saith *Simon Steven*) being exercised in the Old *Histories*, did see this forme of Book-keeping (meaning his owne) before it was perfected in the Presse; he was of judgement that it had not been used in *Italy*, but about two hundred years: But that the same, or one in many parts very like this, was used in the time of *Julius Cæsar*, and in Rome long before; and that some Reliques of Ancient time are come to the hands of them, that of late have received it again.

Which Opinion I thought not to be un-beseeming, the rather, because it seemeth strange, that so exquisite a Deep-diving-Science should be invented so lately: But be it as it will, I will enter the Opinion of my abovesaid Friend, who saith, that

In place of the proper words now used in the Italian-book-keeping, formerly other of the like signification were used: as these,

For	Debt-book, Great-book, or Leager	*Tabula accepti & expensi.*
	Debitor and Creditor	*Acceptum & expensum.*
	Parcells transported into the Leager	*Nomina translata in Tabulas.*
	Parcells not transported	*Nomen jacens.*
	Waste-book, or perhaps Journall	*Adversaria.*

All which (saith he) is apparent in innumerable places of the Latine Writers; but especially *ex Oratione Ciceronis pro Roscio Comœdo.* And that the one side of their Book was used for *Debitor*, the other for *Creditor*, is manifest (saith he) in a certain place, *Naturalis historiæ Plinii, lib. 2. cap. 7.* where he speaking of Fortune, saith thus:

Huic omnia EXPENSA.
Huic omnia FERUNTUR ACCEPTA, *& in tota* RATIONE *Mortalium sola* UTRAMQUE PAGINAM *facit.*

If others took regard unto this matter, perhaps further certainty might be found, and that this forme of Book-keeping, not onely by the Romans, but might have been in use before them amongst the Grecians: for being the Romans were no great Inventors, but had their exquisite Art from the Grecians, it is in reason most probable to come from them; whereof further certainty might be found in reading the Greek Histories. Thus much in *Simon Steven, fol.* 105, 106. A JUDICIOUS

Briefe CONTENTS of the chiefest Points contained in this Book.

The Contents of the Book.

INTRODUCTION.

THE FIRST PLACE.

SPEAKERS,

Philo-Mathy. School-Partner.

Phil. HOw now School Partner? Whither away thus solitary? it seems you are in some serious Meditation.

Sch. Surely you have judged aright: for I was musing upon our Masters Instructions of Book-keeping, taught us by way of Questions aud Answers; whereof I have forgotten much, because I frequent not the daily examination.

Phil. Very likely: *For Exercise is the Preserver of Art*; therefore do I daily resort to the
2 examination, which (you know) our Master continually useth: the which not onely confirmeth what we have, but it is likewise *an Augmenter of Knowledg*, according to the Motto of James Peel. *Practice procureth perfection*

Sch. Surely you say truth: Therefore I intreat you (seeing we have time and opportunity) to question me in such things as at present are readiest in your mind, beginning with the first grounds of our Masters Instructions, and so in brief sort to wade through them all, for the refreshing of my memory.

Phil. Very gladly: for in questioning of you I shall be the better confirmed in that which
3 already I have obteined. But seeing that all good gifts (even in mean Mechanical matters) proceed from the *All-giver*, as in *Exod.* 31. Ver. 2, 3, 4, 6, 7. appeareth, therefore do I humbly intreat my understandings illumination from thee:

O! al-verbullend' Een, die alles scheppe zyt,
Self-standigh weezen, zonder Stof, of form, of Tydt,
Of yet dat ons begrip, bedenken kan, of vaten:
Al-schoon, Almatigh, Wys, end' Goedigh boven maten!
Onnoemelike-Al, All-hærschende Natuur!
Wéét-oorzaaks milde Born! Stort ghy te dezer uur,
Of Strael, of Kracht, of Ghæst! sont my wisdom, and zeeghe,
Dat ick den grond uyt-vind', end' onder wyz' ter dæghe,
Ons wéét maer stuck-werk is, vol onghelt adighæden,
Wy sluyten huyden a'ers vaak dan my ghilstren dæden,
Meest als de Mensch hoogh vlieght (end' must uw' Hulp O Hær)
Hy snevelt on-bewaand met Icarus ter neer!
Ach! Laat zelf achtings Liefd, of waan my doe gheen schennis,
Schéést my een scherp begrip, Goed oordeel, ware kennis
Der dinghen onderscheid doorn, uyt my te Leeren,
Teschiften Goed, end Quaad, valt dit! wat mach my deeren?

B 2 Taking

Taking now my beginning from our Masters grounds, I intend in order (according to capacity) to passe through them all · and being that Book-writing, by way of Debitor and Creditor, after the (so termed) Italian manner, is renowned to be an exquisite knowledg, shew me its event

Sch The Event or End is (saith one) that which moveth to *Action*, and the End finall is ever better then that which is for the End; yet this End cannot be attained, but by another thing intended, as a means thereunto So, that all things which (as means) are for, and conduce to the End, are not intended, nor prosecuted, but out of a deliberate and full intention of the End.

In like manner.

The End of Book-writing is to give contentment unto the Book-owner, and to shew him (or them, whom they do concern) at all times, and in every degree, how his Estate standeth in the so written Books. For, the view of a well established Estate in a mans Books, procureth contentment unto the possessor; yet this contentment (for no rest without former labour) cannot be attained, but by another thing intended as a means thereunto: to wit, *Book-keeping knowledge* and being known, prosecuted, and affected; the same being very Requisite, Usefull, and Commodious for the writing.

Of
- Princely Revenues, findings of Customes, and the like duties; of which at present I intend not to treat, but may hereafter have some occasion to shew the necessity thereof in Princely Courts, as well as in Merchants passages Of the which there is a worthy work compiled in Dutch for Prince Maurice, Conte of Nassaw, which he learned of the Compiler, Simon Stevin his Mathematician, and exercised the same in his Court, which still (as I have been informed) is there in use, as also in the Swethian Court, and elsewhere.
- Merchants-trading; being for *Proper*, *Factorage*, or *Company* accounts: of this I intend to speak at present.

And this Mirrour of Estate is not to be seen in any Book, but onely in the Leager, whose proper office it is to shew the Estate of the same to the Book-owner.

Of needlesse Books

This reproveth the keeping of a mans Estate in many Books: as in a Book of Buying, another of Selling, another of Receipts, another of Shipping, and what not? All these Books cannot shew a mans Estate, nor Case of standing with any man, or in any Commodity, untill all matters are drawn to a head upon a paper in form of a Leager; so that they have every way as much trouble in writing their imperfect form, as we in making our work compleat at once: but the generality want capacity to apprehend the manner, and rectifie their own defects · therefore they affect this form but with small affection.

4 *Phil.* Being that the tenor of our speech concerneth *Books*, I take it not unfitting that you rehearse those Books that are most requisite for Merchants use, to avoid all those needlesse Books.

Of the Cash-Book, and Banck-Book.

Sch. A Merchant in Amsterdam useth a Cash Book, and a Banck-Book, because his Journall and Leager are (in posting) behind-hand, else the Leager might cause the avoiding for those two Books.

Of the Specie-Book.

A Merchant useth likewise a Specie-Book, More usefull for the Low-Countries then for England, because of the variety of Coines there in use; as likewise in times of controversie to approve what Coins passed in Receipt of Payment: whereof John Coutereels of Antwerp

werp hath shewed a worthy example in his Book called Den Stile van Bockh uen.

Of the petty Expences-Book.

More, he useth a Book of petty Expences for house-keeping, and small disbursements upon Merchandizing; the which are posted once a moneth, or quarter of a year, into the Journall, of which the said John Coutereels N°. B. *fol.* 9, 10, 11. hath lively instances. Simon Stevin in his Princely Book-keeping, *fol.* 52. writeth concerning this Book, thus:

This Book of Expences is likewise a kind of a Cash-Book, and is onely for charges, which generally are posted once a moneth in one summe into the Journall: partly, for brevity, to post many petties into one summe: partly, because in great mens houses, its the proper office of some one man to administrate those petty expences, rendring an account of each particular, as well for Mustard and Matches to kindle the fire, as of things of greater importance, unto which end there is kept a Particular-Book.

Copy Book of Letters.

More, he keepeth a Copy Book of Letters, which informeth his memory of what he hath written unto others; and this Book is very requisite against controversies of advices, the Letters sometimes not being well understood by the receiver.

Of the Memoriall.

A Merchant may use a Memoriall, there to note some things that properly appertain to no other Book: as for instance; I lent unto a man a shilling, or a pound, for a day or a week, its sufficient to note a word or two *per* memory, without making any Journall parcell of the same. yea not in the Clad or Waste-Book, for that hath another office. *Simon Stevin, fol.* 21. Some enter such things in the Clad, but the same is so large, that by prolongation of time its hard to be found; and causeth likewise a doubt in the Accomptant whether it shall be posted, or not.

Copy Book for Accounts.

Some use likewise a Copy Book for Accounts, sent, or delivered to any man, because the Leager agreeth not compleatly in each particular parcell in order, or day, with the sent Account; else that Book, and the writing thereof might be avoided, Of which form, if any man desire an instance, may have it in the Book of John Coutereels, *lit.* O. *fol.* 6. & 7.

Four other principall Books doth a Merchant use in his Traffique, to wit:

A { *Waste-book*, fore-runner of the Journall
Journall, or Day-book, fore-runner of the Leager.
Leager, or Gather-book, Mirrour of a mans Estate.
Factor book, for the entring of each particular received, pack or parcell of wares alone, that cometh into his hands to sell, either in Commission, or for Company Account. Of these last four Books I intend to treat, and to explain their proper offices, as much as the *All-Comprizer* shall please to impart to my present memories apprehension. For,

On thee, O God, I do depend,
Ever me with thy Shield defend,
That Jesus my Redeeming Lord
May Mercies sentence me afford:
And that the Illuminating Sp'rit
Grant that I may know my self aright,
To put my confidence alone
In Trinity, but else-where none.
For none but thou didst wisdome give
Unto Bezaleel, Uri's *sonne:*

And

And even of love thou didst relieve
Him with another chosen One.
LORD, so infuse thy gifts in me,
And aid me in this work of mine,
That it to many usefull be,
The praise thereof shall all be thine.

WASTE-BOOK:

So called, because when the matter is written into the Journall, then is this book void, and of no esteem; especially in Holland, where the buying people firme not the Waste-book, as here our Nation do in England.

5 *Phil.* Explaine the office and dependances of the Waste-book.
Sch. Two things are to be noted in the Waste-book.

The { *Form* / *Office* } thereof.

The *Forme* is, that this book is lined towards the left hand with one line (but some use two) and towards the right hand with three; leaving towards the left hand a Margine or whiteness of an inch or lesse, according to the books largenesse, to enter therein the Day, Moneth, Mark of the Commodity, or all: and between the three lines towards the right hand, there to enter the mony, as by severall instances shall be made plain.

The *Office* of this book is, that onely the Daily-trading ought to be written therein, even as it is truly acted:

AS

Buying, Selling, Receiving, Paying, Drawing, Remitting, Assignments, Shipping, &c. and this must be entred immediately upon the action of the thing acted, to the end no passing parcells be forgotten, according to the Dutch Proverb: Dat men schryft, Dat blyft, That which is written, Remaineth. In this book ought neither Inventory nor Ballance of the Leager to be entred; for that is against the office of this book · it being onely to write Traficking passages in. In this book may write Master, Accomptant, or any Servant of the house, by whom the thing is acted, or by advice and order of another. In this book must the matter be entred in plain sincerity as it is acted, without Debitor, or Creditor forme; for that is the proper office of the Journall · likewise many people understand the Waste-book entrances, that apprehend not the Journall forme. In this book ought the parcels to be entred close under each other as they were acted, without leaving of any empty paper, to avoid suspicion of *Forging* any parcells betwixt them, upon any omitted occasion: and each parcell ought to be separated with a line from the other before written, and ensuing parcel. In this book ought the acted matter to be first entred; partly, because it is a fore-runner of the Journal especially when the Merchant useth an Accomptant that dwelleth without his house; for he may sometime be absent when such matters are acted. Again, there may be an error committed in Weight, Measure, Quantity or Casting. Again, because the matter or condition may be changed, by diminishing or augmenting of any thing, or by wholly leaving out of any matter, the bargain being broken, and so that parcell cancelled there. for Blotching or Racing out of any parcell in the Journall is unbeseeming.

6 *Phil.* What considerations else are to be observed in this Waste-book?
Sch Five other things must be duely observed in this book:

1. The Year, Moneth, Day, Town or Place where such matters are acted.

2. The Name and Surname of the Party with whom we trade · or, if it be Factorage, then unto the former name must be added the Owners name for whom the thing is effected, as likewise the place of his Residence · and whether the Bargain be for Time or Ready mony, that's alike, in respect of Booking the same unto him whose Commodities they are.

3. The

3. The quantity or quality of the thing traded for: as, Ells, Pieces, Colours; Weight, Mark, Number, Exchanges, Assignments, or the like.

4. The value of price of the thing traded for: whether Wares, Exchanges, or the like.

5. The conditions or circumstances that were used about the matter: as Time, Suretiship, Bonds given, or taken, Brokeridge, &c.

The Waste Book parcells are of tenour, as the ensuing examples.

	Anno 1630, the 25. of March, in London.	L	s	d
	Marmaduke Grimston of Northampton, lendeth me 68. l. untill the first of May next coming: which summe (by his assignment) my Cashier receiveth of *Arthur Manering*, in consideration whereof I am to allow him certain mony; being, with principall	69	15	7
Day. 27	Assigned *Sybrant Johnson* upon *Thomas Coster*, for the accompt of *Seager Solt*, to receive, 495. l. the remainer hath my Cashier received of *John Sybrantson*, by assignment of the said *Coster*, with 7. l. 10. for six weeks time forbearance: the whole being	951	9	—
1630. March 30.	Agreed with *Jacob Johnson* of Marken, to let him have 3000. Florines for Franckford, at 81. d. Flemish, to be repayd to me, or Assignes, the first of June next; as the Exchange shall then return from Franckford: this being mony for the Company of *Edward Denis* at Northampton and me, each one halfe, producing	1012	10	—
	In part of payment of the same, I deliver him 18. Lasts, 7. Mudde of Rye, being in Company ½ for *Edward Denis*, and ½ for me; at 15 0. gl. each Last ready-mony, is gl. 3834. 8. 12. The remainer have I made good in Banck (for him) upon the accompt of *John Johnson* Vinck, abating 22. ½ gl. for Banck-mony, at one *per Cent.* the whole produceth	1012	10	—

Phil. What use have those slanting strokes that are drawn in the Margine?

7 *Sch.* They have two uses: 1. They shew how far is posted out of the Waste-book into the Journall; and they are a sure mark that a man omit no parcell, being called away from his posting: neither to enter one thing twice upon the said calling away. 2. They shew how many Journal parcells are included in such a Waste Book parcel: insomuch, that in re-pointing of the Waste-Book, a man may the easier see the quantity of the included parcells, when the Waste and Journall shall be compared against each other. Some draw those strokes on the right hand, where the mony is; but that multitude of Strokes darkneth the mony summes: *each his choice.* The Waste-Book parcells ought with all convenient speed to be posted into the Journall, and Leager, to the end the Book owner may the better discern how his case standeth with each man, and matter. Thus much of the Waste-Book in *Form*, *Office*, and *Circumstances*: Now,

OF THE JOURNALL.

It being the first exquisite Book, wherein carefully must be observed, that each parcel have its Charge, and Discharge · that is, the true *Debttor*, and *Creditor*, wherewith each Journal parcel ought to begin: which being well apprehended, and with fit words (according to the nature of the matter) expressed, *is one of the chiefest principles belonging*

belonging unto book-keeping. Mark well; he that can discern the true *Debitor* and *Creditor*, in any propounded proposition (concerning this Art) hath the right (Theorick) *inward-ground-knowledge* and contemplation of the matters: and he, and *onely* he (with the help of Arithmetick) goeth firm in his action, to give each man his due, and book his matters under due and true Titles. It is very requisite (if possible it may be effected) that the Journall be written by one man: for in times of controversie he can best answer for his own postings.

8 *Phil.* What things are most requisite in the Journall to be noted?

Sch. Three Notable things are to noted in the Journall:

1. The *Matter* whereof it is made.
2. The *Form* thereof.
3. The *Office* whereunto it is used.

OF THE JOURNALLS MATTER.

9 *Phil.* Proceed to the Explication of the first member.

Sch. The *Matter* whereof the Journall is made, may be drawn to five chief branches: for it

proceedeth:
1. From the Inventary: as in the 10. and so to 61. place.
2. From Traffickes continuall Exercise: as in 62. place (including 205.)
3. From transporting of full accounts in the Leager unto a new leaf, See 206. place.
4. From the equalizing of Over, or Under-weights, Measures, or the like. See 212. place.
5. From the Leagers Conclude, or Ballancing of the Leager. See 215. place

10 *Phil.* Go on with the first branch.

Sch. An usuall Inventary generally consisteth in

Stocks,
- Increasing: improperly by means of
  1. Ready-mony, and that in Cash, in Banck, or both.
  2. Wares remaining unsould for proper accompt. under this second member is included Houses, Lands, Rents, Ships-parts; as also Wares unsould for Factorage, or Company-accompts, and those that were formerly shipt unto another place, being as yet unsould for Proper, Factorage, or Company accompts.
  3. Debitors, and them againe in
     1. People unto whom we formerly sould: or, that promised us payment of exchanges, and the like.
     2. Factors, 3. Partners, 4. Masters, } that have not as yet given us full satisfaction.
- Decreasing: improperly by means of
  4. Debt-demanders; and them in
     1. People of whom we have bought, or whose Bills we have accepted.
     2. Factors, 3. Partners, 4. Masters, } unto whom we as yet have not given full content.
     5. Wares, partly sould for Factorage, of Company-accounc

11 *Phil.* In the above-standing Table you speak of Stockes Increasing, and Decreasing Improperly; explain the word Improper.

Sch. Simon Stevin, discoursing of Merchants Book-keeping, *fol.* 55. with *Prince Mau-*

rus

ries, concerning Stockes Increasing, and Decreasing: the Prince saith, that, *Monies*, *Wares*, and *Debitors*, Increase Stock · for the more a man hath of them, the greater will his Stock be. Contrarily, *Debt-demanders* Decrease Stock. Simon Stevin replyeth, to be of another Opinion; expressing himself with the ensuing Instance: If (saith he) in former Books I bought of Peter a Bale of Pepper upon Time; that Pepper augmenteth not my Stock: for Peter demandeth of me the value, time being expired. In like manner, my Stock decreaseth not, because Peter is a *Debt-demander*: for its as much augmented by the Pepper. But if a Bale of Pepper be given me, that, truly augmenteth my Stock: for I enter, *Pepper-debitor* to Stock. And, *fol* 54. A Merchant giving certain hundreds to Marriage with his *Daughter*, that decreaseth Stock. By this may easily be discerned, what Stock Augmenter, and Diminisher properly is.

12 *Phil.* Speaking of Stocks Increasing, and Decreasing, you rehearsed in how many parts the substance of an Inventary did consist; but let me now hear you *nominate* the true *Debitors* and *Creditors* of the same *onely*, without any other Circumstances of Dictations.

Sch To give you the better content, I will speake of each in order as they stand: and first,

OF THE READY MONY.

13 *Phil.* How Book you the Ready mony after the way of Debitor and Creditor?
Sch. *Cash* Debitor to *Stock*.

14 *Phil.* Why make you *Cash* Debitor?

Sch Because *Cash* (having received my mony into it) is obliged to restore it again at my pleasure: for *Cash* representeth (to me) a man, to whom I (onely upon confidence) have put my mony into his keeping; the which by reason is obliged to render it back, or, to give me an account what is become of it · even so, if *Cash* be broken open, it giveth me notice what's become of my mony, else it would redound it wholly back to me.

15 *Phil.* Why do you use the word *Cash*, being the word *Mony* is in use amongst our Nation?

Sch. Simon Stevin treating of this word with *Prince Maurits* of *Nassau*, in the fift Head point of his Princely Book-keeping, *fol* 52. saith, that he could give none other reason, *but onely*, that this word is in *Use*, which if it were not, I account it better (saith he) to have said, *Mony is Debitor*.

Our Master usually alledged the difference between private, and generall discourses, shewing that many words are usually among Dutch, French, and other Nations, with whom a Merchant doth traffick therefore he thought it fittest to use generall words, as being generally known, and most usefull in Book keeping; else (said he) why should not *Mony* bear its *own Name* as well as other commodities?

16 *Phil.* One other Question I have to demand before you proceed, which is, Why is *Stock* made *Creditor*?

Sch. Because the word *Stock* containeth in it, all what a man possesseth; whether *Money*, *Wares*, *Debts* due to us, or the like: and (marke this well) *Cash*, yea, each particular thing that I possesse, is but a member of that whole body *Stocke*; therefore by the joynt meeting of all those members, the body (*Stock*) is made compleat.

17 *Phil.* Having passed the first part of Ready-mony, treat now somewhat

OF THE MONY IN BANCKE.

For in the hands of the Honourable *Lords* of the Bancke, I have a certain summe of money; how shall I Book that?

NOTE —Pages 23 to 43, 10 to 14, 24 to 44, 48, 49 and 53 of the text are omitted, because they give questions and answers setting forth how journal entries under differing circumstances are made They do not present any argumentation or theory, nor do they show why they are made, and therefore are practically nothing but repetitions of what has been said in other pages

40 *Phil.* Let me hear you enter this according to the nature of the Inventary.

Sch They were sent before, and therefore I enter now.

Edward Denis of Northampton his account at Roan in France, in the Administration of *P. D.* Debitor to Stock; for the charges by me done at the first sending. See 46. place.

41 *Phil.* But suppose the charges that you did at the first sending were writ off from his above-named Roan account, unto his account currant, being that I would have all disbursed money upon one account; and therefore that account hath no charge now upon it.

Sch. Edward Denis of Northampton, his account at Roan in France, in the Administration of *P. D* is Debitor to Stock: *Nota*, for a Blank summe, both in Debit and Credit; and must be so carried to each account *per Formam*, because there must not be a Debitor without a Creditor, nor the contrary.

42 *Phil.* Suppose *P D.* had in the former books made sale of part, or whole; whereof you had advice then, but no Returns. See 46. place.

Sch. P. D. at Roan, for the proper account of *E. D.* at *N. N.* Debitor to Stock; for as much as the known sales import and so I pass forward, according to the Tables tenour, unto.

Wares abroad, unsold, for Company-Account.

43 *Phil.* I perceive you cleave close to the Table.

Sch. School men (as I have read) say, that a good Disputant ought never to digresse from the propounded Proposition, untill it be discussed. Neither ought any Writer to commit a digression from the grounds of his intended subject, as is here the before-entred Table in the 10. place, as also the ensuing three Tables; to wit, The Table of Accounts *Proper* in the 63. place · the Table of *Factorage*-accounts in the 122. place: and the Table of *Company*-accounts in the 174. place. From these I intend not to stray; but in order will work upon them (as the Table shall deliver matter thereunto:) the more, because any one which shall have occasion to seek a matter in any of those particular Tables, whether in the *Inventaries*, *Proper*, *Factorage*, or, *Company*-Tables, may presently know what goeth before, or, followeth his desired matter.

44 *Phil.* But to our intended purpose; rehearse some Instances of Company unsold Wares.

Sch. { Voyage to Roan, consigned to *Pierre du Pont*, being in Company for *James Bartram*, and me, each ½ ———————
Voyage to Lisborne, consigned to *Pedro del Verdo*, being in Company, ½ for *Robert Clifton*, and Partner, ⅛ for *James Joyner*; and, for me. ——————— } Debitor to Stock.

45 *Phil.* Having in order waded through the second branch of the Inventary-Table, in the 10. place, proceed to the third branch of Stocks increasing: being

DEBITORS, OF WHOM WE ARE TO HAVE.

Sch. Four in number are they comprehended under, in the third branch of the 10. place, and may all be joyned as under one, yet in brief I will touch each apart. as

{ 1. *B. C.* to whom we formerly sold, or, that he had accepted our Exchanges, Debitor to Stock.
2. *C. D.* at Venice my account currant, Debitor to Stock.

3. Partner,

3. Partner,
Who hath part of My estate in his hands, to be imployed, by him for the good of our Company · *N. N.* my account by him in Company, Debitor to Stock.
Whose part of Stock is in my hands to be by me imployed, and I am for him in disburse: *N N* his account by me in Company, Debitor to Stock.
4. *M. M.* at Colchester his account Currant, Debitor to Stock.

By the word *Currant*, do not I understand the account that is opposite to an account of *Time*, (For I distinguish them by the name of *Time*, and Ready-mony) but by *Currant*, I understand, a *Running* account, (*Conte-Courante*) upon the which all things may passe, as well for time, as Ready-mony.

46 *Phil.* Thus I see you have passed through the three branches of Stocks Increasing, with the dependances of the same in a briefe manner: what followeth next to treat of?

DEBT-DEMANDERS.

Sch. In the 10. place is shewed, that Stock hath (Improperly) a Decreasing part; and that again is divided into five Sub divisions of these in briefe likewise, after a plain manner as thus,

Stocke is Debitor to
1. *D. E.* Of whom we formerly bought, or whose Bills in former Books we accepted, and presently Booked them, but not due to be paid in those Books.
2. *E. F.* at Constantinople, my account *Currant*; for that he hath made me more Returns then my sold Wares did import.
3. Partner,
My account by him in Company, he having paid out more then his part doth import.
His account by me in Company. I having received into my hands mony for sold Wares, and detain his part thereof, where he ought to have it.
4. *F. G.* His account *Currant*; the credit of which being heavier then his Debit: but whether it be in Ready-mony, or, for Wares sold upon time, thats not materiall, in respect of his *Running-accounts* form.
5. *G. H.* His account of Kersies, for so much as was sold upon that account in the former Book: See 36. place.
Durances in Company, $\frac{1}{2}$ for *A. B.* $\frac{1}{3}$ for *B. C.* and $\frac{1}{6}$ for me for so much as in the former Book was sold upon that account: See 37. place, it being compared with this.
Edward Denis of Northampton, his account at *Roan in France*, in the Administration of *P. D.* for as much as the known Sales import. *Nota*, in the 42. place, the Factor was made Debitor to Stock, for the like summe: therefore our Stock standeth well in the like case with others. Again, we have our first charges done us good unto our Stock in the 40. place.

Stock Debitor to Voyage to Lisborne, consigned unto *Pedro del Vergo*, being in Company, $\frac{1}{2}$ for *Robert Clifton*, and Partner $\frac{1}{6}$ for *James Joyner*, and $\frac{1}{3}$ for me: for as much as the known Sales import. You must conceive, that *Pedro del Vergo*, our account, being in Company, $\frac{1}{2}$ for *Robert Clifton*, and Partner; $\frac{1}{6}$ for *I. I.* and $\frac{1}{3}$ for me. either *standeth*, or, *should stand* Debitor to Stock, for the like summe, that Stock standeth Debitor to the Voyage for the Sales; for the *Voyage* cannot have a Credit, but by one, or more Debitours that *even* Counter-poize that Credit.

47 *Phil.* I have seen your *Dexterity* in the handling of the Inventary-Table, as also in the Booking of a mans known estate; but if a Merchant will not have his estate known, how

how will you behave your self therein? Ha! I think I have pos'd you now. Now you are stall'd, I trow

Sch. In such difficult Questions you cannot debarre me, to take the aid of some Renowned Authors: for in the first place of our Dialogue I feared my weaknesse, because I frequented not the daily Examination; but although I frequent not the School, I am yet not ignorant of what the Authors passages are upon this Subject: and therefore I will decide your Question, with the Solution of Master *Henry Waninghen* in the first Chapter, the 17. Questions answer, his words are these: *Cash must be entred in place of Stocke, making all that is due to us Debitor to Cash. contrarily, Cash Debitor to all them that are to have of us.*

With him (in the very same words) agreeth his Disciple *Joannes Buingha*, who now at Amsterdam, after the death of his before-named Master, succeedeth his place in Schoolmastership. See the 38. page of his Book, printed 1627.

J. Carpenter Gent. in his *Most Excellent Instruction*, printed in London 1632. is a direct *Imitator* of both the former *See fol.* 20.24. of his Book: and no mervaile; for the greatest part of his published Book, is nothing else but a generall copy of *Henry Waninghens* Book, both in words, and number of the Questions. *J. C.* in his Epistle to the Reader, pretendeth Ignorance, of not knowing the Author, who in the French Language many years agone was easie to be found.

48 *Phil.* Shew me some Instances how they would Book their passages.

Sch. In briefe I will: and first,

OF THE WARES.

Grograines,
Kersies
Durances, } Debitor to Cash.

Of the People that owe to us.

Robin Good-fellow,
Herman Hard-head,
John Gentleman, } Debitor to Cash.

Of the People that we owe unto.

Cash Debitor to { *Rowland Red-beard.* *Ralph Would-well.* *Reynst Reach-farre.*

49 *Phil.* Suppose a man at the making of his Inventary hath some mony, how shall he Book that?

Sch. The before-named in the places of their Books mentioned, say, *The Ready-mony is not to be entred, till you disburse the same.*

50 *Phil.* Suppose with part of that concealed mony you bought *Wares*, and with other part, paid them unto whom you are indebted: how enter you that?

Wares,
People, } Debitor to Cash.

51 *Phil.* This being thus rehearsed, what will you conclude; have these (think you) digressed?

Sch. Suppose they had, what's that to me? But because you should not flout at me, thinking my capacity to be so stupid, that it is void of distinction, I will in some briefe notes onely touch the same.

Firstly,

Firſt, let me conſider whether the Book-owner be more indebted then his Eſtate is worth; which if he be, then is their entrance good, for his Eſtates concealment *for the Debit ſide of Caſh ought to be heavieſt, or, having no mony, it muſt be even, becauſe all is paid out*: but if he have any Eſtate, then is the *Credit* of his Caſh (who ſtandeth in *Stocks* ſtead) heavieſt: and therefore an *Errour*, being there is more paid, then was received.

Secondly, the commodities that we have at the making of our Inventary, were bought in *former* Books, and there made *Debitors*; and that we now enter them again *Debitors* to *Caſh*, is to re-buy them: and conſequently, in place of *book-reforming, book deforming*, and an *undefendable Errour.*

Thirdly, the People whom we now make *Debitors* to *Caſh*, are *abſolutely* our *Debitors*; and do we *pay* them, who are to *pay* us? many men would deſire to be *our* Debitors.

Fourthly, As ſenſeleſſe is it, to make Caſh *Debitor* to People that are to have of us; will they that are to have of us 100. l. for a Bill of Exchange by us accepted, ſay, *Come my Friend,* you have accepted an Exchange, to pay at time expired, which is now: ſend your man to my houſe, and the mony ſhall incontinently be paid to him? *I think nothing leſſe.*

☞ Fifthly, Caſh may never be ☞ *named. Nota, not named,* but when *money* is either truly, and really paid, or, received, as in the 17. place is mentioned. But if theſe People enter *forged* Imaginaries in the *Fore-front* of their Books what is not to be expected before the *End?*

Sixthly, The *Stock* which they ſeek to *conceale*, is manifeſt in the *difference* of Caſh it ſelf. For let then tranſport their *Caſh*, and they ſhall find (if as before is ſaid, that their Eſtate ſtand well) that *Caſh* is, and in tranſporting forward, alwayes remaineth *Creditor*. Ballance that *Caſh*, and tell me what ſhall be done with the *difference*. Carry it to a new account, what then? there it will prove to be *Stock* Carry it to Profit and Loſſe, there it will prove to be *Stockes Augmentor. Wonder is it,* that theſe and many other *Forrain bred-defects* muſt now be *cloathed in Engliſh Attire*, and paſſe for currant amongſt us! Surely, our Judgement is weak in the *diſcerning of this Art.*

Phil. I perceive their paſſages in Booking of their Matters, doth not digeſt with you; is
52 there a more plain way? diſcover that.

Sch. If we were as *Exact Diſcuſſors*, as we are *Imitators*; we had not been ſo *beſotted*, as to entertain thoſe Forrain defects, having *better at home.*

Look into *James Peele*, whoſe well-entrances, through neglecting Age (or diſdain of Domeſtick Writers, and extolling of Forrain) are as ſtrange to us, as though (as the ſaying is) they were written in Heathen Greek.. He ſheweth us the fit ground-work, how to conceale a mans Eſtate, in the Booking of his private accounts, and matters manifeſted for Merchandizing.

Phil. Inſtance ſome particulars, how to Book the manifeſted part.

53 *Sch.* You ſpeak of *part*; whether he bring in *part*, or, *All*, who can certainly know that? being that we can but *Aime* at it, as the Blind at the *colour of Cloth*. And for that which he manifeſteth, may be

entred
Caſh,
Banck,
Perpetuanes,
Marmaduke Man,
John Knoll at Lisborn, my account Proper,
Debitor unto the *Private* account.

Phil. How ſhall the Maſter, or Book-owner, enter into his *private* Books the things
54 manifeſted for Merchandizing?

Sch. Generall account for Traffick, Debitor to
Caſh,
Banck,
Perpetuanes,
Marmaduke Man,
John Knoll at Lisborn, my account Proper.

D

Phil.

55 *Phil.* Suppose there is gained upon Wares sould.
Sch. Wares Debitor to Private account, for the Gaines; do the like in Factor accounts, and all other, upon which Gaines ariseth.

56 *Phil.* Suppose I lose by Wares, or Exchanges.
Sch. Private account, Debitor to Wares, Exchanges, or, unto that account; upon which Losse ariseth.

57 *Phil.* At the Conclude of my Book, I surrender *Monies, Debts*, and *Unsould-Wares.*
Sch. Private account Debitor to Cash, Men, and Wares, each *name* severally.

58 *Phil.* How shall the Book-owner enter back in his private Books the *surrendred* severall matters?
Phil. Cash, Men, Wares, each *name* severally, Debitor to Generall account for Traffick.

59 *Phil.* How shall the Book-owner enter into his Private Book, the Gaines that are found upon his Book of Traffick?
Sch. Generall account for Traffick, Debitor to Profit and Losse.

60 *Phil.* But if he lost in his Book for Traffick.
Sch. Profit, and Losse Debitor to Generall account for traffick; because it hath *surrendred* back lesse, then formerly was confidented unto the same: Judge of the Gaines likewise, that the Generall account for Traffick yielded more, then the first in-laid Principall. Here you see the matter *plainly discursed.* Here you see the ground-work, by which they are *confuted*, gathered from *one* of our *own Nation*; which to their mis-entrings might rather have been

A worthy Refutation,
Then, by their Approbation
To bring them to our Nation.

But it seeemeth that this Absurdity (and many more, which upon due Examination of their works apparently *I can make* appear) was not *discerned*, or, being *discerned*, how to amend it, *Experience had not befriended them.*

61 *Phil.* Rehearse some other Instances of their Mis-entrances, that (for the Reader) they may be as *Buoyes* in this *Sea*, to keep him from Ignorances Ship-wrack.
Sch. Very loth am I to *pry* any further into their Books: for their *Adsurdities* are many in divers matters. And if I should dive into them all, it would be thought that I onely uttered *Satyricall Snarlings*, where my *plain meaning* is, to stirre them up to a more *serious study*, that the *silly* beginner be not frustrate of his Expectation: seeking in them (as one saith) *Sapientia*, but finding *Apedia*: therefore let me proceed towards our intended purpose.

62 *Phil.* Well; for this time let us do as you desire: What followeth next to treat of, seeing the *Inventory*, with the Dependances (which is the *first matter* whereof the Journall is made) are discussed?
Sch. The second matter whereof the *Journall* is made, is the next thing in order that we are to treat upon; and proceedeth from

TRAFFICKES CONTINUALL EXERCISE,

as in the Ninth place is rehearsed: wherein is to be considered three Principall accounts, consisting

In

In { *Proper* / *Factorage* / *Company* } Accounts: and each of these again, in { *Domestick-affaires*: for so I terme those things, which I in actuall Administration, administrate as chiefe Manager in the matter; whether in *Proper*, *Factorage*, or, *Company* accounts. / *Forraine-affaires*. for so do I nominate those matters, that another administrateth as chiefe Actor in the matter, without hand-action of me, or, mine: and thus do my——— { *Factor* / *Partner* } { With the Wares, Bills, and Monies that I send to him, to be imployed for me. } / *Friend*: unto whom I sent my Masters Wares, because they were not *Vendible* here, as in the 39. place is expressed: the said *Friend* is to be countable for the Sales thereof to me, and I to my Master, with whose order I sent them thither; he not having any acquaintance with the man, nor Trading for that place. Of these I intend to treat in *Order*, as they are entred in the above-standing Table: but first I will Book some exquisite

Rules of aide, very requisite in Trades continuance, to be learned without Book.

1. Whatsoever commeth unto us (whether Mony, or Wares) for Proper, Factorage, or Company account, the same is ——— *Debtor.*

2. Whosoever Promiseth, the Promiser is ——— *Debitor.*

3. Unto whom we pay (whether with Mony, Wares, Exchanges, Assignations) being for his own account: that man is ——— *Debitor.*

4. Unto whom we pay (as above) for another mans account:
The man for whose account we pay, is ——— *Debitor.*

5. When we buy Wares for another mans account (whether we pay them presently, or not, that is all one in the entrance) and send them unto him, or unto another by his order.
The man for whose account we bought, and sent them, is for the Wares, and Charges, ——— *Debitor.*

6. If we deliver an Assignation unto any man (whether it be our own, or anothers) that man for whose account we deliver that Assignation in payment, is ——— *Debitor.*

NOTA,

This is much like the third Article, but this is here thus entred, because this Article is here more largely explained, for the better understanding of Assignation.

7. When we, or any other man for us, sendeth commodities unto another Land, or Towne, to be sould, for *Proper* or *Company* account, then is

1. Whatsoever goeth from us (whether Mony, or Wares) for Proper, Factorage, or Company account, the same is ——— *Creditor.*

2. Unto whom we Promise, the Promised man is ——— *Creditor.*

3. Of whom we receive (whether Mony, Wares, Exchanges, Assignations) being for his own account: that man is ——— *Creditor.*

4. Of whom we receive (as above) for another mans account:
The man for whose account we receive, is ——— *Creditor.*

5 When we buy for our selves, or for another man, and pay not presently.
The man of whom we bought those Wares, is ——— *Creditor.*

6. Whosoever delivereth an Assignation unto us upon any man, for his own account: the man of whom we received it, is *Creditor.*

OR,

Upon whom I deliver mine Assignation, to be paid by him for his own account, that man is ——— *Creditor*

OR,

Whosoever (to pleasure, or accommodate me) payeth my Assignation, the accommodating man, is ——— *Creditor.*

7. When we receive advice from our Factor, that those sent commodities, or part of them are sould, or lost then is

D2 Voyage

Voyage to ſuch a place conſigned to ſuch a man——————————*Debitor.*	Voyage to ſuch a place conſigned to ſuch a man——————————*Creditor.*
8 When we pay Cuſtome, Inſurance, or other charges, upon the ſending of thoſe commodities, then is Voyage (as above)——————*Debitor.*	8. Caſh, or charges of Merchandizing is *Creditor. Nota,* divers Merchants keep ſuch an account of charges of Merchandizing, eſpecially thoſe that have Caſhiers within their own houſe.
9. When we cauſe the ſent goods to be inſured, but pay it not preſently, then is Voyage (as above)——————*Debitor.*	9. The Inſurer is——————*Creditor.*
10 When we enſure any mans ſent Wares, and receive the mony preſently, then is Caſh——————————*Debitor.*	10. Inſurance-reckoning, Or Profit, and Loſſe.— } is *Creditor.* Chuſe of theſe which you pleaſe.
11. When we Inſure any mans ſent Wares, and receive not the mony preſently, then is the man, for whoſe account we Inſured thoſe Wares,——————*Debitor.*	11 As above——————————*Creditor.* *Nota,* Merchants that trade much in this kinde, uſe an account in their Books, called *Inſurance-reckoning.*
12. When we receive advice, that the former ſent Wares, or part of them are ſold, then is The Factor that ſold them for our account——————————*Debitor.*	12. When we receive *Returnes,* either in Mony or Wares, in lieu of thoſe ſould Wares, then is The Factor that payeth us, or cauſeth us to be paid,——————————*Creditor.*
13. If any man draw Exchanges upon us for himſelf, or for any other man, the man for whoſe account the ſame was drawn, is——————————*Debitor.*	13. If we draw Exchanges upon any man for himſelf, or for any other man, the man for whoſe account we draw, the ſame is——————————*Creditor.*
14. If we remit Exchanges unto any man, for himſelf, for me, or any other man: The Factor, *If for me,* or the man for whoſe account it was remitted, is——*Debitor.*	14. If any man remitteth Exchanges unto us for himſelf, for me, or for another man; The Factor, if for me, or the man for whoſe account the ſame was remitted to me is——————————*Creditor.*
15. When we loſe by gratuities given, whether great, or ſmall, or howſoever, then is Profit and Loſſe——————*Debitor.*	15. When we gain by gratuities received, whether great, or ſmall, or howſoever, then is Profit, and Loſſe——*Creditor.*

63 *Phil.* Having thus placed your *Rules of aide,* proceed (as was determined) to the firſt of your before-mentioned Principall accounts.

Sch. The firſt nominated Principall account (for plain apprehenſions ſake) I will *diſplay* under the form of account.

Proper,

Proper, in
- *Domestick-affaires*, whose parts may be
  - *Buying*, upon severall conditions. See the *64*. place.
  - *Shipping of Wares* to another Towne, or Land, to be sould for my account: See the 85. place.
  - *Selling* upon severall conditions. See the 92. place.
  - *Abatements* upon
    - *Wares*: See the 103. place.
    - *Mony*: See the 109. place.
  - *Receiving*: See the 108. place, having 12. branches.
  - *Gratuity*: See the 110. place.
  - *Paying*: See the 111. place.
- *Forrain-affaires*, consisting in
  - *Advice*, that the sent goods, or, part of them are
    - Sould: See the 113. place.
    - Lost: See the 117. place.
  - *Returnes* in
    - *Wares*: See the 119. place.
    - *Mony*. See the 121. place.

64 *Phil.* The Table being entred in briefe as above, requireth an explaining; therefore let me see your Entrances upon each member apart.

Sch. The parts being divided into Affaires *Domestick*, and *Forraine*, I intend to treat first of the first; and therein again of the branches orderly as they follow, whose beginning is with

BUYING.

65 *Phil.* I *buy* Wheat, and pay for the same presently, even upon the receit thereof: How shall I enter that?

Sch. Wheat Debitor to Cash. *Nota*, Some will, that of the like Passages should be made a double Entrance, because upon all Occasions the mans name might be found upon the Alphabet: each do his pleasure; I account this way clear, and evident. For afterward if any controversie should arise, that Book (from whence the Question ariseth) will shew the Year, and Moneth; then is it upon my Book easie to be found. *Nota*, All accounts of *Commodities* must have lines *within*, to keep the quantity of *Ells*, *Measure*, *Weight*, and the like.

66 *Phil* I Buy Rye Contant, but pay not instantly.

Sch Rye Debitor to the *Man* of whom I bought it. *Nota*, the word *Contant* signifieth, *upon Demand*; and that again, for 1 2.3. daies, or 1 2 or three weeks: generally, it is included under one moneths time; for that which is contained under the *nomination of moneths*, is 1.2 3. or more moneths.

67 *Phil.* I buy upon two moneths time a little parcell of Pepper, Ginger, Cloves, or the like; some one parcell to the value of 10 l. and some lesse.

Sch. Groceries, Debitor to the *Man* of whom I bought them · understand my meaning, which is not, that I should make the Commodity Debitor to the *Mans servant*, because I bought it of him; but unto the Principall, or Man, *to whom it belongeth*, in respect of my knowledge. *Nota*, the Entrance of that which I buy, upon 2. Daies, 2 Moneths, 2 Years, is all as one · for my acknowledged man must be known upon my Books, as well for 2. Daies, as for 2. Years.

68 *Phil.* I buy Latton-wyre upon 3. moneths paying $\frac{1}{67}$, part presently.

Sch. Latton wyre Debitor to the *Man Principall*, from whence it came. And then, *Man Principall*, Debitor to Cash, for the $\frac{1}{67}$ part now paid I enter this thus in $\frac{1}{67}$ parts, because some make the Bought Wares Debitor to the Selling man, for the part upon Time: and Wares Debitor to Cash, for the part paid. Here you see Wares are divided into two parts, (which is unseemly) and therefore must have two Journall parcells so there is every way as much writing, as to make the Wares Debitor to the man for the whole; and then, him Debitor to Cash for the paid part. But if I buy severall Wares to pay $\frac{1}{6}$, part in money, what brave divisions would then arise? For each parcell must have two Debitors, and Creditors,

Creditors, which will be no small trouble; or else they must learn to place their parcels with more judgment.

69 *Phil* I buy Cloth upon 9. moneths Time, which is to ride out ;, then to discount for 6. moneths · paying for them in Banck, and *enjoy* Banck-monies allowance in hand.

Sch. Cloth Debitor to the *Man*, for the whole cost upon 9. Moneths : *and then*, the Man Debitor to Cloth for the Discount; *and then*, the Man Debitor to Banck for the summe writ in *and then*, Cash Debitor to Profit and Losse; because the mony by me written in Banck, and the Discount, counter-vailed the first Principall upon 9 moneths.

70 *Phil* I buy Barly upon 8. moneths time, discounting instantly; paying part in Mony, part by Assignement, part with Rye the remainer in Banck, *abating* so much as the Banck-monies allowance is worth.

Sch. Barly Debitor to the *Man*, for the whole upon 8. moneths . 2. the Man Debitor to Cash for the summe payd 3. the Man Debitor unto him, who was to pay my Assignation for his own account 4. The Man Debitor to Rye, for the delivered value: 5. The Man Debitor to Banck for the summe made good, either upon his account, or, upon the account of another, by his order. 6. The Man Debitor to Profit, and Losse, for Banck-monies allowance; because this, and the Banck-mony, make both but one compleat part of payment · but if I had writ in Banck his compleat part of payment, and he made good the mony for Banck allowance to me, by paying it in hand; then must we enter, Cash Debitor to Profit, and Losse . 7. The Man Debitor to Barly for the 8. moneths discount. *Nota, Henry Waningben, Chapter* 2. *Question* 14 entereth the Man Debitor to Profit, and Losse, for the discount. *Passcher Goossens*, zu Hamburgh, printed 1594. *parcell* 44. 47. and others, entreth the like. *Johannes Buingha, folio* 39. *Question* 7. entreth the like. *J. Carpenter, fol.* 34. his Booking is with *Henry Waninghen* the 14. *parcell* alike; and .. -nely an Imitator. and so of other Authors. But *premeditation* sheweth, that the *Rebates* of commodities should *not be* carried unto Profit, and Losse, as our printed Authors in generall do, without any further in-sight into the nature of the matter · For *Barly*, which before was *Barly* upon *Time*, is now become *Barly* for *Ready-mony*; which at the buying (in respect of the Time I was to stand out, and have the use of the mony in *mine own* hands) cost me *more* then it now will yeld me *Ready mony*; the while then *Barly* upon 8. moneths was more charged at the buying, then it now is worth *Contant*, reason requireth that *Barly* should be *discharged*, because I have disbursed my mony. *See Ralph Handson upon Abatements in his Table.*

This must be well regarded in *Rebates*, to the end, that each *Horse* may bear his own Burthen; well *noting*, that the *Rebates* are not made good in *mony* · *See Ralph Handson.*

☞ But if we buy sundry commodities, and have an allowance upon the whole buying, then must we enter,

The man of whom I bought, Debitor to Profit, and Losse Proper: for *no one* commodity may *enjoy the allowance* made upon the whole Cargo, or Parcell, and to make a division *pro rato*, of each commodities Capitall, would be a troublesome (but true) worke: therefore Profit and Losse is the briefest carriage in such matters, being the *Facit* after either of the wayes, redoundeth unto our finall advance for the Abatement. This in briefe.

Buying { For Ready-mony, and presently pay: See the 65. place.
Upon time, the conditions being severall: See 66, 67, 68, 69, 70.

BARTER, OR TRUCKE.

71 *Phil.* I buy Wares, for other Wares; value being equall.

Sch In bought Wares (what name soever) Debitor to the Deliverd Wares: this is seldome seen. ☞ But if writing be not tedious unto us, or we not paper-penurious, the best, and most uniforme Booking (in respect of the generall varieties) of giving, or receiving of diversities (being Wares, and Mony, or severall Wares) is to have the received Wares Debitor to the Trucking Man, and then, the Trucking Man Debitor to the Delivered Wares.

Phil.

72 *Phil.* You have related your minde in things of an Equall value; but if I buy Wares paying with *other* Wares and Mony.

Sch. Henry Waninghen, Chapter 2. unto the 6. *Question*, answereth in Dutch; 'T goet datmen koopt Debitaen Cassa, Daernaer, Cassa Debitaen't goet datmen toeghæft, *I English it:* The Wares that we buy, Debitor to Cash; *afterwards*, Cash Debitor to the Wares that we deliver: *as thus*, The Wares that I buy are worth 100. l. and the Wares that I deliver are worth 90. l. Consequently, *I paying the Man*, he must have 90. l. in Wares, and 10. l. in *Mony*; so that *Cash* is for the 10. l. paid, more *Credit* then *Debit*; therefore Cash hath its due. With *Henry Waninghen* agreeth *J. Carpenter, fol.* 2. *parcell* 8. as bove; he writeth, the goods bought, owe unto Cash for the whole summe: *and after*, Cash oweth unto the goods, which you have delivered to the Seller, for the value of them.

73 *Phil.* Seeing you *Imitate* in entring of their words; have they your *Approbation*?

Sch. I have related their words, not as an *affectionate-Follower*, but as an *Admirer* of their *Imitation*. For as in the 17. and 51. place by this ☞ is said; Cash may not be *named* (no not *Named*) but where *Mony* is either *Really paid*, or *received*: *Nota*, and the while that it is absolutely false, that Cash hath in the above-mentioned 72. place not *paid* out 100. l. but onely 10. l. nor hath it *received* any peny of the 90. l. therefore for the 90. l. on each side, I say *Cash* is an *Asse*.

74 *Phil.* But in the conclusion, it cometh all to one purpose.

Sch. That is not meteriall: why many words, when few may suffice? For *J. Carpenter fol* 32. *parcell* 7. answereth *direct* to the number; *The goods which you buy, owe to the Seller:* And contrarily, *He oweth to Cash, and to the goods which you have delivered him.* This is somewhat like a mans mony: But as in the 71. place is said; Idlenesse in writing, or Penuriousnesse in paper, is the cause of these *Folly entrances*. For not onely in this, but in Exchanges, and the like, because we will not have (as some terme it) *a Book full of names*, we must have our passages smothered under the covert of *Imaginary obscurity*; whereas we may have them delectably Booked, if we were not sparing in writing. Daer en is niet, sonder becomst, *Nothing without trouble.* But I have no time to discusse other mens works; therefore let me proceed.

75 *Phil.* I buy Wares, delivering a great value; and receiving the *Over-plus* back in Mony

Sch. In-bought Wares Debitor to the Selling Man, for their value; 2. The Man Debitor to Delivered Wares, for their value 3. Cash Debitor to the Man, for the Received mony, to equall the Truck. So, in brief; if the Wares are of an equall value, *then enter* Bought Wares, Debitor to the Trading man 2 Trading Man Debitor to Delivered Wares; because the value is equall. If un-equall, and Mony given; *then enter*, In-bought Wares Debitor to the Trading Man: *and then*, Trading Man Debitor to Delivered Wares, and to Cash. But if un-equall, and Mony *Received*; In-bought Wares, and Cash, Debitor to the Trading Man: *and then*, Trading Man Debitor to *Delivered* Wares. And so I proceed to Wares bought, which are to be

Delivered mee, 2. 3. Weekes, or Moneths after *the agreement.*

76 *Phil.* I buy Wares, agreeing now for Quantity, and Price; but am to receive them 2. moneths hence

Sch. The *Promising Man* is Debitor to *Promise-reckoning*.

77 *Phil.* I have already by this one parcell conceived, that you digresse from divers Printed Authors: for,

Passchier Goessens of Brussel, in the German Language.
Pieter Nicolaeson Daventriensis.
John Willemson of Leuven.

John

Transporting of Accounts in the Leager from one Leafe *unto* another.

207 *Phil.* What are the *Motives* ?

Sch. They may be *two*, the one, when the *Leaves* of the Leager are full written in the Debitor, or Creditor side, or both. The other, because the *former* accounts are concluded, so that upon foot of that account, generally there remaineth a remainer due to me, or from me; and we will have the account begunne again upon a *New* Leafe.

208 *Phil* Is this all ?

Sch. Herein again is to be observed, whether those accounts that are to be Transported, be *Commodities-accounts*, which in *New* leaves are to be continued as upon the former. *or*, whether they are *Ships-parts*, Houses, Rents, Lands, Interests, Insurances, *Factor-accounts*, or the like: of which (for that time) we make no *estimation of Estate*, but onely a transport for Tradings further continuance, untill a Generall Ballance be made

209 *Phil.* How must Commodities-reckonings fitly be transported, to make *true Journal* parcells of them ?

Sch In all transports (if possible) must heedfully be heeded, that not any parcell be posted with *Blinde-summes*, or Blancks, *as some tearme them* · that is, *Not without Mony-summes.* Many in their Books transport with *Blankes* in their Leager, yet have Mony to transport, if they had *Art* to carry them *handsomely* forwards; to which end observe the ensuing Documents.

Suppose the *Wares* were Cambrix-cloth, and the whole *Debitor-side* contained 400. Peeces, which cost 765.l'.8 s. and that the whole sale in the *Creditor-side* were 278. Peeces; producing in mony 789.l'.10.s *Nota,* these cannot be substracted from each other to make Journall parcells, but in the one will be Wares without Mony; and in the other Mony without Wares. which kind of Transports are very absurd, though used by many.

Their *forme is as this Instance.*

	Debitor		L				*Creditor.*				
2	June, cost of Peeces. 400.	7	765	8	—	3	July, sales of Peeces. 278.	—	789	10	—
7	August, carried to new account.————	9	.24	2	—	7	August, carried to new account ———— 122	.9	—	—	—
	Peeces 400. 789.l'. 10.						Peeces 400. 789. l'. 10.				

To avoid the above-entred absurdity of *Wares* in one Journall parcell, but *no Mony*; and *Mony* in the other Journall parcell, but *no Wares* · enter as the ensuing Journall instance instanceth.

Cambrix-cloth upon *folio* 30. Debitor to Cambrix-cloth upon *folio* 12. 765. l'. 8. s. for the present costs of 400. Peeces, being the whole Debitor-side, in Wares, and Mony for want of place transported to a new leafe, the mony is 765.l'.8.s.

And then

Cambrix cloth upon *folio* 12 Debitor to Cambrix-cloth upon *folio* 30. 789. l'. 10. s. for the sales of 278. Peeces, being the whole Creditor-side, in Wares, and Mony, transported for want of place to a new leafe, the mony being———————789.l'.10.s.

Thus ought each Journall parcell in Wares transporting truly to be Journalized, then the Leager will stand as this ensuing instance instanceth.

Fol. 12.

	Fol.12. *Debitor.*	£				*12. Creditor.*	£		
2	June, costs of Peeces. 400	7765	8	—	3	July, sales of Peeces 278.	—789	10	—
7	August, carried to new account Peeces,————278	30789	10	—	7	August, carried to new account.————400	30765	8	—
	Peeces 678. 1554. l. 18. s.					Peeces. 678. 1554. l. 18 s.			

And folio 30. will stand

7. Aug. costs of Peeces 400. 765. l. 8 s   7. Aug. sales of Peeces 278. 789 l. 10 s.

Here you see the Leager stand again as formerly it did, to be continued in writing, as before: here you see each Journall parcell compleately carried. and thus ought Factor-accounts to be crossed: Forrain-mony, under Forrain-mony, as here Peeces under Peeces: and Inlandish-mony under Inlandish-mony, as before is instanced. *Nota*, Do the like in Houses, Lands, Rents, Legacies, Interests, Ships-parts, Insurances, and the like · because the principall (by Deduction) should not be Diminished untill the finall finishing of those accounts.

210 *Phil.* Is this an usuall course in the transporting of all kinds of accounts?
Sch. No: In your Generall accounts with Common-trading-people, as also in *Cash*, Bank, Stock, Profit and Losse, *or the like*: deduct the *Lesser* from the *Greater*, and make a Journall parcell for the *difference*, as thus:

If the *Debitor-side* of any of the above-named accounts (which are to be transported) be heaviest, then for the *difference* make the

New account Debitor to the old

If the *Creditor-side* be heaviest, then for the *difference* of any of those accounts, make the

old account Debitor to the New.

211 *Phil.* What Observations arise from hence?
Sch. Hence is it manifest, that in the Leager ought to be neither *Debitor*, nor *Creditor*, but such as have their

Originall from the Journall,

whose proper Office it is, to explain why the *one man*, or *thing* is Indebted unto the other, as hereafter in the Explication of the Journall Office shall appear in the 244. place: and so I end with the *Third Ground matter*, of which the Journall is made.

212 *Phil.* Explicate the *fourth Ground-matter*, of which the Journall is made.
Sch. The *fourth Member* of the 9. place, saith, that it proceedeth from the

Equalizing, or, even-making of over, or, under-measures,
Weight, Leackage, Pounds, Ells,
or the like.

213 *Phil.* Instance some matters in *Proper-accounts.*
Sch. When we find any *under-measure* in Corn, or *Leakage* in Wine, or *Shortnesse* in Length. *then enter*, Profit and Losse Debitor to the *wanting-matter*; rating it as you please: for that rating neither augmenteth, nor diminisheth your Estate; but is onely done for decentnesse, to have mony in the Debit, and Credit of such Journall parcell.

Phil.

214 *Phil.* Rehearse some instances in *Factorage* accounts.

Sch. If in weight I find in any commodity lesse by sales, because of drines, or the like; *enter, John Knoll* his account Curiant, Debitor to *John Knoll* his account of Saffron; rating them as before, to bring them into the *true* form of *Debitor* and *Creditor*, in Journall and Leager. Hence may easily be gathered how to deal in Company-accounts; which I now passe, and so proceed to the next matter in order.

215 *Phil.* Whence ariseth the *Fift Ground-matter*, that maketh a Member of the Journall?

Sch. In the 9 place it is said to arise from the

Leagers-Conclusion, or Ballancing of the Leager.

216 *Phil* What Causes may move a man to a Generall Ballance?

Sch. The same may be either of these three

1. When the Journall, and Leager are full written; so that there must be New-Books — Then is a Ballance requisite
2. When a Merchant ceaseth from Trading — Then is a Ballance requisite
3. When the book-Owner departeth this world. — Then is a Ballance requisite

217 *Phil* What understand you by the word *Ballance*?

Sch. By *Ballance* I understand, *An Equall-making in Equivalent manner all the Open-standing Leager-accounts*; transporting all those Open-standing Leager differences under One last framed accounts Title, whose name Generally we call *Ballance*: for being that that account *includeth* all the Leagers remaining differences; so it *concludeth* with *One* solely it self. *Nota*, the word *Ballance* seemeth to be borrowed from a pair of Scales: for as true Scales ought neither to be heavier then other; so a true taked Generall Ballance ought not to differ the least naming value: for the Generall Debitor and Creditor must justly counter-poize each other in even-monies nomination; *else*, the Book is out of square; the summes ill taken, or amisse added. In place of the word *Ballance*, I should rather enter *Estate reckoning*: for by drawing the whole Book to a head, I draw with *One* an account of my *Estate* Simon Stevin in his *Princely Book-keeping*, carrieth the *Leagers* difference at the Years end, unto the *first begun* Stock when he *began* his Books: but he contradicteth himself. For he began well the *First* day of January, in making all that owed to him *Debitors* to Stock; and Stock *Debitor* to them who were *Debt-demanders*: but at his Leagers *concluding*, the 31 of December, he entreth Stock *Debitor* to his *Debitors*; and he entreth his *Debt demanders*, as *Augmentors* of his Stock. Such entrances made by him are but a *mistake onely*; in me they were *meer* Absurdities.

Ballance is either a *Triall*, or *True-ballance*.

Of the Tryall ballance.

218 *Phil.* Relate the *manner* of making a Tryall-ballance.

Sch. Add the Debitor summes of all the Leager *Un-equall-open-standing-accounts* upon a Paper together, or in a Book thereto prepared: *then*, add all the Creditor parcels in the whole Leager together by themselves; because the *Uniformity* of the *Generall Additions* should be manifested; if they be to each other *equivalent*, then (if no whole parcell be left out) are the Journall *mony parcells* truely transported into the Leager.

219 *Phil.* What more is to be said of the Tryall-ballance.

Sch. The *Tryall-ballanse* is of *two* sorts The first is a Survay (as above) of the Leager accounts,

accounts, so soon as all the parcells are transported out of the *Waste-book* into the Journall, and from thence into the Leager *Nota*, before any *unsold wares*, or *Gain*, and *Losse* of any accounts be medled with. Of such matter is the first ballance of the *three-fold-mony-ballance* in my Great Waste-Book, printed 1621. at Amsterdam in English, and Dutch; and shall be in this Book.

220 *Phil.* Instance the second sort.

Sch. The second sort of the *Tryall-ballance* is seen, when all *unsould Wares*, and *Out-landish monies* are rated all *Abatements*, as likewise *Gaines* or *Losses* are known. Of such matter is the second *Three-double-mony-ballance* in my Great Waste-Book; and shall be in this. In this *second* ballance is also comprised the parcells appertaining to the *true* ballance· *else*, that second ballance could not be even weighty.

Of the True-ballance.

221 *Phil.* Proceed to the same.

Sch. The *true-ballance* ariseth from the *Remainers* of Leager accounts; as well in *Mony*, Unsold Wares, *Voyages* not wholly sold, *Houses*, *Lands*, *People*, *&c.* not yet compleatly perfected· and are therefore transported to the New-Books, to be there fully finished: Leaving the *Old Books* to their perpetuall rest, except some *Scrupulous* matter molest them. Of such matter is the *Third* ballance of the *Three-double-mony-ballance* in my Great Waste-Book, and shall be in this.

Observations in ballancing of the Leager.

But for a preparative, first *note*, that *even* as the Monies, Wares, Voyages, Houses, Lands, and people were in their accounts (whether Debitors, or Creditors) even so must they stand in your Ballance:, and so of each other matter. Reason, for Ballance representeth in that onely account, all that the other represent through the whole Book: for if they were Debitors, Ballance is a Debitor in their place: if they were Creditors, Ballance is likewise a Creditor.

222 *Phil.* Go forwards in this matter.

Sch. There ought to be observed *A Decent Order* in Leagers ballancing*: that is,* Which account ought *first* to be concluded, and which last; both in *Debitor* and *Creditor* side. this is not of Necessity, but for Decentnesse in Order.

223 *Phil.* Prosecute your opinion in the Order.

Sch. First, ballance the accounts of the People of whom you bought: or to whom you sould. *Reason*: because all Discounts, Abatements, Mis-castings, or Omissions that have happened, may be rectified to the end each account may bear its own burthen. take then the difference of each mans account (being found to agree) and enter them into your Ballance-Book (as in the 218. place is mentioned) untill the finall Ballance be found even-weighty.

224 *Phil.* Which next?

Sch. Secondly, ballance the Peoples accounts with whom you had to deal for Exchanges, Assignations, or the like entring the differences into your Ballance Book thereunto prepared,

225 *Phil.* What followeth:

Sch. Thirdly, ballance your *Factors* accounts· first for *Proper*, and then for *Company*, (but there is no necessity in this Order, as it said) the Remainers being well found, your Gain,

4. VOYAGE.

Debitor.	*Creditor.*
For 100. Pieces of Cambrix shipt at 3. l. each Piece, is——300.l.——	For Sales of 80. Pieces, at 2. l 16, s. is ——————— 224. l.———
	Unsold, 20. Pieces, at 3. l. *per* Piece,———————60. l.———
	Lost by Sales,——————16. l.———
	Summe—300. l ———

235 *Phil.* Go forward in the order of your Leagers Ballancing.
Sch. Fifthly, ballance your *Commodities-accounts*; first for *Proper*: then, for *Company.*

236 *Phil.* Suppose them all sold; and there is Gaines
Sch The first Voyage is a President.

237 *Phil.* Suppose your Commodities to be sold in part.
Sch. The second Voyage is an Instance.

238 *Phil.* Suppose that none of your Commodities are sold.
Sch. The third Voyage sheweth the form.

239 *Phil.* Suppose losse upon the Sale of part of your Commodities, or upon the whole.
Sch If losse upon part Sales, the Fourth Voyage is an Instance: If losse upon the Sale of a whole parcell: See

THE FORME.

Debitor	*Creditor.*
For 16. Butts of Sack cost with charges. ———————134. l. 8.	For Sale of 16. Butts, at 8. l 6. is ————————132 l 16,
	Lost by the Sale—————1. l 12.
	Summe 134. l. 8.

Under the name of *Commodities* in the second branch of the 10. place, is included *Houses, Lands, Ships-parts*; upon which if you will see the yearly Gain, or Losse, *then* rate them as they cost; entring them in Credit as in the second Voyage: *then*, in your House, and Land will appear what is gained by the Rents, above reparation, and maintaining of them; and in your Ships parts will be made plain what is advanced by their Voyages, more then her victualling carrying your Proper Gains or Loss, to Profit and Loss proper; and Companies Gain, or Loss, to Profit and Loss in Company. But if you will let them run on untill the finall ending of them; then *cross* them, as is shewed in the second Instance of Cambrix-cloth, in the 209 place.

240 *Phil* What followeth next in the Ballance order?
Sch. Sixthly, ballance your Company Profit and Loss, imparting to each Partner his due upon fit account: and your part upon Profit and Loss proper.

Seventhly, ballance your Partners account, transporting the difference unto your Ballance book (as in the 218. place is mentioned) untill the finall ballance be found Eavenweighty

Eighthly, ballance Cash, and Bank, carrying their differences to your Ballance-book.

Ninthly, conclude your Profit and Loss proper, carrying the difference to your Stock-account.

Tenthly, conclude your Stock-account, transporting that difference (which is the summe

summe of your Estate) unto your Ballance-book. then ought your Ballance accodnt to be equall-weighty.

NOTA,

Having drawn all your Leager to a head in your Ballance-Book, and found it to b eright taken · then may you take your Journall in hand, and post them as they in order follow upon your Ballance-book, unto your Ballance-account in the Leager.

Or if you will not make a Ballance-account in your Leager, you may let your Ballance-book be your private contentment; and transport each Ballance-parcell out of the Old Leager into the New · avoiding your Ballance-writing into the Journall, both at the End of the Old Leager, or beginning of the New · entring into the Old Leager the *folio* whither carried into the New; and in the New Leager the *leaf* from whence that remainer is brought out of the Old Leager; and so avoid (perhaps) the writing of two or three hundred Journall-parcels in both Leagers.

Particular Observations upon each side of the true-ballance in Debit, and Credit, for the Memories refreshing.

241 *Phil.* Rehearse first the Observations that arise upon the *Debitor-side* of the *True-ballance.*

Sch. In a much-Trafficking Merchants-Books are five things to be regarded:

Firstly, of *Debitors*, and them in
- *People*—unto whom we sold, or that have promised us payment of Exchanges, or Assignations, and the like.
- *Partners*—unto whom we have delivered Mony or Wares, to be by them imployed for the Companies good.
- *Factors*—that serve us in Commission,—
- *Masters*—whom we serve in Commission,——————

who as yet have not given us full satisfaction: Again, the first of these two may arise from Proper, Factorage, or Company-accounts.

Secondly, of the Unsold Wares, formerly shipt to another Town, or Land, there to be sold for *Proper*, *Factorage*, or *Company-account*

Thirdly, of Matters as yet remaining *Unsold* under our own Administration · consisting again in *Wares*, *Houses*, *Lands*, *Jewels*, *Ships-parts*, and the like whereof some of those *Wares* may be for *Proper*, *Factorage*, or *Company-accounts* · and those *Ships parts* for Proper, or Company-accounts.

Fourthly, of the *Ready-mony* in Cash, in Bank, or in both.

Lastly, of Company Gain, and Losse; of the which we still keep an open-standing-account, because the Company continueth in Trading, upon unchangeable terms. And these in substance are all that concern the Contents of Ballances-Debitor-side

242 *Phil.* Proceed to the observations in the Creditor-side of the *True ballance.*

Sch. Four things are heedfully to be regarded

Firstly, *Debt-demanders*; and them in
- *People*—of whom we bought, as also, whose Exchanges we accepted; or whose Assignments we promised unto their Creditor, having entred their Creditor into my book in place of them.
- *Partners*—of whom we have received Mony, or Wares, to imploy for Company-account,
- *Masters*-whom we serve in Commission,——————
- *Factors*-that serve us in Commission,

unto whom (as yet) we have not given full content: The last of these may arise, either from *Proper*, *Factorage*, or *Company-accounts.*

H 2 *secondly,*

Secondly, Unsold-*Wares*, *Houses*, *Lands*, *Jewels*, *Rents*, *Voyages*, and the like upon which accounts the Gains or Loss (at present) is not desired to be known; but are deferred untill the finall finishing of that account, then to know the Generall *Gain*, or *Loss* upon the same and these for *Proper*, some for *Factorage*, and some for *Company-accounts*

Thirdly, in Companies Profit and Loss Reckonings, because the division is not made in these Old-books, but prosecuted untill the Companies finall finishing.

Lastly, in *Stock account*, whose difference must be carried to *Ballance*; for that difference must make your Ballance-account *Eaven weighty* in the *Generall* Addition · *Nota*, for in it is contained the *true* difference between the *Ready mony*, *Wares*, *Houses*, &c. *Debitors* in your Ballance debit-side, and the *Debt-demanders* in the Creditor side of your Ballance-account. Or more plain; take the whole Debit-side of your *Ballance*, deduct from that all that you owe: and the differing mony will be *Equall-weighty*, with the difference brought from your *Stock account*. And thus much of the *fifth matter*, of which the Journal is made.

Of the Journalls Form.

243 *Phil.* This is the *second branch* in the Eight place: of which let me heare your Explication.

Sch The *Form* is generally in folio, or the full bigness of the Paper, be it small, or large: Ruled towards the *left-hand* with *one line*, and towards the *right-hand* with *three* entring between them l. s. d. as in the Waste book is, and in the Journals Instances sha'l be made plain.

Some use two lines towards the *left-hand*, as doth Simon Stevin in his *Princely-book-keeping Journall* use three entring therein the *Day*, and *Moneth* · but that maketh the Journall between line, and line, too narrow. My manner of my *day*, and *Moneths* entrances shall be shewed in the Explication of the Journals Office.

This Book is by *some* numbred on each leaves-side: the beginning-side with 1. the second with 2. and so through all the Book · of which I approve, and use it. For in a Great-trafficking book (as an *East*, *West*, *Turky*, or the like Company) severall sides are oftimes filled in one day so that the Margin of the Leager quoteth *directly* to the side of that Journall-leaf, where the desired parcell is: and so avoideth the perusall of needlesse sides.

Of the Journalls Office.

244 *Phil.* Let me know that: for that is the third *Notable* matter mentioned in the Eighth place

Sch. The Journalls *Proper Office* is, to have the *Matter* (thereunto appertaining) entred in *Book-keepings true method*, with *words* suitable to the *Action*; plainly expressing what ever was obscurely booked in other books.

Book-keepings Office is, to book the acted matter in the true *Nomination* of *Debitor* and *Creditor*, with the *brief* (yet plain) Circumstances of the Action. Heedfully in this Journall must be observed, that the *Debitor*, that is, the *Man*, or *Thing*, that ought to be *charged*, be first named, and placed towards the *left hand*, as thus ·

James Mirth is Debitor.

Then enter the Creditor, Man, or Thing, that ought to be discharged, as thus

James Mirth is Debitor to *John Melody*.

Unto them annex the quantity of Mony, as thus:

James Mirth is Debitor to *John Melody* 300.l.12.s.8.d.

There-unto adde the reason why the One Man, or Thing is indebted to the other: and this is gathered from the acted matter.

245 *Phil.* As how ·

Sch. Compare the Wastebook parcels in the 6. place, with the ensuing Journall parcels framed out of them, and the *Reasons* may appear by the Circumstances.

Anno

		li	s	d
$\frac{5}{6}$	*Dito* is Debitor to Bank 369. l. 13. 10. $\frac{1}{2}$ d. written by his order upon the account of *John Johnson Vinck*, being the full of the before-mentioned exchange, the summe written in, is	369	13	10 $\frac{1}{2}$
$\frac{5}{3}$	*Dito* is Debitor to Profit and Loss 3. l. 14. 8. d. for Bank-mony of gl. 2240. 11. 4. pen. at one *per centum*, is	.3	14	.8
$\frac{6}{5}$	*Edward Denis* of Northampton, *his* account by me in Company, is Debitor to Dito *Edward his* account of *Ready-mony*, 213. l. — 5 $\frac{5}{8}$ d. for his $\frac{1}{3}$ of gl. 3834. 8. 12 pen. product of 18. Last, 7. Mudde of Company Rye, sold to *Iacob Johnson*, as above; $\frac{1}{3}$ thereof is	213	—	.5

246 *Phil.* What signifie those Fractions $\frac{1}{2}$ $\frac{2}{3}$, and the like, in the Margine?

Sch. Fractions they are none but signifying-figures concerning the Leager: for the Figures above the stroke, shew upon what Leager-Leafe the Debitors are to be found; and the Figures under the stroke, point unto the Creditors in the said Leager.

247 *Phil.* Why are some pointed, and not other some?

Sch. Those that are pointed, are transported into the Leager, the other not.

248 *Phil.* Some do not point at all.

Sch. They are subject to mistake, or they must enter each figure above, and under, when they have entred the parcell into their Leager, and that is tedious. The points are very requisite to avoid Omissions, or not to charge one summe twice, if a man should be called from his posting.

249 *Phil.* When do you enter the figures above, or under the stroke?

Sch. I lay the Journall open before me, making first the straight strokes that are between the figures against each parcell, on both sides of the Journall: then do I enter the folio, or leaves, or those figures, before I touch the Leager.

250 *Phil.* How then?

Sch. Then setting my Journall before me, I transport all the *Debitors* and *Creditors* (that correspond upon one Leager-leafe) one after another into the Leager; then *removing* my hand from the Leager, immediately I set point by that Debitor, or Creditor, that is posted into the Leager, without removing of my Journall.

Thus much in brief of the Matter, Form, and Office of the Journall mentioned in the ninth place.

sent payment for Company-use, being—— —— — 146 | 11 | —

117. *Thomas Trust* at Antwerp for company of *Randoll Rice* ½, and ½ for me, our account of Time, debitor to Voyage to Antwerp, consigned to dito *Thomas* for our company ½, and ½ li. 1515. 7. s. for

12. | the ensuing Wares sold by him. the particulars are, *viz.*

10. | 8. Bales of Pepper, producing clear Ready-mony, as by the account —— —— ——gl. 2753.9.4.

30. Butts of Serresé to *Iaques Gerritsm*; part at 2. moneths, producing (whereof ½ is received) as by the account, clear mony—— ——gl. 12400.——

gl. 15153.9.4. pen. reduced at 10. gl. or 33.s.4.d. are—— — 1515 | .7 | —

118. *Dito Thomas* for our company, as above, our account of Ready-mony, debitor to the said *Thomas* for company *R.R.* ½, and ½ me our account of Time li. 1102.—4.d. for gl. 11020.3.9. pen. by him

13 | received of the before entred mony, is here—— —— — 1102 | — | .4

10. |

The 15. *day of* June. 1634.

119. *Debitors* to *Iacob Symonson* his account of Cambrix-cloth, li.405. for 60. Pieces sold joyntly to the ensuing parties, at 6 li. 15. s. upon an equall share, at 4. moneths time, *viz.*

James Wilkinson 20. Pieces————li.135.

4 | *George Pinchback* 20. Pieces————li.135.

3. | *Andrew Hitchcock* 20. Pieces——————li.135. —— ——

11. | The Rule in the 244. place

8. | is *contra-dicted.* 405 | — | —

120. *Jacob Symonson* his account of Cambrix-cloth, debitor to

8. | Cash li.1.7.s. for Brokage of li.405. at ⅓ *per centum*, is—— —— .1. | 7 | —

1. | 121. *Dito* to Profit and Loss li.8.12 s. for the ensuing particulars, *viz.*

For Ware-house-room at 2.d. *per* Piece li.—10.
For Provision of Sales at 2. *per* C.———li.8.2.

7. | —— .8 | 12 | —

122. *Dito* to *Jacob Symonson* his account Currant li. 390.14.s. for the neat proceed made good there, without my prejudice of debts,

2. | yet standing out upon 4. moneths time: the sum now transported, is 390 | 14 | —

123. *Jean du Boys* for company *Randell Rice* ½, and ½ for me, our account Currant, debitor to *Thomas Trust* for dito company ½, and ½ our account of Ready-mony li.1092.17.10.d. for gl. 11020. re-

6. | mitted in his own Bills, dated their 2. present. payable by, and un-

13. | to himself, exchange at 121.d. are ₘᵥ 3642. 58.6.d. and here at 72.d.—— —— —— —— — 1092 | 17 | 10

The 23. *day of June* 1624.

6. | 124. *Randoll Rice* his account Currant, debitor to *Diego*

12 | *del Varino* his account of Fruits li. 541. 4. s. 9. d. for severall

M sorts

		l.	s.	d.
6.	185. *Randoll Rice* his account by me in company debitor to Ballance l.991.7.6.d. for so much due to him upon this account——	991	.7	.6
10.	186. *Hendrick vander Linden* $\frac{1}{2}$, *John van Does* $\frac{1}{6}$, *Jaques Reinst* $\frac{1}{3}$, their account of commodities, debitor to *Ballance* l.194.12.1.d. for 160. Pieces of Figs, and 4. Bales of Pepper sold, being the whole Wares in Credit, transported thus to have the account compleat in new books, as it here standeth: the mony is—— —— ——	194	12	.1
10.	187. *Dito Company* their account of Ready-mony debitor to *Ballance* l.99.7.7.d. for conclude due to them—— —— —— ——	99	.7	.7
13. 13.	188. *Dito Company* their account of Time, debitor to *Ballance* l.93.19.8.d. due to them for conclude of this account, being——	93	19	.8
13 / 1.	189. *Ballance* debitor to Cash l.947.2.1 d. and is for so much by conclude remaining therein, and transported, being—— ——	947	2	.1
7. / 1.	190. *Profit and Loss* debitor to Stock l.1046.8.10.d. for gaines in this handle, transported to conclude this account, being—— ——	1046	.8	10
1. / 13.	191. *Stock* debitor to Ballance l.2902.12.7.d. for the difference of that account, being my present Estate; and transported thither to conclude this, being—— —— —— ——	2902	12	.7

End of the Journall

A.

1634.

OF THE LEAGER.

HAving (in form as is instanced) entred all the trading-parcels of Merchandizing into the Journall in such after-following manner as they daily happened; then hath the *Book owner* his whole Trading, with all the Circumstances in writing: but not in such sort, that he is able to confer with any man about his accounts: for each mans severall Parcels are dispersed through the whole Journall; neither doth it (in drawing an account to a Head upon a Paper) content the mind, fearing that any Parcels might be mistaken or omitted. Upon the like Reason we may conjecture the Obscurity in knowing what mony is in Cash, what weight, measure, and quantity of any Commodity might be in the Ware-house, what Profit or Losse there is upon any sort of Wares, or Matter, what Weekly, or Monethly debts are to be received, or payd for Wares, or Exchanges: and many such like.

For the avoyding of all such diffidences, the Journall Parcels must be transported into the *Leager* in such manner, that all what doth concern one mans particular, must (under one accounts Title) be gathered together, *to wit*, all his *Debit* parcels upon the Left-hand; and all his *Credit* parcels upon the Right-hand of the *Open lying Leager*; of the which many instances follow in the Leager: the like manner must be used in each sort, as *Mony, Wares, People*, or what ever else; each must be gathered together in an Exquisite form, with few words.

The thing charged, or *Debitor*, must have its discharge, or *Creditor*, even opposite against it selfe when the Leager lieth open. In this Leager, where *Fol.* standeth between the lines before the L, both upon the Right and Left hand, are many Arithmetical Characters. The Character, Characters, or Figures that stand between the two lines upon the *Debitor* side, point (as with a finger) unto the Folio where each severall lines *Creditor* standeth in the said Book, whether it be upon the same Leafe, or else where: Contrarily, the Figures that stand between the two lines upon the *Creditor*-side, point at the Folio where each severall lines *Debitor*

Debitor ſtandeth in the ſaid Book, whether upon the ſame Leafe or elſe-where.

In Brief,

The Owner, *or the* Owing thing,
Or what-ſo-ever comes to thee:
Upon the Left-hand ſee thou bring;
For there the ſame muſt placed be.

But

they unto whom thou doeſt owe,
Upon the Right let them be ſet;
Or what-ſo-ere doth from thee go,
To place them there do not forget.

THIS

Book ſheweth our *true Eſtate* in each particular account; whether Bought, Sold, Sent, or Received, Commodity: People with-in, or without the Land; Exchanges which way-ſo-ever, and the Coynes of theſe ſeverall places; *Factorage*, *Company*, or what account elſe belongeth to *Traffick*: So that the *Leager* is the *Mirrour* by which onely the Eſtate can *truly*, and *plainly* be diſcerned.

O2

	Jour.	Day		Fol	L	S	D
			Cash is Debitor.				
	1	1	Janu. To Stock, for feverall coynes of mony—— —	1	1000	15	7
	5	27	Febr. To *Iacob Symonson* his account Currant— —	2	328	10	11
1634.	9	22	April To *George Pinchback*, received in full—— —	3	9	11	2
	10	8	May To Figs $\frac{1}{3}$ *R. R.* $\frac{2}{3}$ for me—— ——	9	525	—	—
	12	22	Dito to *Iames Wilkinson*, received to clear a truck——	4	102	16	1
	14	23	June To *Diego del Varino* his account of Cash—— —	12	25	10	7
	14	—	Dito To Profit and Losse, gained by *Diego's* fruits——	7	13	4	—
	14	2	July To *George-Pincback* received by his Assignment—	3	485	6	5
	16	11	Dito To *Iacob Symonson* his account Currant— —	2	28	1	7
	16	20	Dito To *Randoll Rice* his account Currant—— —	6	284	16	8
	16	20	Dito To *Andrew Hitchcock* received in part— ——	11	100	—	—
			Summe—	L	2903	13	—

	Jour.	Day		Fol	L	S	D
			Stock is Debitor.				
1633.	1	1	Janu. To *Iacob Symonson* his account Currant— —	2	150	—	—
1634.	19	20	July To *Ballance*, for conclude carried thither—— —	13	2902	12	7
			Summe—	L	3052	12	7

	Jour.	Day		L	R	Fol	L	S	D
			Wares are Debitors.						
1633.	1	1	Janu. To Stock, resting unsold—— ——	60	90	1	477	10	—
1634.	20	20	July To Profit and Losse gained			7	92	10	—
			Summe—	60	90	L	570	—	—

	Jour.	Dy		Fol	L	s	d
			Cash is Creditor.				
	2	. 4	Janu. By *George Pinchback*, paid in part— —	3	144	-	—
	2	. 9	Dito By *James Wilkinson*, paid in part— —	4	120	—	—
	3	30	Dito By *George Pinchback*, paid him— —	3	135	16	. 8
	4	. 9	Febr. By *Iac. Symonson*. his account of Couchaneille, payd	3	. . 5	. 5	. 4
	4	21	Dito by voyage to Lisborn, consigned to *Diego del Varno* for company $\frac{1}{3}$, and $\frac{2}{3}$ paid— —	5	594	—	—
	5	13	March by Dansick-exchange for *Arthur Mump*. and me $\frac{1}{2}$	8	200	—	—
	5	—	Dito By Kersies in Company $\frac{1}{3}$ *Iacob Symonson*, $\frac{2}{3}$ for me	4	. . 2	. 8	. 6
	9	—	Dito By *Iacob Symonson* his Cambrix cloth— —	8	. . 4	. 7	—
	6	22	Dito By *Iacob Symonson* his account Currant— —	2	. 9	7	9
	6	—	Dito By Figs in company $\frac{1}{3}$ *R. R.* $\frac{2}{3}$ for me — —	9	. . 8	. 7	. 6
1634.	6	29	Dito By *Hendrick vander Linden*, and Company their account of commodities, for charges— —	10	. .	12	. 5
	7	. 7	April By Silver, for charges of 8. Barrs— —	10	. . 4	7	. 2
	10	. 8	May By *Randoll Rice* his account Currant— —	6	. 99	19	. 1
	11	13	Dito By Amsterdam-exchange $\frac{1}{2}$ for *Iacob Symonson*—	11	504	19	. 6
	12	. 7	June By *Diego del varno* his account of Cash— —	12	25	10	. 7
	12	. 7	Dito By Figs in Company $\frac{1}{3}$ *R. R.* $\frac{2}{3}$ for me— —	. 9	23	. 8	. 9
	12	. 7	Dito By *Andrew Hitchcock* paid him— —	11	. 73	16	. 8
	13	15	Dito By *Iacob Symonson* his account of Cambrix cloth--	. 8	. 1	. 7	—
	19	20	July By *Ballance*, transported thither to conclude this--	13	947	2	1
			Summe—	L	2903	13	—

	Jour.	Dy		Fol	L	s	d
			stock is Debitor.				
1633.	1	. 1	Janu. By Cash, for severall coynes of mony— —	. 1	1000	15	. 7
	1	—	Dito By Wares for sundry sorts unsold— —	1	477	10	—
	1	—	Dito By Kettles for 5. Barrels unsold— — —	2	. 55	—	. 6
	1	-	Dito By *Iean du Boys* at Roan my account Currant—	2	240	—	—
	1	—	Dito By *Iacob Symonson* my account by him in company	2	229	—	—
	1	—	Dito By *Iacob Symonson* his account of Couchaneille—	3	. . 3	17	. 8
1634	19	20	July By Profit and Losse, gained by this handle— —	7	1046	. 8	10
			Summe—	L	3052	12	. 7

	Jour.	Dy		L	l	Fol	L	s	d
			Wares are Creditors.						
	2	13	Janua. By Kersies in company, by me layd in--	. .	90	4	270	—	—
1633.	6	21	March By *Iacob Symonson*, sold to him— —	60	. .	2	300	—	—
			Summe—	60	90	L	570	—	—

		Day		Fol	li	s	d
			Profit and Losse **in company** $\frac{1}{3}$ **for** ***Randoll Rice*****, and** $\frac{2}{3}$ **for me, Debitor.**				
	3	23	Janu. To Profit and Losse for charges of a Remise——	7	2	11	11
1634.	7	29	March. To *Iean du Boys*, for his Provision, and Brokage—	6	2	11	3
	17	20	July To *Thomas Trust*, our account of Ready-mony, lost- -	13	9	2	6
	18	—	Dito To *Ran. Rice*, his account by me in comp. for $\frac{1}{3}$ gains	6	444	9	8
	18	—	Dito To Profit and Losse, for my part gains—— —	7	296	6	5
			Summe—	li	755	1	9

		Day		Fol	li	s	d
			Profit and Losse**, Debitor.**				
1633.	4	17	Febru. To *Iacob Symonson* my account of Ready-mony, for his charges, being Brokage, and Provision — —	3	—	10	1
1634.	17	20	July To *Iac. Symonson* my account of Ready-mony, lost-	3	25	—	11
	17	20	Dito To Silver, lost by the sale of 8. Barres.————	10	3	9	1
	19	20	Dito To Stock, gained by this handle.————-	1	1046	8	10
			Summe—	li	1075	8	11

		Day		Fol	li	s	d
			Ballance**, Debitor.**				
1634.	18	20	July To *Jacob Symonson* my account by him in company	2	301	—	8
	18	20	Dito To *Jean du Boys*, for company *R.R.* $\frac{1}{3}$, me $\frac{2}{3}$ Curiant-	6	1092	17	10
	18	20	Dito To *Hen. van. Linden*, and comp. their commodies-	10	194	12	1
	18	20	Dito To Voyage to Antw. in comp. *R. R.* $\frac{1}{3}$, and $\frac{2}{3}$ me——	10	189	12	—
	18	20	Dito To *Andrew Hitchcock* due to me by conclude——	11	446	12	9
	18	20	Dito To *Arthur Mumperson* my account by him in comp.	12	402	12	1
	18	20	Dito To *Tho. Trust*, for comp. *R.R.* $\frac{1}{3}$, me $\frac{2}{3}$ our Time acco.	12	413	6	8
	18	20	Dito To Figs in comp. for *Iacob Symonson* $\frac{2}{3}$, and $\frac{1}{3}$ for me-	13	806	6	11
	19	20	Dito To Cash, resting therein, and brought hither——	1	947	2	1
			Summe——	li	4794	3	1

	Day	*Contra*, Creditor.	Fol	L	S	D
17	20	July By Voyage to Lisborn for dito company gained—	5	14	2	8
17	20	Dito By *Iean du Boys*, for dito company, gained—	6	80	11	7
17	20	Dito By *Iacob Symonson*, for dito company, gained—	9	60	—	6
17	20	Dito By Voyage to Antwerp, for dito company, gained-	10	600	7	—
		Summe—	L	75	1	9

			contra, Creditor.				
1633.	3	23	Janu By Profit and Losse in company $\frac{1}{3}$ *R.R.* $\frac{2}{3}$ me—	7	2	11	11
	4	9	Febru. By *Iacob Symonson* his Couchaneille, for provision	3	31	12	2
	5	13	March By Kersies in comp. $\frac{1}{4}$ and $\frac{3}{4}$ for provision & gains	4	128	5	—
1634.	8	15	April By *Iacob Symonson* my acco. by him in comp. gained	2	50	—	—
	9	22	Dito By Dansick-exchange, gained by the same—	8	10	19	9
	11	22	May By *George Pinchback* upon Sugar gained— —		36	5	—
	13	15	June By *Iacob Symonson* his Cambrix for provision—	8	8	12	—
	14	23	Dito By Cash, for provision of *Piego* his Fruits— —	1	13	4	—
	15	2	July By Amsterdam-exchange in company, gained—	11	23	—	8
	15	11	Dito By Figs $\frac{1}{3}$, and $\frac{2}{3}$ in comp. for provision and gaines—	9	114	15	5
	17	20	Dito By Wares gained thereby— — —	1	92	10	—
	17	—	Dito By Kettles, gained thereby— — —	2	20	—	2
	17	20	Dito By *Iean du Boys* my account Currant gained—	2	56	5	6
	17	20	Dito By Voyage to Amsterdam consigned to *I.S.* gained	4	111	17	—
	17	20	Dito By Interest-reckoning, gained thereby— —	5	16	6	2
	17	20	Dito By Voyage to Lisborn $\frac{2}{3}$, and $\frac{1}{3}$ for my gaines—	8	63	17	9
	18	—	Dito By Profit and Losse $\frac{1}{3}$, and $\frac{2}{3}$ for my $\frac{2}{3}$ gaines— —	7	296	6	5
			Summe—	L	1075	8	11

			Ballance, Creditor.				
1634.	18	20	July By *Iacob Symonson* his account by me in company-	5	512	3	8
	19	20	Dito By *Randoll Rice* his account by me in company—	6	991	7	6
	19	20	Dito By *Hend. vander Lind.* and comp. their commodities	10	194	12	1
	19	20	Dito By *Hend. vand. Linden*, and comp. their ready-mony	10	99	7	7
	19	20	Dito By *Hend. vand. Lind.* and comp their Time account-	13	93	19	8
	19	20	Dito By Stock, for difference there, being my pres. estate-	1	2902	12	7
			Summe—	L	4794	3	1

SURVEY OF THE Generall Ballance, or Estate-reckoning.

	Debitor	Thus ought your accounts to stand at the first view of the Bookes, when every thing is transported out of the Waste Book into the Leager. Gul.	st.	p.	Thus ought your Second, or Triall-Ballance to stand with the Losses. Gul.	st.	p.	Thus ought your True-Ballance to stand, which you transport into your New-Books. Gul.	st.	p.
23	Dito. To Banck, as in fol. 1. appeareth—	13688	17	8	5555	2	—	5555	2	—
—	Dito. To House King *David*, fol. 2 —	6213	15	—						
—	Dito. To *Susanna Peeters Orphans* —	5573	16	8	713	14	8	713	14	8
—	Dito. To *Jack Pudding* my account Currant — — —	11328	6	8	2648	6	8	2648	6	8
—	Dito. To Wines, for 15 Butts unsold	1260	—	—	1260	—	—	1260	—	—
—	Dito. To French Aquavitæ, for 58. Hogsheads — — — —	5568	—	—						
—	Dito To Rye, for 18. Last, 7 Mudde, fol. 3. — — — —	2877	15	8	1533	15	8	1533	15	8
—	Dito. To Couchaneillie, as in fol. 4 —	10080	—	—	36	—	—			
—	Dito. To Brasil, as in fol. — —	10888	3	—	70	11	—			
—	Dito. To Interest-reckoning, fol —	44	14	—						
—	Dito. To Profit and Losse, fol. —	320	2	8						
—	Dito To Voyage to London, consigned to *Jack Pudding*, fol. — —	7810	—	—	2600	—	—	2600	—	—
—	Dito. To Voyage to Hambrough, fol	2353	3	—						
—	Dito. To Voyage to Dansick, fol. —	1967	1	—						
—	Dito. To Insurance-reckoning, fol. —	3463	2	8						
—	Dito. To Cash, as appeareth in fol. —	29561	11	—	27153	8	—	27153	8	—
—	Dito To Cambrix, 11. Peeces unsold	8900	—	—	440	—	—	440	—	—
—	Dito. To Ship the Rain-bow, fol. —	1043	12	8						
—	Dito. To *Hans van Essen* at Hambrough, my account Currant, fol. —	3780	—	—	60	—	—			
—	Dito. To *Peeter Brasseur* at Dansick, my account Currant, fol — —	3805	14	8	53	12	8			
—	Dito. To *Jack Pudding* at London, his account Currant, fol. — —	917	—	—						
	Summe gl. —	130544	15	—	42124	10	—	41904	6	8

	SURVEY OF THE Generall-Ballance, or Estate-reckoning.	Thus ought your accounts to stand at the first view of your Books, when each parcel is transported out of the Waste-Book into the Journall and Leager.			Thus ought your *Second*, or *Tryall-Ballance* to stand with the Gains.			Thus ought your *True Ballance* to stand, which you transport to *New-Books*		
	Creditor.	Guil.	sti.	p.	Guil.	sti.	p.	Guil.	sti.	p.
23	Dito. By Banck, as in fol. 1. appeareth-	8133	15	8						
—	Dito. By House King *David*, fol. 2. —	7538	15	—	1325	—	—			
—	Dito. By *Susanna Peeters Orphans* —	4860	. 2	—						
—	Dito. By *Jack Pudding* my account Currant -- — — ——	9145	—	—	.465	—	—			
—	Dito. By French Aqua-vitæ 58. Hogsheads sold — — — —	6960	—	—	1392	—	—			
—	Dito. By Rye, for 16. Last sold, fol. 3	1788	12	8	444	12	8			
—	Dito. By Couchaneille, as in fol. 4. -	13950	—	—	3906	—	—			
—	Dito. By Brasil, as in fol 4. — —	10817	12	—						
—	Dito. By Interest-reckoning, fol. —	102	16	8	58	2	8			
—	Dito. By Profit and Losse, fol. ——	394	. 7	8	74	5	—			
—	Dito. By Voyage to London, fol. —	8350	—	—	3140	—	—			
—	Dito. By Voyage to Hambrough —	3816	. 6	—	1463	. 3	—			
—	Dito. By Voyage to Dansick, fol. —	3805	14	8	1838	13	8			
—	Dito. By Insurance-reckoning, fol. -	3576	6	—	113	3	8			
—	Dito. By Cash, as appeareth in fol. -	2408	3	—						
—	Dito. By Cambrix-Cloth, fol. ——	8105	12	—	545	12	—			
—	Dito. By Ship the Rain-bow, fol. —	1432	12	8	389	—	—			
—	Dito. By *Hans van Essen* my account-	3720	—	—						
—	Dito. By *Peeter Brasseur* my account-	3752	2	—						
—	Dito. By *Jack Pudding* at London, his account Currant — — ——	3294	18	—	2377	18	—	2377	18	—
—	Dito. By Stock, for my just Estate —	24592	—	—	24592	—	—	39526	.8	8
	Summe gl. ——	130544	15	—	42124	10	—	41904	6	8

Afterword

To the reader's own judgment have been left the many conclusions that are to be drawn from these reproductions of bookkeeping's earliest exponents.

The author in no sense desired to intrude too strongly his own ideas upon his reader. It has been his intent to show clearly how the ideas expressed by Pacioli in the early Italian vernacular came down through many translations into German, into Dutch, into French and lastly into English, withstanding all the many changes of language, surviving the "Dark Ages" of history and retaining unchanged through the centuries their clarity of thought and purpose until today the modern bookkeeper and the professional accountant are to be found trudging faithfully in the footsteps of the Franciscan Friar of medieval times.

Natural prejudice or partiality toward heralding abroad the imprint left by the early authors of his mother country on his own profession in its making is to be expected from the writer as an Hollander-born and for this reason, if no other, he has been diffident to drive home the conclusions he himself has formed. It is devoutly to be hoped that the reader will experience the same pleasure in the reading that the author has taken in the making of this contribution to his fellows.

Lightning Source UK Ltd.
Milton Keynes UK
176376UK00007B/74/P

9 781176 447509

Cisco Networking Academy Pr

HP IT Essentials I: PC Hardware and Software Lab Companion

Second Edition

Cisco Systems, Inc.
Cisco Networking Academy Program

Cisco Press
800 East 96th Street
Indianapolis, IN 46240 USA

Cisco Networking Academy Program

HP IT Essentials I: PC Hardware and Software Lab Companion

Second Edition

Cisco Systems, Inc.
Cisco Networking Academy Program

Course Sponsored by Hewlett-Packard Company

Published by:
Cisco Press
800 East 96th Street
Indianapolis, IN 46240 USA

Printed in the United States of America 1 2 3 4 5 6 7 8 9 0
First Printing June 2004
ISBN: 1-58713-138-2

Warning and Disclaimer

This book is designed to provide information about PC and hardware setup, configuration, and troubleshooting. Every effort has been made to make this book as complete and as accurate as possible, but no warranty or fitness is implied.
The information is provided on an "as is" basis. The author, Cisco Press, and Cisco Systems, Inc. shall have neither liability nor responsibility to any person or entity with respect to any loss or damages arising from the information contained in this book or from the use of the programs that might accompany it.
The opinions expressed in this book belong to the author and are not necessarily those of Cisco Systems, Inc.

This book is part of the Cisco Networking Academy® Program series from Cisco Press. The products in this series support and complement the Cisco Networking Academy Program curriculum. If you are using this book outside the Networking Academy program, then you are not preparing with a Cisco trained and authorized Networking Academy provider.

For information on the Cisco Networking Academy Program or to locate a Networking Academy, please visit http://www.cisco.com/edu.

Trademark Acknowledgments

All terms mentioned in this book that are known to be trademarks or service marks have been appropriately capitalized. Cisco Press or Cisco Systems, Inc. cannot attest to the accuracy of this information. Use of a term in this book should not be regarded as affecting the validity of any trademark or service mark.
The logo of the CompTIA Authorized Curriculum Program and the status of this or other training material as "Authorized" under the CompTIA Authorized Curriculum Program signifies that, in CompTIA's opinion, such training material covers the content of the CompTIA's related certification exam. CompTIA has not reviewed or approved the accuracy of the contents of this training material and specifically disclaims any warranties of merchantability or fitness for a particular purpose. CompTIA makes no guarantee concerning the success of persons using any such "Authorized" or other training material in order to prepare for any CompTIA certification exam.

Corporate and Government Sales

Cisco Press offers excellent discounts on this book when ordered in quantity for bulk purchases or special sales.
For more information, please contact: U.S. Corporate and Government Sales 1-800-382-3419
corpsales@pearsontechgroup.com
For sales outside the U.S. please contact: International Sales international@pearsoned.com

Feedback Information

At Cisco Press, our goal is to create in-depth technical books of the highest quality and value. Each book is crafted with care and precision, undergoing rigorous development that involves the unique expertise of members of the professional technical community.

Readers' feedback is a natural continuation of this process. If you have any comments regarding how we could improve the quality of this book, or otherwise alter it to better suit your needs, you can contact us at networkingacademy@ciscopress.com. Please be sure to include the book title and ISBN in your message.

We greatly appreciate your assistance.

Publisher	John Wait
Editor-in-Chief	John Kane
Executive Editor	Mary Beth Ray
Cisco Representative	Anthony Wolfenden
Cisco Press Program Manager	Nannette M. Noble
Production Manager	Patrick Kanouse
Development Editor	Deb Doorley
Senior Editor	Sheri Cain
Technical Editors	Jim Drennen, Frank Mann
Copy Editor	Kris Simmons

Printed in the USA

Table of Contents

Introduction

The *HP IT Essentials I: PC Hardware and Software Lab Companion*, Second Edition, is a complete collection of all the labs and worksheets from the Cisco Networking Academy Program online course. The labs complement the theory and foundational concepts introduced in the course and the *HP IT Essentials I: PC Hardware and Software Companion Guide*, Second Edition. This book is useful in its own right as a hardware and software basics lab manual, providing opportunities for hands-on practice and thought-provoking review questions. The easy-to-follow exercises further prepare you to pass the CompTIA A+ Certification exam.

HP IT Essentials I: PC Hardware and Software, Second Edition, covers the internal components of a computer used to successfully assemble a computer system, install an operating system, and troubleshoot using system tools and diagnostic software. You also work with architectures to connect to the Internet and to share resources in a network environment.

You will find that your studies are best complemented by a text that describes the theory and foundational concepts introduced in the hands-on lab exercises. To that end, *HP IT Essentials I: PC Hardware and Software Companion Guide*, Second Edition, includes thorough treatments of the topics discussed in this lab manual.

Who Should Read This Book

This book is intended for the student in high school, technical school, community college, or a four-year institution who wants to pursue a career in information technology (IT) or who wants to have the working knowledge of how a computer works, how to assemble a computer, and how to troubleshoot hardware and software issues. Ideally, this student is enrolled in the HP IT Essentials I course within a Cisco Networking Academy Program.

This Book's Organization

This book is divided into chapters corresponding to the chapters in the Companion Guide:

- Chapter 1, "Information Technology Basics"—Labs and worksheets include Windows basics; number conversions, including binary, decimal, and hexadecimal; and lab safety.
- Chapter 2, "How Computers Work"—Labs and worksheets identify the internal components of a computer, including the motherboard, ROM and BIOS chips, video card, and power supply.
- Chapter 3, "Assembling a Computer"—This chapter focuses on assembling a computer system. The labs provide hands-on experience for connecting the power supply, motherboard, and drives.
- Chapter 4, "Operating System Fundamentals"—You install the operating system in this chapter. The worksheets focus on the fundamentals and navigation, and the labs deal with DOS and creating a boot disk.

- Chapter 5, "Windows 9*x* Operating Systems"—The worksheets provide a review of the Windows file system, printers management, and hard drive preparation. The labs actually prepare the hard drive and install the operating system. Troubleshooting skills include installing drivers and creating a Windows startup disk.

- Chapter 6, "Windows NT/2000 Operating Systems"—This chapter details the differences between Windows 9*x* and Windows 2000. The labs demonstrate the upgrade to Windows 2000 and the steps to create an emergency startup disk. In addition, you gain experience by creating user accounts and assigning permissions.

- Chapter 7, "Windows XP Operating System"—These labs focus on the XP operating system. You perform a demonstration of the installation process. You then work with the enhancements, including file sharing, Remote Desktop Connection, the Internet Firewall Connection, the XP Start menu, and Windows Explorer.

- Chapter 8, "Multimedia Capabilities"—Multimedia is the focus of this chapter. The labs and worksheets include both sound and video. You install a sound card and update the video card. Additionally, you review the terminology as it relates to CDs and DVDs.

- Chapter 9, "Advanced Hardware Fundamentals for Servers"—The worksheets in this chapter review the concepts of Redundant Array of Independent Disks (RAID) and the steps to add a processor to a server and to upgrade a server adapter.

- Chapter 10, "Networking Fundamentals"—Networking is detailed in this chapter. You install and configure the network interface card (NIC) in the labs, plus you troubleshoot by using the ping command. The worksheets review the types of networks and topology and connecting to the Internet.

- Chapter 11, "Printers and Sharing"—In this chapter, you complete labs to manage files in a printer queue and to allow print sharing. The worksheet provides the information required to clear a paper jam.

- Chapter 12, "Preventive Maintenance"—The labs in this chapter focus on preventive maintenance, including using a digital multimeter, cleaning computer components, and using system tools. The worksheets cover environmental issues, electrostatic discharge (ESD), and general preventive maintenance.

- Chapter 13, "Troubleshooting PC Hardware"—This chapter details the troubleshooting basics. The labs cover the steps of the troubleshooting cycle and identifying power-on self-test (POST) errors. The worksheets cover troubleshooting printers and a hardware overview.

- Chapter 14, "Troubleshooting Software"—Troubleshooting as it relates to software is the focus of this chapter. In the labs, you boot to Safe Mode, use the Windows 2000 Recovery Console, and back up the Windows Registry.

This Book's Features

This book contains several elements that help you learn about the basics of hardware and software for the PC:

- **Objectives and scenarios**—Each of the labs in this manual provide an objective or a goal of the lab. It lists the equipment required, and a scenario allows you to relate the exercise to real-world environments.

- **Demonstrations**—These labs show the step-by-step procedures for installing different operating systems. Not all lab environments can accommodate the installation of all operating systems discussed throughout the course. Combined with the actual installation, the demonstration helps to prepare the technician for any situation.

- **Reflection questions**—To demonstrate an understanding of the concepts covered, each lab provides a reflection question at the end. Also, it includes questions that are designed to elicit particular points of understanding. These questions help verify your comprehension of the technology.

The conventions that present command syntax in this book are the same conventions used in the Cisco IOS Command Reference:

- **Bold** indicates commands and keywords that are entered literally as shown. In examples (not syntax), bold indicates user input (for example, a **show** command).

- *Italic* indicates arguments for which you supply values.

- Braces ({ }) indicate a required element.

- Square brackets ([ ]) indicate an optional element.

- Vertical bars (|) separate alternative, mutually exclusive elements.

- Braces and vertical bars within square brackets (such as [x {y | z}]) indicate a required choice within an optional element. You do not need to enter what is in the brackets, but if you do, you have some required choices in the braces.

CompTIA Authorized Quality Curriculum

The contents of this training material were created for the CompTIA A+ Certification exam covering the upgraded Core Hardware Exam Objectives and the upgraded OS Technologies Exam Objectives that were current as of November 2003.

How To Become CompTIA Certified

This training material can help you prepare for and pass a related CompTIA certification exam or exams. To achieve CompTIA certification, you must register for and pass a CompTIA certification exam(s).

To become CompTIA certified, you must

1. Select a certification exam provider.
2. Register for and schedule a time to take the CompTIA certification exam at a convenient location.
3. Read and sign the Candidate Agreement, which is presented at the time of the exam. The text of the Candidate Agreement appears on the CompTIA website.
4. Take and pass the CompTIA certification exam.

Everything you need to find an exam provider and to register is on the CompTIA website: http://comptia.org/certification/A/default.asp. The site also provides information about other CompTIA certifications, industry acceptance, benefits, and program news.

CompTIA is a nonprofit IT trade association. CompTIA's certifications are designed by subject-matter experts from across the IT industry. Each CompTIA certification is vendor-neutral, covers multiple technologies, and requires demonstration of skills and knowledge widely sought after by the IT industry.

To contact CompTIA with any questions or comments, please call + 1 630 268 1818 or e-mail questions@comptia.org.

Chapter 1

Information Technology Basics

Lab 1.3.8: Getting to Know Windows

Estimated Time: 10 Minutes

Objective

In this lab, you learn the proper way to shut down Windows and navigate the Windows interface, as well as use Windows Help features.

Equipment

The following equipment is required for this lab:

- Lab computer with Windows 98 installed

Scenario

To help a friend with Windows, you need to become more familiar with the Windows graphical user interface (GUI).

Procedures

Knowing how to use the Windows interface will help in nearly any job today. Most computers in the workplace have a version of Microsoft Windows installed on them. To work in a Windows environment, the user should have a firm grasp of several skills. Examples include resizing windows, creating and deleting icons, working with files and folders, and navigating the Start menu (Shut Down, Run, Search, Settings, Documents, and Programs).

Step 1

If the lab computer is not already on, boot it up now. If you are prompted for a login name and password when Windows boots, use the username and password assigned by the instructor.

Step 2

At the Windows desktop, become familiar with the Windows interface to make troubleshooting faster and easier. Take a minute to click the **Start** button and look through the items that are listed in the menu.

What options are listed under the Find menu?

____
____
____
____

Step 3

Run the Calculator program by selecting **Start** > **Programs** > **Accessories** > **Calculator**. Enter a few simple test calculations to see how it works. Use both the mouse and the numeric keypad. When finished, click the **X** on the top-right corner of the Calculator program to close it.

Step 4

Now, try the help system that is built into Windows. Help is organized into separate books and includes a search feature so that you can locate specific topics quickly. To begin, click the **Start** button and then click **Help**. This move opens a window with a list of categories that outline the major areas that Help covers.

Click the **Search** tab, and enter one or more words relating to the topic that needs research. Do a search for the word **resize**.

After completing a search for **resize**, what topics does Help display?

____
____
____
____

An **Index** tab lists all help items alphabetically.

Step 5

There are different ways of resizing a window to minimize it or maximize it. To see more of a help item in one screen, resize the window. The fastest way to view a window in full screen is to click the **Maximize** button. The Maximize button is the middle button on the top-right corner of the window.

To return the window to its original size, click the **Restore** button. The Restore button replaces the Maximize button when the window is in full screen, as shown in Figure 1-1.

To resize the window to a custom size, grab the edges or corners of a window by first moving the mouse cursor to the edge or corner of the window. When the double arrow appears, click and hold the mouse button and drag the window to the desired size.

Figure 1-1 Restoring and Maximizing

Step 6

To properly shut down Windows, click the **Start** button and select **Shut Down** from the menu. Select **Shut Down** from the list and click the **OK** button. You should always shut the computer down using this method. Important data that is stored in memory while the system is running needs to be written to the hard disk before the computer shuts off. Do not turn the computer off until a message displays indicating that it is safe to do so. Newer operating systems automatically turn off power when the shutdown process is complete.

Troubleshooting

The Windows Help feature is a valuable tool when the technician needs information on a specific topic. If there is something in Windows that you need to research, using the Help feature can answer a lot of questions.

Reflection

What is the proper way to shut down Windows?

____

____

____

____

Why is it important to shut down Windows properly instead of just pressing the power button?

____

____

____

____

Lab 1.5.3: Boolean Operations

Estimated Time: 25 Minutes

Objective

In this lab, you are introduced to the AND, OR, NOR, and NOT Boolean operations. You also calculate the output of different combinations of Boolean operations based on input.

Equipment

This is a written lab. No equipment is necessary.

Scenario

You receive a circuit board diagram. To figure out what each logic gate does, you must understand how Boolean operations function.

Procedures

This lab helps you learn to work with Boolean operations. Computers use Boolean operations to make calculations based on inputs of 0 (off) and 1 (on). 0s and 1s are represented in computer microchips and the bus on the motherboard by the presence or absence of voltage. You perform some basic calculations using the AND, OR, NOR, and NOT Boolean operations to get a better idea of how computers work internally. Computers constantly perform complex combinations of these operations within millionths of a second.

Step 1

The Boolean operations of AND, OR, NOR, and NOT work as follows:

0 OR 0 is 0.	0 AND 0 is 0.	0 NOR 0 is 1.	NOT 0 is 1.
0 OR 1 is 1.	0 AND 1 is 0.	0 NOR 1 is 0.	NOT 1 is 0.
1 OR 0 is 1.	1 AND 0 is 0.	1 NOR 0 is 0.	
1 OR 1 is 1.	1 AND 1 is 1.	1 NOR 1 is 0.	

Note: AND, OR, and NOR are called binary operations (not to be confused with binary numbers) because the operations require two inputs. NOT is called a unary operation because it has only one input.

Look at the following combination of Boolean operations and determine the output:

(1 AND 0) OR (0 AND 1)

Compute the operations in parentheses first. 1 AND 0 is 0. 0 AND 1 is 0. The solution is 0 OR 0, which is 0.

As a second example, compute the following Boolean operations:

NOT [(1 AND 0) NOR (0 OR 1)] AND 1

Work from the inner parentheses toward the outer parentheses. Also, the NOT applies to the expression that follows it. (The NOT does not apply to anything that appears after the].) So, following these instructions, the result is NOT [0 NOR 1] AND 1, which is equivalent to NOT [0] AND 1, which is the same as 1 AND 1. This gives the result of 1.

Step 2

For each of the following combinations of Boolean operations, compute the final output based on the rules for AND, OR, NOR, and NOT. Refer to the table of Boolean operations in Step 1 for help on how to compute the following.

Solve for the output. The answer should be 0 or 1.

Input: (1 AND 0) AND 1

Output: ______________________________

Input: 1 NOR {NOT [0 OR (1 NOR 1)]}

Output: ______________________________

Input: 0 AND {1 AND [1 OR (0 NOR 0)] AND 0} (Remember to work left to right through the expression.)

Output: ______________________________

Input: 1 AND NOT {[0 OR (1 OR 0)] NOR [1 AND NOT (0)]}

Output: ______________________________

Troubleshooting

For a PC technician, understanding how data is stored in a computer can be a great trouble-shooting tool.

Reflection

How are Boolean operations used in computer systems?

Lab 1.5.9: Converting Numbers Overview

Estimated Time: 25 Minutes

Objective

In this lab, you identify the places in binary and decimal numbers and know the value of each. Also, you work with powers of 10 and relate them to decimal places, as well as work with powers of 2 and relate them to binary places. Finally, you manually convert between simple binary numbers and decimal numbers and describe the differences between binary and decimal number systems.

Equipment

This is a written lab. No equipment is necessary.

Scenario

Having sharp skills in number systems can aid you in a career as an IT professional. With the ability to convert numbers without the use of a calculator, you can solve problems quickly and easily.

Procedures

This lab helps you learn to work with the binary number system. You convert binary numbers (base 2) to decimal numbers (base 10) and then from decimal to binary. Computers and networking equipment, such as routers, use binary numbers. A binary number is a series of *bits* (short for binary digits) that are either on (a binary 1) or off (a binary 0). They are encoded internally in the PC on microchips and on the computer motherboard bus as electrical voltages. Understanding binary numbers and how they relate to decimal numbers is critical to understanding how computers work internally.

Step 1

The decimal number system is based on powers of 10. This lab helps you develop and understand how the decimal number system is constructed. With base 10, the rightmost place has a value of 1 (as with base 2). Each place moving to the left is valued 10 times more. Ten to the zero power is one ($10^0=1$), 10 to the first power is 10 ($10^1=10$), 10 to the second power is 100 ($10^2=10 \text{ x } 10=100$), 10 to the third power is 1000 ($10^3=1000$), and so on. Just multiply the number in each place with the value of each place (for example, 400=4 x $10^{2=4\text{ x }100}$). Remember that any number (other than 0) to the 0 power is 1.

The following chart shows how the decimal number system represents the number 352,481. This helps in understanding the binary number system.

Exponent	10^5	10^4	10^3	10^2	10^1	10^0
Expanded	100,000	10,000	1000	100	10	1
Numeral	3	5	2	4	8	1
	3 x 100,000	5 x 10,000	2 x 1000	4 x 100	8 x 10	1 x 1

The number 352,481, if read from left to right in expanded decimal form, is (3 x 100,000) + (5 x 10,000) + (2 x 1,000) + (4 x 100) + (8 x 10) + (1 x 1), for a total of 352,481 (a six-digit number).

Here is another way to look at it that makes it easier to add up the decimal number values.

Position of Digit (from Right)	Value of Bit Position (10^X or Ten to the Power of)	Number Value from 0 to 9	Calculation	Decimal Value
1st Decimal Digit	10^0 or 1	1	1 x 1	1
2nd Decimal Digit	10^1 or 10	8	8 x 10	80
3rd Decimal Digit	10^2 or 100	4	4 x 100	400
4th Decimal Digit	10^3 or 1,000	2	2 x 1,000	2,000
5th Decimal Digit	10^4 or 10,000	5	5 x 10,000	52,000
6th Decimal Digit	10^5 or 100,000	3	3 x 100,000	300,000
Decimal Value (Total of 6 Digits)				**352,481**

Step 2

Binary means "two," and each digit in a binary number can have only two values (0 or 1). Understanding binary numbers is key to understanding how computers work. The value of each binary digit, or bit, is based on powers of two.

This lab helps you develop an understanding of powers of two, which is what all computers and data communications use. With base 2, the rightmost place has a value of 1 (as with base 10). Each place moving to the left is valued two times more. Two to the zero power is one (2^0=1), two to the first power is two (2^1=2), two to the second power is four (2^2=4), two to the third power is eight (2^3=8), and so on. Just multiply the number in each place (either a 0 or a 1) by the value of each place (for example, 8=2^3=1 x 8) and add up the total. Remember that any number (except zero) to the zero power is one.

Binary Number Conversion Example

The following table shows the detailed calculations (starting from the right side) to convert the binary number 10011100 into a decimal number.

Position of Digit (from Right)	**Value of Bit Position (2 to the Power of)**	**Is Bit a One (On) or a Zero (Off)?**	**Calculation**	**Decimal Value**
1st Binary Digit	$2^0=1$	0	0 x 1	0
2nd Binary Digit	$2^1=2$	0	0 x 2	0
3rd Binary Digit	$2^2=4$	1	1 x 4	4
4th Binary Digit	$2^3=8$	1	1 x 8	8
5th Binary Digit	$2^4=16$	1	1 x 16	16
6th Binary Digit	$2^5=32$	0	0 x 32	0
7th Binary Digit	$2^6=64$	0	0 x 64	0
8th Binary Digit	$2^7=128$	1	1 x 128	128
Decimal Value (Sum Total of 8 Bits)				156

Step 3

Look at the binary number bit status. If there is a 1 in a given position, add the value shown. If there is a 0 in a given position, then do not add it.

Solve for the decimal value.

Exponent	2^7	2^6	2^5	2^4	2^3	2^2	2^1	2^0
Bit Position	8	7	6	5	4	3	2	1
Value	128	64	32	16	8	4	2	1
Binary Number Bit	1	0	0	1	1	1	0	0

Decimal value: ______________________________

Exponent	2^7	2^6	2^5	2^4	2^3	2^2	2^1	2^0
Bit Position	8	7	6	5	4	3	2	1
Value	128	64	32	16	8	4	2	1
Binary Number Bit Status	1	1	1	0	0	0	1	1

Decimal value: ______________________________

Exponent	2^7	2^6	2^5	2^4	2^3	2^2	2^1	2^0
Bit Position	8	7	6	5	4	3	2	1
Value	128	64	32	16	8	4	2	1
Binary Number Bit Status	0	1	1	1	0	0	0	0

Decimal value: ______________________________

Exponent	2^7	2^6	2^5	2^4	2^3	2^2	2^1	2^0
Bit Position	8	7	6	5	4	3	2	1
Value	128	64	32	16	8	4	2	1
Binary Number Bit Status	1	1	0	1	1	0	1	0

Decimal value: ______________________________

Step 4

Convert the decimal values of 209, 114, 58, and 165 to binary. To do so, look at the decimal value and then subtract binary values starting from 128 (the highest value binary bit for these number). If the number is larger than 128, put a 1 in the 128 (or 2^7) column. Subtract 128 from the number and see if there is 64 or greater left over. If there is, put a 1 there. Otherwise, put a 0 and see if there is 32 or greater left over. Continue until all 8 bits are defined as either a 0 or a 1.

Exponent	2^7	2^6	2^5	2^4	2^3	2^2	2^1	2^0
Bit Position	8	7	6	5	4	3	2	1
Value	128	64	32	16	8	4	2	1
Binary Number Bit Status								

Binary value of 209: ______________________________

Exponent	2^7	2^6	2^5	2^4	2^3	2^2	2^1	2^0
Bit Position	8	7	6	5	4	3	2	1
Value	128	64	32	16	8	4	2	1
Binary Number Bit Status								

Binary value of 114: ____

Exponent	2^7	2^6	2^5	2^4	2^3	2^2	2^1	2^0
Bit Position	8	7	6	5	4	3	2	1
Value	128	64	32	16	8	4	2	1
Binary Number Bit Status								

Binary value of 58: ____

Exponent	2^7	2^6	2^5	2^4	2^3	2^2	2^1	2^0
Bit Position	8	7	6	5	4	3	2	1
Value	128	64	32	16	8	4	2	1
Binary Number Bit Status								

Binary value of 165: ____

Step 5

Check the answers by converting the numbers back to decimal.

Troubleshooting

Learning how to calculate binary numbers without the use of a calculator is an important skill in the IT industry. The ability to perform number conversions can save time, especially in the field where calculators are not always available.

Reflection

Using the system you learned to solve decimal to binary conversion, convert the decimal number 255 to binary.

Worksheet 1.3.8: Windows Navigation and Settings

Worksheets enhance the material covered in the IT Essentials online course and the companion guide. Use the space provided to answer the questions. Refer to this information when preparing for the A+ exam.

1. It is extremely important not to power off the computer while the operating system is still running using the _________________ _________________.

2. The main display screen in Windows is known as the _________________.

3. The _________________ contains the start button, quick launch buttons, and the clock.

4. The _________________ menu allows you to access virtually every program and function on the PC.

5. To adjust the date and time, double-click the _________________ on the right side of the_________________.

6. Most applications have three tiny icons in the upper-right corner of the screen that are used to _________________ the screen, _________________ the screen, or _________________ the application.

7. To adjust the screen display, first_________________ all windows that are open. Right-click an empty space on the _________________ and choose **Properties**.

8. To access the volume control, click the _________________ icon on the right side of the _________________.

9. To move a desktop icon to another position on the desktop, click it and then _________________ it to the desired location.

10. After you highlight them, you can rename icons, like folders, by clicking the _________________ and then typing in a new one.

11. To create a new folder, _________________ the desktop and then select **New > Folder**.

12. The ____________________ bar displays the name of the document and application.

13. The ____________________ bar contains menus for manipulating the document, such as creating new documents, copying text, inserting images, and so on.

14. The ____________________ bar shows useful information, such as page number, whether the file is being saved, how to access the Help feature, and so on.

15. The ____________________ bars appear when the document is too large for it to fit on the screen and you use them for moving the image or text through the window.

Worksheet 1.5.9: Number Systems Exercises

1. Define the following:

   Decimal: ______________________________

   Binary: ______________________________

   Hexadecimal: ______________________________

2. Explain how binary and hexadecimal numbers are used with computers.

____
____
____
____
____
____
____

3. Without using a calculator, convert the binary numbers into decimal numbers.

   a. 01111011 ____________ b. 00000111 ____________

   c. 11110000 ____________ d. 10101010 ____________

   e. 01010101 ____________ f. 10010011 ____________

   g. 00111001 ____________ h. 11111111 ____________

   i. 11010101 ____________ j. 10000000 ____________

4. Convert the decimal numbers into binary numbers.

   a. 23 ____________ b. 131 ____________

   c. 3 ____________ d. 234 ____________

   e. 79 ____________ f. 199 ____________

5. Convert the decimal numbers into hexadecimal numbers.

   a. 16 ____________ b. 131 ____________

   c. 3 ____________ d. 234 ____________

   e. 65 ____________ f. 255 ____________

6. Convert the hexadecimal numbers into decimal numbers.

a. 27 ________________ b. AA ________________

c. 3 ________________ d. F1 ________________

e. 241 ________________ f. 255 ________________

Worksheet 1.6.6: Lab Safety Checklist

1. Near the workbench, power outlets should be available to accommodate the system unit power and the power needs of other electrical devices. In addition, the workspace for an IT technician should be large enough to accommodate the following.

   a. ______________________________

   b. ______________________________

   c. ______________________________

   d. ______________________________

Fill in the blanks in the following lines.

2. The workspace should maintain a humidity level of ______________ percent to reduce the likelihood of ESD.

3. The workbench should be a ______________________ surface. Additionally, it should have a flat cleanable surface.

4. The workspace should be distant from areas of heavy ______________ equipment or concentrations of ________________.

5. The workspace should be free of ________________. __________________ can contaminate the workspace, causing premature damage to computer components. The work area should have a filtered air system to reduce _________ and contaminants.

6. Lighting should be adequate to see small details. Two different illumination forms are preferred, such as an adjustable ________ with a shade and ______________ lighting.

7. Extreme variations of ____________________ can affect a computer's components. ________________ should be maintained consistent with the component's specifications.

8. Properly ___________ AC electrical current is essential. Power outlets should be tested with an outlet tester for proper grounding.

Chapter 2

How Computers Work

Lab 2.3.6: Motherboard Identification

Estimated Time: 30 Minutes

Objective

This lab focuses on identifying motherboards, removing motherboards, replacing motherboards, and using the motherboard manuals to identify a number of the system components.

Equipment

The following equipment is required for this lab:

- A system board (either mounted in a case or not)
- Internet access
- Motherboard manuals
- ID software or local vendor contact

Scenario

A student has just been hired by a PC repair center and has begun your training. PC technicians need to be able to remove and replace motherboards either in an upgrade situation or because of a motherboard failure.

Procedures

If you need to replace the system board, you must follow a few guidelines. Place the system on an antistatic mat and use an antistatic wrist strap. Verify that the system power cord is not attached.

Carefully follow all necessary safety precautions concerning power supplies and electrostatic discharge.

Step 1

Gain access to the motherboard. If the motherboard is installed in a case, remove the case cover.

Step 2

If necessary, remove components and cabling to gain access to the motherboard manufacturer's name and ID number. Be sure to carefully record these connections so you can replace them.

Note: These numbers might be difficult to find and hard to read, so look carefully. As you become familiar with different manufacturers, it becomes easier.

Check with the instructor about the system. Due to variations in motherboards, not all the following information is available.

Step 3

Record the following information from the motherboard of the computer.

Components	Available? (Y/N)	Name and Type (If Applicable)
1. Motherboard manufacturer		
2. Motherboard model number		
3. Form factor (physical size and layout)		
4. Type of CPU Installed		
5. Types of CPUs supported (socket or slot)		
6. Chipset		
7. BIOS manufacturer		
8. BIOS battery		
9. ISA or EISA (number and type)		
10. PCI (number and type)		
11. AGP or AGP Pro (number and type)		
12. Jumpers		
13. DIP settings		

Troubleshooting

A quick check on the motherboard manufacturer's website provides information regarding the motherboard BIOS and whether there is an upgrade available.

Reflection

The ability to properly identify all the components of a motherboard will prove to be useful when troubleshooting in the field.

Where is the first place to look to determine the manufacturer of a motherboard?

____

Lab 2.3.8: Identifying ROM and BIOS Chips

Estimated Time: 30 Minutes

Objective

This lab focuses on the student's ability to locate and identify the ROM chip, BIOS chip, and BIOS manufacturer on a motherboard.

Equipment

The following equipment is required for this lab:

- A complete motherboard
- Motherboard manuals
- Internet access for research

Note: Be sure to observe proper care concerning power supplies and electrostatic discharge (ESD).

Scenario

A client from a few months ago recently purchased a used computer. The client wants to install an expansion card into the machine to add some video-editing capabilities. Before purchasing an expansion card, the client wants to make sure that the BIOS will support it.

Procedures

The Basic Input-Output System (BIOS) is a ROM chip that has built-in commands, which allow the system to power up and perform a self-test of its hardware before turning over control to the operating system.

Read-Only Memory (ROM), as its name implies, can be read but not changed. It stores basic information that the computer needs to operate (for example, the BIOS).

Determine the manufacturer and version number of the BIOS. Research the BIOS manufacturer's website to see whether newer versions are available. Also, examine the physical ROM chip to help answer the following questions.

Step 1

Describe the physical appearance of the ROM chip and its location on the board.

____

____

____

Step 2

What type of BIOS is used?

Manufacturer	
Version/type	
Battery type	
Rewriteable?	

Step 3

If an Internet connection is available, visit the manufacturer's website and list the version number and any new features that are supported.

Step 4

Can the BIOS be upgraded?

Step 5

What are the steps that you must take to upgrade the BIOS?

Troubleshooting

Use extreme caution when flashing the BIOS. Make sure to use the correct file and ensure that it is not corrupt. If you flash the BIOS with the incorrect BIOS type or with a corrupt file, you might render the board inoperable.

Reflection

How many BIOS manufacturers are in the list?

____

Why is the BIOS needed?

____
____
____

Lab 2.3.9: Identifying Computer Expansion Slots

Estimated Time: 20 Minutes

Objective

In this lab, you identify safety issues, specifications, and components relating to expansion slots. You also list the advantages and disadvantages of each expansion slot.

Equipment

The following equipment is required for this lab:

- Motherboard and motherboard manuals
- Expansion cards
- Internet access for research

Scenario

Bob has purchased a used computer and is trying to determine what type of video card and other expansion cards he can install. Help Bob figure out what is currently installed so that he can make an educated decision when he is ready to buy new expansion cards.

Procedures

An expansion slot is a long, thin, socket connection, located on a motherboard or riser board, that lets you add various cards to a computer. These cards can include devices such as modems, sound cards, and network interface cards (NICs). Expansion slots let you extend the life of a computer because you can add new technology as it becomes available.

Verify that the power cord is disconnected and that the antistatic wrist strap is in place. Remove the system case from the computer.

Step 1

Locate the expansion slots on the motherboard (or riser card) and list them.

1.	4.
2.	5.
3.	6.

Step 2

Using the available resources, identify any expansion cards that are installed.

1.	4.
2.	5.
3.	6.

Troubleshooting

Occasionally when a PC is shipped from one location to another, an expansion card might become unseated. Verify that all expansion cards are properly seated and that all connectors are properly plugged in before turning the unit on.

Reflection

What type of expansion card would you install in a Peripheral Component Interconnect (PCI) slot?

____

____

____

____

____

____

What is the speed difference between PCI and the Industry Standard Architecture (ISA) expansion slots?

____

____

____

____

____

____

Lab 2.4.2: Identifying RAM and RAM Sockets

Estimated Time: 40 Minutes

Objective

This lab focuses on the identification of various types of RAM and RAM sockets.

Equipment

The following equipment is required for this lab:

- A functioning computer system with two DIMMs installed and the proper tools to remove the computer cover.
- Manual for the motherboard used in the computer.
- (Optional) RAM tester. If unsure of the operation of the RAM tester, ask the instructor for further instruction.

Scenario

Fred wants to upgrade the amount of RAM in his PC, but he is not sure how to locate it or how to determine how much RAM is installed. Help him determine how much RAM he has so he can figure out how much more to buy.

Procedure

Random Access Memory (RAM) is memory used by the CPU to store open files and active applications temporarily. RAM is volatile, meaning that any information stored in it is lost when you power down the system. RAM comes in small expansion board forms with varying numbers of edge connectors. The RAM boards (also called sticks) are made in 30-, 72-, 168-, or 184-pin configurations. They are referred to as SIMMs or DIMMs, depending on the chip density. Many times, the only information you can gain visually is the manufacturer's name—which is the reason that a quality RAM tester is a critical piece of diagnostic equipment for PC repair shops.

Observe proper care concerning power supplies and ESD.

Step 1

Boot the system and record the power-on self test (POST) amount of RAM.

____

____

____

____

Step 2

Shut down the system and follow all the safety steps in removing the cover of the computer.

Step 3

After gaining access to the motherboard, note the position of the RAM slots and whether they are in use, making notes in the journal.

Slot type	
Total number of slots	
Number of slots open	
Total RAM capacity	

Step 4

Record the information about the installed RAM sticks in the following table. You might have to remove RAM to read the information. Remove the RAM to read the labels, and reinstall the RAM when finished.

Note: RAM labeling is inconsistent, and some of this information is only available from the manufacturer's website.

Manufacturer	
Type	
Capacity (each)	
Speed	
Total capacity installed	
Position	

Step 5

Refer to the motherboard manual or search the Internet for the type and range of RAM chips that you can install on this computer.

Step 6

If there are two sticks of RAM installed, remove one of the RAM sticks, noting the location and orientation of the stick.

Step 7

Put the cover of the computer back on the computer and plug in the power cords. Restart the computer system. Note the POST RAM amount.

____
____
____
____

Step 8

Shut down the system and follow all the safety steps in removing the computer cover.

Step 9

Reinstall the RAM stick that you removed in Step 6.

Step 10

Put the cover of the computer back on the computer and plug in the power cords. Restart the computer system. Note the POST RAM amount.

____
____
____
____

Step 11

Reflect in the journal about any special considerations as you install the RAM memory.

Attach copies of any additional research material used in completing this worksheet before handing in this assignment.

Troubleshooting

Take extreme caution when working with RAM. ESD is one of the most common problems when working on computers. Make sure to have on an antistatic wrist strap at all times, and make sure to be properly grounded. The chips on a RAM module are built for 3.3 volts. If a static discharge is large enough to see a spark, it is 3000 volts.

Reflection

Did you use an antistatic wrist strap while working with RAM modules?

What other types of RAM are there besides the type installed in the PC that you worked on?

Lab 2.5.2: Video Card Identification

Estimated Time: 35 Minutes

Objective

This lab discusses the major features and specifications of different video cards. In this lab, you identify the video card by any markings on the card. These markings might include a manufacturer's name or part number. You can identify some cards only by the physical layout of the card.

Equipment

The following equipment is required for this lab:

- ESD wrist strap
- Standard tool kit
- Lab workstation with Accelerated Graphics Port (AGP) video card installed
- Internet access
- Manufacturer manuals

Scenario

Suppose that you are an avid gamer and you want to compare the features of all the video cards available. Because you need the latest and greatest video card for the latest and greatest games, you must pay special attention to the manufacturer and performance specifications of each video card.

Procedures

A video adapter, or card, is an expansion card that allows the computer to display images on a monitor. It also determines the monitor depth and resolution. The need for the video card is determined by the intended use of the system. For example, a system used for gaming needs a more advanced card than one for word processing.

Step 1

After removing the system case, remove the video card from the expansion slot. When working with video cards, as with any other component on the inside of a computer, take special care to be grounded and make sure to use an antistatic wrist strap. If you damage the video card, the computer is useless until you install a new video card.

Research and supply the following information.

Manufacturer	
Model number	
URL	
Key features	
System requirements	
Cost	

Terms

Research the following terms using these and other Internet resources:

- http://www.techweb.com/encyclopedia
- http://www.webopedia.com/

AGP port

____

____

____

____

Extended Data Out (EDO) RAM

____

____

____

____

pixel

____

____

____

____

refresh rate

____
____
____
____

resolution

____
____
____
____

Troubleshooting

When working with video cards, as with any other component on the inside of a computer, take special care to be grounded and make sure to use an antistatic wrist strap. If you damage the only video card, the computer is useless until you install a new video card.

Reflection

Did any of the video cards have a heat sink or a fan on the Graphics Processing Unit (GPU)?

____
____
____
____

Are video cards with a heat sink or fan on the GPU available?

____
____
____
____

Why would having a separate processor on a video card help performance?

____
____
____
____

Worksheet 2.3.2: PC Power Supply

Worksheets enhance the material covered in the IT Essentials online course and the companion guide. Use the space provided to answer the questions. Refer to this information when preparing for the A+ exam.

1. The most basic function of the PC power supply is to convert ____________ current to ___________ current.

2. What is the purpose of the cover panels?

____

____

3. Drives, like CD-ROMs and DVD-ROMs, are inserted into bays or racks that are typically _________ inches wide.

4. What are some factors to consider when purchasing a computer case?

   a. ____

   b. ____

   c. ____

   d. ____

   e. ____

   f. ____

   g. ____

5. In Europe, the standard outlet delivers ________________volts AC, and in North America, the standard wall outlet delivers ________________volts AC.

6. What rating do computer power supplies have?

____

____

7. What are the two most common power supply types?

   a. ____

   b. ____

8. What is the importance of the power supply fan?

____

____

Worksheet 2.3.8: BIOS/ROM

1. The BIOS serves as the interface between the ____________________ and the ________________________.

2. The detailed instructions needed for system start-up are stored in

    ____

3. What does BIOS stand for?

    ____

4. What does ROM stand for?

    ____

5. What special characteristic do EPROM, EEPROM, and Flash ROM have?

    ____

    ____

6. What differentiates RAM from ROM?

    ____

    ____

    ____

Worksheet 2.3.9: Expansion Slots

1. What are expansion slots?

____

2. Expansion bus is also referred to as a(n) ________________ or ________________.

3. You use an expansion bus to add ______________________ to existing systems.

4. List six different types of expansion slots:

   a. ____

   b. ____

   c. ____

   d. ____

   e. ____

   f. ____

5. Define the term Plug and Play.

____

____

6. Name three common types of expansion cards.

   a. ____

   b. ____

   c. ____

7. Name the three bus types.

   a. ____

   b. ____

   c. ____

8. An ISA bus was developed with both _________ bit and ________ bit bus speeds.

9. Which bus type supports bidirectional communication?

____

10. What does PCI stand for?

____

Worksheet 2.4.2: RAM and RAM Sockets

1. Memory chips in a computer system are referred to as ____________________.

2. RAM is the industry standard abbreviation for ___________________________.

3. Define volatile as it applies to RAM.

____

____

____

4. Name the two basic types of RAM: _________________ and __________________.

5. Which type of RAM needs to be re-energized constantly to retain its contents?

____

6. Define RAM parity.

____

____

7. _________________ refers to the process by which the computer rewrites data to RAM.

8. Describe the physical difference between a SIMM and DIMM chip.

____

____

9. Define memory caching.

____

____

Worksheet 2.5.2: Video Cards

1. A video card converts a _________________________ signal into a __________________ signal.

2. Video cards are also known as ____________________ or ________________________.

3. The video card receives its data from the __________________ and sends it to the ________________.

4. ___________________ provides video during bootup until the necessary video drivers can take over.

5. The abbreviation CRT stands for ______________________________________.

6. List the three colors mixed together within the CRT to produce all other colors:

   a. ____

   b. ____

   c. ____

7. How closely the pixels are grouped, which translates to how sharp the picture appears, is referred to as _________________________.

8. VGA and SVGA video adapters use a standard _______________-pin connector to connect to the monitor.

9. The term pixel stands for what?

____

10. The term VGA stands for what?

____

Worksheet 2.7.1: Floppy Drives

1. Explain what a floppy drive is used for in a computer.

____

____

2. Define the following parts of a floppy disk drive.

read/write head

____

____

logic board

____

____

stepper motor

____

____

case

____

____

hub

____

____

lever

____

____

3. List the different parts of a floppy disk.

   a.____

   b.____

   c.____

   d.____

4. What type of cable do you use to connect the floppy drive to the motherboard?

____

5. How many floppy drives can a computer support on a ribbon cable? ________________

6. What type of power supply connector do you use to supply power to the floppy drive?

____

Worksheet 2.7.2: Hard Drive Identification

1. Explain what a hard drive is used for in a computer.

____

2. Define the following parts of a hard drive.

cover-mounting screw holes

____

____

spindle

____

____

read/write heads

____

____

platter

____

____

actuator

____

____

actuator arm

____

____

base casting

____

____

disk platters

____

____

3. In revolutions per minute (rpm), how fast do hard drives spin?

____

4. Flux is the ______________ ______________ ______________ in the media.

5. What is RLL?

____

____

Worksheet 2.7.3: CD-ROM Identification

Explain how a CD-ROM is used.

____

Define the following components of a CD-ROM.

spindle

____

____

tray motor

____

____

laser lens

____

____

spindle motor

____

____

tracking drive

____

____

laser pickup assembly

____

____

3. List three common CD-ROM speeds found in computers and identify their transfer rate:

   a. ____

   b. ____

   c. ____

4. What type of power connection is used on a CD-ROM drive?

____

5. What is the audio out cable on a CD-ROM connected to in the computer?

____

6. How much information can you store on a CD-ROM?

____

7. Which type of interface controller used by CD-ROM is capable of faster transfer rates, IDE or SCSI?

____

Chapter 3

Assembling a Computer

Lab 3.3.4: The Computer Case and Power Supply

Estimated Time: 45 Minutes

Objective

In this lab, identify the type of computer case to be used, the form factor of the unit, and the voltage selector switch on the power supply. You also check the inventory of all the components that you will install in the computer case. Finally, you install motherboard standoffs to prepare the case for the installation of the motherboard.

Equipment

The following equipment is required for this lab:

- Electrostatic discharge (ESD) wrist strap
- Toolkit and screws
- Computer case with power supply
- Motherboard standoffs and screws
- Motherboard and manual
- Devices that will not be installed yet, but are referenced:
    - CD-ROM, sound card, modem, network interface card (NIC), RAM, hard drive with IDE cable, floppy drive with cable, mouse, keyboard, monitor

Scenario

You are assembling a personal computer for a friend, and you are ready to prepare the case for the installation of the motherboard.

Procedures

Be sure to wear the antistatic wrist strap during the entire installation process. One end should be looped snugly around the wrist, with the other end attached to an unpainted metallic part of the computer case. This strap prevents electrostatic discharge, which can be hazardous to computer devices.

Step 1

The first step in the assembly process is to create an inventory of all computer components that you will install into the computer.

Lay out the computer components that you will use in the labs for this module.

Gather all the information necessary to fill out the following inventory sheet.

Computer Identification	Name: ______________________ Number: ______________________
Case	Number of 3.5" bays _____5.25" bays _____ Manufacturer: __________________
Motherboard	Manufacturer: __________________ Model: ________________________ Bus Speed_________ MHz Form Factor _______AT _______ATX Chipset Manufacturer:______________ Model: ______________ BIOS Manufacturer:_______________ Version: _______________ Does the CPU use a socket or a slot? ________ How many CPU socket/slots are there? _______ How many ISA slots are there? ________ How many PCI slots are there? ________ How many EIDE connectors are there? _______ How many floppy connectors are there? _______ How many serial ports are there? _____ How many parallel ports are there? _____ Is there an AGP slot? _______ How many USB ports are there? ______ How many other ports or slots are there? _______ What kind(s) are they? _______
CPU	Manufacturer: ______________ Model: ___________________ Speed ________________ MHz
Memory	______ 30-pin SIMMs ______ 72-pin SIMMs ______ 168-pin DIMMs _____ 160 pin RIMMs ______ 184-pin RIMMs ______ Others: ___________ How many memory slots are there? _________ What is the fastest type of memory supported? ______ What is the maximum memory supported? _______

Hard Drive	Manufacturer: ___________________ Model: __________________ Size _______ Cylinders _________ Heads _________ SPT _______ Interface Type ________ IDE ________ SCSI
CD-ROM	Manufacturer: ____________________ Model: __________________ Speed: __________________ Interface Type __________ IDE ___________ SCSI
Floppy Disk Drive	Manufacturer: ____________________
Monitor	Manufacturer: ________________ Model Number: _______________
Video Card	Manufacturer: ________________ Model: _____________________ Memory ___________ MB ISA ______________ PCI ______________ On Board_______________
Sound Card	Manufacturer: __________ Model: ________________ ISA _____________ PCI _____________ On Board ______________
Mouse	Type __________ PS/2 __________ Serial ________________ USB
Keyboard	Connector _______ 5-pin DIN or ________ 6-pin mini DIN _______ USB (Make sure that it matches the connector on the motherboard.)
Power Supply	AT __________ ATX _________ Other _________ Power Supply Wattage _______

Step 2

Examine the screws that you will use for the case.

Are the screws Phillips, Flathead, Posidriver, or Torx? ___________________________________

Examine the computer case. Is it an AT or ATX case? ____________________________________

Briefly describe the difference between an AT and an ATX case:

____
____
____

Is the case a desktop, minitower, mid-tower, or a full tower?

____

Step 3

Most computer cases come complete with a power supply. However, not all cases are built for the United States market and therefore might not be set for the correct voltage. Look in the back of the case for the voltage selector switch. If in the United States, make sure that the switch is set to 115 volts. Adhere to the local power requirements when selecting the voltage for the power supply.

Step 4

Power supplies are rated by wattage, which is usually between 250 and 300 watts. What is the power-supply rating for the case? ______________________________

Step 5

Attach the motherboard standoffs to the case. Standoffs are small pegs made of a nonconductive material that helps avoid short circuits by preventing the motherboard from touching the case. Look at the holes on the motherboard to help place the standoffs in the proper locations.

Troubleshooting

An equipment list can help solve problems before they start. If there is an item missing, you discover it before the job is half done.

Reflection

Were you able to fill out all areas of the inventory list? ______________________

Explain any difficulties with the installation.

____
____
____
____
____

Lab 3.5.3: Motherboard Installation

Estimated Time: 45 Minutes

Objective

In this lab, you place the motherboard into the case and secure it. You also install the CPU, the heat sink, the LEDs, and the memory.

Equipment

The following equipment is required for this lab:

- ESD wrist strap and antistatic mat
- Toolkit and screws
- Motherboard and manual
- CPU with fan and heat sink
- Thermal grease
- RAM (use the appropriate type for the motherboard)

Scenario

The case for a friend's computer should be ready for the next step. Continue to work on installing the CPU and RAM.

Procedures

Be sure to wear an antistatic wrist strap for this lab and use extreme care. One discharge of static electricity could render a motherboard useless. In this lab, continue to work on the PC that you are building and properly install the motherboard, CPU, heat sink, CPU fan, and RAM.

Step 1

Lay the motherboard down on the antistatic mat. Identify the CPU socket on the motherboard. The CPU socket is keyed so that you can install the CPU only one way.

What CPU type does the motherboard support? ______________________________________

Step 2

Pick up the CPU and locate pin 1. Note that you can insert the CPU only one way into the CPU socket.

Install the CPU into the CPU socket. If you are installing the CPU into a Zero Insertion Force (ZIF) socket, no force is necessary. If you must apply any force, the CPU is not lined up correctly.

After the CPU is seated, adjust the CPU socket lever until it is in the locked position. When the lever is locked, the CPU is secure.

Who is the manufacturer of the CPU? ______________________________

Step 3

Attach the cooling fan to the heat sink. Use the four screws that came with the cooling fan to attach the fan securely to the top of the heat sink.

Note: Some heat sinks are already equipped with a fan and do not need to be secured with screws.

Is the heat sink attached with screws? ______________________________

Step 4

To attach the fan-heat-sink assembly to the CPU, lay the heat sink down on the CPU and align the heat sink clips to their correct positions on the CPU socket. If necessary, rock the heat sink into position until one side of the heat sink is locked down to the outside of the CPU socket. Next, push down the other clip until it locks. After you clip both sides of the heat sink, the heat sink is secured to the CPU.

Caution: Using a screwdriver might be necessary to secure the heat sink clips, but do not apply excessive force. If the screwdriver slips off the clips, it can damage the motherboard.

Step 5

Attach the power connection for the heat sink fan to the motherboard. Use the motherboard manual to identify the fan power pins on the motherboard. Connect the fan power leads to these pins and make sure that they are secure and in the correct orientation.

Step 6

Install the memory. When installing the memory, the first step is to identify the memory sockets. Use the motherboard manual to identify the memory sockets.

Examine the memory sockets and the memory chips. Memory and associated sockets are keyed to ensure proper installation.

Take the memory and line it up with the socket. Slowly seat the memory into socket 1. It might help to rock the memory into the socket until it is secure by gently pushing alternately on the ends of the chip.

Remember, just as with the installation of the CPU, if you exert too much force, you can damage or destroy the motherboard.

If you are to install more than one memory chip, follow the instructions in the manual for the motherboard to add more. It is common to place the next memory chip in socket 2. Refer to the motherboard manual for specific information.

Step 7

Install the motherboard. Align the motherboard with the standoffs and set it in the case. You might have to push the motherboard back slightly against the I/O plate to get it to line up correctly. After the motherboard is seated, use the proper screws to secure it to the case. Do not overtighten the screws or you might damage the board.

Step 8

Connect the front-panel LEDs to the motherboard. The motherboard connects to the LEDs on the front panel of the computer case to give the operational status of the computer. For example, a green LED on the front panel indicates that the computer is running.

Use the video demonstration and the manual for the motherboard to identify all the LED pinouts.

Connect each LED wire to the appropriate pinouts.

Troubleshooting

Proper installation of the cooling fan is absolutely necessary with newer processors. Newer processors run at high temperatures that can cause diminished performance or risk destruction if they do not cool properly.

Reflection

What would happen if the CPU fan stopped during normal computer operations?

____

____

____

____

What was the most difficult component to install? Why?

____

____

____

____

Lab 3.6.4: Floppy Drive, Hard Drive, DVD, and CD-ROM Installation

Estimated Time: 45 Minutes

Objective

In this lab, you install the floppy drive, hard drive, and CD-ROM drive. You also install the ribbon cables for each drive and the audio cable for the CD-ROM.

Equipment

The following equipment is required for this lab:

- The same computer case that you have been working on
- ESD wrist strap
- Safety glasses
- Toolkit and screws
- Floppy drive with ribbon cable
- Hard drive with ribbon cable
- CD-ROM with ribbon cable and audio cable
- DVD-ROM

Scenario

Continue to install the components necessary to complete a friend's computer.

Procedures

When installing devices that use ribbon cables to communicate with the motherboard, such as hard drives and floppy drives, it is important to note the location of pin 1. Examine the ribbon cable and find the red stripe on one side of the cable. Pin 1 is on the side of the ribbon with the red stripe. The motherboard documentation should show the location of pin 1 for each connector, and pin 1 is also usually labeled on the motherboard for each connector.

Step 1

Locate a 3.5-inch bay that is accessible from the front of the computer case. It is where you install the floppy drive. If there is a cover for this 3.5-inch bay, reach inside the case and push out the cover.

Step 2

Install the floppy drive and line it up with the 3.5-inch bay. Slide it in until the front of the drive lines up with the front of the computer case and the screw holes on the floppy drive line up with the side rails on the case. Use the proper screws and secure the floppy drive to the case. You might need a long screwdriver to reach the back side of the floppy drive.

Step 3

Install the hard drive.

Note: You do not have to remove the 3.5-inch cover for the hard drive bay. Line up the hard drive with the lower 3.5-inch bay. Slide the hard drive in until the screw holes line up with the case rails. Use the proper screws and secure the hard drive to the case.

Step 4

Install the CD-ROM into any of the 5.25-inch bays. In most computer cases, the 5.25inch bays are the upper bays.

Locate the 5.25-inch bay that you will use for the CD-ROM. If there is a cover for this bay, reach inside the case and push out the cover. Retrieve the CD-ROM from the parts inventory and slide it in from the front of the case. Push it back until it is flush with the case and the screw holes line up with the case rails. Use the proper screws and secure the CD-ROM to the case.

Step 5

The floppy drive is connected to the motherboard with a 34 pin, 2-connector ribbon cable that has a twist in it. The twist identifies one of the floppy drives as drive A:\. You use only one floppy drive during this installation. You could connect a second floppy drive to the second connector on the ribbon cable, and it would be assigned as the B:\ drive.

Select the proper ribbon cable for the floppy drive. Take one end of the ribbon cable and connect it to the back of the floppy drive. Take the other end and connect it to the floppy connector on the motherboard. Do not use excessive force when inserting the ribbon cable. Also, make sure that the plug is oriented correctly according to pin 1.

Step 6

You attach the CD-ROM using an IDE, 40-pin, 40-conductor ribbon cable. The CD-ROM cable typically has three connectors, one for the motherboard and two for devices. First, check to make sure that the jumper is seated in the slave location. Next, select the proper ribbon cable for the CD-ROM. Take one end of the ribbon cable and connect it to the back of the CD-ROM. Take the other end and connect it to the IDE2 connector on the motherboard. Do not bend the motherboard with excessive force when inserting the ribbon cable.

Step 7

Connect the audio cable that came with the CD-ROM. Attach one end of the cable to the CD-ROM and the other end to the motherboard. Usually, the audio cable connectors are notched and plug in only one way. If this is not the case, simply insert the connectors whichever way they can go in.

If no sound comes out after you power on the computer and test the CD-ROM, make sure that the volume is turned up on the speakers; otherwise, simply go back in the box, pull out the audio cable, and reverse the sides. Always consult the manuals that come with components for additional direction on installations.

Step 8

You also attach the DVD-ROM using an IDE, 40-pin, 40-conductor ribbon cable. Using the same cable as the CD-ROM, connect the DVD-ROM using the last connection on the IDE cable available.

Step 9

You attach the hard drive using an IDE, 40-pin, 80-conductor ribbon cable. The hard-drive ribbon cable looks similar to the CD-ROM cable. However, for each conductor, it has an associated ground wire, which is why it has 80 (instead of 40) conductors. This cable can fit into a CD-ROM and visa versa, but the hard drive does not work properly if they are switched. The easiest way to tell the difference between the CD-ROM ribbon cable and the hard drive cable is to feel them. Because the hard drive cable has 80 conductors, it is not as coarse as the CD-ROM cable.

First, make sure that the jumper is seated in the "master" location. Next, select the proper ribbon cable for the hard drive. Take one end of the ribbon cable and connect it to the back of the hard drive. Take the other end and connect it to the IDE1 connector on the motherboard. Do not bend the motherboard when inserting the ribbon cable.

Step 10

You attach the power cables to the motherboard and each drive. Examine the power cables that extend from the power supply. There is one large connector and several smaller connectors. The large 20-pin (ATX 1) attaches to the motherboard; the smaller connectors attach to the drives.

Most power supplies support four IDE drives and two floppy drives. The connectors for the floppy drives and for the IDE drives (CD-ROM, DVD-ROM, and hard drive) are different. Examine the back of each drive.

Find the power connectors on the back of each drive and connect the correct power cable to each one. Next, connect the ATX power connector. Use caution when attaching the ATX cable. Do not bend the motherboard.

Troubleshooting

If the floppy ribbon cable is keyed (it can plug in only one way), but the floppy drive does not have a keyed slot, check for a punch-out on the drive that can be removed to make room for the keyed slot. Otherwise, you need a nonkeyed floppy ribbon cable, and you can purchase one at a local computer-supply store.

Reflection

Briefly summarize the differences between the floppy drive and hard drive ribbon cables.

____
____
____
____
____

Write one tip that you learned from the material or in class that helped with the installation of the components in this lab.

____
____
____
____
____

Lab 3.7.1: Video Card Installation and System Booting

Estimated Time: 30 Minutes

Objective

In this lab, you install the video card. You also connect the mouse, keyboard, and monitor. If everything is installed properly, you should be able to turn on the computer at the end of this lab.

Equipment

The following equipment is required for this lab:

- ESD wrist strap
- Toolkit and screws
- Video card
- PS/2 mouse
- PS/2 keyboard
- 15-inch monitor
- 3.5-inch" DOS boot floppy
- Motherboard manual

Scenario

A friend cannot wait any longer for the computer to be finished. It is time to put the finishing touches on the machine and start it up.

Procedure

Before powering up a computer, it is extremely important to properly seat all the expansion cards. If a card is not properly seated when you turn on the computer, it malfunctions. Also, using excessive force when seating an expansion card can damage the motherboard, so you must do the job carefully.

Step 1

Recall from Chapter 2, "How Computers Work," that video cards are built for either the PCI slot or the AGP slot. Check the video card that is included in the equipment inventory.

In the following space, describe the video card. Include how much video RAM is on the card and whether it is a PCI or an AGP card.

____
____
____
____
____

To install the video card, first remove the slot protector from the back of the computer case. Locate the AGP slot or an available PCI slot. Remove the slot protector by removing the screw that holds it in place.

Step 2

Insert the video card into the AGP or PCI slot. If necessary, rock it gently until it is seated on the motherboard. After the video card is seated, line up the hole in the video card bracket with its corresponding hole in the computer case. Use a case screw to secure the video card to the computer case.

Note: Never leave a slot open without a card in it. Leaving a slot open causes poor air circulation in the case and some components can overheat.

Step 3

Before closing the computer case, review the following checklist:

____ Are there any loose screws in the computer case?

____ Have you removed all tools from the computer case?

____ Is the voltage selector switch in the correct position?

____ Is the CPU seated completely?

____ Is the fan secured?

____ Is the fan plugged in?

____ Is the memory in the correct slot, and is it fully seated?

____ Are all the drives in the correct positions and secured to the chassis?

____ Are the ribbon cables fully seated and connected to the correct drives?

____ Is the audio cable correctly connected to the CD-ROM drive?

____ Is the ATX 1 power cable in the right position, and did you latch it down?

After completing the checklist, put the computer case together. Attach all the case panels and secure them with the appropriate screws.

Step 4

Locate the two PS/2 ports on the back of the computer. One port is designated for the mouse and the other for the keyboard. Look closely at these ports. On newer motherboards, there is an icon for the mouse and keyboard. Also, each port might be color-coded. It is purple for the keyboard and green for the mouse. Plug the mouse and keyboard into their respective ports by lining up the pins and pinholes and pushing on the connections. Do not push too hard, but make sure they are inserted all the way.

Step 5

Locate the monitor and place it near the computer. Examine the video card adapter that was installed in Step 1. It is a 15-pin female connector. Examine the monitor connector. It is a 15-pin male connector. Line up the pins to the pinholes and connect the monitor cable to the video adapter. Most cables come with monitor screws already attached. Tighten these screws evenly until the monitor cable is attached to the video card.

Step 6

Now plug in the computer power cable. On ATX models, there is a power switch on the back of the computer and a power button on the front. Turn on the power switch first. The computer does not power up unless both the switch and the button are on.

Now, push the power button on the front panel of the computer. This move powers up the computer. Some front panel LEDs turn on, and the power supply fan starts spinning.

Step 7

Press the appropriate key to cause the computer to go into the BIOS setup mode. Some BIOS manufacturers use a different key, or key combination, to enter BIOS configuration mode. When first powering up the computer, you see a message that says something similar to "Press **F3** to enter Setup." If this message does not appear, consult the manual for the motherboard for the correct button or sequence of keys to push.

When the computer goes into BIOS setup, the main menu screen displays. Run through the BIOS settings and then boot the computer from a bootable floppy disk.

Move around the screen using the arrow keys until the Standard CMOS (**c**omplementary **m**etal **o**xide **s**emiconductor) menu item is highlighted. Press the **Enter** key to open the Standard CMOS features screen. In this screen, you can change the time, date, and the type of drive this computer recognizes.

Check whether the BIOS recognizes Drive A.

Does it show Drive A as a 1.44 MB, 3.5-inch floppy? ______________________________

Check whether there is a Drive B. Because you did not connect a second floppy drive when you built the system, you should not find one.

To leave the BIOS setup, press the **Esc** key. A prompt asks, “Do you want to quit without saving?” Press the **Y** key for yes.

Step 8

In this step, you boot the computer from a floppy disk. Restart the computer and insert the 3.5-inch bootable floppy disk. If you did not alter the standard BIOS settings, the computer looks for the operating system in the following order:

1. Removable media
2. Hard drive
3. CD-ROM

During normal operations, you boot the computer without a floppy disk. Therefore, the computer skips the floppy drive and finds the operating system on the hard drive.

Recall from Chapter 2 that DOS is a command-line operating system. After the computer boots, the screen displays an A:\> prompt. There are not any windows or icons visible.

Use the DOS boot disk to check some basic functions of the computer. Run the following DOS commands and write out the results of each:

Type **dir**, and then press **Enter**.

What are the results of typing this command?

____

____

Troubleshooting

Did the computer boot correctly? ____

If not, go over the checklist again. Have the instructor or lab aide look over the system. How many beeps do you hear? ____

If the computer did not boot correctly, what steps did you take to troubleshoot it?

____

____

____

____

Reflection

Did everything go as expected? If not, why not?

____

____

____

____

____

What would have made the construction of the computer easier? Describe a tip or technique that you learned when building this computer that you could use in the future.

____

____

____

____

____

Worksheet 3.3.4: Power Supplies

Worksheets enhance the material covered in the HP IT Essentials online course and companion guide. Use the space to answer the questions. Refer to this information to prepare for the A+ exam.

1. Depending on the type of case and motherboard selected, the power supply must adhere to the same ________ ___________ requirements to fit inside the case and correctly power the motherboard and other devices.

2. Some fans can change direction to allow air to be blown directly on the ________ and to regulate the quality of the air entering the case.

3. The two basic types of power supplies are ________ and ________.

4. Match each component with the voltage from the power supply unit that it uses.

1. ____	Motherboard	a. –5V
2. ____	Disk drives	b. +3.3V
3. ____	Serial port circuits	c. 0V
4. ____	ISA bus cards	d. +12V
5. ____	Most newer CPUs	e. +5V
6. ____	Ground	f. –12V

5. An AT power supply produces how many different levels of DC voltage?

____

6. An ATX power supply produces how many different levels of DC voltage?

____

7. Match each voltage with the correct color wire.

1. ____	Yellow	a. 0V
2. ____	Red	b. –5V
3. ____	Blue	c. +3.3V
4. ____	White	d. +12V
5. ____	Black	e. +5V
6. ____	Orange	f. –12V

8. Never attempt to repair a defective power supply. _______________ inside a power-supply box store electricity and discharge through the body if touched.

9. The ATX motherboard is a _____-pin keyed connector.

10. The AT motherboard has two _____-pin connectors.

11. The ATX motherboard directs air _________________ of the computer case.

12. The AT motherboard directs air ________________of the computer case.

Worksheet 3.9.1: What Is BIOS?

1. The acronym BIOS stands for what?

____

2. The BIOS code is typically embedded in a ________ chip on the motherboard.

3. ____________ BIOS allows the upgrade of the BIOS software from a disk provided by the manufacturer without replacing the chip.

4. Configuration of the BIOS on a computer is called the ________ setup or ___________ setup.

5. Without the correct code and_____________ _______________, the system either does not boot properly or works inconsistently with frequent errors.

6. The acronym POST stands for what?

____

7. Any problems during the POST are indicated by the BIOS displaying

____

8. BIOS initially runs basic device test programs and then seeks to _______________ these devices.

9. Circle all that are correct:

   a. BIOS contains the software required to test hardware at bootup.

   b. BIOS contains the software required to execute Windows applications and access user files.

   c. BIOS contains the software required to support the transfer of data between hardware components.

   d. BIOS contains the software required to support hard drive and floppy drive data storage.

   e. BIOS contains the software required to start the operating system.

10. BIOS is saved in the chip on the motherboard (even when the power is turned off) by a ______________.

Chapter 4

Operating System Fundamentals

Lab 4.2.3: Basic DOS Commands

Estimated Time: 30 Minutes

Objective

In this lab, you navigate the DOS command line. You also perform basic file-management tasks such as creating directories and files, navigating through directories, displaying the contents of directories, and displaying and changing file attributes.

Equipment

The following equipment is required for this lab:

- A computer with a version of DOS running

Scenario

A manager has asked you to create a directory structure using the DOS command line. The manager wants a directory created in which she will keep documents for the upcoming inventory. The directory structure the manager wants created is **C:\IT\pcs**. She has also asked that you create a read-only test file.

Procedures

The following steps detail the process of managing files by using the DOS command line. You use basic DOS commands to carry out the task presented by the manager. At the end, you safely delete the newly created directories and files that you created.

Step 1

There are a few different ways to access the DOS prompt (command line). The most common way is to boot into a version of Windows, press **Start** > **Run**, then type **command**. You can also access it by pressing **Start** > **Programs** > **Accessories** and selecting **Command Prompt**. If Windows does not load, you can access the DOS prompt by pressing **F8** during the boot process and then selecting **Safe Mode with Command Prompt**.

As illustrated in Figure 4-1, when you access DOS, the window displays the C prompt (C:\>).

Figure 4-1 DOS Prompt

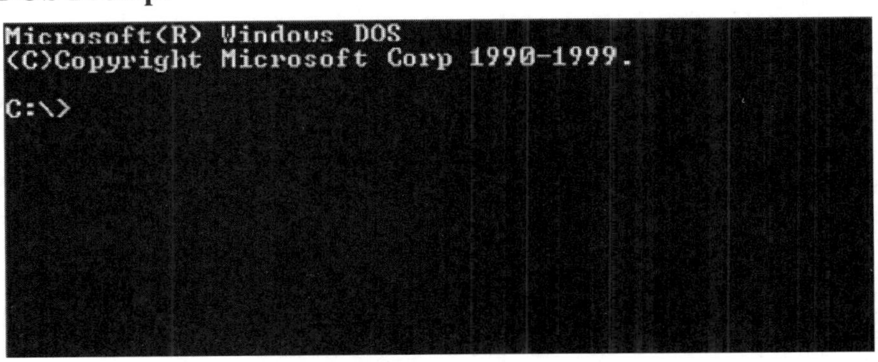

Step 2

At the C prompt, type **dir** to show a list of the directories on this drive.

As seen in Figure 4-2, the **dir** command lists directories and various files. Directories are specified with the <DIR> notation that precedes the file/directory. The **dir** command also displays the volume name, free space, and total files and directories present.

Figure 4-2 Using the dir Command

```
C:\>dir

 Volume in drive C has no label
 Volume Serial Number is 3608-11F7
 Directory of C:\

SOURCE         <DIR>          01-07-02 10:30a SOURCE
COMMAND  COM          93,890  04-23-99 10:22p COMMAND.COM
WIN98          <DIR>          01-07-02 10:47a WIN98
NETLOG   TXT          31,966  01-07-02 11:23a NETLOG.TXT
CONFIG   SYS               0  01-07-02 11:42a CONFIG.SYS
AUTOEXEC BAT               0  01-07-02 11:26a AUTOEXEC.BAT
SCANDISK LOG           5,412  02-26-02 10:59a SCANDISK.LOG
MYDOCU~1       <DIR>          01-07-02 11:43a My Documents
PROGRA~1       <DIR>          01-07-02 10:47a Program Files
         5 file(s)        131,268 bytes
         4 dir(s)   1,674,170,368 bytes free

C:\>_
```

Step 3

To create directories in DOS, use the **md directory_name** or **mkdir directory_name** command. Type **md IT** to create the IT directory:

`C:\>`**`md IT`**

Step 4

Next, display the IT directory using the **dir** command at the root (C:\>). Figure 4-3 shows the newly created IT directory.

Step 5

To change directories, use the **cd directory_name** or **chdir directory_name** command. For example, to access the IT directory, type C:\>**cd IT**. Typing this command changes the C prompt to C:\IT>.

Step 6

The command prompt should now be C:\IT>. The next task is to create another directory called **pcs**.

What command should you use to make this directory?

____

____

____

Figure 4-3 Creating a Directory in DOS

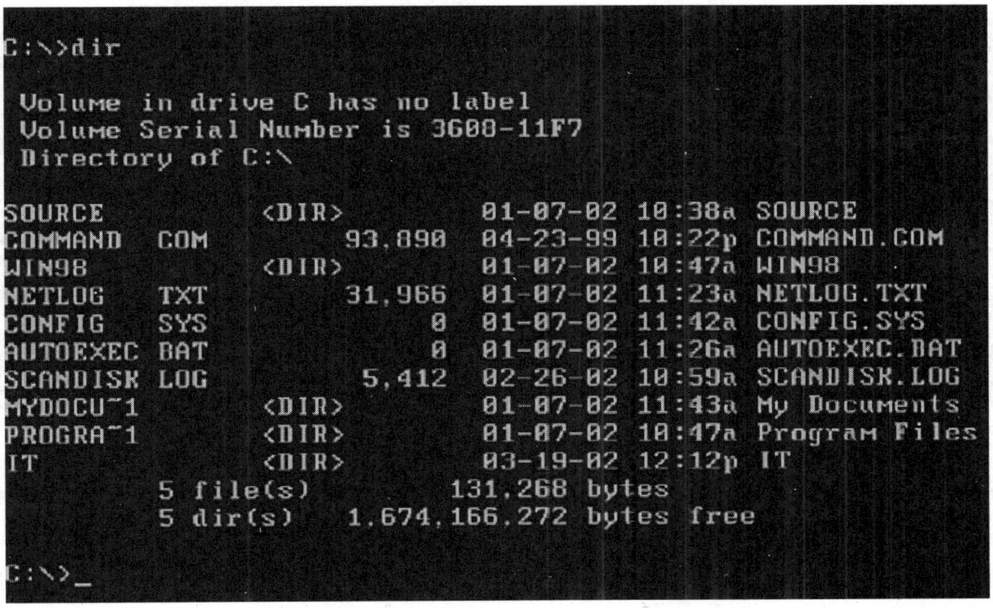

```
C:\>dir

 Volume in drive C has no label
 Volume Serial Number is 3608-11F7
 Directory of C:\

SOURCE         <DIR>        01-07-02 10:38a SOURCE
COMMAND  COM          93,890 04-23-99 10:22p COMMAND.COM
WIN98          <DIR>        01-07-02 10:47a WIN98
NETLOG   TXT          31,966 01-07-02 11:23a NETLOG.TXT
CONFIG   SYS               0 01-07-02 11:42a CONFIG.SYS
AUTOEXEC BAT               0 01-07-02 11:26a AUTOEXEC.BAT
SCANDISK LOG           5,412 02-26-02 10:59a SCANDISK.LOG
MYDOCU~1       <DIR>        01-07-02 11:43a My Documents
PROGRA~1       <DIR>        01-07-02 10:47a Program Files
IT             <DIR>        03-19-02 12:12p IT
         5 file(s)        131,268 bytes
         5 dir(s)   1,674,166,272 bytes free

C:\>_
```

Step 7

Navigate to the newly created pcs directory.

What command do you use to change to the pcs directory?

____

____

____

What does the command line look like?

____

____

____

Step 8

To create a file in DOS, use the **copy con** *filename* command. This command copies a file from the console (con) and places it in the directory. The console in this case is the screen. After you type this command, you see a blank line on the command prompt. Next, type in text that will be saved in the newly created file. When finished typing in the message, hold down the Control key (<**Ctrl**>), press the **Z** key, and then press the **Enter** key. This key combination ends the message and DOS displays "1 file(s) copied":

```
C:\IT\pcs>copy con sample.txt
This is an inventory test document
<Ctrl>+Z
<Enter>
1 file(s) copied
```

Step 9

Display the contents of the pcs directory. The newly created sample.txt in the directory appears. Figure 4-4 shows the DOS output for dir command in the pcs directory.

Figure 4-4 dir Command Showing the Newly Created File

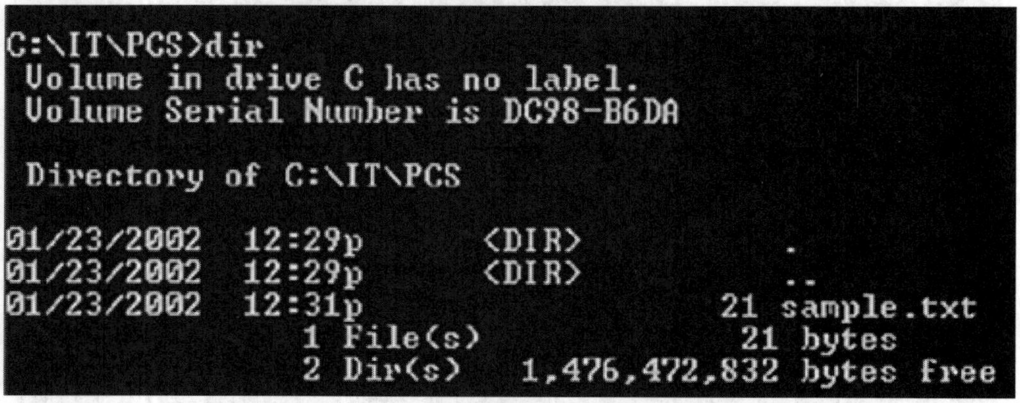

Step 10

Display the attributes for the sample.txt file. To display the attributes of a file, type in **attrib** *filename.* Valid attribute values are

- **R**—Read Only file attribute
- **A**—Archive file attribute
- **S**—System file attribute
- **H**—Hidden file attribute

What command do you type to display the attributes of sample.txt?

What are the attributes of sample.txt?

____

Step 11

To change or remove an attribute, use the **attrib [-/+]** *attribute_value filename* command. The minus (-) option removes an attribute value from a file and the plus (+) option adds an attribute value to a file. As discussed earlier, valid attribute values are R (read-only), A (archive), S (system), and H (hidden).

What command changes the attribute value of the sample.txt file to a read-only file?

____

Troubleshooting

In case a command is unclear or you forget what command to use, DOS can provide useful command information. DOS can provide general command syntax or detailed information about a specific command. The command to list all available commands is c:\>**help**. You can use this command at any level within the DOS structure. To find specific information about a command, including proper syntax and optional parameters, use the command c:\>**command /?**.

Reflection

What is the command to make a directory?

____

What is the command to delete or remove a directory?

____

List the four different attributes that you can assign a file.

____

____

____

____

Lab 4.2.4: Creating a DOS Boot Disk

Estimated Time: 25 Minutes

Objective

In this lab, you learn which files are necessary to make a floppy disk bootable. You also learn the commands necessary to create a boot disk.

Equipment

The following equipment is required for this lab:

- Operational computer with Windows 98 or earlier installed
- A blank floppy disk

Note: This lab does not work with Windows Me, Windows 2000, or Windows XP.

Scenario

As a computer technician, you need to create a boot disk to prepare a computer for installation. This disk will include utilities such as FDISK and FORMAT so that you can prepare a hard drive for an operating system.

Procedures

Formatting prepares the disk for use. For DOS, make a bootable disk using the same version of DOS that is on the hard drive.

Note: Use caution to not accidentally format the hard drive.

Step 1

If the computer is not already booted and showing a DOS prompt, boot it now. Put a floppy disk into the drive and format the floppy disk using the following command:

```
C:\> format A:/S
```

Which three files are necessary to make the disk bootable?

____________________ ____, ______________________ ___, __________________________

Step 2

Leave the disk in the drive and reboot the system. This process tests the disk to make sure that it is bootable.

Did the system successfully boot to a prompt? ____

What does the prompt look like? ____

Step 3

When the system boots using Microsoft DOS, the five files involved are AUTOEXEC.BAT, COMMAND.COM, CONFIG.SYS, IO.SYS, and MSDOS.SYS.

Assuming all five files are available on a bootable disk, what order are these files accessed when the system is booted?

1. ______________________________

2. ______________________________

3. ______________________________

4. ______________________________

5. ______________________________

Step 4

In addition to the five files mentioned earlier, certain utilities can be helpful when working with a computer that does not have an operating system:

- DEFRAG.EXE
- EDIT.COM (which may also require QBASIC.EXE if using an older version of DOS)
- FDISK.EXE
- FORMAT.COM
- MEM.EXE
- SCANDISK.EXE
- SYS.COM
- UNDELETE.EXE

Troubleshooting

You might restart a computer without removing the floppy disk from the floppy drive. If the disk is not bootable (it does not have IO.SYS, MSDOS.SYS, and COMMAND.COM), then an error message says "Non-System disk or disk error. Replace and strike any key when ready." It is possible that you did not use the /S switch if you receive this message after formatting a disk. Double-check that the disk has the proper files on it to make it bootable.

Reflection

List any other utilities that would be useful on a boot disk:

____

____

____

____

____

Worksheet 4.1.3: Operating System Fundamentals

Worksheets enhance the material covered in the HP IT Essentials online course and the companion guide. Use the space provided to answer the questions. Refer to this information when preparing for the A+ exam.

True or false:

1. ______ Two or more users running programs and sharing peripheral devices, such as a printer, at the same time is known as multitasking.
2. ______ Multitasking is a computer's capability to run multiple applications at the same time.
3. ______ When a computer has two or more CPUs that programs share, it is known as multiprocessing.
4. ______ Multithreading is not the capability for a program to be broken into smaller parts that can be loaded as needed by the operating system.
5. ______ Multithreading allows individual programs to be multitasked.
6. ______ UNIX has been around since the 1960s.
7. ______ Computers that are not capable of handling concurrent users and multiple jobs are often called network servers or simply servers.
8. ______ The file management system is what the OS uses to organize and manage files.

Worksheet 4.2.3: DOS Commands

Match each command with the function it performs.

1. ____DIR	a. Copies a file
2. ____CD	b. Displays memory properties
3. ____MD	c. Displays the status of a disk
4. ____RD	d. Changes the attributes of a file
5. ____DEL	e. Copies one floppy disk to another
6. ____REN	f. Formats a disk
7. ____SET	g. Displays the contents of a directory
8. ____MEM	h. Sets the system time
9. ____COPY	i. Prints a text document
10. ____TYPE	j. Opens a file for editing
11. ____FDISK	k. Removes a directory
12. ____TIME	l. Deletes a file
13. ____DATE	m. Creates a new directory
14. ____CHKDSK	n. Renames a file
15. ____DISKCOPY	o. Displays the contents of the environment variables
16. ____EDIT	p. Changes to a specified directory
17. ____FORMAT	q. Program used to format and partition fixed disks
18. ____PRINT	r. Displays the contents of a text file
19. ____ATTRIB	s. Sets the system date

Worksheet 4.2.7: DOS

True or false:

1. ____ DOS is an acronym for Data Operating Service.
2. ____ All generations of Windows to date support DOS commands.
3. ____ DOS is user friendly.
4. ____ DOS can run only a single program at a time.
5. ____ DOS can run very large programs.
6. ____ DOS is an essential tool used extensively for troubleshooting.
7. ____ DOS files on a disk are stored in what are known as folders.
8. ____ DOS records the location of every directory and file on a disk in a table called the FAT.
9. ____ DOS files are referred to by filenames comprising up to 8 characters and an extension.
10. ____ DOS filenames and their extensions are separated by a dash (-).
11. ____ DOS has a main directory on the disk known as the tree directory.
12. ____ The root of the C drive is represented by C:\.
13. ____ The directory name and filename are separated by a slash (/).

Chapter 5

Windows 9*x* Operating Systems

Lab 5.1.6: Changing File Views in Windows (Showing File Extensions)

Estimated Time: 20 Minutes

Objective

In this lab, you change the file view based on needs or preferences.

Equipment

The following equipment is required for this lab:

- A computer running Windows (95, 98, 2000, or XP)

Scenario

While navigating through some folders, you realize that the files and subfolders could be arranged better. You decide that the default display is not the best visual display for the files. In this lab, you change the file view to the preferred view.

Procedures

Changing the file view in Windows can reveal important information about files and subfolders. Users can find information on file size, file type, and the time and date of the last modifications. Also, you can configure the view based on personal preferences. View preferences include thumbnails, list, and large or small icons. Configuring the file view is especially helpful when a folder contains numerous files and subfolders. You can neatly display folder contents according to preference or needs, making navigation easier.

Step 1

Start the computer in the Windows desktop environment.

Step 2

Double-click the **My Computer** icon on the desktop to open the window.

Step 3

While the cursor is pointed at a blank space in the My Computer window, right-click and then select the **View** option. Figure 5-1 displays the right-click menu.

When selecting the **View** option, what parameters are available?

____

____

Figure 5-1 Selecting the View Option

Step 4

Select the **View** parameter for the files. Notice how icons in the folder change when you select a different view.

What information is displayed when you select the Details option?

____

____

Step 5

After selecting the View option, set this view for all folders. To do so, select **Tools** > **Folder Options**. Figure 5-2 displays this process.

Figure 5-2 Selecting the Folder Options

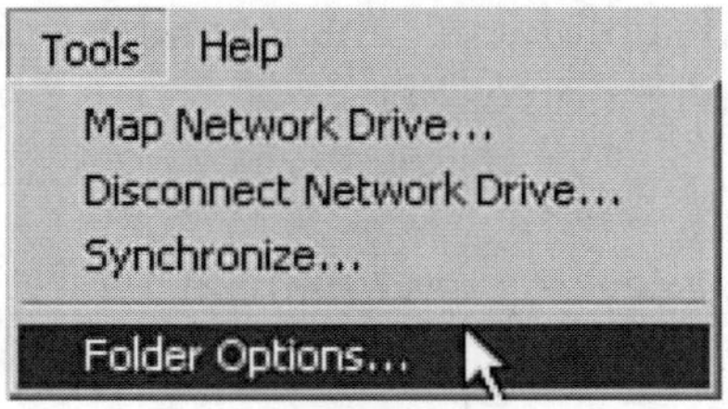

After you select **Folder Options** from the Tool menu, the Folder Options dialog box appears. Figure 5-3 shows the Folder Options dialog box.

Step 6

Select the **View** tab. What options are available in the View tab?

____

____

Step 7

From the View tab, select the **Like Current Folder** command button as shown in Figure 5-4. Selecting this button makes the view in the current folder global throughout the drive.

Figure 5-3 Folder Options

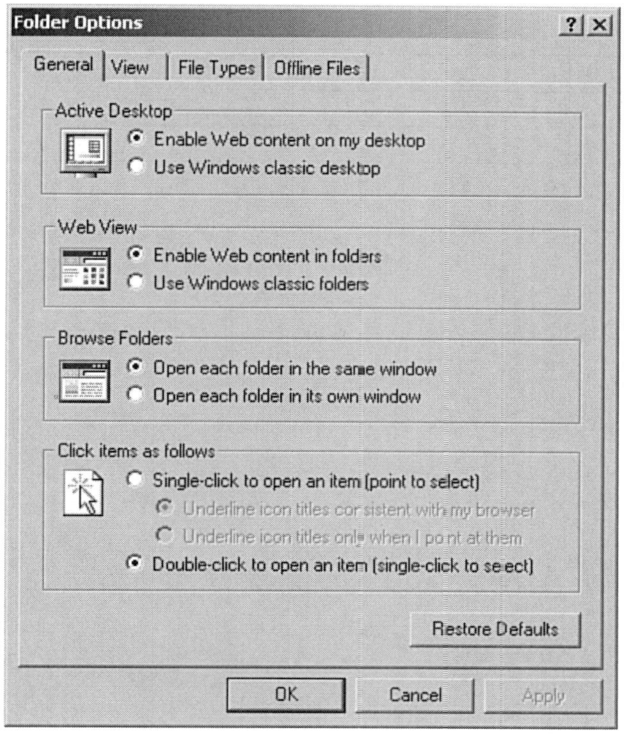

Figure 5-4 Folder Views

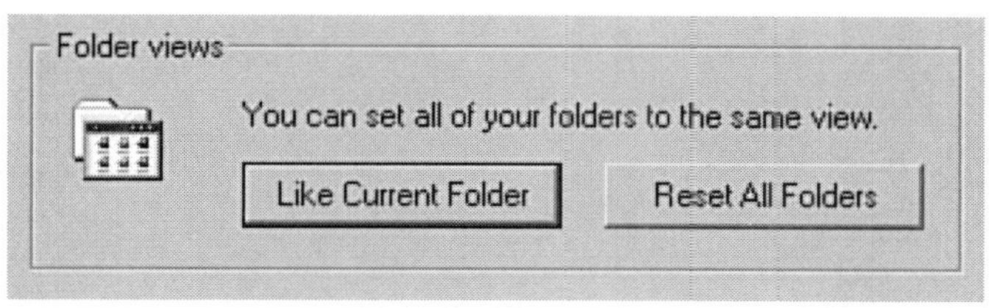

Troubleshooting

Changing a file view customizes the preferences. Also, you can view important details and system files using advanced options in the Folder Options window. System files are usually hidden to protect against accidental deletion, but sometimes, it is necessary to configure these files.

Reflection

How can you rearrange files in a folder?

____

____

____

____

____

Why would a user want to change the folder view settings?

Lab 5.1.7: Text Editing and File Management

Estimated Time: 30 Minutes

Objective

In this lab, you create a file in Notepad, save it to the hard drive, and then create a folder on a floppy disk and move the file from the hard drive to the floppy disk.

Equipment

The following equipment is required for this lab:

- Lab computer with Windows 98 or earlier installed
- 3.5-inch floppy disk

Scenario

You need to edit a text file for testing an installed floppy drive. To do so, you create, edit, and move a file from one location to another.

Procedures

Users manage and create files with an operating system (OS). Some of these tasks include updating, renaming, moving, and deleting files.

Step 1

From the Windows desktop, click the **Start** button, move the cursor to **Programs** > **Accessories**, and then click **Notepad**.

Step 2

Once Notepad is open and on the desktop, type any message within the editing area. Type just a few sentences and then click on the **File** menu and select **Save As**. This move opens a new window, which allows you to choose the location of the text file.

The default location is My Documents. If the My Documents folder is not the default, use the Save In drop-down box to choose My Documents. With My Documents as the folder, type **testfile.txt** within the File Name text box and then click the **Save** button.

Step 3

The file is now saved on the computer. You can close Notepad without losing any data.

To manage files on the computer, open a file-manager application such as Windows Explorer. This application appears in the Programs menu when you click on the **Start** button and then select **Programs** and **Windows Explorer**.

Note: An alternate way to open Windows Explorer is to right-click the **Start** button and choose **Explore**.

Step 4

Using the left window in Windows Explorer, locate the **My Documents** folder where the text file testfile.txt is saved.

Locate the **My Documents** folder and click it to display the contents on the right window. As with most things in Windows, there is more than one way to rename a file.

The more conventional way to rename a file is to select the file by clicking it once. Then, with the file testfile.txt selected, go to the **File** menu of Windows Explorer and select **Rename**. This move outlines the filename with a box and highlights the name of the file. Now, type a new file name for the file, such as **newname.txt**. After the file is renamed, press the **Enter** key to complete the changes.

The other way to rename a file in Windows is to right-click the filename itself and select **Rename** from the drop-down menu. Use this method to rename the file back to the original name **testfile.txt**.

Both methods work equally well. It is a matter of personal preference as to which way you use.

Step 5

Insert a formatted floppy disk into the floppy drive. Navigate Windows Explorer to the 3.5-inch floppy drive icon in the left window. When you select it, the contents of the floppy disk display in the right windowpane. There are two ways to create a new folder on the floppy disk.

The first way is to go to the **File** menu, select **New**, and then in the submenu that appears, click **Folder**. This move creates an empty folder that you need to name. In the same way that the text file was renamed, name the folder **my test folder** and press **Enter** to complete the process.

The second way to create a folder is to right-click in the right window, select **New**, and then select **Folder**.

Step 6

Moving a file from one location to another is a simple process. There are several ways to accomplish this move.

To move the text file that you created earlier to the folder that you created on the floppy disk, navigate Windows Explorer to the **My Documents** folder on the computer. From there, select the **testfile.txt** file and then go to the **Edit** menu and select **Cut**.

Now, navigate Windows Explorer to the folder that you created on the 3.5-inch floppy. Highlight the folder that you created, go to the **Edit** menu, and select **Paste**.

The file moves from the My Documents folder to the floppy disk. To verify that it moved, navigate Windows Explorer back to the **My Documents** folder to make sure that the file is not there anymore. Then, navigate back to the floppy and make sure that the document testfile.txt appears on the floppy.

Troubleshooting

Knowing how to cut, copy, and paste quickly saves a lot of time when working within the Windows environment. There are shortcuts to many of the commands within Windows. To cut a file without clicking the Edit menu or right-clicking, simply select a file and type the key combination **Ctrl-X**. Holding the **Ctrl** key and pressing **X** when a file is selected does the same thing as selecting **Cut** from the Edit menu.

Try this with all the shortcut commands.

Reflection

List a method used to copy or move files from one location to another by using the mouse only.

____
____
____
____
____

Lab 5.4.2: Hard-Drive Preparation Using FDISK and FORMAT

Estimated Time: 30 Minutes

Objective

In this lab, you partition the hard drive. You also install the three system files onto the hard drive to make it a bootable drive.

Note: This procedure erases any current information on the hard drive of the lab computer. Before proceeding, make sure to use only components that you can erase and copy to.

Equipment

The following equipment is required for this lab:

- A lab computer
- Bootable floppy disk with DOS FDISK and FORMAT files

Scenario

You need to prepare a new hard drive for the operating system. You use the DOS FDISK and FORMAT commands.

Procedures

After you install a hard drive into a computer, you must prepare it for the computer to communicate with it during the boot process. Using the DOS commands FDISK and FORMAT, you can partition the hard drive and prepare it for communication and usage.

Step 1

Boot up the computer using a bootable floppy disk with the FDISK and FORMAT files on it.

Step 2

To create and remove partitions, first start the FDISK program. Type **FDISK** at the prompt and then press **Enter**. Once the application starts, select option 4 to check and verify current partitions before attempting to delete any partitions.

Now, select the partition type to delete from the menu that appears. They are Primary DOS Partition, Extended DOS Partition, Logical DOS Drives in the Extended Partition, and a Non-DOS Partition, as shown in Figure 5-5.

If there are logical drives defined in the extended partition, you need to remove them before removing the extended partition. To delete any partition, simply select the option that correlates with the partition to be removed and follow the directions onscreen.

Step 3

After you remove all the partitions from the drive, return to the main menu and select option 1 to create a DOS partition. Then, from the next menu, select option 1 to create a primary DOS partition. From there, follow the onscreen directions to finish creating the primary DOS partition.

Figure 5-5 FDISK Options

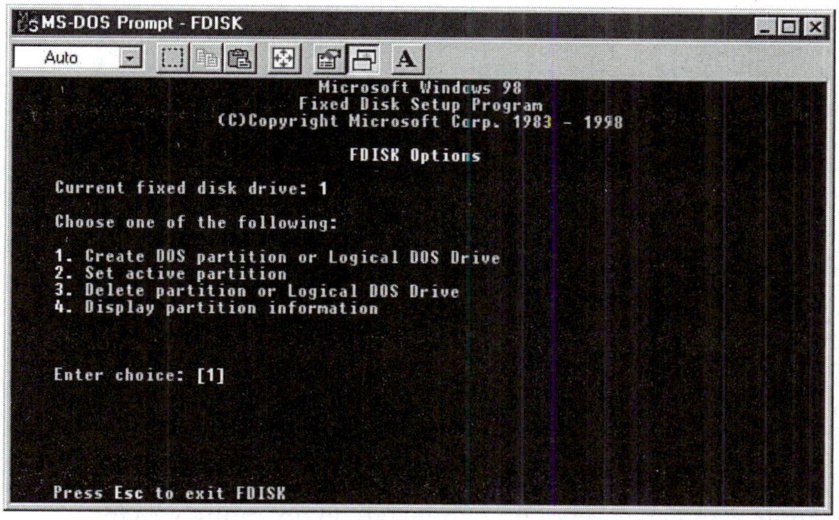

At this point, exit FDISK and then restart the computer with the floppy disk still in the drive.

Note: Make sure to set the primary drive to **Active**.

Step 4

After the computer restarts, it is time to format the partition that you just created. To do so, type **format C: /s** from the command prompt. This line tells the format program to make the C drive usable for DOS. The /s copies system files to the hard drive during formatting so that it is bootable.

The program gives the option of formatting the drive. This option erases anything that is on the drive. Because the drive is empty, type **Y** for yes and press **Enter** to continue.

Step 5

When the format is complete, enter your name when asked to enter a volume label. When the format is complete and the command prompt returns, restart the computer without the bootable floppy inserted to make sure that the computer will boot from the hard drive.

Troubleshooting

Sometimes, you need a third-party formatting application when dealing with certain partition types. If a hard drive does not let you remove a partition, consider purchasing a third-party product such as Power Quest's Partition Magic. It is available in most computer software stores.

Reflection

List the three files required for booting a DOS formatted disk:

______________________________, ______________________________, ______________________________

What other DOS commands will transfer these system files from one drive to another?

____

Lab 5.5.5: Windows OS Installation

Estimated Time: 60 Minutes

Objective

In this lab, you to install Windows 98.

Equipment

The following equipment is required for this lab:

- A computer with a partitioned and formatted hard drive
- A bootable floppy disk with CD-ROM drivers or a bootable CD-ROM drive
- Windows 98 Second Edition Install CD

Scenario

A friend has a computer and is not sure how to install an operating system.

Procedures

For a computer to be useful, it needs an operating system installed. The most commonly used operating system is Microsoft Windows. This lab takes about an hour to complete. Follow the steps to install Windows 98.

Note: You can use the same procedures to install other versions of Windows. However, there might be some significant differences during the setup process.

Step 1

Depending on whether the computer supports bootable CDs, you need to insert a bootable floppy disk with CD-ROM support to get started. If the computer supports bootable CDs, simply insert the Windows 98 installation CD and boot the computer. If a message prompts you to press any key to boot from the CD, press any key to get started.

Step 2

If you need to boot the computer from a floppy disk, insert the disk and turn on the computer. After the computer boots, you should see a DOS prompt that looks like A:\>. To begin the installation, change the directory to the CD-ROM drive by typing **D:** and then pressing **Enter**. Then, type **setup** and press **Enter** to begin the installation.

Note: The CD-ROM drive letter might be different depending on the computer, so make any necessary adjustments.

Step 3

The Microsoft Windows 98 Setup screen displays a few different options:

- To set up Windows now, press **Enter**.
- To learn more about Setup before continuing, press **F1**.
- To quit Setup without installing Windows, press **F3**.

Press **Enter** to install Windows 98.

Step 4

Prior to the installation, Windows Setup needs to run Scandisk to make sure that there are not any problems with the hard drive. Press **Enter** to continue and wait for the graphical setup interface to display.

Once the Windows 98 Setup screen displays, most of the installation is automated. However, the following steps walk you through the areas that require you to gather information.

Step 5

After Windows Setup runs Scandisk, a series of prompts lead you through the installation process. When the Windows 98 Setup Wizard displays, select the directory where Windows 98 is installed. Select the check box that says **C:\WINDOWS**.

Windows then prepares this directory.

Step 6

You see a series of setup options for the installation of Windows 98.

What are the available options for installing Windows 98?

____

____

____

____

For the purpose of this lab, select **Typical** and then press **Next**.

Step 7

Windows then prompts you with options for installing system components. Select the check box to install the most common components and then press **Next**.

Step 8

Setup then gives the option to identify the computer.

What parameters can you define to identify the computer?

____

____

____

____

You can either leave the default computer identification or enter custom information.

Step 9

The Windows 98 Setup Wizard then asks for the location. Make the appropriate selection and continue.

Step 10

Setup then prompts you to start copying files. Press **Next** to continue.

Step 11

At this point, a bar graph appears and begins to count up to 100 percent. Speed varies with system hardware. Carefully read the software license. Select **Yes** to agree with the license. Windows Setup then prompts for the CD-KEY. This information is with the Certificate of Authenticity on the CD case.

Enter the key exactly and click **Next** to continue. Click **Finish** to start using Windows 98.

Step 12

Windows runs through a series of automatic hardware detection features. This process of detecting hardware usually takes a few minutes. When Windows finishes detecting your hardware, select date and time properties. Continue through the Setup, and when prompted, reboot the machine.

Troubleshooting

It is possible for Windows Setup to not finish the installation properly. If, for some reason, there is a problem, try running setup again. Additional help and resources are available on Microsoft website at http://www.microsoft.com/.

Reflection

Did the Windows installation complete successfully? ________________________________

Make note of any tips or tricks learned during the installation.

Lab 5.6.1: Troubleshooting 101

Estimated Time: 20 Minutes

Objective

In this lab, you learn some basic troubleshooting skills.

Equipment

This lab requires a pen or pencil.

Scenario

The questions assist you with solving problems.

Procedures

Troubleshooting is an important part of a technician's job. You must approach troubleshooting in a systematic way. One way to do so is by looking at the most obvious things first. Overlooking the obvious can cost time and money. Remember that every time a technician goes into the computer, there is a risk of damaging the computer.

Step 1

Write down the steps a technician should take if a printer is not printing. Put them in order, starting with what a technician should check first.

____

____

____

____

____

____

Step 2

Write down the steps a technician should take if a file cannot be saved onto a floppy disk. Put them in order, starting with what a technician should check first.

____

____

____

____

____

Step 3

Write down the steps a technician should take if a monitor is not displaying anything. Put them in order, starting with what a technician should check first.

____

____

____

____

____

____

Step 4

Write down the steps a technician should take if the computer will not turn on. Put them in order, starting with what a technician should check first.

____

____

____

____

____

____

Troubleshooting

When approaching a computer that is reportedly broken, rule out the obvious first. Make sure the unit is turned on and that all components are plugged in properly. Also, it might help to ask the user of the system about the last thing done on the computer before it failed.

Reflection

Troubleshooting requires a systematic approach to solve problems. Choose a problem that is not computer related. An example might be that the toaster does not toast bread. List the steps that you should take to solve this problem. Is a systematic approach useful in solving non-computer–related problems?

____

____

____

____

____

____

Lab 5.6.4: Installing a Driver

Estimated Time: 20 Minutes

Objective

In this lab, the student installs the driver for a rollerball mouse. You use the same process when installing any new device on a system.

Equipment

The following equipment is required for this lab:

- Lab computer with Windows 98 or earlier operating system
- A rollerball mouse with the driver disk

Scenario

You need to install a new rollerball mouse.

Procedures

Make sure that the proper drivers for the operating system are installed. Drivers built for Windows 95 might install properly on a Windows 98 platform but could cause undesirable results.

Step 1

From the Windows 9*x* Desktop, go to **Start** > **Settings** > **Control Panel**.

Step 2

On the Control Panel, double-click the **Add New Hardware** icon. This move starts the Add New Hardware Wizard. Read the onscreen display and click the **Next** button to continue.

Step 3

The Hardware Wizard searches for Plug and Play devices. Click the **Next** button to continue. When the search is complete, the wizard asks whether it can search for devices that are not Plug and Play compatible. Select **No, I want to select the hardware from a list** and then click **Next**.

Step 4

You see a list of hardware devices to choose from. Select the device that most closely matches the device being installed, which would be a **Mouse** in this lab. Click **Next**.

Step 5

If the latest driver is on a CD-ROM or floppy disk, insert it into the computer. Click the **Have Disk** button and then either type the path to the driver or click the browse button to find the exact location of the driver. After you select the driver, click **OK** to continue.

At this time, the wizard displays a list consisting of any number of devices, which should match the device being installed. Select the one that the device most closely matches and then click **Next**.

Step 6

Follow the rest of the onscreen instructions to complete the installation process. When the driver is installed, you must restart Windows for the changes to take effect. If a dialog box displays to restart, click **Yes**. Otherwise, click the **Start** button, select the **Shut Down** option, and then shut down the computer.

Step 7

Once the computer is shut down, remove the current mouse and plug the new rollerball mouse into the PS/2 port. When it is plugged in properly, turn on the computer. Test the new device at the Windows desktop. If the device does not respond, see the troubleshooting section of this lab.

Troubleshooting

It is important to use the correct driver when installing a device. For example, a new sound card will most likely not work or will work improperly if you install the wrong drivers.

Also, using the latest driver is a good practice to follow. When installing a new device, check the manufacturer's website for the latest drivers available for its product.

If there are problems with the mouse pointer, verify that it is properly connected and that the mouse pointer is clean and free of any dust or debris. If the problem still exists after verifying the connection and cleaning, restart the machine. Rebooting the machine refreshes and reloads the mouse pointer drivers. This action should resolve most problems associated with the mouse pointer devices. However, if the problem still exists, you might need to update the driver. To update the driver, simply repeat the steps outlined in this lab with the latest driver found on the Internet.

Reflection

Were there any problems installing the drivers for this device?

____

____

If so, explain how you solved the problem.

____

____

____

____

____

____

Lab 5.6.5: Creating a Startup Disk

Estimated Time: 15 Minutes

Objective

In this lab, you create a Windows startup disk.

Equipment

The following equipment is required for this lab:

- Computer with Windows 98 or earlier installed
- One 3.5-inch blank disk

Scenario

The Windows operating system is installed, but you did not make a Windows startup disk during the installation.

Procedures

Once the operating system is up and running, create a Windows 98 startup disk. If for some reason Windows does not load, the boot disk might be necessary to begin the troubleshooting process.

Note: In this lab, use the built-in functionality of Windows to create a Windows startup disk. You can make a boot disk by copying the necessary startup files onto a floppy disk.

Step 1

From the Windows desktop, go to **Start** > **Settings** > **Control Panel**.

What is the general purpose of the Control Panel?

____

____

____

____

____

____

Step 2

Once the Control Panel displays, double-click the **Add/Remove Programs** icon. In the Add/Remove Programs Properties window, select the **Startup Disk** tab.

Step 3

Click the **Create Disk** button. A status bar indicates that it is preparing the files needed for the startup disk. If the .CAB files (cabinet files) are not available, Windows prompts for the Windows installation CD.

Step 4

When the files for the startup disk have been collected, Windows prompts you to label a disk and insert it into the drive. Click the **OK** button.

Step 5

After the startup disk is created, write-protect the disk by moving the switch to the open position. The switch is located on the back of the disk at the top-left corner.

Why is it important to write-protect a bootable floppy disk?

____

____

____

____

Step 6

To finish the process, reboot the system to make sure that the disk works.

Troubleshooting

You often need a bootable floppy disk while working on computers. If the operating system does not start, you use a floppy disk to view the contents of the hard drive and begin the troubleshooting.

Reflection

What three files do you need for a floppy disk to boot properly?

____

____

____

Worksheet 5.1.10: Windows Files and Folders

Worksheets enhance the material covered in the HP IT Essentials online course and the companion guide. Use the space provided to answer the questions. Refer to this information when preparing for the A+ exam.

1. A __________________ and a ________________ are equivalent terms for the same concept. They are places to store files.

2. The ___________ directory is the master folder that contains all the other folders.

3. Names of early Windows 3.1 and DOS filenames are limited to _____ letters plus a ______ letter extension, but Windows 98 and later allow extended filenames of up to _________ characters.

4. Drive letters use the 26 letters of the alphabet followed by a colon. _____ and _____ are reserved for floppy drives, whereas _____ is for the hard drive.

5. When you __________-click an item on the desktop or in Explorer, you see options such as Copy, Move, or Create Shortcuts.

6. ________________ give immediate clues as to the creation or last-modified date of a file or folder, type of item, and size of the file.

7. To highlight several files at one time, hold down the ______ key and click those files you want to select.

8. To unselect a file within a group of selected files, hold the ______ key and then click the highlighted file you want to deselect.

9. To select all files, select ___________ from the menu on the toolbar, and click Select All.

10. _______________-click a file to open it.

11. To copy a file or folder onto a floppy disk, ______________-click the file and click_____________ _______; then click 3 ½ Floppy.

12. Until you _____________ the Recycle Bin, the files are still in the folder on the hard drive.

13. Files can be ___________________ from the Recycle Bin to the original folder that stored the file.

14. _____________-clicking the Recycle Bin brings up a menu, which allows easy emptying.

Worksheet 5.2.2: Managing Printers

1. To add a new printer, you need to click the **Start** button, go to **Settings**, choose **Printers**, and then select ______________________________.

2. The six steps to adding the local printer using the Add Printer Wizard in Windows 98 follow:

   Step 1: Select ___________ printer.

   Step 2: Locate the __________________ on the manufacturer and model list.

   Step 3: Select the printer _________.

   Step 4: _____________ the new printer, especially if there are many printers.

   Step 5: If you want, you can set this printer to be the __________________ printer, if it is the one most commonly used printer.

   Step 6: Print a ____________ page.

3. You can access the print manager by clicking the _______________ icon on the right side of the taskbar.

4. You can access the print manager by going to the ________________ folder under Settings on the Start menu and then _______________-click the printer you are using.

5. Sometimes, you encounter a printer ________________. Then, a pop-up _____________ appears to let you know what it is.

Worksheet 5.4.2: Preparing the Hard Drive

Match each vocabulary word with its correct definition.

1. _____ Primary partition	a. The collective name for all tracks having the same number in a hard disk drive when several disks are stacked and rotate on a common spindle.
2. ____ Extended partition	b. The area on each logical DOS disk where the information to boot the operating system is recorded.
3. _____ Active partition	c. A special file that is created and located in the disk's sector 0 where DOS stores information about the disk's directory structure.
4. _____ Logical drive	d. The first partition on a DOS disk (usually contains an operating system).
5. _____ FDISK	e. A 512-byte "chunk" of space on a DOS disk.
6. _____ Boot sector	f. The partition DOS refers to at bootup.
7. _____ Partition table	g. The process that creates a blank file allocation table and root directory structure on a DOS disk.
8. _____ Track	h. A physical separation of information within an extended partition.
9. _____ Sector	i. The process that marks off the disk into sectors and cylinders and defines their placement on the disk.
10. _____ Cluster	j. The partitioning program for MS-DOS.
11. _____ Cylinder	k. The partition that is normally assigned all the available space left on a DOS drive.

12. _____ FAT	l. Concentric circles on the disk surface created by formatting a hard drive.
13. _____ Low-level format	m. Two or more sectors on a single track.
14. _____ High-level format	n. A record of the starting point of each logical drive, active partition, and master boot record.

Worksheet 5.6.6: Troubleshooting Windows Installation

1. Isolate the problem as either ____________________ or ____________________ related.
2. After installing the OS and not receiving a successful boot, first attempt to restart the machine using the ______________________ button.
3. To learn more about setup errors, refer to the __________________ .txt file that comes with the Windows installation disks or CD.
4. The computer's System Properties gives __________ categories of information, each represented by a tab.
5. The ___________________ ______________________ in Windows provides a graphical interface representation of the devices configured in the system.
6. A device ___________________ is software specially designed to enable the computer to use the hardware or devices installed within the system.
7. What is a Windows startup disk?

____

____

8. To create a Windows 98 startup disk, double-click ___________________ from the Control Panel window.
9. In addition to the critical operating system files copied to the Windows 98 startup disk during creation, what three important disk utilities for troubleshooting are added?

____ SCANDISK.EXE	____ MSD.EXE	____ MEM.EXE
____ WIN.COM	____ AUTOEXEC.BAT	____ FORMAT.EXE
____ WIN.INI	____ SYSTEM.INI	____ FDISK.EXE
____ CONFIG.SYS	____ BOOTLOG.TXT	____ SETUP.TXT

10. When you select the Save Uninstall Information option during Windows 98 setup, Setup creates the _________________ .dat and _________________ .ini files that contain the uninstall information.

Chapter 6

Windows NT/2000 Operating Systems

Lab 6.2.1a: Creating Users Accounts in Windows 2000

Estimated Time: 30 Minutes

Objective

In this lab, you create users and groups as well as assign properties to each.

Equipment

The following equipment is required for this lab:

- A computer with Windows 2000 Professional installed

Scenario

A coworker needs to use a shared computer that contains sensitive files. In this case, it is a good idea to set up a user account for her.

Procedures

Being able to create users and then organizing those users into groups is an essential task when working with Windows 2000. A user account enables a system administrator to log in and access the resources of the computer as well as have a custom environment to work in. A group is simply a collection of users. In this lab, you create both users and groups.

Step 1

From the Control Panel, select the **Users and Passwords** applet. Click the **Advanced** tab, and then click the **Advanced** button. What is the title of the window that opens?

____

Step 2

In the Local Users and Groups window, select the **Users** folder in the left pane. From the Action menu, select **New User**.

What options are available in the New User dialog box?

____

____

____

____

____

____

Step 3

In the New User dialog box, fill out the information for a new user named **LocalUser1**, full name **John Doe**, and in the Description box, type **User**. For the password, just use the word

password. Uncheck the box **User Must Change Password at Next Logon**, and then click the **Create** button.

Using the same process, create a second user named **LocalUser2**, full name **Jane Doe**, and in the Description box, type **User**. For the password, just use the word **password**. Uncheck the box **User Must Change Password at Next Logon**, and then click the **Create** button. When finished, click the **Close** button.

Step 4

Test the user account by logging off the current user and then logging back in using the username that you just created.

Did the user account work properly? ____

If the user account did not log in properly, see the troubleshooting section.

Troubleshooting

If the user account was not created or if it is disabled, retrace the steps necessary to create a new user account and double-check that everything is set up properly.

Reflection

Why is it necessary to have separate user accounts on a local machine?

____
____
____
____
____
____

Lab 6.2.1b: Assigning Permissions in Windows 2000

Estimated Time: 30 Minutes

Objective

In this lab, you learn how to assign NTFS permissions to folders.

Equipment

The following equipment is required for this lab:

- A computer running Windows 2000 formatted with NTFS

Scenario

The boss needs a folder structure created and permissions assigned to the folders.

Procedures

Managing folders and assigning access rights is an important capability of operating systems. This capability helps ensure data integrity by defining the level of user access.

Step 1

First, open **My Computer** and then open the **C:** drive by double-clicking them. Create a folder and name it **Chemistry.** Within the **Chemistry** folder, create an **Experiments** and a **Laboratory** folder. Within the **Chemistry\Experiments** folder, create a **Week3** folder. Refer to Lab 6.2.1 to create the **LocalUser1** and **LocalUser2** user accounts. In the first part of the lab, assign permissions to folders based on these folders, users, and groups. In the second part of the lab, log on to the system as one of the users and test these NTFS permissions.

The following table shows the final structure that you create.

Folder Name and Path	Groups	Permissions
Chemistry	Users group	Read & Execute
	Administrators group	Full Control
Chemistry\Experiments	Users group	Read & Execute
	Administrators group	Full Control
Chemistry\Experiments\Week3	Users group	Read & Execute
	Administrators group	Full Control
	LocalUser2	Modify
Chemistry\Laboratory	Users group	Read & Execute
	Administrators group	Full Control

Step 2

Log on with the administrator account or with an account that has administrator rights, and navigate to the folders that you created according to the scenario.

When at the folder, right-click the folder on which you need to modify permissions, and then click **Properties**. The Properties box should appear for the folder with the General tab view.

Click the **Security** tab.

Step 3

Next, click the **Add** button to add permissions to user accounts or groups. The **Add** button window displays the Select Users, Computers, or Groups window. Verify that the correct computer name is entered.

In the name box, select the name of one of the user accounts or groups listed in the scenario, and then click the **Add** button. You must repeat this process for each user account and group that is listed (for the appropriate folder) in the previously mentioned table.

Step 4

Click **OK** when finished. The Properties dialog box for the folder reappears.

If the Properties box contains user accounts and groups that are not listed in the scenario, remove them by selecting them and then clicking **Remove**.

Step 5

This step specifies the permissions for the folders in the scenario. For all user accounts and groups that are listed for the folder in the scenario, select the user account or group that corresponds to the folder under Name. Then under Permissions, select the **Allow** box or the **Deny** box next to the appropriate permissions that are listed for that folder in the scenario.

Click **OK** to save the changes and close the Properties box.

Repeat this procedure and continue to assign permissions for each folder in the scenario.

Close all the boxes and log off of Windows.

Step 6

Log on as **LocalUser1** and navigate to the **Chemistry\Experiments\Week3** folder. Try to create a file in the Week3 folder.

Could you create this file?

___

Log off of Windows and log back on as **LocalUser2**; then, navigate to the **Chemistry\Experiments\Week3** folder. Try to create a file in the Week3 folder.

Could you create this file?

___

Log off of Windows and log back on as **Administrator**, and then navigate to the **Chemistry\Experiments** folder. Try to create a file in the Experiments folder.

Could you create this file?

____

Log off Windows and log back on as **LocalUser1**; then, navigate to the **Chemistry\ Experiments** folder. Try to create a file in the Experiments folder.

Were you able to create this file?

____

Log off of Windows and log back in as **LocalUser2**, and then navigate back to the **Chemistry\ Experiments** folder. Try to create a file in the Experiments folder.

Could you create this file?

____

Troubleshooting

Assigning NTFS permissions can be a confusing task when dealing with large amounts of data that can be spread out over large volumes. It is a good idea to keep the process as simple as possible. When a drive or volume is formatted with NTFS, the Full Control permission is assigned to the Everyone group. Change this default permission and assign other appropriate NTFS permissions to control access to the folders and files on the network.

Reflection

Why would you use permissions on a computer?

____

____

____

____

____

____

Lab 6.2.4: Creating an Emergency Repair Disk in Windows 2000

Estimated Time: 20 Minutes

Objective

In this lab, you learn how to create and use an emergency repair disk.

Equipment

The following equipment is required for this lab:

- A computer system running Windows 2000
- A blank 3.5-inch floppy disk

Scenario

You need to create an emergency repair disk so that you can use it in the event of a computer malfunction. The disk also has to repair the file systems if they become damaged.

Procedures

In the first part of this lab, you create the emergency repair disk. In the second part of the lab, you use the emergency repair disk.

Step 1

Run the Backup program. Go to **Start** > **Programs** > **Accessories** > **System Tools** > **Backup**. Click the **Emergency Repair Disk** button on the Welcome tab.

Insert a blank formatted disk into Drive A.

Check the box labeled **Also Backup the Registry to the Repair Directory**.

Click **OK**. Remove the disk, label it **Emergency Repair Disk**, and include the current date.

Step 2

Insert the Windows 2000 CD and boot from the CD.

Press **R** to use the emergency repair disk.

When presented with a Fast or Manual option, press **F** to select the Fast option. Press **Enter** to use the emergency repair disk. Insert the emergency repair disk and press **Enter**.

After the files are repaired, reboot the operating system.

Troubleshooting

If the disk is not the proper type, there might be some difficulty during the emergency repair disk creation process. Make sure to use a 3.5-inch HD formatted floppy disk.

Reflection

Why is the emergency repair disk important in the troubleshooting process?

____

____

____

____

Lab 6.4.3: Installation Demonstration of Windows 2000

Estimated Time: 90 Minutes

Objective

In this lab, you learn how to install the Windows 2000 operating system.

Equipment

The following equipment is required for this lab:

- A computer with a blank hard disk
- Windows 2000 installation CD

Scenario

The computer file system has become corrupt because the user installed software that was infected with a virus. During installation of the software, the virus deleted all the files on the hard drive. You must reinstall the operating system.

Procedures

In this lab, you learn how to install the Windows 2000 Professional operating system.

Step 1

Insert the CD into the CD-ROM drive.

Next, configure the system BIOS boot sequence to boot from the CD-ROM first. Keep the CD in the drive and restart the computer.

When the system starts up, watch for the message "Press Any Key to Boot from CD". When the message appears, press any key on the keyboard and boot the system from the CD.

In Figure 6-1, the Windows 2000 Setup screen appears and loads the necessary files.

Figure 6-1 Windows 2000 Setup Screen

This screen displays for a few minutes while the files are copied to the hard drive.

The Welcome to Setup screen displays as shown in Figure 6-2 with options to install, repair, or quit. Press **Enter** to proceed with the installation.

Figure 6-2 Welcome to Windows 2000 Screen

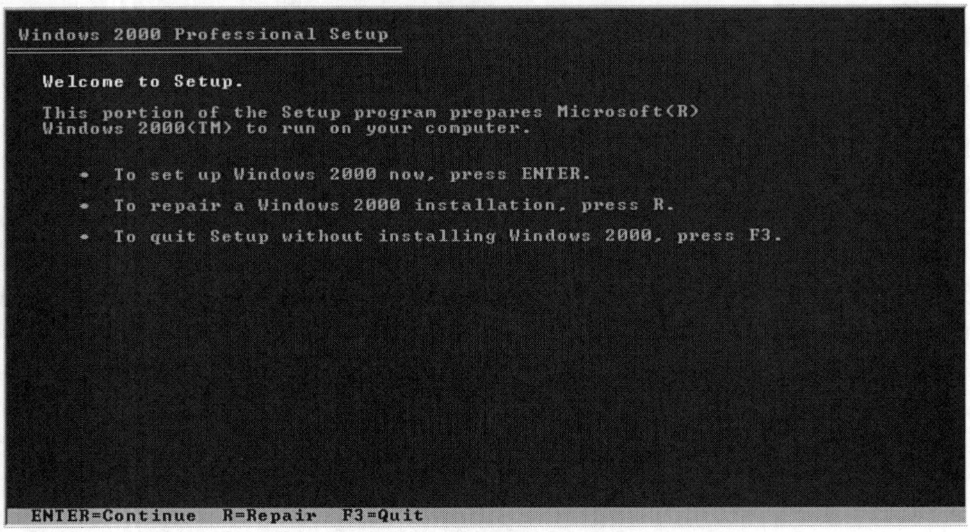

The next step is to partition and format the drive if needed. This step is not always required. For this lab, create a small partition (2 GB) for installing Windows 2000. This step makes the installation a faster process.

Select the option to partition the drive first, and then select the option to format the drive with NTFS.

Setup begins formatting the partition.

When partitioning and formatting is complete, the Windows 2000 Professional Setup screen appears and starts copying the system files to the hard drive, as shown in Figure 6-3.

The system restarts automatically after the files are copied. When the system restarts, you see the message "Press Any Key to Boot from CD" again. Do not press any keys at this time.

Figure 6-4 shows the Windows 2000 splash screen that displays.

This step prepares the system for device installation. The next step, shown in Figure 6-5, will detect and install required devices including the keyboard and mouse.

Figure 6-3 Windows 2000 Setup Copying Files to the Installation Folder

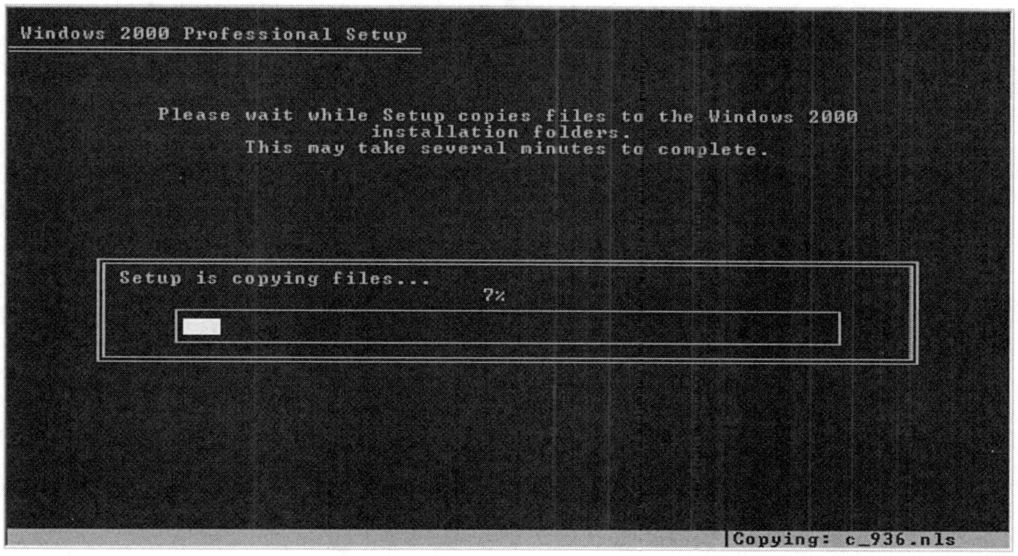

Figure 6-4 Windows 2000 Splash Screen

Figure 6-5 Windows 2000 Installing Devices Screen

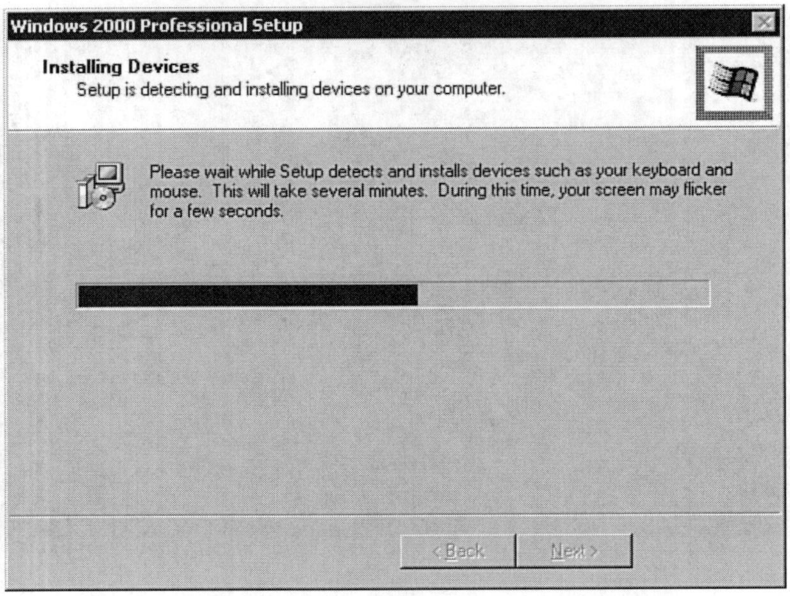

When the system is done installing the devices, Setup proceeds to the Regional Setting screen.

You can change these settings if required. However, for the purposes of this lab, press **Next**.

On this screen, enter the username and the name of the company. Click **Next**.

Enter the Microsoft product registration key when prompted. Click **Next** to continue.

The Computer Name And Administrator Password screen displays next, as shown in Figure 6-6. Enter the computer name and the administrator password.

Figure 6-6 Windows 2000 Computer Name and Administrator Password Screen

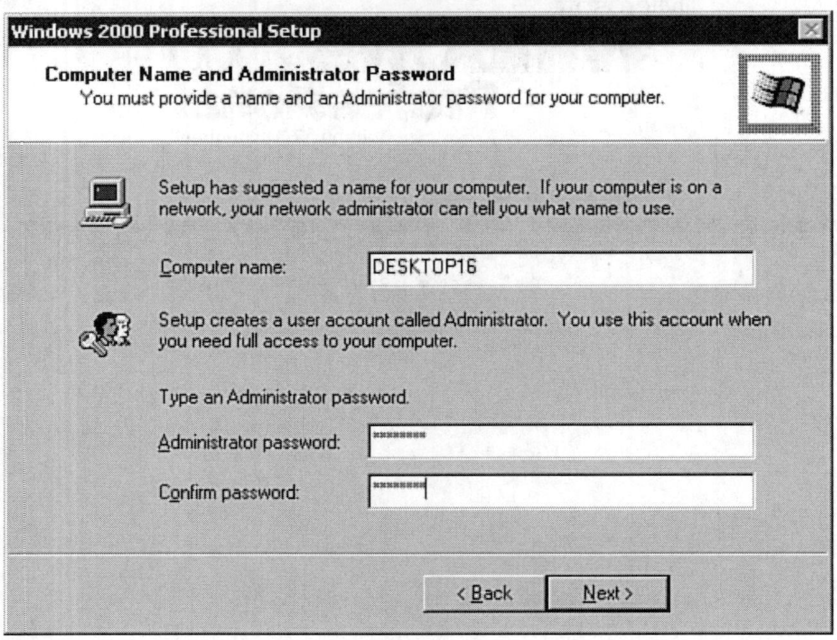

Accept the name suggested by Setup, or enter the name assigned to this computer by the network administrator. Enter the word **password** for the password. Click **Next**.

Enter the appropriate date and time settings for the region. Click **Next**.

Setup now proceeds to the Network Settings screen, as shown in Figure 6-7.

Figure 6-7 Windows 2000 Network Settings Installation Screen

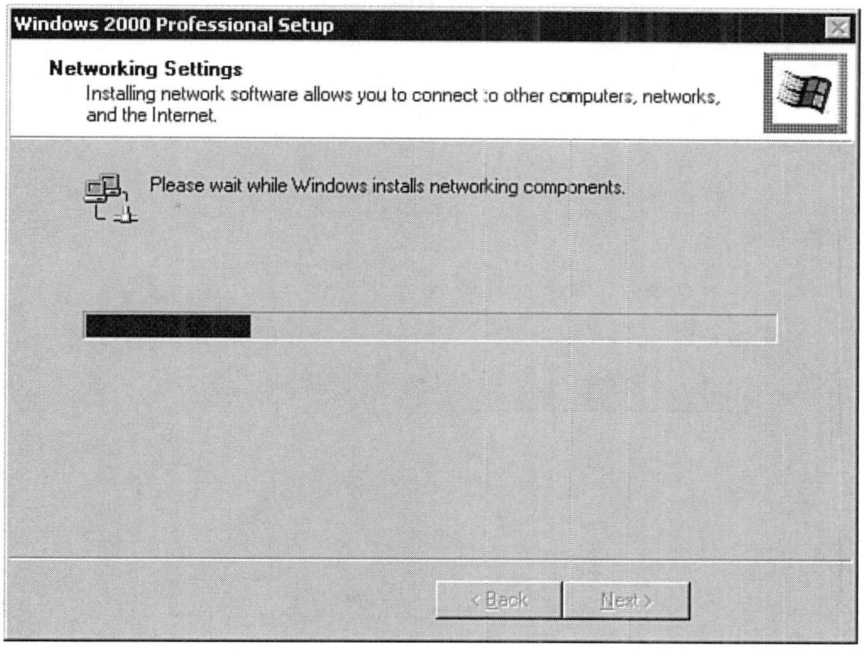

The networking components are installed during this phase of setup. When complete, click **Next** to proceed with the installation. Figure 6-8 shows the options for the next step.

Figure 6-8 Windows 2000 Network Settings Screen

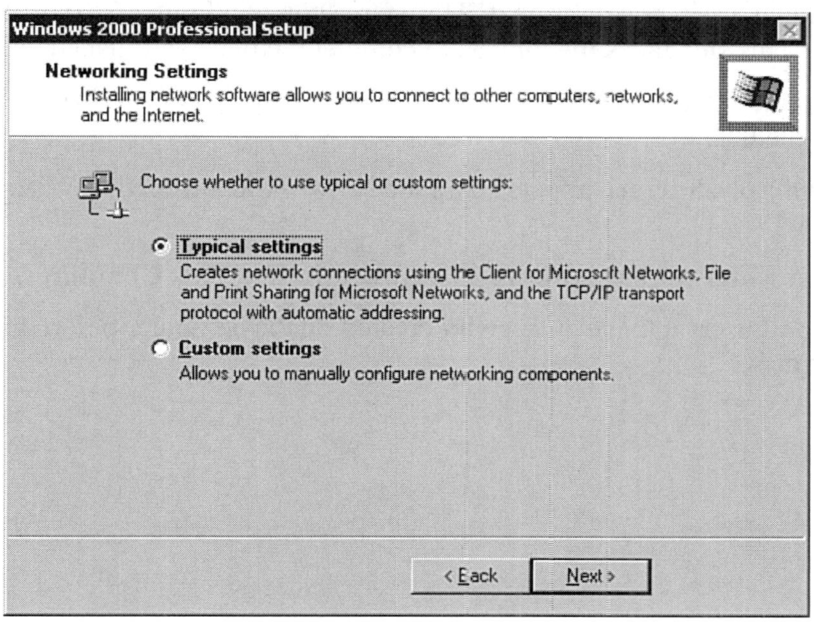

Select the **Typical Settings** radio button to install the default network settings; click **Next**. Custom Settings allows you to install other network components that are not used in this lab. The Workgroup or Computer Domain screen, shown in Figure 6-9, allows the user to join a domain. This step is important when the computer is on a network and requires a domain name and password.

Figure 6-9 Windows 2000 Workgroup or Computer Domain Screen

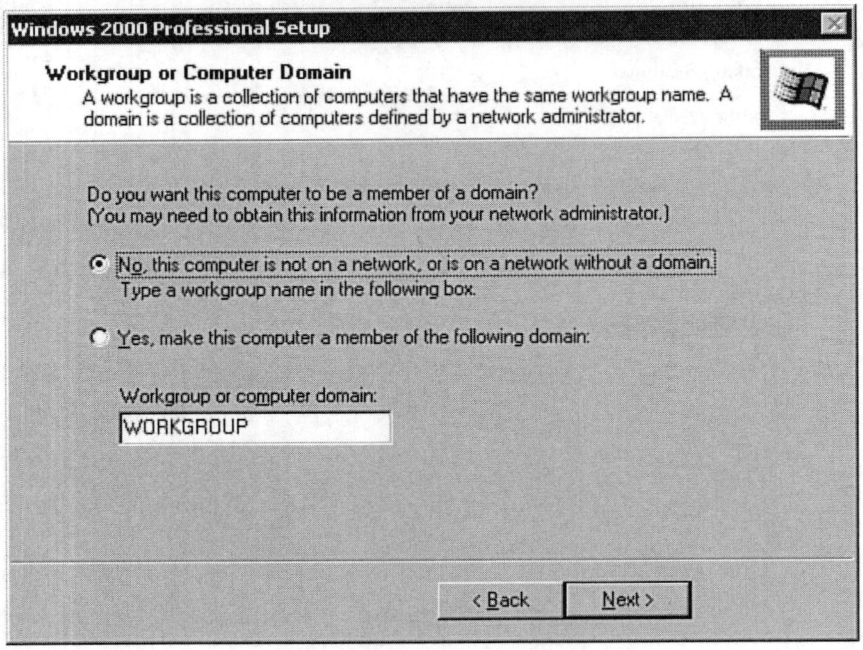

For this lab, select "**No, This Computer Is Not on a Network, or Is on a Network Without a Domain**. Click **Next**. If you were to assign this computer to a domain or group, you would need to provide the exact name of the group and a password.

The Performing Final Tasks screen is next. This step, shown in Figure 6-10, is the final step of the setup process. This step takes the longest to complete. After it is finished, click **Next**.

The computer automatically restarts. Ignore the "Press Any Key to Boot from CD" message and do not boot from the CD.

The Windows 2000 splash screen appears, and the Network Identification Wizard starts, as shown in Figure 6-11.

Select **Users Must Enter a Username and Password to Use This Computer**.

This step requires all users to have an account created on the computer before they are allowed to log on. Click **Next**.

Figure 6-10 Windows 2000 Performing Final Tasks

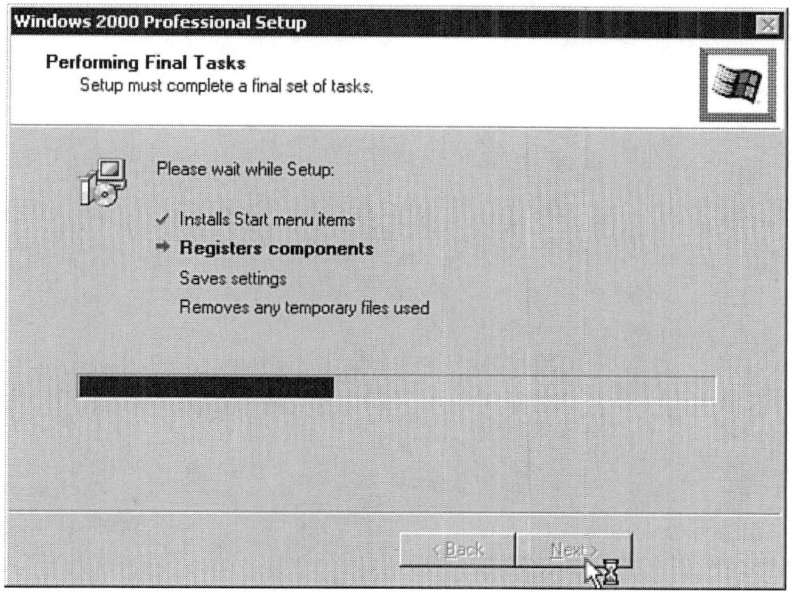

Figure 6-11 Windows 2000 Network Identification Wizard

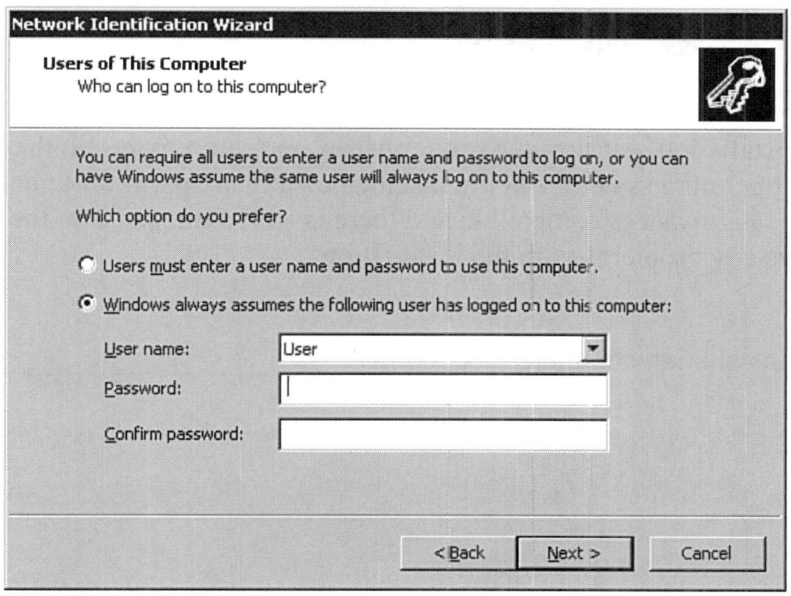

To complete the Network Identification Wizard, click **Finish**.

The log on box appears. Log on with the administrator account and password that you created during setup.

The system now logs on and launches the Windows 2000 desktop, as shown in Figure 6-12.

Figure 6-12 Windows 2000 Desktop After Completing the Installation

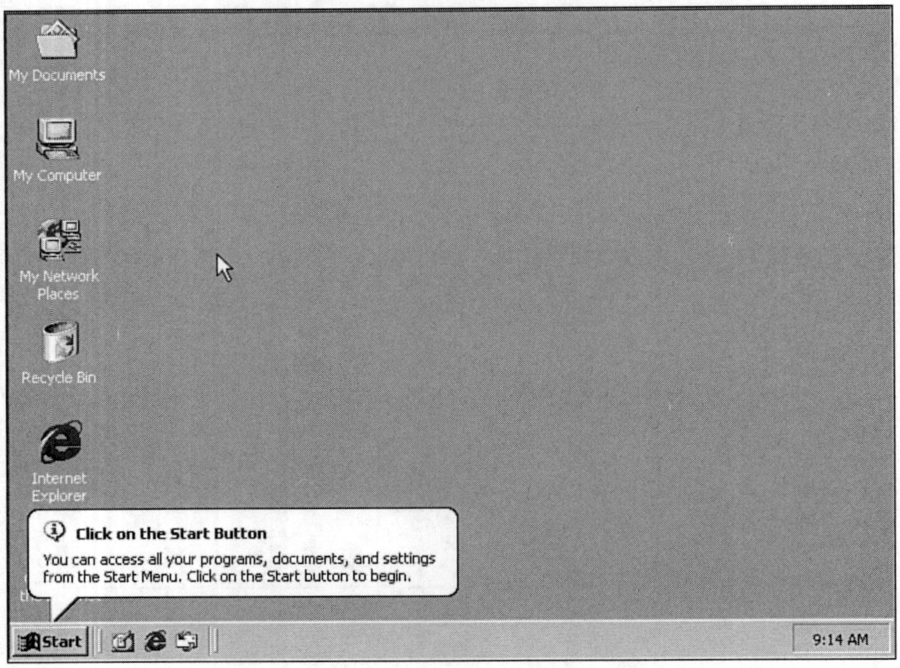

Windows 2000 is now successfully installed.

Troubleshooting

Before doing the installation, confirm the proper hardware requirements on the system. Also make sure that the operating system is being installed on a blank partition or hard drive that has enough space. If the hardware is compatible and there is sufficient space on the drive or partition, you should not have any problems with the installation.

Reflection

Did the Windows installation complete successfully? ______________________________________

Chapter 7

Windows XP Operating System

Lab 7.3.2: Installation of Windows XP

Estimated Time: 90 Minutes

Objective

In this lab, you learn how to install the Windows XP Professional operating system (OS). You can use this lab to install Windows XP or to demonstrate the installation.

Equipment

The following equipment is required for this lab:

- A computer with a blank hard disk
- Windows XP Professional installation CD

Scenario

The IT department has decided to perform an upgrade of all the end-user computers to Windows XP Professional. You need to install the operating systems.

Procedures

In this lab, you install the Windows XP Professional operating system.

Note: Some system hardware requires that you use a manufacturer-supplied recovery disk and procedure for installing the operating system. Refer to manufacturer-supplied documentation for specific instructions.

Step 1

Insert the CD into the CD-ROM drive.

Step 2

Next, configure the system BIOS boot sequence to boot from the CD-ROM first. Keep the CD in the drive and restart the computer.

When the system starts up, watch for the message "Press Any Key to Boot from CD." When the message appears, press any key on the keyboard to boot the system from the CD. The system begins inspecting the hardware configuration, as shown in Figure 7-1.

Step 3

Next, the Windows XP Setup Screen displays and prepares the installation program to load the necessary files, as displayed in Figures 7-2 through 7-4.

Figure 7-1 Windows XP Setup Inspecting the Computer Screen

Figure 7-2 Windows XP Setup screen Displayed As It Is Loading Files

The screens in Figures 7-3 and 7-4 display for a few minutes while the files are copied to the hard drive. Note that the status is displayed on the bottom of the screen.

Figure 7-3 Windows XP Setup

Figure 7-4 Windows XP Setup Loading Files

Step 4

The Welcome to Setup screen appears next, as shown in Figure 7-5. Press **Enter** to continue with the installation.

Figure 7-5 Windows XP Welcome Screen

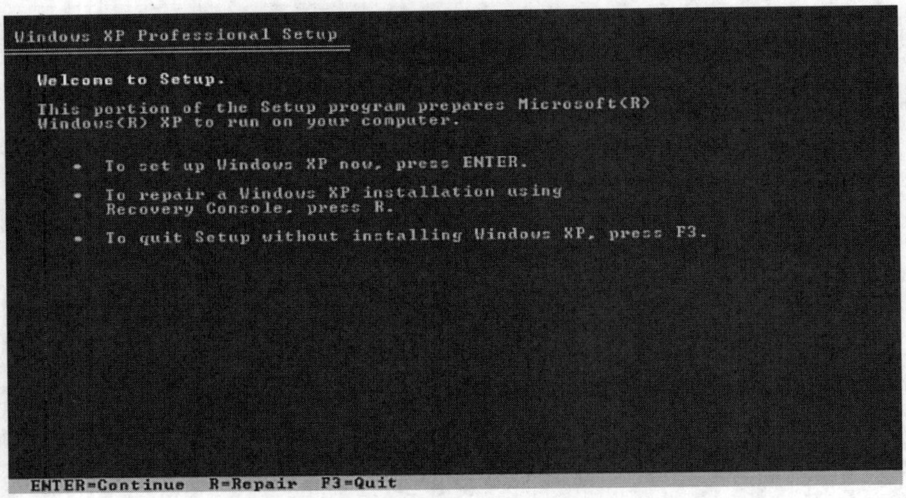

Step 5

After the Windows XP Licensing Agreement screen displays, as shown in Figure 7-6, press **F8** to agree with the Licensing Agreement and continue with the installation.

Figure 7-6 Windows XP Licensing Agreement Screen

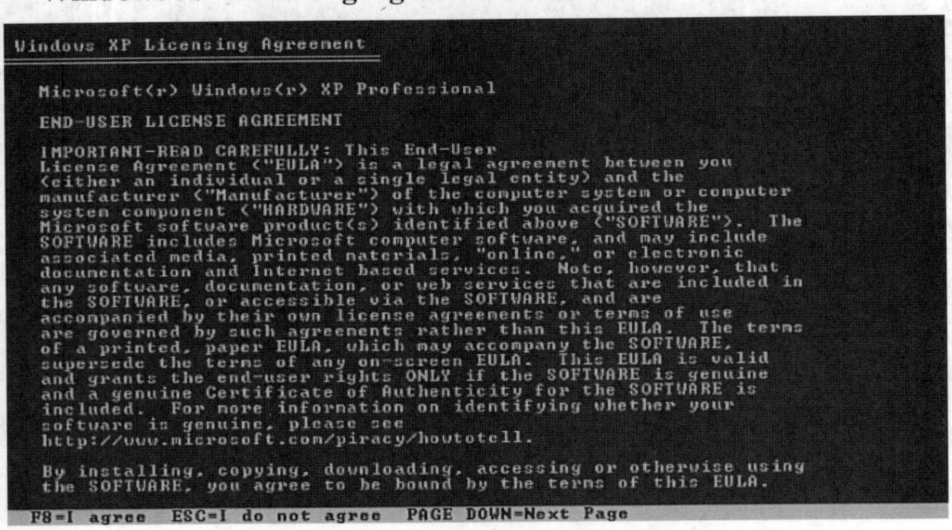

Step 6

In this step, you partition and format the hard drive. *This step is not always required.* If you have a partition already created, use the arrow keys to scroll to that partition. Then, press **Enter** to install the operating system on that partition. If you do not need to create a partition, create a small partition (4 GB) to install Windows XP. This step makes the installation process faster.

To begin the partition setup process, press **C** to create a new partition in the unpartitioned space. Figure 7-7 shows the space available to create a partition.

Figure 7-7 Windows XP Starting the Partition Setup Process

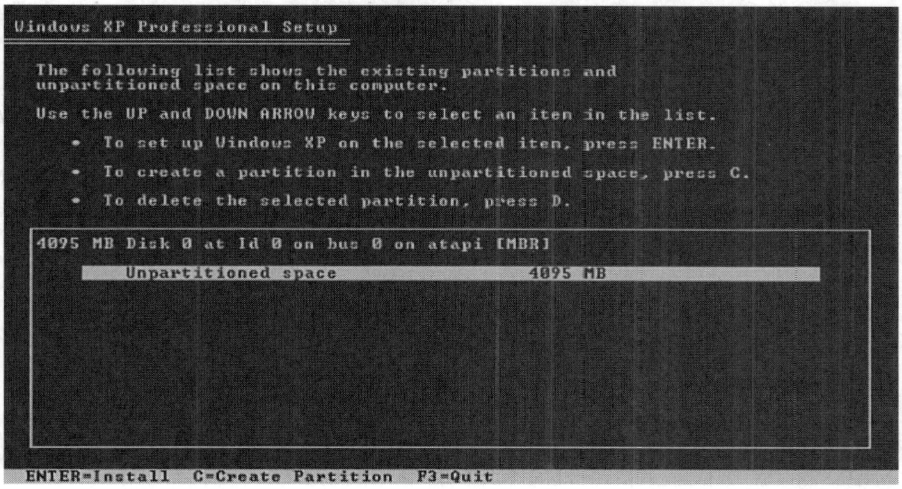

Step 7

In the space provided, type **4087** to create a 4 GB (4087 B) partition. Then, press **Enter** to continue with the installation. Figure 7-8 shows where the user can create the size of the partition.

Figure 7-8 Windows XP Partitioning Screen

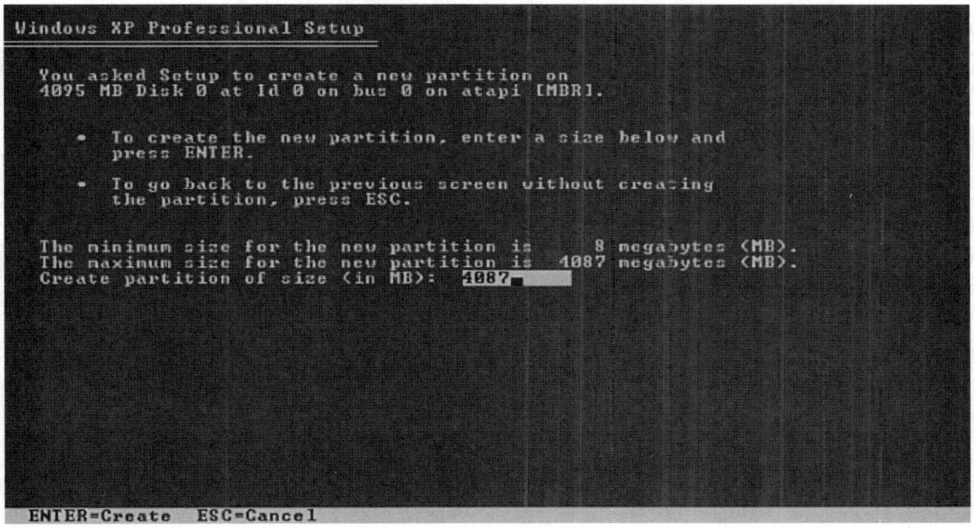

Step 8

For this step, press **Enter** to select the option to install the operating system on the partition that was just created, which should be the **C** drive. Figure 7-9 shows where the user can choose the partition to install the OS.

Figure 7-9 Windows XP Choosing the Partition to Install the OS

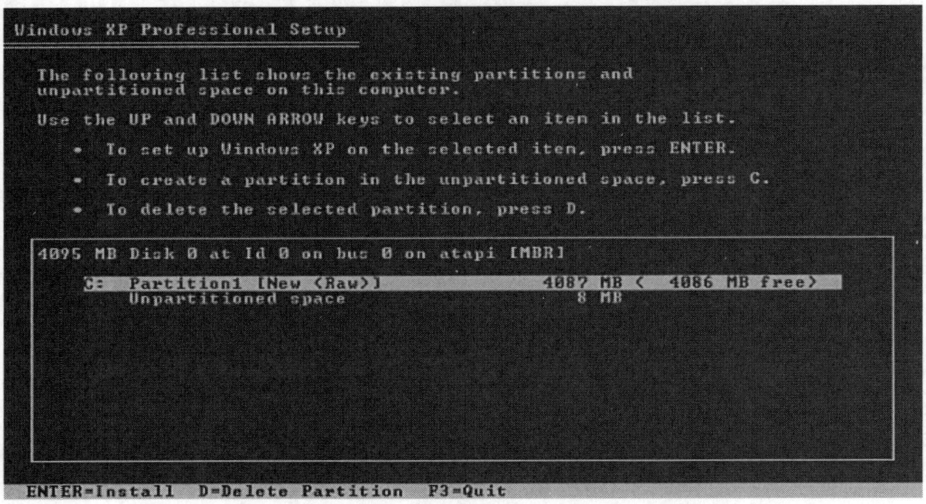

Step 9

Next, select the option to format the partition using the NTFS file system. Do not use the quick method because it does not verify the integrity of the sectors. A full format identifies and tracks bad sectors so they cannot be used for storing data, as shown in Figure 7-10.

Figure 7-10 Windows XP Choosing the Partition Format Type

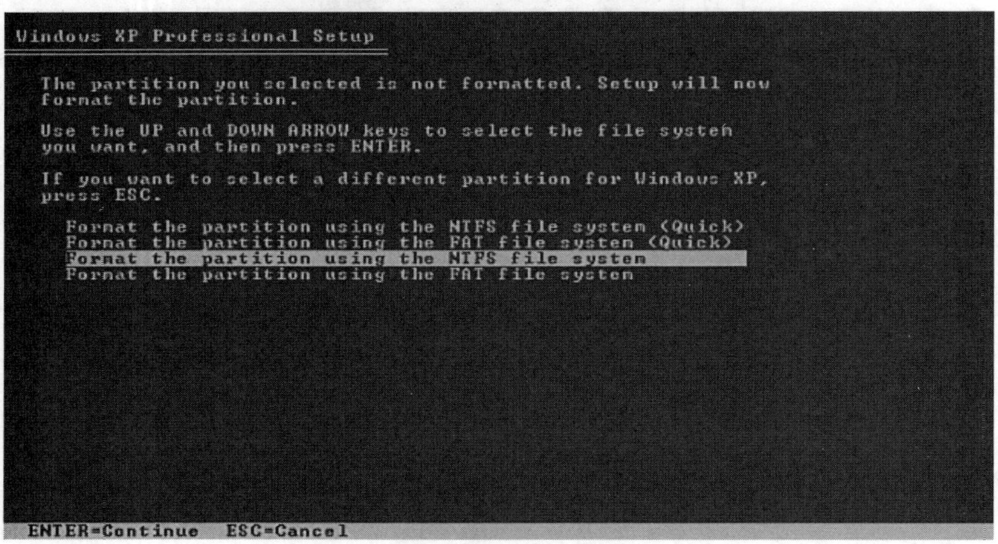

Setup begins formatting the partition, as shown in Figure 7-11.

Figure 7-11 Windows XP Formatting the Partitioned Space

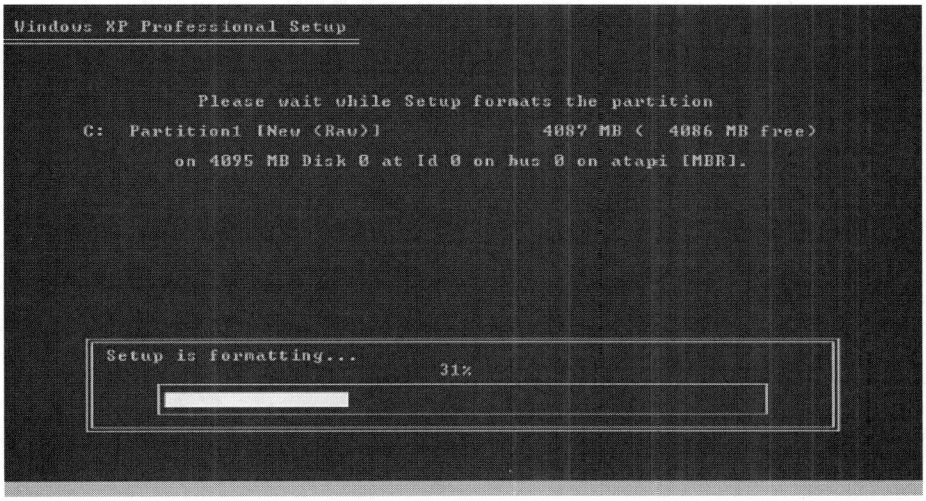

When partitioning and formatting is complete, the Windows XP Professional Setup screen appears and starts copying the system files to the hard drive, as shown in Figures 7-12 and 7-13.

Figure 7-12 Windows XP Preparing to Copy Files

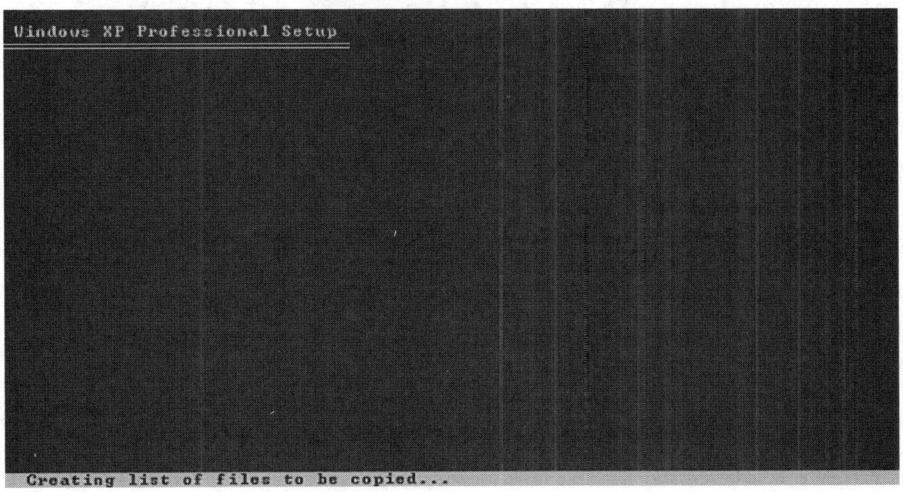

The system restarts automatically after the files are copied. When the system restarts, the message "Press Any Key to Boot from CD" appears again. Do not press any keys at this time or you will have to repeat all previous steps.

Figure 7-13 Windows XP Coping Files

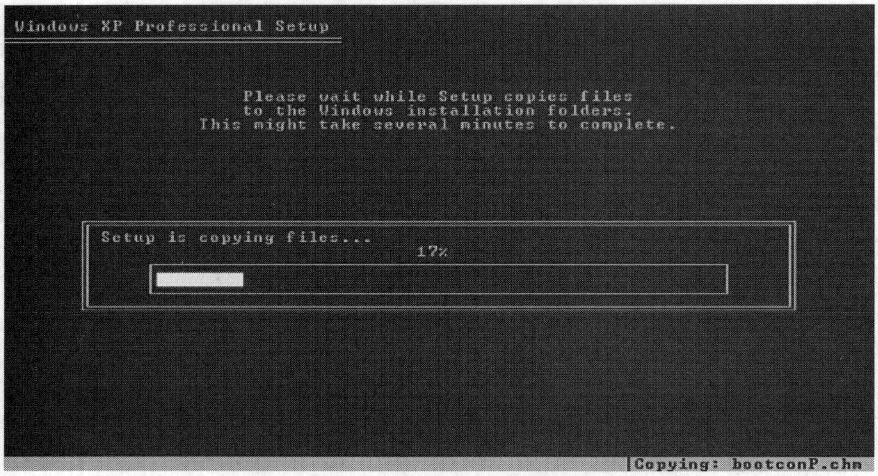

The Windows XP splash screen then displays, as shown in Figure 7-14.

Figure 7-14 Windows XP Splash Screen

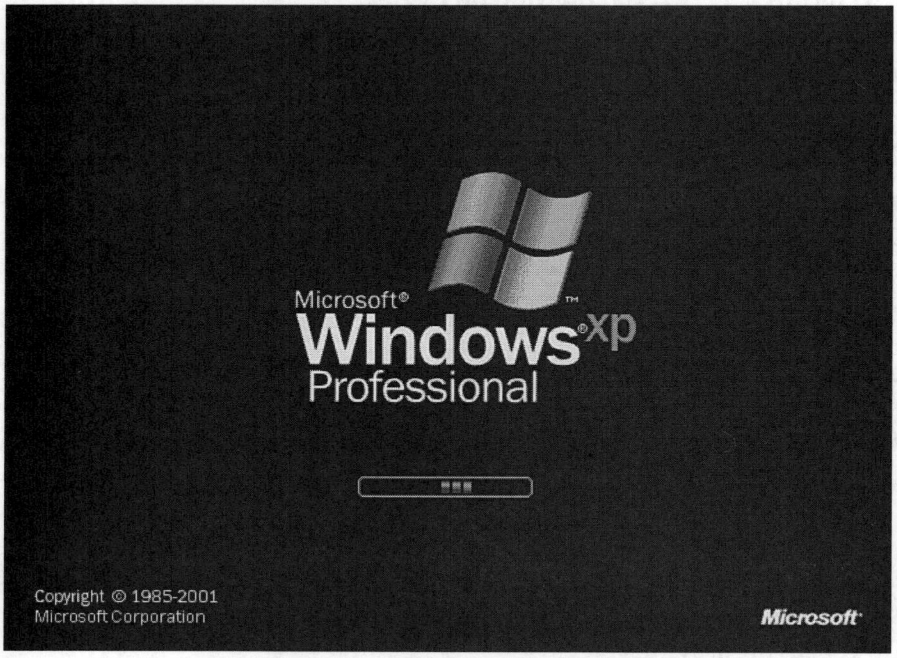

The Windows XP installation screen appears and begins installing the operating system, as shown in Figure 7-15.

Figure 7-15 Windows XP Beginning the Installation of the OS

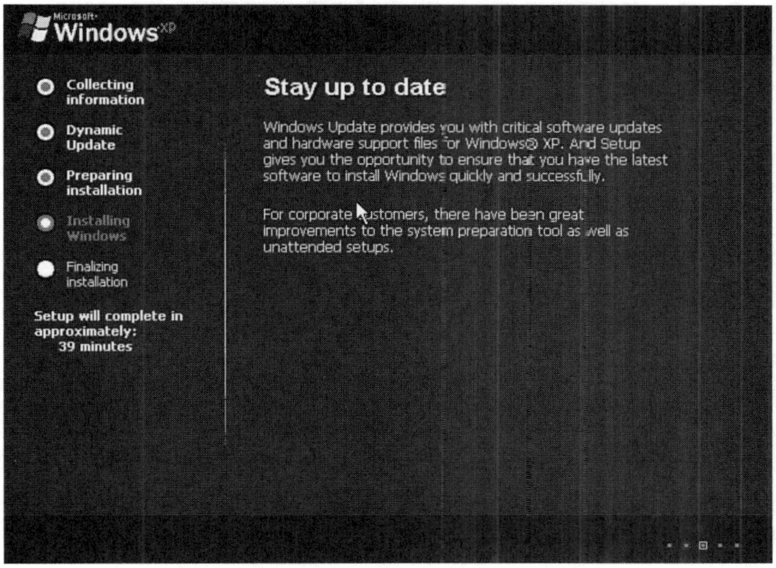

Step 10

The next step of the installation begins installing the hardware devices. Setup proceeds to the screen shown in Figure 7-16.

Figure 7-16 Windows XP Installing Hardware Devices

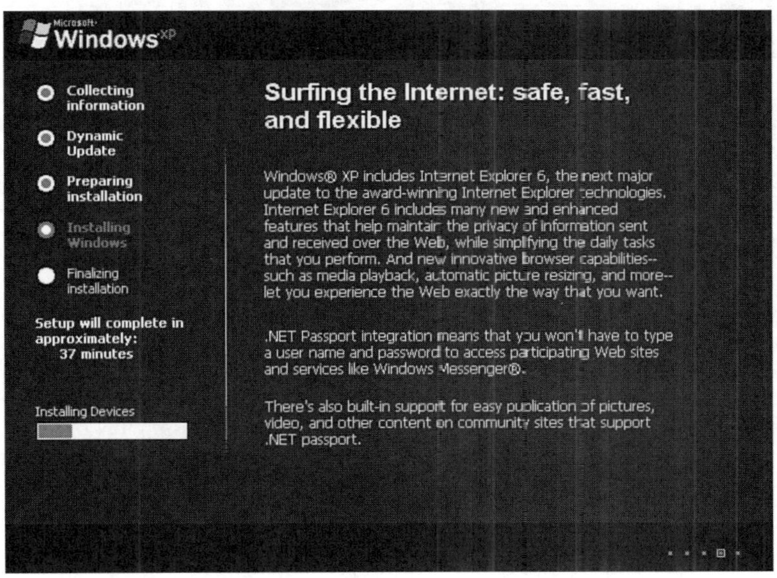

After the devices are initialized and installed, Setup proceeds to the Regional and Language Options screen, as shown in Figure 7-17. This screen is where you can customize the installation based on which country you live in or language you speak.

Figure 7-17 Windows XP Regional and Language Options

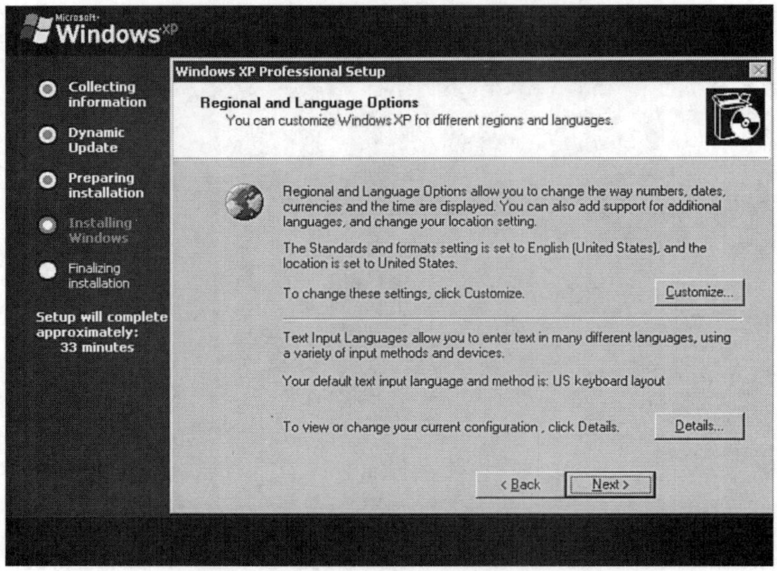

After making the proper selections, press **Enter** and proceed to the Personalization screen shown in Figure 7-18.

Figure 7-18 Windows XP Personalize Your Software Screen

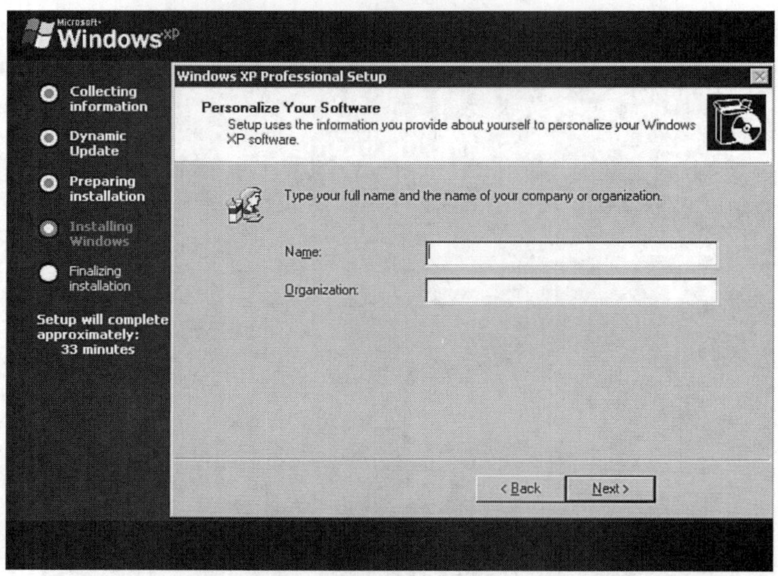

Step 11

When this screen appears, type in the username on the first line and the organization in the second line. Check with the instructor when you reach this point. He or she might have a specified name and organization for you to type.

Press the **Next** button when finished. The next page to appear is the Product Key page.

Enter the Windows XP product key that came with the installation CD. Then, press the **Next** button to continue.

Step 12

The next screen to appear is the Computer Name and Administrator Password page, shown in Figure 7-19.

Figure 7-19 Windows XP Computer Name and Administrator Password Screen

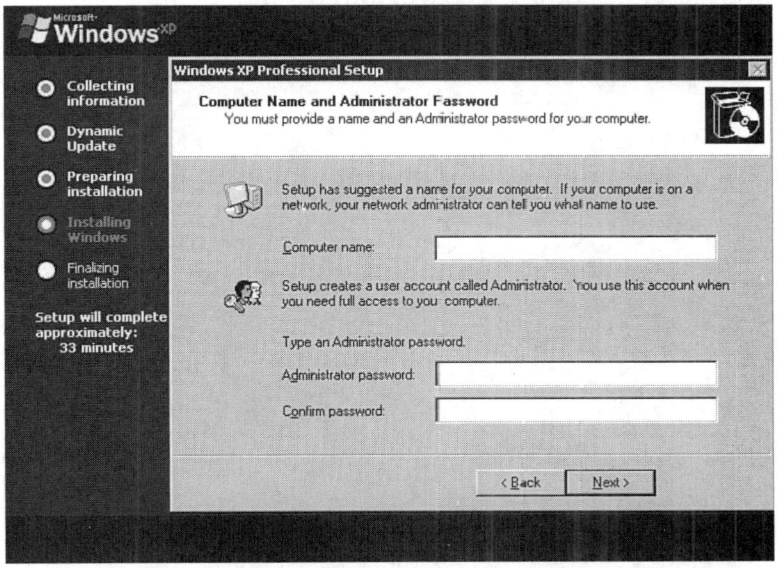

Enter the computer name on the top line and the administrator password on the bottom two lines. Click **Next**.

Step 13

The next page to appear is the Date and Time Settings page, shown in Figure 7-20.

Figure 7-20 Windows XP Date and Time Settings

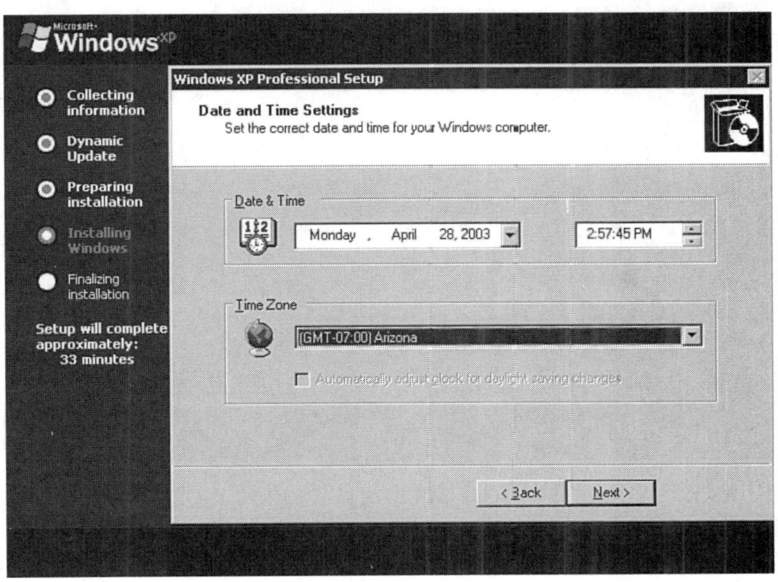

Enter the correct date and time. Then, select the correct time zone.

Click **Next** to continue.

Step 14

The next screen, shown in Figure 7-21, automatically installs the networking components. The setup process first installs the network.

Figure 7-21 Windows XP Installing Networking Components

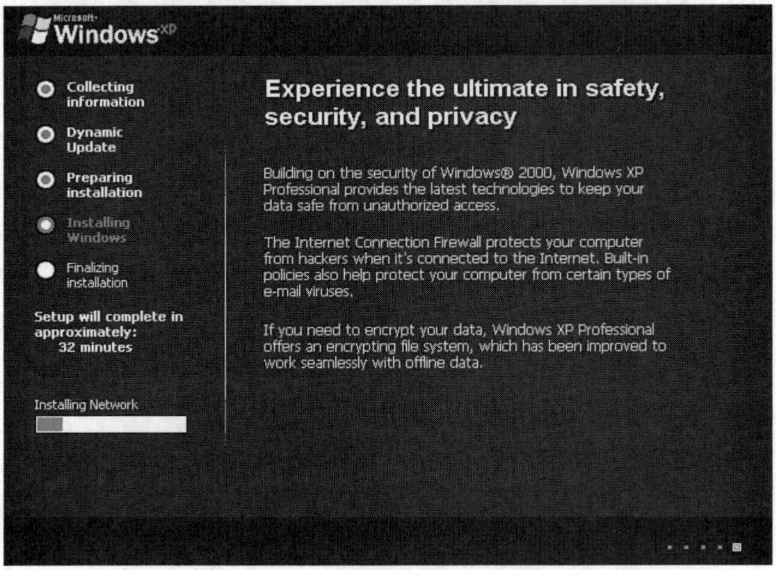

Next, it prompts you to choose the **Typical** or **Custom** settings, as in Figure 7-22.

Figure 7-22 Windows XP Network Settings

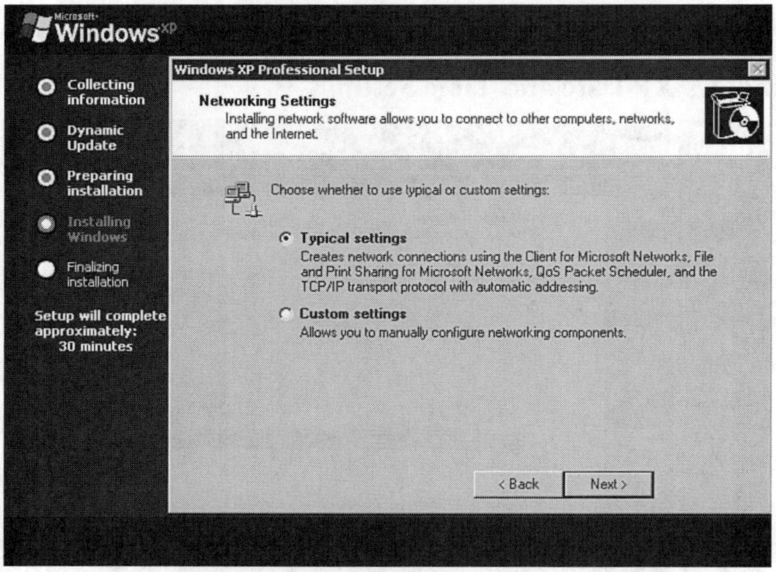

For the purposes of this lab, select **Typical Settings**. It is the most common selection and automatically configures the network settings. If you choose **Custom Settings**, you must manually configure the networking components. Click **Next** to continue to the next step.

Step 15

The last part of the network configuration in the installation process involves assigning workgroup or domain membership. Figure 7-23 shows where you can join a domain.

Figure 7-23 Windows XP Workgroup or Computer Domain Screen

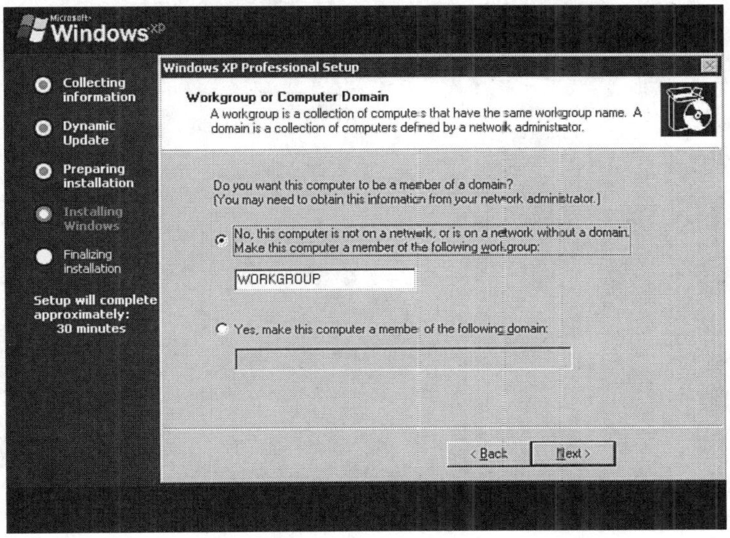

The Workgroup or Computer Domain screen allows you to join a domain. This step is important when the computer is on a network and requires a domain name and password.

Select **No, This Computer Is Not on a Network, or Is on a Network Without a Domain Radio**. Then, click the **Next** button.

This step completes the user involvement in the setup of the installation process. It is the final step of the setup process. This part takes the longest to complete. After it is finished, click **Next**.

Step 16

The next steps are all automated and proceed through copying files, as shown in Figure 7-24.

Figure 7-24 Windows XP Copying Files

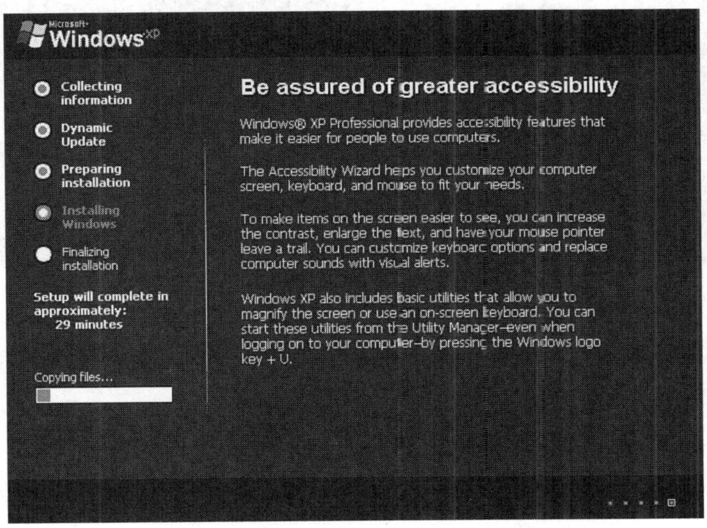

Figure 7-25 shows the screen as it is completing the installation process.

Figure 7-25 Windows XP Completing the Installation

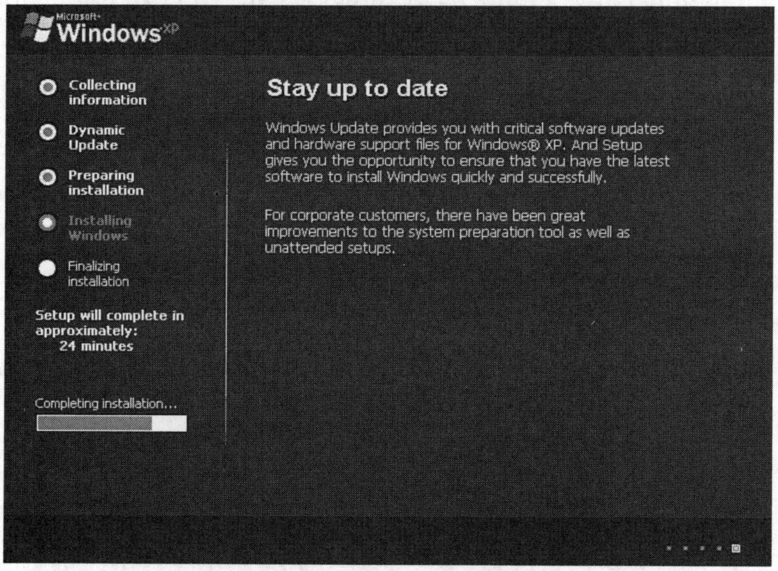

Step 17

This step first shows a series of screens, beginning with Figure 7-26, Installing Start Menu items.

Figure 7-26 Windows XP Installing Start Menu Items

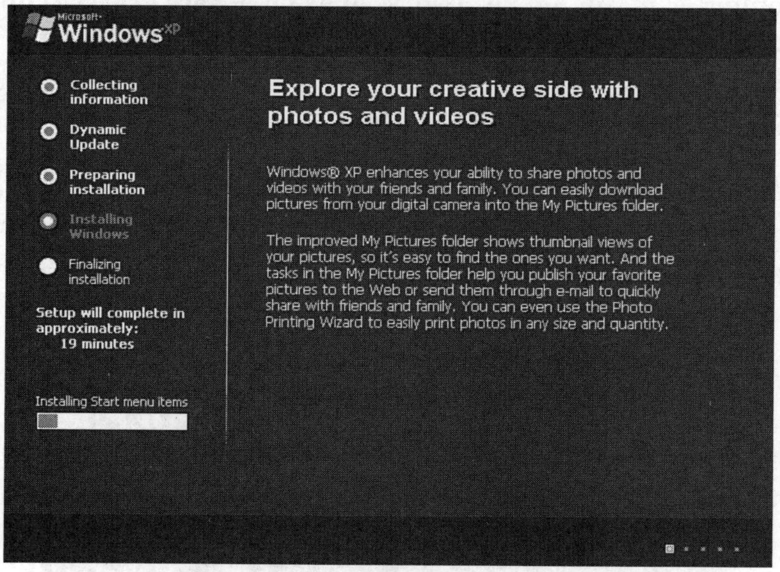

Figure 7-27 shows the screen for registering components.

Then, Figure 7-28 shows the screen that appears when finalizing the installation and saving the configuration settings.

Figure 7-27 Windows XP Registering Components

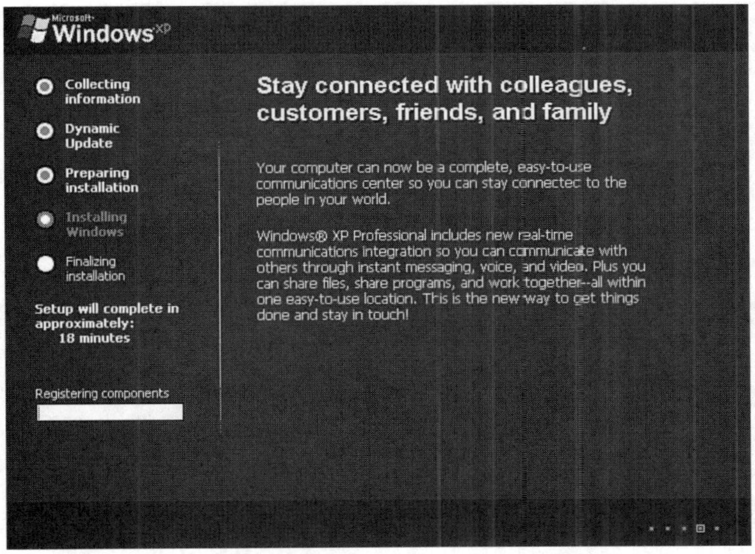

Figure 7-28 Windows XP Saving Settings

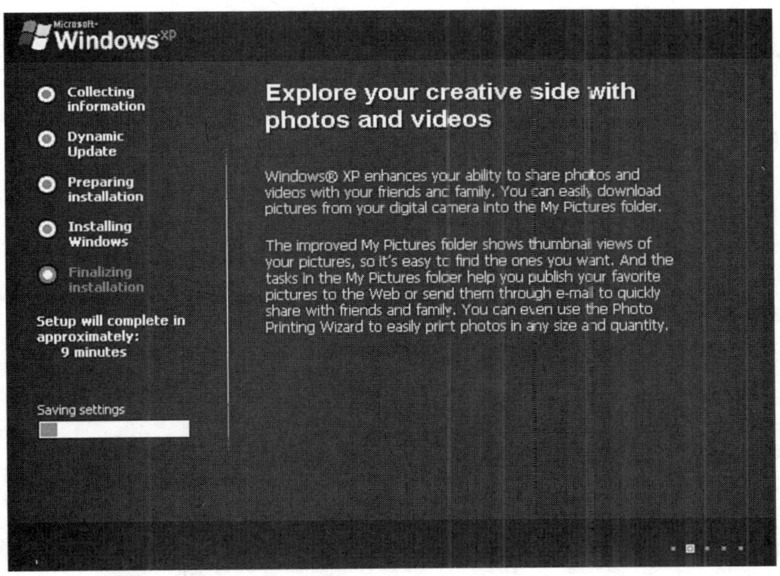

At this point, the computer automatically restarts.

Ignore the "Press any Key to Boot from CD" message. Do not boot from the CD again.

The log on box appears, as shown in Figure 7-29. Log on with the administrator account and password that you created during setup.

Figure 7-29 Windows XP Log On Screen

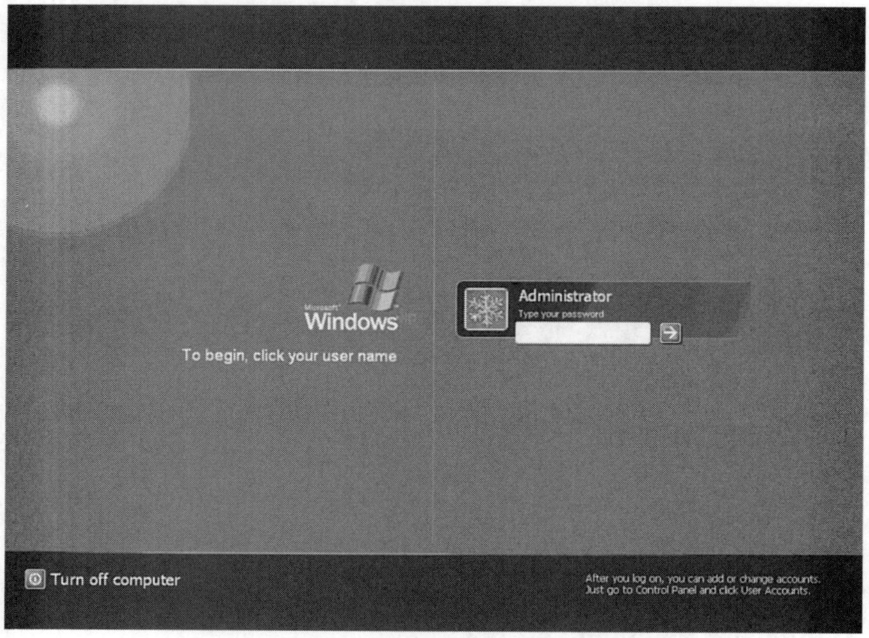

The system now logs on and launches the Windows XP Professional desktop, as shown in Figure 7-30.

Figure 7-30 Windows XP Desktop

Windows XP is successfully installed.

Troubleshooting

Before beginning the installation, confirm the proper hardware requirements of the system. Also, make sure that the operating system is being installed on a blank partition or hard drive that has enough space. If the hardware is compatible and there is sufficient space on the drive or partition, there should not be any problems with the installation.

Reflection

Did the Windows installation complete successfully? ______________________________

Lab 7.5.2: Using Simple File Sharing to Share Files

Estimated Time: 30 Minutes

Objective

In this lab, you use the simple file sharing techniques and tools that are new to Windows XP. This lab helps you become familiar with the easy and simplified method for sharing resources in a Windows XP network.

Equipment

The following equipment is required for this lab:

- A computer with Windows XP Professional installed

Scenario

The IT department has purchased some computers with Windows XP Professional as the operating system on the machines. It wants you to learn how to share files in the file system so you can help other employees.

Procedures

You can share files in the Windows XP Professional file system in the same way as with Windows 2000; however, Windows XP Professional added a few extra features that you can use to make this process a little easier, faster, and more user friendly. This lab shows you how to use these new features.

Step 1: Turning on File Sharing

The first step of this lab provides a series of instructions to show how to turn on the file-sharing feature. File sharing is on by default in Windows XP. To begin, proceed with the following:

1. First, click **Start** (Start Menu) and then click **My Documents** to open the window.
2. Next, click the **Tools** button on the menu list at the top of the screen. Then, scroll down and select **folder options**. This step opens the folder options dialog box.
3. Now, click the **View** tab. This step allows you to select various advanced folder settings. Scroll through these options and read them to become familiar with some of the options that are available and what they do. At the bottom, you see the setting Use Simple File Sharing (Recommended).
4. The Simple File Sharing radio button should be checked because it is the default setting. If you decide at a later date that you do not want to use simple file sharing, then you uncheck this radio box to disable it.
5. Click the **OK** button to close the folder options box.

Step 2: Creating Shared Files on a Computer with Multiple Users

For this step, leave the My Documents window open. Create a new folder called **Shared Files** within My Documents (instructions follow). You use simple file sharing to share a folder with other users who have local user accounts on that computer. To proceed with this step, perform the following:

1. Right-click an open area of the **My Documents** window and select **New** > **Folder**. The new folder appears in the My Documents window. Rename it **Shared Files**.
2. Next, right-click the **Shared Files** folder and select **Properties**. This step opens the properties dialog box for the Shared Files folder. Choose the **Sharing** tab. Read through the entire dialog in both the Local sharing and security and Network sharing and security sections to understand the available options.
3. Do not choose the Make This Folder Private radio button because it disables access to the folder.
4. Click **OK** to close the properties box of the Shared Files folder. Now, locate the Shared Documents folder on the left panel of the My Documents folder. To drag the Shared Files folder to this folder, left-click the **Shared Files** folder and hold it down while dragging it over to the Shared Documents folder.
5. Now, click the **Shared Documents** link on the left panel. Once this folder opens, you see the Shared Files folder in there. Other users who have local accounts on this computer can access any files that you put into the Shared Files folders.
6. If you decide not to share the folder or files, simply delete or move them from this folder.

Step 3: Creating Shared Files on a Network

For this step, leave the My Documents window open. Use the existing Shared Files folder to share. This step enables the users on a network to share files:

1. Right-click the **Shared Files** folder and select **Properties**. This move opens the properties dialog box for the Shared Files folder. Choose the **Sharing** tab. Read through the entire dialog in both the Local sharing and security and Network sharing and security sections to understand the options.
2. On the Network sharing and security section, click the link that states that you understand the implications of sharing this on the network. Then, select **Just Enable File Sharing**. Sometimes, this step is necessary. If you see a **Share This Folder on the Network** dialog box, then select this box and click **Apply**.
3. Click the **OK** button. Now, other users who have access to the network workgroup or domain can access files located within this folder.
4. Look at the Shared Files folder. There should be a little hand holding the folder. This icon indicates that the folder is being shared on the network.

Reflection

You just learned how to use Windows XP simple file sharing to share files locally on the computer and across the network. In what ways is this feature easier or better than the more traditional way of doing it Windows 2000? How might it be worse? What are some of the advantages of using the traditional way of sharing files?

Lab 7.5.3a: Remote Desktop Connection

Estimated Time: 30 Minutes

Objective

In this lab, you use Windows XP Remote Desktop Connection to establish a remote connection to another computer.

Equipment

The following equipment is required for this lab:

- Two computer systems with Windows XP Professional installed

Scenario

You are the system administrator for the XYZ Company. You just upgraded some of the client PCs on the network to Windows XP Professional. You want to set up the client PC for Remote Desktop Administration. This move will enable the IT department to provide desktop support remotely.

Procedures

The instructor will have set up two computers using a cross-over cable so that they are connected and configured with usable IP addresses and subnet masks. Make sure that the computers can communicate by using the **ping** command. Gather the IP configuration data from both PCs. The first part of the lab shows how to set up the remote computer that you will monitor. The second part of the lab shows how to set up the client computer, which is the computer that makes the remote connection.

Step 1: Setting Up the Remote Computer

First, enable Remote Desktop on the remote computer. The Remote Desktop Connection software is pre-installed with Windows XP. To run it, click **Start**, click **All Programs**, click **Accessories**, click **Communications**, and then click **Remote Desktop Connection**. You can also find this software package on the Windows XP Professional and Windows XP Home Edition product CDs and install it on any supported Windows platform.

To install from the CD, insert the disc into the target machine's CD-ROM drive, select **Perform Additional Tasks**, and then click **Install Remote Desktop Connection**. Next, gather the IP information for both computers and record it for Step 2:

1. Log on with the administrator account or as a user that is a member of the Administrators group.
2. Click **Start**, click **Control Panel**, and then double-click the **System** icon. In the System Properties dialog box, click the **Remote** tab.
3. Under the Remote Desktop section, select **Allow Users to Connect Remotely to This Computer**.

Note here that as long as an account has a logon password and that account is logged on, it can remotely connect to the computer. The administrator or any user who is a member of the Administrators or local Remote Desktop Users group can remotely connect to the computer as well.

4. Click the **Select Remote Users** button to change the person who has permission to remotely connect to the computer.
5. Next, select **Add**. In the empty box, type the username of the account that is used to log into the computer and select **OK**.
6. Now, gather the IP information. To do so, click the **Start** menu. Then, click the **Run** button. In the blank space, type **cmd** and click **OK**. This command brings up the DOS prompt. At the prompt, type **ipconfig/all**. This command displays the IP configuration for the computer. Write down the host name and IP address. Keep this information for Step 2.
7. At this point, the remote computer is set up to receive incoming remote connections.

Step 2: Setting Up the Client Computer When the Client Computer Is Running Windows XP

It is important to note that a *user does not* have to be using Windows XP Professional on the client computer to remotely connect to the remote computer. However, the remote computer must be running Windows XP Professional, regardless of what version of Windows the client computer is running. In some cases, such as when the remote computer is running Windows 2000 Server or Advanced Server, you can turn on terminal services to remotely administer the server. For the purposes of this course, Windows 2000 Professional does not have terminal services and therefore cannot be the remote computer:

1. Open the **Start** menu and select **All Programs** > **Accessories** > **Communications** > **Remote Desktop Connection**.
2. In the space, type in the IP address of the remote computer that you recorded in Step 1. Then, click the **Options** tab.
3. In the username space, type the username of the account that has administrative access to the remote computer.
4. Click **Connect**. At this point, the client computer attempts to make a connection. When a connection is made, a logon screen appears. The username should be there. Type in the password, and then click the **OK** button.

Step 3: Setting Up the Client Computer When the Client Computer Is Running Windows 2000

1. If the client computer is using a different operating system other than Windows XP Professional, it still can remotely connect to a Windows XP system. To do so, install the files from the Windows XP Professional installation CD.
2. Insert the CD into the CD-ROM drive. When the XP menu appears, select **Perform Additional Tasks**, and then select **Set Up Remote Desktop Connection**.

3. The necessary files are copied to the hard drive and the setup process is complete.
4. To make the remote connection, simply follow the steps in Step 2 of this lab.

Troubleshooting

For the computers to be able to connect to each other, they must be able to establish contact, communicate, and find each other on the network prior to running Remote Desktop Connection. You must gather and record the IP configurations for both computers by typing **ipconfig/all** at the command prompt. Use the **ping** command to establish that the computers will be able to connect when using Remote Desktop Connection.

Reflection

Use the Remote Desktop Connection utility to connect to your work computer from home or vice versa. This task requires a more advanced knowledge of computer networking because it involves establishing a virtual private network (VPN) through the Internet, and you must configure the routers and firewalls on both ends to open the proper port numbers to allow a remote desktop connection to be established. Windows XP also provides a means of making a remote desktop connection to your PC through the Internet over the web connection.

What are some advantages of using Remote Desktop Connection?

____

____

____

____

What are some disadvantages or security concerns when using Remote Desktop Connection?

____

____

____

____

____

____

Lab 7.5.3b: Internet Connection Firewall

Estimated Time: 30 Minutes

Objective

In this lab, you learn how to use the integrated firewall that is included with the latest releases of Microsoft's operating systems, including Windows XP. You select the proper settings, which allows a user or administrator to secure the integrity of the operating system from intruders.

Equipment

The following equipment is required for this lab:

- A computer system running Windows XP

Scenario

The IT department has purchased some new computers with Windows XP installed on them. These new computers are going to be used by people in the finance and accounting departments of the company. It is important that these computers be as secure as possible and that all the data be protected from intruders. Although proper firewalls, filters, and access lists have been placed on the corporate network incoming gateways, these computers need to be secure from internal threats and intruders who might reside within the network boundaries. The IT department manager has instructed you to implement Windows XP's integrated firewall on these computers to block them from intruders.

Procedures

Before beginning this lab, you need to be logged in as the administrator or as a member of the Administrators group. It is also important to understand that the management tasks covered in this lab apply to other computers that are part of the network, and these settings affect only the individual computer on which they are configured.

Step 1

The first step in configuring the Windows XP integrated firewall is to locate and open the Network Connections settings in the Control Panel:

1. Open the Control Panel using the Start menu. Left-click the **Start** button located in the lower-left side of the screen. Then, click the **Control Panel** button to open the Control Panel.
2. Double-click the **Network Connection** icon in the Control Panel to open the dialog box.
3. At this point, click the **Local Area Connection** icon once to reveal the list of network tasks on the left side of the network connection screen.

Step 2

In Step 2, you learn about these various settings and how to open the Internet Connection Firewall settings dialog box:

1. First, click the **View** status of this connection.
2. On the General tab, you can see the various status settings related to the network connection, such as status, duration, and speed. You can also disable the network connection by clicking the Disable button; however, do not do so in this lab.
3. Next, click the **Support** tab. You see useful information about the network connection, such as the address type, IP address, subnet mask, and default gateway. Using this information and the information from the previous step will help in determining what sort of firewall settings to select, which you do in the next section of this lab.

Step 3

In this step, you configure the proper Internet Connection Firewall settings for this computer:

1. First, click the **General** tab and then click the **Properties** button. You see the local area connection properties dialog box where you can make various configurations and settings on the network connection.
2. Next, click the **Advanced** tab in the Local Area Connection Properties dialog box. At this point, you should see the Internet Connection Firewall settings. The first thing you might want to do is to click the **Learn More About Internet Connection Firewall** link.
3. After reading though the material, close that page and return to the Local Area Connection Properties dialog box. Click the check box next to the **Protect My Computer and Network by Limiting or Preventing Access to This Computer from the Internet** settings.
4. You see a Settings button appear in the bottom-right corner of the Local Area Connection Properties dialog box. Click this **Settings** button to bring up the ICF (Internet Connection Firewall) Advanced Settings screen.

   There are three tabs on this screen. First, you configure the Services tab.
5. Click the **Services** tab. Select all the boxes that you see. As you select each one, a pop-up box appears to allow you to select the name or IP address of the computer that is hosting these services on the network. If this were an actual production environment instead of a lab, you would need to put the correct computer/hostname of the computer that is hosting these services on the network. Also, note the internal and external port number on these pop-up windows. They are the actual ports numbers that close when you click these boxes. By clicking all these boxes, you are essentially closing most of the well-known or popular ports that intruders can use to access the computer. If this computer were acting as a gateway through which other computers gained Internet access, closing these ports would also disable the access to the other computers that use this computer as a gateway.
6. Next, click the **Security Logging** tab. This tab allows you to log events such as attempts or connections made to the computer.

7. Click both the **Log Dropped Packets** and **Log Successful Connections** boxes to enable security logging.

8. Next click the **ICMP** tab. Internet Control Message Protocol (ICMP) is commonly used to for error checking and testing the connectivity of remote computers. Sometimes, intruders or hackers use ICMP to access or do damage to remote computers. Using this tab, it is possible to disable ICMP events or connections from being received and interpreted by this computer.

9. Select all the boxes in the ICMP tab window. Notice that as you select them, descriptions of these various ICMP tasks appear on the bottom of the ICMP tab window. Read them as you select to become more familiar with what each one does.

10. After you select them all, click the **OK** button to save these settings and close the Advance Settings box. Then, click **OK** on the Local Area Connection Properties dialog box to save the settings and close that box. Also, click the **Close** button on the Local Area Connection Status dialog box to close it. Close the Network Connection window in Control Panel.

    You now successfully configured the Internet Connection Firewall in Windows XP.

Troubleshooting

Sometimes, when you configure these settings, they actually tighten or shut off too much access, and sometimes, they actually prohibit users from doing their jobs or accessing network resources that they otherwise need.

In this case, it might be necessary to "tweak" these ICF settings so that users have the proper access they require. You must pay careful attention whenever configuring any type of firewall or security setting.

Reflection

What other security tasks would you have to implement to help protect a computer besides using the ICF?

____

____

____

____

____

____

Lab 7.5.5: Using the Windows XP Start Menu and Windows Explorer

Estimated Time: 30 Minutes

Objective

In this lab, you explore the basic features of the Windows XP Start menu and Windows Explorer Navigation tools.

Equipment

The following equipment is required for this lab:

- A computer system with Windows XP Professional installed

Scenario

The IT department of XYZ Company has installed a computer with Windows XP Professional. The company has asked you to run a few tasks to explore the features of the new Start menu to ensure that it is running properly. It also wants you to learn to navigate the file system so that you can help other employees.

Procedures

Before beginning this lab, make sure that the Windows XP Professional machine is on and that you can log in. Windows XP Professional includes many new features. Some features such as the Start menu and Control Panel have undergone some drastic changes, which the user will need to explore. Navigating the Windows XP Professional file system is almost the same as with Windows 2000; however, Windows XP Professional added a few extra features that help you navigate the file system easier and faster. This lab shows how to use the new features of Windows XP to navigate the file system.

Part 1: Using the Windows XP Start Menu

Step 1

After the system boots, the Windows XP welcome screen appears. Click the proper username, and then log in with the password.

Press **Enter**. If you type the password correctly, the system authenticates you and grants you access.

Step 2

After the system authenticates you, the desktop environment appears, as shown in Figure 7-35.

Notice that the Windows XP Professional desktop environment is different from that of Windows 2000. By default, the My Computer, My Documents, My Network Places, and Internet Explorer icons do not appear on the desktop. You can enable these icons to appear on the desktop if you want. You do so later in the lab.

Figure 7-35 Desktop Environment After Authentication

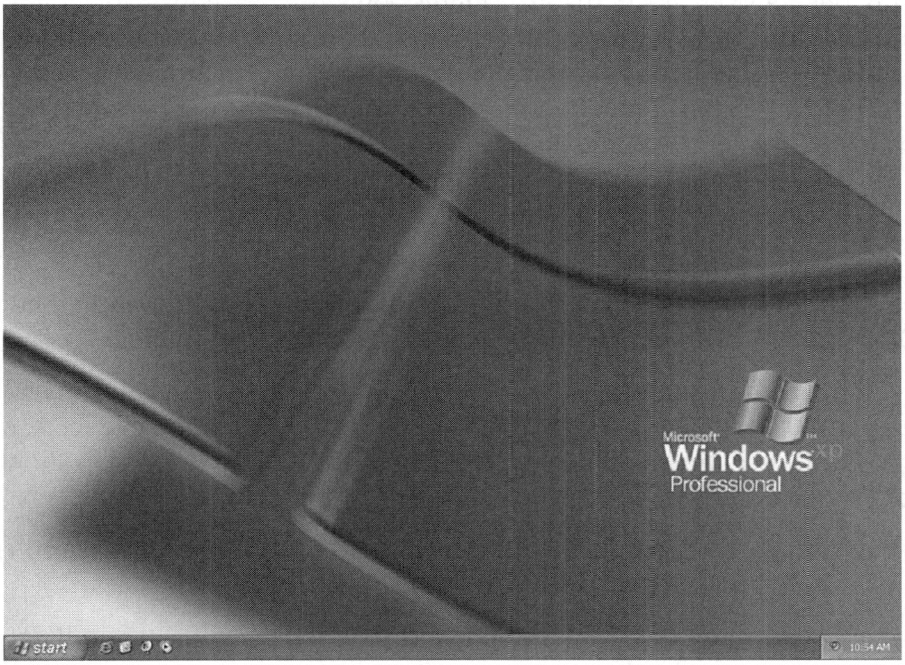

Step 3: Using the New Windows XP Start Menu

The new XP Start menu can be a little confusing when using it for the first time. However, after you become familiar with the new Start menu, you see the changes that Microsoft made will help you navigate the GUI more easily. The following tasks help you become familiar with the new Start menu:

1. To get an idea of what the new Start menu looks like, click the **Start** menu icon in the bottom-left corner of the screen. Notice that the icons that are missing from the desktop now appear in the Start menu. You also see that the Start menu is divided into two parts. The left side shows a list of the programs that you use frequently. The right side shows what is in My Computer and My Network Places. It also contains the Control Panel, Printers and Faxes, and the Search and Run function icons.
2. Click a few of the programs and open a few windows to simulate a typical environment that a user would have when working on the computer.
3. Now, access My Computer by using the Start menu. Click the **Start** icon, and then click the **My Computer** icon. You don't have to close all the windows and then click the icon on the desktop; it is in the Start menu so that you can access it more quickly.
4. Now, examine some of the options that are available to customize the Windows XP Start menu. First, right-click the **Start** menu icon in the lower-left of the screen and select **Properties**.
5. Click the **Taskbar** tab. You see several options to to change how the Start menu and taskbar work. Click some of the radio boxes to select or deselect certain options until the Start menu is the way you like it. When you are finished, click the **Start** menu tab.

6. Notice that Windows XP provides the option of using the Classic Start menu that came with previous releases of Microsoft Windows operating systems. Now, click the **Customize** button. This button provides a new interface to manipulate the Start menu. First, change the setting to use **Small Icons** rather than the large ones. Second, deselect the **Internet** and **E-mail** radio buttons on the bottom of the dialog box. They no longer appear in the Start menu. Remember, you can always go back and select these boxes if you want the options to be quickly available in the Start menu.
7. Look at the Programs section of this screen. Notice that it is possible to change how many programs are available for quick selection on the Start menu. Change the amount to **11**, and then click **OK**. The first box should disappear. Click the **Apply** button and then the **OK** button. You should see the new changes on the Start menu.
8. Keep in mind that the majority of the GUI operations involve the Start menu as the starting place. Users quickly learn that there is really no need to have icons on the desktop. For those who like the icons on the desktop, Step 4 of this lab shows how to add the icons to the desktop.

Step 4: Enabling the My Computer, My Documents, My Network Places, and Internet Explorer Icons

1. Move the mouse pointer to the desktop and right-click the mouse. Scroll down and click the **Properties** button. This move displays the system Display Properties dialog box.
2. Select the **Desktop** tab. This step brings you to the menu that lets you change the desktop feature.
3. Now, click the **Customize Desktop** button in the bottom-left corner of the properties box. You see a dialog box that allows you to make further adjustments to the desktop. From this point, you can select which icons you want to display on the desktop. You can also change what the icon looks like or run the desktop cleanup tool. The **Web** tab lets you display web pages on the desktop. You can also lock the desktop items to prevent the moving or resizing of web items on the desktop.

Part 2: Using the Windows XP Windows Explorer Navigation Tool

Step 1

The first feature that you want to become familiar with concerns navigating to any window without having to close windows or even using Windows Explorer:

1. Click the **Start** menu and then click **My Computer**. Notice how the icons are arranged differently.
2. First, click the **Tools** menu on the top of the screen and select **Folder** options. After the Folder Options box opens, select the **View** tab. Then, scroll down until you come to the **Show Control Panel in My Computer** box and make sure it is checked. If it is not selected, select it because it is not checked by default. Next, click the **Apply** button. This button allows you to put the Control Panel icon in the My Computer window.

Step 2

1. For this step, leave the My Computer window open. Look down the left side of the screen to see the Other Places menu. It shows the other directories that you can navigate to from this window without having to close the current window.
2. First, click the **My Documents** icon in the Other Places menu. It takes you to the My Documents window. Do the same thing to navigate back to the My Computer window or change to a different window from here as well.
3. Double-click the **C:** drive and open a folder. Use the Other Places menu to navigate to different folders and back again, all from one window.
4. Click the **Start** menu icon, and then, click the **Control Panel** icon. By default, the icons are grouped together by category.
5. Now, choose an item from the Control Panel list such as Performance and Maintenance. You have the option to select one of the tasks from the list or you can select one of the icons to compete a specific task.

Reflection

In what circumstances might this way of navigating the file system be easier?

____

____

____

____

____

____

Chapter 8

Multimedia Capabilities

Lab 8.2.3: Upgrading the Video Accelerator

Estimated Time: 30 Minutes

Objective

In this lab, you install a video card with advanced capabilities such as 3D, more memory, or Advanced Graphics Port (AGP). Also, you remove the old video drivers and install new ones.

Equipment

The following equipment is required for this lab:

- Electrostatic discharge (ESD) wrist strap
- The lab computer with Windows 98 installed
- Standard Phillips-head screwdriver that is not magnetic
- AGP video card and driver installation software
- Motherboard manual

Scenario

A computer has limited video capabilities built onto the motherboard or has a basic video card installed. You must install an advanced graphics board to use 3D graphics, to use a larger desktop, or to use programs that require more video memory.

Procedures

This lab involves working with delicate components inside the computer case that are sensitive to static electricity. After you remove the computer cover, touch an unpainted metal part of the chassis. Before touching *anything* else inside the case, be sure that the ESD wrist strap is on. If the motherboard has video capabilities built in, be sure to consult the motherboard manual for instructions on disabling this feature in the BIOS. You might need to manipulate jumpers on the motherboard before proceeding.

Step 1

Before installing a new adapter, it is typically necessary to change the current video card drivers to basic Windows drivers. To accomplish this step, go to **Start** > **Settings** > **Control Panel**. Double-click **System**, click the **Device Manager** tab, and locate the video adapter. Click the + next to the item to show the name of the device. Next, double-click the device to show its properties and click the **Driver** tab and **Update Driver**. When prompted, click **Display a List of All the Drivers in a Specific Location, so You Can Select the Driver You Want**, click **Show All Hardware**, locate **[Standard Display Adapters]**, and install **[Standard VGA 640x480]**. Close any open windows and shut down the computer by clicking **Start**, click **Shut Down**, select the **Shut Down** option, and click **OK**.

Step 2

Unplug the computer from the wall outlet to make sure it is not turned on by accident. Finally, unplug the monitor cable from the computer.

Step 3

Open the computer case, lay it on its side, and locate the expansion slots.

Step 4

Remove the screw holding the expansion card access cover in place. Remove the cover and set it aside.

Step 5

Remove the existing video card from the expansion slot and place it either in an antistatic bag or on an antistatic mat. Next, remove the replacement card from its antistatic bag. Hold the card by the edges, being careful not to touch any of the components on the card.

Step 6

With one hand, grasp the top of the card by the metal end that will be attached to the chassis by a screw and use the other hand for the top corner of the circuit board. Next, place the card edge connector into the PCI or AGP expansion slot, depending on the type of video card that you have. Be sure to line up the metal guide on the bottom of the card with the small opening where the expansion card access cover was removed.

Step 7

If you use a back-and-forth rocking motion and a little bit of pressure, the card should seat into the socket fairly easily. Do not use too much force to insert the card edge connector. If the card will not seat correctly, remove it and make sure to align everything correctly. Then, try again. When the card is properly seated, the metal tab lines up perfectly with the screw hole. In addition, notice that the card is evenly seated in the expansion slot.

Step 8

Secure the tab either with the screws from the access cover or with the screws provided with the card. Remove the ESD strap from the computer and fit the case back together.

Step 9

After the computer is back together, plug the monitor cable into the new graphics card. Next, plug the computer back into the power outlet and make sure all connecting cables are secure.

Step 10

Turn on the computer and follow the onscreen instructions. The Windows 9*x* operating system should find new Plug and Play hardware and try to install the device drivers for it. When prompted, insert the disk that came with the video card to complete the software installation. Click **Yes** when prompted to reboot the computer for changes to take effect. For video cards that come with a manual, follow the installation instructions of the manufacturer.

Step 11

After the computer reboots, the video card should be ready for use. Test the card by changing the resolution of the monitor or running a 3D application.

Troubleshooting

If you cannot change the resolution to the expected range, or a 3D application does not run, check the device manager to make sure that there is no conflict with the new adapter. Reinstall the standard VGA driver, reboot, and reinstall the new drivers for the video card.

Reflection

What was the most challenging part of this lab? Why?

____

____

____

Lab 8.3.4: Sound Card Installation

Estimated Time: 30 Minutes

Objective

In this lab, you install a sound card in a computer, attach the speakers and microphone, and install the proper drivers.

Equipment

The following equipment is required for this lab:

- ESD wrist strap
- Your lab computer with Windows 98 installed
- Standard Phillips-head screwdriver that is not magnetic
- Sound card and driver installation software
- Speakers
- Microphone
- Motherboard manual

Scenario

The computer either has sound capabilities built onto the motherboard or has no sound ability at all. You want to add a sound card to enjoy the full capabilities of the computer's multimedia files.

Procedures

This lab involves working with delicate components inside the computer case that are sensitive to static electricity. After you remove the computer cover has been removed, touch an unpainted metal part of the chassis. Before touching anything else inside the case, be sure that you are using your ESD wrist strap. If the motherboard has sound capabilities built in, consult the motherboard manual for instructions on disabling this feature in the BIOS (or a jumper on the motherboard) before proceeding.

Step 1

Shut down the computer by clicking **Start** > **Shut Down**; then select **Shut Down** and click **OK**. Next, unplug the computer from the wall outlet to make sure it is not be turned on by accident. Also, unplug any speakers or microphone from the motherboard if it is equipped with onboard sound.

Step 2

Open the computer case and lay it on its side, locating the expansion slots. You can now install the sound card.

Step 3

Locate an empty expansion slot, and using a screwdriver, remove the screw holding the expansion card access cover in place. Remove the cover and set it aside.

Step 4

The next step is to remove the sound card from the antistatic bag. Hold the card by the edges, being careful not to touch any of the components on the card.

Step 5

Grasp the top of the card by the metal end that will be attached to the chassis with one hand and the top corner of the circuit board with the other hand. Next, place the card edge connector into the chosen expansion slot. Be sure to line up the metal guide on the bottom of the card with the small opening where you removed the expansion card access cover.

Step 6

If you use a back-and-forth rocking motion and a little bit of pressure, the card should seat into the socket fairly easily. Do not use too much force to insert the card edge connector. If the card does not seat correctly, remove it and make sure to align everything correctly. Then, try again. When the card is properly seated, the metal tab lines up with the screw hole. In addition, notice that the card is evenly seated in the expansion slot.

Step 7

Secure the tab with the screw used to remove the access cover. If you have not installed the CD audio cable yet, attach it at this time.

Step 8

Remove the ESD strap from the computer and fit the case back together.

After the computer is back together, plug the speakers into the sound card in the port labeled "speakers" or labeled with a small picture of a speaker. Next, plug the microphone into the port labeled "mic" or labeled with a small picture of a microphone. Now, plug the computer back into the wall socket and make sure that all connecting cables are secure.

Step 9

Turn on the computer. The Windows 9*x* operating system should find new Plug and Play hardware and try to install the device drivers for it. When prompted, insert the disk that came with the sound card to complete the software installation. The sound card should now be ready to use.

Step 10

To test the sound card, click **Start** > **Control Panel**. Once the Control Panel appears, double-click the **Sounds** icon. Click any sound that has a small speaker icon next to it and click the small **play** button next to the preview speaker. If sound is audible, you installed the card correctly. If you do not hear the sound, double-click the **System** icon in the Control Panel and click the **Device Manager** tab.

Search for the sound card in the hardware list. Make sure that the sound card is listed and does not have any conflicts.

Troubleshooting

Double-check all connections to the sound card, making sure that the plugs are inserted all the way. If the speakers are powered externally, make sure that they are plugged into the wall and turned on. Double-click the speaker icon on the right side of the taskbar to bring up the operating system's volume controls. Make sure that the controls are turned up and that none of them is muted. If there is a problem in the device manager, remove the sound card from the list and restart the computer. This step forces Windows to re-install the sound card into the list and re-install the drivers. Also, if the speakers are not self-powered, you might need to set a jumper on the sound card to the amplified position.

Reflection

What was the most challenging part of this lab? Why?

____

____

____

____

Worksheet 8.1.6: Multimedia Devices

Worksheets enhance the material covered in the HP IT Essentials online course and the companion guide. Use the space provided to answer the questions. Refer to this information when preparing for the A+ exam.

Match each device with its appropriate description:

1. _____Video card	a. Transforms digital information into analog signals and applies them to an audio preamplifier.
2. _____Microphone	b. Takes pictures and movies that can be broadcast on the Internet or sent to someone through e-mail.
3. _____Speakers	c. An interface used by a computer to communicate with a musical instrument.
4. _____Web cam	d. A device used to read and write data to compact disks.
5. _____DVD	e. A device used to input and record sounds to a computer.
6. _____Video capture card	f. An integrated circuit card in a computer or, in some cases, a monitor that provides digital-to-analog conversion.
7. _____Sound card	g. Changes analog signals into sound waves.
8. _____MIDI	h. An optical recording media used for storing enormous amounts of data.
9. _____CD-RW drive	i. A device used to record from video sources outside the computer.

Worksheet 8.2.5: Video Accelerators

1. RAMDAC is an acronym for

____

____

2. The RAMDAC converts ____________________ signals into ____________________ signals.
3. The video card receives data from the ____________ and sends it to the ____________.
4. CRT is an acronym for

____

5. A CRT uses ____________, ________________, and __________________ to produce all other colors.
6. VGA is an acronym for ____
7. AGP is an acronym for ____
8. The AGP interface is a variation of the _________ bus design that has been modified to handle the larger data throughput associated with three-dimensional _______________.
9. What is refresh rate?

____

____

____

Worksheet 8.3.3: Sound Cards

1. The RAMDAC receives the processed __________________ information and converts it to an __________________ signal.
2. Two computer peripheral devices that send a signal to the sound card are the ______________________ and the ________________________.
3. The quality of the sound card depends on the number of _________ used to hold each sound sample, or the sample size.
4. Sound cards generally have sampling rates from about ______________ to ___________________ samples per second.
5. Two of the methods used to convert digitally stored sound into realistic analog sound are ____________________ ____________________ synthesis and ___________________ synthesis.

Worksheet 8.4.7: CD and DVD Terminology

1. CD-ROM is an acronym for ____________________ _______________ ______________ ________________ ____________________________.

2. DVD is an acronym for _______________________ ______________________ __________________.

3. With a CD-R, data is written _______________ on a light-sensitive material by a powerful, highly focused _______________ ______________.

4. Single-speed drives transfer data at a rate of __________ KB per second.

5. A CD-RW drive labeled 48x24x16 is capable of______________ data at 48x, ______________ data at 24x, and ______________data at 16x.

6. A typical DVD has a capacity that ranges from _______ GB to _________GB.

7. Match each recording format with its media.

1. ____ Yellow book	a. Interactive CD
2. ____ Red book	b. Enhanced CDs
3. ____ Orange book	c. Digital computer data
4. ____ Green book	d. Digital music CD
5. ____ Blue book	e. Magneto optical, write once, and rewritable drives

Chapter 9

Advanced Hardware Fundamentals for Servers

Lab 9.1.2: Basic Disk to Dynamic Disk Conversion

Estimated Time: 20 Minutes

Objective

In this lab, you convert a hard drive from a basic disk to a dynamic disk.

Equipment

You need the following items to complete this lab:

- A PC with Windows 2000 Professional installed

Scenario

You are setting up RAID 0 on the newly purchased home server. Windows 2000 Professional is the operating system. You have one 20 GB hard drive, and you are purchasing another one to set up RAID 0.

Procedures

In this lab, you convert the hard drive from a basic disk to dynamic disk to enable configuration of RAID 0 striping on the PC.

Step 1

Right-click **My Computer** and click **Manage**.

What window opens when you click **Manage**?

____

Step 2

In the left window, click **Storage**. In the right window, double-click the **Disk Management (local)** snap in.

How many disks does the computer have?

____

How many partitions does it have, and what are they named?

___

What other devices appear in the window?

___

Step 3

Right-click the local disk (Disk 0) and click **Upgrade to Dynamic Disk**. In the window Upgrade to Dynamic Disk, put a check in the box next to **Disk 0**, if it does not already have one, and click **OK**.

Step 4

In the window Disk to Upgrade, verify that it is Disk 0 and that Will Upgrade has a **Yes** underneath it.

Step 5

In the same window, click **Details** in the lower-left corner. What does it say?

___

Are any volumes contained on Disk 0?

___

Step 6

Click **OK** to return to the Disk to Upgrade window. Now, click **Upgrade**. A warning window asks whether you are sure; click **Yes**. The last warning window appears; read it and click **Yes**.

Step 7

A window reports that a reboot will take place to finish; click **OK**.

Step 8

After the computer reboots, it displays "Windows 2000 Has Finished Installing New Devices. The User Must Restart Their Computer Before the New Settings Will Take Effect." Click **Yes**.

Step 9

Right-click **My Computer** and click **Manage**. Click **Storage** and then **Disk Management (local)**.

Did it convert to dynamic disk? ___

Troubleshooting

Click **Action** in the upper-left corner and click **Restore Basic Disk Configuration**. A warning appears; click **Yes**.

Reflection

Can you convert back to basic disk without losing any information? Why?

____

____

____

Worksheet 9.1.4: RAID

Worksheets enhance the material covered in the HP IT Essentials online course and the companion guide. Use the space provided to answer the questions. Refer to this information when preparing for the A+ exam.

1. What is hardware-based RAID?

____

____

2. What is software-based RAID?

____

____

3. Below each of the pictures that follow, indicate whether it is RAID 0, RAID 1 mirroring, RAID 1 duplexing, RAID 5, or RAID 1/0.

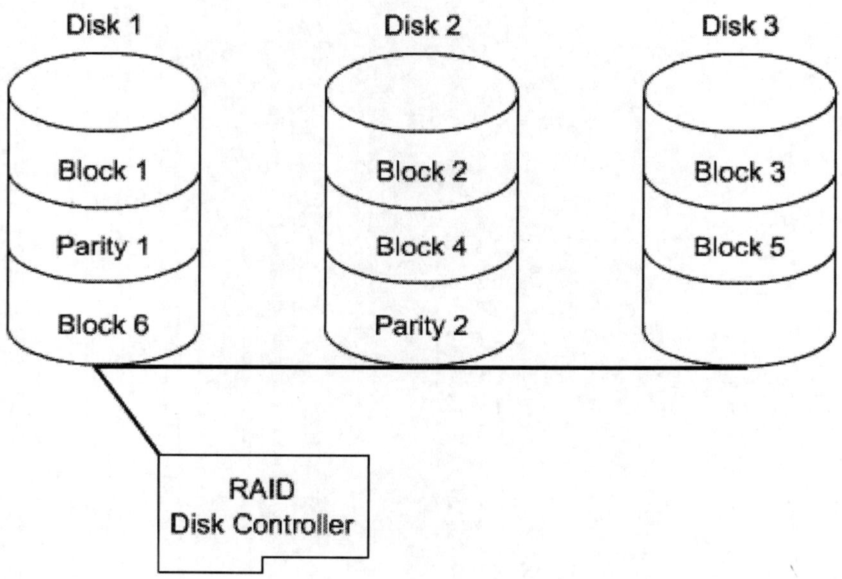

____

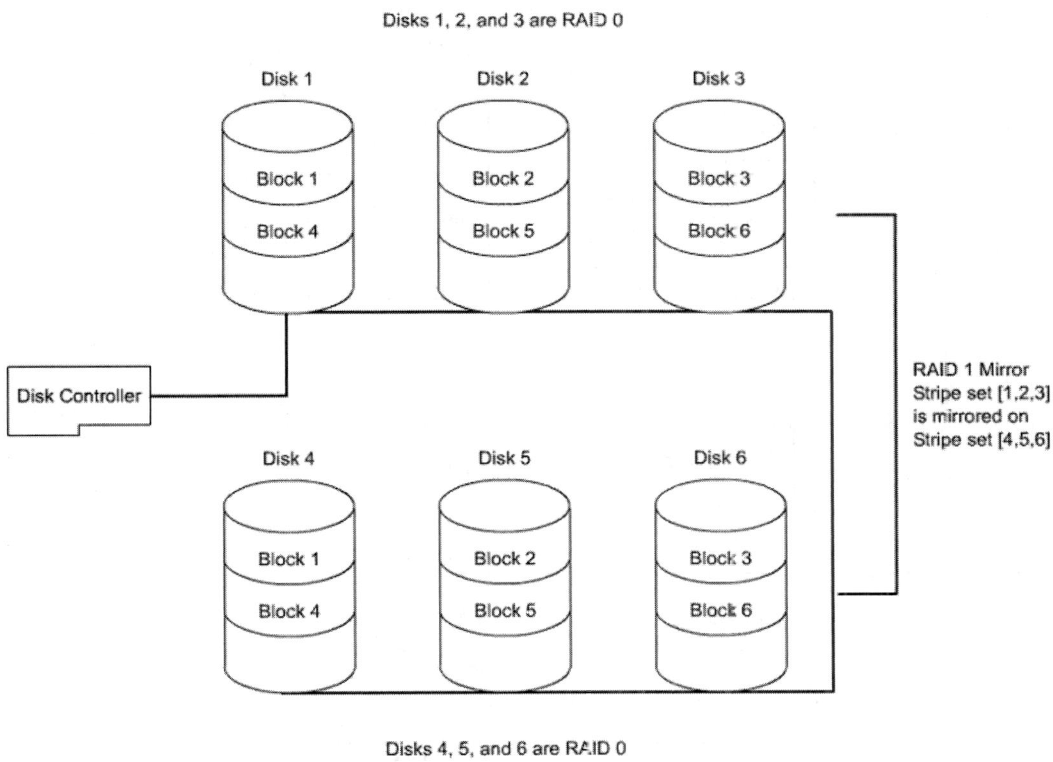
Disks 1, 2, and 3 are RAID 0
Disk 1
Disk 2
Disk 3
Block 1
Block 4
Block 2
Block 5
Block 3
Block 6
Disk Controller
RAID 1 Mirror
Stripe set [1,2,3]
is mirrored on
Stripe set [4,5,6]
Disk 4
Disk 5
Disk 6
Block 1
Block 4
Block 2
Block 5
Block 3
Block 6
Disks 4, 5, and 6 are RAID 0

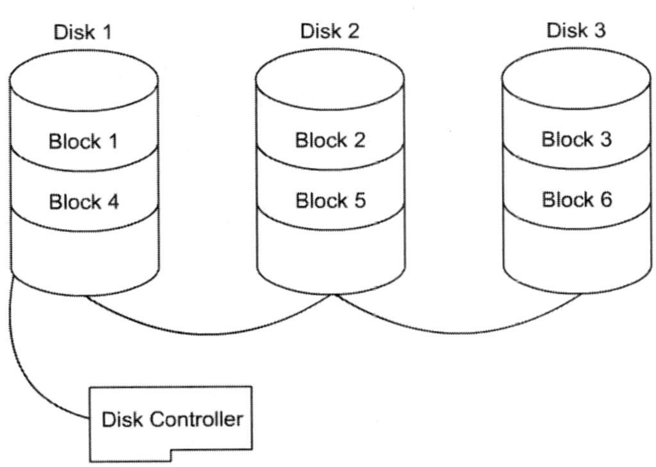
Disk 1
Disk 2
Disk 3
Block 1
Block 4
Block 2
Block 5
Block 3
Block 6
Disk Controller

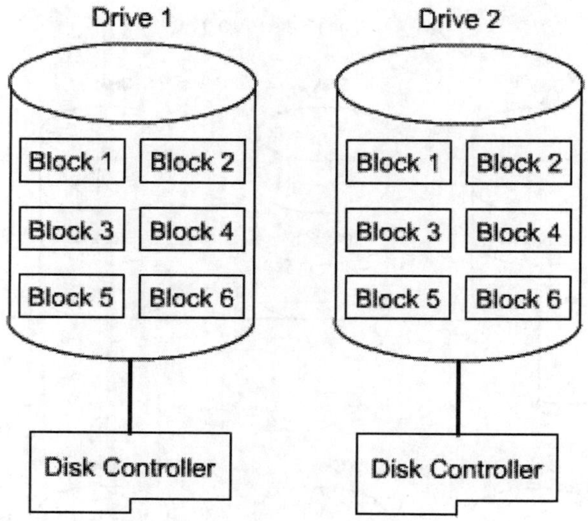
Drive 1
Drive 2
Block 1
Block 2
Block 3
Block 4
Block 5
Block 6
Block 1
Block 2
Block 3
Block 4
Block 5
Block 6
Disk Controller
Disk Controller

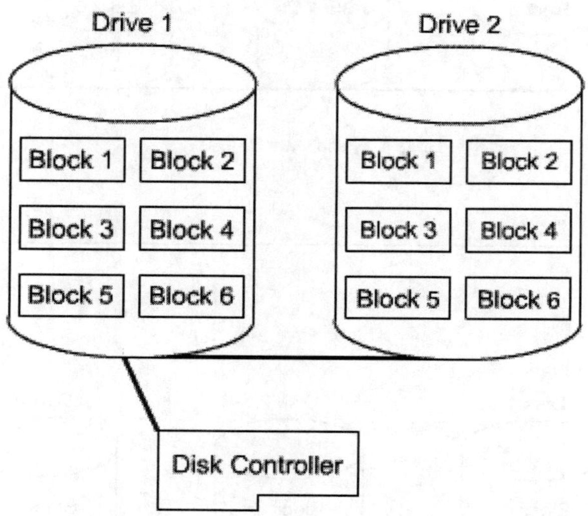
Drive 1
Drive 2
Block 1
Block 2
Block 3
Block 4
Block 5
Block 6
Block 1
Block 2
Block 3
Block 4
Block 5
Block 6
Disk Controller

Worksheet 9.4.3: Adding Processors

1. How do you check the motherboard to see whether it can support a faster clock speed?

____

2. To add another processor to a multiprocessor-capable network server, the new processor must meet what criteria?

____

____

____

3. The seven steps for adding additional processors are

   Step 1: ____

   Step 2: ____

   Step 3: ____

   Step 4: ____

   Step 5: ____

   Step 6: ____

   Step 7: ____

4. On a Windows NT and Windows 2000 Server, you must update the ____________ before you add multiple processors.

5. What number from the processor label can you use to look up Intel websites to identify the processor currently in your network server?

____

6. When upgrading a single processor to a faster single processor, you need to upgrade the BIOS. True or false? ____

7. In what two ways is the processor identification utility available?

____

____

8. Can Novell support multiple processors? ____________________________________

9. What steps do you take to enable multiple processors in Novell?

____

____

10. What must you do in Linux to be able to support multiple processors?

____

11. What command shows you the current processor information?

____

Chapter 10

Networking Fundamentals

Lab 10.3.1: NIC Installation

Estimated Time: 30 Minutes

Objective

In this lab, you install a network interface card (NIC) into a PC. You also configure that NIC to use an IP address.

Equipment

The following equipment is required for this lab:

- PC with Windows 98 or earlier
- NIC with appropriate drivers
- Antistatic wrist strap
- Toolkit
- Windows 98 installation CD-ROM or cab files

Scenario

The boss has decided to install a network using the existing company PCs. You must install the necessary hardware on each computer for them to be networked.

Procedures

A PC technician is responsible for upgrading and maintaining PCs for the company. As part of this job, a technician often upgrades existing PCs with new hardware to fit the company's changing needs. To allow a PC to be networked, one of the first things a technician must do is install a NIC. A NIC allows a PC to access the networking media (cabling, wireless) and communicate with other PCs.

Step 1: Ensuring ESD Prevention

To properly install an NIC, it is important to note several items. First, to prevent the NIC from being damaged by electrostatic discharge (ESD), it is important to ensure that the technician is properly grounded. Wear an ESD wrist-strap that is fastened to the metal frame of the PC whenever handling computer components. Also, when handling the NIC, only hold it by the edges, and do not touch the gold metal contacts along the bottom of the card.

Examine the NIC. Who manufactured the card?

____

Can you identify a model number? If so, what is it?

____

Can you determine the speed at which the NIC operates? If so, what speed?

____

Looking at the end of the card, what type of media connects to it?

____

What slot type does the NIC fit into?

____

Step 2: Proceeding with the Installation of the NIC

After you examine the NIC, it is time to proceed with the installation. Make sure that the PC is shut down and unplugged.

Remove the cover from the PC. Choose a slot on the motherboard to install the NIC. You might need to remove a small metal cover from the back of the expansion slot for the NIC to install properly. The NIC installs only one way. Make sure it is lined up properly. Remember that it is possible to damage the NIC or the motherboard if you use too much force when pushing the NIC into place.

Step 3: Proceeding with the Installation of the NIC

After the card is installed, secure the card with a screw and ensure that the card does not dislodge when you plug in a patch cord. When finished with the card, replace the cover and plug the machine back in.

Step 4: Installing Software

After the hardware is installed, it is time to install the software. This step requires the correct driver for the NIC. A driver is a piece of software that allows an operating system to access a piece of hardware, such as the NIC. Depending on the age of the NIC, Windows might already have a driver for it. If not, go to the NIC manufacturer's website and download it. Use the information in Step 1 to ensure that you are using the right driver.

Boot the PC.

Did Windows find new hardware? If not, refer to the troubleshooting section for suggestions.

____

Step 5: Installing the Driver

After Windows finds new hardware, it brings up the Add New Hardware Wizard screen. Click **Next**. Windows asks to search for the best driver or to display a list of drivers that it includes.

Choose **Search for the Best Driver for Your Device** and click **Next**. Now specify where the driver is located.

If it is on a CD, then click **CD-ROM drive**; if it is on a floppy disk, click **Floppy disk drives**.

If you know the exact location, click **Specify a Location** and type in the path to the driver, or click **Browse** and highlight the folder the driver resides in. After you make a selection, click **Next**. Windows shows the name of the device and where the driver is located.

Click **Next**; Windows installs the driver and displays when it finishes installing the software. Then, click **Finish**, and Windows prompts to reboot. Select **OK** to continue.

Note: Windows might require the Windows 98 installation CD-ROM to complete the installation.

Step 6: Verifying NIC Installation

After the driver is installed, verify that the NIC was properly installed. To do so, use the following directions:

1. Right-click over the **My Computer** icon on the desktop.
2. Click **Properties**.
3. Click the **Device Manager** tab.
4. Click the + sign next to Network Adapters.

Is the name of the adapter listed here?

____

Is anything else listed here? If so, what?

____

Step 7: Setting Up TCP/IP

Now that the NIC is installed, it is time to set up TCP/IP. To do so, complete the following steps:

1. Right-click Network Neighborhood.
2. Click **Properties**.
3. Where The Following Network Components Are Installed appears, scroll down to TCP/IP. If TCP/IP is not listed, you must install it by following the directions here. Otherwise, skip to Step 8.
4. Click the **Add** tab.
5. Click **Protocol** and **Add**.
6. Click **Microsoft** and then scroll down and highlight TCP/IP.
7. Click **OK**.

There might be a prompt for the location of Windows setup files. If you are unsure of their location, ask the instructor for directions.

After TCP/IP is installed, return to the Network Neighborhood properties and configure the IP address.

Step 8: Configuring the IP Address

Double-click the TCP/IP listing that also has the NIC listed next to it.

Make sure that the IP address screen is displayed, and then click **Specify an IP Address**.

Enter an IP address and subnet mask that will work within the network. Ask the instructor for directions about which addresses to use.

After you enter the IP address and subnet mask, click **OK**.

Click **OK** on the Network screen, and when Windows prompts to restart, click **Yes**.

Troubleshooting

Sometimes Windows does not detect a new hardware device. If that happens, you must install the device manually. To do so, complete the following steps:

1. Click **Start > Settings > Control Panel**.
2. Double-click **Add New Hardware**.
3. Click **Next** to begin installing software for the device.

4. Click **Next** to let Windows search for new hardware.

   If Windows still does not detect the new device, it asks to search for a non "plug-and-play" device. Either choose to let Windows search, or choose the hardware from a list.

5. Select **No, I Want to Select It from a List**.

6. Click **Next**.

7. Select **Network Adapters**.

8. Click **Next**.

9. Select **Have Disk** and specify the location of the driver.

If a problem still exists, shut off the computer and make sure that the NIC is physically installed correctly.

A common mistake made by many technicians is accidentally installing the wrong device driver. If this happens, the device usually does not work. The easiest solution is to do the following:

1. Right-click **My Computer**.

2. Click **Properties**.

3. Click Device Manager.

4. Click the + sign next to network adapters and highlight the NIC.

5. Click **Properties**.

6. Click the **Driver** tab at the top of the screen.

7. Click Update Driver.

Follow the prompts . to install the correct driver.

Reflection

As a group, research and list as many NIC card manufacturers and their websites as possible.

____

____

____

____

As a group, research and discuss how a subnet mask is used within a network.

Lab 10.3.3: Configuring the NIC to Work with a DHCP Server

Estimated Time: 10 Minutes

Objective

In this lab, you configure a NIC to utilize Dynamic Host Configuration Protocol (DHCP).

Equipment

The following equipment is required for this lab:

- The network created from the previous sections in this chapter with Windows 98 or earlier and TCP/IP enabled.
- A DHCP server accessible on the network

Scenario

The company wants to expand the number of users it currently has. The company is changing to a dynamic addressing scheme and needs to begin making the necessary changes to the host computers.

Procedures

There is a choice between two types of address management within a network, static or dynamic.

Static addressing requires an administrator to physically enter a unique IP address into each host on the network. The larger the network becomes, the more difficult it can be to keep track of assigned addresses. This point is especially true if hosts are changing to new subnets periodically.

You use DHCP to automatically assign IP addresses to hosts within the network. A DHCP server is configured to automatically assign an address from a range of addresses known as a *scope*. The hosts request an IP address from the DHCP server, which then assigns a unique address. This process enables PCs to move around within a network and have their addresses changed automatically as needed. It also allows the administrator to manage thousands of addresses in the network.

Step 1: Viewing Network Neighborhood Properties

View the Network Neighborhood properties as described. Right-click **Network Neighborhood**. Click **Properties**.

Is TCP/IP listed as an installed component? If so, what is the name and model number of the NIC it is bound to?

____
____

Is TCP/IP listed with any other items? If so, list those items.

____
____

Step 2: Viewing the Settings of TCP/IP

View the settings of TCP/IP as described.

Highlight **TCP/IP**. (Make sure it is the one listed with the NIC.)

Click **Properties**.

Is an IP address currently assigned? If so, write down the address along with the subnet mask.

____
____

Step 3: Changing the Address from Static to Dynamically Assigned

Follow the instructions to change the address from being static to dynamically assigned.

Click the radio button labeled **Obtain an IP Address Automatically**.

Did anything change on the TCP/IP screen? If so, what?

____
____

Step 4: Saving the New Configuration

Follow these instructions to save the new configuration.

1. Click **OK** on the TCP/IP properties page.
2. Click **OK** on the Network Properties page.
3. Click **Yes** when prompted to restart the computer.

If asked to insert a Windows disk to install files, ask the instructor for further directions.

Step 5: Verifying the New IP Address

After rebooting the machine, follow these instructions to verify the new IP address:

1. Click **Start** > **Run**.

2. Type the command **winipcfg** and click **OK**.

3. Click the arrow next to NIC adapter.

4. Highlight the NIC and click the tab that says **More Info**.

Note: Check the lights on back of the card. These lights blink when there is network activity taking place. Blinking lights on the NIC is an indication that the computer is successfully establishing a network connection.

What is the new IP address and subnet mask?

____

____

What is the IP address of the DHCP server?

____

____

What date was the lease for the address obtained, and when does it expire?

____

____

Troubleshooting

When you configure DHCP on a client computer, the computer might display an error stating that the server is unavailable. Should this happen, the easiest solution is to finish rebooting the machine and then follow these instructions:

1. Click **Start**.

2. Click **Run**.

3. Type the command **winipcfg** and click **OK**.

4. Click the arrow and choose an adapter.

5. Click **Release**, which clears an address.

6. Click **Renew**, which requests a new address.

The machine should now be able to join the network after rebooting.

Reflection

As a group, think of situations where static addressing would be preferred over DHCP.

Determine any other commands that would show the IP address under Windows 98 or Windows NT when using DHCP.

A network or PC technician might be required to manage a company's addressing scheme. Static addressing requires a great deal of management on the technician's part. The technician must track what addresses are available and which ones are in use. Depending on the size of your network, this task could become complicated and time-consuming. DHCP allows the creation of a range of addresses and allows a server to determine which address a host receives. If you move a host to a new network, DHCP assigns a new address without the administrator's intervention.

Lab 10.7.2: Troubleshooting a NIC Using the Ping Command

Estimated Time: 15 Minutes

Objective

In this lab, you use the **ping** command to test connectivity and troubleshoot problems based on **ping** command results.

Equipment

The following equipment is required for this lab:

- Several Windows 98 or earlier PCs with networking installed and configured
- One hub or switch
- One PC with Internet access

Scenario

Suppose that you often receive calls from users with complaints about the network. One morning, a user calls and complains that he is unable to reach anything on the network. Because the user is in an office in another building, you decide to try troubleshooting the problem remotely before visiting his office.

Procedures

When working with computers that have networking installed, technicians are asked to troubleshoot a variety of problems. Depending on the size of the company, this task can become quite challenging. If the users are spread out across multiple floors, buildings, or even cities, it can be time-consuming to visit every office for every problem. Luckily, some utilities allow a technician to begin troubleshooting a problem without leaving the office.

There are a wide variety of troubleshooting tools available to a technician. Many of these tools can be expensive to purchase. However, a few utilities are free and come with almost every operating system. One of the most commonly used utilities is the Packet Internet Groper (**ping**) command. You use the **ping** command to test connectivity between two hosts (PCs). When you ping a device, a signal is sent to the device, which then replies. If the ping is successful, then the connection between the two devices is good. If the ping fails, then there is a problem between the devices.

Step 1: Pinging the NIC IP Address

Open a command prompt as described:

1. Click **Start** > **Run**.

2. Type the word **command** and click **OK**

3. Type the command **ping a.b.c.d** (where a.b.c.d is the IP address of the NIC).

Did you receive a reply?

____

How many times did the NIC reply?

____

How many bytes were used?

____

How much time did it take to receive a reply?

____

What was the maximum Time-To-Live (TTL)?

____

Step 2: Pinging the Loopback IP Address

You can ping the NIC in a workstation by using its IP address or something called the *loopback address*. The address 127.0.0.1 is reserved as the loopback address and is not used on the Internet. Instead, the loopback is an address that pings the NIC installed in the workstation you are currently using.

Type the command **ping 127.0.0.1**.

Did you receive a reply?

____

Are the values for bytes, time, and TTL the same as last time? If not, what changed?

____

Step 3: Testing Hosts Within the Network

If you can successfully ping the PC address and the loopback, then the NIC and TCP/IP have been successfully installed. Now, it is time to test whether you can reach the other hosts within the network.

Type **ping A.B.C.D**. (This time, A.B.C.D is the address of another workstation within the network.)

Did you receive a reply? If not, what was the error message?

Are the values the same for bytes, time, and TTL as they were in Step 1? If not, what changed?

Step 4: Testing Hosts on the Outside of the Network

If you can successfully ping another workstation, that means there is a good connection between the two machines. However, sometimes using the **ping** command results in a problem.

Type the command **ping A.B.C.D**. (A.B.C.D is an IP address for a workstation outside of the network.)

What message did you received?

What might this message mean?

Now, using a PC with an Internet connection, open a DOS prompt and type **ping 1.1.1.1**.

What message did you received this time?

What might this message mean?

Troubleshooting

If you have trouble pinging the IP address of the workstation, or if you are unable to ping the loopback address, then you need to check the TCP/IP settings. If the TCP/IP was not set properly, then the ping function will not work. Make sure that the protocol is correctly installed and bound to the NIC.

If you have trouble pinging other hosts within the network, check the cable and make sure that it is correctly plugged into the hub or switch. Check the IP address and the subnet mask to make sure they were entered correctly.

Reflection

Once you install a PC on a network, you spend much of your time troubleshooting network problems. It is important that you save as much time as possible. Ping is a great utility to begin troubleshooting a problem. Ping will help you determine whether the network problem is related to a bad cable, an incorrect TCP/IP setting, or a problem with a remote device. Make sure to be comfortable using the ping command and its responses.

Worksheet 10.2.5: Types of Networks

1. What is the definition of a network?

____

____

____

2. What is the definition of a computer network?

____

____

____

3. Provide a brief definition for each of the terms.

LAN

____

____

____

WAN

____

____

____

Circuit-switched network

____

____

____

Packet-switched network

____

____

____

Client/server network

____

____

____

Peer to peer

Hybrid network

4. On a LAN, what are the rules for coordinating the use of the medium called?

5. Define CSU/DSU.

6. A data channel, over which you can send data, can operate in one of three ways; name the three ways.

Worksheet 10.4.2: Network Topology

1. What is the difference between physical topology and logical topology?

____
____
____

2. Describe the following topology.

Bus

____
____
____

Star

____
____
____

Extended star

____
____
____

Ring

____
____
____

Mesh

____
____
____

Hybrid

____
____
____
____

3. What is the definition of networking media?

4. What does the term "architecture" refer to?

5. In a Token Ring implementation, what is the purpose of the "monitor of the ring?"

Worksheet 10.6.5: OSI Model, TCP/IP, Protocols

1. What does OSI stand for?

____

____

____

2. How does the OSI model work? Include an example:

____

____

____

3. Explain the purpose of each of the seven layers of the OSI model.

Application

____

____

____

Presentation

____

____

____

Session

____

____

____

Transport

____

____

____

Network

____

____

____

Data Link

Physical

4. What is a protocol?

5. For what purpose was the original TCP/IP designed?

6. How does TCP/IP differ from the OSI model?

7. Explain application protocols.

8. Explain transport protocols.

9. Explain network protocols.

Worksheet 10.8.7: Connecting to the Internet

1. Explain the difference between synchronous and asynchronous.

____

____

____

2. What is the definition of a modem?

____

____

____

3. List the four main types of modems.

____

____

____

4. Three activities occur during the local command and online state of a modem. List them.

____

____

____

5. What are AT commands?

____

____

____

6. What does ISP stand for, and what role does an ISP play in the Internet?

____

____

____

7. What does vBNS stand for, and what role does the vBNS play in the Internet?

____

____

____

8. Explain the major differences between DSL and cable modems.

____

____

____

Chapter 11

Printers and Sharing

Lab 11.3.7: Adding an Inkjet Printer to a Computer

Estimated Time: 30 Minutes

Objective

In this lab, you connect a printer to a PC, install the correct printer driver, and verify communication between computer and printer by printing a test page.

Equipment

The following equipment is required for this lab:

- A computer with Windows 98 installed
- Inkjet printer with ink cartridges installed
- Communication cable (Universal Serial Bus [USB] or parallel)
- Printer drivers

Scenario

A PC technician is responsible for installing printers throughout an organization. The goal is to properly install and configure an inkjet printer with the proper drivers.

Procedures

A printer is one of the essential components of a computer system. Whether it is a laser printer for high-quality text printouts or an inkjet printer for publishing digital-camera photographs, it is important to know how to install a printer.

Step 1

Connect the communication cable to the printer.

What type of cable do you use to connect the printer to the PC (USB or parallel)?

____

Which end of the cable do you connect to the printer (USB-A, USB-B, DB-25, or Centronics)?

____

Step 2

Connect the communication cable to the computer.

Which end of the cable do you connect to the computer (USB-A, USB-B, DB-25, or Centronics)?

____

Step 3

Power on the printer and make sure it is functioning properly. Turn the computer power on and log in to Windows.

Step 4

After initial logon, Windows should detect the printer. If the computer does not find the printer, start the Add Printer Wizard by going to **Start** > **Settings** > **Printers**. Double-click the **Add Printer** icon.

If Windows finishes loading the desktop and does not detect new hardware, what might be the cause?

____

____

Step 5

Begin the Found New Hardware Wizard by clicking **Next** at the bottom of the window. This wizard leads you through the entire printer installation process.

Step 6

The next screen in the wizard asks whether the printer is a local or network printer. Select **local** and click **Next**.

This action opens a window with a list of printer manufacturers and devices. If the drivers for the printer are in possession, click the **Have Disk** button and browse for the location of the drivers.

What type of media contains the printer driver?

____

____

Why are printer drivers rarely located on a floppy disk?

____

____

Step 7

Windows searches the selected medium for appropriate printer drivers. Driver files found show up in the Driver File Search Results screen. From this screen, select the proper driver for the printer and choose **Next**.

Why do manufacturers usually include multiple printer drivers on a single CD-ROM?

____

____

Windows is now installing the printer driver files. An installation progress message might appear during this phase.

What are common device-driver file extensions?

____

Step 8

The next window prompts for the port that the printer is connected to. If you used a parallel cable, select LPT1.

What ports are listed other than LPT1?

____

Step 9

The Add Printer Wizard now prompts for the printer name. Use either the default name suggested by the system or another name to help identify the printer. The name might indicate the type of printer, the printer location, or anything else that helps identify the printer on the local system.

Choose whether to make this printer the default printer. If more than one printer is in use, the default printer should be the one you use most often.

What name did you give to the printer?

____

____

Step 10

The final step is to print a test page. Click **Yes** to print a test page and then click **Finish**. Depending on the printer being installed, a printer initialization program might run. These programs set the print orientation, check the type of ink cartridge, and so on.

Step 11

Click **Finish** or **Close** if the wizard has not already closed. When the test page finishes printing, a dialog box asks whether the test page printed properly. If it did, click **Yes**. If the results are not readable, click **No** and follow the printer troubleshooter to help solve the problem.

Step 12

Check to be sure that the printer is installed on the computer. From the Windows Desktop, choose **Start** > **Settings** > **Printers**. This move opens the Printers folder.

Is an icon visible for the printer that you just installed? If not, see the troubleshooting section of this lab.

____

____

Which printer is set as the default printer? How can you check this information?

____

____

Step 13

Double-click the printer icon. This move opens the print queue.

Are any print jobs listed in the print queue? Why or why not?

____

____

Step 14

Right-click the printer icon and choose **Properties**. The printer properties dialog box opens.

What "tabs" are available?

____

List two user-selectable options from a tab.

____

Step 15

Click the **General** tab. The Print Test Page is near the bottom of the page. Click the **Print Test Page** button.

After you clicked the Print Test Page button, what question did Windows ask? How was it answered?

____

Step 16

You successfully installed the inkjet printer on the Windows computer. If you are not able to print a test page, see the troubleshooting section of this lab.

Troubleshooting

If Windows begins the Found New Hardware Wizard but is unable to locate a suitable device driver, check the printer driver media. Also, you might need to download a newer, updated printer driver from the manufacturer website.

If you are able to install the printer but unable to print a test page using either method in the lab, check the communication cable. The cable might be in sufficient condition to allow the computer to know it is connected to a printer but might not be good enough to pass printer data.

You might also need to configure the BIOS for the printer to function correctly. Some computers require the parallel port to be set to EPP. To accomplish this step, you need to configure the BIOS.

Reflection

What is an advantage of a laser printer over an inkjet printer?

____

____

____

Lab 11.4.4: Setting Up Print-Sharing Capabilities

Estimated Time: 20 Minutes

Objective

In this lab, you verify communication between the server and the client, set up the print server, configure the client, and test the client's print capability.

Equipment

The following equipment is required for this lab:

- A functional network with at least two computers running Windows.
- A printer installed on one Windows computer.

Scenario

The sales department in your small company currently has a single printer connected to one computer. Because the other sales reps need access to a printer, the manager has asked you to make the printer available to the entire sales department.

Procedures

The strength of a computer network is the ability to share resources. An example of a resource is a printer. Windows allows users to connect and install a printer on one computer (the print server) and share it with the other computers (clients) on the network. This lab details the steps that you follow to set up print sharing using Windows.

Step 1

On the computer with the printer attached (the server), click **Start** and **Run**. In the Run dialog box, type **Command** and press **Enter**. This move opens a command-line session window.

Step 2

Type **IPCONFIG** if running Windows 2000. Type **WINIPCFG** if running Windows 98. This command presents information about the IP address of the computer.

What is the IP address of the server?

Step 3

On the client computer, click **Start** > **Run**, type **Command**, and press **Enter**. At the command-line prompt, ping the server IP address (for example: **ping 192.168.10.1**).

What is the purpose of using the **ping** command?

Were the ping attempts successful? If not, ensure that both computers are properly configured and connected to the network.

Step 4

It is important to know the network identification information for the server. To see this information, right-click **My Computer**, choose **Properties**, and select the **Network Identification** tab.

What is the full computer name of the server?

What is the workgroup of the server?

Step 5

For several computers to use the same printer, you need to install print-sharing software needs on the server. To do so, return to the desktop, right-click **Network Neighborhood**, choose **Properties**, and then click the **File and Print Sharing** button. Make sure there is a check next to the **I want to be able to allow others to print from my printer(s)** option. After you check that, click the **OK** button. Then, click **OK** on the network properties window. The computer prompts you to restart the machine. Click **Yes**.

Step 6

Now that the print sharing software is installed, it is time to configure the particular printer for print sharing. From the desktop, click **Start** > **Settings** > **Printers** to open the Printers folder.

Is the printer available in the folder?

Step 7

Right-click the icon of the printer to be shared with the client computer. Choose **Properties**, and select the **Sharing** tab.

Step 8

You use the sharing options to make the printer available to clients and give the printer a unique name on the network. Choose **Shared as** and then type a unique name for the printer.

Why must the name for the printer be unique to the network?

____

What name did you give the printer?

____

Step 9

When finished with the sharing options, click **OK**.

After you click **OK** and return to the Printers folder, what has changed regarding the look of the printer icon and what does this change signify?

____
____
____

Step 10

You are now ready to begin installing the printer on the client. On the client computer, click **Start** > **Settings** > **Printers** to open the Printers folder.

Step 11

Double-click the **Add Printer** icon to begin the Add Printer Wizard. This wizard walks you through the process of selecting the shared printer.

Step 12

Click **Next** to get to the printer type screen. On this screen, choose **Network Printer** and click **Next**. This step leads to the wizard that allows you to browse the network for the printer or enter the path to the printer.

Step 13

On this screen, type in the path to the printer and choose **Next**. The path is formatted like this: *server_name**printer_name* where the *server_name* is the full computer name of the server and *printer_name* is the name given to the printer.

What is the path to the printer?

____

After you click the **Next** button and return to the Printers folder, is there an icon for the printer?

____

Step 14

The printer is installed on the client computer. Now, test the communication between the client and the printer.

What are two methods for printing a test page from the client computer?

____

Troubleshooting

If you turn off the computer that a printer is connected to or remove it from the network, the resources that are being shared from that computer are no longer available. Many times, it is necessary to have a dedicated print server so that anyone can print to a computer at any time.

There are various ways to set up a print server. Some network-capable printers have print servers built into them. Other print servers are small and can be easily hide between the printer and a desk or wall.

Reflection

Why would a company install a network printer instead of purchasing a printer for every end user?

____

____

____

Lab 11.5.4: Managing Files in a Printer Queue

Estimated Time: 20 Minutes

Objective

In this lab, you learn how to manipulate print jobs held in a printer queue. After you place jobs in the queue, this lab covers how to delete single jobs, prioritize jobs, and purge the entire printer queue. These skills become necessary when someone sends a print job to the queue, but it is not the correct document to print.

In this lab, you do the following:

- Open the printer queue.
- Add jobs to the printer queue.
- Delete a job from the printer queue.
- Rearrange jobs in the printer queue.
- Purge all jobs held in the printer queue.

Equipment

The following equipment is required for this lab:

- A computer with Windows 98 installed
- An installed printer

Scenario

If a document does not immediately print, many computer users click the print button again. They keep clicking the print button until the document prints. This behavior can lead to massive amounts of wasted resources.

Procedures

You manipulate the print jobs held in the printer so that only one of the duplicate print jobs is completed. This move frees up resources for other jobs that are in the queue. In addition, you verify the status of the jobs that are waiting, pause, cancel, and resume the queue.

Step 1

Each installed printer uses a queue to hold print jobs. This queue is an area of memory and hard drive that feeds information to the printer. Click **Start** > **Settings** > **Printers** to open the Printers folder. Double-click the printer being used in this lab. This move opens the queue.

Which printer do you use for this lab?

____

What jobs are currently in the printer queue?

____

Step 2

In the printer queue menu bar, click **File** and choose **Pause Printing**. This move causes the printer queue to hold all print jobs without sending any information to the printer. Minimize the printer queue window.

Step 3

To add jobs to the printer queue, create some documents to print. Click **Start** > **Programs** > **Accessories** and choose **Notepad**.

Step 4

Using Notepad, type **Document 1** and save it to the desktop as **low.txt**.

Step 5

Add this document to the printer queue by choosing **File** > **Print**. Open the printer queue window. (It is minimized and available on the taskbar.)

Is the print job listed in the printer queue?

____

Who is the owner of the print job?

____

What is the progress of the print job?

____

How long will this job stay in the queue?

____

Step 6

Use Notepad to create and print two more documents. Type in **Document 2**, save it to the desktop as **medium.txt**, and print the document. Type in **Document 3**, save it to the desktop as **high.txt**, and print the document.

How many jobs are now being held in the printer queue?

____

Step 7

Sometimes, it is necessary to cancel print jobs while they are being held in the printer queue. In the printer queue window, right-click **medium.txt**.

What options are available in the context-sensitive menu?

____

____

Step 8

Choose **Cancel Printing**.

How many jobs are now being held in the printer queue?

____

Step 9

By default, the printer queue handles jobs using first in, first out (FIFO). Sometimes, it is necessary to give priority to certain print jobs. In the printer queue window, drag low.txt to an area below high.txt and release it.

What is the order of the print jobs held in the printer queue?

____

____

When the printer is set to resume printing, which print job will the printer queue release first?

____

____

Step 10

To delete all jobs held in the printer queue, either delete each single job or choose to purge the entire queue. To purge the printer queue, open the printer queue window, choose **Printer** from the menu bar, and click **Purge Print Documents**.

How many jobs are now being held in the printer queue?

____

Step 11

Choose the **Printer** menu and click **Pause Printing** to release the printer from its paused state. Close the printer queue window and delete the low, medium, and high documents from the desktop.

Troubleshooting

If you are unable to place jobs in the printer queue using Notepad, check to ensure that the printer queue being viewed is the queue for the current default printer. Notepad is a simple application and only prints to the default printer.

Reflection

As a network administrator, how would being able to control the print queue help with the conservation of resources?

____

____

Worksheet 11.6.1: Paper Jams

Answer true or false.

1. ____ Fragments of paper that are torn in the printing process often must be removed from the paper path.

2. ____ Failing parts that drive paper movement might cause paper to crumple or z-fold in the process of moving through the path.

3. ____ Paper clumping is when one page sticks to another because the toner was not fused to the paper correctly.

4. ____ A paper jam cannot occur when you use the wrong type of paper because the printer does not accept it through the registration rollers.

5. ____ Most of the problems in laser printers that require service are rooted in the paper dust that is accumulated in the paper path.

6. ____ Because there are static charges present in the laser printing process, dust does not accumulate outside the paper path.

7. ____ If there is toner residue on the printer, use a wet towel to clean the affected area.

8. ____ Stepper motors are usually trouble-free.

9. ____ Poor solder connections on stepper motors have been known to cause intermittent operations.

10. ____ Very few paper jams are caused by improper paper type or weight.

Chapter 12

Preventive Maintenance

Lab 12.1.2: Using a Digital Multimeter

Estimated Time: 30 Minutes

Objective

This lab concentrates on your ability to identify and record power-supply specifications and connecter types. It also focuses on the use of a multimeter to safely test and record voltage readings.

Equipment

The following equipment is required for this lab:

- Personal computer (no peripherals will be needed)
- PC hand toolkit
- Multimeter

Scenario

You are an on-call help desk engineer for a small computer sales store. A client, who purchased a computer, as well as an extended warranty, is having problems with her PC. Based on her description of the behavior of the PC, you suspect the power supply.

Procedures

For this lab, you need to compile power-supply information as well as test procedures. Observe various types of power-supply form factors and characteristics. If at any time you are unsure of the procedure, ask the instructor.

Note: This lab deals with electrical power supplies. You should take proper care whenever working with a power supply. Also, do not wear a grounding strap when testing the power supply.

Step 1

Remove the cover of the computer and properly store the screws.

Review the precautions and directions on the side of the air can. Use the air sparingly to blow the dust out of the power supply and off all visible surfaces inside the case.

Step 2

Record the following power-supply information (found on the power-supply label).

Manufacturer	
Model number	
Operating range	
Current at 115 V	
Current at 230 V	
Wattage rating	

Step 3

Sketch the power supply and identify the four main external components of a power supply by labeling them on your drawing.

Step 4

Name the specific type of motherboard connector that the power supply is using.

Step 5

How many large drive connectors are available on your power supply?

Step 6

How many small drive connectors are available on your power supply?

Step 7

Identify the large drive connector leads and then measure their voltage values. (You must turn on the computer for this step. Ask the instructor if you have any questions related to how to proceed with voltage measurements.)

Lead Color	Expected Voltage	Actual Voltage

Step 8

Identify the small drive connector leads, and then measure their voltage values. (Ask the instructor if you have any questions related to how to proceed with voltage measurements.)

Lead Color	Expected Voltage	Actual Voltage

Step 9

Why is it important for a technician to know the different colors and their values?

___

___

___

___

Step 10

With the multimeter, measure the voltage on each colored wire of the motherboard connectors. Most motherboard connectors have either two connectors or one long connector.

Use the following table to record the lead colors and their measured voltage.

Note: Do not measure the black leads because they are the ground wires

Note the meter lead polarity: red is positive (+) and black is negative (-).

Lead color	Voltage reading
Lead color	Voltage reading
Lead color	Voltage reading
Lead color	Voltage reading
Lead color	Voltage reading
Lead color	Voltage reading
Lead color	Voltage reading
Lead color	Voltage reading
Lead color	Voltage reading

Lead color	Voltage reading
Lead color	Voltage reading
Lead color	Voltage reading
Lead color	Voltage reading
Lead color	Voltage reading
Lead color	Voltage reading
Lead color	Voltage reading
Lead color	Voltage reading
Lead color	Voltage reading
Lead color	Voltage reading
Lead color	Voltage reading

Step 11

Check the continuity from the ground of the power cord socket to the metal base of the computer.

Step 12

For this step, you must turn off the computer and unplug it from the AC source. Check the continuity of all three conductors of a power cord from the plug end to the female end.

1. Neutral ______________________
2. Hot ______________________
3. Ground ______________________

Step 13

Why measure voltage when troubleshooting a power supply? Please explain.

____

____

____

____

____

Troubleshooting

One way to determine whether a power supply is not functioning properly is to compare the test results from what the connector should be reading. Never open a malfunctioning power supply. Replace the component with a new one of the same power capacity.

Reflection

What did you learn from this lab that you did not know before?

____
____
____

How can the knowledge from this lab help in the future?

____
____
____

Lab 12.3.5: Cleaning Computer Components

Estimated Time: 25 Minutes

Objective

In this lab, you learn the proper procedure to clean computer components.

Equipment

The following items are needed to complete this lab:

- A computer with a keyboard, mouse, and monitor
- Mild detergent (a little soap, a lot of water)
- Cleaning rag
- Container for the detergent (bucket or spray bottle)
- Can of compressed air
- Toolkit
- Keyboard cap puller (optional)

Scenario

As a PC repair technician, you have been sent to fix a computer that has stopped working. A good practice to follow when repairing PCs is to clean the computer before leaving it.

Procedures

When cleaning electrical components, it is critical to unplug the device before working with it. If there is power running to a computer system and you run a damp cloth over it, the results could be deadly.

Step 1: Cleaning the Inside of the Computer Case

The first thing that you should clean is the inside of the computer case.

To begin, unplug the power cord if it is not already unplugged. Next, remove the case cover either by removing the appropriate screws or latch. When the case is open, it is a good idea to keep the case standing vertical or even angled so that when you blow the dust out, it does not settle back inside.

Review the precautions and directions on the side of the air can. Use the air sparingly to blow the dust out of the power supply and off all visible surfaces inside the case. Once all surfaces are clean, reattach the case cover.

Have you thoroughly cleaned the inside of the case? ______________________________

Step 2: Cleaning the Monitor

When cleaning the monitor, the first and most important step is to turn off the unit and unplug it from the wall.

After it is unplugged, it is safe to clean the surfaces with a cloth that is dampened with a mild detergent. If the cloth leaves streaks on the screen, there is too much liquid. A damp or moist cloth has only enough cleaner to help remove dust and clean the surface. Using a dry cloth, wipe down the screen and sides to remove any residual cleaning fluid.

When all sides of the monitor are clean, it is a good idea to let it sit and dry for at least a half hour, just in case something might have dripped inside.

Have you thoroughly cleaned the monitor? ______________________________

Step 3: Cleaning the Keyboard

The keyboard is the component that has the most physical contact with the user. The two areas of the keyboard that you should clean are the surface of the keys and the area below the keys. It is not necessary to pry the keyboard apart.

The fastest way to remove dust and other loose objects from below the keys is to blow it out with a can of air. Hold the keyboard upside down but away from eyes and face. Start at one side of the keyboard and spray the air from on side to the other side until the dust buildup is removed.

Step 4: Dealing with Liquid Spills at the Keyboard

If someone spilled a liquid such as soda on the keyboard, you must remove the keys to clean it out. Using a keyboard cap puller, remove the keys in the area where the spill occurred and use a cloth to clean up the mess. When the keys are thoroughly cleaned, you can replace them by positioning them in the correct spots and then pressing them down.

Have you thoroughly cleaned the keyboard? ______________________________

Step 5: Cleaning the Mechanical Mouse

The mouse is one of the most frequently cleaned components on a computer. An optical mouse requires less cleaning than a mechanical mouse.

To clean a mechanical mouse, remove the locking ring on the bottom. The proper direction to turn the ring should be indicated by an arrow. After you remove it, turn the mouse over and catch the ring and ball.

Observe the two posts that are inside the mouse, which are the x-axis and the y-axis. If there is a buildup of dirt on either one of these, use a Q-Tip and some denatured alcohol to remove the dirt.

Caution: Denatured alcohol is a poisonous substance. Observe safety precautions when using it.

Step 6: Inspecting the Mouse Ball for Cleaning

After you remove the dirt from the posts, inspect the ball to make sure it is clean. If it needs to be cleaned, use a mild cleanser and a clean lint-free rag to clean off the dirt.

After the ball is clean and dry, put the ball back into the mouse and return the ring to the locked position.

Have you thoroughly cleaned the mouse? ____

Troubleshooting

If dust builds up in a power supply, it could cause the system to malfunction or shut down. If the fans stop and the system overheats, internal components can be damaged as well. Preventive maintenance can prolong the life of not only the power supply, but also the entire system.

Reflection

How often should a computer system be entirely cleaned?

____
____
____

Why should computer systems be cleaned?

____
____
____

Lab 12.4.1: Using the Scandisk and Defrag Utilities

Estimated Time: 30 Minutes

Objective

In this lab, you scan a hard drive, defragment the drive to check for errors, and defragment files using the Scandisk and Defrag utilities.

Equipment

The following equipment is required for this lab:

- A computer with Windows 98 or 2000 Professional installed

Scenario

The manager expects you, as a system administrator, to perform routine maintenance on all computer systems as necessary. Run the Scandisk and Defrag utilities on the appropriate machines to keep them running smoothly.

Procedures

If you do not perform system maintenance on a computer that is used on a regular basis, system stability decreases. As files are created, used, and deleted, their storage media might become fragmented. Also, if a file is not properly closed, it can leave behind corrupted pieces of data. To resolve these problems, the two utilities Scandisk and Defrag are included with the Windows operating system.

Step 1: Running Scandisk

The first utility to run is Scandisk. This utility ensures that any problem files are fixed before the Defrag utility organizes the drive. To start the Scandisk utility, open **My Computer**, right-click the drive to be checked, and choose **Properties**. Select the **Tools** tab and then click the **Check Now** button. This move starts the Scandisk utility (referred to as Error-Checking in Windows 2000).

What types of tests are available in the Scandisk program?

____

____

Which test type is the default?

____

Step 2: Beginning Scanning

To begin the scanning, click the **Start** button. When it is finished, click the **Close** button. If there are errors, see the troubleshooting section of this lab.

Step 3: Starting the Defrag Utility

After Scandisk successfully finishes, you can run the Defrag utility to reorganize the files on the disk. To start the Defrag utility, open **My Computer**, right-click the drive to be defragged, and choose **Properties**. Select the **Tools** tab and then click the **Defragment Now** button. This move starts the Defrag utility.

Note: Make sure that you disable the screensaver and any other programs that automatically start, or they can interrupt the defragmenting process.

Troubleshooting

If Scandisk reports a cross-linked file or fragments of a file, it might ask how it should resolve the problem. There is an option to convert recovered data to a text file. However, this option clutters the drive with many text files of garbled information. Select the option to discard the information and continue.

Reflection

List any other utilities that come with Windows that can help in the preventative maintenance of a system.

____

____

____

____

____

Worksheet 12.1.4: Environmental Considerations

1. Explain why batteries need special disposal guidelines.

____
____
____

2. Explain why monitors need special disposal guidelines.

____
____
____

3. Explain why chemical solvents and aerosol cans need special disposal guidelines.

____
____
____

4. Inkjet printer cartridges and laser printer toner cartridges can be ______________ and ______________.

5. MSDS is an acronym for

____

6. What do you use the MSDS for?

____
____
____

7. MSDS contains information on

   a. ____

   b. ____

   c. ____

   d. ____

Worksheet 12.2.1: ESD

1. ESD is an acronym for _________________ _________________.

2. Most computer chips run on less than ________ volts of electricity.

3. Always use _________________ _________________ to temporarily store computer parts and components until they you ready to reinstall them.

4. Devices such as grounding _____________ __________ form a connection between a person and to the earth, which gives a place for the static to go before it attacks a sensitive computer component.

5. When the humidity is _________, the potential for ESD increases dramatically.

6. If the temperature is cool or if there is carpeting on the floor, there is a ___________ _________________ potential for static electricity.

7. When working on a computer, one of the first things you should do when you open the case is to _________________ yourself to the case by touching an exposed unpainted metal part of the computer case.

8. A good working area should have a climate control system that maintains the relative humidity between ________ % and ________ %.

9. When working on high voltage equipment, such as a power supply or a CRT monitor, you should *not* use a ______________ ______________.

Worksheet 12.3.5: Preventive Maintenance for Components

1. The majority of preventive maintenance involves keeping the components ______________________.

2. A problem with dust is its capability to be ______________ charged.

3. If you use the wrong types of cleaners, damage from ________________ could occur over time.

4. ___________ __________ can be a useful tool to quickly and easily clean out a dusty computer.

5. To fully protect your files from virus infection, you must make sure that the virus ________________ list is up to date.

6. If you are going to work on a laser printer that has been in use, let it ___________ for a while before coming in contact with the internal components.

7. Define the following terms.

   a. blackout

   ____

   ____

   b. brownout

   ____

   ____

   c. electrical noise

   ____

   ____

   d. spike

   ____

   ____

   e. surge

   ____

   ____

f. surge suppressor

g. standby power supply

h. uninterruptible power supply

Chapter 13

Troubleshooting PC Hardware

Lab 13.1.7: The Steps of the Troubleshooting Cycle

Estimated Time: 25 Minutes

Objective

In this lab, you describe the importance of, and identify the steps involved in, the troubleshooting cycle.

Equipment

This is a written lab. No equipment is necessary.

Scenario

You have just started a new job as a computer technician with a small consulting group. The company has approximately 50 employees with varying levels of computer expertise. As a computer technician, your primary responsibility is to provide desktop support to these employees.

You have recently gone through job orientation and received training on the procedures for responding to computer problems. The training included an introduction to the hardware and software in use, common errors, common symptoms, and using the troubleshooting cycle to effectively solve problems.

The end user is complaining that his computer has stopped responding. It is your responsibility to troubleshoot and resolve this problem.

Procedures

The troubleshooting steps can be useful in solving computer problems. Sometimes, a problem requires common sense and the solution is straightforward. Other times, the solution requires a broad level of technical knowledge. In this lab, you follow the troubleshooting cycle as an example of solving computer problems. The lab begins with Step 1, which is identifying the problem from the end user.

Step 1: Defining the Problem

After arriving on scene, begin the troubleshooting cycle by defining the problem. Start by identifying the general symptoms and then determine the possible causes for the existing problem.

For future reference, you bring along a notebook to document the findings.

Upon arrival, what environmental factors can you assess? How is an assessment of the environment beneficial?

____

____

Step 2: Gathering End User Information

The next step is to gather pertinent information from the end user. Initially, ask general questions with the goal of obtaining a broad idea about the computer problem. Questions should gain focus as you obtain information from the end user.

What questions could you ask to obtain a broad idea about the problem?

____

____

After questioning, you learn that the computer is not producing any sound. Everything else appears to be functioning correctly.

You can now assume that the problem is related to the multimedia (sound) capabilities of the computer. What questions could you ask or actions could you take to better define the problem?

____

____

During questioning, you determine that the end user has been having problems ever since a recent sound card upgrade. You attempt to reproduce the error by playing an audio file. The audio file does not produce any sound. You inspect the audio player and it appears to function correctly. Then, you visually inspect the speaker cables and verify that the speakers are turned on. You see no apparent problems with the connected devices, and the speakers are turned on.

Gathering information is by far the most important step of the troubleshooting cycle.

Step 3: Assessing the Problem

Given the preceding scenario, what are the most likely causes of the malfunctioning sound card?

____

____

The user has stated that he is having problems producing sound from his machine, and there has been a recent upgrade performed on his soundcard. From this information, you can infer that the problem is related to the recent upgrade of the sound card.

You have also verified that both the audio player and speakers are functioning properly. You have verified that the speakers are connected correctly. Since verifying the speakers and audio player are working, you conclude it is unlikely they are causing the problem. You continue the troubleshooting cycle by creating solutions for the apparently bad sound card installation.

Step 4: Beginning to Develop a Solution

Effectively developing a solution involves gathering correct information, knowledge of the computer components, and the ability to recognize symptoms.

The problem has been isolated to a bad installation of the sound card.

Give an example of a solution that might solve this user's problem.

____

____

The solution should focus on the different aspects of the sound card installation. Based on experience, you are aware that most sound card problems result from a bad or outdated driver, improperly installed sound card, or system resource conflicts.

For example, one solution might be verifying the proper installation of the sound card in the PCI slot. If the problem still exists, check for system resource conflicts. Finally, update or reinstall the driver.

Step 5: Verifying the Appropriate Solution Through Testing

The first aspect of the solution involves simply checking the installation of the sound card.

What precautions do you need to take before working inside the computer case?

____

____

You verify that the sound card has been properly inserted and has good connections. It appears to be properly inserted. Experience has taught you to check for obvious solutions first. If the problem still exists, move onto the second aspect of the solution, which is to check whether there are any system resource conflicts.

The user is running Windows 98 and you check resource conflicts in the Device Manager.

In the Device Manager for Windows 98, what indicates a system resource conflict?

____

____

You do not notice any problems and move on to updating or installing the device driver for the sound card. To get the latest device driver for the sound card, you visit the website for the sound card manufacturer. You conduct a search for the sound card driver and locate a new driver. This driver is different from the one the user installed because it includes a Windows 98 patch that resolves known compatibility issues. You install the new driver and then reboot the machine.

Step 6: Assessing the Solution: Ensuring That the Problem Was Resolved

The fifth step is determining whether the problem has been solved. If the problem appears to be solved, then you have successfully completed the troubleshooting process. If the problem is not fixed, then you must return to previous steps and continue the troubleshooting process. Sometimes, it might be necessary to undo changes made to the system and revert to the old configuration. In either case, be certain to properly document the results. Documenting the results helps you work productivity in the future.

After bootup, play an audio file and hear sound out of the speakers. The problem has been resolved and the troubleshooting cycle has come to an end.

Troubleshooting

What are the six steps in the troubleshooting cycle?

Step 1: ____________________

Step 2: ____________________

Step 3: ____________________

Step 4: ____________________

Step 5: ____________________

Step 6: ____________________

Reflection

It has been stated that troubleshooting is cyclical. What does this mean?

____

____

Why are the steps in the troubleshooting cycle useful for solving computer problems?

____

____

What is the most important step in the troubleshooting cycle, and why is it so important?

____

____

If the problem exists after the solution is implemented, what steps should you take?

____

____

Lab 13.2.2: Identifying POST Errors

Estimated Time: 20 Minutes

Objective

In this lab, you identify common power-on self-test (POST) errors. The ability to identify POST errors is essential for troubleshooting computers.

Equipment

To complete this lab, you need

- An operating computer
- A mouse
- A keyboard

Scenario

You are working as a technician for a small medical billing office. The office has just bought new computers. The newly purchased computers are all the same make and model. You are to familiarize yourself with the computer and document the POST errors for the major components.

Procedures

To become familiar with POST errors, remove several key components from the computer system and then listen for the audible POST errors. POST errors are a series of beeps that indicate a failure during startup. If you hear a POST error, you then document the findings.

Note: POST errors depend on the BIOS. POST errors are not the same universally.

Step 1: Rebooting the System

First, remove the keyboard connector from the back of the computer case and reboot the system. Listen for any abnormal beeps during startup.

Did you hear any POST error?

____

If you heard a POST error, what was the pattern of the beep?

____

Note: One beep during startup indicates normal operation.

Step 2: Listening for POST Errors

Plug the keyboard connector back into the back of the computer case. Next, unplug the computer and remove the computer case to expose the internal components. Identify the RAM on the motherboard and remove the RAM sticks. Reboot the machine and listen for POST errors.

Did you hear any POST error?

____

If you heard a POST error, what was the pattern of the beep?

____

Step 3: Rebooting to Ensure No POST Errors

Reinstall the RAM and reboot the machine. You should hear one beep, which indicates normal operation during the boot process. If you hear any POST errors, verify that the RAM was properly replaced and try again.

Step 4: Rebooting Again to Ensure No POST Errors

After the machine boots normally, turn the power off and unplug the computer. Identify and disconnect the floppy drive. Remove the connectors for both the ribbon cable and the power supply that connect to the floppy drive. Reboot the machine and listen for POST errors.

Did you hear any POST error?

____

If you heard a POST error, what was the pattern of the beep?

____

Step 5: Reattaching Connectors and Rebooting

Unplug the computer, reattach the floppy drive connectors, and reboot the machine. You should hear one beep, which indicates normal operation, during the boot process. If you hear any POST errors, verify that the floppy drive is properly connected and try again.

Step 6: Removing the Video Card and Rebooting to Test for POST Errors

After the machine boots normally, turn the power off and unplug the computer. Identify and remove the video card from the motherboard. Reboot the machine and listen for POST errors.

Did you hear any POST error?

____

If you heard a POST error, what was the pattern of the beep?

___

Step 7: Testing Again for POST Errors with the Video Card Replaced

Unplug the computer, replace the video card, and reboot the machine. You should hear one beep, which indicates normal operation, during the boot process. If you hear one beep, replace the computer case. If you hear a POST error, verify that the video card was properly replaced and try again.

Troubleshooting

Computer technicians need to be familiar with POST errors and their implications. Technicians need to be aware of any unusual sounds during the boot process because it could be an indication of a failure during initial diagnostic tests. In many cases, these unusual sounds are the first sign that a failure has occurred.

Reflection

When do POST errors occur?

___

What sound do you hear during a normal boot process?

___

Are POST errors dependant on the BIOS installed?

___

Worksheet 13.1.2: Troubleshooting Basics

This worksheet reviews the troubleshooting process, as discussed in Chapter 13.

1. Troubleshooting is a process of diagnosing a ___________ and finding and implementing the correct ___________, which results in restoring the system to its original operational state.

2. Please complete the process description appropriately by filling in the blanks. The troubleshooting cycle:

a. _______ the problem.

b. Gather _______ .

c. _______ a solution.

d. _______ a solution.

e. Is the problem solved?

- Yes: Document your observations and results.
- No: undo changes and _______ Steps a–d.

f. ___________ .

3. Why is using the structured approach provided by the troubleshooting cycle beneficial in solving computer-related problems?

____

____

____

Worksheet 13.3.2: Troubleshooting Printers

For each of the following statements relating to printers, enter T for true or F for false.

True or false:

1. ____ Problems with dot-matrix printers related to the print quality are some of the most difficult to identify.

2. ____ Because dot-matrix printers are relatively simple devices, only a few problems usually arise.

3. ____ With dot-matrix printers, a common cause of a paper jam is a piece of paper that has torn off and lodged in the paper path.

4. ____ Stepper motors are not sensitive to stray voltages.

5. ____ In a dot-matrix printer, lines of print are unevenly spaced if the main motor is damaged.

6. ____ Print quality is the most common problem associated with ink jet printers.

7. ____ Black lines present in every line of text on a printed page are caused by a plugged hole in at least one of the small, pinhole ink nozzles in the print cartridge.

8. ____ Failure of the high-voltage power supply (HVPS) is not the cause of a laser printer printing blank pages.

9. ____ If there is toner inside the toner cartridge, you will be able to hear it when you shake it.

10. ____ The corona wire (or roller) is an inexpensive part and can be easily replaced.

11. ____ Because the drum is grounded, it has no charge and nothing with a charge (such as toner) will stick to it.

12. ____ Toner spilled inside the printer or by a crack or chip in the EP drum can cause repetitive marks.

13. ____ Foreign matter caught on the transfer corona wire causes vertical white lines to run down the printed page.

14. ____ Image smudging is caused by a fuser problem.

Worksheet 13.3.4: Troubleshooting Hardware

This worksheet reviews the information discussed on troubleshooting computer hardware.

1. What is a field replaceable unit (FRU)?

____

____

2. What is POST used for?

____

____

3. Describe what beep codes indicate.

____

____

4. Explain one main reason for a CPU failure.

____

____

____

5. What is the first place you should check when troubleshooting memory?

____

____

____

6. How can you tell whether you have a motherboard problem?

____

____

____

7. List two types of video problems.

a. ____

b. ____

8. The first three steps when diagnosing any disk drive problems are

   a. Check the _______ cable.

   b. Check the _______ cable.

   c. Check the device _______.

9. Most sound card problems are __________________ conflicts.

Chapter 14

Troubleshooting Software

Lab 14.7.4: Booting into Safe Mode

Estimated Time: 25 Minutes

Objective

In this lab, you boot the PC using the advanced troubleshooting options of Windows 2000.

Equipment

The following equipment is required for this lab:

- An operational computer that is running Windows 2000

Scenario

You are the system administrator for the XYZ Company, and upon arriving at work in the morning, you receive a call from an end user stating that he sees a "system boot failure" error message.

Procedures

Booting the computer into Safe Mode bypasses the normal startup sequence of Windows. Part of this process involves timing. When the black and white Starting Windows bar is onscreen, press the **F8** key before the system begins loading Windows.

Step 1: Powering Up the Computer

Power on the computer.

Step 2: Entering Safe Mode in Windows 2000

When the computer is running through the boot process, a series of different startup screens appear. To get into Safe Mode in Windows 2000, press **F8** while the black and white Starting Windows bar appears at the bottom of the screen. The Starting Windows bar appears after the BIOS loads.

What is the name of the menu that displays?

____

What are the options that are available on this menu?

Step 3: Loading to the Safe Mode

Next, select the **Safe Mode** option by using the arrow keys up or down, and press **Enter**. Windows loads to the Safe Mode environment. Read the window carefully and press **OK**.

Step 4: Beginning to Check Video Settings

Windows loads into the Safe Mode desktop environment. However, because Windows loads only basic drivers in Safe Mode, the graphics are in VGA mode.

Does the desktop appear to be in VGA mode?

How do you check the video settings?

Step 5: Accessing the Device Manager

Access the Device Manager to check the loaded drivers. To access the Device Manager, click **Start** > **Settings** > **Control Panel** > **System** > **Hardware** > **Device Manager**. The Device Manager opens, displaying the hardware components.

Step 6: Checking for Conflicting Devices

After the Device Manager is open, check whether any devices are conflicting. Conflicting devices have yellow exclamation points next to them.

Are there any conflicting devices?

Step 7: Verifying That There Are No Network Drivers

Verify that no network drivers are installed. To verify the network drivers, click the plus sign (+) next to Network Adapters. A list of devices should appear. Right-click a device, select Properties, and a Device Properties window appears.

What does the Device Properties window display for Device Status?

____

____

____

Troubleshooting

Computer technicians often boot a PC into Safe Mode when they are troubleshooting a problem. Safe Mode helps technicians identify and diagnose problems. If the problem is not present in Safe Mode, then it is probably related to settings or drivers.

Safe Mode loads only generic drivers during the loading of the operating system (OS). It loads basic drivers for the mouse, video display, mass storage, keyboard, and default services. Booting a PC into Safe Mode does not load network devices or connections by default. However, you can boot the PC using Safe Mode with Networking to establish a network connection.

Reflection

What key do you push to enter into Safe Mode in Windows 2000?

____

What is the main difference between Safe Mode and normal operation?

____

Why might Safe Mode be an effective troubleshooting tool?

____

Lab 14.7.5: Using the Windows 2000 Recovery Console

Estimated Time: 30 Minutes

Objective

In this lab, you learn how to use and implement the Windows 2000 Recovery Console.

Equipment

The following equipment is required for this lab:

- A computer system running Windows 2000

Scenario

You are the system administrator for the XYZ Company, and upon arriving at work in the morning, you receive a call from an end user stating that she sees a "system boot failure" error message. To fix the problem, run the Windows 2000 Recovery Console to repair any boot file that might be damaged.

Procedures

In the first step of this lab, you need to create the system boot failure. In the second step of the lab, you use the Recovery Console to repair the system boot failure that you created in the first step. In the third part of the lab, you install the Recovery Console and use some of the Recovery Console commands.

Step 1: Disabling System Protection

First, turn off or disable system protection. Double-click **My Computer**, and then select **Tools> Folder Options**.

In the Folders Options display box, click the **View** tab.

With the View tab selected, change the defaults for viewing hidden and system files. To do so, click the **Show Hidden Files and Folders** radio button. Also, uncheck **Hide Protected Operating System Files (Recommended)**.

Next, rename the Ntldr file to Oldntldr. To do so, click **Start >Search >for Files and Folders**. In the Search for files and folders named: field, type **ntldr**.

When the file shows up on the right screen, right-click the file and select **Rename**. Rename it to **Oldntldr**.

Restart the computer. You should receive an error message when the computer restarts.

Step 2: Ensuring That the Windows 2000 Installation CD Is in the Drive

Make sure that the Windows 2000 installation CD is in the CD-ROM drive and then restart the computer. Change the BIOS settings to boot from the CD-ROM.

When the Setup Notification message appears, Setup displays the Welcome to Setup screen.

Press **R** to repair a Windows 2000 installation using the Recovery Console. The Windows 2000 Repair Options screen displays.

Press **C** to start the Recovery Console. Next, type **1** and then press **Enter**. At the prompt, enter the administrator's password and then press **Enter**.

A C:\Winnt command prompt appears. Type **cd ..** then press **Enter**. The prompt changes to the root folder (C:\).

Type **copy Oldntldr Ntldr** at the command prompt and press **Enter**.

Type **exit** and press **Enter**. The computer reboots and should start normally.

Step 3: Logging On

Log on to the system with the administrator account.

Insert the Windows 2000 Professional CD into the CD-ROM drive. Close the Windows 2000 window when it displays.

Go to **Start** > **Run** and in the box, type **D:\i386\winnt32 /cmdcons** and then click **OK**. The Windows 2000 Setup message box appears. Note that the CD-ROM drive letter might vary depending on the system configuration.

Click **Yes** to install the Windows 2000 Recovery Console. Windows 2000 Setup installs the Windows 2000 Recovery Console to the hard disk.

Click **OK** to close the Setup dialog box.

Step 4: Restarting and Disabling the Alerter Service

Restart the computer and select Microsoft Windows 2000 Recovery Console from the boot loader menu.

The Windows 2000 Recovery Console starts and prompts for the Windows 2000 installation to log on to. There should only be one choice at this point. Enter the administrator password when prompted and then press **Enter**.

Type **help** and press **Enter** to see the list of available commands. Find the **Listsvc** command and use it to view all the available services.

Type **Listsvc** at the command prompt (at the end of the list) and press **Enter** to view a list of available services. Press **Esc** to stop.

Type **disable /?** and then press **Enter**. This command disables any Windows system service or driver.

Type **disable alerter** and then press **Enter**.

The Alerter Service is now disabled.

Note: Some lines of text advise that the "Alerter service" has been changed.

Type **exit** and then press **Enter** to restart the computer. Boot into Windows 2000.

Now that the Alerter Service is disabled, you need to restart it.

Step 5: Restarting

Log on to the system with the administrator account.

Navigate to the Computer Management window. There are two ways to access the Computer Management window:

Go to **Start** > **Programs** > **Administrative Tools** >**Computer Management**.

Or go to **Start** > **Settings** > **Control Panel** > **Administrative Tools** >**Computer Management**.

Next, expand Services and Applications by clicking the plus (+) sign and then click **Services**.

Double-click **Alerter**, change the Startup Type option to **Automatic**, and then click **OK**.

Right-click **Alerter**, and then click **Start**. Close the Computer Management window.

Troubleshooting

The Recovery Console is a useful tool when troubleshooting problems. If the system stops responding or does not boot properly, it is a good place to go while troubleshooting the issue.

Reflection

Give an example of a problem that you could solve using the Recovery Console:

____
____
____
____

Lab 14.10.3: Windows Registry Backup and Recovery

Estimated Time: 20 Minutes

Objective

In this lab, you learn how to back up and perform a recovery of the Registry. These files are also referred to as the *system state* files.

Equipment

The following equipment is required for this lab:

- A computer system running Windows 2000

Scenario

As the system administrator for the XYZ Company, you are to deploy a new software package onto a manager's system. This software has not been tested; however, it is known that it makes changes to the Registry. The first step is making a backup of the system state files in case the software corrupts the system.

Procedures

The first step is to use the Windows Back Up Wizard to select the files that are to be backed up and to perform the back up. Second, modify the Registry. It is possible that the system will not work after you make these changes to the Registry. Lastly, use the backup to restore the system state and Registry files.

Step 1: Enabling the Backup Wizard

Log on to the server with the administrator account

When the systems boots up, click **Start**, and then click **Run**.

In the Run dialog box, type **ntbackup** and then click **OK**. The Backup dialog box should appear.

Take a minute to read the three descriptions under the Welcome tab, and then click the **Backup Wizard** button. The Backup Wizard should start.

Click **Next** to display the What to Back Up screen. Select the type of backup to be performed.

Click the **Only Back Up the System State Data** button, and then click **Next**. At this point, the Where to Store the Backup screen appears. Select a place to save the file when prompted. It should be a predesignated folder for backup files.

The Completing the Backup Wizard screen should appear. This screen shows the details of the backup that will be performed. At this point, you can make additional changes. Click the **Advanced** button.

Step 2: Setting Up for Backing Up Data

When the Type of Backup screen appears, make sure that **Normal** is selected and that the **Backup Migrated Remote Storage Data** box is not checked.

Click **Next**. The How to Backup screen should display. Verify the backed-up data after performing the backup.

Select the **Verify Data After Backup** check box, and then click **Next**.

The Media Options page appears. Specify whether to append this backup job to existing media or overwrite existing backup data on the destination media at the prompt.

Click the **Replace the Data on the Media with this Backup** button.

Step 3: Labeling the Backup

Click **Next**. Now the Backup Label screen displays. Supply a label for the backup job and for the backup media. Windows supplies a backup label and media label by using the current date and time by default.

In the Backup Label text box, type **System State Set Created on *xxx*** (where *xxx* is today's date and time). Do not change anything in the Media Label text box. Click **Next**.

Step 4: Choosing the Timing of the Backup

When the When to Back Up screen displays, choose whether to run the backup job now or to schedule this backup job. For this lab, select the **Now** radio button. Click **Next**.

Step 5: Starting the Actual Backup Job

When the Completing the Backup Wizard screen displays, click **Finish** to start the backup job.

Windows Backup displays the Selection Information dialog box, showing the system scanning for the files to be placed in the backup.

Windows Backup displays the Backup Progress dialog box, which shows the status of the backup operation, statistics on estimated and actual amount of data being processed, the time that has elapsed, and the estimated time that remains for the backup to complete.

Step 6: Completing the Backup

When the backup is complete, click the **Report** button. A backup report appears. The backup report contains key details about the backup operation, such as the time it started and how many files were backed up. When finished, close Notepad.

Close the Backup Progress dialog box and the Backup dialog box as well.

Step 7: Choosing the Registry Editor Box

Go to **Start** > **Run**. Type **Regedt32** in the box. The Registry Editor window should open.

Expand the **HKEY_LOCAL _MACHINE** Registry key.

Right-click the **Hardware** folder and select **Edit** and then **Delete**.

Close the Registry Editor box. The system is officially broken. In reality, only a virus would be able to damage the Registry in this way. The point is that changes to the system can result in changes to the Registry. With the backup, you can restore the system.

Step 8: Retrieving the Backup Files

Locate the backup file that you saved in Step 1 of this lab.

Double-click that file. The Backup Utility Wizard displays.

Click the **Restore Wizard** button. The Welcome to the Restore Wizard screen displays. Click **Next**.

The What to Restore wizard screen displays. Expand the file. Find the backup file that was created with the proper date and time and expand that as well. Click the **System State** check box. Click **Next**.

On the Completing the Restore wizard screen, click **Advanced**.

Step 9: Replacing and Restoring

On the Where to Restore screen, make sure that **Original Location** is selected. Click **Next**. The Restoring System State will always overwrite files unless restored to a different location from what the screen displays. Click **OK**.

Click the **Replace Existing Files if They Are Older Than the Backup Files** radio button. Click **Next**.

Verify that all three radio buttons are selected, and then click **Next** and **Finish**.

The restore begins by copying the files back to the system and showing the progress results.

When the restore wizard completes, you can view the report by clicking the **Report** button. Then, click **Close**.

When prompted to restart the system, click **Yes**. The system restarts.

Troubleshooting

Always back up the Registry when installing new software. If a change to the Registry affects the system, using the backup to fix it can save hours of troubleshooting.

Reflection

How can backing up the system state files save time?

____

____

____

____

Worksheet 14.4.5: Troubleshooting Software

This worksheet is a review of the software used to troubleshoot related errors. Match each term with its description.

____ 1. Clean boot	a. A file that has a list of DOS statements that are executed when the computer first starts
____ 2. Patch	b. An error that occurs when two programs that are running at the same time try to use the same area in memory
____ 3. Boot disk	c. Software that is still in the initial phase of testing within the software production house
____ 4. CONFIG.SYS	d. A diagnostic state of Windows that allows you to fix problems that prevent you from starting Windows normally
____ 5. AUTOEXEC.BAT	e. Software used to "quick-fix" a bug in a program
____ 6. REM	f. Memory and hard-drive space used by Windows
____ 7. Safe mode	g. A disk containing a rudimentary operating system used to start a computer
____ 8. Registry	h. A way of starting a computer with a minimal set of drivers and programs
____ 9. Device Manager	i. The second release of a program intended for the public to test
____ 10. Resources	j. A file that contains statements for loading memory drivers and that tells the operating system where key DOS files are located
____ 11. GPF	k. A command used to make remarks in DOS startup files
____ 12. Beta release	l. Files that contain information about user settings and configuration information for applications
____ 13. Alpha release	m. A part of Windows that provides you with a visual presentation of physical devices that are used in your system

Notes

Notes

Notes

Notes

Notes

Notes

Notes

Notes

Notes

Notes

Mastering MATLAB® 7

Duane Hanselman
Bruce Littlefield
Department of Electrical and Computer Engineering
University of Maine

ISBN 978-81-317-0743-2

First Impression, 2007
Second Impression, 2008
Third Impression, 2008

Published by Dorling Kindersley (India) Pvt. Ltd., licensees of Pearson Education in South Asia.

Head Office: 482, F.I.E., Patparganj, Delhi 110 092, India.
Registered Office: 14 Local Shopping Centre, Panchsheel Park, New Delhi 11

Printed in India by S P Printers.

Contents

Preface

This text is about MATLAB®. If you use MATLAB or are considering using it, this book is for you. This text represents an alternative to learning MATLAB on your own with or without the help of the documentation that comes with the software. The informal style of this book makes it easy to read and, as the title suggests, it provides the tools you need to master MATLAB. As a programming language and data visualization tool, MATLAB offers a rich set of capabilities for solving problems in engineering, scientific, computing, and mathematical disciplines. The fundamental goal of this text is to help you increase your productivity by showing you how to use these capabilities efficiently. Because of the interactive nature of MATLAB, the material is generally presented in the form of examples that you can duplicate by running MATLAB as you read this book.

This text covers only topics that are of use to a general audience. The material presented generally applies to all computer platforms. None of the *Toolboxes, Blocksets,* and other *Libraries* that are available for additional cost are discussed, although some are referred to in appropriate places. There are simply too many additional product items to consider in one book. However, based on user feedback, this book does discuss linking MATLAB to programs written in C, FORTRAN, and Java. Furthermore, it demonstrates how MATLAB can be dynamically linked to other applications on the PC platform.

Since MATLAB continues to evolve as a software tool, this text focuses on MATLAB Version 7. For the most part, the material applies to 6.x and 5.x versions of MATLAB as well. When appropriate, distinctions between versions are made.

Many thanks to the folks at the MathWorks, specifically Penny Anderson, Rich Ellis, Tim Farajian, Paul Fricker, Steve Lord, Bob Gilmore, and Peter Webb. They carefully reviewed and offered many helpful suggestions that have improved the presentation of this book.

We the authors encourage you to give us feedback on this book. What are the best features of the text? What areas need more work? What topics should be left out? What topics should be added? We can be reached at the e-mail address *mm@eece.maine.edu.* In addition, errata, all examples in the text, and other related material can be found at *http://www.eece.maine.edu/mm.*

DUANE HANSELMAN
BRUCE LITTLEFIELD

1

Getting Started

1.1 INTRODUCTION

This text assumes that you have some familiarity with matrices and computer programming. Matrices and arrays, in general, are at the heart of MATLAB, since all data in MATLAB are stored as arrays. Besides offering common matrix algebra operations, MATLAB offers array operations that allow you to quickly manipulate sets of data in a wide variety of ways. In addition to its matrix orientation, MATLAB offers programming features that are similar to those of other computer programming languages. Finally, MATLAB offers graphical user interface (GUI) tools that enable you to use MATLAB as an application development tool. This combination of array data structures, programming features, and GUI tools makes MATLAB an extremely powerful tool for solving problems in many fields. In this text, each of these aspects of MATLAB is discussed in detail. To facilitate learning, detailed examples are presented.

1.2 TYPOGRAPHICAL CONVENTIONS

The following conventions are used throughout this book:

Bold italics	New terms or important facts
Boxed text	Important terms and facts
Bold Initial Caps	Keyboard key names, menu names, and menu items
`Constant width`	Computer user input, function and file names, commands, and screen displays

`Boxed constant width`	Contents of a script, function, or data file
`Constant width italics`	User input that is to be replaced and not taken literally, such as » `help` *`functionname`*
Italics	Window names, object names, book titles, toolbox names, company names, example text, and mathematical notations

1.3 WHAT'S NEW IN MATLAB 7

MATLAB 7 is yet another evolutionary change in MATLAB. The *Command* window remains the primary user interface, *Figure* windows are used to display graphical information and to create graphical user interfaces (GUIs), and a text editor is provided for writing and editing MATLAB code. The *MATLAB Desktop* coordinates the position and visibility of a number of other windows, such as *Workspace*, *Editor*, *Help*, *Command History*, etc.

Under the surface, several numerical and operational changes have been made to the software. In addition to having added or modified several internal numerical algorithms, MATLAB now supports mathematical operations on data types other than double-precision arrays, which have always been at the heart of MATLAB. Perhaps even more importantly, the MATLAB command interpreter now includes acceleration features, collectively called *The MATLAB JIT-Accelerator*. This accelerator, which first appeared in MATLAB 6.5, dramatically increases the speed of loop operations by interpreting and executing code within a loop as a whole, rather than line by line, as was done previously. This acceleration eliminates the need to *vectorize* some code, which requires you to create and maximize the use of arrays and array mathematics to achieve optimal performance. To make use of the JIT-Accelerator, loop operation code must follow specific guidelines, which are covered in this text. When these guidelines are not followed, loop operation code is interpreted at the much slower line-by-line rate.

In sum, MATLAB 7 represents an evolutionary change in MATLAB. The basic operation of MATLAB and its capabilities haven't changed in any dramatic way. In almost all cases, MATLAB code written for MATLAB 6 will run without change in MATLAB 7. For the most part, the new and changed features of MATLAB 7 can increase your productivity in solving problems with MATLAB.

1.4 WHAT'S IN *MASTERING MATLAB 7*

MATLAB documentation, in both hard copy and electronic format, exceeds 5000 pages of information and help text. Given this exhaustive documentation and help, *Mastering MATLAB 7* does not attempt to be a comprehensive tutorial or reference, which just isn't possible in a single book containing less than 1000 pages. *Mastering MATLAB 7* does not even attempt to document all functions within the base product of MATLAB. This too is impossible, as there are more than 300 built-in functions in MATLAB, and approximately 1000 more M-file functions that are part of the base product of MATLAB. In light of this documentation set, the goals of *Mastering MATLAB 7* include the following: (1) introduce MATLAB to the novice user, (2) illustrate all key features and capabilities of MATLAB, and (3) demonstrate by example how to write efficient MATLAB code.

This text is intended to be a valuable resource when the MATLAB documentation set is unavailable. It follows the rule of providing 80 percent of the information needed in 20 percent of the space required to cover everything. The book is also intended to be a valuable resource when the MATLAB documentation set is available. In this case, it supplies numerous examples of efficient MATLAB coding that demonstrate how the many features of MATLAB come together to solve real problems.

Equally important is what's not included in *Mastering MATLAB 7*. The book does not discuss all of the windows, menus, menu items, submenus, and dialog boxes of the MATLAB user interface. While these user-interface aspects of MATLAB are very important, there is no room for them in this text. Moreover, they are difficult to cover effectively in a text and are best learned by hands-on exploration. Rather, this text focuses on the mathematical, programming, and graphical features that facilitate problem solution.

This book was written using information about MATLAB Version 7.0. As MATLAB evolves between Versions 7.0 and 8.0, some things are bound to change. As a result, there may be isolated areas in this book where information about new features is missing and, worse yet, isolated areas where information is incorrect. The authors have no control over MATLAB. We also cannot rewrite the text to reflect minor MATLAB releases. We are thankful that the makers of MATLAB are very careful when introducing new features and when changing old features. Historically, old features are grandfathered for one major release, and sometimes for additional releases. As a result, even though the book reflects MATLAB Version 7.0, it will undoubtedly be useful for all future 7.x versions as well.

To support this text, the authors maintain the Mastering MATLAB website at *http://www.eece.maine.edu/mm*. At the site, you can find errata for the text, as well as MATLAB script M-files for creating all of the figures in the book. The authors also encourage constructive feedback about the text at the e-mail address *mm@eece.maine.edu*.

2

Basic Features

Running MATLAB creates one or more windows on your computer monitor. One of these windows, entitled MATLAB, is commonly called the ***MATLAB desktop***. This window is the primary graphical user interface for MATLAB. Within the *MATLAB* window, there is a window called the ***Command*** window, which is the primary place wherein you interact with MATLAB. The prompt >> is displayed in the *Command* window, and when the *Command* window is active, a blinking cursor appears to the right of the prompt. This cursor and prompt signify that MATLAB is waiting to perform a mathematical operation.

2.1 SIMPLE MATH

Just like a calculator, MATLAB can do basic math. Consider the following simple example: Mary goes to the office supply store and buys four erasers at 25 cents each, six memo pads at 52 cents each, and two rolls of tape at 99 cents each. How many items did Mary buy, and how much did they cost?

To solve this problem with a calculator, you enter

```
4 + 6 + 2 = 12 items
4 × 25 + 6 × 52 + 2 × 99 = 610 cents
```

In MATLAB, this problem can be solved in a number of different ways. First, the calculator approach can be taken:

```
>> 4+6+2
ans =
    12
```

```
>> 4*25 + 6*52 + 2*99

ans =

   610
```

Note that MATLAB doesn't care about spaces, for the most part, and that multiplication takes precedence over addition. Note also that MATLAB calls the result ans, which is short for *answer* for both computations.

As an alternative, the problem can be solved by storing information in ***MATLAB variables***:

```
>> erasers = 4

erasers =
     4

>> pads = 6

pads =

     6

>> tape = 2;
>> items = erasers + pads + tape

items =

    12
>> cost = erasers*25 + pads*52 + tape*99

cost =

   610
```

Here, we created three MATLAB variables—erasers, pads, and tape—to store the number of each item. After entering each statement, MATLAB displayed the results, except in the case of tape. The semicolon at the end of the line tells MATLAB to evaluate the line, but not to display the answer. Finally, rather than calling the results ans, we told MATLAB to call the number of items purchased items, and the total price paid cost. At each step, MATLAB remembered past information. Because MATLAB remembers things, let's ask what the average cost per item was:

```
>> average_cost = cost/items

average_cost =
   50.833
```

Since the term "average cost," is two words and MATLAB variable names must be one word, an underscore was used to create the single MATLAB variable average_cost.

In all, MATLAB offers the following basic arithmetic operations:

Operation	Symbol	Example
Addition	+	`3 + 22`
Subtraction	−	`54.4 - 16.5`
Multiplication	*	`3.14 * 6`
Division	/ or \	`19.54/7` or `7\19.54`
Exponentiation	^	`2^8`

The order in which these operations are evaluated in a given expression is determined by the usual rules of precedence, summarized as follows:

> Expressions are evaluated from left to right, with the exponentiation operation having the highest precedence, followed by multiplication and division, having equal precedence, and then by addition and subtraction, having equal precedence.
>
> Parentheses can be used to alter this ordering, in which case these rules of precedence are applied within each set of parentheses, by starting with the innermost set and proceeding outward.

More information about precedence rules can be displayed by typing `help precendence` at the MATLAB prompt.

2.2 THE MATLAB WORKSPACE

As you work in the *Command* window, MATLAB remembers the commands you enter, as well as the values of any variables you create. These commands and variables are said to reside in the ***MATLAB workspace*** or ***Base workspace***, and they can be recalled whenever you wish. For example, to check the value of `tape`, all you have to do is ask MATLAB for it by entering its name at the prompt:

```
>> tape
tape =
     2
```

If you can't remember the name of a variable, you can ask MATLAB for a list of the variables it knows by using the MATLAB command `who`:

```
>> who
Your variables are:
```

```
ans             cost      items    tape
average_cost    erasers   pads
```

Note that MATLAB doesn't tell you the value of all of the variables; it merely gives you their names. To find their values, you must enter their names individually at the MATLAB prompt.

To recall previous commands, MATLAB responds to the **Cursor** keys on your keyboard. For example, pressing the ↑ key once recalls the most recent command to the MATLAB prompt. Repeatedly pressing ↑ scrolls back through prior commands, one at a time. In a similar manner, pressing the ↓ key scrolls forward through commands. By pressing the → or ← keys, you can maneuver within a given command at the MATLAB prompt, thereby editing the command in much the same way that you edit text in a word-processing program. Other standard editing keys, such as **Delete** or **Backspace**, **Home**, and **End**, perform their commonly assigned tasks. The **Tab** key is useful for variable-name completion. Once a scrolled command is acceptable, pressing the **Return** key with the cursor *anywhere* in the command tells MATLAB to process it. Finally, and perhaps most useful, the **Escape** key erases the current command at the prompt. For those of you familiar with the EMACS editor, MATLAB also accepts common EMACS editing control-character sequences, such as **Control-U** to erase the current command.

2.3 ABOUT VARIABLES

Like any other computer language, MATLAB has rules about variable names. Earlier, it was noted that variable names must be a single word containing no spaces. More specifically, MATLAB variable-naming rules are listed, as follows:

Variable-Naming Rules	Comments/Examples
Variable names are case sensitive.	`Cost`, `cost`, `CoSt`, and `COST` are all different MATLAB variables.
Variable names can contain up to 63 characters. Any characters beyond the 63rd are ignored.	`Howaboutthisvariablename`
Variable names must start with a letter, followed by any number of letters, digits, or underscores.	`how_about_this_variable_name` `X51483`
Punctuation characters are not allowed, because many of them have special meanings in MATLAB.	`a_b_c_d_e`

There are some specific exceptions to these naming rules. MATLAB has several names that cannot be used for variables. These names are ***keywords*** and form a ***reserved word list*** for MATLAB:

Reserved Word List
`for end if while function return elseif case otherwise`
`switch continue else try catch global persistent break`

This list is returned as an output of the `iskeyword` function. MATLAB will report an error if you try to use a reserved word as a variable. However, you can use words similar to keywords by capitalizing one or more letters. The function `isvarname('teststring')` returns True (1) if the character string argument `'teststring'` is a valid variable name; otherwise, it returns False (0).

In addition, just as your calculator stores constants such as π, MATLAB has a number of special variables:

Special Variables	Description
`ans`	Default variable name used for results
`beep`	Makes computer sound a beep
`pi`	Ratio of the circumference of a circle to its diameter
`eps`	Smallest number that, when added to 1, creates a number greater than 1 on the computer
`inf`	Stands for infinity (e.g., `1/0`)
`NaN` or `nan`	Stands for Not-a-Number (e.g., `0/0`)
`i` or `j`	Stands for $\sqrt{-1}$
`nargin`	Number of function input arguments
`nargout`	Number of function output arguments
`realmin`	Smallest usable positive real number
`realmax`	Largest usable positive real number
`bitmax`	Largest usable positive integer stored in double-precision format
`varargin`	Variable number of function input arguments
`varargout`	Variable number of function output arguments

If you reuse a variable (such as `tape`, in the earlier example) or assign a value to one of the special variables from the preceding list, the prior value of the variable is overwritten and lost. However, any other expressions computed with the prior values do not change. Consider the following example:

```
>> erasers = 4;
>> pads = 6;
>> tape = 2;
```

```
>> items = erasers + pads + tape
items =
    12
>> erasers = 6
erasers =
      6
>> items
items =
    12
```

Here, using the first example again, we found the number of items Mary purchased. Afterward, we changed the number of erasers to six, overwriting its prior value of 4. In doing so, the value of items has not changed. Unlike a common spreadsheet program, MATLAB does not recalculate the number of items based on the new value of erasers. ***When MATLAB performs a calculation, it does so using the values that it knows at the time the requested command is evcluated.*** In the preceding example, if you wish to recalculate the number of items, the total cost, and the average cost, it is necessary to recall the appropriate MATLAB commands and ask MATLAB to evaluate them again.

The special variables given earlier follow this guideline, also, with the exception of the fact that the special values can be restored. When you start MATLAB, the variables have their original values; when you change their values, the original special values are lost. To restore a special value, all you have to do is ***clear*** the overwritten value. For example,

```
>> pi
ans =
        3.1416
>> pi = 1.23e-4
pi =
      0.000123
>> clear pi
>> pi
ans =
        3.1416
```

shows that `pi` has the special value of `3.1416`, to five significant digits; is overwritten with the value of `1.23e-4`; and then, after being cleared using the `clear` function, has its original special value once again.

2.4 COMMENTS, PUNCTUATION, AND ABORTING EXECUTION

As we saw earlier, placing a semicolon at the end of a command suppresses printing of the computed results. This feature is especially useful for suppressing the results of intermediate calculations. For instance,

```
>> erasers

erasers =

     6

>> items = erasers + pads + tape;

>> cost = erasers*25 + pads*52 + tape*99;

>> average_cost = cost/items

average_cost =

      47.143
```

displays the average cost of the items that Mary bought when she purchased six erasers, rather than the original four. The intermediate results `items` and `cost` were not printed, because semicolons appear at the ends of the commands defining them.

In addition to semicolons, MATLAB uses other punctuation symbols. For example, all text after a percent sign (%) is taken as a comment statement:

```
>> tape = 2  % number of rolls of tape purchased
```

The variable `tape` is given the value of 2, and MATLAB simply ignores the percent sign and all text following it.

If they are separated by commas or semicolons, multiple commands can be placed on one line:

```
>> erasers = 6, pads = 6; tape = 2

erasers =

     6

tape =

     2
```

Commas tell MATLAB to display results; semicolons suppress printing.

Sometimes expressions or commands are so long, that it is convenient to continue them onto additional lines. In MATLAB, statement continuation is denoted by three periods in succession, as shown in the following code:

```
>> average_cost = cost/items  % command as done earlier

average_cost =

      47.143
```

```
>> average_cost = cost/... % command with valid continuation
items
average_cost =
      47.143
>>average_cost = cost... % command with valid continuation
/items
average_cost =
      47.143
>>average_cost = cost... command with valid continuation (no % needed)
/items
average_cost =
      47.143
>>average_cost = cost/it... % command with INvalid continuation
ems
??? ems
    |
Error: Missing MATLAB operator.
```

Note that statement continuation works if the three periods appear between variable names and mathematical operators, but not in the middle of a variable name. That is, variable names cannot be split between two lines. Furthermore, all text after the three periods is considered to be a comment, so no percent symbol is needed. In addition, since comment lines are ignored, they cannot be continued either, as the following example shows:

```
>> % Comments cannot be continued...
>> either
??? Undefined function or variable 'either'.
```

In this case, the (...) in the comment line is part of the comment and is not processed by MATLAB.

Finally, MATLAB processing can be interrupted at any time by pressing **Control-C** (that is, pressing the **Ctrl** and **C** keys simultaneously).

2.5 COMPLEX NUMBERS

One of the most powerful features of MATLAB is that it does not require any special handling for complex numbers. Complex numbers are formed in MATLAB in several ways. Examples of complex numbers include the following:

```
>> c1 = 1-2i % the appended i signifies the imaginary part
c1 =
   1.0000 - 2.0000i
>> c1 = 1-2j  % j also works
c1 =
   1.0000 - 2.0000i
>> c1 = complex(1,-2) % a function that creates complex numbers
c1 =
   1.0000 - 2.0000i
>> c2 = 3*(2-sqrt(-1)*3)
c2 =
   6.0000 - 9.0000i
>> c3 = sqrt(-2)
c3 =
        0 + 1.4142i
>> c4 = 6+sin(.5)*1i
c4 =
   6.0000 + 0.4794i
>> c5 = 6+sin(.5)*1j
c5 =
   6.0000 + 0.4794i
```

In the last two examples, multiplication by `1i` and `1j` are used to form the imaginary part. Multiplication by `1i` or `1j` is required in these cases, since `sin(.5)i` and `sin(.5)j` have no meaning in MATLAB. Termination with the characters `i` and `j`, as shown in the first two examples, works only with numbers and not with expressions.

Some programming languages require special handling for complex numbers, wherever they appear. In MATLAB, no special handling is required. Mathematical operations on complex numbers are written the same way as those on real numbers:

```
>> c6 = (c1+c2)/c3  % from the above data
c6 =
  -7.7782 - 4.9497i
>> c6r = real(c6)
c6r =
  -7.7782
```

```
>> c6i = imag(c6)

c6i =

   -4.9497

>> check_it_out = 1i^2 % sqrt(-1) squared must be -1!

check_it_out =

   -1
```

In general, operations on complex numbers lead to complex number results. However, in the last case, MATLAB is smart enough to drop the zero imaginary part of the result. In addition, the foregoing shows that the functions `real` and `imag` extract the real and imaginary parts of a complex number, respectively.

As a final example of complex arithmetic, consider the Euler identity that relates the polar form of a complex number to its rectangular form $M\angle\theta = Me^{j\theta} = a + b\text{j}$, where the polar form is given by a magnitude M and an angle θ and the rectangular form is given by $a + b\text{j}$. The relationships among these forms are $M = \sqrt{a^2 + b^2}$, $\theta = \tan^{-1}(b/a)$, $a = M\cos(\theta)$, and $b = M\sin(\theta)$.

In MATLAB, the conversion between polar and rectangular forms makes use of the functions `real`, `imag`, `abs`, and `angle`:

```
>> c1

c1 =

   1.0000 - 2.0000i

>> mag_c1 = abs(c1) % magnitude

mag_c1 =

   2.2361

>> angle_c1 = angle(c1) % angle in radians

angle_c1 =

  -1.1071

>> deg_c1 = angle_c1*180/pi % angle in degrees

deg_c1 =

  -63.4349

>> real_c1 = real(c1) % real part

real_c1 =

   1

>> imag_c1 = imag(c1) % imaginary part

imag_c1 =

   -2
```

The MATLAB function abs computes the magnitude of complex numbers or the absolute value of real numbers, depending on which one you assign it to compute. Likewise, the MATLAB function angle computes the angle of a complex number in radians. ***MATLAB does not natively perform trigonometric operations with units of degrees; however, basic trigonometric functions supporting angles in degrees are provided in MATLAB 7.***

2.6 FLOATING-POINT ARITHMETIC

In almost all cases, numerical values in MATLAB are represented in double-precision arithmetic, using a binary (base 2) representation internally. Such representation is the most common representation used by computers and is a native format for numerical coprocessors. Because of this representation, not all numbers can be represented exactly. There are limiting values that can be represented, and there is a recognizable lower limit for addition.

The largest positive real number that can be represented is

```
>> format long  % tell MATLAB to display more precision
>> realmax
ans =
   1.797693134862316e+308
```

The smallest positive number that can be represented is

```
>> realmin
ans =
   2.225073858507201e-308
```

The smallest number that can be added to 1 to produce a number larger than 1 in double precision is

```
>> eps
ans =
   2.220446049250313e-016
```

Generalizing this concept, eps(x) is the smallest increment that can be added to x to produce a number larger than x, as the following examples show:

```
>> eps(1) % same as eps by itself
ans =
   2.220446049250313e-016
```

```
>> eps(10)
ans =
     1.776356839400251e-015

>> eps(1e10)
ans =
     1.907348632812500e-006
```

As the magnitude of a number increases, the distance between values that can be represented in finite precision (which is what eps(x) returns) increases as well.

The consequences of the limitations of finite-precision arithmetic are sometimes strange. For example, as shown here, addition is not *exactly* commutative:

```
>> 0.42 - 0.5 + 0.08
ans =
  -1.387778780781446e-017

>> 0.08 - 0.5 + 0.42  % rearrange order
ans =
     0

>> 0.08 + 0.42 - 0.5  % rearrange order again
ans =
     0
```

All three of these results should be zero, but they are not. In each case, the arithmetic was performed from left to right. The issue here is that not all of the numbers can be represented exactly in double-precision arithmetic. In fact, only 0.5 has an exact representation. When numbers cannot be represented exactly, they are approximated with as much precision as possible—leading to inevitable errors in computed results. For the most part, these errors are minor; otherwise, double-precision arithmetic wouldn't be used in modern computers. In practice, the problems with double-precision arithmetic occur most often when asking MATLAB to compare two numbers for equality or inequality. Clearly, within MATLAB, $0.42 - 0.5 + 0.08$ does not equal $0.08 - 0.5 + 0.42$, even though our brains can do the exact arithmetic to show that it does.

A second drawback of finite-precision arithmetic appears in function evaluation. Not only is finite-precision arithmetic unable to always represent function arguments exactly, but also most functions cannot themselves be represented exactly as the following code shows:

```
>> sin(0)
ans =
    0
>> sin(pi)
ans =
    1.224646799147353e-016
```

Here, both results should be zero, but $\sin(\pi)$ is not. It is interesting to note that the error here and the error in the previous example are both less than **eps**.

Finally, when using double-precision, floating-point arithmetic to represent integers, only integers up to a limit can be represented *exactly*. The limiting value is $2^{53} - 1$, which is returned by MATLAB as follows:

```
>> bitmax
ans =
    9.007199254740991e+015
```

2.7 MATHEMATICAL FUNCTIONS

Lists of the common functions that MATLAB supports are shown in the tables on page 17. Most of these functions are used in the same way you would write them mathematically:

```
>> x = sqrt(2)/2
x =
    0.7071
>> y = asin(x)
y =
    0.7854
>> y_deg = y*180/pi
y_deg =
    45.0000
```

These commands find the angle where the sine function has a value of $\sqrt{2}/2$. Note, again, that MATLAB uses radians, not degrees, in trigonometric functions. Other examples include the following:

```
>> y = sqrt(3^2 + 4^2) % show 3-4-5 right triangle relationship
y =
    5
```

```
>> y = rem(23,4)  % remainder function, 23/4 has a remainder of 3
y =
    3
>> x = 2.6, y1 = fix(x), y2 = floor(x), y3 = ceil(x), y4 = round(x)
x =
    2.6000
y1 =
    2
y2 =
    2
y3 =
    3
y4 =
    3
```

Trigonometric Function	Description
acos	Inverse cosine
acosd	Inverse cosine returning degrees
acosh	Inverse hyperbolic cosine
acot	Inverse cotangent
acotd	Inverse cotangent returning degrees
acoth	Inverse hyperbolic cotangent
acsc	Inverse cosecant
acscd	Inverse cosecant returning degrees
acsch	Inverse hyperbolic cosecant
asec	Inverse secant
asecd	Inverse secant returning degrees
asech	Inverse hyperbolic secant
asin	Inverse sine
asind	Inverse sine returning degrees
asinh	Inverse hyperbolic sine
atan	Inverse tangent
atand	Inverse tangent returning degrees
atanh	Inverse hyperbolic tangent
atan2	Four-quadrant inverse tangent

Trigonometric Function	Description
cos	Cosine
cos	Cosine with argument in degrees
cosh	Hyperbolic cosine
cot	Cotangent
cot	Cotangent with argument in degrees
coth	Hyperbolic cotangent
csc	Cosecant
csc	Cosecant with argument in degrees
csch	Hyperbolic cosecant
sec	Secant
sec	Secant with argument in degrees
sech	Hyperbolic secant
sin	Sine
sin	Sine with argument in degrees
sinh	Hyperbolic sine
tan	Tangent
tan	Tangent with argument in degrees
tanh	Hyperbolic tangent

Exponential Function	Description
^	Power
exp	Exponential
expm1	Exponential minus 1 [i.e., $\exp(x) - 1$]
log	Natural logarithm
log10	Base 10 logarithm
log1p	Natural logarithm of $x + 1$ [i.e., $\log(x + 1)$]
log2	Base 2 logarithm and floating-point number dissection
nthroot	n^{th} real root of real numbers
pow2	Base 2 power and floating-point number scaling
reallog	Natural logarithm limited to real nonnegative values
realpow	Power limited to real-valued arguments
realsqrt	Square root limited to real-valued values
sqrt	Square root
nextpow2	Next-higher power of 2

Complex Function	**Description**
abs	Absolute value or magnitude
angle	Phase angle in radians
conj	Complex conjugate
imag	Imaginary part
real	Real part
unwrap	Unwrap phase angle
isreal	True for real values
cplxpair	Sort vector into complex conjugate pairs
complex	Form complex number from real and imaginary parts

Rounding and Remainder Function	**Description**
fix	Round toward zero
floor	Round toward negative infinity
ceil	Round toward positive infinity
round	Round toward nearest integer
mod	Modulus or signed remainder
rem	Remainder after division
sign	Signum function

Coordinate Transformation Function	**Description**
cart2sph	Cartesian to spherical
cartpol	Cartesian to cylindrical or polar
pol2cart	Cylindrical or polar to Cartesian
sph2cart	Spherical to Cartesian

Number Theoretic Function	**Description**
factor	Prime factors
isprime	True for prime numbers
primes	Generate list of prime numbers
gcd	Greatest common divisor
lcm	Least common multiple

Number Theoretic Function	Description
`rat`	Rational approximation
`rats`	Rational output
`perms`	All possible combinations
`nchoosek`	All combinations of *N* elements taken *K* at a time

Specialized Function	Description
`airy`	Airy function
`besselj`	Bessel function of the first kind
`bessely`	Bessel function of the second kind
`besselh`	Bessel function of the third kind
`besseli`	Modified Bessel function of the first kind
`besselk`	Modified Bessel function of the second kind
`beta`	Beta function
`betainc`	Incomplete beta function
`betaln`	Logarithm of beta function
`ellipj`	Jacobi elliptic function
`ellipke`	Complete elliptic integral
`erf`	Error function
`erfc`	Complementary error function
`erfcx`	Scaled complementary error function
`erfinv`	Inverse error function
`expint`	Exponential error function
`gamma`	Gamma function
`gammainc`	Incomplete gamma function
`gammaln`	Logarithm of gamma function
`legendre`	Associated Legendre function
`cross`	Vector cross product
`dot`	Vector dot product

3

The MATLAB Desktop

As stated in the preceding chapter, running MATLAB creates one or more windows on your computer monitor. One of these windows, entitled *MATLAB*, is commonly called the *MATLAB* desktop. This window contains or manages all other windows that are part of MATLAB. Depending on how you set up MATLAB, some windows associated with the desktop may or may not be visible, and some may or may not reside within (i.e., be ***docked*** in) the *MATLAB* window. Management of the *MATLAB* desktop window and its associated windows is not discussed in this text. If you are familiar with other window-based programs, manipulation of windows in MATLAB will be familiar to you. The *MATLAB* desktop menu items change, depending on which window is active. In addition, there are many helpful contextual menus (which are accessed by pressing the right mouse button over an item). If you are not familiar with window-based programs, it may be beneficial to seek general assistance in this area from other sources. In any case, to find out which windows are associated with the desktop, investigate the items on the **Desktop** menu within the *MATLAB* desktop window.

3.1 MATLAB WINDOWS

The windows used in MATLAB include the (1) *Command*, (2) *Command History*, (3) *Current Directory* (browser), (4) *Workspace* (browser), (5) *Help* (browser), (6) *Editor*, and (7) *Profiler*. The following table gives an overview of the purpose of each of these windows:

Window	Description
Command	Issues commands to MATLAB for processing
Command History	Running history of prior commands issued in the *Command* window
Current Directory	GUI for directory and file manipulation in MATLAB
Workspace	GUI for viewing, editing, loading, and saving MATLAB variables
Help	GUI for finding and viewing on-line documentation
Editor	Text editor for creating M-files
Profiler	Tool for optimizing M-file performance

3.2 MANAGING THE MATLAB WORKSPACE

Within the *MATLAB* desktop, actions taken in all windows support computations performed in the *Command* window. As a result, the rest of this chapter provides more detailed information about the *Command* window.

The data and variables created in the *Command* window reside in what is called the ***MATLAB workspace*** or ***Base workspace***. In addition to viewing variables in the *Workspace* window, you can see what variable names exist in the MATLAB workspace by issuing the command `who`:

```
>> who
Your variables are:
angle_c1      c4            cost       pads
ans           c5            deg_c1     real_c1
average_cost  c6            erasers    tape
c1            c6i           imag_c1
c2            c6r           items
c3            check_it_out  mag_c1
```

The variables you see may differ from those just listed, depending on what you've asked MATLAB to do since you opened the program. For more detailed information, use the command `whos`:

```
>> whos
  Name          Size          Bytes  Class
  angle_c1      1x1               8  double array
  ans           1x1               8  double array
```

```
  average_cost        1x1          8  double array
  c1                  1x1         16  double array (complex)
  c2                  1x1         16  double array (complex)
  c3                  1x1         16  double array (complex)
  c4                  1x1         16  double array (complex)
  c5                  1x1         16  double array (complex)
  c6                  1x1         16  double array (complex)
  c6i                 1x1          8  double array
  c6r                 1x1          8  double array
  check_it_out        1x1          8  double array
  cost                1x1          8  double array
  deg_c1              1x1          8  double array
  erasers             1x1          8  double array
  imag_c1             1x1          8  double array
  items               1x1          8  double array
  mag_c1              1x1          8  double array
  pads                1x1          8  double array
  real_c1             1x1          8  double array
  tape                1x1          8  double array
Grand total is 21 elements using 216 bytes
```

Here, each variable is listed, along with its size, the number of bytes used, and its class. Since MATLAB is array oriented, all of the variables belong to the class of double-precision arrays, even though all of the above variables are scalars. Later, as other data types or classes are introduced, the information in this last column will become more useful. The preceding list is also displayed in the *Workspace* window, which can be viewed by typing workspace at the MATLAB prompt or by choosing the **Workspace** menu item on the **Desktop** menu of the *MATLAB* desktop.

The command `clear` deletes variables from the MATLAB workspace. For example,

```
>> clear real_c1 imag_c1 c*
>> who
Your variables are:
angle_c1        deg_c1     mag_c1
ans             erasers    pads
average_cost    items      tape
```

deletes the variables `real_c1`, `imag_c1`, and all variables starting with the letter `c`. Other options for the `clear` function can be identified by asking for information with the command `help` or `helpwin`:

```
>> help clear
 CLEAR  Clear variables and functions from memory.
    CLEAR removes all variables from the workspace.
    CLEAR VARIABLES does the same thing.
    CLEAR GLOBAL removes all global variables.
    CLEAR FUNCTIONS removes all compiled M- and MEX-functions.
    CLEAR ALL removes all variables, globals, functions and MEX links.
    CLEAR ALL at the command prompt also removes the Java packages import
    list.

    CLEAR IMPORT removes the Java packages import list at the command
    prompt. It cannot be used in a function.
    CLEAR CLASSES is the same as CLEAR ALL except that class definitions
    are also cleared. If any objects exist outside the workspace (say in
    userdata or persistent in a locked m-file) a warning will be issued and
    the class definition will not be cleared. CLEAR CLASSES must be used if
    the number or names of fields in a class are changed.
    CLEAR JAVA is the same as CLEAR ALL except that java classes on the
    dynamic java path (defined using JAVACLASSPATH) are also cleared.

    CLEAR VAR1 VAR2 ... clears the variables specified. The wildcard
    character '*' can be used to clear variables that match a pattern. For
    instance, CLEAR X* clears all the variables in the current workspace
    that start with X.

    CLEAR -REGEXP PAT1 PAT2 can be used to match all patterns using regular
    expressions. This option only clears variables. For more information on
    using regular expressions, type "doc regexp" at the command prompt.
    If X is global, CLEAR X removes X from the current workspace, but
    leaves it accessible to any functions declaring it global.
    CLEAR GLOBAL X completely removes the global variable X.
```

```
CLEAR GLOBAL -REGEXP PAT removes global variables that match regular
expression patterns.
Note that to clear specific global variables, the GLOBAL option must
come first. Otherwise, all global variables will be cleared.

CLEAR FUN clears the function specified. If FUN has been locked by
MLOCK it will remain in memory. Use a partial path (see PARTIALPATH) to
distinguish between different overloaded versions of FUN.  For
instance, 'clear inline/display' clears only the INLINE method for
DISPLAY, leaving any other implementations in memory.

CLEAR ALL, CLEAR FUN, or CLEAR FUNCTIONS also have the side effect of
removing debugging breakpoints and reinitializing persistent variables
since the breakpoints for a function and persistent variables are
cleared whenever the m-file changes or is cleared.

Use the functional form of CLEAR, such as CLEAR('name'), when the
variable name or function name is stored in a string.

Examples for pattern matching:
    clear a*                % Clear variables starting with "a"
    clear -regexp ^b\d{3}$  % Clear variables starting with "b" and
                            %     followed by 3 digits
    clear -regexp \d        % Clear variables containing any digits

See also who, whos, mlock, munlock, persistent.
```

Obviously, the `clear` command does more than just delete variables. Its other uses will become apparent as you become familiar with more of MATLAB's features.

3.3 MEMORY MANAGEMENT

MATLAB allocates memory for variables as they are created and for M-file functions as they are used. Depending on the computer on which the program is installed, it is possible for MATLAB to run out of memory, making it impossible to do any further work. When you eliminate variables by using the `clear` command, MATLAB frees up the memory used by the variables cleared. Over time, however, it is possible for memory to become fragmented, leaving MATLAB's memory space populated by variables surrounded by numerous small fragments of free memory. Since MATLAB always stores variables in contiguous chunks of memory, these fragments of free memory may not be reusable. To alleviate this problem, the `pack` command performs memory garbage collection. The command saves all MATLAB workspace variables to disk, clears all variables from the workspace, and then reloads the variables back into the workspace. On completion, all fragments of free memory are consolidated into one large, usable block. Depending on how much memory is allocated to MATLAB on your computer, how long you've been running a particular MATLAB session, and how many variables you've created, you may or may not ever need to use the `pack` command.

3.4 NUMBER DISPLAY FORMATS

When MATLAB displays numerical results, it follows several rules. By default, if a result is an integer, MATLAB displays it as an integer. Likewise, when a result is a real number, MATLAB displays it with approximately four digits to the right of the decimal point. If the significant digits in the result are outside of this range, MATLAB displays the result in scientific notation, similar to the display of a scientific calculator. You can override this default behavior by specifying a different numerical format. From the *Command* window **File** menu, choose the **Preferences** menu. Alternatively, type the appropriate MATLAB `format` command at the prompt. With the special variable `pi`, the numerical display formats produced by different `format` selections are as follows:

MATLAB Command	pi	Comments
`format short`	3.1416	5 digits
`format long`	3.14159265358979	16 digits
`format short e`	3.1416e+000	5 digits plus exponent
`format long e`	3.14159265358979e+000	16 digits plus exponent
`format short g`	3.1416	Best of `format short` or `format short e`
`format long g`	3.14159265358979	Best of `format long` or `format long e`
`format hex`	400921fb54442d18	Hexadecimal, floating point
`format bank`	3.14	2 decimal digits
`format +`	+	Positive (+), negative (−), or zero (0)
`format rat`	355/113	Rational approximation

`format debug`	`Structure address = 1214830`
	`m = 1`
	`n = 1`
	`pr = 11d60d0`
	`pi = 0`
	`3.1416`
		Internal storage information in addition to `short g`

> Note: In MATLAB, the internal representation of a number does not change when different display formats are chosen; only the display changes. All calculations using double-precision numbers are performed using double-precision arithmetic.

3.5 KEEPING A SESSION LOG

Sometimes it is useful to keep a log of all work performed during a MATLAB session. The *Command History* window keeps a chronological log of the functions and commands executed during current and past MATLAB work sessions, but does not show the results. MATLAB provides a command `diary`, which saves all *Command* window activity to a text file in the current directory. The help text for `diary` describes its use:

```
>> help diary
 DIARY Save text of MATLAB session.
    DIARY filename causes a copy of all subsequent command window input
    and most of the resulting command window output to be appended to the
    named file.  If no file is specified, the file 'diary' is used.
    DIARY OFF suspends it.
 DIARY ON turns it back on.
 DIARY, by itself, toggles the diary state.
```

3.6 SYSTEM INFORMATION

MATLAB provides a number of commands that provide information about the computer in use, as well as about the MATLAB version in use. The command `computer` returns a character string identifying the computer in use:

```
>> computer
ans =
PCWIN
```

In this case, the computer is a PC that is running *Windows XP*. The command `version` returns a character string identifying the MATLAB version:

```
>> version
ans =
7.0.0.151483 (R14)
```

Note that the command `ver` returns information about MATLAB, as well as installed toolboxes:

```
> ver
-------------------------------------------------------------------------------
MATLAB Version 7.0.0.051483 (R14)
MATLAB License Number: 9754
Operating System: Microsoft Windows XP Version 5.2 (Build 2600: Service Pack 1)
Java VM Version: Java 1.4.2 with Sun Microsystems Inc. Java HotSpot(TM) Client VM
-------------------------------------------------------------------------------
MATLAB                                  Version 7.0        (R14)
Mastering MATLAB Toolbox                Version 6.0
```

MATLAB licensing information can be found by using the commands `license` and `hostid`:

```
>> hostid
   '9754'

>> license
ans =
9754
```

Of course, your results from entering these commands will most likely be different from those shown because your computer and MATLAB version will probably differ from those used to produce this text.

3.7 THE MATLAB SEARCH PATH

MATLAB uses a ***search path*** to find information stored in files on disk. MATLAB's files are organized into numerous directories and subdirectories.

> The list of all directories where MATLAB's files are found is called the MATLAB search path or simply MATLAB path.

Use of the MATLAB search path is described next. When you enter `cow` at the MATLAB prompt by typing `>>cow`, MATLAB does the following: (1) It checks to see if `cow` is a ***variable*** in the MATLAB workspace. (2) If not, it checks to see if `cow` is a built-in function. (3) If not, it searches for a file named `cow.m` in the ***current directory***. (4) If none exists, it checks to see if `cow.m` exists anywhere on the ***MATLAB search path*** by searching in the order in which the path is specified. (5) If `cow` isn't found at this point, MATLAB reports an error.

MATLAB takes appropriate action according to this search strategy. If `cow` is a variable, MATLAB uses the variable. If `cow` is a built-in function, it is called. If `cow.m` is a file (either in the current directory or anywhere on the MATLAB search path) the file `cow.m` is opened, and MATLAB acts on what is found in the file. As is documented in Chapters 4 and 12, MATLAB has two basic file types that are of common use; both are simple text files containing MATLAB commands. (See Chapters 4 and 12 for further information regarding these ***M-files***).

In reality, the search procedure is more complicated than that just described, because of advanced features in MATLAB. For the most part, however, this search procedure provides sufficient detail for basic MATLAB work. (More detailed information regarding the MATLAB search path can be found in Chapter 12.)

When MATLAB starts up, it defines a default MATLAB search path that points to all of the directories in which MATLAB stores its files. This search path can be displayed and modified in several ways. The easiest way is to use the ***Path Browser***, which is a graphical user interface designed for viewing and modifying the MATLAB search path. The path browser is made available by choosing **Set Path ...** from the **File** menu on the *MATLAB* desktop window. Since the MATLAB search path already points to all directories where MATLAB stores its files, the primary purpose for accessing the path browser is to add your own MATLAB file storage directories to the search path.

To display the MATLAB search path in the *Command* window, MATLAB provides the function `matlabpath`. In addition, the features of the path browser can be duplicated in the *Command* window by using the functions `path`, `addpath`, and `rmpath`. For more information regarding these functions, see the on-line documentation.

4

Script M-Files

For simple problems, entering your requests at the MATLAB prompt in the *Command* window is fast and efficient. However, as the number of commands increases, or when you wish to change the value of one or more variables and reevaluate a number of commands, typing at the MATLAB prompt quickly becomes tedious. MATLAB provides a logical solution to this problem. It allows you to place MATLAB commands in a simple text file and then tell MATLAB to open the file and evaluate the commands exactly as it would have if you had typed the commands at the MATLAB prompt. These files are called ***script files*** or ***M-files***. The term "script" signifies that MATLAB simply reads from the script found in the file. The term *M-file* means that script filenames must end with the extension `'.m'`, as in, for example, `example1.m`.

4.1 SCRIPT M-FILE USE

To create a script M-file, click on the blank page icon on the MATLAB desktop toolbar, or choose **New** from the **File** menu and select **M-file**. This procedure brings up a text editor window wherein you can enter MATLAB commands. The following script M-file shows the commands from an example considered earlier:

```
% script M-file example1.m
  erasers = 4; % number of each item
  pads = 6;
  tape = 2;
```

```
items = erasers + pads + tape
cost = erasers*25 + pads*52 + tape*99
average_cost = cost/items
```

This file can be saved to disk and executed immediately by (1) choosing **Save and Run** from the **Debug** menu, (2) pressing the **Save and Run** button on the *Editor* toolbar, or (3) simply pressing the function key **F5**. Alternatively, you can save this file as the M-file `example1.m` on your disk by choosing **Save** from the **File** menu; then, at the MATLAB prompt, it's just a matter of typing the name of the script file without the `.m` extension:

```
>> example1
items =
    12
cost =
   610
average_cost =
       50.833
```

When MATLAB interprets the `example1` statement, it follows the search path described in Chapter 3. In brief, MATLAB prioritizes current MATLAB variables ahead of M-file names. If `example1` is not a current MATLAB variable or built-in function name, MATLAB opens the file `example1.m` (if it can find it) and evaluates the commands found there just as if they had been entered directly at the *Command* window prompt. As a result, commands within the M-file have access to all of the variables in the MATLAB workspace, and all of the variables created by the M-file become part of the workspace. Normally, the M-file commands are not displayed as they are evaluated. The `echo on` command tells MATLAB to display, or echo, commands to the *Command* window as they are read and evaluated. You can probably guess what the `echo off` command does. Similarly, the command `echo` by itself toggles the echo state.

This ability to create script M-files makes it simple to answer "what if?" questions. For example, you could repeatedly open the `example1.m` M-file, change the number of `erasers`, `pads`, or `tape`, and then save and execute the file.

The utility of MATLAB comments is readily apparent when you use script files, as shown in `example1.m`. Comments allow you to document the commands found in a script file, so that you do not forget the commands when you view them in the future. In addition, the use of semicolons at the ends of lines to suppress the display of results allows you to control script-file output, so that only important results are shown. Because of the utility of script files, MATLAB provides several functions that are particularly helpful when used in M-files:

Function	Description
beep	Makes computer beep
disp(variablename)	Displays results without identifying variable names
echo	Controls *Command* window echoing of script file contents as they are executed
input	Prompts user for input
keyboard	Temporarily gives control to keyboard. (Type return to return control to the executing script M-file.)
pause or pause(n)	Pauses until user presses any keyboard key, or pauses for n seconds and then continues
waitforbuttonpress	Pauses until user presses mouse button or any keyboard key

When a MATLAB command is not terminated by a semicolon, the results are displayed in the *Command* window, with the variable name identified. For a prettier display, it is sometimes convenient to suppress the variable name. In MATLAB, this is accomplished with the command disp:

```
>> items

items =

    12

>> disp(items)

    12
```

Rather than repeatedly edit a script file for computations for a variety of cases, you can employ the input command to prompt for input as a script file is executed. For example, reconsider the example1.m script file, with the following modifications:

```
% script M-file example1.m

erasers = 4; % Number of each item

pads = 6;

tape = input('Enter the number of rolls of tape purchased > ');

items = erasers + pads + tape

cost = erasers*25 + pads*52 + tape*99

average_cost = cost/items
```

Running this script M-file produces this result:

```
>> example1
Enter the number of rolls of tape purchased > 3
items =
    13
cost =
   709
average_cost =
        54.538
```

In response to the prompt, the number 3 was entered and the **Return** or **Enter** key was pressed. The remaining commands were evaluated as before. The function `input` accepts any valid MATLAB expression for input. For example, running the script file again and providing different input gives the following result:

```
>> example1
Enter the number of rolls of tape purchased > round(sqrt(13))-1
items =
    13
cost =
   709
average_cost =
        54.538
```

In this case, the number of rolls of tape was set equal to the result of evaluating the expression

```
round (sqrt(13))-1.
```

To see the effect of the echo command, add it to the script file and execute it:

```
% script M-file example1.m
echo on
erasers = 4;  % Number of each item
pads = 6;
tape = input('Enter the number of rolls of tape purchased > ');
items = erasers + pads + tape
```

```
cost = erasers*25 + pads*52 + tape*99
average_cost = cost/items
echo off
```

```
>> example1
erasers = 4;  % Number of each item
pads = 6;
tape = input('Enter the number of rolls of tape purchased > ');
Enter the number of rolls of tape purchased > 2
items = erasers + pads + tape
items =
    12
cost = erasers*25 + pads*52 + tape*99
cost =
   610
average_cost = cost/items
average_cost =
       50.833
echo off
```

As you can see, the echo command made the result much harder to read. On the other hand, the echo command can be very helpful when debugging more complicated script files.

4.2 BLOCK COMMENTS AND CODE CELLS

In prior versions of MATLAB, comments were line oriented. That is, comments began with an initial percent sign and continued to the end of the current line. To continue the comments on the next line required another initial percent sign. Therefore, a block of comments would all start with initial percent signs, as shown here:

```
% This is an example of multiple line comments
% in an M-file. Each line requires an initial % sign or MATLAB
% assumes the line contains code to be executed.
```

While the block of comments is visually simple, it can become cumbersome to manage later, when comment text is augmented or edited. In this case, the percent signs must remain at the beginnings of the lines, and the comment text must flow after the initial percent signs on each line. In the past, to make it less cumbersome, the MATLAB editor included commands for adding or removing the initial percent signs on a highlighted block of lines. Now, MATLAB 7 supports *block comments* through the use of the syntax %{ and %}. These symbols mark the beginning and end, respectively, of a block of text to be treated as comments by MATLAB. For example, using block comment syntax on the previous example produces

```
%{
This is an example of multiple line comments
in an M-file. Each line requires an initial % sign or MATLAB
assumes the line contains code to be executed.
(Now lines can be added and edited as desired without having to
place percent signs at the beginning of each line.)
%}
```

In addition to their utility in composing multiline comments, block comments will allow you to rapidly turn on and off the interpretation and execution of any number of lines of code in an M-file. This feature is particularly helpful in creating and debugging large M-files. Simply adding %{ before and %} after a block of MATLAB code turns the enclosed code into comments that are not processed by MATLAB. When this feature is used, different sections of a script file can be executed at different times during the editing and debugging processes.

In the past, the MATLAB editor offered commands for executing a block of highlighted code in an editor window. In MATLAB 7, the editor now supports the selective execution of M-file code through the use of ***code cells***. A code cell is simply a block of M-file code that starts with a comment line containing two percent signs followed by a space (i.e., %%). The code cell continues to the end of the M-file or to the beginning of another code cell. From within the MATLAB editor, cells can be created, individually executed, and sequentially executed, thereby enabling effective M-file debugging. The **Cell** menu in the *Editor* window facilitates these operations. It is important to note that the syntax for code cells is interpreted by the editor, not by the MATLAB command interpreter. As a result, when an M-file is executed after its name has been entered in the *Command* window, code-cell syntax is ignored, and all executable lines in the file are processed.

4.3 SETTING EXECUTION TIME

When the name of an M-file is typed at the *Command* window prompt, the M-file is executed immediately. In some circumstances (such as large programming projects, or situations wherein the data to be manipulated becomes available only over a long period of time while MATLAB is running), it is convenient to specify execution times for M-files. In MATLAB, this capability is accomplished by using ***timer objects***. A timer object is created with the function `timer`. For example,

```
>> my_timer = timer('TimerFcn','MfileName','StartDelay',100)
```

creates the timer object stored in the variable `my_timer`, which executes the M-file *`MfileName`* 100 seconds after the timer has been started by using the `start` function:

```
>> start(my_timer) % start the timer in the variable my_timer
```

In general terms, timer function syntax has the form

```
>> t=timer('PropertyName1',PropertyValue1,'PropertyName2',PropertyValue2,...)
```

where the arguments identify property names as character strings paired with corresponding property values.

Neither MATLAB nor the computer operating system is held up while a timer is running, but not executing code. MATLAB and other programs can be used during this idle time. When the timer object initiates code execution, the timer takes control of MATLAB and executes the code, just as if the code had been typed at the MATLAB prompt. When this execution ends, MATLAB returns control to the *Command* window prompt.

The timer object has many more features. For example, '*MfileName*' can be any statement executable at the MATLAB prompt. It can be a script M-file, a function handle or function M-file, or a set of MATLAB commands. You also can specify that timer code be executed on a periodic basis or executed a specified number of times. You can specify four different M-files or code sequences to be executed under different conditions. For example,

```
>> my_timer = timer('TimerFcn','Mfile1',...
                    'StartFcn','Mfile2',...
                    'StopFcn,, 'Mfile3',...
                    'ErrorFcn','Mfile4');
```

creates a timer function that executes (1) `'Mfile1'` as the primary timer code that may be repeatedly executed, (2) `'Mfile2'` when the timer is started with the `start` function, (3) `'Mfile3'` when the timer is stopped with the `stop` function, and (4) `'Mfile4'` if a MATLAB error occurs while any of these functions are executing. (See the MATLAB documentation for more complete information about timer objects.)

4.4 STARTUP AND FINISH

When MATLAB starts up, it executes two script M-files, matlabrc.m and startup.m. The first, matlabrc.m, comes with MATLAB and generally should not be modified. The commands in this M-file set the default *Figure* window size and placement, as well as a number of other default features. The default MATLAB search path is set by retrieving the script file pathdef.m from matlabrc.m. The *Path Browser* and *Command* window functions for editing the MATLAB search path maintain the file pathdef.m, so there is no need to edit it with a text editor.

Commands in matlabrc.m check for the existence of the script M-file startup.m on the MATLAB search path. If the M-file exists, the commands in it are executed. This optional M-file startup.m typically contains commands that add personal default features to MATLAB. For example, it is common to put one or more addpath or path commands in startup.m to append additional directories to the MATLAB search path. Similarly, the default number-display format can be changed (e.g., format compact). Since startup.m is a standard script M-file, there are no restrictions as to what commands can be placed in it. (However, it's probably not wise to include the command quit in startup.m!) On single-user installations, startup.m is commonly stored in the toolbox/local subdirectory on the MATLAB path. On network installations, a convenient location for your startup.m file is the default directory where you start MATLAB sessions.

When you terminate MATLAB via the **Exit MATLAB** item on the **File** menu in the *MATLAB* desktop window (or by typing exit or quit at the MATLAB prompt) MATLAB searches the MATLAB path for a script M-file named finish.m. If one is found, the commands in it are executed before MATLAB terminates. For example, the following finish.m prompts the user for confirmation before quitting, and the command quit cancel provides a way to cancel quitting:

```
%FINISH Confirm Desire for Quitting MATLAB

question = 'Are You Sure You Want To Quit?';
button = questdlg(question,'Exit Request','Yes','No','No');

switch button
case 'No'
   quit cancel;  % how to cancel quitting!
end
% 'Yes' lets script and MATLAB end.
```

5

Arrays and Array Operations

All of the computations considered to this point have involved single numbers called scalars. Operations involving scalars are the basis of mathematics. At the same time, when we wish to perform the same operation on more than one number at a time, performing repeated scalar operations is time consuming and cumbersome. To solve this problem, MATLAB defines operations on data arrays.

5.1 SIMPLE ARRAYS

Consider the problem of computing values of the sine function over one half of its period, namely, $y = \sin(x)$ over $0 \le x \le \pi$. Since it is impossible to compute $\sin(x)$ at all points over this range (there are an infinite number of them), we must choose a finite number of points. In doing so, we sample the function. To pick a number, let's evaluate $\sin(x)$ every 0.1π in this range; that is, let $x = 0, 0.1\pi, 0.2\pi, \ldots, 1.0\pi$. If you were using a scientific calculator to compute these values, you would start by making a list, or an array, of the values of x. Then, you would enter each value of x into your calculator, find its sine, and write down the result as the second array y. Perhaps you would write the arrays in an organized fashion, as follows:

x	0	0.1π	0.2π	0.3π	0.4π	0.5π	0.6π	0.7π	0.8π	0.9π	π
y	0	0.31	0.59	0.81	0.95	1	0.95	0.81	0.59	0.31	0

As shown, x and y are ordered lists of numbers; that is, the first value or element in y is associated with the first value or element in x, the second element in y is associated with the second element in x, and so on. Because of this ordering, it is common to refer to individual values or elements in x and y by using subscripts; for example, x_1 is the first element in x, y_5 is the fifth element in y, and x_n is the nth element in x.

MATLAB handles arrays in a straightforward, intuitive way. Creating arrays is easy—just follow the preceding visual organization to create the following arrays:

```
>> x = [0 .1*pi .2*pi .3*pi .4*pi .5*pi .6*pi .7*pi .8*pi .9*pi pi]
x =
  Columns 1 through 7
         0    0.3142    0.6283    0.9425    1.2566    1.5708    1.8850
  Columns 8 through 11
    2.1991    2.5133    2.8274    3.1416
>> y = sin(x)
y =
  Columns 1 through 7
         0    0.3090    0.5878    0.8090    0.9511    1.0000    0.9511
  Columns 8 through 11
    0.8090    0.5878    0.3090    0.0000
```

To create an array in MATLAB, all you have to do is start with a left bracket, enter the desired values separated by spaces (or commas), and then close the array with a right bracket. Notice that finding the sine of the values in x follows naturally. MATLAB understands that you want to find the sine of each element in x and place the results in an associated array called y. This fundamental capability makes MATLAB different from other computer languages.

Since spaces separate array values, complex numbers entered as array values cannot have embedded spaces, unless the expressions are enclosed in parentheses. For example, `[1 -2i 3 4 5+6i]` contains five elements, whereas the identical arrays `[(1 - 2i) 3 4 5+6i]` and `[1-2i 3 4 5+6i]` contain four.

5.2 ARRAY ADDRESSING OR INDEXING

In the previous example, since x has more than one element, (it has 11 values separated into columns), MATLAB gives you the result with the columns identified. As shown, x is an array having one row and 11 columns; or, in mathematical jargon, it is a row vector, a 1-by-11 array, or simply an array of length 11.

In MATLAB, individual array elements are accessed by using subscripts; for example, x(1) is the first element in x, x(2) is the second element in x, and so on. The following code is illustrative:

```
>> x(3)  % The third element of x
ans =
    0.6283
```

```
>> y(5)  % The fifth element of y
ans =
    0.9511
```

To access a block of elements at one time, MATLAB provides ***colon notation***:

```
>> x(1:5)
ans =
         0    0.3142    0.6283    0.9425    1.2566
```

These are the first through fifth elements in x. The notation 1:5 says, start with 1 and count up to 5. The code

```
>> x(7:end)
ans =
        1.885      2.1991      2.5133        2.8274        3.1416
```

starts with the seventh element and continues to the last element. Here, the word end signifies the last element in the array x. In the code

```
>> y(3:-1:1)
ans =
    0.5878    0.3090         0
```

the results contain the third, second, and first elements in reverse order. The notation 3:-1:1 says, start with 3, count down by 1, and stop at 1. Similarly, the results in the code

```
>> x(2:2:7)
ans =
    0.3142    0.9425    1.5708
```

consists of the second, fourth, and sixth elements in x. The notation 2:2:7 says, start with 2, count up by 2, and stop when you get to 7. (In this case, adding 2 to 6 gives 8, which is greater than 7, and so the eighth element is not included.) The code

```
>> y([8 2 9 1])
ans =
    0.8090    0.3090    0.5878         0
```

uses another array, [8 2 9 1], to extract the elements of the array y in the order we wanted them! The first element taken is the eighth, the second is the second, the third is the ninth, and the fourth is the first. In reality, [8 2 9 1] itself is an array that addresses the desired elements of y. Note that in the code

```
>> y([1 1 3 4 2 2])
ans =
        0         0    0.5878    0.8090    0.3090    0.3090
```

there is no requirement that the array used as an index contain unique elements. This allows you to rearrange and duplicate array elements arbitrarily. Using this feature leads to efficient MATLAB coding.

Addressing one array with another works, as long as the addressing array contains integers between 1 and the length of the array. In contrast, consider the following code:

```
>> y(3.2)
??? Subscript indices must either be real positive integers or logicals.
>> y(11.6)
??? Subscript indices must either be real positive integers or logicals.
>> y(11)
??? Index exceeds matrix dimensions.
```

In these examples, MATLAB simply returns an error when the index is noninteger and returns a statement that no such value exists when the index exceeds the dimensions of the variable. In all cases, no numerical output appears.

5.3 ARRAY CONSTRUCTION

Earlier, we entered the values of x by typing each individual element in x. While this is fine when there are only 11 values in x, what if there were 111 values? Two other ways of entering x are as follows:

```
>> x = (0:0.1:1)*pi
x =
  Columns 1 through 7
        0    0.3142    0.6283    0.9425    1.2566    1.5708    1.8850
  Columns 8 through 11
   2.1991    2.5133    2.8274    3.1416
>> x = linspace(0,pi,11)
x =
  Columns 1 through 7
```

```
     0    0.3142    0.6283    0.9425    1.2566    1.5708    1.8850
 Columns 8 through 11
  2.1991    2.5133    2.8274    3.1416
```

In the first case, the colon notation (0:0.1:1) creates an array that starts at 0, increments (or counts) by 0.1, and ends at 1. Each element in the array is then multiplied by π to create the desired values in x. In the second case, the MATLAB function linspace is used to create x. This function's arguments are described by

```
linspace(first_value,last_value,number_of_values)
```

Both of these array creation forms are common in MATLAB. The colon notation form allows you to directly specify the increment between data points, but not the number of data points. Using linspace, on the other hand, allows you to directly specify the number of data points, but not the increment between the data points.

Both of these array creation forms result in arrays in which the individual elements are linearly spaced with respect to each other. For the special case where a logarithmically spaced array is desired, MATLAB provides the logspace function:

```
>> logspace(0,2,11)
ans =
  Columns 1 through 7
   1.0000    1.5849    2.5119    3.9811    6.3096   10.0000   15.8489
  Columns 8 through 11
  25.1189   39.8107   63.0957  100.0000
```

Here, we created an array starting at 10^0, ending at 10^2, and containing 11 values. The function arguments are described by

```
logspace(first_exponent,last_exponent,number_of_values)
```

Although it is common to begin and end at integer powers of 10, logspace works equally well when nonintegers are used as the first two input arguments.

When using colon notation, or the functions linspace or logspace, there is often a temptation to enclose expressions in brackets:

```
>> a = [1:7]
a =
     1     2     3     4     5     6     7
>> b = [linspace(1,7,5)]
b =
          1          2.5            4          5.5            7
```

Although using brackets does not change the results and may add clarity to the statements, the added brackets force MATLAB to do more work and take more time, because brackets signify a concatenation operation. In the preceding examples, no concatenation is performed, and so there's no need ask MATLAB to take the time to consider that possibility.

Parentheses do not signify concatenation and therefore do not slow MATLAB down. As a result, parentheses can be used as needed:

```
>> a = (1:7)' % change row to column

a =

     1
     2
     3
     4
     5
     6
     7
```

Sometimes, an array is required that is not conveniently described by a linearly or logarithmically spaced element relationship. There is no uniform way to create these arrays. However, array addressing and the ability to combine expressions can help eliminate the need to enter individual elements, one at a time. For example,

```
>> a = 1:5, b = 1:2:9

a =

     1     2     3     4     5

b =

     1     3     5     7     9
```

creates two arrays. Remember that multiple statements can appear on a single line if they are separated by commas or semicolons. The code

```
>> c = [b a]

c =

     1     3     5     7     9     1     2     3     4     5
```

creates an array c composed of the elements of b, followed by those of a, while the code

```
>> d = [a(1:2:5) 1 0 1]

d =

     1     3     5     1     0     1
```

creates an array d composed of the first, third, and fifth elements of a, followed by three additional elements.

The simple array construction features of MATLAB are summarized in the following table:

Array Construction Technique	Description
`x=[2 2*pi sqrt(2) 2-3j]`	Creates row vector x containing arbitrary elements
`x=first:last`	Creates row vector x starting with `first`, counting by 1, and ending at or before `last` (Note that `x=[first:last]` produces the same result, but takes longer, since MATLAB considers both bracket and colon array-creation forms.)
`x=first:increment:last`	Creates row vector x starting with `first`, counting by increment, and ending at or before `last`
`x=linspace(first,last,n)`	Creates linearly spaced row vector x starting with `first`, ending at `last`, having n elements
`x=logspace(first,last,n)`	Creates logarithmically spaced row vector x starting with 10^{first}, ending at 10^{last}, and having n elements

5.4 ARRAY ORIENTATION

In the preceding examples, arrays contained one row and multiple columns. As a result of this row orientation, the arrays are commonly called row vectors. It is also possible for an array to be a column vector, having one column and multiple rows. In this case, all of the previous array manipulation and mathematics apply without change. The only difference is that results are displayed as columns, rather than as rows.

Since the array creation functions previously illustrated all create row vectors, there must be some way to create column vectors. The most straightforward way to create a column vector is to specify it, element by element, by using ***semicolons*** to separate values:

```
>> c = [1;2;3;4;5]
c =
     1
     2
     3
     4
     5
```

According to this example, separating elements by spaces or commas specifies elements in different columns, whereas separating elements by semicolons specifies elements in different rows.

To create a column vector using the colon notation `start:increment:end` or the functions `linspace` and `logspace`, you must ***transpose*** the resulting row into a column by using the MATLAB transpose operator ('). For example,

```
>> a = 1:5
a =
     1     2     3     4     5
```

creates a row vector using the colon notation format. The code

```
>> b = a'
b =
     1
     2
     3
     4
     5
```

uses the transpose operator to change the row vector a into the column vector b:

```
>> w = b'
w =
     1     2     3     4     5
```

This statement applies the transpose again and changes the column back into a row.

In addition to performing the simple transpose operations just described, MATLAB also offers a transpose operator with a preceding dot. In this case, the ***dot-transpose operator*** is interpreted as the noncomplex conjugate transpose. When an array is complex, the transpose (') gives the complex-conjugate transpose; that is, the sign on the imaginary part is changed, as part of the transpose operation. On the other hand, the dot-transpose (.') transposes the array, but does not conjugate it. The code

```
>> c = a.'
c =
     1
     2
     3
     4
     5
```

shows that .' and ' are identical for real data, while the code

```
>> d = complex(a,a)
d =
  Columns 1 through 4
   1.0000 + 1.0000i    2.0000 + 2.0000i    3.0000 + 3.0000i    4.0000 + 4.0000i
  Column 5
   5.0000 + 5.0000i
```

creates a simple complex row vector from the array a by using the function complex. The code

```
>> e = d'
e =
   1.0000 - 1.0000i
   2.0000 - 2.0000i
   3.0000 - 3.0000i
   4.0000 - 4.0000i
   5.0000 - 5.0000i
```

creates a column vector e that is the complex conjugate transpose of d, while the code

```
>> f = d.'
f =
   1.0000 + 1.0000i
   2.0000 + 2.0000i
   3.0000 + 3.0000i
   4.0000 + 4.0000i
   5.0000 + 5.0000i
```

creates a column vector f that is the transpose of d.

If an array can be a row vector or a column vector, it makes intuitive sense that arrays can have both multiple rows and multiple columns. That is, arrays can also be in the form of matrices. The creation of matrices follows the creation of row and column vectors. ***Commas or spaces are used to separate elements in a specific row, and semicolons are used to separate individual rows:***

```
>> g = [1 2 3 4;5 6 7 8]
g =
     1     2     3     4
     5     6     7     8
```

Here, g is an array or matrix having 2 rows and 4 columns; that is, it is a 2-by-4 matrix, or it is a matrix of dimension 2 by 4. The semicolon tells MATLAB to start a new row between the 4 and the 5. Note the use of line breaks in the following code:

```
>> g = [1 2 3 4
5 6 7 8
9 10 11 12]
g =
     1     2     3     4
     5     6     7     8
     9    10    11    12
```

Thus, in addition to using semicolons, pressing the **Return** or **Enter** key while entering an array tells MATLAB to start a new row. MATLAB strictly enforces the fact that all rows must contain the same number of columns:

```
>> h = [1 2 3;4 5 6 7]
??? Error using ==> vertcat
All rows in the bracketed expression must have the same
number of columns.
```

5.5 SCALAR–ARRAY MATHEMATICS

In the first array example given, the array x is multiplied by the scalar π. Other simple mathematical operations between scalars and arrays follow the same natural interpretation. Addition, subtraction, multiplication, and division by a scalar simply apply the operation to all elements of the array. For example, the code

```
>> g-2
ans =
    -1     0     1     2
     3     4     5     6
     7     8     9    10
```

subtracts 2 from each element in g, while the code

```
>> 2*g - 1
ans =
     1     3     5     7
     9    11    13    15
    17    19    21    23
```

multiplies each element in g by 2 and subtracts 1 from each element of the result. Finally, the code

```
>> 2*g/5 + 1
ans =
         1.4          1.8          2.2          2.6
           3          3.4          3.8          4.2
         4.6            5          5.4          5.8
```

multiplies each element of g by 2, then divides each element of the result by 5, and finally adds 1 to each element.

Note that scalar–array mathematics uses the same order of precedence used in scalar expressions to determine the order of evaluation.

5.6 ARRAY–ARRAY MATHEMATICS

Mathematical operations between arrays are not quite as simple as those between scalars and arrays. Clearly, array operations between arrays of different sizes or dimensions are difficult to define and are of dubious value. However, when two arrays have the same dimensions, addition, subtraction, multiplication, and division apply on an element-by-element basis in MATLAB, as in the following example:

```
>> g  % recall previous array
g =
     1     2     3     4
     5     6     7     8
     9    10    11    12
>> h = [1 1 1 1;2 2 2 2;3 3 3 3]  % create new array
h =
     1     1     1     1
     2     2     2     2
     3     3     3     3
>> g + h  % add h to g on an element-by-element basis
ans =
     2     3     4     5
     7     8     9    10
    12    13    14    15
>> ans - h  % subtract h from the previous answer to get g back
```

```
ans =

     1     2     3     4
     5     6     7     8
     9    10    11    12

>> 2*g - h  % multiplies g by 2 and subtracts h from the result

ans =

     1     3     5     7
     8    10    12    14
    15    17    19    21

>> 2*(g-h)  % use parentheses to change order of operation

ans =

     0     2     4     6
     6     8    10    12
    12    14    16    18
```

Note that array–array mathematics uses the same order of precedence used in scalar expressions to determine the order of evaluation. Note also that parentheses can be used as desired to change the order of operation.

Element-by-element multiplication and division work similarly, but use slightly unconventional notation:

```
>> g.*h

ans =

     1     2     3     4
    10    12    14    16
    27    30    33    36
```

Here, we multiplied the arrays g and h, element by element by using the dot multiplication symbol .*.

> The dot preceding the standard asterisk multiplication symbol tells MATLAB to perform element-by-element array multiplication. Multiplication without the dot signifies matrix multiplication, which is discussed later.

For this particular example, matrix multiplication is not defined:

```
>> g*h
??? Error using ==> *
Inner matrix dimensions must agree.
```

Element-by-element division, or dot division, also requires use of the dot symbol as follows:

```
>> g./h
ans =
    1.0000    2.0000    3.0000    4.0000
    2.5000    3.0000    3.5000    4.0000
    3.0000    3.3333    3.6667    4.0000
>> h.\g
ans =
    1.0000    2.0000    3.0000    4.0000
    2.5000    3.0000    3.5000    4.0000
    3.0000    3.3333    3.6667    4.0000
```

As with scalars, division is defined by using both forward and backward slashes. In both cases, the array *below* the slash is divided into the array *above* the slash.

> The dot preceding the forward or backward slash symbol tells MATLAB to perform element-by-element array division. Division without the dot signifies matrix inversion, which is discussed later.

Array or dot division also applies if the numerator is a scalar. Consider the following example:

```
>> 1./g
ans =
            1          0.5      0.33333         0.25
          0.2      0.16667      0.14286        0.125
      0.11111          0.1     0.090909     0.083333
```

In this case, the scalar 1 in the numerator is expanded to an array the same size as the denominator, and then element-by-element division is performed. That is, the preceding code represents a shorthand way of computing

```
>> f=[1 1 1 1; 1 1 1 1; 1 1 1 1] % create numerator
f =
     1     1     1     1
     1     1     1     1
     1     1     1     1
>> f./g
```

```
ans =

           1         0.5     0.33333        0.25
         0.2     0.16667     0.14286       0.125
     0.11111         0.1    0.090909    0.083333

>> f./h

ans =

           1           1           1           1
         0.5         0.5         0.5         0.5
     0.33333     0.33333     0.33333     0.33333
```

This process of automatically expanding scalar values so that element-by-element arithmetic applies is called ***scalar expansion***. Scalar expansion is used extensively in MATLAB.

Division without the dot is the matrix division or matrix inversion operation, which is an entirely different operation, as the following code shows:

```
>> g/h
Warning: Rank deficient, rank = 1  tol =   5.3291e-015.

ans =

           0           0     0.83333
           0           0      2.1667
           0           0         3.5

>> h/g
Warning: Rank deficient, rank = 2  tol =   1.8757e-014.

ans =

      -0.125           0       0.125
       -0.25           0        0.25
      -0.375           0       0.375
```

Matrix division gives results that are not necessarily the same size as g and h. (Matrix operations are discussed in Chapter 17.)

Array exponentiation is defined in several ways. As used with multiplication and division, ^ is reserved for matrix exponentiation, and .^ is used to denote element-by-element exponentiation. When the exponent is a scalar, the scalar is applied to each element of the array. For example,

```
>> g, h  % recalls the arrays used earlier

g =

     1     2     3     4
```

```
     5     6     7     8
     9    10    11    12
h =
     1     1     1     1
     2     2     2     2
     3     3     3     3
```

```
>> g.^2
ans =
     1     4     9    16
    25    36    49    64
    81   100   121   144
```

squares the individual elements of g, whereas

```
>> g^2
??? Error using ==> mpower
Matrix must be square.
```

is matrix exponentiation, which is defined only for square matrices—that is, matrices with equal row and column counts. The code

```
>> g.^-1
ans =
          1          0.5      0.33333       0.25
        0.2      0.16667      0.14286      0.125
    0.11111          0.1     0.090909   0.083333
```

finds the reciprocal of each element in g. The code

```
>> 1./g
ans =
          1          0.5      0.33333       0.25
        0.2      0.16667      0.14286      0.125
    0.11111          0.1     0.090909   0.083333
```

produces the same result as the scalar expansion approach seen earlier.

When the exponent is an array operating on a scalar, each element of the array is applied to the scalar. For example, the code

```
>> 2.^g
ans =
        2        4        8       16
       32       64      128      256
      512     1024     2048     4096
```

raises 2 to the power of each element in the array g.

If both components are arrays of the same size, exponentiation is applied element by element. Thus,

```
>> g.^h
ans =
        1        2        3        4
       25       36       49       64
      729     1000     1331     1728
```

raises the elements of g to the corresponding elements in h. In this case, the first row is unchanged, since the first row of h contains ones, the second row is squared, and the third row is cubed.

The following example shows that scalar and array operations can be combined:

```
>> g.^(h-1)
ans =
     1     1     1     1
     5     6     7     8
    81   100   121   144
```

The two forms of exponentiation that have scalar parts are further examples of scalar expansion. The results make intuitive sense if the scalars involved are first expanded to the size of the array and element-by-element exponentiation is then applied.

The following table summarizes basic array operations:

Element-by-Element Operation	**Representative Data** A = [a1 a2 ... an], B = [b1 b2 ... bn], c = <a *scalar*>
Scalar addition	A+c = [a1+c a2+c ... an+c]
Scalar subtraction	A-c = [a1-c a2-c ... an-c]
Scalar multiplication	A*c = [a1*c a2*c ... an*c]
Scalar division	A/c = c\A = [a1/c a2/c ... an/c]

Array addition	`A+B = [a1+b1 a2+b2 ... an+bn]`
Array multiplication	`A.*B = [a1*b1 a2*b2 ... an*bn]`
Array right division	`A./B = [a1/b1 a2/b2 ... an/bn]`
Array left division	`A.\B = [a1\b1 a2\b2 ... an\bn]`
Array exponentiation	`A.^c = [a1^c a2^c ... an^c]`
	`c.^A = [c^a1 c^a2 ... c^an]`
	`A.^B = [a1^b1 a2^b2 ... an^bn]`

5.7 STANDARD ARRAYS

Because of the general utility of standard arrays, MATLAB provides functions for creating a number of them. Standard arrays include those containing all ones or all zeros, identity matrices, arrays of random numbers, diagonal arrays, and arrays whose elements are a given constant. The following are examples:

```
>> ones(3)
ans =
     1     1     1
     1     1     1
     1     1     1
>> zeros(2,5)
ans =
     0     0     0     0     0
     0     0     0     0     0
>> size(g)
ans =
     3     4
>> ones(size(g))
ans =
     1     1     1     1
     1     1     1     1
     1     1     1     1
```

When called with a single input argument, `ones(n)` or `zeros(n)`, MATLAB creates an `n`-by-`n` array containing ones or zeros, respectively. When called with two input arguments, `ones(r,c)` or `zeros(r,c)`, MATLAB creates an array having `r` rows and `c` columns. To create an array of ones or zeros that is the same size as another array, use the `size` function (discussed later in this chapter) in the argument of ones or `zeros`.

In the code

```
>> eye(4)
ans =
     1     0     0     0
     0     1     0     0
     0     0     1     0
     0     0     0     1
>> eye(2,4)
ans =
     1     0     0     0
     0     1     0     0
>> eye(4,2)
ans =
     1     0
     0     1
     0     0
     0     0
```

the function eye produces identity matrices by using the same syntax style as that used to produce arrays of zeros and ones. An identity matrix or array is all zeros, except for the elements `A(i,i)`, where `i = 1:min(r,c)`, in which `min(r,c)` is the minimum of the number of rows and columns in `A`. In the code

```
>> rand(3)
ans =
    0.9501    0.4860    0.4565
    0.2311    0.8913    0.0185
    0.6068    0.7621    0.8214
>> rand(1,5)
ans =
    0.4447    0.6154    0.7919    0.9218    0.7382
>> b = eye(3)
b =
     1     0     0
```

```
     0     1     0
     0     0     1
>> rand(size(b))
ans =
    0.1763    0.9169    0.0579
    0.4057    0.4103    0.3529
    0.9355    0.8937    0.8132
```

the function rand produces uniformly distributed random arrays whose elements lie between 0 and 1. On the other hand, the function randn produces arrays whose elements are samples from a ***zero-mean, unit-variance*** normal distribution:

```
>> randn(2)
ans =
   -0.4326    0.1253
   -1.6656    0.2877
>> randn(2,5)
ans =
   -1.1465    1.1892    0.3273   -0.1867   -0.5883
    1.1909   -0.0376    0.1746    0.7258    2.183
```

The function diag creates diagonal arrays in which a vector can be placed at any location parallel to the main diagonal of an array:

```
>> a = 1:4  % start with a simple vector
a =
     1     2     3     4
>> diag(a)  % place elements on the main diagonal
ans =
     1     0     0     0
     0     2     0     0
     0     0     3     0
     0     0     0     4
>> diag(a,1)  % place elements 1 place up from diagonal
ans =
     0     1     0     0     0
     0     0     2     0     0
```

```
     0     0     0     3     0
     0     0     0     0     4
     0     0     0     0     0
>> diag(a,-2) % place elements 2 places down from diagonal

ans =
     0     0     0     0     0     0
     0     0     0     0     0     0
     1     0     0     0     0     0
     0     2     0     0     0     0
     0     0     3     0     0     0
     0     0     0     4     0     0
```

With the preceding standard arrays, there are several ways to create an array whose elements all have the same value. Some of them are as follows:

```
>> d = pi;  % choose pi for this example
>> d*ones(3,4)  % slowest method (scalar-array multiplication)
ans =
    3.1416    3.1416    3.1416    3.1416
    3.1416    3.1416    3.1416    3.1416
    3.1416    3.1416    3.1416    3.1416
>> d+zeros(3,4) % slower method (scalar-array addition)
ans =
    3.1416    3.1416    3.1416    3.1416
    3.1416    3.1416    3.1416    3.1416
    3.1416    3.1416    3.1416    3.1416
>> d(ones(3,4))  % fast method (array addressing)
ans =
    3.1416    3.1416    3.1416    3.1416
    3.1416    3.1416    3.1416    3.1416
    3.1416    3.1416    3.1416    3.1416
>> repmat(d,3,4)  % fastest method (optimum array addressing)
ans =
    3.1416    3.1416    3.1416    3.1416
    3.1416    3.1416    3.1416    3.1416
    3.1416    3.1416    3.1416    3.1416
```

For small arrays, all of the methods used in this example are fine. However, as the array grows in size, the multiplications required in the scalar multiplication approach slow the procedure down. Since addition is often faster than multiplication, the next-best approach is to add the desired scalar to an array of zeros. Although they are not intuitive, the last two methods explained are the fastest for large arrays. They both involve array indexing, as described earlier.

The solution `d(ones(r,c))` creates an `r`-by-`c` array of ones and then uses this array to index and duplicate the scalar `d`. Creating the temporary array of ones takes time and uses memory, thereby slowing down this approach, despite the fact that no floating-point mathematics are used. The solution `repmat(d,r,c)` calls the function `repmat`, which stands for replicate matrix. For scalar `d`, this function performs the following steps:

```
D(r*c) = d;             % a row vector whose (r*c)-th element is d
D(:) = d;               % scalar expansion to fill all elements of D with d
D = reshape(D,r,c); % reshape the vector into the desired r-by-c shape
```

This MATLAB code uses scalar expansion to create a vector having `r*c` elements all equal to `d`. The vector is then reshaped, by using the function `reshape`, into an `r`-by-`c` array. (The functions `repmat` and `reshape` are discussed in more detail later.)

5.8 ARRAY MANIPULATION

Because arrays are fundamental to MATLAB, there are many ways to manipulate them in MATLAB. Once arrays are formed, MATLAB provides powerful ways to insert, extract, and rearrange subsets of arrays by identifying subscripts of interest. Knowledge of these features is a key to using MATLAB efficiently. To illustrate the array manipulation features of MATLAB, consider the following examples:

```
>> A = [1 2 3;4 5 6;7 8 9]
A =
     1     2     3
     4     5     6
     7     8     9
>> A(3,3) = 0  % set element in 3rd row, 3rd column to zero
A =
     1     2     3
```

```
     4     5     6
     7     8     0
```

The preceding code changes the element in the third row and third column to zero. The code

```
>> A(2,6) = 1  % set element in 2nd row, 6th column to one
A =
     1     2     3     0     0     0
     4     5     6     0     0     1
     7     8     0     0     0     0
```

places the number one in the second row, sixth column. Since A does not have six columns, the size of A is increased as necessary, and filled with zeros, so that the array remains rectangular.

The code

```
>> A(:,4) = 4
A =
     1     2     3     4     0     0
     4     5     6     4     0     1
     7     8     0     4     0     0
```

sets the fourth column of A equal to 4. Since 4 is a scalar, it is expanded to fill all of the elements specified. This is another example of scalar expansion. MATLAB performs scalar expansion to simplify statements that can be interpreted unambiguously. For example, the preceding statement is equivalent to the following, more cumbersome, statement:

```
>> A(:,4) = [4;4;4]
A =
     1     2     3     4     0     0
     4     5     6     4     0     1
     7     8     0     4     0     0
>> A(:,4) = [4 4 4]  % but a row can't be squeezed into a column!

??? In an assignment  A(:,matrix) = B, the number of elements in
the subscript of A and the number of columns in B must be the same.
```

Let's start over and look at other array manipulations. The code

```
>> A = [1 2 3;4 5 6;7 8 9];  % restore original data

>> B = A(3:-1:1,1:3)
B =
     7     8     9
     4     5     6
     1     2     3

>> B = A(end:-1:1,1:3)  % same as above
B =
     7     8     9
     4     5     6
     1     2     3
```

creates an array B by taking the rows of A in reverse order. The word end automatically denotes the final or largest index for a given dimension. In this example, end signifies the largest row index 3. The code

```
>> B = A(3:-1:1,:)
B =
     7     8     9
     4     5     6
     1     2     3
```

does the same as the previous example. The final single colon means take all columns. That is, : is equivalent to 1:3 in this example, because A has three columns. The code

```
>> C = [A B(:,[1 3])]
C =
     1     2     3     7     9
     4     5     6     4     6
     7     8     9     1     3
```

creates C by appending, or concatenating, all rows in the first and third columns of B to the right of A. Similarly, the code

```
>> B = A(1:2,2:3)
```

```
B =

     2     3
     5     6

>> B = A(1:2,2:end)  % same as above
B =

     2     3
     5     6
```

creates B by extracting the first two rows and last two columns of A. Once again, colon notation is used to create index vectors that identify the array elements to extract. In the second instance just shown, end is used to denote the final or largest column index. The statement

```
>> C = [1 3]
C =
     1     3
>> B = A(C,C)
B =
     1     3
     7     9
```

uses the array C to index the array A, rather than specify them directly by using the colon notation `start:increment:end` or `start:end`. In this example, B is formed from the first and third rows and first and third columns of A. The code

```
>> B = A(:)
B =
     1
     4
     7
     2
     5
     8
     3
     6
     9
```

builds B by stretching A into a column vector and taking its columns one at a time, in order, which is the simplest form of reshaping an array into an array that has different dimensions, but the same number of total elements.

In MATLAB, the statement

```
>> B = B.'
B =
     1     4     7     2     5     8     3     6     9

>> B = reshape(A,1,9)  % reshape A into 1-by-9
B =
     1     4     7     2     5     8     3     6     9
>> B = reshape(A,[1 9])
B =
     1     4     7     2     5     8     3     6     9
```

illustrates the dot-transpose operation introduced earlier, as well as the function `reshape`. In this case, `reshape` works with the indices, supplied as separate function arguments, or supplied as a single vector argument. The code

```
>> B = A  % copy A into B
B =
     1     2     3
     4     5     6
     7     8     9
>> B(:,2) = []
B =
     1     3
     4     6
     7     9
```

redefines B by throwing away all rows in the second column of the original B. When you set something equal to the empty matrix or empty array [], it is deleted, causing the array to collapse into what remains. Note that you must delete whole rows or columns, so that the result remains rectangular.
The statement

```
>> C = B.'
C =
     1     4     7
     3     6     9
```

```
>> reshape(B,2,3) % reshape is not equivalent to transpose
ans =
     1     7     6
     4     3     9
```

illustrates the transpose of an array and demonstrates that reshape is not the same as transpose. The transpose operator converts the *i*th row to the *i*th column of the result, and so the original 3-by-2 array becomes a 2-by-3 array.
The code

```
>> C(2,:) = []
C =
     1     4     7
```

throws out the second row of C, leaving a row vector, while the code

```
>> A(2,:) = C
A =
     1     2     3
     1     4     7
     7     8     9
```

replaces the second row of A with C. The MATLAB code

```
>> B = A(:,[2 2 2 2]) % create new B array
B =
     2     2     2     2
     4     4     4     4
     8     8     8     8
>> B = A(:,2+zeros(1,4))  % [2 2 2 2]=2+zeros(1,4)
B =
     2     2     2     2
     4     4     4     4
     8     8     8     8
>> B = repmat(A(:,2),1,4)  % replicate 2nd column into 4 columns
B =
     2     2     2     2
     4     4     4     4
     8     8     8     8
```

creates B three ways by duplicating all rows in the second column of A four times. The last approach is fastest for large arrays. The statement

```
>> A, C  % show A and C again
A =
     1     2     3
     1     4     7
     7     8     9
C =
     1     4     7
>> A(2,2) = []
???  Indexed empty matrix assignment is not allowed.
```

shows that you can throw out only entire rows or columns. MATLAB simply does not know how to collapse an array when partial rows or columns are thrown out. Finally

```
>> C = A(4,:)
???  Index exceeds matrix dimensions.
```

produces an error since A does not have a fourth row. According to this result, indices must adhere to the following guidelines:

> If A(r,c) appears on the left-hand side of an equal sign and one or more elements specified by (r,c) do not exist, then zeros are added to A as needed, so that A(r,c) addresses known elements. However, on the right-hand side of an equal sign, all elements addressed by A(r,c) must exist or an error is returned.

Continuing on, consider the following:

```
>> C(1:2,:) = A
??? Subscripted assignment dimension mismatch.
```

This example shows that you can't squeeze one array into another array of a different size.

However, the statement

```
>> C(3:4,:) = A(2:3,:)
C =
     1     4     7
     0     0     0
```

```
    1     4     7
    7     8     9
```

reveals that you can place the second and third columns of A into the same-size area of C. Since the second through fourth rows of C did not exist, they are created as necessary. Moreover, the second row of C is unspecified, and so it is filled with zeros.

The code

```
>> A = [1 2 3;4 5 6;7 8 9]  % fresh data
A =
    1     2     3
    4     5     6
    7     8     9
>> A(:,2:3)          % a peek at what's addressed next
ans =
    2     3
    5     6
    8     9
>> G(1:6) = A(:,2:3)
G =
    2     5     8     3     6     9
```

creates a row vector G by extracting all rows in the second and third columns of A. Note that the shapes of the matrices are different on both sides of the equal sign. The elements of A are inserted into the elements of G by going down the rows of the first column and then down the rows of the second column.

When (:) appears on the left-hand side of the equal sign, it signifies that elements will be taken from the right-hand side and placed into the array on the left-hand side without changing its shape. In the following example, this process extracts the second and third columns of A and inserts them into the column vector H:

```
>> H = ones(6,1);    % create a column array
>> H(:) = A(:,2:3)  % fill H without changing its shape
H =
    2
    5
    8
    3
```

```
     6
     9
```

Of course, for this code to work, both sides must address the same number of elements.

When the right-hand side of an assignment is a scalar and the left-hand side is an array, ***scalar expansion*** is used. For example, the code

```
>> A(2,:) = 0
A =
     1     2     3
     0     0     0
     7     8     9
```

replaces the second row of A with zeros. The single zero on the right-hand side is expanded to fill all the indices specified on the left. This example is equivalent to

```
>> A(2,:) = [0 0 0]
A =
     1     2     3
     0     0     0
     7     8     9
```

Scalar expansion occurs whenever a scalar is used in a location calling for an array. MATLAB automatically expands the scalar to fill all requested locations and then performs the operation dictated. The code

```
>> A(1,[1 3]) = pi
A =
    3.1416    2.0000    3.1416
         0         0         0
    7.0000    8.0000    9.0000
```

is yet another example in which the scalar π is expanded to fill two locations. Consider again what the function `reshape` does with scalar input. Let's create a 2-by-4 array containing the number 2:

```
>> D(2*4) = 2  % create array with 8 elements
D =
     0     0     0     0     0     0     0     2
>> D(:) = 2  % scalar expansion
```

```
D =
     2     2     2     2     2     2     2     2
>> D = reshape(D,2,4)  % reshape
D =
     2     2     2     2
     2     2     2     2
```

The first line `D(2*4) = 2` causes a row vector of length 8 to be created and places 2 in the last column. Next, `D(:) = 2` uses scalar expansion to fill all elements of `D` with 2. Finally, the result is reshaped into the desired dimensions.

Sometimes, it is desirable to perform some mathematical operation between a vector and a two-dimensional (2-D) array. For example, consider these arrays:

```
>> A = reshape(1:12,3,4)'
A =
     1     2     3
     4     5     6
     7     8     9
    10    11    12
>> r = [3 2 1]
r =
     3     2     1
```

Suppose that we wish to subtract `r(i)` from the `i`th column of `A`. One way of accomplishing it is as follows:

```
>> Ar = [A(:,1)-r(1) A(:,2)-r(2) A(:,3)-r(3)]
Ar =
    -2     0     2
     1     3     5
     4     6     8
     7     9    11
```

Alternatively, we can use indexing:

```
>> R = r([1 1 1 1],:) % duplicate r to have 4 rows
R =
     3     2     1
     3     2     1
```

```
     3     2     1
     3     2     1
>> Ar = A - R % now use element by element subtraction
Ar =
    -2     0     2
     1     3     5
     4     6     8
     7     9    11
```

The array R can also be computed faster and more generally by using the functions `ones` and `size` or by using the function `repmat`, all of which are discussed later. Consider the following example:

```
>> R = r(ones(size(A,1),1),:) % historically this is Tony's trick
R =
     3     2     1
     3     2     1
     3     2     1
     3     2     1
>> R = repmat(r,size(A,1),1)  % often faster than Tony's trick
R =
     3     2     1
     3     2     1
     3     2     1
     3     2     1
```

In this example, `size(A,1)` returns the number of rows in A.

Sometimes, it is more convenient to address array elements with a single *index*. ***When a single index is used in MATLAB, the index counts down the rows, proceeding column by column, starting with the first column***. Here is an example:

```
>> D = reshape(1:12,3,4)  % new data
D =
     1     4     7    10
     2     5     8    11
     3     6     9    12
```

```
>> D(2)
ans =
     2
>> D(5)
ans =
     5

>> D(end)
ans =
    12
>> D(4:7)
ans =
     4     5     6     7
```

The MATLAB functions sub2ind and ind2sub perform the arithmetic to convert to and from a single index to row and column subscripts:

```
>> sub2ind(size(D),2,4)   % find single index from row and column
ans =
    11
>> [r,c] = ind2sub(size(D),11)   % find row and column from single index
r =
     2
c =
     4
```

The element in the second row, fourth column is the 11th indexed element. Note that these two functions need to know the size of the array to search (i.e., size(D), rather than the array D itself).

> ***Subscripts*** refer to the row and column locations of elements of an array; for instance, A(2,3) refers to the element in the second row and third column of A. The ***index*** of an element in an array refers to its position relative to the element in the first row, first column, having index 1. Indices count down the rows first and then proceed across the columns of an array. That is, the indices count in the order in which the subscripts appear; for example, if D has three rows, D(8) is the second element in the third column of D.

In addition to addressing arrays on the basis of their subscripts, ***logical arrays*** that result from logical operations (to be discussed more thoroughly later) can also be used if the size of the array is equal to that of the array it is addressing.

In this case, True (1) elements are retained, and False (0) elements are discarded. For example,

```
>> x = -3:3  % Create data
x =
    -3    -2    -1     0     1     2     3
>> abs(x)>1
ans =
     1     1     0     0     0     1     1
```

returns a logical array with ones (True), where the absolute value of x is greater than one and zeros (False) elsewhere. (The chapter on logical expressions contains more detailed information.)

The statement

```
>> y = x(abs(x)>1)
y =
    -3    -2     2     3
```

creates y by taking those values of x where its absolute value is greater than 1.

Note, however, that even though abs(x)>1 produces the array [1 1 0 0 0 1 1], it is not equivalent to a numerical array containing those values; that is, the code

```
>> y = x([1 1 0 0 0 1 1])
??? Subscript indices must either be real positive integers or logicals.
```

gives an error, even though the abs(x)>1 and [1 1 0 0 0 1 1] appear to be the same vector. In the second case, [1 1 0 0 0 1 1] is a ***numeric array*** as opposed to a ***logical array***. The difference between these two visually equal arrays can be identified by using the function class:

```
>> class(abs(x)>1)   % logical result from logical comparison
ans =
logical
>> class([1 1 0 0 0 1 1]) % double precision array
ans =
double
```

Alternatively, the functions islogical and isnumeric return logical True (1) or False (0) to identify data types:

```
>> islogical(abs(x)>1)
ans =
     1
>> islogical([1 1 0 0 0 1 1])
ans =
     0
>> isnumeric(abs(x)>1)
ans =
     0
>> isnumeric([1 1 0 0 0 1 1])
ans =
     1
```

Because of the differences between logical and numeric arrays, MATLAB generates an error when executing `x([1 1 0 0 0 1 1])`, because MATLAB arrays do not have indices at zero.

Quite naturally, MATLAB provides the function `logical` for converting numeric arrays to logical arrays:

```
>> y = x(logical([1 1 0 0 0 1 1]))
y =
    -3    -2     2     3
```

Once again, we have the desired result.

To summarize:

> Specifying array subscripts with numerical arrays extracts the elements having the given numerical indices. On the other hand, specifying array subscripts with logical arrays, which are returned by logical expressions and the function `logical`, extracts elements that are logical True (1).

Just as the functions `ones` and `zeros` are useful for creating numeric arrays, the functions `true` and `false` are useful for creating arrays of logical arrays containing True and False values, respectively:

```
>> true
ans =
     1
>> true(2,3)
```

```
ans =
     1     1     1
     1     1     1
>> false
ans =
     0
>> false(1,6)
ans =
     0     0     0     0     0     0
```

Although these results appear to be equal to results returned by equivalent statements that use ones and zeros, they are *logical* arrays, not numeric.

Logical arrays work on two-dimensional arrays, as well as on vectors:

```
>> B = [5 -3;2 -4]   % new data
B =
     5    -3
     2    -4
>> x = abs(B)>2   % logical result
x =
     1     1
     0     1
>> y = B(x)   % grab True values
y =
     5
    -3
     4
```

However, the final result is returned as a column vector, since there is no way to define a two-dimensional array having only three elements. No matter how many elements are extracted, MATLAB extracts all of the true elements by using single-index order and then forms or reshapes the result into a column vector.

The preceding array-addressing techniques are summarized in the following table:

Array Addressing	Description
A(r,c)	Addresses a subarray within A defined by the index vector of desired rows in r and an index vector of desired columns in c

Array Addressing	Description
A(r,:)	Addresses a subarray within A defined by the index vector of desired rows in r and all columns
A(:,c)	Addresses a subarray within A defined by all rows and the index vector of desired columns in c
A(:)	Addresses all elements of A as a column vector taken column by column. If A(:) appears on the left-hand side of the equal sign, it means to fill A with elements from the right hand-side of the equal sign without changing A's shape.
A(k)	Addresses a subarray within A defined by the single index vector k, as if A were the column vector A(:)
A(x)	Addresses a subarray within A defined by the logical array x. Note that x should be the same size as A. If x is shorter than A, the missing values in x are assumed to be False. If x is longer than A, all extra elements in x must be False.

5.9 ARRAY SORTING

Given a data vector, a common task required in numerous applications is sorting. In MATLAB, the function sort performs this task:

```
>> x = randperm(8)  % new data

x =

     7     5     2     1     3     6     4     8

>> xs = sort(x)  % sort ascending by default

xs =

     1     2     3     4     5     6     7     8

>> xs = sort(x,'ascend')  % sort ascending

xs =

     1     2     3     4     5     6     7     8

>> [xs,idx] = sort(x)  % return sort index as well

xs =

     1     2     3     4     5     6     7     8

idx =

     4     3     5     7     2     6     1     8
```

As shown, the sort function returns one or two outputs. The first is an ascending sort of the input argument, and the second is the sort index—for example, xs(k) = x(idx(k)).

> Note that, when a MATLAB function returns two or more variables, they are enclosed by square brackets on the left-hand side of the equal sign. This syntax is different from the array manipulation syntax discussed previously, in which `[a,b]` on the right-hand side of the equal sign builds a new array, with `b` appended to the right of `a`.

In prior versions of MATLAB, sorting in the descending direction required turning around the `sort` function output by using array-indexing techniques. For example, consider the following code:

```
>> xsd = xs(end:-1:1)
xsd =
     8     7     6     5     4     3     2     1
>> idxd = idx(end:-1:1)
idxd =
     8     1     6     2     7     5     3     4
```

With MATLAB Version 7, the sort direction can be specified when calling the `sort` function:

```
>> xs = sort(x,'descend')  % sort descending
xs =
     8     7     6     5     4     3     2     1
```

When presented with a two-dimensional array, `sort` acts differently. For example, in the code

```
>> A = [randperm(6);randperm(6);randperm(6);randperm(6)] % new data
A =
     1     2     5     6     4     3
     4     2     6     5     3     1
     2     3     6     1     4     5
     3     5     1     2     4     6
>> [As,idx] = sort(A)
As =
     1     2     1     1     3     1
     2     2     5     2     4     3
     3     3     6     5     4     5
     4     5     6     6     4     6
```

```
idx =
     1     1     4     3     2     2
     3     2     1     4     1     1
     4     3     2     2     3     3
     2     4     3     1     4     4
```

the sort function sorts, in ascending order, each column independently of the others, and the indices returned are those for each column. In many cases, we are more interested in sorting an array on the basis of the sort of a specific column. In MATLAB, this task is easy. For example, in the code

```
>> [tmp,idx] =  sort(A(:,4)); % sort 4-th column only

>> As = A(idx,:) % rearrange rows in all columns using idx
As =
     2     3     6     1     4     5
     3     5     1     2     4     6
     4     2     6     5     3     1
     1     2     5     6     4     3
```

the rows of As are just the rearranged rows of A, in which the fourth column of As is sorted in ascending order.

MATLAB is a flexible program. Rather than sort each column, it is also possible to sort each row. By using a second argument to sort, you can specify in which direction to sort:

```
>> As = sort(A,2) % sort across 2-nd dimension
As =
     1     2     3     4     5     6
     1     2     3     4     5     6
     1     2     3     4     5     6
     1     2     3     4     5     6
>> As = sort(A,1)  % same as sort(A)
As =
     1     2     1     1     3     1
     2     2     5     2     4     3
     3     3     6     5     4     5
     4     5     6     6     4     6
```

Since in A(r,c), the row dimension appears first, sort(A,1) means to sort down the rows. Because the column dimension appears second, sort(A,2) means to sort across the columns. Although not shown, 'descend' can be appended to the function calls (e.g., sort(A,1,'descend')), to return a descending sort. (The chapter on data analysis contains much more information about the sort function.)

5.10 SUBARRAY SEARCHING

Many times it is desirable to know the indices or subscripts of the elements of an array that satisfy some relational expression. In MATLAB, this task is performed by the function find, which returns the subscripts when a relational expression is True, as for example, in the following code:

```
>> x = -3:3
x =
    -3    -2    -1     0     1     2     3
>> k = find(abs(x)>1)  % finds those subscripts where abs(x)>1
k =
     1     2     6     7
>> y = x(k)  % creates y using the indices in k.
y =
    -3    -2     2     3
>> y = x(abs(x)>1) % creates the same y vector by logical addressing
y =
    -3    -2     2     3
```

The find function also works for two-dimensional arrays:

```
>> A = [1 2 3;4 5 6;7 8 9] % new data
A =
     1     2     3
     4     5     6
     7     8     9
>> [i,j] = find(A>5) % i and j are not equal to sqrt(-1) here
i =
     3
     3
     2
     3
```

```
j =

     1
     2
     3
     3
```

Here, the indices stored in `i` and `j` are the associated row and column indices, respectively, where the relational expression is True. That is, `A(i(1),j(1))` is the first element of A, where A>5, and so on.

Alternatively, `find` returns single indices for two-dimensional arrays:

```
>> k = find(A>5)
k =

     3
     6
     8
     9
```

Of the two index sets returned for two-dimensional arrays, this latter single-index form is often more useful:

```
>> A(k)  % look at elements greater than 5
ans =

     7
     8
     6
     9

>> A(k) = 0  % set elements addressed by k to zero
A =

     1     2     3
     4     5     0
     0     0     0

>> A = [1 2 3;4 5 6;7 8 9]  % restore data
A =

     1     2     3
     4     5     6
     7     8     9
```

```
>> A(i,j)  % this is A([3 3 2 3],[1 2 3 3])
ans =
     7     8     9     9
     7     8     9     9
     4     5     6     6
     7     8     9     9
>> A(i,j) = 0  % this is A([3 3 2 3],[1 2 3 3]) also
A =
     1     2     3
     0     0     0
     0     0     0
```

These A(i,j) cases are not as easy to understand as the preceding single-index cases. To assume that A(k) is equivalent to A(i,j) is a common MATLAB indexing mistake. Rather, A(i,j) in the previous example is equivalent to

```
>> [A(3,1) A(3,2) A(3,3) A(3,3)
    A(3,1) A(3,2) A(3,3) A(3,3)
    A(2,1) A(2,2) A(2,3) A(2,3)
    A(3,1) A(3,2) A(3,3) A(3,3)]
ans =
     7     8     9     9
     7     8     9     9
     4     5     6     6
     7     8     9     9
```

where the first-row index in i is coupled with all of the column indices in j to form the first row in the result. Then, the second-row index in i is coupled with the column indices in j to form the second row in the result, and so on. Given the form in this example, the diagonal elements of A(i,j) are equal to those of A(k). Therefore, the two approaches are equal if the diagonal elements of A(i,j) are retained. In the code

```
>> diag(A(i,j))
ans =
     7
     8
     6
     9
```

while diag (A(i,j)) = A(k), simply entering A(k) is preferred, as it does not create an intermediate square array.

Similarly, A(i,j) = 0 is equivalent to

```
>> A(3,1)=0; A(3,2)=0; A(3,3)=0; A(3,3)=0; % i(1) with all j
>> A(3,1)=0; A(3,2)=0; A(3,3)=0; A(3,3)=0; % i(2) with all j
>> A(2,1)=0; A(2,2)=0; A(2,3)=0; A(2,3)=0; % i(3) with all j
>> A(3,1)=0; A(3,2)=0; A(3,3)=0; A(3,3)=0  % i(4) with all j
A =
     1     2     3
     0     0     0
     0     0     0
```

Based on the above equivalents, it is clear that A(i,j) is not generally as useful as A(k) for subarray searching using find.

When you only need to find a few indices, the find function offers an alternative syntax that avoids searching the entire array. For example, in the code

```
>> x = randperm(8) % new data
x =
     8     2     7     4     3     6     5     1
>> find(x>4) % find all values greater than 4
ans =
     1     3     6     7
>> find(x>4,1) % find first value greater than 4
ans =
     1
>> find(x>4,1,'first') % same as above
ans =
     1
>> find(x>4,2) % find first two values greater than 4
ans =
     1     3
>> find(x>4,2,'last') % find last two values greater than 4
ans =
     6     7
```

find(expr,n), find(expr,n,'first') and find(expr,n,'last'), where the expression expr is True, return up to n indices. That is, n defines the maximum number of indices returned. If fewer indices satisfying expr exist, fewer are returned.

The preceding concepts are summarized in the following table:

Array Searching	Description
i=find(X)	Return single *indices* of the array X, where its elements are nonzero or True
[r,c]=find(X)	Return row and column *subscripts* of the array X, where its elements are nonzero or True
find(X,n) or find(X,n,'first')	Starting at the beginning of the array X, returns up to n indices, where X is nonzero or True
find(X,n,'last')	Starting at the end of the array X, returns up to n indices, where X is nonzero or True

In addition to using the function find to identify specific values within an array, using the maximum and minimum values and their locations within an array is often helpful. MATLAB provides the functions max and min to accomplish these tasks:

```
>> v = rand(1,6)   % new data
v =
    0.3046    0.1897    0.1934    0.6822    0.3028    0.5417

>> max(v)   % return maximum value
ans =
    0.6822

>> [mx,i] = max(v)   % maximum value and its index
mx =
    0.6822
i =
    4

>> min(v)   % return minimum value
ans =
    0.1897

>> [mn,i] = min(v)   % minimum value and its index
```

```
mn =

   0.1897

i =

   2
```

For two-dimensional arrays, `min` and `max` behave a little differently. For example, in the code

```
>> A = rand(4,6)  % new data
A =

   0.1509   0.8537   0.8216   0.3420   0.7271   0.3704
   0.6979   0.5936   0.6449   0.2897   0.3093   0.7027
   0.3784   0.4966   0.8180   0.3412   0.8385   0.5466
   0.8600   0.8998   0.6602   0.5341   0.5681   0.4449

>> [mx,r] = max(A)

mx =

   0.8600   0.8998   0.8216   0.5341   0.8385   0.7027

r =

   4   4   1   4   3   2

>> [mn,r] = min(A)

mn =

   0.1509   0.4966   0.6449   0.2897   0.3093   0.3704

r =

   1   3   2   2   2   1
```

`mx` is a vector containing the maximum of each column of `A`, and `r` is the row index where the maximum appears. The same principle applies to `mn` and `r`, relative to the function `min`. To find the overall minimum or maximum of a 2-D array, one can take one of two approaches:

```
>> mmx = max(mx)  % apply max again to prior result

mmx =

   0.8998

>> [mmx,i] = max(A(:)) % reshape A as a column vector first

mmx =

   0.8998

i =

   8
```

The first of these is essentially max(max(A)), which requires two function calls. The second is preferred in many situations, because it also returns the single index where the maximum occurs (i.e., mmx = A(i)). (The latter approach also works for multidimensional arrays, which are discussed in the next chapter.)

When an array has duplicate minima or maxima, the indices returned by min and max are the first ones encountered. To find all minima and maxima requires the use of the find function:

```
>> x = [1 4 6 3 2 1 6]
x =
     1     4     6     3     2     1     6
>> mx = max(x)
mx =
     6
>> i = find(x==mx) % indices of values equal to mx
i =
     3     7
```

(The chapter on data analysis contains more information about the functions min and max.)

5.11 ARRAY MANIPULATION FUNCTIONS

In addition to the arbitrary array-addressing and manipulation capabilities described in the preceding sections, MATLAB provides several functions that implement common array manipulations. Many of these manipulations are easy to follow:

```
>> A = [1 2 3;4 5 6;7 8 9]  % fresh data
A =
     1     2     3
     4     5     6
     7     8     9
>> flipud(A)  % flip array in up-down direction
ans =
     7     8     9
     4     5     6
     1     2     3
>> fliplr(A)  % flip array in the left-right direction
```

```
ans =
     3     2     1
     6     5     4
     9     8     7
>> rot90(A)  % rotate array 90 degrees counterclockwise
ans =
     3     6     9
     2     5     8
     1     4     7
>> rot90(A,2)  % rotate array 2*90 degrees counterclockwise
ans =
     9     8     7
     6     5     4
     3     2     1

>> A = [1 2 3;4 5 6;7 8 9] % recall data
A =
     1     2     3
     4     5     6
     7     8     9
>> circshift(A,1) % circularly shift rows down by 1
ans =
     7     8     9
     1     2     3
     4     5     6
>> circshift(A,[0 1]) % circularly shift columns right by 1
ans =
     3     1     2
     6     4     5
     9     7     8
>> circshift(A,[-1 1]) % shift rows up by 1 and columns right by 1
ans =
     6     4     5
     9     7     8
     3     1     2
```

```
>> B = 1:12  % more data
B =
     1     2     3     4     5     6     7     8     9    10    11    12
>> reshape(B,2,6)  % reshape to 2 rows, 6 columns, fill by columns
ans =
     1     3     5     7     9    11
     2     4     6     8    10    12

>> reshape(B,[2 6]) % equivalent to above
ans =
     1     3     5     7     9    11
     2     4     6     8    10    12
>> reshape(B,3,4)  % reshape to 3 rows, 4 columns, fill by columns
ans =
     1     4     7    10
     2     5     8    11
     3     6     9    12
>> reshape(B,3,[]) % MATLAB figures out how many columns are needed
ans =
     1     4     7    10
     2     5     8    11
     3     6     9    12

>> reshape(B,[],6) % MATLAB figures out how many rows are needed
ans =
     1     3     5     7     9    11
     2     4     6     8    10    12
>> reshape(A,3,2)  % A has more than 3*2 elements, OOPS!
??? Error using ==> reshape
To RESHAPE the number of elements must not change.
>> reshape(A,1,9)  % stretch A into a row vector
ans =
     1     4     7     2     5     8     3     6     9

>> A(:)' % convert to column and transpose; same as the above
```

```
ans =
     1     4     7     2     5     8     3     6     9

>> reshape(A,[],3) % MATLAB figures out how many rows are needed
ans =
     1     2     3
     4     5     6
     7     8     9
```

The following functions extract parts of an array to create another array:

```
>> A  % remember what A is
A =
     1     2     3
     4     5     6
     7     8     9
>> diag(A)  % extract diagonal using diag
ans =
     1
     5
     9
>> diag(ans)  % remember this? same function, different action
ans =
     1     0     0
     0     5     0
     0     0     9
>> triu(A)  % extract upper triangular part
ans =
     1     2     3
     0     5     6
     0     0     9
>> tril(A)  % extract lower triangular part
ans =
     1     0     0
     4     5     0
     7     8     9
```

```
>> tril(A) - diag(diag(A)) % lower triangular part with no diagonal
ans =
     0     0     0
     4     0     0
     7     8     0
```

The following functions create arrays from other arrays:

```
>> a = [1 2;3 4]  % a smaller data array
a =
     1     2
     3     4
>> b = [0 1;-1 0]  % another smaller data array
b =
     0     1
    -1     0
>> kron(a,b)  % the Kronecker tensor product of a and b
ans =
     0     1     0     2
    -1     0    -2     0
     0     3     0     4
    -3     0    -4     0
```

The preceding kron(a,b) is equivalent to

```
>> [1*b 2*b
    3*b 4*b]
ans =
     0     1     0     2
    -1     0    -2     0
     0     3     0     4
    -3     0    -4     0
```

Now consider

```
>> kron(b,a)  % the Kronecker tensor product of b and a
ans =
     0     0     1     2
```

```
     0     0     3     4
    -1    -2     0     0
    -3    -4     0     0
```

The preceding kron(b,a) is equivalent to

```
>> [0*a 1*a
   -1*a 0*a]
ans =
     0     0     1     2
     0     0     3     4
    -1    -2     0     0
    -3    -4     0     0
```

So, kron(a,b) takes each element of its first argument, multiplies it by the second argument, and creates a block array.

One of the most useful array manipulation functions is repmat, which was introduced earlier:

```
>> a  % recall data
a =
     1     2
     3     4
>> repmat(a,1,3) % replicate a once down, 3 across
ans =
     1     2     1     2     1     2
     3     4     3     4     3     4
>> repmat(a,[1 3]) % equivalent to above
ans =
     1     2     1     2     1     2
     3     4     3     4     3     4
>> [a a a] % equivalent to above
ans =
     1     2     1     2     1     2
     3     4     3     4     3     4

>> repmat(a,2,2) % replicate a twice down, twice across
```

```
ans =
     1     2     1     2
     3     4     3     4
     1     2     1     2
     3     4     3     4
>> repmat(a,2) % same as repmat(a,2,2) and repmat(a,[2 2])
ans =
     1     2     1     2
     3     4     3     4
     1     2     1     2
     3     4     3     4
>> [a a; a a] % equivalent to above
ans =
     1     2     1     2
     3     4     3     4
     1     2     1     2
     3     4     3     4
```

As illustrated, the functions repmat and reshape accept indexing arguments in two ways. The indexing arguments can be passed as separate input arguments, or they can be passed as individual elements in a single-vector argument. In addition, for repmat, a single second-input argument repmat(A,n) is interpreted as repmat(A,[n n]).

Finally, to replicate a scalar to create an array that is the same size as another array, one can simply use repmat(d,size(A)):

```
>> A = reshape(1:12,[3 4]) % new data
A =
     1     4     7    10
     2     5     8    11
     3     6     9    12
>> repmat(pi,size(A)) % pi replicated to be the size of A
ans =
    3.1416    3.1416    3.1416    3.1416
    3.1416    3.1416    3.1416    3.1416
    3.1416    3.1416    3.1416    3.1416
```

(Note that the function size is discussed in the next section.)

5.12 ARRAY SIZE

In cases where the size of an array or vector is unknown, and is needed for some mathematical manipulation, MATLAB provides the utility functions `size`, `length`, and `numel`:

```
>> A = [1 2 3 4;5 6 7 8]
A =
     1     2     3     4
     5     6     7     8
>> s = size(A)
s =
     2     4
```

With one output argument, the `size` function returns a row vector whose first element is the number of rows, and whose second element is the number of columns:

```
>> [r,c] = size(A)
r =
     2
c =
     4
```

With two output arguments, `size` returns the number of rows in the first variable and the number of columns in the second variable:

```
>> r = size(A,1)   % number of rows
r =
     2
>> c = size(A,2)   % number of columns
c =
     4
```

Called with two input arguments, `size` returns either the number of rows or columns. The correspondence between the second argument to `size` and the number returned follows the order in which array elements are indexed. That is, `A(r,c)` has its row index `r` specified first and hence `size(A,1)` returns the number of rows. Likewise, `A(r,c)` has its column index `c` specified second and so `size(A,2)` returns the number of columns.

The function `numel` returns the total number of elements in an array:

```
>> numel(A)
ans =
     8
```

The function `length` returns the number of elements along the largest dimension. For example, the code

```
>> length(A)
ans =
     4
```

returns the number of rows or the number of columns, whichever is larger. For vectors, `length` returns the vector length:

```
>> B = -3:3
B =
    -3    -2    -1     0     1     2     3
>> length(B) % length of a row vector
ans =
     7
>> length(B') % length of a column vector
ans =
     7
```

The functions `size` and `length` also work for an array of zero dimension:

```
>> c = [] % you can create an empty variable!
c =
     []
>> size(c)
ans =
     0     0
>> d = zeros(3,0) % an array with one dimension nonzero!
d =
   Empty matrix: 3-by-0
>> size(d)
ans =
     3     0
```

```
>> length(d)
ans =
     0

>> max(size(d)) % maximum of elements of size(d)
ans =
     3
```

As shown, MATLAB allows arrays to have one zero and one nonzero dimension. For these arrays, length and maximum dimension are not the same.

These array size concepts are summarized in the following table:

Array Size	Description
`s=size(A)`	Returns a row vector `s` whose first element is the number of rows in `A`, and whose second element is the number of columns in `A`
`[r,c]=size(A)`	Returns two scalars, `r` and `c`, containing the number of rows and columns, respectively
`r=size(A,1)`	Returns the number of rows in `A`
`c=size(A,2)`	Returns the number of columns in `A`
`n=length(A)`	Returns `max(size(A))` for nonempty `A`, 0 when `A` has either zero rows or zero columns and the length of `A` if `A` is a vector
`n=max(size(A))`	Returns `length(A)` for nonempty `A`, and for empty `A` returns the length of any nonzero dimension of `A`
`n=numel(A)`	Returns the total number of elements in `A`

5.13 ARRAYS AND MEMORY UTILIZATION

In most modern computers, data transfer to and from memory is more time consuming than floating-point arithmetic, which has been fully integrated into most processors. Memory speed just hasn't kept pace with processor speed, and this has forced computer manufacturers to incorporate multiple levels of memory cache into their products in an attempt to keep processors supplied with data. In addition, computer users work with increasingly larger data sets (variables), which can easily exceed cache capacity. Consequently, efficient memory utilization is critical to effective computing.

MATLAB itself does not perform any explicit memory management. Memory allocation and deallocation within MATLAB use calls to standard C functions (`malloc`, `calloc`, `free`). Therefore, MATLAB relies on the compiler's implementation of these library functions to take appropriate, efficient, system-specific steps for memory allocation and deallocation. Given that there is an inherent tradeoff between memory use and execution speed, MATLAB purposely chooses to use more memory when doing so increases execution speed. Since MATLAB uses memory to gain performance, it is beneficial to consider how memory is allocated in the program and what can be done to minimize memory overuse and fragmentation.

When a variable is created with an assignment statement such as

```
>> P = zeros(100);
```

MATLAB requests a contiguous chunk of memory to store the variable, letting the compiler and the operating system determine where that chunk is allocated. If a variable is reassigned, as in

```
>> P = rand(5,6);
```

the original memory is deallocated, and a new allocation request is made for the new variable in its new size. Once again, it is up to the compiler and the operating system to figure out how to implement these tasks. Clearly, when the reassigned variable is larger than the original, a different chunk of contiguous memory is required to store the new data.

In a case where the variable reassignment just so happens to use exactly the same amount of memory, MATLAB still goes through the memory allocation and deallocation process:

```
>> P = zeros(5,6); % same size as earlier
>> P = ones(6,5);  % same number of elements as earlier
```

As a result, reusing variable names does not eliminate memory allocation or deallocation overhead. However, it does clear the memory used by prior data that are no longer needed. The exception to this reallocation is with scalars. For example, `a = 1` followed by `a = 2` simply copies the new value into the old memory location.

On the other hand, if an assignment statement addresses indices that already exist in a variable, the associated memory locations are updated, and no allocation or deallocation overhead is incurred. For example,

```
>> P(3,3) = 1;
```

does not force any memory-allocation calls, because `P(3,3)` already exists. The variable size remains the same, and hence, there's no need to find a different contiguous chunk of memory to store it. However, if an assignment statement increases the size of a variable, as in the code

```
>> P(8,1) = 1;
>> size(P)
ans =
     8     5
```

which makes P grow from 6-by-5 or 30 elements to 8-by-5 or 40 elements, MATLAB requests memory for the revised variable, copies the old variable into the new memory, and then deallocates the old memory chunk, thereby incurring allocation or deallocation overhead.

When all the indices of a variable are addressed in an assignment statement, such as

```
>> P(:) = ones(1,40);
```

the number of elements on the left- and right-hand sides must be equal. When this is true, MATLAB simply copies the data on the right-hand side into the memory that already exists on the left-hand side. No allocation or deallocation overhead is incurred. Furthermore, the dimensions of P remain unchanged:

```
>> size(P)
ans =
     8     5
```

In MATLAB, variables can be declared global in scope by using the `global` command. (This is discussed elsewhere in the text.) From a memory-management point of view, global variables do not behave any differently than ordinary variables. So there is neither benefit from, nor penalty for, using them.

One interesting thing that MATLAB does to improve performance is a feature called ***delayed copy***.

For example, in the code

```
>> A = zeros(10);
>> B = zeros(10);
>> C = B;
```

the variables A and B each have memory for 100 elements allocated to them. However, the variable C does not have any memory allocated to it. It shares the memory allocated to B. Copying of the data in B to a chunk of memory allocated to C does not take place until either B or C is modified. That is, a simple assignment, such as that shown does *not* immediately create a copy of the right-hand-side array in the left-hand-side variable. When an array is large, it is advantageous to delay the copy. That is, future references to C simply access the associated contents of B, and so to the user it appears that C is equal to B. Time is taken to copy the array B into the variable C only if the contents of B are about to change, or if the contents of C are about to be assigned new values by some MATLAB statement. While the time saved by this delayed-copy feature is insignificant for smaller arrays, it can lead to significant performance improvements for very large arrays.

The delayed-copy scheme applies to functions as well. When a function is called, for example, `myfunc(a,b,c)`, the arrays a, b, and c are not copied into the workspace of the function, unless the function modifies them in some way. By implementing a delayed copy, memory-allocation overhead is avoided, unless the function modifies the variable. As a result, if that function only reads data from the array, there is no performance penalty for passing a large array to a function. (This feature is covered in the chapter on M-file functions as well.)

When you call a function, it is common to pass the result of a computation or a function output directly to another function. For example, in the code

```
>> prod(size(A))
ans =
   100
```

the results from the function `size(A)` are passed directly to the function `prod`, without explicitly storing the result in a named variable. The memory used to execute this statement is identical to

```
>> tmp=size(A);
>> prod(tmp)
ans =
   100
```

In other words, even though the first statement did not explicitly create a variable to store the results from `size(A)`, MATLAB created an implicit variable and then passed it to the function `prod`. The only benefit gained by the first approach is that the implicit variable is automatically cleared after the function call.

In many applications, it is convenient to increase the size of an array as part of a computational procedure. Usually, this procedure is part of some looping structure, but for now, let's consider a simpler example:

```
>> A=1:5
A =
     1     2     3     4     5
>> B=6:10;
>> A=[A;B]
A =
     1     2     3     4     5
     6     7     8     9    10
>> C=11:15;
>> A=[A;C]
A =
```

```
     1     2     3     4     5
     6     7     8     9    10
    11    12    13    14    15
```

Every time the variable A is reassigned, new memory is allocated, old data is copied, and old memory is deallocated. If the arrays involved are large or the reassignment occurs numerous times, then memory overhead can significantly reduce algorithm speed. To alleviate the problem, you should ***preallocate*** all the memory required and then fill it as required. Doing so for the preceding example gives

```
>> A=zeros(3,5)  % grab all required memory up front
A =
     0     0     0     0     0
     0     0     0     0     0
     0     0     0     0     0
>> A(1,:)=1:5;     % no memory allocation here
>> B=6:10;
>> A(2,:)=B;       % no memory allocation here
>> C=11:15;
>> A(3,:)=C        % no memory allocation here
A =
     1     2     3     4     5
     6     7     8     9    10
    11    12    13    14    15
```

While this example is somewhat silly, it serves to illustrate that the memory-allocation process for the variable A is performed only once, rather than once at every reassignment of A.

The following table summarizes the facts discussed in this section:

Syntax	Description
`P=zeros(100);` `P=rand(5,6);`	Reassignment of a variable incurs memory allocation and deallocation overhead.
`P(3,3)=1;`	If the indices on the left exist, no memory allocation and deallocation is performed.
`P(8,1)=1;`	If the indices on the left do not exist, memory allocation and deallocation occurs.

`P=zeros(5,6);`	Reassignment of a variable incurs memory allocation and deallocation overhead, even if the reassignment does not change the number of elements involved.
`P(:)=rand(1,30)`	If `P` exists, contents from the right-hand side are copied into the memory allocated on the left. No memory allocation and deallocation is performed.
`B=zeros(10);` `C=B;`	Delayed copy. `C` and `B` share the memory allocated to `B` until either `B` or `C` is modified.

`prod(size(A))`
 	
`tmp=size(A);`
`prod(tmp)`
	Implicit and explicit variables require the same memory allocation. However, the implicit variable is automatically cleared.

`myfunc(a,b,c)`	Delayed copy. The variables `a`, `b`, and `c` are not copied into the function workspace, unless the function modifies them. No memory allocation and deallocation overhead is incurred if the variables are not modified within the function.

`A=zeros(3,5);`
`A(1,:)=1:5;`
`A(2,:)=6:10;`
`A(3,:)=11:15;`
	Preallocate all memory for a variable that grows as an algorithm progresses. Memory allocation and deallocation overhead is incurred only once, rather than once per iteration or reassignment.

6

Multidimensional Arrays

In the previous chapter, 1- and 2-D arrays and their manipulation were illustrated. Since MATLAB Version 5 appeared several years ago, MATLAB has added support for arrays of arbitrary dimensions. For the most part, MATLAB supports multidimensional arrays (i.e., *n*-D arrays) by using the same functions and addressing techniques that apply to 1- and 2-D arrays. In general, the third dimension is numbered by ***pages***, while higher dimensions have no generic name. Thus, a 3-D array has rows, columns, and pages. Each page contains a 2-D array of rows and columns. In addition, just as all of the columns of a 2-D array must have the same number of rows and vice versa, all of the pages of a 3-D array must have the same number of rows and columns. One way to visualize 3-D arrays is to think of the residential listings (white pages) in a phone book. Each page has the same number of columns and the same number of names (rows) in each column. The stack of all of the pages forms a 3-D array of names and phone numbers.

Even though there is no limit to the number of dimensions, 3-D arrays are predominately used as examples in this chapter, because they are easily visualized and displayed.

6.1 ARRAY CONSTRUCTION

Multidimensional arrays can be created in several ways:

```
>> A = zeros(4,3,2)
A(:,:,1) =
 0     0     0
```

```
0     0     0
0     0     0
0     0     0
A(:,:,2) =
0     0     0
0     0     0
0     0     0
0     0     0
```

This is an array of zeros, having four rows, three columns, and two pages. The first page is displayed first, followed by the second page. The other common array-generation functions `ones`, `rand`, and `randn` work the same way, simply by adding dimensions to the input arguments.

Direct indexing also works, as in the following example:

```
>> A = zeros(2,3)  % start with a 2-D array
A =
     0     0     0
     0     0     0
>> A(:,:,2) = ones(2,3)  % add a second page to go 3-D!
A(:,:,1) =
     0     0     0
     0     0     0
A(:,:,2) =
     1     1     1
     1     1     1
>> A(:,:,3) = 4  % add a third page by scalar expansion
A(:,:,1) =
     0     0     0
     0     0     0
A(:,:,2) =
     1     1     1
     1     1     1
A(:,:,3) =
     4     4     4
     4     4     4
```

This approach starts with a 2-D array, which is the first page of a 3-D array. Then, additional pages are added by straightforward array addressing.

The functions reshape and repmat can also be used to create n-D arrays. For example, in the code

```
>> B = reshape(A,2,9) % 2-D data, stack pages side-by-side
B =
     0     0     0     1     1     1     4     4     4
     0     0     0     1     1     1     4     4     4

>> B = [A(:,:,1) A(:,:,2) A(:,:,3)] % equivalent to above
B =
     0     0     0     1     1     1     4     4     4
     0     0     0     1     1     1     4     4     4

>> reshape(B,2,3,3) % recreate A
ans(:,:,1) =
     0     0     0
     0     0     0
ans(:,:,2) =
     1     1     1
     1     1     1
ans(:,:,3) =
     4     4     4
     4     4     4

>> reshape(B,[2 3 3]) % alternative to reshape(B,2,3,3)
ans(:,:,1) =
     0     0     0
     0     0     0
ans(:,:,2) =
     1     1     1
     1     1     1
ans(:,:,3) =
     4     4     4
     4     4     4
```

reshape can change any dimensional array into any other dimensional array.

The code

```
>> C = ones(2,3) % new data
C =

    1    1    1
    1    1    1

>> repmat(C,1,1,3) % this form not allowed above 2-D!
??? Error using ==> repmat
Too many input arguments.

>> repmat(C,[1 1 3]) % this is how to do it
ans(:,:,1) =
    1    1    1
    1    1    1
ans(:,:,2) =
    1    1    1
    1    1    1
ans(:,:,3) =
    1    1    1
    1    1    1
```

replicates C once in the *row* dimension, once in the *column* dimension, and three times in the *page* dimension.

The cat function creates *n*-D arrays from lower dimensional arrays:

```
>> a = zeros(2); % new data
>> b = ones(2);
>> c = repmat(2,2,2);
>> D = cat(3,a,b,c)  % conCATenate a,b,c along the 3rd dimension
D(:,:,1) =
    0    0
    0    0
D(:,:,2) =
    1    1
    1    1
```

```
D(:,:,3) =

     2     2
     2     2

>> D = cat(4,a,b,c)  % try the 4th dimension!
D(:,:,1,1) =
     0     0
     0     0
D(:,:,1,2) =
     1     1
     1     1
D(:,:,1,3) =
     2     2
     2     2

>> D(:,1,:,:)  % look at elements in column 1
ans(:,:,1,1) =
     0
     0
ans(:,:,1,2) =
     1
     1
ans(:,:,1,3) =
     2
     2

>> size(D)
ans =
     2     2     1     3
```

Note that D has two rows, two columns, one page, and three fourth-dimension parts.

6.2 ARRAY MATHEMATICS AND MANIPULATION

As additional dimensions are created, array mathematics and manipulation become more cumbersome. Scalar-array arithmetic remains straightforward, but array–array arithmetic requires that the two arrays have the same size in all dimensions. Since scalar-array and array–array arithmetic remains unchanged from the 2-D case presented in the previous chapter, further illustrations are not presented here.

MATLAB provides several functions for the manipulation of n-D arrays. The function squeeze eliminates ***singleton dimensions***; that is, it eliminates dimensions of size 1. For example, in the code

```
>> E = squeeze(D)  % squeeze dimension 4 down to dimension 3
E(:,:,1) =
     0     0
     0     0
E(:,:,2) =
     1     1
     1     1
E(:,:,3) =
     2     2
     2     2
>> size(E)
ans =
     2     2     3
```

E contains the same data as D, but has two rows, two columns, and three pages.

How about a 3-D vector? This case is shown as follows:

```
>> v(1,1,:) = 1:6  % a vector along the page dimension
v(:,:,1) =
     1
v(:,:,2) =
     2
v(:,:,3) =
     3
v(:,:,4) =
     4
v(:,:,5) =
     5
v(:,:,6) =
     6
```

```
>> squeeze(v) % squeeze it into a column vector
ans =
     1
     2
     3
     4
     5
     6

>> v(:) % this always creates a column vector
ans =
     1
     2
     3
     4
     5
     6
```

The function reshape allows you to change the row, column, page, and higher order dimensions, without changing the total number of elements:

```
>> F = cat(3,2+zeros(2,4),ones(2,4),zeros(2,4)) % new 3-D array
F(:,:,1) =
     2     2     2     2
     2     2     2     2
F(:,:,2) =
     1     1     1     1
     1     1     1     1
F(:,:,3) =
     0     0     0     0
     0     0     0     0

>> G = reshape(F,[3 2 4]) % change it to 3 rows, 2 columns, 4 pages
G(:,:,1) =
     2     2
     2     2
     2     2
```

```
G(:,:,2) =
     2     1
     2     1
     1     1
G(:,:,3) =
     1     1
     1     0
     1     0
G(:,:,4) =
     0     0
     0     0
     0     0

>> H = reshape(F,[4 3 2]) % or 4 rows, 3 columns, 2 pages
H(:,:,1) =
     2     2     1
     2     2     1
     2     2     1
     2     2     1
H(:,:,2) =
     1     0     0
     1     0     0
     1     0     0
     1     0     0

>> K = reshape(F,2,12) % 2 rows, 12 columns, 1 page
K =
     2     2     2     2     1     1     1     1     0     0     0     0
     2     2     2     2     1     1     1     1     0     0     0     0
```

Reshaping can be confusing until you become comfortable with visualizing arrays in *n*-D space. In addition, some reshaping requests make more practical sense than others. For example, in the previously displayed code, G has little practical value, whereas K is much more practical, because it stacks the pages of F side by side as additional columns.

The reshaping process follows the same pattern as that for 2-D arrays. Data are gathered first by rows, followed by columns, then by pages, and so on into higher dimensions. That is, all the rows in the first column are gathered, then all the rows in the second column, and so on. Thus, when the first page has been gathered, MATLAB moves on to the second page and starts over with all the rows in the first column.

The order in which array elements are gathered is the order in which the functions `sub2ind` and `ind2sub` consider single-index addressing:

```
>> sub2ind(size(F),1,1,1) % 1st row, 1st column, 1st page is element 1

ans =

     1

>> sub2ind(size(F),1,2,1) % 1st row, 2nd column, 1st page is element 3

ans =

     3

>> sub2ind(size(F),1,2,3) % 1st element, 2nd column, 3rd page is element 19

ans =

    19

>> [r,c,p] = ind2sub(size(F),19) % inverse of above

r =

     1

c =

     2

p =

     3
```

The *n*-D equivalent to `flipud` and `fliplr` is `flipdim`:

```
>> M = reshape(1:18,2,3,3) % new data
M(:,:,1) =
     1     3     5
     2     4     6
M(:,:,2) =
     7     9    11
     8    10    12
M(:,:,3) =
    13    15    17
    14    16    18
```

```
>> flipdim(M,1) % flip row order
ans(:,:,1)
     2     4     6
     1     3     5
ans(:,:,2) =
     8    10    12
     7     9    11
ans(:,:,3) =
    14    16    18
    13    15    17
>> flipdim(M,2) % flip column order
ans(:,:,1) =
     5     3     1
     6     4     2
ans(:,:,2) =
    11     9     7
    12    10     8
ans(:,:,3) =
    17    15    13
    18    16    14

>> flipdim(M,3) % flip page order
ans(:,:,1) =
    13    15    17
    14    16    18
ans(:,:,2) =
     7     9    11
     8    10    12
ans(:,:,3) =
     1     3     5
     2     4     6
```

The function shiftdim shifts the dimensions of an array. That is, if an array has r rows, c columns, and p pages, a shift by one dimension creates an array with c rows, p columns, and r pages, as shown in the following example:

```
>> M  % recall data
M(:,:,1) =
     1     3     5
     2     4     6
M(:,:,2) =
     7     9    11
     8    10    12
M(:,:,3) =
    13    15    17
    14    16    18

>> shiftdim(M,1) % shift one dimension
ans(:,:,1) =
     1     7    13
     3     9    15
     5    11    17
ans(:,:,2) =
     2     8    14
     4    10    16
     6    12    18
```

Shifting dimensions by 1 causes the first row on page 1 to become the first column on page 1, the second row on page 1 to become the first column on page 2, and so on.

In the code

```
>> shiftdim(M,2) % shift two dimensions
ans(:,:,1) =
     1     2
     7     8
    13    14
ans(:,:,2) =
     3     4
     9    10
    15    16
ans(:,:,3) =
     5     6
    11    12
    17    18
```

the first column on page 1 of M becomes the first row on page 1, the first column on page 2 becomes the second row on page 1, and so on. If you are like the authors of this text, shifting dimensions is not immediately intuitive. For the 3-D case, it helps if you visualize M forming a rectangular box with page 1 on the front, followed by page 2 behind page 1, and then page 3 forming the back of the box. Hence, shifting dimensions is equivalent to rotating the box so that a different side faces you.

The function shiftdim also accepts negative shifts. In this case, the array is pushed into higher dimensions, leaving singleton dimensions behind, as in this example:

```
>> M % recall data
M(:,:,1) =
     1     3     5
     2     4     6
M(:,:,2) =
     7     9    11
     8    10    12
M(:,:,3) =
    13    15    17
    14    16    18
>> size(M) % M has 2 rows, 3 columns, and 3 pages
ans =
     2     3     3

>> shiftdim(M,-1) % shift dimensions out by 1
ans(:,:,1,1) =
     1     2
ans(:,:,2,1) =
     3     4
ans(:,:,3,1) =
     5     6
ans(:,:,1,2) =
     7     8
ans(:,:,2,2) =
     9    10
ans(:,:,3,2) =
    11    12
```

```
ans(:,:,1,3) =
    13    14
ans(:,:,2,3) =
    15    16
ans(:,:,3,3) =
    17    18
>> size(ans)
ans =
     1     2     3     3
```

The result now has four dimensions. The reader is left to figure out the correspondence between the original data and the shifted result.

In 2-D arrays, the transpose operator swapped rows and columns, converting an r-by-c array into a c-by-r array. The functions permute and ipermute are the *n*-D equivalents of the transpose operator. By itself, permute is a generalization of the function shiftdim. In the following code example:

```
>> M  % recall data
M(:,:,1) =
     1     3     5
     2     4     6
M(:,:,2) =
     7     9    11
     8    10    12
M(:,:,3) =
    13    15    17
    14    16    18

>> permute(M,[2 3 1]) % same as shiftdim(M,1)
ans(:,:,1) =
     1     7    13
     3     9    15
     5    11    17
ans(:,:,2) =
     2     8    14
     4    10    16
     6    12    18
```

```
>> shiftdim(M,1)
ans(:,:,1) =
     1     7    13
     3     9    15
     5    11    17
ans(:,:,2) =
     2     8    14
     4    10    16
     6    12    18
```

[2 3 1] instructs the function to make the second dimension the first, the third dimension the second, and the first dimension the third.

Now, in the simpler code

```
>> permute(M,[2 1 3])
ans(:,:,1) =
     1     2
     3     4
     5     6
ans(:,:,2) =
     7     8
     9    10
    11    12
ans(:,:,3) =
    13    14
    15    16
    17    18
```

[2 1 3] instructs `permute` to transpose the rows and columns, but to leave the third dimension alone. As a result, each page in the result is a conventional transpose of the original data.

The second argument to `permute`, called `ORDER`, must be a permutation of the dimensions of the array, passed as the first argument; otherwise, the requested permutation doesn't make sense, as shown in the following example:

```
>> permute(M,[2 1 1])
??? Error using ==> permute
ORDER cannot contain repeated permutation indices.
```

```
>> permute(M,[2 1 4])
??? Error using ==> permute
ORDER contains an invalid permutation index.
```

The function permute can also be used to push an array into higher dimensions. For example, shiftdim(M,−1), shown earlier, is equivalent to

```
>> permute(M,[4 1 2 3])
ans(:,:,1,1) =
     1     2
ans(:,:,2,1) =
     3     4
ans(:,:,3,1) =
     5     6
ans(:,:,1,2) =
     7     8
ans(:,:,2,2) =
     9    10
ans(:,:,3,2) =
    11    12
ans(:,:,1,3) =
    13    14
ans(:,:,2,3) =
    15    16
ans(:,:,3,3) =
    17    18
```

An array always has a unit dimension beyond its size; for example, a 2-D array has one page. That is, all dimensions past the nonunity size of an array are singletons. As a result, in the preceding example, the singleton fourth dimension in M is made the first dimension of the result shown.

For 2-D arrays, issuing the transpose operator a second time returns the array to its original form. Because of the added generality of *n*-D arrays, the function ipermute is used to undo the actions performed by permute:

```
>> M % recall data
M(:,:,1) =
```

```
     1     3     5
     2     4     6
M(:,:,2) =
     7     9    11
     8    10    12
M(:,:,3) =
    13    15    17
    14    16    18
>> permute(M,[3 2 1]) % sample permutation
ans(:,:,1) =
     1     3     5
     7     9    11
    13    15    17
ans(:,:,2) =
     2     4     6
     8    10    12
    14    16    18
>> ipermute(ans,[3 2 1]) % back to original data
ans(:,:,1) =
     1     3     5
     2     4     6
ans(:,:,2) =
     7     9    11
     8    10    12
ans(:,:,3) =
    13    15    17
    14    16    18
```

6.3 ARRAY SIZE

As demonstrated in the prior chapter and earlier in this chapter, the function `size` returns the size of an array along each of its dimensions. The functionality of `size` is unchanged from the features demonstrated in the last chapter. In addition, the function `numel` remains unchanged. Consider the following example:

```
>> size(M)  % return array of dimensions
ans =
     2     3     3
>> numel(M) % number of elements
ans =
    18
>> [r,c,p] = size(M) % return individual variables
r =
     2
c =
     3
p =
     3
>> r = size(M,1) % return just rows
ans =
     2
>> c = size(M,2) % return just columns
c =
     3
>> p = size(M,3) % return just pages
p =
     3
>> v = size(M,4) % default for all higher dimensions
v =
     1
```

When the number of dimensions is unknown or variable, the function ndims is useful:

```
>> ndims(M)
ans =
     3
>> ndims(M(:,:,1)) % just the 2-D first page of M
ans =
     2
```

In this last example, `M(:,:,1)` is a 2-D array, because it has only one page. That is, it has a singleton third dimension. The function `ndims` is equivalent to the following simple code fragment:

```
>> length(size(M))
ans =
     3
```

The following table summarizes the functions illustrated in this chapter:

n-D Function	Description

`ones(r,c, ...)`
`zeros(r,c, ...)`
`rand(r,c, ...)`
`randn(r,c, ...)`
	Basic *n*-D array creation

`reshape(B,2,3,3)` `reshape(B,[2 3 3])`	Reshape array into arbitrary dimensions
`repmat(C,[1 1 3])`	Replicate array into arbitrary dimensions
`cat(3,a,b,c)`	Concatenate array along a specified dimension
`squeeze(D)`	Eliminate dimensions of size equal to 1 (i.e., singleton) dimensions
`sub2ind(size(F),1,1,1)` `[r,c,p]=ind2sub(size(F),19)`	Subscript to single-index conversion, and single-index to subscript conversion
`flipdim(M,1)`	Flip order along a given dimension; *n*-D equivalent to `flipud` and `fliplr`
`shiftdim(M,2)`	Shift dimensions; circular shift for positive second argument; push-out for negative second argument
`permute(M,[2 1 3])` `ipermute(M,[2 1 3])`	Arbitrary permutation and inverse of dimensions; generalization of transpose operator to *n*-D arrays

`size(M)`
`[r,c,p]=size(M)`
`r=size(M,1)`
`c=size(M,2)`
`p=size(M,3)`
	Size of *n*-D array along its dimensions

`ndims(M)`	Number of dimensions in an array
`numel(M)`	Number of elements in an array

7

Numeric Data Types

In the preceding chapters, numeric variables were real or complex arrays containing values stored in double precision. Historically, all data in MATLAB was stored in double-precision format. Character strings and logical data were stored as double-precision, 8 byte, real arrays. Needless to say, this resulted in very inefficient memory usage. Character strings need, at most, two bytes per character, and logical arrays require only one bit per element to distinguish between True and False.

Over time, these storage inefficiencies were eliminated. First, character strings became a separate *data type* or *variable class* and were changed to a two-bytes-per-character representation. More recently, logical arrays became a separate data type and were changed to a one-byte-per-value representation. Most recently, single-precision data types and a variety of signed and unsigned integer data types were introduced.

Prior to MATLAB 7, arithmetic operations on single-precision and integer data were undefined. However, sorting, searching, logical comparisons, and array manipulation were supported. To perform arithmetic operations on these data types, it was necessary to convert the data to double precision before performing the desired operation. Then, if desired, the result could be converted back to the original data type. With the release of MATLAB Version 7, most operations on these data types are performed natively, without explicit conversions.

7.1 INTEGER DATA TYPES

MATLAB supports signed and unsigned integer data types having 8-, 16-, 32-, and 64-bit lengths. These data types are summarized in the following table:

Data Type	Description
`uint8`	Unsigned 8-bit integer in the range 0 to 255 (or 0 to 2^8)
`int8`	Signed 8-bit integer in the range −128 to 127 (or -2^7 to $2^7 - 1$)
`uint16`	Unsigned 16-bit integer in the range 0 to 65,535 (or 0 to 2^{16})
`int16`	Signed 16-bit integer in the range −32,768 to 32,767 (or -2^{15} to $2^{15} - 1$)
`uint32`	Unsigned 32-bit integer in the range 0 to 4,294,967,295 (or 0 to 2^{32})
`int32`	Signed 32-bit integer in the range −2,147,483,648 to 2,147,483,647 (or -2^{31} to $2^{31} - 1$)
`uint64`	Unsigned 64-bit integer in the range 0 to 18,446,744,073,707,551,615 (or 0 to 2^{64})
`int64`	Signed 64-bit integer in the range −9,223,372,036,854,775,808 to 9,223,372,036,854,775,807, (or -2^{63} to $2^{63} - 1$)

With the exception of the range of definition, each of these integer data types has the same properties. The upper and lower limits of their ranges are given by the `intmax` and `intmin` functions, as shown in the following example:

```
>> intmax('int8')
ans =
   127
>> intmin('uint32')
ans =
   0
```

Variables containing integer data can be created in a number of ways. When an array of zeros or ones is desired, the functions `zeros` and `ones` can be used:

```
>> m = zeros(1,6,'int8') % specify data type as last argument
m =
   0    0    0    0    0    0
>> class(m) % confirm class of result
ans =
int8
>> n = ones(4,'uint16') % again specify data type as last argument
n =
      1     1     1     1
      1     1     1     1
```

```
    1    1    1    1
    1    1    1    1

>> class(n) % confirm class of result
ans =
uint16
```

For other values, one must convert or cast results into the desired data type:

```
>> k = 1:7 % create default double precision
k =
   1    2    3    4    5    6    7
>> class(k)
ans =
double
>> kk = uint8(k) % convert using uint8 function
kk =
  1   2   3   4   5   6   7
>> class(kk)
ans =
uint8
>> kkk = cast(k,'uint8') % use more general cast function
kkk =
  1   2   3   4   5   6   7
>> class(kkk)
ans =
uint8
```

Once a variable of a given data type exists, it retains that data type even if other data are inserted into it:

```
>> kkk(3:5) = ones(1,3) % insert double precision values
kkk =
  1   2   1   1   1   6   7

>> class(kkk) % class remains unchanged
ans =
uint8
```

```
>> kkk(5:7) = zeros(1,3,'uint16') % insert uint16 data
kkk =
    1    2    1    1    0    0    0

>> class(kkk) % class remains unchanged
ans =
uint8

>> kk(1:2:end) = pi % insert a noninteger value!
Kkk =
    3    2    3    1    3    0    3
>> class(kkk) % class remains unchanged
ans =
uint8
```

Note that, when a noninteger is inserted, it is first rounded to the nearest integer and then inserted into the array.

Mathematical operations on integer data types of the same kind are defined as in the following code:

```
>> k = int8(1:7) % create new data
k =
    1    2    3    4    5    6    7
>> m = int8(randperm(7)) % more new data
m =
    7    2    3    6    4    1    5

>> k+m % addition
ans =
    8    4    6   10    9    7   12
>> k-m % subtraction
ans =
   -6    0    0   -2    1    5    2
>> k.*m % element by element multiplication
ans =
    7    4    9   24   20    6   35
```

```
>> k./m % element by element division
ans =
     0     1     1     1     1     6     1

>> k % recall data
k =
     1     2     3     4     5     6     7

>> k/k(2)
ans =
     1     1     2     2     3     3     4
```

Addition, subtraction, and multiplication are straightforward. However, in many cases, integer division does not produce an integer result. As shown, MATLAB performs the integer division as if the arrays were double precision and then rounds the result to the nearest integer.

> When dividing integers, MATLAB effectively performs the operation in double precision, rounds the result to the nearest integer, and converts the result back to the integer data type involved.

Mathematical operations between variables of different integer data types are not defined. However, mathematical operations between a double-precision scalar and an integer data type implicitly convert the double-precision scalar to the corresponding integer type and then perform the requested operation, as the following code illustrates:

```
>> m % recall data and data type
m =
    7    2    3    6    4    1    5
>> class(m)
ans =
int8
>> n = cast(k,'uint16') % new data of type uint16
n =
      1      2      3      4      5      6      7
>> m+n % try mixed type addition
??? Error using ==> plus
```

```
Integers can only be combined with integers of the same class, or scalar doubles.
>> n+3 % try adding default double precision constant 3
ans =
     4     5     6     7     8     9    10
>> class(ans)
ans =
uint16

>> n-(1:7) % try nonscalar double precision subtraction
??? Error using ==> minus
Integers can only be combined with integers of the same class, or scalar doubles.
```

> MATLAB supports mixed mathematical operations between a **scalar** double-precision value and an integer data type, but does not support operations between an array of double-precision values and an integer array.

Given the limited range of each integer data type, mathematical operations may produce results that exceed the data type's range. In this case, MATLAB implements saturation. That is, when the result of an operation exceeds that specified by `intmin` and `intmax`, the result becomes either `intmin` or `intmax`, depending on which limit is exceeded:

```
>> k = cast('hellothere','uint8') % convert a string to uint8
k =
  104  101  108  108  111  116  104  101  114  101
>> double(k)+150 % perform addition in double precision
ans =
   254   251   258   258   261   266   254   251   264   251
>> k+150 % perform addition in uint8, saturate at intmax('uint8')=255
ans =
  254  251  255  255  255  255  254  251  255  251
>> k-110 % perform subtraction in uint8, saturation at intmin('uint8')=0
ans =
    0    0    0    0    1    6    0    0    4    0
```

In sum, MATLAB supports a variety of integer data types. Except for the 64-bit types, these data types are more storage efficient than double-precision data.

Mathematical operations on identical integer data types produce results in the same data type. Operations between mixed data types are defined only between a double-precision scalar and the integer data types. Although not illustrated previously, the double-precision values `inf` and `NaN` do not exist for integer data types. In addition, mathematical operations on 64-bit integers are not defined in MATLAB 7, but may be in future versions.

7.2 FLOATING-POINT DATA TYPES

The default data type in MATLAB is double precision, or simply double. This floating-point data type conforms to the IEEE standard for double-precision arithmetic. MATLAB supports arrays containing single-precision data as a storage-saving alternative. Mathematical operations on single-precision data are defined and perform similarly to the integer data types illustrated in the preceding section. As shown in the following example, the values of `realmin`, `realmax`, and `eps` reflect the reduced range and precision of single-precision data:

```
>> realmin('single')
ans =
    1.175494350822288e-038
>> realmax('single')
ans =
    3.402823466385289e+038
>> eps('single')
ans =
    1.192092895507813e-007

>> realmin('double') % compare to corresponding double values
ans =
    2.225073858507201e-308
>> realmax('double')
ans =
    1.797693134862316e+308
>> eps % same as eps(1) and eps('double')
ans =
    2.220446049250313e-016
```

The creation of single-precision data follows the approach used for integer data types:

```
>> a = zeros(1,5,'single') % specify data type as last argument
a =
     0     0     0     0     0
>> b = eye(3,'single') % specify data type as last argument
b =
     1     0     0
     0     1     0
     0     0     1
>> c = single(1:7) % convert default double precision to single
c =
     1     2     3     4     5     6     7
>> d = cast(6:-1:0,'single') % use more general cast function
d =
     6     5     4     3     2     1     0
```

Mathematical operations between single-precision data and between single- and double-precision data produce single-precision results:

```
>> c.^d % element by element exponentiation of singles
ans =
     1    32    81    64    25     6     1
>> c*pi % multiplication by a scalar double
ans =
    3.1416    6.2832    9.4248    12.566    15.708    18.85    21.991
>> d.*rand(size(d)) % element by element multiplication by a double array
ans =
    4.879    0.049307    0.55556    0.6083    0.39744    0.60379    0
>> class(ans)
ans =
single
```

> MATLAB supports mathematical operations between arrays of double- and single-precision arrays, returning single-precision results.

Single-precision data share the special floating-point values of `inf` and `NaN` that are well known in double precision:

```
>> c % recall data
c =
     1     2     3     4     5     6     7
>> c(1:2:end) = 0 % inserting double precision does not change data type
c =
     0     2     0     4     0     6     0
>> c./c % create 0/0 values
Warning: Divide by zero.
Ans =
   NaN     1   NaN     1   NaN     1   NaN
>> 1./c % create 1/0 values
Warning: Divide by zero.
Ans =
     Inf     0.5     Inf     0.25     Inf     0.16667     Inf
```

7.3 SUMMARY

The following table identifies functions that pertain to the numeric data types supported in MATLAB 7:

Function	Description
`double`	Double-precision data type creation and conversion
`single`	Single-precision data type creation and conversion
`int8, int16, int32, int64`	Signed integer data type creation and conversion
`uint8, uint16, uint32, uint64`	Unsigned integer data type creation and conversion
`isnumeric`	True for integer or floating-point data types
`isinteger`	True for integer data types
`isfloat`	True for single or double data types
`isa(x,'type')`	True if x has class `'type'`, including `'numeric'`, `'integer'`, and `'float'`

Function	Description
`cast(x,'type')`	Cast x to class 'type'
`intmax('type')`	Maximum integer value for class 'type'
`intmin('type')`	Minimum integer value for class 'type'
`realmax('type')`	Maximum floating-point real value for class 'type'
`realmin('type')`	Minimum floating-point real value for class 'type'
`eps('type')`	eps value for floating-point value for class 'type'
`eps(x)`	Distance between x and next larger representable value of same type as x
`zeros(...,'type')`	Create array containing zeros for class 'type'
`ones(...,'type')`	Create array containing ones for class 'type'
`eye(...,'type')`	Create identity array for class 'type'

8

Cell Arrays and Structures

MATLAB Version 5 introduced two container data types called ***cell arrays*** and ***structures***. These data types allow the grouping of dissimilar, but related, arrays into a single variable. Data management then becomes easier, since groups of related data can be organized and accessed through a cell array or structure. Because cell arrays and structures are *containers* for other data types, mathematical operations on them are not defined. The *contents* of a cell or structure must be addressed to perform mathematical operations.

One way to visualize cell arrays is to imagine a collection of post office boxes covering a wall at the post office. The collection of boxes is the cell array, with each box being one cell in the cell array. The contents of each post office box are different, just as the contents of each cell in a cell array are different types or sizes of MATLAB data, such as character strings or numerical arrays of varying dimensions. Just as each post office box is identified by a number, each cell in a cell array is indexed by a number. When you send mail to a post office box, you identify the box number you want them put in. When you put data in a particular cell, you identify the cell number you want them put in. The number is also used to identify which box or cell to take data out of.

Structures are almost identical to cell arrays, except that the individual post office boxes (or data-storage locations) are not identified by number. Instead, they are identified by name. Continuing the post office box analogy, the collection of post office boxes is the structure, and each box is identified by its owner's name, rather than by a number. To send mail to a post office box, you identify the name of the box you want it put in. To place data in a particular structure element, you identify the name (i.e., field) of the structure element to put the data in.

8.1 CELL ARRAY CREATION

Cell arrays are MATLAB arrays whose elements are cells. Each cell in a cell array can hold any MATLAB data type, including numerical arrays, character strings, symbolic objects, other cell arrays, and structures. For example, one cell of a cell array might contain a numerical array; another, an array of character strings; and another, a vector of complex values. Cell arrays can be created with any number of dimensions, just as numerical arrays can. However, in most cases, cell arrays are created as a simple vector of cells.

Cell arrays can be created by using assignment statements or by preallocating the array with the `cell` function and then assigning data to the cells. If you have trouble with these examples, it is very likely that you have another variable of the same name in the workspace. If any of the examples that follow give unexpected results, clear the array from the workspace and try again.

> If you assign a cell to an existing variable that is not a cell, MATLAB will stop and report an error.

Like other kinds of arrays, cell arrays can be built by assigning data to individual cells, one at a time. There are two different ways to access cells. If you use standard array syntax to index the array, you must enclose the cell contents in curly braces, {}. These curly braces construct a cell array. They act like a call to the `cell` function:

```
>> clear A  % make sure A is not being used
>> A(1,1) = { [1 2 3; 4 5 6; 7 8 9] };
>> A(1,2) = { 2+3i };                % semicolons suppress display
>> A(2,1) = { 'A character string' };
>> A(2,2) = { 12:-2:0 } % no semicolon, so display requested
A =
            [3x3 double]    [2.0000+ 3.0000i]
    'A character string'         [1x7 double]
```

Note that MATLAB shows that A is a 2-by-2 cell array, but it does not show the contents of all cells. Basically, MATLAB shows the cell contents if they do not take up much space, but only describes the cell contents if they do take up significant space. The curly braces on the right side of the equal sign indicate that the right-hand side expression returns a cell, rather than numerical values. This is called ***cell indexing***. Alternatively, the following statements create the same cell array:

```
>> A{1,1} = [1 2 3; 4 5 6; 7 8 9];
>> A{1,2} = 2+3i;
```

```
>> A{2,1} = 'A character string';
>> A{2,2} = 12:-2:0
A =
                [3x3 double]     [2.0000+ 3.0000i]
    'A character string'               [1x7 double]
```

Here, the curly braces appear on the left-hand side of the equal sign. The term `A{1,1}` indicates that `A` is a cell array and that the contents of the first row and first column of the cell array are on the right-hand side of the equal sign. This is called ***content addressing***. Both methods can be used interchangeably.

As the example demonstrates, curly braces `{ }` are used to access or specify the contents of cells, whereas parentheses `( )` are used to identify cells, but not their contents. To apply the post office box analogy, curly braces are used to look at the contents of post office boxes, whereas parentheses are used to identify post office boxes without looking inside at their contents.

> The two commands `A(i,j) = {x};` and `A{i,j} = x;` both tell MATLAB to store the content of variable `x` in the `(i,j)` element of the cell array `A`. The notation `A(i,j)` is called **cell indexing**, and the notation `A{i,j}` is called **content addressing**. That is, curly braces `{ }` access the contents of cells, whereas parentheses `( )` identify cells without looking at their contents.

The `celldisp` function forces MATLAB to display the contents of cells in the usual manner:

```
>> celldisp(A)
A{1,1} =
    1     2     3
    4     5     6
    7     8     9
A{2,1} =
    A character string
A{1,2} =
    2.0000+  3.0000i
A{2,2} =
    12    10     8     6     4     2     0
```

If a cell array has many elements, `celldisp` can produce a lot of output to the *Command* window. As an alternative, requesting the contents of the cell by using content addressing displays the contents of a single cell. This is different from cell indexing, which identifies the cell, but not its contents:

```
>> A{2,2} % content addressing
ans =
   12   10    8    6    4    2    0
>> A(2,2) % cell indexing
ans =
   [1x7 double]

>> A{1,:} % address contents of the first row
ans =
    1    2    3
    4    5    6
    7    8    9
ans =
   2.0000 + 3.0000i
>> A(1,:)
ans =
   [3x3 double]    [2.0000+ 3.0000i]
```

Note that the contents of all of the cells shown are generically named ans, because the cells store data that do not have associated variable names.

Square brackets were used in previous chapters to create numerical arrays. Curly braces work the same way for cells. In the following example, commas separate columns, and semicolons separate rows:

```
>> B = { [1 2], 'John Smith'; 2+3i, 5 }
B =
        [1x2 double]    'John Smith'
   [2.0000+ 3.0000i]    [         5]
```

When dealing with numerical arrays, it is common to preallocate an array with zeros and then fill the array as needed. The same can be done with cell arrays. The `cell` function creates a cell array and fills it with empty numerical matrices as shown in the following []:

```
>> C = cell(2,3)
C =
   []    []    []
   []    []    []
```

Once the cell array has been defined, both cell indexing and content addressing can be used to populate the cells. In the code

```
>> C(1,1) = 'This doesn''t work'
??? Conversion to cell from char is not possible.
```

the left-hand side uses cell indexing. As a result, the right-hand side must be a cell, but it is not, because it lacks curly braces surrounding its contents. This problem can be resolved by addressing the cell correctly:

```
>> C(1,1) = { 'This does work' }
C =
    'This does work'      []       []
                  []      []       []
>> C{2,3} = 'This works too'
C =
    'This does work'      []                     []
                  []      []       'This works too'
```

Because curly braces appear on the left-hand side of the last statement, MATLAB makes the character string the contents of the addressed cell. Once again, this is an example of content addressing, whereas the prior statement is an example of cell indexing.

8.2 CELL ARRAY MANIPULATION

The numerical array manipulation techniques presented in preceding chapters apply to cell arrays as well. In a sense, cell array manipulation is just a natural extension of these techniques to a different type of array. If you assign data to a cell outside of the dimensions of the current cell array, MATLAB automatically expands the array and fills the intervening cells with the empty numerical array [].

Square brackets are used to combine cell arrays into larger cell arrays, just as they are used to construct larger numerical arrays:

```
>> A  % recall prior cell arrays
A =
              [3x3 double]     [2.0000+ 3.0000i]
     'A character string'           [1x7 double]
>> B
B =
          [1x2 double]     'John Smith'
     [2.0000+ 3.0000i]     [         5]
```

```
>> C = [A;B]
C =
             [3x3 double]     [2.0000+ 3.0000i]
    'A character string'          [1x7 double]
             [1x2 double]     'John Smith'
    [   2.0000+ 3.0000i]      [              5]
```

A subset of cells can be extracted to create a new cell array by conventional array addressing techniques:

```
>> D = C([1 3],:) % first and third rows
D =
    [3x3 double]     [2.0000+ 3.0000i]
    [1x2 double]     'John Smith'
```

An entire row or column of a cell array can be deleted by using the empty array:

```
>> C(3,:) = []
C =
             [3x3 double]     [2.0000+ 3.0000i]
    'A character string'          [1x7 double]
    [   2.0000+ 3.0000i]      [              5]
```

Note that curly braces do not appear in either of the preceding expressions, because we are working with the cell array itself, not the contents of the cells. Once again, curly braces are used to address the contents of cells, whereas parentheses are used to identify the cells without regard for their content.

The reshape function can be used to change the configuration of a cell array, but cannot be used to add or remove cells. For example, in the code

```
>> X = cell(3,4);
>> size(X) % size of the cell array, not the contents
ans =
     3     4

>> Y = reshape(X,6,2);
>> size(Y)
ans =
     6     2
```

So the function reshape naturally reshapes any array, without regard to its type. Similarly, the size function returns the size of any array type.

The function repmat also works, even though its name implies that it replicates matrices. The function repmat was created when matrices were MATLAB's only data type. If MATLAB had been written after the introduction of cell arrays and other array types, perhaps this function would have been called reparray. The following example is illustrative:

```
>> Y  % recall data
Y =
     []     []
     []     []
     []     []
     []     []
     []     []
     []     []
>> Z = repmat(Y,1,3)
Z =
     []     []     []     []     []     []
     []     []     []     []     []     []
     []     []     []     []     []     []
     []     []     []     []     []     []
     []     []     []     []     []     []
     []     []     []     []     []     []
```

8.3 RETRIEVING CELL ARRAY CONTENT

To retrieve the contents of a cell in a cell array, you must apply content addressing, which involves the use of curly braces. For instance, in the code

```
>> B  % recall cell array
B =
            [1x2 double]    'John Smith'
    [2.0000+ 3.0000i]    [          5]
>> x = B{2,2} % content addressing uses { }
x =
     5
```

the variable x now contains the numerical value 5, making x a numerical array (a scalar, in this case). The class function can be used to confirm that this is true, as in the following example:

```
>> class(x) % return argument's data type
ans =
     double
```

Because numerical arrays are double precision, `class` returns a character string that identifies `x` as being `double`. If cell indexing had been used mistakenly, the result would be different:

```
>> y = B(2,2)   % cell indexing uses ( )
y =
    [5]
>> y = B(4)     % same as above using single index
y =
    [5]

>> class(y)     % y is not a double, but a cell!
ans =
cell
>> class(y{1})  % but the contents of y is a double!
ans =
double
```

By now, you are either bored with this distinction between cell indexing and content addressing, or your head is spinning from the confusion.

There are also other functions for testing variable types. The following examples return logical results, where True = 1 and False = 0:

```
>> iscell(y)        % yes, y is a cell
ans =
     1
>> iscell(y{1})     % contents of y is NOT a cell
ans =
     0
>> isa(y,'cell')  % yes, y is a cell
ans =
     1
>> isdouble(y{1})  % this function doesn't exist (yet?)
??? Undefined function or variable 'isdouble'
```

```
>> isnumeric(y{1}) % contents of y is numerical
ans =
     1
>> isfloat(y{1}) % contents of y is floating point
ans =
     1
>> isa(y{1},'double')  % contents of y is a double
ans =
     1
>> isa(y{1},'numeric') % contents of y is also numeric
ans =
     1
>> isa(y{1},'cell')    % contents of y is NOT a cell
ans =
     0
```

While you can display the contents of more than one cell array at a time, it is not possible to assign more than one at a time to a variable by using a standard assignment statement. Consider the following code:

```
>> B{:,2}
ans =
John Smith
ans =
     5
>> d = B{:,2}
??? Illegal right hand side in assignment. Too many elements.
```

If you think about it, this error message makes sense. How can two pieces of data be assigned to a single variable? If the method applied in the preceding example did work, d would be a 2-by-1 array with a character string in its first location and a scalar in its second. Extracting data from multiple cells at one time simply cannot be done so casually.

When addressing the contents of a single cell, it is possible to further address a subset of the contents by simply appending the desired subscript range:

```
>> A  % recall prior data
A =
                  [3x3 double]     [2.0000+ 3.0000i]
```

```
    'A character string'          [1x7 double]
>> celldisp(A) % display contents
A{1,1} =
     1     2     3
     4     5     6
     7     8     9
A{2,1} =
A character string
A{1,2} =
   2.0000 + 3.0000i
A{2,2} =
    12    10     8     6     4     2     0
>> A{1,1}(3,:)  % third row of 3-by-3 array
ans =
     7     8     9
>> A{4}(2:5)     % second through fifth elements of A{2,2}
ans =
    10     8     6     4
>> A{1,2}(2)     % second element doesn't exist
??? Index exceeds matrix dimensions.
>> A{2,1}(3:11) % extract part of the character string
ans =
character
```

8.4 COMMA-SEPARATED LISTS

To extract the contents of more than one cell at a time, MATLAB provides comma-separated list syntax. This syntax applies in any place where variables or constants appear in a list separated by commas. For example, comma-separated lists appear in array construction:

```
>> a = ones(2,3);
>> b = zeros(2,1);
>> c = (3:4)';
>> d = [a,b,c] % same as [a b c]
```

```
d =
 1    1    1    0    3
 1    1    1    0    4
```

They also appear in function input and output argument lists:

```
>> d = cat(2,a,b,c)
d =
     1     1     1     0     3
     1     1     1     0     4
>> [m,n] = size(d)
m =
 2
n =
 5
```

Comma-separated list syntax is implemented as follows: Placing a content-addressed cell array in locations where comma-separated lists appear causes MATLAB to extract the contents of the addressed cell arrays and place them sequentially, separated by commas. In the code

```
>> F = {a b c} % create a cell array
F =
    [2x3 double]    [2x1 double]    [2x1 double]
>> d = cat(2,F{:}) % same as cat(2,a,b,c)
d =
     1     1     1     0     3
     1     1     1     0     4
>> d = cat(2,F(:)) % not content addressing
d =
    [2x3 double]
    [2x1 double]
    [2x1 double]
```

`cat(2,F{:})` is interpreted by MATLAB as `cat(2,F{1},F{2},F{3})`, which is equal to `cat(2,a,b,c)`. That is, comma-separated list syntax dictates that `F{:}` is interpreted as a listing of all addressed parts of `F{:}`, separated by commas. Note that content addressing must be used. Cell indexing, as shown in the second case in the preceding example, acts on the cells, not on their contents. As a result, there is no comma-separated list in the second case, `cat(2,F(:))`. Consider this example:

```
>> d = [F{:}]
d =
     1     1     1     0     3
     1     1     1     0     4
>> d = [F{1},F{2},F{3}] % what is implied by the above
d =
     1     1     1     0     3
     1     1     1     0     4
>> e = [F{2:3}] % can also content address any subset
e =
     0     3
     0     4
>> e = [F{2},F{3}] % what is implied by the above
e =
     0     3
     0     4
```

At first, comma-separated list syntax may seem strange. However, once you become familiar with it, you will recognize its power. (For more information, see the on-line help for `lists`, or search for the phrase `comma separated list`.)

Given comma-separated list syntax, the function `deal` provides a way to extract the contents of numerous cells into separate variables. If you have ever used playing cards, you know that "to deal" means to pass out the cards in some organized way. The function `deal` does just that; it passes out cell array contents to individual variables. In the code

```
>> celldisp(F) % recall data
F{1} =
     1     1     1
     1     1     1
F{2} =
     0
     0
F{3} =
     3
     4
```

```
>> [r,s,t] = deal(F{:}) % deal out contents of F
r =
     1     1     1
     1     1     1
s =
     0
     0
t =
     3
     4
```

the variables r, s, and t are numerical variables, with r = F{1}, s = F{2}, t = F{3}. Hence, this example is equal to

```
>> [r,s,t] = deal(F{1},F{2},F{3})
r =
     1     1     1
     1     1     1
s =
     0
     0
t =
     3
     4
```

So, the function deal is, in reality, pretty simple. It just assigns the contents of the first input argument to the first output argument, the second to the second, and so on. Despite its simplicity, deal is a very powerful tool for extracting data from multiple cells with one statement.

Because the output of deal is also a comma-separated list, deal can be used to assign the contents of multiple cells in one statement:

```
>> [G{:}] = deal(a,b,c)
??? Error using ==> deal
The number of outputs should match the number of inputs.

>> [G{1:3}] = deal(a,b,c)
G =
    [2x3 double]    [2x1 double]    [2x1 double]
```

```
>> F = {a b c}
F =
    [2x3 double]    [2x1 double]    [2x1 double]
>> isequal(F,G) % True since F = G
ans =
     1
```

The first statement produced an error, as `G{:}` doesn't identify how many cell array elements to separate by commas. The second statement identifies the three cell array elements needed. Since the syntax `{a b c}` produces the same cell array, using `deal` to populate multiple cells with one statement is unnecessary (and slower).

8.5 CELL FUNCTIONS

Besides the functions `celldisp`, `cell`, `iscell`, `isa`, and `deal`, there are several other functions that are useful when dealing with cell arrays. The function `cellfun` provides a way to apply certain functions to all cells in a cell array, thereby eliminating the need to apply them to each cell individually:

```
>> A  % recall data
A =
               [3x3 double]    [2.0000+ 3.0000i]
    'A character string'             [1x7 double]

>> cellfun('isreal',A) % True=1 where not complex
ans =
     1     0
     1     1
>> cellfun('length',A) % length of contents
ans =
     3     1
    18     7
>> cellfun('prodofsize',A) % number of elements in each cell
ans =
     9     1
    18     7
>> cellfun('isclass',A,'char') % True for character strings
```

```
ans =

     0     0
     1     0
```

(The function `cellfun` offers other functions as well. For more information, see online help.)

Another function that is sometimes useful is `num2cell`. This function takes an array of any type (not just numbers, as the function name suggests) and fills a cell array with its components:

```
>> a = rand(3,6) % new numerical data
a =
   0.7266   0.2679   0.6833   0.6288   0.6072   0.5751
   0.4120   0.4399   0.2126   0.1338   0.6299   0.4514
   0.7446   0.9334   0.8392   0.2071   0.3705   0.0439
>> c = num2cell(a)   % c{i,j}=a(i,j)
c =
   [0.7266]   [0.2679]   [0.6833]   [0.6288]   [0.6072]   [0.5751]
   [0.4120]   [0.4399]   [0.2126]   [0.1338]   [0.6299]   [0.4514]
   [0.7446]   [0.9334]   [0.8392]   [0.2071]   [0.3705]   [0.0439]
>> d = num2cell(a,1) % d{i}=a(:,i)
d =
  Columns 1 through 4
   [3x1 double]   [3x1 double]   [3x1 double]   [3x1 double]
  Columns 5 through 6
   [3x1 double]   [3x1 double]
>> e = num2cell(a,2)  % e{i}=a(i,:)
e =
   [1x6 double]
   [1x6 double]
   [1x6 double]
```

With numerical data as input, `num2cell(a)` isn't useful in many applications, but packing larger pieces of an array into cells is often more useful, as illustrated in the last two cases.

8.6 CELL ARRAYS OF STRINGS

Although a rigorous discussion of character strings doesn't occur until the next chapter, the use of character strings and their storage in cell arrays are described in this section. If the concept of a character string is foreign to you, read the next chapter and then come back to this material.

In MATLAB, character strings are formed by enclosing characters within quotes. For example, in the code

```
>> s = 'Rarely is the question asked: is our children learning?'
s =
Rarely is the question asked: is our children learning?
```

the variable s contains a string of characters. In many applications, groups of character strings are associated with each other. When this occurs, it is convenient to group them into a cell array rather than store them in individual variables. In the code

```
>> cs = {'My answer is bring them on.'
s
'I understand small business growth. I was one.'}
cs =
   'My answer is bring them on.'
   'Rarely is the question asked: is our children learning?'
   'I understand small business growth. I was one.'

>> size(cs)  % a column cell array
ans =
     3     1
>> iscell(cs) % yes, it is a cell array
ans =
     1
```

the cell array cs has three cells, each containing a character string. In MATLAB, this is simply called a ***cell array of strings***. Because cell arrays are commonly used to store sets of character strings, MATLAB provides several functions to support them, like the one in the following example:

```
>> iscellstr(cs)
ans =
1
```

The function iscellstr returns logical True (1) if all the cells in its cell array argument contain character strings; otherwise, it returns logical False (0).

Before cell arrays were introduced in MATLAB 5, groups of character strings were stored in character string arrays—2-D arrays just like the numerical arrays discussed earlier—with each string occupying a separate row in the array. Each character in the ***string array*** occupies its own location and is indexed just like a numerical array.

MATLAB provides functions to convert a cell array of strings to a string array and vice versa:

```
>> cs  % recall previous cell array of strings

cs =

'My answer is bring them on.'

    'Rarely is the question asked: is our children learning?'

    'I understand small business growth. I was one.'

>> sa = char(cs) % convert to a string array

sa =

My answer is bring them on.
Rarely is the question asked: is our children learning?
I understand small business growth. I was one.
>> ischar(sa) % True for string array

ans =

     1

>> iscell(sa) % True for cell array

ans =

     0

>> size(sa)   % size of string array

ans =

     3    34

>> size(cs)   % size of cell array

ans =

     3     1

>> cst = cellstr(sa) % convert back to cell array

cst =

    'My answer is bring them on.'

    'Rarely is the question asked: is our children learning?'

    'I understand small business growth. I was one.'

>> iscell(cst)       % True for cell array
```

```
ans =
     1
>> isequal(cs,cst)   % True for equal variables
ans =
     1
>> isequal(cs,sa)    % cell array not equal to string array
ans =
     0
```

So, the MATLAB functions `char` and `cellstr` are inverses of each other. In addition, since a string array must have the same number of columns in each row, blank spaces are added to rows, as necessary, to make the string array rectangular.

8.7 STRUCTURE CREATION

Structures are like cell arrays in that they allow you to group collections of dissimilar data into a single variable. However, instead of addressing elements by number, structure elements are addressed by names called ***fields***. Like cell arrays, structures can have any number of dimensions, but a simple scalar or vector array is the most common type.

Whereas cell arrays use curly braces to access data, structures use dot notation to access data in fields. Creating a structure can be as simple as assigning data to individual fields. For example, in the code

```
>> circle.radius = 2.5;      % semicolon, no display
>> circle.center = [0 1];
>> circle.linestyle = '--';
>> circle.color = 'red'      % no semicolon, so display
circle =
       radius: 2.5
       center: [0 1]
    linestyle: '--'
        color: 'red'
```

the data are stored in a structure variable called `circle`. The case-sensitive fields are entitled `radius`, `center`, `linestyle`, and `color`. Structure field names have the same restrictions as variable names: They can contain up to 63 characters, and they must begin with a letter. For example, in the statement

```
>> size(circle)
ans =
     1     1
```

```
>> whos
  Name        Size         Bytes  Class

  ans         1x2             16  double array
  circle      1x1            530  struct array

Grand total is 14 elements using 546 bytes
```

circle is a scalar structure, since size says that it is a 1-by-1 array. The whos command shows its size, the fact that it is a structure array, and the fact that it uses 530 bytes of memory. If there is more than one circle, it can be stored as a second element in the circle variable. For example, in the code

```
>> circle(2).radius = 3.4;
>> circle(2).color = 'green';
>> circle(2).linestyle = ':';
>> circle(2).center = [2.3 -1.2]
circle =
1x2 struct array with fields:
    radius
    center
    linestyle
    color
```

circle is a structure array having two elements. The (2) appears immediately after the variable name, because it is the variable that is having an element added to it. The .fieldname suffix identifies the field where data is to be placed. Note that the structure fields are filled in a different order this time and that the size of the data differs between the two elements. That is, the color fields are 'red' and 'green'. There are no restrictions on what can be placed in fields from one array element to the next. For instance, in the MATLAB statement

```
>> circle(2).radius = 'sqrt(2)'
circle =
1x2 struct array with fields:
    radius
    center
    linestyle
```

```
>> circle.radius  % display radius contents
ans =
         2.5
ans =
sqrt(2)
```

Here, `circle(1).radius` holds numerical data and `circle(2).radius` holds a character string.

If the value of structures is not apparent to you, consider how the data would be stored without structures:

```
>> Cradius = [2.5 3.4]; % ignore sqrt(2) change above
>> Ccenter = [0 1 ; 2.3 -1.2];
>> Clinestyle = {'--' ':'};  % cell array of strings
>> Ccolor = {'red' 'green'};
```

Now, rather than having a single variable storing the information for two circles, there are four variables that must be indexed properly to extract data for each circle. It's easy to add another circle to the structure, but more cumbersome to add them to the four variables. Now, consider the following example:

```
>> circle(3).radius = 25.4;
>> circle(3).center = [-1 0];
>> circle(3).linestyle = '-.';
>> circle(3).color = 'blue'    % third circle added
circle =
1x3 struct array with fields:
   radius
   center
   linestyle
   color
>> Cradius(3) = 25.4
Cradius =
         2.5          3.4          25.4
>> Ccenter(3,:) = [-1 0]
Ccenter =
           0            1
         2.3         -1.2
```

```
            -1              0
>> Cradius(3) = 25.4
Cradius =
          2.5           3.4           25.4

>> Clinestyle{3} = '-.'
Clinestyle =
     '--'    ':'    '-.'
>> Ccolor(3) = {'blue'}
Ccolor =
  'red'   'green'    'blue'
```

The clarity provided by structures should be readily apparent. In addition, consider passing the circle data to a function. For example, as a structure, the data are passed simply as `myfunc(circle)`, whereas the other approach requires `myfunc(Cradius,Ccenter,Clinestyle,Ccolor)`.

Suppose that, at some later date, you wanted to add another field to `circle`, as in

```
>> circle(1).filled = 'yes'
circle =
1x3 struct array with fields:
     radius
     center
     linestyle
     color
     filled
>> circle.filled  % display all .filled fields
ans =
yes
ans =
     []
ans =
     []
```

Now, all of the elements of `circle` have the field `filled`. Those not assigned by default contain the empty array `[]`. The other `filled` fields are easily assigned:

```
>> circle(2).filled = 'no';
>> circle(3).filled = 'yes';
>> circle.filled
ans =
yes
ans =
no
ans =
yes
```

When structure creation by direct assignment isn't possible, MATLAB provides the function `struct`. For example, to re-create the previous structure, the following code is used:

```
>> values1 = {2.5 'sqrt(2)' 25.4}; % cell arrays with field data
>> values2 = {[0 1] [2.3 -1.2] [-1 0]};
>> values3 = {'--' ':' '-.'};
>> values4 = {'red' 'green' 'blue'};
>> values5 = {'yes' 'no' 'yes'};
>> CIRCLE = struct('radius',values1,'center',values2,...
           'linestyle',values3,'color',values4,'filled',values5)
CIRCLE =
1x3 struct array with fields:
    radius
    center
    linestyle
    color
    filled
>> isequal(circle,CIRCLE) % True since structures are equal
ans =
     1
```

8.8 STRUCTURE MANIPULATION

Structures are arrays and therefore can be combined and indexed like numerical arrays and cell arrays. When combining structure arrays, the only restriction is that the arrays combined must share the same fields. Thus, in the code

```
>> square.width = 5;  % a new structure
>> square.height = 14;
>> square.center = zeros(1,2);
>> square.rotation = pi/4
square =
       width: 5
      height: 14
      center: [0 0]
    rotation: 0.7854
>> A = [circle CIRCLE]
A =
1x6 struct array with fields:
    radius
    center
    linestyle
    color
    filled
>> B = [circle square]
??? Number of fields does not match in [] concatenation.
```

the structures `circle` and `CIRCLE` are both 1 by 3 and share the same fields; hence, concatenating them produces a 1-by-6 structure array. However, the structure `square` and `circle` do not have the same fields and therefore cannot be concatenated.

It is also possible to address a subarray of a structure. For example, in the code

```
>> C = [circle(1:2) CIRCLE(3)]
C =
1x3 struct array with fields:
    radius
    center
    linestyle
    color
    filled
>> isequal(C,circle) % True since equal
ans =
     1
```

C and circle are equal because CIRCLE(3) = circle(3). Once again, basic array addressing and concatenation apply to structure arrays as well. For concatenation, field names must match exactly.

Although they are not as useful in this case, structures can also be manipulated with the functions reshape and repmat:

```
>> Aa = reshape(A,3,2)
Aa =
3x2 struct array with fields:
    radius
    center
    linestyle
    color
    filled
>> Aaa = reshape(A,1,2,3)
Aaa =
1x2x3 struct array with fields:
    radius
    center
    linestyle
    color
    filled
```

Since there is seldom a practical reason to have anything other than a structure array with vector orientation, reshape is seldom needed or used with structures. However, it is often convenient to create a structure array with default data in all fields of all array elements. The function repmat performs this task with ease:

```
>> S = repmat(square,3,1)
S =
3x1 struct array with fields:
    width
    height
    center
    rotation
>> S.width  % look at all width fields
ans =
    5
```

```
ans =
     5
ans =
     5
```

All three elements of the structure S contain the data originally assigned to the structure square. At this point, the structure fields can be modified, as needed, to describe different squares.

8.9 RETRIEVING STRUCTURE CONTENT

When you know the names of the fields associated with a structure array, retrieving the data in a particular structure element and field simply requires identifying them. For example, in the code

```
>> rad2 = circle(2).radius
rad2 =
sqrt(2)

>> circle(1).radius
ans =
          2.5

>> area1 = pi*circle(1).radius^2
area1 =
       19.635
```

circle(1).radius identifies the value 2.5, which is used to compute the area of the first circle.

When the contents of a field are an array, it is also possible to retrieve a subset of that field by appending an array index to the structure request:

```
>> circle(1).filled          % the entire field
ans =
yes
>> circle(1).filled(1)       % first element of field
ans =
y
>> circle(1).filled(2:end) % rest of fielc
ans =
es
```

As is true for cell arrays, retrieving the contents of more than one structure array element and field cannot be accomplished by direct addressing. For example, the command

```
>> col = circle.color

??? Illegal right hand side in assignment. Too many elements.
```

attempted to extract three pieces of data and store them in one variable, but failed. However, MATLAB solves this problem the same way it does for cell arrays by using comma-separated lists and `deal`.

When the structure field to be accessed is stored in a character string, MATLAB provides *dynamic addressing* to gain access to the data:

```
>> fldstr = 'color';  % store desired field in variable

>> circle.(fldstr)    % get all color fields
ans =
red
ans =
green
ans =
blue

>> fldstr = 'radius';
>> area=pi*circle(1).(fldstr)^2  % compute area of first circle
area =
      19.635
```

Dynamic addressing is similar to using subscripts to identify specific elements in an array. Both methods use parentheses to hold the chosen elements. For example, `A(r,c)` uses the information in variables `r` and `c` to identify the desired rows and columns of array `A`, whereas `circle.(fldstr)` uses the information in variable `fldstr` to identify the desired field in the structure `circle`.

8.10 COMMA-SEPARATED LISTS (AGAIN)

To extract the contents of more than one structure array element at a time, MATLAB provides comma-separated list syntax. This syntax applies in any place where variables or constants appear in a list, separated by commas. For example, it appears in array construction:

```
>> a = ones(2,3);
>> b = zeros(2,1);
>> c = (3:4)';
>> d = [a,b,c] % same as [a b c]
d =
 1    1    1    0    3
 1    1    1    0    4
```

It also appears in function input and output argument lists:

```
>> d = cat(2,a,b,c)
d =
     1     1     1     0     3
     1     1     1     0     4
>> [m,n] = size(d)
m =
 2
n =
 5
```

Building on this idea, comma-separated list syntax is implemented as follows: Placing a structure array with appended field name in locations where comma-separated lists appear causes MATLAB to extract the contents of the addressed fields and place them sequentially, separated by commas. In the code

```
>> cent = cat(1,circle.center) % comma-separated list syntax
cent =
          0            1
        2.3         -1.2
         -1            0
>> cent = cat(1,circle(1).center,circle(2).center,circle(3).center)
cent =
          0            1
        2.3         -1.2
         -1            0
>> some = cat(1,circle(2:end).center)
```

```
some =
        2.3          -1.2
         -1             0
```

the cat function concatenates the circle centers into rows of the numerical array cent. According to comma-separated list syntax, the first two statements in the preceding example are identical. The third statement shows that you can index and extract a subarray as well.

Since the color fields of the structure circle are character strings of different lengths, they cannot be extracted into a string array, but they can be extracted into a cell array, as in the following example:

```
>> circle.color
ans =
red
ans =
green
ans =
blue

>> col = cat(1,circle.color) % elements have different lengths
??? Error using ==> cat
CAT arguments dimensions are not consistent.
>> col = [circle.color] % no error but not much use!
col =
redgreenblue
>> col = {circle.color} % cell array of strings
col =
    'red'    'green'    'blue'

>> col = char(col) % if needed, convert to string array
col =
red
green
blue
```

MATLAB does not provide tools for extracting all the fields of a single structure array element. For instance, there is no way to retrieve the radius, center, linestyle, color, and filled fields of the first circle in one statement. In a sense, there is no need to have such a function, because each of these fields can be directly addressed and used in computations, such as area1 = pi*circle(1).radius^2.

Given comma-separated list syntax, the function deal provides a way to extract the contents of numerous structure elements into separate variables as in the following example:

```
>> [c1,c2,c3] = deal(circle.color) % get all colors
c1 =
red
c2 =
green
c3 =
blue
>> [rad1,rad3]=deal(circle([1 3]).radius) % 1st and 3rd radius
rad1 =
        2.5
rad3 =
       25.4
```

Because the output of deal is also a comma-separated list, deal can be used to assign the contents of multiple structure array elements, with a single field in one statement. For example, consider the following code:

```
>> [circle.radius] = deal(5,14,83)
circle =
1x3 struct array with fields:
    radius
    center
    linestyle
    color
    filled
>> circle.radius  % confirm assignments
ans =
     5
ans =
    14
```

```
ans =
    83
>> [triangle(:).type] = deal('right','isosceles','unknown')
??? Error using ==> deal
The number of outputs should match the number of inputs.
>> [triangle(1:3).type] = deal('right','isosceles','unknown')
triangle =
1x3 struct array with fields:
    type
>> triangle.type
ans =
right
ans =
isosceles
ans =
unknown
```

In the first statement, the structure `circle` already existed and has three elements. Therefore, the output argument was expanded into three elements. In the second statement containing `deal`, the structure `triangle` didn't exist. Because it wasn't possible to determine how many elements to create in a comma-separated list, an error was returned. However, in the last statement containing `deal`, the number of elements was given explicitly, and the `type` property of the newly created structure `triangle` was populated with the given data.

8.11 STRUCTURE FUNCTIONS

In the *Command* window, it is easy to identify the field names of a given structure by simply entering the structure name at the MATLAB prompt:

```
>> circle
circle =
1x3 struct array with fields:
    radius
    center
    linestyle
    color
    filled
```

```
>> square
square =
      width: 5
     height: 14
     center: [0 0]
   rotation: 0.7854
```

When a structure is passed to a function—for example, `myfunc(circle)`—the function internally must know or have some way to obtain the field names of the structure. (Writing functions in MATLAB is covered in Chapter 12.) In MATLAB, the function `fieldnames` provides this information:

```
>> fieldnames(circle)
ans =
    'radius'
    'center'
    'linestyle'
    'color'
    'filled'
```

The output of `fieldnames` is a cell array of strings identifying the fields that are associated with the input structure.

It is also possible to guess the field names and ask whether they exist by using the logical function `isfield`:

```
>> isfield(circle,'color') % True
ans =
     1
>> isfield(circle,'width') % False
ans =
     0
```

If you don't know whether a variable is a structure or not, the functions `class` and `isstruct` are helpful, as the following example shows:

```
>> class(square)     % ask for the class of variable square
ans =
struct
```

```
>> isstruct(circle) % True for structures
ans =
     1
>> d = pi;
>> isstruct(d)       % False for doubles
ans =
     0
```

When the field names of a structure are known, the function `rmfield` allows you to remove one or more fields from the structure. For example, the code

```
>> fnames = fieldnames(circle)
fnames =
    'radius'
    'center'
    'linestyle'
    'color'
    'filled'
```

stores the `fnames` field names of `circle` in a cell array. Arbitrarily choosing the last field name, we can remove the `filled` field from the structure by calling `rmfield`:

```
>> circle2 = rmfield(circle,fnames{5})
circle2 =
1x3 struct array with fields:
    radius
    center
    linestyle
    color
```

This code removes the field `filled` from `circle` and assigns the result to a new structure `circle2`.

Similarly,

```
>> circle3 = rmfield(circle,fnames{1:3})
circle3 =
1x3 struct array with fields:
    'color'
    'filled'
```

removes the fields `radius`, `center`, and `linestyle` from `circle`, and assigns the result to a new structure `circle3`.

In some cases, it is beneficial to rearrange the order in which the field names of a structure are presented. The function `orderfields` performs this task and places the fields in ASCII order:

```
>> circleA = orderfields(circle)
circleA =
1x3 struct array with fields:
    center
    color
    filled
    linestyle
    radius
```

Other orderings are possible as well, as in the following code:

```
>> circleB = orderfields(circleA,CIRCLE) % match fields of structure CIRCLE
circleB =
1x3 struct array with fields:
    radius
    center
    linestyle
    color
    filled
>> circleC = orderfields(circle,[2 5 1 4 3]) % provide permutation vector
circleC =
1x3 struct array with fields:
    center
    filled
    radius
    color
    linestyle
>> circleD = orderfields(circle,fnames(end:-1:1)) % reverse original order
circleD =
1x3 struct array with fields:
    filled
```

```
color
linestyle
center
radius
```

Finally, given the similarity between cell arrays and structures and applying the post office box analogy, it's not hard to believe that MATLAB provides the functions `cell2struct` and `struct2cell` to convert cell arrays to structures and back in an organized fashion. (More detailed explanations of these functions can be found in the on-line documentation.)

8.12 SUMMARY

MATLAB supports arrays with an unlimited number of dimensions. Cell arrays and structures can store any array type, including cell arrays and structures. So, it is possible to have a cell in a cell array that contains a structure with a field that contains another structure that has a field containing a cell array, of which one cell contains another cell array. Needless to say, there comes a point where the power of cell arrays and structures becomes indecipherable and of little practical use. Thus, to end this chapter, try to decipher the following legal MATLAB statements:

```
>> one(2).three(4).five = {circle}
one =
1x2 struct array with fields:
    three
>> test = {{{circle}}}
test =
    {1x1 cell}
```

How many structures are involved in the first statement? What is the total number of structure elements, including empty arrays, created by the statement? Can the structure `circle` be extracted from the second statement with a single MATLAB statement?

9

Character Strings

MATLAB's true power is in its ability to crunch numbers. However, there are times when it is desirable to manipulate text, such as when putting labels and titles on plots. In MATLAB, text is referred to as character strings, or simply strings. Character strings represent another variable class or data type in MATLAB.

9.1 STRING CONSTRUCTION

Character strings in MATLAB are special numerical arrays of ASCII values that are displayed as their character-string representation, as in the following code:

```
>> t = 'How about this character string?'
t =
How about this character string?
>> size(t)
ans =
     1    32
>> whos
  Name      Size          Bytes  Class

  ans       1x2              16  double array
  t         1x32             64  char array
Grand total is 34 elements using 80 bytes
```

A character string is simply text surrounded by single quotes. Each character in a string is one element in an array that requires 2 bytes per character for storage, which is different from the 8 bytes per element that are required for numerical or double arrays.

To see the underlying ASCII representation of a character string, you need only perform some arithmetic operation on the string or use the dedicated function `double`, as in the following code:

```
>> u = double(t)
u =
  Columns 1 through 12
    72   111   119    32    97    98   111   117   116    32   116   104
  Columns 13 through 24
   105   115    32    99   104    97   114    97    99   116   101   114
  Columns 25 through 32
    32   115   116   114   105   110   103    63
>> abs(t)
ans =
  Columns 1 through 12
    72   111   119    32    97    98   111   117   116    32   116   104
  Columns 13 through 24
   105   115    32    99   104    97   114    97    99   116   101   114
  Columns 25 through 32
    32   115   116   114   105   110   103    63
```

The function `char` performs the inverse transformation:

```
>> char(u)
ans =
How about this character string?
```

Numerical values less than 0 produce a warning message when converted to character; values greater than 255 simply address characters in the font beyond `char(255)`:

```
>> a = double('a')
a =
    97
```

```
>> char(a)
ans =
a
>> char(a+256) % adding 256 does change the result
ans =
š
>> char(a-256) % negative value produces a blank character
Warning: Out of range or non-integer values truncated during conversion
to character.
ans =
```

Since strings are arrays, they can be manipulated with all the array-manipulation tools available in MATLAB, For example, in the coce

```
>> u = t(16:24)
u =
character
```

strings are addressed just as arrays are. Here, elements 16 through 24 contain the word `character`.

```
>> u = t(24:-1:16)
u =
retcarahc
```

The result here is the word `character` spelled backwards.

Using the transpose operator changes the word `character` to a column:

```
>> u = t(16:24)'
u =
c
h
a
r
a
c
t
```

```
e
r
```

Single quotes within a character string are symbolized by two consecutive quotes:

```
>> v = 'I can''t find the manual!'
v =
I can't find the manual!
```

Also, string concatenation follows directly from array concatenation:

```
>> u = 'If a woodchuck could chuck wood,';
>> v = ' how much wood could a woodchuck chuck?';

>> w = [u v]
w =
If a woodchuck could chuck wood, how much wood could a woodchuck chuck?
```

The function disp allows you to display a string without printing its variable name:

```
>> disp(u)
If a woodchuck could chuck wood,
```

Note that the u = statement is suppressed. This feature is useful for displaying help text within a script file.

Like other arrays, character strings can have multiple rows, but each row must have an equal number of columns. Therefore, blanks are explicitly required to make all rows the same length, as in the following code:

```
>> v = ['Character strings having more than'
        'one row must have the same number '
        'of columns just like arrays!      ']
v =
Character strings having more than
one row must have the same number
of columns just like arrays!
```

The functions char and strvcat create multiple-row string arrays from individual strings of varying lengths:

```
>> legends = char('Wilt','Russel','Kareem','Bird','Magic','Jordan')
```

```
legends =
Wilt
Russel
Kareem
Bird
Magic
Jordan
>> legends = strvcat('Wilt','Russel','Kareem','Bird','Magic','Jordan')
legends =
Wilt
Russel
Kareem
Bird
Magic
Jordan
>> size(legends)
ans =
     6     6
```

The only difference between `char` and `strvcat` is that `strvcat` ignores empty string inputs, whereas `char` inserts blank rows for empty strings, as in the following example:

```
>> char('one','','two','three')
ans =
one

two
three

>> strvcat('one','','two','three')
ans =
one
two
three
```

Horizontal concatenation of string arrays that have the same number of rows is accomplished by the function `strcat`. Padded blanks are ignored. The following code is illustrative:

```
>> a = char('apples','bananas')
a =
apples
bananas
>> b = char('oranges','grapefruit')
b =
oranges
grapefruit
>> strcat(a,b)
ans =
applesoranges
bananasgrapefruit
```

Once a string array is created with padded blanks, the function `deblank` is useful for eliminating the extra blanks from individual rows extracted from the array:

```
>> c = legends(4,:)
c =
Bird

>> size(c)
ans =
     1     6

>> c = deblank(legends(4,:))
c =
Bird

>> size(c)
ans =
     1     4
```

9.2 NUMBERS TO STRINGS TO NUMBERS

There are numerous contexts in which it is desirable to convert numerical results to character strings and to extract numerical data from character strings. MATLAB provides the functions int2str, num2str, mat2str, sprintf, and fprintf for converting numerical results to character strings. Examples of the first three functions are in the following code:

```
>> int2str(eye(3)) % convert integer arrays
ans =
1 0 0
0 1 0
0 0 1

>> size(ans) % it's a character array, not a numerical matrix
ans =
     3     7

>> num2str(rand(2,4)) % convert noninteger arrays
ans =
0.95013     0.60684     0.8913     0.45647
0.23114     0.48598     0.7621     0.01850

>> size(ans) % again it is a character array
ans =
     2    40

>> mat2str(pi*eye(2)) % convert to MATLAB input syntax form!
ans =
[3.14159265358979 0; 0 3.14159265358979]

>> size(ans)
ans =
     1    40
```

The following code illustrates the two functions sprintf and fprintf:

```
>> fprintf('%.4g\n',sqrt(2)) % display in Command window
1.414
```

```
>> sprintf('%.4g',sqrt(2)) % create character string
ans =
1.414
>> size(ans)
ans =
     1     5
```

The functions `sprintf` and `fprintf` are general-purpose conversion functions that closely resemble their ANSI C language counterparts. As a result, these two functions offer the most flexibility. Normally `fprintf` is used to convert numerical results to ASCII format and append the converted results to a data file. However, if no file identifier is provided as the first argument to `fprintf` or if a file identifier of 1 is used, the resulting output is displayed in the *Command* window. The functions `sprintf` and `fprintf` are identical, except that `sprintf` simply creates a character array that can be displayed, passed to a function, or modified like any other character array. Because `sprintf` and `fprintf` are nearly identical, consider the usage of `sprintf` in the following example:

```
>> radius = sqrt(2);
>> area = pi * radius^2;

>>s = sprintf('A circle of radius %.5g has an area of %.5g.',radius,area)
s =
A circle of radius 1.4142 has an area of 6.2832.
```

Here, `%.5g`, the format specification for the variable `radius` indicates that five significant digits in general-conversion format are desired. The most common usage of `sprintf` is to create a character string for the purposes of annotating a graph, displaying numerical values in a graphical user interface, or creating a sequence of data file names. A rudimentary example of this last usage is as follows:

```
>> i = 3;
>> fname = sprintf('mydata%.0f.dat',i)
fname =
mydata3.dat
```

In the past, the functions `int2str` and `num2str` were nothing more than a simple call to `sprintf`, with `%.0f` and `%.4g` as format specifiers, respectively. In MATLAB 5, `int2str` and `num2str` were enhanced to work with numerical arrays. As a result of these functions' former simplicity, in prior versions of MATLAB it was common to use the following code:

```
s = ['A circle of radius ' num2str(radius) ' has an area of ' ...
num2str(area) '.']
s =
A circle of radius 1.4142 has an area of 6.2832.
```

Even though we obtain the same result when using `int2str` and `num2str` as we do when using `sprintf`, the latter form requires more computational effort, is more prone to typographical errors (such as missing spaces or single quotes), and requires more effort to read. As a result, it is suggested that usage of `int2str` and `num2str` be limited to the conversion of arrays, as illustrated earlier in this section. In almost all other cases, it is more productive to use `sprintf` directly.

The help text for `sprintf` concisely describes its use:

```
>> help sprintf
 SPRINTF Write formatted data to string.
    [S,ERRMSG] = SPRINTF(FORMAT,A,...) formats the data in the real
    part of matrix A (and in any additional matrix arguments), under
    control of the specified FORMAT string, and returns it in the
    MATLAB string variable S. ERRMSG is an optional output argument
    that returns an error message string if an error occurred or an
    empty matrix if an error did not occur. SPRINTF is the same as
    FPRINTF except that it returns the data in a MATLAB string
    variable rather than writing it to a file.

    FORMAT is a string containing C language conversion specifications.
    Conversion specifications involve the character %, optional flags,
    optional width and precision fields, optional subtype specifier, and
    conversion characters d, i, o, u, x, X, f, e, E, g, G, c, and s.
    See the Language Reference Guide or a C manual for complete details.

    The special formats \n,\r,\t,\b,\f can be used to produce linefeed,
    carriage return, tab, backspace, and formfeed characters respectively.
    Use \\ to produce a backslash character and %% to produce the percent
    character.

    SPRINTF behaves like ANSI C with certain exceptions and extensions.
    These include:
    1. The following non-standard subtype specifiers are supported for
       conversion characters o, u, x, and X.
```

```
t  - The underlying C datatype is a float rather than an
     unsigned integer.
b  - The underlying C datatype is a double rather than an
     unsigned integer.
For example, to print out in hex a double value use a format like
'%bx'.
2. SPRINTF is "vectorized" for the case when A is nonscalar. The
   format string is recycled through the elements of A (columnwise)
   until all the elements are used up. It is then recycled in a similar
   manner through any additional matrix arguments.

Examples
   sprintf('%0.5g',(1+sqrt(5))/2)      1.618
   sprintf('%0.5g',1/eps)              4.5036e+15
   sprintf('%15.5f',1/eps)             4503599627370496.00000
   sprintf('%d',round(pi))             3
   sprintf('%s','hello')               hello
   sprintf('The array is %dx%d.',2,3)  The array is 2x3.
   sprintf('\n') is the line termination character on all platforms.

See also FPRINTF, SSCANF, NUM2STR, INT2STR.
```

The following table shows how pi is displayed under a variety of conversion specifications:

Command	**Result**
sprintf('%.0e',pi)	3e+000
sprintf('%.1e',pi)	3.1e+000
sprintf('%.3e',pi)	3.142e+000
sprintf('%.5e',pi)	3.14159e+000
sprintf('%.10e',pi)	3.1415926536e+000
sprintf('%.0f',pi)	3
sprintf('%.1f',pi)	3.1
sprintf('%.3f',pi)	3.142
sprintf('%.5f',pi)	3.14159
sprintf('%.10f',pi)	3.1415926536

`sprintf('%.0g',pi)`	3
`sprintf('%.1g',pi)`	3
`sprintf('%.3g',pi)`	3.14
`sprintf('%.5g',pi)`	3.1416
`sprintf('%.10g',pi)`	3.141592654
`sprintf('%8.0g',pi)`	`       3`
`sprintf('%8.1g',pi)`	`       3`
`sprintf('%8.3g',pi)`	`    3.14`
`sprintf('%8.5g',pi)`	`  3.1416`
`sprintf('%8.10g',pi)`	3.141592654

In the preceding table, the format specifier `e` signifies exponential notation, `f` signifies fixed-point notation, and `g` signifies the use of `e` or `f`, whichever is shorter. Note that, for the `e` and `f` formats, the number to the right of the decimal point indicates how many digits to the right of the decimal point are to be displayed. On the other hand, in the `g` format, the number to the right of the decimal specifies the total number of digits that are to be displayed. In addition, note that, in the last five entries, a width of eight characters is specified for the result, and the result is right justified. In the very last case, the 8 is ignored because more than eight digits were specified.

Although it is not as common, sometimes it is necessary to convert or extract a numerical value from a character string. The MATLAB functions `str2num`, `sscanf`, and `str2double` provide this capability:

```
>> s = num2str(pi*eye(2)) % create string data
s =
3.1416          0
     0     3.1416

>> ischar(s) % True for string
ans =
     1

>> m = str2num(s) % convert string to number
m =
         3.1416             0
              0        3.1416

>> isdouble(m)  % Oops, this function doesn't exist
??? Undefined function or variable 'isdouble'.
```

```
>> isnumeric(m) % True for numbers
ans =
     1

>> isfloat(m) % True for floating point numbers
ans =
     1

>> pi*eye(2) - m % accuracy is lost
ans =
 -7.3464e-006            0
            0 -7.3464e-006
```

The function str2num can contain expressions, but not variables, in the workspace:

```
>> x = pi; % create a variable
>> ss = '[sqrt(2) j; exp(1) 2*pi-x]' % string with variable x
ss =
[sqrt(2) j; exp(1) 2*pi-x]

>> str2num(ss) % conversion fails because of x
ans =
     []

>> ss = '[sqrt(2) j; exp(1) 2*pi-6]' % replace x with 6
ss =
[sqrt(2) j; exp(1) 2*pi-6]

>> str2num(ss) % now it works
ans =
 1.4142                    0 +          1i
 2.7183              0.28319

>> class(ans)  % yes, its a double
ans =
double
```

The function sscanf is the counterpart to sprintf. The function sscanf reads data from a string under format control:

```
>> v = version       % get MATLAB version as a string
v =
7.0.0.51483 (R14)

>> sscanf(v,'%f')  % get floating point numbers
ans =
         7
         0
    0.51483

>> sscanf(v,'%f',1) % get just one floating point number
ans =
     7

>> sscanf(v,'%d')   % get an integer
ans =
     7

>> sscanf(v,'%s')   % get a string
ans =
7.0.0.51483(R14)
```

You can specify the format under which sscanf operates; this capability makes sscanf a very powerful and flexible function. (See the on-line help text under sscanf for more thorough information about the capabilities of this function.)

When the conversion to a single double-precision value is required, the function str2double is useful. While the function str2num performs this task as well, str2double is generally quicker because of its more limited scope:

```
>> str2double('Inf') % It does convert infinity
ans =
   Inf

>> class(ans)
ans =
double
```

```
>> str2double('34.6 - 23.2j') % complex numbers work
ans =
          34.6 -       23.2i

>> str2double('pi') % variables and expressions don't work
ans =
 NaN
```

9.3 STRING EVALUATION

There are some applications in which it is convenient to evaluate a character string as if it were a MATLAB expression. This is a generalization of what `str2num` and `str2double` do. These functions are limited to extracting numerical values from strings. The MATLAB functions `eval` and `evalc` bring in the entire MATLAB interpreter to evaluate any string that conforms to MATLAB syntax. For example, in the code

```
>> funs = char('ceil','fix','floor','round')
funs =
ceil
fix
floor
round
>> [deblank(funs(1,:)) '(pi)']  % display string to evaluate
ans =
ceil(pi)
>> f = eval([deblank(funs(1,:)) '(pi)'])
f =
     4
>> class(f) % data type of output is numeric double
ans =
double

>> fc = evalc([deblank(funs(1,:)) '(pi)']) % try evalc
fc =
ans =
     4
```

```
>> class(fc) % output of evalc is a character string
ans =
char
>> size(fc)
ans =
     1    13
```

the function `eval` uses the MATLAB command interpreter to evaluate a character-string input and return the results into its output argument. The function `evalc` also evaluates an input string, but its output is the character-string representation of the output. In other words, it returns the results seen in the *Command* window.

If at all possible, for the most part, the use of `eval` and `evalc` should be avoided. Since these functions bring in the entire MATLAB intepreter to evaluate a string expression, they incur significant overhead. In addition, the functions cannot be compiled by the MATLAB compiler, which is a MATLAB add-on product that converts MATLAB code into executable C code.

9.4 STRING FUNCTIONS

MATLAB provides a variety of string-related functions, some of which have been discussed already. The following table briefly describes many of the string functions in MATLAB:

Function	Description
`char(S1,S2,...)`	Create character array from strings or cell arrays
`double(S)`	Convert string to ASCII representation
`cellstr(S)`	Create cell array of strings from character array
`blanks(n)`	Create string of `n` blanks
`deblank(S)`	Remove trailing blanks
`eval(S), evalc(S)`	Evaluate string expression with MATLAB interpreter
`ischar(S)`	True for string array
`iscellstr(C)`	True for cell array of strings
`isletter(S)`	True for letters of the alphabet
`isspace(S)`	True for white-space characters
`isstrprop(S, 'property')`	True for elements that have specified property
`strcat(S1,S2,...)`	Concatenate strings horizontally
`strvcat(S1,S2,...)`	Concatenate strings vertically, ignoring blanks
`strcmp(S1,S2)`	True if strings are equal

Function	Description
strncmp(S1,S2,n)	True if n characters of strings are equal
strcmpi(S1,S2)	True if strings are equal, ignoring case
strncmpi(S1,S2,n)	True if n characters of strings are equal, ignoring case
strtrim(S1)	Trim leading and trailing white space
findstr(S1,S2)	Find shorter string within longer string
strfind(S1,S2)	Find S2 string in S1 string
strjust(S1,type)	Justify string array left, right, or center
strmatch(S1,S2)	Find indices of matching strings
strrep(S1,S2,S3)	Replace occurrences of S2 in S1 with S3
strtok(S1,D)	Find tokens in string given delimiters
upper(S)	Convert to uppercase
lower(S)	Convert to lowercase
num2str(x)	Convert number to string
int2str(k)	Convert integer to string
mat2str(X)	Convert matrix to string for eval
str2double(S)	Convert string to double-precision value
str2num(S)	Convert string array to numerical array
sprintf(S)	Create string under format control
sscanf(S)	Read string under format control

Now consider some other examples of the usage of some of the functions that were defined in the preceding table. For instance, the function `findstr` returns the starting indices of one string within another:

```
>> b = 'Peter Piper picked a peck of pickled peppers';

>> findstr(b,' ')     % find indices of spaces
ans =
     6    12    19    21    26    29    37
>> findstr(b,'p')     % find the letter p
ans =
     9    13    22    30    38    40    41

>> find(b=='p')     % for single character searches find works too
ans =
     9    13    22    30    38    40    41
>> findstr(b,'cow')  % cow does not exist
```

```
ans =

     []

>> findstr(b,'pick') % find the string pick

ans =

    13    30
```

Note that `findstr` is case sensitive and returns the empty matrix when no match is found. `findstr` does not work on string arrays with multiple rows.

Tests on character strings include the following:

```
>> c = 'a2 : b_c'

c =

a2 : b_c

>> ischar(c)    % it is a character string

ans =

     1

>> isletter(c) % where are the letters?

ans =

     1     0     0     0     0     1     0     1

>> isspace(c)   % where are the spaces?

ans =

     0     0     1     0     1     0     0     0


>> isstrprop(c,'wspace') % same as above

ans =

     0     0     1     0     1     0     0     0

>> isstrprop(c,'digit') % True for digits

ans =

     0     1     0     0     0     0     0     0
```

To illustrate string comparison, consider the situation where a user types (perhaps into an editable text `uicontrol`) a string that must match, at least in part, one of a list of strings. The function `strmatch` provides this capability:

```
>> S = char('apple','banana','peach','mango','pineapple')

S =

apple
```

```
banana
peach
mango
pineapple
>> strmatch('pe',S)    % pe is in 3rd row
ans =
     3
>> strmatch('p',S)        % p is in 3rd and 5th rows
ans =

     3

     5

>> strmatch('banana',S) % banana is in 2nd row
ans =
     2
>> strmatch('Banana',S) % but Banana is nowhere
ans =
     []
>> strmatch(lower('Banana'),S) % changing B to b finds banana
ans =
     2
```

9.5 CELL ARRAYS OF STRINGS

The fact that all rows in string arrays must have the same number of columns is sometimes cumbersome, especially when the nonblank portions vary significantly from row to row. This issue of cumbersomeness is eliminated by using cell arrays. All data forms can be placed in cell arrays, but their most frequent use is with character strings. A cell array is simply a data type that allows you to name a group of data of various sizes and types, as in the following example:

```
>> C = {'How';'about';'this for a';'cell array of strings?'}
C =
    'How'
    'about'
    'this for a'
    'cell array of strings?'
```

```
>> size(C)
ans =
     4     1
```

Note that curly brackets { } are used to create cell arrays and that the quotes around each string are displayed. In this example, the cell array C has four rows and one column. However, each element of the cell array contains a character string of different length.

Cell arrays are addressed just as other arrays are:

```
>> C(2:3)
ans =
    'about'
    'this for a'
>> C([4 3 2 1])
ans =
    'cell array of strings?'
    'this for a'
    'about'
    'How'
>> C(1)
ans =
    'How'
```

Here, the results are still cell arrays. That is, C(indices) addresses given cells, but not the contents of those cells. To retrieve the contents of a particular cell, use curly brackets, as in the following example:

```
>> s = C{4}
s =
cell array of strings?
>> size(s)
ans =
     1    22
```

To extract more than one cell, the function **deal** is useful:

```
>> [a,b,c,d] = deal(C{:})
a =
How
```

```
b =
about
c =
this for a
d =
cell array of strings?
```

Here, C{:} denotes all the cells as a list. That is, it's the same as

```
>> [a,b,c,d] = deal(C{1},C{2},C{3},C{4})
a =
How
b =
about
c =
this for a
d =
cell array of strings?
```

Partial cell array contents can also be dealt, as in the following code:

```
>> [a,b] = deal(C{2:2:4}) % get 2nd and 4th cell contents
a =
about
b =
cell array of strings?
```

A subset of the contents of a particular cell a [illegible] can be addressed as well:

```
>> C{4}(1:10) % 4th cell, elements 1 through 10
ans =
cell array
```

The multipurpose function char converts the contents of a cell array to a conventional string array, as in the following example:

```
>> s = char(C)
s =
How
```

```
about
this for a
cell array of strings?
>> size(s)  % result is a standard string array with blanks
ans =
     4    22
>> ss = char(C(1:2))  % naturally you can convert subsets
ss =
How
about
>> size(ss)  % result is a standard string array with blanks
ans =
     2     5
```

The inverse conversion is performed by the function cellstr, which deblanks the strings as well:

```
>> cellstr(s)
ans =
     'How'
     'about'
     'this for a'
     'cell array of strings?'
```

You can test whether a particular variable is a cell array of strings by using the function iscellstr:

```
>> iscellstr(C)      % True for cell arrays of strings
ans =
     1
>> ischar(C)         % True for string arrays not cell arrays of strings
ans =
     0
>> ischar(C{3})      % Contents of 3rd cell is a string array
ans =
     1
>> iscellstr(C(3)) % but 3rd cell itself is a cell
```

```
ans =
     1
>> ischar(C(3))      % and not a string array
ans =
     0

>> class(C)          % get data type or class string
ans =
cell
>> class(s)          % get data type or class string
ans =
char
```

Most of the string functions in MATLAB work with either string arrays or cell arrays of strings. In particular, the functions `deblank`, `strcat`, `strcmp`, `strncmp`, `strcmpi`, `strncmpi`, `strmatch`, and `strrep` all work with either string arrays or cell arrays of strings. (Further information regarding cell arrays in general can be found in Chapter 8).

9.6 SEARCHING WITH REGULAR EXPRESSIONS

The standard string functions, like `findstr`, are useful for searching for specific sequences of characters within strings and for replacing specific character sequences. More generally, you may want to find such *patterns* in strings as repeated characters, all uppercase letters, any capitalized words, or all dollar amounts (i.e., strings of digits preceded by a dollar sign and containing a decimal point). MATLAB supports ***regular expressions***, which is a powerful tool for searching for character strings within character strings. A regular expression is a formula for matching strings that follow some pattern. The Unix world has used regular expressions in many of its tools (such as `grep`, `awk`, `sed`, `vi`, and others) for years. Programmers who use Perl and other languages make extensive use of regular expressions. MATLAB's implementation of regular expressions is very comprehensive and includes many features, including some called *extended regular expressions*. And, if you are familiar with regular expressions, MATLAB's implementation will seem to you to follow naturally. If you are new to regular expressions, you can make use of the simpler features immediately and the more complex features later on.

Here are a few simple rules to get you started. A formula string, or *expression*, that describes the criteria for identifying matching portions of a character string is created. The expression consists of characters and optional modifiers that define the criteria to be used for the substring match. The simplest expression is a string of literal characters, as in the following code:

```
>> str = 'Peter Piper picked a peck of pickled peppers.'; % create a string

>> regexp(str,'pe')         % return the indices of substrings matching 'pe'
ans =
     9    22    38    41
```

Here, we found the letter combination `'pe'` in the words `Piper` and `peck` and twice in the word `peppers`.

Character classes are used to match a specific type of character—such as a letter, a number, or a white-space character—or to match a specific set of characters. The most useful character class is a period (.), which represents *any single character*. Another useful character class is a list of characters, or range of characters, within square brackets (`[]`) that matches *any member of the list or range of characters in the set*. For example, consider searching for a sequence of three characters consisting of a `p`, followed by any single character, followed by the letter `c` or the letter `r`:

```
>> regexpi(str,'p.[cr]')
ans =
     9    13    22    30    41
>> regexp(str,'p.[cr]','match')            % list the substring matches
ans =
    'per'    'pic'    'pec'    'pic'    'per'
```

You could also use a range of characters to find all uppercase letters in the string:

```
>> regexp(str,'[A-Z]')                     % match any uppercase letter
ans =
     1     7
```

The character expressions in the following table match a single character with the indicated characteristics:

Character expression	Description and usage
	Any single character (including white space)
`[abcd35]`	Any single character in the set enclosed by square brackets `[]`
`[a-zA-Z]`	Any single character in the range `a-z` or `A-Z`; the dash `-` between characters defines an inclusive range of characters
`[^aeiou]`	Any single character NOT in the set of lowercase vowels; the `^` used as the first character in the set negates the sense of the set

Character expression	Description and usage
`\s`	Any white-space character (space, tab, form feed, new line, or carriage return); equivalent to the set `[ \t\f\n\r]`
`\S`	Any nonwhite-space character: `[^ \t\f\n\r]`
`\w`	Any "word character" (an upper- or lowercase letter, a digit, or an underscore): `[a-zA-Z_0-9]`
`\W`	Any character that is not a "word character": `[^a-zA-Z_0-9]`
`\d`	Any numeric digit: `[0-9]`
`\D`	Any nondigit character: `[^0-9]`
`\xN or \x{N}`	The character with hexadecimal value N
`\oN or \o{N}`	The character with octal value N
`\a`	The alarm, bell, or beep character: \o007 or \x07
`\b`	The backspace character: \o010 or \x08
`\t`	The horizontal tab character: \o011 or \x09
`\n`	The line-feed or newline character: \o012 or \x0A
`\v`	The vertical tab character: \o013 or \x0B
`\f`	The form-feed character: \o014 or \x0C
`\r`	The carriage-return character: \o015 or \x0D
`\e`	The escape character: \o033 or \x1B
`\`	Use a backslash to force a literal match on the next character. This enables matching on characters that have special meaning in regular expressions; for example, the characters `\.\*\?\\` represent a literal period, asterisk, question mark, and backslash, respectively.

The character expressions in the preceding table can be modified by using regular expression *modifiers* or *quantifiers*. Here is an example of using the \w class, along with a modifier, to find all of the words in the string:

```
>> regexp(str,'\w+','match')                  % find all individual words
ans =
      'Peter'    'Piper'    'picked'    'a'    'peck'    'of'
'pickled'    'peppers'
```

This example shows how the + modifier changes the sense of the expression. Without the modifier, the \w expression matches any single "word character." Adding the modifier changes the expression to match all words (groups of one or more "word characters") in the string.

Character modifiers are listed in the following table:

Modifier	Description and usage
?	Match the preceding element zero or one times
*	Match the preceding element zero or more times
+	Match the preceding element one or more times
{n}	Match the preceding element exactly n times
{n,}	Match the preceding element at least n times
{n,m}	Match the preceding element at least n times, but no more than m times

Character modifiers are considered *greedy* (i.e., they match the longest string they can). For example, in the code

```
>> regexp(str,'p.*p','match')
ans =
    'per picked a peck of pickled pepp'
```

the modifier matches a lowercase p, followed by zero or more of any character, followed by a lowercase p. This behavior can be changed by using the quantifier expressions listed in the following table:

Quantifier	Description and usage
q	Match as much of the string as possible (a *greedy quantifier*). This is the default. Here, q represents one of the modifiers in the previous table (e.g., ?, *, +, {n,m}).
q+	Match as many components of the string as possible, without rescanning any portions of the string should the initial match fail (a *possessive quantifier*). Again, q represents one of the modifiers in the previous table (e.g., ?, *, +, {n,m}).
q?	Match as little of the string as possible, while scanning the string (a *lazy quantifier*). Again, q represents one of the modifiers in the previous table (e.g., ?, *, +, {n,m}).

The following code matches shorter strings bracketed by lowercase p characters:

```
>> regexp(str,'p.*?p','match')
ans =
    'per p'    'peck of p'    'pep'
```

Notice that the string `'picked a p'` was not returned. Lazy quantifiers cause the string to be scanned from beginning to end. If a match is found, scanning continues, beginning with the next character in the string; previous portions are not rescanned.

Parentheses can be used to group patterns. For example, the expression in the following example matches a p, followed by one or more characters that are not the letter i:

```
>> regexp(str,'p[^i]+','match')
ans =
     'per p'    'peck of p'    'peppers'
```

The modifier applies to the preceding character. The sense of the expression changes slightly when parentheses are added. The expression in the following example matches one or more sequences of a p followed by a character that is not the letter i:

```
>> regexp(str,'(p[^i])+','match')
ans =
    'pe'    'pe'    'pepp'
```

The modifier now applies to the two-character sequence within the parentheses.

Matches can be made conditional to the context of a regular-expression match. MATLAB supports both *logical* operators and *lookaround* operators. Lookaround operators can be used to condition a match only if the string is preceded or followed by the presence or absence of another string match. The next example matches all words preceded by words ending in d:

```
>> regexp(str,'(?<=d\s)\w+','match')
ans =
     'a'    'peppers'
```

The expression matches groups of word characters only if preceded by the character d, followed by a white-space character.

The lookaround operators are listed in the following table:

Lookaround operator	Description and usage
`p(?=q)`	Lookahead. Match pattern p only if followed by a match for pattern q
`p(?!q)`	Negative lookahead. Match pattern p only if not followed by a match for pattern q
`(?<=q)p`	Lookbehind. Match pattern p only if preceded by a match for pattern q
`(?<!q)p`	Negative lookbehind. Match pattern p only if not preceded by a match for pattern q

Logical operators are also available. The following example matches words containing the string `'ip'` or the string `'ck'`:

```
>> regexp(str,'\w*(ip|ck)\w*','match')

ans =
      'Piper'    'picked'    'peck'    'pickled'
```

Logical operators are listed in the following table:

Logical operator	**Description and usage**
p|q	Match the pattern p or the pattern q
^p	Match the pattern p only if it occurs at the beginning of the string
p$	Match the pattern p only if it occurs at the end of the string
\<p	Match the pattern p only if it occurs at the beginning of a word
p\>	Match the pattern p only if it occurs at the end of a word
\<p\>	Match the pattern p only if it exactly matches a word

Repeated sequences can be matched by using tokens. When expressions contain parentheses, the string matching the expression within the parentheses (a *token*) is stored and can be reused in the expression. Up to 255 tokens can be used in an expression. Tokens can be referenced by using the syntax \d, where d is the index of the desired token. For example, \1 represents the first token, \2 represents the second token, and so on. The following example matches any doubled-word character:

```
>> regexp(str,'(\w)\1','match')

ans =

      'pp'
```

The next example matches any character followed by zero or more word characters, followed by a white-space character, followed by the same initial character, followed by zero or more word characters, followed by the same white space character:

```
>> regexp(str,'(.)\w*(\s)\1\w*\2','match')
ans =

      'Peter Piper '
```

Notice that the string `'pickled peppers'` did not match, since there is no space after the string `'peppers'`

The following table lists the token expressions available in MATLAB:

Expression	Description and usage
(p)	Capture all characters matched by expression p in a token
(?:p)	Group all characters matched by expression p, but do not save in a token
(?>p)	Group atomically, but do not save in a token
(?#A Comment)	Insert a comment into an expression (The comment is ignored.)
\N	Match the Nth token in this expression (e.g., \1 is the first token, \2 is the second token, and so on)
$N	Insert a match for the Nth token in a replacement string (regexprep function only)
(?<name>p)	Capture all characters matched by the pattern p in a token and assigns a name to the token
\k<name>	Match the token referred to by name
(?(T)p)	If token T is generated (i.e., the match for token T was successful), then match pattern p. This is an IF/THEN construction. The token can be a named token or a positional token.
(?(T)p|q)	If token T is generated, then match pattern p; otherwise, match pattern q. This is an IF/THEN/ELSE construction. The token can be a named token or a positional token.

There are three different regular expression functions in MATLAB. The preceding examples used regexp. The regexpi function ignores cases when matching, whereas the regexprep function replaces strings by using regular expressions.

The following example searches for words beginning with the string 'pi', reverses the words, and returns the resulting string:

```
>> regexprep(str,'(pi\w*)(.*)(pi\w*)','$3$2$1')
ans =
        'Peter Piper pickled a peck of picked peppers'
```

This example generates three tokens: Token 1 is the string 'picked', token 2 is ' a peck of ', and token 3 is 'pickled'. The replacement string '$3$2$1' instructs regexprep to remove the part of the original string matched by the first argument, and replace it with a string consisting of the values of the tokens, in the reverse order. The rest of the original string is returned unchanged. Numbered tokens are referenced in the search pattern by using the \N notation. The $n notation is used to reference the tokens in the replacement string.

The regular expression functions are listed in the following table:

Function	Description and usage
`regexp`	Search for substrings by using regular expressions
`regexpi`	Search for substrings by using regular expressions, ignoring case
`regexprep`	Search and replace substrings by using regular expressions

There are many options available for applying and modifying the regular expression functions. One option is the `'match'` argument illustrated earlier. The `regexprep` function is normally case sensitive and replaces all matches it finds. Options are available to change that default behavior.

All three functions operate on cell arrays of strings, as well as on individual strings. One pattern can be used to search many strings, or different patterns can be used for different strings. Any or all of the input parameters can be a cell array of strings. (For more thorough information about these extremely powerful and complex capabilities, see the MATLAB help documentation.)

10

Relational and Logical Operations

In addition to traditional mathematical operations, MATLAB supports relational and logical operations. You may be familiar with these if you've had some experience with other programming languages. The purpose of these operators and functions is to provide answers to True/False questions. One important use of this capability is to control the flow or order of execution of a series of MATLAB commands (usually in a M-file) based on the results of True/False questions.

> As inputs to all relational and logical expressions, nonzero values are considered True, and zero values are considered False. The output of all relational and logical expressions produces logical arrays with True (1) and False (0).

Logical arrays are a special type of numerical array that can be used for logical array addressing, as shown in the chapter on arrays, as well as in any numerical expression. Internally, logical arrays are a separate variable class that uses one byte of storage per value.

10.1 RELATIONAL OPERATORS

MATLAB relational operators include all common comparisons, as shown in the following table:

Relational Operator	Description
<	Less than
<=	Less than or equal to
>	Greater than
>=	Greater than or equal to
==	Equal to (not to be confused with =)
~=	Not equal to

MATLAB relational operators can be used to compare two arrays of the same size or to compare an array with a scalar. In the latter case, scalar expansion is used to compare the scalar with each array element, and the result has the same size as the array. For example, the code

```
>> A = 1:9, B = 9-A
A =
     1     2     3     4     5     6     7     8     9
B =
     8     7     6     5     4     3     2     1     0
>> tf = A>4
tf =
     0     0     0     0     1     1     1     1     1
```

finds elements of A that are greater than 4. Zeros appear in the result where A<=4, and ones appear where A>4.

The code

```
>> tf = (A==B)
tf =
     0     0     0     0     0     0     0     0     0
```

finds elements of A that are equal to those in B.

> Note that = and == mean two different things: == compares two variables and returns ones (True) where they are equal and zeros (False) where they are not; =, on the other hand, is used to assign the output of an operation to a variable.

Note that testing for equality sometimes produces confusing results for floating point numbers:

```
>> tf = (-0.08 + 0.5 -0.42)==(0.5 - 0.42 - 0.08) % equal ?
tf =
     0
>> tf = (-0.08 + 0.5 -0.42)~=(0.5 - 0.42 - 0.08) % not equal ?
tf =
     1
>> (-0.08 + 0.5 -0.42)-(0.5 - 0.42 - 0.08) % not exactly equal!
ans =
  -1.3878e-017
```

This is the example we used in Chapter 2 to illustrate that arithmetic is not *exactly* commutative when using finite precision. We would expect the result to be True = 1; but it is not, because the two expressions differ by a number smaller than eps. On the MATLAB newsgroup, this fundamental fact of finite-precision arithmetic is regularly posed as a ***bug*** in MATLAB.

It is possible to combine relational expressions with mathematical expressions. For example, the code

```
>> tf = B - (A>2)
tf =
     8     7     5     4     3     2     1     0    -1
```

finds where A>2 and subtracts the resulting vector from B. The code

```
>> B = B + (B==0)*eps
B =
  Columns 1 through 7
   8.0000    7.0000    6.0000    5.0000    4.0000    3.0000    2.0000
  Columns 8 through 9
   1.0000    0.0000
```

is a demonstration of how to replace zero elements in an array with the special MATLAB number eps, which is approximately 2.2e-16 for double-precision values. This particular expression is sometimes useful to avoid dividing by zero, as in the code

```
>> x = (-3:3)/3
x =
  -1.0000   -0.6667   -0.3333         0    0.3333    0.6667    1.0000
```

```
>> sin(x)./x
Warning: Divide by zero.
ans =
   0.8415    0.9276    0.9816       NaN    0.9816    0.9276    0.8415
```

Computing the function sin(x)/x gives a warning because the fifth data point is zero. Since sin(0)/0 is undefined, MATLAB returns NaN (meaning Not-a-Number) at that location in the result. This can be avoided by replacing the zero with eps, as in the code

```
>> x = x + (x==0)*eps;
>> sin(x)./x
ans =
   0.8415    0.9276    0.9816    1.0000    0.9816    0.9276    0.8415
```

Now sin(x)/x for x=0 gives the correct limiting answer. Alternatively, you can avoid the computation at x=0, for example, by using the code

```
>> x = (-3:3)/3 % recreate x
x =
  Columns 1 through 6
        -1    -0.66667    -0.33333         0     0.33333     0.66667
  Column 7
         1
>> y = ones(size(x)) % create default output
y =
     1     1     1     1     1     1     1
>> tf = x~=0  % find nonzero locations
tf =
     1     1     1     0     1     1     1
>> y(tf) = sin(x(tf))./x(tf) % operate only on nonzeros
y =
  Columns 1 through 6
   0.84147     0.92755     0.98158           1     0.98158     0.92755
  Column 7
   0.84147
```

While this approach may seem cumbersome compared with adding eps to x, the concept of avoiding computations with selected components of an array is used often in efficient MATLAB programming.

10.2 LOGICAL OPERATORS

Logical operators provide a way to combine or negate relational expressions. MATLAB logical operators include those shown in the following table:

Logical Operator	Description
&	Element-by-element AND for arrays
|	Element-by-element OR for arrays
~	NOT
&&	Scalar AND with short-circuiting
||	Scalar OR with short-circuiting

The next four examples illustrate the use of logical operators. The code

```
>> A = 1:9; B = 9-A; % recall data
>> tf = A>4
tf =
     0     0     0     0     1     1     1     1     1
```

finds where A is greater than 4.

The code

```
>> tf = ~(A>4)
tf =
     1     1     1     1     0     0     0     0     0
```

negates the preceding result; that is, it swaps the positions of the logical ones and zeros.

The code

```
>> tf = (A>2) & (A<6)
tf =
     0     0     1     1     1     0     0     0     0
```

returns True where A is greater than 2 and less than 6.

The code

```
>> tf= A<2 | A>7
tf =
     1     0     0     0     0     0     0     1     1
```

returns True where A is less than 2 or greater than 7.

The scalar short-circuiting logical operators permit an early exit from logical comparisons where the operator arguments are scalars. That is, when a logical result is known before performing all relational tests, unneeded comparisons are skipped. The following code is illustrative:

```
>> a=0; b=pi; % new data
>> a==0 || b~=1 % a=0 so this is True and b~=1 is not evaluated

ans =

     1
>> b==1 && a==0 % b~=1 so this is False and a==0 is not evaluated
ans =
     0
>> a==0 || (1/a)<1 % a==0 so 1/a is not computed

ans =

     1
```

This last example demonstrates the utility of short circuiting. Since a is equal to zero, the second expression is never evaluated because it does not change the True result. Therefore, `1/a` is not computed. If it was, a divide-by-zero error would have been returned.

10.3 OPERATOR PRECEDENCE

When evaluating an expression, MATLAB follows a set of rules governing operator precedence. Operators having higher precedence are evaluated before operators of lower precedence. Operators of equal precedence are evaluated left to right. The following table illustrates the operator precedence rules used by MATLAB:

Operator	**Precedence Level**
Parentheses ( )	Highest
Transpose (.'), conjugate transpose ('), power (.^), matrix power (^)	
Unary plus (+), unary minus (-), negation (~)	
Multiplication (.*), matrix multiplication (*), right division (./), left division (.\), matrix right division (/), matrix left division (\)	
Addition (+), subtraction (-), logical negation (~)	
Colon operator (:)	
Less than (<), less than or equal to (<=), greater than (>), greater than or equal to (>=), equal to (==), not equal to (~=)	

Operator	Precedence Level
Element-wise logical AND (&)	
Element-wise logical OR (|)	
Short-circuiting logical AND (&&)	
Short-circuiting logical OR (||)	Lowest

This order of precedence is similar, or exactly equal, to the order used by most computer programming languages. As a result, you are probably already comfortable with writing expressions that conform to these rules. As in other programming languages, parentheses can and should be used to control the order in which an expression is evaluated. Within each level of parentheses, the rules hold; for example, the code

```
>> 3|2&0

ans =

     1

>> 3|(2&0)

ans =

     1

>> (3|2)&0

ans =

     0
```

points out that the preceding order of precedence table is different from the tables included in MATLAB versions prior to Version 6. In Version 5 and prior versions of MATLAB, logical AND and logical OR shared the same order of precedence, whereas logical AND now has higher precedence than logical OR.

10.4 RELATIONAL AND LOGICAL FUNCTIONS

In addition to basic relational and logical operators, MATLAB provides a number of other relational and logical functions, including the following:

Function	Description
`xor(x,y)`	Exclusive OR operation. Returns True for each element where either x or y is nonzero. Returns False where both x and y are zero, or both are nonzero.
`any(x)`	Returns True if any element in a vector x is nonzero. Returns True for each column in an array x that has any nonzero elements.
`all(x)`	Returns True if all elements in a vector x are nonzero. Returns True for each column in an array x that has all nonzero elements.

In addition to these functions, MATLAB provides numerous functions that test for the existence of specific values or conditions and return logical results as shown in the following table:

Function	Description
`ispc`	True for the PC (Windows) version of MATLAB
`isstudent`	True for MATLAB student edition
`isunix`	True for the UNIX version of MATLAB
`ismember`	True for set member
`isglobal`	True for global variables
`mislocked`	True if an M-file cannot be cleared
`isempty`	True for an empty matrix
`isequal`	True if arrays are numerically equal
`isequalwithequalnans`	True if arrays are equal with NaNs considered equal
`isfinite`	True for finite elements
`isfloatpt`	True for floating-point numbers
`isscalar`	True for a scalar
`isinf`	True for infinite elements
`islogical`	True for a logical array
`isnan`	True for Not-a-Number
`isnumeric`	True for a numeric array
`isreal`	True for a real array
`isprime`	True for prime numbers
`issorted`	True if an array is sorted
`automesh`	True if the inputs should be automatically meshgridded
`inpolygon`	True for points inside a polygonal region
`isvarname`	True for a valid variable name
`iskeyword`	True for keywords or reserved words
`issparse`	True for a sparse matrix
`isvector`	True for a vector
`isappdata`	True if application-defined data exists
`ishandle`	True for graphics handles
`ishold`	True if the graphics hold state is On
`figflag`	True if a figure is currently displayed on screen
`iscellstr`	True for a cell array of strings
`ischar`	True for a character string array
`isletter`	True for letters of the alphabet

Function	Description
isspace	True for white-space characters
isa	True if an object is a given class
iscell	True for a cell array
isfield	True if a field is in structure array
isjava	True for Java object arrays
isobject	True for objects
isstruct	True for structures
isvalid	True for serial port objects that can be connected to hardware

10.5 NANS AND EMPTY ARRAYS

NaNs (Not-a-Numbers) and empty arrays ([]) require special treatment in MATLAB, especially when used in logical or relational expressions. According to IEEE mathematical standards, almost all operations on NaNs result in NaNs. Consider the following example:

```
>> a = [1 2 nan inf nan]  % note that NaN is not case-sensitive
a =
      1      2    NaN     Inf    NaN

>> b = 2*a
b =
      2      4    NaN     Inf    NaN
>> c = sqrt(a)
c =
    1.0000    1.4142        NaN        Inf        NaN
>> d = (a==nan)
d =
      0      0      0      0      0
>> f = (a~=nan)
f =
      1      1      1      1      1
```

The first two computations give NaN results for NaN inputs. However, the final two relational computations produce somewhat surprising results: (a==nan) produces all zeros or False results even when NaN is compared with NaN; at the same time, (a~=nan) produces all ones or True results. **Thus, individual NaNs are not equal to each other**. Because of this property of NaNs, MATLAB has a built-in logical function for finding NaNs, called isnan:

```
>> g = isnan(a)
g =
     0     0     1     0     1
```

Moreover, the `isnan` function makes it possible to find the indices of NaNs with the `find` command:

```
>> i = find(isnan(a))  % find indices of NaNs
i =
     3     5
>> a(i) = zeros(size(i))  % changes NaNs in a to zeros
a =
     1     2     0   Inf     0
```

Whereas NaNs are well-defined mathematically by IEEE standards, empty arrays are defined by the creators of MATLAB and have their own interesting properties. Empty arrays are just that: They are MATLAB variables having zero length in one or more dimensions, as in the following code:

```
>> size([])  % simplest empty array
ans =
     0     0
>> c = zeros(0,5)  % how about an empty array with multiple columns!
c =
   Empty matrix: 0-by-5

>> size(c)
ans =
     0     5
>> d = ones(4,0)  % an empty array with multiple rows!
d =
   Empty matrix: 4-by-0
>> size(d)
ans =
     4     0
>> length(d)  % it's length is zero even though it has 4 rows
ans =
     0
```

This may seem strange, but allowing an empty array to have zero length in any dimension is sometimes useful. [] is just the simplest empty array.

In MATLAB, many functions return empty arrays when no other result is appropriate. Perhaps the most common example is the `find` function;

```
>> x = -2:2  % new data
x =
    -2    -1     0     1     2
>> y = find(x>2)
y =
Empty matrix: 1-by-0
```

In this example, `x` contains no values greater than 2, and so, there are no indices to return. To test for empty results, MATLAB provides the logical function `isempty`:

```
>> isempty(y)
ans =
     1
```

When performing relational tests where empty arrays may appear, it is important to use `isempty`, as the following code shows:

```
>> c==[] % comparing 0-by-5 to 0-by-0 arrays produces an error
??? Error using ==> eq
Matrix dimensions must agree.

>> isempty(c) % isempty returns the desired result.
ans =
     1
>> a = []; % create an empty variable

>> a==[]  % comparing equal size empties gives empty results
ans =
     []

>> b=1; % create nonempty variable
>> b==[] % comparing nonempty to empty produces an empty result.
ans =
     []
```

```
>> b~=[] % even not equal comparison produces and empty result.

ans =

    []
```

The general rule is that relational operations on empty arrays produce either an error or an empty array result. Therefore, it is important to use `isempty` to consider the empty array case whenever it may appear.

11

Control Flow

Computer programming languages and programmable calculators offer features that allow you to control the flow of command execution using decision-making structures. If you have used these features before, this section will be very familiar to you. On the other hand, if control flow is new to you, the material may seem complicated the first time through.

Control flow is extremely powerful, since it lets past computations influence future operations. MATLAB offers five decision-making or control-flow structures: (1) For Loops, (2) While Loops, (3) If-Else-End constructions, (4) Switch-Case constructions, and (5) Try-Catch blocks. Because these constructions often encompass numerous MATLAB commands, they frequently appear in M-files, rather than having to be typed directly at the MATLAB prompt.

11.1 FOR LOOPS

For Loops allow a group of commands to be repeated for a fixed, predetermined number of times. The general form of a For Loop is

```
for x = array
    (commands)
end
```

The *(commands)* between the `for` and `end` statements are executed once for every **column** in `array`. At each iteration, `x` is assigned to the next column of `array`; that is, during the nth time through the loop, `x = array(:,n)`. For example, in the code

```
>> for n = 1:10
      x(n) = sin(n*pi/10);
   end
>> x
x =
  Columns 1 through 7
    0.3090    0.5878    0.8090    0.9511    1.0000    0.9511    0.8090
  Columns 8 through 10
    0.5878    0.3090    0.0000
```

the first statement says, "For n equals 1 to 10, evaluate all statements until the next end statement." The first time through the For Loop, n=1; the second time, n=2; and so on through the n=10 case. After the n=10 case, the For Loop ends, and any commands after the end statement are evaluated, which in this case results in the computed elements of x.

Since the loop variable is assigned to successive columns of the array on the right-hand side of the equal sign, arbitrary indexing, or inadvertent errors, can occur. For example, in the code

```
>> for n = 10:-1:1   % decrementing loop
      x(n) = sin(n*pi/10);
   end
>> x
x =
  Columns 1 through 6
    0.30902      0.58779      0.80902      0.95106            1      0.95106
  Columns 7 through 10
    0.80902      0.58779      0.30902   1.2246e-016
```

the loop variable n counts down from 10 to 1. The expression 10:-1:1 is a standard array-creation statement that creates a row vector with multiple columns. Any numerical array can be used. In the code

```
>> i = 0; % count loop iterations
>> for n = (1:10)'
      i = i+1;
      x(n) = sin(n*pi/10);
   end
```

```
>> i  % Only one time through the loop!
i =
     1
>> x
x =
  Columns 1 through 6
     0.30902     0.58779     0.80902     0.95106           1     0.95106
  Columns 7 through 10
     0.80902     0.58779     0.30902  1.2246e-016
```

the For Loop executes only one pass! The expression `(1:10)'` is a column vector, and so `n` is set equal to the entire array `(1:10)'` on its first pass. Since there are no additional columns in the right-hand side array, the loop terminates. In the code

```
>> array = randperm(10)
array =
     8     2    10     7     4     3     6     9     5     1
>> for n = array
      x(n) = sin(n*pi/10);
   end
>> x
x =
  Columns 1 through 6
     0.30902     0.58779     0.80902     0.95106           1     0.95106
  Columns 7 through 10
     0.80902     0.58779     0.30902  1.2246e-016
```

the loop variable `n` takes on the numbers 1 to 10 in the random order given by `array`.

A For Loop cannot be terminated by reassigning the loop variable `n` within the loop:

```
>> for n = 1:10
      x(n) = sin(n*pi/10);
      n = 10;
   end
```

```
>> x
x =
   Columns 1 through 6
      0.30902      0.58779      0.80902      0.95106            1      0.95106
   Columns 7 through 10
      0.80902      0.58779      0.30902  1.2246e-016
```

To repeat, the right-hand-side array in the For Loop statement can be any valid array-creation statement:

```
>> i = 1;
>> for x = rand(4,5)
      y(i) = sum(x);
      i = i+1;
   end
>> y
y =
   1.7325      2.3954      1.6326      1.7201      2.0872
```

Here, the loop variable *x* is assigned to the successive 4-by-1 columns of a random array. Since the For Loop has no natural loop index, i was added.

Naturally, For Loops can be nested as desired:

```
>> for n = 1:5
      for m = 5:-1:1
         A(n,m) = n^2 + m^2;
      end
      disp(n)
   end
      1
      2
      3
      4
      5
>> A
A =
      2     5    10    17    26
      5     8    13    20    29
```

```
    10    13    18    25    34
    17    20    25    32    41
    26    29    34    41    50
```

Just because the preceding examples were used to illustrate For Loop usage, it doesn't mean that they are examples of efficient MATLAB programming. Historically, For Loops represented poor programming practice whenever an equivalent array approach existed. The equivalent array approach, called a ***vectorized*** solution, often is orders of magnitude faster than the scalar approaches just shown. For example, in the code

```
>> n = 1:10;
>> x = sin(n*pi/10)
x =
  Columns 1 through 6
     0.30902     0.58779     0.80902     0.95106           1     0.95106
  Columns 7 through 10
     0.80902     0.58779     0.30902  1.2246e-016
```

the two statements duplicate the repeated example of computing the sine function at 10 angles. In addition to being orders of magnitude faster, the preceding vectorized solution is more intuitive, is easier to read, and requires less typing.

The earlier nested For Loop is equivalent to the following vectorized code:

```
>> n = 1:5;
>> m = 1:5;
>> [nn,mm] = meshgrid(n,m);
>> A = nn.^2 + mm.^2
A =
     2     5    10    17    26
     5     8    13    20    29
    10    13    18    25    34
    17    20    25    32    41
    26    29    34    41    50
```

As discussed in Chapter 5, arrays should be preallocated before a For Loop (or While Loop) is executed. Doing so minimizes the amount of memory allocation required. For example, in the first case considered in this section, every time the commands within the For Loop are executed, the size of the variable x is increased by 1, which forces MATLAB to take the time to allocate more memory for x every time it goes through the loop. To eliminate this step, the For Loop example should be rewritten, as follows:

```
>> x = zeros(1,10); % preallocated memory for x
>> for n = 1:10
      x(n) = sin(n*pi/10);
   end
```

In this case, only the values of x(n) need to be changed each time through the loop. Memory allocation occurs once outside the loop, so no memory allocation overhead bogs down the operations within the loop.

Starting with MATLAB 6.5, improvements were made to the MATLAB interpreter to minimize the processing overhead involved in executing loops. These improvements are collectively known as the ***JIT-Accelerator***. As stated in the documentation, such improvements will appear over a series of MATLAB releases. At this time, the JIT-Accelerator offers significant improvements for a subset of MATLAB syntax, data types, and array sizes. MATLAB code containing loops benefits from JIT-acceleration if it has the following features and properties:

1. The loop structure is a For Loop.
2. The loop contains only logical, character string, double-precision, and less than 64-bit integer data types.
3. The loop uses arrays that are three dimensional or less.
4. All variables within a loop are defined prior to loop execution.
5. Memory for all variables within the loop are preallocated, and maintain constant size and data type for all loop iterations.
6. Loop indices are scalar quantities, such as the index i in for i=1:N.
7. Only built-in MATLAB functions are called within the loop.
8. Conditional statements with *if-then-else* or *switch-case* constructions (introduced later in this chapter) involve scalar comparisons.
9. All lines within the block contain no more than one assignment statement.

JIT-acceleration provides the greatest benefit when the arrays that are addressed within the loop are relatively small. As array sizes increase, computational time increases and the percentage of time spent on processing overhead decreases, thereby leading to less dramatic improvements in overall execution time.

The following code demonstrates the capabilities of the JIT-Accelerator:

```
N = 1e5;
% generate sin(x) at 1e5 points by using array mathematics
% this is often called a 'vectorized' solution.
```

```
x = linspace(0,2*pi,N);
y = sin(x);     % vectorized solution requires two lines
% redo above using JIT-acceleration.
i = 0;
y = zeros(1,N);  % initialize all variables within loop
x = zeros(1,N);  % and allocate all memory
for i=1:N                  % scalar loop variable
   x(i) = 2*pi*(i-1)/N; % only built-in function calls
   y(i) = sin(x(i));
end
```

With JIT-acceleration, both approaches take approximately the same time to execute. However, prior to the existence of the JIT-Accelerator, the For Loop approach would have been orders of magnitude slower than the vectorized solution. For this particular case, the array mathematics approach is much shorter and much easier to read, so the JIT-acceleration approach has little value for solving this problem. JIT-acceleration proves its value in more substantial problems where it is difficult or impossible to compose a vectorized solution by using array mathematics.

11.2 WHILE LOOPS

As opposed to a For Loop that evaluates a group of commands a fixed number of times, a While Loop evaluates a group of statements an indefinite number of times.

The general form of a While Loop is

```
while expression
   (commands)
end
```

The *(commands)* between the `while` and `end` statements are executed as long as *all* elements in *expression* are True. Usually, evaluation of *expression* gives a scalar result, but array results are also valid. In the array case, *all* elements of the resulting array must be True.

One way of computing the double-precision value `eps`, which is the smallest number that can be added to 1 such that the result is greater than 1, using finite precision is

```
>> num = 0; EPS = 1;
>> while (1+EPS)>1
     EPS = EPS/2;
     num = num+1;
   end
```

```
>> num

num =

    53

>> EPS=2*EPS

EPS =

   2.2204e-16
```

Here, we used uppercase EPS so that the MATLAB value eps is not overwritten. In this example, EPS starts at 1. As long as (1+EPS)>1 is True (nonzero), the commands inside the While Loop are evaluated. Since EPS is continually divided in two, it eventually gets so small that adding EPS to 1 is no longer greater than 1. (Recall that this happens because a computer uses a fixed number of digits to represent numbers. Double precision specifies approximately 16 digits, so we would expect eps to be near 10^{-16}.) At this point, (1+EPS)>1 is False (zero) and the While Loop terminates. Finally, EPS is multiplied by 2, because the last division by 2 made it too small by a factor of 2.

For array expressions, the While Loop continues only when *all* elements in *expression* are True. If you want the While Loop to continue when *any* element is True, simply use the function any. For instance, while any(*expression*) returns a scalar logical True whenever any of its contents are True.

11.3 IF-ELSE-END CONSTRUCTIONS

Many times, sequences of commands must be conditionally evaluated on the basis of a relational test. In programming languages, this logic is provided by some variation of an If-Else-End construction. The simplest If-Else-End construction is

```
if expression
    (commands)
end
```

The *(commands)* between the if and end statements are evaluated if *all* elements in expression are True (nonzero).

> In cases where *expression* involves several logical subexpressions, only the minimum number required to determine the final logical state are evaluated. For example, if *expression* is (*expression1* | *expression2*), then *expression2* is evaluated only if *expression1* is False. Similarly, if *expression* is (*expression1* & *expression2*), then expression2 is not evaluated if expression1 is False. Note that this short circuiting occurs in If-Else-End constructions even if the specific short-circuiting operators || or && are not used.

The following example is illustrative:

```
>> apples = 10;                  % number of apples
>> cost = apples*25              % cost of apples
cost =
   250

>> if apples>5                   % give 20% discount for larger purchases
      cost = (1-20/100)*cost;
  end
>> cost
cost =
   200
```

In cases where there are two alternatives, the If-Else-End construction is

```
if expression
    (commands evaluated if True)
else
    (commands evaluated if False)
end
```

Here, the first set of commands is evaluated if *expression* is True; the second set is evaluated if *expression* is False.

When there are three or more alternatives, the If-Else-End construction takes the form

```
if expression1
    (commands evaluated if expression1 is True)
elseif expression2
    (commands evaluated if expression2 is True)
elseif expression3
    (commands evaluated if expression3 is True)
elseif expression4
    (commands evaluated if expression4 is True)
elseif expression5
```

```
else
    (commands evaluated if no other expression is True)
end
```

In this last form, only the commands associated with the first True expression encountered are evaluated; ensuing relational expressions are not tested; and the rest of the If-Else-End construction is skipped. Furthermore, the final `else` command may or may not appear.

Now that we know how to make decisions with If-Else-End constructions, it is possible to show a legal way to break out of For Loops and While Loops:

```
>> EPS = 1;
>> for num = 1:1000
      EPS = EPS/2;
      if (1+EPS)<=1
         EPS = EPS*2
         break
      end
   end
EPS =
   2.2204e-16

>> num
num =
   53
```

This example demonstrates another way of estimating the double-precision value `eps`. In this case, the For Loop is instructed to run some sufficiently large number of times. The If-Else-End structure tests to see if `EPS` has gotten small enough. If it has, `EPS` is multiplied by 2, and the `break` command forces the For Loop to end prematurely, which, in this case is at `num=53`.

Furthermore, when the `break` statement is executed, MATLAB jumps to the next statement outside of the loop in which the `break` statement appears. Therefore, it returns to the MATLAB prompt and displays `EPS`. If a `break` statement appears in a nested For Loop or While Loop structure, MATLAB only jumps out of the immediate loop in which the `break` statement appears. It does not jump all the way out of the entire nested structure.

MATLAB Version 6 introduced the command `continue` for use in For Loops and While Loops. When MATLAB encounters a `continue` statement inside of a For Loop or While Loop, it immediately jumps to the `end` statement of the loop, bypassing all of the commands between the `continue` command and the `end` statement.

In doing so, the `continue` command moves immediately to the expression test for the next pass through the loop:

```
>> EPS = 1;
>> for num = 1:1000
      EPS = EPS/2;
      if (1+EPS)>1
         continue
      end
      EPS = EPS*2
      break
   end
EPS =
   2.2204e-016
```

Here, the previous example is rewritten to use the `continue` command. Note that the `continue` command has no affect on the If-End construction.

11.4 SWITCH-CASE CONSTRUCTIONS

When sequences of commands must be conditionally evaluated on the basis of repeated use of an equality test with one common argument, a Switch-Case construction is often easier. Switch-Case constructions have the form

```
switch expression
   case test_expression1
      (commands1)
   case {test_expression2,test_expression3,test_expression4}
      (commands2)
   otherwise
      (commands3)
end
```

where *expression* must be either a scalar or a character string. If *expression* is a scalar, *expression==test_expressionN* is tested by each case statement. If *expression* is a character string, *strcmp(expression,test_expression)* is tested. In this example, `expression` is compared with *test_expression1* at the first case statement. If they are equal, *(commands1)* are evaluated, and the rest of the statements before the end statement are skipped. If the first comparison is not true, the second is considered. In this example, *expression* is compared with *test_expression2*, *test_expressior3*, and *test_expression4*, which are contained in a cell array. If any of these are equal to *expression*, *(commands2)* are evaluated, and the rest of the statements before end are skipped. If all case comparisons are False, *(commands3)* following the optional otherwise statement are executed. ***Note that this implementation of the Switch-Case construction allows at most one of the command groups to be executed.***

A simple example demonstrating the Switch-Case construction is

```
x = 2.7;
units = 'm';
switch units  % convert x to centimeters
   case {'inch','in'}
      y = x*2.54;
   case {'feet','ft'}
      y = x*2.54*12;
   case {'meter','m'}
      y = x/100;
   case {'millimeter','mm'}
     y = x*10;
   case {'centimeter','cm'}
      y = x;
   otherwise
      disp(['Unknown Units: ' units])
      y = nan;
end
```

Executing this code gives a final value of y=0.027.

11.5 TRY-CATCH BLOCKS

A Try-Catch block provides user-controlled error-trapping capabilities. That is, with a Try-Catch block, errors found by MATLAB are captured, giving the user the ability to control the way MATLAB responds to errors. Try-Catch blocks have the form

```
try
   (commands1)
catch
   (commands2)
end
```

Here, all MATLAB expressions in *(commands1)* are executed. If no MATLAB errors are generated, control is passed to the end statement. However, if a MATLAB error appears while executing *(commands1)*, control is immediately passed to the catch statement and subsequent expressions in *(commands2)*. The code within *(commands2)* can make use of the functions lasterr and lasterror to access information about the error and act accordingly.

Consider the following example, implemented in a script M-file for convenience:

```
x = ones(4,2);
y = 4*eye(2);
try
   z = x*y;
catch
   z = nan;
   disp('X and Y are not conformable.')
end
z
```

With the preceding data for x and y, this code segment produces the following output:

```
z =
     4     4
     4     4
     4     4
     4     4
```

In this case, only the code in the Try block was executed. Changing the variable y creates an error:

```
x = ones(4,2);
y = 4*eye(3);  % now wrong size
try
   z = x*y;
catch
   z = nan;
   disp('X and Y are not conformable.')
end
z
```

Executing the code this time generates the following output in the *Command* window:

```
X and Y are not conformable.
z =
   NaN
```

In addition, the function `lasterr` describes the error found:

```
>> lasterr
ans =
Error using ==> *
Inner matrix dimensions must agree.
```

More detailed information is returned by the structure output of the function `lasterror`:

```
>> errstr = lasterror
errstr =
         message: [1x53 char]
      identifier: 'MATLAB:innerdim'
>> errstr.message
ans =
Error using ==> *
Inner matrix dimensions must agree.
```

Here, the content of the `message` field is the same as the output from `lasterr`. The `indentifier` field describes the message identifier, which in this case classifies the error type as being generated by an inner-dimension error in MATLAB.

The Catch block also may perform tasks and then reissue the original error by using the `rethrow` function. For example, revising and rerunning the code from the previous example produces

```
x = ones(4,2);
y = 4*eye(3);  % now wrong size
try
   z = x*y;
catch
   z = nan;
   disp('X and Y are not conformable.')
```

```
    rethrow(lasterror) % process error as if Try-Catch did not happen.
end
z
```

In this case, the *Command* window displays

```
X and Y are not conformable.
??? Error using ==> *
Inner matrix dimensions must agree.
```

The `rethrow` function reissues the error, terminates execution, and therefore does not display the contents of `z` as requested by the last code line.

12

Functions

When you use MATLAB functions such as `inv`, `abs`, `angle`, and `sqrt`, MATLAB takes the variables that you pass to it, computes the required results using your input, and then passes these results back to you. The commands evaluated by the function, as well as any intermediate variables created by these commands, are hidden. All you see is what goes in and what comes out. In other words, a function is a black box.

This property makes functions very powerful tools for evaluating commands that encapsulate useful mathematical functions or sequences of commands that often appear when you are solving some larger problem. Because of the usefulness of this power, MATLAB provides several structures that enable you to create functions of your own. These structures include ***M-file*** functions, ***anonymous*** functions, and ***inline*** functions. Of these, M-file functions are the most common. M-file functions are text files that contain MATLAB code and a function header. The function `mmempty` is a good example of an M-file function:

```
function d=mmempty(a,b)
%MMEMPTY Substitute Value if Empty.
% MMEMPTY(A,B) returns A if A is not empty,
% otherwise B is returned.
%
% Example: The empty array problem in logical statements
% let a=[]; then use MMEMPTY to set default logical state
% (a==1) is [], but MMEMPTY(a,1)==1 is true
% (a==0) is [], but MMEMPTY(a,0)==0 is true
```

```
% Also:
% sum(a) is 0,  but sum(MMEMPTY(a,b))=sum(b)
% prod(a) is 1, but prod(MMEMPTY(a,b))=prod(b)
%
% See also ISEMPTY, SUM, PROD, FIND
if isempty(a)
     d=b;
else
     d=a;
end
```

A function M-file is similar to a script M-file in that it is a text file having a `.m` extension. Like script M-files, function M-files are not entered in the *Command* window, but rather are external text files created with a text editor (probably the Editor/Debugger that comes with MATLAB). A function M-file is different from a script file in that a function communicates with the MATLAB workspace only through the variables passed to it and through the output variables it creates. Intermediate variables within the function do not appear in, or interact with, the MATLAB workspace. As can be seen in the previous example, the first line of a function M-file defines the M-file as a function and specifies its name, which is the same as its filename without the `.m` extension. The first line also defines the M-file's input and output variables. The next continuous sequence of comment lines comprises the text displayed in response to the help command `help mmempty` or `helpwin mmempty`. The first help line, called the H1 line, is the line searched by the `lookfor` command. Finally, the remainder of the M-file contains MATLAB commands that create the output variables. Note that there is no `return` command in `mmempty`; the function simply terminates after it executes the last command. However, you can use the `return` command to terminate execution before reaching the end of the M-file.

12.1 M-FILE FUNCTION CONSTRUCTION RULES

Function M-files must satisfy a number of criteria and should have a number of desirable features:

1. The function M-file name and the function name (e.g., `mmempty`) that appear in the first line of the file should be identical. In reality, MATLAB ignores the function name in the first line and executes functions on the basis of the file name stored on disk.
2. Function M-file names can have up to 63 characters. This maximum may be limited by the operating system, in which case the lower limit applies. MATLAB ignores characters beyond the 63rd or the operating system limit, and so

longer names can be used, provided the legal characters point to a unique file name.

3. Function M-file names are case sensitive on UNIX platforms, and in MATLAB 7 they are now case sensitive on Windows platforms as well. To avoid platform dependencies across MATLAB versions, it is beneficial to use only lowercase letters in M-file names.
4. Function names must begin with a letter. Any combination of letters, numbers, and underscores can appear after the first character. Function names cannot contain spaces or punctuation characters. This naming rule is identical to that for variables.
5. The first line of a function M-file is called the ***function-declaration line*** and must contain the word `function` followed by the calling syntax for the function in its most general form. The input and output variables identified in the first line are variables local to the function. The input variables contain data passed to the function, and the output variables contain data passed back from the function. It is not possible to pass data back through the input variables.
6. The first set of contiguous comment lines after the function-declaration line are the help text for the function. The first comment line is called the H1 line and is the line searched by the `lookfor` command. The H1 line typically contains the function name in uppercase characters and a concise description of the function's purpose. Comment lines after the first describe possible calling syntaxes, algorithms used, and simple examples, if appropriate.
7. Function names appearing in the help text of a function are normally capitalized only to give them visual distinction. Functions are called by matching the exact case of the letters making up their filenames.
8. All statements following the first set of contiguous comment lines compose the body of the function. The body of a function contains MATLAB statements that operate on the input arguments and produce results in the output arguments.
9. A function M-file terminates after the last line in the file is executed or whenever a `return` statement is encountered. If an M-file contains nested functions, each function in the M-file requires a terminating end statement.
10. A function can abort operation and return control to the *Command* window by calling the function `error`. This function is useful for flagging improper function usage, as shown in the following code fragment:

```
if length(val) > 1
   error('VAL must be a scalar.')
end
```

When the function `error` in the preceding code is executed, the string `'VAL must be a scalar.'` is displayed in the *Command* window, after a line identifying the file that produced the error message. Passing an empty string to `error` (e.g., `error('')`) causes no action to be taken. After being issued, the error character string is passed to the functions `lasterror` and `lasterr` for later recall. It is also possible to pass numerical data to the displayed error string by using the function `error` as one would use the function `sprintf`. For example, the previous example could be revised as follows:

```
val = zeros(1,3);
if length(val) > 1
   error('VAL has %d elements but must be a scalar.',length(val))
end
??? VAL has 3 elements but must be a scalar.
```

The %d specification indicates that an integer format should be used to insert the value of `length(val)` into the given place in the error string. When MATLAB identifies an error, it also creates an error message identifier string that is returned by the function `lasterror`, as in the following code:

```
>> eig(eye(2,4))
??? Error using ==> eig
Matrix must be square.
>> lasterror
ans =
       message: [1x42 char]
    identifier: 'MATLAB:square'
```

Here, the `identifier` field identifies the error source as coming from MATLAB and having to do with square matrices. To include this information in an M-file function, simply add it as a first argument to the `error` function, as illustrated in the following code:

```
>> val = zeros(1,3);
>> msg = 'VAL has %d elements but must be a scalar.';
if length(val) > 1
   error('MyToolbox:scalar',msg,length(val))
end
??? VAL has 3 elements but must be a scalar.
>> lasterror
ans =
       message: 'VAL has 3 elements but must be a scalar.'
    identifier: 'MyToolbox:scalar'
```

The `identifier` field now shows that this error was flagged by a function in `MyToolbox`, rather than by MATLAB itself, and that the error was related to a scalar.

11. A function can report a warning and then continue operation by calling the function `warning`. This function has the same calling syntax as the function `error`. Warnings can contain simple character strings, strings containing formatted data, and an optional initial message-identifier string. The difference between the `warning` and `error` functions is that warnings can be turned Off globally, or have warnings associated with specific message identifiers turned Off. Warning states can also be queried. (See MATLAB documentation for more thorough information about the features of the function `warning`.)

12. Function M-files can contain calls to script files. When a script file is encountered, it is evaluated in the function's workspace, not in the MATLAB workspace.

13. Multiple functions can appear in a single function M-file. Additional functions, called subfunctions or local functions, are simply appended to the end of the primary function. Subfunctions begin with a standard function statement line and follow all function construction rules.

14. Subfunctions can be called by the primary function in the M-file, as well as by other subfunctions in the same M-file, but subfunctions cannot be called directly from outside the M-file. Like all functions, subfunctions have their own individual workspaces.

15. Subfunctions can appear in any order after the primary function in an M-file. Help text for subfunctions can be displayed by entering `>> helpwin` *`func/subfunc`*, where *`func`* is the main function name and *`subfunc`* is the subfunction name.

16. It is suggested that subfunction names begin with the word `local`, for example, `local_myfun`. This practice improves the readability of the primary function, because calls to local functions are clearly identifiable. All local function names can have up to 63 characters. The following function `mmclass` demonstrates the use of subfunctions:

```
function c=mmclass(arg)
%MMCLASS MATLAB Object Class Existence.
% MMCLASS returns a cell array of strings containing the
% names of MATLAB object classes available with this license.
%
% MMCLASS('ClassName') returns logical True (1) if the class
% having the name 'ClassName' exists with this license.
% Otherwise logical False (0) is returned.
%
% MMCLASS searches the MATLABPATH for class directories.
```

```
% Classes not on the MATLABPATH are ignored.
%
% See also CLASS, ISA, METHODS, ISOBJECT
persistent clist  % save data for future calls

if isempty(clist) % clist contains no data, so create it
   clist=local_getclasslist;
end
if nargin==0
   c=clist;
elseif ischar(arg)
   c=~isempty(strmatch(arg,clist));
else
   error('Character String Argument Expected.')
end

function clist=local_getclasslist
%LOCAL_GETCLASSLIST Get list of MATLAB classes
%
% LOCAL-GETCLASSLIST returns a list of all MATLAB classes
% in a cell array of strings.
clist=cell(0);
cstar=[filesep '@*'];
dlist=[pathsep matlabpath];
sidx=findstr(pathsep,dlist)+1;       % path segment starting indices
eidx=[sidx(2:end)-2 length(dlist)]; % path segment ending indices

for i=1:length(sidx)-1    % look at each path segment
   cdir=dir([dlist(sidx(i):eidx(i)) cstar]); % dir @* on segment
   clist=[clist {cdir.name}];                 % add results to list
end
cstr=char(clist);            % convert to string array
cstr(:,1)=[];                % eliminate initial '@'
cstr=unique(cstr,'rows');% alphabetize and make unique
clist=cellstr(cstr);        % back to a cell array
% end of subfunction
```

17. In addition to subfunctions, M-files can call private M-files, which are standard function M-files that reside in a subdirectory of the calling function entitled `private`. Only functions in the immediate parent directory of private M-files have access to private M-files. Private subdirectories are meant to contain utility functions useful to several functions in the parent directory. Private function M-file names need not be unique, because of their higher precedence and limited scope.
18. It is suggested that private M-file names begin with the word `private`, for example, `private_myfun`. This practice improves the readability of the primary function, because calls to private functions are clearly identifiable. Like other function names, the names of all private M-files can have up to 63 characters.

12.2 INPUT AND OUTPUT ARGUMENTS

MATLAB functions can have any number of input and output arguments. The features of, and criteria for, these arguments are as follows:

1. Function M-files can have zero input arguments and zero output arguments.
2. Functions can be called with fewer input and output arguments than are specified in the function-definition line in the M-file. Functions cannot be called with more input or output arguments than the M-file specifies.
3. The number of input and output arguments used in a function call can be determined by calls to the functions `nargin` and `nargout`, respectively. Since `nargin` and `nargout` are functions, not variables, one cannot reassign them with statements such as `nargin = nargin - 1`. The function `mmdigit` illustrates the use of `nargin`:

```
function y=mmdigit(x,n,b,t)
%MMDIGIT Round Values to Given Significant Digits.
% MMDIGIT(X,N,B) rounds array X to N significant places in base B.
% If B is not given, B=10 is assumed.
% If X is complex the real and imaginary parts are rounded separately.
% MMDIGIT(X,N,B,'fix') uses FIX instead of ROUND.
% MMDIGIT(X,N,B,'ceil') uses CEIL instead of ROUND.
% MMDIGIT(X,N,B,'floor') uses FLOOR instead of ROUND.

if nargin<2
   error('Not enough input arguments.')
elseif nargin==2
   b=10;
```

```
   t='round';
elseif nargin==3
   t='round';
end
n=round(abs(n(1)));
if isempty(b), b=10;
else          b=round(abs(b(1)));
end
if isreal(x)
    y=abs(x)+(x==0);
    e=floor(log(y)./log(b)+1);
    p=repmat(b,size(x)).^(n-e);
    if strncmpi(t,'round',1)
        y=round(p.*x)./p;
    elseif strncmpi(t,'fix',2)
        y=fix(p.*x)./p;
    elseif strncmpi(t,'ceil',1)
        y=ceil(p.*x)./p;
    elseif strncmpi(t,'floor',2)
        y=floor(p.*x)./p;
    else
        error('Unknown rounding requested')
    end
else % complex input
    y=complex(mmdigit(real(x),n,b,t),mmdigit(imag(x),n,b,t));
end
```

In `mmdigit`, `nargin` is used to assign default values to input arguments not supplied by the user.

4. When a function is called, the input variables are not copied into the function's workspace, but their values are made ***readable*** within the function. However, if any values in the input variables are changed, the array is then copied into the function's workspace. Thus, to conserve memory and increase speed, it is better to extract elements from large arrays and then modify them, rather than

to force the entire array to be copied into the function's workspace. Note that using the same variable name for both an input and an output argument causes an immediate copying of the contents of the variable into the function's workspace. For example, `function y=myfunction(x,y,z)` causes the variable `y` to be immediately copied into the workspace of `myfunction`.

5. If a function declares one or more output arguments, but no output is desired, simply do not assign the output variable (or variables) any values. Alternatively, the function `clear` can be used to delete the output variables before terminating the function.
6. Functions can accept a variable and an unlimited number of input arguments by specifying `varargin` as the last input argument in the function-declaration line. The argument `varargin` is a predefined cell array whose *i*th cell is the *i*th argument, starting from where `varargin` appears. For example, consider a function having the following function-declaration line:

```
function a=myfunction(varargin)
```

If this function is called as `myfunction(x,y,z)`, then `varargin{1}` contains the array `x`, `varargin{2}` contains the array `y`, and `varargin{3}` contains the array `z`. Likewise, if the function is called as `myfunction(x)`, then `varargin` has length 1 and `varargin{1}=x`. Every time `myfunction` is called, it can be called with a different number of arguments.

In cases where one or more input arguments are fixed, `varargin` must appear as the last argument:

```
function a=myfunction(x,y,varargin)
```

If this function is called as `myfunction(x,y,z)`, then, inside of the function, `x` and `y` are available, and `varargin{1}` contains `z`. In any case, the function `nargin` returns the actual number of input arguments used. (For further information on cell arrays, see Chapter 8.)

7. Functions can accept a variable, unlimited number of output arguments by specifying `varargout` as the last output argument in the function-declaration line. The argument `varargout` is a predefined cell array whose *i*th cell is the *i*th argument, starting from where `varargout` appears. For example, consider a function having the following function-declaration line:

```
function varargout=myfunction(x)
```

If this function is called as `[a,b]=myfunction(x)`, then, inside of the function, the contents of `varargout{1}` must be assigned to the data that become the variable `a`, and the contents of `varargout{2}` must be assigned to the data that become the variable `b`. As with `varargin` discussed previously, the length of `varargout` is equal to the number of output arguments used and `nargout` returns this length. In cases where one or more output arguments are fixed, `varargout` must appear as the last argument in the function-declaration line, that is, `function [a,b,varargout]=myfunction(x)`. (For further information on cell arrays, see Chapter 8.)

8. The functions `nargchk` and `nargoutchk` provide simple error checking for the number of valid input and output arguments, respectively. Since functions automatically return an error if called with more input or output arguments than appear in their function definitions, these functions have limited value. They may be useful, however, when a function definition declares an arbitrary number of input or output arguments.

12.3 FUNCTION WORKSPACES

As stated earlier, functions are black boxes. They accept inputs, act on these inputs, and create outputs. Any and all variables created within the function are hidden from the MATLAB or base workspace. Each function has its own temporary workspace that is created with each function call and deleted when the function completes execution. MATLAB functions can be called recursively, and each call has a separate workspace. In addition to furnishing input and output arguments, MATLAB provides several techniques for communicating among function workspaces and the MATLAB or base workspace:

1. Functions can share variables with other functions, the MATLAB workspace, and recursive calls to themselves if the variables are declared `global`. To gain access to a global variable within a function or the MATLAB workspace, the variable must be declared `global` within each desired workspace—for example, `global myvariable`.

> As a matter of programming practice, the use of global variables is discouraged whenever possible. However, if they are used, it is suggested that global variable names be long, contain all capital letters, and optionally start with the name of the M-file where they appear; for example, MYFUN_ALPHA. If followed, these suggestions will minimize unintended conflicts among global variables.

2. In addition to sharing data through global variables, function M-files can have restricted access to variables for repeated or recursive calls to themselves by declaring a variable `persistent`, such as `persistent myvariable`. Persistent variables act like global variables whose scope is limited to the function where they are declared. Persistent variables exist as long as an M-file remains in memory in MATLAB. The function `mmclass` illustrates the use of persistent variables:

```
function c=mmclass(arg)
%MMCLASS MATLAB Object Class Existence.
% MMCLASS returns a cell array of strings containing the
```

```
% names of MATLAB object classes available with this license.
%
% MMCLASS('ClassName') returns logical True (1) if the class
% having the name 'ClassName' exists with this license.
% Otherwise logical False (0) is returned.
%
% MMCLASS searches the MATLABPATH for class directories.
% Classes not on the MATLABPATH are ignored.
%
% See also CLASS, ISA, METHODS, ISOBJECT
persistent clist % save data for future calls

if isempty(clist) % clist contains no data, so create it
   clist=cell(0);
   cstar=[filesep '@*'];
   dlist=[pathsep matlabpath];
   sidx=findstr(pathsep,dlist)+1;      % path segment starting indices
   eidx=[sidx(2:end)-2 length(dlist)]; % path segment ending indices
   for i=1:length(sidx)-1     % look at each path segment
      cdir=dir([dlist(sidx(i):eidx(i)) cstar]); % dir @* on segment
      clist=[clist {cdir.name}];                % add results to list
   end
   cstr=char(clist);           % convert to string array
   cstr(:,1)=[];               % eliminate initial '@'
   cstr=unique(cstr,'rows'); % alphabetize and make unique
   clist=cellstr(cstr);        % back to a cell array
end
if nargin==0
   c=clist;
elseif ischar(arg)
   c=~isempty(strmatch(arg,clist));
else
   error('Character String Argument Expected.')
end
```

In mmclass, the variable clist is declared persistent. The first time mmclass is called during a MATLAB session, clist is created as an empty array. When the function finds it empty, it fills it with data in the first If-End construction in the function. In future calls to mmclass, clist exists because of its persistence, and re-creating clist in the future is unnecessary. For these subsequent function calls, the data previously stored in clist is simply reused.

3. MATLAB provides the function evalin to allow you to reach into another workspace, evaluate an expression, and return the result to the current workspace. The function evalin is similar to eval, except that the string is evaluated in either the ***caller*** or the ***base*** workspace. The caller workspace is the workspace where the current function was called from. The base workspace is the MATLAB workspace in the *Command* window. For example, A=evalin('caller', '*expression*') evaluates '*expression*' in the caller workspace and returns the results to the variable A in the current workspace. Alternatively, A=evalin('base', '*expression*') evaluates '*expression*' in the MATLAB workspace and returns the results to the variable A in the current workspace. The function evalin also provides error trapping with the syntax evalin('*workspace*', '*try*', '*catch*'), where '*workspace*' is either 'caller' or 'base'; '*try*' is the first expression evaluated; and '*catch*' is an expression that is evaluated in the ***current*** workspace if the evaluation of '*try*' produces an error.

4. Since you can evaluate an expression in another workspace, it makes sense that you can also assign the results of some expression in the current workspace to a variable in another workspace. The function assignin provides this capability. For example, assignin('*workspace*', '*vname*', *X*), where '*workspace*' is either 'caller' or 'base', assigns the contents of the variable *X* in the current workspace to a variable named '*vname*' in the 'caller' or 'base' workspace.

5. The function inputname provides a way to determine the variable names used when a function is called. For example, suppose a function is called as

```
>> y = myfunction(xdot,time,sqrt(2))
```

Issuing inputname(1) inside of myfunction returns the character string 'xdot', inputname(2) returns 'time', and inputname(3) returns an empty array, because sqrt(2) is not a variable, but rather an expression that produces an unnamed temporary result.

The function mmswap illustrates the use of evalin, assignin, and inputname:

```
function mmswap(x,y)
%MMSWAP Swap Two Variables.
% MMSWAP(X,Y) or MMSWAP X Y  swaps the contents of the
% variable X and Y in the workspace where it is called.
```

```
% X and Y must be variables not literals or expressions.
%
% For example: Rat=ones(3); Tar=pi; MMSWAP(Rat,Tar) or MMSWAP Rat
Tar
% swaps the contents of the variables named Rat and Tar in the
% workspace where MMSWAP is called giving Rat=pi and Tar=ones(3).
if nargin~=2
  error('Two Input Arguments Required.')
end
if ischar(x) & ischar(y)    % MMSWAP X Y 'string input arguments'

  % check existence of arguments in caller
  estr=sprintf('[exist(''%s'',''var'')
exist(''%s'',''var'')]',x,y);
  t=evalin('caller',estr);
  if all(t)                       % both x and y are valid
    xx=evalin('caller',x);        % get contents of x
    yy=evalin('caller',y);        % get contents of y
    assignin('caller',y,xx)       % assign contents of x to y
    assignin('caller',x,yy)       % assign contents of y to x

  elseif isequal(t,[0 1])         % x is not valid
    error(['Undefined Variable: ''' x ''''])

  elseif isequal(t,[1 0])         % y is not valid
    error(['Undefined Variable: ''' y ''''])

  else                            % neither is valid
    error(['Undefined Variables: ''' x ''' and ''' y ''''])
  end
else                          % MMSWAP(X,Y) 'numerical input arguments'
  xname=inputname(1);         % get x argument name if it exists
  yname=inputname(2);         % get x argument name if it exists
```

```
    if ~isempty(xname) & ~isempty(yname)    % both x and y are valid
       assignin('caller',xname,y)           % assign contents of y to x
       assignin('caller',yname,x)           % assign contents of x yo y
    else
       error('Arguments Must be Valid Variables.')
    end
end
```

6. The name of the M-file being executed is available within a function in the variable `mfilename`. For example, when the M-file `myfunction.m` is being executed, the workspace of the function contains the variable `mfilename`, which contains the character string `'myfunction'`. This variable also exists within script files, in which case it contains the name of the script file being executed.

12.4 FUNCTIONS AND THE MATLAB SEARCH PATH

Function M-files and their powerful features are among the fundamental strengths of MATLAB. They allow you to encapsulate sequences of useful commands and apply them over and over. Since M-files exist as text files on disk, it is important that MATLAB maximize the speed at which the files are found, opened, and executed. The following are the techniques that MATLAB uses to maximize speed:

1. The first time MATLAB executes a function M-file, it opens the corresponding text file and ***compiles*** the commands into an internal pseudocode representation in memory that speeds execution for all later calls to the function. If the function contains references to other M-file functions and script M-files, they too are compiled into memory.
2. The function `inmem` returns a cell array of strings containing a list of functions and script files that are currently compiled into memory.
3. Issuing the command `mlock` within an M-file locks the compiled function so that it cannot be cleared from memory. For example, `clear functions` does not clear a locked function from memory. By locking an M-file, persistent variables declared in a function are guaranteed to exist from one call to the next. The function call `munlock('FUN')` unlocks the function `FUN`, so that it can be cleared from memory. The function `mislocked('FUN')` returns True if the function `FUN` is currently locked in memory. By default, function M-files are unlocked.

4. It is possible to store the compiled pseudocode, or P-code, version of a function M-file to disk by using the pcode command. When this is done, MATLAB loads the compiled function, rather than the M-file, into memory. For most functions, this step does not significantly shorten the amount of time required to execute a function for the first time. However, it can speed up large M-files associated with complex graphical user-interface functions. P-code files are created by issuing the command

```
>> pcode myfunction
```

where *myfunction* is the M-file name to be compiled. P-code files are encrypted, platform-independent binary files that have the same name as the original M-file, but end in .p rather than in .m. P-code files provide a level of security, since they are visually indecipherable and can be executed without the corresponding M-file. Furthermore, it is not possible to convert a P-code file into an M-file. Because of their binary nature, P-code files are not backward compatible across MATLAB versions. That is, a P-code file created by using MATLAB 7.0 will not run on MATLAB 6.X. However, a P-code file created using MATLAB 6.X will generally run on MATLAB 7.0.

5. When MATLAB encounters a name it doesn't recognize, it follows a set of precedence rules to determine what to do. For example, when you enter cow at the MATLAB prompt, or if MATLAB encounters a reference to cow in a script or function M-file,

   a. MATLAB checks to see if cow is a ***variable*** in the current workspace; if not,
   b. it checks to see if cow is a ***subfunction*** in the file in which cow appears; if not,
   c. it checks to see if cow is a ***private*** function to the file in which cow appears; if not,
   d. it checks to see if cow exists in the ***current directory***; if not,
   e. it checks to see if cow exists in each directory specified on the ***MATLAB search path***, by searching in the order in which the search path is specified.

   MATLAB uses the first match it finds. In addition, in steps d and e, it prioritizes by type by considering MEX-files first, followed by P-code files, followed by M-files. So if cow.*mex*, cow.p, and cow.m exist, MATLAB uses cow.*mex*, where *mex* is replaced by the platform-dependent MEX-file extension. If cow.p and cow.m exist, MATLAB uses cow.p. If cow.m exists and cow is a *built-in* function, the built-in function is executed. If cow.m exists and is not a built-in function, the M-file is executed.

6. When MATLAB is started, it ***caches*** the name and location of all M-files stored within the toolbox subdirectory and within all subdirectories of the toolbox directory. This allows MATLAB to find and execute function M-files much faster.

M-file functions that are cached are considered read-only. If they are executed and then later altered, MATLAB simply executes the function that was previously compiled into memory, ignoring the changed M-files. Moreover, if new M-files are added within the `toolbox` directory after MATLAB is already running, their presence will not be noted in the cache, and thus they will be unavailable for use.

As a result, as you develop M-file functions, it is best to store them outside of the `toolbox` directory, perhaps in the `MATLAB` directory, until you consider them to be complete. When they are complete, move them to a subdirectory inside of the read-only `toolbox` directory. Finally, make sure the MATLAB search path cache is changed to recognize their existence.

7. When new M-files are added to a ***cached*** location, MATLAB finds them only if the cache is refreshed by the command `rehash toolbox`. On the other hand, when cached M-files are modified, MATLAB recognizes the changes only if a previously compiled version is dumped from memory as a result of issuing the `clear` command; for example, `>> clear` *`myfun`* clears the M-file function *`myfun`* from memory. Alternatively, `>> clear functions` clears all unlocked, compiled functions from memory.
8. MATLAB keeps track of the modification date of M-files outside of the `toolbox` directory. As a result, when an M-file function that was previously compiled into memory is encountered, MATLAB compares the modification date of the compiled M-file with that of the M-file on disk. If the two dates are the same, MATLAB executes the compiled M-file. On the other hand, if the M-file on disk is newer, MATLAB dumps the previously compiled M-file and compiles the newer, revised M-file for execution.
9. It is possible to check all of the file dependencies for a function M-file by using the function `depfun`. This function rigorously parses an M-file for all calls to other M-file functions, built-in functions, and function calls in `eval` strings and callbacks, and identifies variable and Java classes used. This function is helpful for identifying function dependencies in M-files that are being shared with others who may not have the same *Toolboxes* installed. The function `depdir` uses `depfun` to return a listing of the dependent directories of an M-file.

12.5 CREATING YOUR OWN TOOLBOX

It is common to organize a group of M-files into a subdirectory on the MATLAB search path. If the M-files are considered complete, the subdirectory should be placed in the `toolbox` directory so that the M-file names are cached, as described earlier. When a `toolbox` subdirectory is created, it is beneficial to include two additional script M-files containing only MATLAB comments (i.e., lines that begin with a percent sign %). These M-files, named `Readme.m` and `Contents.m`, have the following properties:

1. The script file `Readme.m` typically contains comment lines that describe late-breaking changes or descriptions of undocumented features. Issuing the

command >> `whatsnew` *`MyToolbox`* (where *`MyToolbox`* is the name of the directory containing the group of M-files) displays this file in the *Help* window. If the Toolbox is posted to *MATLAB Central* at *The Mathworks* website, the `Readme.m` file should include a disclaimer, such as the following, to avoid legal problems:

```
% These M-files are User Contributed Routines that are being redistributed
% by The Mathworks, upon request, on an "as is" basis. A User Contributed
% Routine is not a product of The Mathworks, Inc. and The Mathworks assumes
% no responsibility for any errors that may exist in these routines.
```

2. The script file `Contents.m` contains comment lines that list all the M-files in the Toolbox. Issuing the command >> `helpwin` *`MyToolbox`* (where *`MyToolbox`* is the name of the directory containing the group of M-files) displays the file listing in the *Help* window. The first line in the `Contents.m` file should specify the name of the Toolbox, and the second line should state the Toolbox version and date, as follows:

```
% Toolbox Description
% Version xxx dd-mmm-yyyy
```

This information is used by the `ver` command, which lists installed toolbox information.

3. When writing a collection of M-files to form a Toolbox, it is sometimes convenient to allow the user to maintain a set of preferences for Toolbox use or to set preferences for one or more functions in the Toolbox. While it is always possible to store this information in a MAT-file and retrieve it in later MATLAB sessions, doing so requires choosing a directory location for the preferences file and guaranteeing that the file isn't moved or deleted between sessions. To eliminate these weaknesses of the data file approach, MATLAB provides the functions `getpref`, `setpref`, `addpref`, and `rmpref`. These functions allow you to get, set, add, and remove preferences, respectively. Preferences are organized in groups so that preferences for multiple activities are supported. Within each group, individual preferences are named with character strings, and the values stored can be any MATLAB variable. This is similar to the way structures work. For example, `group.prefname=values` is a way to store `values` for `prefname` in a structure named `group`. When these functions are used, the handling of preference files is hidden from the user. Where they are stored is system dependent, and they remain persistent from one MATLAB session to the next.

12.6 COMMAND-FUNCTION DUALITY

In addition to creating function M-files, it is also possible to create MATLAB ***commands***. Examples of MATLAB commands include `clear`, `who`, `dir`, `ver`, `help`, and `whatsnew`. MATLAB commands are very similar to functions. In fact, there are only two differences between commands and functions:

1. Commands do not have output arguments.
2. Input arguments to commands are not enclosed in parentheses.

For example, `clear functions` is a command that accepts the input argument `functions` without parentheses, performs the action of clearing all compiled functions from memory, and produces no output. A function, on the other hand, usually places data in one or more output arguments, and must have its input arguments separated by commas and enclosed in parentheses (e.g., `a=atan2(x,y)`).

In reality, MATLAB commands are function calls that obey the two differences. For example, the command `whatsnew` is a function M-file. When called from the MATLAB prompt as

```
>> whatsnew MyToolbox
```

MATLAB interprets the command as a call to the function `whatsnew` with the following syntax:

```
>> whatsnew('MyToolbox')
```

In other words, as long as there are no output arguments requested, MATLAB interprets command arguments as character strings, places them in parentheses, and then calls the requested function. This interpretation applies to all MATLAB commands.

Both command and function forms can be entered at the MATLAB prompt, although the command form generally requires less typing. A function M-file can also be interpreted as a function, if it obeys the rules for calling functions. For example, the command

```
>> which fname
```

displays the directory path string to the M-file *fname*, and the function call

```
>> s = which('fname')
```

returns the directory path string in the variable `s`. At the same time, the code

```
>> s = which fname
??? s = which fname
                |

Error: Missing MATLAB operator.
```

causes an error because it mixes function and command syntaxes. ***Whenever MATLAB encounters an equal sign, it interprets the rest of the statement as a function, which requires a comma-separated list of arguments enclosed in parentheses.***

To summarize, both commands and functions call functions. Commands are translated into function calls by interpreting command arguments as character strings, placing them in parentheses, and then calling the requested function. Any function call can be made in the form of a command if it produces no output and if it requires only character-string input.

12.7 FUNCTION HANDLES AND ANONYMOUS FUNCTIONS

There are a number of occasions when the identity of a function must be passed to another function for evaluation. For example, many of the numerical analysis functions in MATLAB evaluate a function provided by the user as part of the function's input arguments. For example, Chapter 24 discusses the function `quad`, which, when called as `quad(Fun, low, high)`, computes the area under the function `Fun` over the range from `low` to `high`. Historically, the function argument `Fun` was specified by the character-string name of the function to be evaluated (e.g., *sin*(x) was denoted as `'sin'`). This method works for both built-in functions and M-file functions. Alternatively, MATLAB 5 introduced *inline functions*, which create functions from character-string expressions. For example, in the code

```
>> il_humps = inline('1./((x-.3).^2 +.01) + 1./((x-.9).^2 +.04) - 6','x')

il_humps =

     Inline function:
     il_humps(x) = 1./((x-.3).^2 +.01) + 1./((x-.9).^2 +.04) - 6
```

the function `inline` creates an inline function object from the character string, with `x` as the variable. Using an inline function definition, `Fun` in `quad(Fun,low,high)` is simply replaced by the name of the inline function (e.g., `quad(il_humps,low,high)`).

To evaluate functions specified by their character-string name or inline function object, MATLAB provides the function `feval`. For example, in the code

```
>> y = feval('sin',pi*(0:4)/4)
y =
            0     0.70711           1     0.70711  1.2246e-016
>> z = feval(il_humps,[-1 0 1])
z =
      -5.1378       5.1765          16
```

`feval` simply evaluates the function described by its first argument, using whatever data are supplied as additional arguments. The preceding example demonstrates the use of `feval` with one vector input argument and one vector output argument. In general, any number of input or output arguments can be used.

In MATLAB 7, the use of strings identifying function names (e.g., `'sin'`) and the use of in-line functions (e.g., `il_humps`) remain supported, but are discouraged in favor of using ***anonymous functions*** and their corresponding ***function handles***.

Anonymous functions were introduced in MATLAB 7 as a replacement for inline functions and are created as shown in the following example:

```
>> af_humps =@(x) 1./((x-.3).^2 +.01) +1./((x-.9).^2 +.04) -6;
```

Here, the `@` symbol identifies that the left-hand side is to be a *function handle*. The `(x)` defines the list of function arguments, and the remainder of the line describes the function expression. Evaluation of this function can use `feval`, as in the code

```
>> z = feval(af_humps,[-1 0 1])
z =
   -5.1378     5.1765    16
```

However, the function `feval` is no longer needed or recommended. It is preferable to use the function handle name itself to perform function evaluation:

```
>> z = af_humps([-1 0 1])
z =
   -5.1378     5.1765    16
```

The definition of an anonymous function can access any MATLAB function, as well as the present content of variables that exist in the workspace where the anonymous function is created. For example, in the code

```
>> a = -.3; b = -.9;
>> af_humpsab = @(x) 1./((x+a).^2 + .01) + 1./((x+b).^2 + .04) - 6;
>> af_humpsab([-1 0 1])
ans =
   -5.1378     5.1765    16
```

the values of the previously defined values of `a` and `b` become part of the anonymous function definition. If the values of `a` or `b` change, the anonymous function does not change. The function handle `af_humpsab` captures and holds a snapshot of the function at the time it is created:

```
>> a = 0; % changing the value of a does not change the function
>> af_humpsab([-1 0 1]) % evaluate again, get the same results
ans =
   -5.1378     5.1765    16
```

The concept of creating function handles applies to built-in and M-file functions as well. For example, in the code

```
>> fh_Mfile = @humps % function handle for M-file function
fh_Mfile =
    @humps

>> fh_Mfile(1) % evaluate humps(1)
ans =
    16
>> fh_builtin = @cos % function handle for built-in function
fh_builtin =
    @cos

>> fh_builtin(pi) % evaluate cos(pi)
ans =
    -1
```

a function handle for an M-file function or built-in function is created by using the @ symbol, followed immediately by the name of the function to be converted. Function handles can also be placed in cell arrays and evaluated by using the same approach:

```
>> fhan = {@humps @cos}
fhan =
    [@humps]    [@cos]
>> fhan{1}(1) % evaluate humps(1)
ans =
    16
>> fhan{2}(pi) % evaluate cos(pi)
ans =
    -1
```

Here, the cell array `fhan` contains a function handle to the M-file function `humps.m` and a function handle to the built-in function cos. Evaluation of the two functions follows the approach outlined earlier, with `fhan{1}` and `fhan{2}` addressing the first and second function handles, respectively. In MATLAB 6, function handles were standard arrays, so the preceding handles could be created using standard brackets, as in `fhan = [@humps @cos]`. This standard-array format for function handles is no longer supported.

To support function handles, MATLAB offers a number of useful functions:

```
>> functions(fh_Mfile)
ans =
    function: 'humps'
        type: 'simple'
        file: 'C:\matlab7\toolbox\matlab\demos\humps.m'


>> functions(fh_builtin)
ans =
    function: 'cos'
        type: 'simple'
        file: 'C:\matlab7\toolbox\matlab\elfun\cos.m'


>> functions(af_humps)
ans =
     function: '@(x) 1./((x-.3).^2 +.01) +1./((x-.9).^2 +.04) -6'
         type: 'anonymous'
         file: ''
    workspace: [1x1 struct]
```

The function `functions` returns information about the function handle. (For the most part, this information is used for debugging purposes only. MATLAB warns that the content of the structure returned by `functions` is subject to change.)

When the name of a function is stored in a character-string variable, the function `str2func` provides a means for creating a function handle:

```
>> myfunc = 'humps' % place name of humps.m in a string variable
myfunc =
humps
>> fh2 = @myfunc % this doesn't work!
??? Error: "myfunc" was previously used as a variable,
conflicting with its use here as the name of a function.
>> fh2 = str2func(myfunc) % this works
```

```
fh2 =
    @humps

>> isequal(fh2,fh_Mfile) % these are equal function handles
ans =
     1
```

The inverse operation of `str2func` is `func2str`. As shown next, it simply extracts the name of the function or the string identifying the anonymous function:

```
>> func2str(fh2) % M-file function
ans =
humps
>> func2str(af_humps) % anonymous function
ans =
@(x) 1./((x-.3).^2 +.01) +1./((x-.9).^2 +.04) -6
>> class(ans) % output is a character string
ans =
char

>> isa(fh2,'function_handle') % True for function handles
ans =
     1
```

Function handles are an extremely powerful and beneficial feature in MATLAB. First, they capture all of the information needed to evaluate the function at the time of function handle creation. As a result, when a function defined by a function handle is evaluated, MATLAB does not need to search for it on the MATLAB path. It immediately evaluates it. For example, as shown before, the file location for `humps.m` is stored as part of the function handle `fh_Mfile`. The overhead time required to find the function is eliminated, which improves performance, especially when a function is evaluated repeatedly.

Another powerful and beneficial feature of function handles is that they can point to subfunctions, private functions, and nested functions (to be discussed next) that normally are not visible from outside of the functions where they appear or are referenced. That is, if the output of a function contains a function handle to a subfunction, private function, or nested function that is visible or within the scope of the function returning the function handle, the returned function handle can be evaluated. For example, the following M-file function skeleton demonstrates returning a function handle to a subfunction:

```
function out=myfunction(select)
%MYFUNCTION Return function handle to a subfunction.
% Example function demonstrating function handles to subfunctions.

switch select
case 'case1'
   out=@local_subfun1;
case 'case2'
   out=@local_subfun2;
otherwise
   out=[];
   error('Unknown Input.')
end
function a=local_subfun1(b,c)
%LOCAL_SUBFUN Some function operation.
% code that operates on the input arguments b and c
% and returns content in the variable a

% end of local_subfun1
function d=local_subfun2(e,f)
%LOCAL_SUBFUN Some function operation.
% code that operates on the input arguments e and f
% and returns content in the variable d
% end of local_subfun2
```

On the basis of this function skeleton, the following sample code creates a function handle to a subfunction in `myfunction` and then evaluates the subfunction outside of the context of the original function `myfunction`:

```
>> h_subfun = myfunction('case2'); % handle to local_subfun2
>> dout = h_subfun(x,y); % execute local_subfun2(e,f)
```

This works because all of the information required to execute either subfunction is captured by the function handle when it is created. Therefore, the subfunction `local_subfun2` can be evaluated, because `h_subfun` has complete knowledge of the content and location of `local_subfun2`.

12.8 NESTED FUNCTIONS

Nested functions are new in MATLAB 7. If you are unfamiliar with the concept of nested functions, they can appear to be strange and confusing, and they can promote poor programming practice. Indeed, they can be all of these things if used improperly. However, they can also be immensely helpful in some situations.

Fundamentally, nested functions provide a way to pass information to and from a function without using global variables, and without passing information through the input and output arguments. The following is the basic form of a simple nested function:

```
function out=primary_function (...)
%PRIMARYFUNCTION primary function.

% code in primary function
% this code can call nested functions

  function nout1=nested_function1(...)
  % Code in nested_function1.
  % In addition to variables passed through the input arguments
  % this nested function has access to all variables in existence
  % in the primary function at the point where this function
  % definition appears. This access permits reading and writing
  % to all variables available.

  end % required to mark the end of nested_function1
% other code in primary_function, including other
% nested functions terminated with end statements

end % end statement required here for primary_function
```

As shown in the preceding code, nested functions are functions that are fully contained within the definition of another function, with end statements marking the end of each nested function and the primary function as well. As opposed to subfunctions, which are functions appended to the primary function, nested functions have access not only to data passed through the nested function input arguments, but also to variables in the parent function. A nested function has its own workspace that includes read and write access to the primary function workspace. In addition, the primary function has read and write access to variables defined in functions nested within it.

In general, a primary function can have any number of nested functions. In addition, nested functions can have nested functions within them. Arbitrary nesting is permitted, but usually is not that useful. In addition, a nested function has access to variables passed to it, and to the workspaces of all functions in which it is nested. If this sounds confusing to you, you are not alone. Nested functions add a level of complexity that can make M-file debugging difficult. Moreover, it may not be clear what beneficial purpose this apparent complexity provides.

The example that follows illustrates a prime use for nested functions. In this rational polynomial example, the primary function returns a function handle to a nested function, which obtains data directly from the primary function workspace:

```
function fhandle=nestexample(num,den)
%NESTEXAMPLE Example Nested Function.
%  NESTEXAMPLE(Num,Den) returns a function handle to a function that can
%  be used to evaluate a rational polynomial. Num and Den are vectors
%  containing the numerator and denominator polynomial coefficients.
%
%  For example, ratpoly=nestexample([1 2],[1 2 3]) returns a function
%  handle that facilitates evaluation of the rational polynomial
%
%      x + 2
%  ------------
%  x^2 + 2x + 3
if ~isnumeric(num) || ~isnumeric(den)
   error('Num and Den Must be Numeric Vectors.')
end
```

```
num=reshape(num,1,[]); % make num into a row vector
den=reshape(den,1,[]); % make den into a row vector
fhandle=@nested_ratpoly; % create function handle for return
   function out=nested_ratpoly(x)
   % Nested function that evaluates a rational polynomial, where the
   % numerator and denominator coefficients are obtained from the primary
   % function workspace. Only the evaluation points x appear as an input
   % argument.

   out = polyval(num,x)./polyval(den,x);

end % nested function terminated with an end statement
end % primary function terminated with an end statement too!
```

Using this function, function handles to specific rational polynomials can be created as demonstrated by the following code:

```
>> ratpoly1 = nestexample([1 2],[1 2 3]) % (x + 2)/(x^2 + 2x + 3);
>> ratpoly2 = nestexample([2 1],[3 2 1]) % (2x +1)/(3x^2 + 2x +1);
>> x = linspace(-10,10); % independent variable data
>> y1 = ratpoly1(x);      % evaluate first rational polynomial
>> y2 = ratpoly2(x);      % evaluate second rational polynomial
>> plot(x,y1,x,y2) % plot created data
>> xlabel('X')
>> ylabel('Y')
>> title('Figure 12.1: Rational Polynomial Evaluation')
```

The two calls to `nestexample` in the preceding code return function handles to two different rational polynomials. Because each rational polynomial obtained its coefficients from the input arguments to `nestexample`, and these coefficients were available to the nested function through a shared workspace, the coefficients are not needed for evaluating the rational polynomials. The coefficients are contained in their respective function handles.

Figure 12.1: Rational Polynomial Evaluation

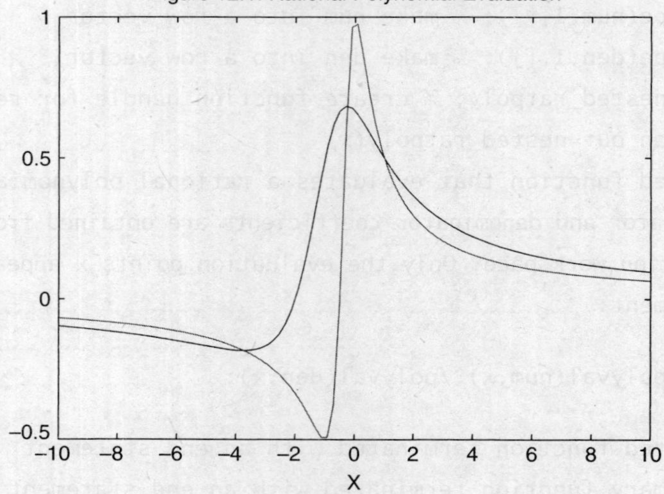

Prior to the existence of nested functions, rational polynomial evaluation using function handles could have been implemented with the following function:

```
function out=ratpolyval(num,den,x)
%RATPOLYVAL Evaluate Rational Polynomial.
% RATPOLYVAL(Num,Den,X) evaluates the rational polynomial, whose
% numerator and denominator coefficients are given by the vectors
% Num and Den respectively, at the points given in X.
if ~isnumeric(num) || ~isnumeric(den)
   error('Num and Den Must be Numeric Vectors.')
end
num=reshape(num,1,[]); % make num into a row vector
den=reshape(den,1,[]); % make den into a row vector
out=polyval(num,x)./polyval(den,x);
```

Evaluation of the two rational polynomials used earlier proceeds as follows:

```
>> yy1 = ratpolyval([1 2],[1 2 3],x); % same as y1 above

>> yy2 = ratpolyval([2 1],[3 2 1],x); % same as y2 above
```

In this case, the numerator and denominator polynomials are required every time a rational polynomial is evaluated. While this is straightforward and common in MATLAB, the nested function approach allows you to encapsulate all information required for a particular rational polynomial into a function handle that is easily evaluated.

Because rational polynomial evaluation can be written as a single statement, this example can also be implemented by using anonymous functions, while retaining the features of the nested function approach. That is, the two function handles ratpoly1 and ratpoly2 could be created by the following statements:

```
>> num = [1 2]; den = [1 2 3]; % specify numerator and denominator
>> ratpoly1 = @(x) polyval(num,x)./polyval(den,x); create anonymous fun

>> num = [2 1]; den = [3 2 1]; % redefine numerator and denominator
>> ratpoly2 = @(x) polyval(num,x)./polyval(den,x); create anonymous fun

>> y1 = ratpoly1(x);       % evaluate first rational polynomial
>> y2 = ratpoly2(x);       % evaluate second rational polynomial
```

This process of creating handles to nested functions and using function handles to evaluate functions is extremely powerful. It allows you to create multiple instances of a function, each with a shared purpose (such as rational polynomial evaluation), while permitting distinct properties as well (such as different numerator and denominator coefficients). Equally important is the fact that each instance has its own workspace, and therefore, each operates independently of all others.

13

M-File Debugging and Profiling

In the process of developing function M-files, it is inevitable that errors (i.e., ***bugs***) appear. MATLAB provides a number of approaches and functions to assist in ***debugging*** M-files. MATLAB also provides a tool to help you improve the execution speed of M-files. In ***profiling*** the execution of an M-file, MATLAB identifies which lines of code take the most time to complete.

13.1 DEBUGGING TOOLS

Two types of errors can appear in MATLAB expressions: syntax errors and run-time errors. Syntax errors (such as misspelled variables or function names or missing quotes or parentheses) are found when MATLAB evaluates an expression or when a function is compiled into memory. MATLAB flags these errors immediately and provides feedback on the type of error encountered and the line number in the M-file where the error occurred. Given this feedback, these errors are usually easy to spot. An exception to this situation occurs in syntax errors within GUI callback strings. These errors are not detected until the strings themselves are evaluated during the operation of the GUI.

Run-time errors, on the other hand, are generally more difficult to find, even though MATLAB flags them also. When a run-time error is found, MATLAB returns control to the *Command* window and the MATLAB workspace. Access to the function workspace where the error occurred is lost, and so you cannot interrogate the contents of the function workspace in an effort to isolate the problem.

According to the authors' experience, the most common run-time errors occur when the result of some operation leads to empty arrays or to NaNs. All operations on NaNs return NaNs, so if NaNs are a possible result, it is good to use the logical function isnan to perform some default action when NaNs occur. Addressing arrays that are empty always leads to an error, since empty arrays have a zero dimension. The find function represents a common situation where an empty array may result. If the empty array output of the find function is used to index some other array, the result returned will also be empty. That is, empty matrices tend to propagate empty matrices, as, for example, in the following code:

```
>> x = pi*(1:4)  % example data
x =
    3.1416    6.2832    9.4248   12.5664
>> i = find(x>20)  % use find function
i =
   Empty matrix: 1-by-0
>> y = 2*x(i)  % propagate the empty matrix
y =
   Empty matrix: 1-by-0
```

Clearly, when y is expected to have a finite dimension and values, a run-time error is likely to occur. When performing operations or using functions that can return empty results, it helps to use the logical function isempty to define a default result for the empty matrix case, thereby avoiding a run-time error.

There are several approaches to debugging function M-files. For simple problems, it is straightforward to use a combination of the following:

1. Remove semicolons from selected lines within the function so that intermediate results are displayed in the *Command* window.
2. Add statements that display variables of interest within the function.
3. Place the keyboard command at selected places in the M-file to give temporary control to the keyboard. By doing so, the function workspace can be interrogated and values changed as necessary. Resume function execution by issuing a return command, K>>return, at the keyboard prompt.
4. Change the function M-file into a script M-file by placing a % before the function definition statement at the beginning of the M-file. When executed as a script file, the workspace is the MATLAB workspace, and thus it can be interrogated after the error occurs.

When the M-file is large, recursive, or highly nested (that is, it calls other M-file functions that call still other functions, and so on), it is more convenient to use the MATLAB graphical debugging functions found on the **Debug** and **Breakpoints** menus of the Editor/Debugger. *Command* window equivalents of these functions exist, but are more cumbersome to use. If you insist on using these functions rather than the graphical debugger, see the on-line help text for debug—that is,

```
>> doc debug
```

The graphical debugging tools in MATLAB allow you to stop at user-set breakpoints, at MATLAB warnings and errors, and at expressions that create `NaNs` and `Infs`. You can also set conditional breakpoints on the basis of some condition tested in the breakpoint itself. When a breakpoint is reached, MATLAB stops execution before the affected line completes execution and returns results. While the program is stopped, the *Command* window keyboard prompt `K>>` appears, allowing you to interrogate the function workspace, change the values of variables in the workspace, and so on, as required to track down the bug. In addition, the *Editor/Debugger* window shows the line where execution stopped and provides the means for stepping into the workspace of other functions that were called by the M-file being debugged. When you are ready to move beyond a breakpoint, the Editor/Debugger provides menu items for single-stepping, continuing until the next breakpoint, continuing until the cursor position is reached, or terminating the debugging activity.

Describing the use of the graphical debugging tools is difficult because of their graphical nature, and because the process of debugging is unique to each debugging session. However, the authors have found the debugging tools to be intuitive and easy to use. Once the basic steps are mastered, the graphical debugging features of MATLAB are extremely powerful and productive in assisting the process of creating good MATLAB code.

13.2 SYNTAX CHECKING AND FILE DEPENDENCIES

During the process of creating and debugging an M-file, it is advantageous to check the code for syntax errors and runtime errors. In the past, this was accomplished by executing the M-file and watching for warnings and errors reported in the *Command* window. Alternatively, it was done by using the `pcode` command to create a P-code file from the M-file. In MATLAB 7, the function `mlint` parses M-files for syntax errors and other possible problems and inefficiencies. For example, `mlint` will point out variables that are defined but never used, input arguments that are not used, output arguments that are not assigned, obsolete usages, statements that are unreachable, etc. In addition, `mlint` will make suggestions to improve execution time. This function is commonly called as a command—for example,

```
>> mlint myfunction
```

where *`myfunction`* is the name of an M-file anywhere on the MATLAB search path. This function can also be called using function syntax, in which case the output can be captured in a number of different ways. For example, the function

```
>> out = mlint('myfunction','-struct');
```

returns the output of `mlint` in the structure variable `out`. In addition to checking a single function by using `mlint`, the function `mlintrpt` accepts a directory name as an input argument, applies `mlint` to all M-files in the directory, and provides a report for each function in a separate HTML-based window. This feature is also available as a choice from the *Current Directory* window in the MATLAB desktop.

Given the ease with which M-files can be transferred electronically, it is not uncommon to run an M-file only to find out that it fails to run because it calls one or more M-file functions not found on your MATLAB path. MATLAB provides the function `depfun`, which parses an M-file for file dependencies. This function recursively searches for all function dependencies, including the dependencies within functions called by the function in question as well as any dependencies found in the callbacks of Handle Graphics objects. Because of the large amount of output produced by this function, it is difficult to demonstrate here and is best explored firsthand.

13.3 PROFILING M-FILES

Even when a function M-file works correctly, there may be ways to fine-tune the code to avoid unnecessary calculations or function calls. Performance improvements can be obtained by simply storing the result of a calculation to avoid a complex recalculation, by using vectorization techniques to avoid an iterative procedure such as a For Loop, or by using MATLAB JIT-acceleration features. When writing a function, it is difficult to guess where most execution time is spent. In today's high-speed processors, with integrated floating-point units, it may be faster to calculate a result more than once than to store it in a variable and recall it again later. There is an inherent tradeoff between memory usage and the number of computations performed. Depending on the data being manipulated, it may be faster to use more memory to store intermediate results, or it may be faster to perform more computations. Furthermore, the trade-off between memory and computations is almost always dependent on the size of the data set being considered. If a function operates on large data sets, the optimum implementation may be much different from that of a small data set. Complicating things even further is the fact that the best computer implementation of a given algorithm is often much different from how one writes the algorithm on paper.

MATLAB provides ***profiling*** tools to optimize the execution of M-file functions. These tools monitor the execution of M-files and identify which lines consume the greatest amount of time relative to the rest of the code. For example, if one line (or function call) consumes 50 percent of the time in a given M-file, the attention paid to this line (or function call) will have the greatest impact on overall execution speed. Sometimes, you can rewrite the code to eliminate the offending line or lines. Other times, you can minimize the amount of data manipulated in the line, thereby speeding it up. And still other times, there may be nothing you can do to increase speed. In any case, a great deal of insight is gained by profiling the operation of M-file functions.

In addition to using the profiler through the *Profiler* window on the MATLAB desktop, MATLAB uses the `profile` command to determine which lines of code in an M-file take the most time to execute. Using `profile` is straightforward. For example, the execution profile of myfunction is found by executing the following commands:

```
>> profile on

>> for i=1:100
      out = myfunction(in);
   end

>> profile viewer
```

First, the profiler is turned On; then, myfunction is executed some sufficient number of times to gather sufficient data; finally, a profile report is generated. The profile report is an HTML file, displayed in the *Profiler* window in the MATLAB Desktop, which in turn is displayed by choosing it from the **Desktop** menu or by issuing the last command in the preceding example. The profile report generates a variety of data. Clicking on various links in the window gives different information.

14

File and Directory Management

MATLAB opens and saves data files in a variety of file formats. Some are formats custom to MATLAB, others are industry standards, and still others are file formats custom to other applications. The techniques used to open and save data files include GUIs, as well as *Command* window functions.

Like most modern applications, MATLAB uses the current directory as the default location for data files and M-files. Implementing directory management tools and changing the current directory are accomplished through GUIs, as well as through the *Command* window functions.

This chapter covers file and directory management features in MATLAB.

14.1 NATIVE DATA FILES

Variables in the MATLAB workspace can be saved in a format native to MATLAB by using the save command. For example,

```
>> save
```

stores all variables in the the MATLAB workspace, in MATLAB binary format, and in the file matlab.mat in the current directory. These native binary MAT-files maintain full double precision, as well as the names of the variables saved. MAT-files are not platform-independent, but are completely cross-platform compatible. Variables saved on one platform can be opened on other MATLAB platforms without any special treatment.

The save command can be used to store specific variables as well. For example, the code

```
>> save var1 var2 var3
```

saves just the variables var1, var2, and var3 to matlab.mat. The file name can be specified as a first argument to save, as in the code

```
>> save filename var1 var2 var3
```

which saves var1, var2, and var3 to the file named filename.mat.

Using command-function duality, the preceding command form can alsobe written in function form as

```
>> save('filename','var1','var2,','var3')
```

This particular format is useful if the file name is stored in a MATLAB character string:

```
>> fname = 'myfile';
>> save(fname,'var1','var2,','var3')
```

Here, the named variables are stored in a file named myfile.mat.

In addition to these above simple forms, the save command supports options for saving in compressed format and in ASCII text format, and the command can be used to append data to a file that already exists. (For help with these features refer to the on-line help.)

The complement to save is the load command. This command opens data files that were created by the save command or that are compatible with the save command. For example,

```
>> load
```

loads all variables found in matlab.mat, wherever it is first found in the current directory or on the MATLAB search path. The variable names originally stored in matlab.mat are restored in the workspace, and they overwrite any like-named variables that may exist there.

To load specific variables from a MAT-file, you must include the file name and a variable list:

```
>> load filename var1 var2 var3
>> load('filename','var1','var2','var3')
```

Here, filename.mat is opened, and variables var1, var2, and var3 are loaded into the workspace. The second statement demonstrates the functional form of the load command, which allows the data file to be specified as a character string. Although not shown, the `filename` string can include a complete or a partial directory path, thereby restricting `load` to a search in a specific directory for the data file.

The latter example provides a way to open a sequence of enumerated data files, such as `mydata1.mat`, `mydata2.mat`, and so on, as in the following example:

```
for i=1:N
    fname=sprintf('mydata%d',i);
    load(fname)
end
```

This code segment uses `sprintf` to create file-name strings inside of a For Loop, so that a sequence of data files is loaded into the workspace.

When you do not wish to overwrite workspace variables, you can write the `load` command in function form and give it an output argument. For example,

```
>> vnew = load('filename','var1','var2');
```

opens the file `filename.mat` and loads the variables `var1` and `var2` into a ***structure*** variable named `vnew` that has fields `var1` and `var2`—that is, `vnew.var1 = var1` and `vnew.var2 = var2`.

The `load` command can also open ASCII text files. In particular, if the data file consists of MATLAB comment lines and rows of space-separated values, the syntax

```
>> load filename.ext
```

opens the file `filename.ext` and loads the data into a single double-precision data array named `filename`. (For further information regarding the load command, see the on-line help.)

To find out whether a data file exists and what variables it holds, the MATLAB commands `exist` and `whos` are valuable. For example, the command

```
>> exist('matlab.mat','file')
```

returns 0 if the file doesn't exist and 2 if it does, and the command

```
>> whos -file matlab.mat
```

returns the standard `whos` *Command* window display for the variables contained in the file `matlab.mat`. Alternatively, the code

```
>> w = whos('-file','matlab.mat')
w =
3x1 struct array with fields:
    name
```

```
size
bytes
class
```

returns a structure array with fields named for the columns of the whos display. Used in this way, the variable names, sizes, memory, and class are stored in variables.

Last, but not least, data files can be deleted by using the *Command* window command `delete`. For example,

```
>> delete filename.ext
```

deletes the file named `filename.ext`.

In MATLAB Version 7, data file management functions can be accessed from the *Workspace* browser, as well as from the *Import* wizard. The *Workspace* browser can be viewed by choosing **Workspace** from the **View** menu on the *MATLAB* desktop. The *Import* wizard, which appears by selecting **Import Data...** from the **File** menu or by typing `uiimport` in the *Command* window, is a general-purpose GUI that facilitates loading data in a variety of formats, not just MATLAB's native MAT-file format.

14.2 DATA IMPORT AND EXPORT

In addition to supporting MATLAB's native MAT-file format and conventional ASCII text format, MATLAB supports a variety of industry standard formats and other custom file formats. Some formats are restricted to reading, others to writing. Some formats are restricted to images, others to multimedia or spreadsheets. These data import and export functions and capabilities make it possible for MATLAB to exchange data with other programs.

Figure window images can be saved in a native MATLAB FIG-file format using the **Save** item on the *Figure* window **File** menu. In addition, *Figure* window images can be exported to a variety of formats by selecting **Export...** on the **File** menu of a *Figure* window. The *Command* window function `saveas` provides an alternative to this GUI-based approach. (For assistance in using `saveas`, see the on-line documentation.)

Data-specific import and export functions available in MATLAB include those listed in the following table:

Function	**Description**
`dlmread`	Reads delimited text file.
`dlmwrite`	Writes delimited text file.
`textread`	Reads formatted text from file.
`textscan`	Reads formatted text from file after opening with `fopen`.

wk1read	Reads spreadsheet file.
wk1write	Writes spreadsheet file.
xlsread	Reads spreadsheet file.
aviread	Reads movie file.
imread	Reads image file.
imwrite	Writes image file.
auread	Reads Sun sound file.
auwrite	Writes Sun sound file.
wavread	Reads Microsoft sound file.
wavwrite	Writes Microsoft sound file.
hdf	Gateway to HDF file capabilities.
cdfepoch	Constructs object for Common Data File (CDF) format export.
cdfinfo	Gets information about a CDF file.
cdfread	Reads from a CDF file.
cdfwrite	Writes to a CDF file.

(The help text for each of these functions provides information on their use.)

The functions imread and imwrite in particular support multiple formats, including JPEG, TIFF, BMP, PNG, HDF, PCX, and XWD. The help text for fileformats provides a more complete listing of the file formats supported by MATLAB, such as the following:

```
>> help fileformats
  Readable file formats.
   Data formats                         Command    Returns
    MAT  - MATLAB workspace             load       Variables in file.
    CSV  - Comma separated numbers      csvread    Double array.
    DAT  - Formatted text               importdata Double array.
    DLM  - Delimited text               dlmread    Double array.
    TAB  - Tab separated text           dlmread    Double array.

   Spreadsheet formats
    XLS  - Excel worksheet              xlsread    Double array and cell array.
    WK1  - Lotus 123 worksheet          wk1read    Double array and cell array.
   Scientific data formats
    CDF  - Common Data Format           cdfread    Cell array of CDF records
```

```
  FITS - Flexible Image                     fitsread  Primary table data
  HDF  - Hierarchical Data Format           hdfread   HDF or HDF-EOS data set
  Movie formats
  AVI  - Movie                              aviread   MATLAB movie.
 Image formats
  TIFF - TIFF image                         imread    image.
  PNG  - PNG image                          imread    image.
  HDF  - HDF image                          imread    Truecolor or indexed image(s).
  BMP  - BMP image                          imread    Truecolor or indexed image.
  JPEG - JPEG image                         imread    Truecolor or grayscale image.
  GIF  - GIF image                          imread    Indexed image.
  PCX  - PCX image                          imread    Indexed image.
  XWD  - XWD image                          imread    Indexed image.
  CUR  - Cursor image                       imread    Indexed image.
  ICO  - Icon image                         imread    Indexed image.
  RAS  - Sun raster image                   imread    Truecolor or indexed.
  PBM  - PBM image                          imread    Grayscale image.
  PGM  - PGM image                          imread    Grayscale image.
  PPM  - PPM image                          imread    Truecolor image.

 Audio formats
  AU   - NeXT/Sun sound                     auread    Sound data and sample rate.
  SND  - NeXT/Sun sound                     auread    Sound data and sample rate.
  WAV  - Microsoft Wave sound               wavread   Sound data and sample rate.
See also IOFUN
```

14.3 LOW-LEVEL FILE I/O

Because an infinite variety of file types exists, MATLAB provides low-level file I/O functions for reading or writing any binary or formatted ASCII file imaginable. These functions closely resemble their ANSI C programming language counterparts, but do not necessarily exactly match their characteristics. In fact, many of the special-purpose file I/O commands described previously use these commands internally. The low-level file I/O functions in MATLAB are given in the following table:

Category	Function	Description/Syntax Example
File opening and closing	`fopen`	Opens file `fid= fopen('filename','permission')`
	`fclose`	Closes file `status= fclose(fid)`
Binary I/O	`fread`	Reads part or all of a binary file `A= fread(fid, num, precision)`
	`fwrite`	Writes array to a binary file `count= fwrite(fid, array, precision)`
Formatted I/O	`fscanf`	Reads formatted data from file `A= fscanf(fid, format, num)`
	`fprintf`	Writes formatted data to file `count= fprintf(fid, format, A)`
	`fgetl`	Reads line from file; discard newline character `line= fgetl(fid)`
	`fgets`	Reads line from file, keep newline character `line= fgets(fid)`
String conversion	`sprintf`	Writes formatted data to string `S= sprintf(format, A)`
	`sscanf`	Reads string under format control `A= sscanf(string, format, num)`
File positioning	`ferror`	Inquires about file I/O status `message= ferror (fid)`
	`feof`	Tests for end of file `TF= feof(fid)`
	`fseek`	Sets file position indicator `status= fseek(fid, offset, origin)`
	`ftell`	Gets file position indicator `position= ftell(fid)`
	`frewind`	Rewinds file `frewind(fid)`

In this table, `fid` is a file identifier number and `permission` is a character string identifying the permissions requested. Possible strings include `'r'` for reading only, `'w'` for writing only, `'a'` for appending only, and `'r+'` for both reading and writing. Since the PC distinguishes between text and binary files, a `'b'` must often be appended when you are working with binary files—for example, `'rb'`. In the preceding table, `format` is a character string defining the desired formatting. Note that `format` follows ANSI standard C very closely. (More information regarding the use of these functions can be found in the on-line documentation for each function.)

14.4 DIRECTORY MANAGEMENT

With all the windows in MATLAB, it makes sense to have management of the current directory and its files available in a GUI. The *Current Directory* window, displayed by choosing **Current Directory** from the **View** menu in the *MATLAB* desktop window, performs these tasks. In addition to traversing the directory tree, this GUI allows you to preview the files in the current directory, see their modification dates, search for text in M-files, create new directories and new M-files, and so on. Because of the fundamental utility of knowing the current directory, the *Current Directory* window is also displayed in a pop-up menu in the *MATLAB* desktop window. Therefore, the current directory always can be known simply by looking at the toolbar on the desktop.

Prior to MATLAB Version 6, directory management was conducted through the use of *Command* window functions. Although these functions are not as important now, they still serve a valuable purpose. In particular, most functions have the capability of returning directory and file information in MATLAB variables, thereby allowing complex manipulation of files and directories to be completed within function M-files. The *Command* window directory management functions available in MATLAB are summarized in the following table:

Function	**Description**
`cd, pwd`	Show present working directory
`S = cd;`	Return present working directory as a string in S
`cd` *`dirname`*	Change present working directory to *`dirname`*
`copyfile (`*`oldname, dirname`*`)`	Copy file *`oldname`* to directory *`dirname`*
`copyfile (`*`oldname, newname`*`)`	Copy file *`oldname`* to *`newname`*
`delete` *`filename.ext`*	Delete file *`filename.ext`*
`dir, ls`	Display files in current directory
`S = dir;`	Return directory information in structure S
`fileattrib`	Get or set file attributes
`mkdir` *`dirname`*	Make directory *`dirname`* in current directory
`movefile(`*`source, destination`*`)`	Move source file or directory to a new destination
`rmdir` *`dirname`*	Remove directory *`dirname`*

`what`	Display an organized listing of all MATLAB files in the current directory
`S = what;`	Return listing information in structure S
`which filename`	Display directory path to *filename*
`S = which ('filename');`	Return directory path to *filename* as a string in S
`who`	Display variables in workspace
`who -file filename`	Display variables in MAT-file *filename.mat*
`S = who('-file','filename');`	Return variables names in *filename.mat* in a cell array S
`whos`	Display variables, size, and class in workspace
`whos -file filename`	Display variables, size, and class in MAT-file *filename.mat*
`S = whos ('-file','filename');`	Return variables, size, and class in *filename.mat* in structure S
`help filename`	Display help text for *filename* in *Command* window
`S = help('filename');`	Return help text for *filename* in a character string S
`type filename`	Display M-file *filename* in *Command* window

Most of these functions require only partial path information to locate a particular file. That is, `filename` may or may not include part of its directory path. If no directory path is included in `filename`, then the MATLAB search path is used to find the requested file. If some part of the directory path is provided, MATLAB traverses the MATLAB search path to find the subdirectory and file specified. For example, if *filename* = `'mystuff/myfile'`, MATLAB restricts its search to a subdirectory named `mystuff` on the MATLAB path.

To illustrate the usefulness of these functions, consider the function `mmbytes`:

```
function y=mmbytes(arg)
%MMBYTES Variable Memory Usage.
% MMBYTES and MMBYTES('base') returns the total memory in bytes
% currently used in the base workspace.
% MMBYTES('caller') returns the total memory in bytes currently
% used in the workspace where MMBYTES is called from.
% MMBYTES('global') returns the total memory in bytes currently
% used in the global workspace.
```

```
if nargin==0
    arg='base';
end
if strcmp(arg,'global')
    x=evalin('base','whos("global")');
else
    x=evalin(arg,'whos');
end
y=sum(cat(1,x.bytes));
```

This function uses the whos function to gather information about the variables that exist within MATLAB. The output of the whos function generates a structure array x. The bytes field of this structure contains the memory allocated to all variables. The final statement in the function concatentates all of the memory-allocated numbers into a vector, which is summed using the sum function.

Because of its varied uses, the function `exist` was not listed in the preceding table. This function tests for the existence of variables, files, directories, and so on. The help text for this function describes its many uses:

```
>> help exist
 EXIST  Check if variables or functions are defined.
    EXIST('A') returns:
      0 if A does not exist
      1 if A is a variable in the workspace
     2 if A is an M-file on MATLAB's search path.  It also returns 2 when
          A is the full pathname to a file or when A is the name of an
            ordinary file on MATLAB's search path
      3 if A is a MEX-file on MATLAB's search path
      4 if A is a MDL-file on MATLAB's search path
      5 if A is a built-in MATLAB function
      6 if A is a P-file on MATLAB's search path
      7 if A is a directory
      8 if A is a Java class
  EXIST('A') or EXIST('A.EXT') returns 2 if a file named 'A' or 'A.EXT'
```

```
exists and the extension isn't a P or MEX function extension.
EXIST('A','var') checks only for variables.
EXIST('A','builtin') checks only for built-in functions.
EXIST('A','file') checks for files or directories.
EXIST('A','dir') checks only for directories.
EXIST('A','class') checks only for Java classes.
EXIST returns 0 if the specified instance isn't found.
```

To facilitate the manipulation of character strings containing directory paths and filenames, MATLAB provides several useful functions, summarized in the following table:

Function	Description
`addpath('`*`dirname`*`')`	Prepend directory *dirname* to the MATLAB search path
`[path,name,ext] = ... fileparts(`*`filename`*`)`	Return path, name, and extension for file *filename*
`filesep`	Return file separator character for this computer platform. The file separator is the character used to separate directories and the file name. For example, on the PC the file separator is '\'.
`fullfile (`*`d1, d2, ..., filename`*`)`	Return full path and file specification for *filename* by using directory tree strings, *d1, d2, ...*.
`matlabroot`	Return a string containing the path to the root of directory MATLAB
`mexext`	Return MEX-file extension for this computer platform
`pathsep`	Return path separator for this platform. The path separator is the character used to separate entries on the MATLAB search path string
`prefdir`	Return MATLAB preferences directory for this platform
`rmpath('`*`dirname`*`')`	Remove directory *dirname* from the MATLAB search path
`tempdir`	Return name of a temporary directory for this platform
`tempname`	Return name of a temporary file for this platform

These functions, along with those in the preceding table, facilitate the creation of file and directory management functions as M-files. (More assistance for each function can be found by consulting the on-line help.)

14.5 FTP FILE OPERATIONS

MATLAB 7 now includes built-in FTP capabilities. From within MATLAB, the function `ftp` creates an ***FTP server object*** that acts like the file identifier used in low-level file I/O. For example,

```
>> ftp_object = ftp('ftp.somewhere.org')
```

establishes an FTP connection to the site `ftp.somewhere.org` and returns an identifier to this site in the variable `ftp_object`. Once this FTP session is established, common FTP commands can be used to change directories and perform file operations. Many of these operations use the same functions used for local file and directory manipulation. For instance,

```
>> dir(ftp_object)
```

returns a directory listing of the default directory. Once FTP operations are completed, the function `disconnect` closes the FTP session. For example,

```
>> disconnect(ftp_object)
```

terminates the ftp session at *ftp.somewhere.org*.

The following table identifies a list of FTP functions available in MATLAB:

Function	**Description**
`ascii`	Set FTP transfer type to ASCII
`binary`	Set FTP transfer type to binary
`cd`	Change current directory
`connect`	Open connection that timed out
`delete`	Delete file
`dir`	List directory contents
`disconnect`	Close connection
`disp`	Set display format
`ftp`	Connect to FTP server
`isconnected`	Detect if connection is valid
`mget`	Download file
`mkdir`	Create new directory
`mput`	Upload file or directory
`rename`	Rename file
`rmdir`	Remove directory

15

Set, Bit, and Base Functions

15.1 SET FUNCTIONS

Since arrays are ordered collections of values, they can be thought of as sets. With that understanding, MATLAB provides several functions for testing and comparing sets. The simplest test is for equality, as in the following code:

```
>> a = rand(2,5);   % random array
>> b = randn(2,5); % a different random array
>> isequal(a,b)     % a and b are not equal
ans =
     0
>> isequal(a,a)     % but a is certainly equal to a
ans =
     1

>> isequal(a,a(:)) % a with a as a column
ans =
     0
```

For two arrays to be equal, they must have the same dimensions and the same contents. This function applies to all MATLAB data types, not just numerical arrays:

```
>> a = 'a string';
>> b = 'a String';
>> isequal(a,b)  % character string equality
ans =
     0
>> a = {'one' 'two' 'three'};
>> b = {'one' 'two' 'four'};
>> isequal(a,b)  % cell array equality
ans =
     0
>> isequal(a,a)
ans =
     1
>> a.one = 'one';
>> a.two = 2;
>> a.three = pi;
>> b.two = 2;
>> b.one = 'one';
>> b.three = pi;
>> isequal(a,b) % structure equality
ans =
     1
>> isequal(a,a)
ans =
     1
```

MATLAB variables are equal if they have the same size and exactly the same content.

The function `unique` removes duplicate items from a given set:

```
>> a = [2:2:8;4:2:10] % new data
a =
     2     4     6     8
     4     6     8    10
```

```
>> unique(a) % unique elements sorted into a column
ans =
     2
     4
     6
     8
    10
```

The `unique` function returns a sorted column vector because removal of duplicate values makes it impossible to maintain the array dimensions. The function `unique` also applies to cell arrays of strings, as in the following example:

```
>> c = {'Shania' 'Britney' 'Dixie' 'Shania' 'Faith'};
>> unique(c)
ans =
    'Britney'    'Dixie'    'Faith'    'Shania'
```

Set membership is determined with the function `ismember`, as in the following code:

```
>> a = 1:9
a =
     1     2     3     4     5     6     7     8     9
>> b = 2:2:9
b =
     2     4     6     8
>> ismember(a,b) % which elements in a are in b
ans =
     0     1     0     1     0     1     0     1     0
>> ismember(b,a) % which elements in b are in a
ans =
     1     1     1     1
```

For vector arguments, `ismember` returns a logical array the same size as its first argument, with ones appearing at the indices where the two vectors share common values:

```
>> A = eye(3);  % new data
>> B = ones(3);
```

```
>> ismember(A,B) % those elements in A that are also in B
ans =
     1
     0
     0
     0
     1
     0
     0
     0
     1
>> ismember(B,A)
ans =
     1
     1
     1
     1
     1
     1
     1
     1
     1
```

For 2-D arrays, `ismember` returns a column vector, with ones appearing at the *single* indices of the first argument where the two arguments share common values. The function `ismember` also applies to cell arrays of strings:

```
>> ismember(c,'Dixie')
ans =
     0     0     1     0     0
```

Set arithmetic is accomplished with the functions `union`, `intersect`, `setdiff`, and `setxor`. Examples of the use of these functions include the following:

```
>> a,b                  % recall prior data
a =
     1     2     3     4     5     6     7     8     9
```

```
b =

     2     4     6     8

>> union(a,b) % union of a and b

ans =

     1     2     3     4     5     6     7     8     9

>> intersect(a,b) % intersection of a and b

ans =

     2     4     6     8

>> setxor(a,b)      % set exclusive or of a and b

ans =

     1     3     5     7     9

>> setdiff(a,b)     % values in a that are not in b

ans =

     1     3     5     7     9

>> setdiff(b,a)     % values in b that are not in a

ans =

     []

>> union(A,B,'rows') % matrix inputs produce combined rows with no repetitions

ans =

     0     0     1
     0     1     0
     1     0     0
     1     1     1
```

Like prior functions discussed in this chapter, these set functions also apply to cell arrays of strings.

15.2 BIT FUNCTIONS

In addition to the logical operators discussed in the last chapter, MATLAB provides functions that allow logical operations on individual bits of any unsigned integer data. For backward compatibility, these bit functions also work on floating-point integers, namely integers stored in double-precision floating-point variables. The MATLAB bitwise functions `bitand`, `bitcmp`, `bitor`, `bitxor`, `bitset`, `bitget`, and `bitshift` work on integers. Examples of bit operations include:

```
>> format hex
>> intmax ('uint16') % largest unsigned 16-bit number
ans =
    ffff
>> a = uint16 (2^10 -1) % first data value
a =
    03ff
>> b = uint16 (567) % second data value
b =
    0237
>> bitand (a, b) % (a & b)
ans =
    0237
>> bitor (a, b) % (a | b)
ans =
    03ff
>> bitcmp (a) % complement a
ans =
    fc00
>> bitxor (a,b) % xor (a, b)
ans =
    01c8
>> bitget (b, 7) % get 7th bit of b
ans =
    0000
>> bitset (b, 7) % set 7th bit to 1
ans =
    0277
>> format short g % reset display format
```

15.3 BASE CONVERSIONS

MATLAB provides a number of utility functions for converting decimal numbers to other bases ***in the form of character strings***. Conversions between decimals and binary numbers are performed by the functions dec2bin and bin2dec, as in the following example:

```
>> a = dec2bin(17) % find binary representation of 17

a =

10001

>> class(a) % result is a character string

ans =

char

>> bin2dec(a) % convert a back to decimal

ans =

    17

>> class(ans) % result is a double precision decimal

ans =

double
```

Conversions between decimals and hexadecimals are performed by dec2hex and hex2dec, as in the following example:

```
>> a = dec2hex(2047) % hex representation of 2047

a =

7FF

>> class(a) % result is a character string

ans =

char

>> hex2dec(a) % convert a back to decimal

ans =

          2047

>> class(ans) % result is a double precision decimal

ans =

double
```

Conversions between decimals and any base between 2 and 36 are performed by dec2base and base2dec:

```
>> a = dec2base(26,3)
a =
222
>> class(a)
ans =
char
>> base2dec(a,3)
ans =
    26
```

Base 36 is the maximum usable base, because it uses the numbers 0 through 9 and the letters A through Z to represent the 36 distinct digits of a base 36 number.

16

Time Computations

MATLAB offers a number of functions to manipulate time. You can do arithmetic with dates and times, print calendars, and find specific days. MATLAB does this by storing the date and time as a double-precision number representing the number of days since the beginning of year zero. For example, midnight, January 1, 2000, is represented as 730486, and the same day at noon is 730486.5. This format may make calculations easier for a computer, but it is difficult to interpret visually. That's why MATLAB supplies a number of functions to convert between date numbers and character strings, and to manipulate dates and times.

16.1 CURRENT DATE AND TIME

The function `clock` returns the current date and time in an array:

```
>> T = clock
T =
        2004          2          2         18          4     27.893
```

This was the time when this part of the text was written. The preceding data are organized as `T = [year month day hour minute seconds]`, so the time shown is the year 2004, the 2nd month, 2nd day, 18th hour, 4th minute, and 27.893 seconds.

The function `now` returns the current date and time as a double-precision date number, or simply a date number:

```
>> format long

>> t = now
```

```
t =

    7.319797537603473e+005

>> format short g
```

Both T and t represent essentially the same information.

The function date returns the current date as a character string in the dd-mmm-yyyy format:

```
>> date
ans =
02-Feb-2004
>> class(ans)
ans =
char
```

16.2 DATE FORMAT CONVERSIONS

In general, mathematics with time involves converting times to date number format, performing standard mathematical operations on the date numbers, and then converting the result back to a format that makes human sense. As a result, converting time among different formats is very important. MATLAB supports three formats for dates: (1) double-precision date number, (2) date (character) strings in a variety of styles, and (3) numerical date vector, where each element contains a different date component—that is, [year,month,day,hour,minute,seconds].

The function datestr converts the date number to a date string. The syntax for using datestr is datestr(date,dateform), where dateform is described by the help text for datestr:

```
>> help datestr
 DATESTR String representation of date.
    DATESTR(D,DATEFORM) converts D, a date vector (as returned by DATEVEC)
    or serial date number (as returned by DATENUM), or a free format date
    string into a date string with a format specified by format number or
    string DATEFORM (see table below). By default, DATEFORM is 1, 16, or 0
    depending on whether D contains dates, times or both. Date strings
    with 2 character years are interpreted to be within the 100 years
    centered around the current year.

    DATESTR(D,DATEFORM,PIVOTYEAR) uses the specified pivot year as the
    starting year of the 100-year range in which a two-character year
```

resides. The default pivot year is the current year minus 50 years.

DATEFORM = -1 uses the default format.

DATEFORM number	DATEFORM string	Example
0	'dd-mmm-yyyy HH:MM:SS'	01-Mar-2000 15:45:17
1	'dd-mmm-yyyy'	01-Mar-2000
2	'mm/dd/yy'	03/01/00
3	'mmm'	Mar
4	'm'	M
5	'mm'	03
6	'mm/dd'	03/01
7	'dd'	01
8	'ddd'	Wed
9	'd'	W
10	'yyyy'	2000
11	'yy'	00
12	'mmmyy'	Mar00
13	'HH:MM:SS'	15:45:17
14	'HH:MM:SS PM'	3:45:17 PM
15	'HH:MM'	15:45
16	'HH:MM PM'	3:45 PM
17	'QQ-YY'	Q1-96
18	'QQ'	Q1
19	'dd/mm'	01/03
20	'dd/mm/yy'	01/03/00
21	'mmm.dd,yyyy HH:MM:SS'	Mar.01,2000 15:45:17
22	'mmm.dd,yyyy'	Mar.01,2000
23	'mm/dd/yyyy'	03/01/2000
24	'dd/mm/yyyy'	01/03/2000
25	'yy/mm/dd'	00/03/01
26	'yyyy/mm/dd'	2000/03/01
27	'QQ-YYYY'	Q1-1996
28	'mmmyyyy'	Mar2000
29 (ISO 8601)	'yyyy-mm-dd'	2000-03-01
30 (ISO 8601)	'yyyymmddTHHMMSS'	20000301T154517
31	'yyyy-mm-dd HH:MM:SS'	2000-03-01 15:45:17

```
See also DATE, DATENUM, DATEVEC, DATETICK.
```

Some examples of datestr usage include the following:

```
>> t = now
t =
   7.319797588851968e+005
>> datestr(t)
ans =
02-Feb-2004 18:12:48

>> class(ans)
ans =
char
>> datestr(t,12)
ans =
Feb04
>> datestr(t,23)
ans =
02/02/2004
>> datestr(t,25)
ans =
04/02/02
>> datestr(t,13)
ans =
18:12:48
>> datestr(t,29)
ans =
2004-02-02
```

The function datenum is the inverse of datestr. That is, datenum converts a date string to a date number using the form datenum(str). Alternatively, it converts individual date specifications using the form datenum(year,month,day) or datenum(year,month,day,hour,minute,second), as in the following example:

```
>> t = now
t =
   7.319797588851968e+005
```

```
>> ts = datestr(t)

ts =

02-Feb-2004 18:12:48

>> datenum(ts)

ans =

   7.319797588888889e+005

>> datenum(2004,5,14,16,48,07)

ans =

   7.320817000810185e+005

>> datenum(2004,5,14)

ans =

      732081
```

The `datevec` function converts a date string using `datestr` formats 0, 1, 2, 6, 13, 14, 15, or 16 to a numerical vector containing the date components. Alternatively, it converts a date number to a numerical vector of date components, as in the following code:

```
>> c = datevec('12/24/1984')

c =

   1984     12     24      0      0      0

>> [yr,mo,day,hr,min,sec] = datevec('24-Dec-1984 08:22')

yr =

   1984

mo =

   12

day =

   24

hr =

   8

min =

   22

sec =

   0
```

16.3 DATE FUNCTIONS

The numerical day of the week can be found from a date string or a date number by using the function weekday (***MATLAB uses the convention that Sunday is day 1 and Saturday is day 7***):

```
>> [d,w] = weekday(728647)
d =
     2
w =
     Mon

>> [d,w] = weekday('21-Dec-1994')
d =
     4
w =
     Wed
```

The last day of any month can be found by using the function eomday. Because of leap year, both the year and the month are required, as in the following example:

```
>> eomday(1996,2) % divisible by 4 is a leap year
ans =
    29

>> eomday(1900,2) % divisible by 100 not a leap year
ans =
    28

>> eomday(2000,2) % divisible by 400 is a leap year
ans =
    29
```

MATLAB can generate a calendar for any month you request and display it in the *Command* window or place it in a 6-by-7 matrix by using the function calendar:

```
>> calendar(date)
                          Feb 2004
     S       M       Tu      W       Th      F       S
     1       2       3       4       5       6       7
     8       9       10      11      12      13      14
     15      16      17      18      19      20      21
     22      23      24      25      26      27      28
     29      0       0       0       0       0       0
     0       0       0       0       0       0       0
>> calendar(1954,9)
                          Sep 1954
     S       M       Tu      W       Th      F       S
     0       0       0       1       2       3       4
     5       6       7       8       9       10      11
     12      13      14      15      16      17      18
     19      20      21      22      23      24      25
     26      27      28      29      30      0       0
     0       0       0       0       0       0       0
>> x = calendar(2004,2)
x =
     1       2       3       4       5       6       7
     8       9       10      11      12      13      14
     15      16      17      18      19      20      21
     22      23      24      25      26      27      28
     29      0       0       0       0       0       0
     0       0       0       0       0       0       0
>> class(x)
ans =
double
```

16.4 TIMING FUNCTIONS

The functions `tic` and `toc` are used to time a sequence of MATLAB operations. The function `tic` starts a stopwatch, while `toc` stops the stopwatch and displays the elapsed time:

```
>> tic; plot(rand(50,5)); toc
elapsed_time =
    0.33

>> tic; plot(rand(50,5)); toc
elapsed_time =
    0.11
```

Note the difference in elapsed times for identical `plot` commands. The second `plot` was significantly faster, because MATLAB had already created the *Figure* window and compiled the functions it needed into memory.

The function `cputime` returns the amount of central processing unit (CPU) time, in seconds, that MATLAB has used since the current session was started. The function `etime` calculates the elapsed time between two time vectors, in six-element row vector form such as that returned by the functions `clock` and `datevec`. Both `cputime` and `etime` can be used to compute the time it takes for an operation to be completed. In fact, the functions `tic` and `toc` simply automate the use of `clock` and `etime` to compute elapsed time. Usage of `cputime` and `etime` are demonstrated by the following examples, in which `myoperation` is a script file containing a number of MATLAB commands:

```
>> t0 = cputime; myoperation; cputime-t0
ans =
    0.149999999999991

>> t1 = clock; myoperation; etime(clock,t1)
ans =
    11.284853
```

16.5 PLOT LABELS

Sometimes it is useful to plot data and use dates or time strings for one or more of the axis labels. The `datetick` function automates this task. ***Use of this function requires that the axis to be marked be plotted with a vector of date numbers, such as the output of the `datenum` function***. The following code is illustrative:

```
>> t = (1900:10:1990)';
>> p = [ 75.995;  91.972; 105.711; 123.203; 131.669;
         150.697; 179.323; 203.212; 226.505; 249.633];
>> plot(datenum(t,1,1),p)
>> datetick('x','yyyy')    % use 4-digit year on the x-axis
>> title('Figure 16.1: Population by Year')
```

Figure 16.1: Popu ation by Year

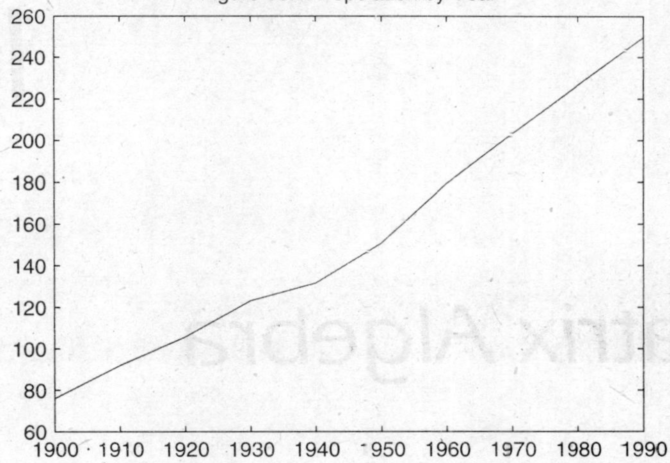

Next, we create a bar chart of company sales from November 1998 to December 1999:

```
>> y = [1998 1998 1999*ones(1,12)]';
>> m = [11 12 (1:12)]';
>> s = [1.1 1.3 1.2 1.4 1.6 1.5 1.7 1.6 1.8 1.3 1.9 1.7 1.6 1.95]';
>> bar(datenum(y,m,1),s)
>> datetick('x','mmmyy')
>> ylabel('$ Million')
>> title('Figure 16.2: Monthly Sales')
```

Figure 16.2: Monthly Sales

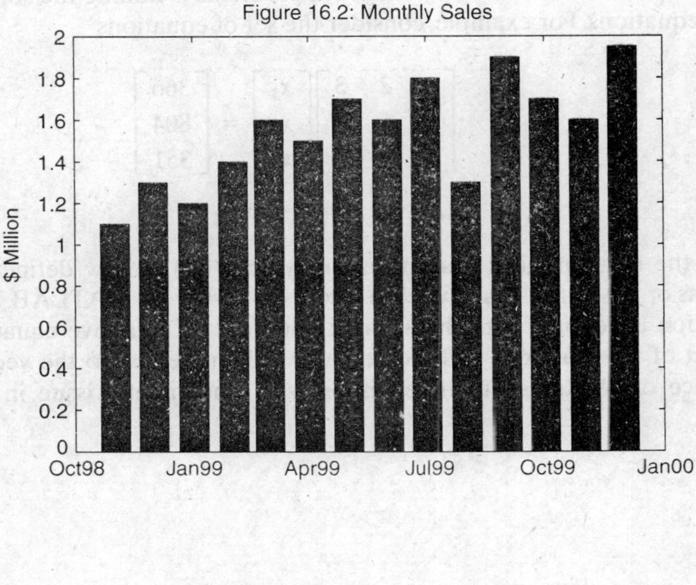

17

Matrix Algebra

MATLAB was originally written to provide an easy-to-use interface to professionally developed numerical linear algebra subroutines. As it has evolved over the years, other features, such as graphics and graphical user interfaces, have made the numerical linear algebra routines less prominent. Nevertheless, MATLAB offers a wide range of valuable matrix algebra functions.

> It is important to note that, while MATLAB supports n-dimensional arrays, matrix algebra is defined only for 2-D arrays—that is, vectors and matrices.

17.1 SETS OF LINEAR EQUATIONS

One of the most common linear algebra problems is finding the solution of a linear set of equations. For example, consider the set of equations

$$\begin{bmatrix} 1 & 2 & 3 \\ 4 & 5 & 6 \\ 7 & 8 & 0 \end{bmatrix} \begin{bmatrix} x_1 \\ x_2 \\ x_3 \end{bmatrix} = \begin{bmatrix} 366 \\ 804 \\ 351 \end{bmatrix}$$

$$\boldsymbol{A} \cdot \boldsymbol{x} = \boldsymbol{y}$$

where the mathematical multiplication symbol ($\cdot$) is now defined in the matrix sense, as opposed to the array sense discussed earlier. In MATLAB, this matrix multiplication is denoted with the asterisk notation *. The above equations define the product of the matrix $\boldsymbol{A}$ and the vector $\boldsymbol{x}$ as being equal to the vector $\boldsymbol{y}$. The very existence of solutions of this equation is a fundamental issue in linear algebra.

Moreover, when a solution does exist, there are numerous approaches to finding that solution, such as Gaussian elimination, LU factorization, or the direct use of A^{-1}. Clearly, it is beyond the scope of this text to discuss the many analytical and numerical issues of matrix algebra. We wish only to demonstrate how MATLAB can be used to solve problems like the one in the preceding example.

To solve the problem at hand, it is necessary to enter $\boldsymbol{A}$ and $\boldsymbol{y}$:

```
>> A = [1 2 3;4 5 6
7 8 0]
A =
        1      2      3
        4      5      6
        7      8      0
>> y = [366;804;351]
y =
    366
    804
    351
```

As discussed earlier, the entry of the matrix A shows the two ways that MATLAB distinguishes between rows. The semicolon between the 3 and 4 signifies the start of a new row, as does the new line between the 6 and 7. The vector y is a column, because each semicolon signifies the start of a new row.

If you have a background in linear algebra, you will find it easy to see that this problem has a unique solution if the rank of A and the rank of the augmented matrix [A y] are both equal to 3. Alternatively, you can check the condition number of A. If the condition number is not excessively large, then A has an inverse with good numerical properties. Testing this problem produces the following result:

```
>> rank(A)
ans =
    3
>> rank([A y])
ans =
    3

>> cond(A) % close to one is best
ans =
        35.106
```

Since the rank and condition number tests hold, MATLAB can find the solution of $A \cdot x = y$ in two ways, one of which is preferred. The less favorable method is to take $x = A^{-1} \cdot y$ literally, as in the following code:

```
>> x = inv(A)*y % Avoid this approach if possible

x =

    25

    22

    99
```

Here, inv(A) is a MATLAB function that computes A^{-1}, and the multiplication operator * is matrix multiplication. The preferable solution is found by using the matrix left-division operator, or backward slash, as in this example:

```
>> x = A\y % Recommended approach to solving sets of equations

x =

    25

    22

    99
```

This equation uses an LU factorization approach and expresses the answer as the left division of A into y. The left-division operator \ has no preceding dot, as this is a matrix operation, not an element-by-element array operation. There are many reasons to prefer this second solution. Of these, the simplest is that the latter method requires fewer floating-point operations and, as a result, is significantly faster. In addition, this solution is generally more accurate, especially for larger problems. In either case, if MATLAB cannot find a solution or cannot find one accurately, it displays a warning message.

If the transpose of the above set of linear equations is taken (i.e., $(A \cdot x)' = y'$) then the previous set of linear equations can be written as $x' \cdot A' = y'$, where x' and y' are now row vectors. As a result, it is equally valid to express a set of linear equations in terms of the product of a row vector and a matrix being equal to another row vector—for example, $u \cdot B = v$. In MATLAB, this case is solved by the same internal algorithms, by using the matrix right-division operator, or forward slash, as in u = v/B.

It is important to note that when MATLAB encounters a forward slash (/) or backward slash (\), it checks the structure of the coefficient matrix to determine what internal algorithm to use to find the solution. In particular, if the matrix is upper or lower triangular or a permutation of an upper or lower triangular matrix, MATLAB does not refactor the matrix, but rather just performs the forward or backward substitution steps required to find the solution. As a result, MATLAB makes use of the properties of the coefficient matrix to compute the solution as quickly as possible.

When the structure of the coefficient matrix is known ahead of time, the function `linsolve` solves the set of equations by using matrix structure information provided by the user. By using this function, MATLAB does not spend time analyzing the structure of the coefficient matrix and thereby minimizes the time required to solve the set of equations. The calling syntax for this function is `linsolve(A,y,options)`, where `options` is a structure containing fields that can be set to True or False to identify the structure of the A matrix.

If you've studied linear algebra rigorously, you know that when the number of equations and number of unknowns differ, a single unique solution usually does not exist. However, with further constraints, a practical solution can usually be found. In MATLAB, when rank(A) = min(r,c), where r and c are the number of rows and columns in $\boldsymbol{A}$, respectively, and there are more equations than unknowns ($r > c$) (i.e., the ***overdetermined*** case), a division operator / or \ automatically finds the solution that minimizes the norm of the squared residual error $\boldsymbol{e} = \boldsymbol{A} \cdot \boldsymbol{x} - \boldsymbol{y}$. This solution is of great practical value and is called the ***least-squares solution***. The following example is illustrative:

```
>> A = [1 2 3;4 5 6;7 8 0;2 5 8]  % 4 equations in 3 unknowns
A =
     1     2     3
     4     5     6
     7     8     0
     2     5     8
>> y = [366 804 351 514]'  % a new r.h.s. vector
y =
   366
   804
   351
   514
>> x = A\y        % least squares solution
x =
       247.98
      -173.11
       114.93
>> e = A*x-y    % this residual has the smallest norm.
e =
  -119.4545
    11.9455
     0.0000
    35.8364
```

```
>> norm(e)
ans =
   125.2850
```

In addition to the least squares solution that is computed with the left- and right-division operators, MATLAB offers the functions `lscov` and `lsqnonneg`. The function `lscov` solves the weighted least-squares problem when the covariance matrix (or weighting matrix) of the data is known, and `lsqnonneg` finds the nonnegative least squares solution where all solution components are constrained to be positive.

When there are fewer equations than unknowns ($r < c$) (i.e., the ***underdetermined*** case) an infinite number of solutions exist. Of these solutions, MATLAB computes two in a straightforward way. Use of the division operator gives a solution that has a maximum number of zeros in the elements of $\boldsymbol{x}$. Alternatively, computing `x=pinv(A)*y` gives a solution where the length or norm of `x` is smaller than all other possible solutions. This solution, based on the *pseudoinverse*, also has great practical value and is called the ***minimum norm solution***:

```
>> A = A'   % create 3 equations in 4 unknowns
A =
     1     4     7     2
     2     5     8     5
     3     6     0     8
>> y = y(1:3) % new r.h.s. vector
y =
   366
   804
   351
>> x = A\b  % solution with maximum zero elements
x =
         0
 -165.9000
   99.0000
  168.3000
>> xn = pinv(A)*b % minimum norm solution
xn =
   30.8182
 -168.9818
   99.0000
  159.0545
```

```
>> norm(x)  % norm of solution with zero elements
ans =
   256.2200
>> norm(xn) % minimum norm solution has smaller norm!
ans =
   254.1731
```

17.2 MATRIX FUNCTIONS

In addition to the solution of linear sets of equations, MATLAB offers numerous matrix functions that are useful for solving numerical linear algebra problems. A thorough discussion of these functions is beyond the scope of this text. In general, MATLAB provides functions for all common, and some uncommon, numerical linear algebra problems. A brief description of many of the matrix functions is given in the following table:

Function	Description
/ and \	Solve Ax=y (much better than using inv(A)*y)
accumarray(ind,val)	Construct array with accumulation
A^n	Exponentiation, e.g., A^3 = A*A*A
balance(A)	Scale to improve eigenvalue accuracy
[V,D]=cdf2rdf(V,D)	Complex diagonal form to real block diagonal form
chol(A)	Cholesky factorization
cholinc(A,DropTol)	Incomplete Cholesky factorization
cholinc(A,Options)	
cholupdate(R,X)	Rank 1 update to Cholesky factorization
cond(A)	Matrix condition number using singular value decomposition
condest(A)	1-norm condition number estimate
[V,D,s]=condeig(A)	Condition number with respect to repeated eigenvalues
det(A)	Determinant
dmperm(A)	Dulmage–Mendelsohn permutation
eig(A)	Vector of eignenvalues
[V,D]=eig(A)	Matrix of eignenvectors, and diagonal matrix containing eigenvalues
expm(A)	Matrix exponential
funm(A)	General matrix function
gsvd(A,B)	Generalized singular values

Function	Description
[U,V,X,C,S]=gsvd(A)	Generalized singular value decomposition
hess(A)	Hessenburg form of a matrix
inv(A)	Matrix inverse (use only when / or \ won't do)
linsolve(A,y,options)	Solve Ax=y quickly when structure of A is given by options
logm(A)	Matrix logarithm
lscov(A,y,V)	Weighted least squares with covariance matrix
lsqnonneg(A,y)	Nonnegative least squares solution
[L,U,P]=lu(A)	LU decomposition
minres(A,y)	Minimum residual method
norm(A,type)	Matrix and vector norms
null(A)	Null space
orth(A)	Orthogonal range space using singular value decomposition
pinv(A)	Pseudoinverse using singular value decomposition
planerot(X)	Plane rotation
poly(A)	Characteristic polynomial
polyeig(A0,A1,. . .)	Polynomial eigenvalue solution
polyvalm(A)	Evaluate matrix polynomial
qr(A)	Orthogonal-triangular decomposition
qrdelete(Q,R,J)	Delete column or row from QR factorization
qrinsert(Q,R,J,X)	Insert column or row into QR factorization
qrupdate(Q,R,U,V)	Rank 1 update to QR factorization
qz(A,B)	Generalized eigenvalues
rank(A)	Matrix rank using singular value decomposition
rcond(A)	LAPACK reciprocal condition estimator
rref(A)	Reduced row echelon form
rsf2csf(A)	Real Schur form to complex Schur form
schur(A)	Schur decomposition
sqrtm(A)	Matrix square root
subspace(A,B)	Angle between two subspaces
svd(A)	Singular values
[U,S,V]=svd(A)	Singular value decomposition
trace(A)	Sum of matrix diagonal elements

17.3 SPECIAL MATRICES

MATLAB offers a number of special matrices; some of them are general utilities, while others are matrices of interest to specialized disciplines. These and other special matrices include those given in the following table (use the on-line help to learn more about these matrices):

Matrix	Description
`[ ]`	Empty matrix
`blkdiag(a0,a1,...)`	Block diagonal concatenation of input arguments
`compan(P)`	Companion matrix to polynomial
`eye(r,c)`	Identity matrix
`gallery`	More than 50 test matrices
`hadamard(n)`	Hadamard matrix of order `n`
`hankel(C)`	Hankel matrix
`hilb(n)`	Hilbert matrix of order `n`
`invhilb(n)`	Inverse Hilbert matrix of order `n`
`magic(n)`	Magic matrix of order `n`
`ones(r,c)`	Matrix containing all ones
`pascal(n)`	Pascal matrix of order `n`
`rand(r,c)`	Uniformly distributed random matrix with elements between 0 and 1
`randn(r,c)`	Normally distributed random matrix with elements having zero mean and unit variance
`rosser`	Classic symmetric eigenvalue test problem
`toeplitz(C,R)`	Toeplitz matrix
`vander(C)`	Vandermonde matrix
`wilkinson(n)`	Wilkinson's eigenvalue test matrix of order `n`
`zeros(r,c)`	Matrix containing all zeros

17.4 SPARSE MATRICES

In many practical applications, matrices are generated that contain only a few nonzero elements. As a result, these matrices are said to be ***sparse***. For example, circuit simulation and finite element analysis programs routinely deal with matrices containing less than 1 percent nonzero elements. If a matrix is large—for example, `max(size(A)) > 100`—and has a high percentage of zero elements, it is wasteful, both of computer storage to store the zero elements, and of computational power to perform arithmetic operations by using the zero elements. To eliminate the storage of zero elements, it is common to store only the nonzero elements of a sparse matrix and two sets of indices identifying the row and column positions of these elements.

Similarly, to eliminate arithmetic operations on the zero elements, special algorithms have been developed to solve typical matrix problems (such as solving a set of linear equations in which operations involving zeros are minimized, and intermediate matrices have minimum nonzero elements).

The techniques used to optimize sparse matrix computations are complex in implementation, as well as in theory. Fortunately, MATLAB hides this complexity. In MATLAB, sparse matrices are stored in variables, just as regular, full matrices are. Moreover, most computations with sparse matrices use the same syntax as that used for full matrices. In particular, all of the array manipulation capabilities of MATLAB work equally well on sparse matrices. For example, `s(i,j) = value` assigns `value` to the `i`th row and `j`th column of the sparse matrix `s`.

In this text, only the creation of sparse matrices and the conversion to and from sparse matrices are illustrated. In general, operations on full matrices produce full matrices and operations on sparse matrices produce sparse matrices. In addition, operations on a mixture of full and sparse matrices generally produce sparse matrices, unless the operation makes the result too densely populated with nonzeros to make sparse storage efficient.

Sparse matrices are created using the MATLAB function sparse. For example, the code

```
>> As = sparse(1:10,1:10,ones(1,10))
As =
   (1,1)         1
   (2,2)         1
   (3,3)         1
   (4,4)         1
   (5,5)         1
   (6,6)         1
   (7,7)         1
   (8,8)         1
   (9,9)         1
  (10,10)        1
```

creates a 10-by-10 identity matrix. In this usage, `sparse(i,j,s)` creates a sparse matrix whose *k*th nonzero element is `s(k)`, which appears in the row `i(k)` and column `j(k)`. Note the difference in how sparse matrices are displayed. Nonzero elements and their row and column positions are displayed. The preceding sparse matrix can also be created by conversion. For example, the code

```
>> As = sparse(eye(10))
As =
   (1,1)         1
```

```
      (2,2)        1
      (3,3)        1
      (4,4)        1
      (5,5)        1
      (6,6)        1
      (7,7)        1
      (8,8)        1
      (9,9)        1
     (10,10)       1
```

creates the 10-by-10 identity matrix again, this time by converting the full matrix eye(10) to sparse format. While this method of creating a sparse matrix works, it is seldom used in practice, because the initial full matrix wastes a great deal of memory.

Given a sparse matrix, the function full generates the conventional full matrix equivalent. The following example converts the sparse matrix As back to its full form:

```
>> A = full(As)
A =
     1     0     0     0     0     0     0     0     0     0
     0     1     0     0     0     0     0     0     0     0
     0     0     1     0     0     0     0     0     0     0
     0     0     0     1     0     0     0     0     0     0
     0     0     0     0     1     0     0     0     0     0
     0     0     0     0     0     1     0     0     0     0
     0     0     0     0     0     0     1     0     0     0
     0     0     0     0     0     0     0     1     0     0
     0     0     0     0     0     0     0     0     1     0
     0     0     0     0     0     0     0     0     0     1
```

To compare sparse matrix storage to full matrix storage, consider the following example:

```
>> B = eye(200);
>> Bs = sparse(B);
>> whos
  Name        Size            Bytes  Class
```

```
  B        200x200          320000  double array
  Bs       200x200            3204  sparse array

Grand total is 40200 elements using 323204 bytes
```

Here, the sparse matrix Bs contains only 0.5 percent nonzero elements and requires 3204 bytes of storage. On the other hand, B, the same matrix in full matrix form, requires two orders of magnitude more bytes of storage!

17.5 SPARSE MATRIX FUNCTIONS

MATLAB provides numerous sparse matrix functions. Many involve different aspects of, and techniques for, the solution of sparse simultaneous equations. A discussion of these functions is beyond the scope of this text. The functions available are listed in the following table:

Sparse Matrix Function	Description
bicg	Biconjugate gradient iterative linear equation solution
bicgstab	Biconjugate gradient stabilized iterative linear equation solution
cgs	Conjugate gradients squared iterative linear equation solution
cholinc	Incomplete Cholesky factorization
colamd	Column approximate minimum degree reordering method
colamdtree	colamd followed by column elimination tree postordering
colmmd	Column minimum degree reordering method
colperm	Column permutation
condest	1-norm condition number estimate
dmperm	Dulmage–Mendelsohn reordering method
eigs	A few eigenvalues using ARPACK
etree	Elimination tree
etreeplot	Plot elimination tree
find	Find indices of nonzero elements
full	Convert sparse matrix to full matrix
gmres	Generalized minimum residual iterative linear equation solution
gplot	Construct graph theory plot
issparse	True for sparse matrix

lsqr	LSQR implementation of conjugate gradients on normal equations
luinc	Incomplete LU factorization
minres	Minimum residual iterative linear equation solution
nnz	Number of nonzero matrix elements
nonzeros	Nonzero matrix elements
normest	Estimate of matrix 2-norm
nzmax	Storage allocated for nonzero elements
pcg	Preconditioned conjugate gradients iterative linear equation solution
qmr	Quasi-minimal residual iterative linear equation solution
randperm	Random permutation
spalloc	Allocate space for sparse matrix
sparse	Create sparse matrix
spaugment	Form least squares augmented system
spconvert	Import from sparse matrix external format
spdiags	Sparse matrix formed from diagonals
speye	Sparse identity matrix
spfun	Apply function to nonzero elements
spones	Replace nonzeros with ones
spparms	Set parameters for sparse matrix routines
sprand	Sparse uniformly distributed matrix
sprandn	Sparse normally distributed matrix
sprandsym	Sparse random symmetric matrix
sprank	Structural rank
spy	Visualize sparsity pattern
svds	A few singular values
symbfact	Symbolic factorization analysis
symamd	Symmetric approximate minimum degree reordering method
symamdtree	symamd followed by symmetric elimination tree postordering
symmd	Symmetric minimum degree reordering method
symmlq	Symmetric LQ iterative linear equation solution
symrcm	Symmetric reverse Cuthill–Mckee reordering method
treelayout	Lay out tree or forest
treeplot	Plot tree

18

Data Analysis

Because of its array orientation, MATLAB readily performs statistical analyses on data sets. While MATLAB, by default, considers data sets stored in column-oriented arrays, data analysis can be conducted along any specified dimension.

> Unless specified otherwise, each column of an array represents a different measured variable and each row represents individual samples or observations.

18.1 BASIC STATISTICAL ANALYSIS

For example, let's assume that the daily high temperature (in Celsius) of three cities over a 31-day month was recorded and assigned to the variable `temps` in a script M-file. Running the M-file puts the variable `temps` in the MATLAB workspace. When this work is done, the variable `temps` contains the following data:

```
>> temps
temps =
    12     8    18
    15     9    22
    12     5    19
    14     8    23
    12     6    22
```

```
11    9   19
15    9   15
 8   10   20
19    7   18
12    7   18
14   10   19
11    8   17
 9    7   23
 8    8   19
15    8   18
 8    9   20
10    7   17
12    7   22
 9    8   19
12    8   21
12    8   20
10    9   17
13   12   18
 9   10   20
10    6   22
14    7   21
12    5   22
13    7   18
15   10   23
13   11   24
12   12   22
```

Each row contains the high temperatures for a given day. Each column contains the high temperatures for a different city. To visualize the data, plot it with the following code:

```
>> d = 1:31;    % number the days of the month
>> plot(d,temps)

>> xlabel('Day of Month'), ylabel('Celsius')
>> title('Figure 18.1: Daily High Temperatures in Three Cities')
```

Figure 18.1: Daily High Temperatures in Three Cities

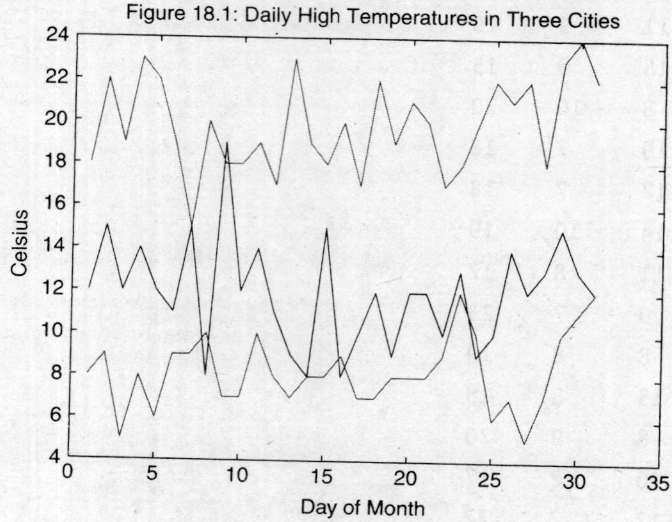

The `plot` command in this example illustrates yet another form of `plot` command usage. The variable `d` is a vector of length 31, whereas `temps` is a 31-by-3 matrix. Given this data, the `plot` command plots each column of `temps` versus `d`.

To illustrate some of the data-analysis capabilities of MATLAB, consider the following commands based on the temperature data stored in `temps`:

```
>> avg_temp = mean(temps)
avg_temp =
   11.968    8.2258    19.871
```

This result shows that the third city has the highest average temperature. Here, MATLAB found the average of each column individually. Taking the average again gives

```
>> avg_avg = mean(avg_temp)
avg_avg =
   13.3548
```

which returns the overall average temperature of the three cities.

> When the input to a data analysis function is a row or column vector, MATLAB simply performs the operation on the vector, returning a scalar result.

Alternatively, you can specify the dimension to work on:

```
>> avg_temp = mean(temps,1)  % same as above, work down the rows
avg_temp =
     11.968      8.2258     19.871
>> avg_tempr = mean(temps,2)  % compute means across columns
avg_tempr =
     12.667
     15.333
         12
         15
     13.333
         13
         13
     12.667
     14.667
     12.333
     14.333
         12
         13
     11.667
     13.667
     12.333
     11.333
     13.667
         12
     13.667
     13.333
         12
     14.333
         13
     12.667
         14
         13
     12.667
```

```
        16
        16
    15.333
```

This output lists the three-city average temperature on each day. The scalar second argument to mean dictates the dimension to be analyzed; for example, 1 is the row dimension number, so MATLAB performs the analysis accumulating information down the rows; 2 is the column dimension number, so MATLAB performs the analysis accumulating information across the columns.

If temps were n-dimensional, the mean and other statistical functions could be used along any dimension, as in the following example:

```
>> temps2 = temps+round(2*rand(size(temps))-1);
>> temps3 = cat(3,temps,temps2);
>> size(temps3)
ans =
    31     3     2
>> mean(temps3)  % same as mean(temps3,1)
ans(:,:,1) =
      11.968       8.2258       19.871
ans(:,:,2) =
      11.677       8.0968       19.903

>> squeeze(mean(temps3))' % squeeze to two dimensions
ans =
      11.968       8.2258       19.871
      11.677       8.0968       19.903

>> reshape(mean(temps3),3,2)' % alternate squeeze
ans =
      11.968       8.2258       19.871
      11.677       8.0968       19.903
>> mean(temps3,3)
ans =
          12            8           18
        14.5            9         22.5
          12          5.5           19
          14          7.5         23.5
```

```
   11.5    6.5   21.5
   10.5    9.5   18.5
     15    8.5   15.5
      8    9.5     20
   18.5    6.5   18.5
   11.5    6.5     18
   13.5     10     19
     11    7.5     17
    8.5    7.5   22.5
      8    7.5   18.5
     15    7.5   17.5
      8    9.5     20
     10      7   17.5
   11.5      7     22
      9      8   19.5
     12      8     21
     12      8     20
    9.5      9     17
     13   11.5     18
      9    9.5   20.5
     10      6   21.5
     14    7.5     21
     12    5.5   21.5
   12.5      7     18
     15    9.5     23
     13   11.5   24.5
   12.5   11.5     22
```

Here, `temps2` contains randomly generated data for the temperatures in the three cities for a second month. The variable `temps3` contains the first month's temperatures on page 1 and the second month's temperatures on page 2. The function call `mean(temps3)` computes the means down each column on each page, giving a result that has one row, three columns, and two pages. This data can be squeezed into two rows and three columns by using `squeeze` or `reshape`. The function call `mean(temps3,3)` computes the mean along the page dimension, which is the month-to-month mean of the temperatures on a given day, in a given city. The result is an array having 31 rows, three columns, and one page (i.e., a 2-D array).

Going back to the 2-D case, consider the problem of finding the daily deviation from the mean of each city. That is, avg_temp(i) must be subtracted from column i of temps. You cannot simply issue the statement

```
>> avg_temp
avg_temp =
      11.968        8.2258        19.871

>> temps - avg_temp
??? Error using ==> -
Matrix dimensions must agree.
```

because the operation is not a defined array operation (temps is 31 by 3, and avg_temp is 1 by 3). Perhaps the most straightforward approach is to use a For Loop:

```
>> for c=1:3
      tdev(:,c) = temps(:,c) - avg_temp(c);
   end
```

While this approach works, it was much slower before the introduction of JIT-Acceleration in MATLAB. An alternative is to use the array manipulation features of MATLAB. In this case, you duplicate avg_temp to make it the size of temps and then do the subtraction:

```
>> tdev = temps - repmat(avg_temp,31,1)
tdev =
     0.0323   -0.2258   -1.8710
     3.0323    0.7742    2.1290
     0.0323   -3.2258   -0.8710
     2.0323   -0.2258    3.1290
     0.0323   -2.2258    2.1290
    -0.9677    0.7742   -0.8710
     3.0323    0.7742   -4.8710
    -3.9677    1.7742    0.1290
     7.0323   -1.2258   -1.8710
     0.0323   -1.2258   -1.8710
     2.0323    1.7742   -0.8710
    -0.9677   -0.2258   -2.8710
```

```
-2.9677   -1.2258    3.1290
-3.9677   -0.2258   -0.8710
 3.0323   -0.2258   -1.8710
-3.9677    0.7742    0.1290
-1.9677   -1.2258   -2.8710
 0.0323   -1.2258    2.1290
-2.9677   -0.2258   -0.8710
 0.0323   -0.2258    1.1290
 0.0323   -0.2258    0.1290
-1.9677    0.7742   -2.8710
 1.0323    3.7742   -1.8710
-2.9677    1.7742    0.1290
 0.0323   -3.2258    2.1290
 1.0323   -1.2258   -1.8710
 3.0323    1.7742    3.1290
 1.0323    2.7742    4.1290
 0.0323    3.7742    2.1290
```

Here, `repmat(avg_temp,31,1)` replicates the row vector `avg_temp`, 31 times in the row dimension and once in the column dimension, creating a 31-by-3 matrix the same size as `temps`. The first column of `repmat(avg_temp,31,1)` contains `avg_tmp(1)`, the second column contains `avg_temp(2)`, and the third column contains `avg_temp(3)`.

MATLAB can also find minima and maxima. For example, the code

```
>> max_temp = max(temps)
max_temp =
    19    12    24
```

finds the maximum high temperature of each city over the month, while

```
>> [max_temp,maxday] = max(temps)
max_temp =
    19    12    24
maxday =
     9    23    30
```

finds the maximum high temperature of each city and the row index `maxday` where the maximum appears. In this example, `maxday` identifies the day of the month when the highest temperature occurred.

The code

```
>> min_temp = min(temps)
min_temp =
     8     5    15
```

finds the minimum high temperature of each city, and the code

```
>> [min_temp,minday] = min(temps)
min_temp =
     8     5    15
minday =
     8     3     7
```

finds the minimum high temperature of each city and the row index `minday` where the minimum appears. For this example, `minday` identifies the day of the month when the lowest high temperature occurred.

Other standard statistical measures are also provided in MATLAB, including the following:

```
>> s_dev = std(temps) % standard deviation in each city
s_dev =
    2.5098    1.7646    2.2322
>> median(temps) % median temperature in each city
ans =
    12     8    20
>> cov(temps) % covariance
ans =
        6.2989      0.04086     -0.13763
       0.04086        3.114     0.063441
      -0.13763     0.063441       4.9828
>> corrcoef(temps) % correlation coefficients
ans =
             1    0.0092259    -0.024567
     0.0092259            1     0.016106
     -0.024567     0.016106            1
```

You can also compute differences from day to day by using the function diff:

```
>> daily_change = diff(temps)
daily_change =

     3     1     4
    -3    -4    -3
     2     3     4
    -2    -2    -1
    -1     3    -3
     4     0    -4
    -7     1     5
    11    -3    -2
    -7     0     0
     2     3     1
    -3    -2    -2
    -2    -1     6
    -1     1    -4
     7     0    -1
    -7     1     2
     2    -2    -3
     2     0     5
    -3     1    -3
     3     0     2
     0     0    -1
    -2     1    -3
     3     3     1
    -4    -2     2
     1    -4     2
     4     1    -1
    -2    -2     1
     1     2    -4
     2     3     5
    -2     1     1
    -1     1    -2
```

This function computes the difference between daily high temperatures and describes how much the daily high temperature varied from day to day. For example, between the first and second days of the month, the first row of `daily_change` is the amount that the daily high changed. As with other functions, the difference can be computed along other dimensions as well:

```
>> city_change = diff(temps,1,2)
city_change =
    -4    10
    -6    13
    -7    14
    -6    15
    -6    16
    -2    10
    -6     6
     2    10
   -12    11
    -5    11
    -4     9
    -3     9
    -2    16
     0    11
    -7    10
     1    11
    -3    10
    -5    15
    -1    11
    -4    13
    -4    12
    -1     8
    -1     6
     1    10
    -4    16
    -7    14
    -7    17
    -6    11
    -5    13
```

```
    -2    13
     0    10
```

Here, diff(temps,1,2) says to compute a first-order difference along dimension 2. Therefore, the result is the city difference. The first column is the difference between city 2 and city 1; the second column is the difference between city 3 and city 2.

It is common to use the value NaN to signify missing data. When this is done, most statistical functions require special treatment, because operations on NaNs generally produce NaNs, as in the following example:

```
>> temps4 = temps;     % copy data
>> temps4(5,1) = nan; % insert some NaNs
>> temps4(29,2) = nan;
>> temps4(13:14,3) = nan
temps4 =
    12     8    18
    15     9    22
    12     5    19
    14     8    23
   NaN     6    22
    11     9    19
    15     9    15
     8    10    20
    19     7    18
    12     7    18
    14    10    19
    11     8    17
     9     7   NaN
     8     8   NaN
    15     8    18
     8     9    20
    10     7    17
    12     7    22
     9     8    19
    12     8    21
    12     8    20
    10     9    17
    13    12    18
```

```
       9    10    20
      10     6    22
      14     7    21
      12     5    22
      13     7    18
      15   NaN    23
      13    11    24
      12    12    22
>> max(temps4) % max and min ignore NaNs
ans =
    19    12    24
>> mean(temps4) % other statistical functions propagate NNs
ans =
   NaN   NaN   NaN
>> std(temps4)
ans =
   NaN   NaN   NaN
```

One solution to this NaN problem is to write your own functions that exclude NaN elements:

```
>> m = zeros(1,3); % preallocate memory for faster results

>> for j=1:3 % find mean column by column
       idx = ~isnan(temps4(:,j));
       m(j)=mean(temps4(idx,j));
   end
>> m
m =

          13       7.3333       19.667
```

Here, the function isnan is used to locate elements containing NaN. Then, the mean down each column is found by indexing only non-NaN elements. It is not possible to exclude NaN elements over all columns simultaneously, because not all columns have the same number of NaN elements.

An alternative to the preceding approach is to replace the NaNS with zeros, and compute the mean accordingly, as in the following example:

```
>> lnan = isnan(temps4); % logical array identifying NaNs
>> temps4(lnan) = 0;     % change all NaNs to zero
```

```
>> n = sum(~lnan);        % number of nonNaN elements per column

>> m = sum(temps4)./n     % find mean for all columns
m =
        13          7.3333          19.667
```

In this example, a logical array `lnan` containing True where the elements of `temps4` are `NaN` was found. The `NaN` values were then set to zero. Then the mean was computed by dividing the column sums by the number of nonNaN elements per column.

18.2 BASIC DATA ANALYSIS

In addition to statistical data analysis, MATLAB offers a variety of general-purpose data analysis functions. For example, the temperature data `temps` can be filtered by using the function `filter(b,a,data)`:

```
>> filter(ones(1,4),4,temps)
ans =
         3            2          4.5
      6.75         4.25           10
      9.75          5.5        14.75
     13.25          7.5         20.5
     13.25            7         21.5
     12.25            7        20.75
        13            8        19.75
      11.5          8.5           19
     13.25         8.75           18
      13.5         8.25        17.75
     13.25          8.5        18.75
        14            8           18
      11.5            8        19.25
      10.5         8.25         19.5
     10.75         7.75        19.25
        10            8           20
     10.25            8         18.5
     11.25         7.75        19.25
      9.75         7.75         19.5
     10.75          7.5        19.75
```

```
    11.25        7.75       20.5
    10.75        8.25      19.25
    11.75        9.25         19
       11        9.75      18.75
     10.5        9.25      19.25
     11.5        8.75      20.25
    11.25           7      21.25
    12.25        6.25      20.75
     13.5        7.25         21
    13.25        8.25      21.75
    13.25          10      21.75
```

Here, the filter implemented is $4y_n = x_n + x_{n-1} + x_{n-2} + x_{n-3}$, or, equivalently, $y_n = (x_n + x_{n-1} + x_{n-2} + x_{n-3})/4$. In other words, each column of `temps` is passed through a ***moving-average filter*** of length 4. Any realizable filter structure can be applied by specifying different coefficients for the input and output coefficient vectors.

The function `y=filter(b,a,x)` implements the following general tapped delay-line algorithm:

$$\sum_{k=0}^{N} a_{k+1} y_{n-k} = \sum_{k=0}^{M} b_{k+1} x_{n-k}$$

Here, the vector a is the tap weight vector a_{k+1} on the output, and the vector b is the tap weight vector b_{k+1} on the input. For $N = 2$ and $M = 3$, the preceding equation is equivalent to

$$a_1 y_n + a_2 y_{n-1} + a_3 y_{n-2} = b_1 x_n + b_2 x_{n-1} + b_3 x_{n-2} + b_4 x_{n-3}$$

The `filter` function uses a difference equation description of a filter. When a state space description of a filter is known, the built-in function `ltitr` is useful. The help text of this function contains the following text:

```
LTITR   Linear time-invariant time response kernel.

 X = LTITR(A,B,U) calculates the time response of the system:
         x[n+1] = Ax[n] + Bu[n]
 to input sequence U.  The matrix U must have as many columns as
 there are inputs u.  Each row of U corresponds to a new time
 point.  LTITR returns a matrix X with as many columns as the
 number of states x, and with LENGTH(U) rows.
```

```
LTITR(A,B,U,Xo) can be used if initial conditions Xo exist.

Here is what it implements, in high speed:
  for i=1:n
      x(:,i) = xo;
      xo = a * xo + b * u(i,:).';
  end
  x = x.';
```

In this case, if the state space output equation is $y[n] = Cx[n] + Du[n]$, where C and D are matrices of appropriate dimensions, `x=ltitr(A,B,u)` can be used to compute the state response $x[n]$, followed by

```
y = x*C.' + u*D.';
```

to obtain the filter output. Here, the array y will have as many columns as there are outputs and as many rows as there are time points.

In MATLAB, data can also be sorted:

```
>> data = rand(10,1) % create some data
data =
        0.61543
        0.79194
        0.92181
        0.73821
        0.17627
        0.40571
        0.93547
         0.9169
        0.41027
        0.89365
>> [sdata,sidx] = sort(data) % sort in ascending order
sdata =
        0.17627
        0.40571
        0.41027
```

```
        0.61543
        0.73821
        0.79194
        0.89365
         0.9169
        0.92181
        0.93547
sidx =
        5
        6
        9
        1
        4
        2
       10
        8
        3
        7
```

The second output of the sort function is the sorted index order. That is, the fifth element in data has the lowest value, and the seventh element in data has the highest value.

Sometimes, it is important to know the ***rank*** of the data. For example, what is the rank or position of the *i*th data point in the unsorted array with respect to the sorted array? With MATLAB array indexing, the rank is found by the single statement

```
>> ridx(sidx) = 1:10 % ridx is
ridx =
    4    6    9    5    1    2   10    8    3    7
```

That is, the first element of the unsorted data appears fourth in the sorted data, and the last element is seventh. If a descending sort is required, it is simply a matter of calling the sort function as [sdata, sidx] = sort (data, 'descend').

When the array to be sorted is a matrix, as temps in the preceding example, each column is sorted, and each column produces a column in the optional index matrix. As with the other data analysis functions, the dimension to analyze can be specified as a second input argument before the optional final 'ascend' or 'descend' argument.

Very often, it is desirable to use the results of sorting one column of an array by applying that sort order to all remaining columns, as in the following example:

```
>> newdata = randn(10,4) % new data for sorting
newdata =
     -0.43256     -0.18671      0.29441     -0.39989
      -1.6656      0.72579      -1.3362         0.69
      0.12533     -0.58832      0.71432      0.81562
      0.28768       2.1832       1.6236      0.71191
      -1.1465      -0.1364     -0.69178       1.2902
       1.1909      0.11393        0.858       0.6686
       1.1892       1.0668        1.254       1.1908
    -0.037633     0.059281      -1.5937      -1.2025
      0.32729    -0.095648       -1.441     -0.01979
      0.17464     -0.83235      0.57115     -0.15672
>> [tmp,idx] = sort(newdata(:,2)); % sort second column
>> newdatas = newdata(idx,:) % shuffle rows using idx from 2nd column
newdatas =
      0.17464     -0.83235      0.57115     -0.15672
      0.12533     -0.58832      0.71432      0.81562
     -0.43256     -0.18671      0.29441     -0.39989
      -1.1465      -0.1364     -0.69178       1.2902
      0.32729    -0.095648       -1.441     -0.01979
    -0.037633     0.059281      -1.5937      -1.2025
       1.1909      0.11393        0.858       0.6686
      -1.6656      0.72579      -1.3362         0.69
       1.1892       1.0668        1.254       1.1908
      0.28768       2.1832       1.6236      0.71191
```

Here, the second column of the random array is sorted in increasing order. Then, the sort index is used to shuffle the rows in all columns. For example, the last row of newdata is now the first row in newdatas, because the last element in the second column is the smallest element in the second column.

A vector is strictly monotonic if its elements either always increase or always decrease as one proceeds down the array. The function diff is useful for determining monotonicity:

```
>> A = diff(data) % check randon data
A =
        0.1765
```

```
      0.12988
     -0.18361
     -0.56194
      0.22944
      0.52976
    -0.018565
     -0.50663
      0.48338
>> mono = all(A>0) | all(A<0) % as expected, not monotonic
mono =
     0
>> B = diff(sdata) % check random data after sorting
B =
      0.22944
     0.004564
      0.20516
      0.12277
      0.05373
      0.10171
     0.023255
    0.0049085
     0.013657
>> mono = all(B>0) | all(B<0) % as expected, monotonic
mono =
     1
```

Furthermore, a monotonic vector is equally spaced if

```
>> all( diff( diff(sdata) )==0 ) % random data is not equally spaced
ans =
     0
>> all( diff( diff(1:25) )==0 ) % but numbers from 1 to 25 are equally
spaced
ans =
     1
```

18.3 DATA ANALYSIS AND STATISTICAL FUNCTIONS

By default, data analysis in MATLAB is performed on column-oriented matrices. Different variables are stored in individual columns, and each row represents a different observation of each variable. Many data analysis functions work along any dimension, provided that the dimension is specified as an input argument. The data analysis and statistical functions in MATLAB are listed in the following table:

Function	Description
`corrcoef(A)`	Correlation coefficients
`cov(A)`	Covariance matrix
`cplxpair(v)`	Sorts vector into complex conjugate pairs
`cumprod(A)`	Cumulative product of elements
`cumsum(A)`	Cumulative sum of elements
`cumtrapz(A)`	Cumulative trapezoidal integration
`del2(A)`	Discrete Laplacian (surface curvature)
`diff(A)`	Differences between elements
`gradient(Z,dx,dy)`	Approximate surface gradient
`histc(X,edges)`	Histogram count and bin locations using bins marked by edges
`issorted(A)`	True if A is sorted
`max(A)`	Maximum values
`median(A)`	Median values
`mean(A)`	Mean values
`min(A)`	Minimum values
`prod(A)`	Product of elements
`sort(A)`	Sorts in ascending or descending order
`sortrows(A)`	Sorts rows in ascending order, i.e., dictionary sort
`std(A)`	Standard deviation
`sum(A)`	Sum of elements
`trapz(A)`	Trapezoidal integration
`var(A)`	Variance, i.e., square of standard deviation

19

Data Interpolation

Interpolation is a way of estimating values of a function between those given by some set of data points. In particular, interpolation serves as a valuable tool when you cannot quickly evaluate the function at the desired intermediate points—for example, when the data points are the result of some experimental measurements or lengthy computational procedure. MATLAB provides tools for interpolating in any number of dimensions by using multidimensional arrays. To illustrate interpolation, only 1- and 2-D interpolations are considered in depth here. However, the functions used for higher dimensions are briefly discussed.

19.1 ONE-DIMENSIONAL INTERPOLATION

Perhaps the simplest example of interpolation is MATLAB plots. By default, MATLAB draws straight lines connecting the data points used to make a plot. This linear interpolation guesses that intermediate values fall on a straight line between the entered points. Certainly, as the number of data points increases and the distance between them decreases, linear interpolation becomes more accurate:

```
>> x1 = linspace(0,2*pi,60);
>> x2 = linspace(0,2*pi,6);
>> plot(x1,sin(x1),x2,sin(x2),'--')
>> xlabel('x'),ylabel('sin(x)')
>> title('Figure 19.1: Linear Interpolation')
```

Of the two plots of the sine function shown, the one using 60 points is much more accurate between the data points than the one using only 6 points.

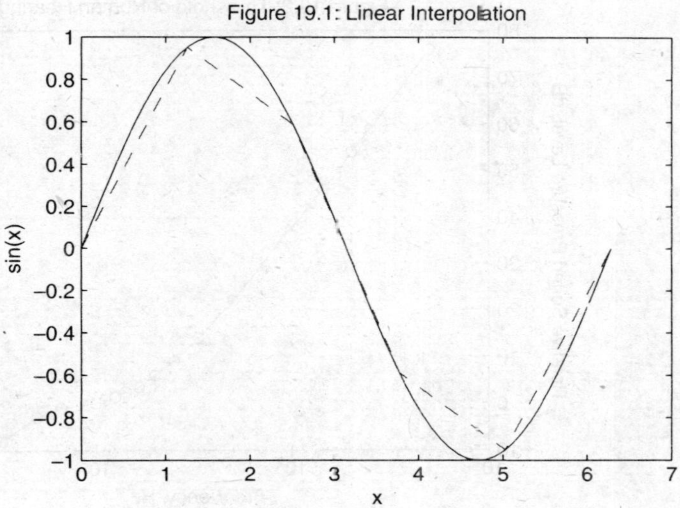

To understand 1-D interpolation, consider the following illustration: The threshold of audibility (i.e., the lowest perceptible sound level) of the human ear varies with frequency. Typical data are as follows:

```
>> Hz=[20:10:100 200:100:1000 1500 2000:1000:10000]; % frequencies in Hertz
>> spl =[76 66 59 54   49  46  43 40 38 22 ...   % sound pressure level in dB
     14  9  6 3.5 2.5 1.4 0.7  0 -1 -3 ...
     -8 -7 -2   2   7   9  11 12];
```

The sound pressure levels are normalized, so that 0 dB appears at 1000 Hz. Since the frequencies span such a large range, plot the data using a logarithmic x-axis:

```
>> semilogx(Hz,spl,'-o')
>> xlabel('Frequency, Hz')
>> ylabel('Relative Sound Pressure Level, dB')
>> title('Figure 19.2: Threshold of Human Hearing')
>> grid on
```

According to this plot, the human ear is most sensitive to tones around 3 kHz. Given these data, let's use the function `interp1` to estimate the sound pressure level in several different ways at a frequency of 2.5 kHz:

```
>> s = interp1(Hz,spl,2.5e3)              % linear interpolation
s =
     -5.5
```

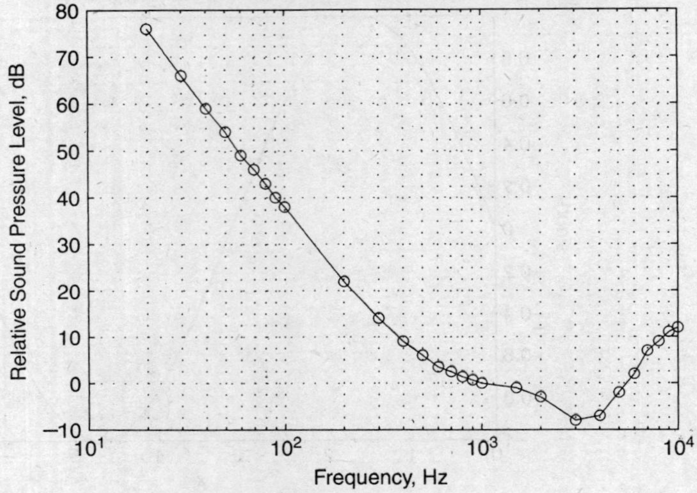


```
>> s = interp1(Hz,spl,2.5e3,'linear')  % linear interpolation again
s =
      -5.5
>> s = interp1(Hz,spl,2.5e3,'cubic')   % cubic interpolation
s =
     -6.0488
>> s = interp1(Hz,spl,2.5e3,'spline')  % cubic spline interpolation
s =
      -5.869
>> s = interp1(Hz,spl,2.5e3,'nearest') % nearest neighbor interpolation
   s =
        -8
```

Note the differences in these results. The first two results return exactly what is shown in the figure at 2.5 kHz, since MATLAB linearly interpolates between data points on plots. Cubic and spline interpolation fit cubic, that is, third-order, polynomials to each data interval by using different constraints. Cubic interpolation maintains data monotonicity, whereas spline interpolation exhibits the greatest smoothness. The crudest interpolation in this case is the nearest-neighbor method, which returns the input data point nearest the given value.

So how do you choose an interpolation method for a given problem? In many cases, linear interpolation is sufficient. In fact, that's why it is the default method. While the nearest-neighbor method produced poor results here, it is often used when speed is important or when the data set is large. The most time-consuming method is `'spline'`, but it frequently produces the most desirable results.

While the preceding case considered only a single interpolation point, `interp1` can handle any arbitrary number of points. In fact, one of the most common uses of cubic or spline interpolation is to smooth data. That is, given a set of data, use interpolation to evaluate the data at a finer interval:

```
>> Hzi = linspace(2e3,5e3);   % look closely near minimum
>> spli = interp1(Hz,spl,Hzi,'spline');  % interpolate near minimum
>> i = find(Hz>=2e3 & Hz<=5e3);  % find original data indices near minimum
>> semilogx(Hz(i),spl(i),'--o',Hzi,spli)  % plot old and new data
>> xlabel('Frequency, Hz')
>> ylabel('Relative Sound Pressure Level, dB')
>> title('Figure 19.3: Threshold of Human Hearing')
>> grid on
```

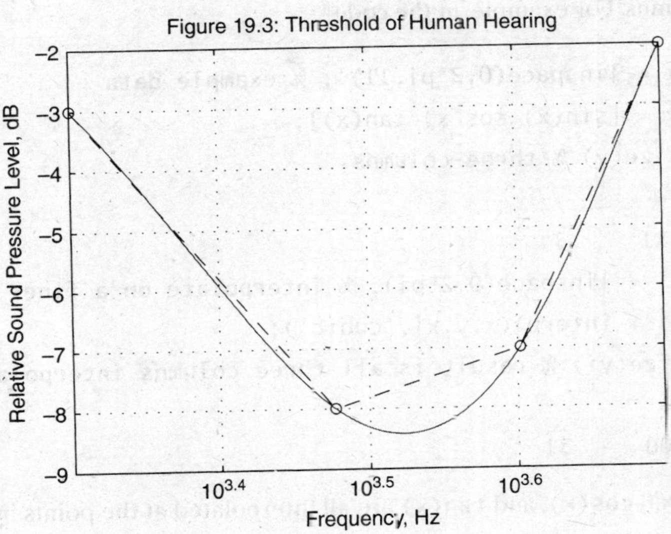

In the plot, the dashed line is the linear interpolation, the solid line is the cubic interpolation, and the original data are marked with `'o'`. By asking for a finer resolution on the frequency axis, and by using spline interpolation, we have a smoother estimate of the sound pressure level. In particular, note how the slope of the spline solution does not change abruptly at the data points.

With these data, we can make a better estimate of the frequency of greatest sensitivity, using for example, the following code:

```
>> [spl_min,i] = min(spli) % minimum and index of minimum
spl_min =
      -8.4245
i =
    45
>> Hz_min = Hzi(i)   % frequency at minimum
Hz_min =
      3333.3
```

According to this analysis, the human ear is most sensitive to tones near 3.33 kHz.

It is important to recognize the major restriction enforced by `interp1`, namely, that the independent variable must be monotonic. That is, the first variable must always increase or must always decrease. In our example, `Hz` is monotonic.

Finally, it is possible to interpolate more than one data set at a time, because the function `interp1` supports multidimensional input (for example, if `y` is a column-oriented data array). That is, if `x` is a vector, either `y` can be a vector, as shown previously, or it can be an array having `length(x)` rows and any number of columns. For example, in the code

```
>> x = linspace(0,2*pi,11)'; % example data
>> y = [sin(x) cos(x) tan(x)];
>> size(y) % three columns
ans =
    11     3
>> xi = linspace(0,2*pi); % interpolate on a finer scale
>> yi = interp1(x,y,xi,'cubic');
>> size(yi) % result is all three columns interpolated
ans =
   100     31
```

`sin(x)`, `cos(x)`, and `tan(x)` are all interpolated at the points in `xi`.

19.2 TWO-DIMENSIONAL INTERPOLATION

Two-dimensional interpolation is based on the same underlying ideas as 1-D interpolation. However, as the name implies, 2-D interpolation interpolates functions of two variables: $z = f(x, y)$. To illustrate this added dimension, consider the following illustration: An exploration company is using sonar to map the ocean floor. At points every 0.5 km on a rectangular grid, the ocean depth in meters is recorded for later analysis. A portion of the data collected is entered into MATLAB in the script M-file ocean.m, as shown in the following:

```
% ocean.m, example test data

% ocean depth data

x = 0:.5:4;   % x-axis (varies across the rows of z)
y = 0:.5:6;   % y-axis (varies down the columns of z)

z=[100   99  100   99  100   99   99   99  100
   100   99   99   99  100   99  100   99   99
    99   99   98   98  100   99  100  100  100
   100   98   97   97   99  100  100  100   99
   101  100   98   98  100  102  103  100  100
   102  103  101  100  102  106  104  101  100
    99  102  100  100  103  108  106  101   99
    97   99  100  100  102  105  103  101  100
   100  102  103  101  102  103  102  100   99
   100  102  103  102  101  101  100   99   99
   100  100  101  101  100  100  100   99   99
   100  100  100  100  100   99   99   99   99
   100  100  100   99   99  100   99  100   99];
```

A plot of this data can be displayed by entering

```
>> mesh(x,y,z)
>> xlabel('X-axis, km')
>> ylabel('Y-axis, km')
>> zlabel('Ocean Depth, m')
>> title('Figure 19.4: Ocean Depth Measurements')
```

With these data, the depth at arbitrary points within the rectangle can be found by using the function interp2, as in the following code:

```
>> zi = interp2(x,y,z,2.2,3.3)
```

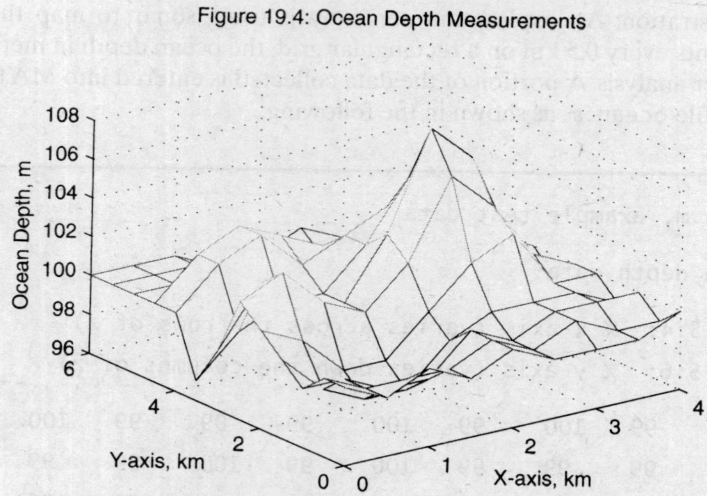


```
zi =
      103.92
>> zi = interp2(x,y,z,2.2,3.3,'linear')
zi =
      103.92
>> zi = interp2(x,y,z,2.2,3.3,'cubic')
zi =
      104.19
>> zi = interp2(x,y,z,2.2,3.3,'nearest')
zi =
   102
```

As was the case with 1-D interpolation, several interpolation methods are available, with the default method being linear.

Once again, we can interpolate on a finer scale, or mesh, to smooth the plot:

```
>> xi = linspace(0,4,30);  % finer x-axis
>> yi = linspace(0,6,40);  % finer y-axis
```

For each value in `xi`, we wish to interpolate at all values in `yi`. That is, we wish to create a grid of all combinations of the values of `xi` and `yi`, and then interpolate at all of these points. The function `meshgrid` accepts two vectors and produces two arrays, each containing duplicates of its inputs, so that all combinations of the inputs are considered:

```
>> xtest = 1:5
xtest =
     1     2     3     4     5

>> ytest = 6:9
ytest =
     6     7     8     9

>> [xx,yy] = meshgrid(xtest,ytest)
xx =
     1     2     3     4     5
     1     2     3     4     5
     1     2     3     4     5
     1     2     3     4     5
yy =
     6     6     6     6     6
     7     7     7     7     7
     8     8     8     8     8
     9     9     9     9     9
```

As shown in this code, xx has `length(ytest)` rows, each containing `xtest`, and yy has `length(xtest)` columns, each containing `ytest`. With this structure, `xx(i,j)` and `yy(i,j)` for all `i` and `j` cover all combinations of the original vectors, `xtest` and `ytest`.

Applying `meshgrid` to our ocean depth example produces

```
>> [xxi,yyi] = meshgrid(xi,yi);  % grid of all combinations of xi and yi
>> size(xxi) % xxi has 40 rows each containing xi
ans =
   40    30
>> size(yyi) % yyi has 30 columns each containing yi
ans =
   40    30
```

Given `xxi` and `yyi`, the ocean depth can now be interpolated on the finer scale by entering

```
>> zzi = interp2(x,y,z,xxi,yyi,'cubic');  % interpolate
>> size(zzi) % zzi is the same size as xxi and yyi
```

```
ans =
    40    30
>> mesh(xxi,yyi,zzi)  % plot smoothed data
>> hold on
>> [xx,yy] = meshgrid(x,y); % grid original data
>> plot3(xx,yy,z+0.1,'ok')  % plot original data up a bit to show nodes
>> hold off

>> xlabel('X-axis, km')
>> ylabel('Y-axis, km')
>> zlabel('Ocean Depth, m')
>> title('Figure 19.5: 2-D Smoothing')
```

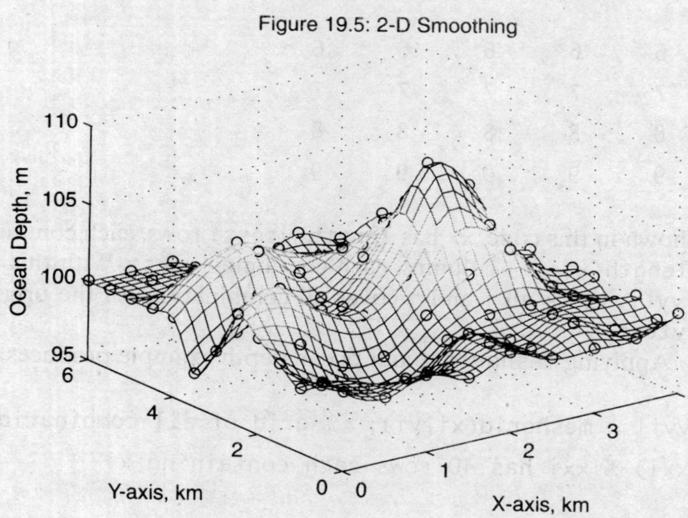

Using these data, we can now estimate the peak and its location:

```
>> zmax = max(max(zzi))
zmax =
        108.05
>> [i,j] = find(zmax==zzi);
>> xmax = xi(j)
xmax =
        2.6207
```

```
>> ymax = yi(i)
ymax =
       2.9231
```

The concepts discussed in these first two sections extend naturally to higher dimensions, where `ndgrid`, `interp3`, and `interpn` apply. The function `ndgrid` is the multidimensional equivalent of `meshgrid`. Multidimensional interpolation uses multidimensional arrays in a straightforward way to organize the data and perform the interpolation. The function `interp3` performs interpolation in 3-D space, and `interpn` performs interpolation in higher order dimensions. Both `interp3` and `interpn` offer method choices of `'linear'`, `'cubic'`, and `'nearest'`. (For more information regarding these functions, see the MATLAB documentation and the on-line help.)

19.3 TRIANGULATION AND SCATTERED DATA

In a number of applications, such as those involving geometric analysis, data points are often scattered, rather than appearing on a rectangular grid, like the ocean data in the example discussed in the last section. For example, consider the following 2-D random data:

```
>> x = randn(1,12);
>> y = randn(1,12);
>> z = zeros(1,12); % no z component for now
>> plot(x,y,'o')
>> title('Figure 19.6: Random Data')
```

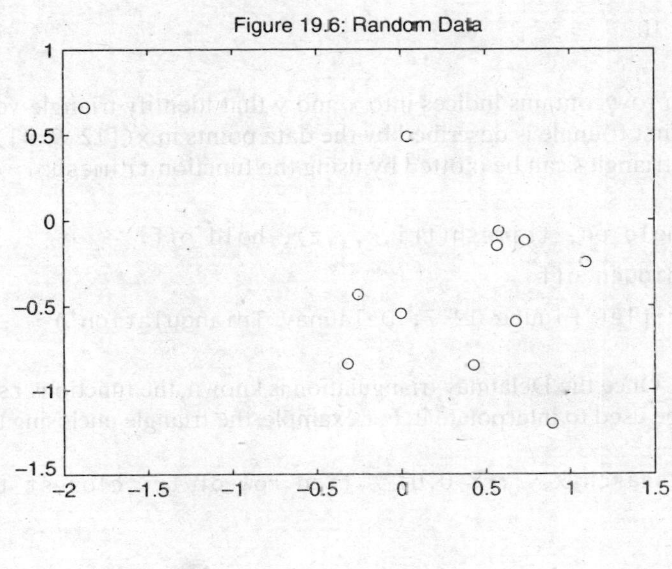

Given these scattered data, it is common to apply ***Delaunay triangulation***, which returns a set of triangles connecting the data points such that no data points are contained within any triangle. The MATLAB function `delaunay` accepts data points and returns a list of indices that identify the triangle vertices. For the random data, `delaunay` returns

```
>> tri = delaunay(x,y)
tri =
    12     9     4
    12     2     4
     7     9     3
     8    12     9
     8     7     9
     8     7    11
     5     2     6
     1     8    12
     1     8    11
     1    12     2
     1     5     2
    10     7    11
    10     1    11
    10     1     5
    10     7     3
    10     6     3
    10     5     6
```

Each row contains indices into `x` and `y` that identify triangle vertices. For example, the first triangle is described by the data points in `x([12 9 4])` and `y([12 9 4])`. The triangles can be plotted by using the function `trimesh`:

```
>> hold on, trimesh(tri,x,y,z), hold off
>> hidden off
>> title('Figure 19.7: Delaunay Triangulation')
```

Once the Delaunay triangulation is known, the functions `tsearch` and `dsearch` can be used to interpolate it. For example, the triangle enclosing the origin is

```
>> tsearch(x,y,tri,0,0) % find row of tri closest to (0,0)
```

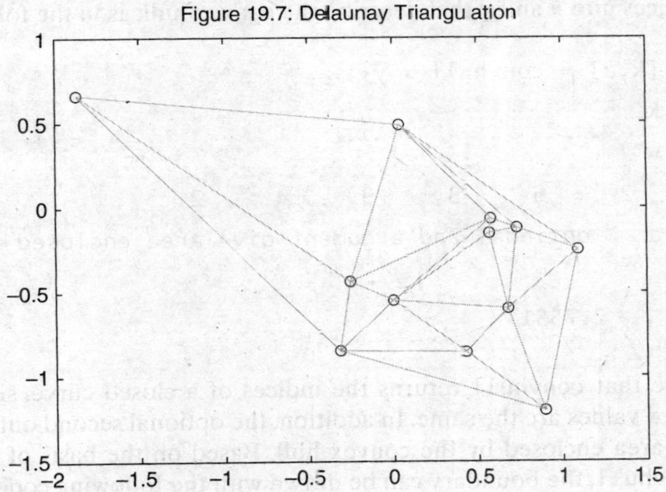


```
ans =

     4

>> tri(ans,:) % vertices of triangle closest to (0,0)

ans =

     8    12     9
```

Naturally, tsearch accepts multiple values—for example,

```
>> tsearch(x,y,tri,[-.5 1],[.1 .5])

ans =

     1   NaN
```

Here, the first triangle encloses the point $(-0.5, 0.1)$, and no triangle encloses the point $(1, 0.5)$.

Rather than returning the triangle enclosing one or more data points, the function dsearch returns the indices into x and y that are closest to the desired points:

```
>> dsearch(x,y,tri,[-.5 1],[.1 .5])

ans =

    12     7
```

Here, the point (x(12),y(12)) is closest to the point $(-0.5, 0.1)$, and the point (x(7),y(7)) is closest to $(1, 0.5)$.

In addition to interpolating the data, it is often useful to know which points form the outer boundary or ***convex hull*** for the set. The function convhull returns indices into x and y that describe the convex hull, as in the following example:

```
>> [k,a] = convhull(x,y);
>> k'
k =
     2     6     3     9     4     2
>> a   % optional 2nd argument give area enclosed
a =
     2.7551
```

Note that convhull returns the indices of a closed curve, since the first and last index values are the same. In addition, the optional second output argument returns the area enclosed by the convex hull. Based on the basis of the data returned by convhull, the boundary can be drawn with the following code:

```
>> plot(x,y,'o',x(k),y(k))
>> title('Figure 19.8: Convex Hull')
```

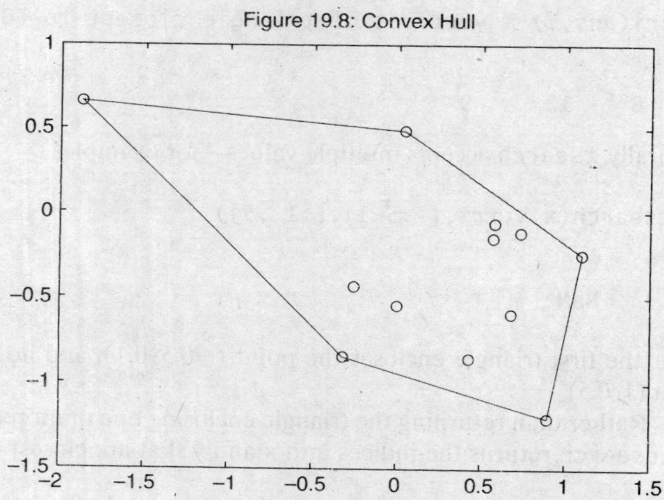

It is also possible to define and draw the lines that separate regions in the plane that are closest to a particular data point. These lines form what is called a ***Voronoi polygon***. In MATLAB, these lines are drawn by the function voronoi:

```
>> voronoi(x,y)
>> title('Figure 19.9: Voronoi Diagram')
```

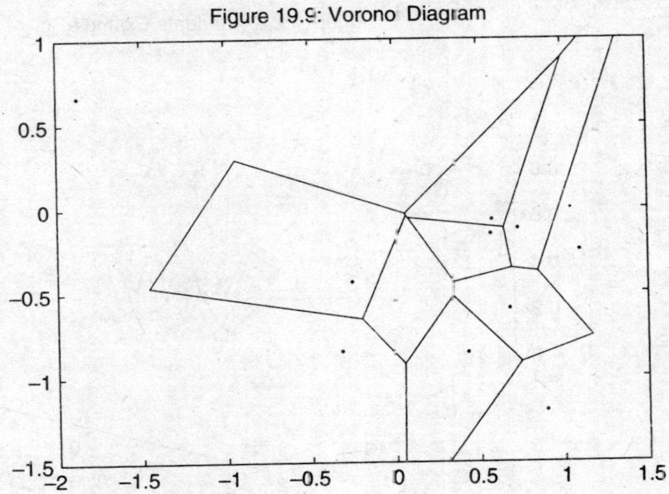

Finally, it is possible to interpolate a Delaunay triangulation to produce interpolated points on a rectangular grid by using the function `griddata`. In particular, this step is required to use functions such as `surf` and other standard plotting routines. These plotting routines require data that contain information at a complete sequence of points along two coordinate axes, rather than the scattered data that `trimesh` uses. Think about a map analogy. Delaunay triangulation allows you to identify specific scattered points on a map. The function `griddata` uses this information to construct an approximation to the rest of the map, filling in data in a user-specified rectangular region in two coordinate directions:

```
>> z = rand(1,12); % now use some random z axis data
>> xi = linspace(min(x),max(x),30);  % x interpolation points
>> yi = linspace(min(y),max(y),30);  % y interpolation points

>> [Xi,Yi] = meshgrid(xi,yi);        % create grid of x and y

>> Zi = griddata(x,y,z,Xi,Yi);       % grid data at Xi,Yi points

>> mesh(Xi,Yi,Zi)
>> hold on
>> plot3(x,y,z,'ko')  % show original data as well
>> hold off
>> title('Figure 19.10: Griddata Example')
```

Figure 19.10: Griddata Example

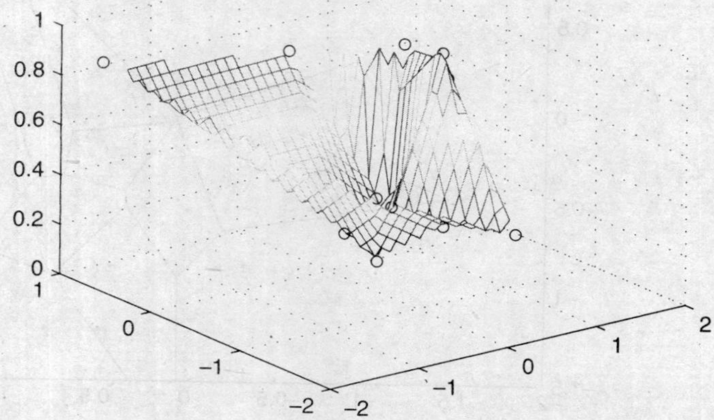

In this example, the information at the 12 scattered data points was interpolated to produce an array of data on a 30-by-30 grid in the x-y plane. The variable `Zi` contains a 30-by-30 array of points linearly interpolated from the triangulation of the data in `x`, `y` and `z`. Just as `interp1` and `interp2` support other interpolations, `griddata` also supports others:

```
>> Zi = griddata(x,y,z,Xi,Yi,'linear')  % same as above (default)
>> Zi = griddata(x,y,z,Xi,Yi,'cubic')   % triangle based cubic interpolation
>> Zi = griddata(x,y,z,Xi,Yi,'nearest') % triangle based nearest neighbor
```

19.4 SUMMARY

In MATLAB, the triangulation functions discussed in this chapter have n-dimensional forms as well. Many of the data interpolation functions have other features and options that cannot be covered here. The data interpolation functions in MATLAB are summarized in the following table:

Function	Description
`convhull`	Convex hull
`convhulln`	*n*-D convex hull
`delaunay`	Delaunay triangulation
`delaunay3`	3-D Delaunay tesselation
`delaunayn`	*n*-D Delaunay tesselation

dsearch	Nearest point search in Delaunay triangulation
griddata	2-D rectangular gridding
griddata3	3-D rectangular gridding
griddatan	*n*-D rectangular gridding
interp1	1-D interpolation
interp1q	1-D quick interpolation (no error checking)
interp2	2-D interpolation
interp3	3-D interpolation
interpft	1-D interpolation using FFT method
interpn	*n*-D interpolation
meshgrid	Generate X and Y matrices for 3-D functions
ndgrid	Generate arrays for multidimensional functions
tetramesh	Tetrahedron mesh plot
trimesh	Triangular mesh plot
triplot	2-D triangular plot
trisurf	Triangular surface plot
tsearch	Closest triangle search
tsearchn	n-D closest triangle search
voronoi	Voronoi diagram
voronoin	n-D Voronoi diagram

20

Polynomials

MATLAB provides a number of functions for manipulating polynomials. Polynomials are easily differentiated and integrated, and it is straightforward to find polynomial roots. However, higher-order polynomials pose numerical difficulties in a number of situations and therefore should be used with caution.

20.1 ROOTS

Finding the roots of a polynomial—that is, the values for which the polynomial is zero—is a problem common to many disciplines. MATLAB solves this problem and provides other polynomial manipulation tools as well. In MATLAB, a polynomial is represented by a row vector of its coefficients in descending order. For example, the polynomial $x^4 - 12x^3 + 0x^2 + 25x + 116$ is entered as

```
>> p = [1 -12 0 25 116]
p =
     1   -12     0    25   116
```

Note that terms with zero coefficients must be included. MATLAB has no way of knowing which terms are zero unless you specifically identify them. Given this form, the roots of a polynomial are found by using the function `roots`:

```
>> r = roots(p)
r =
   11.7473
    2.7028
```

```
  -1.2251 + 1.4672i
  -1.2251 - 1.4672i
```

Since in MATLAB both a polynomial and its roots are vectors, MATLAB adopts the convention that ***polynomials are row vectors and roots are column vectors.***

Given the roots of a polynomial, it is also possible to construct the associated polynomial. In MATLAB, the command `poly` performs this task:

```
>> pp = poly(r)
pp =
            1         -12 -1.7764e-014          25         116
>> pp(abs(pp)<1e-12) = 0  % change small element to zero!
pp =
            1         -12            0          25         116
```

Because of truncation errors, it is not uncommon for the results of `poly` to have near-zero components or to have components with small imaginary parts. As already shown, near-zero components can be corrected by array manipulation. Similarly, eliminating spurious imaginary parts is simply a matter of using the function `real` to extract the real part of the result.

20.2 MULTIPLICATION

Polynomial multiplication is supported by the function `conv` (which performs the convolution of two arrays). Consider the product of the two polynomials $a(x) = x^3 + 2x^2 + 3x + 4$ and $b(x) = x^3 + 4x^2 + 9x + 16$:

```
>> a = [1 2 3 4];   b = [1 4 9 16];
>> c = conv(a,b)
c =
     1     6    20    50    75    84    64
```

This result is $c(x) = x^6 + 6x^5 + 20x^4 + 50x^3 + 75x^2 + 84x + 64$. Multiplication of more than two polynomials requires repeated use of `conv`.

20.3 ADDITION

MATLAB does not provide a direct function for adding polynomials. Standard array addition works if both polynomial vectors are the same order, as in the code

```
>> d = a + b
d =
     2     6    12    20
```

which represents $d(x) = 2x^3 + 6x^2 + 12x + 20$. When two polynomials are of different orders, the polynomial of lower order must be padded with leading zeros so that it has the same effective order as the higher-order polynomial. Consider the addition of the preceding polynomials c and d:

```
>> e = c + [0 0 0 d]
e =
     1     6    20    52    81    96    84
```

The resulting polynomial is $e(x) = x^6 + 6x^5 + 20x^4 + 52x^3 + 81x^2 + 96x + 84$. Leading zeros, rather than trailing zeros, are required, because coefficients associated with like powers of x must line up. The following M-file function automates polynomial addition:

```
function p=mmpadd(a,b)
%MMPADD Polynomial Addition.
% MMPADD(A,B) adds the polynomials A and B.

if nargin<2
   error('Not Enough Input Arguments.')
end
a=reshape(a,1,[]); % make sure inputs are polynomial row vectors
b=b(:).';          % this makes a row as well
na=length(a);  % find lengths of a and b
nb=length(b);
p=[zeros(1,nb-na) a]+[zeros(1,na-nb) b]; % pad with zeros as necessary
```

To illustrate the use of mmpadd, consider again the preceding example

```
>> f = mmpadd(c,d)
f =
     1     6    20    52    81    96    84
```

which is the same as our earlier e. Of course, mmpadd can also be used for subtraction, as in

```
>> g = mmpadd(c,-d)
g =
     1     6    20    48    69    72    44
```

The resulting polynomial is $g(x) = x^6 + 6x^5 + 20x^4 + 48x^3 + 69x^2 + 72x + 44$.

20.4 DIVISION

In some special cases, it is necessary to divide one polynomial into another. In MATLAB, this is accomplished with the function deconv:

```
>> [q,r] = deconv(c,b)
q =
     1     2     3     4
r =
     0     0     0     0     0     0     0
```

This result says that b divided into c gives the quotient polynomial q and the remainder r, which is zero in this case, since the product of b and q is exactly c. Another example gives a remainder:

```
>> [q,r] = deconv(f,b)
q =
     1     2     3     6
r =
     0     0     0     0    -2    -6   -12
```

Here, b divided into f gives the quotient polynomial q and the remainder r. The leading zeros in r simply make r the same length as f. In this case, the quotient is $q(x) = x^3 + 2x^2 + 3x + 6$ and the remainder term is $r(x) = -2x^2 - 6x - 12$.

20.5 DERIVATIVES AND INTEGRALS

Because differentiation of a polynomial is simple to express, MATLAB offers the function polyder for polynomial differentiation:

```
>> g  % recall polynomial
g =
     1     6    20    48    69    72    44
```

```
>> h = polyder(g)
h =
     6    30    80   144   138    72
```

Similarly, the integral of a polynomial is easy to express. Given an integration constant, the function polyint returns the integral:

```
>> polyint(h,44) % get g back from h=polyder(g)
ans =
     1     6    20    48    69    72    44
```

20.6 EVALUATION

Given that you can add, subtract, multiply, divide, and differentiate polynomials on the basis of row vectors of their coefficients, you should be able to evaluate them also. In MATLAB, this is accomplished with the function polyval, as in the following example:

```
>> p = [1 4 -7 -10];      % the polynomial
>> x = linspace(-1,3); % evaluation points
>> v = polyval(p,x);      % evaluate p at points in x
>> plot(x,v)              % plot results
>> title('Figure 20.1: x{^3} + 4x{^2} - 7x -10')
>> xlabel('x')
```

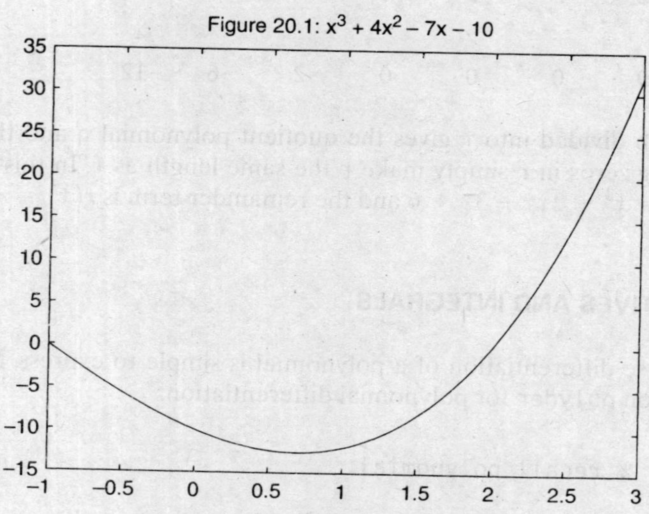

20.7 RATIONAL POLYNOMIALS

Sometimes one encounters ratios of polynomials—for example, transfer functions and Pade approximations to functions. In MATLAB, these are manipulated by considering the numerator and denominator polynomials separately, as in the following example:

```
>> n = [1 -10 100]  % a numerator

n =

     1   -10   100

>> d = [1 10 100 0]  % a denominator

d =

     1    10   100     0

>> z = roots(n)  % the zeros of n(x)/d(x)

z =

           5 +     8.6603i
           5 -     8.6603i

>> p = roots(d)  % the poles of n(x)/d(x)

p =

           0
          -5 +     8.6603i
          -5 -     8.6603i
```

The derivative of this rational polynomial with respect to x is found by using `polyder`:

```
>> [nd,dd] = polyder(n,d)

nd =

        -1          20        -100       -2000      -10000

dd =

  Columns 1 through 6

         1          20         300        2000       10000           0

  Column 7

         0
```

Here, nd and dd are the respective numerator and denominator polynomials of the derivative.

Another common operation is to find the partial-fraction expansion of a rational polynomial—for example,

```
>> [r,p,k] = residue(n,d)
r =

   9.7954e-17 +       1.1547i
   9.7954e-17 -       1.1547i
            1

p =

           -5 +       8.6603i
           -5 -       8.6603i
            0

k =

     []
```

In this case, the `residue` function returns the residues or partial-fraction expansion coefficients `r`, their associated poles `p`, and the direct term polynomial `k`. Since the order of the numerator is less than that of the denominator, there are no direct terms. For this example, the partial fraction expansion of the rational polynomial is

$$\frac{n(x)}{d(x)} = \frac{1.1547i}{x + 5 - 8.6603i} + \frac{-1.1547i}{x + 5 + 8.6603i} + \frac{1}{x}$$

Given this information, the original rational polynomial is found by using `residue` yet again:

```
>> [nn,dd] = residue(r,p,k)
nn =
           1           -10           100
dd =
           1            10           100            0
```

So, in this case, the function `residue` performs two operations that are inverses of one another depending on how many input and output arguments are used.

20.8 CURVE FITTING

In numerous application areas, you are faced with the task of fitting a curve to measured data. Sometimes the chosen curve passes through the data points, but at other times the curve comes close to, but does not necessarily pass through, the data points. In the most common situation, the curve is chosen so that the sum of the squared errors at the data points is minimized. This choice results in a ***least squares*** curve fit. While least squares curve fitting can be done by using any set of basis functions, it is straightforward and common to use a truncated power series—that is, a polynomial.

In MATLAB, the function `polyfit` solves the least squares polynomial curve-fitting problem. To illustrate the use of this function, let's start with the following data:

```
>> x = [0 .1 .2 .3 .4 .5 .6 .7 .8 .9 1];
>> y = [-.447 1.978 3.28 6.16 7.08 7.34 7.66 9.56 9.48 9.30 11.2];
```

To use `polyfit`, we must supply this data and the order, or degree, of the polynomial we wish to best fit to the data. If we choose $n = 1$ as the order, the best straight line approximation will be found. This is often called ***linear regression***. On the other hand, if we choose $n = 2$ as the order, a quadratic polynomial will be found. For now, let's choose a quadratic polynomial:

```
>> n = 2;
>> p = polyfit(x,y,n)
p =
   -9.8108   20.1293   -0.0317
```

The output of `polyfit` is a row vector of the polynomial coefficients. Here the solution is $y(x) = -9.8108x^2 + 20.1293x - 0.0317$. To compare the curve-fit solution to the data points, let's plot both:

```
>> xi = linspace(0,1,100);
>> yi = polyval(p,xi);
>> plot(x,y,'-o',xi,yi,'-')
>> xlabel('x'), ylabel('y=f(x)')
>> title('Figure 20.2:  Second Order Curve Fitting')
```

This plot contains the original data `x` and `y`, marking the data points with `'o'` and connecting them with straight lines. In addition, the evaluated polynomial data `xi` and `yi` are plotted with a dashed line (`'--'`).

The choice of polynomial order is somewhat arbitrary. It takes two points to define a straight line or first-order polynomial. (If this isn't clear to you, mark two points and draw a straight line between them.) It takes three points to define a quadratic, or second-order, polynomial. Following this progression, it takes $n + 1$ data points to uniquely specify an nth-order polynomial. Thus, in the preceding case, where there are 11 data points, we could choose up to a 10th-order polynomial. However, given the poor numerical properties of higher order polynomials, you

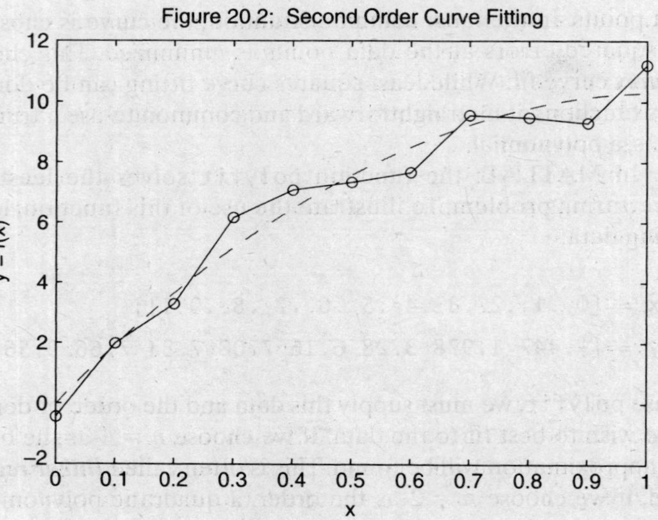

should not choose a polynomial order that is any higher than necessary. In addition, as the polynomial order increases, the approximation becomes less smooth, since higher order polynomials can be differentiated more times before they become zero. For example, consider choosing a 10th-order polynomial:

```
>> pp = polyfit(x,y,10);
>> pp.'  % display polynomial coefficients as a column
ans =
  -4.6436e+005
   2.2965e+006
  -4.8773e+006
   5.8233e+006
  -4.2948e+006
   2.0211e+006
  -6.0322e+005
   1.0896e+005
        -10626
        435.99
        -0.447
```

Note the size of the polynomial coefficients in this case, compared with those of the earlier quadratic fit. Note also the seven orders of magnitude difference between the smallest (−0.447) and largest (−4.6436e+005) coefficients and the alternating signs on the coefficients. To see how this polynomial differs from the quadratic fit shown earlier, consider a plot of both:

```
>> y10 = polyval(pp,xi);   % evaluate 10th order polynomial
>> plot(x,y,'o',xi,yi,'--',xi,y10) % plot data
>> xlabel('x'), ylabel('y=f(x)')
>> title('Figure 20.3: 2nd and 10th Order Curve Fitting')
```

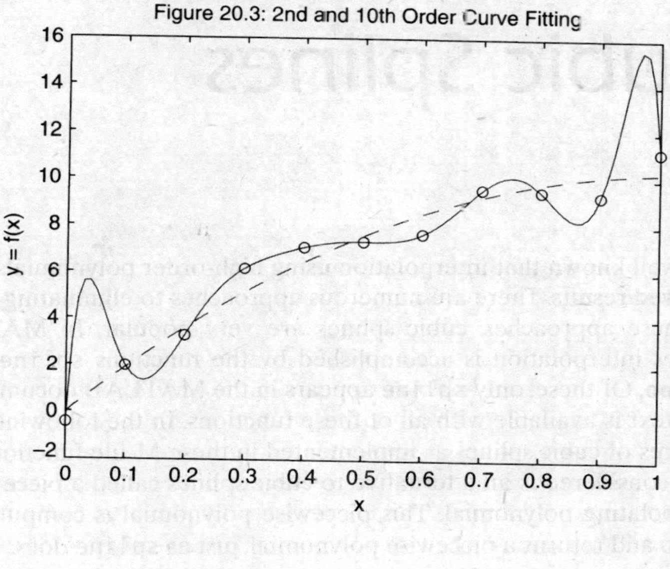

In this plot, the original data are marked with `'o'`, the quadratic curve fit is dashed, and the 10th-order fit is solid. Note the wavelike ripples that appear between the data points at the left and right extremes in the 10th-order fit. This example clearly demonstrates the difficulties with higher order polynomials.

21

Cubic Splines

It is well known that interpolation using high-order polynomials often produces ill-behaved results. There are numerous approaches to eliminating this poor behavior. Of these approaches, cubic splines are very popular. In MATLAB, basic cubic splines interpolation is accomplished by the functions `spline`, `ppval`, `mkpp`, and `unmkpp`. Of these, only `spline` appears in the MATLAB documentation. However, help text is available with all of these functions. In the following sections, the basic features of cubic splines as implemented in these M-file functions is demonstrated. Also considered is an alternative to cubic splines called a piecewise cubic Hermite interpolating polynomial. This piecewise polynomial is computed by the function `pchip` and returns a piecewise polynomial, just as `spline` does.

21.1 BASIC FEATURES

In cubic splines, cubic polynomials are found to approximate the curve between each pair of data points. In the language of splines, these data points are called breakpoints. Since a straight line is uniquely defined by two points, an infinite number of cubic polynomials can be used to approximate a curve between two points. Therefore, in cubic splines, additional constraints are placed on the cubic polynomials to make the result unique. By constraining the first and second derivatives of each cubic polynomial to match at the breakpoints, all internal cubic polynomials are well defined. Moreover, both the slope and curvature of the approximating polynomials are continuous across the breakpoints. However, the first and last cubic polynomials do not have adjoining cubic polynomials beyond the first and last breakpoints. As a result, the remaining constraints must be determined by some other means. The most common approach, which is adopted by the function `spline`, is to adopt a ***not-a-knot*** condition. This condition forces the third derivative of the first and second cubic polynomials to be identical, and likewise for the last and second-to-last cubic polynomials.

Based on this description, you could guess that finding cubic spline polynomials requires solving a large set of linear equations. In fact, given n breakpoints, there are $n - 1$ cubic polynomials to be found, each having 4 unknown coefficients. Thus, the set of equations to be solved involves $4(n - 1)$ unknowns. By writing each cubic polynomial in a special form and by applying the constraints, the cubic polynomials can be found by solving a reduced set of n equations in n unknowns. Thus, if there are 50 breakpoints, there are 50 equations in 50 unknowns. Luckily, these equations can be concisely written and solved using sparse matrices, which describes what the function `spline` uses to compute the unknown coefficients.

21.2 PIECEWISE POLYNOMIALS

In its most simple use, `spline` takes data `x` and `y` and desired values `xi`, finds the cubic spline interpolation polynomials that fit `x` and `y`, and then evaluates the polynomials to find the corresponding `yi` values for each `xi` value. This approach matches the use of `yi = interp1(x,y,xi,'spline')`:

```
>> x = 0:12;
>> y = tan(pi*x/25);
>> xi = linspace(0,12);

>> yi = spline(x,y,xi);

>> plot(x,y,'o',xi,yi)
>> title('Figure 21.1: Spline Fit')
```

This approach is appropriate if only one set of interpolated values is required. However, if more values are needed from the same set of data, it doesn't make sense to recompute the same set of cubic spline coefficients a second time. In this situation, one can call `spline` with only the first two arguments:

```
>> pp = spline(x,y)
pp =
      form: 'pp'
    breaks: [0 1 2 3 4 5 6 7 8 9 10 11 12]
     coefs: [12x4 double]
    pieces: 12
     order: 4
       dim: 1
```

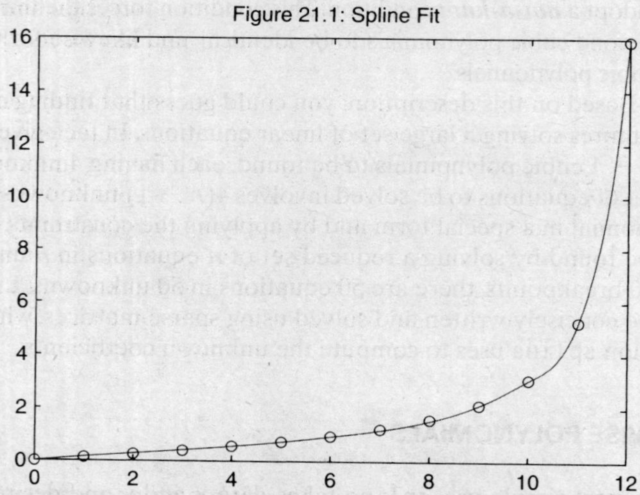

When called in this way, spline returns a structure containing the ***pp-form***, or piecewise polynomial form, of the cubic splines. This structure contains all of the information necessary to evaluate the cubic splines for any set of desired interpolation values. The pp-form structure is also compatible with the optional *Spline Toolbox* available with MATLAB. Given the pp-form, the function ppval evaluates the cubic splines. For example,

```
>> yi = ppval(pp,xi);
```

computes the same yi values computed earlier. Similarly,

```
>> xi2 = linspace(10,12);
>> yi2 = ppval(pp,xi2);
```

uses the pp-form again to evaluate the cubic splines over a finer spacing, restricted to the region between 10 and 12. The code

```
>> xi3 = 10:15;

>> yi3 = ppval(pp,xi3)
yi3 =
     3.0777    5.2422   15.8945   44.0038   98.5389  188.4689

>> yi4 = ppval(xi3,pp) % can be called with arguments reversed
yi4 =
     3.0777    5.2422   15.8945   44.0038   98.5389  188.4689
```

shows that cubic splines can be evaluated outside of the region over which the cubic polynomials were computed. When data appears beyond the last or before the first breakpoint, the last and first cubic polynomials are used, respectively, to find interpolated values. In addition, this example shows that `ppval` can be called with its input arguments reversed. This permits creating a function handle for `ppval` and passing it as an argument to functions that evaluate a user-supplied function as part of their work. For example, the function

```
>> quad(@ppval,0,10,[],[],pp)
ans =
        9.3775
```

computes the area under the spline given by pp over the range 0 to 10. (More information about the function quad can be found in Chapter 24.)

The cubic splines pp-form just given stores the breakpoints and polynomial coefficients, as well as other information regarding the cubic splines representation. This form is a convenient data structure in MATLAB, since all information is stored in a single structure. When a cubic spline representation is evaluated, the various fields in the pp-form must be extracted. In MATLAB, this process is conveniently performed by the function `unmkpp`. Using this function on the preceding pp-form gives

```
>> [breaks,coefs,npolys,ncoefs,dim] = unmkpp(pp)
breaks =
  Columns 1 through 12
     0     1     2     3     4     5     6     7     8     9    10    11
  Column 13
    12
coefs =
    0.0007   -0.0001    0.1257         0
    0.0007    0.0020    0.1276    0.1263
    0.0010    0.0042    0.1339    0.2568
    0.0012    0.0072    0.1454    0.3959
    0.0024    0.0109    0.1635    0.5498
    0.0019    0.0181    0.1925    0.7265
    0.0116    0.0237    0.2344    0.9391
   -0.0083    0.0586    0.3167    1.2088
    0.1068    0.0336    0.4089    1.5757
   -0.1982    0.3542    0.7967    2.1251
```

```
    1.4948   -0.2406    0.9102    3.0777
    1.4948    4.2439    4.9136    5.2422
npolys =
    12
ncoefs =
     4
dim =
     1
```

Here, breaks contains the breakpoints, coefs is a matrix whose ith row is the ith cubic polynomial, npolys is the number of polynomials, ncoefs is the number of coefficients per polynomial, and dim is the spline dimension. Note that this pp-form is sufficiently general that the spline polynomials need not be cubic. This fact is useful when the spline is integrated or differentiated.

In MATLAB versions prior to version 6, the pp-form was stored in a single numerical array rather than in a structure. As a result, unmkpp was valuable in separating the parts of the pp-form from the numerical array. Given the simplicity of the structure form, you can easily address the fields directly and avoid using unmkpp entirely. However, unmkpp continues to support the prior numerical array pp-form, thereby making the process of extracting the parts of a pp-form transparent to the user.

Given the broken-apart form, the function mkpp restores the pp-form:

```
>> pp = mkpp(breaks,coefs)
pp =
      form: 'pp'
    breaks: [0 1 2 3 4 5 6 7 8 9 10 11 12]
     coefs: [12x4 double]
    pieces: 12
     order: 4
       dim: 1
```

Since the size of the matrix coefs determines npolys and ncoefs, they are not needed by mkpp to reconstruct the pp-form.

21.3 CUBIC HERMITE POLYNOMIALS

When the underlying data to be interpolated represents a smooth function, cubic splines return appropriate values. However, when the underlying data are not so smooth, cubic splines can predict minima and maxima that do not exist and can destroy monotonicity. Therefore, for nonsmooth data, a different piecewise polynomial interpolation is called for. In MATLAB, the function pchip returns a piecewise cubic polynomial that has the properties described in the following help text:

```
>> help pchip

  PCHIP  Piecewise Cubic Hermite Interpolating Polynomial.
   PP = PCHIP(X,Y) provides the piecewise polynomial form of a certain
   shape-preserving piecewise cubic Hermite interpolant, to the values
   Y at the sites X, for later use with PPVAL and the spline utility UNMKPP.
   X must be a vector.
   If Y is a vector, then Y(j) is taken as the value to be matched at X(j),
   hence Y must be of the same length as X.
   If Y is a matrix or ND array, then Y(:,...,:,j) is taken as the value to
   be matched at X(j),  hence the last dimension of Y must equal length(X).
   YY = PCHIP(X,Y,XX) is the same as YY = PPVAL(PCHIP(X,Y),XX), thus
   providing, in YY, the values of the interpolant at XX.
   The PCHIP interpolating function, p(x), satisfies:
   On each subinterval,  X(k) <= x <= X(k+1),  p(x) is the cubic Hermite
      interpolant to the given values and certain slopes at the two endpoints.
   Therefore, p(x) interpolates Y, i.e., p(X(j)) = Y(:,j), and
      the first derivative, Dp(x), is continuous, but
      D^2p(x) is probably not continuous; there may be jumps at the X(j).
   The slopes at the X(j) are chosen in such a way that
     p(x) is "shape preserving" and "respects monotonicity". This means that,
   on intervals where the data is monotonic, so is p(x);
   at points where the data have a local extremum, so does p(x).
  Comparing PCHIP with SPLINE:
   The function s(x) supplied by SPLINE is constructed in exactly the same way,
   except that the slopes at the X(j) are chosen differently, namely to make
   even D^2s(x) continuous. This has the following effects.
   SPLINE is smoother, i.e., D^2s(x) is continuous.
   SPLINE is more accurate if the data are values of a smooth function.
   PCHIP has no overshoots and less oscillation if the data are not smooth.
```

```
PCHIP is less expensive to set up.
The two are equally expensive to evaluate.
```

The following example demonstrates the similarities and differences between `spline` and `pchip`:

```
>> x = [0 2 4 5 7.5 10];% sample data
>> y = exp(-x/6).*cos(x);

>> cs = spline(x,y);     % cubic spline
>> ch = pchip(x,y);      % cubic Hermite

>> xi = linspace(0,10);
>> ysi = ppval(cs,xi);  % interpolate spline
>> yhi = ppval(ch,xi);  % interpolate Hermite

>> plot(x,y,'o',xi,ysi,':',xi,yhi)
>> legend('data','spline','hermite')
>> title('Figure 21.2: Spline and Hermite Interpolation')
```

Figure 21.2: Spline and Hermite Interpolation

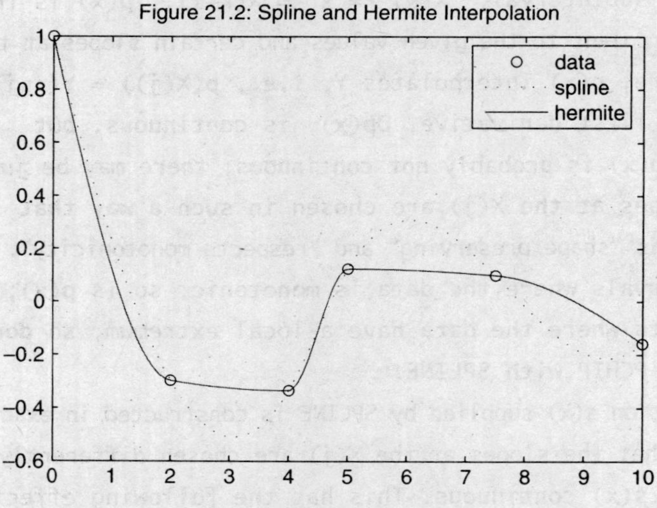

21.4 INTEGRATION

In many situations, it is desirable to know the area under a function described by piecewise polynomials as a function of the independent variable x. That is, if the piecewise polynomials are denoted $y = s(x)$, we are interested in computing

$$S(x) = \int_{x_1}^{x} s(x)\,dx + C$$

where x_1 is the first breakpoint and C is the integration constant. Since $s(x)$ is composed of connected cubic polynomials, with the kth cubic polynomial being

$$s_k(x) = a_k(x - x_k)^3 + b_k(x - x_k)^2 + c_k(x - x_k) + d_k, \quad x_k \leqslant x \leqslant x_{k+1}$$

and whose integral or area over the range $[x_k, x]$, where $x_k \leq x \leq x_{k+1}$, is

$$S_k(x) = \int_{x_k}^{x} s_k(x)\,dx = \frac{a_k}{4}(x - x_k)^4 + \frac{b_k}{3}(x - x_k)^3 + \frac{c_k}{2}(x - x_k)^2 + d_k(x - x_k)$$

the area under a piecewise polynomial is easily computed as

$$S(x) = \sum_{i=1}^{k-1} S_i(x_{i+1}) + S_k(x)$$

where $x_k \leq x \leq x_{k+1}$. The summation term is the cumulative sum of the areas under all preceding cubic polynomials. As such, it is readily computed and forms the constant term in the polynomial describing $S(x)$, since $S_k(x)$ is a polynomial. With this understanding, the integral itself can be written as a piecewise polynomial. In this case, it is a quartic piecewise polynomial, because the individual polynomials are of order four.

Because the pp-form used in MATLAB can support piecewise polynomials of any order, the preceding piecewise polynomial integration is embodied in the function mmppint. The body of this function is as follows:

```
function ppi=mmppint(pp,c)
%MMPPINT Cubic Spline Integral Interpolation.
% PPI=MMPPINT(PP,C) returns the piecewise polynomial vector PPI
% describing the integral of the cubic spline described by
% the piecewise polynomial in PP and having integration constant C.

if prod(size(c))~=1
   error('C Must be a Scalar.')
end
[br,co,npy,nco]=unmkpp(pp);                % take apart pp
```

```
sf=nco:-1:1;                                 % scale factors for integration
ico=[co./sf(ones(npy,1),:) zeros(npy,1)];   % integral coefficients
nco=nco+1;                              % integral spline has higher order
ico(1,nco)=c;                           % integration constant
for k=2:npy                             % find constant terms in polynomials
    ico(k,nco)=polyval(ico(k-1,:),br(k)-br(k-1));
end
ppi=mkpp(br,ico);                            % build pp form for integral
```

Consider the following example using mmppint:

```
>> x = (0:.1:1)*2*pi;
>> y = sin(x); % create rough data
>> pp = spline(x,y);         % pp-form fitting rough data
>> ppi = mmppint(pp,0);      % pp-form of integral
>> xi = linspace(0,2*pi); % finer points for interpolation
>> yi = ppval(pp,xi);        % evaluate curve
>> yyi = ppval(ppi,xi);      % evaluate integral
>> plot(x,y,'o',xi,yi,xi,yyi,'--') % plot results
>> title('Figure 21.3: Spline Integration')
```

Note that this plot qualitatively shows the identity

$$\int_0^x \sin(x)\,dx = 1 - \cos(x)$$

21.5 DIFFERENTIATION

Just as you may be interested in piecewise polynomial integration, you may find that the derivative or slope of a function described by piecewise polynomials is also useful. Given that the kth cubic polynomial is

$$s_k(x) = a_k(x - x_k)^3 + b_k(x - x_k)^2 + c_k(x - x_k) + d_k, \quad x_k \leqslant x \leqslant x_{k+1}$$

Figure 21.3: Spline Integration

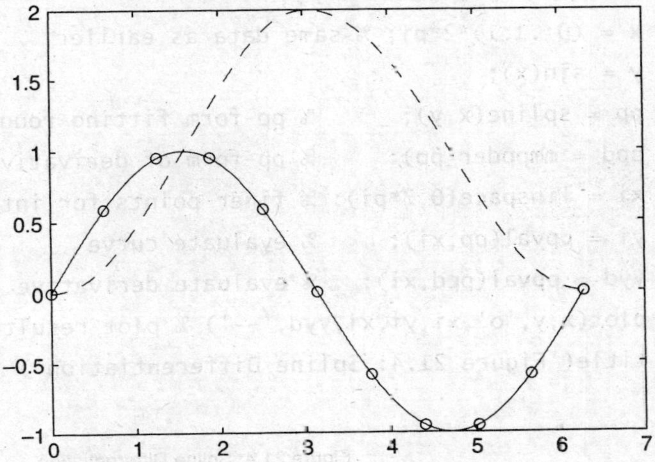

the derivative of $s_k(x)$ is easily written as

$$\frac{ds_k(x)}{dx} = 3a_k(x - x_k)^2 + 2b_k(x - x_k) + c_k$$

where $x_k \le x \le x_{k+1}$. As with integration, the derivative is also a piecewise polynomial. However, in this case it is a quadratic piecewise polynomial, since the order of the polynomial is two.

Based on this expression, the function mmppder performs piecewise polynomial differentiation. The body of this function is as follows:

```
function ppd=mmppder(pp)
%MMPPDER Cubic Spline Derivative Interpolation.
% PPD=MMPPDER(PP) returns the piecewise polynomial vector PPD
% describing the cubic spline derivative of the curve described
% by the piecewise polynomial in PP.
[br,co,npy,nco]=unmkpp(pp);                  % take apart pp
sf=nco-1:-1:1;                          % scale factors for differentiation
dco=sf(ones(npy,1),:).*co(:,1:nco-1); % derivative coefficients
ppd=mkpp(br,dco);                            % build pp form for derivative
```

To demonstrate the use of mmppder, consider the following example:

```
>> x = (0:.1:1)*2*pi; % same data as earlier
>> y = sin(x);
>> pp = spline(x,y);         % pp-form fitting rough data
>> ppd = mmppder(pp);        % pp-form of derivative
>> xi = linspace(0,2*pi); % finer points for interpolation
>> yi = ppval(pp,xi);        % evaluate curve
>> yyd = ppval(ppd,xi);      % evaluate derivative
>> plot(x,y,'o',xi,yi,xi,yyd,'--') % plot results
>> title('Figure 21.4: Spline Differentiation')
```

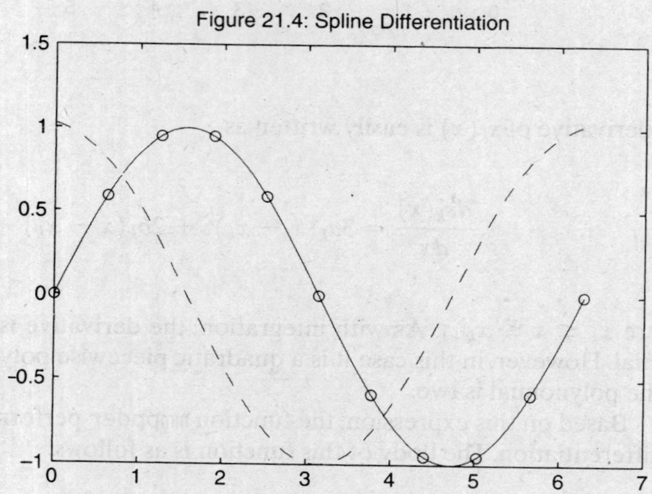

Note that this plot qualitatively shows the identity

$$\frac{d}{dx}\sin(x) = \cos(x)$$

21.6 SPLINE INTERPOLATION ON A PLANE

Spline interpolation, as implemented by the function spline, assumes that the independent variable is monotonic. That is, the spline $y = s(x)$ describes a continuous function. When it is not monotonic, there is no one-to-one relationship between x and y, and the function ppval has no way of knowing what y value to return for a given x. A common situation where this occurs is a curve defined on a plane—for example,

```
>> t = linspace(0,3*pi,15);
>> x = sqrt(t).*cos(t);
>> y = sqrt(t).*sin(t);

>> plot(x,y)
>> xlabel('X')
>> ylabel('Y')
>> title('Figure 21.5: Spiral Y=f(X)')
```

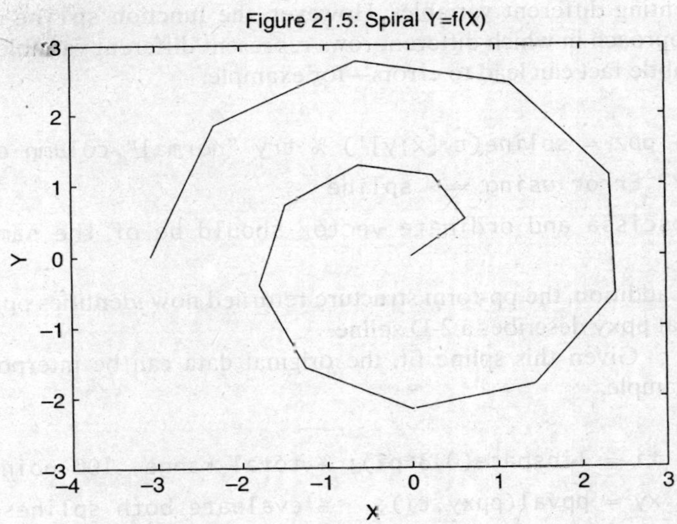

It is not possible to compute a cubic spline for the spiral as a function of x, since there are multiple y values for each x near the origin. However, it is possible to compute a spline for each axis with respect to the variable or parameter t. This can be accomplished in two ways in MATLAB. First, you could make two calls to spline to fit a spline to $x(t)$ and then make another call to fit a spline to $y(t)$. Alternatively, the spline function can fit both splines simultaneously and return a single pp-form structure containing both fits. The following example demonstrates the latter approach:

```
>> ppxy = spline(t,[x;y])
ppxy =
      form: 'pp'
    breaks: [1x15 double]
     coefs: [28x4 double]
    pieces: 14
     order: 4
       dim: 2
```

Here, the second argument to `spline` is an array containing two ***rows***, each of which is fit with a spline by using the independent variable `t`, which is monotonic. Elsewhere in MATLAB, data arrays are column-oriented, with different columns representing different variables. However, the function `spline` adopts a row-oriented approach in which different rows represent different variables. Not recognizing this subtle fact can lead to errors—for example,

```
>> ppz = spline(t,[x;y]') % try "normal" column oriented data
??? Error using ==> spline
Abscissa and ordinate vector should be of the same length.
```

In addition, the pp-form structure returned now identifies `ppxy.dim = 2`, meaning that `ppxy` describes a 2-D spline.

Given this spline fit, the original data can be interpolated as desired—for example,

```
>> ti = linspace(0,3*pi); % total range, 100 points
>> xy = ppval(ppxy,ti);   % evaluate both splines
>> size(xy)               % results are row-oriented too!
ans =
     2   100
>> plot(x,y,'d',xy(1,:),xy(2,:))
>> xlabel('X')
>> ylabel('Y')
>> title('Figure 21.6: Interpolated Spiral Y=f(X)')
```

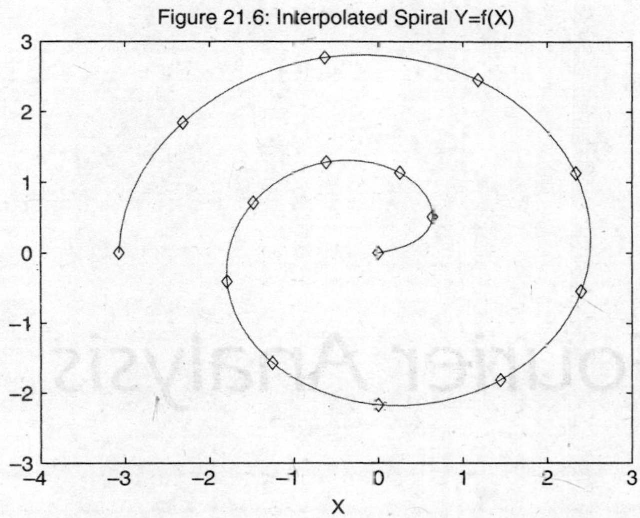

In the example, the results of ppval are also row-oriented, the first row being associated with the first spline, and so on. Therefore, to plot y versus x, the second row xy(2,:) is plotted versus the first row xy(1,:).

Finally, the preceding approach is not limited to two dimensions. The pp-form structure and MATLAB piecewise polynomial functions all handle n-dimensional splines.

22

Fourier Analysis

Frequency-domain tools, such as Fourier series, Fourier transforms, and their discrete time counterparts, form a cornerstone in signal processing. These transforms decompose a signal into a sequence or continuum of sinusoidal components that identify the frequency-domain content of the signal. MATLAB provides the functions `fft`, `ifft`, `fft2`, `ifft2`, `fftn`, `ifftn`, `fftshift`, and `ifftshift` for Fourier analysis. This collection of functions performs the discrete Fourier transform and its inverse in one or more dimensions. (More extensive signal-processing tools are available in the optional *Signal Processing Toolbox*.)

Because signal processing encompasses such a diverse area, it is beyond the scope of this text to illustrate even a small sample of the type of problems that can be solved using the discrete Fourier transform functions in MATLAB. Therefore, only one example of using the function `fft` to approximate the Fourier transform of a continuous time signal is illustrated. In addition, the use of the function `fft` to approximate the Fourier series of a periodic continuous time signal is demonstrated.

22.1 DISCRETE FOURIER TRANSFORM

In MATLAB, the function `fft` computes the discrete Fourier transform of a signal. In cases where the length of the data is a power of 2, or a product of prime factors, fast Fourier transform (FFT) algorithms are employed to compute the discrete Fourier transform.

> Because of the substantial increase in computational speed that occurs when data length is a power of 2, whenever possible it is important to choose data lengths equal to a power of 2, or to pad data with zeros to give it a length equal to a power of 2.

The fast Fourier transform implemented in MATLAB follows that commonly used in engineering texts:

$$F(k) = FFT\{f(n)\} = \sum_{n=0}^{N-1} f(n)e^{-j2\pi nk/N} \quad k = 0, 1, \ldots, N-1$$

Since MATLAB does not support zero indices, the values are shifted by one index value to

$$F(k) = FFT\{f(n)\} = \sum_{n=1}^{N} f(n)e^{-j2\pi(n-1)(k-1)/N} \quad k = 1, 2, \ldots, N$$

The inverse transform follows accordingly as

$$f(n) = FFT^{-1}\{F(k)\} = \frac{1}{N}\sum_{k=1}^{N} F(k)e^{j2\pi(n-1)(k-1)/N} \quad n = 1, 2, \ldots, N$$

Specific details on the use of the `fft` function are described in its help text:

```
>> help fft
 FFT Discrete Fourier transform.
    FFT(X) is the discrete Fourier transform (DFT) of vector X.  For
    matrices, the FFT operation is applied to each column. For N-D
    arrays, the FFT operation operates on the first non-singleton
    dimension.

    FFT(X,N) is the N-point FFT, padded with zeros if X has less
    than N points and truncated if it has more.
    FFT(X,[],DIM) or FFT(X,N,DIM) applies the FFT operation across the
    dimension DIM.
    For length N input vector x, the DFT is a length N vector X,
    with elements
                     N
       X(k) =       sum  x(n)*exp(-j*2*pi*(k-1)*(n-1)/N), 1 <= k <= N.
                    n=1

    The inverse DFT (computed by IFFT) is given by
                     N
       x(n) = (1/N) sum  X(k)*exp( j*2*pi*(k-1)*(n-1)/N), 1 <= n <= N.
                    k=1

    See also IFFT, FFT2, IFFT2, FFTSHIFT.
```

To illustrate the use of the FFT, consider the problem of estimating the continuous Fourier transform of the signal

$$f(t) = 2e^{-3t} \quad t \geq 0$$

Analytically, the Fourier transform of $f(t)$ is given by

$$F(\omega) = \frac{2}{3 + j\omega}$$

Although using the FFT has little real value in this case (since the analytical solution is known), this example illustrates an approach to estimating the Fourier transform of less common signals, especially those whose Fourier transform is not readily found analytically. The following MATLAB statements estimate $|F(\omega)|$ by using the FFT and graphically compare it to the preceding analytical expression:

```
N = 128;                 % choose a power of 2 for speed
t = linspace(0,3,N);     % time points for function evaluation
f = 2*exp(-3*t);         % evaluate function, minimize aliasing: f(3) ~ 0
Ts = t(2) - t(1);        % the sampling period
Ws = 2*pi/Ts;            % the sampling frequency in rad/sec
F = fft(f);              % compute the fft
Fc = fftshift(F)*Ts;     % shift and scale

W = Ws*(-N/2:(N/2)-1)/N;% frequency axis
Fa = 2./(3+j*W);         % analytical Fourier transform
plot(W,abs(Fa),W,abs(Fc),'.') % generate plot, 'o' marks fft
xlabel('Frequency, Rad/s')
ylabel('|F(\omega)|')
title('Figure 22.1: Fourier Transform Approximation')
```

The function `fftshift` flips the halves of `F` so that the $(N/2) + 1$ element of `Fc` is the DC component of the result. Elements less than this are negative frequency components, while those greater are positive frequency components. Using this fact, `W` creates the appropriate analog frequency axis with `W(N/2 + 1) = 0`. Graphically, the FFT approximation is good at low frequencies, but demonstrates some aliasing at higher frequencies near the Nyquist frequency.

The FFT-related functions in MATLAB include those listed in the following table:

Function	Description
conv	Convolution
conv2	2-D convolution
convn	*n*-D convolution
deconv	Deconvolution
filter	Discrete time filter
filter2	2-D discrete time filter
fft	Discrete Fourier transform
fft2	2-D discrete Fourier transform
fftn	*n*-D discrete Fourier transform
ifft	Inverse discrete Fourier transform
ifft2	2-D inverse discrete Fourier transform
ifftn	*n*-D inverse discrete Fourier transform
fftshift	Shift FFT results so that negative frequencies appear first
ifftshift	Undo actions performed by fftshift
abs	Magnitude of complex array
angle	Radian angle of complex array
unwrap	Remove phase angle jumps
cplxpair	Sort vector into complex conjugate pairs
nextpow2	Next higher power of 2

Figure 22.1: Fourier Transform Approximation

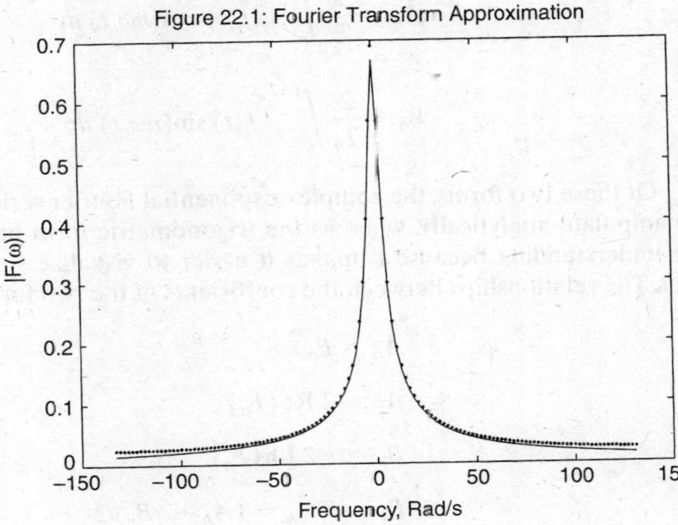

22.2 FOURIER SERIES

MATLAB itself offers no functions specifically tailored to Fourier series analysis and manipulation. However, these functions can be easily added when you understand the relationship between the discrete Fourier transform of samples of a periodic signal and its Fourier series.

The Fourier series representation of a real-valued periodic signal *f(t)* can be written in complex exponential form as

$$f(t) = \sum_{n=-\infty}^{\infty} F_n e^{jn\omega_o t}$$

where the Fourier series coefficients are given by

$$F_n = \frac{1}{T_o}\int_t^{t+T_o} f(t)e^{-jn\omega_o t}\, dt$$

and the fundamental frequency is $\omega_o = 2\pi/T_o$, where T_o is the period. The complex exponential form of the Fourier series can be rewritten in trigonometric form as

$$f(t) = A_o + \sum_{n=1}^{\infty}\{A_n \cos(n\omega_o t) + B_n \sin(n\omega_o t)\}$$

where the coefficients are given by

$$A_o = \frac{1}{T_o}\int_t^{t+T_o} f(t)\, dt$$

$$A_n = \frac{2}{T_o}\int_t^{t+T_o} f(t)\cos(n\omega_o t)\, dt$$

$$B_n = \frac{2}{T_o}\int_t^{t+T_o} f(t)\sin(n\omega_o t)\, dt$$

Of these two forms, the complex exponential Fourier series is generally easier to manipulate analytically, whereas the trigonometric form provides a more intuitive understanding because it makes it easier to visualize sine and cosine waveforms. The relationships between the coefficients of the two forms are

$$A_o = F_o$$

$$A_n = 2\,\mathrm{Re}\{F_n\}$$

$$B_n = -2\,\mathrm{Im}\{F_n\}$$

$$F_n = F^*_{-n} = (A_n - \mathrm{j}B_n)/2$$

Using these relationships, you can use the complex exponential form analytically and then convert results to the trigonometric form for display.

The discrete Fourier transform can be used to compute the Fourier series coefficients, provided that the time samples are appropriately chosen and the transform output is scaled. For example, consider computing the Fourier series coefficients of the sawtooth waveform shown next.

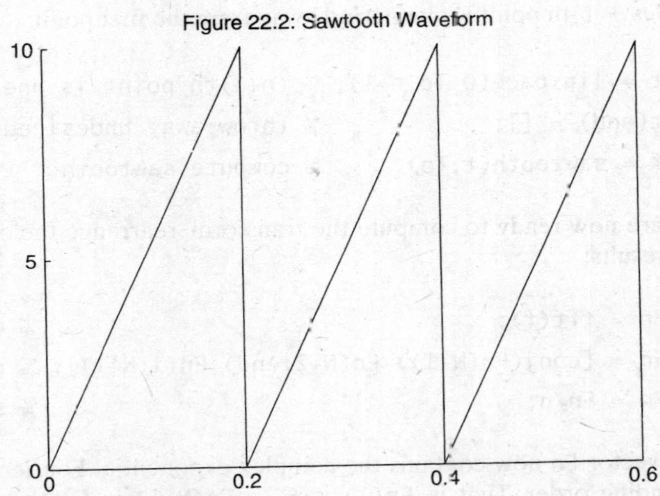

First, you must create a function to evaluate the sawtooth at arbitrary points:

```
function f=sawtooth(t,To)
%SAWTOOTH Sawtooth Waveform Generation.
% SAWTOOTH(t,To) computes values of a sawtooth having
% a period To at the points defined in the vector t.
f = 10*rem(t,To)/To;
f(f==0 | f==10) = 5; % must average value at discontinuity!
```

To minimize aliasing, it is necessary to compute enough harmonics so that the highest harmonic amplitude is negligible. In this case, choose

```
>> N = 25;    % number of harmonics
>> To = 0.2; % choose period
```

The number of terms to consider in the discrete Fourier transform is twice the number of harmonics, since the discrete Fourier transform computes both positive and negative harmonics:

```
>> n = 2*N;
```

The function must be evaluated at n points over one period in such a manner that the $(n + 1)$th point is one period away from the first point:

```
>> t = linspace(0,To,n+1); % (n+1)th point is one period away
>> t(end) = [];            % throw away undesired last point
>> f = sawtooth(t,To);     % compute sawtooth
```

We are now ready to compute the transform, rearrange the components, and scale the results:

```
>> Fn = fft(f);                                   % compute FFT
>> Fn = [conj(Fn(N+1)) Fn(N+2:end) Fn(1:N+1)]; % rearrange values
>> Fn = Fn/n;                                     % scale results
```

The vector Fn now contains the complex exponential Fourier series coefficients in ascending order. That is, Fn(1) is F_{-25}; Fn(N+1) is F_o, the DC component; and Fn(2*N+1) is F_{25}, the 25th harmonic component.

From these data, the trigonometric Fourier series coefficients are as follows:

```
>> A0 = Fn(N+1) % DC component
A0 =
     5
>> An = 2*real(Fn(N+2:end)) % Cosine terms
An =
   1.0e-015 *
  Columns 1 through 7
   -0.1176   -0.0439   -0.2555    0.3814    0.0507   -0.2006    0.1592
  Columns 8 through 14
   -0.1817    0.0034         0    0.0034   -0.1141   -0.1430   -0.0894
  Columns 15 through 21
   -0.0685   -0.0216    0.0537   -0.0496   -0.0165         0   -0.0165
  Columns 22 through 25
   -0.0079    0.2405    0.3274    0.2132
```

```
>> Bn = -2*imag(Fn(N+2:end)) % Sine terms
Bn =

  Columns 1 through 7
   -3.1789   -1.5832   -1.0484   -0.7789   -0.6155   -0.5051   -0.4250
  Columns 8 through 14
   -0.3638   -0.3151   -0.2753   -0.2418   -0.2130   -0.1878   -0.1655
  Columns 15 through 21
   -0.1453   -0.1269   -0.1100   -0.0941   -0.0792   -0.0650   -0.0514
  Columns 22 through 25
   -0.0382   -0.0253   -0.0126         0
```

Since the sawtooth waveform has odd symmetry (except for its DC component), it makes sense that the cosine coefficients An are negligible. (Note that they are scaled by 10^{-15}.) Comparing the actual Fourier series coefficients for this sawtooth waveform with the preceding Bn terms gives a relative error of

```
>> idx = -N:N;              % harmonic indices
>> Fna = 5j./(idx*pi); % complex exponential terms
>> Fna(N+1) = 5;
>> Bna = -2*imag(Fna(N+2:end)); % sine terms

>> Bn_error = (Bn-Bna)./Bna      % relative error
Bn_error =

  Columns 1 through 7
   -0.0013   -0.0053   -0.0119   -0.0211   -0.0331   -0.0478   -0.0653
  Columns 8 through 14
   -0.0857   -0.1089   -0.1352   -0.1645   -0.1971   -0.2330   -0.2723
  Columns 15 through 21
   -0.3152   -0.3620   -0.4128   -0.4678   -0.5273   -0.5917   -0.6612
  Columns 22 through 25
   -0.7363   -0.8174   -0.9051   -1.0000
```

As with the earlier Fourier transform example, aliasing causes errors that increase with increasing frequency. Since all practical signals are not band-limited, aliasing is inevitable, and a decision must be made about the degree of aliasing that can be tolerated in a given application. As the number of requested harmonics increases, the degree of aliasing decreases. Therefore, to minimize aliasing, you can

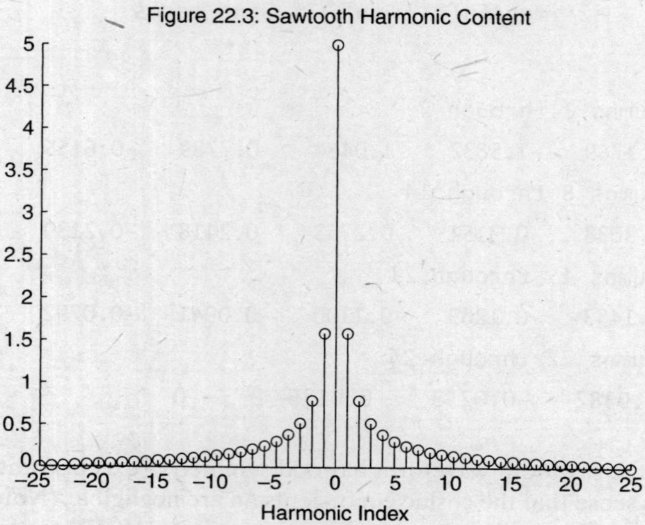

request a larger number of harmonics and then choose a subset of them to view and further manipulate.

Finally, the line spectra of the complex exponential Fourier series can be plotted using the stem function:

```
>> stem(idx,abs(Fn))
>> xlabel('Harmonic Index')
>> title('Figure 22.3: Sawtooth Harmonic Content')
>> axis tight
```

23

Optimization

Optimization in the context of this chapter refers to the process of determining where a function $y = g(x)$ takes on either specific or extreme values. When a function is defined simply, the corresponding inverse function $x = g^{-1}(y)$ can often be found, in which case you can determine what x values produce a given y by evaluating the inverse function. On the other hand, many functions, including many simple ones, have no inverse. When this is the case, you must estimate the x that produces a known y by some iterative procedure. In practice, this iterative procedure is called ***zero finding***, because finding x such that $y = g(x)$ for some y is equivalent to finding x such that $f(x) = 0$, where $f(x) = y - g(x)$.

In addition to knowing where a function takes on specific values, it is also common to know its extreme values—that is, where it achieves maximum or minimum values. As before, there are numerous times when these extreme values must be estimated by some iterative procedure. Since a function maximum is the minimum of its negative (i.e., $\max f(x) = \min\{-f(x)\}$), iterative procedures for finding extreme values typically find only minimum values, and the procedures are called ***minimization*** algorithms.

In this chapter, the optimization functions available in basic MATLAB are covered. (Many more functions are available in the optional *Optimization Toolbox*.)

23.1 ZERO FINDING

Finding a zero of a function can be interpreted in a number of ways, depending on the function. When the function is 1-D, the MATLAB function `fzero` can be used to find a zero. The algorithm used by this function is a combination of bisection and inverse quadratic interpolation. When the function is multidimensional—that is, the function definition consists of multiple scalar functions of a vector variable—you

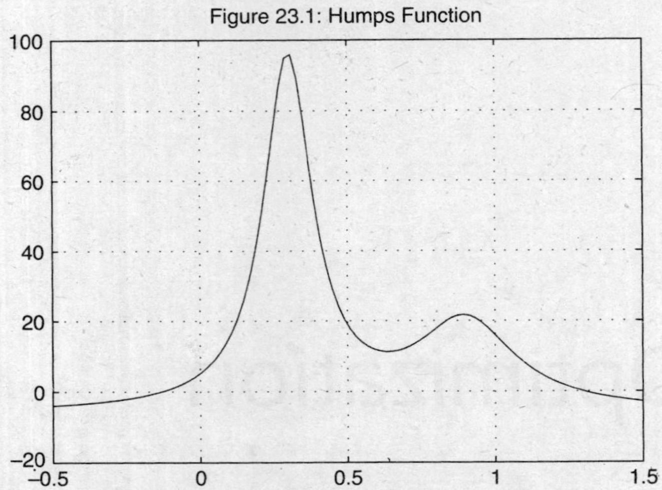

must look beyond basic MATLAB for a solution. The *Optimization Toolbox* or other third-party toolbox is required to solve the multidimensional case.

To illustrate the use of the function fzero, consider the function humps:

```
>> x = linspace(-.5,1.5);
>> y = humps(x);
>> plot(x,y)
>> grid on
>> title('Figure 23.1: Humps Function')
```

The humps M-file evaluates the function

$$humps(x) = \frac{1}{(x - 0.3)^2 + 0.01} + \frac{1}{(x - 0.9)^2 + 0.04} - 6$$

which crosses zero near $x = -0.2$ and $x = 1.3$. The function fzero provides a way to find a better approximation to these zero crossings:

```
>> format long  % display more precision

>> H_humps = @humps;  % create function handle to humps.m function.

>> x = fzero(H_humps,1.3)
x =

   1.29954968258482

>> humps(x) % how close is it to 0?
```

```
ans =

     0

>> H_humps(x) % evaluate humps through its handle as well

ans =

     0

>> [x,value] = fzero(H_humps,-0.2)
x =
   -0.13161801809961
value =
    8.881784197001252e-016
```

Here, the two zeros of the function were found. The first zero is very close to 1.3, and evaluation of function at the zero produced zero. The second zero was found to be close to −0.13. In this call to `fzero`, a second output argument was supplied, which returned the function evaluated at the zero. Therefore, it wasn't necessary to call `humps(x)` to check the accuracy of the solution found by `fzero`. It is important to note that `fzero` returns just one zero—the zero found closest to the initial guess. So, if a function has more than one zero, it is up to the user to call `fzero` multiple times with different initial guesses.

When initially called, the function `fzero` searches on either side of the initial guess for a sign change in the function. When a sign change is found, the two endpoints that produced the sign change form a ***bracket*** on the number line. If a function is continuous, it must cross through zero somewhere in the bracket. Knowing this, the function `fzero` then searches for the zero crossing and returns the value of x that comes closest to making this happen.

In many cases, supplying an initial guess or estimate of the zero is unnecessary, because a bracket is already known from the properties of the problem to be solved. When this occurs, you can simply supply `fzero` with the bracket rather than with an initial guess of the zero location:

```
>> [x,value] = fzero(H_humps,[-2 0])
Zero found in the interval: [-2, 0].
x =
   -0.13161801809961
value =

     0

>> [x,value] = fzero(H_humps,[0 1.2])
??? Error using ==> fzero
The function values at the interval endpoints must differ in sign.
```

In the first example, `[-2 0]` is a bracket around the zero near −0.13. As a result, `fzero` finds the zero. In the second example, `[0 1.2]` is not a bracket around a zero, forcing `fzero` to report an error and abort its search. So, if a two-element array is supplied to `fzero`, it must bracket a zero, or else the function terminates without doing a zero search.

In the preceding examples, the function to be searched was provided to `fzero` as a function handle, which uniquely identifies the function M-file. As discussed in Chapter 12, the function to be searched can also be supplied as an ***anonymous function***, an ***in-line function*** object, or a ***string expression***. While all three of these work, the use of function handles is encouraged. In-line function objects and string expression definitions are obsolete, but remain operable in MATLAB for the time being. (To learn more about these alternatives, see the MATLAB documentation.)

All functions in this chapter have various settable parameters. These functions, as well as those in the *Optimization Toolbox*, share the same format for managing parameters. The functions `optimset` and `optimget` are used, respectively, to set and get parameters for all functions. For `fzero`, there are two settable parameters, `'Display'` and `'TolX'`. The first parameter controls the amount of detail returned while the function is working; the second sets a tolerance range for accepting the final answer. The following code is illustrative:

```
>> options = optimset('Display','iter'); % show iteration history
>> [x,value] = fzero(H_humps,[-2 0],options)
 Func-count    x          f(x)             Procedure
    1            -2       -5.69298          initial
    2             0        5.17647          initial
    3      -0.952481      -5.07853          interpolation
    4      -0.480789      -3.87242          interpolation
    5      -0.240394      -1.94304          bisection
    6      -0.120197       0.28528          bisection
    7      -0.135585     -0.09443           interpolation
    8      -0.131759   -0.0033840           interpolation
    9      -0.131618  1.63632e-006          interpolation
   10      -0.131618 -7.14819e-010          interpolation
   11      -0.131618             0          interpolation
Zero found in the interval: [-2, 0].
x =

  -0.13161801809961

value =

   0
```

```
>> options = optimset('Display','final'); % display successful interval

>> [x,value] = fzero(H_humps,[-2 0],options)
Zero found in the interval: [-2, 0].
x =

  -0.13161801809961
value =

   0

>> options = optimset('TolX',0.1);

>> [x,value] = fzero(H_humps,[-2 0],options)
x =

  -0.24039447250762
value =
  -1.94303825972565

>> options = optimset('Display','iter','TolX',0.1); % set both
>> [x,value] = fzero(H_humps,[-2 0],options)
 Func-count    x          f(x)        Procedure
    1           -2      -5.69298       initial
    2            0       5.17647       initial
    3    -0.952481      -5.07853       interpolation
    4    -0.480789      -3.87242       interpolation
    5    -0.240394      -1.94304       bisection
Zero found in the interval: [-2, 0].
x =

  -0.24039447250762

value =
  -1.94303825972565
```

In the preceding code, an options structure was created with the desired parameters and then passed as a third argument to `fzero`. The `'Display'` option has four settings: `'final'`, `'iter'`, `'notify'`, and `'off'`. The setting `'notify'` is the default, and it means "Display information only if no solution is found." The `'TolX'` option sets the tolerance for the final answer, which is equal to eps by default. (See the online help for `optimset` and `optimget` for more information regarding parameters for MATLAB optimization functions.)

23.2 MINIMIZATION IN ONE DIMENSION

In addition to the visual information provided by plotting, it is often necessary to determine other, more specific attributes of a function. Of particular interest in many applications are function extremes—that is, a function's maxima (peaks) and minima (valleys). Mathematically, these extremes are found analytically by determining where the derivative (slope) of a function is zero. This idea can be readily understood by inspecting the slope of the humps plot at its peaks and valleys. Clearly, when a function is simply defined, this process often works. However, even for many simple functions that can be differentiated readily, it is often impossible to find where the derivative is zero. In these cases and in cases where it is difficult or impossible to find the derivative analytically, it is necessary to search for function extremes numerically. MATLAB provides two functions that perform this task, `fminbnd` and `fminsearch`. These two functions find minima of 1-D and *n*-D functions, respectively. The function `fminbnd` employs a combination of golden-section search and parabolic interpolation. Since a maximum of *f(x)* is equal to a minimum of $-f(x)$, `fminbnd` and `fminsearch` can be used to find both minima and maxima. If this notion is not clear, visualize the preceding humps(x) plot flipped upside down. In the upside-down state, peaks become valleys and valleys become peaks.

To illustrate 1-D minimization and maximization, consider the preceding humps(x) example once again. From the figure, there is a maximum near $x = 0.3$ and a minimum near $x = 0.6$. With `fminbnd`, these extremes can be found with more accuracy:

```
>> H_humps=@humps;  % create handle to humps.m function.

>> [xmin,value] = fminbnd(H_humps,0.5,0.8)
xmin =
   0.63700821196362
value =
  11.25275412587769
>> options=optimset('Display','iter');
>> [xmin,value] = fminbnd(H_humps,0.5,0.8,options)
 Func-count       x            f(x)          Procedure
     1        0.61459        11.4103          initial
     2        0.68541        11.9288          golden
     3        0.57082        12.7389          golden
     4       0.638866        11.2538          parabolic
     5       0.637626        11.2529          parabolic
     6       0.637046        11.2528          parabolic
     7       0.637008        11.2528          parabolic
     8       0.636975        11.2528          parabolic
```

```
Optimization terminated successfully:
the current x satisfies the termination criteria using
OPTIONS.TolX of 1.000000e-004
xmin =
   0.63700821196362
value =
   11.25275412587769
```

In this example, in the two calls to `fminbnd`, 0.5 and 0.8 denote the range over which to search for minimum. In the second case, options were set to display the iterations performed by `fminbnd`.

To find the maximum near $x = 0.3$, we can either modify the `humps.m` file to negate the expression, or we can create an anonymous function. The following example demonstrates the latter approach:

```
>> AH_humps = @(x) -1./((x-.3).^2 +.01) - 1./((x-.9).^2 +.04) + 6;
>> [xmax,value] = fminbnd(AH_humps,0.2,0.4,options)
 Func-count     x          f(x)         Procedure
     1       0.276393    -91.053        initial
     2       0.323607    -91.4079       golden
     3       0.352786    -75.1541       golden
     4       0.300509    -96.5012       parabolic
     5       0.300397    -96.5014       parabolic
     6       0.300364    -96.5014       parabolic
     7       0.300331    -96.5014       parabolic
Optimization terminated successfully:
the current x satisfies the termination criteria using
OPTIONS.TolX of 1.000000e-004
xmax =
   0.30036413790024
value =
  -96.50140724387050
```

On termination, the maximum is found to be very close to 0.3, and the peak has an amplitude of +96.5. The value returned by `fminbnd` is the negative of the actual value, because `fminbnd` computes the minimum of $-\text{humps}(x)$.

23.3 MINIMIZATION IN HIGHER DIMENSIONS

As described previously, the function `fminsearch` provides a simple algorithm for minimizing a function of several variables. That is, `fminsearch` attempts to find the minimum of $f(\boldsymbol{x})$, where $f(\boldsymbol{x})$ is a scalar function of a vector argument $\boldsymbol{x}$. The function `fminsearch` implements the Nelder-Mead simplex search algorithm, which modifies the components of $\boldsymbol{x}$ to find the minimum of $f(\boldsymbol{x})$. This algorithm is not as efficient on smooth functions as some other algorithms are, but, on the other hand, it does not require gradient information that is often expensive to compute. It also tends to be more robust on functions that are not smooth, where gradient information is less valuable. If the function to be minimized is inexpensive to compute, the Nelder-Mead algorithm usually works very well.

To illustrate usage of `fminsearch`, consider the banana function, also called Rosenbrock's function:

$$f(x) = 100(x_2 - {x_1}^2)^2 + (1 - x_1)^2$$

This function can be visualized by creating a 3-D mesh plot with x_1 as the x-dimension, and x_2 as the y-dimension:

```
x = [-1.5:0.125:1.5];   % range for x1 variable
y = [-.6:0.125:2.8];    % range for x2 variable
[X,Y] = meshgrid(x,y); % grid of all x and y
Z = 100.*(Y-X.*X).^2 + (1-X).^2; % evaluate banana
mesh(X,Y,Z)
hidden off
xlabel('x(1)')
ylabel('x(2)')
title('Figure 23.2: Banana Function')
hold on
plot3(1,1,1,'k.','markersize',30)
hold off
```

As shown in the plot, the banana function has a unique minimum of zero at $\boldsymbol{x}$ = [1; 1]. To find the minimum of this function, it must be rewritten in terms of x_1 = `x(1)` and x_2 = `x(2)`, as shown before mathematically. It can be entered as the M-file

Figure 23.2: Banana Function

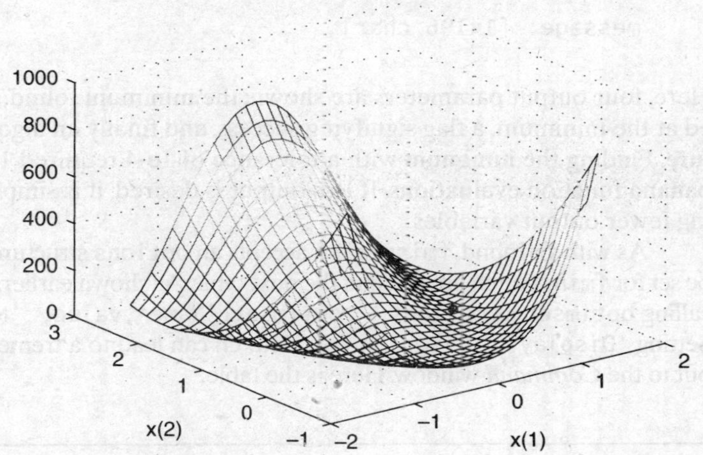


```
function f=banana(x)
% Rosenbrock's banana function
    f=100*(x(2)-x(1)^2)^2 + (1-x(1))^2;
```

or as the anonymous function

```
>> AH_banana = @(x) 100*(x(2)-x(1)^2)^2 + (1-x(1))^2;
```

Using either of these representations, `fminsearch` produces

```
>> [xmin,value,flag,output] = fminsearch(AH_banana,[-1.9,2])
xmin =
    1.00001666889480    1.00003447386277
value =
    4.068551535063419e-010
flag =
    1
output =
    iterations: 114
     funcCount: 210
```

```
    algorithm: 'Nelder-Mead simplex direct search'
    message: [1x196 char]
```

Here, four output parameters are shown: the minimum found, the function evaluated at the minimum, a flag signifying success, and finally an algorithm statistics structure. Finding the minimum with a tolerance of 1e-4 required 114 iterations and 210 banana function evaluations. If less output is desired, it is simply a matter of providing fewer output variables.

As with `fminbnd`, `fminsearch` accepts an `options` structure. The options that can be set for `fminsearch` are listed in the next table. As shown earlier, preferences are set by calling `optimset` as `options = optimset('Name',value, 'Name',value, ...)`. Setting `'Display'` to `'iter'` in `fminsearch` can lead to a tremendous amount of output to the *Command* window. Here is the table:

Option Name	**Description**	**Default Value**
`'Display'`	Displays frequency, `'iter'`, `'final'`, `'notify'`, or `'off'`	`'notify'` (displays information only if no solution is found)
`'MaxFunEvals'`	Maximum function evaluations	`200*length(x)`
`'MaxIter'`	Maximum algorithm iterations	`200*length(x)`
`'TolFun'`	Function solution tolerance	`1.00E-004`
`'TolX'`	Variable solution tolerance	`1.00E-004`

To demonstrate how to use the options shown in the table, consider finding the solution to the previous problem with tighter function and variable tolerances:

```
>> options = optimset('TolFun',1e-8,'TolX',1e-8);
>> [xmin,value,flag,output] = fminsearch(AH_banana,[-1.9,2],options)
xmin =
   1.00000000126077    1.00000000230790
value =
    6.153858843361103e-018
flag =
    1
output =
    iterations: 144
     funcCount: 266
     algorithm: 'Nelder-Mead simplex direct search'
       message: [1x196 char]
```

With the tighter tolerances, `xmin` is now within 1e-8 of the actual minimum, the function evaluates to well within `eps` of the minimum of zero, and the number of algorithm iterations and function evaluations increases by approximately 26 percent. From this information, it is clear that `fminsearch` requires a lot of function evaluations and therefore can be slow for functions that are computationally expensive.

23.4 PRACTICAL ISSUES

Iterative solutions, such as those found by `fzero`, `fminbnd`, and `fminsearch`, all make some assumptions about the function to be iterated. Since there are essentially no limits to the function provided, it makes sense that these ***function functions*** may not converge or may take many iterations to converge. At worst, these functions can produce a MATLAB error that terminates the iteration without producing a result. And even if they do terminate promptly, there is no guarantee that they have stopped at the desired result. To make the most efficient use of these function functions, consider applying the following points:

1. Start with a good initial guess. This is the most important consideration. A good guess keeps the problem in the neighborhood of the solution, where its numerical properties are hopefully stable.
2. If components of the solution (e.g., in `fminsearch`) are separated by several orders of magnitude or more, consider scaling them to improve iteration efficiency and accuracy. For example, if `x(1)` is known to be near `1`, and `x(2)` is known to be near `1e6`, scale `x(2)` by `1e-5` in the function definition, and then scale the returned result by `1e6`. When you do so, the search algorithm uses numbers that are all around the same order of magnitude.
3. If the problem is complicated, look for ways to simplify it into a sequence of simpler problems that have fewer variables.
4. Make sure your function cannot return complex numbers, `Inf`, or `NaN`, which usually results in convergence failure. The functions `isreal`, `isfinite`, and `isnan` can be used to test results before returning them.
5. Avoid functions that are discontinuous. Functions such as `abs`, `min`, and `max` all produce discontinuities that can lead to divergence.
6. Constraints on the allowable range of x can be included by adding a penalty term to the function to be iterated, such that the algorithm is persuaded to avoid out-of-range values.

24

Integration and Differentiation

Integration and differentiation are fundamental tools in calculus. Integration computes the area under a function, and differentiation describes the slope or gradient of a function. MATLAB provides functions for numerically approximating the integral and slope of a function. Functions are provided for making approximations when functions exist as M-files and as anonymous functions, as well as when functions are tabulated at uniformly spaced points over the region of interest.

24.1 INTEGRATION

MATLAB provides four functions for computing integrals of functions: `quad`, `quadl`, `dblquad`, and `triplequad`.

To illustrate integration, consider the function humps(x), as shown in Figure 24.1. As is apparent in the figure, the sum of the trapezoidal areas approximates the integral of the function. Clearly, as the number of trapezoids increases, the fit between the function and the trapezoids gets better, leading to a better integral or area approximation.

Using tabulated values from the `humps` function, the MATLAB function `trapz` approximates the area using the trapezoidal approximation. Duplicating the trapezoids shown in the preceding figure produces

```
>> x = -1:.17:2;
>> y = humps(x);
>> area = trapz(x,y)
```

Figure 24.1: Integration Approximation with Trapezoids

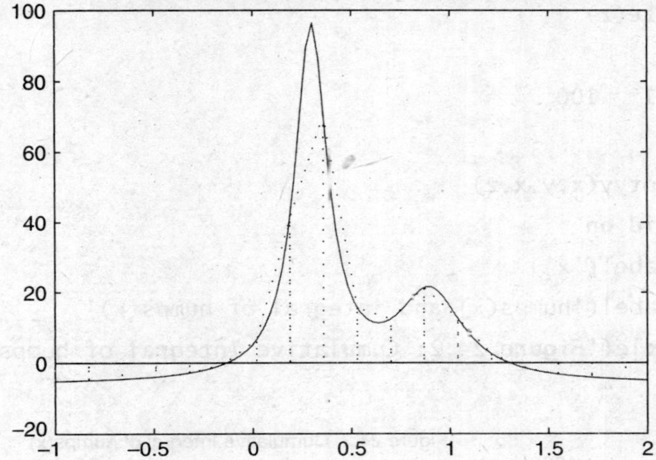


```
area =

     25.917
```

In comparison to the figure, this is probably not a very accurate estimate of the area. However, when a finer discretization is used, more accuracy is achieved:

```
>> x = linspace(-1,2,100);
>> y = humps(x);
>> format long
>> area = trapz(x,y)
area =

     26.34473119524596
```

This area agrees with the analytical integral through five significant digits.

Sometimes, we are interested in the integral as a function of x—that is,

$$\int_{x_1}^{x} f(x)\, dx$$

where x_1 is a known lower limit of integration. The definite integral from x_1 to any point x is then found by evaluating the function at x. Using the trapezoidal rule, tabulated values of the cumulative integral are computed using the function `cumtrapz`, as in the following example:

```
>> x = linspace(-1,2,100);
>> y = humps(x);
```

```
>> z = cumtrapz(x,y);
>> size(z)
ans =
     1   100

>> plotyy(x,y,x,z)
>> grid on
>> xlabel('x')
>> ylabel('humps(x) and integral of humps(x)')
>> title('Figure 24.2: Cumulative Integral of humps(x)')
```

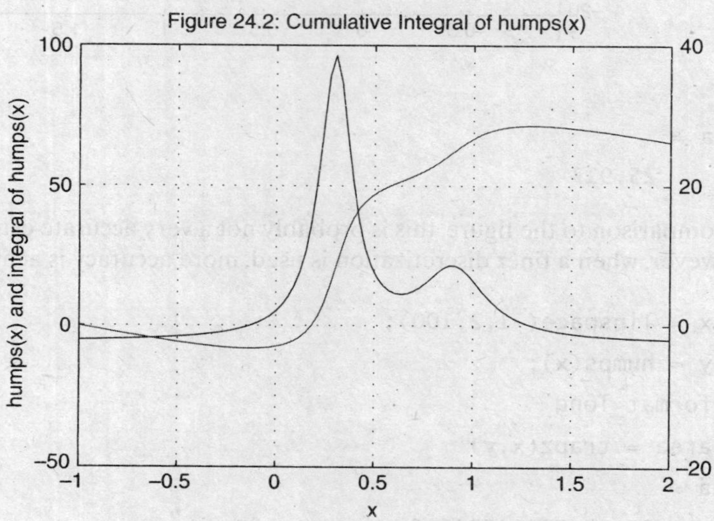

Depending on the properties of the function at hand, it may be difficult to determine an optimum trapezoidal width. Clearly, if you could somehow vary the individual trapezoid widths to match the characteristics of the function, much greater accuracy could be achieved.

The MATLAB functions quad and quadl, which are based on a mathematical concept called quadrature, take this approach. These integration functions operate in the same way. Both evaluate the function to be integrated at whatever intervals are necessary to achieve accurate results. Moreover, both functions make higher order approximations than a simple trapezoid, with quadl being more rigorous than quad. As an example, consider computing the integral of the humps function again:

```
>> z(end)             % cumtrapz result
ans =
  26.34473119524596

>> H_humps = @humps;  % create function handle

>> quad(H_humps,-1,2)
ans =
  26.34496050120123

>> quadl(H_humps,-1,2)
ans =
  26.34496047137897
```

For this example, quad and quadl both return the same result to eight significant digits, with these digits exhibiting eight-digit accuracy with respect to the true solution. On the other hand, cumtrapz achieves only five significant digit accuracy.

The function to be integrated (i.e., the integrand) must support a vector input argument. That is, the integrand must return a vector of outputs for a vector of inputs. Doing so means using dot-arithmetic operators, .*, ./, .\, and .^. For example, the function in humps.m is given by the statement

```
y = 1./((x-.3).^2 + .01) + 1./((x-.9).^2 + .04) - 6;
```

The functions quad and quadl also allow you to specify an absolute error tolerance as a fourth input argument, with the default absolute tolerance being 10^{-6}.

In addition to 1-D integration, MATLAB supports 2-D integration with the function dblquad. That is, dblquad approximates the integral

$$\int_{y_{min}}^{y_{max}} \int_{x_{min}}^{x_{max}} f(x, y)\, dx\, dy$$

To use dblquad, you must first create a function that evaluates $f(x,y)$. For example, consider the function myfun.m:

```
function z=myfun(x,y)
%MYFUN(X,Y) an example function of two variables
z = sin(x).*cos(y) + 1; % must handle vector x input
```

This function can be plotted by issuing the commands

```
>> x = linspace(0,pi,20);    % xmin to xmax
>> y = linspace(-pi,pi,20); % ymin to ymax

>> [xx,yy] = meshgrid(x,y); % create grid of point to evaluate at

>> zz = myfun(xx,yy);         % evaluate at all points

>> mesh(xx,yy,zz)
>> xlabel('x'), ylabel('y')
>> title('Figure 24.3: myfun.m plot')
```

Figure 24.3: myfun.m plot

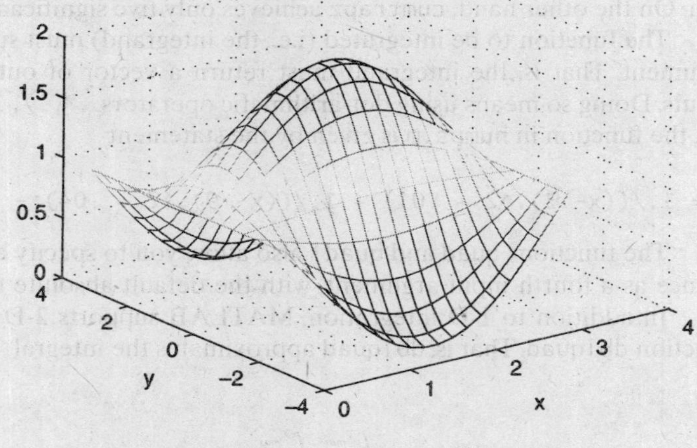

The volume under this function is computed by calling dblquad as

```
>> area = dblquad(@myfun,0,pi,-pi,pi)
area =
   19.73920880609102
>> relerr = (area-2*pi^2)/(2*pi^2)
relerr =
   1.981996941074027e-010
```

Here, dblquad is called as dblquad(Fname,xmin,xmax,ymin,ymax). Based on the relative error computed above, we can say that the results produced by dblquad are highly accurate, even though the function quad is called by dblquad to do the actual integration.

The function triplequad extends the above quadrature integration schemes to triple integration, or volume integration. In this case, triplequad(Fname, xmin,xmax,ymin,ymax,zmin,zmax) integrates the function *Fname*(*x,y,z*) over the limits specified by the remainder of the triplequad arguments. (For further information regarding these integration function, see the MATLAB documentation.)

24.2 DIFFERENTIATION

As opposed to integration, numerical differentiation is much more difficult. Integration describes an overall or macroscopic property of a function, whereas differentiation describes the slope of a function at a point, which is a microscopic property of a function. As a result, integration is not sensitive to minor changes in the shape of a function, whereas differentiation is. Any small change in a function can easily create large changes in its slope in the neighborhood of the change.

Because of this inherent sensitivity in differentiation, numerical differentiation is avoided whenever possible, especially if the data to be differentiated is obtained experimentally. In this case, it is best to perform a least-squares curve fit to the data and then differentiate the resulting polynomial. Alternatively, you could fit cubic splines to the data and then find the spline representation of the derivative, as discussed in Chapter 21. For example, consider again the example from Chapter 20:

```
>> x = [0 .1 .2 .3 .4 .5 .6 .7 .8 .9 1];
>> y = [-.447 1.978 3.28 6.16 7.08 7.34 7.66 9.56 9.48 9.30 11.2];
>> n = 2; % order of fit
>> p = polyfit(x,y,n)  % find polynomial coefficients
p =
  -9.8108    20.1293    -0.0317

>> xi = linspace(0,1,100);
>> yi = polyval(p,xi); % evaluate polynomial

>> plot(x,y,'-o',xi,yi,'-')
>> xlabel('x'), ylabel('y=f(x)')
>> title('Figure 24.4: Second Order Curve Fitting')
```

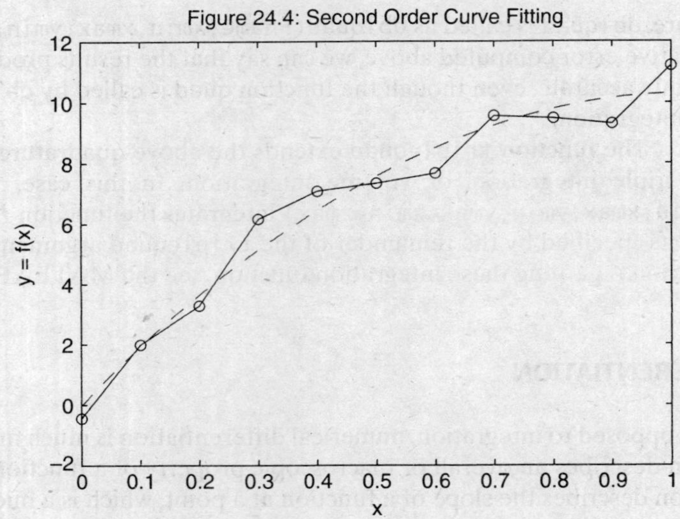

The derivative in this case is found by using the polynomial derivative function `polyder`:

```
>> pd = polyder(p)
pd =
   -19.6217   20.1293
```

The derivative of $y(x) = -9.8108x^2 + 20.1293x - 0.0317$ is $dy/dx = -19.6217x + 20.1293$. Since the derivative of a polynomial is yet another polynomial of the next-lowest order, the derivative can also be evaluated at any point. In this case, the polynomial fit is second order, making the resulting derivative first order. As a result, the derivative is a straight line, meaning that it changes linearly with x.

MATLAB provides a function for computing an approximate derivative, given tabulated data describing some function. This function, named `diff`, computes the difference between elements in an array. Since differentiation is defined as

$$\frac{dy}{dx} = \lim_{\Delta x \to 0} \frac{f(x + \Delta x) - f(x)}{\Delta x}$$

the derivative of $y = f(x)$ can be approximated by

$$\frac{dy}{dx} \approx \frac{\Delta y}{\Delta x} = \frac{f(x + \Delta x) - f(x)}{\Delta x}$$

which is the *forward* finite difference in *y* divided by the finite difference in *x*. Since diff computes differences between array elements, differentiation can be approximated in MATLAB. Continuing with the previous example, we have

```
>> dyp = polyval(dp,x);      % poly derivative for comparison

>> dy = diff(y)./diff(x);  % compute differences and use array division
>> xd = x(1:end-1);          % new x axis array since dy is shorter than y

>> plot(xd,dy,x,dyp,':')
>> ylabel('dy/dx'), xlabel('x')
>> title('Figure 24.5: Forward Difference Derivative Approximation')
```

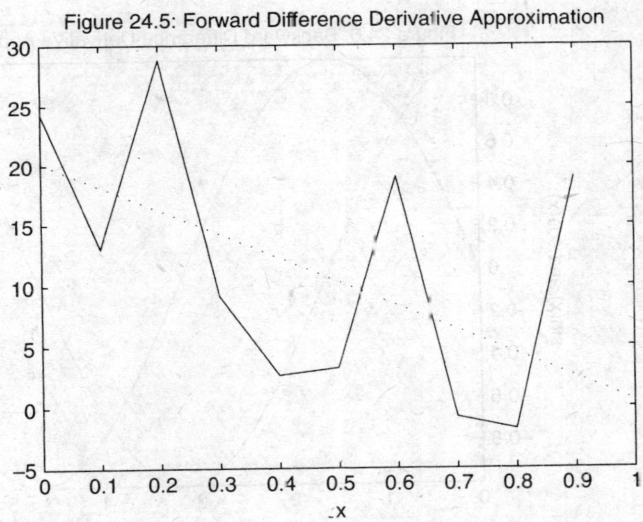

Since diff computes the difference between elements of an array, the resulting output contains one less element than the original array. Thus, to plot the derivative, one element of the x array must be thrown out. When the first element of x is thrown out, the this procedure gives a *backward* difference approximation, which uses information at x(n−1) and x(n) to approximate the derivative at x(n). On the other hand, throwing out the last element gives a *forward* difference approximation, which uses x(n+1) and x(n) to compute results at x(n). Comparing the derivative found using diff with that found from polynomial approximation, it is overwhelmingly apparent that approximating the derivative by finite differences can lead to poor results, especially if the data originates from experimental or noisy measurements.

When the data used do not have uncertainty, the results of using `diff` can be acceptable, especially for visualization purposes, as in this example:

```
>> x = linspace(0,2*pi);
>> y = sin(x);

>> dy = diff(y)/(x(2)-x(1));
>> xd = x(2:end);

>> plot(x,y,xd,dy)
>> axis tight
>> xlabel('x'), ylabel('sin(x) and cos(x)')
>> title('Figure 24.6: Backward Difference Derivative Approximation')
```

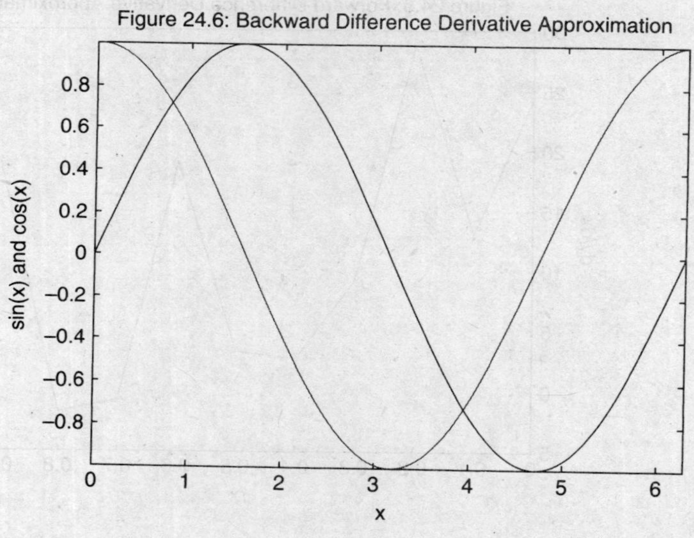

Here, x was linearly spaced, so dividing by x(2)−x(1) gives the same answer as diff(x), which is required if x is not linearly spaced. In addition, the first element in x is thrown out, making the result a backward-difference derivative approximation. Visually, the derivative in this example is quite accurate. In fact, the maximum error is

```
>> max(abs(cos(xd)-dy))
ans =
    0.0317
```

When forward- or backward-difference approximations are not sufficient, *central* differences can be computed by performing the required array operations directly. The first central difference for equally spaced data is given by

$$\frac{dy(x_n)}{dx} \approx \frac{f(x_{n+1}) - f(x_{n-1})}{x_{n+1} - x_{n-1}}$$

Therefore, the slope at x_n is a function of its neighboring data points. Repeating the previous example gives

```
>> dy = (y(3:end)-y(1:end-2)) / (x(3)-x(1));
>> xd = x(2:end-1);
>> max(abs(cos(xd)-dy))
ans =
   0.00067086
```

In this case, the first and last data points do not have a central-difference approximation, because there are no data at `n = 0` and `n = 101`, respectively. However, at all intermediate points, the central-difference approximation is nearly two orders of magnitude more accurate than the forward- or backward-difference approximations.

When dealing with 2-D data, the function `gradient` uses central differences to compute the slope in each direction at each tabulated point. Forward differences are used at the initial points, and backward differences are used at the final points, so that the output has the same number of data points as the input. The function `gradient` is used primarily for graphical data visualization:

```
>> [x,y,z] = peaks(20);    % simple 2-D function
>> dx = x(1,2) - x(1,1); % spacing in x direction
>> dy = y(2,1) - y(1,1); % spacing in y direction
>> [dzdx,dzdy] = gradient(z,dx,dy);

>> contour(x,y,z)
>> hold on
>> quiver(x,y,dzdx,dzdy)
>> hold off
>> title('Figure 24.7: Gradient Arrow Plot')
```

In this example, `gradient` computes *dz/dx* and *dz/dy* from the tabulated data output of `peaks`. These data are supplied to the function `quiver`, which draws arrows normal to the underlying surface, with lengths scaled by the slope at each point.

Figure 24.7: Gradient Arrow Plot

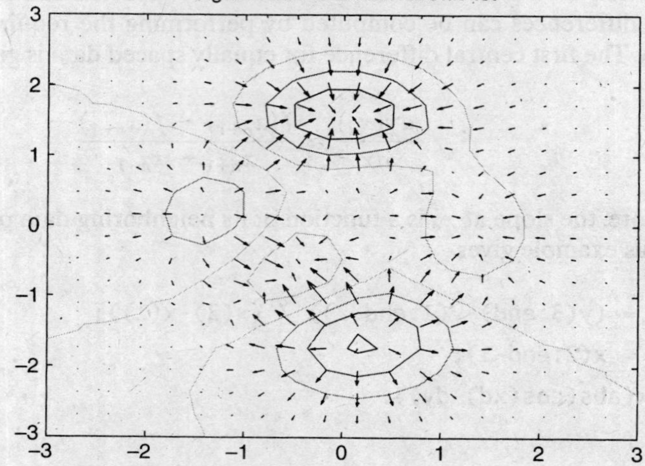

In addition to the gradient, it is sometimes useful to know the curvature of a surface. The curvature, or change in slope, at each point is calculated by the function `del2`, which computes the discrete approximation to the Laplacian:

$$\nabla^2 z(x, y) = \frac{d^2 z}{dx^2} + \frac{d^2 z}{dy^2}$$

In its simplest form, this value is computed by taking each surface element and subtracting from it the average of its four neighbors. If the surface is flat in each direction at a given point, the element does not change. Since MATLAB version 5, central second differences have been used at interior points to produce more accurate results. In the following example, the absolute surface curvature influences the color of the surface:

```
>> [x,y,z] = peaks; % default output of peaks
>> dx = x(1,2) - x(1,1); % spacing in x direction
>> dy = y(2,1) - y(1,1); % spacing in y direction
```

```
>> L = del2(z,dx,dy);
>> surf(x,y,z,abs(L))
>> shading interp
>> title('Figure 24.8: Discrete Laplacian Color')
```

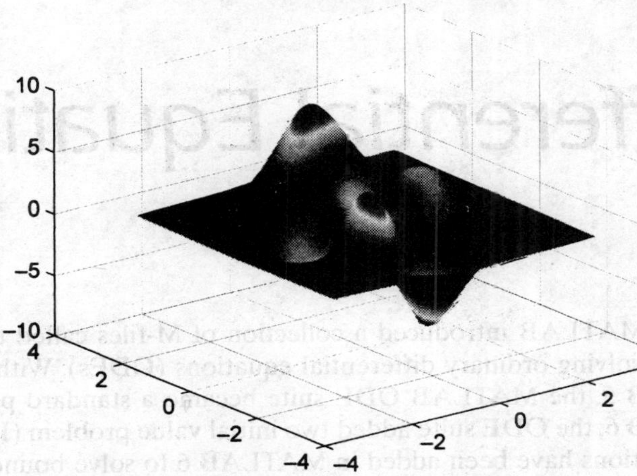

Figure 24.8: Discrete Laplacian Color

25

Differential Equations

In 1995, MATLAB introduced a collection of M-files called the MATLAB ODE suite for solving ordinary differential equations (ODEs). With the introduction of MATLAB 5, the MATLAB ODE suite became a standard part of MATLAB. In MATLAB 6, the ODE suite added two initial value problem (IVP) solvers. In addition, functions have been added in MATLAB 6 to solve boundary value problems (BVPs) and partial differential equations (PDEs). Since MATLAB 6, the ODE suite has added the ability to solve delay differential equations (DDEs) and to solve implicit differential equations.

Taken as a whole, MATLAB now has the capability to solve a wide variety of problems involving differential equations. However, discussing each of these is beyond the scope of this text. Because initial value problems appear most often in applications, they are discussed here.

25.1 IVP FORMAT

The initial value problem solvers in MATLAB compute the time history of a set of coupled first-order differential equations with known initial conditions. In mathematical terms, these problems have the form

$$\dot{\boldsymbol{y}} = \boldsymbol{f}(t, \boldsymbol{y}) \qquad \boldsymbol{y}(t_o) = \boldsymbol{y}_o$$

which is vector notation for the set of differential equations

$$\begin{aligned}
\dot{y}_1 &= f_1(t, y_1, y_2, \ldots, y_n) & y_1(t_o) &= y_{1o} \\
\dot{y}_2 &= f_2(t, y_1, y_2, \ldots, y_n) & y_2(t_o) &= y_{2o} \\
&\vdots & &\vdots \\
\dot{y}_n &= f_n(t, y_1, y_2, \ldots, y_n) & y_n(t_o) &= y_{no}
\end{aligned}$$

where $\dot{y}_i = dy_i/dt$, n is the number of first-order differential equations, and y_{io} is the initial condition associated with the ith equation. When an initial value problem is not specified as a set of first-order differential equations, it must be rewritten as one. For example, consider the classic van der Pol equation

$$\ddot{x} - \mu(1 - x^2)\dot{x} + x = 0$$

where μ is a parameter greater than zero. If we choose $y_1 = x$ and $y_2 = dx/dt$, the van der Pol equation becomes

$$\dot{y}_1 = y_2$$
$$\dot{y}_2 = \mu(1 - y_1^2)y_2 - y_1$$

This initial value problem is used throughout this chapter to demonstrate aspects of the IVP solvers in MATLAB.

25.2 ODE SUITE SOLVERS

The MATLAB ODE suite offers eight initial value problem solvers. Each has characteristics appropriate for different initial value problems. The calling syntax for each solver is identical, making it relatively easy to change solvers for a given problem. A description of each solver is given in the following table:

Solver	Description
`ode23`	An explicit one-step Runge-Kutta low-order (2nd- to 3rd-order) solver. Suitable for problems that exhibit mild stiffness, problems where lower accuracy is acceptable, or problems where $f(t,y)$ is not smooth (e.g., discontinuous).
`ode23s`	An implicit one-step modified Rosenbrock solver of order two. Suitable for stiff problems where lower accuracy is acceptable or where $f(t,y)$ is discontinuous. ***Stiff problems are generally described as problems in which the underlying time constants vary by several orders of magnitude or more.***
`ode23t`	An implicit, one-step trapezoidal rule using a *free* interpolant. Suitable for moderately stiff problems. Can be used to solve differential-algebraic equations (DAEs).
`ode23tb`	An implicit trapezoidal rule followed by a backward differentiation of order two. Similar to `ode23s`. Can be more efficient than `ode15s` for crude tolerances.
`ode45`	An explicit one-step Runge Kutta medium-order (4th- to 5th-order) solver. Suitable for nonstiff problems that require moderate accuracy. ***This is typically the first solver to try on a new problem.***
`ode113`	A multistep Adams-Bashforth-Moulton PECE solver of varying order (1st- to 13th-order). Suitable for nonstiff problems that require moderate to high accuracy involving problems where $f(t,y)$ is expensive to compute. Not suitable for problems where $f(t,y)$ is not smooth.

Solver	Description
`ode15s`	An implicit, multistep numerical differentiation solver of varying order (1st- to 5th-order). Suitable for stiff problems that require moderate accuracy. ***This is typically the solver to try if* `ode45` *fails or is too inefficient.***
`ode15i`	A solver of varying order (1st- to 5th-order) for solving fully implicit differential equations.

This table uses terminology—for example, *explicit, implicit*, and *stiff*—that requires a substantial theoretical background to understand. If you understand the terminology, the table describes the basic properties of each solver. If you don't understand the terminology, just follow the guidelines presented in the table, and apply `ode45` and `ode15s`, respectively, as the first and second solvers to be tried on a given problem.

It is important to note that the MATLAB ODE suite is provided as a set of M-files that can be viewed. In addition, these same solvers are included internally in SIMULINK for the simulation of dynamic systems.

25.3 BASIC USE

Before a set of differential equations can be solved, they must be coded in a function M-file as `ydot=odefile(t,y)`. That is, the file must accept a time `t` and a solution `y` and return values for the derivatives. For the van der Pol equation, this ODE file can be written as follows:

```
function ydot=vdpol(t,y)
%VDPOL van der Pol equation.
% Ydot=VDPOL(t,Y)
% Ydot(1) = Y(2)
% Ydot(2) = mu*(1-Y(1)^2)*Y(2)-Y(1)
% mu = 2

mu = 2;
ydot = [y(2); mu*(1-y(1)^2)*y(2)-y(1)];
```

Note that the input arguments are `t` and `y`, but that this particular function does not use `t`. Note also that the output `ydot` must be a column vector.

Given the preceding ODE file, this set of ODEs is solved by using the following commands:

```
>> tspan = [0 20];   % time span to integrate over

>> yo = [2; 0];      % initial conditions (must be a column)
>> [t,y] = ode45(@vdpol,tspan,yo);
>> size(t)           % number of time points
ans =
   333     1
>> size(y)           % (i) th column is y(i) at t(i)
ans =
   333     2
>> plot(t,y(:,1),t,y(:,2),'--')
>> xlabel('time')
>> title('Figure 25.1: van der Pol Solution')
```

Note that the use of function handles is appropriate in this case, since differential equations are written as M-files, and they are evaluated many times in the process of generating a solution over a reasonable time span.

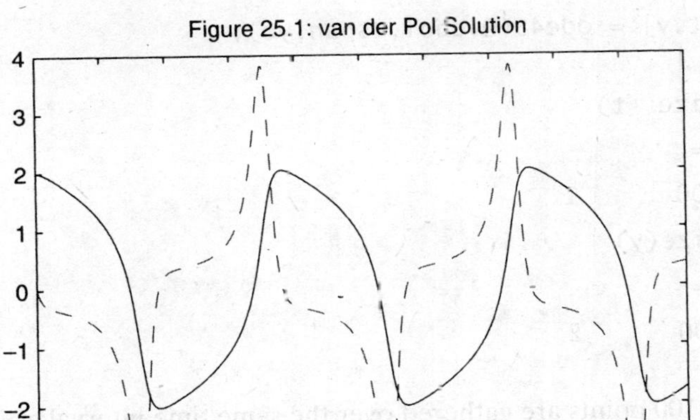

By default, if a solver is called with no output arguments (e.g., `ode45(@vdpol, tspan,yo)`) the solver generates no output variables, but generates a time plot similar to that shown in the previous figure. Alternatively, if a solver is called with one output argument, that argument is a structure containing all of the information needed to evaluate the solution at arbitrary time points by using the function deval:

```
>> sol = ode45(@vdpol, tspan,yo)
sol =

          x: [1x84 double]
          y: [2x84 double]
     solver: 'ode45'
      idata: [1x1 struct]
```

The help text for deval provides information about the contents of the output variable sol. It is also possible to use this solution structure to extend or extrapolate the solution by using the function odextend.

In addition to specifying the initial and final time points in tspan, you can identify the desired specific solution time points by simply adding them to tspan, as in the following example:

```
>> yo = [2; 0];
>> tspan = linspace(0,20,100);

>> [t,y] = ode45(@vdpol,tspan,yo);

>> size (t)
ans =
   100     1
>> size(y)
ans =
   100     2
```

Here, 100 points are gathered over the same time interval as in the earlier example. When called in this way, the solver still uses automatic step-size control to maintain accuracy. ***The solver does not use fixed step integration.*** To gather the solution at the desired points, the solver interpolates its own solution in an efficient way that does not deteriorate the solution's accuracy.

Sometimes the set of differential equations to be solved contains a set of parameters that the user wishes to vary. Rather than open the ODE file and change the parameters before each call to a solver, the parameters can be added to the solver and ODE file input arguments:

```
function ydot=vdpol(t,y,mu)
%VDPOL van der Pol equation.
% Ydot=VDPOL(t,Y,mu)
% Ydot(1) = Y(2)
% Ydot(2) = mu*(1-Y(1)^2)*Y(2)-Y(1)

% mu = ?; now passed as an input argument

if nargin<3 % supply default if not given
  mu=2;
end
ydot = [y(2); mu*(1-y(1)^2)*y(2)-y(1)];
```

```
>> mu = 10 % set mu in Command window
mu =
    10
>> ode45(@vdpol, tspan,yo,[],mu)
>>title('Figure 25.2 van der Pol Solution, \mu=10')
```

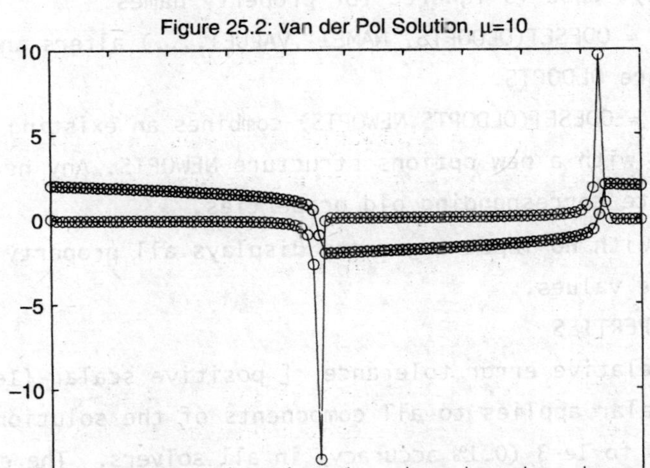

The preceding solves the van der Pol equation with $\mu = 10$. Here, mu is added as a third input argument to vdpol.m. Then the differential equations are solved by adding two input arguments to the ode45 function call. The first added argument is an empty array; this tells the function to use default solver options. The second added argument contains the value of the parameter. Since no output arguments were specified, the plotted solution is automatically created. While the above example describes the use of one parameter, any number of parameters can be added after the first one shown. In addition, each parameter can be an array of any data type.

25.4 SETTING OPTIONS

Up to this point, we have just accepted all default tolerances and options. When these are not sufficient, an options structure can be passed to a solver as a fourth input argument. The MATLAB ODE suite contains the functions odeset and odeget to manage this options structure. The function odeset works similarly to the Handle Graphics set function, in that parameters are specified in name/value pairs—for example, options = odeset('Name1',Value1,'Name2',Value2,...);. The available parameter names and values are described in the on-line help for odeset:

```
>> help odeset
 ODESET Create/alter ODE OPTIONS structure.
    OPTIONS = ODESET('NAME1',VALUE1,'NAME2',VALUE2,...) creates an integrator
    options structure OPTIONS in which the named properties have the
    specified values. Any unspecified properties have default values. It is
    sufficient to type only the leading characters that uniquely identify the
    property. Case is ignored for property names.
    OPTIONS = ODESET(OLDOPTS,'NAME1',VALUE1,...) alters an existing options
    structure OLDOPTS.
    OPTIONS = ODESET(OLDOPTS,NEWOPTS) combines an existing options structure
    OLDOPTS with a new options structure NEWOPTS. Any new properties
    overwrite corresponding old properties.
    ODESET with no input arguments displays all property names and their
    possible values.
ODESET PROPERTIES
RelTol - Relative error tolerance  [ positive scalar {1e-3} ]
   This scalar applies to all components of the solution vector, and
   defaults to 1e-3 (0.1% accuracy) in all solvers.  The estimated error in
   each integration step satisfies e(i) <= max(RelTol*abs(y(i)),AbsTol(i)).
```

```
AbsTol - Absolute error tolerance  [ positive scalar or vector {1e-6} ]
   A scalar tolerance applies to all components of the solution vector.
   Elements of a vector of tolerances apply to corresponding components of
   the solution vector. AbsTol defaults to 1e-6 in all solvers. See RelTol.
NormControl -  Control error relative to norm of solution  [ on | {off} ]
   Set this property 'on' to request that the solvers control the error in
   each integration step with norm(e) <= max(RelTol*norm(y),AbsTol). By
   default the solvers use a more stringent component-wise error control.
Refine - Output refinement factor  [ positive integer ]
   This property increases the number of output points by the specified
   factor producing smoother output. Refine defaults to 1 in all solvers
   except ODE45, where it is 4. Refine does not apply if length(TSPAN) > 2
   or the ODE solver returns the solution as a structure.
OutputFcn - Installable output function  [ function ]
   This output function is called by the solver after each time step. When
   a solver is called with no output arguments, OutputFcn defaults to the
   function odeplot. Otherwise, OutputFcn defaults to [].
OutputSel - Output selection indices  [ vector of integers ]
   This vector of indices specifies which components of the solution vector
   are passed to the OutputFcn. OutputSel defaults to all components.
Stats - Display computational cost statistics  [ on | {off} ]
Jacobian - Jacobian function [ function | constant matrix ]
   Set this property to a function FJac (if FJac(t,y) returns dF/dy) or to
   the constant value of dF/dy.
JPattern - Jacobian sparsity pattern [ sparse matrix ]
   Set this property to a sparse matrix S with S(i,j) = 1 if component i of
   F(t,y) depends on component j of y, and 0 otherwise.
Vectorized - Vectorized ODE function  [ on | {off} ]
   Set this property 'on' if the ODE function F is coded so that
   F(t,[y1 y2 ...]) returns [F(t,y1) F(t,y2) ...].
Events - Locate events  [ function ]
   To detect events, set this property to the event function.
Mass - Mass matrix [ constant matrix | function ]
   For problems M*y' = f(t,y) set this property to the value of the constant
```

```
   mass matrix. For problems with time- or state-dependent mass matrices,
   set this property to a function that evaluates the mass matrix.
MStateDependence - Dependence of the mass matrix on y [ none | {weak} | strong ]
   Set this property to 'none' for problems M(t)*y' = F(t,y). Both 'weak' and
   'strong' indicate M(t,y), but 'weak' will result in implicit solvers
   using approximations when solving algebraic equations.
MassSingular - Mass matrix is singular  [ yes | no | {maybe} ]
   Set this property to 'no' if the mass matrix is not singular.
MvPattern - dMv/dy sparsity pattern [ sparse matrix ]
   Set this property to a sparse matrix S with S(i,j) = 1 if for any k, the
   (i,k) component of M(t,y) depends on component j of y, and 0 otherwise.
InitialSlope - Consistent initial slope yp0 [ vector ]
   yp0 satisfies M(t0,y0)*yp0 = F(t0,y0).
InitialStep - Suggested initial step size  [ positive scalar ]
   The solver will try this first.  By default the solvers determine an
   initial step size automatically.
MaxStep - Upper bound on step size  [ positive scalar ]
   MaxStep defaults to one-tenth of the tspan interval in all solvers.
BDF - Use Backward Differentiation Formulas in ODE15S  [ on | {off} ]
   This property specifies whether the Backward Differentiation Formulas
   (Gear's methods) are to be used in ODE15S instead of the default
   Numerical Differentiation Formulas.
MaxOrder - Maximum order of ODE15S  [ 1 | 2 | 3 | 4 | {5} ]
```

The following examples use the preceding options:

```
>> odeset
          AbsTol: [ positive scalar or vector {1e-6} ]
          RelTol: [ positive scalar {1e-3} ]
     NormControl: [ on | {off} ]
       OutputFcn: [ function ]
       OutputSel: [ vector of integers ]
          Refine: [ positive integer ]
           Stats: [ on | {off} ]
     InitialStep: [ positive scalar ]
```

```
         MaxStep: [ positive scalar ]
             BDF: [ on | {off} ]
        MaxOrder: [ 1 | 2 | 3 | 4 | {5} ]
        Jacobian: [ matrix | function ]
        JPattern: [ sparse matrix ]
      Vectorized: [ on | {off} ]
            Mass: [ matrix | function ]
MStateDependence: [ none | weak | strong ]
       MvPattern: [ sparse matrix ]
    MassSingular: [ yes | no | {maybe} ]
    InitialSlope: [ vector ]
          Events: [ function ]
```

Invoking odeset without input or output arguments returns an option listing, their possible values, and default values in braces:

```
>> tspan = [0 20]; % set time span to solve
>> yo = [2; 0];    % intial conditions
>> mu = 10;        % parameter mu
>> options = odeset('AbsTol',1e-12,'RelTol',1e-6);

>> [t,y] = ode45(@vdpol,tspan,yo,[],mu);  % default tolerances
>> length(t)
ans =
   593
>> [t,y] = ode(@vdpol,tspan,yo,options,mu); % tight tolerances
>> length(t)
ans =
        1689

>> [t,y] = ode15s(@vdpol,tspan,yo,[],mu); % new solver, default tols
>> length(t)
ans =
   232
```

```
>> [t,Y] = ode15s(@vdpol,tspan,yo,options,mu);  %  new solver, tight tols
>> length(t)
ans =
   651
```

Here, the steps needed to integrate the first 20 seconds are shown. Default tolerances, (i.e., `AbsTol=1e-6` and `RelTol=1e-3`) forces `ode45` to take 593 time steps. Decreasing the tolerances to `AbsTol=1e-12` and `RelTol=1e-6` takes 1689 time steps. However, changing to the stiff solver `ode15s` requires only 651 steps at the tighter tolerances.

The stiff solvers `ode15s`, `ode23s`, `ode23t`, and `ode23tb` allow you to specify an analytical Jacobian, rather than a numerically computed approximation, which is the default. The Jacobian is a matrix of partial derivatives that has the form

$$\begin{bmatrix} \frac{\partial f_1}{\partial y_1} & \frac{\partial f_1}{\partial y_2} & \cdots & \frac{\partial f_1}{\partial y_n} \\ \frac{\partial f_2}{\partial y_1} & \frac{\partial f_2}{\partial y_2} & \cdots & \frac{\partial f_2}{\partial y_n} \\ \vdots & \vdots & \ddots & \vdots \\ \frac{\partial f_n}{\partial y_1} & \frac{\partial f_n}{\partial y_2} & \cdots & \frac{\partial f_n}{\partial y_n} \end{bmatrix}$$

This matrix or a numerical approximation of it is used by the stiff solvers to compute the solution of a set of nonlinear equations at each time step. If at all possible, an analytical Jacobian should be supplied, as shown in the following code:

```
function jac=vdpoljac(t,y,mu)
%VDPOLJAC van der Pol equation Jacobian.

% mu = ?; passed as an input argument
if nargin<3 % supply default if not given
   mu=2;
end
jac = [        0                         1
       (-2*mu*y(1)*y(2)-1) (mu*(1-y(1)^2))];
```

```
>> options = odeset(options,'Jacobian',@vdpoljac);
>> [t,y] = ode15s(@vdpol,tspan,yo,options,mu);
>> length (t)
ans =
    670
```

In this example, the function handle of the M-file that computes the Jacobian is added to the options structure set discussed earlier. Running the solver now shows that it takes 670 steps. While this is more than the 651 steps shown earlier, providing the analytical Jacobian still significantly increases execution speed.

When it is not possible to supply an analytical Jacobian, it is beneficial to supply a ***vectorized*** ODE file. Vectorizing the ODE file usually means replacing `y(i)` with `y(i,:)` and using array operators. Doing so allows computation of the numerical Jacobian to proceed as fast as possible, as in this example:

```
function ydot=vdpol(t,y,mu)
%VDPOL van der Pol equation.
% Ydot=VDPOL(t,Y)
% Ydot(1) = Y(2)
% Ydot(2) = mu*(1-Y(1)^2)*Y(2)-Y(1)

% mu = ?; now passed as an input argument
if nargin<3 % supply default if not given
   mu=2;
end
ydot = [y(2,:); mu*(1-y(1,:)^2)*y(2,:)-y(1,:)];
```

The `'Refine'` property determines how much output data to generate. It does not affect the step sizes chosen by the solvers, or the solution accuracy. It merely dictates how many intermediate points to interpolate the solution at within each integration step, as in the following example:

```
>> options = odeset('Refine',1);
>> [t,y] = ode45(@vdpol,tspan,yo,options,mu);
>> length (t) % # of time points
ans =
    149
```

```
>> options = odset('Refine',4);
>> [t,y] = ode45(@vdpol,tspan,yo,options,mu);
>> length(t)  % # of time points
ans =
   593
```

With 'Refine' set to 1, 149 time points are returned over the 20-second time span. Setting 'Refine' to 4 increases the number of time points returned to 593.

The 'Events' property allows you to flag one or more events that occur as an ODE solution evolves in time. For example, a simple event could be when some solution component reaches a maximum, a minimum, or crosses through zero. Optionally, the occurrence of an event can force a solver to stop integrating. To make use of this feature, you must simply supply a function handle that computes the values of the events to be tracked. At each time step, the solver computes the events and marks in time those that cross through zero—for example,

```
function [value,isterminal,direction]=vdpolevents(t,y,mu)
%VDPOLEVENTS  van der Pol equation events.
value(1)=abs(y(2))-2; % find where |y(2)|=2
isterminal(1)=0;      % don't stop integration
direction(1)=0;       % don't care about crossing direction
```

```
>> mu = 2;
>> options = odeset('Events',@vdpolevents);
>> [t,y,te,ye] = ode45(@vdpol,tspan,yo,options,mu);
>> plot (t,y,te,ye(:,2),'o')
>> title('Figure 25.3: van der Pol Solution, |y(2)|=2')
```

The function vdpolevents receives the same three arguments as the other functions and returns three numerical vectors. The first is the value of the events, the second is a logical array dictating whether the solver should terminate execution on a zero crossing in one or more of the computed events, and the third gives the user the ability to specify whether the direction of event crossing should be considered. In the preceding example, the points where $\text{abs}(y_2(t)) = 2$ are selected as the only event. The solver is told to not halt on sensing events and to not care about the direction of event crossing. The generated plot shows the system solution and the points where the chosen events occur.

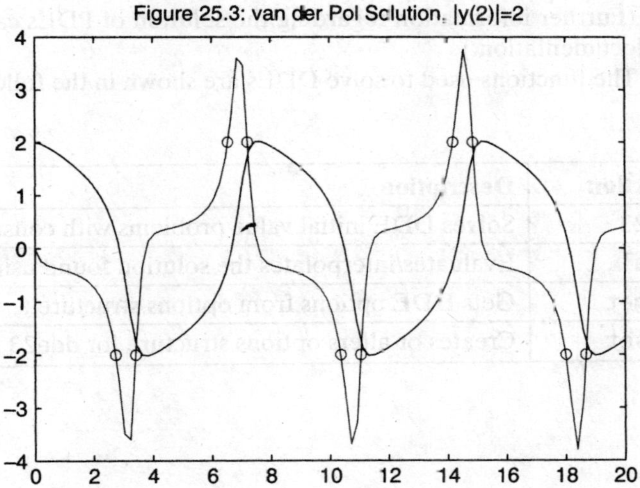

25.5 BVPs, PDEs, AND DDEs

In addition to the seven MATLAB solvers for solving initial value ordinary differential equations, MATLAB includes functions for the solution of boundary value problems (BVPs), partial differential equations (PDEs) and delay differential equations (DDEs). The functions used to solve BVPs are shown in the following table:

Function	Description
bvp4c	BVP solver
bvpget	Gets BVP options structure
bvpinit	Forms the initial solution guess, which is refined by bvp4c
bvpset	Sets the BVP options structure
deval	Evaluates/interpolates the solution found by using bvp4c

(Further information regarding the solution of BVPs can be found in the MATLAB documentation.)

The functions used to solve PDEs are shown in this table:

Function	Description
pdepe	Solves IVPs for parabolic-elliptic PDEs in one dimension
pdeval	Evaluates/interpolates the solution found using pdepe

(Further information regarding the solution of PDEs can be found in the online documentation.)

The functions used to solve DDEs are shown in the following table:

Function	Description
dde23	Solves DDE initial value problems with constant delays
deval	Evaluates/interpolates the solution found using dde23
ddeget	Gets DDE options from options structure
ddeset	Creates or alters options structure for dde23

26

Two-Dimensional Graphics

Throughout this text, several of MATLAB's graphics features have been introduced. In this and the next several chapters, the graphics features in MATLAB are more rigorously illustrated. Many of the features and capabilities illustrated here are available as menu items from the top of a *Figure* window. They are also available as buttons on the *Figure* or *Camera* toolbar, which appears by default when plots are generated or can be chosen via the **View** menu in a *Figure* window.

The general rule is to use the toolbar and menu features of *Figure* windows if you want to customize a single *Figure*. Otherwise, use *Command* window functions to automate the process of customizing plots. This text concentrates on the *Command* window functions, since they perform the actions taken when menu and toolbar items are used.

26.1 THE plot FUNCTION

As you have seen in earlier examples, the most common function for plotting 2-D data is the `plot` function. This versatile function plots sets of data arrays on appropriate axes and connects the points with straight lines:

```
>> x = linspace(0,2*pi,30);
>> y = sin(x);
>> plot(x,y), title('Figure 26.1: Sine Wave')
```

This example creates 30 data points over $0 \leq x \leq 2\pi$ to form the horizontal axis of the plot and creates another vector `y` containing the sine of the data points in `x`. The `plot` function opens a graphics window, called a *Figure* window, scales the

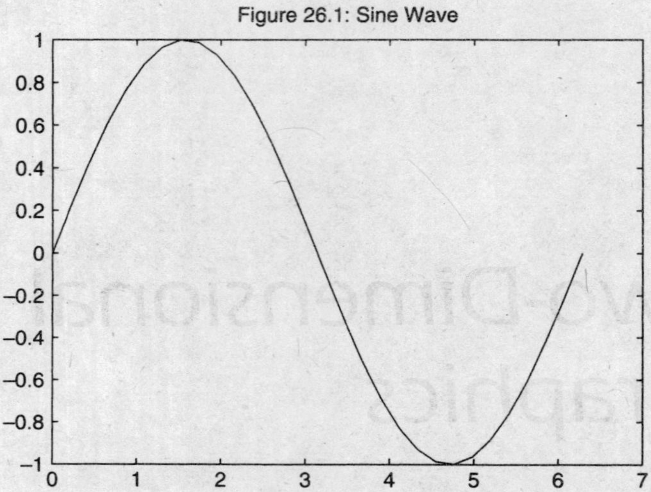

axes to fit the data, plots the points, and then connects the points with straight lines. It also adds numerical scales and tick marks to the axes automatically. If a *Figure* window already exists, `plot` generally clears the current *Figure* window and draws a new plot.

The following code plots more than one curve or line:

```
>> z = cos(x);
>> plot(x,y,x,z)
>> title('Figure 26.2: Sine and Cosine')
```

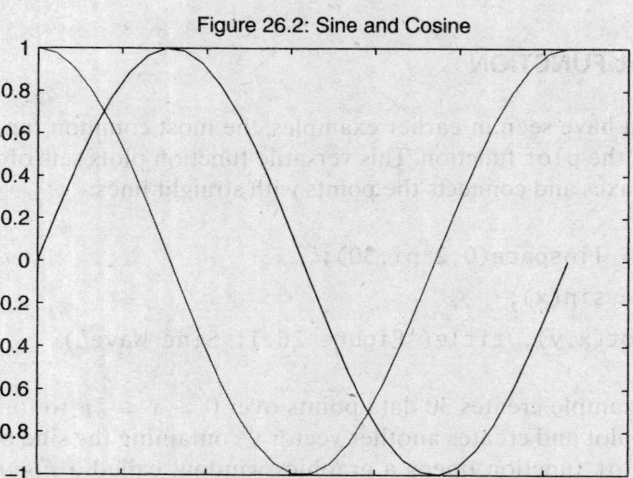

Just giving plot another pair of arguments instructs it to generate a second line. This time, sin(x) versus x, and cos(x) versus x were plotted on the same plot. Although the figure doesn't show color, plot automatically draws the second curve in a different color. The function plot generates as many curves as it receives pairs of input arguments.

If one of the arguments is a matrix and the other a vector, the plot function plots each column of the matrix versus the vector. For example, the code

```
>> W = [y;z]; % create a matrix of the sine and cosine
>> plot(x,W)  % plot the columns of W vs. x
```

reproduces the preceding plot.

If you change the order of the arguments, the orientation of the plot changes accordingly:

```
>> plot(W,x) % plot x vs. the columns of W
>> title('Figure 26.3: Change Argument Order')
```

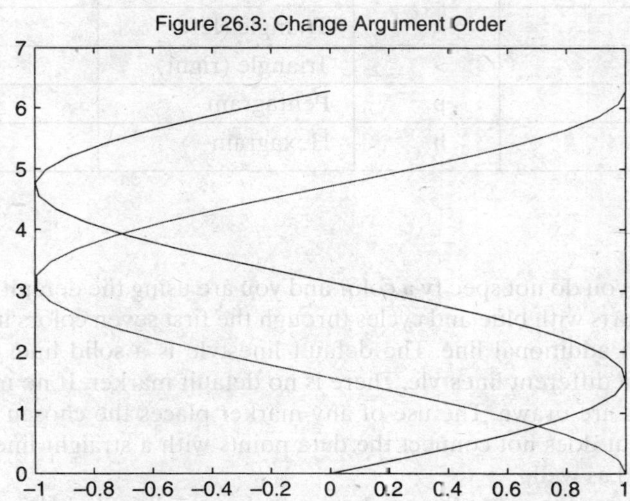

When the plot function is called with only one argument (e.g., plot(Y)) the plot function acts differently, depending on the data contained in Y. If Y is a ***complex-valued*** vector, plot(Y) is interpreted as plot(real(Y),imag(Y)). In all other cases, the imaginary components of the input vectors are *ignored*. On the other hand, if Y is ***real-valued***, then plot(Y) is interpreted as plot(1:length(Y),Y); that is, Y is plotted versus an index of its values. When Y is a matrix, this interpretation is applied to each column of Y.

26.2 LINESTYLES, MARKERS, AND COLORS

In the previous examples, MATLAB chose the solid linestyle, and the colors blue and green, for the plots. You can specify your own colors, markers, and linestyles by giving `plot` a third argument after each pair of data arrays. This optional argument is a character string consisting of one or more characters from the following table:

Symbol	Color	Symbol	Marker	Symbol	Linestyle
b	Blue		Point	-	Solid line
g	Green	o	Circle	:	Dotted line
r	Red	x	Cross	-.	Dash-dot line
c	Cyan	+	Plus sign	--	Dashed line
m	Magenta	*	Asterisk		
y	Yellow	s	Square		
k	Black	d	Diamond		
w	White	v	Triangle (down)		
		^	Triangle (up)		
		<	Triangle (left)		
		>	Triangle (right)		
		p	Pentagram		
		h	Hexagram		

If you do not specify a color and you are using the default color scheme, MATLAB starts with blue and cycles through the first seven colors in the preceding table for each additional line. The default linestyle is a solid line, unless you explicitly specify a different linestyle. There is no default marker. If no marker is selected, no markers are drawn. The use of any marker places the chosen symbol at each data point, but does not connect the data points with a straight line unless a linestyle is specified as well.

If a color, a marker, and a linestyle are all included in the string, the color applies to both the marker and the line. To specify a different color for the marker, plot the same data with a different specification string:

```
>> plot(x,y,'b:p',x,z,'c-',x,1.2*z,'m+')
>> title('Figure 26.4: Linestyles and Markers')
```

As with many of the plots in this section, your computer displays color, but the figures shown here do not. If you are following along in MATLAB, just enter the commands listed in the examples to see the effects of color.

Figure 26.4: Linestyles and Markers

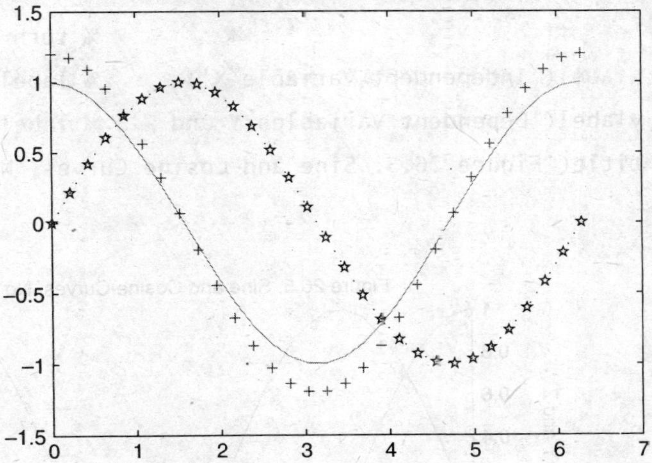

26.3 PLOT GRIDS, AXES BOX, AND LABELS

The `grid on` command adds grid lines to the current plot at the tick marks. The `grid off` command removes the grid. The command `grid` with no arguments alternately turns the grid lines on and off—that is, it ***toggles*** them. By default, MATLAB starts up with `grid off` for most plots. If you like to have grid lines on all of your plots by default, add the following lines to your `startup.m` file:

```
set(0,'DefaultAxesXgrid','on')
set(0,'DefaultAxesYgrid','on')
set(0,'DefaultAxesZgrid','on')
```

These lines illustrate the use of Handle Graphics features in MATLAB and the setting of default behavior. (More information on these topics can be found in Chapter 30.)

Normally, 2-D axes are fully enclosed by solid lines called an ***axes box***. This box can be turned off with `box off`. The command `box on` restores the axes box. The box command toggles the state of the axes box. Horizontal and vertical axes can be labeled with the `xlabel` and `ylabel` functions, respectively. The `title` function adds a line of text at the top of the plot. The following example is illustrative:

```
>> x = linspace(0,2*pi,30);
>> y = sin(x);
>> z = cos(x);
```

```
>> plot(x,y,x,z)
>> box off                                  % turn off the axes box
>> xlabel('Independent Variable X')         % label horizontal axis
>> ylabel('Dependent Variables Y and Z') % label vertical axis
>> title('Figure 26.5: Sine and Cosine Curves, No Box') % title
```

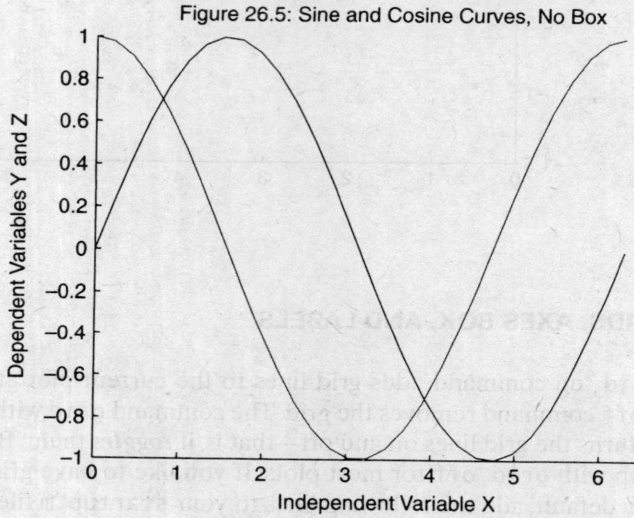

You can add a label or any other text string to any specific location on your plot with the `text` function. The syntax for `text` is `text(x,y,'string')`, where `(x,y)` represents the coordinates of the center left edge of the text string in units taken from the plot axes. For example, the following code segment places the text `'sin(x)'` at the location $x = 2.5$, $y = 0.7$:

```
>> grid on, box on % turn axes box and grid lines on
>> text(2.5,0.7,'sin(x)')
>> title('Figure 26.6: Sine and Cosine Curves, Added Label')
```

If you want to add a label, but don't want to stop to figure out the coordinates to use, you can place a text string with the mouse. The `gtext('text')` function switches to the current *Figure* window, puts up a cross-hair that follows the mouse, and waits for a mouse click or key press. When either one occurs, the string argument to `gtext` is placed with the lower left corner of the first character at that location.

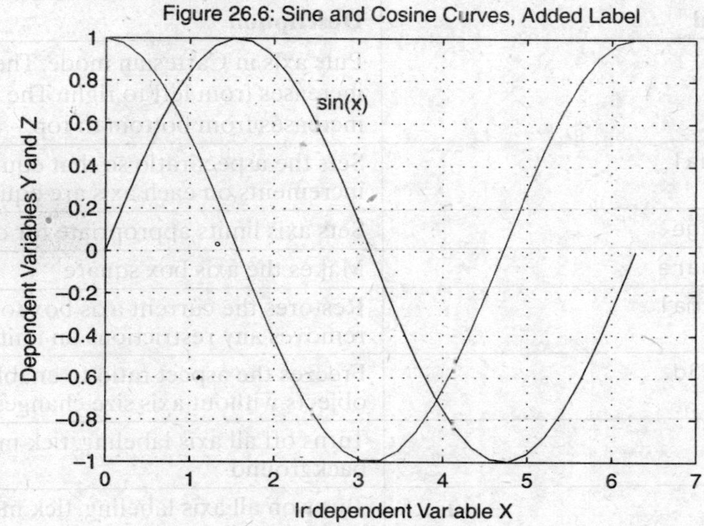

26.4 CUSTOMIZING PLOT AXES

MATLAB gives you complete control over the scaling and appearance of both the horizontal and vertical axes of your plot with the `axis` command. Because this command has so many features, only the most useful are described here. The primary features of the `axis` command are given in the following table:

Command	Description
`axis([xmin xmax ymin ymax])`	Sets axis limits on the current plot
`V = axis`	Returns a row vector containing the current axis limits
`axis auto`	Returns axis scaling to automatic defaults
`axis manual`	Freezes axis scaling so that if `hold` is on, subsequent plots use the same axis limits
`axis tight`	Sets axis limits to the range of the plotted data
`axis fill`	Sets the axis limits and aspect ratio so that the axis fills the allotted space. This option has an effect only if `PlotBoxAspectRatio` or `DataAspect RatioMode` is `'manual'`.
`axis ij`	Puts axis in ***matrix*** mode. The horizontal axis increases from left to right. The vertical axis increases from top to bottom.

Command	Description
`axis xy`	Puts axis in Cartesian mode. The horizontal axis increases from left to right. The vertical axis increases from bottom to top.
`axis equal`	Sets the aspect ratio so that equal tick mark increments on each axis are equal in size
`axis image`	Sets axis limits appropriate for displaying an image
`axis square`	Makes the axis box square
`axis normal`	Restores the current axis box to full size and removes any restrictions on unit scaling
`axis vis3d`	Freezes the aspect ratio to enable rotation of 3-D objects without axis size changes
`axis off`	Turns off all axis labeling, tick marks, and background
`axis on`	Turns on all axis labeling, tick marks, and background

Multiple commands to `axis` can be given at once. For example, `axis auto on xy` is the default axis scaling. The `axis` command affects only the current plot. Therefore, it is issued after the `plot` command, just as `grid`, `xlabel`, `ylabel`, `title`, `text`, and so on, are issued after the plot is on the screen:

```
x = linspace(0,2*pi,30);
y = sin(x);
plot(x,y)
title('Figure 26.7: Fixed Axis Scaling')
axis([0 2*pi -1.5 2])  % change axis limits
```

Note that by specifying the maximum x-axis value to be `2*pi`, the plot axis ends at exactly `2*pi` rather than rounding the axis limit up to 7. The simplest way to see what the various `axis` command arguments do is to generate a simple plot, then issue multiple `axis` commands, and, finally view the resulting changes.

When you simply want to change the axis limits on a single axis, the `axis` command is cumbersome because it requires you to enter limits for all axes. To solve this problem, MATLAB provides the functions `xlim`, `ylim`, and `zlim`, which are described by the help text for `xlim`, with the obvious change for `ylim` and `zlim`:

```
>> help xlim
 XLIM X limits.
    XL = XLIM             gets the x limits of the current axes.
    XLIM([XMIN XMAX])     sets the x limits.
```

```
XLMODE = XLIM('mode') gets the x limits mode.
XLIM(mode)            sets the x limits mode.
                        (mode can be 'auto' or 'manual')
XLIM(AX,...)          uses axes AX instead of current axes.
XLIM sets or gets the XLim or XLimMode property of an axes.
See also PBASPECT, DASPECT, YLIM, ZLIM.
```

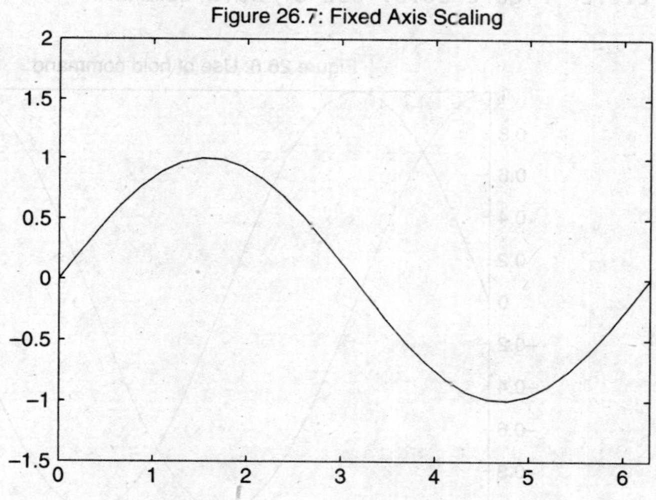

26.5 MULTIPLE PLOTS

You can add new plots to an existing plot by using the `hold` command. When you enter `hold on`, MATLAB does not remove the existing axes when new `plot` functions are issued. Instead, it adds new curves to the current axes. However, if the new data does not fit within the current axes limits, the axes are rescaled. Entering `hold off` releases the current *Figure* window for new plots. The `hold` command, without arguments, toggles the `hold` setting:

```
>> x = linspace(0,2*pi,30);
>> y = sin(x);
>> z = cos(x);
>> plot(x,y)
>> hold on
```

```
>> ishold  % return 1 (True) if hold is ON
ans =
     1
>> plot(x,z,'m')
>> hold off
>> ishold  % hold is no longer ON
ans =
     0
>> title 'Figure 26.8: Use of hold command'
```

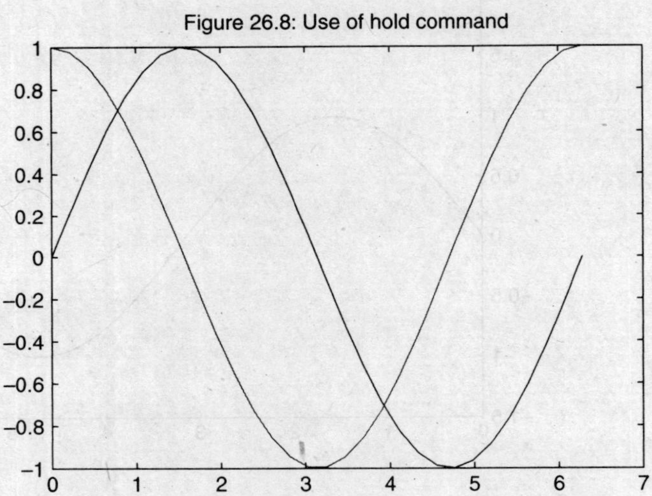

Notice that this example specifies the color of the second curve. Since there is only one set of data arrays in each `plot` function, the line color for each `plot` function would otherwise default to the first color in the color order list, resulting in two lines plotted in the same color on the plot. Note also that the title text is not enclosed in parentheses, but the effect remains unchanged. In the alternative form shown, `title` is interpreted as a command rather than a function. In addition, in MATLAB 7, the command `hold all` holds both the current plot and the next line color to be used. Therefore, if `hold on` in the previous example is replaced by `hold all`, and no explicit color is specified for the second plot, then, by default, `plot(x,z)` would have produced a green line.

26.6 MULTIPLE FIGURES

It is possible to create multiple *Figure* windows and plot different data sets in different ways in each one. To create new *Figure* windows, use the `figure` command in the *Command* window or the **New Figure** selection from the **File** menu in the *Command* or *Figure* window. You can choose a specific *Figure* window to be the active, or current, figure by clicking on it with the mouse or by using `figure(n)`, where `n` is the number of the window. The current *Figure* window is the window that is active for subsequent plotting functions.

Every time a new *Figure* window is created, a number identifying it—that is, its ***handle***—is returned and stored for future use. The figure handle is also displayed in the *Figure* window title bar. When a new *Figure* window is created, it is placed in the default figure position on the screen. As a result, when more than one *Figure* window is created, each new window covers all preceding *Figure* windows. To see the windows simultaneously, simply drag them around by using the mouse on the *Figure* window title bar.

To reuse a *Figure* window for a new plot, it must be made the active, or current, figure. Clicking on the figure of choice with the mouse makes it the current figure. From within MATLAB, `figure(h)` where `h` is the figure handle, makes the corresponding figure active or current. Only the current figure is responsive to the `axis`, `hold`, `xlabel`, `ylabel`, `title`, and `grid` commands.

Figure windows can be deleted by closing them with the mouse, similar to the way you may close windows on your computer. Alternatively, the command `close` can be issued. For example,

```
>> close
```

closes the current *Figure* window,

```
>> close(h)
```

closes the *Figure* window having handle `h`, and

```
>> close all
```

closes all *Figure* windows.

If you simply want to erase the contents of a *Figure* window without closing it, use the command `clf`. For example,

```
>> clf
```

clears the current *Figure* window, and

```
>> clf reset
```

clears the current *Figure* window and resets all properties, such as `hold`, to their default states.

26.7 SUBPLOTS

One *Figure* window can hold more than one set of axes. The `subplot(m,n,p)` command subdivides the current *Figure* window into an m-by-n matrix of plotting areas and chooses the pth area to be active. The subplots are numbered left to right along the top row, then along the second row, and so on.

The following code is illustrative:

```
x = linspace(0,2*pi,30);
y = sin(x);
z = cos(x);
a = 2*sin(x).*cos(x);
b = sin(x)./(cos(x)+eps);

subplot(2,2,1) % pick the upper left of a 2-by-2 grid of subplots
plot(x,y), axis([0 2*pi -1 1]), title('Figure 26.9a: sin(x)')

subplot(2,2,2) % pick the upper right of the 4 subplots
plot(x,z), axis([0 2*pi -1 1]), title('Figure 26.9b: cos(x)')

subplot(2,2,3) % pick the lower left of the 4 subplots
plot(x,a), axis([0 2*pi -1 1]), title('Figure 26.9c: 2sin(x)cos(x)')

subplot(2,2,4) % pick the lower right of the 4 subplots
plot(x,b), axis([0 2*pi -20 20]), title('Figure 26.9d: sin(x)/cos(x)')
```

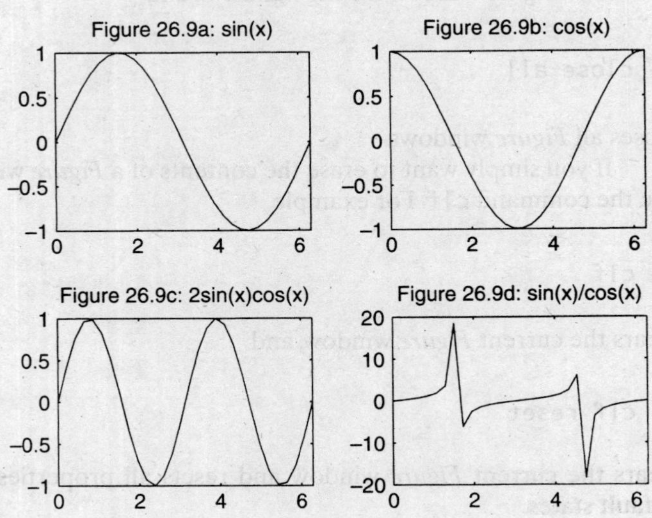

Note that when a particular subplot is active, it is the only subplot or axis that is responsive to the `axis`, `hold`, `xlabel`, `ylabel`, `title`, `grid`, and `box` commands. The other subplots are not affected. In addition, the active subplot remains active until another `subplot` or `figure` command is issued. When a new `subplot` command changes the number of subplots in the *Figure* window, previous subplots are erased to make room for the new orientation. To return to the default mode and use the entire *Figure* window for a single set of axes, use the command `subplot(1,1,1)`. When you print a *Figure* window containing multiple plots, all of them are printed on the same page. For example, when the current *Figure* window contains four subplots and the orientation is landscape mode, each of the plots uses one-quarter of the printed page.

26.8 INTERACTIVE PLOTTING TOOLS

Before the *Figure* window menu bar and toolbars existed, MATLAB offered several functions for annotating plots interactively. These functions are described in this section, and most are available from the *Figure* menu bar and toolbars.

Rather than individual text strings, a legend can be used to identify the data sets on your plot. The `legend` command creates a legend box on the plot, keying any text you supply to each line in the plot. If you wish to move the legend, simply click and hold down the mouse button near the lower left edge of the legend and drag the legend to the desired location. The command `legend off` deletes the legend. The following example is illustrative:

```
>> close % close figure containing subplots

>> x = linspace(0,2*pi,30);

>> y = sin(x);
>> z = cos(x);
>> plot(x,y,x,z)
>> legend('sin(x)', 'cos(x)')
>> title('Figure 26.10: Legend Example')
```

MATLAB provides an interactive tool to expand sections of a 2-D plot to see more detail or to ***zoom in*** on a region of interest. The command `zoom on` turns on the zoom mode. Clicking the left mouse button within the *Figure* window expands the plot by a factor of 2 centered around the point under the mouse pointer. Each time you click, the plot expands. Click the right mouse button to open a contextual menu to zoom out or select other properties. You can also click and drag a rectangular area to zoom in on a specific area. The `zoom out` command returns the plot to its initial state. The command `zoom off` turns off the zoom mode. Just `zoom` with no arguments toggles the zoom state of the active *Figure* window. The *Figure* toolbar and *Figure* window menus offer a GUI approach to implementing this feature as well.

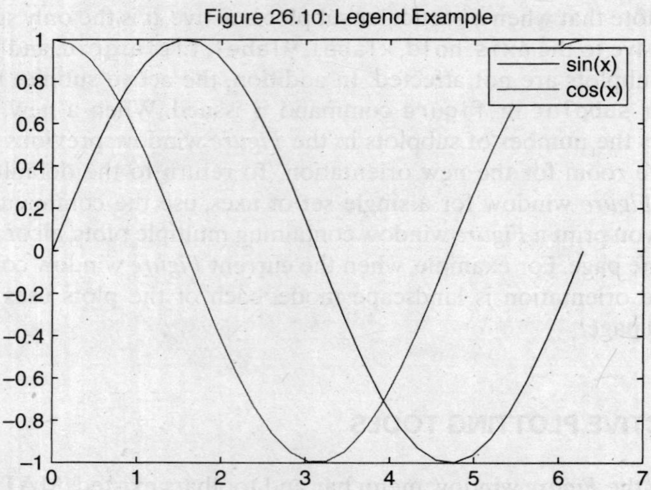

In some situations, it is convenient to select coordinate points from a plot in a *Figure* window. In MATLAB, this feature is embodied in the `ginput` function. The form `[x,y]=ginput(n)` gets `n` points from the current plot or subplot based on mouse click positions within the plot or subplot. If you press the **Return** or **Enter** key before all `n` points are selected, `ginput` terminates with fewer points. The points returned in the vectors `x` and `y` are the respective *x* and *y* data coordinate points selected. The returned data are not necessarily points from the plotted data, but rather the explicit *x*- and *y*-coordinate values where the mouse was clicked. If points are selected outside of the plot or subplot axes limits—for example, outside the plot box—the points returned are extrapolated values.

This function can be somewhat confusing when used in a *Figure* window containing subplots. The data returned is with respect to the current or active subplot. Thus, if `ginput` is issued after a `subplot(2,2,3)` command, the data returned is with respect to the axes of the data plotted in `subplot(2,2,3)`. If points are selected from other subplots, the data is still with respect to the axes of the data in `subplot(2,2,3)`. When an unspecified number of data points are desired, the form `[x,y]=ginput` without an input argument can be used. Here, data points are gathered until the **Return** key is pressed. The `gtext` function (described earlier in this chapter) uses the function `ginput` along with the function `text` for placing text with the mouse.

26.9 SCREEN UPDATES

Because screen rendering is relatively time-consuming, MATLAB does not always update the screen after each graphics command. For example, if the following commands are entered at the MATLAB prompt, MATLAB updates the screen after each graphics command (`plot`, `axis`, and `grid`):

```
>> x = linspace(0,2*pi); y = sin(x);
>> plot(x,y)
>> axis([0 2*pi -1.2 1.2])
>> grid
```

However, if the same graphics commands are entered on a single line, such as

```
>> plot(x,y), axis([0 2*pi -1.2 1.2]), grid
```

then MATLAB renders the figure only once—when the MATLAB prompt reappears. A similar procedure occurs when graphics commands appear as part of a script or function M-file. In this case, even if the commands appear on separate lines in the file, the screen is rendered only once—when all commands are completed and the MATLAB prompt reappears.

In general, six events cause MATLAB to render the screen:

1. A return to the MATLAB prompt
2. Encountering a function that temporarily stops execution, such as `pause`, `keyboard`, `input`, and `waitforbuttonpress`
3. Execution of a `getframe` command
4. Execution of a `drawnow` command
5. Execution of a `figure` command
6. Resizing of a *Figure* window

Of these, only the `drawnow` command specifically allows one to force MATLAB to redraw the screen at arbitrary times.

26.10 SPECIALIZED 2-D PLOTS

Up to this point, the basic plotting function `plot` has been illustrated. In many situations, plotting lines or points on linearly scaled axes does not convey the desired information. As a result, MATLAB offers other basic 2-D plotting functions, as well as specialized plotting functions that are embodied in function M-files.

In addition to `plot`, MATLAB provides the functions `semilogx` for plotting with a logarithmically scaled x-axis, `semilogy` for plotting with a logarithmically scaled y-axis, and `loglog` for plotting with both axes logarithmically spaced. All of the features discussed previously with respect to the function `plot` apply to these functions as well.

The `area` function is useful for building a stacked area plot. The function `area(x,y)` is the same as `plot(x,y)` for vectors `x` and `y`, except that the area under the plot is filled in with color. The lower limit for the filled area may be specified, but defaults to zero. To stack areas, use the form `area(X,Y)`, where `Y` is a matrix and `X` is a matrix or vector whose length equals the number of rows in `Y`. If `X` is omitted, as in the following for example, `area` uses the default value `X=1:size(Y,1)`;

```
>> z = -pi:pi/5:pi;
>> area([sin(z);cos(z)])
>> title('Figure 26.11: Stacked Area Plot')
```

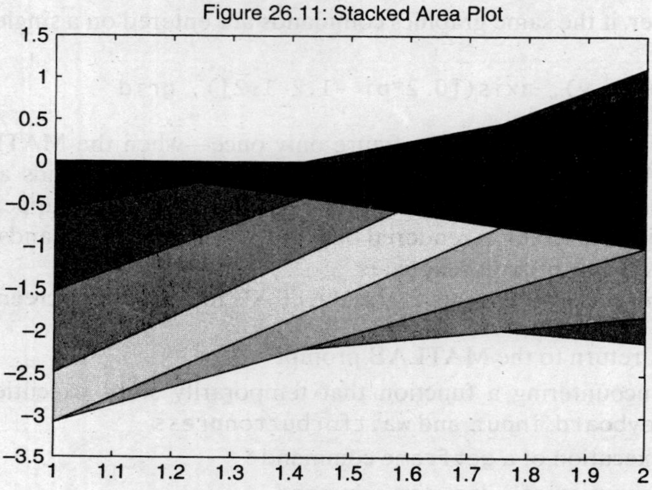

Filled polygons can be drawn by using the `fill` function. The function `fill(x,y,'c')` fills the 2-D polygon defined by the column vectors `x` and `y` with the color specified by `c`. The vertices of the polygon are specified by the pairs `(xi,yi)`. If necessary, the polygon is closed by connecting the last vertex to the first. Like the `plot` function, `fill` can have any number of pairs of vertices and associated colors. Moreover, when `x` and `y` are matrices of the same dimension, the columns of `x` and `y` are assumed to describe separate polygons. In the code

```
>> t = (1:2:15)'*pi/8;
>> x = sin(t);
>> y = cos(t);
>> fill(x,y,'r') % a filled red circle using only 8 data points
>> axis square off
>> text(0,0,'STOP', ..
   'Color',[1 1 1], ...
   'FontSize',80, ...
   'FontWeight','bold', ...
   'HorizontalAlignment','center')
>> title('Figure 26.12: Stop Sign')
```

Figure 26.12: Stop Sign

the text(x,y,'string') function is used with extra arguments. The Color, FontSize, FontWeight, and HorizontalAlignment arguments tell MATLAB to use Handle Graphics to modify the text. Handle Graphics is the name of MATLAB's underlying graphics functions. You can access this rich set of powerful, versatile graphics functions yourself. (See Chapter 31 for more information on these features.)

Standard pie charts can be created by using the pie(a,b) function, where a is a vector of values and b is an optional logical vector describing a slice or slices to be pulled out of the pie chart. The pie3 function renders the pie chart with a 3-D appearance:

```
>> a = [.5 1 1.6 1.2 .8 2.1];
>> pie(a,a==max(a));   % chart a and pull out the biggest slice
>> title('Figure 26.13: Example Pie Chart )
```

Figure 26.13: Example Pie Chart

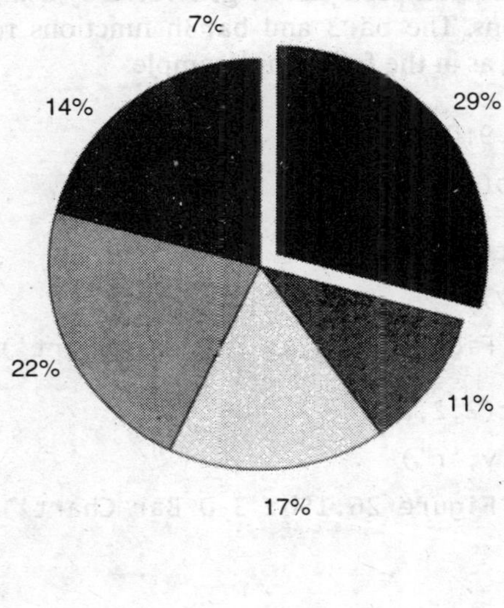

Sometimes it is desirable to plot two different functions on the same axes by using different y-axis scales. The function `plotyy` does just that:

```
>> x = -2*pi:pi/10:2*pi;
>> y = sin(x);
>> z = 3*cos(x);
>> subplot(2,1,1), plot(x,y,x,z)
>> title('Figure 26.14a: Two plots on the same scale.');
>> subplot(2,1,2), plotyy(x,y,x,z)
>> title('Figure 26.14b: Two plots on different scales.');
```

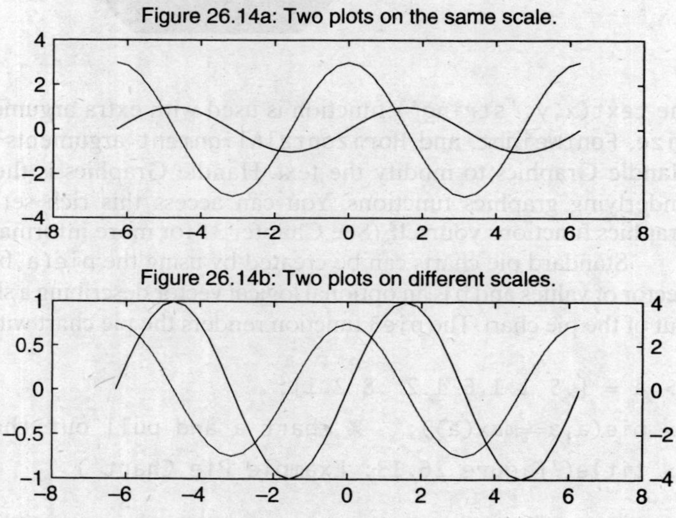

Bar and stair plots can be generated by using the `bar`, `barh`, and `stairs` plotting functions. The `bar3` and `bar3h` functions render the bar charts with a 3-D appearance, as in the following example:

```
>> x = -2.9:0.2:2.9;
>> y = exp(-x.*x);

>> subplot(2,2,1)
>> bar(x,y)
>> title('Figure 26.15a: 2-D Bar Chart')

>> subplot(2,2,2)
>> bar3(x,y,'r')
>> title('Figure 26.15b: 3-D Bar Chart')
```

```
>> subplot(2,2,3)
>> stairs(x,y)
>> title('Figure 26.15c: Stair Chart')

>> subplot(2,2,4)
>> barh(x,y)
>> title('Figure 26.15d: Horizontal Bar Chart')
```

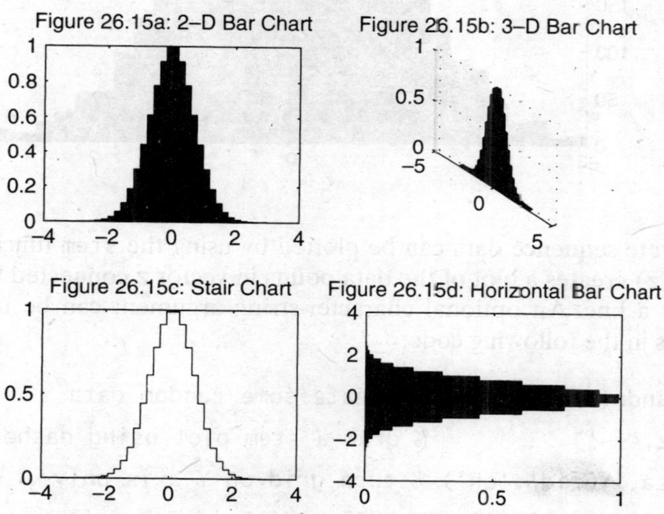

The various bar functions accept a single-color argument for all bars. Bars can be grouped or stacked as well. The form `bar(x,Y)` for vector `x` and matrix `Y` draws groups of bars corresponding to the columns of `Y`. The form `bar(x,Y,'stacked')` draws the bars stacked vertically. The functions `barh`, `bar3`, and `bar3h` have similar options.

Histograms illustrate the distribution of values in a vector. The function `hist(y)` draws a 10-bin histogram for the data in vector `y`. The function `hist(y,n)`, where `n` is a scalar, draws a histogram with `n` bins. The function `hist(y,x)`, where `x` is a vector, draws a histogram using the bins specified in `x`:

```
>> x = -2.9:0.2:2.9;  % specify the bins to use
>> y = randn(5000,1); % generate 5000 random data points

>> hist(y,x)          % draw the histogram
>> title('Figure 26.16: Histogram of Gaussian Data')
```

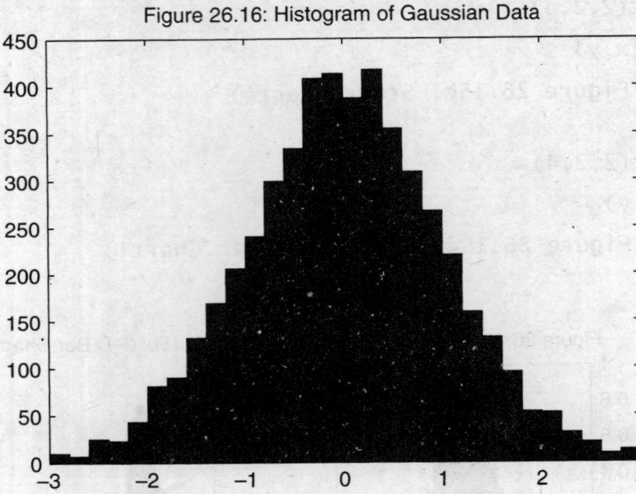

Discrete sequence data can be plotted by using the stem function. The function stem(z) creates a plot of the data points in vector z connected to the horizontal axis by a line. An optional character-string argument can be used to specify linestyle, as in the following code:

```
>> z = randn(30,1);          % create some random data
>> stem(z,'--')              % draw a stem plot using dashed linestyle
>> set(gca,'YGrid','on') % turn grid on Y-axis only
>> title('Figure 26.17: Stem Plot of Random Data')
```

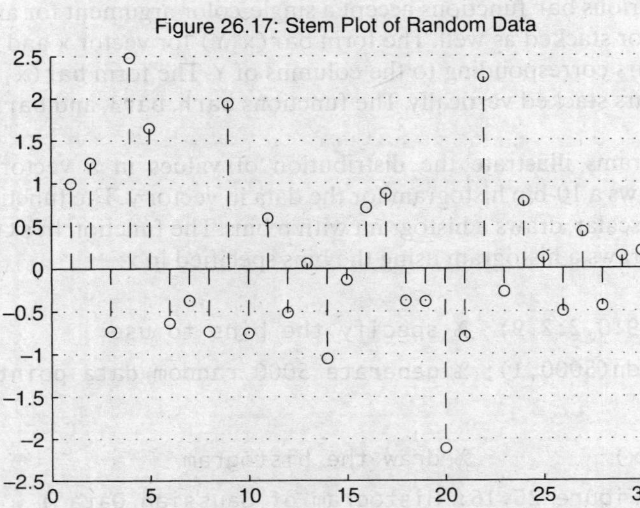

The function stem(x,z) plots the data points in z at the values specified in x.

A plot can include error bars at the data points. The function errorbar(x,y,e) plots the graph of vector x versus vector y with error bars specified by vector e:

```
>> x = linspace(0,2,21); % create a vector
>> y = erf(x);           % y is the error function of x
>> e = rand(size(x))/10; % e contains random error values

>> errorbar(x,y,e)       % create the plot
>> title('Figure 26.18: Errorbar Plot')
```

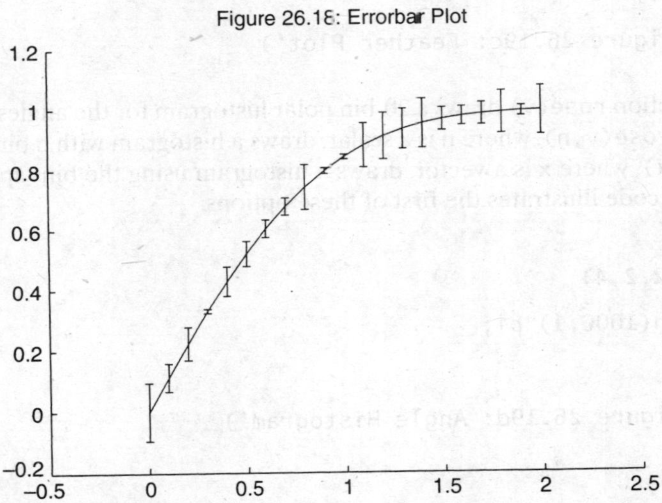

Note that all vectors must be the same length. For each data point (xi,yi), an error bar is drawn a distance ei above and ei below the point:

Plots in polar coordinates can be created by using the polar(t,r,S) function, where t is the angle vector in radians, r is the radius vector, and S is an optional character string describing color, marker symbol, and/or linestyle:

```
>> t = linspace(0,2*pi);
>> r = sin(2*t).*cos(2*t);
>> subplot(2,2,1)
>> polar(t,r), title('Figure 26.19a: Polar Plot')
```

Complex data can be plotted by using compass and feather. The function compass(z) draws a plot that displays the angle and magnitude of the complex elements of z as arrows emanating from the origin. The function `feather(z)` plots the same data by using arrows emanating from equally spaced points on a horizontal line. The functions `compass(x,y)` and `feather(x,y)` are equivalent to `compass(x+i*y)` and `feather(x+i*y)`, respectively. The following example is illustrative:

```
>> z = eig(randn(20));
>> subplot(2,2,2)
>> compass(z)
>> title('Figure 26.19b: Compass Plot')
>> subplot(2,2,3)
>> feather(z)
>> title('Figure 26.19c: Feather Plot')
```

The function `rose(v)` draws a 20-bin polar histogram for the angles in vector v. The function `rose(v,n)`, where n is a scalar, draws a histogram with n bins. The function `rose(v,x)`, where x is a vector, draws a histogram using the bins specified in x. The following code illustrates the first of these options:

```
>> subplot(2,2,4)
>> v = randn(1000,1)*pi;
>> rose(v)
>> title('Figure 26.19d: Angle Histogram')
```

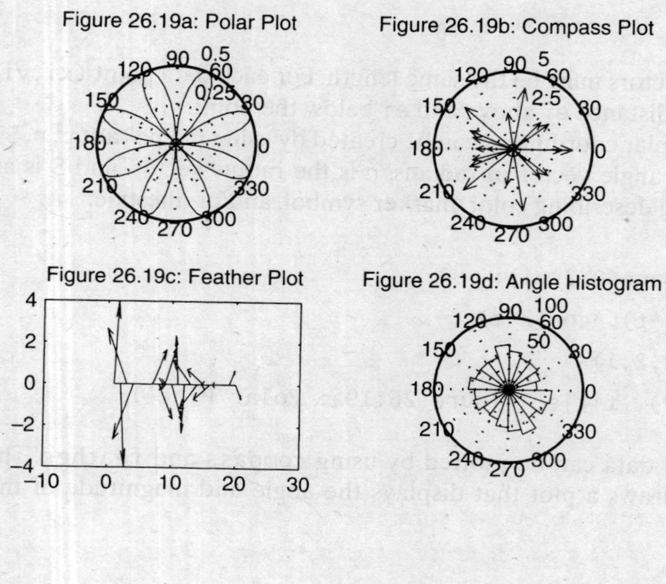

The function `scatter` generates a scatter plot—that is, a plot of circles at data points, where the circle size or color can vary, point by point:

```
>> x = rand(40,1);
>> y = randn(40,1);
>> area = 20+(1:40);
>> scatter(x,y,area)
>> box on
>> title('Figure 26.20: A scatter plot')
```

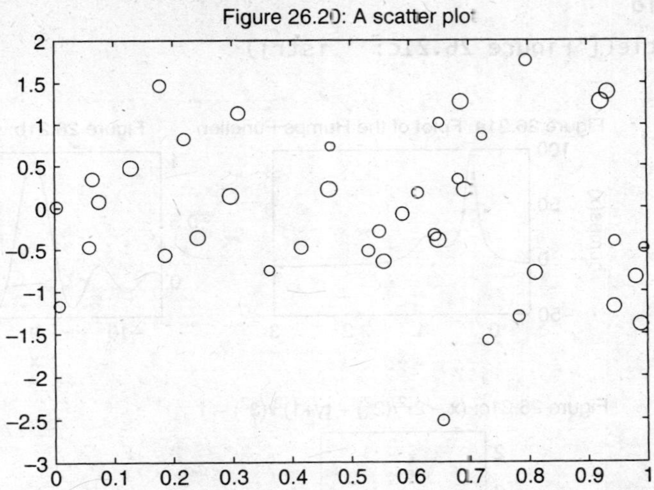

26.11 EASY PLOTTING

When you don't want to take the time to specify the data points explicitly for a plot, MATLAB provides the functions `fplot`, `ezplot`, and `ezpolar`. The function `fplot` plots functions defined by M-file names or function handles. The functions `ezplot` and `ezpolar` plot functions defined by function handles, string expressions, or symbolic math objects, with the obvious difference in plot type. These functions simply spare the user from having to define the data for the independent variable, as the following code indicates:

```
>> subplot(2,2,1)
>> fplot(@humps,[-.5 3])
>> title('Figure 26.21a: Fplot of the Humps Function')
>> xlabel('x')
>> ylabel('humps(x)')
```

```
>> subplot(2,2,2)
>> f_hdl=@(x) sin(x)/x;
>> ezplot(f_hdl,[-15,15])
>> title(['Figure 26.21b: ' sin(x)/x])

>> subplot(2,2,3)
>> istr = '(x-2)^2/(2^2) + (y+1)^2/(3^2) - 1';
>> ezplot(istr,[-2 6 -5 3])
>> axis square
>> grid
>> title(['Figure 26.21c: ' istr])
```

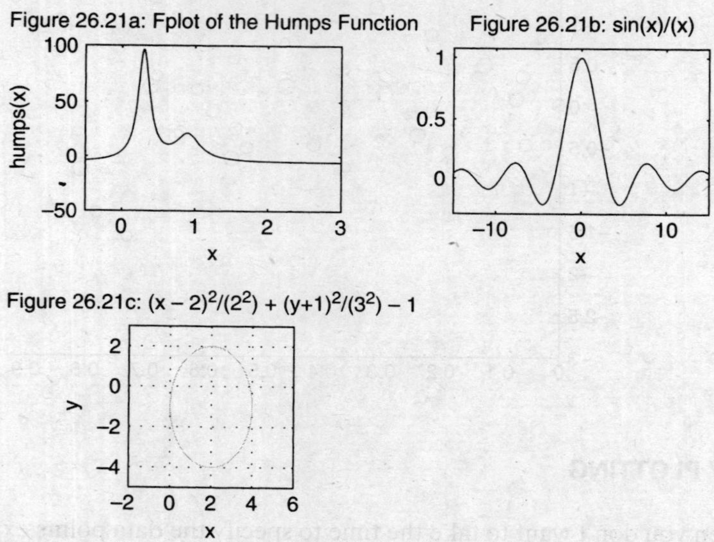

The last example shows that `ezplot` can be used to plot implicit functions. In this case, the string expression is that of an ellipse centered at (2, −1).

26.12 TEXT FORMATTING

Multiline text can be used in any text string, including titles and axis labels, as well as the `text` and `gtext` functions. Simply use string arrays or cell arrays for multiline text. For example,

```
>> xlabel({'This is the first line','and this is the second.'});
```

labels the *x*-axis with two lines of text. Note that the string separator can be a space, a comma, or a semicolon; each style produces the same result. (See Chapter 9 for more details on cell arrays of strings.)

A selection of more than 75 symbols, including Greek letters and other special characters, can be included in MATLAB text strings by embedding commands within the string. The available symbols and the character strings used to define them are listed in the following table (this information can also be found by viewing the `string` property of the *text* Handle Graphics object in the online documentation):

Character Sequence	**Symbol**	**Character Sequence**	**Symbol**	**Character Sequence**	**Symbol**
`\alpha`	α	`\rfloor`	$\rfloor$	`\cong`	$\cong$
`\beta`	β	`\lfloor`	$\lfloor$	`\approx`	$\approx$
`\gamma`	γ	`\perp`	$\perp$	`\Re`	$\Re$
`\delta`	δ	`\wedge`	$\wedge$	`\oplus`	$\oplus$
`\epsilon`	ε	`\rceil`	$\rceil$	`\cup`	$\cup$
`\zeta`	ζ	`\vee`	$\vee$	`\subseteq`	$\subseteq$
`\eta`	η	`\langle`	$\langle$	`\in`	$\in$
`\theta`	θ	`\upsilon`	υ	`\lceil`	$\lceil$
`\vartheta`	ϑ	`\phi`	ϕ	`\cdot`	$\cdot$
`\iota`	ι	`\chi`	χ	`\neg`	$\neg$
`\kappa`	κ	`\psi`	ψ	`\times`	$\times$
`\lambda`	λ	`\omega`	ω	`\surd`	$\surd$
`\mu`	μ	`\Gamma`	Γ	`\varpi`	ϖ
`\nu`	ν	`\Delta`	Δ	`\rangle`	$\rangle$
`\xi`	ξ	`\Theta`	Θ	`\sim`	$\sim$
`\pi`	π	`\Lambda`	Λ	`\leq`	$\leq$
`\rho`	ρ	`\Xi`	Ξ	`\infty`	∞
`\sigma`	σ	`\Pi`	Π	`\clubsuit`	$\clubsuit$
`\varsigma`	ς	`\Sigma`	Σ	`\diamondsuit`	♦
`\tau`	τ	`\Upsilon`	Υ	`\heartsuit`	♥
`\equiv`	$\equiv$	`\Phi`	Φ	`\spadesuit`	$\spadesuit$
`\Im`	$\Im$	`\Psi`	Ψ	`\leftrightarrow`	$\leftrightarrow$
`\otimes`	$\otimes$	`\Omega`	Ω	`\leftarrow`	$\leftarrow$
`\cap`	$\cap$	`\forall`	$\forall$	`\uparrow`	$\uparrow$
`\supset`	$\supset$	`\exists`	$\exists$	`\rightarrow`	$\rightarrow$
`\int`	$\int$	`\ni`	$\ni$	`\downarrow`	$\downarrow$

Character Sequence	Symbol	Character Sequence	Symbol	Character Sequence	Symbol
\circ	°	\neq	≠	\nabla	∇
\pm	±	\aleph	ℵ	\ldots	...
\geq	≥	\wp	℘	\prime	′
\propto	∝	\oslash	Ø	\0	Ø
\partial	∂	\supseteq	⊇	\mid	|
\bullet	•	\subset	⊂	\copyright	©
\div	÷	\o	ο		

In several previous versions of MATLAB, only a limited subset of TEX formatting commands was available. In MATLAB 7, all TEX formatting commands are available. Complete information regarding these commands can be found online. Some of the common and important commands include the following: Superscripts and subscripts are specified by ^ and _, respectively; text font and size are chosen by using the \fontname and \fontsize commands; and a font style are specified by using the \bf, \it, \sl, or \rm command to select a boldface, italic, oblique (or slant), or normal Roman font, respectively. To print the special characters used to define TeX strings, prefix them with the backslash (\) character. The characters affected are the backslash (\), left and right curly braces { }, underscore (_), and carat (^). The following example illustrates the use of TeX formatting commands:

```
>> close % close last Figure window and start over
>> axis([0 1 0 0.5])
>> text(0.2,0.1,'\itE = M\cdotC^{\rm2}')
>> text(0.2,0.2,'\fontsize{16} \nabla \times H = J + \partialD/\partialt')
>> text(0.2,0.3,'\fontname{courier}\fontsize{16}\bf x_{\alpha}+y^{2\pi}')
>> fsstr='f(t) = A_o + \fontsize{30}_\Sigma\fontsize{10}';
>> text(0.2,0.4,[fsstr '[A_ncos(n\omega_ot) + B_nsin(n\omega_ot)]'])
>> title('Figure 26.22: TeX Formatting Examples')
```

Figure 26.22: TeX Formatting Examples

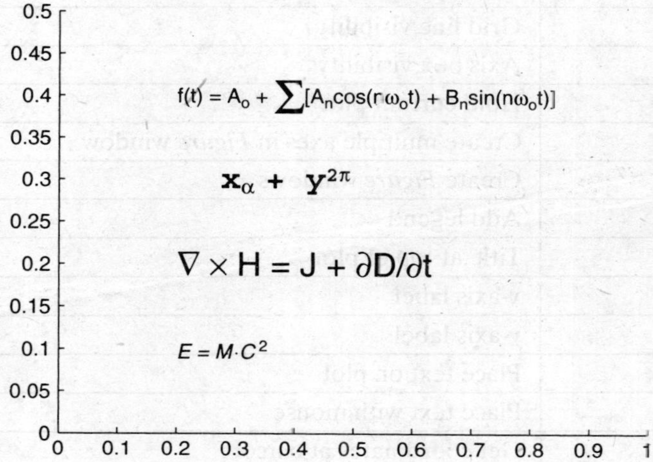

26.13 SUMMARY

The following table lists MATLAB functions for 2-D plotting:

Function	**Description**
`plot`	Linear plot
`loglog`	Log-log plot
`semilogx`	Semilog *x*-axis plot
`semilogy`	Semilog *y*-axis plot
`polar`	Polar coordinate plot
`plotyy`	Linear plot with two *y*-axes
`axis`	Controls axis scaling and appearance
`xlim`	*x*-axis limits
`ylim`	*y*-axis limits
`zlim`	*z*-axis limits
`daspect`	Set and get data aspect ratio, i.e , `axis equal`
`pbaspect`	Set and get plot box aspect ratio, i.e., `axis square`
`zoom`	Zoom in and out

Function	Description
grid	Grid line visibility
box	Axis box visibility
hold	Hold current plot
subplot	Create multiple axes in *Figure* window
figure	Create *Figure* windows
legend	Add legend
title	Title at top of plot
xlabel	*x*-axis label
ylabel	*y*-axis label
text	Place text on plot
gtext	Place text with mouse
ginput	Get coordinates at cursor
area	Filled area plot
bar	Bar graph
barh	Horizontal bar graph
bar3	3-D bar graph
bar3h	3-D horizontal bar graph
compass	Compass graph
errorbar	Linear plot with error bars
ezplot	Easy line plot of string expression
ezpolar	Easy polar plot of string expression
feather	Feather plot
fill	Filled 2-D polygons
fplot	Plot function
hist	Histogram
pareto	Pareto chart
pie	Pie chart
pie3	3-D pie chart
plotmatrix	Scatter plot matrix
ribbon	Linear plot with 2-D lines as ribbons
scatter	Scatter plot
stem	Discrete sequence or stem plot
stairs	Stairstep plot

27

Three-Dimensional Graphics

MATLAB provides a variety of functions to display 3-D data. Some functions plot lines in three dimensions, while others draw surfaces and wire frames. In addition, color can be used to represent a fourth dimension. When color is used in this manner, it is called ***pseudocolor***, since color is not an inherent or natural property of the underlying data in the way that color in a photograph is a natural characteristic of the image. To simplify the discussion of 3-D graphics, the use of color is postponed until the next chapter. In this chapter, the fundamental concepts of producing useful 3-D plots are discussed.

27.1 LINE PLOTS

The `plot` function from the 2-D world is extended into three dimensions with `plot3`. The format is the same as the 2-D `plot`, except that the data is supplied in triplets rather than pairs. The general format of the function call is `plot3(x1,y1,z1,S1,x2,y2,z2,S2,...)`, where `xn`, `yn`, and `zn` are vectors or matrices and `Sn` are optional character strings specifying color, marker symbol, and or linestyle. The function `plot3` is commonly used to plot a 3-D function of a single variable, as in the following example:

```
>> t = linspace(0,10*pi);
>> plot3(sin(t),cos(t),t)
>> xlabel('sin(t)'), ylabel('cos(t)'), zlabel('t')
>> text(0,0,0,'Origin')
>> grid on
```

```
>> title('Figure 27.1: Helix')
>> v = axis
v =
    -1     1    -1     1     0    35
```

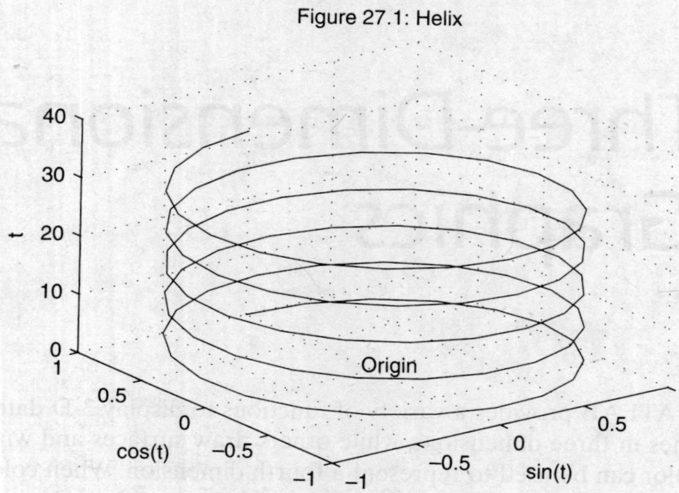

From this simple example, it is apparent that all of the basic features of 2-D graphics exist in 3-D graphics also. The `axis` command extends to 3-D by returning the *z*-axis limits (0 and 35) as two additional elements in the axis vector. There is a `zlabel` function for labeling the *z*-axis. The `grid` command toggles a 3-D grid underneath the plot, and the `box` command creates a 3-D box around the plot. The defaults for `plot3` are `grid off` and `box off`. The function `text(x,y,z,'string')` places a character string at the position identified by the triplet `x,y,z`. In addition, subplots and multiple *Figure* windows apply directly to 3-D graphics functions.

In the last chapter, multiple lines or curves were plotted on top of one another by specifying multiple arguments to the `plot` function or by using the `hold` command. The function `plot3` and the other 3-D graphics functions offer the same capabilities. For example, the added dimension of `plot3` allows multiple 2-D plots to be stacked next to one another along one dimension, rather than directly on top of one another:

```
>> x = linspace(0,3*pi);  % x-axis data
>> z1 = sin(x);           % plot in x-z plane
>> z2 = sin(2*x);
>> z3 = sin(3*x);
>> y1 = zeros(size(x));   % spread out along y-axes
>> y3 = ones(size(x));    % by giving each curve different y-axis values
```

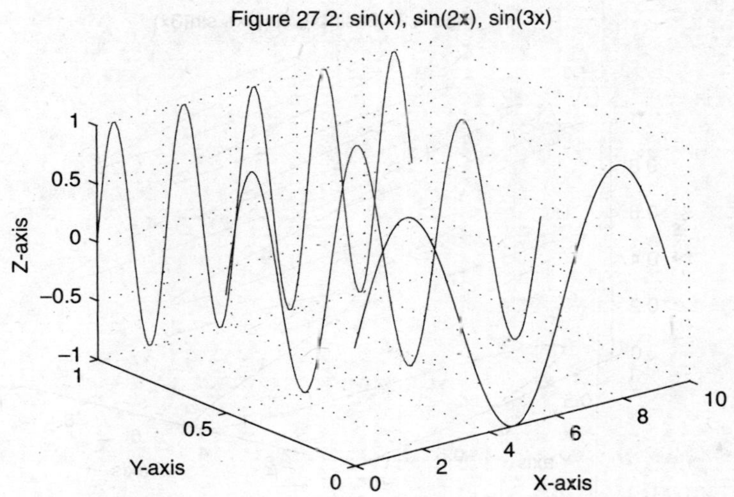


```
>> y2 = y3/2;
>> plot3(x,y1,z1,x,y2,z2,x,y3,z3)
>> grid on
>> xlabel('X-axis'), ylabel('Y-axis'), zlabel('Z-axis')
>> title('Figure 27.2: sin(x), sin(2x), sin(3x)')
>> pause(5)
>> plot3(x,z1,y1,x,z2,y2,x,z3,y3)
>> grid on
>> xlabel('X-axis'), ylabel('Y-axis'), zlabel('Z-axis')
>> title('Figure 27.3: sin(x), sin(2x), sin(3x)')
```

27.2 SCALAR FUNCTIONS OF TWO VARIABLES

As opposed to generating line plots with `plot3`, it is often desirable to visualize a scalar function of two variables—that is,

$$z = f(x, y)$$

Here, each pair of values for x and y produces a value for z. A plot of z as a function of x and y is a surface in three dimensions. To plot this surface in MATLAB, the values for z are stored in a matrix. As described in the section on 2-D interpolation, given that x and y are the independent variables, z is a matrix of the dependent variable and the association of x and y with z is

`z(i,:) = f(x,y(i))` and `z(:,j) = f(x(j),y)`

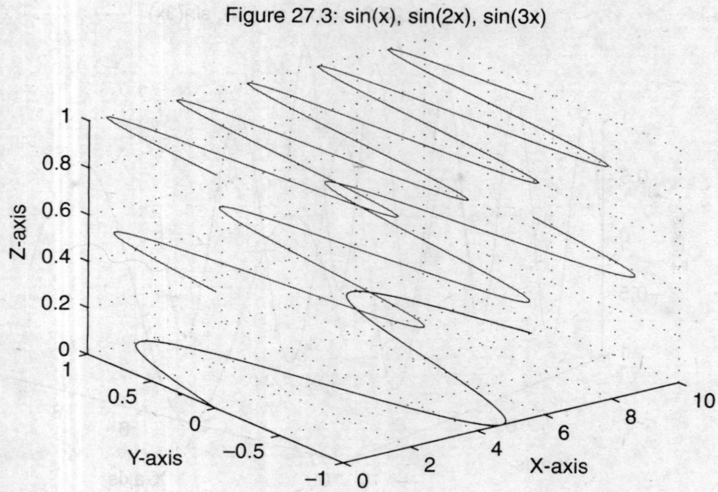

That is, the *i*th row of z is associated with the *i*th element of y, and the *j*th column of z is associated with the *j*th element of x.

When z=f(x,y) can be expressed simply, it is convenient to use array operations to compute all of the values of z in a single statement. To do so requires that we create matrices of all *x*- and *y*-values in the proper orientation. This orientation is sometimes called ***plaid*** by *The Mathworks Inc.* MATLAB provides the function meshgrid to perform this step:

```
>> x = -3:3;  % choose x-axis values
>> y = 1:5;   % y-axis values
>> [X,Y] = meshgrid(x,y)
X =
    -3    -2    -1     0     1     2     3
    -3    -2    -1     0     1     2     3
    -3    -2    -1     0     1     2     3
    -3    -2    -1     0     1     2     3
    -3    -2    -1     0     1     2     3
Y =
     1     1     1     1     1     1     1
     2     2     2     2     2     2     2
     3     3     3     3     3     3     3
     4     4     4     4     4     4     4
     5     5     5     5     5     5     5
```

As you can see, `meshgrid` duplicated `x` for each of the five rows in `y`. Similarly, it duplicated `y` as a column for each of the seven columns in `x`.

> An easy way to remember which variable is duplicated which way by `meshgrid` is to think about 2-D plots. The x-axis varies from left to right, just as the `X` output of `meshgrid` does. Similarly the y-axis varies from bottom to top, just as the `Y` output of `meshgrid` does.

Given `X` and `Y`, if $z = f(x,y) = (x + y)^2$, then the matrix of data values defining the 3-D surface is given simply as

```
>> Z = (X+Y).^2
Z =
     4     1     0     1     4     9    16
     1     0     1     4     9    16    25
     0     1     4     9    16    25    36
     1     4     9    16    25    36    49
     4     9    16    25    36    49    64
```

When a function cannot be expressed simply, you must use For Loops or While Loops to compute the elements of `Z`. In many cases, it may be possible to compute the elements of `Z` rowwise or columnwise. For example, if it is possible to compute `Z` rowwise, the following script file fragment can be helpful:

```
x= ???  % ostatement defining vector of x axis values
y= ???  % statement defining vector of y axis values

nx = length(x);     % length of x is no. of rows in Z
ny = length(y);     % length of y is no. of columns in Z
Z = zeros(nx,ny);   % initialize Z matrix for speed

for r=1:nx
   (preliminary commands)
   Z(r,:)= {a function of y and x(r) cefining r-th row of Z}
end
```

On the other hand, if `Z` can be computed columnwise, the following script file fragment can be helpful:

```
x= ??? % statement defining vector of x axis values
y= ??? % statement defining vector of y axis values

nx = length(x);    % length of x is no. of rows in Z
ny = length(y);    % length of y is no. of columns in Z
Z = zeros(nx,ny);  % initialize Z matrix for speed

for c=1:ny
  (preliminary commands)
  Z(:,c)= {a function of y(c) and x defining c-th column of Z}
end
```

Only when the elements of Z must be computed element by element does the computation usually require a nested For Loop, such as in the following script file fragment:

```
x= ??? % statement defining vector of x axis values
y= ??? % statement defining vector of y axis values
nx = length(x);    % length of x is no. of rows in Z
ny = length(y);    % length of y is no. of columns in Z
Z = zeros(nx,ny);  % initialize Z matrix for speed
for r=1:nx
  for c=1:ny
    (preliminary commands)
    Z(r,c)= {a function of y(c) and x(r) defining (r,c)-th element}
  end
end
```

27.3 MESH PLOTS

MATLAB defines a ***mesh*** surface by the z-coordinates of points above a rectangular grid in the x-y plane. It forms a mesh plot by joining adjacent points with straight lines. The result looks like a fishing net with knots at the data points. The following example is illustrative:

```
>> [X,Y,Z] = peaks(30);
>> mesh(X,Y,Z)
>> xlabel('X-axis'), ylabel('Y-axis'), zlabel('Z-axis')
>> title('Figure 27.4: Mesh Plot of Peaks')
```

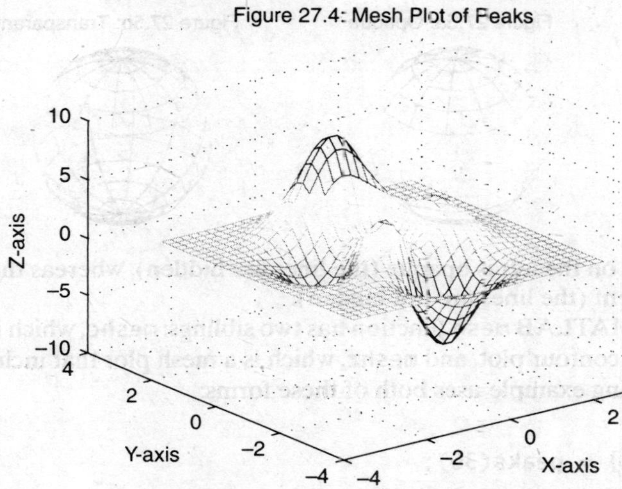

Note on your monitor how the line colors are related to the height of the mesh. In general, mesh accepts optional arguments to control color use in the plot. (This ability to change how MATLAB uses color is discussed in the next chapter.) The use of color is called pseudocolor, since color is used to add a fourth effective dimension to the graph. Note also that the plot was drawn with a grid. ***Most 3-D plots, other than*** **`plot3`** ***and a few other exceptions, default to*** **`grid on`**.

In addition to these input arguments, mesh and most 3-D plot functions can also be called with a variety of input arguments. The syntax used here is the most specific, in that information is supplied for all three axes. The function mesh(Z) plots the matrix z versus its row and column indices. The most common variation is to use the vectors that were passed to meshgrid for the *x*- and *y*- axes—for example, mesh(x,y,Z).

As shown in the previous figure, the areas between the mesh lines are opaque rather than transparent. The MATLAB command hidden controls this aspect of mesh plots:

```
>> [X,Y,Z]=sphere(12);
>> subplot(1,2,1)
>> mesh(X,Y,Z), title('Figure 27.5a: Opaque')
>> hidden on
```

```
>> axis square off
>> subplot(1,2,2)
>> mesh(X,Y,Z), title('Figure 27.5b: Transparent')
>> hidden off
>> axis square off
```

Figure 27.5a: Opaque   Figure 27.5b: Transparent

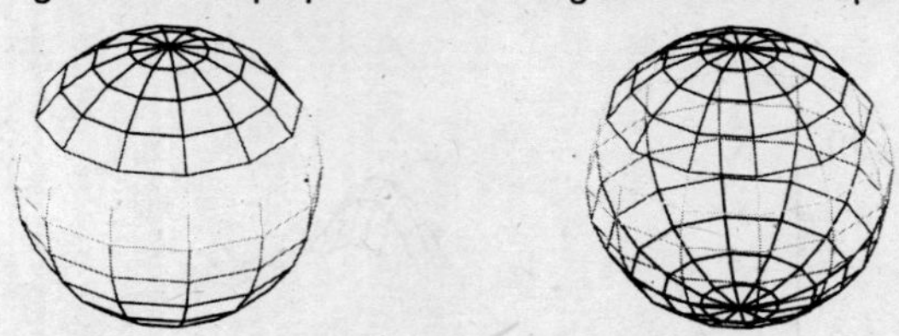

The sphere on the left is opaque (the lines are hidden), whereas the one on the right is transparent (the lines are not hidden).

The MATLAB mesh function has two siblings: meshc, which is a mesh plot and underlying contour plot, and meshz, which is a mesh plot that includes a zero plane. The following example uses both of these forms:

```
>> [X,Y,Z] = peaks(30);
>> meshc(X,Y,Z)  % mesh plot with underlying contour plot
>> title('Figure 27.6: Mesh Plot with Contours')
>> pause(5)
>> meshz(X,Y,Z)  % mesh plot with zero plane
>> title('Figure 27.7: Mesh Plot with Zero Plane')
```

Figure 27.6: Mesh Plot with Contours

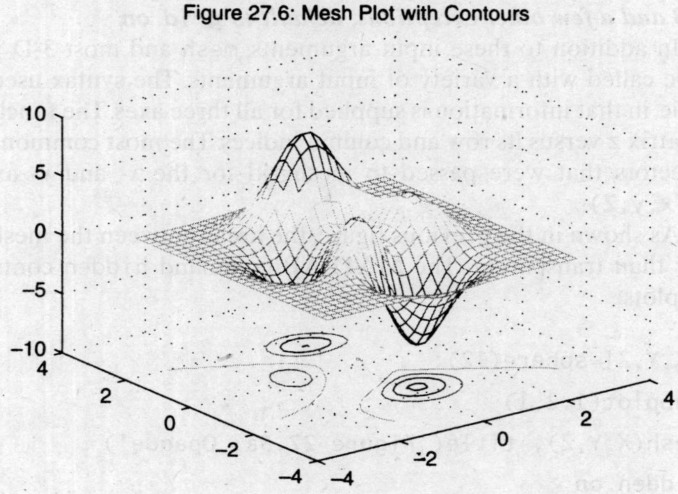

Figure 27.7: Mesh Plot with Zero Plane

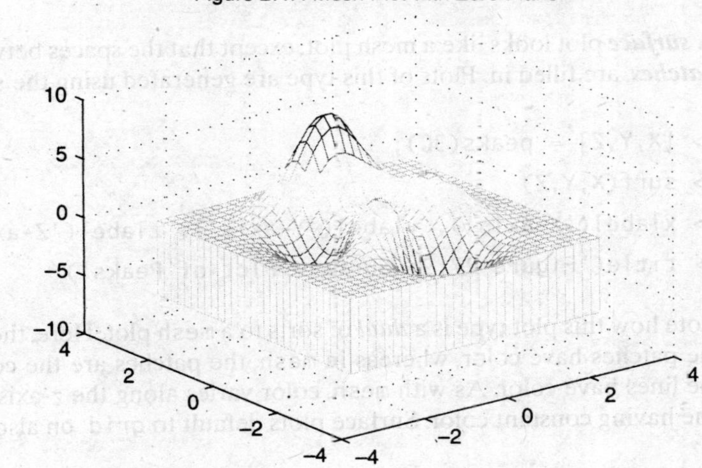

The function `waterfall` is identical to `mesh`, except that the mesh lines appear only in the *x*-direction:

```
>> waterfall(X,Y,Z)
>> xlabel('X-axis'), ylabel('Y-axis'), zlabel('Z-axis')
>> title('Figure 27.8: Waterfall Plot')
```

Figure 27.8: Waterfall Plot

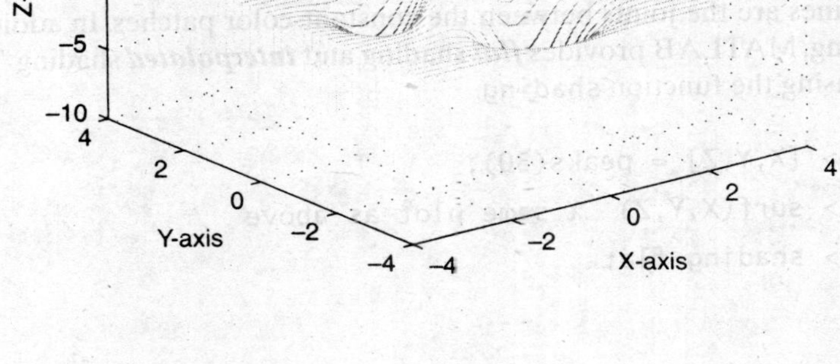

27.4 SURFACE PLOTS

A ***surface*** plot looks like a mesh plot, except that the spaces between the lines, called ***patches***, are filled in. Plots of this type are generated using the `surf` function:

```
>> [X,Y,Z] = peaks(30);
>> surf(X,Y,Z)
>> xlabel('X-axis'), ylabel('Y-axis'), zlabel('Z-axis')
>> title('Figure 27.9: Surface Plot of Peaks')
```

Note how this plot type is a *dual* of sorts to a `mesh` plot. Here, the lines are black and the patches have color, whereas in `mesh`, the patches are the color of the axes and the lines have color. As with `mesh`, color varies along the z-axis, with each patch or line having constant color. Surface plots default to `grid on` also.

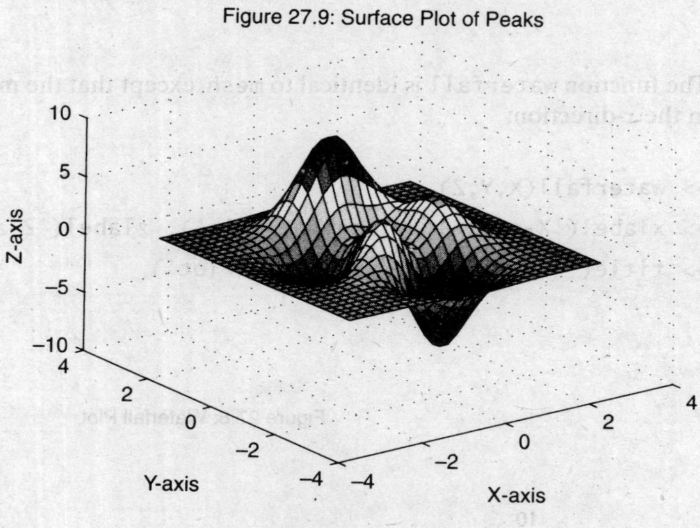

In a surface plot, one does not think about hidden line removal as in a `mesh` plot, but rather about different ways to shade the surface. In the preceding `surf` plot, the shading is ***faceted*** like a stained-glass window or object, where the black lines are the joints between the constant-color patches. In addition to faceted shading, MATLAB provides ***flat*** shading and ***interpolated*** shading. These are applied by using the function `shading`:

```
>> [X,Y,Z] = peaks(30);
>> surf(X,Y,Z)  % same plot as above
>> shading flat
```

Figure 27.10: Surface Plot with Flat Shading

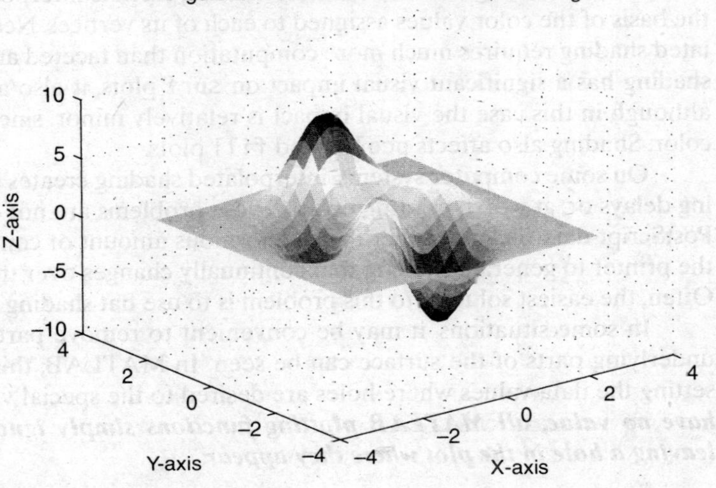


```
>> xlabel('X-axis'), ylabel('Y-axis'), zlabel('Z-axis')
>> title('Figure 27.10: Surface Plot with Flat Shading')
>> pause(5)
>> shading interp
>> title('Figure 27.11: Surface Plot with Interpolated Shading')
```

In flat shading, the black lines are removed and each patch retains its single color, whereas in interpolated shading, the lines are also removed but each patch is given

Figure 27.11: Surface Plot with Interpolated Shading

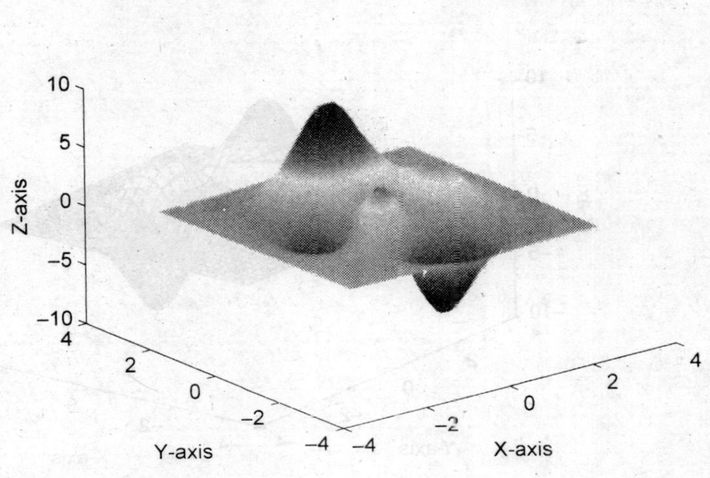

interpolated shading. That is, the color of each patch is interpolated over its area on the basis of the color values assigned to each of its vertices. Needless to say, interpolated shading requires much more computation than faceted and flat shading. While shading has a significant visual impact on `surf` plots, it also applies to `mesh` plots; although in this case the visual impact is relatively minor, since only the lines have color. Shading also affects `pcolor` and `fill` plots.

On some computer systems, interpolated shading creates extremely long printing delays or, at worst, printing errors. These problems are not due to the size of the PostScript data file, but rather to the enormous amount of computation required in the printer to generate shading that continually changes over the surface of the plot. Often, the easiest solution to this problem is to use flat shading for printouts.

In some situations, it may be convenient to remove part of a surface so that underlying parts of the surface can be seen. In MATLAB, this is accomplished by setting the data values where holes are desired to the special value NaN. ***Since NaNs have no value, all MATLAB plotting functions simply ignore NaN data points, leaving a hole in the plot where they appear:***

```
>> [X,Y,Z] = peaks(30);
>> x = X(1,:);                 % vector of x axis
>> y = Y(:,1);                 % vector of y axis
>> i = find(y>.8 & y<1.2);     % find y axis indices of hole
>> j = find(x>-.6 & x<.5);     % find x axis indices of hole
>> Z(i,j) = nan;               % set values at hole indices to NaNs
>> surf(X,Y,Z)
>> xlabel('X-axis'), ylabel('Y-axis'), zlabel('Z-axis')
>> title('Figure 27.12: Surface Plot with a Hole')
```

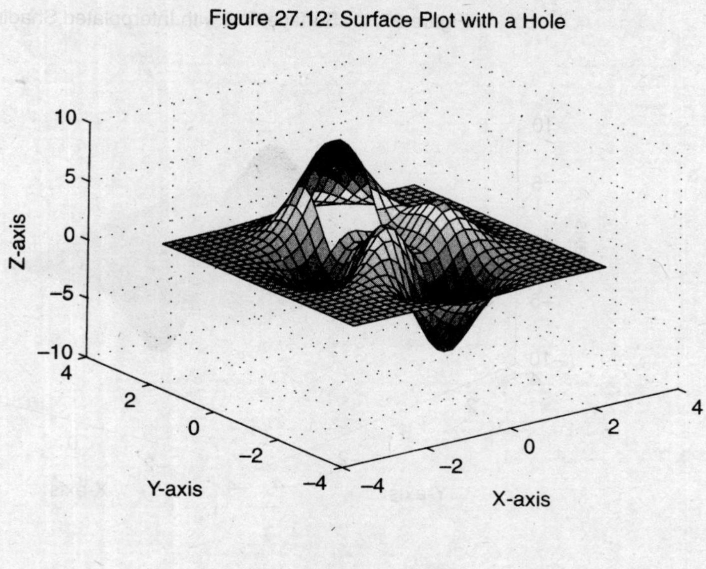

The MATLAB surf function also has two siblings: surfc, which is a surface plot and underlying contour plot, and surfl, which is a surface plot with lighting. Both are used in the following code:

```
>> [X,Y,Z] = peaks(30);
>> surfc(X,Y,Z)  % surf plot with contour plot
>> xlabel('X-axis'), ylabel('Y-axis'), zlabel('Z-axis')
>> title('Figure 27.13: Surface Plot with Contours')
>> pause(5)
>> surfl(X,Y,Z)    % surf plot with lighting
>> shading interp  % surfl plots look best with interp shading
>> colormap pink   % they also look better with shades of a single color
>> xlabel('X-axis'), ylabel('Y-axis'), zlabel('Z-axis')
>> title('Figure 27.14: Surface Plot with Lighting')
```

The function surfl makes a number of assumptions regarding the light applied to the surface. It does not use the *light* object. Rather, it simply modifies the color of the surface to give the appearance of lighting. (The next chapter provides more rigorous information regarding light properties.) Also, in the preceding commands, colormap is a MATLAB function for applying a different set of colors to a figure. (This function is discussed in the next chapter as well.)

The surfnorm(X,Y,Z) function computes surface normals for the surface defined by X, Y, and Z; plots the surface; and plots vectors normal to the surface at the data points:

Figure 27.13: Surface Plot with Contours

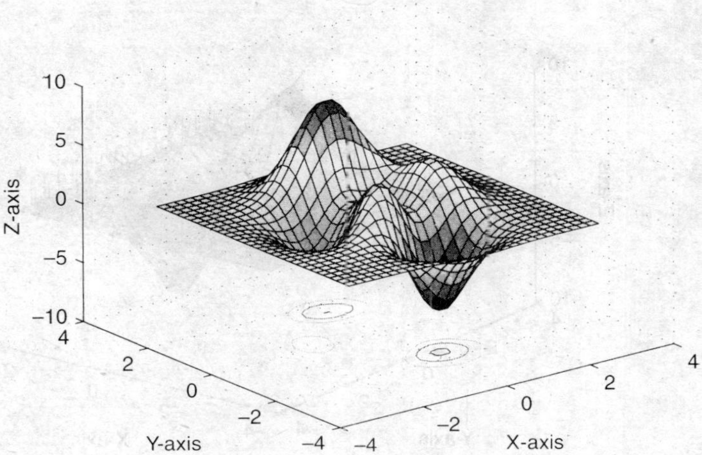

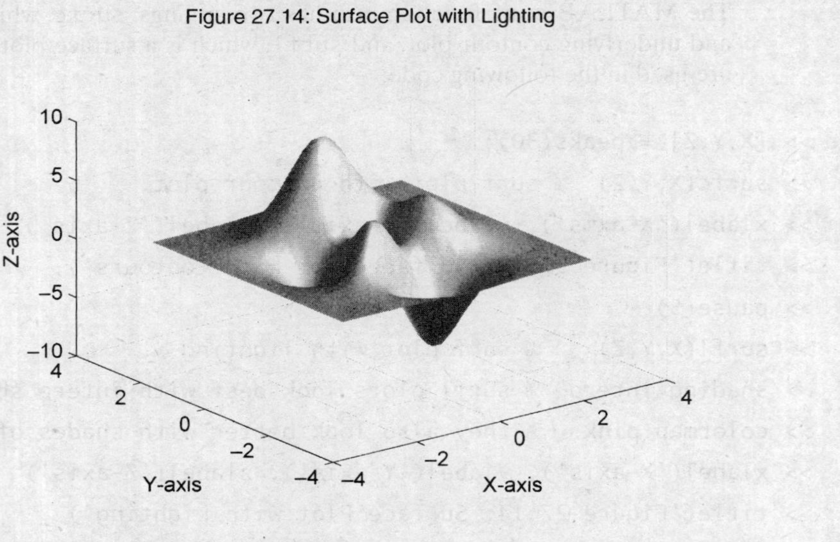


```
>> [X,Y,Z] = peaks(15);
>> surfnorm(X,Y,Z)
>> xlabel('X-axis'), ylabel('Y-axis'), zlabel('Z-axis')
>> title('Figure 27.15: Surface Plot with Normals')
```

Note that the surface normals are unnormalized and valid at each vertex. The form `[Nx,Ny,Nz]=surfnorm(X,Y,Z)` computes the 3-D surface normals and returns their components, but does not plot the surface.

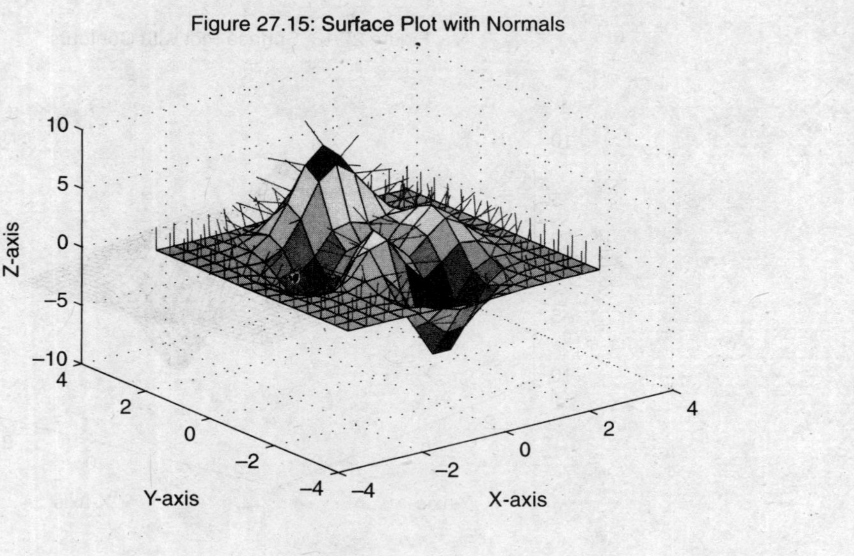

27.5 MESH AND SURFACE PLOTS OF IRREGULAR DATA

Irregular or nonuniformly spaced data can be visualized using the functions `trimesh`, `trisurf`, and `voronoi`:

```
>> x = rand(1,50);
>> y = rand(1,50);
>> z = peaks(x,y*pi);
>> t = delaunay(x,y);
>> trimesh(t,x,y,z)
>> hidden off
>> title('Figure 27.16: Triangular Mesh Plot')
>> pause(5)
>> trisurf(t,x,y,z)
>> title('Figure 27.17: Triangular Surface Plot')
>> pause(5)
>> voronoi(x,y)
>> title('Figure 27.18: Voronoi Plot')
```

(See Chapter 19 for more information on Delaunay triangulation and Voronoi diagrams.)

Figure 27.16: Triangular Mesh Plot

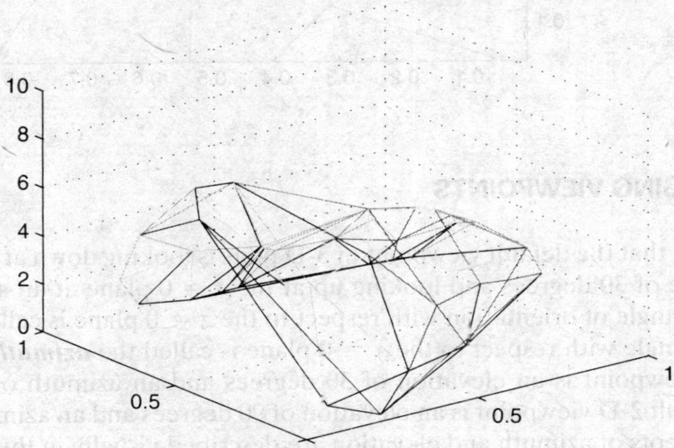

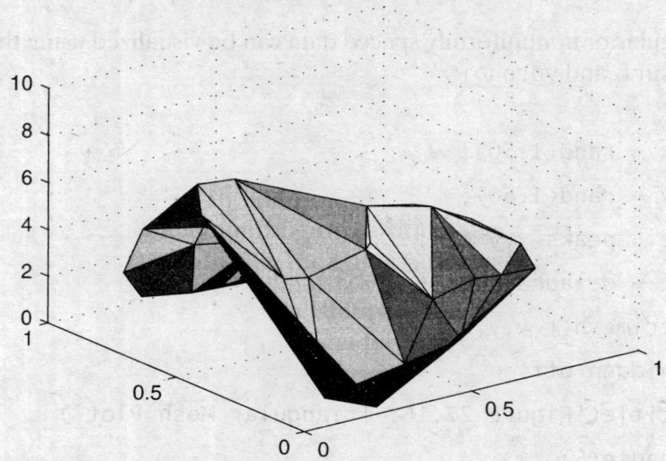

Figure 27.17: Triangular Surface Plot

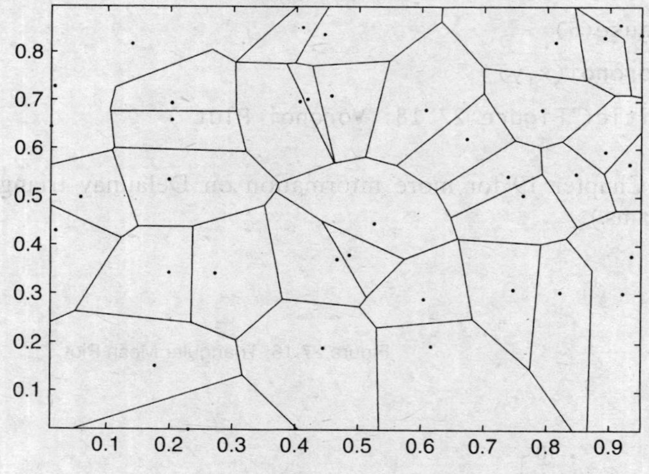

Figure 27.18: Voronoi Plot

27.6 CHANGING VIEWPOINTS

Note that the default viewpoint of 3-D plots is looking down at the $z = 0$ plane at an angle of 30 degrees and looking up at the $x = 0$ plane at an angle of 37.5 degrees. The angle of orientation with respect to the $z = 0$ plane is called the ***elevation***, and the angle with respect to the $x = 0$ plane is called the ***azimuth***. Thus, the default 3-D viewpoint is an elevation of 30 degrees and an azimuth of −37.5 degrees. The default 2-D viewpoint is an elevation of 90 degrees and an azimuth of 0 degrees. The concepts of azimuth and elevation are described visually in the following figure.

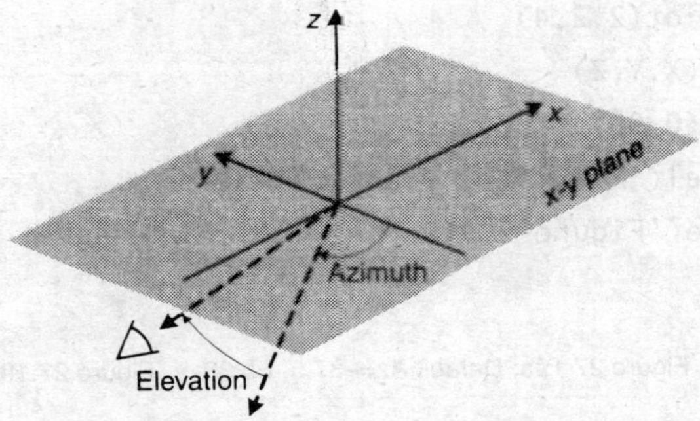

In MATLAB, the function `view` changes the graphical viewpoint for all types of 2-D and 3-D plots. The forms `view(az,el)` and `view([az,el])` change the viewpoint to the specified azimuth az and elevation `el`:

```
>> x = -7.5:.5:7.5; y = x;                % create a data set
>> [X,Y] = meshgrid(x,y);
>> R = sqrt(X.^2+Y.^2)+eps;
>> Z = sin(R)./R;
>> subplot(2,2,1)
>> surf(X,Y,Z)
>> view(-37.5,30)
>> xlabel('X-axis'), ylabel('Y-axis'), zlabel('Z-axis')
>> title('Figure 27.19a: Default Az = -37.5, El = 30')

>> subplot(2,2,2)
>> surf(X,Y,Z)
>> view(-37.5+90,30)
>> xlabel('X-axis'), ylabel('Y-axis'), zlabel('Z-axis')
>> title('Figure 27.19b: Az Rotated to 52.5')

>> subplot(2,2,3)
>> surf(X,Y,Z)
>> view(-37.5,60)
>> xlabel('X-axis'), ylabel('Y-axis'), zlabel('Z-axis')
>> title('Figure 27.19c: El Increased to 60')
```

```
>> subplot(2,2,4)
>> surf(X,Y,Z)
>> view(0,90)
>> xlabel('X-axis'), ylabel('Y-axis')
>> title('Figure 27.19d: Az = 0, El = 90')
```

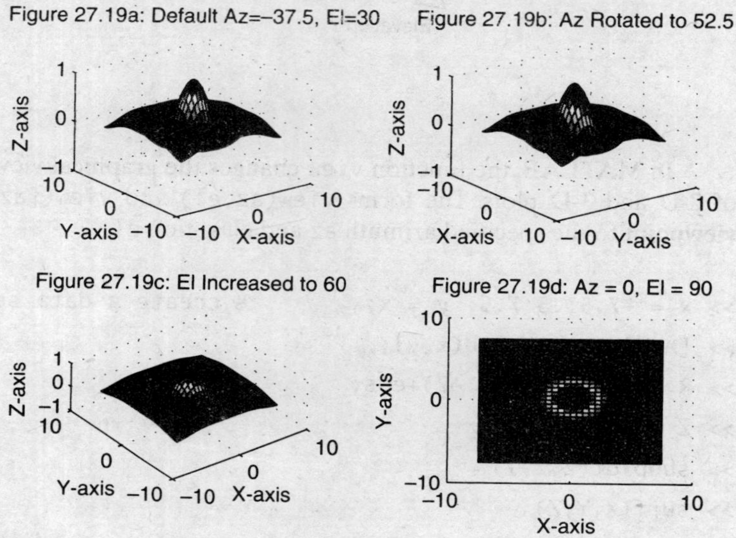

In addition to these forms, `view` offers additional features that are summarized in its online documentation and in its help text:

```
>> help view
 VIEW   3-D graph viewpoint specification.
   VIEW(AZ,EL) and VIEW([AZ,EL]) set the angle of the view from which an
   observer sees the current 3-D plot.  AZ is the azimuth or horizontal
   rotation and EL is the vertical elevation (both in degrees). Azimuth
   revolves about the z-axis, with positive values indicating counter-
   clockwise rotation of the viewpoint. Positive values of elevation
   correspond to moving above the object; negative values move below.
   VIEW([X Y Z]) sets the view angle in cartesian coordinates. The
   magnitude of vector X,Y,Z is ignored.

   Here are some examples:
```

```
AZ = -37.5, EL = 30 is the default 3-D view.
AZ = 0, EL = 90 is directly overhead and the default 2-D view.
AZ = EL = 0 looks directly up the first column of the matrix.
AZ = 180 is behind the matrix.

VIEW(2) sets the default 2-D view, AZ = 0, EL = 90.
VIEW(3) sets the default 3-D view, AZ = -37.5, EL = 30.

[AZ,EL] = VIEW returns the current azimuth and elevation.

VIEW(T) accepts a 4-by-4 transformation matrix, such as
the perspective transformations generated by VIEWMTX.

T = VIEW returns the current general 4-by-4 transformation matrix.

See also VIEWMTX, the AXES properties View, Xform.
```

In addition to the `view` function, the viewpoint can be set interactively with the mouse by using the function `rotate3d`. The function `rotate3d on` turns on mouse-based view rotation, `rotate3d off` turns it off, and `rotate3d` with no arguments toggles the state. This functionality is also available on the **Tools** menu in a *Figure* window, as well as on a button on the *Figure* toolbar. In reality, the **Rotate 3D** menu item and toolbar button both call `rotate3d` to do the requested work.

27.7 CAMERA CONTROL

The viewpoint control provided by the `view` function is convenient, but limited in capabilities. To provide complete control of a 3-D scene, camera capabilities are needed. That is, one must have all of the capabilities available when filming a movie with a camera. Alternatively, one must have all of the capabilities available in a 3-D computer or console game environment. In this environment, there are two 3-D coordinate systems to manage: one at the camera and one at what the camera is pointed at (i.e., the camera target). The camera functions in MATLAB manage and manipulate the relationships between these two coordinate systems and provide control over the camera lens.

Use of the camera functions in MATLAB is generally not easy for a novice. Therefore, to simplify the use of these functions, most are made available interactively from the **Tools** menu or from the *Camera* toolbar in a *Figure* window. To view the *Camera* toolbar, choose it from the **View** menu in the *Figure* window. By using the interactive camera tools, you avoid dealing with the input and output arguments that the *Command* window functions require. Given the ease with which the interactive tools can be used, the complexity involved in using and describing the camera functions, and the relatively small number of potential users, camera functions are not described in this text. The MATLAB documentation contains a rigorous discussion of these functions and their use. The camera functions available in MATLAB are listed at the end of this chapter.

27.8 CONTOUR PLOTS

Contour plots show lines of constant elevation or height. If you've ever seen a topographical map, you know what a contour plot looks like. In MATLAB, contour plots in 2-D and 3-D are generated by using the `contour` and `contour3` functions, respectively:

```
>> [X,Y,Z] = peaks;
>> subplot(1,2,1)
>> contour(X,Y,Z,20)            % generate 20 2-D contour lines
>> axis square
>> xlabel('X-axis'), ylabel('Y-axis')
>> title('Figure 27.20a: 2-D Contour Plot')
>> subplot(1,2,2)
>> contour3(X,Y,Z,20)           % the same contour plot in 3-D
>> xlabel('X-axis'), ylabel('Y-axis'), zlabel('Z-axis')
>> title('Figure 27.20b: 3-D Contour Plot')
```

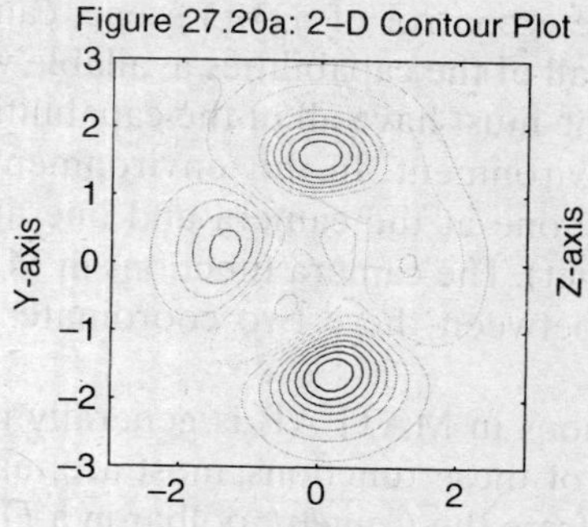

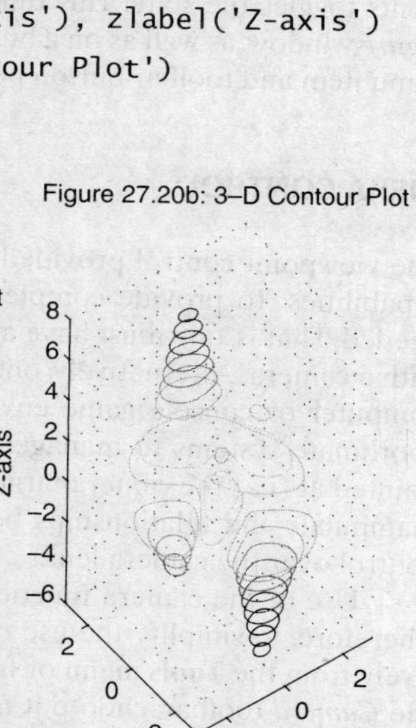

The pcolor function maps height to a set of colors and presents the same information as the contour plot, at the same scale:

```
>> subplot(1,2,1)
>> pcolor(X,Y,Z)
>> shading interp  % remove the grid lines
>> axis square
>> title('Figure 27.21a: Pseudocolor Plot')
```

Combining the idea of a pseudocolor plot with a 2-D contour produces a filled contour plot. In MATLAB, this plot is generated by the function contourf:

```
>> subplot(1,2,2)
>> contourf(X,Y,Z,12)          % filled contour plot with 12 contours
>> axis square
>> xlabel('X-axis'), ylabel('Y-axis')
>> title('Figure 27.21b: Filled Contour Plot')
```

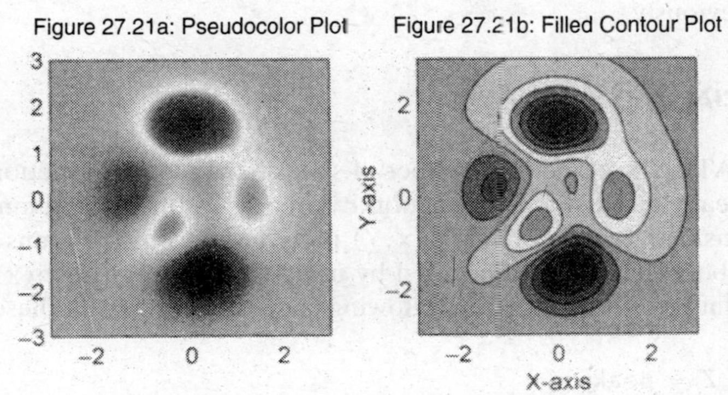

Contour lines can be labeled by using the clabel function, which requires a matrix of lines and optional text strings that are returned by contour, contourf, and contour3:

```
>> C = contour(X,Y,Z,12);
>> clabel(C)
>> title('Figure 27.22: Contour Plot With Labels')
```

Alternatively, inline labels are generated by using two arguments returned by the contour functions. For example, modifying the preceding MATLAB code to [C,h]=contour(X,Y,Z,12); clabel(C,h) produces inline labels that follow the

Figure 27.22: Contour Plot With Labels

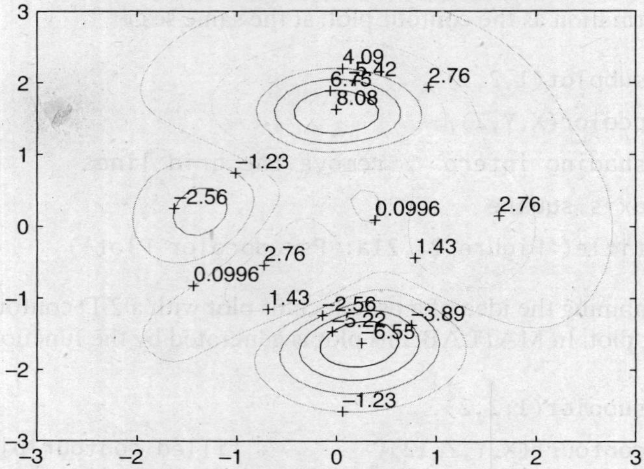

contours. Finally, by using the mouse, you can select which contours to label by providing `'manual'` as the last input argument to `clabel`. Inline or horizontal labels are used, depending on the presence of the second argument `h`, as illustrated previously.

27.9 SPECIALIZED 3-D PLOTS

MATLAB provides a number of specialized plotting functions in addition to those already discussed. The function `ribbon(Y)` plots the columns of `Y` as separate ribbons. The function `ribbon(x,Y)` plots `x` versus the columns of `Y`. The width of the ribbons can also be specified by using the syntax `ribbon(x,Y,width)`, where the default width is 0.75. The following code uses the first of these forms:

```
>> Z = peaks;
>> ribbon(Z)
>> title('Figure 27.23: Ribbon Plot of Peaks')
```

The function `quiver(x,y,dx,dy)` draws directional or velocity vectors `(dx,dy)` at the points `(x,y)`:

```
>> [X,Y,Z] = peaks(16);
>> [DX,DY] = gradient(Z,.5,.5);
>> contour(X,Y,Z,10)
>> hold on
>> quiver(X,Y,DX,DY)
```

Figure 27.23: Ribbon Plot of Feaks

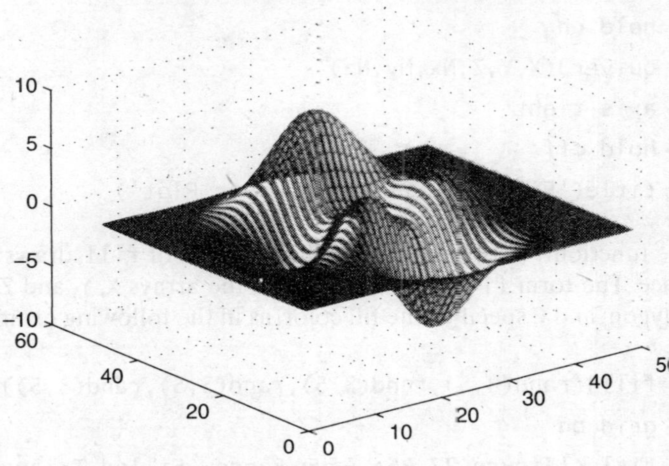


```
>> hold off
>> title('Figure 27.24: 2-D Quiver Plot')
```

Three-dimensional quiver plots of the form `quiver3(x,y,z,Nx,Ny,Nz)` display the vectors `(Nx,Ny,Nz)` at the points `(x,y,z)`:

```
>> [X,Y,Z] = peaks(20);
>> [Nx,Ny,Nz] = surfnorm(X,Y,Z);
```

Figure 27.24: 2–D Quive⁻ Plot

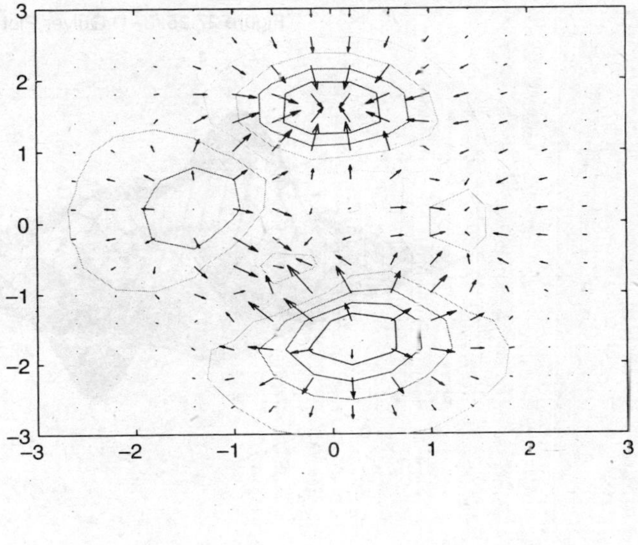

```
>> surf(X,Y,Z)
>> hold on
>> quiver3(X,Y,Z,Nx,Ny,Nz)
>> axis tight
>> hold off
>> title('Figure 27.25: 3-D Quiver Plot')
```

The function `fill3`, being the 3-D equivalent of `fill`, draws filled polygons in 3-D space. The form `fill3(X,Y,Z,C)` uses the arrays `X`, `Y`, and `Z` as the vertices of the polygon; and `C` specifies the fill color, as in the following example:

```
>> fill3(rand(3,5),rand(3,5),rand(3,5),rand(3,5))
>> grid on
>> title('Figure 27.26: Five Random Filled Triangles')
```

The 3-D equivalent of `stem` plots discrete sequence data in 3-D space. The form `stem3(X,Y,Z,C,'filled')` plots the data points in `(X,Y,Z)` with lines extending to the *x–y* plane. The optional argument `C` specifies the marker style or color, and the optional `'filled'` argument causes the marker to be filled in. The `stem3(Z)` function plots the points in `Z` and automatically generates `X` and `Y` values. The following code uses `stem3` with three arguments:

```
>> Z = rand(5);
>> stem3(Z,'ro','filled');
>> grid on
>> title('Figure 27.27: Stem Plot of Random Data')
```

Figure 27.25: 3–D Quiver Plot

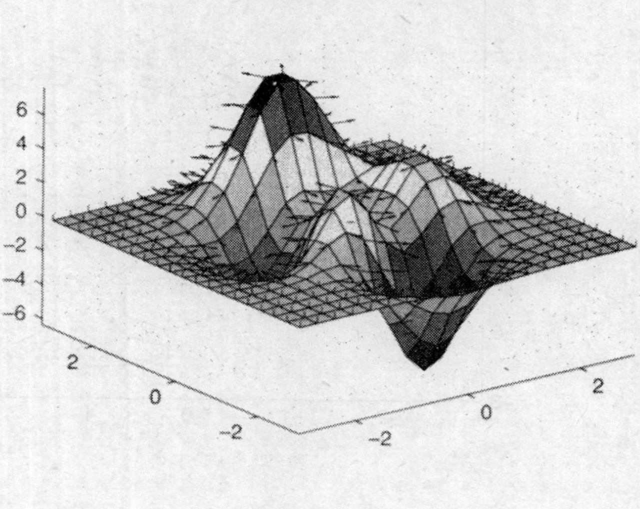

Figure 27.26: Five Random Filled Triangles

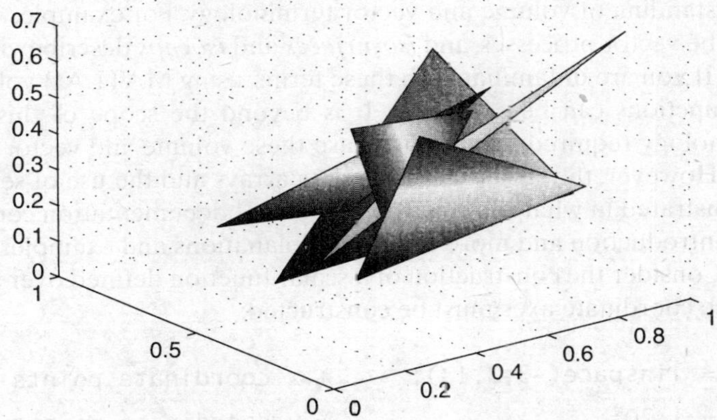

Figure 27.27: Stem Plot of Random Data

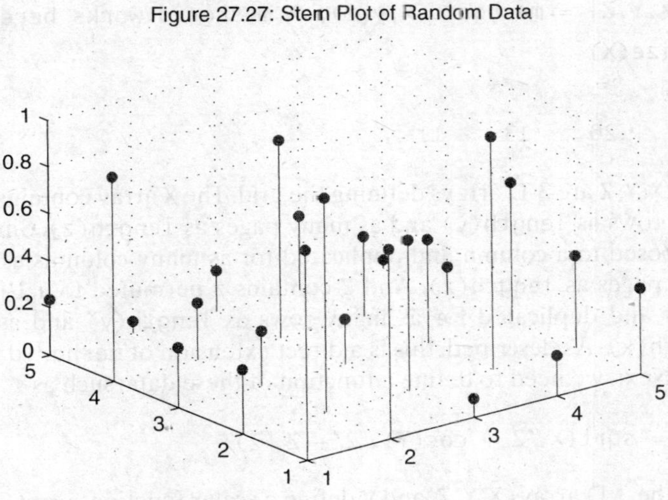

27.10 VOLUME VISUALIZATION

In addition to the common mesh, surface, and contour plots, MATLAB offers a variety of more complex volume and vector visualization functions. These functions construct plots of scalar and vector quantities in 3-D space. Because they generally construct volumes rather than surfaces, their input arguments are 3-D arrays, one for each axis x, y, and z. The points in each 3-D array define a grid of coordinates or data at the coordinates. For scalar functions, four 3-D arrays are required, one for each of the three coordinate axes, plus one for the scalar data at the coordinate points. These arrays are commonly identified as X, Y, Z, and V, respectively. For vector functions, six 3-D arrays are required, one for each of the three coordinate axes, plus one for each axis component of the vector at the coordinate points. These arrays are commonly identified as X, Y, Z, U, V, and W, respectively.

Use of the volume and vector visualization functions in MATLAB requires an understanding of volume and vector terminology. For example, *divergence* and *curl* describe vector processes, and *isosurfaces* and *isocaps* describe visual aspects of volumes. If you are unfamiliar with these terms, using MATLAB volume and visualization functions can be confusing. It is beyond the scope of this text to cover the terminology required to rigorously use these volume and vector visualization functions. However, the structure of the data arrays and the use of several functions are demonstrated in what follows. The MATLAB documentation contains a more thorough introduction and more rigorous explanations and examples.

Consider the construction of a scalar function defined over a volume. First, the volume coordinate axes must be constructed:

```
>> x = linspace(-3,3,13);          % x coordinate points
>> y = 1:20;                       % y coordinate points
>> z = -5:5;                       % z coordinate points
>> [X,Y,Z] = meshgrid(x,y,z); % meshgrid works here too!
>> size(X)
ans =
       20     13     11
```

Here, X, Y, Z are 3-D arrays defining the grid. The X array contains x duplicated for as many rows as `length(y)` and as many pages as `length(z)`. Similarly, Y contains y transposed to a column and duplicated for as many columns as `length(x)` and as many pages as `length(z)`. And Z contains z permuted to a 1-by-1-by-`length(z)` vector and duplicated for as many rows as `length(y)` and as many columns as `length(x)`. As described, this is a direct extension of `meshgrid` to 3-D.

Next, we need to define a function of these data, such as

```
>> V = sqrt(X.^2 + cos(Y).^2 + Z.^2);
```

Now, the 3-D arrays X, Y, Z, and V define a scalar function $v = f(x,y,z)$ defined over a volume. To visualize what this looks like, we can look at slices along planes:

```
>> slice(X,Y,Z,V,[0 3],[5 15],[-3 5])
>> xlabel('X-axis')
>> ylabel('Y-axis')
>> zlabel('Z-axis')
>> title('Figure 27.28: Slice Plot Through a Volume')
```

This plot shows slices on planes defined by $x = 0$, $x = 3$, $y = 5$, $y = 15$, $z = -3$, and $z = 5$, as shown by the last three arguments to the function `slice`. The color of the plot is mapped to the values in V on the slices.

Figure 27.28: Slice Plot Through a Volume

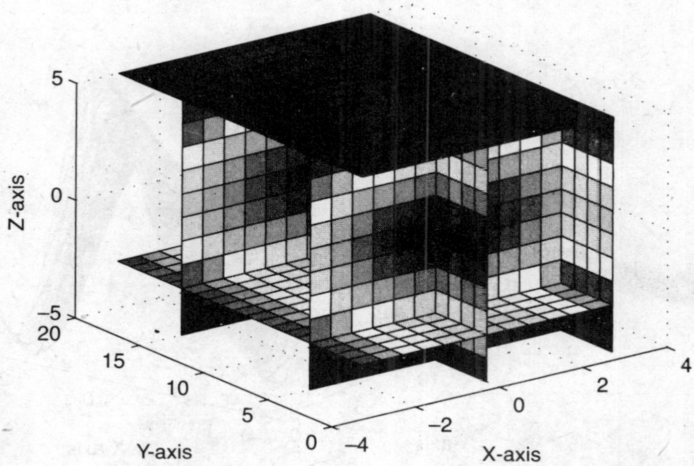

The slices displayed need not be planes. They can be any surface, as generated by the following code:

```
>> [xs,ys] = meshgrid(x,y);
>> zs = sin(-xs+ys/2); % a surface to use
>> slice(X,Y,Z,V,xs,ys,zs)
>> xlabel('X-axis')
>> ylabel('Y-axis')
>> zlabel('Z-axis')
>> title('Figure 27.29: Slice Plot Using a Surface')
```

Here, xs, ys, and zs define a surface to slice through the volume.

Going back to the original slice plot, it is possible to add contour lines to selected planes by using the contourslice function:

```
>> slice(X,Y,Z,V,[0 3],[5 15],[-3 5])
>> hold on
>> h = contourslice(X,Y,Z,V,3,[5 15],[]);
>> set(h,'EdgeColor','k','Linewidth',1.5)
>> xlabel('X-axis')
>> ylabel('Y-axis')
>> zlabel('Z-axis')
>> title('Figure 27.30: Slice Plot with Selected Contours')
>> hold off
```

Figure 27.29: Slice Plot Using a Surface

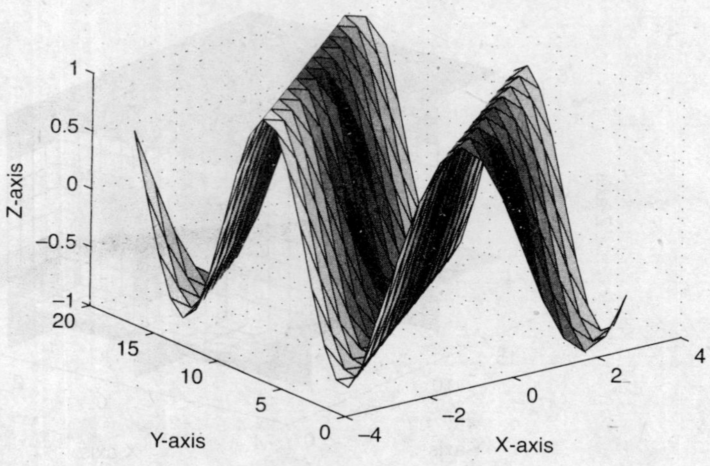

Here, contour lines are added to the $x = 3$, $y = 5$, and $y = 15$ planes. With the use of Handle Graphics features, the contour lines are set to black and their width is set to 1.5 points.

In addition to looking at slices through a volume, surfaces where the scalar volume data `V` has a specified value can be plotted by using the `isosurface` function. This function returns triangle vertices in a manner similar to Delaunay triangulation, the results being in the form required by the `patch` function, which plots the triangles:

Figure 27.30: Slice Plot with Selected Contours

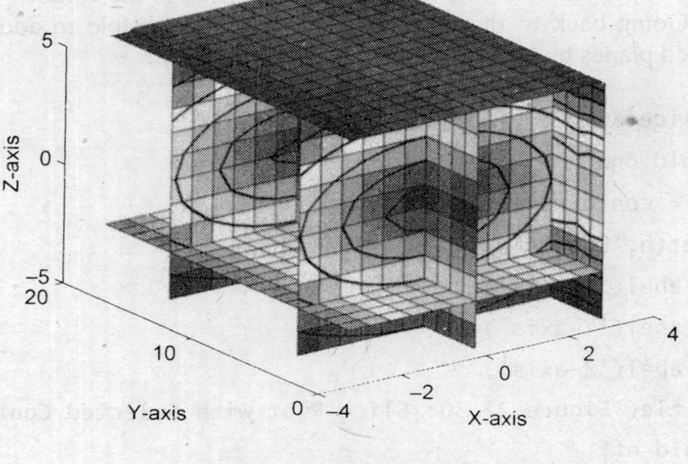

```
>> [X,Y,Z,V] = flow(13);                 % get flow data
>> fv = isosurface(X,Y,Z,V,-2);          % find surface of value -2

>> subplot(1,2,1)
>> p = patch(fv);                        % plot V = -2 surface
>> set(p,'FaceColor',[.5 .5 .5],'EdgeColor','Black'); % modify patches
>> view(3), axis equal tight, grid on % pretty it up
>> title({'Figure 27.31a:' 'Isosurface Plot, V = 2'})

>> subplot(1,2,2)
>> p = patch(shrinkfaces(fv,.3));        % shrink faces to 30% of original
>> set(p,'Facecolor',[.5 .5 .5],'EdgeColor','Black'); % modify patches
>> view(3), axis equal tight, grid on % pretty it up
>> title({'Figure 27.31b:' 'Shrunken Face Isosurface Plot, V = 2'})
```

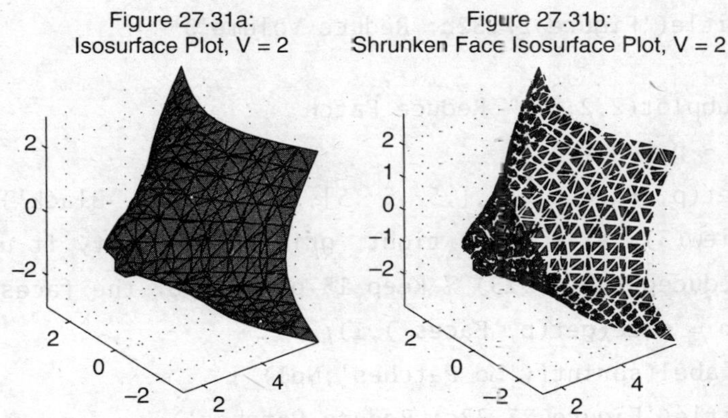

The preceding plots also demonstrate the use of the function `shrinkfaces`, which does exactly what its name suggests.

Sometimes volume data contain too many points for efficient display. The functions `reducevolume` and `reducepatch` represent two ways to improve the display of an isosurface. The function `reducevolume` eliminates data before the isosurface is formed, whereas `reducepatch` seeks to eliminate patches while minimizing distortion in the underlying surface. The following code is illustrative:

```
>> [X,Y,Z,V] = flow;
>> fv = isosurface(X,Y,Z,V,-2);
>> subplot(2,2,1) % Original
```

```
>> p = patch(fv);
>> Np = size(get(p,'Faces'),1);
>> set(p,'FaceColor',[.5 .5 .5],'EdgeColor','Black');
>> view(3), axis equal tight, grid on  % pretty it up
>> zlabel(sprintf('%d Patches',Np))
>> title('Figure 27.32a: Original')

>> subplot(2,2,2) % Reduce Volume
>> [Xr,Yr,Zr,Vr] = reducevolume(X,Y,Z,V,[3 2 2]);
>> fvr = isosurface(Xr,Yr,Zr,Vr,-2);
>> p = patch(fvr);
>> Np = size(get(p,'Faces'),1);
>> set(p,'FaceColor',[.5 .5 .5],'EdgeColor','Black');
>> view(3), axis equal tight, grid on  % pretty it up
>> zlabel(sprintf('%d Patches',Np))
>> title('Figure 27.32b: Reduce Volume')

>> subplot(2,2,3) % Reduce Patch
>> p = patch(fv);
>> set(p,'FaceColor',[.5 .5 .5],'EdgeColor','Black');
>> view(3), axis equal tight, grid on  % pretty it up
>> reducepatch(p,.15) % keep 15 percent of the faces
>> Np = size(get(p,'Faces'),1);
>> zlabel(sprintf('%d Patches',Np))
>> title('Figure 27.32c: Reduce Patches')

>> subplot(2,2,4) % Reduce Volume and Patch
>> p = patch(fvr);
>> set(p,'FaceColor',[.5 .5 .5],'EdgeColor','Black');
>> view(3), axis equal tight, grid on  % pretty it up
>> reducepatch(p,.15) % keep 15 percent of the faces
>> Np = size(get(p,'Faces'),1);
>> zlabel(sprintf('%d Patches',Np))
>> title('Figure 27.32d: Reduce Both')
```

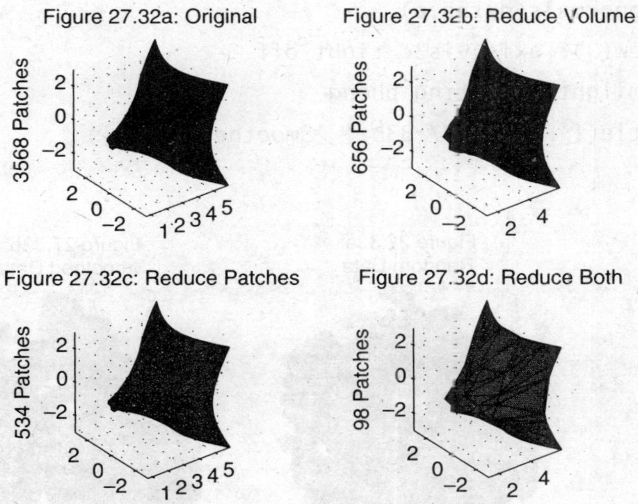

Three-dimensional data can also be smoothed by filtering it with the `smooth3` function, as in the following code:

```
>> data = rand(10,10,10);                % random data
>> datas = smooth3(data,'box',3); % smoothed data

>> subplot(1,2,1) % random data
>> p = patch(isosurface(data,.5), ...
   'FaceColor','Blue','EdgeColor','none');
>> patch(isocaps(data,.5), ...
   'FaceColor', 'interp', 'EdgeColor', 'none');
>> isonormals(data,p)
>> view(3); axis vis3d tight off
>> camlight; lighting phong
>> title({'Figure 27.33a:' 'Random Data'})

>> subplot(1,2,2) % smoothed random data
>> p = patch(isosurface(datas,.5), ...
   'FaceColor','Blue','EdgeColor','none');
>> patch(isocaps(datas,.5), ...
   'FaceColor', 'interp', 'EdgeColor', 'none');
```

```
>> isonormals(datas,p)
>> view(3); axis vis3d tight off
>> camlight; lighting phong
>> title({'Figure 27.33b:' 'Smoothed Data'})
```

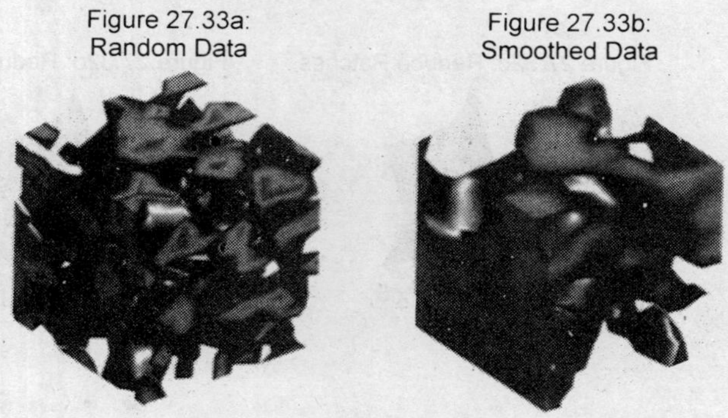

This example demonstrates the use of the functions isocaps and isonormals. The function isocaps creates the faces on the outer surfaces of the block. The function isonormals modifies properties of the drawn patches, so that lighting works correctly.

27.11 EASY PLOTTING

For those occasions when you don't want to take the time to specify the data points explicitly for a 3-D plot, MATLAB provides the functions ezcontour, ezcontour3, ezmesh, ezmeshc, ezplot3, ezsurf, and ezsurfc. These functions construct plots like their equivalents without the ez prefix. However, the input arguments are functions defined by function handles, string expressions, or symbolic math objects and, optionally, the axis limits over which the plot is to be generated. Internally, the functions compute the data and generate the desired plot, as in the following example:

```
>> fstr = ['3*(1-x).^2.*exp(-(x.^2) - (y+1).^2)' ...
   ' - 10*(x/5 - x.^3 - y.^5).*exp(-x.^2-y.^2)' ...
   ' - 1/3*exp(-(x+1).^2 - y.^2)'];

>> subplot(2,2,1)
>> ezmesh(fstr)
>> title('Figure 27.34a: Mesh of peaks(x,y)')
>> subplot(2,2,2)
```

```
>> ezsurf(fstr)
>> title('Figure 27.34b: Surf of peaks(x,y)')
>> subplot(2,2,3)
>> ezcontour(fstr)
>> title('Figure 27.34c: Contour of peaks(x,y)')
>> subplot(2,2,4)
>> ezcontourf(fstr)
>> title('Figure 27.34d: Contourf of peaks(x,y)')
```

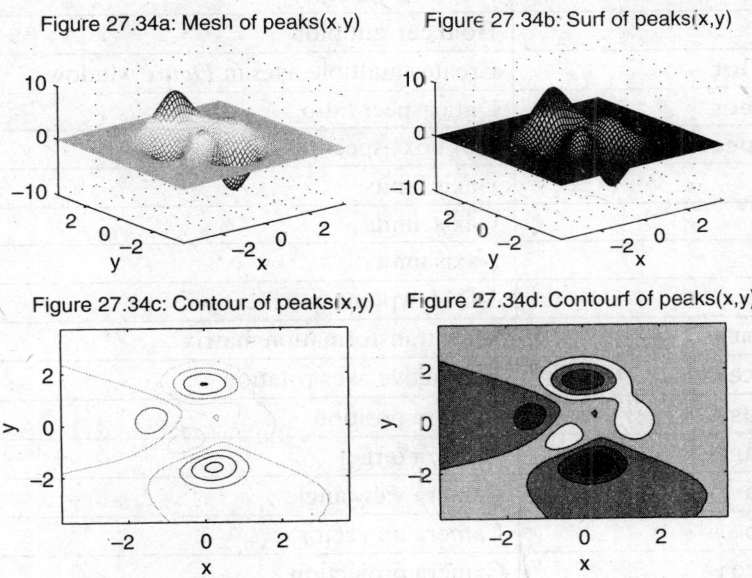

27.12 SUMMARY

The following table documents MATLAB functions for 3-D plotting:

Function	Description
`plot3`	Plot lines and points in 3-D space
`mesh`	Mesh surface
`meshc`	Mesh with underlying contour plot
`meshz`	Mesh with zero plane
`surf`	Surface plot

Function	Description
`surfc`	Surface plot with underlying contour plot
`surfl`	Surface plot with basic lighting
`fill3`	Filled 3-D polygons
`shading`	Color shading mode
`hidden`	Mesh hidden line removal
`surfnorm`	Surface normals
`axis`	Control axis scaling and appearance
`grid`	Grid line visibility
`box`	Axis box visibility
`hold`	Hold current plot
`subplot`	Creates multiple axes in *Figure* window
`daspect`	Data aspect ratio
`pbaspect`	Plot box aspect ratio
`xlim`	*x*-axis limits
`ylim`	*y*-axis limits
`zlim`	*z*-axis limits
`view`	3-D viewpoint specification
`viewmtx`	View transformation matrix
`rotate3d`	Interactive axes rotation
`campos`	Camera position
`camtarget`	Camera target
`camva`	Camera view angle
`camup`	Camera up vector
`camproj`	Camera projection
`camorbit`	Camera orbit
`campan`	Pan camera
`camdolly`	Dolly camera
`camzoom`	Zoom camera
`camroll`	Roll camera
`camlookat`	Look at specific object
`camlight`	Camera lighting creation and placement
`title`	Plot title
`xlabel`	*x*-axis label
`ylabel`	*y*-axis label
`zlabel`	*z*-axis label

Function	Description
`text`	Places text on plot
`gtext`	Places text with mouse
`contour`	Contour plot
`contourf`	Filled contour plot
`contour3`	3-D contour plot
`clabel`	Contour labeling
`pcolor`	Pseudocolor plot
`voronoi`	Voronoi diagram
`trimesh`	Triangular mesh plot
`trisurf`	Triangular surface plot
`scatter3`	3-D scatter plot
`stem3`	3-D stem plot
`waterfall`	Waterfall plot
`ezmesh`	Easy mesh plot of string expression
`ezmeshc`	Easy mesh plot with contour plot of string expression
`ezplot3`	Easy 3-D linear plot of string expression
`ezsurf`	Easy surface plot of string expression
`ezsurfc`	Easy surface plot with contour plot of string expression
`ezcontour`	Easy contour plot of string expression
`ezcontourf`	Easy filled contour plot of string expression
`vissuite`	Help for visualization suite
`isosurface`	Isosurface extractor
`isonormals`	Isosurface normals
`isocaps`	Isosurface end caps
`isocolors`	Isosurface and patch colors
`contourslice`	Contours in slice planes
`slice`	Volumetric slice plot
`streamline`	Streamlines from data
`stream3`	3-D streamlines
`stream2`	2-D streamlines
`quiver3`	3-D quiver plot
`quiver`	2-D quiver plot
`divergence`	Divergence of a vector field
`curl`	Curl and angular velocity of a vector field
`coneplot`	Cone plot

Function	Description
streamtube	Stream tube
streamribbon	Stream ribbon
streamslice	Streamlines in slice planes
streamparticles	Display stream particles
interpstreamspeed	Interpolate streamline vertices from speed
subvolume	Extract subset of volume data set
reducevolume	Reduce volume data set
volumebounds	Return volume and color limits
smooth3	Smooth 3-D data
reducepatch	Reduce number of patch faces
shrinkfaces	Reduce size of patch faces

28

Using Color and Light

MATLAB provides a number of tools for displaying information visually in two and three dimensions. For example, the plot of a sine curve presents more information at a glance than a set of data points could. The technique of using plots and graphs to present data sets is known as ***data visualization***. In addition to being a powerful computational engine, MATLAB excels in presenting data visually in interesting and informative ways.

Often, however, a simple 2-D or 3-D plot cannot display all of the information you would like to present at one time. Color can provide an additional dimension. Many of the plotting functions discussed in previous chapters accept a *color* argument that can be used to add that additional dimension.

This discussion begins with an investigation of colormaps—how to use them, display them, alter them, and create them. Next, techniques for simulating more than one colormap in a *Figure* window or for using only a portion of a colormap are illustrated. Finally, lighting models are discussed, and examples are presented. As in the preceding chapters, the figures in this chapter do not exhibit color, although they do have color on a computer screen. As a result, if you are not following along in MATLAB, it may take some imagination to understand the concepts covered in this chapter.

28.1 UNDERSTANDING COLORMAPS

MATLAB uses a numerical array with three columns to represent color values. This array is called a ***colormap***, and each row in the matrix represents an individual color by using numbers in the range 0 to 1. The numbers in each row indicate the intensity of red, green, and blue that make up a specific color. The following table illustrates the correspondence between numerical values in a colormap and colors:

Red	Green	Blue	Color
1	0	0	Red
0	1	0	Green
0	0	1	Blue
1	1	0	Yellow
1	0	1	Magenta
0	1	1	Cyan
0	0	0	Black
1	1	1	White
0.5	0.5	0.5	Medium gray
0.67	0	1	Violet
1	0.4	0	Orange
0.5	0	0	Dark red
0	0.5	0	Dark green

The first column in a colormap is the intensity of red, the second column is the intensity of green, and the third column is the intensity of blue. Colormap values are restricted to the range from 0 to 1.

A colormap is a sequence of rows containing red-green-blue (RGB) values that vary in some prescribed way from the first row to the last. MATLAB provides a number of predefined colormaps, as shown in the following table:

Colormap Function	Description
`hsv`	Hue-saturation-value colormap, begins and ends with red
`jet`	Variant of `hsv` that starts with blue and ends with red
`hot`	Black to red to yellow to white
`cool`	Shades of cyan and magenta
`summer`	Shades of green and yellow
`autumn`	Shades of red and yellow
`winter`	Shades of blue and green
`spring`	Shades of magenta and yellow
`white`	All white
`gray`	Linear gray scale
`bone`	Gray with a tinge of blue
`pink`	Pastel shades of pink
`copper`	Linear copper tone
`prism`	Alternating red, orange, yellow, green, blue, and violet
`flag`	Alternating red, white, blue, and black
`lines`	Alternating plot line colors
`colorcube`	Enhanced color cube

By default, each of these colormaps generates a 64-by-3 array specifying the RGB descriptions of 64 colors. Each of these functions accepts an argument specifying the number of rows to be generated. For example, `hot(m)` generates an `m`-by-3 matrix containing the RGB values of colors ranging from black, through shades of red, orange, and yellow, to white.

28.2 USING COLORMAPS

The statement `colormap(M)` installs the matrix `M` as the colormap to be used in the current *Figure* window. For example, `colormap(cool)` installs a 64-entry version of the `cool` colormap. The form `colormap default` installs the default colormap, usually `hsv` or `jet`.

Line plotting functions, such as `plot` and `plot3`, do not use colormaps; they use the colors listed in the `plot` color and linestyle table. The sequence of colors used by these functions varies, depending on the plotting style you have chosen. Most other plotting functions, such as `mesh`, `surf`, `contour`, `fill`, `pcolor`, and their variations, use the current colormap to determine color sequences.

Plotting functions that accept a *color* argument usually accept the argument in one of three forms:

(1) a character string representing one of the colors in the `plot` color and linestyle table—for example, `'r'` or `'red'` for red;

(2) a three-entry row vector representing a single RGB value—for example, `[.25 .50 .75]`;

(3) an array. If the color argument is an array, the elements are scaled and used as indices into the current colormap.

28.3 DISPLAYING COLORMAPS

Colormaps can be viewed in a number of ways. One way is to view the elements in a colormap matrix directly:

```
>> hot(8)

ans =

    0.33333          0          0

    0.66667          0          0

          1          0          0

          1    0.33333          0

          1    0.66667          0

          1          1          0
```

```
             1          1          0.5
             1          1          1
>> gray(5)
ans =
             0          0          0
          0.25       0.25       0.25
           0.5        0.5        0.5
          0.75       0.75       0.75
             1          1          1
```

This example shows two standard colormaps. The first is an eight-element `hot` colormap, and the second is a five-element `gray` colormap. The gray colormap increments all three components equally, thereby producing various shades of gray.

A colormap is best visualized graphically. The `pcolor` and `rgbplot` functions are useful in this case, as in the following example:

```
>> n = 21;
>> map = copper(n);
>> colormap(map)
>> subplot(2,1,1)
>> [xx,yy] = meshgrid(0:n,[0 1]);
>> c = [1:n+1;1:n+1];
>> pcolor(xx,yy,c)
>> set(gca,'Yticklabel','')
>> title('Figure 28.1a: Pcolor of Copper')
>> subplot(2,1,2)
>> rgbplot(map)
>> xlim([0,n])
>> title('Figure 28.1b: RGBplot of Copper')
```

These figures show how a copper colormap varies, from its first row (shown on the left) to its last row (shown on the right). The function `rgbplot` simply plots the three columns of the colormap in red, green, and blue, respectively, thereby dissecting the three components visually.

Figure 28.1a: Pcolor of Copper

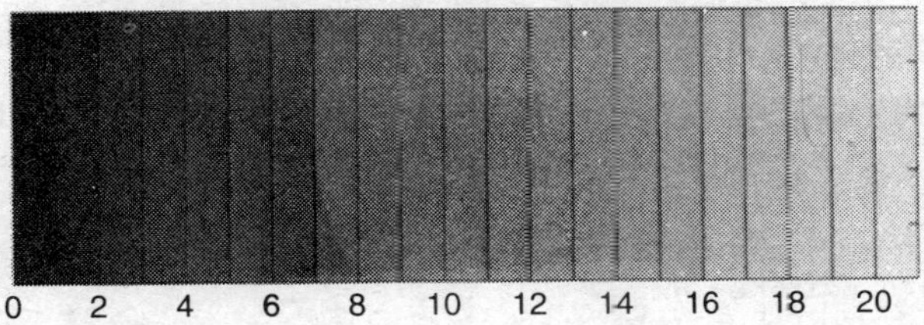

Figure 28.1b: RGBplot of Copper

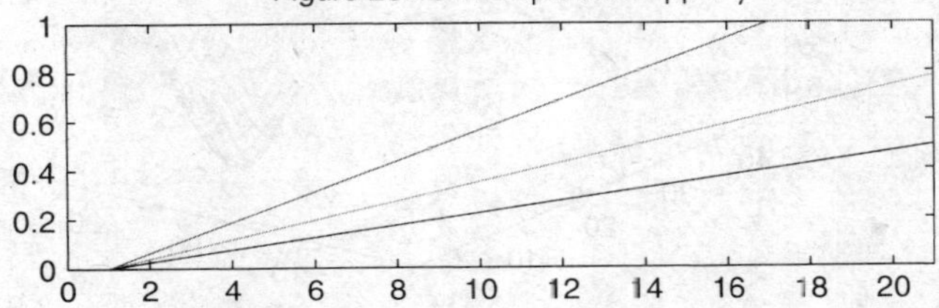

When a 3-D plot is made, the color information in the plot can be displayed as auxiliary information in a colorbar by using the `colorbar` function. For example, consider the following:

```
>> mesh(peaks)
>> axis tight
>> colorbar
>> title('Figure 28.2: Colorbar Added')
```

In this plot, color is associated with the z-axis, and the colorbar associates z-coordinate values with the colors in the colormap.

28.4 CREATING AND ALTERING COLORMAPS

The fact that colormaps are arrays means that you can manipulate them exactly like other arrays. The function `brighten` takes advantage of this feature to adjust a given colormap to increase or decrease the intensity of the colors. The form `brighten(beta)` brightens (`0 < beta ≤ 1`) or darkens (`-1 ≤ beta < 0`) the current colormap. The form `brighten(beta)` followed by `brighten(-beta)` restores the original colormap. The command `newmap=brighten(beta)` creates a brighter or darker version of the current colormap without changing the current map. The command `mymap=brighten(cmap,beta)` creates an adjusted version of the specified colormap without affecting either the current colormap or the specified colormap `cmap`.

Colormaps can be created by generating an `m`-by-3 array `mymap` and installing it with `colormap(mymap)`. Each value in a colormap matrix must be between 0 and 1.

Figure 28.2: Colorbar Added

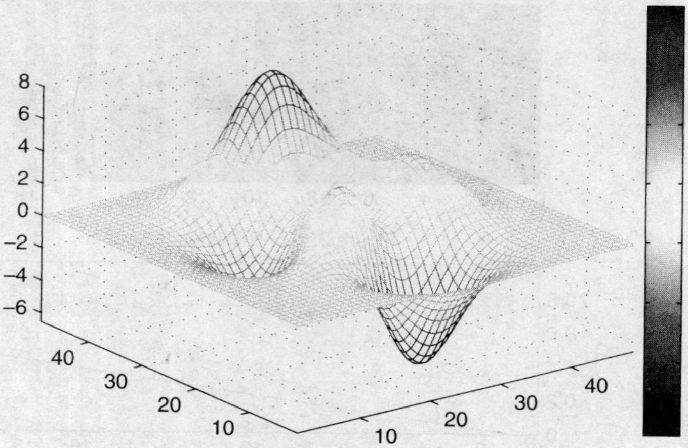

If you try to use a matrix with more or fewer than three columns, or one containing any values less than 0 or greater than 1, `colormap` will report an error.

Colormaps can be converted between the red-green-blue (RGB) standard and the hue-saturation-value (HSV) standard by using the `rgb2hsv` and `hsv2rgb` functions. MATLAB, however, always interprets colormaps as RGB values. Colormaps can be combined as well, as long as the result satisfies the size and value constraints. For example, the colormap called `pink` is simply

```
pinkmap = sqrt(2/3*gray + 1/3*hot);
```

Again, the result is a valid colormap only if all elements of the `m`-by-3 matrix are between 0 and 1 inclusive.

Normally, a colormap is scaled to extend from the minimum to the maximum values of your data—that is, the entire colormap is used to render your plot. You may occasionally wish to change the way these colors are used. The `caxis` function, which stands for *color axis*, allows you to use the entire colormap for a subset of your data range or to use only a portion of the current colormap for your entire data set.

The statement `[cmin, cmax] = caxis` returns the minimum and maximum data values mapped to the first and last entries of the colormap, respectively. These are normally set to the minimum and maximum values of your data. For example, `mesh(peaks)` creates a mesh plot of the `peaks` function and sets `caxis` to `[-6.5466, 8.0752]`, the minimum and maximum `z` values. Data points between these values use colors interpolated from the colormap.

The function `caxis([cmin,cmax])` uses the entire colormap for data in the range between `cmin` and `cmax`. Data points greater than `cmax` are rendered with the color associated with `cmax`, and data points less than `cmin` are rendered with the color associated with cmin. If cmin is less than min(data), or cmax is greater than max(data), the colors associated with cmin or cmax will never be used. Only the portion of the colormap associated with data will be used. The function caxis('auto') or the command form caxis auto restores the default values of cmin and cmax. The following example illustrates color axis settings:

```
>> N = 17;
>> data = [1:N+1;1:N+1]';

>> subplot(1,3,1)
>> colormap(hsv(N))
>> pcolor(data)
>> set(gca,'XtickLabel','')
>> title('Figure 28.3: Auto Limits')
>> caxis auto       % automatic limits (default)

>> subplot(1,3,2)
>> pcolor(data)
>> axis off
>> title('Extended Limits')
>> caxis([-5,N+5]) % extend the color limits

>> subplot(1,3,3)
>> pcolor(data)
>> axis off
>> title('Restricted Limits')
>> caxis([5,N-5]) % restrict the color limits
```

The first plot on the left is the default plot. This plot covers the complete colormap. In the center plot, the color axis is extended, forcing all plotted values to use a subset of the colormap. In the plot on the right, the color axis is restricted, forcing the colormap to cover a region in the center of the plot. The plot extremes simply use the colormap extremes.

28.5 USING COLOR TO DESCRIBE A FOURTH DIMENSION

Surface plots such as mesh and surf vary color along the z-axis, unless a color argument is given—for example, surf(X,Y,Z) is equivalent to surf(X,Y,Z,Z).

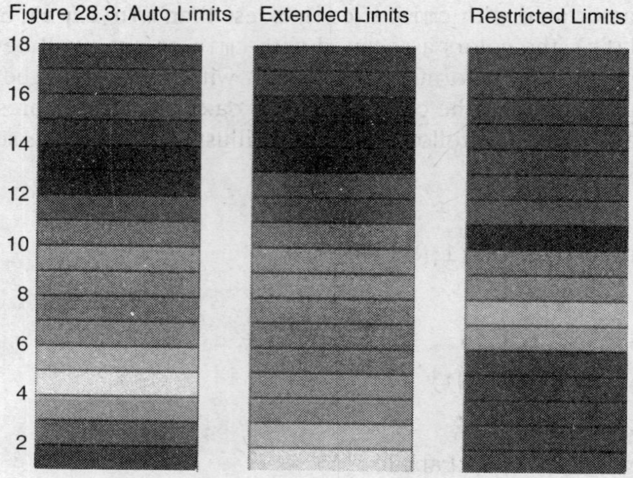

Applying color to the z-axis produces a colorful plot, but does not provide additional information, since the z-axis already exists. To make better use of color, it is suggested that color be used to describe some property of the data not reflected by the three axes. To do so requires specifying different data for the color argument to 3-D plotting functions.

If the color argument to a plotting function is a vector or a matrix, it is scaled and used as an index into the colormap. This argument can be any real vector or matrix that is the same size as the other arguments. The following code is illustrative:

```
>> x = -7.5:.5:7.5;                 % data
>> [X Y] = meshgrid(x);             % create plaid data
>> R = sqrt(X.^2 + Y.^2)+eps; % create sombrero
>> Z = sin(R)./R;

>> subplot(2,2,1)
>> surf(X,Y,Z,Z)      % default color order
>> colormap(gray)
>> shading interp
>> axis tight off
>> title('Figure 28.4a: Default, Z')

>> subplot(2,2,2)
>> surf(X,Y,Z,Y)    % Y axis color order
```

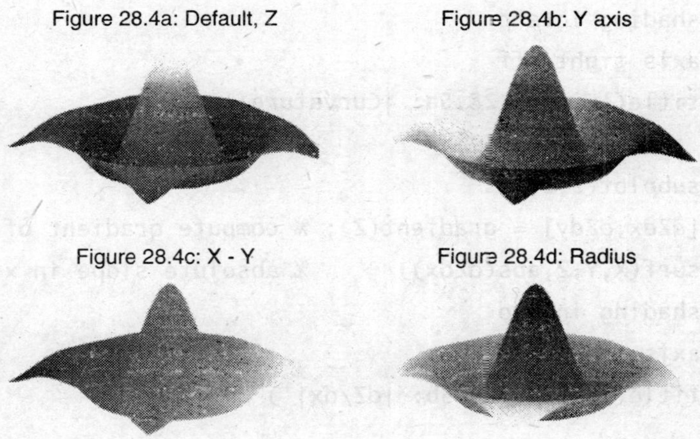


```
>> shading interp
>> axis tight off
>> title('Figure 28.4b: Y axis')

>> subplot(2,2,3)
>> surf(X,Y,Z,X-Y) % diagonal color order
>> shading interp
>> axis tight off
>> title('Figure 28.4c: X - Y')

>> subplot(2,2,4)
>> surf(X,Y,Z,R)   % radius color order
>> shading interp
>> axis tight off
>> title('Figure 28.4d: Radius')
```

These subplots demonstrate four simple ways to use color as a fourth dimension. Whatever data are provided as the fourth argument to `surf` is used to interpolate the colormap. Any function of the first three arguments can be provided, or some completely independent variable works as well. Using the functions `del2` and `gradient` allows one to apply color with respect to curvature and slope, respectively:

```
>> subplot(2,2,1)
>> surf(X,Y,Z,abs(del2(Z)))   % absolute Laplacian
>> colormap(gray)
```

```
>> shading interp
>> axis tight off
>> title('Figure 28.5a: |Curvature|')

>> subplot(2,2,2)
>> [dZdx,dZdy] = gradient(Z); % compute gradient of surface
>> surf(X,Y,Z,abs(dZdx))      % absolute slope in x-direction
>> shading interp
>> axis tight off
>> title('Figure 28.5b: |dZ/dx|')

>> subplot(2,2,3)
>> surf(X,Y,Z,abs(dZdy))      % absolute slope in y-direction
>> shading interp
>> axis tight off
>> title('Figure 28.5c: |dZ/dy|')

>> subplot(2,2,4)
>> dR = sqrt(dZdx.^2 + dZdy.^2);
>> surf(X,Y,Z,abs(dR))        % absolute slope in radius
>> shading interp
>> axis tight off
>> title('Figure 28.5d: |dR|')
```

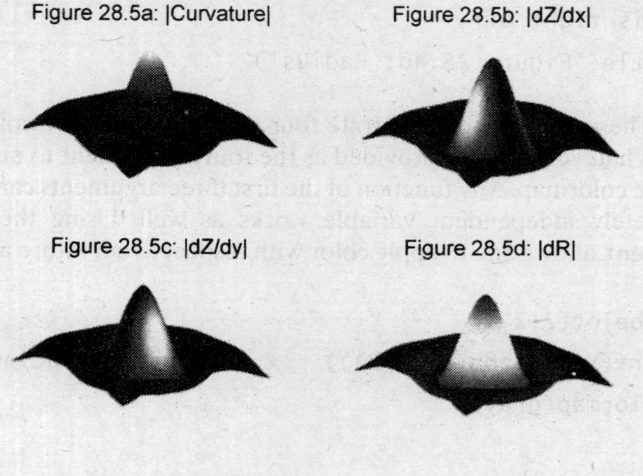

Note how color in these subplots provides an additional dimension to the plotted surface. The function `del2` is the discrete Laplacian function that applies color based on the curvature of the surface. The function `gradient` approximates the gradient, or slope, of the surface with respect to the two coordinate directions.

28.6 LIGHTING MODELS

The graphics functions `pcolor`, `fill`, `fill3`, `mesh`, and `surf` discussed in the previous chapters render objects that appear to be well lit from all sides by very diffuse light. This technique emphasizes the characteristics of the objects in the *Figure* window and enhances the user's ability to visualize the data being analyzed. Although the data can be visualized quite clearly, the realism of the scene can be enhanced or diminished by creating different lighting effects.

The `shading` function selects faceted, flat, or interpolated shading. (Examples of each of these were illustrated in the chapter on 3-D graphics.) Although requiring more computational power and subsequently more time to render, interpolated shading of the objects in a scene can enhance the realism of the scene being rendered.

One or more light sources can be added to simulate the highlights and shadows associated with directional lighting. The function `light` creates a white light source infinitely far away along the vector [1 0 1]. Once the light source has been created, the `lighting` function allows you to select from four different lighting models: none (which ignores any light source), `flat` (the default when a light source is created), phong, and gouraud. Each of these models uses a different algorithm to change the appearance of the object. Flat lighting uses a uniform color for each face of the object. Gouraud lighting interpolates the face colors from the vertices. Phong lighting interpolates the normals at the vertices across each face and calculates the reflectance at each pixel. While colormaps are properties of *Figure* windows, light is a property, or child, of the axes. Therefore, each axis in a *Figure* window can be separately lit, as in the following example:

```
>> subplot(2,2,1)
>> sphere
>> light
>> shading interp
>> axis square off
>> lighting none
>> title('Figure 28.6a: No Lighting')

>> subplot(2,2,2)
>> sphere
>> light
```

```
>> shading interp
>> axis square off
>> lighting flat
>> title('Figure 28.6b: Flat Lighting')

>> subplot(2,2,3)
>> sphere
>> light
>> shading interp
>> axis square off
>> lighting gouraud
>> title('Figure 28.6c: Gouraud Lighting')

>> subplot(2,2,4)
>> sphere
>> light
>> shading interp
>> axis square off
>> lighting phong
>> title('Figure 28.6d: Phong Lighting')
```

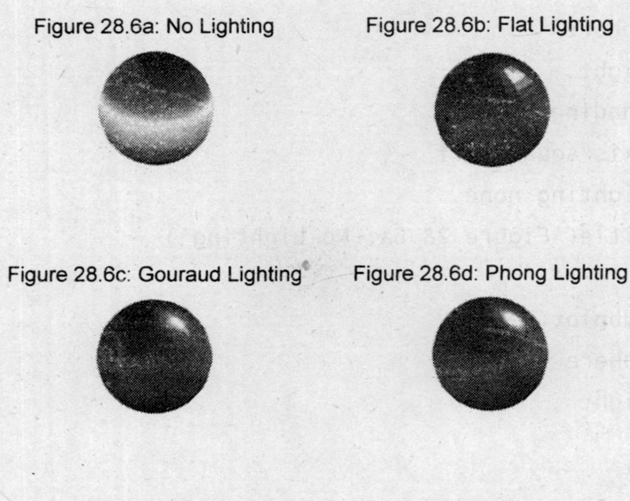

In addition to lighting, the appearance of objects in an axis can be changed by modifying the apparent reflective characteristics, or ***reflectance***, of surfaces. Reflectance is made up of a number of components:

- ***Ambient light***—strength of the uniform directionless light in the figure
- ***Diffuse reflection***—intensity of the soft directionless reflected light
- ***Specular reflection***—intensity of the hard directional reflected light
- ***Specular exponent***—controls the size of the specular "hot spot" or spread
- ***Specular color reflectance***—determines the contribution of the surface color to the reflectance

Some predefined surface reflectance properties are available by using the `material` function. Options include `shiny`, `dull`, `metal`, and `default` for restoring the default surface reflectance properties. The form `material([ka kd ks n sc])`, where `n` and `sc` are optional, sets the ambient strength, diffuse reflectance, specular reflectance, specular exponent, and specular color reflectance of objects in an axis. The following code illustrates the first four options:

```
>> subplot(2,2,1)
>> sphere
>> colormap(gray)
>> light
>> shading interp
>> axis square off
>> material default
>> title('Figure 28.7a: Default Material')

>> subplot(2,2,2)
>> sphere
>> light
>> shading interp
>> axis square off
>> material shiny
>> title('Figure 28.7b: Shiny Material')

>> subplot(2,2,3)
>> sphere
>> light
>> shading interp
```

```
>> axis square off
>> material dull
>> title('Figure 28.7c: Dull Material')

>> subplot(2,2,4)
>> sphere
>> light
>> shading interp
>> axis square off
>> material metal
>> title('Figure 28.7d: Metal Material')
```

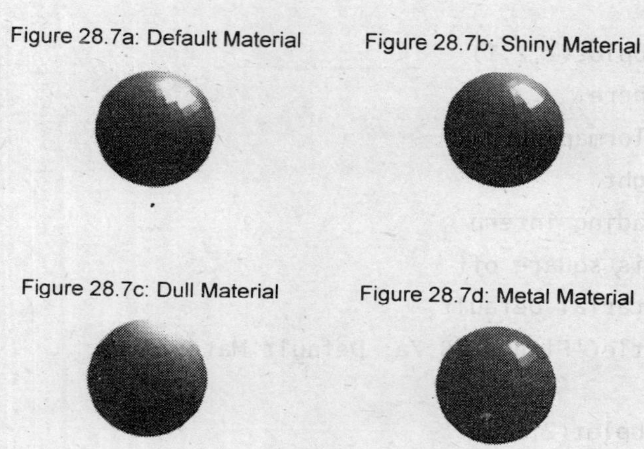

Note that the function `light` is fairly limited. It creates white light emanating from an infinite distance away along a given direction. In reality, `light` is a Handle Graphics object creation function. The function `light` offers a variety of properties that can be set. For example, the light color, position, and style can be set, with style meaning that the light can be a point source at a given position or can be infinitely far away along some vector:

```
>> Hl = light('Position',[x,y,z],'Color',[r,g,b],'Style','local');
```

This command creates a light source at position `(x,y,z)` using light color `[r,g,b]` and specifies that the position is a location (`'local'`) rather than a vector ('infinite'). It also saves the handle of the *light* object (Hl), which can be used to change the properties of the light source at a later time. For example,

```
>> set(Hl,'Position',[1 0 1],'Color',[1 1 1],'Style','infinite');
```

sets the light source defined by the handle Hl back to its original default characteristics. (For more information about Handle Graphics, see Chapter 31.)

28.7 SUMMARY

The following table documents MATLAB functions for color and lighting:

Function	Description
light	Light object creation function
lighting	Set lighting mode (flat, gouraud, phong, or none)
lightangle	Position light object in spherical coordinates
material	Set material reflectance (default, shiny, dull, or metal)
camlight	Set light object with respect to camera
brighten	Brighten or darken colormap
caxis	Set or get color axis limits
diffuse	Find surface diffuse reflectance
specular	Find surface specular reflectance
surfnorm	Compute surface normals
colorbar	Create colorbar
colordef	Define default color properties
colormap	Set or get *Figure* window colormap
colormapeditor	GUI for creating colormaps
hsv2rgb	Convert hue-saturation-value color values to red-green-blue model
rgb2hsv	Convert red-green-blue color values to hue-saturation-value model
rgbplot	Plot colormap
shading	Surface shading (flat, faceted, or interp)
spinmap	Spin colormap
whitebg	Change plot axes background color
graymon	Set graphics defaults for grayscale monitors
autumn	Colormap with shades of red and yellow

Function	Description
bone	Gray-scale colormap with a tinge of blue
cool	Colormap with shades of cyan and magenta
copper	Colormap with linear copper tone
flag	Colormap with alternating red, white, blue, and black
gray	Colormap with linear gray scale
hot	Colormap with black, red, yellow, and white
hsv	Colormap based on hue, saturation, and value progression
jet	Colormap variant of hsv that starts with blue and ends with red
lines	Colormap based on line colors
prism	Colormap with alternating red, orange, yellow, green, blue, and violet
spring	Colormap with shades of magenta and yellow
summer	Colormap with shades of green and yellow
winter	Colormap with shades of blue and green

29

Images, Movies, and Sound

MATLAB provides commands for displaying several types of images. Images can be created and stored as standard double-precision floating-point numbers (`double`) and, optionally, as 8-bit (`uint8`) or 16-bit (`uint16`) unsigned integers. MATLAB can read and write image files in a number of standard graphics file formats, as well as use `load` and `save` to save image data in MAT-files. MATLAB provides commands for creating and playing animations as movies (sequences of frames). Sound functions are available as well for computers that support sound.

29.1 IMAGES

Images in MATLAB consist of a data matrix and usually an associated colormap matrix. There are three types of image data matrices, each interpreted differently: indexed images, intensity images, and truecolor, or RGB, images.

An ***indexed image*** requires a colormap and interprets the image data as indices into the colormap matrix. The colormap matrix is a standard colormap—any `m`-by-3 array containing valid RGB data. Given an image data array `X(i,j)` and a colormap array `cmap`, the color of each image pixel P_{ij} is `cmap(X(i,j),:)`. This implies that the data values in `X` are integers within the range `[1 length(cmap)]`. This image can be displayed by using

```
>> image(X); colormap(cmap)
```

An ***intensity image*** scales the image data over a range of intensities. This form is normally used with images to be displayed in grayscale or one of the other monochromatic colormaps, but other colormaps can be used if desired. The image data are not required to be in the range [1 length(cmap)], as is the case with indexed images. The data are scaled over a given range, and the result is used to index into the colormap. For example,

```
>> imagesc(X,[0 1]); colormap(gray)
```

associates the value 0 with the first colormap entry, and the value 1 with the last colormap entry. Values in X between 0 and 1 are scaled and used as indices into the colormap. If the scale is omitted, it defaults to [min(min(X)) max(max(X))].

A ***truecolor***, or ***RGB image*** is created from an m-by-n-by-3 data array containing valid RGB triples. The row and column dimensions specify the pixel location, and the page of third dimension specifies each color component. For example, pixel P_{ij} is rendered in the color specified by X(i,j,:). A colormap is not required, because the color data are stored within the image data array itself. For example,

```
>> image(X)
```

where X is an m-by-n-by-3 truecolor, or RGB, image, displays the image. The image X can contain uint8, unit16, or double data.

If images are displayed on default axes, the aspect ratio will often be incorrect and the image will be distorted. Issuing

```
>> axis image off
```

sets the axis properties so that the aspect ratio matches the image and the axis labels and ticks are hidden. To force each pixel in the image to occupy one pixel on the display requires setting *figure* and *axes* object properties, as in the following example:

```
>> load clown          % sample image
>> [r,c] = size(X); % pixel dimensions
>> figure('Units','Pixels','Position',[100 100 c r])
>> image(X)
>> set(gca,'Position',[0 0 1 1])
>> colormap(map)
```

Here, the *figure* is set to display exactly the same number of pixels as the image by setting its width and height equal to that of the image. Then, the *axes* position is set to occupy the entire figure in normalized units.

MATLAB installations have a number of sample images in addition to clown.mat used in the preceding example. The demos subdirectory on the MATLAB path contains cape.mat, clown.mat, detail.mat, durer.mat, flujet.mat, gatlin.mat, mandrill.mat, and spine.mat. Each of these images can be displayed by issuing

```
>> load filename
>> image(X), colormap(map)
```

```
>> title(caption)
>> axis image off
```

29.2 IMAGE FORMATS

The image and imagesc commands can display 8- and 16-bit images without first converting them to the double format. However, the range of data values for uint8 data is [0 255], as supported in standard graphics file formats, and the range of data values for uint16 is [0 65535].

For indexed images, image maps the value 0 to the first entry in a 256-entry colormap and maps the value 255 to the last entry, by automatically supplying the proper offset. Since the normal range of double data for indexed images is [1 length(cmap)], converting between uint8 and double or uint16 and double requires shifting the values by 1. Before MATLAB 7, mathematical operations on uint8 and uint16 arrays were not defined. As a result, to perform mathematical operations on unsigned integers in previous versions of MATLAB required that they must be converted to the double format. For example, the code

```
>> Xdouble = double(Xuint8) + 1;
>> Xuint8 = uint8(Xdouble - 1);
```

converts the uint8 data in Xuint8 to double and back, taking into account the offset of 1. With the introduction of arithmetic for integer data types in MATLAB 7, it is now possible to perform operations without conversion to double precision. This facilitates easier image manipulation in MATLAB.

For 8-bit intensity and RGB images, the range of values is normally [0 255] rather than [0 1]. To display 8-bit intensity and RGB images, use the following commands:

```
>> imagesc(Xuint8,[0 255]); colormap(cmap)
>> image(Xuint8)
```

Conversions to double can also be normalized, as in the following code:

```
>> Xdouble = double(Xuint8)/255;
>> Xuint8 = uint8(round(Xdouble*255));
```

The 8-bit color data contained in an RGB image is automatically scaled when it is displayed. For example, the color white is normally [1 1 1] when doubles are used. If the same color is stored as 8-bit data, the color white is represented as [255 255 255].

The optional *Image Processing Toolbox* available for MATLAB contains many functions for manipulating images. This Toolbox is valuable if you regularly manipulate images.

29.3 IMAGE FILES

Image data can be saved to files and reloaded into MATLAB by using many different file formats. The normal MATLAB save and load functions support image data in double, uint8, or uint16 format in the same way that they support any other MATLAB variable and data type. When saving indexed images or intensity images with nonstandard colormaps, be sure to save the colormap as well as the image data, using, for example, the command

```
>> save myimage.mat X map
```

MATLAB also supports several industry-standard image file formats using the imread and imwrite functions. Information about the contents of a graphics file can be obtained with the imfinfo function. The help text for imread gives extensive information regarding image read formats and features. Following is part of this help text:

```
Supported file types
--------------------
JPEG  Any baseline JPEG image; JPEG images with some
      commonly used extensions; 8-bit and 12-bit lossy
      compressed RGB and grayscale images; 8-bit and 12-bit
      lossless compressed RGB images; 8-bit, 12-bit, and
      16-bit lossless compressed grayscale images

TIFF  Any baseline TIFF image, including 1-bit, 8-bit, and
      24-bit uncompressed images; 1-bit, 8-bit, and 24-bit
      images with packbits compression; 1-bit images with
      CCITT compression; 16-bit grayscale, 16-bit indexed,
      and 48-bit RGB images; 24-bit and 48-bit ICCLAB
      and CIELAB images; 32-bit and 64-bit CMYK images; and
      8-bit tiled TIFF images with any compression and colorspace
      combination listed above.

GIF   Any 1-bit to 8-bit GIF image

BMP   1-bit, 4-bit, 8-bit, 16-bit, 24-bit, and 32-bit uncompressed
      images; 4-bit and 8-bit run-length encoded (RLE) images

PNG   Any PNG image, including 1-bit, 2-bit, 4-bit, 8-bit,
      and 16-bit grayscale images; 8-bit and 16-bit
      indexed images; 24-bit and 48-bit RGB images
```

```
HDF   8-bit raster image datasets, with or without an
      associated colormap; 24-bit raster image datasets

PCX   1-bit, 8-bit, and 24-bit images

XWD   1-bit and 8-bit ZPixmaps; XYBitmaps; 1-bit XYPixmaps

ICO   1-bit, 4-bit, and 8-bit uncompressed images

CUR   1-bit, 4-bit, and 8-bit uncompressed images

RAS   Any RAS image, including 1-bit bitmap, 8-bit indexed,
      24-bit truecolor and 32-bit truecolor with alpha.

PBM   Any 1-bit PBM image.  Raw (binary) or ASCII (plain) encoded.

PGM   Any standard PGM image.  ASCII (plain) encoded with
      arbitrary color depth.  Raw (binary) encoded with up
      to 16 bits per gray value.

PPM   Any standard PPM image.  ASCII (plain) encoded with
      arbitrary color depth. Raw (binary) encoded with up
      to 16 bits per color component.
```

The calling syntax for imwrite varies, depending on the image type and file format. The help text for imwrite, shown in part as follows, gives extensive information regarding image save formats and features:

```
Table: summary of supported image types
---------------------------------------

BMP   1-bit, 8-bit and 24-bit uncompressed images

TIFF  Baseline TIFF images, including 1-bit, 8-bit, 16-bit,
      and 24-bit uncompressed images; 1-bit, 8-bit, 16-bit,
      and 24-bit images with packbits compression; 1-bit
      images with CCITT 1D, Group 3, and Group 4 compression;
      CIELAB, ICCLAB, and CMYK images

JPEG  Baseline JPEG images
```

PNG 1-bit, 2-bit, 4-bit, 8-bit, and 16-bit grayscale images; 8-bit and 16-bit grayscale images with alpha channels; 1-bit, 2-bit, 4-bit, and 8-bit indexed images; 24-bit and 48-bit truecolor images; 24-bit and 48-bit truecolor images with alpha channels

HDF 8-bit raster image datasets, with or without associated colormap; 24-bit raster image datasets; uncompressed or with RLE or JPEG compression

PCX 8-bit images

XWD 8-bit ZPixmaps

RAS Any RAS image, including 1-bit bitmap, 8-bit indexed, 24-bit truecolor and 32-bit truecolor with alpha.

PBM Any 1-bit PBM image, ASCII (plain) or raw (binary) encoding.

PGM Any standard PGM image. ASCII (plain) encoded with arbitrary color depth. Raw (binary) encoded with up to 16 bits per gray value.

PPM Any standard PPM image. ASCII (plain) encoded with arbitrary color depth. Raw (binary) encoded with up to 16 bits per color component.

PNM Any of PPM/PGM/PBM (see above) chosen automatically.

29.4 MOVIES

Animation in MATLAB takes one of two forms. First, if the computations needed to create a sequence of images can be performed quickly enough, *figure* and *axes* properties can be set so that screen rendering occurs sufficiently quickly so that animation is visually smooth. On the other hand, if computations require significant time or the resulting images are complex enough, you must create a movie.

In MATLAB, the functions `getframe` and `movie` provide the tools required to capture and play movies. The `getframe` command takes a snapshot of the current *figure*, and movie plays back the sequence of frames after they have been captured. The output of getframe is a structure containing all of the information needed by movie. Capturing multiple frames is simply a matter of adding elements to the structure. The following code is illustrative:

```
% moviemaking example: rotate a 3-D surface plot
[X,Y,Z]=peaks(50);          % create data
surfl(X,Y,Z)                % plot surface with lighting
axis([-3 3 -3 3 -10 10])    % fix axes so that scaling does not change
axis vis3d off              % fix axes for 3D and turn off axes ticks etc.
shading interp              % make it pretty with interpolated shading
colormap(copper)            % choose a good colormap for lighting
for i=1:15                  % rotate and capture each frame
   view(-37.5+15*(i-1),30)% change the viewpoint for this frame
   m(i)=getframe;           % add this figure to the frame structure
end
cla       % clear axis for movie
movie(m)  % play the movie
```

The preceding script file creates a movie by incrementally rotating the peaks surface and capturing a frame at every increment. Finally, the movie is played after clearing the *axes*. The variable m contains a structure array, with each array element containing a single frame:

```
>> m
m =
1x15 struct array with fields:
    cdata
    colormap

>> size(m(1).cdata)
ans =
   342   306     3
```

The color data holding the image cdata make up a truecolor, or RGB, bitmap image. As a result, the complexity of contents of the *axes* does not influence the bytes required to store a movie. The size of the *axes* in pixels determines the size of the image and therefore the number of bytes required to store a movie.

29.5 IMAGE UTILITIES

Conversion between indexed images and movie frames is possible with the `im2frame` and `frame2im` functions. For example,

```
>> [X,cmap] = frame2im(M(n))
```

converts the `n`th frame of the movie matrix `M` into an indexed image `X` and associated colormap `cmap`. Similarly,

```
>> M(n) = im2frame(X,cmap)
```

converts the indexed image `X` and colormap `cmap` into the `n`th frame of the movie matrix `M`. Note that `im2frame` can be used to convert a series of images into a movie in the same way that `getframe` converts a series of *figures* or *axes* into a movie.

29.6 SOUND

In addition to the high level `audiorecorder` and `audioplayer` functions now available, MATLAB supports sound by using a variety of lower-level functions. The function `sound(y,f,b)` sends the signal in vector `y` to the computer's speaker at sample frequency `f`. Values in `y` outside of the range `[-1 1]` are clipped. If `f` is omitted, the default sample frequency of 8192 Hz is used. MATLAB plays the sound by using `b` bits persecond, if possible. Most platforms support `b=8` or `b=16`. If `b` is omitted, `b=16` is used.

The `soundsc` function is the same as `sound`, except that the values in `y` are *scaled* to the range `[-1 1]` rather than clipped. This results in a sound that is as loud as possible without clipping. An additional argument is available that permits mapping a range of values in `y` to the full sound range. The format is `soundsc(y,...,[smin smax])`. If omitted, the default range is `[min(y) max(y)]`.

Two industry-standard sound file formats are supported in MATLAB. NeXT/Sun audio format (*`file.au`*) files and Microsoft WAVE format (*`file.wav`*) files can be written and read.

The NeXT/Sun Audio sound storage format supports multichannel data for 8-bit mu-law, 8-bit linear, and 16-bit linear formats. The most general form of `auwrite` is `auwrite(y,f,n,'`*`method`*`', '`*`filename`*`')`, where `y` is the sample data, `f` is the sample rate in hertz, `b` specifies the number of bits in the encoder, `'`*`method`*`'` is a string specifying the encoding method, and `'`*`filename`*`'` is a string specifying the name of the output file. Each column of `y` represents a single channel. Any value in `y` outside of the range `[-1 1]` is clipped prior to writing the file. The `f`, `n`, and `'`*`method`*`'` arguments are optional. If omitted, `f=8000`, `n=8`, and `method='mu'`. The `method` argument must be either `'linear'` or `'mu'`. If the file name string contains no extension, `'.au'` is appended.

Conversion between mu-law and linear formats can be performed by using the `mu2lin` and `lin2mu` functions. (More information about the exact conversion processes involved with these two functions can be found by using the on-line help.)

Multichannel 8-bit or 16-bit WAVE sound storage format sound files can be created with the `wavwrite` function. The most general form is `wavwrite(y,f,n,'`*`filename`*`')`, where `y` is the sample data, `f` is the sample rate in hertz, `b` specifies the number of bits in the encoder, and `'`*`filename`*`'` is a string specifying the name of the output file. Each column of `y` represents a single channel. Any value in `y` outside of the range `[-1 1]` is clipped prior to writing the file. The `f` and `n` arguments are optional. If omitted, `f=8000` and `n=16`. If the file name string contains no extension, `'.wav'` is appended.

Both `auread` and `wavread` have the same syntax and options. The most general form is `[y,f,b]=auread('`*`filename`*`',n)`, which loads a sound file specified by the string `'`*`filename`*`'` and returns the sampled data into `y`. The appropriate extension (`.au` or `.wav`) is appended to the file name if no extension is given. Values in `y` are in the range `[−1 1]`. If three outputs are requested, as previously illustrated, the sample rate in hertz and the number of bits per sample are returned in `f` and `b`, respectively. If `n` is given, only the first `n` samples are returned from each channel in the file. If `n=[n1 n2]`, only samples from `n1` through `n2` are returned from each channel. The form `[samples,channels]=wavread('`*`filename`*`','`*`size`*`')` returns the size of the audio data in the file, rather than the data itself. This form is useful for preallocating storage or estimating resource use.

29.7 SUMMARY

The following table summarizes the image, movie, and sound capabilities in MATLAB:

Function	Description
`image`	Create indexed or truecolor (RGB) *image* object
`imagesc`	Create intensity *image* object
`colormap`	Apply colormap to *image*
`axis image`	Adjust axis scaling for *image*
`uint8`	Conversion to unsigned 8-bit integer
`uint16`	Conversion to unsigned 16-bit integer
`double`	Conversion to double precision
`imread`	Read image file
`imwrite`	Write image file
`imfinfo`	Image file information
`getframe`	Place movie frame in structure

Function	Description
movie	Play movie from movie structure
frame2im	Convert movie frame to image
im2frame	Convert image to movie frame
avifile	Create avi movie file
addframe	Add frame to avi movie file
close	Close avi movie file
aviread	Read avi movie file
aviinfo	Information about an avi movie file
movie2avi	Convert movie in MATLAB format to avi format
audiorecorder	Audio recorder object
audioplayer	Audio player object
audiodevinfo	Audio device information
sound	Play vector as sound
soundsc	Autoscale and play vector as sound
wavplay	Play WAVE format sound file
wavrecord	Record sound using Windows audio input device
wavread	Read WAVE format sound file
wavwrite	Write WAVE format sound file
auread	Read NeXT/SUN sound file
auwrite	Write NeXT/SUN sound file
lin2mu	Convert linear audio to mu-law
mu2lin	Convert mu-law audio to linear

30

Printing and Exporting Graphics

MATLAB graphics are very effective tools for data visualization and analysis. Therefore, it is often desirable to create hard-copy output or to use these graphics in other applications. MATLAB provides a very flexible system for printing graphics and creating output in many different graphics formats, including EPS and TIFF. Most other applications can import one or more of the graphics file formats supported by MATLAB.

Perhaps the most important issue to recognize when printing or exporting graphics is that the *figure* is ***rerendered*** in the process. That is, what you see on the screen is *not* what you get on a printed page or in an exported file. By default, MATLAB can choose a different renderer (`painters`, `zbuffer`, or `OpenGL`), can change the *axes* tick-mark distribution, and can change the size of the *figure* being printed and exported. Naturally, MATLAB provides the capability to enforce what-you-see-is-what-you-get (WYSIWYG), but this is not the default action taken.

In general, printing and exporting are not simple, because there is an almost uncountable number of possible combinations involving printer drivers, printer protocols, graphics file types, renderers, bit-mapped versus vector graphics descriptions, dots-per-inch selection, color versus black and white, compression, platform limitations, and so on. Most of this complexity is hidden when default output is requested. However, when very specific printed characteristics are required, or when exporting a *figure* for insertion into a word processing or presentation document, the complexities of printing and exporting must be understood. In these cases, it is not uncommon to spend a significant amount of time tweaking output until it matches the characteristics desired.

This chapter introduces the printing and exporting capabilities of MATLAB. As in other areas, MATLAB provides menu items, as well as *Command* window functions, for printing and exporting. The menu approach offers convenience, but limited flexibility, whereas the function approach offers complete flexibility, but requires much more knowledge on the part of the user.

> Accessing the on-line documentation for the function `print` by issuing `>> doc print` provides a great deal of information about printing and exporting.

30.1 PRINTING AND EXPORTING USING MENUS

When graphics are displayed in a *Figure* window, the top of the window contains a menu bar and possibly one or more toolbars. The menu bar has a number of menus, including **File, Edit, View, Insert, Tools, Desktop, Window**, and **Help**. Of these, the **File** menu lists menu items for printing and exporting the current *figure*. In addition, the **Edit** menu on the Windows platform contains menu items for exporting the current *figure* to the system clipboard. The **File** menu includes the menu items **Export Setup, Page Setup, Print Setup, Print Preview**, and **Print**. Each of these items offers dialog boxes for setting various aspects of printing and exporting.

The **Export Setup** menu item makes it possible to save the current *figure* in one of many graphics formats. The **Export Setup** dialog box presents an **Export...** dialog, where the user chooses a directory, file name, and file type for the current *figure*. The size and features of the saved *figure* can be set from the dialog box.

Choosing the **Page Setup** menu item (or the `pagesetupdlg` command) opens a tabbed dialog box for setting a number of features that can be used when a *figure* is rendered for printing or exporting. This dialog box is the primary place to specify the size, orientation, placement, and many of the other features of the rendered *figure*.

Choosing the **Print Setup** menu item (or the `print -dsetup` command) on the Windows platform opens a standard dialog box with selections for a printer and options such as paper size, paper source, and orientation. On UNIX systems, the **Print Setup** menu item (or the `printdlg -setup` command) opens a dialog box identical to the **Print** dialog box, except for the title of the box and the fact that the **OK** button closes the dialog box, but does not send the *figure* to the printer or to a file. The UNIX **Print Setup** dialog box includes options for selecting a printer (or a filename) and a printer driver, *figure* size, axes and tick options. This dialog box also offers an **Options** button providing access to a dialog box for setting many additional options, including choosing a renderer and setting the output resolution. On both platforms, options chosen in this dialog box persist during a MATLAB session and override any like settings made in the **Page Setup** dialog box.

The **Print Preview** menu item (or the `printpreview` command) opens a window showing how the *figure* will be rendered on the printed page. Buttons are provided to call the **Page Setup** dialog box to make any necessary changes and to call the **Print** dialog box to print the *figure*.

The **Print** menu item (or the `printdlg` command) opens a standard **Print** dialog box on PC systems. From this dialog box, the printer and the number of copies can be chosen. The option to print to a file is available here as well. On UNIX systems, the printer or the filename, the printer driver, and options to freeze the axes and tick marks can be chosen. An **Options** button provides access to a dialog box that is useful for setting a variety of additional options, all of which also appear in the **Page Setup** dialog box.

> **Page Setup** options apply to the current *figure* and are saved with the current *figure*. **Print Setup** options persist through the current MATLAB session and override any like **Page Setup** options for the current *figure*. **Print** options apply only to the current *figure* and override any like options in **Page Setup** or **Print Setup** for the current *figure*.

On the Windows platform, the **Edit** menu provides export capabilities through the system clipboard. The **Copy Figure** menu item places the current *figure* on the clipboard based on the options set in the preferences dialog box opened by selecting the **Copy Options** menu item. The current *figure* can be copied in either bitmap (BMP) or enhanced meta file (EMF) format. A template can be used to change line widths and font sizes, as well as to set other default options for copy operations. These options apply only when a *figure* is copied to the clipboard by using the **Copy Figure** menu item. They have no effect when printing or exporting a *figure* to a graphics file.

30.2 COMMAND LINE PRINTING AND EXPORTING

The function `print` handles all printing and exporting from the *Command* window. This single function offers numerous options that are specified as additional input arguments. The syntax for the command form of `print` is

```
>> print -device -option -option filename
```

where all parameters or arguments are optional. The parameter *-device* specifies the device driver to be used, *-option* specifies one or more options, and `filename` specifies the name of an output file if the output is not sent directly to a printer. Because of command-function duality, `print` can be called as a function as well. For example,

```
>> print('-device','-option','-option','filename')
```

is equivalent to the preceding `print` command statement.

In general, print options including *-device* can be specified in any order. Recognized print *-option* strings are described in the following table:

-option	**Description**
-adobecset	Select PostScript default character set encoding (early PostScript printer drivers and EPS file formats only)
-append	Append *figure* to existing file (PostScript printer drivers only)
-cmyk	Print with CMYK colors instead of RGB colors (PostScript printer drivers and EPS file format only)
-device	Printer driver to be used
-dsetup	Display the **Print Setup** dialog box (Windows only)
-*fhandle*	Specify numerical `handle` of *figure* to print or export
-loose	Use *loose* PostScript bounding box (PostScript, EPS, and GhostScript only)
-noui	Suppress printing of *uicontrol* objects
-opengl	Render using OpenGL algorithm (bitmap format)
-painters	Render using Painter's algorithm (vector format)
-P*printer*	Specify name of printer to use (UNIX only)
-r*number*	Specify resolution in dots per inch (dpi). Settable for most devices for printing. Settable for built-in MATLAB file formats except EMF and ILL. Not settable for many GhostScript export formats. Default export resolution is 150 dpi for Z-buffer and OpenGL renderers, and 864 dpi for Painter's renderer.
-s*windowtitle*	Specify name of SIMULINK system window to print or export
-v	Verbose. Display the **Print** dialog box (Windows only)
-zbuffer	Render using Z-buffer algorithm (bitmap format)

30.3 PRINTERS AND EXPORT FILE FORMATS

The `print` function supports a number of output devices (printers and file types). Many of these printers are supported through the use of GhostScript printer drivers, which convert PostScript printer code to native printer code. This conversion process is transparent to the user, but limits printable fonts to those supported in PostScript.

The function `print` also supports exporting to a file or to the clipboard in a number of graphics formats. Export file formats are also specified by the *-device* option to `print`. Some of the supported file formats are shown in the following table.

-device	**Description**
-dbmp16m	24-bit BMP (Windows only) (uses GhostScript)
-dbmp256	8-bit BMP with fixed colormap (Windows only) (uses GhostScript)
-dbmp	24-bit BMP (Windows only)

-dmeta	EMF (Windows only)
-deps	EPS level 1, black and white, including grayscale
-depsc	EPS level 1, color
-deps2	EPS level 2, black and white, including grayscale
-depsc2	EPS level 2, color
-hdf	HDF, 24-bit (Windows only)
-dill	Adobe Illustrator
-djpeg	JPEG, 24-bit, quality setting of 75 (rendered using Z-buffer)
-djpeg*NN*	JPEG, 24-bit, quality setting of *NN*
-dpbm	PBM plain format (UNIX only) (uses GhostScript)
-dpbmraw	PBM raw format (UNIX only) (uses GhostScript)
-dpcxmono	PCX, 1-bit (Windows only) (uses GhostScript)
-dpcx24b	PCX, 24-bit color (Windows only) (uses GhostScript)
-dpcx256	PCX, 8-bit color (Windows only) (uses GhostScript)
-dpcx16	PCX, 16 colors (Windows only) (uses GhostScript)
-dpcx	PCX, 8-bit color (Windows only)
-dpgm	PGM portable graymap, plain (UNIX only) (uses GhostScript)
-dpgmraw	PGM portable graymap, raw (UNIX only) (uses GhostScript)
-dpng	PNG 24 bit
-dppm	PPM portable pixmap, plain (UNIX only) (uses GhostScript)
-dppmraw	PPM portable pixmap, raw (UNIX only) (uses GhostScript)
-dtiff	TIFF (rendered using Z-buffer)
-tiff	Add TIFF preview to EPS formats only—must be used in addition to an EPS device specification

MATLAB also provides methods for exporting images to graphics files. The functions `getframe`, `imwrite`, `avifile`, and `addframe` provide the capability to create and save image files from *figures*. (See Chapter 29 for more information.)

30.4 POSTSCRIPT SUPPORT

All PostScript devices as well as devices that use GhostScript, offer limited font support. This includes both devices that print and those that save images. The following table shows the supported fonts, in addition to common Windows fonts that map into standard PostScript fonts (Note that fonts not listed in the table are mapped to `Courier` and that the Windows devices `-dwin` and `-dwinc` use standard Windows printer drivers and therefore support all installed fonts):

PostScript Font	Windows Equivalent
AvantGarde	
Bookman	
Courier	Courier New
Helvetica	Arial
Helvetica-Narrow	
NewCenturySchlBk	New Century Schoolbook
Palatino	
Symbol	
Times-Roman	Times New Roman
ZapfChancery	
ZapfDingbats	

If your printer supports PostScript, a built-in PostScript driver should be used. Level 1 PostScript is an older specification and is required for some printers. Level 2 PostScript produces smaller and faster code and should be used if possible.

If you are using a color printer, a color driver should be used. Black-and-white or grayscale printers can use either driver. However, when a color driver is used for a black-and-white printer, the file is larger and colors are dithered, making lines and text less clear in some cases. When colored lines are printed by using a black-and-white driver, they are converted to black. When colored lines are printed by using a color driver on a black-and-white printer, the lines are printed in grayscale. In this case, unless the lines have sufficient width, they often do not have sufficient contrast with the printed page.

As implemented in MATLAB, PostScript supports *surfaces* and *patches* (only with triangular faces) that have interpolated shading. When printed, the corresponding PostScript files contain color information at the *surface* or *patch* vertices, requiring the printer to perform the shading interpolation. Depending on the printer characteristics, this may take an excessive amount of time, possibly leading to a printer error. One way to solve this problem is to use flat shading along with a finer meshed surface. Another alternative that ensures that the printed output matches the screen image is to print by using either the Z-buffer or OpenGL renderer with a sufficiently high resolution. In this case, the output is in bitmap format and may result in a large output file, but no interpolation is required by the printer.

30.5 CHOOSING A RENDERER

A renderer processes graphics data such as arrays of vertices and color data into a format suitable for display, printing, or export. There are two major categories of graphics formats: bitmap (or raster) graphics and vector graphics.

Bitmap graphics formats contain information such as color at each point in a grid. As the divisions between points decrease, and the total number of points increases, the resolution of the resulting graphic increases, and the size of the resulting file increases. Increasing the number of bits used to specify the color of each point in the grid increases the total number of possible colors in the resulting graphic, and also increases the size of the resulting file. Increasing the complexity of the graphic has no effect on the size of the resulting output file.

Vector graphics formats contain instructions for recreating the graphic by using points, lines, and other geometric objects. Vector graphics are easily resized and usually produce higher-resolution results than bitmap graphics. However, as the number of objects in the graphic increases, the number of instructions required to recreate the graphic increases, and the size of the resulting file increases. At some point, the complexity of the instructions can become too much for an output device to handle, and the graphic simply cannot be output on the specific output device.

MATLAB supports three rendering methods: OpenGL, Z-buffer, and Painter's. Painter's uses vector format, while OpenGL and Z-buffer produce bitmaps. By default, MATLAB automatically selects a renderer based on the characteristics of the *figure* and the printer driver or file format used.

> The renderer MATLAB selects for printing or exporting is not necessarily the same renderer used to display a *figure* on the screen.

MATLAB's default selection can be overridden by the user, and this is often done to make the printed or exported *figure* look the same as it does on the screen or to avoid imbedding a bitmap in a vector-format output file, such as PostScript or EPS.

Examples of some situations that require specific renderers are as follows:

- If the *figure* uses RGB color rather than a single color for surface or patch objects, the graphic must be rendered by using a bitmap method to properly capture color.
- HPGL (`-dhpgl`) and Adobe Illustrator (`-cill`) output formats use the Painter's renderer.
- JPEG (`-djpeg`) and TIFF (`-dtiff`) output formats always use Z-buffer rendering.
- Lighting effects cannot be reproduced by using the vector-format Painter's renderer, and so a bitmap method must be used in this case as well.
- The OpenGL renderer is the only method that supports transparency.

The renderer used for printing and exporting can be chosen by using dialog boxes or options to the `print` command, or by setting Handle Graphics properties. The dialog box opened by selecting the **Options** button in the **Print Setup** and **Print** dialog boxes on UNIX platforms and the **Axes and Figures** tab in the **Page Setup** dialog box on all platforms can be used to select a renderer. The `-zbuffer`, `-opengl`, and `-painters` options to the `print` command select a specific renderer when printing or exporting that overrides any other selections made.

30.6 HANDLE GRAPHICS PROPERTIES

A number of Handle Graphics properties influence the way graphics are printed or exported. Many of the options selected from printing and exporting dialog boxes make changes to these properties for the current *figure*. The following table lists the *figure* properties that influence printing and exporting:

<table>
<tr><th>'PropertyName'</th><th>'PropertyValue' choices, {default}</th><th>Description</th></tr>
<tr><td>Color</td><td>[RGB vector]</td><td>Sets figure background color</td></tr>
<tr><td>InvertHardcopy</td><td>[{on} | off]</td><td>Determines whether figure background color is printed or exported. When set to on, forces a white figure background independent of the Color property.</td></tr>
<tr><td>PaperUnits</td><td>[{inches} | centimeters | normalized | points]</td><td>Units used to measure the size of a printed or exported figure</td></tr>
<tr><td>PaperOrientation</td><td>[{portrait} | lanscape | rotated]</td><td>Orientation of figure with respect to paper</td></tr>
<tr><td>PaperPosition</td><td>[left bottom width height] vector</td><td>Position of figure on paper or in exported file. width and height determine the size of the figure printed or exported.</td></tr>
<tr><td>PaperPositionMode</td><td>[auto | {manual}]</td><td>Determines whether PaperPosition width and height are used. When set to auto, the figure is printed or exported using the Figure window displayed width and height (i.e., output is WYSIWYG)</td></tr>
<tr><td>PaperSize</td><td>[width height] vector</td><td>Paper size measured in PaperUnits</td></tr>
<tr><td>PaperType</td><td>[{usletter} | uslegal | A0 | A1 | A2 | A3 | A4 | A5 | B0 | B1 | B2 | B3 | B4 | B5 | arch-A | arch-B | arch-C | arch-D | arch-E | A | B | C | D | E | tabloid | <custom</td><td>Type of paper used. Selecting a paperType sets the PaperSize accordingly</td></tr>
</table>

Renderer	[{painters} | zbuffer | OpenGL]	Displays renderer
RendererMode	[{auto} manual]	Determines how the renderer is chosen. When set to auto, MATLAB chooses the renderer automatically and independently for display, printing, and export. When set to manual, the renderer set by the Renderer property is used for display, printing, and export.

Certain *axes* properties also influence printing and exporting. Particularly important are the *axes* tick mode properties:

```
XTickMode [ {auto} | manual ]
YTickMode [ {auto} | manual ]
ZtickMode [ {auto} | manual ]
```

When a *figure* is printed or exported, the resulting graphic is normally rendered at a different size than the *figure* on the screen. Since the width and height are different, MATLAB can rescale the number and placement of tick marks on each axis to reflect the new size. Setting the tick mode properties to 'manual' prevents MATLAB from changing the tick marks on the *axes* when the *figure* is printed or exported.

Some *line* properties can be used to advantage for output as well:

```
Color: [ 3-element RGB vector ]
LineStyle: [ {-} | – | : | -. | none ]
LineWidth: [ scalar ]
Marker: [ + | o | * | . | x | square | diamond | v | ^ | > | < | pentagram
    | hexagram | {none} ]
MarkerSize: [ scalar ]
MarkerEdgeColor: [ none | {auto} ] -or- a ColorSpec.
MarkerFaceColor: [ {none} | auto ] -or- a ColorSpec.
```

When colored lines are printed, the result depends on the capabilities of the output device and the printer driver. If a color printer and a color printer driver are used, the result is in color, as expected. If a black-and-white printer driver is used, the result is black and white. If a color printer driver is used with a black-and-white printer, the result is grayscale. This can be a problem, since grayscale is printed by using dithering, which may lead to lines that are not distinct. A different, but related, problem can occur when printing in black and white. When multiple solid lines are printed in black, they lose the distinction that color provides on the screen. In this case, the line properties `'Color'`, `'LineStyle'`, `'LineWidth'`, and `'Marker'` can be used to add distinction to plotted lines.

Finally, it is often advantageous to modify *text* when printing or exporting *figures*. Useful *text* properties include the following:

```
Color: [ 3-element RGB vector ]
FontAngle: [ {normal} | italic | oblique ]
FontName: [ font name ]
FontSize: [ scalar ]
FontUnits: [ inches | centimeters | normalized | {points} | pixels ]
FontWeight: [ light | {normal} | demi | bold ]
```

Increasing the size of *text* strings such as titles and *axes* labels when printing or exporting to a smaller-sized graphic can often make the text easier to read. If the font used in the *figure* is not one of the 11 previously listed fonts supported by MATLAB for PostScript output, changing the font to one of these 11 can prevent unwanted font substitution. Sometimes a bold font shows up better in printed output than a normal-weight font. Changes such as these can often improve the appearance of the printed or exported output. Font characteristics are particularly important when exporting graphics for inclusion in presentation software, where fonts must be large and distinct enough to be readable from across a large room.

30.7 SETTING DEFAULTS

MATLAB sets the following factory default options for printing and exporting:

- *Figure* size is 8-by-6 inches (may be different outside of the United States).
- Orientation is portrait.
- *Figure* and *axes* background colors are inverted to white.
- U.S. letter (8.5-by-11 inch) paper is used if available (may be different outside of the United States).
- *Figure* is centered on the paper.
- *Figure* is cropped.
- Output is RGB (not CYMK).
- Tick marks are recalculated.
- MATLAB chooses the renderer.
- Uicontrols print.
- Print device is `-dps2` on UNIX and `-dwin` on the PC platform.

The default print device is set in the `$TOOLBOX/local/printopt.m` file. Edit this file to change the default print device across MATLAB sessions. If you do not have write access to this file, edit the file by using the command `edit printopt.m`, make your changes, save the `printopt.m` file into a local directory, and make sure the local directory is in the MATLABPATH before `$TOOLBOX/local`. For example, if you use a color PostScript printer for printed output on a UNIX platform, edit `printopt.m` and add the line `dev = '-dpsc2';` to the file at the location specified in the file.

Other option defaults can be changed by setting default properties in the `startup.m` file. For example, `set(0,'DefaultFigurePaperType','A4');` changes the default paper type to A4. The handle 0 addresses the *root* object. The `'DefaultFigurePaperType'` property sets the default value for the *figure* property `'PaperType'`. Adding the prefix `'Default'` to any Handle Graphics property name specifies that the accompanying property value should be used as the default. Default properties for a given object must be set at a higher level in the Handle Graphics hierarchy. For example, default *figure* properties must be set at the *root* object level, and default *axes* properties must be set at the *figure* object or *root* object level. Therefore, defaults are usually set at the *root* level. For example, the code

```
set(0,'DefaultFigurePaperOrientation','landscape');
set(0,'DefaultFigurePaperPosition',[0.25 0.25 10.5 8]);
set(0,'DefaultAxesXGrid','on','DefaultAxesYGrid','on');
set(0,'DefaultAxesLineWidth','1');
```

tells MATLAB to use the landscape mode, fill the page with the plot, print (and display) *x*- and *y*-axis grids, and display and print lines that are 1 point wide, as defaults in all *figures* and *axes*.

Many other options can be set using Handle Graphics properties. Most printing and exporting properties are *figure* and *axes* properties. (For more information on Handle Graphics properties and default values, see the next chapter.)

30.8 PUBLISHING

MATLAB provides additional options for publishing your formatted results, including graphics, to a number of different formats. Publishing in MATLAB provides the ability to execute M-files and capture the output in a formatted document. Document formats supported by MATLAB include HTML, XML, and LaTeX. On PC platforms, publishing to Microsoft Word or Powerpoint (if installed) is also supported. The MATLAB Notebook is another option for publishing on PC platforms. (See Chapter 36 for an example using the MATLAB Notebook.)

Publishing requires that the user define *Cells* (sections of code) in the M-file to be executed. (See the documentation on the MATLAB Editor for additional information on defining Cells.) When an M-file is published, the M-file is executed and the output—including the source code in each Cell, along with any *Command* Window output and graphical output—is formatted and published into document files in the selected format. Text markup is also supported. Additions can include an overall title, section titles, descriptive text, and equations and symbols using TeX formatting. Text may be formatted by using bold text, indented or preformatted text, bulleted lists, monospaced text, or even HTML links.

In addition to the **Publish** entries in the **File** menu of the MATLAB Editor, the `publish` function is available in the *Command* Window. Publishing preferences can be set in the Editor/Debugger section of the MATLAB **Preferences** menu. Specific instructions and examples of publishing are available in the on-line documentation.

30.9 SUMMARY

MATLAB provides a very flexible system for printing graphics and creating output in many different graphics formats. Most other applications can import one or more of the graphics file formats supported by MATLAB, but many have limited ability to edit the resulting graphic. The best results are achieved if the *figure* is edited and appropriate options are set before the *figure* is printed or exported. The most widely used, flexible output formats are PostScript, EPS, EMF, and TIFF. MATLAB contains native support for all of these formats and uses Ghostscript to translate them into many others.

MATLAB also provides the ability to publish a document that includes portions of an M-file—along with *Command* Window output, graphics output, descriptive text, and comments—in a number of document formats, including HTML, XML, LaTeX, Microsoft Word, and Powerpoint.

31

Handle Graphics

Handle Graphics is the name given to a large collection of low-level graphics features that specify how graphics behave and are displayed in MATLAB. Through interaction with Handle Graphics *objects* and their associated properties, you can gain almost infinite control over the graphical features available in MATLAB. As MATLAB continues to evolve, many Handle Graphics features can be manipulated interactively by using the numerous menus, contextual menus, toolbars, palettes, browsers, and editors available within *Figure* windows. These interactive tools make it possible to customize graphics while requiring minimal knowledge of Handle Graphics. As a result, detailed knowledge of Handle Graphics is required only when noninteractive graphics customization is desired. In this case, Handle Graphics function calls are commonly placed in an M-file.

Because of the diversity and breadth of the graphics features in MATLAB, there are well over one thousand pages of MATLAB-supplied documentation on graphics. As a result, it is simply not possible to provide a comprehensive survey of Handle Graphics in this text. Doing so would at least double the size of this text.

Given the space limitations and broader goals of the text, this chapter develops a basic understanding of Handle Graphics features that provides a basis for learning the many more specific aspects of graphics in MATLAB.

31.1 OBJECTS

Handle Graphics is based on the idea that every component of a MATLAB graphic is an ***object***, that each object has a unique identifier, or ***handle***, associated with it, and that each object has ***properties*** that can be modified as desired. Here, the term *object* is defined as a closely related collection of data and functions that form a unique whole. In MATLAB, a graphics object is a distinct component that can be manipulated individually.

All plotting and graphics in MATLAB create graphics objects. Some produce ***composite objects***, and some produce ***core objects***. Graphical objects in MATLAB are arranged in a hierarchy of parent objects and associated child objects, as shown in the following diagram:

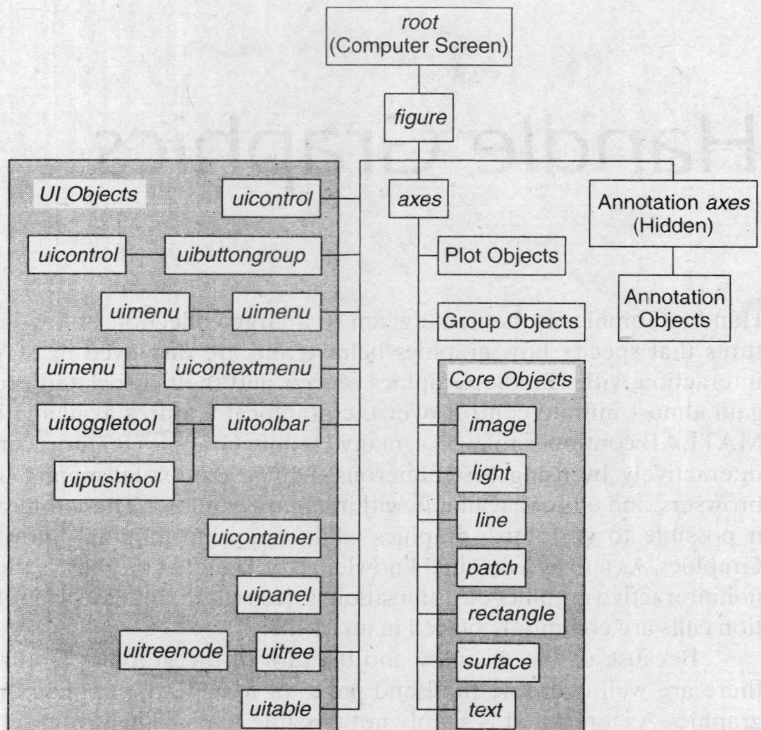

The computer screen itself is the *root* object and the parent of everything else. One or more *figure* objects are children of the *root*. The objects *axes*, annotation *axes*, and the collection of UI objects are children of *figures*. Plot objects, group objects, and the collection of core objects are children of *axes*. All objects that are children of the *figure* object in the hierarchy, except for the core objects, are called composite objects.

This hierarchy is new to MATLAB 7. In MATLAB 6, the graphics hierarchy did not document the hidden annotation *axes* and did not have ***plot*** objects or ***group*** objects. Core objects and some UI objects existed, but were simply not grouped and named. UI objects and core objects behave in the same way in MATLAB 7 as they did in previous MATLAB versions, whereas plot objects and group objects are new in MATLAB 7.

31.2 OBJECT HANDLES

In MATLAB, each object has an associated identifier, called a *handle*, which is a double-precision number. Each time an object is created, a unique handle is created for it. The handle of the *root* object, the computer screen, is always zero. The `Hf_fig=figure` command creates a new *figure* and returns its handle in the `Hf_fig` variable. *Figure* handles are normally integers and are usually displayed in the *Figure* window title bar. Other object handles are typically noninteger numbers in full MATLAB precision. All object creation functions return the handles of the objects they create.

Before MATLAB 7, the high-level graphics functions (discussed in Chapters 26 and 27) returned a column vector of handles to the core objects they created. For example, `Hl=plot(...)` returned handles to all *line* objects created by the `plot` function. Similarly, `Hs=surf(...)` returned a handle to a *surface* object. Now, in MATLAB 7, many high-level graphics creation functions return handles to plot objects. That is, `Hls=plot(...)` returns handles to *lineseries* plot objects. In the presence of these changes in the graphics hierarchy, fundamental operations using Handle Graphics remain unchanged. As a result, before these new features are addressed, the fundamental creation and manipulation of Handle Graphics objects through use of their handles is discussed.

> It is suggested that variable names used to store handles start with an upper case `H`, followed by one or more letters identifying the object type, then an underscore, and finally one or more descriptive characters. Thus, `Hf_fig` is a handle to a *figure*, `Ha_ax1` is a handle to an *axes* object, and `Ht_title` is a handle to a *text* object. When an object type is unknown, the letter `x` is used, as in `Hx_obj`. While handles can be given any name, following this convention makes it easy to spot object handle variables in an M-file.

31.3 OBJECT PROPERTIES

All objects have a set of ***properties*** that define their characteristics. It is by setting these properties that you modify how graphics are displayed. The properties associated with each object type (e.g., *axes*, *line*, and *surface*) are unique, although a number of property names are common to all objects. Object properties include characteristics such as an object's position, color, object type, parent object handle, child object handles, and many others. Each distinct object has properties associated with it that can be changed without affecting other objects of the same type.

Object properties consist of property ***names*** and their associated property ***values***. Property names are character strings. They are typically displayed in mixed case, with the initial letter of each word capitalized. For example, the property name `'LineStyle'` identifies the line style for a *line* object. When identifying a property name in an M-file or at the *Command* window prompt, MATLAB recognizes properties regardless of case. In addition, you need use only enough characters to uniquely identify the property name. For example, the position property of an *axes* object can be called `'Position'`, `'position'`, or even `'pos'`.

When an object is created, it is initialized with a full set of default property values that can be changed in either of two ways. The object-creation function can be issued with `('Property-name',Property-value)` pairs, or property values can be changed after the object is created. For example,

```
>> Hf_1 = figure('Color','yellow')
```

creates a new *figure* with default properties, except that the background color is set to yellow rather than to the default color.

In addition to the *Figure* window menu and toolbar features in MATLAB, the function `inspect` provides a GUI for inspection and modification of object properties. To use this function, simply issue `inspect(H)`, where `H` is the handle of the desired object.

31.4 get AND set

The two functions `get` and `set` are used to obtain or change Handle Graphics object properties. The function `get` returns the current value of one or more properties of an object. The most common syntax is `get(handle,'PropertyName')`. For example,

```
>> p = get(Hf_1,'Position')
```

returns the position vector of the *figure* having the handle `Hf_1`. Similarly,

```
>> c = get(Hl_a,'Color')
```

returns the color of an object identified by the handle `Hl_a`.

The function `set` changes the values of Handle Graphics object properties and uses the syntax `set(handle,'PropertyName',PropertyValue)`. For example,

```
>> set(Hf_1,'Position',p_vect)
```

sets the position of the *figure* having the handle `Hf_1` to that specified by the vector `p_vect`. Likewise,

```
>> set(Hl_a,'Color','r')
```

sets the color of the object having the handle `Hl_a` to red. In general, the `set` function can have any number of `('PropertyName',PropertyValue)` pairs. For instance,

```
>> set(Hl_a,'Color',[1 0 0],'LineWidth',2,'LineStyle','--')
```

changes the color of the *line* having the handle `Hl_a` to red, its line width to 2 points, and its line style to dashed.

In addition to these primary purposes, the `get` and `set` functions provide feedback about object properties. For example, `set(handle,'PropertyName')` returns a list of values that can be assigned to the object described by `handle`. For example,

```
>> set(Hf_1,'Units')
[ inches | centimeters | normalized | points | {pixels} | characters ]
```

shows that there are six allowable character-string values for the `'Units'` property of the *figure* referenced by `Hf_1` and that `'pixels'` is the default value.

If you specify a property that does not have a fixed set of values, MATLAB informs you of that fact:

```
>> set(Hf_1,'Position')
A figure's 'Position' property does not have a fixed set of property values.
```

In addition to the `set` command, Handle Graphics object-creation functions accept multiple pairs of property names and values. For example,

```
>> figure('Color','blue','NumberTitle','off','Name','My Figure')
```

creates a new *figure* with a blue background entitled `'My Figure'`, rather than the default window title `'Figure 1'`.

As an illustration of the preceding concepts, consider the following example:

```
>> Hf_fig = figure  % create a figure
Hf_fig =
     1
>> Hl_light = light % add default light to an axes in the figure
Hl_light =
           107
>> set(Hl_light)    % find settable properties of light
     Position
     Color
     Style: [ {infinite} | local ]

     ButtonDownFcn: string -or- function handle -or- cell array
     Children
     Clipping: [ {on} | off ]
     CreateFcn: string -or- function handle -or- cell array
     DeleteFcn: string -or- function handle -or- cell array
```

```
    BusyAction: [ {queue} | cancel ]
    HandleVisibility: [ {on} | callback | off ]
    HitTest: [ {on} | off ]
    Interruptible: [ {on} | off ]
    Parent
    Selected: [ on | off ]
    SelectionHighlight: [ {on} | off ]
    Tag
    UIContextMenu
    UserData
    Visible: [ {on} | off ]

>> get(Hl_light)    % get all properties and names for light
    Position = [1 0 1]
    Color = [1 1 1]
    Style = infinite

    BeingDeleted = off
    ButtonDownFcn =
    Children = []
    Clipping = on
    CreateFcn =
    DeleteFcn =
    BusyAction = queue
    HandleVisibility = on
    HitTest = on
    Interruptible = on
    Parent = [108]
    Selected = off
    SelectionHighlight = on
    Tag =
    Type = light
    UIContextMenu = []
    UserData = []
    Visible = on
```

The *light* object was used because it contains the fewest properties of any MATLAB object. A *figure* was created and returned a handle. A *light* object was then created that returned a handle of its own. An *axes* object was also created, since *light* objects are children of *axes*; the *axes* handle is available in the 'Parent' property of the *light*.

Note that the property lists for each object are divided into two groups. The first group lists properties that are unique to the particular object type, and the second group lists properties common to all object types. Note also that the set and get functions return slightly different property lists. The function set lists only properties that can be changed with the set command, while get lists all visible object properties. In the previous example, get listed the 'Type' property, while set did not. This property can be read but not changed; that is, it is a read-only property.

The number of properties associated with each object type is fixed in each release of MATLAB, but the number varies among object types. As already shown, a *light* object lists 3 unique and 18 common properties, or 21 properties in all. On the other hand, an *axes* object lists 103 properties. Clearly, it is beyond the scope of this text to thoroughly describe and illustrate all of the properties of all object types!

As an example of the use of object handles, consider the problem of plotting a line in a nonstandard color. In this case, the line color is specified by using an RGB value of [1 .5 0], a medium orange color:

```
>> x = -2*pi:pi/40:2*pi;  % create data
>> y = sin(x);            % find sine of x
>> Hls_sin = plot(x,y)    % plot sine and save lineseries handle
Hls_sin =
   59.0002
>> set(Hls_sin,'Color',[1 .5 0],'LineWidth',3) % Change color and width
```

Now add a cosine curve in light blue:

```
>> z = cos(x);            % find cosine of x
>> hold on                % keep sine curve
>> Hls_cos = plot(x,z);   % plot cosine and save lineseries handle
>> set(Hls_cos,'Color',[.75 .75 1]) % color it light blue
>> hold off
```

It's also possible to do the same thing with fewer steps:

```
>> Hls_line = plot(x,y, x,z);       % plot both curves and save handles
>> set(Hls_line(1),'Color',[1 .5 0],'LineWidth', 3)
>> set(Hls_line(2),'Color',[.75 .75 1])
```

How about adding a title and making the font size larger than normal?

```
>> title('Handle Graphics Example') % add a title
>> Ht_text = get(gca,'Title')        % get handle to title
>> set(Ht_text,'FontSize',16)        % customize font size
```

The last example illustrates an interesting point about *axes* objects. Every object has a `'Parent'` property, as well as a `'Children'` property, which contains handles to descendant objects. A *lineseries* object on a set of axes has the handle of the *axes* object in its `'Parent'` property and the empty array in the `'Children'` property. At the same time, the *axes* object has the handle of its *figure* in its `'Parent'` property and the handles of *lineseries* objects in the `'Children'` property. Even though *text* objects created with the `text` and `gtext` commands are children of *axes* and their handles are included in the `'Children'` property, the handles associated with the title string and axis labels are not. These handles are kept in the `'Title'`, `'XLabel'`, `'YLabel'`, and `'ZLabel'` properties of the *axes*. These *text* objects are always created when an *axes* object is created. The `title` command simply sets the `'String'` property of the title *text* object within the current *axes*. Finally, the standard MATLAB functions `title`, `xlabel`, `ylabel`, and `zlabel` return handles and accept property and value arguments. For example, the following command adds a 24-point green title to the current plot and returns the handle of the title *text* object:

```
>> Ht_title = title('This is a title.','FontSize',24,'Color','green')
```

In addition to `set` and `get`, MATLAB provides several other functions for manipulating objects and their properties. Objects can be ***copied*** from one parent to another using the `copyobj` function. For instance,

```
>> Ha_new = copyobj(Ha_ax1,Hf_fig2)
```

makes copies of the *axes* object with handle `Ha_ax1` and all of its children, assigns new handles, and places the objects in the *figure* with handle `Hf_fig2`. A handle to the new *axes* object is returned in `Ha_new`. Any object can be copied into any valid parent object based on the hierarchy described earlier. Either one or both arguments to `copyobj` can be vectors of handles.

Note that any object can be ***moved*** from one parent to another simply by changing the `'Parent'` property value to the handle of another valid parent object. For example,

```
>> figure(1)
>> set(gca,'Parent',2)
```

moves the current *axes* and all of its children from the *figure* having handle 1 to the *figure* having handle 2. Any existing objects in *figure* 2 are not affected, except that they may become obscured by the relocated objects.

Any object and all of its children can be ***deleted*** using the `delete(handle)` function. Similarly, `reset(handle)` resets all object properties associated with `handle`, except for the `'Position'` property, to the defaults for that object type. If `handle` is a column vector of object handles, all referenced objects are affected by `set`, `reset`, `copyobj`, and `delete`.

The `get` and `set` functions return a structure when an output is assigned. Consider the following example:

```
>> lprop = get(Hl_light)
lprop =
          BeingDeleted: 'off'
            BusyAction: 'queue'
         ButtonDownFcn: ''
              Children: [0x1 double]
              Clipping: 'on'
                 Color: [1 1 1]
             CreateFcn: ''
             DeleteFcn: ''
      HandleVisibility: 'on'
               HitTest: 'on'
         Interruptible: 'on'
                Parent: 108
              Position: [1 0 1]
              Selected: 'off'
    SelectionHighlight: 'on'
                 Style: 'infinite'
                   Tag: ''
                  Type: 'light'
         UIContextMenu: []
              UserData: []
               Visible: 'on'
>> class(lprop) % class of get(Hl_light)
ans =
struct

>> lopt = set(Hl_light)
lopt =
```

```
           BusyAction: {2x1 cell}
        ButtonDownFcn: {}
             Children: {}
             Clipping: {2x1 cell}
                Color: {}
            CreateFcn: {}
            DeleteFcn: {}
     HandleVisibility: {3x1 cell}
              HitTest: {2x1 cell}
        Interruptible: {2x1 cell}
               Parent: {}
             Position: {}
             Selected: {2x1 cell}
   SelectionHighlight: {2x1 cell}
                Style: {2x1 cell}
                  Tag: {}
        UIContextMenu: {}
             UserData: {}
              Visible: {2x1 cell}
>> class(lopt) % class of set(Hl_light)
ans =
struct
```

The field names of the resulting structures are the object property-name strings and are assigned alphabetically. Note that even though property names are not case sensitive, these field names are:

```
>> lopt.BusyAction
ans =
    'queue'
    'cancel'
>> lopt.busyaction
??? Reference to non-existent field 'busyaction'.
```

Combinations of property values can be set by using structures as well. For example,

```
>> newprop.Color = [1 0 0];
>> newprop.Position = [-10 0 10];
```

```
>> newprop.Style = 'local';
>> set(Hl_light,newprop)
```

changes the 'Color', 'Position', and 'Style' properties, but has no effect on any other properties of the *light* object. Note that you cannot simply obtain a structure of property values using get and use the same structure to set values:

```
>> light_prop = get(Hl_light);
>> light_prop.Color = [1 0 0];  % change the light color to red
>> set(Hl_light,light_prop);    % reapply the property values
??? Error using ==> set
Attempt to modify read-only light property: 'Type'.
```

Since 'Type' is the only read-only property of a *light* object, you can work around the problem by removing the 'Type' field from the structure:

```
>> light_prop = rmfield(light_prop,'Type');
>> set(Hl_light,light_prop)
```

For objects with more read-only properties, all read-only properties must be removed from the structure before using it to set property values.

A cell array can also be used to query a selection of property values. To do so, create a cell array containing the desired property names in the desired order and pass the cell array to get. The result is returned as a cell array as well:

```
>> plist = {'Color','Position','Style'}
plist =
    'Color'    'Position'    Style'
>> get(Hl_light,plist)
ans =
    [ double]    [1x3 double]    'local'
>> class(ans) % cell array in, cell array out
ans =
cell
```

One more point about the get function should be noted. If H is a vector of handles, get(H,'Property') returns a cell array rather than a vector. Consider the following example, given a *Figure* window with four subplots:

```
>> Ha = get(gcf,'Children')            % get axes handles
Ha =
       15.0002
       13.0002
```

```
     11.0002
      9.0002
>> Ha_kids = get(Ha,'Children')  % get handles of axes children
Ha_kids =
    [    16.0002]
    [4x1 double]
    [    12.0002]
    [2x1 double]]
>> class(Ha_kids)
ans =
    cell
>> Hx = cat(1,Ha_kids{:})        % convert to column vector
Hx =
     16.0002
     26.0002
     24.0002
     18.0002
     22.0002
     12.0002
     14.0002
     10.0002
>> class(Hx)
ans =
    double
```

Now Hx can be used as an argument to Handle Graphics functions expecting a vector of object handles.

31.5 FINDING OBJECTS

As has been shown, Handle Graphics provides access to objects in a *figure* and allows the user to customize graphics by using the get and set commands. The use of these functions requires that you know the handles of the objects to be manipulated. In cases where handles are unknown, MATLAB provides a number of functions for finding object handles. Two of these functions, gcf and gca, were introduced earlier. For example,

```
>> Hf_fig = gcf
```

returns the handle of the current *figure*, and

```
>> Ha_ax = gca
```

returns the handle of the current *axes* in the current *figure*.

In addition to the above, MATLAB includes gco, a function to obtain the handle of the current object. For example,

```
>> Hx_obj = gco
```

returns the handle of the current object in the current *figure*; alternatively,

```
>> Hx_obj = gco(Hf_fig)
```

returns the handle of the current object in the *figure* associated with the handle Hf_fig.

The current object is defined as the last object clicked on with the mouse within a *figure*. This object can be any graphics object except the *root*. When a *figure* is initially created, no current object exists, and gco returns an empty array. The mouse button must be clicked while the pointer is within a *figure* before gco can return an object handle.

Once an object handle has been obtained, the object type can be found by querying an object's 'Type' property, which is a character-string object name such as 'figure', 'axes', or 'text'. The 'Type' property is common to all objects. For example,

```
>> x_type = get(Hx_obj,'Type')
```

is guaranteed to return a valid object string for all objects.

When something other than the 'CurrentFigure', 'CurrentAxes', or 'CurrentObject' is desired, the function get can be used to obtain a vector of handles to the children of an object. For example,

```
>> Hx_kids = get(gcf,'Children');
```

returns a vector containing handles of the children of the current *figure*.

To simplify the process of finding object handles, MATLAB contains the built-in function findobj, which returns the handles of objects with specified property values. The form Hx=findobj(Handles,'flat','PropertyName',PropertyValue) returns the handles of all objects in Handles whose 'PropertyName' property contains the value PropertyValue. Multiple ('PropertyName', PropertyValue) pairs are allowed, and all must match. When Handles is omitted, the *root* object is assumed. When no ('PropertyName',PropertyValue) pairs are given, all objects match and all Handles are returned. When 'flat' is omitted, all objects in Handles ***and all descendants of these objects***, including axes titles and labels, are searched. When no objects are found to match the specified criteria, findobj returns an empty array. As an example, finding all green *line* objects is easily accomplished with the following statement:

```
>> Hl_green = findobj(0,'Type','line','Color',[0 1 0]);
```

It is possible to hide specific handles by using the 'HandleVisibility' property common to all objects. This property is convenient, because it keeps the user from inadvertently deleting or changing the properties of an object. When an object has its 'HandleVisibility' property set to 'off' or to 'callback', findobj does not return handles to these objects when called from the *Command* window. Hidden handles do not appear in lists of children or as the output of gcf, gca, or gco. However, when the property is set to 'callback', these handles can be found during the execution of a callback (which is discussed in the next chapter).

31.6 SELECTING OBJECTS WITH THE MOUSE

The gco command returns the handle of the current object, which is the last object clicked on with the mouse. When a mouse click is made near the intersection of more than one object, MATLAB uses rules to determine which object becomes the current object. Each object has a selection region associated with it. A mouse click within this region selects the object. For *line* objects, the selection region includes the *line* and all of the area within a 5-pixel distance from the *line*. The selection region of a *surface*, *patch*, or *text* object is the smallest rectangle that contains the object. The selection region of an *axes* object is the *axes* box itself, plus the areas where labels and titles appear. Objects within *axes*, such as *lines* and *surfaces*, are higher in the stacking order, and clicking on them selects the associated object rather than the *axes*. Selecting an area outside of the *axes* selection region selects the *figure* itself.

When a mouse click is within the border of two or more objects, the ***stacking order*** determines which object becomes the current object. The stacking order determines which overlapping object is on *top* of the others. Initially, the stacking order is determined when the object is created, with the newest object at the top of the stack. For example, when you issue two figure commands, two *figures* are created. The second *figure* is drawn on top of the first. The resulting stacking order has *figure* 2 on top of *figure* 1, and the handle returned by gcf is 2. If the figure(1) command is issued or if *figure* 1 is clicked on, the stacking order changes. *Figure* 1 moves to the top of the stack and becomes the current *figure*.

In the preceding example, the stacking order was apparent from the window overlap on the computer screen. However, this is not always the case. When two *lines* are plotted, the second *line* drawn is on top of the first at the points where they intersect. If the first *line* is clicked on with the mouse at some other point, the first *line* becomes the current object, but the stacking order does not change. A click on the intersecting point continues to select the second *line* until the stacking order is explicitly changed.

The stacking order is given by the order in which `'Children'` handles appear for a given object. That is, `Hx_kids=get(handle,'Children')` returns handles of child objects, in the stacking order. The first element in the vector `Hx_kids` is at the top of the stack, and the last element is at the bottom of the stack. The stacking order can be changed by changing the order of the `'Children'` property value of the parent object. For example,

```
>> Hf = get(0,'Children');
>> if length(Hf) > 1
     set(0,'Children',Hf([end 1:end-1]);
   end
```

moves the bottom *figure* to the top of the stack, where it becomes the new current *figure*.

31.7 POSITION AND UNITS

The `'Position'` property of *figure* objects and of most other Handle Graphics objects is a four-element row vector. As shown in the following figure, the values in this vector are `[left, bottom, width, height]`, where `[left, bottom]` is the position of the lower left corner of the object relative to its parent and `[width, height]` is the width and height of the object.

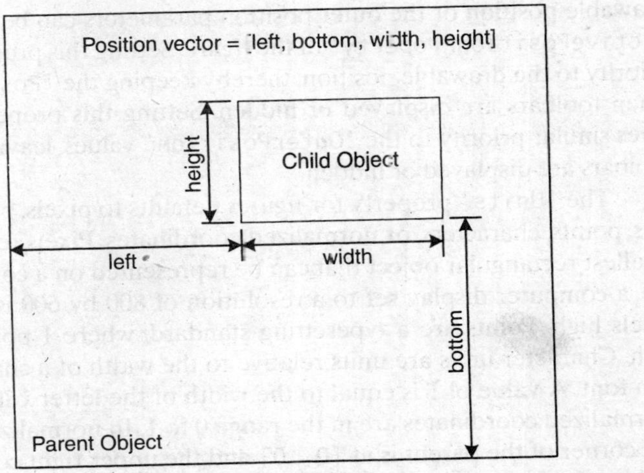

These position vector values are in units specified by the `'Units'` property of the object. For example, the code

```
>> get(gcf,'Position')
ans =
```

```
   920   620   672   504
>> get(gcf,'units')
ans =
pixels
```

shows that the lower left corner of the current *figure* object is 920 pixels to the right and 620 pixels above the lower left corner of the screen and that the *figure* object is 672 pixels wide and 504 pixels high. ***Note that the*** **`'Position'`** ***vector for a figure gives the drawable area within the figure object itself and does not include window borders, scroll bars, menus, or the title bar of the Figure window.***

Alternatively, *figures* have an undocumented `'OuterPosition'` property that does include the window borders:

```
>> get(gcf,'Position')        % drawable position
ans =
   920   620   672   504
>> get(gcf,'OuterPosition') % outside position
ans =
   916   616   680   531
```

Here, the outer position contains the left, bottom, width, and height of the outer boundary of the *Figure* window. When the *Figure* or *Camera* toolbar is displayed or hidden in response to a choice from the **View** menu in a *Figure* window, either the drawable position or the outer position parameters can be maintained by setting the `'ActivePositionProperty'` of the *figure*. Setting this property to `'Position'` gives priority to the drawable position, thereby keeping the `'Position'` values unchanged when toolbars are displayed or hidden. Setting this property to `'OuterPosition'` gives similar priority to the `'OuterPosition'` values, leaving them unchanged when toolbars are displayed or hidden.

The `'Units'` property for *figures* defaults to pixels, but can be inches, centimeters, points, characters, or normalized coordinates. Pixels represent screen pixels, the smallest rectangular object that can be represented on a computer screen. For example, a computer display set to a resolution of 800 by 600 is 800 pixels wide and 600 pixels high. Points are a typesetting standard, where 1 point is equal to 1/72 of an inch. Character units are units relative to the width of a character in the default system font. A value of 1 is equal to the width of the letter *x* in the default system font. Normalized coordinates are in the range 0 to 1. In normalized coordinates, the lower left corner of the parent is at `[0, 0]` and the upper right corner is at `[1, 1]`. Inches and centimeters are self-explanatory.

To illustrate various `'Units'` property values, consider again the preceding example:

```
>> set(gcf,'units','inches')      % INCHES
>> get(gcf,'position')
```

```
ans =
        7.9224        5.3362        5.7931        4.3448

>> set(gcf,'units','cent')        % CENTIMETERS
>> get(gcf,'position')
ans =
        20.108        13.544        14.703        11.027

>> set(gcf,'units','normalized')% NORMALIZED
>> get(gcf,'position')
ans =
       0.57438       0.51583          0.42          0.42
>> set(gcf,'units','points')      % POINTS
>> get(gcf,'position')
ans =
        570.41        384.21         417.1        312.83
>> set(gcf,'units','char')        % CHARACTERS
>> get(gcf,'position')
ans =
        153.17        38.688           112          31.5
```

All of these values represent the same *figure* position relative to the computer screen for a particular monitor and screen resolution.

The positions of *axes* objects are also four-element vectors having the same form, `[left, bottom, width, height]`, but specifying the object position relative to the lower left corner of the parent *figure*. ***In general, the* `'Position'` *property of a child is relative to the position of its parent.***

To be more descriptive, the computer screen, or *root* object, position property is not called `'Position'`, but rather `'ScreenSize'`. In this case, `[left, bottom]` is always `[0, 0]`, and `[width, height]` are the dimensions of the computer screen in units specified by the `'Units'` property of the *root* object.

31.8 DEFAULT PROPERTIES

MATLAB assigns default properties to each object as it is created. The built-in defaults are referred to as *factory* defaults. To override these defaults, you must set or get the values using `set` and `get`. In cases where you want to change the same properties every time, MATLAB allows you to set your own default properties. It lets you change the default properties for individual objects and for object types at any point in the object hierarchy. When an object is created, MATLAB looks for a default value at the ***parent*** level. If no default is found, the search continues up the object hierarchy until a default value is found or until it reaches the built-in factory default.

You can set your own default values at any level of the object hierarchy by using a special property-name string consisting of 'Default', followed by the object type and the property name. The handle you use in the set command determines the point in the object parent-child hierarchy at which the default is applied. For example,

```
>> set(0,'DefaultFigureColor',[.5 .5 .5])
```

sets the default background color for all new *figure* objects to medium gray rather than the MATLAB default. This property applies to the *root* object (whose handle is always zero), and so all new *figures* will have a gray background. Other examples include the following:

```
>> set(0,'DefaultAxesFontSize',14)          % larger axes fonts - all figures
>> set(gcf,'DefaultAxesLineWidth',2)        % thick axis lines - this figure only
>> set(gcf,'DefaultAxesXColor','y')         % yellow X axis lines and labels
>> set(gcf,'DefaultAxesYGrid','on')         % Y axis grid lines - this figure
>> set(0,'DefaultAxesBox','on')             % enclose axes - all figures
>> set(gca,'DefaultLineLineStyle',':')      % dotted linestyle - these axes only
```

When a default property is changed, only objects created *after* the change is made are affected. Existing objects already have property values assigned and do not change.

When working with existing objects, it is always a good idea to restore them to their original state after they are used. If you change the default properties of objects in an M-file, save the previous settings and restore them when exiting the routine:

```
oldunits = get(0,'DefaultFigureUnits');
set(0,'DefaultFigureUnits','normalized');

    <MATLAB statements>

set(0,'DefaultFigureUnits',oldunits);
```

To customize MATLAB to use user-defined default values at all times, simply include the desired set commands in your startup.m file. For example, the code

```
set(0,'DefaultAxesXGrid','on')
set(0,'DefaultAxesYGrid','on')
```

```
set(0,'DefaultAxesZGrid','on')
set(0,'DefaultAxesBox','on')
set(0,'DefaultFigurePaperType','A4')
```

creates all axes with grids, and an enclosing box is turned on and sets the default paper size to A4. Defaults set at the *root* level affect every object in every *Figure* window.

There are three special property value strings that reverse, override, or query user-defined default properties. They are 'remove', 'factory', and 'default'. If you've changed a default property, you can reverse the change, thereby resetting it to the original defaults using 'remove':

```
>> set(0,'DefaultFigureColor',[.5 .5 .5])  % set a new default
>> set(0,'DefaultFigureColor','remove')    % return to MATLAB defaults
```

To temporarily override a default and use the original MATLAB default value for a particular object, use the special property value 'factory':

```
>> set(0,'DefaultFigureColor',[.5 .5 .5])   % set a new user default
>> figure('Color','factory')   % figure using default color
```

The third special property value string is 'default'. This value forces MATLAB to search up the object hierarchy until it encounters a default value for the desired property. If one is found, MATLAB uses this default value. If the *root* object is reached and no user-defined default is found, the MATLAB factory default value is used. This feature is useful when you want to set an object property to a default property value after it was created with a different property value, as in the following code:

```
>> set(0,'DefaultLineColor','r') % set default at the root level
>> set(gcf,'DefaultLineColor','g') % current figure level default
>> Hl_rand = plot(rand(1,10));     % plot a line using 'ColorOrder' color
>> set(Hl_rand,'Color','default') % the line becomes green
>> close(gcf)                      % close the window
>> Hl_rand = plot(rand(1,10));     % plot a line using 'ColorOrder' color again
>> set(Hl_rand,'Color','default') % the line becomes red
```

Note that the plot command does not use *line* object defaults for the line color. If a color argument is not specified, the plot command uses the *axes* 'ColorOrder' property to specify the color of each *line* it generates.

A list of all of the factory defaults can be obtained by issuing

```
>> get(0,'factory')
```

Default properties that have been set at any level in the object hierarchy can be listed by issuing

```
>> get(handle,'default')
```

The *root* object contains default values for a number of color properties and the *figure* position at startup:

```
>> get(0,'default')
ans =
           defaultTextColor: [0 0 0]
          defaultAxesXColor: [0 0 0]
          defaultAxesYColor: [0 0 0]
          defaultAxesZColor: [0 0 0]
      defaultPatchFaceColor: [0 0 0]
      defaultPatchEdgeColor: [0 0 0]
           defaultLineColor: [0 0 0]
 defaultFigureInvertHardcopy: 'on'
         defaultFigureColor: [0.8 0.8 0.8]
           defaultAxesColor: [1 1 1]
      defaultAxesColorOrder: [7x3 double]
      defaultFigureColormap: [64x3 double]
    defaultSurfaceEdgeColor: [0 0 0]
      defaultFigurePosition: [920 620 672 504]
```

Other defaults are not listed until they have been created by the user:

```
>> get(gcf,'default')
ans =
0x0 struct array with fields:
>> set(gcf,'DefaultLineMarkerSize',10)
>> get(gcf,'default')
ans =
    defaultLineMarkerSize: 10
```

31.9 COMMON PROPERTIES

All Handle Graphics objects share the common set of object properties shown in the following table:

Property	Description
BeingDeleted	Set to 'on' when object is about to be deleted
BusyAction	Controls how MATLAB handles callback interuptions
ButtonDownFcn	Callback code executed when the mouse button is pressed over the object
Children	Handles of visible children
Clipping	Enable or disable clipping of *axes* children
CreateFcn	Callback code executed immediately *after* an object is created
DeleteFcn	Callback code executed immediately *before* an object is deleted
BusyAction	Determines how callbacks to this object are interrupted by other callbacks
HandleVisibility	Determines whether the object handle is visible in the *Command* window or while executing callbacks
HitTest	Determines whether the object can be selected with the mouse and then become the current object
Interruptible	Determines whether callbacks to this object are interruptible
Parent	Handle of parent object
Selected	Determines whether an object has been selected as the current object
SelectionHighlight	Determines whether a selected object shows visible selection handles or not
Tag	User-defined character string used to identify or *tag* the object. Often useful in association with findobj. For example, findobj(0,'tag','mytagstring').
Type	Character string identifying object type
UIContextMenu	Handle of contextual menu associated with an object
UserData	Storage of any user-defined variable associated with an object
Visible	Visibility of object

Three of these properties contain *callbacks*: 'ButtonDownFcn', 'CreateFcn', and 'DeleteFcn'. Callbacks identify MATLAB code to be executed when the action described by the property occurs. In many cases, the code is a function call. The 'Parent' and 'Children' properties contain handles of other objects in the hierarchy. Objects drawn on the *axes* are clipped at the *axes* limits if 'Clipping' is 'on', which is the default for all axes children except *text* objects. 'Interruptible' and 'BusyAction' control the behavior of callbacks if a later callback is triggered while a previous callback is currently executing. 'Type' is a string specifying the object type. 'Selected' is 'on' if this object is the 'CurrentObject' of the *figure*, and 'SelectionHighlight' determines whether the object changes appearance when selected. 'HandleVisibility' specifies whether the object handle is visible, invisible, or visible only to callbacks. The *root* 'ShowHiddenHandles' property overrides the 'HandleVisibility' property of all objects, if needed. If 'Visible' is set to 'off', the object disappears from view. It is still there, and the object handle is still valid, but it is not rendered on the computer screen. Setting 'Visible' to 'on' restores the object to view. The 'Tag' and 'UserData' properties are reserved for the user. The 'Tag' property is typically used to tag an object with a user-defined character string. For example,

```
>> set(gca,'Tag','My Axes')
```

attaches the string 'My Axes' to the current *axes* in the current *figure*. This string does not display in the *axes* or in the *figure*, but you can query the 'Tag' property to identify the object. For instance, when there are numerous *axes*, you can find the handle to the above *axes* object by issuing the command

```
>> Ha_myaxes = findobj(0,'Tag','My Axes');
```

The 'UserData' property can contain any variable you wish to put into it. A character string, a number, a structure, or even a multidimensional cell array can be stored in any object's 'UserData' property. No MATLAB function changes, or makes assumptions about, the values contained in these properties.

The properties listed for each object using the get and set commands are the documented properties. There are also undocumented, or hidden, properties used by MATLAB developers. Some of them can be modified, but others are read-only. Undocumented properties are simply hidden from view. These properties still exist and can be modified. The undocumented *root* property 'HideUndocumented' controls whether get returns all properties or only documented properties. For example,

```
>> set(0,'HideUndocumented','off')
```

makes undocumented object properties visible within MATLAB.

> Since undocumented properties have been purposely left undocumented, one must be cautious when using them. They are sometimes less robust than documented properties and are always subject to change. Undocumented properties may appear, disappear, change functionality, or even become documented in future versions of MATLAB.

31.10 PLOT OBJECTS

As stated earlier, MATLAB 7 introduces plot objects and group objects. Plot objects are objects associated with the high-level graphics functions discussed in Chapters 26 and 27. Plot objects were created in MATLAB 7 as a way to group the core objects created by high-level graphics functions, so that the overall properties of the graphics are more easily identified and modified. That is, plot objects have additional properties that do not exist in the core objects used in their creation. These additional properties specify properties specific to the type of graphic created. For example, consider the creation of a bar graph:

```
>> hbs_mm7 = bar(randn(1,6));
>> title('Figure 31.1 Random Bar Graph')
>> get(hbs_mm7,'type')
ans =
hggroup
>> hx_hbs = get(hbs_mm7,'children');
>> get(hx_hbs,'type')
ans =
patch
```

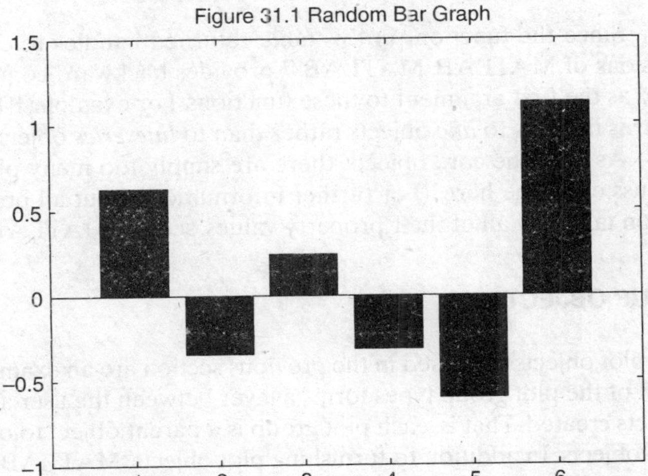

This bar graph contains a composite *barseries* plot object whose handle type is designated hggroup. The children of this object are single *patch* objects. Rather than have all of the properties of the *patch* object, the *barseries* object has properties such as 'BaseLine', 'BarLayout', and 'BarWidth', which directly specify aspects of the created bar chart. Changing these properties in turn changes the appropriate properties of the underlying *patch* object. By adding this layer on top of the *patch* object, manipulation of the bar chart is much easier. You do not need to know how to manipulate *patch* object properties to make changes in the bar chart.

The plot objects in MATLAB 7 are shown in the following table (also included is the `'type'` property returned when `get(H,'type')` is called, where `H` is a handle of the corresponding plot object):

Plot Object	`Get(H,'type')`	**Created by the graphics functions**
`areasseries`	`hggroup`	`area`
`barseries`	`hggroup`	`bar, bar3, bar3h.`
`contourgroup`	`hggroup`	`contour, contour3, contourf`
`errorbarseries`	`hggroup`	`errorbar`
`lineseries`	`line`	`plot, plot3, semilogx, semilogy, loglog`
`quivergroup`	`hggroup`	`quiver, quiver3`
`scattergroup`	`hggroup`	`scatter, scatter3`
`stairseries`	`hggroup`	`stairs`
`stemseries`	`hggroup`	`stem, stem3`
`surfaceplot`	`surface`	`surf, mesh`

Since the functions in this table returned handles to core objects in previous versions of MATLAB, MATLAB 7 provides backward compatibility when `'v6'` is used as the first argument to these functions. For example, `Hl = plot('v6', ...)` returns handles to *line* objects rather than to *lineseries* objects.

As with the core objects, there are simply too many plot object properties to discuss each one here. (For further information about all object properties and the action taken by all of their property values, see the MATLAB documentation.)

31.11 GROUP OBJECTS

The plot objects discussed in the previous section are an example of grouped objects. Each of the plot group types forms a layer between the user and the underlying core objects created. That is, each plot group is a parent object to one or more underlying core objects. In addition to furnishing plot objects, MATLAB 7 provides this grouping capability through the function `hggroup`. That is, you can group any number of *axes* object children into a group. These children can include any of the core objects, plot objects, or other objects grouped with the use of the `hggroup` function. As such, a group object has an *axes* object, or another group object, as its parent object.

By grouping Handle Graphics objects and giving them a single group handle, the visibility and selectability of the group are determined globally. That is, setting the `'visible'` property of the group sets the individual `'visible'` properties of all underlying group children. In addition, it is possible to select all members in a group by clicking on any group member with the mouse. While the plot objects created as part of MATLAB have different or additional property names and property values than their underlying core objects, MATLAB does not provide this capability for groups created by means of the hggroup function. Group objects have all of the common object properties listed in section 31.9. In addition, they have an 'EraseMode' property that controls the 'EraseMode' property of all core objects in the group.

To illustrate the creation of a group object, consider the following code segment:

```
Ha = newplot; % create new axes object

Hl = line(1:6,[rand(1,6);1:6]);  % create 2 core line objects
Hp = patch([3 5 4],[2 2 5],'w'); % create a core patch object

Hg_mm7 = hggroup; % create a new group object and return handle

set(Hl,'Parent',Hg_mm7) % place lines in group
set(Hp,'Parent',Hg_mm7) % place patch in group

get(Hg_mm7) % look at group properties
	EraseMode = normal
	HitTestArea = off

	BeingDeleted = off
	ButtonDownFcn =
	Children = [ (3 by 1) double array]
	Clipping = on
	CreateFcn =
	DeleteFcn =
	BusyAction = queue
	HandleVisibility = on
	HitTest = on
	Interruptible = on
	Parent = [151.017]
	Selected = off
	SelectionHighlight = on
	Tag =
```

```
Type = hggroup
UIContextMenu = []
UserData = []
Visible = on
```

The children of the group object having handle `Hg_mm7` are the two *line* objects and one *patch* object. The properties of the lines and patch are hidden under group object, and the group `'type'` property is `hggroup`.

There are many cases where it is desirable to rotate, translate, or scale a group of objects within an axes. While the `hggroup` function does not provide this capability, the group function `hgtransform` does. Like the `hggroup` function, `hgtransform` creates a group object that becomes the parent of any number of *axes* object children. These children can include any of the core objects, plot objects, or other objects grouped by means of the `hgtransform` function. As such, a group object has an *axes* object, or another group object, as its parent object. The construction of a `hgtransform` group object follows that of the `hggroup` function. Group objects created by using the `hgtransform` function have all of the common object properties listed in section 31.9. In addition, they have a `'Matrix'` property that specifies a graphical transformation matrix to be applied to all members of the group object. The content of this transformation matrix is constructed following standard graphics transformation practice. The function `makehgtform` facilitates the construction of this matrix. (For further information see the MATLAB documentation and other resources on graphics transformations.)

31.12 ANNOTATION *AXES*

The annotation *axes* shown in the Handle Graphics hierarchy at the beginning of this chapter is simply a core object *axes* with its handle visibility turned Off. This object contains all of the annotations added to a *figure*, using the numerous menus, toolbars, palettes, browsers, and editors available within *Figure* windows. The `'units'` property of this axes is set to `'normalized'`, and its position is set to [0 0 1 1], so that it covers the entire drawing area of the *figure*. Lines, arrows, rectangles, text boxes, etc., can be created by the use of the interactive aspects of *Figure* windows; in addition, they can be created with the `annotation` function. Because annotations added to a *figure* exist in this separate *axes*, they do not change in response to additions or modifications to any underlying data plots. Therefore, it is important to create annotations after the underlying plots are finalized.

31.13 LINKING OBJECTS

In some situations it is desirable to link identical properties of a number of objects, so that changing a linked property of any one of the objects makes the same change to all linked objects. To support this capability, MATLAB provides the functions `linkprop` and `linkaxes`. The function `linkprop` provides general object-property linking, whereas `linkaxes` is an M-file function that uses `linkprop` to specifically link axis limits on two or more *axes* objects.

To demonstrate the use of these functions, consider the following code:

```
>> H_a1 = subplot(2,1,1);       % create axes object
>> plot(rand(1,30))             % plot some random data
>> H_a2 = subplot(2,1,2);       % create a second axes
>> plot(randn(1,30))            % plot random data on second axes

>> linkaxes([H_a1 H_a2],'xy') % link x and y axis limits
```

After this code is executed, the axis limits on the two *axes* are linked. Using the pan or zoom features on the *Figure* window toolbar, panning or zooming one *axes* performs the identical function on the other *axes*. Alternatively, issuing an `axis` command on one *axes* applies the command to all linked *axes* objects.

The previous example can also be implemented with the use of `linkprop` by executing the following code:

```
>> close                        % close current figure to start over
>> H_a1 = subplot(2,1,1);       % create axes object
>> plot(rand(1,30))             % plot some random data
>> H_a2 = subplot(2,1,2);       % create a second axes
>> plot(randn(1,30))            % plot random data on second axes

>> H_link = linkprop([H_a1 H_a2],{'Xlim','Ylim'})
H_link =
        graphics.linkprop

>> class(H_link)
ans =
graphics.linkprop

>> methods(H_link)
Methods for class graphics.linkprop:
addprop     addtarget     linkprop     removeprop     removetarget
```

The output `H_link` of the `linkprop` function is a handle to a *linkprop* object named `graphics.linkprop`. This object is an object-oriented class created by using

MATLAB's object-oriented programming features (as discussed in Chapter 33). As shown, this class has five methods that facilitate manipulation of *linkprop* objects. Once properties are linked via the function `linkprop`, the returned handle `H_link` must remain in existence. In the preceding example, `H_link` exists in the base workspace. If `H_link` is deleted or destroyed by being overwritten, the linked properties are unlinked. Modifying a *linkprop* object requires passing the associated object handle to one of its methods. For example,

```
>> addprop(H_link,'Zlim')
```

adds z-axis limit linking to the object in `H_link`. (See the MATLAB documentation for more information on linking Handle Graphics object linking.)

31.14 NEW PLOTS

When a new graphics object is created by using a low-level command such as `line` or `text`, the object appears on the current *axes* in the current *figure* by default. High-level graphics functions like `mesh` and `plot`, however, clear the current *axes* and reset most *axes* properties to their defaults before displaying a plot. As discussed earlier, the `hold` command can be used to change this default behavior. Both *figures* and *axes* have a `'NextPlot'` property used to control how MATLAB reuses existing *figures* and *axes*. The `hold`, `newplot`, `reset`, `clf`, and `cla` functions all affect the `'NextPlot'` property of *figures* and *axes*. `'NextPlot'` has three possible values:

```
>> set(gcf,'NextPlot')
    [ {add} | replace | replacechildren ]
>> set(gca,'NextPlot')
    [ add | {replace} | replacechildren ]
```

The default setting for *figures* is `'add'`; the default for *axes* is `'replace'`. When `'NextPlot'` is set to `'add'`, a new plot is added without clearing or resetting the current *figure* or *axes*. When the value is `'replace'`, a new object causes the *figure* or *axes* to remove all child objects and reset all properties except `'Position'` and `'Units'` to their defaults before drawing the new plot. The default settings clear and reset the current *axes* and reuse the current *figure*.

The third possible setting for `'NextPlot'` is `'replacechildren'`. This setting removes all child objects, but does not change the current *figure* or *axes* properties. The command `hold on` sets both *figure* and *axes* `'NextPlot'` properties to `'add'` The command `hold off` sets the *axes* `'NextPlot'` property to `'replace'`.

The `newplot` function creates a new *axes* by following the `'NextPlot'` guidelines. This function is meant to be called to create an *axes* that will contain children created by a core object-creation function such as `line`, `patch`, and so on, as opposed to a high-level graphics function such as `plot` or `surf`. The `newplot` function contains code similar to the following code segment:

```
function Ha = newplot
Hf = gcf;                              % get current figure or create one
next = lower(get(Hf,'NextPlot'));
switch next
  case 'replacechildren', clf;         % delete figure children
  case 'replace', clf('reset');        % delete children and reset properties
end
Ha = gca;                              % get current axes or create one
next = lower(get(Ha,'NextPlot'));
switch next
  case 'replacechildren', cla;         % delete axes children
  case 'replace', cla('reset');        % delete children and reset properties
end
```

31.15 RENDERING SPEED

There are many applications in which you either wish to show the evolution of a graphical solution as one or more properties of the solution change or to dynamically modify a graphical image in response to mouse feedback. In both of these cases, it is desirable to maximize the screen rendering speed and eliminate flicker. MATLAB *figure*, *axes*, *line*, *patch*, *rectangle*, and *surface* objects offer properties that influence rendering speed and flicker.

MATLAB *figures* have three properties that influence rendering speed: `'Renderer'`, `'DoubleBuffer'`, and `'BackingStore'`. `'Renderer'` refers to the underlying algorithm used to create or render a graphical image on the screen. This property has three possible values—`'painters'`, `'zbuffer'`, and `'openGL'`. Normally, MATLAB selects among the three renderers automatically on the basis of the complexity of the graphics objects to be rendered and on the capabilities of the computer being used. For the most part, MATLAB makes the optimum choice for each *figure*. However, in special cases, the renderer can be specified by setting this property as desired.

`'BackingStore'` is normally set to `'on'` and controls the existence of a duplicate copy of the *Figure* window data. When multiple overlapping windows appear on a computer screen, having `'BackingStore'` set to `'on'` allows obscured or partially obscured *Figure* windows to be refreshed quickly from the off-screen copy when uncovered. When `'BackingStore'` is set to `'off'`, no off-screen copy is created, thereby increasing rendering speed, but forcing a recomputation of graphical data when a *figure* is uncovered.

The *figure* 'DoubleBuffer' property is normally set to 'off'. Setting this property to 'on' instructs MATLAB to draw graphics objects into an off-screen buffer and then dump the data to the screen when the buffer is fully updated. By drawing into an off-screen buffer rather than directly updating the screen, the rendering progress is hidden from the user. MATLAB sets this property to 'off' because it is applicable only to graphics rendered with the Painter's algorithm. In addition, it produces flicker-free rendering only for simple graphics, such as those produced by the function plot. Graphics containing *surface* or *patch* objects generally do not benefit from double buffering.

When an *axes* is rendered with the Painter's algorithm, the amount of behind-the-scenes work done to render objects such as *lines* can be controlled by the 'DrawMode' *axes* property. By default, this property is set to 'normal'. However, setting it to 'fast' sacrifices rendering accuracy for added speed. For Z-buffer and OpenGL rendering, the property has no effect.

The graphics drawing objects *line*, *patch*, *rectangle*, and *surface* all have an 'EraseMode' property that allows the user to specify how they are erased and rerendered. The default value for this property is 'normal', with 'none', 'background', and 'xor' being alternatives. This property determines how these objects are rendered when they are redrawn because of a change in their own properties or the placement of other objects on top of them. For example, when 'EraseMode' is set to 'none', the original object is not erased when its properties are changed, the modified object is simply rendered. In most cases, this leaves the *axes* with undesirable ghosts. Setting 'EraseMode' to 'background' erases the original object by setting the pixels it occupies to the *axes* background color. This damages objects appearing beneath the original object. Setting 'EraseMode' to 'xor' erases and redraws the *line* by applying an exclusive OR operation on the color underneath the object. This does not damage objects beneath the changed object, but can affect the color of the changed object. Given these property value descriptions, rendering speed is increased most dramatically with 'EraseMode' set to 'none', but this results in ghosts that are undesirable in most cases. Setting 'EraseMode' to 'xor' or 'background' offers a compromise between speed and rendering accuracy. In most cases, 'xor' is the best choice for creating animations.

31.16 CALLBACKS

All Handle Graphics objects have the properties 'ButtonDownFcn', 'CreateFcn', and 'DeleteFcn'. In addition, *figures* have the properties 'CloseRequestFcn', 'KeyPressFcn', 'WindowButtonDownFcn', 'WindowButtonMotionFcn', and 'WindowButtonUpFcn', and the user interface functions have a property 'CallBack'. The property names associated with each of these properties are called ***callbacks***. These callbacks identify code to be executed when the specific user actions associated with a property name are taken. In the simplest case, callbacks are character strings that are evaluated by eval in the *Command* window workspace. These strings can contain any sequence of valid MATLAB statements. In most cases, callbacks are function calls, often to the same function where the callbacks are defined. The setting of callbacks tells MATLAB to perform certain tasks in response to an action taken by the user. These callbacks form the basis for MATLAB's GUI features to be discussed in the next chapter.

The simplest callback is the close request callback, which, by default, is not empty:

```
>> get(gcf,'CloseRequestFcn')
ans =
closereq
>> class(ans)
ans =
char
```

By default, when a *Figure* window is closed by clicking the close box in the *figure* title bar, the string `closereq` is passed to `eval`. This string is the name of a function in MATLAB that simply deletes the current *figure*. So, by default, clicking the close box deletes the associated *Figure* window. This behavior can be changed simply by replacing the preceding string with another to be evaluated on a close request—for example,

```
>> set(gcf,'CloseRequestFcn','')
```

This replacement disables closure via the close box. The close request function is an empty string, and so no action is taken. This callback string can be any valid sequence of MATLAB statements. Therefore, the string could prompt the user for confirmation of the close request before actually doing it.

31.17 M-FILE EXAMPLES

There are many, many examples of Handle Graphics usage in MATLAB itself. Almost all of the specialized plotting functions in the `specgraph` directory (`>> doc specgraph`) are composed of Handle Graphics functions. Even the M-file function `axis` is implemented by using Handle Graphics function calls. This section provides further illustrations of Handle Graphics usage.

This function `mmis2d` returns logical True if an axis is a 2-D view of the *x-y* plane:

```
function [tf,xa,ya]=mmis2d(H)
%MMIS2D True for Axes that are 2D.
% MMIS2D(H) returns True if the axes having handle H displays
% a 2D viewpoint of the X-Y plane where the X- and Y-axes are
% parallel to the sides of the associated figure window.
```

```
%
% [TF,Xa,Ya]=MMIS2D(H) in addition returns the angles of x- and y-axes
%
% e.g., if the x-axis increases from right-to-left Xa=180
% e.g., if the y-axis increases from left-to-right Ya=0
% e.g., if the x-axis increases from bottom-to-top Xa=90

if ~ishandle(H)
      error('H Must be a Handle.')
end
if ~strcmp(get(H,'Type'),'axes')
      error('H Must be a Handle to an Axes Object.')
end
v = get(H,'view');
az = v(1);
el = v(2);
tf = rem(az,90)==0 && abs(el)==90;

if nargout==3
      xdir = strcmp(get(H,'Xdir'),'reverse');
      ydir = strcmp(get(H,'Ydir'),'reverse');
      s = sign(el);

      xa = mod(-s*az - xdir*180,360);
      ya = mod(s*(90-az) - ydir*180,360);
end
```

This function makes use of the function `ishandle`, which returns logical True for arguments that are valid object handles. It checks to see if the supplied handle is that of an *axes* by getting the `'Type'` property. If successful, it then gets the `'View'` property to determine the requested output.

The function `mmgetpos` finds the position of an object in a specific set of units. This function does the right thing, in that it gets the current `'Units'` property, sets the units to the `'Units'` of the desired output. gets the `'Position'` property in the desired units, and then resets the `'Units'` property:

```
function p=mmgetpos(H,u,cp)
%MMGETPOS Get Object Position Vector in Specified Units.
% MMGETPOS(H,'Units') returns the position vector associated with the
% graphics object having handle H in the units specified by 'Units'.
% 'Units' is one of: 'pixels', 'normalized', 'points', 'inches', 'cent',
% or 'character'.
% 'Units' equal to 'data' is valid for text objects only.
%
% MMGETPOS does the "right thing", i.e., it: (1) saves the current units,
% (2) sets the units to those requested, (3) gets the position, then
% (4) restores the original units.
%
% MMGETPOS(H,'Units','CurrentPoint') returns the 'CurrentPoint' position
% of the figure having handle H in the units specified by 'Units'.
%
% MMGETPOS(H,'Units','Extent') returns the 'Extent' rectangle of the text
% object having handle H.
%
% 'Uimenu', 'Uicontextmenu', 'image', 'line', 'patch', 'surface',
% 'rectangle' and 'light' objects do NOT have position properties.

if ~ischar(u)
   error('Units Must be a Valid String.')
end
if ~ishandle(H)
         error('H is Not a Valid Handle.')
end
Htype = get(H,'Type');
if nargin==3 && ~isempty(cp) && ischar(cp)
      if strcmp(Htype,'figure') && lower(cp(1))=='c'
            pname = 'CurrentPoint';
      elseif strcmp(Htype,'text') && lower(cp(1))=='e'
            pname = 'Extent';
```

```
    else
            error('Unknown Input Syntax.')
    end

elseif H~=0
    pname = 'Position';

elseif H==0  % root object
    pname = 'ScreenSize';
else
    error('Unknown Input Syntax.')
end

hu = get(H,'units'); % get original units
set(H,'units',u)     % set to desired units

p = get(H,pname);    % get position in desired units
set(H,'units',hu)    % set units back to original units
```

The mmzap function illustrates a technique that is very useful when writing Handle Graphics function M-files: It uses a combination of waitforbuttonpress and gco to get the handle to an object selected using the mouse. The command waitforbuttonpress is a built-in MATLAB function that waits for a mouse click or key press. Following is its help text:

```
>> help waitforbuttonpress

 WAITFORBUTTONPRESS Wait for key/buttonpress over figure.
    T = WAITFORBUTTONPRESS stops program execution until a key or
    mouse button is pressed over a figure window.  Returns 0
    when terminated by a mouse buttonpress, or 1 when terminated
    by a keypress.  Additional information about the terminating
    event is available from the current figure.
```

After a mouse button is pressed with the mouse pointer over a *figure*, gco returns the handle of the selected object. This handle is then used to manipulate the selected object:

```
function mmzap(arg)
%MMZAP Delete Graphics Object Using Mouse.
% MMZAP waits for a mouse click on an object in
% a figure window and deletes the object.
% MMZAP or MMZAP text erases text objects.
% MMZAP axes  erases axes objects.
% MMZAP line  erases line objects.
% MMZAP surf  erases surface objects.
% MMZAP patch  erases patch objects.
%
% Clicking on an object other than the selected type, or striking
% a key on the keyboard aborts the command.

if nargin<1
   arg='text';
end
Hf = get(0,'CurrentFigure');
if isempty(Hf)
   error('No Figure Window Exists.')
end
if length(findobj(0,'Type','figure'))==1
      figure(Hf) % bring only figure forward
end
key = waitforbuttonpress;

if key  % key on keyboard pressed
      return
      else    % object selected
            object = gco;
            type = get(object,'Type');
            if strncmpi(type,arg,4)
                  delete(object)
            end
end
```

The functions `xlim`, `ylim`, and `zlim` in MATLAB allow you to set and get axis limits for the three plot axes independently. There are no equivalent functions for grid lines. The function `grid` turns grid lines on and off along all three axes. To add this feature the function `mmgrid` allows you to turn grid lines on and off along any individual axis:

```
function mmgrid(varargin)
%MMGRID  Individual Axis Grid Lines on the Current Axes.
% V is a single character X, Y, or Z denoting the desired axis.
% MMGRID V toggles the major grid lines on the V-axis.
% MMGRID V ON adds major grid lines to the V-axis.
% MMGRID V ON MINOR adds minor grid lines to the V-axis.
% MMGRID V OFF removes major grid lines from the V-axis.
% MMGRID V OFF MINOR removes minor grid lines from the V-axis.
%
% See also GRID

ni = nargin;
if ni==0
   error('At Least One Input Argument Required.')
end
if ~iscellstr(varargin)
   error('Input Arguments Must be Strings.')
end
Hf = get(0,'CurrentFigure'); % get current figure if it exists
if isempty(Hf) % no figure so do nothing
   return
end
Ha = get(Hf,'CurrentAxes'); % get current axes if it exists
if isempty(Ha) % no axes so do nothing
   return
end
% parse input and do work
V = varargin{1};
idx = strfind('xXyYzZ',V(1));
```

```
if isempty(idx)
   error('Unknown Axis Selected.')
end
VGrid = [upper(V(1)) 'Grid']; % XGrid, YGrid, or ZGrid

if ni==1  % MMGRID V      Toggle Grid
   Gstate = get(Ha,VGrid);
   if strcmpi(Gstate,'on')
      set(Ha,VGrid,'off')
   else
      set(Ha,VGrid,'on')
   end
elseif ni==2  % MMGRID V ON  or MMGRID V OFF
   OnOff = varargin{2};
   if strcmpi(OnOff,'on')
      set(Ha,VGrid,'on')
   elseif strcmpi(OnOff,'off')
      set(Ha,VGrid,'off')
   else
      error('Second Argument Must be On or OFF.')
   end
elseif ni==3  % MMGRID V ON MINOR  or MMGRID V OFF MINOR
   if ~strcmpi(varargin{3},'minor')
      error('Unknown Third Argument.')
   end
   VGrid = [upper(V(1)) 'MinorGrid'];
   OnOff = varargin{2};
   if strcmpi(OnOff,'on')
      set(Ha,VGrid,'on')
   elseif strcmpi(OnOff,'off')
      set(Ha,VGrid,'off')
   else
      error('Second Argument Must be On or OFF.')
   end
end
```

Rather than use the functions `gcf` and `gca` to get the current *figure* and *axes*, respectively, Handle Graphics calls are used to get the `'CurrentFigure'` and `'CurrentAxes'` properties. By doing so, no automatic creation of a *figure* or *axes* is performed. This allows the function to terminate without performing any action, if no *figure* or *axes* exists. The rest of the function simply modifies the `'XGrid'`, `'YGrid'`, `'ZGrid'`, `'XMinorGrid'`, `'YMinorGrid'`, or `'ZMinorGrid'` properties of the current *axes*, as directed by the input arguments.

31.18 SUMMARY

Handle Graphics functions provide the ability to fine-tune the appearance of visual aspects of MATLAB. Each graphics object has a handle associated with it that can be used to manipulate the object. The following table documents pertinent Handle Graphics functions in MATLAB:

Function	Description
`get`	Get object properties
`set`	Set object properties
`gcf`	Get current *figure*
`gca`	Get current *axes*
`gco`	Get current object
`findobj`	Find visible objects having specified properties
`findall`	Find visible and invisible objects having specified properties
`findfigs`	Return visible *figure* windows to the computer screen
`allchild`	Get visible and invisible children handles for an object
`copyobj`	Copy object to new parent
`inspect`	Open Handle Graphics property inspector GUI
`root`	Root computer object, handle = 0
`figure`	*figure* object creation
`axes`	*axes* object creation
`image`	*image* object creation
`light`	*light* object creation
`line`	*line* object creation
`patch`	*patch* object creation
`rectangle`	*rectangle* object creation
`surface`	*surface* object creation
`text`	*text* object creation

Function	Description
linkaxes	Create a link object for linking axis limits on two or more *axes* objects
linkprop	Create a link object for linking listed properties of two or more Handle Graphics objects
uibuttongroup	User interface container object for managing 'radiobutton' and 'togglebutton' style *uicontrol* objects
uicontainer	User interface *container* object creation
uicontrol	User interface *uicontrol* object creation
uimenu	User interface *uimenu* object creation
uicontextmenu	User interface *uicontextual menu* object creation
uipanel	User interface *uipanel* object creation
uitoolbar	User interface *uitoolbar* object creation
uipushtool	Momentary contact pushbutton for a *uitoolbar*
uitoggletool	On/Off pushbutton for a *uitoolbar*
uitable	User interface *uitable* object creation
uitree	User interface *uitree* object creation
uitreenode	User interface *uitreenode* object creation
areasseries	Plot object created by the function area
barseries	Plot object created by the functions bar, bar3, bar3h
contourgroup contourf	Plot object created by the functions contour, contour3,
errorbarseries	Plot object created by the function errorbar
lineseries	Plot object created by the functions plot, plot3, semilogx, semilogy, loglog
quivergroup	Plot object created by the functions quiver, quiver3
scattergroup	Plot object created by the functions scatter, scatter3
stairseries	Plot object created by the function stairs
stemseries	Plot object created by the functions stem, stem3
surfaceplot	Plot object created by the functions surf, mesh
hggroup	Create group object
hgtransform	Create group object
makehgtform	Create transformation matrix for hgtransform group object
annotation	Create annotation *axes* object
reset	Reset object properties to default values
clf	Clear current *figure*
cla	Clear current *axes*

Function	Description
`ishandle`	True for arguments that are object handles
`delete`	Delete object
`close`	Close *figure* using close request function
`refresh`	Refresh *figure*
`gcbo`	Get current callback object
`gcbf`	Get current callback *figure*
`closereq`	Default *figure* `'CloseRequestFcn'` callback
`newplot`	Create *axes* with knowledge of `'NextPlot'` properties

32

Graphical User Interfaces

This chapter introduces the graphical user interface features available in MATLAB. These features include predefined dialog boxes, as well as window menus, contextual menus, pushbuttons, scroll bars, radio buttons, toggle buttons, popup menus, list boxes, and toolbars that can be placed in *Figure* windows. In addition to these features, it is possible to dynamically track mouse position and motion, and perform tasks based on this position and motion. These features are so extensive and detailed that entire texts have been devoted exclusively to them. Given the broader goals of this text, the best that can be offered here is a useful introduction and several illustrative examples.

32.1 WHAT'S A GUI?

A user interface is the point of contact or method of interaction between a person and a computer or computer program. It is the method used by the computer and the user to exchange information. The computer displays text and graphics on the computer screen and may generate sounds with a speaker. The user communicates with the computer by using an input device such as a keyboard, mouse, trackball, drawing pad, or microphone. The user interface defines the look and feel of the computer, operating system, or application. Often a computer or program is chosen on the basis of pleasing design and the functional efficiency of its user interface.

A graphical user interface, or GUI (pronounced *goo' ey*), is a user interface incorporating graphics objects such as windows, icons, buttons, menus, and text. Selecting or activating these objects in some way usually causes an action or change to occur. The most common activation method is to use a mouse or other pointing device to control the movement of a pointer on the screen and to press a mouse button to signal object selection or some other action.

In the same way that the Handle Graphics capabilities of MATLAB discussed in the previous chapter let you customize the way MATLAB displays information, the Handle Graphics user interface functions described in this chapter let you customize the way you interact with MATLAB.

This chapter illustrates the use of predefined dialog boxes and the use of Handle Graphics *uicontrol*, *uimenu*, *uicontextmenu*, and *uitoolbar* objects to add graphical user interfaces to MATLAB functions and M-files. *uimenu* objects create drop-down menus and submenus in *Figure* windows. *uicontrol* objects create objects such as buttons, sliders, popup menus, and text boxes. *uicontextmenu* objects create contextual menus that open over objects. *uitoolbar* objects contain pushbuttons (*uipushtool* objects) and toggle buttons (*uitoggletool* objects).

MATLAB includes an excellent example of its GUI capabilities in the `demo` command. To explore these demonstrations, simply issue the command

```
>> demo
```

32.2 PREDEFINED DIALOG BOXES

Essentially, every computer application offers the capability to open and save data files. To navigate the directory structure, operating systems or window managers provide dialog boxes to perform the tasks of identifying file names and directory paths. In MATLAB, these tasks are performed by the functions `uigetfile`, `uiputfile`, and `uigetdir`. None of these functions actually opens or saves a file. All they do is return a file name or a directory path that can be used, along with the low-level file I/O functions discussed in Chapter 14, to perform directory and file manipulation.

When possible, `uigetfile`, `uiputfile`, and `uigetdir` use standard dialog boxes available on your computer platform. As a result, their layout varies from platform to platform, but their functionality does not. These dialog boxes match the operation of standard operating system dialog boxes that identify files for opening and saving and for choosing directories. For example, using `uigetfile` to find the `startup.m` file on the author's computer produces the following results:

```
>> [fname,dirpath] = uigetfile('*.m')
fname =
startup.m
dirpath =
C:\matlabR14\work\
```

Appending the file name to the directory path gives the unique file specfication for `startup.m`:

```
>> myfile = [dirpath fname]
myfile =
C:\matlabR14\work\startup.m
```

It is important to note that `uigetfile` is not limited to directories on the MATLAB search path. The directory path returned will be for whatever directory the dialog box points to just before it is closed.

Using `uiputfile` to save a MAT-file in the work directory on the author's computer produces the following results:

```
>> [fname,dirpath] = uiputfile('*.mat')

fname =

mydata

dirpath =

C:\matlabR14\work\
```

Here, the string `mydata` was entered as the file name in the dialog box. Even though `'*.mat'` specified the file type, `'.mat'` was not automatically appended to the returned `fname`. It is up to the programmer to append the file extension.

Specifying colors in MATLAB based on RGB triples is straightforward, but lacks visual feedback about the actual color specified by a given triple. In addition, most graphics objects have a `'Color'` property that can be set. The function `uisetcolor` provides a GUI for choosing RGB triples or setting the color of a particular graphics object.

As with `uigetfile`, the function `uisetcolor` uses the standard color dialog box available on your computer platform (when one is available). As a result, the layout and features of `uisetcolor` vary from platform to platform, but the functionality does not.

Another built-in function, named `uisetfont`, provides a GUI for selecting fonts and font attributes. Using the function to choose Palatino 12-point italics produces the following results:

```
>> fc = uisetfont

fc =

      FontName: 'Palatino'
     FontUnits: 'points'
      FontSize: 12
    FontWeight: 'normal'
     FontAngle: 'italic'
```

Here, `fc` is a structure containing the features chosen in the `uisetfont` GUI. The results are in the proper form to set the font properties of any *text* object.

32.3 M-FILE DIALOG BOXES

In addition to the built in dialog functions discussed earlier, MATLAB offers a number of dialog boxes implemented as M-file functions. Some of these functions prompt the user for input of some kind. The functions available include `axlimdlg`, `dialog`, `inputdlg`, `menu`, and `msgbox`.

The function axlimdlg provides a rudimentary dialog box for setting plot axes limits. The *Figure* window editing features in MATLAB are much more comprehensive. The function inputdlg creates a set of text edit box *uicontrols* and prompts the user for input into each. This function is useful for prompting the user for a few values. The function Menu offers the user a selection of alternatives using *uicontrol* pushbuttons.

The functions dialog and msgbox are generic dialog-box creation functions. Of these functions, dialog simply creates a *Figure* window with default properties set appropriate for *Figure* windows that do not contain any *axes* objects. *Figure* windows created by using dialog use minimal system resources. For example, they do not allocate memory for a colormap. The function msgbox is used by all message dialog boxes and manages all of the underlying activities required to put up a dialog box and accept input.

The standard message dialog boxes in MATLAB include errordlg, helpdlg, questdlg, and warndlg. These boxes display an appropriate icon, along with at least one pushbutton to acknowledge and dismiss the dialog box. In addition to being helpful in application development, these functions are good examples of GUI construction to study.

32.4 DIALOG BOX SUMMARY

The dialog box functions available in MATLAB are summarized in the following table:

Function	Description
axlimdlg	Axes limits dialog box
dialog	Creates figure for dialog box or GUI
errordlg	Error dialog box
helpdlg	Help dialog box
inputdlg	Input dialog box
listdlg	List selection dialog box
menu	Menu choice selection dialog box
msgbox	Generic message dialog box
pagedlg	Page position dialog box
pagesetupdlg	Page setup dialog box
printdlg	Print dialog box
printpreview	Print preview dialog box
questdlg	Question dialog box
uigetfile	Standard open file dialog box
uiputfile	Standard save file dialog box
uisetcolor	Color selection dialog box
uisetfont	Font and font attributes dialog box
waitbar	Displays wait bar
warndlg	Warning dialog box

32.5 GUI OBJECT HIERARCHY

Graphical user interface creation utilizes a number of MATLAB functions. These functions create Handle Graphics objects that are shown in the UI Objects group in the following figure:

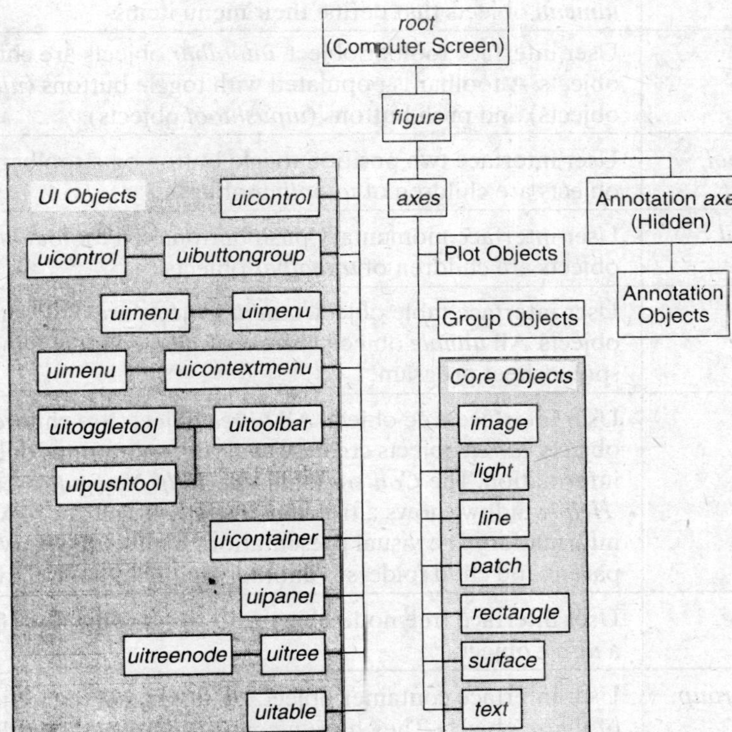

The *UI Objects* group contains numerous types of GUI objects. These features are summarized in the following table:

UI Object	Description
uicontrol	General user interface control object having one of the following styles: `'checkbox'`, `'edit'`, `'frame'`, `'listbox'`, `'popupmenu'`, `'pushbutton'`, `'radiobutton'`, `'slider'`, `'text'`, and `'togglebutton'`. All *uicontrol* objects are the children of *figure* objects.
uimenu	User interface menu object. *uimenu* objects that are children of *figure* objects are menu headings at the top of a *Figure* window. *uimenu* objects that are children of other *uimenu* objects are menu items or submenu items.

UI Object	Description
uicontextmenu	User interface contextual menu object. All *uicontextmenu* objects are children of *figure* objects. The handle of a *uicontextmenu* is placed in the `'UIContextMenu'` property of the Handle Graphics object for which they are to appear. All *uicontextmenu* objects have child *uimenu* objects that define their menu items.
uitoolbar	User interface toolbar object. *uitoolbar* objects are children of *figure* objects. A toolbar is populated with toggle buttons (*uitoggletool* objects) and push buttons (*uipushtool* objects).
uitoggletool	User interface two position toggle button on a toolbar. *uitoggletool* objects are children of *uitoolbar* objects.
uipushtool	User interface momentary push button on a toolbar. *uipushtool* objects are children of *uitoolbar* objects.
uitable	User interface table object. *uitable* objects are children of *figure* objects. All *uitable* objects have rows and columns similar to a spreadsheet program.
uitree	User interface tree object. All *uitree* objects are children of *figure* objects. *uitree* objects create visual representations of hierarchical information. The *Content* tab in the *Help Navigator* section of the *Help* window shows a tree that visually organizes MATLAB help information. The visual presentation of a file directory tree showing parent and child folders is another example of a tree object.
uitreenode	User interface tree node object. *uitreenode* objects define nodes on a *uitree* object.
uibuttongroup	User interface container object. All *uibuttongroup* objects are children of *figure* objects. They have *uicontrol* and other Handle Graphics objects as their children. The primary purpose of *uibuttongroup* objects is to manage the exclusive selection behavior of radio buttons and toggle buttons contained within it.
uicontainer	User interface container object. *uicontainer* objects contain groups of other user interface objects and become their parent. The position of *uicontainer* child objects is relative to the container and therefore move relative to the container.
uipanel	User interface container object. Like *uicontainer* objects, *uipanel* objects contain groups of other user interface objects and become their parent. However, *uipanel* objects have borders and titles that can be set.

There are 10 different styles of *uicontrol* objects. Each of these styles creates a different GUI component. Because these components are fundamental parts of a graphical user interface, they are described in the following table:

uicontrol Style	Description
`'checkbox'`	Check boxes consist of buttons with a label and a small square box to the left of the label text. When activated, the control is toggled between checked and cleared. When checked, the box is filled or contains an x, depending on the platform; when cleared, the box becomes empty. Check boxes are typically used to indicate the state of an option or attribute.
`'edit'`	Editable text boxes display text in a box so that you can modify or replace the text string dynamically, just as you would by using a text editor or word processor. Editable text boxes can contain one or more lines of text. A single-line editable text box accepts one line of text from the user, while a multiline text box accepts more than one line of text. Multiline editable text boxes have a vertical scroll bar. Single-line text entry is terminated by pressing the **Return** key. Multiline text entry is terminated with **Control-Return**.
`'frame'`	Frame *uicontrol* objects are simply opaque, shaded, rectangular regions with a border. Frames are analogous to the `'Separator'` property of *uimenu* objects, in the sense that they provide visual separation. Frames are typically used to logically group radio buttons or other *uicontrol* objects. Frames should be defined before other objects are placed within them. Otherwise, the frame may cover the other *uicontrols*. In MATLAB 7, frame style *uicontrol* objects have been superseded by *uicontainer* and *uipanel* objects, which are much more versatile.
`'listbox'`	List box *uicontrol* objects look like multiline text boxes. However, in this case one or more lines of text text are selectable, but they are not editable.
`'popupmenu'`	Popup menus are used to present a list of mutually exclusive choices to the user. When closed, a popup menu appears as a rectangle or button containing the label of the current selection with a small raised rectangle, or downward-pointing arrow, beside the label to indicate that the object is a popup menu. When the pointer is positioned over a popup control and the mouse button is pressed, other choices appear. Moving the pointer to a different choice and releasing the mouse button closes the popup menu and displays the new selection. MS Windows and some X-Window System platforms allow the user to click on a popup menu to open it and then click again on a menu choice to select it.
`'pushbutton'`	Pushbuttons, sometimes called *command buttons* or just *buttons*, are small, rectangular screen objects that usually contain a text label. Selecting a pushbutton with the mouse by moving the pointer over the object and clicking the mouse button causes MATLAB to perform the action defined by the object's callback string. Immediately after a pushbutton is pressed, it returns to its default up state. Pushbuttons are typically used to perform an action, rather than change a state or set an attribute.

uicontrol Style	Description
`'radiobutton'`	Radio buttons consist of buttons containing a label and a small circle or diamond to the left of the label text. When selected, the circle or diamond is filled; when unselected, the indicator is cleared. Radio buttons are typically used to select one of a group of mutually exclusive options.
`'slider'`	Sliders, or ***scroll bars***, consist of three distinct parts: the trough, or the rectangular area representing the range of valid object values; the indicator within the trough representing the current value of the slider; and arrows at each end of the trough. Sliders are typically used to select a value from a range of values. Slider values can be set in three ways: First, the indicator can be moved by positioning the mouse pointer over the indicator, holding down the mouse button while moving the mouse, and releasing the mouse button when the indicator is in the desired location. The second method is to click the mouse button while the pointer is in the trough, but to one side of the indicator. The indicator moves in that direction over a default distance equal to about 10 percent of the total range of the slider. Finally, clicking on one of the arrows at the ends of the slider moves the indicator by default about 1 percent of the slider range in the direction of the arrow. Sliders are often accompanied by separate text objects used to display labels, the current slider value, and range limits.
`'text'`	Static text boxes are controls that simply display a text string. Static text boxes are typically used to display labels, user information, or current values. Static text boxes are static in the sense that the user cannot dynamically change the text displayed.
`'togglebutton'`	Toggle buttons are identical to pushbuttons, except that they toggle between two states, up and down, when repeatedly pushed by clicking on them with the mouse pointer.

Given the 12 GUI objects and the 10 styles of *uicontrol* objects described in the preceding tables, there are 21 distinct GUI objects that can be used to create graphical user interfaces in MATLAB. Each of these objects has numerous Handle Graphics properties that can be accessed by using the functions `set` and `get`. Taken as a whole, these objects, their property names, and associated property values constitute hundreds of features and options. Discussion of all of these features and options is beyond the scope of this text. The remainder of this chapter introduces some of the main features of GUI creation and ends with several illustrative examples.

32.6 GUI CREATION FUNDAMENTALS

The fundamental steps of GUI creation are as follows:

1. Understand what you want the GUI to do. This is often the most difficult step. In many cases, what you want the GUI to do changes as new ideas and options are discovered during GUI construction.

2. Sketch the GUI layout on a piece of paper. This often skipped step saves time in the long run, because iterating hand sketches of potential GUI layouts on paper is much faster than building and rebuilding GUI prototypes in MATLAB.

3. On the basis of the final sketch, create the GUI using UI objects. This step can be done by directly entering the creation code in to an M-file. Alternatively, the MATLAB graphical user interface development environment (GUIDE), can be used.

4. Create the MATLAB code that is executed when a user interacts with the GUI. This callback code is most often contained in the same M-file as the code that creates the GUI.

5. Test and debug the GUI. In particular, if the GUI will be used by others, try interacting with the GUI in ways that you never intended, yet in ways a less knowledgeable user may actually use it.

32.7 GUI OBJECT SIZE AND POSITION

The `'Position'` and `'Units'` properties of UI objects are used to locate objects within their parent object, which in many cases is a *Figure* window. Given a *Figure* window or container object of some size, GUI layout is a problem in 2-D geometry. When designing a GUI, you must make objects large enough to be seen and to display the text or image that is part of the object. You also must decide if the GUI *figure* is to be resizable.

Often, sizing and placing UI objects is a process of trial and error. Even when you are satisfied with the result, the appearance of the *figure* on another platform may be sufficiently different to require more adjustments. Many times, it is desirable to make objects a bit larger than appears necessary, simply to ensure usability on all computer platforms.

Just because a *figure* has a default size, there is no guarantee that all *figures* on all platforms are that size. If you add UI objects to an existing *figure*, you may find that the *figure* is smaller or larger than the default. In addition, you can resize any *figure* at any time, unless you are prevented from doing so because the *figure* object's `'Resize'` property has been set to `'off'`. Therefore, in general it is a good idea to specifically set the size of a *Figure* window to be used for a GUI.

When you are adding UI objects to a *figure* that may be resized, the `'Units'` property and the restrictions imposed by fixed font-size character strings can be a problem. When the position of each UI object is specified in absolute units such as pixels, inches, centimeters, or points, resizing the *Figure* window does not change the size or placement of the objects. The objects maintain the same absolute position relative to the bottom and left sides of the *figure*. If the *figure* is made smaller, some of the UI Objects objects may move outside of the *figure* and no longer be visible.

When the positions of UI objects are specified in normalized units, the objects maintain their relative relationships to each other and to the *figure* itself when the *figure* is resized. However, there is a drawback in this case as well. If the *figure* is made smaller and the objects are resized accordingly, label strings may become unreadable, since the font size is fixed. Any portion of a label outside of the dimensions of the resized object is clipped.

There is no way to avoid this conflict between readable character strings of fixed size and GUI size. Good GUI layout practice usually leaves sufficient white space around objects so that clipping does not occur in transferring from one computer platform to the next. If a GUI is meant to be resizable, the `'ResizeFcn'` callback property of the GUI *figure* can be used to move and reshape the objects in response to a change in *figure* size.

32.8 CAPTURING MOUSE ACTIONS

GUI functions use the location of the mouse pointer and the status of mouse buttons to control MATLAB actions. This section discusses the interaction between pointer and object locations and mouse button actions and how MATLAB responds to changes or events, such as a button press, a button release, or pointer movement.

All Handle Graphics objects have a `'ButtonDownFcn'` property. Most UI objects have a `'CallBack'` property, and *uicontrol* objects have a `'KeyPressFcn'` property. *figure* objects have `'WindowButtonDownFcn'`, `'WindowButtonUpFcn'`, and `'WindowButtonMotionFcn'` properties, as well as `'KeyPressFcn'`, `'CloseRequestFcn'`, and `'ResizeFcn'` properties. All Handle Graphics objects also have `'CreateFcn'` and `'DeleteFcn'` properties. The value associated with each of these properties is a callback that tells MATLAB what to do when the corresponding action occurs. The mouse pointer location determines which callbacks are involved and the order in which they are invoked when an event occurs.

The previous chapter contained a discussion of stacking order and object selection regions that is relevant to this discussion. MATLAB determines which callback is invoked on the basis of three regions within a *figure*. When the pointer is within a Handle Graphics object, as determined by its `'Position'` property, the pointer is considered to be on the object. If the pointer is not on an object, but is within an object's selection region, the pointer is `near` the object. Finally, if the pointer is within the *figure*, but not `on` or `near` another object, the pointer is `off` the other objects. When objects or their selection regions overlap, the stacking order determines which one is selected.

The selection region of Handle Graphics *line*, *surface*, *patch*, *text*, and *axes* objects was discussed in the previous chapter. *uimenu* objects have no external selection region. Either the pointer is on a *uimenu* object, or it is not. *uicontrols* have a selection region that extends about 5 pixels beyond the control's position in all directions. The pointer can be either `on` or `near` a control.

A ***button click*** is defined as the press and subsequent release of a mouse button while the mouse pointer is over an object. If the mouse pointer is over a *uimenu*, *uicontextmenu*, or *uicontrol* object, a button click triggers execution of the object's `'CallBack'` property string, as long as the `'Enable'` property of the object is set to `'on'`. The button press prepares the *uicontrol* and often changes the *uicontrol* or *uimenu* visually, and the button release triggers callback execution. If the mouse pointer is not on a *uicontrol* or *uimenu*, both button press and button release events are triggered as explained next.

When the mouse button is pressed, a ***button press*** event is created. When this happens with the pointer located within a *Figure* window, a number of different actions can occur, on the basis of the location of the pointer and the proximity of Handle Graphics objects. If an object is selected, it becomes the current object. If no object is selected, the *figure* itself becomes the current object. The *figure* object's `'CurrentPoint'` and `'SelectionType'` properties are also updated. The appropriate callbacks are then invoked.

The following table lists the pointer location options and the callbacks executed for a button press event:

Button Press Pointer Location	**Action Taken**
On a *uimenu* item if the `'Enable'` property is `'on'`.	Change *uimenu* appearance and prepare for a release event
On a *uicontrol* if the `'Enable'` property is `'on'`.	Change *uicontrol* appearance and prepare for a release event
On a *uimenu* item if the `'Enable'` property is `'off'`.	Ignore Button press
On a *uicontrol* if the `'Enable'` property is `'off'` or `'inactive'`	Evaluate *figure's* `'WindowButtonDownFcn'` callback and then *uicontrol's* `'ButtonDownFcn'` callback
On or near any Handle Graphics object except for *uimenus* and *uicontrols*	Evaluate *figure's* `'WindowButtonDownFcn'` callback and then the object's `'ButtonDownFcn'`callback
Within a *figure*, but not on or near any other object	Evaluate *figure's* `'WindowButtonDownFcn'` callback and then *figure's* `'ButtonDownFcn'` callback

Note that a button press event always invokes the *figure's* `'WindowButtonDownFcn'` callback before the selected object's `'ButtonDownFcn'` callback, except when the pointer is on a *uicontrol* or *uimenu* object. When the pointer is near a *uicontrol* or on a *uicontrol* with the `'Enable'` property `'off'` or `'inactive'`, the *uicontrol's* `'ButtonDownFcn'` callback is invoked (rather than the `'CallBack'` property) after the *figure's* `'WindowButtonDownFcn'` callback has finished. The `'ButtonDownFcn'` callback of a *uimenu* is never invoked.

When the mouse button is released, a ***button release*** event is created. When this happens, the *figure* object's `'CurrentPoint'` property is updated and the *figure* object's `'WindowButtonUpFcn'` callback is invoked. If the `'WindowButtonUpFcn'` callback is not defined, the `'CurrentPoint'` property is not updated when the button is released.

When the pointer is moved within a figure, ***pointer movement*** events are created. When this happens, the *figure* object's `'CurrentPoint'` property is updated and the *figure* object's `'WindowButtonMotionFcn'` callback is invoked. If the

'WindowButtonMotionFcn' callback is not defined, the 'CurrentPoint' property is not updated when the pointer moves.

32.9 THE EVENT QUEUE

Because GUIs rely on human actions, GUI execution is based on the concept of an ***event queue***. That is, a GUI is presented to the user. The user in turn interacts with the GUI in an essentially arbitrary way over time, with each interaction creating an event that is placed in the event queue. In addition, other commands that involve *Figure* window input or output generate events. Events include pointer movements and mouse button actions that generate callbacks, waitfor and waitforbuttonpress functions, and commands that redraw graphics such as drawnow, figure, getframe, or pause. MATLAB acts on all of these events in the order in which they appear in the queue. MATLAB manages its event queue in a default manner that is appropriate in most cases. However, the common Handle Graphics object properties 'Interruptible' and 'BusyAction' can be used to specify particular actions.

In all cases, a callback executes until it reaches a waitfor, drawnow, waitforbuttonpress, getframe, pause, or figure command. ***Callbacks that do not contain any of these commands cannot be interrupted.*** When one of these special commands is reached, MATLAB suspends execution of the callback and examines each of the pending events in the event queue. If the 'Interruptible' property of the object with the suspended callback is set to 'on', which is its default value, all pending events are processed before the suspended callback is resumed. If the 'Interruptible' property is set to 'off', then only pending screen-update events are processed. At the same time, if the 'BusyAction' property of the object with the suspended callback is set to 'cancel', the interrupting callback events are discarded. If the 'BusyAction' property is set to 'queue', interrupting callback events are held in the event queue until the interrupted callback finishes. Even if an executing callback is not interruptible, pending screen-update events are still processed when the callback reaches a waitfor, waitforbuttonpress, drawnow, figure, getframe, or pause command.

32.10 CALLBACK PROGRAMMING

Handle Graphics and GUI functions make extensive use of callbacks to perform the tasks associated with user selections in a GUI. Prior to MATLAB 7, callbacks were always character strings evaluated in the *Command* window workspace. In this scenario, a callback string was passed to the function eval each time the callback was invoked. For example,

```
H_p1 = uicontrol('Style','PushButton',...
                 'Callback','myguifcn push1');
```

sets the callback for a pushbutton *uicontrol* object to the string 'myguifcn push1'. When this GUI pushbutton is pressed, this command syntax form is interpreted as the function call myguifcn('push1') and is executed in the *Command* window workspace. In most situations, myguifcn is the name of the function containing the preceding uicontrol statement. That is, callbacks are often directed to call the same function where they are defined. In this way, a single M-file creates the GUI and contains all of the code that is executed when the GUI is run. This approach of placing all GUI callbacks in the same M-file leads to a ***switchyard programming*** structure. For example, suppose a GUI function M-file myguifcn.m creates three pushbuttons—Apply, Revert, and Done—with the callbacks to these buttons being myguifcn('Apply'), myguifcn('Revert'), and myguifcn('Done'), respectively. Then the function myguifcn can implement the switchyard programming callback structure with a Switch-Case construction, shown as follows:

```
function myguifcn(arg)
%MYGUIFCN Sample Switchyard Programming Example.

persistent mydata
if nargin==0
   arg = 'Initialize';
end
switch arg
case 'Initialize'
   % code that creates the GUI and sets the callbacks
   uicontrol('Style','PushButton',...
            'String','Apply',...
            % In a real GUI other properties must be set also
            'Callback','myguifcn Apply')
   uicontrol('Style','PushButton',...
            'String','Revert',...
            % In a real GUI other properties must be set also
            'Callback','myguifcn Revert')
   uicontrol('Style','PushButton',...
            'String','Done',...
            % In a real GUI other properties must be set also
            'Callback','myguifcn Done')

   mydata = ... % data to be stored in the GUI for callback use,
               % most commonly a structure
```

```
case 'Apply'
    % code that performs Apply button callback actions

case 'Revert'
    % code that performs Revert button callback actions

case 'Done'
    % code that performs Done button callback actions

otherwise
    % report error?
end
```

The most difficult aspect of callback programming, as shown, is retrieving data. Even though switchyard programming callbacks call the same function repeatedly, each callback creates a separate instance of the function, each with its own separate workspace. As a result, callback instances do not have access to anything other than the function argument passed to it in the callback string. MATLAB provides a variety of ways to make data available to separate callback instances. The simplest approach is to declare one or more variables associated with needed data `persistent`. In doing so, the declared variables persist and are available whenever the function is called. In the preceding example, the variable `mydata` is declared `persistent` and is assigned data when the GUI is created; then the data stored in `mydata` are available when any switchyard callback is invoked. The only disadvantage of using the `persistent` declaration is that only one instance of the GUI can exist at a given time. If multiple GUIs existed simultaneously, they would all share the same persistent data.

As an alternative to using persistent variables, the `'Tag'` property of Handle Graphics objects can be set to a unique character string. Then, the function `findobj` can be used to search for objects having the specified tag string. Once the object is found, the functions `getappdata`, `setappdata`, `rmappdata`, and `isappdata` can be used to manipulate data stored in the tagged object. The following example demonstrates this approach:

```
function myguifcn(arg)
%MYGUIFCN Sample Switchyard Programming Example.

if nargin==0
   arg = 'Initialize';
end
```

```
switch arg
case 'Initialize'
   % code that creates the GUI and sets the callbacks
   Hf = figure(... % create figure for gui
            % In a real GUI other properties must be set also
            'Tag','MyGuiFcnTag')

   uicontrol('Parent',Hf,...
           'Style','PushButton',...
           'String','Apply',...
           % In a real GUI other properties must be set also
           'Callback','myguifcn Apply')
   uicontrol('Parent',Hf,...
           'Style','PushButton',...
           'String','Revert',...
           % In a real GUI other properties must be set also
           'Callback','myguifcn Revert')
   uicontrol('Parent',Hf,...
           'Style','PushButton',...
           'String','Done',...
           % In a real GUI other properties must be set also
           'Callback','myguifcn Done')
   mydata = ... % data to be stored in the CUI for callback use,
              % most commonly a structure
   setappdata(Hf,'MyGuiFcnData',mydata)

case 'Apply'
   % code that performs Apply button callback actions
   Hf = findobj('Tag','MyGuiFcnTag');
   mydata = getappdata(Hf,'MyGuiFcnData');

case 'Revert'
   % code that performs Revert button callback actions
   Hf = findobj('Tag','MyGuiFcnTag');
   mydata = getappdata(Hf,'MyGuiFcnData');
```

```
case 'Done'
   % code that performs Done button callback actions
   Hf = findobj('Tag','MyGuiFcnTag');
   mydata = getappdata(Hf,'MyGuiFcnData');
otherwise
   % report error?
end
```

As shown `setappdata` is used to store a variable called `mydata` in the GUI *figure* application data property. The GUI figure is given the tag `'MyGuiFcnTag'`. In the code executed by each callback, `findobj` is used to find the handle of the GUI figure. Then `getappdata` is used to retrieve the application data stored in the *figure*.

An alternative to the previous example uses the function `guidata`, which stores and retrieves data in the GUI *figure* `'ApplicationData'` property. Using `guidata`, the previous example simplifies to the following:

```
function myguifcn(arg)
%MYGUIFCN Sample Switchyard Programming Example.

if nargin==0
   arg = 'Initialize';
end
switch arg
case 'Initialize'
   % code that creates the GUI and sets the callbacks
   Hf = figure(...) % create figure for gui

   uicontrol('Parent',Hf,...
            'Style','PushButton',...
            'String','Apply',...
            % In a real GUI other properties must be set also
            'Callback','myguifcn Apply')
```

```
    uicontrol('Parent',Hf,...
        'Style','PushButton',...
        'String','Revert',...
        % In a real GUI other properties must be set also
        'Callback','myguifcn Revert')
    uicontrol('Parent',Hf,...
        'Style','PushButton',...
        'String','Done',...
        % In a real GUI other properties must be set also
        'Callback','myguifcn Done')
    mydata = ... % data to be stored in the GUI for callback use,
                 % most commonly a structure

    guidata(Hf,mydata)

case 'Apply'
    % code that performs Apply button callback actions
    mydata = guidata(gcbo);

case 'Revert'
    % code that performs Revert button callback actions
    mydata = guidata(gcbo);

case 'Done'
    % code that performs Done button callback actions
    mydata = guidata(gcbo);

otherwise
    % report error?
end
```

Object tagging is no longer required. Instead, the function gcbo gets the handle of the **c**all**b**ack **o**bject (thus the reason for calling this function gcbo). That is, it returns the handle of the object that invoked the callback. While this handle is not that of the *figure* containing the data, guidata finds the *figure* by searching through the parent objects of the callback object, as returned by gcbo. The function guidata uses setappdata and getappdata behind the scenes and simplifies the syntax for storing and retrieving data between callback instances.

The definition of callbacks as character strings evaluated in the *Command* window workspace has been around since the introduction of Handle Graphics. This approach has a number of weaknesses, including the facts that callback strings are evaluated each time a callback is invoked and that it is not possible to directly pass data to callbacks. Because of these weaknesses, MATLAB 7 introduces an alternative approach to defining callbacks. MATLAB now supports defining callbacks as function handles rather than as character strings. For example,

```
H_p1 = uicontrol('Style','PushButton',...
                 'Callback',@mycbfcn);
```

defines the callback for this *uicontrol* as a function handle to the function mycbfcn. When this callback is invoked, MATLAB calls the function pointed to by the function handle as mycbfcn(cbo,eventdata). The first argument cbo contains the handle of the callback object—the same handle that is returned by the function gcbo. The second argument contains event data specific to the callback object and the type of callback invoked. As of this writing, the content of this variable is unspecified.

The strength of this function handle approach is that all of the information required to execute the function is created when the function handle is created, namely, at the time the GUI is created. That is, the function pointed to by @mycbfcn can be a subfunction or a nested function within the main GUI creation M-file. In accordance with this approach, the earlier callback examples can be rewritten as follows:

```
function myguifcn
%MYGUIFCN Sample GUI Funcition Using Function Callbacks

% code that creates the GUI and sets the callbacks
Hf = figure(...)% create figure for gui

uicontrol('Parent',Hf,...
        'Style','PushButton',...
        'String','Apply',...
        % In a real GUI other properties must be set also
        'Callback',@Applyfcn)
uicontrol('Parent',Hf,...
        'Style','PushButton',...
        'String','Revert',...
        % In a real GUI other properties must be set also
        'Callback',@Revertfcn)
```

```
uicontrol('Parent',Hf,...
        'Style','PushButton',...
        'String','Done',...
        % In a real GUI other properties must be set also
        'Callback',@Donefcn)

mydata = ... % data to be stored in the GUI for callback use,
             % most commonly a structure

guidata(Hf,mydata)

%-----------------------------------
function Applyfcn(cbo,eventdata)
% subfunction code that performs Apply button callback actions
mydata = guidata(cbo);

%-----------------------------------
function Revertfcn(cbo,eventdata)
% subfunction code that performs Revert button callback actions
mydata = guidata(cbo);

%-----------------------------------
function Donefcn(cbo,eventdata)
% subfunction code that performs Done button callback actions
mydata = guidata(cbo);
```

The switchyard programming structure is no longer needed. Each callback calls its own subfunction. In addition, since the callback object handle is the first argument, the function `guidata` easily retrieves GUI data stored in the GUI creation *figure*.

In addition to this default use of function handles as callbacks, MATLAB supports function handle callbacks that pass additional data variables directly. For example,

```
H_p1 = uicontrol('Style','PushButton',...
                 'Callback',{@mycbfcn, mydata1, mydata2});
```

defines the callback for this *uicontrol* as a cell array containing a function handle to the function `mycbfcn`, plus additional input arguments `mydata1` and `mydata2`.

When this callback is invoked, MATLAB calls the function pointed to by the function handle as

```
mycbfcn(cbo,eventdata,mydata1,mydata2)
```

where the content of the variables mydata1 and mydata2 are set at the time the GUI is created. Any number of additional variables can be passed to callback functions in this way.

In accordance with this approach, this example can be rewritten as follows:

```
function myguifcn
%MYGUIFCN Sample GUI Funcition Using Function Callbacks

% code that creates the GUI and sets the callbacks
Hf = figure(...)% create figure for gui

mydata = ... % data to be stored in the GUI for callback use,
             % most commonly a structure

uicontrol('Parent',Hf,...
      'Style','PushButton',...
      'String','Apply',...
      % In a real GUI other properties must be set also
      'Callback',{@Applyfcn, mydata})
uicontrol('Parent',Hf,...
      'Style','PushButton',...
      'String','Revert',...
      % In a real GUI other properties must be set also
      'Callback',{@Revertfcn, mydata})
uicontrol('Parent',Hf,...
      'Style','PushButton',...
      'String','Done',...
      % In a real GUI other properties must be set also
      'Callback',{@Donefcn, mydata})

%------------------------------------
function Applyfcn(cbo,eventdata,mydata)
% subfunction code that performs Apply button callback actions
```

```
%-----------------------------------------------
function Revertfcn(cbo,eventdata,mydata)
% subfunction code that performs Revert button callback actions

%-----------------------------------------------
function Donefcn(cbo,eventdata,mydata)
% subfunction code that performs Done button callback actions
```

Now it is no longer necessary to retrieve data by using the `guidata` function. The only restriction is that the content of the variable `mydata` must be known before it appears in the callback cell array.

While the above examples demonstrate the use of function handles pointing to subfunctions as callbacks, function handle callbacks can point to any function type that is within scope (i.e., is visible) at the time the function handle is created. Therefore, in addition to subfunctions, function handle callbacks can be nested functions, anonymous functions, or private functions. Once the function handle is created, MATLAB can execute the underlying function even if it goes out of scope or would otherwise be invisible to MATLAB. Clearly, the versatility of function handles and the ability to use them as callbacks increase the productivity of MATLAB GUI programming.

32.11 M-FILE EXAMPLES

It is difficult to illustrate GUI programming with rigorous examples, because GUI M-files are typically very long and their user-interactive nature makes it difficult to illustrate their results on a printed page. The best way to become familiar with GUI programming is to find a preexisting one in MATLAB or on a website, open it in an editor to view the source code, and run it to see what the code produces. Comparing the visual operation of the GUI to the MATLAB code that produces it provides a wealth of information that cannot be gained in any other way.

Given that disclaimer, two GUI examples are illustrated in this section. In the first example, the functions `mmtext6` and `mmtext7` demonstrate the use of the *figure* object callback properties `'WindowButtonDownFcn'`, `'WindowButtonMotionFcn'`, and `'WindowButtonUpFcn'`. These functions interactively place text on an *axes* similar to the MATLAB function `gtext`. The added feature in these functions is the ability to drag the text around the *axes* with the mouse after it has been placed. The function `mmtext6` demonstrates the use of character-string callbacks that were available in MATLAB 6 and earlier, whereas `mmtext7` demonstrates the use of function handle callbacks now available in MATLAB 7. Here is the code:

```
function h=mmtext6(arg)
%MMTEXT6 Place and Drag Text with Mouse.
% MMTEXT6 waits for a mouse click on a text object in the current figure
% then allows it to be dragged while the mouse button remains down.
%
% MMTEXT6('whatever') places the string 'whatever' on the current axes
% and allows it to be dragged with the mouse
%
% Ht = MMTEXT6('whatever') returns the handle to the text object.
%
% MMTEXT6 becomes inactive after the move is complete or no text
% object is selected.

if nargin==0, arg = 0; end

if ischar(arg)  % user entered text to be placed
   Ht = text('Units','normalized',...
             'Position',[.5 .5],...
             'String',arg,...
             'HorizontalAlignment','center',...
             'VerticalAlignment','middle');


   if nargout>0, h=Ht; end
   mmtext6(0)  % call mmtext6 again to drag it
elseif arg==0  % initial call, select text for dragging

   Hf = get(0,'CurrentFigure');
   if isempty(Hf)
      error('No Figure Window Exists.')
   end
   set(Hf,'BackingStore','off',... % speed up rendering
        'DoubleBuffer','on',...  % get rid of screen flicker
        'WindowButtonDownFcn','mmtext6(1)')
```

```
   figure(Hf)  % bring figure forward

elseif arg==1 & strcmp(get(gco,'type'),'text') % text object selected

   set(gco,'Units','data',...
           'HorizontalAlignment','left',...
           'VerticalAlignment','baseline');
   set(gcf,'Pointer','topr',...
           'WindowButtonMotionFcn','mmtext6(2)',...
           'WindowButtonUpFcn','mmtext6(99)')

elseif arg==2  % dragging text object

   cp = get(gca,'CurrentPoint'); % get current mouse point
   set(gco,'Position',cp(1,1:3)) % move text to the current point

else       % mouse button up or incorrect object selected, reset everything
   set(gcf,'WindowButtonDownFcn','',...
           'WindowButtonMotionFcn','',...
           'WindowButtonUpFcn','',...
           'Pointer','arrow',...
           'DoubleBuffer','off',...
           'BackingStore','on')
end
```

The procedure used in `mmtext6` is to set the `'WindowButtonDownFcn'` property of the *figure* to `'mmtext6(1)'`, which is a callback to `mmtext6`. Then, `gco` is used to identify the handle of the selected text. Next, the `'WindowButtonMotionFcn'` property of the *figure* is set to `'mmtext6(2)'`, and `'WindowButtonUpFcn'` is set to `'mmtext6(99)'`. These three different numerical arguments to `mmtext6` cause it to perform the desired operations. Finally, when the text move is completed, the callbacks are all reset to empty strings, thereby disabling text selection and dragging.

The MATLAB 7 equivalent of `mmtext6` is shown as follows as the function `mmtext7`.

```
function h=mmtext7(arg)
%MMTEXT7 Place and Drag Text with Mouse.
% MMTEXT7 waits for a mouse click on a text object in the current figure
% then allows it to be dragged while the mouse button remains down.
%
% MMTEXT7('whatever') places the string 'whatever' on the current axes
% and allows it to be dragged with the mouse
%
% Ht = MMTEXT7('whatever') returns the handle to the text object.
%
% MMTEXT7 becomes inactive after the move is complete or no text
% object is selected.

if nargin==0       % call subfunction to set up string drag
   local_mmtext_init

elseif ischar(arg) % user entered text to be placed

   Ht = text('Units','normalized',...
             'Position',[.5 .5],...
             'String',arg,...
             'HorizontalAlignment','center',...
             'VerticalAlignment','middle');

   if nargout>0, h=Ht; end
   local_mmtext_init      % call subfunction to set up string drag
else
   error('String Input Expected.')
end
%-----------------------------------------------------------------
function local_mmtext_init(cbo,eventdata)
% two input arguments required even if not used
```

```
   Hf = get(0,'CurrentFigure');
   if isempty(Hf)
      error('No Figure Window Exists.')
   end
   set(Hf,'BackingStore','off',... % speed up rendering
          'DoubleBuffer','on',...  % get rid of screen flicker
          'WindowButtonDownFcn',@local_mmtext_down)
   figure(Hf)  % bring figure forward

%-----------------------------------------------------------------
function local_mmtext_down(cbo,eventdata)
% two input arguments required even if not used

if strcmp(get(gco,'type'),'text') % text object selected

   set(gco,'Units','data',...
          'HorizontalAlignment','left',...
          'VerticalAlignment','baseline');
   set(gcf,'Pointer','topr',...
          'WindowButtonMotionFcn',@local_mmtext_drag,...
          'WindowButtonUpFcn',@local_mmtext_up)
else
   local_mmtext_up % reset everything
end

%-----------------------------------------------------------------
function local_mmtext_drag(cbo,eventdata) % dragging text object
% two input arguments required even if not used

cp = get(gca,'CurrentPoint'); % get current mouse point
set(gco,'Position',cp(1,1:3)) % move text to the current point
```

```
%------------------------------------------------------------
function local_mmtext_up(cbo,eventdata) % reset everything
% two input arguments required even if not used

set(gcf,'WindowButtonDownFcn','',...
        'WindowButtonMotionFcn','',...
        'WindowButtonUpFcn','',...
        'Pointer','arrow',...
        'DoubleBuffer','off',...
        'BackingStore','on')
```

This function handle callback case is not dramatically different from the character-string case in mmtext6, but it is generally easier to read. The process of setting and clearing callbacks at the appropriate times is the same in both functions. The primary difference is that the switchyard programming structure has been replaced by callbacks to subfunctions.

The next example creates the following GUI:

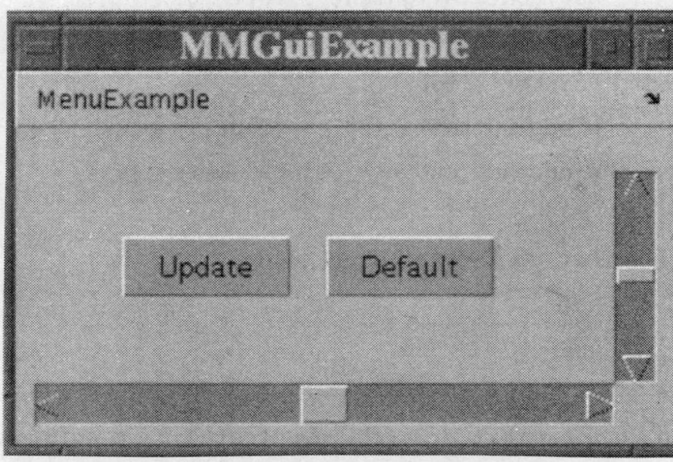

This GUI contains a *uimenu* object, two pushbutton style *uicontrol* objects, and two slider style *uicontrol* objects. Interacting with the horizontal slider moves the *figure* horizontally, and interacting with the vertical slider moves the *figure* vertically. The sliders or scroll bars are made so that the *figure* can be moved all around the current screen. The **Default** button moves the *figure* back to its default size and centered position. If the *figure* is manually dragged with the mouse, pressing the **Update** button updates the slider indicators to reflect the current *figure* position. The **MenuExample** menu contains a single selection named **Close**, which closes the GUI *figure*. The code that creates this GUI is shown as follows:

```
function mmguiexample
%MMGUIEXAMPLE Example GUI in Mastering MATLAB 7

% Build GUI

set(0,'Units','pixels');
Ssize = get(0,'ScreenSize'); % get screen size so gui can be centered

H.gui = dialog('WindowStyle','normal',... % Figure object with good
               'Resize','on',...          % properties for a gui
               'Name','MMGuiExample',...  % Add modifications
               'Units','pixels',...
               'Position',[(Ssize(3)-310)/2 (Ssize(4)-150)/2 310 150]);

DefOutPos = get(H.gui,'OuterPosition'); % undocumented figure property
set(H.gui,'UserData',DefOutPos) % store default outer position here

Hm = uimenu('Parent',H.gui,'Label','MenuExample'); % create top level menu
uimenu('Parent',Hm,... % add 'Close' menu item to top level menu
       'Label','Close',...
       'Callback','close(gcbf)'); % simple string callback

H.Hslider = uicontrol('Style','slider',... % horizontal slider
                      'Parent',H.gui,...
                      'Units','pixels',...
                      'Position',[10 10 270 20],...
                      'Min',20,'Max',Ssize(3)-DefOutPos(3)-20,...
                      'Value',DefOutPos(1),...
                      'Callback',{@local_Hslider,H});
```

```
H.Vslider = uicontrol('Style','slider',... % vertical slider
                      'Parent',H.gui,...
                      'Units','pixels',...
                      'Position',[280 30 20 100],...
                      'Min',20,'Max',Ssize(4)-DefOutPos(4)-20,...
                      'Value',DefOutPos(2),...
                      'Callback',{@local_Vslider,H});

H.Update = uicontrol('Style','pushbutton',... % Update pushbutton
                     'Parent',H.gui,...
                     'Units','pixels',...
                     'Position',[50 70 80 30],...
                     'String','Update',...
                     'Callback',{@local_Update,H});

H.Default = uicontrol('Style','pushbutton',... % Default pushbutton
                      'Parent',H.gui,...
                      'Units','pixels',...
                      'Position',[145 70 80 30],...
                      'String','Default',...
                      'Callback',{@local_Default,H});
%----------------------------------------------------------
% Subfunction callbacks
%----------------------------------------------------------
function local_Hslider(cbo,eventdata,h)
% Callback for horizontal slider
% Move gui figure horizontally
% Slider value contains desired outer left position

SliderValue = get(cbo,'Value');
pos = get(h.gui,'OuterPosition');
set(h.gui,'OuterPosition',[SliderValue pos(2:4)])
```

```
%-------------------------------------------------------------
function local_Vslider(cbo,eventdata,h)
% Callback for vertical slider
% Move gui figure vertically
% Slider value contains desired outer bottom position

SliderValue = get(cbo,'Value');
pos = get(h.gui,'OuterPosition');
set(h.gui,'OuterPosition',[pos(1) SlicerValue pos(3:4)])

%-------------------------------------------------------------
function local_Update(cbo,eventdata,h)
% Callback for Update pushbutton
% Update slider values to reflect current GUI position
% This button is only needed if the user drags the GUI
%  window manually with the mouse

OutPos = get(h.gui,'OuterPosition');
set(h.Hslider,'Value',OutPos(1))
set(h.Vslider,'Value',OutPos(2))

%-------------------------------------------------------------
function local_Default(cbo,eventdata,h)
% Callback for Default pushbutton
% Return GUI position vector to default value

defoutpos = get(h.gui,'UserData'); % retrieve cefault outer position
set(h.gui,'OuterPosition',defoutpos)
set(h.Hslider,'Value',defoutpos(1))
set(h.Vslider,'Value',defoutpos(2))
```

As shown in the code, with the exception of the *uimenu* for closing the GUI *figure*, callbacks are specified as function handles. Comments in the M-file describe the important aspects of the GUI. Given the power of function handle callbacks, no attempt was made to write this function by using only character-string callbacks. It is important to note that the above example reflects just one of many ways that this GUI could be created. While handles for the horizontal and vertical sliders are stored, they are never used, because the variable `cbo` in their callback functions contains their handles. In addition, the `'Userdata'` property of the GUI *figure* was used to store the default figure position vector. Alternatively, this variable could have been passed to the `local_Default` subfunction as an additional input argument.

32.12 GUIDE

GUIDE (Graphical User Interface Design Environment) is a GUI tool that has been designed to make building your own GUIs easier, faster, and more consistent. To create, place, align, and resize UI objects, the function `guide` provides a property editor and inspector that lists object properties and lets the user modify these properties interactively and a menu editor for interactive editing and rearranging user-defined pull-down and contextual menus. GUIDE provides an interactive approach to GUI development and performs well in laying out the geometry of a GUI. It also makes the structure of GUI code consistent from one GUI to the next. GUIDE stores the graphical user interface in a FIG-file, and creates an M-file to initiate the GUI and store the code used for callbacks. GUIDE has improved considerably with every MATLAB release. At this point, GUIDE works well and creates easily debugged and maintainable GUIs. The only weakness of GUIDE (which cannot be eliminated) is the wealth of knowledge required to understand all the nuances involved in creating a well-functioning GUI that does exactly what is desired. For example, Handle Graphics properties such as `'HitTest'`, `'Interruptible'`, and `'BusyAction'` must be understood, as must button-click sequencing, the event queue, and callbacks.

32.13 SUMMARY

Graphical user interface design is not for everyone. However, if you have a need for a GUI, it can be constructed in MATLAB. With the powerful numerical and graphical capabilities available in MATLAB, GUIs can become impressive tools for demonstrating and exploring a wide variety of technical data.

The following table summarizes the GUI functions available in MATLAB, including a number that have not been discussed elsewhere in this chapter (further information regarding GUI construction can be found in the MATLAB documentation):

Function	Description
uibuttongroup	User interface container object for managing 'radiobutton' and 'togglebutton' style *uicontrol* objects
uicontainer	User interface *container* object creation
uicontrol	User interface *uicontrol* object creation
uimenu	User interface *uimenu* object creation
uicontextmenu	User interface *uicontextual menu* object creation
uipanel	User interface *uipanel* object creation
uitoolbar	User interface *uitoolbar* object creation
uipushtool	Momentary contact pushbutton for a *uitoolbar*
uitoggletool	On/Off pushbutton for a *uitoolbar*
uitable	User interface *uitable* object creation
uitree	User interface *uitree* object creation
uitreenode	User interface *uitreenode* object creation
drawnow	Process all pending graphics events and update screen now
gcbf	Get callback *figure* handle
gcbo	Get callback object handle
dragrect	Drag rectangles with the mouse
rbbox	Capture the position of a rubberband box
selectmoveresize	Interactively select, move, and resize *axes* and *uicontrol* objects
waitforbuttonpress	Wait for a key press or a button press over a *figure*
waitfor	Block execution and wait for an event
uiwait	Block execution and wait for resume
uiresume	Resume execution of a blocked M-file
uistack	Control the stacking order of objects
uisuspend	Suspend the interactive state of a *figure*
uirestore	Restore the interactive state of a *figure*
uiclearmode	Clear the current interactive mode
guide	Graphical user interface design environment
inspect	Inspect object properties
ishandle	True if valid object handle
isprop	True if valid object property
align	Align *uicontrols* and *axes*
propedit	Open property editor GUI
makemenu	Create *uimenu* structure
umtoggle	Toggle checked status of a *uimenu* item

Function	Description
`getpixelposition`	Get position of object in pixels
`setpixelposition`	Set position of object in pixels
`getptr`	Get *figure* pointer
`setptr`	Set *figure* pointer
`hidegui`	Hide or unhide GUI
`movegui`	Move *figure* window to a specified part of screen
`guidata`	Store or retrieve application data
`getappdata`	Get application data associated with a GUI
`setappdata`	Set application data associated with a GUI
`rmappdata`	Remove application data associated with a GUI
`isappdata`	True if named application data exists
`guihandles`	Create structure of handles
`overobj`	Get handle of object that pointer is over
`popupstr`	Get popup menu selection string
`remapfig`	Transform positions of objects in a *figure*

33

MATLAB Classes and Object-Oriented Programming

MATLAB has a number of fundamental data types otherwise known as classes. For example, arrays of numbers are commonly double-precision arrays. A variable containing such an array has a class called `double`. Similarly, character strings are another data type or class. Variables containing character strings have a class called `char`. Consider the following example:

```
>> pi           % a simple double

ans =
        3.1416

>> class(pi)
ans =
double

>> s = 'pi'    % a simple string
s =
pi
```

```
>> class(s)
ans =
char
```

Data types or classes in basic MATLAB include `double`, `char`, `logical`, `cell`, and `struct`. These data types are the most commonly used classes in MATLAB. In addition, MATLAB includes the lesser-used classes `function`, `handle`, `inline`, `java`, `single`, and a variety of integer data types.

For each of these classes, MATLAB defines operations that can be performed. For example, addition is a defined operator for elements of the class `double`, but is not defined for elements of the class `char` or for elements of the class `cell`:

```
>> x = pi+2
x =
       5.1416

>> y = 'hello' + 'there'
y =
   220   205   209   222   212

>> {'hello' 'there'}+{'sunny' 'day'}
??? Function 'plus' is not defined for values of class 'cell'.
```

Here, adding two character strings created a numerical array rather than a character string. Rather than report an error, MATLAB chose to convert `'hello'` and `'there'` to their ASCII numerical equivalents, and then perform element-by-element numerical addition. Even though MATLAB produced a result for this character-string example, it did so only after converting the elements on the right-hand side to the class double. MATLAB does this implicit type or class conversion for convenience, not because addition is defined for character strings. On the other hand, trying to add two cell arrays produces an immediate error.

Starting with version 5, MATLAB added the ability to define new operations for the basic data types and, more importantly, added the ability to create user-defined data types or classes. Creating and using data types is called ***object oriented programming*** (OOP), in which variables in each data type or class are called ***objects***. Operations on objects are defined by methods that encapsulate data and overload operators and functions. The vocabulary of OOP includes terms such as *operator* and *function overloading*, *data encapsulation*, *methods*, *inheritance*, and *aggregation*. These terms and the fundamental principles of object-oriented programming in MATLAB are discussed in this chapter.

33.1 OVERLOADING

Before getting involved in the details of OOP and creating new variable classes, consider the process of overloading standard classes in MATLAB. The techniques used to overload standard classes are identical to those used for user-created classes. Once overloading is understood for standard classes, it is straightforward for user-created classes.

When the MATLAB interpreter encounters an operator such as addition, or a function with one or more input arguments, it considers the data type or class of the arguments to the operator or function, and acts according to the rules it has defined internally. For example, addition means to compute the numerical sum of the arguments if the arguments are numerical values or can be converted to numerical values, such as character strings. When the internal rules for an operation or function are redefined, the operator or function is said to be ***overloaded.***

> ***Operator*** and ***function overloading*** allow a user to redefine what actions MATLAB performs when it encounters an operator or function.

In MATLAB, the redefined rules for interpreting operators and functions are simply function M-files stored in ***class directories*** just off of the MATLAB search path.

> The collection of rules or M-files for redefining operators and functions define ***methods***. The files themselves are commonly referred to as method functions.

That is, class directories themselves are not and cannot be on the MATLAB search path, but they are and must be subdirectories of directories that are on the MATLAB search path. To find class subdirectories, MATLAB requires that class directories be named as *@class*, where *class* is the variable class that the M-files in *@class* apply to. In addition, MATLAB supports multiple class directories. That is, there can be multiple *@class* directories for the same data type just off of the MATLAB path. When looking for functions in class directories, MATLAB follows the order given by the MATLAB search path and uses the first matching method function file found.

For example, if a directory `@char` appears just **off** of the MATLAB search path, the M-files contained in this directory can redefine operations and functions on character strings. To illustrate this, consider the function M-file `plus.m`:

```
function s=plus(s1,s2)
% Horizontal Concatenation for char Objects.

if ischar(s1)&ischar(s2)
```

```
    s=cat(2,s1(:).',s2(:).');
elseif isnumeric(s2)
    s=double(s1)+s2;
else
    error('Operator + Not Defined.')
end
```

If this M-file is stored in any `@char` directory just off of the MATLAB search path, addition of character strings is redefined as horizontal concatenation. For example, repeating the statement `y = 'hello' + 'there'` made earlier becomes

```
>> y = 'hello' + 'there'
y =
hellothere
```

MATLAB no longer converts the strings on the right-hand side to their ASCII equivalents and adds the numerical results! What MATLAB did was (1) construe character strings to appear on both sides of the addition symbol (+); (2) look down the MATLAB search path for an `@char` subdirectory; (3) find the one we created and look for a function M-file named `plus.m`; (4) find the previous `plus.m` function, pass the two arguments to the addition operator to the function, and let it determine what action to perform; and (5) finally, return the function output as the result of the addition operation.

> To speed operation, MATLAB ***caches*** class subdirectories at startup. So, for this example to work, you must create the subdirectory and M-file and then restart MATLAB or issue the `rehash` command to get MATLAB to cache the newly created class subdirectory and associated M-files.

When addition is performed between two different data types, such as `char` and `double`, MATLAB considers the precedence and order of the arguments. For variables of equal precedence, MATLAB gives precedence to the leftmost argument to an operator or function as in the following example:

```
>> z = 2 + 'hello'
z =
   106   103   110   110   113
```

The classes `double` and `char` have equal precedence. As a result, MATLAB considers addition to be numerical and applies its internal rules, converting `'hello'` to its

ASCII equivalent and performing numerical addition. On the other hand, if the order of the preceding operands is reversed, as in the code

```
>> z = 'hello' + 2

z =

   106   103   110   110   113
```

then MATLAB considers addition to be a `char` class operation. In this case, the `@char/plus.m` function is called as `plus('hello',2)`. As written, `plus.m` identifies this mixed class call with `isnumeric(s2)` and returns the same result as `z = 2 + 'hello'`.

As illustrated earlier, a function named `plus.m` defines addition in a class subdirectory. To support overloading of other operators, MATLAB assigns the function names shown in the following table to operators:

Operator	Function Name	Description
`a + b`	`plus(a,b)`	Numerical addition
`a - b`	`minus(a,b)`	Numerical subtraction
`-a`	`uminus(a)`	Unary minus
`+a`	`uplus(a)`	Unary plus
`a .* b`	`times(a,b)`	Element-by-element multiplication
`a * b`	`mtimes(a,b)`	Matrix multiplication
`a ./ b`	`rdivide(a,b)`	Element-by-element right division
`a .\ b`	`ldivide(a,b)`	Element-by-element left division
`a / b`	`mrdivide(a,b)`	Matrix right division
`a \ b`	`mldivide(a,b)`	Matrix left division
`a .^ b`	`power(a,b)`	Element-by-element exponentiation
`a ^ b`	`mpower(a,b)`	Matrix exponentiation
`a < b`	`lt(a,b)`	Less than
`a > b`	`gt(a,b)`	Greater than
`a <= b`	`le(a,b)`	Less than or equal to
`a >= b`	`ge(a,b)`	Greater than or equal to
`a ~= b`	`ne(a,b)`	Not equal
`a == b`	`eq(a,b)`	Equal
`a & b`	`and(a,b)`	Logical AND
`a | b`	`or(a,b)`	Logical OR
`~a`	`not(a)`	Logical NOT

Operator	Function Name	Description
`a:d:b`	`colon(a,d,b)`	Colon operator
`a:b`	`colon(a,b)`	
`a'`	`ctranspose(a)`	Conjugate transpose
`a.'`	`transpose(a)`	Transpose
`[a b]`	`horzcat(a,b)`	Horizontal concatenation
`[a; b]`	`vertcat(a,b)`	Vertical concatenation
`a(s1,s2, ...)`	`subsref(a,s)`	Subscripted reference
`a(s1,s2, ...) = b`	`subsasgn(a,s,b)`	Subscripted assignment
`b(a)`	`subsindex(a)`	Subscript index
	`display(a)`	*Command* window output
`end`	`end(a,k,n)`	Subscript interpretation of end

Continuing with the previous char class example, note that subtraction can be overloaded with the following function:

```
function s=minus(s1,s2)
% Subtraction for char Objects.
% Delete occurrences of s2 in s1.

if ischar(s1)&ischar(s2)
   s=strrep(s1,s2,'');
elseif isnumeric(s2)
   s=double(s1)-s2;
else
   error('Operator - Not Defined.')
end
```

As defined, subtraction is interpreted as the deletion of matching substrings:

```
>> z = 'hello' - 'e'
z =
hllo

>> a = 'hello' - 2
```

```
a =

   102    99   106   106   109
```

Again, this mixed-class case returns the MATLAB default action.

When multiple operators appear in a statement, MATLAB adheres to its usual order of precedence rules, working from left to right in an expression, as in the following example:

```
>> a = 'hello' + ' ' + 'there'

a =

hello there


>> a - 'e'

ans =

hllo thr


>> a = 'hello' + ' ' + ('there' - 'e')

a =

hello thr
```

When a statement assigns a character string to an output without a terminating semicolon, MATLAB displays the string in the *Command* window. What is displayed in the *Command* window can be overloaded by using the function `display.m`. While the default character display behavior of MATLAB is convenient, it can be overloaded with a function such as the following:

```
function display(s)
% Display for char objects.

isloose=strcmp(get(0,'FormatSpacing'),'loose');
ssiz=size(s);

if isloose, disp(' '), end
disp(['A Character Array of Size: ' mat2str(ssiz)])
if isloose, disp(' '), end
```

This function redefines how character strings are displayed in the *Command* window, as in the following code:

```
>> 'hello'
A Character Array of Size: [1 5]

>> a = 'hello' + ' ' + 'there'
A Character Array of Size: [1 11]

>> format loose
>> a

A Character Array of Size: [1 11]

>> format compact
>> s=char('hello','there')
A Character Array of Size: [2 5]
```

This discussion concludes how MATLAB overloads operators. Overloading functions follows the same procedure. In this case, the function stored in the class subdirectory has the same name as that of the standard MATLAB function:

```
function s=cat(varargin)
%CAT Concatenate Strings as a Row.

if length(varargin)>1 & ~ischar(varargin{2})
   error('CAT Not Defined for Mixed Classes.')
else
   s=cat(2,varargin{:});
end
```

This function overloads the function cat for character strings. It is called only if the first argument to the cat function is a character string; that is, it is of class char. If the first argument is numerical, the standard cat function is called:

```
>> cat('hello','there') % call overloaded cat
ans =
hellothere
```

```
>> cat('hello',2)          % call overloaded cat
??? Error using ==> char/cat
CAT Not Defined for Mixed Classes.

>> cat(2,'hello')          % call built in cat
ans =
hello
```

In addition to the operator overloading functions listed in this section, MATLAB provides several OOP utility functions. They include `methods`, `isa`, `class`, `loadobj`, and `saveobj`. The functions `isa` and `class` help to identify the data type or class of a variable or object:

```
>> a = 'hello';
>> class(a) % return class of argument
ans =
char
>> isa(a,'double') % logical class test
ans =
     0
>> isa(a,'char') % logical class test
ans =
     1
```

The function `methods` returns a listing of the methods, or overloading operators, and functions associated with a given class:

```
>> methods cell

Methods for class cell:

cell2struct   ismember   regexprep   str2func   strmatch    tril
ctranspose    lower      reshape     strcat     strncmp     triu
diag          permute    setdiff     strcmp     strncmpi    union
display       regexp     setxor      strcmpi    strtok      unique
intersect     regexpi    sort        strfind    transpose   upper
```

This result shows that MATLAB itself has overloading functions that are called when input arguments are cell arrays. These functions extend the functionality of basic MATLAB functions to cell arrays without requiring the basic functions themselves to be rewritten to accept cell array arguments.

Finally, the functions `loadobj` and `saveobj` are called (if they exist) whenever the functions `load` and `save` are called with user-defined classes, respectively. Adding these functions to a class subdirectory allows you to modify a user-defined variable after a load operation or before a save operation.

33.2 CLASS CREATION

Operator and function overloading are key aspects of OOP. MATLAB's implementation relies on a simple scheme whereby the methods associated with a variable class are stored in class directories just off of the MATLAB search path. The methods themselves are contained in standard M-files. (They can be P-file or MEX-file equivalents of M-files as well.) User-defined classes use the same scheme for method creation and storage. This section illustrates the creation of user-defined classes.

A new variable class is created when a class directory *`@classname`* is created and populated by at least two function M-files. The first M-file has the name *`classname.m`*, which is used to define the creation of variables in the new class. This M-file is called the ***constructor***. The second M-file has the name `display.m` and is used to display the new variable in the *Command* window. No variable class is useful without additional method M-files, but the constructor and `display.m` are a minimum requirement.

> In the vocabulary of OOP, the constructor creates an ***instance*** of the class. This instance is an object that utilizes the methods that overload how operators and functions act in the presence of the object.

The constructor function `classname`.m is a standard function call with input arguments containing the data needed to create an output variable of the desired class. For greatest flexibility, the constructor should handle three different sets of input arguments. Just as there are empty strings, arrays, cells, and so on, the constructor should produce an empty variable if no arguments are passed to it. On the other hand, if the constructor is passed a variable of the same class as that created by the constructor, the constructor should simply pass it back as an output argument. Finally, if creation data are provided, a new variable of the desired class should be created. In this last case, the input data can be checked for appropriateness. Inside of the constructor, the data used to create a variable of the desired class are stored in the fields of a structure. Once the structure fields are populated, the new variable is created by a call to the `class` function. For example, the following is the constructor function for a rational polynomial object:

```
function r=mmrp(varargin)
%MMRP Mastering MATLAB Rational Polynomial Object Constructor.
% MMRP(p) creates a polynomial object from the polynomial vector p
% with 'x' as the variable.
% MMRP(p,'s') creates the polynomial object using the letter 's' as
% the variable in the display of p.
% MMRP(n,d) creates a rational polynomial object from the numerator
% polynomial vector n and denominator polynomial d.
% MMRP(n,d,'s') creates the rational polynomial using the letter 's' as
% the variable in the display of p.
%
% All coefficients must be real.
[n,d,v,msg]=local_parse(varargin); % parse input arguments

if isempty(v) % input was mmrp so return it
   r=n;
else
   error(msg) % return error if it exists
   tol=100*eps;
   if length(d)==1 & abs(d)>tol % enforce scalar d=1
      r.n=n/d;
      r.d=1;
   elseif abs(d(1))>tol % make d monic if possible
      r.n=n/d(1);
      r.d=d/d(1);
   else                        % can't be made monic
      r.n=n;
      r.d=d;
   end
   r.v=v(1);

   r=class(r,'mmrp');   % create object from parts
   r=minreal(r);        % perform pole-zero cancellation
end
```

To simplify the function, parsing of the input arguments is handled by a subfunction entitled `local_parse`. This function is not shown in the preceding code, but it returns four outputs, `n`, `d`, `v`, and `msg`. The variables `n` and `d` are numerical row vectors containing the coefficients of the numerator and denominator of the rational polynomial, respectively. The variable `v` contains the string variable used to display the polynomial. Last, `msg` contains an error message if `local_parse` encounters invalid inputs.

Creation of the rational polynomial object is performed by the statement `r=class(r,'mmrp')`. This usage of the function `class` is valid only within the constructor itself. In other contexts, `class` returns the character-string name of the class of its single input argument. The previous constructor considers all three sets of input arguments. If no input arguments exist, `n`, `d`, and `v` are returned to create an empty rational polynomial. If the input argument is a rational polynomial object, it is simply returned as the output argument. Finally, if data are supplied, a rational polynomial object is created. In the simplest case, the denominator is simply equal to 1 and the display variable is `'x'`. The last assignment statement in `mmrp` passes the created rational polynomial to the overloaded but not shown function `minreal`, which returns a minimal realization of the object by canceling like poles and zeros.

Within the constructor M-file, it is important that the structure fields be created in the same order under all circumstances. Violation of this rule may cause the created object to behave erratically.

Given the `mmrp` constructor, we have the following associated `display.m` file:

```
function display(r)
%DISPLAY Command Window Display of Rational Polynomial Objects.

loose=strcmp(get(0,'FormatSpacing'),'loose');
if loose, disp(' '), end
var=inputname(1);
if isempty(var)
    disp('ans =')
else
    disp([var ' ='])
end
nstr=mmp2str(r.n,r.v); % convert polynomial to string
nlen=length(nstr);
if length(r.d)>1 | r.d~=1
    dstr=mmp2str(r.d,r.v);
```

```
else
    dstr=[];
end
dlen=length(dstr);
dash='-';
if loose, disp(' '), end
if dlen % denominator exists
    m=max(nlen,dlen);
    disp('MMRP Rational Polynomial Object:')
    disp([blanks(ceil((m-nlen)/2)) nstr]);
    disp(dash(ones(1,m)));
    disp([blanks(fix((m-dlen)/2)) dstr]);
else
    disp('MMRP Rational Polynomial Object:')
    disp(nstr);
end
if loose, disp(' '), end
```

This `@mmrp/display.m` function calls the function `mmp2str` to convert a numerical polynomial vector and a desired variable to a character-string representation. This `mmp2str` function must exist elsewhere on the MATLAB search path, not in the `@mmrp` directory. In this case, `mmp2str` is not part of the MATLAB installation. If it existed in the class directory, MATLAB would not find it, since the arguments to `mmp2str` are `double` and `char`, respectively, and not of class `mmrp`. As described in the last section, a method function is called only if the leftmost or highest-precedence input argument has a class that matches that of the method.

Within a method function, it is possible to act on objects as shown in the last assignment statement in the constructor `r=minreal(r)`, where the variable `r` on the right-hand side is an object having class `mmrp`. There are two exceptions to this property. ***The overloading functions `subsref` and `subsasgn` are not called when subscripted reference and subscripted assignment appear within a method function.*** This allows the user to more freely access and manipulate a class variable within a method function.

It is also possible to act on the data contained in an object by simply addressing the structure fields of the object, as shown in numerous places within `display.m`. In this case, the class of the data determines how MATLAB acts.

> Outside of method functions (for example, in the *Command* window), it is not possible to gain access to the contents of fields of an object, nor is it possible to determine the number of or names of the fields. This property is called data encapsulation.

The following examples demonstrate the creation and display of rational polynomial objects:

```
>> p = mmrp([1 2 3])
p =
MMRP Rational Polynomial Object:
x^2 + 2x^1 + 3

>> q = mmrp([1 2 3],[4 5 6],'z')
q =
MMRP Rational Polynomial Object:
0.25z^2 + 0.5z^1 + 0.75
-----------------------
  z^2 + 1.25z^1 + 1.5

>> r = mmrp(conv([1 2],[1 4]),conv([1 2],[1 3]))
r =
MMRP Rational Polynomial Object:
x^1 + 4
-------
x^1 + 3
```

Rational polynomial objects have little value unless operators and functions are overloaded. In particular, it is convenient to define arithmetic operations on mmrp objects. The following M-files define addition, subtraction, multiplication, and division for mmrp objects (since multiplication and division offer multiple methods, they are all overloaded with the associated polynomial manipulation):

```
function r=plus(a,b)
%PLUS Addition for Rational Polynomial Objects.

if isnumeric(a)
   rn=mmpadd(a*b.d,b.n); % see chapter 20 for mmpadd
```

```
    rd=b.d;
    rv=b.v;
elseif isnumeric(b)
    rn=mmpadd(b*a.d,a.n);
    rd=a.d;
    rv=a.v;
else % both polynomial objects
    if ~isequal(a.d,b.d)
        rn=mmpadd(conv(a.n,b.d),conv(b.n,a.c));
        rd=conv(a.d,b.d);
    else
        rn=mmpadd(a.n,b.n);
        rd=b.d;
    end
    if ~strcmp(a.v,b.v)
        warning('Variables Not Identical')
    end
    rv=a.v;
end
r=mmrp(rn,rd,rv); % create new MMRP object from results
```

```
function r=minus(a,b)
%MINUS Subtraction for Rational Polynomial Objects.

r=a+(-b); % use plus and uminus to implement minus
```

```
function r=uminus(a)
%UMINUS Unary Minus for Rational Polynomial Objects.

r=mmrp(-a.n,a.d,a.v);
```

```
function r=times(a,b)
%TIMES Dot Times for Rational Polynomial Objects.

a=mmrp(a); % convert inputs to mmrp if necessary
b=mmrp(b);
rn=conv(a.n,b.n);
rd=conv(a.d,b.d);
if ~strcmp(a.v,b.v)
     warning('Variables Not Identical')
end
rv=a.v;
r=mmrp(rn,rd,rv); % create new MMRP object from results
```

```
function r=mtimes(a,b)
%MTIMES Times for Rational Polynomial Objects.
r=a.*b; % simply call times.m
```

```
function r=rdivide(a,b)
%RDIVIDE Right Dot Division for Rational Polynomial Objects.

a=mmrp(a); % convert inputs to mmrp if necessary
b=mmrp(b);
rn=conv(a.n,b.d);
rd=conv(a.d,b.n);
if ~strcmp(a.v,b.v)
     warning('Variables Not Identical')
end
rv=a.v;
r=mmrp(rn,rd,rv); % create new MMRP object from results
```

```
function r=mrdivide(a,b)
%MRDIVIDE Right Division for Rational Polynomial Objects.

r=a./b; % simply call rdivide.m
```

```
function r=ldivide(a,b)
%LDIVIDE Left Dot Division for Rational Polynomial Objects.

r=b./a; % simply call rdivide.m
```

```
function r=mldivide(a,b)
%MLDIVIDE Left Division for Rational Polynomial Objects.

r=b./a; % simply call rdivide.m
```

The preceding method functions are self-explanatory, in that they implement simply polynomial arithmetic. Examples of their use include the following:

```
>> a = mmrp([1 2 3])
a =
MMRP Rational Polynomial Object:
x^2 + 2x^1 + 3

>> b = a + 2                          % addition
b =
MMRP Rational Polynomial Object:
x^2 + 2x^1 + 5

>> a - b                              % subtraction
ans =
MMRP Rational Polynomial Object:
-2
```

```
>> a + b                                   % addition
ans =
MMRP Rational Polynomial Object:
2x^2 + 4x^1 + 8

>> 2*b                                     % multiplication
ans =
MMRP Rational Polynomial Object:
2x^2 + 4x^1 + 10

>> a * b                                   % multiplication
ans =
MMRP Rational Polynomial Object:
x^4 + 4x^3 + 12x^2 + 16x^1 + 15

>> b/2                                     % division
ans =
MMRP Rational Polynomial Object:
0.5x^2 + x^1 + 2.5

>> 2/b                                     % division
ans =
MMRP Rational Polynomial Object:
      2
--------------
x^2 + 2x^1 + 5

>> c = a/b                                 % division
c =
MMRP Rational Polynomial Object:
x^2 + 2x^1 + 3
--------------
x^2 + 2x^1 + 5

>> d = c/(1+c)                             % mixed
```

```
d =
MMRP Rational Polynomial Object:
0.5x^2 + x^1 + 1.5
--------------------
  x^2 + 2x^1 + 4

>> (a/b)*(b/a)                     % mixed
ans =
MMRP Rational Polynomial Object:
1
```

Given the polynomial functions available in MATLAB and the ease with which they can be manipulated, there are many functions that can be overloaded. For example, the basic MATLAB functions roots and zeros can be overloaded by the following method M-files:

```
function [z,p]=roots(r)
%ROOTS Find Roots of Rational Polynomial Objects.
% ROOTS(R) returns the roots of the numerator of R.
% [Z,P]=ROOTS(R) returns the zeros and poles of R in
% Z and P respectively.

z=roots(r.n);
if nargout==2
    p=roots(r.d);
end
```

```
function z=zeros(r)
%ZEROS Zeros of a Rational Polynomial Object.

z=roots(r.n);
```

The method function roots calls the basic MATLAB function roots, because the arguments within the method are of class double. With the creation of the zeros method, the function zeros has two entirely different meanings, depending on what its arguments are. The beauty of OOP is that functions can have multiple meanings or contexts without having to imbed them all in a single M-file. The class of the input arguments dictates which function is called into action.

Mimicking their Handle Graphics usage, it is common to use them to `set` or `get` individual class structure fields, as in the following example:

```
function set(r,varargin)
%SET Set Rational Polynomial Object Parameters.
% SET(R,Name,Value, ...) sets MMRP object parameters of R
% described by the Name/Value pairs:
%
%  Name           Value
% 'Numerator'     Numeric row vector of numerator coefficients
% 'Denominator'   Numeric row vector of denominator coefficients
% 'Variable'      Character Variable used to display polynomial

if rem(nargin,2)~=1
   error('Parameter Name/Values Must Appear in Pairs.')
end
for i=2:2:nargin-1
   name=varargin{i-1};
   if ~ischar(name), error('Parameter Names Must be Strings.'), end
   name=lower(name(isletter(name)));
   value=varargin{i};
   switch name(1)
   case 'n'
      if ~isnumeric(value) | size(value,1)>1
         error('Numerator Must be a Numeric Row Vector.')
      end
      r.n=value;
   case 'd'
      if ~isnumeric(value) | size(value,1)>1
         error('Denominator Must be a Numeric Row Vector.')
      end
      r.d=value;
```

```
  case 'v'
     if ~ischar(value) | length(value)>1
        error('Variable Must be a Single Character.')
     end
     r.v=value;
  otherwise
     warning('Unknown Parameter Name')
  end
end
vname=inputname(1);
if isempty(vname)
  vname='ans';
end
r=mmrp(r.n,r.d,r.v);
assignin('caller',vname,r);
```

```
function varargout=get(r,varargin)
%GET Get Rational Polynomial Object Parameters.
% GET(R,Name) gets the MMRP object parameter of R described by
% one of the following names:
%
%  Name            Description
% 'Numerator'    Numeric row vector of numerator coefficients
% 'Denominator'  Numeric row vector of denominator coefficients
% 'Variable'     Character Variable used to display polynomial
%
% [A,B,...]=get(R,NameA,NameB,...) returns multiple parameters
% in the corresponding output arguments.

if (nargout+(nargout==0))~=nargin-1
   error('No. of Outputs Must Equal No. of Names.')
end
```

```
for i=1:nargin-1
   name=varargin{i};
   if ~ischar(name), error('Parameter Names Must be Strings.'), end
   name=lower(name(isletter(name)));
     switch name(1)
     case 'n'
        varargout{i}=r.n;
     case 'd'
        varargout{i}=r.d;
     case 'v'
        varargout{i}=r.v;
     otherwise
        warning('Unknown Parameter Name')
     end
end
```

These functions allow you to modify an mmrp object or to get data out of one, as the following example shows:

```
>> c  % recall data
c =
MMRP Rational Polynomial Object:
x^2 + 2x^1 + 3
--------------
x^2 + 2x^1 + 5
>> n = get(c,'n') % get numerator vector
n =
           1           2           3
>> set(c,'Numerator',[3 1]) % change numerator
>> c
c =
MMRP Rational Polynomial Object:
```

```
   3x^1 + 1
--------------
x^2 + 2x^1 + 5

>> class(c)  % class and isa know about mmrp objects
ans =
mmrp
>> isa(c,'mmrp')
ans =
     1
```

33.3 SUBSCRIPTS

Because of MATLAB's array orientation, user-defined classes can also make use of subscripts. In particular, `V(...)`, `V{...}`, and `V.field` are all supported. In addition, these constructions can appear on either side of an assignment statement. When they appear on the right-hand side of an assignment statement, they are referencing the variable V; and when they appear on the left-hand side, they are assigning data to some part of the variable V. These indexing processes are called subscripted reference and subscripted assignment, respectively. The method functions that control how they are interpreted when applied to an object are `subsref` and `subasgn`, respectively. These functions are not as straightforward to understand as other operator and function overloading methods. As a result, this section specifically addresses them. To facilitate this discussion, the `mmrp` object created in the preceding section is used in the examples.

When dealing with rational polynomials, there are two obvious interpretations for subscripted reference. For a rational polynomial object R, `R(x)`, where x is a data array, can return the results of evaluating R at the points in x. Alternatively, `R('v')`, where `'v'` is a single character, could change the variable used to display the object to the letter provided.

The part of the help text for `subsref` that describes how to write a `subsref` method is as follows:

```
B = SUBSREF(A,S) is called for the syntax A(I), A{I}, or A.I
when A is an object.  S is a structure array with the fields:
    type -- string containing '()', '{}', or '.' specifying the
            subscript type.
    subs -- Cell array or string containing the actual subscripts.
```

```
For instance, the syntax A(1:2,:) invokes SUBSREF(A,S) where S is a
1-by-1 structure with S.type='()' and S.subs = {1:2,':'}. A colon
used as a subscript is passed as the string ':'.

Similarly, the syntax A{1:2} invokes SUBSREF(A,S) where S.type='{}'
and the syntax A.field invokes SUBSREF(A,S) where S.type='.' and
S.subs='field'.

These simple calls are combined in a straightforward way for
more complicated subscripting expressions.  In such cases
length(S) is the number of subscripting levels.  For instance,
A(1,2).name(3:5) invokes SUBSREF(A,S) where S is 3-by-1 structure
array with the following values:
    S(1).type='()'       S(2).type='.'        S(3).type='()'
    S(1).subs={1,2}      S(2).subs='name'     S(3).subs={3:5}
```

According to the help text, if R is an mmrp object, R(x) creates S.type='()' and S.subs=x, where x contains the values where R is to be evaluated, not indices into an array. Similarly, R('v') creates S.type='()' and S.subs='v'. All other possibilities should produce an error.

Using this information leads to the subsref method function:

```
function y=subsref(r,s)
%SUBSREF(R,S) Subscripted Reference for Rational Polynomial Objects.
% R('z') returns a new rational polynomial object having the same numerator
% and denominator, but using the variable 'z'.
%
% R(x) where x is a numerical array, evaluates the rational polynomial R
% at the points in x, returning an array the same size as x.

if length(s)>1
      error('MMRP Objects Support Single Arguments Only.')
end
```

```
if strcmp(s.type,'()') % R(x) or R('v')
   arg=s.subs{1};
   argc=class(arg);
   if strcmp(argc,'char')
      if strcmp(arg(1),':')
         error('MMRP Objects Do Not Support R(:).')
      else
          y=mmrp(r.n,r.d,arg(1)); % change variables
      end
   elseif strcmp(argc,'double')
      if length(r.d)>1
         y=polyval(r.n,arg)./polyval(r.d,arg);
      else
         y=polyval(r.n,arg);
      end
   else
      error('Unknown Subscripts.')
   end
else % R{ } or R.field
   error('Cell and Structure Addressing Not Supported.')
end
```

Examples using this method include the following:

```
>> c  % recall data
c =
MMRP Rational Polynomial Object:
   3x^1 + 1
--------------
x^2 + 2x^1 + 5

>> c = c('t') % change variable
```

```
c =
MMRP Rational Polynomial Object:
   3t^1 + 1
--------------
t^2 + 2t^1 + 5

>> x = -2:2
x =
    -2     -1     0     1     2
>> c(x)        % evaluate c(x)
ans =
            -1          -0.5          0.2      0.5    0.53846

>> c{3}        % try cell addressing
??? Error using ==> mmrp/subsref
Cell and Structure Addressing Not Supported.

>> c.n         % Try field addressing
??? Error using ==> mmrp/subsref
Cell and Structure Addressing Not Supported.
```

As stated earlier, outside of method functions, the field structure of objects is hidden from view. If it were not, issuing `c.n` above would have returned the numerator row vector from the object `c`. To enable this feature, it must be explicitly included in the `subsref` method:

```
function y=subsref(r,s)
%SUBSREF(R,S) Subscripted Reference for Rational Polynomial Objects.
% R('z') returns a new rational polynomial object having the same numerator
% and denominator, but using the variable 'z'.
%
% R(x) where x is a numerical array, evaluates the rational polynomial R
% at the points in x, returning an array the same size as x.
%
% R.n returns the numerator row vector of R.
```

```
% R.d returns the denominator row vector of R.
% R.v returns the variable associated with R.

if length(s)>1
   error('MMRP Objects Support Single Arguments Only.')
end
if strcmp(s.type,'()') % R( )
   arg=s.subs{1};
   argc=class(arg);
   if strcmp(argc,'char')
      if strcmp(arg(1),':')
         error('MMRP Objects Do Not Support R(:).')
      else
         y=mmrp(r.n,r.d,arg(1));
      end
   elseif strcmp(argc,'double')
      if length(r.d)>1
         y=polyval(r.n,arg)./polyval(r.d,arg);
      else
         y=polyval(r.n,arg);
      end
   else
      error('Unknown Subscripts.')
   end
elseif strcmp(s.type,'.') % R.field
   arg=lower(s.subs);
   switch arg(1)
   case 'n'
      y=r.n;
   case 'd'
      y=r.d;
```

```
  case 'v'
    y=r.v;
  otherwise
    error('Unknown Data Requested.')
  end
else % R{ }
  error('Cell Addressing Not Supported.')
end
```

Examples using this method include the following:

```
>> c.n  % return numerator
ans =
     3     1

>> c.v  % return variable
ans =
x

>> c.nadfdf % only first letter is checked
ans =
     3     1

>> c.t      % not n, d, or v
??? Error using ==> mmrp/subsref
Unknown Data Requested.

>> c.d(1:2) % we didn't include subaddressing in subsref
??? Error using ==> mmrp/subsref
MMRP Objects Support Single Arguments Only.
```

As stated earlier, the overloading functions `subsref` and `subsasgn` are *not* implicitly called when subscripted reference and subscripted assignment appear within a method function. Overloading the MATLAB polynomial evaluation function `polyval` demonstrates this fact, as shown by the following method:

```
function y=polyval(r,x)
%POLYVAL Evaluate Rational Polynomial Object.
% POLYVAL(R,X) evaluates the rational polynomial R at the
% values in X.

if isnumeric(x)
   %y=r(x);          % what we'd like to do, but can't
   S.type='()';
   S.subs={x};
   y=subsref(r,S); % must call subsref explicitly
else
   error('Second Input Argument Must be Numeric.')
end
```

Because of how `subsref` is written for the `mmrp` object, polynomial evaluation is simply a matter issuing `R(x)`, where `R` is an `mmrp` object and `x` contains the values where `R` is to be evaluated. Since this matches the expected operation of `polyval`, simply issuing `y=r(x)` within `polyval` should cause MATLAB to call the `subsref` method to evaluate the rational polynomial. This does not happen, because MATLAB does not call `subsref` or `subsasgn` within methods. However, to force this to happen, one can explicitly call `subsref` with the desired arguments, as previously shown.

When dealing with rational polynomials, there is one obvious interpretation for subscripted assignment. For a rational polynomial object `R`, `R(1,p) = v`, where `p` is a numerical vector identifying variable powers and `v` is a numerical vector of the same length, the elements of `v` become the coefficients of the numerator polynomial associated with the powers in `p`. Likewise, `R(2,q) = w` changes the denominator coefficients for those powers identified in `q`.

The part of the help text for `subsasgn` that describes how to write a `subsasgn` method is as follows:

```
A = SUBSASGN(A,S,B) is called for the syntax A(I)=B, A{I}=B, or
A.I=B when A is an object.  S is a structure array with the fields:
    type -- string containing '()', '{}', or  '.' specifying the
            subscript type.
    subs -- Cell array or string containing the actual subscripts.
```

```
For instance, the syntax A(1:2,:)=B calls A=SUBSASGN(A,S,B) where
S is a 1-by-1 structure with S.type='()' and S.subs = {1:2,':'}. A
colon used as a subscript is passed as the string ':'.

Similarly, the syntax A{1:2}=B invokes A=SUBSASGN(A,S,B) where
S.type='{}' and the syntax A.field=B invokes SUBSASGN(A,S,B) where
S.type='.' and S.subs='field'.

These simple calls are combined in a straightforward way for
more complicated subscripting expressions.  In such cases
length(S) is the number of subscripting levels.  For instance,
A(1,2).name(3:5)=B invokes A=SUBSASGN(A,S,B) where S is 3-by-1
structure array with the following values:
    S(1).type='()'       S(2).type='.'        S(3).type='()'
    S(1).subs={1,2}      S(2).subs='name'     S(3).subs={3:5}
```

On the basis of this help text and the desired subscripted assignment, the following subsasgn method is created:

```
function a=subsasgn(a,s,b)
%SUBSASGN Subscripted assignment for Rational Polynomial Objects.
%
% R(1,p)=C sets the coefficients of the Numerator of R identified
% by the powers in p to the values in the vector C.
%
% R(2,p)=C sets the coefficients of the Denominator of R identified
% by the powers in p to the values in the vector C.
%
% R(1,:) or R(2,:) simply replaces the corresponding polynomial
% data vector.
%
% For example, for the rational polynomial object
```

```
%            2x^2 + 3x + 4
% R(x) = --------------------
%          x^3 + 4x^2 + 5x + 6
%
% R(1,2)=5           changes the coefficient 2x^2 to 5x^2
% R(2,[3 2])=[7 8] changes x^3 + 4x^2 to 7x^3 + 8x^2
% R(1,:)=[1 2 3]   changes the numerator to x^2 + 2x + 3

if length(s)>1
   error('MMRP Objects Support Single Arguments Only.')
end
if strcmp(s.type,'()') % R(1,p) or R(2,p)
   if length(s.subs)~=2
      error('Two Subscripts Required.')
   end
   nd=s.subs{1}; % numerator or denominator
   p=s.subs{2};  % powers to modify
   if ndims(nd)~=2 | length(nd)~=1 | (nd~=1 & nd~=2)
      error('First Subscript Must be 1 or 2.')
   end
   if isnumeric(p) & ...
      (ndims(p)~=2 | any(p<0) | any(fix(p)~=p))
      error('Second Subscript Must Contain Nonnegative Integers.')
   end
   if ndims(b)~=2 | length(b)~=prod(size(b))
      error('Right Hand Side Must be a Vector.')
   end
   b=b(:).';     % make sure b is a row
   p=p(:)';      % make sure p is a row
   if ischar(p) & length(p)==1 & strcmp(p,':') % R(1,:) or R(2,:)
      if nd==1  % replace numerator
         r.n=b;
         r.d=a.d;
      else      % replace denominator
```

```
          r.n=a.n;
          r.d=b;
        end
      elseif isnumeric(p) % R(1,p) or R(2,p)
        plen=length(p);
        blen=length(b);
        nlen=length(a.n);
        dlen=length(a.d);
        if plen~=blen
          error('Sizes Do Not Match.')
        end
        if nd==1  % modify numerator
          r.d=a.d;
          rlen=max(max(p)+1,nlen);
          r.n=zeros(1,rlen);
          r.n=mmpadd(r.n,a.n);
          r.n(rlen-p)=b;
        else       % modify denominator
          r.n=a.n;
          rlen=max(max(p)+1,dlen);
          r.d=zeros(1,rlen);
          r.d=mmpadd(r.d,a.d);
          r.d(rlen-p)=b;
        end
      else
        error('Unknown Subscripts.')
      end
    else % R{ } or R.field
      error('Cell and Structure Addressing Not Supported.')
    end
    a=mmrp(r.n,r.d,a.v);
```

Examples using this method include the following:

```
>> a = mmrp([3 1],[1 2 5 10]) % create test object
a =
MMRP Rational Polynomial Object:
   3x^1 + 1
-----------------------
x^3 + 2x^2 + 5x^1 + 10

>> a(1,:) = [1 2 4]        % replace entire numerator
a =
MMRP Rational Polynomial Object:
     x^2 + 2x^1 + 4
-----------------------
x^3 + 2x^2 + 5x^1 + 10

>> a(2,2) = 12             % replace x^2 coef in denominator
a =
MMRP Rational Polynomial Object:
     x^2 + 2x^1 + 4
-----------------------
x^3 + 12x^2 + 5x^1 + 10

>> a(1,0) = 0              % replace 4x^0 with 0x^0
a =
MMRP Rational Polynomial Object:
       x^2 + 2x^1
-----------------------
x^3 + 12x^2 + 5x^1 + 10

>> a(1,:)=a.d              % subsref and subsasn! (a.n and a.d cancel)
a =
MMRP Rational Polynomial Object:
1
```

33.4 CONVERTER FUNCTIONS

As demonstrated in earlier chapters, the functions `double`, `char`, and `logical` convert their inputs to the data type matching their name. For example, `double('hello')` converts the character string `'hello'` to its numerical ASCII equivalent. Whenever possible, methods for these converter functions should be included in a class directory. For `mmrp` objects, `double` and `char` have obvious interpretations. The `double` method should extract the numerator and denominator polynomials, and the `char` method should create a string representation such as that displayed by `display.m`, as in the following code:

```
function [n,d]=double(r)
%DOUBLE Convert Rational Polynomial Object to Double.
% DOUBLE(R) returns a matrix with the numerator of R in
% the first row and the denominator in the second row.
% [N,D]=DOUBLE(R) extracts the numerator N and denominator D
% from the rational polynomial object R.

if nargout<=1 & length(r.d)>1
   nlen=length(r.n);
   dlen=length(r.d);
   n=zeros(1,max(nlen,dlen));
   n=[mmpadd(n,r.n);mmpadd(n,r.d)];
elseif nargout<=1
     n=r.n;
else % nargout==2
     n=r.n;
     d=r.d;
end
```

```
function [n,d,v]=char(r)
%CHAR Convert Rational Polynomial Object to Char.
% CHAR(R) returns a 3 row string array containing R in the
% format used by DISPLAY.M
% [N,D]=CHAR(R) extracts the numerator N and denominator D
```

```
% as character strings from the rational polynomial object R.
% [N,D,V]=CHAR(R) in addition returns the variable V.

if nargout<=1
   nstr=mmp2str(r.n,r.v);
   nlen=length(nstr);
   if length(r.d)>1
      dash='-';
      dstr=mmp2str(r.d,r.v);
      dlen=length(dstr);
      m=max(nlen,dlen);
      n=char([blanks(ceil((m-nlen)/2)) nstr],...
         dash(ones(1,m)),...
         [blanks(fix((m-dlen)/2)) dstr]);
   else
      n=nstr;
   end
elseif nargout>1
   n=mmp2str(r.n); % converts polynomial to string
   d=mmp2str(r.d);
end
if nargout>2
   v=r.v;
end
```

33.5 PRECEDENCE, INHERITANCE, AND AGGREGATION

MATLAB automatically gives user-defined classes ***higher precedence*** than the built-in classes in MATLAB. Therefore, operators and functions containing a mixture of built-in classes and a user-defined class always call the methods of the user-defined class. While this default precedence is usually sufficient for simple classes, the presence of multiple user-defined classes requires that some mechanism exist to allow the user to control the precedence of classes with respect to one another, or perhaps to force a user-defined class to have lower precedence than a built-in class. The functions `inferiorto` and `superiorto` provide this capability within MATLAB. If you are using them, calls to ***these functions must appear within the constructor***

function for a class. The arguments to both functions contain a list of character strings identifying the classes that have lower or higher precedence than the object created by the constructor. For example, `superiorto('double')` dictates that the object has higher precedence than double-precision variables, and `inferiorto('mmrp','char')` dictates that an object has lower precedence than `mmrp` and `char` objects.

For large programming projects, it may be convenient to create a hierarchy of object types. In this case, it may be beneficial to let one object type inherit methods from another type. In doing so, fewer methods need to be written, and method modifications are more centralized. In the vocabulary of OOP, an object that inherits the properties of another is called a ***child*** class, and the class it inherits from is called the ***parent*** class. In the simplest case, a child class inherits methods from a single parent class. This is called ***simple*** or ***single inheritance***. It is also possible for a child class to inherit methods from multiple classes, which is called ***multiple inheritance***.

In single inheritance, the child class is given all of the fields of the parent class, plus one or more unique fields of its own. As a result, methods associated with the parent can be directly applied to objects of the child class. Quite naturally, methods of the parent class have no knowledge of the fields unique to the child and therefore cannot use them in any way. Similarly, fields of the parent class cannot be accessed by methods of the child. The child must use the methods it inherited from the parent to gain access to the parent fields. The `lti` object in the *Control Toolbox* is an example of a parent class having child classes `tf`, `zpk`, `ss`, `dss`, `frd`.

In multiple inheritance, a child class is given all of the fields of all parent classes, plus one or more unique fields of its own. As in single inheritance, the parents and child do not have direct access to each other's fields. With multiple parents, the complexity of determining which parent methods are called under what circumstances is more difficult to describe. (Information and detailed examples regarding inheritance can be found in the MATLAB documentation.)

In the `mmrp` class used as an example earlier, the object fields contained data that were elements of the MATLAB classes `double` and `char`. In reality, there is no reason object fields cannot contain other data types, including user-defined classes. In the vocabulary of OOP, this is called ***containment*** or ***aggregation***. The rules for operator and function overloading do not change. Within method functions of one class, the methods of the classes of other classes are called as needed to operate on the fields of the original class.

34

MATLAB Programming Interfaces

MATLAB provides a number of ways to interface with external programs. C functions and FORTRAN subroutines can be called from MATLAB by using MEX-files. Furthermore, MATLAB can perform computations and return the results to C or FORTRAN programs by using the *MATLAB **Engine***. MATLAB provides header files and libraries for creating and accessing standard MATLAB MAT-files. Data can be collected and brought directly into MATLAB, using the built-in serial port interface. In addition, MATLAB can use Java classes, objects, and methods and can exchange data with PC applications by using Component Object Model (COM) objects and Dynamic Data Exchange (DDE). MATLAB can also act as a COM Automation server to communicate with Visual Basic (VB) applications or Visual Basic for Applications (VBA)-enabled PC applications, such as Microsoft Excel, PowerPoint, and Word. The use of Java, COM, DDE, and ActiveX are covered in the following chapters. This chapter focuses on interfacing with C and FORTRAN and serial port communications.

MATLAB supplies a rich set of external programming interfaces, many more than can be covered in this text. A comprehensive treatment of the MATLAB application programming interface (API) could easily fill a book by itself. This chapter and the next two chapters provide a constructive introduction, with examples, to the API features in MATLAB. (The MATLAB documentation provides a more comprehensive treatment of this subject.)

The discussions and examples in this chapter are based on the use of an ANSI C compiler on a UNIX platform, with additional discussion of platform-specific differences. The examples were developed and tested by using the GCC compiler version 3.3.3 on a Linux i386 platform, with the 2.6.6 kernel (`glnx86` architecture). The GCC compiler version 3.3 was also used as a test on a Macintosh platform running OS X version 10.3.4 (`mac` architecture). The LCC compiler supplied with MATLAB was used to test the C language examples on a Windows 2000 Pentium PC (win32 architecture), and the G77 FORTRAN compiler version 3.3.3 was used to test FORTRAN code on the Linux platform.

34.1 ACCESSING MATLAB ARRAYS

Anyone writing programs to interface with MATLAB should have a basic understanding of the structure of MATLAB arrays. Any MEX, MAT, or Engine program must access MATLAB arrays to perform useful work. This section explains a little about how MATLAB stores arrays and lists some of the functions available for use in programs to access MATLAB arrays.

The MATLAB Array

MATLAB supports only one type of object: the MATLAB array. All MATLAB variables are stored as MATLAB arrays. MATLAB array elements are composed of one of the fundamental data types (`double`, `sparse`, `char`, `cell`, `object`, `single`, or 8-, 16-, 32-, or 64-bit signed or unsigned integers) or another MATLAB array. All scalars and composite elements such as strings, vectors, matrices, cell arrays, and structures are MATLAB arrays.

MATLAB stores array data in columnwise order. This fact is used later in the `mmcellstr` MEX-file (MEX Example 4) when data is extracted from a string buffer and reassembled into individual strings. The following example illustrates this data organization:

```
>> x = [1 2 3; 4 5 6; 7 8 9]

x =

     1     2     3
     4     5     6
     7     8     9

>> size(x)

ans =

     3     3

>> x(:)'

ans =

     1     4     7     2     5     8     3     6     9
```

Accessing MATLAB Arrays: The `mxArray`

A MATLAB array in C can be considered a new C data type—an object called an `mxArray` built from a C structure. The `mxArray` structure stores information about the type of array (double, sparse, cell, and so on), the array dimensions, and references to the data. The mxArray structure also stores type-specific information, such as the complexity of a numerical array (real or complex), the number and names of fields of a structure or an object, and the indices and maximum number of nonzero elements of a sparse array. The names of the functions used to access the characteristics and the elements of an mxArray all begin with the prefix mx.

Numerical matrices are stored as two vectors of doubles (or any of the other numerical data types); one vector contains the real elements, and the second vector contains the imaginary elements. Two pointers are used to access the data—a pointer to the real vector (pr) and another pointer to the vector of imaginary numbers (pi). The pi pointer is NULL if the array is real. Strings are stored as 16-bit integers (16 bits per character) with no imaginary component. C strings are null terminated, but MATLAB strings are not. The length of a MATLAB string is always available from the array dimensions.

Cell arrays are collections of arrays. The data vector contains pointers to other arrays. There is no imaginary component. Each pointer in the vector of pointers is called a cell. Structures are stored as folded cell arrays in which each element of the data vector is a field. Each field is associated with a name stored in another structure element of the mxArray. Objects are stored as named structures (the class name) with registered collections of methods. There are no imaginary components of cell arrays, structures, or objects.

One of the elements of an mxArray is the size of the array, implemented as a vector of integers. Each integer corresponds to the length of the associated dimension. If the number of elements in the vector is greater than 2, the mxArray is a multidimensional array. If any one of these dimensions is zero, the array is considered to be an empty array. Another mxArray structure element can be used to flag any noncomplex array as a logical array.

Sparse matrices consist of the elements described earlier—two numerical vectors, along with pointers to the vectors. These vectors contain the nonzero elements of the matrix. Sparse arrays also contain the parameters nzmax, ir, and jc, where ir is a pointer to an array of the row indices of the corresponding nonzero elements and jc is a pointer to a vector of column indices. The maximum number of nonzero elements in the sparse matrix is stored in nzmax.

MX Functions

MATLAB provides more than 100 functions and subroutines to access and manipulate mxArrays from C or FORTRAN programs. The logical subroutines (mxIs...) return one (1) for True and zero (0) for False. The mxCreate... functions normally come in two versions: an mxCreate...Matrix function for 2-D mxArrays and an mxCreate...Array version for *n*-D mxArrays. FORTRAN mxCopyPtrTo... functions are used to copy data from an mxArray into a FORTRAN array, and mxCopy...ToPtr subroutines are used to copy data from a FORTRAN array into an mxArray. These subroutines are often used to copy mxArrays into FORTRAN arrays, send the data to subroutines, and copy the resulting FORTRAN arrays back into mxArrays. Examples later in this chapter will illustrate the use of many of these functions and subroutines. Complete lists of MX functions and subroutines, including parameters and return values, are included in the MATLAB documentation.

34.2 CALLING C OR FORTRAN FROM MATLAB

MEX-files are compiled C or FORTRAN functions that can be called from the MATLAB environment, just as if they were M-file functions. Preexisting C functions or FORTRAN subroutines can be modified by adding a few lines of code to manage access to MATLAB data and functions. Compiling the modified code with the `mex` command produces a MEX-file that can be called from within MATLAB. Most computational functions perform faster and more efficiently by using MATLAB M-files. However, a few operations, such as certain For Loops, may be more efficiently implemented in C or FORTRAN. If you cannot eliminate iteration through vectorization, or improve performance sufficiently through loop optimization techniques, MEX-file creation may provide a viable solution.

Compiled MEX-files have platform-specific file name extensions. For example, `dll` is the MEX-file extension on the Windows platform, and `mexsol` is the MEX-file extension for Sun Solaris platforms. On all platforms, the `mexext` function returns the appropriate MEX-file extension.

Each MEX function you create should have an associated M-file (*`myfunc.m`*) to provide help text for the MEX function. The MATLAB documentation provides additional information about using other architectures and other compilers.

Preparing the MEX Environment

The MEX environment must be initialized to access an installed C or FORTRAN compiler. MATLAB supports a number of compilers, including those available for no charge. For example, the GCC compiler (including FORTRAN support) is available by download from many sources on the Internet, including the GCC home page at `http://gcc.gnu.org/`, and is supplied with many operating system distributions. Another option is to use the LCC compiler supplied with MATLAB on the PC platform. Standard third-party ANSI C compilers and FORTRAN compilers are supported, such as the Microsoft and Borland compilers on the PC platform, the GCC compiler on the Linux and BSD platforms, and the vendor-supplied optional ANSI C or FORTRAN compilers on Unix workstations.

Certain compilers do not mask floating-point exceptions by default. MATLAB arrays allow nonfinite values, such as `Inf` and `NaN`, which generate floating-point exceptions if they are not masked. The MATLAB documentation and the compiler documentation contain information describing ways to mask floating-point exceptions when compiling MEX, Engine, and MAT-file programs that use these compilers.

The command » `mex -setup` selects the appropriate initialization or options file for the compiler and computer platform (operating system and architecture). The options file sets certain environment variables and specifies the locations of the appropriate header files and libraries for a platform and compiler. Options files are located in `$MATLAB/bin` on Unix, Linux, and Macintosh platforms and in `$MATLAB\bin\win32\mexopts` on Windows PC platforms. Once the MEX environment has been initialized, the command » `mex myprog.c` compiles the MEX source file `myprog.c` into the compiled MEX-file `myprog.dll` (or `myprog.mexglx`, and so on). The `mex` command line option `-f` can be used to temporarily select a different initialization file if needed. The -f option is used later to compile MATLAB Engine and MAT programs. The -v option can be used to list the compiler settings and to observe the compile and link stages. The command » mex -help provides a list of mex command-line options. Other standard compiler options, such as -c, -g, and -D, are also supported by mex. Debuggers (such as dbx, ddd, or gdb) can be used to debug MEX programs if the -g option is used. The mex command is implemented both as a function to be called from the MATLAB *Command* window and as a batch or script file for use outside of the MATLAB environment. The MATLAB documentation contains more information about the mex command, command-line options, supported compilers, and debugging procedures.

> MEX-files must be designed to operate as standard MATLAB functions using a variable number of input arguments and a variable number of output arguments. Normal MATLAB functions pass data by value rather than by reference. The inputs to a MEX function should never be modified. If the purpose of a function is to change the input, the changed value should be returned as an output. For example, if the function inc increments the value of an input variable b, the function should be called by using the syntax b=inc(b).

MEX Source File Organization

MEX source code files can be divided into ***interface*** and ***subroutine*** sections. The interface section (also known as the ***gateway routine*** in the MATLAB documentation) contains any necessary #include and #define directives, along with code to access MATLAB data and functions from your program. The subroutine section (also known as the ***computational routine*** in the MATLAB documentation) actually performs operations on the data. This section can be written as a separate function or subroutine, or the code can be incorporated into the interface section.

In addition to any other necessary include files, the interface section must contain an #include "mex.h" directive to provide support for MEX functions. The mex prefix designates functions that can be used only within MEX-files and that can operate in the MATLAB workspace. The "mex.h" header file also includes "matrix.h" to provide MX functions to support MATLAB data types, along with the standard header files <stdio.h>, <stdlib.h>, and <stddef.h>. The mx prefix designates functions that operate on MATLAB data types.

The interface section is used to communicate with the MATLAB environment. Every MEX-file requires a mexFunction statement. This is the entry point to the program and corresponds to the main function in a stand-alone C program. The mexFunction function definition is

```
void mexFunction( int nlhs,        mxArray *plhs[],
                  int nrhs, const mxArray *prhs[] )
```

The variable nlhs is an integer containing the number of left-hand-side (output) arguments corresponding to the number returned from the MATLAB nargout function. Similarly, nrhs contains the number of right-hand-side (input) arguments. prhs[] is an array of pointers to the input arguments. prhs[0] is a pointer to the first input argument, prhs[1] is a pointer to the second input argument, and prhs[nrhs-1] is a pointer to the last input argument. All MATLAB data types are MATLAB arrays, and so all input and output arguments to a MEX-file are the mxArray data type.

At the time the compiled MEX function is called, prhs contains pointers to the input arguments, while plhs contains null pointers. It is the responsibility of the programmer to create any output arrays and assign array pointers to the plhs pointer array. An output array can be created even if nlhs contains 0, indicating that no output arguments have been requested. If called from the *Command* window, any output is assigned to the ans variable in the MATLAB base workspace.

Workspace Issues

When a MATLAB M-file function is called, the function operates in a private workspace that is distinct from the MATLAB base workspace or the caller function workspace. Variables in the base or caller workspace are passed by value rather than by reference and are not affected by changes within the called function. The evalin and assignin functions are exceptions; these functions affect variables outside of the current workspace.

MEX functions operate in their own environment, in that the scope of local variables is limited to the MEX function itself. However, this environment is not a MATLAB workspace as such. MX functions (functions with the mx prefix) operate on MATLAB data types. MEX functions (functions with the mex prefix) operate within the MATLAB workspace itself. For example, the mexEvalString and mexCallMATLAB functions evaluate their string arguments in the caller workspace. The mexGetVariable function copies a variable from a specified MATLAB workspace ('base', 'caller', or 'global') into an mxArray. The function mexGetVariablePtr gets a read-only pointer to a MATLAB variable. The function mexPutVariable copies an mxArray into a specified MATLAB workspace. All other mex functions operate in the caller workspace.

Another difference is the use of the mexPrintf function for printing formatted strings. The function mexPrintf must be used, rather than the standard C printf, within MEX-files. This function calls the MATLAB printf function in the base workspace and prints in the *Command* window (and in the diary file if it is in use).

The following is a list of MEX functions available in C programs, FORTRAN programs, or both:

Function	C	F	Purpose
mexAtExit	C	F	Register a function to be called when the MEX-file is cleared
mexCallMATLAB	C	F	Call a MATLAB function, M-file, or MEX-file
mexFunction	C	F	Entry point to the MEX-file
mexFunctionName	C	F	Name of the current MEX function

mexGetVariable	C	F	Get a copy of a variable from another workspace
mexGetVariablePtr	C	F	Get a read-only pointer to a variable from another workspace
mexPutVariable	C	F	Copy an mxArray into a MATLAB workspace
mexEvalString	C	F	Execute a MATLAB command in the caller workspace
mexErrMsgTxt	C	F	Issue an error message and returns to MATLAB
mexErrMsgIdAndTxt	C	F	Issue an error message and identifier, and returns to MATLAB
mexWarnMsgTxt	C	F	Issue a warning message
mexWarnMsgIdAndTxt	C	F	Issue a warning message and identifier
mexLock	C	F	Lock a MEX-file so it cannot be cleared from memory
mexUnlock	C	F	Unlock a MEX-file so it can be cleared from memory
mexIsLocked	C	F	True if the MEX-file is locked
mexIsGlobal	C	F	True if the mxArray has global scope
mexPrintf	C		ANSI C printf-style output routine
mexPrintf		F	Output routine. Optional arguments, such as format strings, are not supported in FORTRAN.
mexSetTrapFlag	C	F	Control the response of mexCallMATLAB to errors
mexMakeArrayPersistent	C	F	Make an mxArray persist after the MEX-file completes
mexMakeMemoryPersistent	C	F	Make memory allocated by mxMalloc and mxCalloc persist
mexGet	C		Get the value of a Handle Graphics property
mexSet	C		Set the value of a Handle Graphics property

MATLAB version 7 has replaced the older mexGetArray, mexGetMatrix, and mexGetFull functions with a single mexGetVariable function. Similarly, the mexPutArray, mexPutMatrix, and mexPutFull functions have been replaced by the mexPutVariable function. Pointer functions have had a similar name change.

The mxGetName function, which returned the MATLAB name of an mxArray (similar to the MATLAB built-in function inputname), has been discontinued in MATLAB 7 and will no longer be supported. For backward compatibility, you can still use the -V5 option in the mex script, but that capability will be removed in the future. The only way to pass a MATLAB variable name into your program without using mxGetName is to pass the arguments as strings containing the variable names, rather than the variables themselves, and use mexGetVariable to get the data, using the variable name.

MEX Example 1: fact

This basic example creates a MEX-file that computes the factorial function (imbedded comments and error checking have been omitted):

```
/*
 * fact.c - returns the factorial of a nonnegative integer.
 *
 *  MATLAB usage:   p=fact(n)
 *
 *  Mastering MATLAB 7 C MEX Example 1
 */

#include "mex.h"

void mexFunction( int nlhs,         mxArray *plhs[],
                  int nrhs, const mxArray *prhs[] )
{
    double n, j, *p;
    int i;

    n=mxGetScalar(prhs[0]);
    plhs[0]=mxCreateDoubleMatrix(1,1,mxREAL);
    p=mxGetPr(plhs[0]);

    j=1.0;
    for (i=n;i>1;i--)
      j=j*i;
    *p=j;
}
```

First, the mex.h header file is included. Then, mexFunction is declared, along with the required parameters. A few variables are declared, and the value of the input argument is obtained by using the mxGetScalar function. An output matrix is created to be a 1-by-1 matrix of real doubles by using the mxCreateDoubleMatrix function, and a C pointer is obtained by using mxGetPr. The calculation is performed, and the result is assigned to the output matrix.

Issuing » mex fact.c creates a MEX-file that can be called from MATLAB. The name of the resulting MEX-file depends on the computer platform: fact.dll on a Windows PC or fact.mexglx on a Linux platform. If the source C file contains an error, compiler error messages are displayed that provide sufficient information to make the necessary corrections to the source code. No MEX output file is created if errors are found.

Running the compiled MEX-file produces output similar to the following:

```
>> x = 5

x =

     5


>> y = fact(x)

y =

   120


>> which fact

/home/work/matlab/fact.mexglx
```

Some of the more common MX and MEX functions are used in these examples, but many more are available. A complete list of MATLAB interface functions, along with descriptions of their arguments and return values (called the MATLAB application programming interface) is available in both HTML and PDF formats.

MEX Example 2: mycalc

This example introduces more elements. The function mycalc includes error checking and uses a subroutine to perform a calculation on the elements of an array. This style can be used to turn an existing C subroutine into a MEX-file by adding an interface section to existing source code, adding the #include "mex.h" directive, and compiling.

The mycalc MEX-file accepts a 2-D array of doubles and returns an array of the same size that contains the results of the calculation on each of the input elements. The interface section is used to do some error checking, determine the dimensions of the input array, create C pointers to the input and output arrays, and call the subroutine to do the calculation. Here is the code:

```
/*
 * mycalc.c - calculates x^2-x+1/x for each element of an array.
 *
 *   MATLAB usage:    p=mycalc(n)
 *
 *  Mastering MATLAB 7 C MEX Example 2:
 *       single 2-D real numeric array input,
 *       single array output.
 */

#include "mex.h"

/* This is the original subroutine that performs the calculation. */
static void mycalc( double p[], double n[], int r, int c)
{
    int i;
    for (i=0;i<r*c;i++)
        p[i]=n[i]*n[i]-n[i]+1.0/n[i];
}

/* This is the interface to MATLAB data types and arguments. */
void mexFunction( int nlhs,       mxArray *plhs[],
                  int nrhs, const mxArray *prhs[] )
{
    double *p, *n;
    int r, c;

    /* Do some error checking. */
    if (nrhs != 1)
     mexErrMsgTxt("One input argument required.");
    else if (nlhs > 1)
     mexErrMsgTxt("Too many output arguments.");
    else if (!mxIsNumeric(prhs[0]))
     mexErrMsgTxt("Input must be numeric.");
    else if (mxIsComplex(prhs[0]))
```

```
    mexErrMsgTxt("Input must be real.");
  else if (mxGetNumberOfDimensions(prhs[0]) > 2)
    mexErrMsgTxt("N-Dimensional arrays are not supported.");

  /* Get the input array dimensions. */
  r=mxGetM(prhs[0]);
  c=mxGetN(prhs[0]);

  /* Create a matrix for the return argument */
  plhs[0]=mxCreateDoubleMatrix(r,c,mxREAL);

  /* Assign pointers to the parameters. */
  p=mxGetPr(plhs[0]);
  n=mxGetPr(prhs[0]);

  /* Do the actual calculation in a subroutine. */
  mycalc(p,n,r,c);
}
```

The subroutine appears first in the MEX C source file to avoid forward references and the necessity for a prototype statement. The `mexErrMsgTxt` function operates in the same way as the MATLAB `error` function. The error message text is printed in the MATLAB *Command* window, and the MEX function exits. Note that the standard C language double quotation marks (") are used to delimit a string argument. The `mexWarnMsgTxt` function can be used to emulate the MATLAB `warning` function, and it prints the text string in the *Command* window without exiting the MEX-file. The `mexWarnMsgIdAndTxt` and `mexErrorMsgIdAndTxt` functions could have been used to return a MATLAB message identifier string along with the text strings if desired. (See the MATLAB documentation for more information on using message identifiers to classify warnings and errors.)

The `mxGetM` and `mxGetN` functions return the number of rows and columns, respectively, of a 2-D `mxArray`. The statement

```
plhs[0]=mxCreateDoubleMatrix(r,c,mxREAL);
```

creates an `r`-by-`c` `mxArray` to contain real elements of MATLAB type `double`. The `mxCOMPLEX` flag, rather than the `mxREAL` flag, could be used to create an array containing complex elements. C-style pointers to the data stored in `mxArrays` are returned by the `mxGetPr` function. The function `mxGetPr` returns a pointer to the real elements of an `mxArray`. (Use `mxGetPi` to get a pointer to the imaginary elements of a complex mxArray.) The final step is to call the subroutine mycalc with the appropriate arguments.

MEX Example 3: count

The following example supports multidimensional arrays, uses #define statements to simplify the source code, and includes MATLAB help text for the count MEX-file:

```
/*
 * count.c - count occurrences of values in an array.
 *
 *   MATLAB usage:   c=count(a,b,tol)
 *
 *  Mastering MATLAB 7 C MEX Example 3
 */

#include <math.h>
#include "mex.h"

/* Define some variables to make life easier. */
#define A   prhs[0] /* Pointer to first right-hand-side argument  */
#define B   prhs[1] /* Pointer to second right-hand-side argument */
#define TOL prhs[2] /* Pointer to third right-hand-side argument  */
#define C   plhs[0] /* Pointer to first left-hand-side argument   */
void  mexFunction( int nlhs,       mxArray *plhs[],
                   int nrhs, const mxArray *prhs[] )
{
   int i, j, sizea, sizeb;
   double tol, vcount;
   double *a, *b, *c;

   /* Do some error checking */
   if (nrhs < 2)
     mexErrMsgTxt("Missing input arguments.");
   else if (nrhs > 3)
     mexErrMsgTxt("Too many input arguments.");
```

```
else if (nlhs > 1)
  mexErrMsgTxt("Too many output arguments.");

/* Get tolerance value if supplied, otherwise use EPS. */
if (nrhs == 3) {
  if (!mxIsNumeric(TOL) || mxIsComplex(TOL) ||
      mxGetNumberOfElements(TOL) != 1 )
    mexErrMsgTxt("TOL must be a real numeric scalar.");
  tol=mxGetScalar(TOL);
  if (tol < mxGetEps())
    mexErrMsgTxt("TOL must be a positive value.");
}
else
  tol=mxGetEps();

/* Make sure input arrays are noncomplex numeric arrays. */
if (!mxIsNumeric(A) || !mxIsNumeric(B) ||
    mxIsComplex(A) || mxIsComplex(B))
  mexErrMsgTxt("Input arguments must be real of type double.");

/* Create the output mxArray the same size as A */
C=mxCreateNumericArray(mxGetNumberOfDimensions(A),
      mxGetDimensions(A),mxDOUBLE_CLASS,mxREAL);

/* Get the number of elements in A and B and create pointers */
/* to the input and output arrays. */
sizea=mxGetNumberOfElements(A);
sizeb=mxGetNumberOfElements(B);
a=(double *) mxGetPr(A);
b=(double *) mxGetPr(B);
c=(double *) mxGetPr(C);

/* Cycle through the elements of the arrays and count values */
```

```
for (i=0;i<sizea;i++) {
  vcount=0.0;
  for (j=0;j<sizeb;j++)
  if ((fabs(a[i]-b[j])) <= tol)
        vcount++;
      c[i]=vcount;
    }
}
```

This example includes the standard `math.h` header file, in addition to the `mex.h` file, to support the `fabs` function used in the calculation section. Four `#define` statements are also used to reduce the amount of typing required and to improve the readability of the resulting code. The line

```
C=mxCreateNumericArray(mxGetNumberOfDimensions(A),
          mxGetDimensions(A),mxDOUBLE_CLASS,mxREAL);
```

is an example of an MX creation function for *n*-D `mxArrays`. Most `mxArray` creation functions have two distinct forms: a 2-D form and an *n*-D form. The 2-D version is

```
C=mxCreateNumericMatrix(mxGetM(A),mxGetN(A),mxDOUBLE_CLASS,mxREAL);
```

The 2-D form (`mxCreate...Matrix`) expects the number of rows and the number of columns as separate arguments. Any other arguments (the numerical class and the real/complex flag in this case) follow. The *n*-D form requires the number of dimensions and a vector of dimension sizes, followed by any other arguments. For example,

```
plhs[0]=mxCreateCellMatrix(3,4);
```

creates an empty 3-by-4 cell `mxArray`, while

```
plhs[0]=mxCreateCellArray(3,{2,3,4});
```

creates a 3-D 2-by-3-by-4 cell `mxArray`.

The `mxGetNumberOfElements` function returns the total number of elements in an `mxArray`. This is the number passed to the subfunction, rather than the dimensions of the arrays, since the subroutine uses single-subscript addressing to process the array elements.

Finally, we create an M-file to provide appropriate MATLAB help text for the `count` function. The file is named `count.m` and is saved in the same directory as the `count.mexglx` MEX-file:

```
function c=count(a,b,tol)
%COUNT Count Occurrences of Values in an Array.
% COUNT(A,B) returns an array the same size as A whose i-th element
% contains the number of times A(i) appears in the array B.
% A and B must be Real arrays.
%
% COUNT implements the following:
%        c = zeros(size(A)));
%        for i=1:prod(size(A))
%            c(i)=sum(A(i)==B);
%        end
```

When MATLAB finds a MEX-file and an M-file in the same directory, the MEX-file is called to execute the function, while the M-file provides help text.

MEX Example 4: mmcellstr

The next example leaves the realm of numbers and enters the world of strings and cells. The `mmcellstr` function is a C MEX-file implementation of the MATLAB `cellstr` function. The function `mmcellstr` creates a cell array of strings from a character array. Each row of the character array is placed in an individual cell of a cell array.

The following example demonstrates a number of new techniques, including allocating memory in a MEX-file, handling empty arrays, and duplicating an array:

```
/*
 *  mmcellstr.c - Create a cell array of strings from a 2-D character
array.
 *
 *   MATLAB usage: c=mmcellstr(s)
 *
 *  Mastering MATLAB 7 C MEX Example 4
 */

#include "mex.h"
```

```
void mexFunction( int nlhs,        mxArray *plhs[],
                  int nrhs, const mxArray *prhs[] )
{
  int m, n, i, j;
  char *buf;
  char **line;

  /* Do some error checking */
  if (nrhs < 1)
    mexErrMsgTxt("Missing input argument.");
  else if (nrhs > 1)
    mexErrMsgTxt("Too many input arguments.");
  else if (mxGetNumberOfDimensions(prhs[0]) != 2)
    mexErrMsgTxt("Input must be 2-D.");
  else if (nlhs > 1)
    mexErrMsgTxt("Too many output arguments.");

/****** Start of Region 1 ******/
  /* If the input is already a cell array, duplicate it. */
  if (mxIsCell(prhs[0]))
    if (mxIsChar(mxGetCell(prhs[0],0))) {
      plhs[0]=mxCreateCellMatrix(mxGetM(prhs[0]),mxGetN(prhs[0]));
      plhs[0]=mxDuplicateArray(prhs[0]);
      return;
    }
/******  End of Region 1  ******/

  /* Make sure the input is a character array. */
  if (!mxIsChar(prhs[0]))
    mexErrMsgTxt("Input must be a character array.");

  /* Handle the empty input case. */
  if (mxIsEmpty(prhs[0])) {
    plhs[0]=mxCreateCellMatrix(1, 1);
```

```
      mxSetCell(plhs[0],0,mxDuplicateArray(prhs[0]));
      return;
    }

    /* Determine the dimensions of the input structure array */
    m=mxGetM(prhs[0]);
    n=mxGetN(prhs[0]);

/****** Start of Region 2 ******/
    /* Stuff the input into a string buffer. */
    /* If mxArrayToString fails to allocate the buffer, the MEX file
terminates. */
    buf=mxArrayToString(prhs[0]);

    /* Create line buffers for the individual strings. */
    line=(char **)mxCalloc(m,sizeof(char*));
    for (i=0;i<m;i++)
      line[i]=mxCalloc(n+1,sizeof(char));
/******  End of Region 2  ******/

    /* Parse the buffer into individual lines. */
    for (j=0;j<n;j++)
      for (i=0;i<m;i++)
        line[i][j]=buf[i+m*j];

    /* Free the string buffer and create the output cell array. */
    mxFree(buf);
    plhs[0]=mxCreateCellMatrix(m, 1);

    for (i=0;i<m;i++) {
      /* For each line, remove trailing blanks... */
      j=n;
      while (--j >= 0)
```

```
    if (line[i][j] != ' ')
      break;
   line[i][j+1]='\0';

   /* insert the line into the output array... */
   mxSetCell(plhs[0],i,mxCreateString(line[i]));

   /* and free the line buffer memory. */
   mxFree(line[i]);
  }
 mxFree(line);
}
```

After the header section and the function definition, some variables are defined. The variable `buf` is a pointer to a character array (a string buffer), while `line` is a pointer to an array of character pointers. Memory is allocated for these buffers later in the function. Next comes some error checking. The next section deserves a closer look:

```
   /****** Start of Region 1 ******/
     /* If the input is already a cell array, duplicate it. */
     if (mxIsCell(prhs[0]))
       if (mxIsChar(mxGetCell(prhs[0],0))) {

   plhs[0]=mxCreateCellMatrix(mxGetM(prhs[0]),mxGetN(prhs[0]));
          plhs[0]=mxDuplicateArray(prhs[0]);
          return;
       }
   /******  End of Region 1  ******/
```

This section handles the case where the input is already a cell array of strings. In this case, the array is duplicated and passed to the output. First, we check that the input is a cell array (`mxIsCell`). If it is, we check the class of the contents of a cell. The function `mxGetCell(prhs[0],0)` returns the contents of cell 0 of the input array; `mxIsChar` then determines whether the element contains character data. The line

```
plhs[0]=mxCreateCellMatrix(mxGetM(prhs[0]),mxGetN(prhs[0]));
```

creates an output array with the same dimensions as the input array. Then, `mxDuplicateArray` makes a ***deep*** copy of the input `mxArray` into the output `mxArray`. A deep copy duplicates all levels of an array; it is essentially a recursive copy. In this case, the line

```
plhs[0]=mxDuplicateArray(prhs[0]);
```

copies the entire contents of the input array into the output array. The function then returns to the calling workspace.

At this point, we have the correct number and type of arguments. In the second section, shown next, we obtain the dimensions of the input character array and then allocate a character buffer of the correct size and copy the character array into the new buffer as one long string by using `mxArrayToString`. The size is one more than the number of characters in the character array, because `mxArrayToString` converts the character array to a C-style null-terminated string. We then allocate a line buffer for each row in the input array. The size of each line buffer is the width of the character array, plus one space for the C string terminator `'\0'`. The code is as follows:

```
/****** Start of Region 2 ******/
  /* Stuff the input into a string buffer. */
  /* If mxArray To String fails to allocate the buffer, the MEX file
terminates.
  buf=mxArrayToString(prhs[0]);

  /* Create line buffers for the individual strings. */
  line=(char **)mxCalloc(m,sizeof(char*));
  for (i=0;i<m;i++)
    line[i]=mxCalloc(n+1,sizeof(char));
/****** End of Region 2 ******/
```

MEX-files should always use `mxCalloc` (or `mxMalloc`) to allocate memory and `mxFree` to return the allocated memory to the heap. These functions register the allocation and deallocation of memory with the MATLAB memory manager, which automatically frees all allocated memory when the function exits. The following code shows how `mxFree` is used:

```
/* Parse the buffer into individual lines. */
  for (j=0;j<n;j++)
    for (i=0;i<m;i++)
      line[i][j]=buf[i+m*j];

  /* Free the string buffer and create the output cell array. */
  mxFree(buf);
  plhs[0]=mxCreateCellMatrix(m, 1);

  for (i=0;i<m;i++) {
    /* For each line, remove trailing blanks... */
    j=n;
    while (--j >= 0)
      if (line[i][j] != ' ')
        break;
    line[i][j+1]='\0';

    /* insert the line into the output array... */
    mxSetCell(plhs[0],i,mxCreateString(line[i]));

    /* and free the line buffer memory. */
    mxFree(line[i]);
  }
  mxFree(line);
}
```

Since MATLAB arrays are stored columnwise, the buffer contains the input-array elements in column order, similar to the result of using the MATLAB colon operator (`buf=chararray(:)`). The remainder of the program extracts the correct elements of `buff` into the line buffers, frees the string buffer memory, and creates the output cell array. Then, each line is processed. A C-string terminator (`'\0'`) is inserted into the buffer after the last nonblank character, and the line is copied and converted from a C string to a MATLAB string by using `mxCreateString` and is inserted into the output cell array by using `mxSetCell`. The line buffer memory is then freed by using `mxFree`, and the next line is processed. After all lines have been processed, `mxFree` is called one final time to free the line pointer array.

Windows PC Considerations

The previous examples were also compiled on a Windows PC, using the LCC compiler supplied with MATLAB. While this compiler does not offer many features, it does produce functional MEX-files. The command

```
» mex myprog.c
```

produces the MEX-file `myprog.dll` in the current directory. Adding the verbose (`-v`) option to the `mex` command line prints the compiler settings and shows the compile and link stages. The appropriate options file for this compiler was chosen previously by using the `mex -setup` command. A different options file for an individual compilation can be specified by using the `-f` option. The `$MATLAB\bin\win32\mexopts` directory contains options files for many different compilers. The MATLAB documentation offers more details about configuring compilers and debugging MEX programs.

FORTRAN Considerations

FORTRAN MEX-files can now create any MATLAB data type. Note that FORTRAN source code is not case sensitive, and so `MXCREATEDOUBLEMATRIX`, `mxcreatedoublematrix`, and `mxCreateDoubleMatrix` are the same function. FORTRAN examples in this chapter continue to use mixed case to maintain consistency and make the FORTRAN code easier to read.

Since few FORTRAN compilers support new data types, MATLAB passes a special identifier of type `integer`, called a ***pointer***, to the FORTRAN program for each input and output variable. These pointers can be used by MEX subroutines to obtain data in an appropriate FORTRAN native data type from the MATLAB arrays. Pointers must be declared as the default `integer` or `integer*4` on all platforms, except those using a 64-bit processor, in which case pointers must be declared as `integer*8`.

Many FORTRAN compilers support the `%val` construct, which can be used to pass values from pointers obtained from functions such as `p=mxGetPr()` to subroutines. Otherwise, `mxCopy...` routines (such as `mxCopyPtrToReal8` and `mxCopyReal8ToPr`) should be used to extract the data from the `mxArray`, pass it to the subroutine, and return the result to the `mxArray`.

In FORTRAN, the `mexFunction` subroutine definition is

```
subroutine mexFunction(nlhs, plhs, nrhs, prhs)
integer plhs(*), prhs(*)
integer nlhs, nrhs
```

where `nlhs` and `nrhs` contain the number of left- and right-hand-side arguments, respectively, and `plhs` and `prhs` are arrays of pointers to the arguments themselves.

The FORTRAN equivalent of the C MEX-file `fact.c` is as follows:

```
C-------------------------------------------------------------
C    fact.f - returns the factorial of a nonnegative integer.
C
C     MATLAB usage:   p=fact(n)
C
C    Mastering MATLAB 7 FORTRAN MEX Example 1

     subroutine mexFunction(nlhs, plhs, nrhs, prhs)
C-------------------------------------------------------------
C    These are pointers: integer*4 (integer*8 on 64-bit CPUs)
C
     integer plhs(*), prhs(*)
     integer mxGetPr, mxCreateDoubleMatrix
     integer y_pr
C-------------------------------------------------------------
     integer nlhs, nrhs
     integer i
     real*8  x, y, mxGetScalar
C-------------------------------------------------------------
     x = mxGetScalar(prhs(1))
     plhs(1) = mxCreateDoubleMatrix(1, 1, 0)
     y_pr = mxGetPr(plhs(1))
C
     y = 1.0
     do 10 i=x,1,-1
        y = y * i
 10  continue
C
     call mxCopyReal8ToPtr(y, y_pr, 1)
     return
     end
```

Note that FORTRAN, like MATLAB, uses one-based array and loop indexing, rather than the zero-based indexing used in C programs. Therefore, the pointer to the first right-hand-side (input) argument (`prhs[0]` in a C program) is `prhs(1)` in a FORTRAN program.

34.3 CALLING MATLAB FROM C OR FORTRAN

Just as you are able to call C or FORTRAN routines from MATLAB, you can also call MATLAB to perform operations in the background as part of some larger C or FORTRAN program. In MATLAB, this is called the MATLAB Engine.

What Is It?

The MATLAB Engine consists of a communication library and a small collection of linkable routines that call MATLAB as a server process without linking in all of MATLAB. The MATLAB Engine allows you to start a MATLAB process, transfer data to MATLAB, execute MATLAB commands, capture the normal *Command* window output if desired, transfer data back to your program, and shut down the MATLAB process—all from within a C or FORTRAN program.

How It Works

The MATLAB Engine process runs in the background, separate from any interactive MATLAB session currently running. It does not interfere with any user running MATLAB. When an Engine process is started, a new MATLAB instance is created. This process is shared by all programs requesting access to a MATLAB Engine process on the specific host computer. An exclusive Engine process can be reserved in C programs, but the process is always shared in FORTRAN programs.

The MATLAB Engine communicates with your C or FORTRAN program by using pipes on Unix platforms and the Component Object Model (COM) interface on Windows PC platforms. You can specify a remote computer as the host of the MATLAB Engine on Unix platforms. See the `engOpen` function for specific syntax.

The `eng` prefix designates a MATLAB Engine function. MATLAB Engine functions available to C and FORTRAN programs are listed in the following table:

Function	C	F	Purpose
`engOpen`	C	F	Start up or shares an instance of the MATLAB Engine
`engOpenSingleUse`	C		Start an exclusive (nonshared) MATLAB Engine session
`engPutVariable`	C	F	Send a MATLAB array (`mxArray`) to the MATLAB Engine
`engGetVariable`	C	F	Get a MATLAB array (`mxArray`) from the MATLAB Engine
`engOutputBuffer`	C	F	Create a buffer to store MATLAB text output

Function	C	F	Purpose
engEvalString	C	F	Execute a MATLAB command within the MATLAB Engine
engGetVisible	C		Determine the visibility setting of a MATLAB Engine session. A visible session runs in a window on a PC desktop and is available for user interaction. An invisible session runs in the background and is hidden from the user.
engSetVisible	C		Set the visibility of a MATLAB Engine session
engClose	C	F	Shut down the MATLAB Engine

Engine Program Structure

The first step in using the MATLAB Engine is to open an Engine session by using `engOpen` or `engOpenSingleUse`. Then, create any `mxArrays` needed by using the appropriate MX functions, such as `mxCreateDoubleMatrix`. Populate the `mxArrays` and place them in the MATLAB environment by using `engPutVariable`. Create a buffer to capture *Command* window output, if desired, by using `engOutputBuffer`, and execute MATLAB commands by using `engEvalString`. Recover any output `mxArrays` from the MATLAB environment by using `engGetVariable`, and continue processing within the C or FORTRAN program. When you are done with the MATLAB environment, terminate the process by using `engClose`, and release allocated memory for `mxArrays` by using `mxDestroyArray`.

Engine Program Description

The `engOpen` function starts a MATLAB Engine session and returns a unique "Engine ID," which can be used to address this particular Engine. The function returns NULL if an error occurs. If the `engOpen` argument is NULL (`'\0'`), the Engine is started on the local computer, using the command `matlab`. On a UNIX or Linux computer, the argument can be a host name. In this case, the Engine is started on the remote host, using `rsh`. The `DISPLAY` environment variable is also set so that any graphics generated by the Engine (such as the result of a `plot` command) appear on the local computer display, rather than on the computer running the Engine process. Appropriate permissions must be set to allow remote execution and to allow the remote computer to display on your computer screen. If the argument to `engOpen` is anything other than a host name (such as a string containing spaces, tabs, or nonalphanumerical characters), the string is executed literally to start an Engine process. You can take advantage of this facility to customize your Engine session, such as by using `ssh` for encrypted communications with the remote host. The `engOpen` argument must be NULL on a Windows PC, since remote execution is not supported on this platform. The MATLAB application installed on the local PC is started to service any Engine requests.

You must create any MATLAB variables to be used within the Engine environment. One way to create a MATLAB variable is to use the `engEvalString` function to evaluate a MATLAB command such as `y=22*pi:pi/25:2*pi;` to create the variable `y` in the MATLAB workspace and assign values to `y`. Another method is to create a MATLAB array within your program and pass the resulting `mxArray` to the MATLAB Engine. For example, given a 1-by-10 array of double-precision data in the C variable `dataset`, the code

```
Engine *mat
mxArray *mydata = NULL;

mat = engOpen(NULL);
mydata = mxCreateDoubleMatrix(1, 10, mxREAL);
memcpy((void *)mxGetPr(mydata), (void *)dataset, sizeof(dataset));
engPutVariable(mat, "newdata", mydata);
engEvalString("sqdata=newdata.^2;");
```

opens a connection to MATLAB on the local computer, creates an `mxArray` called `mydata`, populates the array, assigns a MATLAB variable name `newdata` to the `mydata` array when sending the array to the Engine, squares the elements of the array, and assigns the output to the MATLAB variable `sqdata`. In this example, the C name and the MATLAB name are different, to illustrate how each is used. Normally, the same name is used to avoid confusion.

Once MATLAB performs the desired operations, the results must be passed back into your program. Once again, there are two ways to do this. The first method is to create a text buffer by using the `engOutputBuffer` function (to capture MATLAB text that is normally discarded), use the `engEvalString` function to generate the output text, and then parse the string buffer. For example, the code

```
char buf[256];
engOutputBuffer(mat, buf, 256);
engEvalString("disp(sum(sqdata))");
```

captures the output of the `disp(sum(sqdata))` command, as it would be displayed in the MATLAB *Command* window, into the string buffer `buf`. The buffer can be parsed to extract the desired data.

```
double x;
x=atof(buf+2);
```

Each call to `engEvalString` replaces the data in the MATLAB output string buffer. Note that the first two characters of the output buffer always contain the MATLAB prompt characters ">>", and so the call to the `atof` function skips over these characters.

When the result is more substantial, you can retrieve one or more arrays from the MATLAB workspace. For example, the code

```
mxArray *sqdata = NULL;
double *sptr;

sqdata = engGetVariable(mat,"sqdata");
sptr = mxGetPr(sqdata);
```

makes the mxArray sqdata available to your program. Use mxGetPr to get a C pointer to the real part of the mxArray. The other MX functions are also available to access the sqdata array.

Be sure to release the memory that was allocated to mxArrays when you are finished with them, and close the MATLAB Engine when it is no longer needed.

```
mxDestroyArray(mydata);
mxDestroyArray(sqdata);
engClose(mat);
```

Compiling and Running Engine Programs

Programs that incorporate MATLAB Engine access functions must include the engine.h header file to support the MATLAB Engine functions, in addition to any other necessary header files. The engine.h header file also includes matrix.h for MX function support. The compilation step uses the mex command with the engopts.sh options file, in addition to any other compiler options. For example, if the MATLAB application is installed in /usr/local/matlab, the mex command to compile a C Engine program might be

```
mex -f /usr/local/matlab/bin/engopts.sh myprog.c
```

This command creates an executable program called myprog in the current directory, and can be run from an operating system command prompt or by double-clicking on a Windows PC. If the standard options file does not meet your needs, make a local copy of engopts.sh and modify it as appropriate.

When the compiled Engine program is run, one or more MATLAB shared libraries are loaded as well. The operating system must be told where to look for these libraries. The LD_LIBRARY_PATH environment variable (or the equivalent on your platform) lists additional directories to be searched when the operating system cannot find all of the required shared libraries in the standard system directories. You must add the appropriate system-specific MATLAB shared library directory to this list. If you have a Solaris operating system with MATLAB installed in the /opt/matlab directory and you are using a Bourne shell (sh, bsh, ksh), the commands are

```
LD_LIBRARY_PATH=/opt/matlab/extern/lib/sol2:$LD_LIBRARY_PATH
export LD_LIBRARY_PATH
```

If you are using a C shell (csh, tcsh) on a Linux platform with libc2 C libraries and have MATLAB installed in the /usr/local/matlab directory, the command is

```
setenv LD_LIBRARY_PATH /usr/local/matlab/extern/lib/glnx86:$LD_LIBRARY_PATH
```

The platform-specific library directories (sol2, glnx86, sgi, sgi64, win32, hpux, and others) are located in the $MATLAB/extern/lib directory. Some platforms use a different environment variable to list additional shared library locations. The SGI64 platform uses LD_LIBRARY64_PATH, rather than LD_LIBRARY_PATH. The HPUX platform uses SHLIB_PATH, and the Mac OS X platform uses DYLD_LIBRARY_PATH. The easiest way to set this variable is to add the appropriate command(s) to your shell start-up script (.profile, .cshrc, .bashrc, .tcshrc, and so on).

Engine Example

So far, we have covered the individual elements of MATLAB Engine programs. Now it is time to put it all together. This example builds on the preceding sections to create a complete C program that uses the MATLAB Engine as a back-end computational engine. This program creates an array of data, sends the array to MATLAB, calculates the squares of the elements and the sum of the squares, and returns the results to the C program for printing. Comments have been added to explain how the pieces are combined. The code is as follows:

```
/*
 *  sos.c - Calculate the sum of the squares of the elements of a
vector.
 *
 *  Mastering MATLAB 7 C Engine Example 1
 *
 */

#include <stdio.h>
#include <string.h>
#include "engine.h"
#define  BUFSIZE 256

int main()
{
    Engine *mat;
```

```
mxArray *mydata = NULL, *sqdata = NULL;
int i;
double x, *myptr, *sptr;
char buf[BUFSIZE];
double dataset[10] = { 0.0, 1.0, 2.0, 3.0, 4.0,
                       5.0, 6.0, 7.0, 8.0, 9.0 };

/* Start the MATLAB Engine on the local computer. */
if (!(mat = engOpen(NULL))) {
    fprintf(stderr, "\nCannot open connection to MATLAB!\n");
    return EXIT_FAILURE;
}

/* Create an mxArray and get a C pointer to the mxArray. */
mydata = mxCreateDoubleMatrix(1, 10, mxREAL);
myptr = mxGetPr(mydata);

/* Copy the dataset array to the new mxArray. */
memcpy((void *)myptr, (void *)dataset, sizeof(dataset));

/* Pass the mxArray to the Engine and square the elements. */
engPutVariable(mat, "newdata", mydata);
engEvalString(mat, "sqdata = newdata.^2");

/* Create an output buffer to capture MATLAB text output. */
engOutputBuffer(mat, buf, BUFSIZE);

/* Calculate the sum of the squares and save the result in x. */
engEvalString(mat,"disp(sum(sqdata))");
x=atof(buf+2);

/* Retrieve the array of squares from the Engine, */
if ((sqdata = engGetVariable(mat,"sqdata")) == NULL) {
    fprintf(stderr, "Cannot retrieve sqdata!\n\n");
    return EXIT_FAILURE;
}
```

```
    /* and get a C pointer to the mxArray. */

    sptr = mxGetPr(sqdata);

    /* Print the results to stdout. */

    printf("\nThe inputs are:\n");
    for (i=0;i<10;i++)
      printf("%6.1f ",myptr[i]);
    printf("\n\nThe squares are:\n");
    for (i=0;i<10;i++)
      printf("%6.1f ",sptr[i]);
    printf("\n\nThe sum of the squares is %6.1f \n\n",x);

    /* Free the mxArray memory and quit MATLAB. */

    mxDestroyArray(mydata);
    mxDestroyArray(sqdata);
    engClose(mat);

    return EXIT_SUCCESS;
}
```

This example was compiled and tested on both Linux and Macintosh platforms.

Windows PC Considerations

The previous example also compiles on a Windows PC with the LCC compiler. The command

```
mex -f c:\matlab7\bin\win32\mexcpts\lccengmatopts.bat sos.c
```

produces the executable file `sos.exe` in the current directory. If you are not using the LCC compiler, specify the appropriate options file on the command line. The `$MATLAB\bin\win32\mexopts` directory contains at least eight options files for different versions of the Borland, Microsoft, and Watcom compilers alone. If you have trouble, use the verbose (`-v`) option to the `mex` command to view the compiler settings and the various steps in the compilation process.

MATLAB Engine programs link with DLL libraries in the `$MATLAB\bin\win32` directory. MATLAB adds this directory to your default path during installation so that Windows will be able to find the libraries. When executed from the command line or by double-clicking on the `sos.exe` file, a MATLAB session is run (minimized) to perform the calculations. It does not interfere with any interactive MATLAB session that may be open.

Consult the MATLAB documentation for more details about how to configure your specific programming software to compile MEX and Engine programs and for debugging these programs within your software development environment.

FORTRAN Considerations

The same MATLAB Engine program written in FORTRAN requires only a few changes. Most of the Engine functions return a status value which is tested for errors. Also, the sum of the squares is printed as a character array to avoid extracting the numerical value from the text buffer and then printing it. Here is the code:

```
C
C   sos.f - Calculate the sum of the squares of the elements of a vector.
C
C   Mastering MATLAB 7 FORTRAN Engine Example 1
C
C======================================================================
      program main
C----------------------------------------------------------------------
C     Pointers
C
      integer engOpen, engGetVariable, mxCreateDoubleMatrix, mxGetPr
      integer mat, mydata, sqdata
C----------------------------------------------------------------------
C     Other variable declarations
C
      double precision dataset(10), sqrs(10)
      integer engPutVariable, engEvalString, engClose, engOutputBuffer
      integer temp, status
      character*256 buf
      data dataset / 0.0, 1.0, 2.0, 3.0, 4.0, 5.0, 6.0, 7.0, 8.0, 9.0 /
C----------------------------------------------------------------------
C     Start the MATLAB Engine on the local computer.
C
      mat = engOpen('matlab')
```

```
      if (mat .eq. 0) then
         write(6,*) 'Cannot open connection to MATLAB!'
         stop
      endif
C
C     Create an mxArray, associate a MATLAB variable name with the
C       mxArray, and copy the data into the array.
C
      mydata = mxCreateDouble Matrix(1, 10, 0)
      call mxCopyReal8ToPtr(dataset, mxGetPr(mydata), 10)
C
C     Pass the variable mydata into the MATLAB workspace.
C
      status = engPutVariable(mat, 'newdata', mydata)
      if (status .ne. 0) then
         write(6,*) 'Cannot pass mydata to the Engine!'
         stop
      endif
C
C     Square the elements of the array.
C
      if (engEvalString(mat, 'sqdata = newdata.^2;') .ne. 0) then
         write(6,*) 'engEvalString failed'
         stop
      endif
C
C     Create an output buffer to capture MATLAB text output.
C
      if (engOutputBuffer(mat, buf) .ne. 0) then
         write(6,*) 'engOutputBuffer failed'
         stop
      endif
```

```
C
C     Calculate the sum of the squares and capture the result.
C
      if (engEvalString(mat, 'disp(sum(sqdata))') .ne. 0) then
         write(6,*) 'engEvalString failed'
         stop
      endif
C
C     Retrieve the mxArray of squares from the Engine,
C     copy the data into an array of doubles, and print.
C
      sqdata = engGetVariable(mat, 'sqdata')
      call mxCopyPtrToReal8(mxGetPr(sqdata), sqrs, 10)
C
 20   format(' ', G8.3, G8.3, G8.3, G8.3, G8.3, G8.3,
     & G8.3, G8.3, G8.3, G8.3)
      print *, 'The inputs are:'
      print 20, dataset
      print *, 'The squares are:'
      print 20, sqrs
      print *,  'The sum of the squares is ', buf(3:10)
C
C     Free the mxArray memory and quit MATLAB.
C
      call mxFreeMatrix(mydata)
      call mxFreeMatrix(sqdata)
      status = engClose(mat)
C
      if (status .ne. 0) then
         write(6,*) 'engClose failed'
         stop
      endif
```

```
C
  stop
  end
```

Note that, if your FORTRAN compiler uses shared libraries, you must add the appropriate MATLAB shared library directory to your `LD_LIBRARY_PATH` (or equivalent) before executing any compiled Engine program. If you are using a Windows PC, the `$MATLAB\bin\win32` directory was added to your default path during MATLAB installation so that Windows can find the MATLAB shared libraries (DLLs).

34.4 EXCHANGING DATA WITH MAT-FILES

There are several ways to exchange data between MATLAB and other programs. Most methods involve creating a data file to serve as an exchange medium. Selecting the appropriate method depends on the amount and format of the data to be imported or exported. In this section, reading and writing standard MATLAB MAT-files from C and FORTRAN are considered.

MAT-files

MAT-files are platform-independent, in that platform differences (such as the native byte order) are stored in the MAT-file itself and MATLAB automatically translates the data format when loading data from the MAT-file. By supplying header files and libraries for use in your programs to read and write MAT-files, MATLAB provides these platform-independent features to C and FORTRAN programs, and enables easy data exchange with MATLAB.

MAT Functions

The `mat` prefix designates a MATLAB function that operates on MAT-files. MATLAB MAT functions available to C or FORTRAN programs are listed in the following table:

MAT Function	C	F	Purpose
`matOpen`	C	F	Open a MAT-file
`matClose`	C	F	Close a MAT-file
`matGetDir`	C	F	Get a list of MATLAB arrays from a MAT-file
`matGetFp`	C		Get an ANSI C file pointer to a MAT-file

MAT Function	C	F	Purpose
matGetVariable	C	F	Read a MATLAB array from a MAT-file
matGetVariableInfo	C	F	Load a MATLAB array header from a MAT-file
matGetNextVariable	C	F	Read the next MATLAB array from a MAT-file
matGetNextVariableInfo	C	F	Load the next MATLAB array header from a MAT-file
matPutVariable	C	F	Write a MATLAB array to a MAT-file
matPutVariableAsGlobal	C	F	Write a MATLAB array to a MAT-file as a global variable
matDeleteVariable	C	F	Delete a MATLAB array from a MAT-file

The `matGetVariableInfo` function creates an `mxArray` containing everything in the `mxArray` structure except the actual data itself. The `matGetDir` function creates a list of variable names and returns the number of MATLAB variables contained in the MAT-file. The `matGetVariable` function uses the variable name to access the contents of the variable, while `matGetNextVariable` and `matGetNextVariableInfo` functions access the variables sequentially. The `matPutVariableAsGlobal` function writes an array to the MAT-file as a global variable; that is, when the `load` command is used to load the MAT-file into MATLAB, the variable is loaded into the MATLAB workspace as a global variable.

MAT Program Structure

C or FORTRAN programs that read or write MAT-files use MX functions to create MATLAB data arrays (`mxArrays`) in the same general way that MX functions are used in MEX-files or Engine programs. When creating a MAT-file, you first open the MAT-file by using `matOpen`. Then you create, name, and populate `mxArrays` for each MATLAB variable; write the `mxArrays` to the MAT-file by using `matPutVariable` or `matPutVaribleAsGlobal`; and, finally, close the MAT-file by using `matClose`. When reading data from a MAT-file, you first open the MAT-file by using `matOpen`; get a list of the variables, if desired, by using `matGetDir`; create `mxArrays` by using `matGetVariable` or `matGetNextVariable`; and, finally, close the MAT-file by using `matClose`.

Compiling and Running MAT programs

Programs that incorporate MATLAB MAT-file access functions must include the `mat.h` header file to support the MATLAB MAT-file functions, in addition to any other necessary header files. The `mat.h` header file also includes `matrix.h` for MX function support. The compilation step uses the `mex` command with the `matopts.sh` options file, in addition to any other compiler options you may need. For example, if the MATLAB application is installed in `/usr/local/matlab`, the `mex` command to compile a C MAT program might be

```
mex -f /usr/local/matlab/bin/matopts.sh myprog.c
```

This command creates an executable program called myprog in the current directory and can be run from an operating system command prompt. The shared-library discussions in the Engine section relating to the UNIX and PC platforms apply here as well. An executable program created by the mex command uses shared libraries that must be found by your operating system when the program is run.

The Windows PC version uses the same options file that Engine programs do. Compiling the same myprog.c MAT program by using the LCC compiler might use the command

```
mex -f c:\matlab7\bin\win32\mexopts\lccengmatopts.bat myprog.c
```

The compilation produces the executable file myprog.exe in the current directory, which can be run from a command prompt or by double-clicking on the file. If you are not using the LCC compiler, specify the apprcpriate options file on the command line.

MAT Program Example 1: writemat

The following C program creates a MAT-file containing a string and an array of doubles:

```
/*
 *  writemat.c - Create a binary MAT-file.
 *
 *  Mastering MATLAB 7 C MAT-file Example 1
 *
 */

#include "mat.h"

int makemat(const char *filename,
            double *data, int m, int n,
            char *mmstr)
{
  MATFile *mfile,
  mxArray *mdata, *mstr;
```

```
/* Open the MAT-file for writing. */
mfile = matOpen(filename, "w");
if (mfile == NULL) {
  printf("Cannot open %s for writing.\n", filename);
  return(EXIT_FAILURE);
}

/* Create the mxArray to hold the numeric data.      */
/* Note that the array dimensions are reversed.      */
/* C uses row order while MATLAB uses column order. */
/* The data array will be transposed in MATLAB.      */
mdata = mxCreateDoubleMatrix(n,m,mxREAL);

/* Copy the data to the mxArray. Note that mxGetData is */
/* similar to mxGetPr but returns a void pointer while  */
/* mxGetPr returns a pointer to a double.               */
memcpy((void *)(mxGetData(mdata)), (void *)data,
                 m*n*sizeof(double));

/* Create the string array. */
mstr = mxCreateString(mmstr);

/* Write the mxArrays to the MAT-file. */
matPutVariable(mfile, "mydata", mdata);
matPutVariable(mfile, "mystr", mstr);

/* Free the mxArray memory. */
mxDestroyArray(mdata);
mxDestroyArray(mstr);

/* Close the MAT-file. */
if (matClose(mfile) != 0) {
  printf("Cannot close %s.\n",filename);
  return(EXIT_FAILURE);
}
```

```
  return(EXIT_SUCCESS);
}

int main()
{
  int status;
  char *mmstr = "Mastering MATLAB Rocks!";
  double data[3][4] = {{  1.0,  2.0,  3.0,  4.0 },
                       {  5.5,  6.6,  7.7,  8.8 },
                       { -4.0, -3.0, -2.0, -1.0 }};

  status = makemat("mmtest.mat", *data, 3, 4, mmstr);
  return(status);
}
```

This program was compiled and tested on Linux, Macintosh, and Windows PC platforms. The resulting MAT-files were then loaded into different MATLAB sessions, with the following results:

```
>> clear all

>> load mmtest

>> whos
  Name        Size           Bytes  Class

  mydata      4x3               96  double array
  mystr       1x23              46  char array

Grand total is 35 elements using 142 bytes

>> mydata
mydata =
    1.0000    5.5000   -4.0000
    2.0000    6.6000   -3.0000
    3.0000    7.7000   -2.0000
    4.0000    8.8000   -1.0000
```

```
>> mystr
mystr =
Mastering MATLAB Rocks!
```

Note that the numerical array was transposed when loaded into MATLAB. This is because of the differences in the way that C and MATLAB store arrays—rowwise and columnwise, respectively. The FORTRAN version does not transpose the matrix, since both MATLAB and FORTRAN store arrays in columnwise format. The following is a FORTRAN version of the same program:

```
C
C     writemat.f - Create a binary MAT-file.
C
C     Mastering MATLAB 7 FORTRAN MAT-file Example 1
C
C
      program writemat
C-----------------------------------------------------------------------
C     Pointers.
C
      integer matOpen, mxCreateDoubleMatrix, mxCreateString
      integer matGetVariable, mxGetPr
      integer mfile, mdata, mstr
C-----------------------------------------------------------------------
C     Other variables
C
      integer status, matClose
      double precision dat(12)
      data dat / 1.0, 5.5, -4.0,
     &           2.0, 6.6, -3.0,
     &           3.0, 7.7, -2.0,
     &           4.0, 8.8, -1.0 /
C
```

```
C     Open MAT-file for writing.
C
      mfile = matOpen('mmtest.mat', 'w')
      if (mfile .eq. 0) then
         write(6,*) 'Can''t open ''mmtest.mat'' for writing.'
         stop
      end if
C
C     Create the mxArray to hold the numeric data.
C
      mdata = mxCreateDoubleMatrix(4,3,0)
C
C     Copy the data to the mxArray.
C
      call mxCopyReal8ToPtr(dat, mxGetPr(mdata), 12)
C
C     Create the string array.
C
      mstr = mxCreateString('Mastering MATLAB Rocks!')
C
C     Write the mxArrays to the MAT-file.
C
      call matPutVariable(mfile, 'mydata', mdata)
      call matPutVariable(mfile, 'mystr', mstr)
C
C     Free the mxArray memory.
C
      call mxFreeMatrix(mdata)
      call mxFreeMatrix(mstr)
C
C     Close the MAT-file.
C
      status = matClose(mfile)
```

```
      if (status .ne. 0) then
         write(6,*) 'Cannot close mmtest.mat'
         stop
      end if
C
      stop
      end
```

MAT Program Example 2: whomat

The next example reads a MAT-file, examines its contents, and then prints variable lists in formats similar to the MATLAB who and whos commands:

```
/*
 *   whomat.c - Examine a binary MAT-file and print a list
 *              of the contents (like "who" or "whos").
 *
 *   Mastering MATLAB 7 C MAT-file Example 2
 *
 */

#include "mat.h"
#include <string.h>

int whomat(const char *filename)
{
  MATFile *mfile;
  mxArray *marray;
  char **dir;
  char siz[25], buf[10];
  int i, j, num, nel, elsize, ndim, eltot, btot;
  const int *dims;
```

```
/* Open the MAT-file for reading. */
mfile = matOpen(filename, "r");
if (mfile == NULL) {
  printf("Cannot open %s for reading.\n", filename);
  return(EXIT_FAILURE);
}

 /* Get the directory list and print in "who" format. */
dir = matGetDir(mfile, &num);
if (dir == NULL) {
  printf("Error reading the directory of %s.\n", filename);
  return(EXIT_FAILURE);
} else {
  printf("\n");
  printf("Variables in %s are:\n\n", filename);
  for (i=0; i<num; i++) {
    printf("%-10s",dir[i]);
    if (i>0 && i%4==0) printf("\n");
  }
}

/* Examine each variable and print a "whos" list. */
eltot=btot=0;
printf("\n\n  Name           Size          Bytes  Class\n\n");
for (i=0; i<num; i++) {
  marray=matGetVariable(mfile, dir[i]);
  if (marray == NULL) {
    printf("Cannot read file %s.\n\n", filename);
    return(EXIT_FAILURE);
  }

  /* If marray is a cell array or structure array, then  */
  /* mxGetElementSize returns the size of a pointer, not */
  /* the size of all the elements in each cell or field. */
```

```
    /* To get the correct number of bytes would require    */
    /* traversing the array and summing leaf element sizes.*/
    /* Java arrays return 0x0 array dimensions and 0 size. */

    elsize=mxGetElementSize(marray);
    btot=btot+(nel*elsize);
    nel=mxGetNumberOfElements(marray);
    eltot=eltot+nel;
    ndim=mxGetNumberOfDimensions(marray);
    dims=mxGetDimensions(marray);
    siz[0]='\0';
    for (j=0; j<ndim; j++) {
      sprintf(buf,"%d",dims[j]);
      strcat(siz,buf);
      if (j<(ndim-1))
        strcat(siz,"x");
    }
    printf("  %-12s %-12s %5d  %s array\n", dir[i],
              siz,nel*elsize,mxGetClassName(marray));
    mxDestroyArray(marray);
  }
  printf("\nGrand total is %d elements using %d bytes\n\n",
            eltot,btot);

  /* Release the memory allocated for the directory. */
   mxFree(dir);

  /* Close the MAT-file. */
  if (matClose(mfile) != 0) {
      printf("Cannot close %s.\n",filename);
      return(EXIT_FAILURE);
  }
  return(EXIT_SUCCESS);
}
```

```
int main(int argc, char **argv)
{
  int status;

  if (argc > 1)
    status = whomat(argv[1]);
  else{
    status = EXIT_FAILURE;
    printf("Usage: whomat <matfile>");
  }
  return(status);
}
```

The output of this program, while very similar to the output of the MATLAB who and whos commands with the '-file' argument, reports incorrect results for cell arrays, structures, and Java arrays. If marray is a cell array or structure array, then mxGetElementSize(marray) returns the size of a pointer, not the size of all of the elements in each cell or field. To get the correct number of bytes would require traversing the array and summing leaf element sizes. If marray is a Java array, then mxGetElementSize(marray) returns zero and mxGetDimensions(marray) returns a pointer to a vector of zeros of length mxGetNumberOfDimensions(marray). Adding support for these data types is left as an exercise for the reader.

34.5 SHARED LIBRARIES

Libraries are collections of functions that are available to any program. These functions are precompiled into library files. There are two kinds of libraries. Static libraries are linked with your program at compile time, and the functions referenced in your program are included in your executable. Shared libraries are linked with your program at run time. Because they are not embedded in your executable, the shared libraries must be available at run time. Many different programs running on the same computer can share access to the same shared libraries at the same time. On Unix and Linux systems, these shared libraries are normally located in the standard system library directories (/lib, /usr/lib, /usr/shlib, or /usr/local/lib) and $MATLAB/bin/$ARCH. They are named by using the lib prefix and the .so suffix. (Macintosh systems use the .dylib suffix). On Windows PC systems, the shared libraries are called Dynamic Link Libraries and use the .DLL extension. At run time, the necessary functions from the appropriate shared libraries are loaded into memory and made available to the applications.

The MATLAB interface to shared libraries provides tools to load and unload a shared library, list the functions available in the library (including function name, arguments, and return values), and invoke these functions from within MATLAB. Any shared library can be accessed, as long as it has C-style arguments and types.

MATLAB shared library functions are listed in the following table:

Function	**Purpose**
`loadlibrary`	Load an external library into MATLAB
`unloadlibrary`	Unload an external library from memory
`libisloaded`	Determine if an external library is loaded
`libfunctions`	Return information on the functions in an external library
`libfunctionsview`	Create a window to display function information
`calllib`	Call a function in an external library
`libpointer`	Create a pointer object for use with external libraries
`libstruct`	Create a C-like structure that can be passed to external libraries

MATLAB automatically converts between MATLAB data types and C data types in most cases. For example, MATLAB structures passed as arguments to C library functions are converted to C structures automatically. MATLAB data types passed as values to C functions expecting pointers are converted into pointers automatically. The `libpointer` and `libstruct` functions permit explicit conversions under the control of the user. (For more details about shared library functions and data conversion issues, see the MATLAB documentation.)

34.6 SERIAL COMMUNICATIONS

Data are often gathered by using instruments connected to a serial port. MATLAB provides a built-in interface to manage serial ports and to communicate directly with devices connected to these serial ports. MATLAB supports the RS-232, RS-422, and RS-485 serial communications standards on Linux, Sun Solaris, and Windows platforms. Enhanced support for multifunction I/O boards, GPIB or VESA instrumentation, and additional serial-port functions are available in optional toolboxes. However, the built-in serial interface will suffice for most direct serial communications.

The MATLAB interface to serial ports is an object-based interface. The `serial` function creates an object connected to a specific serial port, with properties that can be queried and set by using the standard `get` and `set` functions. The `serial` function requires the name of a serial device and optional PropertyName and PropertyValue pairs. Serial devices have different names on different platforms. For example, the first serial port is `/dev/term/a` or `/dev/ttya` on a Solaris 7 platform, `/dev/ttyS0` on an i386 Linux platform, and `COM1` on a Windows PC.

Communicating with a serial device normally consists of a fixed sequence of operations. First, create the interface to the serial device with the `serial` function and `set` the appropriate properties. Then, open the device by using `fopen`, write and read by using `fprintf` and `fscanf` respectively, close the device by using `fclose`, and finally `delete` the serial object and `clear` the MATLAB reference to the variable.

Serial Communication Example

This is an interactive example of a communication session with a blood glucose meter. The meter requires serial port settings of 9600,8,N,1 with no handshaking. This means a baud rate of 9600 bits per second, 8-bit data, no parity checking, and one stop bit. The meter does not use hardware handshaking.

First, create a serial object attached to the first serial port, and check its properties:

```
>> s = serial('/dev/ttyS0');
>> get(s)
    ByteOrder = littleEndian
    BytesAvailable = 0
    BytesAvailableFcn =
    BytesAvailableFcnCount = 48
    BytesAvailableFcnMode = terminator
    BytesToOutput = 0
    ErrorFcn =
    InputBufferSize = 512
    Name = Serial-/dev/ttyS0
    ObjectVisibility = on
    OutputBufferSize = 512
    OutputEmptyFcn =
    RecordDetail = compact
    RecordMode = overwrite
    RecordName = record.txt
    RecordStatus = off
    Status = closed
    Tag =
    Timeout = 10
    TimerFcn =
```

```
    TimerPeriod = 1
    TransferStatus = idle
    Type = serial
    UserData = []
    ValuesReceived = 0
    ValuesSent = 0

    SERIAL specific properties:
    BaudRate = 9600
    BreakInterruptFcn =
    DataBits = 8
    DataTerminalReady = on
    FlowControl = none
    Parity = none
    PinStatus = [1x1 struct]
    PinStatusFcn =
    Port = /dev/ttyS0
    ReadAsyncMode = continuous
    RequestToSend = on
    StopBits = 1
    Terminator = LF
```

In this case, most of the default communications parameters are correct. However, the default line terminator is a line feed character, whereas the meter expects a carriage return/line feed sequence:

```
>> set(s,'Terminator','CR/LF');
>> get(s,'Terminator')
ans =
CR/LF
```

Now open the port and send a command to the device. In this case, the command instructs the meter to respond with its serial number and a communications checksum:

```
>> fopen(s);
>> fprintf(s,'DM@');
>> snum = fscanf(s)
```

```
snum =
    @ "RMF99CFBV" 031D
```

The next command zeros the meter's data. Write the command and check for a response:

```
>> fprintf(s,'DMZ')
>> resp = fscanf(s)
resp =
    Z 005A
```

No errors were encountered, so close the connection, delete the port object, and remove the variable from the MATLAB environment:

```
>> fclose(s)
>> delete(s)
>> clear s
```

Serial port objects are similar to graphics objects in that they support events and callbacks. Callbacks are functions to be executed when certain events occur. Functions can be specified either by using function handles or as cell arrays containing function names. Any object property with the string `'Fcn'` in the property name can be configured to execute a callback function when the associated event occurs. Examples of serial events include timer expiration, errors, interrupts (break), output buffer empty, data available in the input buffer, or change of state of a serial line pin (CD, RI, DSR, and/or CTS).

Properties are available to monitor the status of control pins, control the DTR pin, implement data flow control using hardware (RTS/CTS) or software (Xon/Xoff), and automatically record details about the session to a data file. The number and types of data read and written and the event information, as well as all of the data values can be saved to one or more files if desired. (The MATLAB documentation contains more details and additional examples.)

34.7 SOURCE CODE CONTROL SYSTEMS

Large programming projects or projects involving many developers often use source code control systems (SCCS) to manage program source code and revisions. Files are collected into a central repository and are checked out by developers working on the project. Files are then checked back in after revisions. The SCCS ensures consistency and facilitates version rollbacks if needed.

Many existing source code control systems can be accessed from within the MATLAB environment. Supported systems include CVS, RCS, PVCS, CM Synergy, and ClearCase on Unix, Linux, or Macintosh systems, and any system conforming to the Microsoft Common Source Control standard on Windows PC platforms. Custom SCCS systems are also supported on all platforms except Windows PCs.

MATLAB supplies a graphical interface to your existing SCCS system when using the MATLAB Editor, as well as a function interface available from the *Command* window. Select your preferred SCCS in the Preferences window (select **Preferences** from the **File** menu of the *Command* window). A **Source Control** menu is then available from the **File** menu in the MATLAB Editor. Available actions are Check In, Check Out, and Undo Check-Out. SCCS functions are listed in the following table:

Function	Purpose
`cmopts`	Return the name of the selected source code control system
`checkin`	Check a file in to the source code control system
`checkout`	Check a file out of the source code control system
`undocheckout`	Undo the previous check-out
`customverctl`	Custom version control system template
`rcs`	Version control actions using RCS
`cvs`	Version control actions using CVS
`pvcs`	Version control actions using PVCS
`sourcesafe`	Version control actions using SourceSafe
`clearcase`	Version control actions using PVCS

34.8 WEB SERVICES

Now that the Internet is such a big part of computing, MATLAB has extended support for various Internet technologies. MATLAB now includes client support for making remote procedure calls over a network (local networks or the Internet) by using some of these technologies.

First, a little background and terminology are in order. The Standardized Generalized Markup Language (SGML), developed in 1985, is an international standard for defining descriptions of the structure of different types of electronic documents. Extensible Markup Language (XML) is a light-weight version of SGML without much of the overhead associated with the parent standard. Hypertext Markup Language (HTML) is a static subset of SGML describing a very simple class of report-style document and is widely used for Web pages. Simple Object Access Protocol (SOAP) is a lightweight protocol for exchange of information in a decentralized, distributed, networked environment that is based on XML. Web Services Description Language (WSDL) is a specification used to describe and locate networked XML-based services. WSDL provides a simple way for service providers to describe the basic format of requests to their systems, regardless of the underlying protocol (such as SOAP or XML) or encoding (such as Multipurpose Internet Messaging

Extensions or MIME). MATLAB provides support for WSDL and SOAP, but only supports remote procedure call (RPC) Web services.

MATLAB can act as a Web service client by sending requests to a server and handling the responses. The client, MATLAB in this case, initiates a connection with a server by using HTTP. When the server receives the request, which includes the operation to be performed and any necessary parameters, it sends back a response. A list of many of the available services is maintained at the XMethods website `<http://www.xmethods.net>`. The MATLAB documentation provides more information on these protocols, MATLAB Web services support, and examples.

34.9 SUMMARY

The MATLAB programming interfaces described in this chapter provide tools for maximizing MATLAB's productivity. MEX-files can be created to speed up loops that cannot be vectorized or to take advantage of previously written C functions or FORTRAN subroutines by adding a few lines of interface code. The resulting compiled MEX-files can then be called from MATLAB just like M-file functions. MATLAB can be used as a back-end computational engine by your own programs to take advantage of MATLAB's computational speed, efficiency, and visualization functions. You can read and write MATLAB MAT-files from your own programs, and transfer collections of variables and data into and out of MATLAB, by using simple `load` and `save` commands. Shared libraries can be accessed from within MATLAB. Direct control of serial ports and communication with serial devices can be accomplished from within MATLAB. Source code control systems can be accessed directly from MATLAB. XML-based Web services can be accessed by remote procedure calls, using standard protocols. All these ***hooks*** into the MATLAB environment add to the collection of tools you can use to solve problems or extend the capabilities of existing programs. (Much more extensive documentation of the MATLAB API—including a complete list of MX functions and details of the internal structure of MAT-files—and additional examples can be found in the MATLAB documentation.)

35

Extending MATLAB with Java

35.1 JAVA OVERVIEW

MATLAB 7 makes extensive use of the Java programming language. Every installation of MATLAB uses a Java virtual machine (JVM) supplied by the operating system or integrated into MATLAB. This Java interpreter is used extensively within MATLAB, as well as being the foundation of the MATLAB user interface. Because Java is so thoroughly integrated into the MATLAB environment, the Java virtual machine is also available to the MATLAB user. Java classes, objects, and methods can be manipulated within MATLAB, both from the command line and from MATLAB functions. Java integration provides opportunities to extend MATLAB in many different ways.

This chapter discusses the incorporation of Java into MATLAB. It is not an introduction to Java. The user is encouraged to consult a Java programming book to learn the details of the programming language. Only those features of Java that are useful in this chapter are covered here.

Java

Java is a programming language expressly designed for use in distributed environments on different kinds of computers under different operating systems. Java programs are compiled into Java platform-independent ***bytecode*** that can be run on any computer that has a Java virtual machine installed. The Java virtual machine is a program that interprets the bytecode into machine code that runs on the real computer hardware. This means that individual computer platform differences, such as instruction lengths and data storage differences, can be recognized and accommodated at the time the program is executed. Platform-specific versions of Java programs are not required. A single Java program can produce the same results on any computer with a JVM.

Java is an object-oriented programming language. If you have experience with Java, C++, or one of a number of other programming languages, or if you are comfortable with MATLAB classes and objects, the concepts and terms used to describe Java may be quite familiar.

The language of Java includes the following terms:

- **Class**–A Java class consists of data specification (variables) and a collection of operations (methods) available to objects of this class. A Java class is a template definition of a particular kind of object.
- **Object**–A Java object is a specific instance of a particular Java class or subclass in the same way that a MATLAB structure object is an instance of the MATLAB `struct` class. An object contains real values instead of variables, and all of the methods associated with the class can operate on any object instantiated from the class.
- **Method**–A method is a programmed procedure or operation that is defined as part of a class and is available for use by any object of that class. A Java method is analogous to a MATLAB class method—a function that operates only on objects of a specific class.
- **Variable** or **field**–A variable or field is the name associated with a value. Java variables are defined in Java classes. The terms *field* and *variable* are often used interchangeably.
- **Class library, toolkit, or package**–A package is a collection of related Java classes, such as the Abstract Windowing Toolkit (`java.awt.*`), providing windowing and GUI services, or the net class library (`java.net.*`), providing Internet and communications services.
- **Private/public**–*Private fields* are visible only within the class and can be changed only by public or private methods defined for the class. *Private methods* can be called only within the class and are not visible outside of the class. *Public fields* and *public methods* are visible outside of the class.
- **Static/nonstatic**–*Static fields* and *static methods* are associated with classes rather than with objects. Static fields are read-only; the contents cannot be changed. Static methods operate on classes. *Nonstatic fields* are associated with objects and often can be modified.
- **Final**–*Final classes* cannot have subclasses. *Final variables* or fields cannot be changed. *Final methods* cannot be overridden by subclasses. Private methods are effectively final. Variables labeled *public static final* are read-only class variables visible outside of the class. By convention, public static final variable names use all capital letters.

The ability to access arbitrary Java classes in the MATLAB environment opens up almost unlimited possibilities beyond the traditional MATLAB environment. Some of these possibilities are explored in examples later in this chapter.

Why Use Java?

Why would anyone want to use Java? There are a number of reasons. Anyone familiar with object-oriented programming languages or with MEX-file programming in MATLAB should be comfortable using Java. You can access existing Java classes and methods to add functionality to MATLAB. You can use special-purpose prewritten Java classes to add unique functionality. You can also create your own Java classes and access them from within MATLAB. *The MathWorks Inc.* has also made it easy to pass data between MATLAB data types and Java objects by automatically casting between Java and MATLAB data types. MATLAB support for Java arrays makes interaction between MATLAB and Java even easier.

35.2 JAVA CLASSES

Java classes are the foundation of Java. MATLAB makes a number of standard and MATLAB-specific class packages available automatically. Making additional classes or class libraries available entails two steps. First, you must tell MATLAB where to look for the `.class` or `.jar` files containing Java class definitions by adding entries to the `classpath.txt` file. Then, you must refer to a class by using the full class and package name, or `import` the class or package into the MATLAB workspace.

Using Java Classes in MATLAB

The systemwide `classpath.txt` file located in the `$toolbox/local` directory specifies the locations of Java class definitions. This text file can be edited to make additional classes available to all MATLAB users when MATLAB is launched. If this file is copied to your own startup directory, any changes made will affect only one user. To make individual `.class` files available, add the path to the directory containing the `.class` files to the `classpath.txt` file. Add the top directory of a class package directory tree to the `classpath.txt` file to add an entire package. Add the entire path to a `.jar` file (including the file name) to make an entire compressed Java archive available. The `classpath.txt` file is read only at startup, and so changes to the file are not recognized until MATLAB is restarted. MATLAB 7 provides the ability to dynamically change the Java class path during a MATLAB session by using the `javaclasspath`, `javaaddpath`, and `javarmpath` functions.

Once MATLAB knows where to look for Java classes, you can refer to any available class by using the full class name. For example, `java.lang.String` refers to the `String` class contained in the `java.lang` class library.

35.3 JAVA OBJECTS

Java objects are created by using either Java syntax or MATLAB syntax conventions. For example, the code

```
>> myFrameA = java.awt.Frame('A Cool Window');                    % Java syntax
>> myFrameB = javaObject('java.awt.Frame','Another Window'); % MATLAB syntax
```

creates two objects, both instances of the `java.awt.Frame` class. The `javaObject` function is intended for unusual situations within functions and is rarely used. Java syntax is preferred.

The function `import` provides a shortcut method for refering to a given class within MATLAB. For instance, the code

```
>> import java.awt.Frame
>> myFrameA = Frame; myFrameB = Frame;
```

creates two objects of the `java.awt.Frame` class. Future references to `Frame` refer to `java.awt.Frame`. Entire class libraries can be imported in the same manner. For example, the code

```
>> import java.awt.* java.net.* com.mathworks.ide.help.HelpBrowser
```

makes all `java.awt` classes, all `java.net` classes, and the `com.mathworks.ide.help.HelpBrowser` class available in shorthand notation. For instance, the code

```
>> import java.awt.*
>> myButton = Button('Stop');
```

creates an instance of a `java.awt.Button` class. The `import` command with no arguments returns the current import list without adding to it. The `clear import` command clears the import list from the current workspace. Function import lists are cleared when the function returns.

Java Objects are References in MATLAB

It is important to understand that Java objects are **references** in MATLAB and are not copied on assignment or passed by value. A new reference is created whenever a Java object is assigned. When a Java object is passed to a function as an input argument, the variable name in the function is simply another reference to the original object. As an example, consider this short test function:

```
function javatest(obj)
% Test java object references

disp(obj.getLabel)                  % Display the object label
newRef=obj;                         % Create a new reference
set(newRef,'Label','Label One')     % Change the label using set()
disp(newRef.getLabel)               % Display the new label
setLabel(newRef,'Label Two')        % Use the setLabel method
disp(newRef.getLabel)               % Display the label again
newRef.setLabel('Label Three')      % Use Java object method syntax
disp(newRef.getLabel)               % Display the label
```

To illustrate use of the `javatest` function, first create an object of the `Button` class:

```
>> myBut = java.awt.Button('Label Zero')
 myBut =
 java.awt.Button[button1,0,0,0x0,invalid,label=Label Zero]
```

Then, pass the `Button` to the `javatest` function:

```
>> javatest(myBut)
Label Zero
Label One
Label Two
Label Three
```

The `Button` object in the MATLAB base workspace has changed!

```
>> myBut
myBut =
 java.awt.Button[button1,0,0,0x0,invalid,label=Label Three]
```

But the `newRef` reference remains local to the function workspace and is unknown in the base workspace:

```
>> newRef
??? Undefined function or variable 'newRef'.
```

This occurs because Java objects are passed by reference rather than by value, and assignments simply create another reference. Changes made to the object referenced by `newRef` within the function affect the object referenced by `myBut` in the base workspace, since they both refer to the *same* object. This is different from conventional MATLAB, where data is passed and assigned by value, not by reference.

> Java objects are created by object constructor methods and released by the `clear` function. Since every assignment creates a new object reference, Java objects cannot be duplicated. You cannot make a direct copy of any Java object.

Java arrays can be copied, but the elements of the new array are newly created references to the original objects.

35.4 JAVA METHODS

Java classes consist of data definitions and a collection of operations that can be performed on or by objects created from the class. The collection of operations, called methods, are the Java equivalent of operators and functions in MATLAB.

Invoking Methods on Java Objects

In the preceding example, the Button's Label property was changed within the javatest function in three different ways:

```
set(newRef,'Label','Label One')      % Change the label using set()
setLabel(newRef,'Label Two')         % Use the setLabel method
newRef.setLabel('Label Three')       % Use Java object method syntax
```

The first assignment uses the MATLAB set function, overloaded for Java objects by using the functional syntax set(object,property,value). The second assignment uses the java.awt.Button class setLabel method in a hybrid functional syntax: method(object,value). The third assignment uses pure Java syntax: object.method(value). All three variations are used in this example.

There is one more way to invoke a method on a Java object. The javaMethod command uses pure functional notation to invoke a method. For example, the code

```
javaMethod('setLabel',newRef,'Label Four')
```

also invokes the setLabel method on the Button object newRef. The javaMethod function is available for unique situations, but is rarely used. Java or MATLAB syntax is preferred.

Getting Information about Classes and Objects

Classes are collections of variables and methods, and objects are instances of classes or subclasses. Each object inherits the methods and variables of the class. The methods command produces a list of the public methods available for a specific class:

```
>> methods java.lang.Double

Methods for class java.lang.Double:

Double       doubleToLongBits     intValue          parseDouble  strncmp
Number       doubleToRawLongBits  intersect         permute      strncmpi
Object       doubleValue          isInfinite        reshape      toString
byteValue    eq                   isNaN             setdiff      transpose
char         equals               isletter          setxor       tril
compare      eval                 ismember          shortValue   triu
compareTo    evalc                isspace           sort         unique
ctranspose   fieldnames           longBitsToDouble  str2double   valueOf
diag         findstr              longValue         str2num      wait
```

```
disp        floatValue        ne           strcmp
display     getClass          notify       strcmpi
double      hashCode          notifyAll    strmatch
```

Any object of the java.lang.Double class can use any of these methods. The argument to the methods command is the name of a Java class. A second argument '-full' produces a much more detailed list of methods, including information about their arguments and return values:

```
>> methods java.lang.Double -full

Methods for class java.lang.Double:

Double(double)
Double(java.lang.String) throws java.lang.NumberFormatException
Number()
Object()
byte byteValue()
byte byteValue()
char  % Inherited from opaque
static int compare(double,double)
abstract int compareTo(java.lang.Object)
int compareTo(java.lang.Object)
int compareTo(java.lang.Double)
ctranspose  % Inherited from opaque
diag  % Inherited from opaque
disp  % Inherited from opaque
display  % Inherited from opaque
double  % Inherited from opaque
static long doubleToLongBits(double)
static long doubleToRawLongBits(double)
abstract double doubleValue()
double doubleValue()
eq  % Inherited from opaque
boolean equals(java.lang.Object)
boolean equals(java.lang.Object)  % Inherited from java.lang.Object
(...)
```

The `methodsview` function presents the same information about the methods of a Java class by creating a new window displaying the methods and their attributes. When a method that does not exist for a Java class is invoked on an instance of that class, MATLAB will check for a built-in MATLAB function of the same name and try to invoke that function. If no built-in function is found, a message is returned indicating that a method by that name was not found for this class.

As the following code shows, the `fieldnames` command (introduced in the earlier discussion of structures) has been overloaded to return information about the public fields or variables of a Java class or object:

```
>> dObj = java.lang.Double(5.0);

>> fieldnames(dObj)
ans =
     'POSITIVE_INFINITY'
     'NEGATIVE_INFINITY'
     'NaN'
     'MAX_VALUE'
     'MIN_VALUE'
     'TYPE'

>> fieldnames(dObj,'-full')
ans =
     'static final double POSITIVE_INFINITY'
     'static final double NEGATIVE_INFINITY'
     'static final double NaN'
     'static final double MAX_VALUE'
     'static final double MIN_VALUE'
     'static final java.lang.Class TYPE'

>> fieldnames(java.awt.Dimension)
ans =
     'width'
     'height'

>> fieldnames(java.awt.Point,'-full')
ans =
     'int x'
     'int y'
```

Use the object.field syntax to access the public data fields of a Java object:

```
>> dObj.MAX_VALUE
ans =
    1.7977e+308
```

35.5 OBJECT PROPERTIES

Java objects in MATLAB have properties, just as Handle Graphics objects do. The MATLAB get and set methods can be used to access some of the standard Java class methods and to add common properties to Java objects. For example, the java.awt.Frame object has a MATLAB property called 'Background'. The MATLAB get and set methods implement the Java getBackground and setBackground methods to change this property.

For example, create a java.lang.Double object with the code

```
>> dObj = java.lang.Double(6.0)
dObj. =
6.0
```

and examine its properties:

```
>> get(dObj)

        Class = [ (1 by 1) java.lang.Class array]
        Infinite = off
        NaN = off

        BeingDeleted = off
        ButtonDownFcn =
        Children = []
        Clipping = on
        CreateFcn =
        DeleteFcn =
        BusyAction = queue
        HandleVisibility = on
        HitTest = on
        Interruptible = on
        Parent = []
```

```
Selected = off
SelectionHighlight = on
Tag =
Type = java.lang.Double
UIContextMenu = []
UserData = []
Visible = on
```

The common MATLAB object properties are available, including the `'Tag'` and `'UserData'` properties. The three object-specific properties, `'Class'`, `'Infinite'`, and `'NaN'`, are all read-only properties. Object properties can be queried and/or changed by using the `get` and `set` commands:

```
>> get(dObj,'Class')
ans =
class java.lang.Double
>> set(dObj,'Tag','MyDouble')
>> get(dObj,'Tag')
ans =
MyDouble
```

> Java objects do not have handles in the sense that Handle Graphics objects do. Java objects are not children of the *root* window and cannot be found by the `findobj` function or any other MATLAB search technique.

35.6 DATA EXCHANGE

Java classes and objects are distinct from MATLAB classes and variables. Moving data between different classes of objects or variables requires changing the form of the data.

Automatic Data Type Conversions

MATLAB and Java, as in any typed programming language or environment, use ***coercion*** or ***casting***, a familiar concept to most programmers, to transfer data between data types or classes. Each class contains at least one class constructor method used to create an object from a different source data type. For example, arithmetic operations on the MATLAB `integer` data types are performed internally by explicitly casting the integer values into the `double` data type, performing the operation, and casting the result back into the appropriate `integer` data type.

The different integer data types cannot be mixed in an expression, but can be computed by explicit casting:

```
>> x = uint8(95)
x =
    95

>> y = uint16(43)
y =
    43

>> z = x+y
??? Error using ==> plus
Integers can only be combined with integers of the same class, or scalar
doubles.

>> z = y+uint16(x)
z =
    138

>> class(z)
ans =
uint16
```

MATLAB hides most of the complexity of Java data type conversion by automatically casting native MATLAB data types into standard Java classes as needed. In general, MATLAB numerical data types are converted to the most appropriate Java target data type. MATLAB strings and arrays of characters are converted to the `java.lang.String` class. Cell arrays of Java objects are converted to Java arrays of objects. Note that MATLAB arrays and Java arrays are not the same.

Java objects returned to MATLAB from Java methods are generally not automatically converted to MATLAB data types, so that they can continue to be used by Java methods. There is one general exception. Numerical values returned from Java methods are converted to MATLAB data types; scalars are converted to MATLAB `doubles`, and numerical arrays are converted to arrays of the MATLAB type most appropriate to save storage space. `java.lang.String` objects returned to MATLAB can be converted to character arrays, and Java `String` arrays can be converted to cell arrays of strings using the `char` function. Java objects explicitly created in MATLAB retain their original Java object form, including `java.lang.Double` and `java.lang.String` objects.

Explicit Data Type Conversions

Explicit data type conversions are also possible. Java objects belonging to any Java `Numeric` class or subclass, or any other Java class containing a `toDouble` method, can be converted to a MATLAB `double`. Any Java object of the `String` class or any other Java class containing a `toChar` method can be converted to a MATLAB `char`. The following example is illustrative:

```
>> wObj = java.lang.Double(3.12)
wObj =
3.12

>> wObj.intValue
ans =
     3

>> class(ans)
ans =
double
>> class(double(wObj))
ans =
double

>> sObj = java.lang.String('A Java String')
sObj =
A Java String

>> class(sObj)
ans =
java.lang.String
>> sObj.toUpperCase
ans =
A JAVA STRING

>> class(ans)
ans =
java.lang.String
```

```
>> butObj = java.awt.Button('OK')
but =
java.awt.Button[button1,0,0,0x0,invalid,label=OK]

>> butObj.getSize
ans =
java.awt.Dimension[width=0,height=0]

>> class(ans)
ans =
java.awt.Dimension
```

Java objects often have characteristics that are accessible by using field names defined as part of the object. This is very similar to the way MATLAB handles structures. As might be expected, the `struct` function can be used to convert Java objects into MATLAB structures. The MATLAB `cell` function can also be used to convert Java objects or arrays into cell arrays.

Displaying Java Objects

Whenever a Java object is listed by using the `disp` function or by omitting the semicolon on the command line, the `toString` method is used to display the object. The `toString` method for most Java objects returns a string containing the class name and information about some of the variables associated with the object:

```
>> butObj = java.awt.Button('OK')
butObj =
java.awt.Button[button0,0,0,0x0,invalid,label=OK]

>> f = java.awt.Frame('My Frame')
f =
java.awt.Frame[frame0,0,0,0x0,invalid,hidden,layout=java.awt.BorderLayout,
            title=My Frame,resizable,normal] % (line wrapped for printing)
```

Objects of the `Numeric` and `String` classes and subclasses are again exceptions to the rule. `Numeric` Java types are displayed as strings containing the value of the number, and `String` types are displayed as a character array containing the text of the Java `String`.

Java objects are very similar to MATLAB structures in some respects. Java class fields (the same fields listed by the `fieldnames` command) can be converted to MATLAB structures and accessed by using standard MATLAB syntax, as in the following example:

```
>> b = struct(butObj)
b =
         TOP_ALIGNMENT: 0
      CENTER_ALIGNMENT: 0.5000
      BOTTOM_ALIGNMENT: 1
        LEFT_ALIGNMENT: 0
       RIGHT_ALIGNMENT: 1
                 WIDTH: 1
                HEIGHT: 2
            PROPERTIES: 4
              SOMEBITS: 8
             FRAMEBITS: 16
               ALLBITS: 32
                 ERROR: 64
                 ABORT: 128

>> b.PROPERTIES
ans =
     4

>> class(ans)
ans =
double
```

This feature provides a way to capture the names and values of all of the public fields or variables of a Java class; however, the only way to change these values is by using appropriate Java methods on an object of the class—if such methods are available. Note that these particular fields are likely to be public static final (the field names are capitalized) and as such cannot be changed at all.

35.7 JAVA ARRAYS

So far, we have discussed passing singular Java objects between Java methods and the MATLAB environment. Some methods can handle or even expect arrays of objects, while others can return arrays of objects. Java arrays can be returned by Java methods or can be created by MATLAB commands.

Java arrays are based on the C language model and are significantly different from MATLAB arrays in their structure and in the way elements are accessed. Most of the time, the differences do not matter, as MATLAB handles the conversion transparently.

Java Array Structure

Java arrays are always 1-D vectors. 2-D Java arrays are constructed as arrays of arrays. 3-D Java arrays are arrays of arrays of arrays, and *n*-D Java arrays can be constructed in the same manner. This array structure is similar to that of nested cell arrays in MATLAB. Like cell arrays, nested Java arrays can be of different lengths. For example, 2-D MATLAB character arrays must have rectangular dimensions: Each row must have the same number of columns. Cell arrays of strings, however, can contain strings of different lengths. Java arrays can contain arrays of different lengths as well. These types of arrays are sometimes termed ***ragged*** arrays. When methods return ragged, nonrectangular arrays, MATLAB stores them in cell arrays.

Accessing Elements of Java Arrays

Java array indexing, like C, is zero-based, while MATLAB uses one-based indexing. Java programs access elements of an array of length `N` by using the indices `0` through `N-1`. MATLAB accesses the same elements by using the indices `1` through `N`. For example, `myArray(4)` is used to access the fourth element of a Java array in MATLAB, while a Java program accesses the same element of the array by using `myArray[3]`. Similarly, the element of a Java array that is accessed by `myArray[2][4]` in a Java program can be accessed by `myArray(3,5)` within MATLAB. However, MATLAB hides these differences. When a Java method is used or a Java array is accessed in the MATLAB environment, normal MATLAB syntax is used. MATLAB makes the necessary indexing conversions transparently, as the following example shows:

```
>> but1Obj = java.awt.Button('STOP')
but1Obj =
java.awt.Button[button1,0,0,0x0,invalid,label=STOP]

>> but2Obj = java.awt.Button('GO')
but2Obj =
java.awt.Button[button2,0,0,0x0,invalid,label=GO]

>> butArray = [but1Obj,but2Obj]
butArray =
java.awt.Button[]:
```

```
    [java.awt.Button]
    [java.awt.Button]
>> class(butArray)
ans =
java.awt.Button[]

>> size(butArray)
ans =
     2     1

>> getLabel(butArray(1))    % Functional syntax for the getLabel method
ans =
STOP

>> butArray(2).getLabel     % Java syntax for the getLabel method
ans =
GO

>> butArray(2).setLabel('YIELD')

>> but2Obj
but2Obj =
java.awt.Button[button2,0,0,0x0,invalid,label=YIELD]
```

Note that butArray is an array of ***references*** to the but1Obj and but2Obj objects. Changes made to these references change the original object.

Creating Java Arrays

Java arrays can be created as the output of the operation of a Java method, by concatenating objects or arrays, by extracting elements of existing Java arrays, by assignment to an array element, or by using the javaArray function.

As shown in the preceding example, the standard array operators [] (and the cat function) can be used to concatenate Java objects into a Java array. If the objects are of the same class, the resulting array is of the same class as well. If the objects are arrays of the same class, the arrays are stacked. The length of the resulting array is the sum of the lengths of the individual arrays. If the objects are 2-D arrays that differ in the lengths of the second dimension, the result is a ragged array. If the objects are of different classes, the resulting array is of the java.lang.Object class and its length is the number of arrays being combined.

As with normal MATLAB arrays, you can also create a Java array by assigning an object to a specific element of a nonexistent array:

```
>> bigButArray(3,4) = java.awt.Button('YES')
bigButArray =
 java.awt.Button[][]:
    []        []        []                      []
    []        []        []                      []
    []        []        []     [java.awt.Button]
```

Extending an array can produce unexpected results. Because of the structure of Java arrays and the fact that they can be ragged, extending an existing Java array by assignment does not necessarily result in a rectangular array. Consider an example using the bigButArray from the previous example:

```
>> bigButArray(4,5) = java.awt.Button('NO')
bigButArray =
java.awt.Button[][]:
    [4 element array]
    [4 element array]
    [4 element array]
    [5 element array]
```

This adds a fourth element to the top-level Java array containing a five-element Java array of Button objects. Each of the existing elements of the top-level array continue to contain four-element Java arrays of Button objects. Because the resulting array is nonrectangular or ragged, MATLAB stores the result as a cell array of Java arrays.

Similarly, when the empty matrix is assigned to an entire row or column of a MATLAB matrix, MATLAB removes the row or column and collapses the resulting matrix dimensions. Since Java arrays can be ragged, they cannot be handled in the same way. When an entire row or column of a Java array is assigned the empty matrix, the dimensions do not change. The elements are simply assigned the Java null character, which MATLAB represents as the empty matrix.

The javaArray function creates an unpopulated Java array (filled with null values) of a specific class by using the syntax javaArray('java_class',m,n,p,...), where java_class is a fully qualified Java class name (package and class name) and m, n, and p are array dimensions. For example, create a 3-by-4 empty Java array to contain Button objects with the following code:

```
>> buttonArray = javaArray('java.awt.Button',3,4)
buttonArray =
java.awt.Button[][]:
    []    []    []    []
    []    []    []    []
    []    []    []    []
```

Then, use standard MATLAB assignment syntax and a `Button` constructor method to populate the array with new `Button` objects:

```
>> buttonArray(2,2) = java.awt.Button('MAYBE')
buttonArray =
java.awt.Button[][]:
    []                     []    []    []
    []    [java.awt.Button]    []    []
    []                     []    []    []
```

Accessing Java Array Elements

The elements of a Java object array can be accessed by using the normal MATLAB array indexing syntax, as in the following example:

```
>> dArray = javaArray('java.lang.Double',3,4)
dArray =
java.lang.Double[][]:
    []    []    []    []
    []    []    []    []
    []    []    []    []

>> for i = 1:3
     for j = 1:4
       dArray(i,j) = java.lang.Double(i*10+j);
     end
   end

>> dArray
dArray =
java.lang.Double[][]:
    [11]    [12]    [13]    [14]
    [21]    [22]    [23]    [24]
    [31]    [32]    [33]    [34]
```

Notice that the result is a Java array consisting of three elements displayed as rows; each of these elements contains another Java array consisting of four elements displayed as columns. The element referenced by dArray[0][2] in Java is the element referenced by dArray(1,3) in MATLAB:

```
>> dArray(1,3)
ans =
13.0
```

The second element of the top-level dArray is a four-element Java array:

```
>> dArray(2)
ans =
java.lang.Double[]:
    [21]
    [22]
    [23]
    [24]
```

This is *not* the result you get when you use the same syntax on a MATLAB array. Given a 3-by-4 MATLAB array D of doubles, D(4) and D(1,2) refer to the same individual array element.

Subarrays

Subsets of Java arrays can be accessed by using familiar MATLAB array syntax. The following example uses the given Java array dArray and the corresponding MATLAB array D:

```
>> dArray
dArray =
java.lang.Double[][]:
    [11]    [12]    [13]    [14]
    [21]    [22]    [23]    [24]
    [31]    [32]    [33]    [34]

>> D = double(dArray)
D =
    11    12    13    14
    21    22    23    24
    31    32    33    34
```

```
>> dArray(2,2:3)
ans =
java.lang.Double[]:
    [22]
    [23]

>> D(2,2:3)
ans =
    22    23
```

On the other hand, MATLAB uses column-oriented storage for array elements, whereas Java uses row-oriented storage for array elements. A 2-by-2 MATLAB array is stored as `[11 21 12 22]`, while a 2-by-2 Java array (a two-element Java array containing two-element Java arrays) is stored as `[11 12][21 22]`. When using the colon operator (:) to create a vector from an array, the result differs because of these storage differences:

```
>> dArray(:)
ans =
java.lang.Double[]:
    [11]
    [12]
    [13]
    [14]
    [21]
    [22]
    [23]
    [24]
    [31]
    [32]
    [33]
    [34]
>> D(:)
ans =
    11
    21
    31
```

```
    12
    22
    32
    13
    23
    33
    14
    24
    34
```

The colon operator allows assignment to every element of a Java array or subarray with a single statement by treating the array as a single vector:

```
>> dblArray = javaArray('java.lang.Double',3,4)
dblArray =
java.lang.Double[][]:
    []    []    []    []
    []    []    []    []
    []    []    []    []

>> dblArray(:) = java.lang.Double(0)
dblArray =
java.lang.Double[][]:
    [0]    [0]    [0]    [0]
    [0]    [0]    [0]    [0]
    [0]    [0]    [0]    [0]

>> dblArray(2,:) = java.lang.Double(1)
dblArray =
java.lang.Double[][]:
    [0]    [0]    [0]    [0]
    [1]    [1]    [1]    [1]
    [0]    [0]    [0]    [0]
```

```
>> dblArray(:,3) = java.lang.Double(4)
dblArray =
java.lang.Double[][]:
    [0]    [0]    [4]    [0]
    [1]    [1]    [4]    [1]
    [0]    [0]    [4]    [0]
```

Remember that each of these elements is another reference to the same object. The original constructor assignment statement `dblArray(:)=java.lang.Double(0)` creates one `java.lang.Double` object containing the value `0` and a populated `dblArray` with 12 references to this object. Each subsequent assignment statement created one new object and multiple references to this object.

Duplicating Arrays

Assigning Java arrays creates new references as well. For example, the code

```
>> xArray = dArray
xArray =
java.lang.Double[][]:
    [11]    [12]    [13]    [14]
    [21]    [22]    [23]    [24]
    [31]    [32]    [33]    [34]
```

simply creates a new reference to `dArray` named `xArray`. You can also create a new object reference by assigning a name to a single element of an array:

```
>> xObj = dArray(2,3)
xObj =
23.0
```

In this example, `xObj` and `dArray(2,3)` reference the same object.

If you assign a top-level element of an array containing two or more levels, the result is another reference to the array contained in the top-level array:

```
>> yArray = dArray(2)
yArray =
java.lang.Double[]:
    [21]
    [22]
    [23]
    [24]
```

```
>> yArray(2)=java.lang.Double(0)
yArray =
java.lang.Double[]:
    [21]
    [ 0]
    [23]
    [24]

>> dArray
dArray =
java.lang.Double[][]:
    [11]     [12]     [13]     [14]
    [21]     [ 0]     [23]     [24]
    [31]     [32]     [33]     [34]
```

The preceding code creates yArray as a new reference to the second element of the top-level array in dArray.

You can create a new array from elements of a Java array (known as ***cloning*** in Java) by assigning a subset of the original Java array elements to a new variable:

```
>> zArray = dArray(1:2,2:3)
zArray =
java.lang.Double[][]:
    [12]     [13]
    [ 0]     [23]
```

In this example, zArray is a new array of Doubles containing values *which are new references to the original objects*. For example, zArray(1,1) and dArray(1,2) point to the same object. However, if you *replace* an element of zArray with a new object, dArray is not affected:

```
>> zArray(2,2) = java.lang.Double(-1)
zArray =
java.lang.Double[][]:
    [12]     [13]
    [ 0]     [-1]
```

```
>> dArray
dArray =
java.lang.Double[][]:
    [11]     [12]     [13]     [14]
    [21]     [ 0]     [23]     [24]
    [31]     [32]     [33]     [34]
```

Replacing an element of zArray replaces the existing object reference with a new reference to a new object, and therefore does not affect dArray. However, the other elements in zArray are still references. Changes to ***attributes*** of these elements are changes to the original elements.

An entire Java array can be copied by using the colon operator:

```
>> xArray = dArray(:,:)
xArray =
java.lang.Double[][]:
    [11]     [12]     [13]     [14]
    [21]     [ 0]     [23]     [24]
    [31]     [32]     [33]     [34]

>> xArray(2,3) = dArray(3,4)
xArray =
java.lang.Double[][]:
    [11]     [12]     [13]     [14]
    [21]     [ 0]     [34]     [24]
    [31]     [32]     [33]     [34]

>> dArray
dArray =
java.lang.Double[][]:
    [11]     [12]     [13]     [14]
    [21]     [ 0]     [23]     [24]
    [31]     [32]     [33]     [34]
```

The element at xArray(2,3) now contains a new reference to dArray(3,4), while dArray is unaffected.

A new array is also created when you concatenate Java arrays:

```
>> a = dArray(1,3)
a =
13.0
```

```
>> b = dArray(3,2)
b =
32.0

>> c = [a b]
c =
java.lang.Double[]:
    [13]
    [32]

>> c(2) = dArray(3,3)
c =
java.lang.Double[]:
    [13]
    [33]

>> a
a =
13.0
>> b
b =
32.0
```

> In general, a reference is created whenever you assign any Java object or array. A new array is created when you assign a subset of a Java array (or an entire array using the (:,:) notation) or concatenate Java arrays. The new array contains new references to the original array elements.

The statements

```
xArray = dArray;
yArray = dArray(2);
zObj = dArray(2,3);
```

create new references, while the statements

```
xArray = dArray(:.:);
yArray = dArray(2,:);
zArray = [dArray, dArray];
```

create new arrays containing additional references to the specified elements of the original array.

Java Array Size

Some MATLAB functions have been enhanced to support Java arrays, but full MATLAB functionality is not available because of the structure of Java arrays. For example, the `size` and `length` functions operating on a Java array return information about the top-level array only:

```
>> myArray = javaArray('java.lang.Double',3,4)
myArray =
java.lang.Double[][]:
     []       []       []       []
     []       []       []       []
     []       []       []       []

>> size(myArray)
ans =
     3     1

>> length(myArray)
ans =
     3
```

To get information on other dimensions, you must specifically address an element of the top-level array:

```
>> size(myArray(1))
ans =
     4     1

>> length(myArray(2))
ans =
     4
```

The total number of elements in a non-empty Java array can be obtained by using the `length` function:

```
>> length(dblArray(:))              % the dblArray created earlier
ans =
    12
```

```
>> length(myArray(:))        % the 0-by-1 (empty) myArray
ans =
    0

>> size(myArray(:))
ans =
    0     1
```

Since myArray is empty, size(myArray(:)) returns 0-by-1 and length (myArray(:)) returns 0. Similarly, you can use the end keyword when addressing Java arrays, but only in the top-level reference (the first dimension):

```
>> dblArray(2:end)
ans =
java.lang.Double[][]:
    [1]     [1]     [4]     [1]
    [0]     [0]     [4]     [0]
>> dblArray(2,2:end)
ans =
java.lang.Double[][]:
    [0 element array]
```

35.8 JAVA FUNCTIONS

In addition to those mentioned previously, other MATLAB functions have been created or modified to support Java classes, objects, and methods. As noted earlier, import can be used to add to the Java class and package import list and allow shorthand references to Java classes. Java objects can be removed and the import list cleared with the clear function. The inmem function has been enhanced to list the names of all of the Java classes that have been loaded into the MATLAB workspace in an optional third output argument. The exist function now recognizes and identifies Java objects and arrays. The class function recognizes the class of Java objects and arrays, and the isa function can test the class of a Java object or array. The new isjava function can be used to determine whether or not a variable is a Java object.

The fieldnames function returns a list of the public fields of a Java class or object. The methods command lists the names of the methods available to operate on objects of specific Java classes. The which function has been enhanced to return a list of the loaded Java classes that contain a given method or a combination of method and signature, as in the following example:

```
>> which -all resize
java.awt.Button.resize                                    % Button method
```

```
java.awt.TextArea.resize                            % TextArea method
java.awt.Frame.resize                               % Frame method
matlab6/toolbox/matlab/graph2d/@axisobj/resize.p % axisobj method
matlab6/toolbox/matlab/graph2d/@axisobj/resize.m   % Shadowed axisobj method
```

The save and load functions can store and recall Java objects and arrays in normal binary MAT-files. Java objects cannot be saved in ASCII formatted files, however. Java exceptions are automatically caught and converted to normal MATLAB errors. The text of the exception is captured and can be displayed by using lasterr.

The following table summarizes the MATLAB functions that support Java, some of which are standard MATLAB functions that have been overloaded for Java and others of which have been created specifically to support working with Java in MATLAB:

Function	**Description**
methods	List the public methods of a Java class
methodsview	List the public methods of a Java class in a new window
usejava	Determine if a Java feature is supported in MATLAB
fieldnames	List the public fields or variables of a Java class
import	List or add to the Java class and package import list
inmem	Can return a cell array of the names of all Java classes that have been loaded
which	Can return a list of matching methods in loaded Java classes
class	Determine the class of a Java object
clear	Clear Java objects from the workspace, or clear the Java class import list
double	Convert a Java object or array of class Numeric to MATLAB doubles
char	Convert a Java object or array of class String to a MATLAB character array or to a cell array of strings
struct	Create a structure from the public fields of a Java class or object
isjava	True if the argument is a Java object or Java array
isa	Determine if a variable is a Java object of a specific class
exist	Determine the nature of a variable; return 8 if the argument is a Java class
ismethod	Determine if the argument is a method of a Java object
isprop	Determine if the argument is a property of a Java object

Function	Description
`inspect`	Display a graphical interface to list and modify property values
`[] and cat`	Concatenate Java objects or arrays into a Java array
`save`	Store variables including Java objects to a binary MAT-file
`load`	Load variables including Java objects from a binary MAT-file
`size`	Return the size of the top-level array of a Java array
`length`	Determine the length of the top-level array of a Java array
`javaArray`	Create a new Java array and populate it with null values
`javaMethod`	Invoke a Java method on a Java object or Java array (not recommended)
`javaObject`	Create a Java object (not recommended)
`javaaddpath`	Add entries to a dynamic Java class path
`javarmpath`	Remove entries from a dynamic Java class path
`javaclasspath`	Set and get a dynamic Java class path
`javachk`	Generate an error message if a Java feature is not available

35.9 EXAMPLES

This section contains a number of examples that pull together many of the concepts and tools presented in this chapter to illustrate how Java can help to extend the capabilities of MATLAB. We start with few basic examples and proceed to more complete functions.

Example 1: whoami

This example uses elements of the `java.net` class library to return the host name and IP address of the computer running MATLAB:

```
function whoami
% Test function to illustrate the use of the java.net package.
%
% Mastering MATLAB 7 Java Example 1

% Use try and catch to avoid Java exception messages.
try
    me=java.net.InetAddress.getLocalHost;
```

```
catch
    error('Unable to get local host address.');
end

% Find my hostname and IP address
myname=me.getHostName;
myip=me.getHostAddress;

% and print the results.
disp(sprintf('My host name is %s',myname));
disp(sprintf('My IP address is %s',myip));
```

The whoami function produces results similar to the following:

```
>> whoami
My host name is www.phptr.com
My IP address is 204.179.152.74
```

Example 2: random

The next example uses the java.util package to generate a random number:

```
function num=random(varargin)
% Test function to illustrate the use of the java.util package.
%   Generate a random number between given limits (or 0:1).
%
% Mastering MATLAB 7 Java Example 2

% Check any input arguments.
if nargin == 0
  rmin=0; rmax=1;
elseif nargin < 3
  if nargin == 1
    lim = varargin{1};
```

```
  else
    lim = [varargin{1}, varargin{2}];
  end
  if isnumeric(lim) & length(lim) == 2
    rmin = min(lim); rmax = max(lim);
  else
    error('Invalid limits.');
  end
else
  error( Too many arguments.')
end

% Construct a Random object and generate a uniformly-distributed
% random number between the desired limits.
rNum = java.util.Random;
num = rNum.nextDouble * (rmax - rmin) + rmin;
```

The random function parses the input, creates a Random object, and uses the nextDouble method to obtain a uniformly distributed pseudorandom number. The nextGaussian method is available to generate a normally distributed random number. Other Random methods can be used to generate integer, long, or float values, or even a user-specified number of random bytes.

Example 3: hithere

This example creates a simple dialog box containing a line of text and a button. When the button is clicked, the dialog box exits:

```
% script hithere.m
% Example script to illustrate the use of the java.awt package.
%
% Mastering MATLAB 7 Java Example 3

% Create a Frame object and specify a 2x1 grid layout style.
dbox=java.awt.Frame('Hi There!');
dbox.setLayout(java.awt.GridLayout(2,1));
```

```
% Specify the window location, size and color. Use Java syntax
%    for the location, hybrid syntax for the size, and MATLAB
%    syntax to set the background color.
dbox.setLocation(50,50);
resize(dbox,200,100);
set(dbox,'Background',[.7,.8,.9]);

% Create a text label and a bright red button.
txt=java.awt.Label('Click the button to exit.',1);
but=java.awt.Button('Exit Button');
set(but,'Background',[1,0,0]);

% Define a callback for the button.
set(but,'MouseClickedCallback','dbox.dispose')

% Attach the label and button to the window.
dbox.add(txt);
dbox.add(but);

% The window is hidden by default. Make it visible.
dbox.show;
```

This example uses a script M-file, rather than a function, to avoid scoping issues with the `Button` callback. As with Handle Graphics objects, Java callbacks are either function handles or strings that are passed to the `eval` function in the MATLAB base workspace. The following figure is an example of the dialog box generated by the `hithere.m` script:

Example 4: netsearch

This example uses the `java.net` package to manage Internet communication, along with the `java.io` package to read a data stream. The `netsearch` function performs an Internet search and returns a cell array of the uniform resource locator (URL) strings found by the search engine. If no matches are found after contacting one search engine, another is tried. Here is the code:

```
function ulist=netsearch(varargin)
% MATLAB Java Demo function netsearch.m
%
%  Mastering MATLAB 7 Java Example 4
%    Open a connection to an internet search engine using
%    Java networking toolkit objects and return the URLs
%    found by the search in a cell array.

% Import the java.net and java.io toolkits to save typing.
import java.net.* java.io.*

% Define the url for a search command and a target string
%     for each host to try in order.
s_host={
        'http://www.google.com/search?q=',   '<p class=g><a href='
        'http://search.yahoo.com/search?p=', 'H=0/*-href='
        };

nhosts=size(s_host,1);      % Number of search hosts defined
ulist={};                   % Cell array to contain results

% Do some error checking.
if nargin < 1
  error('Nothing to search for.');
end
if nargout > 1
  error('Too many output arguments.');
end

% Create a search string from the input arguments.
for (idx=1:nargin)
  if ~ischar(varargin{idx})
    error('Search terms must be strings');
```

```
    else
      tmp_str=varargin{idx};

      % If this string argument contains spaces, quote the string
      % and replace the spaces with plus sign characters.
      if findstr(tmp_str,' ')
        tmp_str=['%22',strrep(tmp_str,' ','+'),'%22'];
      end


      % Build up the search string.
      if idx == 1
        s_str=tmp_str;
      else
        s_str=[s_str,'+',tmp_str];
      end
    end
  end

  % Start with the initial search host.
  uidx=1;
  hostidx=1;
  while isempty(ulist) & (hostidx <= nhosts)

    % Construct a complete URL using the search string.
    s_url=[s_host{hostidx,1},s_str];

    % Create a URL connection to the search engine.
    s_con=jaca.net.URL(s_url);

    % Open an input stream on the connection.
    s_stream = openStream(s_con);

    % Open an input stream reader to read the stream.
    s_rdr = InputStreamReader(s_stream);
```

```
    % Open a buffered reader to read one line at a time.
    shBuf = BufferedReader(s_rdr);

    end

    % Read the lines of the page returned by the search engine
    %   and extract any target URLs until the the page ends.
    linebuf=shBuf.readLine;
    while ~isempty(linebuf)
      linebuf=char(linebuf);
      found = findstr(linebuf, s_host{hostidx,2});
      if ~isempty(found)
        tmp = strtok(linebuf(found(1)+length(s_host{hostidx,2}):end),'>');
        ulist{uidx}=strrep(tmp,'"','');   % Remove extra quote characters
        uidx=uidx+1;
      end
      linebuf=shBuf.readLine;
    end

    % We are done with this page so close the connection.
    shBuf.close;

    % If a target URL was not found, try the next host.
    if isempty(ulist)
      hostidx=hostidx+1;
    end
  end

  if isempty(ulist)
    ulist=[];
  elseif length(ulist) == 1
    ulist=ulist{1};
  end
```

The `s_host` array consists of two strings for each host. The first string contains the protocol, host, and search command portion of a search URL. The search terms are added to this string in an appropriate format to generate the complete URL string that is used to create a `java.net.URL` object. The `openStream` method is used on the `searchHost` object to open an Internet connection to the search host. An `InputStreamReader` object is created on this connection and passed to a `BufferedReader` to enable line-at-a-time processing of the input stream. The `readLine` method is then used to read one line at a time into a string buffer.

The second element of the `s_host` array is a target string. A Web page is composed of text containing formatting and other codes called ***tags*** delimited by `'<'` and `'>'` characters. Each target URL (or ***hit***) that is found by a particular search engine is normally preceded by a specific character string in the page returned by the search URL. Each line of the Web page is examined for the presence of this target string. If the string is found, the target URL is extracted and copied into the output cell array. When the page has been completely processed, the connection is closed. If no results are found, the next search host is contacted, and the search continues. Note that Web pages change over time, and the strings in `s_host` may have to be modified appropriately.

Example 5: winfun

The next example is an expanded version of the `hithere` script shown in Example 3. This time, a window is created containing some buttons and menus with callbacks. The first time `winfun` is called, a window is constructed from `java.awt` toolkit objects, set to an initial state, and made visible. The function then exits. The Java objects still exist and are visible, but the object references (the variables) do not exist in the base workspace. If a button is pressed or a menu item is selected, the associated object callback is executed. The callback calls the `winfun` function again with a unique argument. When `winfun` is called with an argument, the argument is parsed to service the callback. Finally, if the `winfun` function is called with no arguments, but the Java objects still exist, the window is reset to the initial state and made visible again. The code is as follows:

```
function winfun(varargin)
% MATLAB Java Demo function winfun.m
%
% Mastering MATLAB 7 Java Example 5
%   Create a window with buttons, menus and text objects using
```

```
%   Java windowing toolkit objects within a function. Use a
%   local function to implement callbacks. Use persistent variables
%   to maintain visibility of the Java objects between calls.
%

% Import the entire Java Abstract Window Toolkit.

import java.awt.*

% Make sure we can find the Java objects when servicing callbacks.

persistent win ta mi abt mq ma txt x y h w

if isempty(win)

   % Initial function call: create the necessary objects.
   % Start with some text for the About Box.
   txt=[' Cool Window version 1.4  ';...
        ' MM7 example function by  ';...
        'Mastering MATLAB authors  ';...
        'Hanselman and Littlefield '];
   % Reshape it for use in the textarea as well.
   tstr=reshape(txt',1,prod(size(txt)));

   % Create a window using the flow layout model (the simplest)
   %    and set the title. Set the layout using Java syntax.
   win=Frame('Cool Java Window');
   win.setLayout(FlowLayout);

   % Specify the window location, size and color. Use Java syntax
   %    for the location and size, and use MATLAB syntax to set
   %    the background color.
   x=150; y=150; w=430; h=160;
```

```
win.setLocation(x,y);
win.setSize(w,h);
set(win,'Background',[.8 .8 .8]);

% Create some menus: a 'File' menu and a 'Help'  menu.
mf=Menu('File');
mh=Menu('Help');

% Create a 'Quit' menu item, define a callback to close the window,
%      and attach it to the File menu.
mq=MenuItem('Quit');
set(mq,'ActionPerformedCallback','winfun(''quit'')');
mf.add(mq);

% Create a 4x21 text area with no scroll bars (3).
ta=TextArea(tstr,4,21,3);

% Don't let the user change the text.
ta.setEditable(0);

% Set the text background color.
set(ta,'Background',[1 1 .9]);

% Create a 'Show Info' menu item and attach it to the Help menu.
%     Show or hide the textarea when the menu item is selected.
mi=MenuItem('Show Info');
set(mi,'ActionPerformedCallback','winfun(''info'')');
mh.add(mi);

% Create an 'About' menu item and attach it to the Help menu.
ma=MenuItem('About');
```

```
set(ma,'ActionPerformedCallback','winfun(''about'')');
mh.add(ma);

% Create a menubar object, add the menus, and attach
%   the menubar to the window.
mb=MenuBar;
mb.add(mf); mb.add(mh);
mb.setHelpMenu(mh);       % Move the Help menu to the right side.
win.setMenuBar(mb);

% Create some buttons.
bs=Button('Shrink');
be=Button('Expand');
bl=Button('Left');
bu=Button(' Up ');
bd=Button('Down');
br=Button('Right');
bq=Button('Quit');

% Define callbacks for the buttons.
set(bs,'MouseClickedCallback','winfun(''shrink'')')
set(be,'MouseClickedCallback','winfun(''expand'')')
set(bl,'MouseClickedCallback','winfun(''left'')');
set(bu,'MouseClickedCallback','winfun(''up'')');
set(bd,'MouseClickedCallback','winfun(''down'')');
set(br,'MouseClickedCallback','winfun(''right'')');
set(bq,'MouseClickedCallback','winfun(''quit'')');

% Specify some colors for the buttons.
set(bs,'Background',[.5,1,1]);
set(be,'Background',[.5,1,1]);
set(bq,'Background',[1,.4,.4]);
```

```
set(bl,'Background',[.9,.9,.9]);
set(bu,'Background',[.7,.7,.7]);
set(bd,'Background',[.7,.7,.7]);
set(br,'Background',[.9,.9,.9]);

% Add the first row of buttons to the window. Objects will be
%    positioned in the order in which they are added.
win.add(bs);
win.add(bl);
win.add(bu);
win.add(bd);
win.add(br);
win.add(be);

% Attach the text area to the window, but don't display it yet.
win.add(ta);
ta.setVisible(0);

% Now add the Quit button.
win.add(bq);

% Now that the main window has been created, it is time
%    to create a dialog box for the 'About' menu item.
abt = Dialog(win, 'About Winfun');
set(abt,'Background',[.95 .95 .95]);
abt.setLayout(GridLayout(5,1));

% Add some lines of text
abt.add(Label(txt(1,:)));
abt.add(Label(txt(2,:)));
abt.add(Label(txt(3,:)));
abt.add(Label(txt(4,:)));
```

```
  % and a button bar to close the About box.
  bok = Button('OK');
  set(bok,'ActionPerformedCallback','winfun(''ok'')');
  set(bok,'Background',[.6 .8 .8]);
  abt.add(bok);

  % Set the size of the dialog box but don't make it visible.
  abt.setSize(180,110);

  % All done. Now show the main window and exit.
  win.setVisible(1);

elseif nargin == 0
  % Reset the hidden window to the initial state and show it.
  abt.setVisible(0);
  ta.setVisible(0); mi.setLabel('Show Info');
  x=150; y=150; w=430; h=160;
  win.setLocation(x,y);
  win.setSize(w,h);
  win.setVisible(1);

elseif nargin == 1   % This is a callback.
   switch (varargin{1})
     case 'shrink'   % Shrink width by 4 pixels, height by 2
       w=w-4; h=h-2;
     case 'expand'   % Expand width by 4 pixels, height by 2
       w=w+4; h=h+2;
     case 'left'     % Move 4 pixels to the left
       x=x-4;
     case 'up'       % Move 2 pixels higher
       y=y-2;
     case 'down'     % Move 2 pixels lower
       y=y+2;
```

```
case 'right'    % Move 4 pixels to the right
  x=x+4;
case 'info'     % Toggle visibility of the text area
  if (ta.isVisible)
    ta.setVisible(0); mi.setLabel('Show Info');
  else
    ta.setVisible(1); mi.setLabel('Hide Info');
  end
case 'about'    % Show the About Box to the right and lower
  abt.setLocation(x+w+20,y+10);
  abt.setVisible(1);
case 'ok'       % Hide the About Box
  abt.setVisible(0);
case 'quit'     % Hide the windows
  abt.setVisible(0);
  win.setVisible(0);
  return
otherwise       % Bad argument
  error('Invalid callback');
end
win.setBounds(x,y,w,h); win.setVisible(1);
else   % Should not get here.
  error('Too many arguments.');
end
```

The callback argument determines which `case` statement is executed within the `switch` statement. When the argument is `shrink`, the size of the window object `win` is reduced by 4 pixels in the horizontal (x) direction and 2 pixels in the vertical (y) direction using the `setBounds` method. The `setVisible` method is then used to redraw the window with the changed characteristics. Similarly, the expand argument increases the window size. The `up`, `down`, `left`, and `right` arguments change the window location using the same methods.

When the `info` argument is invoked, the result depends on the state of the `ta` text area object. If `ta` is visible (as determined by the `isVisible` method), the text area is hidden and the menu item label is changed appropriately. If the text area is currently hidden, `ta` is made visible by using the `setVisible` method, and the menu item label is changed again. The function `win.setVisible` is then called to refresh the window.

When the `about` argument is received, the dialog box `abt` is positioned to the right of the `win` window and made visible. When the `ok` argument is received, the `abt` dialog box is hidden. When `quit` is received, both the `win` window and the `abt` dialog box are hidden.

The following figure is an example of the windows generated by the `winfun` function:

35.10 SUMMARY

Java is an object-oriented, platform-independent programming language that can be used to extend the scope of the MATLAB environment. Every installation of MATLAB 7 includes a Java virtual machine integrated into MATLAB and available to the MATLAB user. Java classes, objects, and methods can be manipulated within MATLAB, both from the command line and from MATLAB functions. Java integration provides new opportunities to extend MATLAB in many different ways. While MATLAB currently incorporates Java, it is not possible to call MATLAB functions from Java. It is expected that this feature will appear in a future MATLAB release.

The examples in this chapter explore only a few of the possibilities opened up by the availability of Java objects and methods within MATLAB. The MATLAB documentation contains additional Java examples and more details on some of the topics discussed in this chapter. Perhaps the most important property of Java objects is that they are passed by reference, not by value.

Important: Java objects are references in MATLAB. As a result, Java objects cannot be copied, only modified. In addition, Java objects never really disappear. The `clear` function removes references to these objects from the workspace, but the objects themselves may still exist. The Java `setVisible` method simply makes objects invisible. The Java `dispose` method may remove some attributes of objects, but the objects may still exist. Finally, if you lose all references to a Java object by exiting a workspace or using the `clear` command, they cannot be retreived. There is nothing similar to the `findobj` function for Java objects.

To end this chapter, we note that MATLAB 7 has greatly expanded Java support and that future versions of MATLAB are likely to continue to move toward full Java integration. Handle Graphics objects and Java graphics classes and objects are likely to converge. MATLAB appears to be moving toward a fully integrated development environment implemented in Java. This all suggests that Java will play an increasingly important role in the future development of MATLAB.

36

Windows Application Integration

It is not always necessary to write your own applications in a programming language such as C or FORTRAN to enable direct communication between applications. UNIX and Linux platforms use standard ***pipes*** (the standard output of one program is redirected to the standard input of another) to connect applications. Microsoft Windows operating systems implemented similar functionality with Dynamic Data Exchange (DDE). DDE permits applications to communicate directly with each other to send commands or exchange data. A component framework was built upon DDE and Visual Basic Extensions (VBX) and named Object Linking and Embedding (OLE). Later, some parts of OLE relating to graphical user interfaces (GUI) and the Internet were renamed ActiveX. Microsoft later renamed the entire component framework the ***Component Object Model*** or COM.

A COM object is an instance of a component object class that runs on a server application and is controlled by a client application. A COM object encapsulates all data and methods of the object and uses *interfaces* to access the methods of the object. An interface is a pointer to the methods of an object. COM objects can have multiple interfaces. (Refer to the documentation of the component vendor for details of the interfaces available for a specific component.)

Many commercial applications support COM objects, ActiveX, or DDE for interapplication communication on the Windows PC platform. MATLAB supports COM objects, ActiveX controls, and DDE in a limited capacity. It supports the creation of COM objects within MATLAB to control other applications and can also act as a COM server and respond to requests from other applications. COM and DDE are currently available only on the `win32` platform under a *Microsoft Windows* operating system such as Windows 98, Windows 2000, or Windows XP.

36.1 COM OBJECTS: CLIENT/SERVER COMMUNICATION

The COM protocol specifies an object model and a collection of standard and custom interfaces that define each object's methods, properties, and events. Methods are actions that can be performed on or by an object (similar to MATLAB functions and object methods), properties are variables that determine the state of an object (similar to Handle Graphics properties), and events are notifications of changes in the state of an object that may trigger some action (similar to Handle Graphics or Java callbacks).

Applications that support COM can support server functions (the application responds to client requests), client functions (the application sends requests to a server), or both. ActiveX controls are objects that can be integrated into ***control containers*** (such as MATLAB *Figure* windows) by a COM client application and are used to initiate an action by a COM server application. COM servers are applications that can be controlled in some way by a COM client or by an ActiveX control.

MATLAB COM Support

MATLAB supports a limited set of COM interfaces. It can act as an Automation server by exchanging data with other applications and executing commands in the MATLAB workspace. MATLAB also can act as a COM client by exchanging data with other applications and controlling these Automation server applications (such as Microsoft Word, Excel, and PowerPoint) from the MATLAB command line or through M-files. MATLAB cannot be physically imbedded within other applications, but it can act as a control container by imbedding Automation server controls within MATLAB *Figure* windows, similar to the way *uicontrols* are used.

MATLAB as a COM Client

The `actxserver` function creates a COM object and opens a connection to a COM Automation server. Similarly, the `actxcontrol` function creates a control that can be imbedded in a MATLAB container (such as a *Figure* window) to control a COM Automation server. The functions (methods) that operate on COM objects are shown in the following table:

Function/Method	Description
`actxserver`	Create a COM Automation server
`actxcontrol`	Create an ActiveX control object to imbed within a *Figure* window
`actxcontrollist`	List all ActiveX controls that are currently installed
`fieldnames`	Return the property names of an object
`interfaces`	List the custom interfaces to a COM server
`methods`	List all of the public methods for the control or server

Function/Method	Description
events	Display a list of events the control can trigger
eventlisteners	Return the list of events attached to listeners
addproperty	Add a custom property to an object
deleteproperty	Remove a custom property from an object
invoke	Invoke a method on an interface or object, or displays a list of methods
registerevent	Register an event handler with a control to handle a specific event
unregisterevent	Unregister an event handler with a control
unregisterallevents	Unregister all event handlers with a control
isa	True if an argument is of a given MATLAB or Java class
iscom	True if the argument is a COM object
isevent	True if the argument is an event
isinterface	True if the argument is a COM interface
ismethod	True if the argument is an object method
isprop	True if the argument is an object property
inspect	Display a GUI to list and modify property values
methodsview	Display a GUI to list information about the methods of an object
actxcontrolselect	Display a GUI for creating an ActiveX control
class	Create an object or return the class of an object
set	Set a property value on an object or interface
get	Get a property value from an interface or display a list of properties
propedit	Display the built-in property page of a control if the page exists
release	Release an interface
delete	Delete a COM control object and all of its interfaces
load	Load the property state of a control from a file
save	Save the property state of a control to a file
move	Move or resize a control and return the new position

The actxcontrol, actxserver, get, and invoke functions can all return COM objects (or new ***interfaces*** to objects—essentially separate communication channels to objects), which can be controlled or queried by using other COM functions or methods. The release function should be used to release the resources used by a COM object or interface when it is no longer needed. The delete function closes all connections and releases all resources when the server or control object is no longer needed.

Help text is available by using the appropriate object method. For example, the code

```
>> help COM/delete
```

displays the help text for the `delete` method for COM objects.

A list of properties can be obtained by using the form `get(axhandle)` or `axhandle.get`, where `axhandle` is the COM object handle obtained from an `actxserver` or `actxcontrol` object creation method. The properties of a MS PowerPoint COM server are as follows:

```
>> ppapp = actxserver('powerpoint.application');

ppapp =

    COM.powerpoint_application

>> get(ppapp)

         Presentations: [1x1 Interface.Microsoft_PowerPoint_9.0_Object_Library.Presentations]
               Windows: [1x1 Interface.Microsoft_PowerPoint_9.0_Object_Library.DocumentWindows]
          ActiveWindow: [1x203 char]
    ActivePresentation: [1x196 char]
      SlideShowWindows: [1x1 Interface.Microsoft_PowerPoint_9.0_Object_Library.SlideShowWindows]
           CommandBars: [1x1 Interface.Microsoft_Office_9.0_Object_Library._CommandBars]
                  Path: 'C:\Program Files\Microsoft Office\Office'
                  Name: 'Microsoft PowerPoint'
               Caption: 'Microsoft PowerPoint'
             Assistant: [1x1 Interface.Microsoft_Office_9.0_Object_Library.Assistant]
            FileSearch: [1x1 Interface.Microsoft_Office_9.0_Object_Library.FileSearch]
              FileFind: [1x51 char]
                 Build: '6620'
               Version: '9.0'
       OperatingSystem: 'Windows (32-bit) 5.00'
         ActivePrinter: 'XColor'
               Creator: 1.3479e+009
                AddIns: [1x1 Interface.Microsoft_PowerPoint_9.0_Object_Library.AddIns]
                   VBE: [1x1 Interface.Microsoft_Visual_Basic_for_Applications_Extensibility_5.3.VBE]
```

```
               Left: 99
                Top: 99
              Width: 720
             Height: 546.7500
        WindowState: 'ppWindowNormal'
            Visible: 'msoFalse'
             Active: 'msoFalse'
       AnswerWizard: [1x1 Interface.Microsoft_Office_9.0_Object_Library.AnswerWizard]
          COMAddIns: [1x1 Interface.Microsoft_Office_9.0_Object_Library.COMAddIns]
        ProductCode: '{00010409-78E1-11D2-B60F-0060774499C8E7}'
  DefaultWebOptions: [1x1 Interface.Microsoft_PowerPoint_9.0_Object_Library.DefaultWebOptions]
  LanguageSettings: [1x1 Interface.Microsoft_Office_9.0_Object_Library.LanguageSettings
ShowWindowsInTaskbar: 'msoTrue'
     FeatureInstall: 'msoFeatureInstallNone'
```

A list of methods for the ppapp object, along with the calling syntax, can be obtained by using the invoke function:

```
>> invoke(ppapp)
      Activate = void Activate(handle)
      Help = void Help(handle, Variant(Optional))
      Quit = void Quit(handle)
      Run = Variant Run(handle, string, SafeArray(Variant))
```

All of the methods available, including inherited methods for the COM.powerpoint_application class of objects, can be obtained by using the methods function:

```
>> ppapp.methods

Methods for class COM.powerpoint_application:

Activate        eq              load            str2double
Help            eval            move            str2num
Quit            evalc           ne              strcmp
Run             events          permute         strcmpi
addproperty     fieldnames      propedit        strmatch
char            findstr         release         strncmp
```

```
ctranspose       get          reshape    strncmpi
delete           interfaces   save       transpose
deleteproperty   intersect    send       tril
diag             invoke       set        triu
disp             isletter     setdiff    unique
display          ismember     setxor
double           isspace      sort
```

The `fieldnames` function provides a cell array containing the names of the public data fields available for the ppapp object:

```
>> ppapp.fieldnames

ans =

    'Presentations'
    'Windows'
    'ActiveWindow'
    'ActivePresentation'
    'SlideShowWindows'
    'CommandBars'
    'Path'
    'Name'
    'Caption'
    'Assistant'
    'FileSearch'
    'FileFind'
    'Build'
    'Version'
    'OperatingSystem'
    'ActivePrinter'
    'Creator'
    'AddIns'
    'VBE'
    'Left'
    'Top'
```

```
    'Width'
    'Height'
    'WindowState'
    'Visible'
    'Active'
    'AnswerWizard'
    'COMAddIns'
    'ProductCode'
    'DefaultWebOptions'
    'LanguageSettings'
    'ShowWindowsInTaskbar'
    'FeatureInstall'
```

Finally, the events function lists all of the events that the ppapp object can trigger (the list includes the function prototype used when calling the event handler and does not distinguish between registered and unregistered events):

```
>> ppapp.events
    WindowSelectionChange = void WindowSelectionChange(handle Sel)
    WindowBeforeRightClick = void WindowBeforeRightClick(handle Sel, bool Cancel)
    WindowBeforeDoubleClick = void WindowBeforeDoubleClick(handle Sel, bool Cancel)
    PresentationClose = void PresentationClose(handle Pres)
    PresentationSave = void PresentationSave(handle Pres)
    PresentationOpen = void PresentationOpen(handle Pres)
    NewPresentation = void NewPresentation(handle Pres)
    PresentationNewSlide = void PresentationNewSlide(handle Sld)
    WindowActivate = void WindowActivate(handle Pres, handle Wn)
    WindowDeactivate = void WindowDeactivate(handle Pres, handle Wn)
    SlideShowBegin = void SlideShowBegin(handle Wn)
    SlideShowNextBuild = void SlideShowNextBuild(handle Wn)
    SlideShowNextSlide = void SlideShowNextSlide(handle Wn)
    SlideShowEnd = void SlideShowEnd(handle Pres)
    PresentationPrint = void PresentationPrint(handle Pres)
    AfterNewPresentation = void AfterNewPresentation(handle Pres)
    AfterPresentationOpen = void AfterPresentationOpen(handle Pres)
```

With this introduction, several examples are presented to illustrate the key features of COM and ActiveX in MATLAB.

MATLAB Client Examples

This example uses MATLAB as a COM client and Microsoft Word as a COM Automation server. The MATLAB M-file function wordfig copies the contents of the current (or a specified) *Figure* window to the clipboard, starts a server instance of the Microsoft Word application, opens a selected document (or creates a new document) by using the uiputfile dialog box to specify the filename, pastes the graphic at the end of the document, closes the document, quits the Word application, and deletes the COM server object:

```
function wordfig(filespec,popt)
%WORDFIG Open a MSWord document and paste the current figure into it.
% WORDFIG Paste the current Figure window into a word document.
% WORDFIG(FILESPEC) Paste the current Figure window into the document
%   named FILESPEC. Use the complete path to the document if necessary.
% WORDFIG(FILESPEC,POPT) Paste a Figure window into the document FILESPEC
%   using the print options POPT (e.g. -f2 to select Figure window #2).
% If the FILESPEC argument is missing or empty, the uiputfile dialog box
%   is used to select a file name.

% Create or verify a valid file name.
if nargin < 1 | isempty(filespec) | ~ischar(filespec)
  [fname,dname]=uiputfile('*.doc','Modify or create the file:');
  if isequal(fname,0), return, end
  filespec=fullfile(dname,fname);
end
[dname,fname,fext]=fileparts(filespec);
if isempty(dname), dname=pwd; end
if isempty(fext), fext='.doc'; end
filespec=fullfile(dname,[fname,fext]);

% Copy the current Figure window cnto the clipboard.
if nargin < 2
  print('-dmeta');
else
  print('-dmeta',popt);
end
```

```
% Start a session with MSWord.
wrd=actxserver('word.application');
wrd.Visible=1;  % Watch the action...

% Open or create a document.
if ~exist(filespec,'file')
  doc=invoke(wrd.Documents,'Add');
else
  doc=invoke(wrd.Documents,'Open',filespec);
end

% Insert some text at the end of the document.
myrange=doc.Content;
myrange.InsertParagraphAfter;
invoke(myrange,'InsertAfter','---Figure Top Caption Goes Here---');
myrange.InsertParagraphAfter;
% Paste AFTER the existing text.
invoke(myrange,'Collapse',0);
% Paste with "Picture Format" (1) and "Float Over Text" (3) options.
invoke(myrange,'PasteSpecial',0,0,1,0,3);
mmyrange.InsertParagraphAfter;
invoke(myrange,'InsertAfter','---Figure Bottom Caption Goes Here---');
myrange.InsertParagraphAfter;

% Save and close the document.
if ~exist(filespec,'file')
  invoke(doc,'SaveAs',filespec,1);
else
  doc.Save;
end
doc.Close;

% Quit Word and close the server connection.
wrd.Quit;
delete(wrd);
return
```

The next example uses MATLAB as a COM client and Microsoft PowerPoint as a COM Automation server. The MATLAB M-file function addslide starts a server instance of the Microsoft PowerPoint application and opens a selected presentation (or creates a new presentation) by using the uiputfile dialog box to specify the filename. A new slide is added to the end of the presentation for each valid variable argument. Valid arguments are character strings, cell arrays of strings, 2-D numeric arrays, and figure handles. After the new slides have been added, the presentation is saved to a file and closed, the application is terminated, and the COM server object is deleted. The code is as follows:

```
function addslide(filespec,varargin)
%ADDSLIDE Insert variables into a PowerPoint presentation.
%
% ADDSLIDE(filename,var1,var2,...) Insert variables into
%   new slides at the end of a PowerPoint presentation.
%
%   An invalid or empty filename or a new filename will
%   bring up a dialog box to enable the user to select an
%   existing file or create a new file.
%
%   Inputs can be strings, cell arrays of strings, 2D numeric
%   arrays, and figure handles. Variable sizes should be limited
%   to avoid overfilling the slides.

% Check for missing arguments and initialize variables
narg=nargin;
if narg < 2, error('Missing input arguments.'); end
nl=char(13);

% Make sure we have a valid file name
if ischar(filespec) & exist(filespec,'file')   % a real file
  fullname=filespec;
else
  if ischar(filespec) & ~isempty(filespec)     % use as default file
    [dname,fname,fext]=fileparts(filespec);
    if isempty(fext), fext='.ppt'; end
    defname=fullfile(dname,[fname fext]);
```

```
  else
    defname='*.ppt';                              % use file filter
  end
  [fname,dname]=uiputfile(defname,'Modify or create the file:');
  if isequal(fname,0), return, end
  fullname=fullfile(dname,fname);
end

% Start a session with PowerPoint
ppapp=actxserver('powerpoint.application');
ppapp.Visible=1;                              % Watch the action...

% Open or create a presentation
if ~exist(fullname,'file')
  ppres=invoke(ppapp.Presentations,'Add');
else
  ppres=invoke(ppapp.Presentations,'Open',fullname);
end

% Process the rest of the arguments
for idx=2:narg
  arg=varargin{idx-1};

  if ishandle(arg) & (floor(arg)==arg)    % figure handle
    ppslide=ppres.Slides.Add(ppres.Slides.Count+1,'ppLayoutBlank');
    print('-dmeta',sprintf('-f%d',arg));  % copy plot to clipboard
    ppfig=ppslide.Shapes.Paste;           % paste the clip into the slide
    ppfig.Align(1,-1);                    % center the plot
    ppfig.IncrementTop(200);              % lower the plot
    ppfig.ScaleWidth(1.5,0,1);            % scale width from middle

  elseif isstr(arg)                       % text string
    if length(arg) > 275, warning('possible overfull slide'); end
    ppslide=ppres.Slides.Add(ppres.Slides.Count+1,'ppLayoutTitleOnly');
```

```
    ppslide.Shapes.Title.TextFrame.AutoSize=1;
    ppslide.Shapes.Title.TextFrame.VerticalAnchor=1;
    ppslide.Shapes.Title.TextFrame.TextRange.Text=arg;

  elseif iscellstr(arg)                    % cell array of strings
    ppslide=ppres.Slides.Add(ppres.Slides.Count+1,'ppLayoutTitleOnly');
    str='';
    for idx2=1:length(arg)
      str=[str,arg{idx2},nl];
    end
    if (length(arg) > 5) | (length(str) > 275)
      warning('possible overfull slide');
    end
    ppslide.Shapes.Title.TextFrame.AutoSize=1;
    ppslide.Shapes.Title.TextFrame.VerticalAnchor=1;
    ppslide.Shapes.Title.TextFrame.TextRange.Text=str(1:end-1);

  elseif isnumeric(arg) & ~all(ishandle(arg(:))) & (ndims(arg) <= 2)
    ppslide=ppres.Slides.Add(ppres.Slides.Count+1,'ppLayoutTitleOnly');
    [r,c]=size(arg);
    if numel(arg) > 20, warning('possible overfull slide'); end
    rs=int2str(r); cs=int2str(c);
    str=[sprintf('Array %s', inputname(idx)),nl,nl];
    for idx2=1:r
        str=[str, sprintf('    %5.5f',arg(idx2,:)), nl];
    end
    ppslide.Shapes.Title.TextFrame.AutoSize=1;
    ppslide.Shapes.Title.TextFrame.VerticalAnchor=1;
    ppslide.Shapes.Title.TextFrame.TextRange.Text=str;
  else
   warning([inputname(idx), ' is not an accepted input and will be ignored.'])
  end %if
end %for
```

```
% Save the file and exit
ppres.SaveAs(fullname,1,0);                % save as presentation
ppres.Close;                               % close the presentation
ppapp.Quit;                                % quit PPT
delete(ppapp);                             % done with the COM server
return
```

The final client example illustrates the use of COM events and event handlers. The cdemo function embeds an ActiveX control in a *Figure* window and performs certain actions when events are triggered. MATLAB ships with two very simple ActiveX controls (mwsamp.ocx and mwsamp2.ocx) and associated type libraries (mwsamp.tlb and mwsamp2.tlb) stored in the $MATLAB\bin\win32 directory. The Mwsamp class contains one event (Click) and three variables (Label, Radius, and MMPropertyContainer). The MMPropertyContainer is a Java object containing various properties of the control. The Mwsamp2 class is an expanded version of the Mwsamp class and adds two events (DblClick and MouseDown) and one variable (Ret_IDispatch) containing an interface function.

When an event is triggered by an ActiveX control, MATLAB passes a number of arguments to the event handler, including the name of the object, a numerical event identifier, zero or more event arguments, an event structure containing additional information about the event, and the event name as the final argument. The number and names of the event arguments are specific to the ActiveX control object. (Refer to the MATLAB documentation for more details about these arguments.)

The cdemo function creates a new *Figure* window containing a surf plot, embeds an MWSAMP2 control in the corner of the *Figure* window, sets some control properties, and exits. When a mouse-click event is detected within the control, the cdemo function is called again to service the callback. The control is deleted when the *Figure* window is closed. Following is the code:

```
function cdemo(varargin)
%CDEMO Sample function to manage an ActiveX object.
%  Function to create a sample ActiveX control. The function creates
%  a figure window, adds a nice plot, creates an MWSAMP control,
%  embeds the control in the Figure window, sets the 'Label' and
%  'Radius' properties of the control, and invokes the 'Redraw'
%  method on the control.
```

```
%
% CDEMO is also the event handler for this control. The three events
% fired by the control are 'Click', 'DblClick', and 'MouseDown'.
% The event handler changes the text message in the control when
% a valid event is fired.
% The control is deleted when the figure window is closed.

% Keep track of a few things between calls.
persistent numclicks h

if nargin == 0       % Initial call -- do the setup.

  % Create a new figure window and draw a nice plot.
  f = figure;
  surf(peaks);
  numclicks=0;

  % Embed an MWSAMP2 ActiveX control in the lower left corner
  % of the Figure window and set the callback to recall this
  % function (cdemo).
  h = actxcontrol('MWSAMP.MwsampCtrl.2',[0 0 90 90],f,'cdemo');

  % Set the initial label and circle radius in the control
  % showing two methods of setting the property values.
  set(h, 'Label', 'Click Here');
  h.Radius=28;

  % Tell the control to redraw itself by invoking the Redraw method.
  invoke(h, 'Redraw');

else    % This part handles the callback. For each valid event
        % detected, the last argument will be a string that
        % resolves to the event name.
```

```
  if strcmp(varargin{end},'Click')
    % Increment the click total.
    numclicks = numclicks + 1;
    h.Label=['Click #',num2str(numclicks)];

  elseif strcmp(varargin{end},'DblClick')
    % Decrement the click total by 2. The first of the pair
    % generated a Click event and incremented by 1. The second
    % click within the time limit generated this DblClick event.
    numclicks = numclicks - 2;
    h.Label=['Click #',num2str(numclicks)];

  elseif strcmp(varargin{end},'MouseDown')
    % Display the x,y coordinates of the mouse pointer.
    h.Label=['(x,y)=(',num2str(varargin{5}),',',num2str(varargin{6}),')'];

  else
    error('Invalid input.');
  end
  % Redraw the control.
  h.Redraw;
end
```

MATLAB as COM Server

MATLAB can act as a COM Automation server when called by a COM client such as Visual Basic, Visual Basic for Applications, Visual C++, or even MATLAB itself. Microsoft Excel, Microsoft Access, or another COM client application can be an Automation controller as well. The client application can start and stop an instance of MATLAB, pass arrays to and from the MATLAB workspace, and execute MATLAB commands in the MATLAB workspace. In many ways, this functionality is identical to that provided by the MATLAB Engine. In fact, any application you build by using C or FORTRAN should use the MATLAB Engine interface rather than the COM interface to MATLAB. The COM interface should be reserved for use by applications that cannot access MATLAB as a server in any other way.

The registered MATLAB COM object name is **matlab.application**. MATLAB provides the following Automation methods to COM client applications:

Function	Description
`Execute`	Execute a MATLAB command contained in a string argument in the server
`Feval`	Evaluate a MATLAB command that cannot be contained in a single string in the server; examples include commands that use values contained in local variables unknown in the MATLAB server workspace
`GetCharArray`	Get a character array from the server
`GetFullMatrix`	Get a matrix from the server; returns a SAFEARRAY data type
`GetWorkspaceData`	Get data from the server workspace; returns a variant data type
`MaximizeCommandWindow`	Display the server window on the Windows desktop
`MinimizeCommandWindow`	Minimize the size of the server window
`PutCharArray`	Store a character array in the server
`PutFullMatrix`	Store a matrix in the server
`PutWorkspaceData`	Store data in the server workspace
`Quit`	Terminate the MATLAB server

This list of methods, along with the calling syntax, can be obtained by using the `invoke` function on a `COM.matlab_application` object handle. Properties of a MATLAB COM server can be obtained by using MATLAB as a COM client. Both of these uses are illustrated in the following code:

```
>> mlapp=actxserver('matlab.application')

mlapp =

    COM.matlab_application

>> get(mlapp)
    Visible: 1

>> mlapp.methods
```

```
Methods for class COM.matlab_application:

Execute                   evalc        send
GetCharArray              events       set
GetFullMatrix             fieldnames   setdiff
MaximizeCommandWindow     findstr      setxor
MinimizeCommandWindow     get          sort
PutCharArray              interfaces   str2double
PutFullMatrix             intersect    str2num
Quit                      invoke       strcmp
addproperty               isletter     strcmpi
char                      ismember     strmatch
ctranspose                isspace      strncmp
delete                    load         strncmpi
deleteproperty            move         transpose
diag                      ne           tril
disp                      permute      triu
display                   propedit     unique
double                    release
eq                        reshape
eval                      save

>> mlapp.fieldnames
ans =

    'Visible'
```

A MATLAB COM server does not support any events:

```
>> mlapp.events
```

Example

This is an example of an Excel macro that starts MATLAB as an Automation server, passes the contents of cells B3:E8 to a MATLAB array, squares the contents of the array, passes back the result, and inserts the result in cells B12:E17 in the Excel spreadsheet. It also passes a string value obtained from cell B1 to MATLAB, appends " squared (in MATLAB)" to the string, passes back the result, and inserts this result in cell B10. The MATLAB server is then closed. The code is as follows:

```
Sub Square()
'
' Square Macro
' Square the contents of cells B3:E8 and place the result in B12:E17.
' Also append the phrase " squared (in MATLAB)" to a string from B1
' and place the result in B10.

' First define the variables.
Dim MatLab As Object
Dim Result, NewString As String
Dim MReal(6, 4) As Double
Dim MImag() As Double
Dim RealValue As Double
Dim i, j As Integer

' Invoke MATLAB.
Set MatLab = CreateObject("Matlab.Application")

' Fill the Mreal array with data from the sheet.
For i = 0 To 5
  For j = 0 To 3
    Real(i,j)=ActiveSheet.Range(Cells(i+3,j+2),Cells(i+3,j+2)).Value
  Next j
Next i
```

```
' Send the string and data from the spreadsheet to MATLAB.
Call MatLab.PutCharArray("instr", "base", ActiveSheet.Range("B1:B1").Value)
Call MatLab.PutFullMatrix("a", "base", MReal, Mimag)

' Send MATLAB some commands to execute.
Result = MatLab.Execute("b=a.^2;")
Result = MatLab.Execute("outstr=[instr, ' squared (in MATLAB)']")

' Retrieve the results and stuff them into spreadsheet cells.
Call MatLab.GetFullMatrix("b", "base", MReal, MImag)
ActiveSheet.Range("B12:E17").Value = MReal
ActiveSheet.Range("B10:B10").Value = MatLab.GetCharArray("outstr", "base")
'
End Sub
```

Suppose the Sub Square() macro is applied to the following spreadsheet:

	Input array of numeric values			
	1	2	3	4
	2	3	4	5
	3	4	5	6
	4	5	6	7
	5	6	7	8
	6	7	8	9

The results after the macro is run are as follows:

	Input array of numeric values			
	1	2	3	4
	2	3	4	5
	3	4	5	6
	4	5	6	7
	5	6	7	8
	6	7	8	9
	Input array of numeric values squared (in MATLAB)			
	1	4	9	16
	4	9	16	25
	9	16	25	36
	16	25	36	49
	25	36	49	64
	36	49	64	81

Of course, this example is of very limited practical value. However, it provides a solid foundation for further development.

> An easy way to create a VBA macro is to record a new macro and edit the resulting VBA code. For example, open Excel and select the menu item **Tools/Macro/Record New Macro . . .** Give your macro a name in the dialog box (the previous example used the name "Square") and click on the OK button. Then, click on the Stop Recording button in the next dialog box. This creates an empty macro. Next, select the **Tools/Macro/Macros . . .** menu item and click on the **Edit** button. Now you can edit the macro, save the result, and run the macro whenever you wish.

The Visual Basic environment provides some tools that help determine the appropriate objects and methods for communicating with other COM applications in addition to the MATLAB `get` and `invoke` methods previously illustrated. The Object Browser can be used to determine the objects available in each of the object libraries (such as the Excel library or the MSForms library). The objects and members (properties, events, and functions) are searchable, and context-sensitive help is available.

36.2 DYNAMIC DATA EXCHANGE

Prior to the client/server capabilities of COM, Microsoft created a mostly peer-to-peer interapplication communication protocol called Dynamic Data Exchange. DDE enables two cooperating applications to exchange data and execution strings (commands) by using the Windows clipboard. One application can also register a request for notification of updates when certain data change in the other application. This DDE functionality has been incorporated into the more flexible COM protocol. DDE is still supported for existing code, but COM is normally used for new implementations.

DDE connections between applications are called ***conversations***. Each application has a unique ***service name*** to identify the application. Each conversation is identified by a service name and a ***topic*** known to both applications. Each application supports a System topic, and most support one or more additional topics. The application that initiates a DDE request is designated the ***client***, and the application that answers the request is designated the ***server*** for the duration of the conversation.

A typical DDE conversation starts with application A requesting a conversation with an instance of application B. The conversation consists of a service name/topic pair. If application B (identified by service name) recognizes the topic, then it establishes a conversation with application A. The elements of the conversation are items that are passed between the applications by using the Windows clipboard. All applications support the Text format for data exchange. Some applications support additional data formats, such as Bitmap and MetaFilePict for graphics and XLTable format for Excel spreadsheet data. MATLAB supports only the Text format when operating as a DDE client, but supports Text, XLTable, and MetaFilePict formats when operating as a DDE server.

A COM connection request can invoke an instance of an application (launch the application) to service a client request, but a DDE conversation can be initiated only between applications that are already running.

MATLAB as a DDE Client

The DDE functions supported by MATLAB are listed in the following table:

Function	Description
`ddeadv`	Set up an advisory link between MATLAB and a DDE server application
`ddeexec`	Send an execution string to a DDE server application
`ddeinit`	Initiate a DDE conversation between MATLAB and another application
`ddepoke`	Send data from MATLAB to a DDE server application

ddereq	Request data from a DDE server application
ddeterm	Terminate a DDE conversation between MATLAB and a server application
ddeunadv	Release an advisory link between MATLAB and a DDE server application

These functions are used by MATLAB to manage DDE connections to other applications acting as DDE servers. Examples of DDE servers include Microsoft Excel, Word, Access, PowerPoint, and even another instance of MATLAB.

As a server, Microsoft Excel supports two kinds of topics: the System topic and a topic consisting of the name of a workbook that is open in Excel or the name of a spreadsheet in the open workbook. A Microsoft Excel item is any cell reference—an individual cell or a range of cells. Microsoft Word supports the System topic and the name of an open document in Word. A Microsoft Word item is any bookmark in the open document. (Consult the on-line help or the printed documentation for these and other DDE applications for details about the topics and the items they support.)

The following is an example of a DDE conversation between MATLAB (the client) and an open copy of Excel (the server); first, we request a connection to the System topic (every DDE application supports the System topic):

```
>> xls = ddeinit('excel','system')
>> xls =
     4.7836e-299
```

The return value is the handle assigned to the conversation. A failed request returns a handle value of 0. Next, we request a list of the items available under the System topic by using the standard SysItems item. The optional third argument is a format vector. The first element indicates the clipboard format (1 for Text—the only format supported by MATLAB as a client). The second element determines how the result is stored: as 0 to interpret the data as numerical values (the default) or as 1 to interpret the data as a character string. These requests are for items that return tab-delimited character strings. Here is the code:

```
>> s = ddereq(xls,'SysItems',[1 1])
s =
SysItems    Topics   Status   Formats Selection   Protocols    EditEnvItems
```

Query each of them for more detail:

```
>> t = ddereq(xls,'Topics',[1 1])
t =
[Book1]Sheet1    [Book1]Sheet2    [Book1]Sheet3    System
```

```
>> t = ddereq(xls,'Status',[1 1])
t =
Ready

>> t = ddereq(xls,'Formats',[1 1])
t =
XlTable Microsoft Excel 8.0 Format  BIFF4 Biff3 SYLK Wk1 Csv Unicode Text
Text    Rich Text Format     DIF Bitmap  Picture (Enhanced Metafile)
Printer_Picture Screen Picture EMF

>> t = ddereq(xls,'Selection',[1 1])
t =
[Book1]Sheet1!R1C1

>> t = ddereq(xls,'Protocols',[1 1])
t =
StdFileEditing  Embedding

>> t = ddereq(xls,'EditenvItems',[1 1])
t =
StdHostNames    StdTargetDevice StdDocDimensions
```

Close the connection:

```
>> status = ddeterm(xls)
status =
     1
```

This shows that the open workbook named Book1 contains three worksheets, named Sheet1, Sheet2, and Sheet3; that Excel is ready to converse; that Excel supports many clipboard formats; that the currently selected cell is row 1, column 1; and other details. Excel supports the System topic and one topic for each of the available worksheets. The worksheet topics support only one item type—a range of cells.

The next example opens a conversation with one of the worksheets. First, create a magic square and plot the resulting surface:

```
>> m = magic(10);
>> h = surf(m);
```

Open a connection to a worksheet and insert the data into a range of cells:

```
>> xl = ddeinit('excel','Sheet1');
>> range = 'r1c1:r10c10';
>> status = ddepoke(xl,range,m);
```

Now set up an advisory link between the spreadsheet data and MATLAB to trigger a callback if any data in the range of cells change:

```
>> status = ddeadv(xl,range,'disp(''Spreadsheet data change alert!'')');
```

The third argument is the callback passed to `eval`. Now, anytime a change is made to the contents of one or more of these cells in the spreadsheet, a message is displayed in the *Command* window.

Next, close this link and open another. This time, when a change is made to the spreadsheet, the link passes the range of data back to MATLAB in the variable `z` and the callback updates the plot with the new data. The presence of the fourth argument notifies the server to send back data, in addition to sending a signal to MATLAB to execute the callback. The code is as follows:

```
>> status = ddeunadv(xl,range);
>> status = ddeadv(xl,range,'set(h,''ZData'',z);
          set(h,''CData'',z);','z');
```

Make some extensive changes to the data to see the effect on the plot:

```
>> range1 = 'r1c1:r9c9';
>> status = ddepoke(xl,range1,magic(9));
```

Change some data yourself to see how it affects the plot.

The `ddeexec` function passes a command to the DDE server to be evaluated. For example, the code

```
>> status = ddeexec(xl,'[formula.goto(''r3c5'')]'');
```

makes the cell in row 3, column 5, the current cell. (Consult the documentation for your DDE server application for a list of supported commands.)

When you are finished, close the link and terminate the conversation:

```
>> status = ddeunadv(xl,range);
>> status = ddeterm(xl);
```

MATLAB as a DDE Server

The DDE service name for MATLAB is, naturally enough, **MATLAB**. MATLAB supports two topics, System and Engine, when operating as a DDE server. The valid items for each of these topics are listed in the following table:

Topic	Item	Description
`System`	`SysItems`	A tab-delimited list of items supported under the System topic (`SysItems`, `Format`, and `Topics`)
	`Format`	A tab-delimited list of supported formats (`Text`, `MetaFilePict`, and `XLTable`)
	`Topics`	A tab-delimited list of supported topics (`System` and `Engine`)
`Engine`	`EngEvalString`	Item name (if required by the client calling syntax) when a command is sent for evaluation
	`EngStringResult`	String result of a DDE `execute` command
	`EngFigureResult`	Graphical result of a DDE `execute` command
	`<matrixname>`	The name of the matrix to be created, updated, or returned

DDE client applications open a conversation with MATLAB by using the service name **MATLAB** and either the System or Engine topic. The MATLAB Engine topic supports the following three client request operations: sending data to MATLAB, receiving data from MATLAB, and sending a command to MATLAB to be executed.

The client can send data by using a DDE `poke` operation, where the item is the name of the matrix to create or update and the format of the poke data is Text or XLTable. Text format data should be in tab-delimited ASCII format with CR/LF row delimiters, while XLTable format accepts any Excel binary data format. The client can request data from MATLAB by using the DDE `request` operation in three forms. To request the contents of an array, the item is the name of the matrix to send, and the data format is Text or XLTable. To request the text output from a previous MATLAB command, the item is `EngStringResult`, using the Text format. To request graphical output from a previous MATLAB command, the item is `EngFigureResult` and the format is MetaFilePict. Some clients are able to receive only Text from a `request` operation. For these clients, MATLAB provides the ability to specify item `EngFigureResult` with the Text format. In this case, the result is a status string. If the string is "Yes", the figure is available on the clipboard for the client to retrieve. If the operation fails, the text returned is "No".

The client can send a command to MATLAB by using the DDE `execute` operation. The item is `EngEvalString` and the format of the command is Text. Some clients omit the item and just send the command. MATLAB accepts either form. (Consult the documentation for your DDE client application or programming language for the appropriate syntax for writing DDE programs or functions to connect to an instance of MATLAB.)

36.3 MATLAB NOTEBOOK

Tha MATLAB Notebook is an easy way to create a report or other document and embed MATLAB commands, command output, and graphics. The MATLAB Notebook provides direct access to MATLAB as a COM Automation server from within a Microsoft Word document without requiring that you actually write your own C or FORTRAN programs. Microsoft Word is the only word processor supported by the MATLAB Notebook and must be purchased and installed separately on your Windows PC or Macintosh OS X computer. Using the Notebook, you can create a report with MATLAB commands and the resulting MATLAB output imbedded within the document itself. The Notebook is implemented by using a predefined collection of Microsoft Word macros and COM controls that allow you to connect to a MATLAB session from a Word document called an M-book. This functionality is automatically available when you install MATLAB on a `win32` PC platform along with Microsoft Word or Office

The Notebook uses a Microsoft Word template to embed controls within your document. The command `notebook -setup` initializes the Notebook. You are prompted to select the version of Word you are using (97, 2000, or 2002). MATLAB will then attempt to determine the location of the installation and install the correct version of a template file. If the executable cannot be found, the installation script requests the location of the Microsoft Word program (by using a file requester) and the location of a template file (such as `normal.dot`) by using another file requester. After verification, the correct template file (called `m-book.dot`) is copied into the appropriate directory. The next time you use the `notebook` command, the Microsoft Word application is opened using the `m-book.dot` template. If a filename argument is supplied, Word attempts to open the requested file. If no argument is supplied, a new M-book document is opened.

Notebook support is not enabled in MATLAB 7 on the Macintosh platform; the `notebook` command is PC-specific in this version. The capability is there, however, and we expect that Macintosh support will be added in a future release.

When an M-book is opened by using the `notebook` command from MATLAB or by opening an existing M-book from Microsoft Word, a MATLAB server session is started and a new **Notebook** menu appears next to the **Table** menu in the Word application menus. The **Notebook** menu items enable such operations as defining or undefining MATLAB input statements or ***cells***, grouping and ungrouping these cells, defining calculation zones within the document, and evaluating cells, calculation zones, or the entire M-book. When an input cell is evaluated, the statement is sent to the MATLAB server for evaluation, and the results (either the command-line results, a plot, or both) are inserted into the M-book document following the input statement. Notebook preferences can also be set from the **Notebook** menu.

> To create a new M-book without using the `notebook` command from MATLAB, start Word and select **Templates and Add-Ins . . .** from the **Tools** menu. (If `mbook.dot` is not listed in the **Global templates** area, click on the **Add . . .** button and select the `m-book` file.) Select the `m-book.dot` template (a checkmark will appear) and close the dialog box. The **Notebook** menu will appear and the document becomes an M-book. Save the file and close Word.

For example, consider the following illustrative M-book:

MATLAB Notebook Example 1

Assignment #2

```
Create a 3-by-3 magic square

   m=magic(3)

square the elements of the magic square

   m2=m.^2

and plot the result

   plot(1:9,m2(:))
```

Select one of the MATLAB statements, and then select the **Notebook/Define Input Cell** menu item. This defines the selected text as an *input cell*—a MATLAB statement to be evaluated. After each of the MATLAB statements has been defined as an input cell, the resulting M-book appears as follows:

MATLAB Notebook Example 1

Assignment #2

```
Create a 3-by-3 magic square

      [m=magic(3) ]

square the elements of the magic square

      [m2=m.^2 ]

and plot the result

      [plot(1:9,m2(:)) ]
```

The command text in the input cells changes to a fixed-point font, and the cells are delimited by special bold square brackets. (The brackets do not appear when the document is printed.) If the **Notebook/Evaluate M-book** menu item is then selected, the application connects to an open MATLAB session (or starts a new MATLAB session), evaluates the MATLAB statements, and inserts the results into the M-book:

MATLAB Notebook Example 1

Assignment #2

```
Create a 3-by-3 magic square

      [m=magic(3) ]
```

```
[m =

     8     1     6
     3     5     7
     4     9     2 ]

square the elements of the magic square

          [m2=m.^2 ]

[m2 =

    64     1    36
     9    25    49
    16    81     4 ]

and plot the result

          [plot(1:9,m2(:)) ]
```

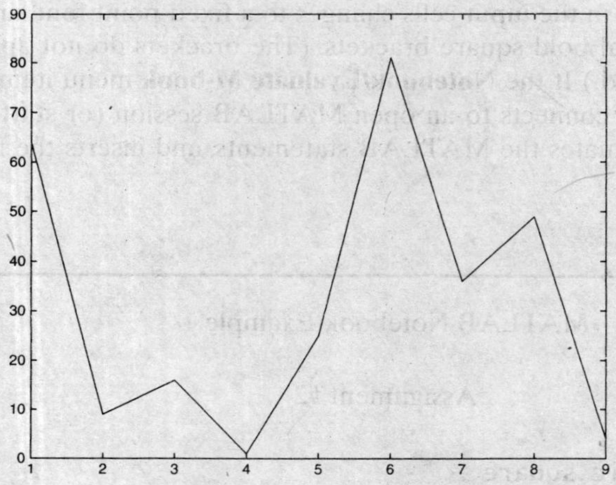

The Notebook can be used to create an annotated record of a MATLAB session (think of it as a *very* fancy `diary` command) or to insert MATLAB examples into a report. Any changes made to an input cell are reflected in the output cell whenever the input cell is evaluated. In that respect, an M-book is a dynamic document.

All M-books in a Word session share a single server instance of MATLAB, and all share the same MATLAB workspace. Thus, if you have multiple documents open, all variables are shared among all M-books; a change to a variable in one M-book is a change to variables of the same name in other M-books. Also, since you can define and undefine input cells and calculation zones, data dependencies can be easily broken by these changes. The **Purge Output Cells** and **Evaluate M-book** menu items should be selected periodically to ensure data consistency. When you evaluate any input cell or an entire M-book, text output is replaced, but graphical output is replicated. For example, if the example M-book document is evaluated a second time without first purging the output cells, the document will contain two graphs at the end.

36.4 MATLAB COM-RELATED TOOLBOXES

The MathWorks Inc. sells a product called *Excel Link* as an extra-cost toolbox that provides functionality similar to that of the MATLAB Notebook for the Microsoft Excel spreadsheet application. Data exchange and MATLAB commands can be easily controlled from within Excel. If your work requires moving large amounts of data between Excel and MATLAB or using MATLAB to perform complex calculations on Excel data, the time saved by purchasing *Excel Link* may be well worth the cost of the toolbox.

Other COM-related toolboxes are available as extra-cost additions to MATLAB. MATLAB COM Builder can be used to convert MATLAB algorithms to Common Object Model (COM) objects that are accessible from any COM-based application. MATLAB Excel Builder converts complex MATLAB algorithms into independent Excel add-ins. The MATLAB Report Generator lets you create standard and customized reports from your MATLAB models and organize data in multiple output formats, including HTML, RTF, XML, and SGML. All of these toolboxes consist of collections of functions built upon the techniques and functions previously described.

36.5 SUMMARY

The simplicity of using pipes to connect the standard input and standard output of applications on UNIX and Linux platforms has enabled widespread interapplication communication for many years. Standardized protocols for communication between applications on the Windows PC platform are now available as well.

MATLAB supports the Microsoft Dynamic Data Exchange and COM protocols to enable MATLAB to operate as a client or as a server for other DDE or COM-enabled applications, such as Microsoft Word, Excel, and PowerPoint. Extra-cost toolboxes are available to enhance your ability to easily integrate MATLAB with other COM-enabled applications.

37

Getting Help

With each major release of the software, the help capabilities of MATLAB have improved significantly. MATLAB 7 is no exception. Historically, help text was simply displayed in the *Command* window by using the function `help` and `lookfor`. As versions have changed, old help functions have changed, too. Some have become obsolete, and others that have been grandfathered now do different things. This chapter introduces the primary help capabilities available in MATLAB, including resources available via the Internet.

37.1 *COMMAND* WINDOW HELP

Before MATLAB included GUI features, help was available in the *Command* window by using the functions `help` and `lookfor`. These basic functions remain available today. For example, the code

```
>> help sqrt

 SQRT   Square root.
    SQRT(X) is the square root of the elements of X. Complex
    results are produced if X is not positive.

    See also SQRTM.
```

shows the help text for the function `sqrt`. In general, the function `help` is useful if you know the name of a particular function, but are unsure of its input or output arguments. In the previous example, function names are capitalized only to give them visual distinction. All functions in MATLAB are case sensitive. For example, the code

```
>> SQRT(2)
??? Undefined command/function 'SQRT'
```

shows that MATLAB does not recognize SQRT as the square root function.

If you are unsure which function performs a given task, but you know a keyword that is related to the function, the function `lookfor` is helpful:

```
>> lookfor inverse
INVHILB Inverse Hilbert matrix.
ACOS    Inverse cosine.
ACOSH   Inverse hyperbolic cosine.
ACOT    Inverse cotangent.
ACOTH   Inverse hyperbolic cotangent.
ACSC    Inverse cosecant.
ACSCH   Inverse hyperbolic cosecant.
ASEC    Inverse secant.
ASECH   Inverse hyperbolic secant.
ASIN    Inverse sine.
ASINH   Inverse hyperbolic sine.
ATAN    Inverse tangent.
ATAN2   Four quadrant inverse tangent.
ATANH   Inverse hyperbolic tangent.
ERFCINV Inverse complementary error function.
ERFINV  Inverse error function.
INV     Matrix inverse.
PINV    Pseudoinverse.
IFFT Inverse discrete Fourier transform.
IFFT2 Two-dimensional inverse discrete Fourier transform.
IFFTN N-dimensional inverse discrete Fourier transform.
IFFTSHIFT Inverse FFT shift.
IPERMUTE Inverse permute array dimensions.
UPDHESS Performs the Inverse Hessian Update.
INVHESS Inverse of an upper Hessenberg matrix.
```

The function `lookfor` opens all of the function M-files on the MATLAB search path, looks for the given keyword on the first comment line (i.e., the H1 help line), and returns the lines where a match is found.

37.2 THE HELP BROWSER

In newer versions of MATLAB, help functions beyond `help` and `lookfor` have been consolidated in the Help Browser or simply in the *Help* window. This window can be opened by choosing **Help** from the **Window** menu on the MATLAB desktop or by typing `helpwin`, `helpdesk`, or `doc` at the MATLAB prompt. In addition to supplying a text area for displaying help text, the *Help* window offers a help navigator that contains user-selectable tabs for *Contents, Index, Search*, and *Demos*. The *Contents* tab provides a table of contents to all on-line documentation for MATLAB and all toolboxes. The *Index* tab provides an index to all on-line help entries. The *Search* tab allows you to search on-line documentation. Finally, the *Demos* tab provides an interface to MATLAB demo functions. These features are easier to explore firsthand than they are to illustrate in a text, so users are encouraged to explore the Help Browser for themselves.

The *Help* window equivalent to the function `help` is `helpwin`. For example, the code

```
>> helpwin mmpadd
```

displays the same help text as `help mmpadd`, but it does so in the *Help* window. Behind the scenes, MATLAB opens the file `mmpadd.m`, reads the help text found there, converts the file to HTML format, and displays the HTML text in the *Help* window. In the process, capitalized function names are converted to lowercase and functions listed on the `See also` line are converted to HTML links to the named functions. In addition, if the function has more extensive on-line documentation, a link to that documentation appears at the top of the displayed help text. If you create your own toolbox or collection of function M-files, `helpwin` will display help text (as described here) for these functions as well. If the argument to `helpwin` is the name of a toolbox directory, the `Contents.m` file in that directory is opened and displayed in the *Help* window.

The function `doc` bypasses M-file help text and goes directly to on-line documentation. For example, the code

```
>> doc print
```

displays the on-line documentation for the function `print`, which contains much more information than is available from `helpwin print`.

The functions `whatsnew` and `whatsnew` *`toolbox`* display release notes and last-minute changes for MATLAB or a selected toolbox in the *Help* window. Behind the scenes, `whatsnew` *`toolbox`* opens and displays the `Readme.m` file for the toolbox in the *Help* window.

37.3 INTERNET RESOURCES

The Mathworks Inc., the makers of MATLAB, was one of the first 100 commercial sites on the Internet. Their website, `http://www.mathworks.com`, provides a wealth of information covering all aspects of MATLAB. There is simply too much on their website to discuss here. In addition, as with most sites, features and links come and go, making it difficult to accurately describe what is available at any given time. Two of the most useful features of *The Mathworks Inc.* website are the solution search engine, which provides answers to common technical support questions, and the repository of user-contributed and Mathworks-contributed function M-files, called *MATLAB Central*. You should be able to find *Mastering MATLAB 7* listed on their website as well.

If you are in the middle of a MATLAB session, you need not leave MATLAB to go to their website. The MATLAB Help Browser accepts URLs and serves as a simple web browser. Alternatively, any other web browser will do.

In addition to the wealth of information on *The Mathworks Inc.* website, the Internet newsgroup `comp.soft-sys.matlab` is an unmoderated forum for discussion of MATLAB topics. Access to this newsgroup requires software and access to newsgroups. Alternatively, the newsgroup can be accessed through *MATLAB Central*. Many very knowledgeable people monitor the MATLAB newsgroup regularly and contribute answers to posted questions. The MATLAB newsgroup is a good place to ask questions that are not easily answered through on-line help. Before posting to the newsgroup, it is beneficial to follow conventional newsgroup etiquette. In addition, many common questions can be answered by consulting the newsgroup Frequently-Asked-Questions (FAQ) list, which can be found at the URL `www.mit.edu/~pwb/cssm/matlab-faq.html`.

37.4 *MASTERING MATLAB 7* HELP

In addition to the help capabilities available in MATLAB, the authors of this text provide two services. First, we maintain the *Mastering MATLAB* website at `http://www.eece.maine.edu/mm`. At this website, you will find a downloadable collection of script M-files to generate all of the figures in the text. These M-files spare you from having to type all of the code found in the text into the *Command* window. In addition, the Java, MEX, and function M-file code that appears in the text is available for downloading. You can also find a listing of errata for the text, as well as links to other MATLAB-related areas on the Internet. Second, the authors provide an email address, `mm@eece.maine.edu`, for your comments and feedback. We encourage you to submit errata, to give us feedback that will help us make the next edition of the text better, and to ask questions about the examples and content of *Mastering MATLAB 7*. You may submit general questions about MATLAB as well, but we might not provide an answer if that answer can be found easily by using the documentation that comes with MATLAB, in the MATLAB FAQ, or in the MATLAB newsgroup archive.

37.5 SUMMARY

The following table summarizes the important aspects of this chapter:

Item	Description
`help` *functionname*	Display help for the function `functionname` in the *Command* window
`lookfor` *keyword*	Keyword search of M-files, using the string `keyword`
`helpwin` *functionname*	Display help for the function `functionname` in the *Help* window
`doc functionname`	Display online help for the function `functionname` in the *Help* window
`helpbrowser, helpdesk`	Open the *Help* window to the documentation homepage
`whatsnew`	Display Release Notes or `Readme.m` toolbox file
`http://www.mathworks.com`	*The Mathworks Inc.* website
`comp.soft-sys.matlab`	The MATLAB newsgroup
`www.mit.edu/~pwb/cssm/matlab-faq.html`	The MATLAB newsgroup FAQ
`http://www.eece.maine.edu/mm`	*Mastering MATLAB 7* website
`mm@eece.maine.edu`	E-mail to *Mastering MATLAB 7* authors

38

Examples, Examples, Examples

It's been said that a picture is worth a thousand words. Likewise, when it comes to software, an example is worth a thousand words. This chapter is devoted to extensive examples. Some of the examples demonstrate ***vectorization***, which is the process of writing code that maximizes the use of array operations. Other examples illustrate creating code that maximizes the benefits achieved from MATLAB's ***JIT-Accelerator*** features. Still other examples demonstrate the solution of typical problems. Before considering the examples, it is beneficial to introduce vectorization and JIT-acceleration.

38.1 VECTORIZATION

Vectorization means to write or rewrite code so that scalar operations on array elements are replaced by array operations. For example, the code

```
>> for i=1:n
      y(i) = sin(2*pi*i/m);
   end
```

is replaced by the *vectorized* code

```
>> i = 1:n;
>> y = sin(2*pi*i/m);
```

The preceding For Loop represents poor programming practice. Not only is the For Loop unnecessary (as shown by its vectorized equivalent), but it's also very slow, since memory is reallocated for the variable y each time through the loop.

Contrary to what some may believe, vectorization does not mean eliminating *all* For Loops. For Loops serve a very useful purpose; after all, MATLAB wouldn't include them as a control flow structure if they didn't. For Loops are a good choice when the loop makes full use of JIT-acceleration features. When that is not possible, For Loops are often a good choice when (1) the amount of code to be interpreted within the loop is small, especially if this code requires substantial floating-point operations; (2) the code within the loop makes minimum calls to M-file functions; (3) no memory is allocated or reallocated after the first pass through the loop; or (4) using a For Loop eliminates the need to create arrays larger than the computer can access with minimum delay. Obviously, the last case is not only platform-dependent, but also dependent on the hardware attributes of an individual platform.

While vectorization leads to efficient MATLAB programming, it does have a down side. That is, vectorized code is often more difficult to read or follow. The previous example is clearly an exception to this fact—the vectorized code is much easier to read than the nonvectorized code. The example represents a simple, easy-to-learn vectorization. Most often, it is the more difficult or less obvious vectorization challenges that lead to code that is more difficult to follow.

Vectorizing code makes use of a small number of MATLAB operators and functions. These operators and functions generally involve the manipulation of indices or the replication of arrays and can be divided into three categories, as shown in the following tables (the first two categories are basic, internal MATLAB capabilities and are therefore fast; the last category consists of optimized M-file code for implementing common array manipulation functions):

Operator	Description
:	Colon notation. `n:m` creates a row array that starts with `n` and ends with `m`. `n:inc:m` creates a row array that starts with `n`, counts by `inc`, and ends at or before `m`. As an array index, `:` means take all elements. Also, `A(:)` on the right-hand side of an equal sign means reshape `A` as a column vector. On the left-hand side of an equal sign, `A(:)` means fill contents of `A` with results of the right-hand side without reallocating memory for `A`.
.'	Nonconjugate transpose. Exchanges rows for columns.
[ ]	Brackets. Array concatenation. Slower than using `cat(...)`.

Built-in Function	Description
`all(x)`	True if all elements of `x` are nonzero
`any(x)`	True if any elements of `x` are nonzero
`cat(Dim,A,B, ...)`	Concatenate `A, B, ...` along dimension `Dim` (faster than `[ ]`)

Built-in Function	Description
`cumsum(x)`	Cumulative sum of elements of vector `x`
`diff(x)`	Difference between elements in `x`
`end`	Last index; inside array index identifies the last element along given dimension
`find(x)`, `find(x,n)` `find(x,n, 'last')`	Find indices where `x` is nonzero (usually slower than using the logical argument `x` directly for array addressing)
`logical(x)`	Convert `x` to logical data type to enable logical array addressing
`permute(A,Order)`	Generalized transpose; rearrange the dimensions of `A` so that they are in the order specified by the vector `Order`
`prod(x)`	Product of elements in `x`
`reshape(A,r,c)`	Reshape array `A` to be `r`-by-`c`
`sort(x)` `sort(x, 'descend')`	Sort array `x` in ascending or descending order
`sum(x)`	Sum of elements in `x`

M-file Functions	Description
`ind2sub(Size,idx)`	Convert single indices in `idx` to array subscripts of an array having dimensions `Size`
`ipermute(A,Order)`	Generalized transpose; inverse of `permute(A,Order)`
`kron(A,B)`	Kronecker tensor product of `A` and `B`
`meshgrid(x,y)`	Mesh domain generation from vectors `x` and `y`
`repmat(A,r,c)`	Replicate array `A` creating an `r`-by-`c` block array
`shiftdim(A,n)`	Shift dimensions of `A` by integer `n`
`squeeze(x)`	Remove singleton dimensions from array A
`sub2ind(Size,r,c)`	Convert array subscripts `r` and `c` of an array having dimensions `Size` to single indices

Using the above operators, built-in functions, and M-file functions, vectorization involves the substitution of scalar operations with equivalent array operations when such operations increase execution speed.

38.2 JIT-ACCELERATION

Starting with MATLAB 6.5, improvements were made to the MATLAB interpreter to minimize the processing overhead involved in executing loops. These improvements are collectively known as the ***JIT-Accelerator***. As stated in the documentation, these improvements will appear over a series of MATLAB releases. At this time, the JIT-Accelerator offers significant improvements for a subset of MATLAB syntax, data types, and array sizes. MATLAB code containing loops benefits from JIT-acceleration if it has the following features and properties:

1. The loop structure is a For Loop.
2. The loop contains only logical data, character string data, double-precision real data, and less than 64-bit integer data.
3. The loop uses arrays that are three-dimensional or less.
4. All variables within a loop are defined prior to loop execution.
5. Memory for all variables within the loop are preallocated, and maintain constant size and data type for all loop iterations.
6. Loop indices are scalar quantities (e.g., the index `i` in `for i=1:N`).
7. Only built-in MATLAB functions are called within the loop.
8. Conditional statements using *if-then-else* or *switch-case* constructions involve scalar comparisons.
9. All lines within the block contain no more than one assignment statement.

JIT-acceleration provides the greatest benefit when the arrays addressed within the loop are relatively small. As array sizes increase, computational time increases and the percentage of time spent on processing overhead decreases, thereby leading to less dramatic improvements in overall execution time.

38.3 UP-DOWN SEQUENCE

As a first example, consider the following simple algorithm: Let N be some positive integer. If N is even, divide it by 2. On the other hand, if it is odd, multiply it by 3 and add 1. Repeat until N becomes 1. This algorithm has some interesting properties. It appears to converge to 1 for all numbers N. Some numbers require many iterations to converge. Others, such as $N = 2^m$, converge very quickly. While it is interesting to study the sequence of values generated by different values of N, let's just compute the number of iterations required to achieve convergence.

First, let N be a scalar. That is, let's write the algorithm for a single number. The following script M-file implements algorithm:

```
% updown1.m
% up-down algorithm

N = 25;       % number to test
count = 0;    % iteration count
```

```
while N>1
  if rem(N,2)==0 % even, since division by 2 gives zero remainder
     N = N/2;
     count = count+1;
  else          % odd
     N = (3*N+1)/2;
     count = count+2;
  end
end
count % display iteration count
```

This code directly implements the algorithm, with one exception. When an odd number is multiplied by 3 and has 1 added, the resulting number is automatically even. As a result, the next pass through the algorithm always divides by 2. Since this always occurs, the divide-by-2 step is included, and the count is incremented by 2 to reflect the fact that two steps are taken.

Next, consider letting N be an array of numbers, for each of which we wish to find the iteration count. The most direct approach is to use a For Loop, as shown in the following script M-file:

```
% updown2.m
% up-down algorithm

Nums = 25:50;  % numbers to test
for i=1:length(Nums)
  N = Nums(i);  % number to test
  count = 0;  % iteration count
    while N>1
     if rem(N,2)==0 % even
        N = N/2;
        count = count+1;
     else          % odd
        N = (3*N+1)/2;
```

```
            count = count+2;
        end
    end
    Counts(i) = count;
end
results = [Nums 'Counts']
```

Here, the earlier scalar algorithm appears within a For Loop. At the beginning of the loop, the *i*th element of the vector Nums is copied into N. The algorithm then runs to completion, and the iteration count is copied into the *i*th element of Counts. Finally, all results are displayed. This code segment violates a key memory allocation guideline—namely, the variable Counts is reallocated to a larger size at every pass through the For Loop. As a result, the previous code does not make use of JIT-acceleration.

To fix this problem, Counts must be preallocated as follows:

```
% updown3.m
% up-down algorithm

Nums = 25:50;                   % numbers to test
Counts = zeros(size(Nums)); % preallocate array
N = Nums(1);                    % predefine N data type and dimension
count = 0;                      % predefine count data type and dimension
for i=1:length(Nums)
   N = Nums(i);  % number to test
   count = 0;  % iteration count
      while N>1
      if rem(N,2)==0 % even
         N = N/2;
         count = count+1;
      else              % odd
         N = (3*N+1)/2;
         count = count+2;
```

```
        end
    end
    Counts(i) = count;
end
results = [Nums' Counts']
```

Now, every time through, the For Loop simply inserts the current count into a preexisting location in Counts. Preallocation is always a first and most important step in any code optimization process. In addition, since N and count are used within the For Loop, their data types and dimensions are predefined. With these changes, updown3.m makes full use of JIT-acceleration.

For comparison purposes, it is beneficial to develop a vectorized version of this algorithm. In a vectorized version, all input data must be processed simultaneously. This eliminates the For Loop. The function rem returns an array the same size as its input, and so all numbers can be tested simultaneously at every iteration of the While Loop. Using this fact leads to the following script M-file:

```
% updown4.m
% up-down algorithm


Nums = 25:50; % numbers to test
N = Nums;                     % duplicate numbers
Counts = zeros(size(N)); % preallocate array

not1 = N>1;                          % True for numbers greater than one

while any(not1)

   odd = rem(N,2)~=0;                % True for odd values

   odd_not1 = odd & not1;            % True for odd values greater than one
   even_not1 = ~odd & not1;          % True for even values greater than one

   N(even_not1) = N(even_not1)/2;              % Process evens
   Counts(even_not1) = Counts(even_not1)+1;
```

```
    N(odd_not1) = (3*N(odd_not1)+1)/2;        % Process odds
    Counts(odd_not1) = Counts(odd_not1)+2;

    not1 = N>1;                       % Find remaining numbers not converged
end
results = [Nums' Counts']
```

When you consider all elements simultaneously, you must find a way to operate only on array elements that have not converged to 1. The statement `not1 = N>1;` logically identifies all elements of `N` that haven't converged. Inside of the While Loop, the nonconverged odd and even values are identified by the `odd_not1` and `even_not1` logical variables, respectively. With the use of these variables, the corresponding elements of `N` are processed, and the `Counts` values are updated.

This vectorized solution makes use of logical array addressing. Addressing by using numerical indices could have been done as well by using the `find` function; for example, the odd indices are given by `find(odd_not1)`. However, use of this function adds more statements to the solution, which makes the code run slower.

Running the profiler on this solution shows that the greatest percentage of time is consumed by the `odd = rem(N,2)~=0;` statement. There are two reasons for this. First, this statement finds the remainder for all elements of `N` every time, not just the remaining of nonconverged numbers. For example, if there are 1000 data points in `N` and only 10 of them are nonconverged, the remainder is computed for 990 elements in `N` that are not required. Second, the remainder function incurs overhead because it is a function call and because it performs internal error checking. Both of these reasons for the time consumed by the call to the `rem` function can be addressed. Eliminating the cause of the first reason requires removing the converged values from `N` as they appear. Implementing this requires substantial complexity. However, the the `rem` function overhead can be minimized by replacing it with its definition, as shown in the following code:

```
% updown5.m
% up-down algorithm

Nums = 25:50;     % numbers to test

N = Nums;                  % duplicate numbers
```

```
Counts = zeros(size(N)); % preallocate array

not1 = N>1;                      % True for numbers greater than one

while any(not1)

   odd = (N-2*fix(N/2))~=0;      % True for odd values


   odd_not1 = odd & not1;        % True for odd values greater than one
   even_not1 = ~odd & not1;      % True for even values greater than one

   N(even_not1) = N(even_not1)/2;          % Process evens
   Counts(even_not1) = Counts(even_not1)+1;

   N(odd_not1) = (3*N(odd_not1)+1)/2;      % Process odds
   Counts(odd_not1) = Counts(odd_not1)+2;

   not1 = N>1;                             % Find remaining numbers
end
results = [Nums' Counts']
```

Running the profiler on this example shows that (N-2*fix(N/2)) is generally faster rem(N,2).

As a final test, it is worth considering the use of integer arithmetic. Since N and Counts are always integers, it is possible to cast them into integer arrays. In this case, (N-2*fix(N/2)) no longer works as a replacement for rem(N,2). However, odd = 2*(N/2)~=N; is an alternative test for odd integers. The code shown next illustrates this integer implementation:

```
% updown6.m
% up-down algorithm

Nums = 25:50; % numbers to test

N = uint32(Nums);                   % duplicate numbers as uint32
```

```
Counts = zeros(size(N),'uint32'); % preallocate array as uint32

not1 = N>1;                       % True for numbers greater than one

while any(not1)

   odd = 2*(N/2)~=N;              % True for odd values

   odd_not1 = odd & not1;         % True for odd values greater than one
   even_not1 = ~odd & not1;       % True for even values greater than one

   N(even_not1) = N(even_not1)/2;              % Process evens
   Counts(even_not1) = Counts(even_not1)+1;

   N(odd_not1) = (3*N(odd_not1)+1)/2;          % Process odds
   Counts(odd_not1) = Counts(odd_not1)+2;

   not1=N>1;                      % Find remaining numbers
end
results = [Nums' Counts']
```

As a comparison, the last four implementations were timed with the profiler by using `Nums = 1:2049;` and with the last line `results = [Nums' Counts']` removed. The following table documents the timing results:

Code	Relative Execution Time	Comments
updown3	1.0	Scalar operations using JIT-acceleration
updown5	1.2	Vectorized operations **without** the function `rem`
updown4	1.5	Vectorized operations with the function `rem`
updown6	2.3	Vectorized operations, using `uint32` integers and without the function `rem`

These results clearly show the power of the JIT-accelerator. Without it, updown3 would have been up to an order of magnitude slower than the vectorized cases. Now it is the fastest. More surprising is the fact that the integer arithmetic case updown6 was slowest, even though it is otherwise identical to updown5.

It is important to note that the preceding timing performance is representative of data computed on the author's computer using the prerelease version of MATLAB 7. Every profiler run produces slightly different results. To generate your own timing information, you can download this code to your computer from the *Mastering MATLAB* website at *http://www.eece.maine.edu/mm*.

38.4 VANDERMONDE MATRIX

There are a number of numerical linear algebra problems that require the generation of a Vandermonde matrix. For a vector $\boldsymbol{x}$ having n elements, a Vandermonde matrix has the following form:

$$V = \begin{bmatrix} x_1^m & x_1^{m-1} & \cdots & x_1 & 1 \\ x_2^m & x_2^{m-1} & \cdots & x_2 & 1 \\ \vdots & \vdots & \ddots & \vdots & \vdots \\ x_n^m & x_n^{m-1} & \cdots & x_n & 1 \end{bmatrix}$$

As shown, the columns of V are element-by-element powers of the components of $\boldsymbol{x}$. Let's consider a variety of approaches to constructing this matrix.

The first approach that comes to mind is the straightforward application of a For Loop, as in the following script M-file:

```
% vander1.m
% construct a Vandermonde matrix.

x = (1:6)';       % column vector for input data
m = 5;            % highest power to compute
V = [];

for i = 1:m+1  % build V column by column
    V = [V x.^(m+1-i)];
end
```

This approach builds V column by column, starting from an empty matrix. There are a number of weaknesses in this implementation, the most obvious being that memory is reallocated for V each time through the loop. So the first vectorization step is to preallocate V, as shown in the following M-file:

```
% vander2.m
% construct a Vandermonde matrix.

x = (1:6)';          % column vector for input data
m = 5;               % highest power to compute
n = length(x);       % number of elements in x
V = ones(n,m+1);     % preallocate memory for result

for i=0:m-1          % build V column by column
   V(:,i+1) = x.^(m-i);
end
```

Here, V is initialized as a matrix containing all ones. Then, the individual columns of V are assigned within the For Loop. The last column is not assigned in the For Loop, since it already contains ones and there is no use in computing `x.^0`. There are still two problems with the preceding code. First, the columns of V are explicitly computed without making use of prior columns; second, the For Loop should be able to be eliminated. The following script M-file solves the first problem:

```
% vander3.m
% construct a Vandermonde matrix.

x = (1:6)';          % column vector for input data
m = 5;               % highest power to compute
n = length(x);       % number of elements in x
V = ones(n,m+1);     % preallocate memory for result

for i=m:-1:1         % build V column by column
   V(:,i) = x.*V(:,i+1);
end
```

Now the columns of V are assigned, starting with the second-to-last column and proceeding backward to the first. This is done because the ith column of V is equal to the $(i + 1)$th column multiplied elementwise by x. This is the implementation found in the MATLAB functions `polyfit` and `vander`.

At this point, the preceding implementation cannot be optimized further without eliminating the For Loop. Eliminating the For Loop requires some ingenuity and a lot of familiarity with the functions in MATLAB. Using the array manipulation tables found earlier in this chapter, the functions repmat and cumprod offer some promise. The following script M-file demonstrates an approach that uses repmat:

```
% vander4.m
% construct a Vandermonde matrix.

x = (1:6)';          % column vector for input data
m = 5;               % highest power to compute
n = length(x);       % number of elements in x

p = m:-1:0;          % column powers

V = repmat(x,1,m+1).^repmat(p,n,1);
```

This implementation uses repmat twice, once to replicate x, creating a matrix of m+1 columns each containing x, and the second time to create a matrix containing the powers to be applied to each element of the matrix containing x. Given these two matrices, element-by-element exponentiation is used to create the desired result. As with vander2.m, this implementation explicitly computes each column without using information from other columns. The function cumprod solves this problem, as shown in the following script M-file:

```
% vander5.m
% construct a Vandermonde matrix.

x = (1:6)';          % column vector for input data
m = 5;               % highest power to compute
n = length(x);       % number of elements in x

V = ones(n,m+1); % preallocate memory for result

V(:,2:end) = cumprod(repmat(x,1,m),2);

V = V(:,m+1:-1:1); % reverse column order
```

Here, the function cumprod is used to compute the columns of V after using repmat to duplicate x. Since cumprod proceeds from left to right, the final result is found by reversing the columns of V. This implementation uses only one M-file function, repmat. Eliminating this function by array addressing should lead to the fastest possible implementation. Doing so leads to the following script M-file:

```
% vander6.m
% construct a Vandermonde matrix.

x = (1:6)';         % column vector for input data
m = 5;              % highest power to compute
n = length(x);      % number of elements in x

V = ones(n,m+1); % preallocate memory for result

V(:,2:end) = cumprod(x(:,ones(1,m)),2); % avoid call to repmat

V = V(:,m+1:-1:1); % reverse column order
```

Among these six implementations, vander3 and vander6 are the fastest. The MATLAB functions polyfit and vander employ the same algrorithm as vander3, which is easier to read and requires less memory than vander6. All of the other algorithms are not as efficient, from either a memory allocation or computational point of view.

38.5 REPEATED VALUE CREATION AND COUNTING

This section considers the following problem: Given a vector $\boldsymbol{x}$ containing data and a vector $\boldsymbol{n}$ of equal length containing nonnegative integers, construct a vector where $x(i)$ is repeated $n(i)$ times for every ith element in the two vectors. For example, $\boldsymbol{x} = [3\,2\,0\,5\,6]$ and $\boldsymbol{n} = [2\,0\,3\,1\,2]$ would produce the result $\boldsymbol{y} = [3\,3\,0\,0\,0\,5\,6\,6]$. Note that since $\boldsymbol{n}(2)$ is zero, $\boldsymbol{x}(2)$ does not appear in the result $\boldsymbol{y}$.

In addition to repeated value creation, the inverse problem of identifying and counting repeated values is also of interest. Thus, given the previous example $\boldsymbol{y}$, find the vectors $\boldsymbol{x}$ and $\boldsymbol{n}$ that describe it.

Consider repeated value creation first. A scalar approach is straightforward, as shown in the following script M-file:

```
% repeat1.m
% repeated value creation and counting

x = [3 2 0 5 6];  % data to repeat
n = [2 0 3 1 2];  % repeat counts

y = [];
for i=1:length(x)
   y = [y repmat(x(i),1,n(i))];
end
```

In this implementation, the result is built by using brackets to concatenate the repeated values next to each other. JIT-acceleration does not work with this example, because memory is reallocated for y every loop iteration and the M-file function repmat appears in the loop. These issues can be resolved by preallocating y and by using indexing, as shown in the following script M-file:

```
% repeat2.m
% repeated value creation and counting

x = [3 2 0 5 6];  % data to repeat
n = [2 0 3 1 2];  % repeat counts

nz = n==0;                % locations of zero elements
n(nz) = [];               % eliminate zero counts
x(nz) = [];               % eliminate corresponding data
y = zeros(1,sum(n));  % preallocate output array
idx = 1;                % pointer into y
for i=1:length(x)
   y(idx:idx+n(i)-1) = x(i); % fill y using scalar expansion
   idx = idx+n(i);              % next pointer location
end
```

In the preceding code, zero counts are eliminated prior to the For Loop, since they do not contribute to the result. In this algorithm, sum(n) is the total number of elements in the result, and the variable idx is used to identify where the next data is to be placed in y.

Once again, it is worthwhile to consider a vectorized solution to this problem. To determine how to proceed, it is beneficial to look at how x is related to y. After eliminating zero counts in the example being considered, x, n, and y are as follows:

```
>> x

x =

     3     0     5     6

>> n

n =

     2     3     1     2

>> y

y =

     3     3     0     0     0     5     6     6
```

If we can create an index vector idx = [1 1 2 2 2 3 4 4], then x is related to y as

```
>> idx = [1 1 2 2 2 3 4 4];
>> y = x(idx)

y =

     3     3     0     0     0     5     6     6
```

So, rather than concentrate on getting the values of x into the correct places in y, if we can generate an index vector for x with the desired values, finding y simplifies to just one statement, y = x(idx). This is a common situation in vectorizing. The indices are often more important than the data.

The relationship between n and idx is straightforward. In addition, since idx looks like a cumulative sum, there's a chance that the cumsum function will be useful. If we can generate an array of ones and zeros at the indices where idx changes value, then idx is indeed a cumulative sum, as in the following example:

```
>> tmp = [1 0 1 0 0 1 1 0]

tmp =

     1     0     1     0     0     1     1     0

>> idx = cumsum(tmp)

idx =

     1     1     2     2     2     3     4     4
```

The nonzero values in tmp are related to n. To discover this relationship, look at its cumulative sum:

```
>> csn = cumsum(n)
csn =
     2     5     6     8
```

If the last value in csn is discarded and 1 is added to the remaining values, then the indices of all 1s in tmp are known, except for the first, which is always 1. Therefore, the indices of all 1s can be computed:

```
>> tmp2 = [1 csn(1:end-1)+1]
tmp2 =
     1     3     6     7
```

That's it. The values in tmp2 identify the 1s to be placed in tmp. All other values in tmp are 0. Now, all that remains is creating tmp. This is easily done, as in the following example:

```
>> tmp = zeros(1,csn(end)) % preallocate with all zeros
tmp =
     0     0     0     0     0     0     0     0
>> tmp(tmp2) = 1           % poke in ones with scalar expansion
tmp =
     1     0     1     0     0     1     1     0
>> idx = cumsum(tmp)       % form the desired cumsum
idx =
     1     1     2     2     2     3     4     4
>> y = x(idx)              % idx does the rest!
y =
     3     3     0     0     0     5     6     6
```

Using this approach, a vectorized implementation of creating repeated values is shown in the following script M-file:

```
% repeat3.m
% repeated value creation and counting

x = [3 2 0 5 6];  % data to repeat
```

```
n = [2 0 3 1 2];  % repeat counts

nz = n==0;                  % locations of zero elements
n(nz) = [];                 % eliminate zero counts
x(nz) = [];                 % eliminate corresponding data
csn = cumsum(n);                    % cumulative sum of counts
tmp = zeros(1,csn(end));            % preallocate memory
tmp([1 csn(1:end-1)+1]) = 1;        % poke in ones
idx = cumsum(tmp);                  % index vector
y = x(idx);                         % let array indexing do the work
```

As a comparison, these implementations were timed with the profiler, using larger x and n data sets than shown in the implementations. The following table documents the timing results:

Code	**Relative Execution Time**	**Comments**
repeat3	1.0	Vectorized solution
repeat2	4.0	Scalar operations using JIT-acceleration
repeat1	55	Nonoptimized solution without variable preallocation

In this case, the vectorized solution is much faster than the JIT-accelerated solution. This is the opposite conclusion as that reached in the Vandermonde matrix construction example illustrated earlier in this chapter. The downside of the vectorized solution is that the code is not transparent. It is almost impossible to tell what the vectorized code does without actually executing it and monitoring the intermediate variables.

Let's move on to the inverse of the above algorithm, namely, repeated value identification and counting. That is, starting with ***y***, find ***x*** and ***n*** (except for any zero-count values, of course). Again, the most obvious solution is nonvectorized and uses a For Loop, as shown in the following script M-file:

```
% repeat4.m
% repeated value creation and counting
% inverse operation
```

```
y = [3 3 0 0 0 5 6 6]; % data to examine

x = y(1);                % beginning data
n = 1;                   % beginning count
idx = 1;                 % index value
for i=2:length(y)
   if y(i)==x(idx) % value matches current x

      n(idx) = n(idx)+1; % increment current count

   else % new value found

      idx=idx+1;         % increment index
      x(idx) = y(i);     % poke in new x
      n(idx) = 1;        % start new count
   end
end
```

Here, a simple If-Else-End construction is used to decide if a particular element of y is a member of the current repeated value. If it is, the count is incremented. If it's not, a new repeat value is created. Although it is not obvious, each time the Else section is executed, memory is reallocated for x and n. As a result, this solution does not benefit from JIT-acceleration.

The next step is to use preallocation, as shown in the following script M-file:

```
% repeat5.m
% repeated value creation and counting
% inverse operation

y = [3 3 0 0 0 5 6 6]; % data to examine

x = zeros(size(y));    % preallocate results
n = zeros(size(y));

x(1) = y(1);             % beginning data
```

```
n(1) = 1;                  % beginning count
idx = 1;                   % index value

for i=2:length(y)

   if y(i)==x(idx) % value matches current x

      n(idx) = n(idx)+1; % increment current count

   else % new value found
      idx = idx+1;          % increment index
      x(idx) = y(i);        % poke in new x
      n(idx) = 1;           % start new count
   end
end
nz = (n==0);  % find elements not used
x(nz) = [];   % delete excess allocations
n(nz) = [];
```

Since the lengths of x and n are unknown (but they cannot be any longer than y) x and n are preallocated to have the same size as y. At the end, the excess memory allocations are discarded.

Eliminating the For Loop to vectorize this algorithm requires study of an example. Consider the y vector that was the result of applying the creation algorithm to the original x and n data:

```
>> y
y =
     3     3     0     0     0     5     6     6
```

Because of the structure of this vector, the MATLAB function `diff` must be useful:

```
>> diff(y)
ans =
     0    -3     0     0     5     1     0
```

If this vector is shifted one element to the right, the nonzero elements line up with places in y that represent new repeated values. In addition, the first element is always a new repeated value. So, using logical operations, the repeated values can be identified, as in the following code:

```
>> y
y =
     3     3     0     0     0     5     6     6
>> tmp = [1 diff(y)]~=0
tmp =
     1     0     1     0     0     1     1     0
```

Given the logical variable tmp, the vector x is found by logical addressing:

```
>> x = y(tmp)
x =
     3     0     5     6
```

Finding the repeat counts n associated with each value in x takes further study. The repeat counts are equal to the distance between the ones in tmp. Therefore, finding the indices associated with tmp is useful, as the following example shows:

```
>> find(tmp)
ans =
     1     3     6     7
>> diff(ans)
ans =
     2     3     1
```

The difference in indices gives the repeat count for all but the last repeated element. The function diff misses this count because there is no marker identifying the end of the array, which marks the end of the last repeated value. Appending one True value to tmp solves this problem:

```
>> find([tmp 1])
ans =
     1     3     6     7     9
>> n = diff(ans)
n =
     2     3     1     2
```

The inverse algorithm is now known. Implementing it leads to the following script file:

```
% repeat6.m
% repeated value creation and counting
% inverse operation

y = [3 3 0 0 0 5 6 6]; % data to examine

tmp = ([1 diff(y)]~=0);
x = y(tmp);
n = diff(find([tmp 1]));
```

The preceding implementation demonstrates the compactness of vectorization. This solution requires 3 lines of code, compared to the 17 used in `repeat5.m`. This implementation also demonstrates the difficulty often encountered in reading vectorized code. These 3 lines are essentially meaningless, unless you execute and view the results of each line with a simple example.

A comparison of these three algorithms by using the profiler shows that `repeat4` is generally the slowest and that `repeat5` and `repeat6` are essentially equal in performance. If there are few repeated values, the lack of preallocation does not slow `repeat4` much. On the other hand, the deletion of the extra elements in the last three lines of `repeat5` can be time consuming if the size of `y` is much greater than the size of `x`.

Before concluding, it is important to note that the preceding implementations fail if `y` contains any `Inf` or `NaN` elements. The function `diff` returns `NaN` for differences between `Inf` elements, as well as for differences containing `NaN` elements. Because of the utility of creating and counting repeated values, these algorithm encapsulated in the function `mmrepeat` shown as follows:

```
function [y,m]=mmrepeat(x,n)
%MMREPEAT Repeat or Count Repeated Values in a Vector.
% MMREPEAT(X,N) returns a vector formed from X where X(i) is repeated
% N(i) times. If N is a scalar it is applied to all elements of X.
% N must contain nonnegative integers. N must be a scalar or have the same
% length as X.
%
% For example, MMREPEAT([1 2 3 4],[2 3 1 0]) returns the vector
% [1 1  2 2 2  3]    (extra spaces added for clarity)
%
```

```
% [X,N]=MMREPEAT(Y) counts the consecutive repeated values in Y returning
% the values in X and the counts in N. Y=MMREPEAT(X,N) and [X,N]=MMREPEAT(Y)
% are inverses of each other if N contains no zeros and X contains unique
% elements.

if nargin==2 % MMREPEAT(X,N) MMREPEAT(X,N) MMREPEAT(X,N) MMREPEAT(X,N)
    xlen=length(x);
    nlen=length(n);
    if ndims(x)~=2 | numel(x)~=xlen
        error('X Must be a Vector.')
    else
        [r,c]=size(x);
    end
    if any(n<0) | any(fix(n)~=n)
        error('N Must Contain NonNegative Integers.')
    end
    if ndims(n)~=2 | numel(n)~=nlen | (nlen>1 & nlen~=xlen)
        error('N Must be a Scalar or Vector the Same Size as X.')
    end
    x=reshape(x,1,xlen); % make x a row vector

    if nlen==1 % scalar n case, repeat all elements the same amount
        if n==0 % quick exit for special case
            y=[];
            return
        end
        y=x(ones(1,n),:); % duplicate x to make n rows each containing x
        y=y(:);           % stack each column into a single column
        if r==1           % input was a row so return a row
            y=y.';
        end
    else % vector n case
```

```
        iz=find(n~=0);      % take out elements to be repeated zero times
        x=x(iz);
        n=n(iz);
        csn=cumsum(n);
        y=zeros(1,csn(end)); % preallocate temp/output variable
        y(csn(1:end-1)+1)=1; % mark indices where values increment
        y(1)=1;              % poke in first index
        y=x(cumsum(y));      % use cumsum to set indices
        if c==1              % input was a column so return a column
           y=y.';
        end
     end
elseif nargin==1 % MMREPEAT(Y) MMREPEAT(Y) MMREPEAT(Y) MMREPEAT(Y)
     xlen=length(x);
     if ndims(x)~=2 | prod(size(x))~=xlen
        error('Y Must be a Vector.')
     else
        [r,c]=size(x);
     end
     x=reshape(x,1,xlen); % make x a row vector
     xnan=isnan(x);
     xinf=isinf(x);
     if any(xnan|xinf) % handle case with exceptions
        ntmp=sum(rand(1,4))*sqrt(realmax); % replacement for nan's
        itmp=1/ntmp;                       % replacement for inf's
        x(xnan)=ntmp;
        x(xinf)=itmp.*sign(x(xinf));
        y=[1 diff(x)]~=0;          % places where distinct values begin
        m=diff([find(y) xlen+1]); % counts
        x(xnan)=nan;               % poke nan's and inf's back in
        x(xinf)=inf*x(xinf);
```

```
    else % x contains only algebraic numbers
        y=[1 diff(x)]~=0;          % places where distinct values begin
        m=diff([find(y) xlen+1]); % counts
    end
    y=x(y); % the unique values
    if c==1
        y=y.';
    end
else
    error('Incorrect Number of Input Arguments.')
end
```

38.6 DIFFERENTIAL SUMS

This section considers computing the differential sum between elements in an array. That is, if $\boldsymbol{x} = [3\,1\,2\,6\,3\,1\,{-1}]$, then the differential sum of $\boldsymbol{x}$ is $\boldsymbol{y} = [4\,3\,8\,9\,4\,0]$. This is the dual, or complement, of the MATLAB function `diff`. Just as with `diff`, we wish to create a function that works along any dimension of its input, no matter how many dimensions the input has. Before generalizing to the *n*-D case, let's consider the vector and matrix cases. The vector case is straightforward:

```
>> x = [3 1 2 6 3 1 -1]
x =
     3     1     2     6     3     1    -1
>> x(1:end-1)
ans =
     3     1     2     6     3     1
>> x(2:end)
ans =
     1     2     6     3     1    -1
>> y = x(1:end-1)+x(2:end)
y =
     4     3     8     9     4     0
```

Simple array addressing is all that is required, and the preceding approach works if x is either a row or a column vector. When the input is a matrix, the default action is to perform a differential sum down the columns, which is along the row dimension, as in the following example:

```
>> x = magic(4) % 2-D data
x =
    16     2     3    13
     5    11    10     8
     9     7     6    12
     4    14    15     1
>> y = x(1:end-1,:)+x(2:end,:)
y =
    21    13    13    21
    14    18    16    20
    13    21    21    13
```

It is also desirable to be able to specify an operation across the columns, which is along the column dimension:

```
>> y = x(:,1:end-1)+x(:,2:end)
y =
    18     5    16
    16    21    18
    16    13    18
    18    29    16
```

Here, the row and column indices are reversed from the preceding row operation. This operation, along the column dimension, can be performed by the preceding row operation if x is transposed first, and then transposed again after the operation:

```
>> tmp = x'; % transpose data
>> y = tmp(1:end-1,:)+tmp(2:end,:);
>> y = y'    % transpose result
y =
    18     5    16
    16    21    18
    16    13    18
    18    29    16
```

This can also be accomplished with the *n*-D functions permute and ipermute, which are generalizations of the transpose operator, as in the following example:

```
>> tmp = permute(x,[2 1])
tmp =
    16     5     9     4
     2    11     7    14
     3    10     6    15
    13     8    12     1
>> y = tmp(1:end-1,:)+tmp(2:end,:);
>> y = ipermute(y,[2 1])
y =
    18     5    16
    16    21    18
    16    13    18
    18    29    16
```

Before extending this to the *n*-D case, consider the 3-D case, since it is relatively easy to visualize:

```
>> x = cat(3,hankel([3 1 6 -1]),pascal(4))
x(:,:,1) =
     3     1     6    -1
     1     6    -1     0
     6    -1     0     0
    -1     0     0     0
x(:,:,2) =
     1     1     1     1
     1     2     3     4
     1     3     6    10
     1     4    10    20
>> y = x(1:end-1,:,:)+x(2:end,:,:) % diff sum along row dimension
y(:,:,1) =
     4     7     5    -1
     7     5    -1     0
     5    -1     0     0
```

```
y(:,:,2) =
     2     3     4     5
     2     5     9    14
     2     7    16    30
```

Note that the same process occurs here, but that added colons are required to reach both pages of x. If the 1:end-1 and 2:end indices are moved to other dimensions, the differential sum moves to that dimension, as in the following example:

```
>> y = x(:,:,1:end-1)+x(:,:,2:end)
y =
     4     2     7     0
     2     8     2     4
     7     2     6    10
     0     4    10    20
```

This is the differential sum between the two pages of x.

The previous example points to one way to generalize this algorithm to *n*-dimensions. The indices into x on the right-hand side are comma-separated lists. Therefore, if we create cell arrays containing the desired indices, the differential sum can be computed by using comma-separated list syntax:

```
>> y = x(1:end-1,:,:)+x(2:end,:,:) % duplicate this case
y(:,:,1) =
     4     7     5    -1
     7     5    -1     0
     5    -1     0     0
y(:,:,2) =
     2     3     4     5
     2     5     9    14
     2     7    16    30

>> c1 = {(1:3) ':' ':'}    % first set of indices
c1 =
    [1x3 double]    ':'    ':'
>> c2 = {(2:4) ':' ':'}    % second set of indices
c2 =
    [1x3 double]    ':'    ':'
```

```
>> y = x(c1{:})+x(c2{:})  % use comma separated list syntax
y(:,:,1) =
     4     7     5    -1
     7     5    -1     0
     5    -1     0     0
y(:,:,2) =
     2     3     4     5
     2     5     9    14
     2     7    16    30
```

The preceding example demonstrates the power of comma-separated list syntax. In the example, the keyword end could not be used because it has meaning only when used directly as an index to a variable. As a result, c1 and c2 contain the actual numerical indices.

The following script file generalizes this implementation for computing differential sums:

```
% diffsum1.m
% compute differential sum along a given dimension

x = cat(3,hankel([3 1 6 -1]),pascal(4)) % data to test
dim = 1  % dimension to work along

xsiz = size(x)
xdim = ndims(x)

tmp = repmat({':'},1,xdim) % cells of ':'
c1 = tmp;
c1{dim} = 1:xsiz(dim)-1    % poke in 1:end-1
c2 = tmp;
c2(dim) = {2:xsiz(dim)}    % poke in 2:end

y = x(c1{:})+x(c2{:})      % comma separated list syntax
```

With no semicolons at the end of the statements, `diffsum1` produces the following output:

```
x(:,:,1) =

     3     1     6    -1

     1     6    -1     0

     6    -1     0     0

    -1     0     0     0

x(:,:,2) =

     1     1     1     1

     1     2     3     4

     1     3     6    10

     1     4    10    20

dim =

     1

xsiz =

     4     4     2

xdim =

     3

tmp =

    ':'    ':'    ':'

c1 =

    [1x3 double]    ':'    ':'

c2 =

    [1x3 double]    ':'    ':'

y(:,:,1) =

     4     7     5    -1

     7     5    -1     0

     5    -1     0     0

y(:,:,2) =

     2     3     4     5

     2     5     9    14

     2     7    16    30
```

Here, x is the input data and dim is the dimension chosen for computing the differential sum. Using information about the size and dimensions of x, repmat can produce a cell array for addressing all elements in all dimensions of x. Then, indices are inserted into the proper cells to create c1 and c2, as shown earlier. Finally, comma-separated list syntax is used to generate the final result.

The preceding algorithm is not the only way to compute differential sums for an arbitrary *n*-D array. The functions permute and ipermute can be used to transpose x so that the desired dimension for computing the sum is the row dimension. Applying this procedure to the previous 3-D example gives the following script M-file:

```
% diffsum2.m
% compute differential sum along a given dimension

x = cat(3,hankel([3 1 6 -1]),pascal(4)) % data to test
dim = 3  % dimension to work along

xsiz = size(x);
n = xsiz(dim);                     % size along desired dim
xdim = ndims(x);                   % # of dimensions

perm = [dim:xdim 1:dim-1]          % put dim first
x = permute(x,perm)                % permute so dim is row dimension
x = reshape(x,n,[])                % reshape into a 2D array

y = x(1:n-1,:)+x(2:n,:)           % Differential sum along row dimension

xsiz(dim) = n-1                    % new size of dim dimension
y = reshape(y,xsiz(perm))          % put result back in original form
y = ipermute(y,perm)               % inverse permute dimensions
```

Here, the variable perm forms a permutation vector for transposing x so that the differential sum is computed along the row dimension. After permuting, x is reshaped into a 2-D array. For 3-D x, this means block-stacking the pages of x as additional columns. Then, the differential sum is computed, and the array result is reshaped and inverse-permuted to its original shape by using the fact that its size along the chosen dimension has decreased by 1. With no semicolons at the end of the statements, diffsum2 produces the following output:

```
x(:,:,1) =

     3     1     6    -1
     1     6    -1     0
     6    -1     0     0
    -1     0     0     0

x(:,:,2) =

     1     1     1     1
     1     2     3     4
     1     3     6    10
     1     4    10    20

dim =

     3

perm =

     3     1     2

x(:,:,1) =

     3     1     6    -1
     1     1     1     1

x(:,:,2) =

     1     6    -1     0
     1     2     3     4

x(:,:,3) =

     6    -1     0     0
     1     3     6    10

x(:,:,4) =

    -1     0     0     0
     1     4    10    20

x =

  Columns 1 through 12

     3     1     6    -1     1     6    -1     0     6    -1     0     0
     1     1     1     1     1     2     3     4     1     3     6    10

  Columns 13 through 16

    -1     0     0     0
     1     4    10    20
```

```
y =

  Columns 1 through 12

     4     2     7     0     2     8     2     4     7     2     6    10

  Columns 13 through 16

     0     4    10    20

xsiz =

     4     4     1

y(:,:,1) =

     4     2     7     0

y(:,:,2) =

     2     8     2     4

y(:,:,3) =

     7     2     6    10

y(:,:,4) =

     0     4    10    20

y =

     4     2     7     0
     2     8     2     4
     7     2     6    10
     0     4    10    20
```

Of these two approaches to generalizing functions, the *n*-D case (the approach taken in `diffsum2`) appears more often in M-File functions distributed with MATLAB. There is no significant difference in the speed of the approaches.

38.7 STRUCTURE MANIPULATION

Structures are a convenient data structure in MATLAB. They allow you to group associated data into a single variable and use descriptive field names to identify different data contained within the structure. Given the utility and convenience of structures, it is often convenient to pack a group of variables into a single structure, and then later extract them back out. To illustrate this, first consider the process of gathering variables and storing them as fields within a single structure, with field names matching variable names. Performing this task in the *Command* window is straightforward: you simply assign fields to like-named variables, as in the following example:

```
>> a = eye(2) % test data
a =
     1     0
     0     1
>> b = 'String'
b =
String
>> c = cell(2)
c =
     []     []
     []     []
>> y.a = a; % store variables in a structure
>> y.b = b;
>> y.c = c
y =
    a: [2x2 double]
    b: 'String'
    c: {2x2 cell}
```

The inverse of this process is alsc straightforward. Using the structure y as an example leads to the following statements:

```
>> a = y.a
a =
     1     0
     0     1
>> b = y.b
b =
String
>> c = y.c
c =
     []     []
     []     []
```

Here, the field names of the structure become the variable names.

This process of packing and unpacking variables is encapsulated in the M-file function mmv2struct:

```
function varargout=mmv2struct(varargin)
%MMV2STRUCT Pack/Unpack Variables to/from a Scalar Structure.
% MMV2STRUCT(X,Y,Z,...) returns a structure having fields X,Y,Z,...
% containing the corresponding data stored in X,Y,Z,...
% Inputs that are not variables are stored in fields named ansN
% where N is an integer identifying the Nth unnamed input.
%
% MMV2STRUCT(S)assigns the contents of the fields of the scalar structure
% S to variables in the calling workspace having names equal to the
% corresponding field names.
%
% [A,B,C,...]=MMV2STRUCT(S) assigns the contents of the fields of the
% scalar structure S to the variables A,B,C,... rather than overwriting
% variables in the caller. If there are fewer output variables than
% there are fields in S, the remaining fields are not extracted. Variables
% are assigned in the order given by fieldnames(S).

if nargin==0
   error('Input Arguments Required.')

elseif nargin==1 % Unpack Unpack Unpack Unpack Unpack Unpack Unpack Unpack

   argin = varargin{1};
   if ~isstruct(argin)||length(argin)~=1
      error('Single Input Must be a Scalar Structure.')
   end
   names = fieldnames(argin);

   if nargout==0 % assign in caller

      for i=1:length(names)
         assignin('caller',names{i},argin.(names{i}))
      end
   else % deal fields into variables in caller
```

```
        varargout = cell(1,nargout); % preallocate output
        for i=1:nargout
            varargout{i} = argin.(names{i});
        end
    end
else % Pack Pack Pack Pack Pack Pack Pack Pack Pack Pack Pack Pack Pack Pack

    args = cell(2,nargin);
    num = 1;

    for i=1:nargin % build cells for call to struct

        args(:,i) = {inputname(i); varargin{i}};

        if isempty(args{1,i})
            args{1,i} = sprintf('ans%d',num);
            num = num+1;
        end
    end
    varargout{1}=struct(args{:}); % create struct using comma-separated list
end
```

Consider the code that unpacks a structure into variables. When called with no output arguments as `mmv2struct(structvar)`, the function uses a For Loop to repeatedly call the function `assignin` to assign values to variables in the workspace that called `mmv2struct`. During each For Loop iteration, variables having names that match the corresponding field names of the structure are created. The statement fragment `arg.(names{i})` addresses the field name string contained in `names{i}` of the structure `argin`, which is equal to `structvar`. The content of `arg.(names{i})` is assigned to a variable named `names{i}` in the workspace of the calling program.

The code that packs variables into a structure creates a cell array containing the arguments required for the `struct` function (e.g. `struct('field1', values1, 'field2', values2, ...)`). For convenience, the arguments to the `struct` function are created with `'field1'`, `'field2'`, etc., as a first row in the variable `args`, and `values1`, `values2`, etc., as a second row in the variable `args`. Then, `args{:}` in the `struct(arg{:})` statement creates a single row of arguments, as needed by the `struct` function, by using comma-separated list syntax.

38.8 INVERSE INTERPOLATION

In Chapter 19, Data Interpolation, 1-D interpolation was demonstrated by using the function `interp1(x,y,xi)`. While this function offers a variety of beneficial features, it assumes that there is one y value for each value in `xi`. If there is not, the function terminates with an error.

In some situations, it is necessary to interpolate in the reverse direction (i.e., to inverse interpolate data), whereby given a value of y, the problem is to find all values of x where $y = f(x)$. To illustrate this situation, consider the following example code and associated plot:

```
>> x = (1:10).';    % sample data
>> y = cos(pi*x);

>> yo = -0.2;       % inverse interpolation point
>> xol = [x(1); x(end)];
>> yol = [yo; yo];

>> plot(x,y,xol,yol)
>> xlabel X
>> ylabel Y
>> set(gca,'Ytick',[-1 yo 0 1])
>> title('Figure 38.1: Inverse Interpolation')
```

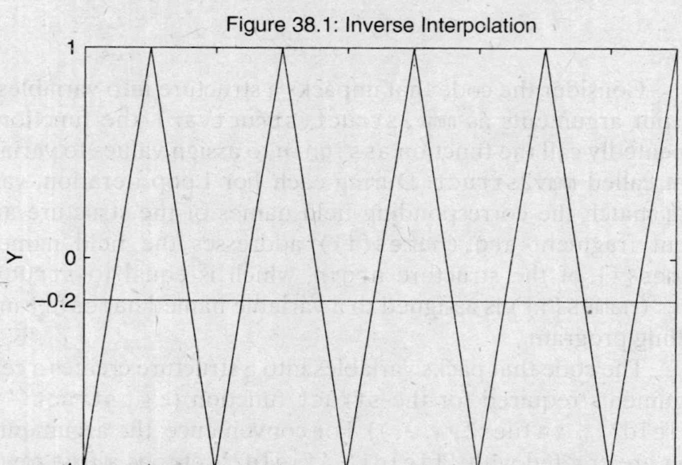

As shown by the triangle waveform in the figure, it is straightforward to use `interp1` to find y values associated with any set of x values, since, for each x value, there is one and only one value of y. On the other hand, in the inverse direction, there are numerous values of x for each value of y between −1 and 1. For example, for the horizontal line drawn yo = −0.2, there are nine corresponding values of y. The function `interp1` cannot be used to find those points:

```
>> interp1(y,x,yo)
??? Error using ==> interp1
The data abscissae should be distinct.
```

Since `interp1` does not work in this case, let's consider the development of an M-file function that performs this task.

To solve this problem, we must find all of the data points that stagger the desired point. As shown in the figure below, in some cases, a data point will appear below the interpolating point y_o and the next point will be above it. In other cases, a data point will appear above y_0 and the next point will be below it. Once the pairs of data points (x_k, y_k) and (x_{k+1}, y_{k+1}) are found, it is simply a matter of linearly interpolating between the data point pairs to find each x_o that corresponds with y_o.

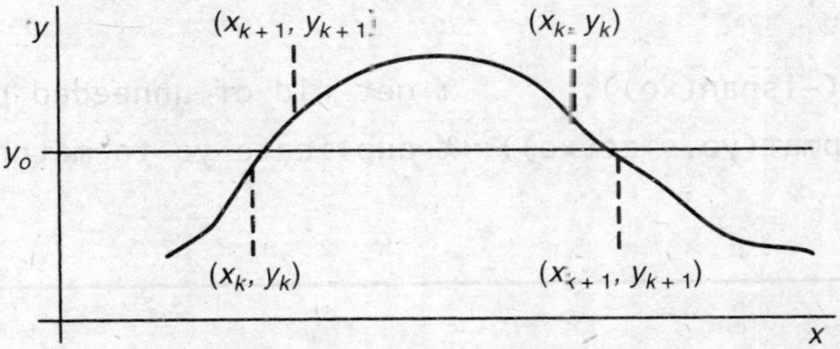

A straightforward, nonvectorized solution is shown in the following code segment:

```
% invinterp1

x = (1:10).';      % sample data
y = cos(pi*x);

yo = -0.2;         % chosen inverse interpolation point

if yo<min(y) || yo>max(y) % quick exit if no values exist
```

```
    xo = [];
else                  % search for the desired points

    n = length(y);
    xo = zeros(size(y))+nan; % preallocate space for found points
    alpha = 0;

    for k=1:n-1 % look through all data pairs

        if ( y(k)<yo && y(k+1)>=yo ) ||... % below then above
           ( y(k)>yo && y(k+1)<=yo )      % above then below

            alpha = (yo-y(k))/(y(k+1)-y(k));    % distance between x(k+1) and x(k)
            xo(k) = alpha*(x(k+1)-x(k)) + x(k); % linearly interpolate using alpha

        end
    end
    xo = xo(~isnan(xo));          % get rid of unneeded preallocated space
    yo = repmat(yo,size(xo)); % duplicate yo to match xo points found
end
```

Note that this code preallocates the interpolation points xo with an array of NaNs. An array of zeros or ones is not appropriate, since zero and one are potential valid points in xo. In some sense, this preallocation is wasteful, because xo typically has many fewer points than the input data. In any case, the unused points are eliminated in the second-to-last statement, and yo is replicated to be the same size as xo in the last statement. This replication makes it simple to plot the interpolated points, as in plot(xo,yo,'o').

It appears that this function can be vectorized, since logical comparisons can be done on an array basis. To investigate this possibility, consider the following example code:

```
>> x = (1:10);    % sample data
>> y = cos(pi*x);
>> yo = -0.2;     % chosen inverse interpolation point
```

```
>> below = y<yo    % True where below yo
below =
     1     0     1     0     1     0     1     0     1     0

>> above = y>=yo   % True where at or above yo
above =
     0     1     0     1     0     1     0     1     0     1
```

Because of the choice of x and y in the foregoing example, alternating elements are below and alternating elements are above. The value yo is bracketed by consecutive data points when below(k) and above(k+1) are True or when above(k) and below(k+1) are True. By shifting the below and above arrays by one, these tests are accomplished:

```
>> n = length(y);
>> below(1:n-1) & above(2:n)   % below(k) and above(k+1)
ans =
     1     0     1     0     1     0     1     0     1

>> above(1:n-1) & below(2:n)   % above(k) and below(k+1)
ans =
     1     0     1     0     1     0     1     0     1
```

Combining these gives the k points. The points immediately after these are the (k+1) points. These are found by the code

```
>> kth = (below(1:n-1)&above(2:n))|(above(1:n-1)&below(2:n)); % True at k points
>> kp1 = [false kth];                                          % True at k+1 points
```

These two logical arrays address the points in y that require interpolation. Using the same interpolation algorithm used earlier, a vectorized inverse interpolation solution is shown in the following code segment:

```
% invinterp2

x = (1:10).';    % sample data
y = cos(pi*x);

yo = -0.2;       % chosen inverse interpolation point
```

```
n = length(y);

if yo<min(y) || yo>max(y) % quick exit if no values exist
   xo = [];
else                         % find the desired points

   below = y<yo;    % True where below yo
   above = y>=yo;  % True where at or above yo

   kth = (below(1:n-1)&above(2:n))|(above(1:n-1)&below(2:n)); % k points
   kp1 = [false; kth];                                          % k+1 points

   alpha = (yo - y(kth))./(y(kp1)-y(kth));% distance between x(k+1) and x(k)
   xo = alpha.*(x(kp1)-x(kth)) + x(kth);  % linearly interpolate using alpha

   yo = repmat(yo,size(xo)); % duplicate yo to match xo points found
end
```

Searching with a For Loop is replaced with logical comparisons and logical manipulation. Again, the `find` function has been avoided, since it requires additional computations, which would slow the implementation down. All linear interpolations are performed with array mathematics. Here, the size of `xo` is determined as the code executes, so there is no need to preallocate it, as with the JIT-accelerated case earlier. The downside of this vectorized case is that it creates a number of potentially large arrays.

Testing both of these algorithms with the profiler shows that they have essentially identical performance. In some cases, the JIT-accelerated algorithm is faster; in others, the vectorized case is faster. Since neither implementation dominates, the following code illustrates M-file function creation, implementing the vectorized solution:

```
function [xo,yo]=mminvinterp(x,y,yo)
%MMINVINTERP 1-D Inverse Interpolation.
% [Xo,Yo]=MMINVINTERP(X,Y,Yo) linearly interpolates the vector Y to find
% the scalar value Yo and returns all corresponding values Xo interpolated
% from the X vector. Xo is empty if no crossings are found. For
% convenience, the output Yo is simply the scalar input Yo replicated so
```

```
% that size(Xo)=size(Yo).
% If Y maps uniquely into X, use INTERP1(Y,X,Yo) instead.
%
% See also INTERP1.

if nargin~=3
   error('Three Input Arguments Required.')
end
n = numel(y);
if ~isequal(n,numel(x))
   error('X and Y Must have the Same Number of Elements.')
end
if ~isscalar(yo)
   error('Yo Must be a Scalar.')
end

x = x(:); % stretch input vectors into column vectors
y = y(:);

if yo<min(y) || yo>max(y) % quick exit if no values exist
   xo = [];
   yo = [];
else                        % find the desired points

   below = y<yo;            % True where below yo
   above = y>=yo;           % True where at or above yo

   kth = (below(1:n-1)&above(2:n))|(above(1:n-1)&below(2:n)); % point k
   kp1 = [false; kth];                                       % point k+1

   alpha = (yo - y(kth))./(y(kp1)-y(kth));% distance between x(k+1) and x(k)
```

```
    xo = alpha.*(x(kp1)-x(kth)) + x(kth);  % linearly interpolate using alpha

    yo = repmat(yo,size(xo)); % duplicate yo to match xo points found
end
```

The preceding function is useful for finding the intersection of two plotted curves. For example, consider the problem of finding the intersection points of the two curves created by the following code:

```
>> x = linspace(0,10);
>> y = sin(x);
>> z = 2*cos(2*x);
>> plot(x,y,x,z)
>> xlabel X
>> ylabel Y
>> title 'Figure 38.2: Intersection of Two Curves'
```

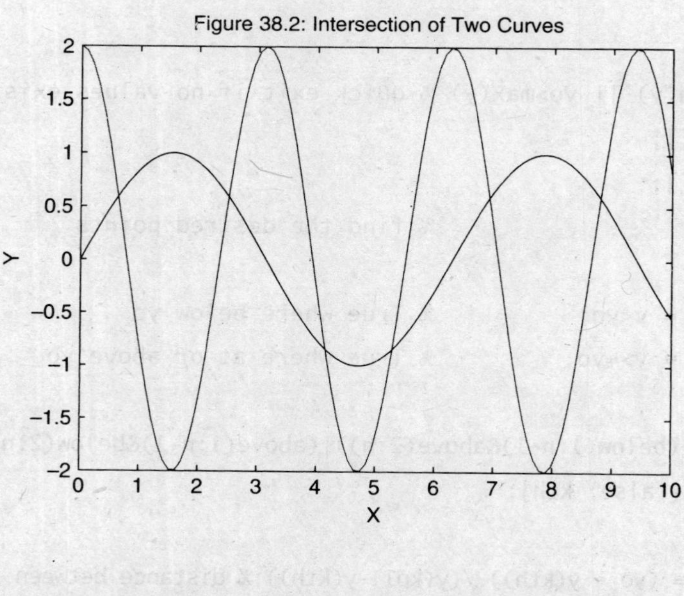

The intersection of these two curves is given by the zero crossings of their difference. Given the preceding data and using mminvinterp, these points are found to be

```
>> xo = mminvinterp(x,y-z,0); % find zero crossings of difference

>> yo = interp1(x,y,xo);      % find corresponding y values

>> plot(x,y,x,z,xo,yo,'o')    % regenerate plot showing intersection points
>> xlabel X
>> ylabel Y
>> title 'Figure 38.3: Intersection Points'
```

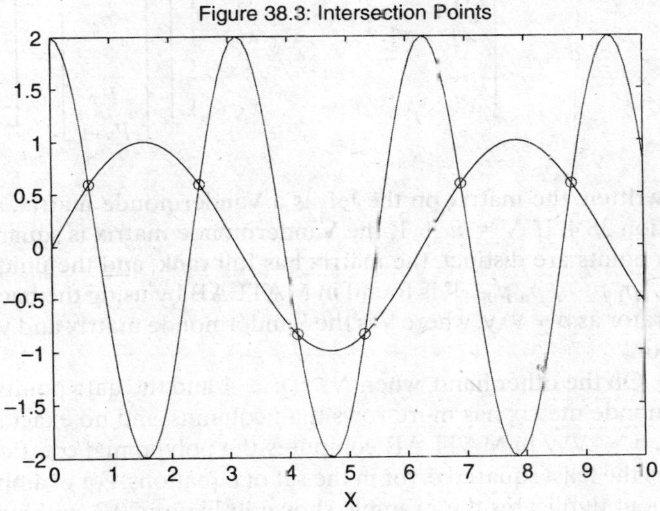

38.9 POLYNOMIAL CURVE FITTING

As discussed in Chapter 20, polynomial curve fitting is performed by using the function `polyfit`. Because polynomial curve fitting is such a basic numerical analysis topic, it is worth exploring more fully. Consider a general polynomial, written as

$$y = p_1 x^n + p_2 x^{n-1} + \cdots + p_n x + p_{n+1}$$

Here, there are $n + 1$ coefficients for an nth order polynomial. For convenience, the coefficients have subscripts that are numbered in increasing order as the power of x decreases. Written in this way, the polynomial can be written as the matrix product

$$y = [x^n \quad x^{n-1} \quad \cdots \quad x \quad 1] \cdot \begin{bmatrix} p_1 \\ p_2 \\ \cdots \\ p_n \\ p_{n+1} \end{bmatrix}$$

In this format, the polynomial coefficients are grouped into a single column vector.

Common polynomial curve fitting uses this form to compute the polynomial coefficients, given a set of data points $\{x_i, y_i\}$ for $i = 1, 2, \ldots N$. Substituting each of these data points into the preceding relationship and grouping the results leads to the matrix equation

$$\begin{bmatrix} x_1^n & x_1^{n-1} & \cdots & x_1 & 1 \\ x_2^n & x_2^{n-1} & \cdots & x_2 & 1 \\ \vdots & \vdots & \cdots & \vdots & \vdots \\ x_N^n & x_N^{n-1} & \cdots & x_N & 1 \end{bmatrix} \cdot \begin{bmatrix} p_1 \\ p_2 \\ \cdots \\ p_n \\ p_{n+1} \end{bmatrix} = \begin{bmatrix} y_1 \\ y_2 \\ \vdots \\ y_N \end{bmatrix}$$

As written, the matrix on the left is a Vandermonde matrix, as discussed earlier in Section 38.4. If $N = n + 1$, the Vandermonde matrix is square. Furthermore, if the data points are distinct, the matrix has full rank, and the unique polynomial vector $p = [p_1\, p_2 \cdots p_n\, p_{n+1}]'$ is found in MATLAB by using the backslash or left-division operator as `p = V\y`, where `V` is the Vandermonde matrix and `y` is the right-hand side vector.

On the other hand, when $N \geq n + 1$ and the data points are distinct, the Vandermonde matrix has more rows than columns, and no exact solution exists. In this case, `p = V\y` in MATLAB computes the polynomial coefficient vector that minimizes the least squared error in the set of equations. For example, the following code segment duplicates the example shown in Figure 20.2, without the use of `polyfit`:

```
% polyfit1.m
% find polynomial coefficients without polyfit

x = [0 .1 .2 .3 .4 .5 .6 .7 .8 .9 1]';  % column vector data
y = [-.447 1.978 3.28 6.16 7.08 7.34 7.66 9.56 9.48 9.30 11.2]';

n = 2; % desired polynomial order

pm = polyfit(x,y,n) % MATLAB polyfit result
```

```
% create Vandermonde matrix using code from vander3.m
m = length(x);   % number of elements in x
V = ones(m,n+1); % preallocate memory for result

for i=n:-1:1     % build V column by column
   V(:,i) = x.*V(:,i+1);
end

p = V\y; % find least squares solution

p = p'   % convert to row vector to match MATLAB's convention for polynomials
```

Running this code shows that both polynomial vectors are equal:

```
>> polyfit1
pm =
      -9.8108      20.129    -0.031671
p =
      -9.8108      20.129    -0.031671
```

From this basic understanding, it is possible to consider potential numerical problems. In particular, because the Vandermonde matrix contains elements ranging from 1 to x^n, it can suffer accuracy problems if the x data points differ a great deal from the number 1. For example, if the desired polynomial order is increased to 4, and the x data is scaled by 10^4, the Vandermonde matrix becomes

```
>> x = 1e4*[0 .1 .2 .3 .4 .5 .6 .7 .8 .9 1]'; % scale x data by 1e4

>> n = 4;                                      % change order to 4
>> m = length(x);  % number of elements in x
>> V = ones(m,n+1); % preallocate memory for result
>> for i=n:-1:1     % build V column by column
   V(:,i) = x.*V(:,i+1);
end
```

```
>> V
V =
               0              0              0              0              1
          1e+012         1e+009         1e+006           1000              1
        1.6e+013         8e+009         4e+006           2000              1
        8.1e+013       2.7e+010         9e+006           3000              1
       2.56e+014       6.4e+010       1.6e+007           4000              1
       6.25e+014      1.25e+011       2.5e+007           5000              1
      1.296e+015      2.16e+011       3.6e+007           6000              1
      2.401e+015      3.43e+011       4.9e+007           7000              1
      4.096e+015      5.12e+011       6.4e+007           8000              1
      6.561e+015      7.29e+011       8.1e+007           9000              1
          1e+016         1e+012         1e+008          10000              1
```

Now the values in V vary in value from 1 to 10^{16}. This disparity causes trouble for the function `polyfit`:

```
>> p = polyfit(x,y,n)
  Warning: Rank deficient, rank = 4,  tol =   3.1633e+001.
  (Type "warning off MATLAB:rankDeficientMatrix" to suppress this warning.)
p =
  3.0675e-015 -4.8147e-011  9.5904e-008    0.0018927          0
```

Since we have reached the limits of double-precision mathematics, to eliminate this problem we must somehow scale the data so that the Vandermonde matrix does not exhibit this disparity in values. Of the numerous ways to scale the data, use of the mean and standard deviation often leads to good results. That is, instead of fitting a polynomial to the data in x, the fit is done with respect to a new independent variable z, given by

$$z = \frac{x - x_m}{s}$$

where x_m and s are the mean and standard deviation, respectively, of the x data. Subtracting by the mean shifts the data to the origin, and dividing by the standard deviation reduces the spread in the data values. Applying this to the previous data that were scaled by 10^4 gives

```
>> xm = mean(x)
>> s = std(x)
>> z = (x - xm)/s;
```

```
>> m = length(z);    % number of elements in x
>> V = ones(m,n+1); % preallocate memory for result
>> for i=n:-1:1      % build V column by column
    V(:,i) = z.*V(:,i+1);
end
>>V
V =
       5.1653      -3.4263      2.2727      -1.5076      1
       2.1157      -1.7542      1.4545      -1.206       1
      0.66942     -0.74007     0.81818     -0.90453      1
      0.13223     -0.21928     0.36364     -0.60302      1
    0.0082645     -0.02741    0.090909     -0.30151      1
            0            0           0            0      1
    0.0082645      0.02741    0.090909      0.30151      1
      0.13223      0.21928     0.36364      0.60302      1
      0.66942      0.74007     0.81818      0.90453      1
       2.1157       1.7542      1.4545        1.206      1
       5.1653       3.4263      2.2727       1.5076      1
```

Now the Vandermonde matrix is numerically well conditioned, and the polynomial curve fit proceeds without difficulty. For this data, the resulting polynomial is

```
>> p = (V\y)'
p =
      0.26689      0.58649     -1.6858       2.4732      7.7391
```

Comparing these polynomial coefficients to those computed before scaling shows that these are much better scaled as well.

While the previous result works well, it changes the original problem to

$$y = p_1 z^n + p_2 z^{n-1} + \cdots + p_n z + p_{n+1}$$

That is, the polynomial is now a function of the variable z. Because of this, evaluation of the original polynomial requires a two-step process. First, using the values of x_m and s used to find z, x data points for polynomial evaluation must be converted to their z data equivalents by using $z = (x - x_m)/s$. Then, the polynomial can be evaluated, as in the following code:

```
>> xi = 1e4*[.25 .35 .45]; % sample data for polynomial evaluation

>> zi = (xi-xm)/s;          % convert to z data


>> yi = polyval(p,zi)       % evaluate using polyval

yi =

      4.752       6.2326       7.326
```

Rather than performing this step manually when data scaling is used, the MATLAB functions polyfit and polyval implement this data scaling through the use of an additional variable. For example, the previous results are duplicated by the following code:

```
>> [p,Es,mu] = polyfit(x,y,n);

>> p

p =

     0.26689      0.58649      -1.6858       2.4732       7.7391

>> yi = polyval(p,xi,Es,mu)

yi =

      4.752       6.2326       7.326
```

The optional polyfit output variable mu contains the mean and the standard deviation of the data used to compute the polynomial. Providing this variable to polyfit directs it to perform the conversion to z before evaluating the polynomial. As shown here, the polynomial p and the interpolated points yi are equal to those just computed by using the Vandermonde matrix.

The structure variable Es (which has not been discussed here) is used to compute error estimates in the solution. (See the documentation for further information regarding this variable.)

Beyond a consideration of data scaling, it is sometimes important to perform weighted polynomial curve fitting. That is, in some situations, there may be more confidence in some of the data points than in others. When this is true, the curve fits procedure should take this confidence into account and return a polynomial that reflects the weight given to each data point.

While polyfit does not provide this capability, it is easy to implement in a number of ways. Perhaps the simplest way is to weigh the data before the Vandermonde matrix is formed. For example, consider the case of a third-order polynomial being fit to five data points. Assuming that the confidence in the third data point is α times that of all other data points, the matrix equation to be solved becomes

$$\begin{bmatrix} x_1^3 & x_1^2 & x_1 & 1 \\ x_2^3 & x_2^2 & x_2 & 1 \\ \alpha \cdot x_3^3 & \alpha \cdot x_3^2 & \alpha \cdot x_3 & \alpha \\ x_4^3 & x_4^2 & x_4 & 1 \\ x_5^3 & x_5^2 & x_5 & 1 \end{bmatrix} \cdot \begin{bmatrix} p_1 \\ p_2 \\ p_3 \\ p_4 \end{bmatrix} = \begin{bmatrix} y_1 \\ y_2 \\ \alpha \cdot y_3 \\ y_4 \\ y_5 \end{bmatrix}$$

By multiplying the third row of the matrix equation by α, the error in this equation is weighted by α. The process of minimizing the least squared error forces the error at this data point to decrease relative to the others. As α increases, the error at the data point decreases.

In general, it is possible to give a weight to each data point, not just to one of them, as previously shown. Implementing this approach in MATLAB is illustrated in the following code segment:

```
% polyfit2.m
% find weighted polynomial coefficients

x = [0 .1 .2 .3 .4 .5 .6 .7 .8 .9 1]';

y = [-.447 1.978 3.28 6.16 7.08 7.34 7.66 9.56 9.48 9.30 11.2]';

n = 3;

pm = polyfit(x,y,n) % MATLAB polyfit result

% create Vandermonde matrix using code from vander3.m

m = length(x);    % number of elements in x

V = ones(m,n+1); % preallocate memory for result

for i=n:-1:1      % build V column by column
   V(:,i) = x.*V(:,i+1);
end

w = ones(size(x)); % default weights of one
w(4) = 2;          % weigh 4th point by 2
w(7) = 10;         % weigh 7th point by 10
```

```
V = V.*repmat(w,1,n+1); % multiply rows by weights
y = y.*w;               % multiply y by weights

p = (V\y)' % find polynomial
```

Running this code shows that the unweighted and weighted polynomials are different:

```
>> polyfit2
pm =
        16.076      -33.924      29.325      -0.6104
p =
        28.576      -50.761      34.104      -0.67441
```

An alternative to this approach uses the MATLAB function `lscov`, which specifically computes weighted least squares solutions. Repeating the previous example by using this function is straightforward, as shown in the following code segment and its associated output:

```
% polyfit3
% find weighted polynomial coefficients using lscov

x = [0 .1 .2 .3 .4 .5 .6 .7 .8 .9 1]';
y = [-.447 1.978 3.28 6.16 7.08 7.34 7.66 9.56 9.48 9.30 11.2]';

n = 3;

pm = polyfit(x,y,n) % MATLAB polyfit result

% create Vandermonde matrix using code from vander3.m

m = length(x);    % number of elements in x
V = ones(m,n+1); % preallocate memory for result

for i=n:-1:1      % build V column by column
   V(:,i) = x.*V(:,i+1);
end
```

```
w = ones(size(x)); % default weights of one
w(4) = 2^2;          % here weights are the square of those used in polyfit2
w(7) = 10^2;

p = lscov(V,y,w)'
```

```
>> polyfit3
pm =
        16.076       -33.924       29.325      -0.6104
p =
        28.576       -50.761       34.104      -0.67441
```

To see how these polynomials differ, they can be plotted over the range of the data:

```
% mm3804.m
% find weighted polynomial coefficients using lscov

x = [0 .1 .2 .3 .4 .5 .6 .7 .8 .9 1]';
y = [-.447 1.978 3.28 6.16 7.08 7.34 7.66 9.56 9.48 9.30 11.2]';
n = 3;
pm = polyfit(x,y,n); % MATLAB polyfit result

% create Vandermonde matrix using code from vander3.m

m = length(x);      % number of elements in x
V = ones(m,n+1); % preallocate memory for result

for i=n:-1:1        % build V column by column
   V(:,i) = x.*V(:,i+1);
end

w = ones(size(x)); % default weights of one
w(4) = 2^2;
w(7) = 10^2;
```

```
p = lscov(V,y,w)';

xi = linspace(0,1,100);
ym = polyval(pm,xi);
yw = polyval(p,xi);

pt = false(size(x)); % logical array pointing to weighted points
pt([4 7]) = true;

plot(x(~pt),y(~pt),'x',x(pt),y(pt),'o',xi,ym,'--',xi,yw)
xlabel('x'), ylabel('y=f(x)')
title('Figure 38.4: Weighted Curve Fitting')
```

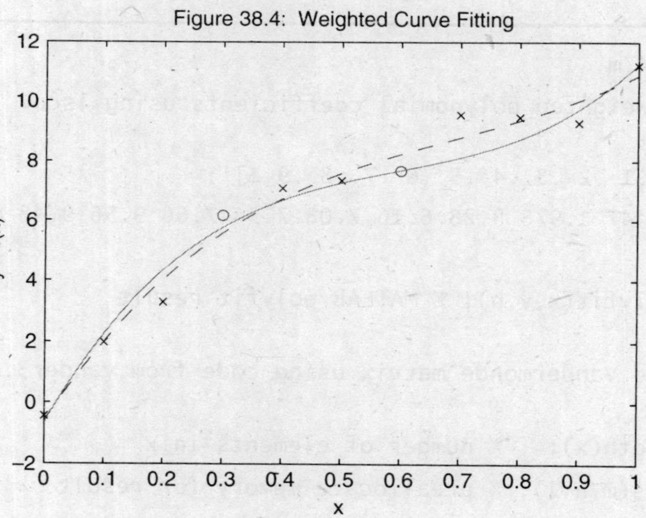

The weighted points are marked with circles in the figure, while the unweighted points are marked with an x. Clearly, the weighted polynomial is closer to the fourth and seventh data points than the original `polyfit` results. In addition, the seventh data point is closer than the fourth because its weight is much higher.

38.10 NONLINEAR CURVE FITTING

The polynomial curve fitting discussed in the previous section is popular in part because the problem can be written in matrix form and solved by using linear least-squares techniques. Perhaps most important, or most convenient, is that no initial guess is required. The optimum solution is found without searching an n-dimensional solution space. In the more general case, where the unknown parameters do not appear linearly (i.e., nonlinear curve fitting), the solution space must be searched, starting with an initial guess. For example, consider fitting data to the function

$$f(t) = a - be^{\alpha t} + ce^{\beta t}$$

If α and β are known constants and a, b, and c are the unknowns to be found, this function can be written as

$$f(t) = [1 \quad e^{\alpha t} \quad e^{\beta t}] \cdot \begin{bmatrix} a \\ b \\ c \end{bmatrix}$$

Substituting a given a set of data points, $\{t_i, y_i = f(t_i)\}$ for $i = 1, 2, \ldots N$, into this expression and gathering the results in matrix format results in the equation

$$\begin{bmatrix} 1 & e^{\alpha t_1} & e^{\beta t_1} \\ 1 & e^{\alpha t_2} & e^{\beta t_2} \\ \vdots & \vdots & \vdots \\ 1 & e^{\alpha t_N} & e^{\beta t_N} \end{bmatrix} \cdot \begin{bmatrix} a \\ b \\ c \end{bmatrix} = \begin{bmatrix} y_1 \\ y_2 \\ \vdots \\ y_N \end{bmatrix}$$

Written in this way, a, b, and c appear linearly, just as the polynomial coefficients did in the previous section. As a result, the backslash operation in MATLAB produces the least-squares solution for the unknown variables. That is, if E is the N-by-3 matrix on the left, p is the vector $[a\,b\,c]'$, and y is the right-hand side vector, then `p = E\y` gives the least-squares solution for p.

When α and β are not known, the linear least-squares solution does not apply, because α and β cannot be separated as a, b, and c are in the preceding equation. In this case, it is necessary to use a minimization algorithm such as `fminsearch` in MATLAB. There are two ways to set up this problem for solution with `fminsearch`. The first is to write $f(t)$ as

$$f(t) = x_3 + x_4\, e^{x_1 t} + x_5\, e^{x_2 t}$$

where the unknown variables have been combined into a vector $x = [x_1\, x_2\, x_3\, x_4\, x_5]'$. Given this form and a set of data points $\{t_i, y_i\}$ for $i = 1, 2, \ldots N$, the least-squares solution minimizes the norm of error between the data points y_i and the function evaluated at t_i, $f(t_i)$. That is, if y is a vector containing the y_i data points and if f is a vector containing the previous function evaluated at the time points t_i, then the least-squares solution is given by

$$\min_x \|y - f\|$$

To use fminsearch, this norm must be computed in a function as follows:

```
function enorm=fitfun1(x,tdata,ydata)
%ENORM Norm of fit to example nonlinear function
% f(t) = x(3)+x(4)*exp(x(1)*t)+x(5)*exp(x(2)*t)
%
% ENORM(X,Tdata,Ydata) returns norm(Ydata-f(Tdata))

f = x(3)+x(4)*exp(x(1)*tdata)+x(5)*exp(x(2)*tdata);

enorm = norm(f-ydata);
```

The following code segment tests this approach by creating some data, making an initial guess, and calling fminsearch to find a solution:

```
% testfitfun1
% script file to test nonlinear least squares problem

% create test data
x1 = -2; % alpha
x2 = -5; % beta
x3 = 10;
x4 = -4;
x5 = -6;

tdata = linspace(0,4,30)';
ydata = x3+x4*exp(x1*tdata)+x5*exp(x2*tdata);

% create an initial guess

x0 = zeros(5,1); % not a good one, but a common first guess

% call fminsearch

fitfun = @fitfun1; % create handle

options = []; % take default options
```

```
x = fminsearch(fitfun,x0,options,tdata,ydata)

% compute error norm at returned solution

enorm = fitfun(x,tdata,ydata)
```

Running this code produces the following output:

```
>> testfitfun1
Exiting: Maximum number of function evaluations has been exceeded
         - increase MaxFunEvals option.
         Current function value: 3.234558
x =
     0.17368
     -1.5111
      13.972
     -2.2059
     -9.4466

enorm =
      3.2346
```

For this initial guess, the algorithm has not converged. Increasing the number of function evaluations and algorithm iterations permitted to 2000 leads to

```
>> options = optimset('MaxFunEvals',2e3,'MaxIter',2e3);

x = fminsearch(fitfun,x0,options,tdata,ydata)
x =
    -0.78361
     -3.7185
      10.061
    -0.80533
     -9.1907
```

```
enorm =
  0.23727
```

The algorithm now converges, but not to the values $x = [-2\ -5\ 10\ -4\ -6]'$ used to create the data. A plot of the data, the actual function, and the fitted solution provides further information, computed and displayed as follows:

```
% testfitfun2
% script file to test nonlinear least squares problem

% create test data
x1 = -2; % alpha
x2 = -5; % beta
x3 = 10;
x4 = -4;
x5 = -6;
tdata = linspace(0,4,30)';
ydata = x3+x4*exp(x1*tdata)+x5*exp(x2*tdata);

% create an initial guess

x0 = zeros(5,1); % not a good one, but a common first guess

% call fminsearch

fitfun = @fitfun1; % create handle
options = optimset('MaxFunEvals',2e3,'MaxIter',2e3);

x = fminsearch(fitfun,x0,options,tdata,ydata);

ti = linspace(0,4); % evaluation points
actual = x3+x4*exp(x1*ti)+x5*exp(x2*ti); % actual function

fitted = x(3)+x(4)*exp(x(1)*ti)+x(5)*exp(x(2)*ti); % fitted solution
subplot(2,1,1)
plot(tdata,ydata,'o',ti,actual,ti,fitted)
xlabel t
title 'Figure 38.5: Nonlinear Curve Fit'
```

```
subplot(2,1,2)
plot(ti,actual-fitted)
xlabel t
ylabel Error
```

Figure 38.5: Nonlinear Curve Fit

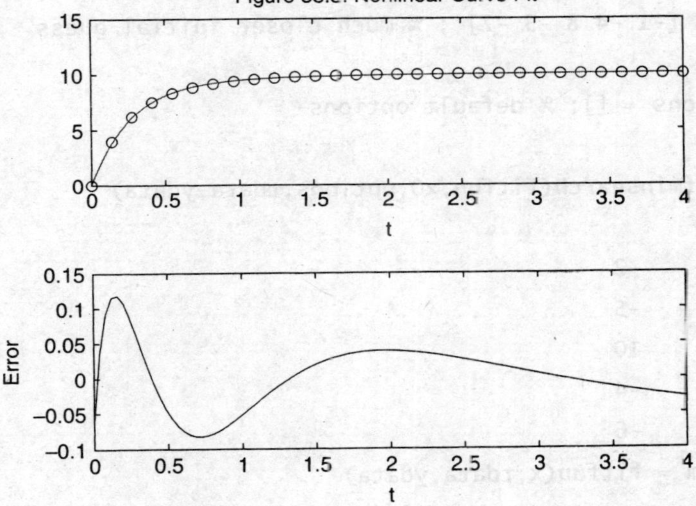

The fitted solution in the upper plot looks good visually. However, the lower error plot shows that there is significant error. If the overall goal of this problem is to minimize the error between the actual coefficients represented by the data and the results returned by `fminsearch`, then this algorithm essentially failed, even though the fitted solution plot looks good visually.

At this point, you must decide whether this solution is satisfactory. Certainly, you can try setting tighter convergence criteria, as in the following code:

```
>> options=optimset('TolX',1e-10,'TolFun',1e-10,'MaxFunEvals',2e3,'MaxIter',2e3);

>> x = fminsearch(fitfun,x0,options,tdata,ydata)
x =
     -0.78359
      -3.7185
       10.061
```

```
      -0.80533
      -9.1907
>> enorm = fitfun(x,tdata,ydata)
enorm =
      0.23727
```

In this case, the solution has not changed. You can also try better initial guesses, such as the following:

```
>> x0 = [-1 -4 8 -3 -7]'; % much closer initial guess

>> options = []; % default options

>> x = fminsearch(fitfun,x0,options,tdata,ydata)
x =
        -2
        -5
        10
        -4
        -6
>> enorm = fitfun(x,tdata,ydata)
enorm =
   3.2652e-006
```

In this case, fminsearch returns coefficients that very closely match those used to create the data. This example illustrates an ambiguity inherent in most nonlinear optimization algorithms. That is, other than having the error norm be zero, there is no set way of knowing when a solution is the best that can be expected.

When a nonlinear curve fitting problem contains a mixture of linear and nonlinear terms, as is true in this example, it is possible to use linear least squares to compute the linear terms and use a function such as fminsearch to compute the nonlinear terms. This leads to better results in almost all cases.

To understand how this is done, consider the problem formulation stated earlier, where α and β were known constants:

$$\begin{bmatrix} 1 & e^{\alpha t_1} & e^{\beta t_1} \\ 1 & e^{\alpha t_2} & e^{\beta t_2} \\ \vdots & \vdots & \vdots \\ 1 & e^{\alpha t_N} & e^{\beta t_N} \end{bmatrix} \cdot \begin{bmatrix} a \\ b \\ c \end{bmatrix} = \begin{bmatrix} y_1 \\ y_2 \\ \vdots \\ y_N \end{bmatrix}$$

In this case, α and β become the variables manipulated by fminsearch. Within the function that evaluates the error norm, this linear least-squares problem is solved by using the current estimates for α and β. That is, if $x_1 = \alpha$, $x_2 = \beta$, and $p = [a\ b\ c]'$, then fitfun1 is rewritten as follows:

```
function [enorm,p]=fitfun2(x,tdata,ydata)
%ENORM Norm of fit to example nonlinear function
% f(t) = p(1)+p(2)*exp(x(1)*t)+p(3)*exp(x(2)*t)
%
% ENORM(X,Tdata,Ydata) returns norm(Ydata-f(Tdata))
%
% [e,p]=ENORM(...) returns the linear least squares
%                  parameter vector p

% solve linear least squares problem given x input supplied by fminsearch

E = [ones(size(tdata)) exp(x(1)*tdata) exp(x(2)*tdata)];
p = E\ydata; % least squares solution for p=[a b c]'

% use p vector to compute error norm
f = p(1)+p(2)*exp(x(1)*tdata)+p(3)*exp(x(2)*tdata);

enorm = norm(f-ydata);
```

Now there are only two parameters for fminsearch to manipulate. The following code segment tests this alternative approach:

```
% testfitfun3
% script file to test nonlinear least squares problem

% create test data
x1 = -2; % alpha
x2 = -5; % beta
p1 = 10;
p2 = -4;
p3 = -6;
```

```
tdata = linspace(0,4,30)';

ydata = p1+p2*exp(x1*tdata)+p3*exp(x2*tdata);

% create an initial guess

x0 = zeros(2,1); % only two parameters to guess now!

% call fminsearch

fitfun = @fitfun2; % create handle to new function

options = []; % take default options

x = fminsearch(fitfun,x0,options,tdata,ydata)

% find p and compute error norm at returned solution

[enorm,p] = fitfun(x,tdata,ydata)
```

Running this code produces the following output:

```
>> testfitfun3
x =
            -2
            -5
enorm =
   7.1427e-006
p =
            10
            -4
            -6
```

Without any difficulty, `fminsearch` finds a minimum very close to the actual values. The incorporation of an internal linear least-squares algorithm within a nonlinear problem reduces dimension of the parameter space to be searched. This almost always improves the speed and convergence of the nonlinear algorithm. In the preceding example, the problem was reduced from five dimensions to two.

Finally, note how the parameter p was included as a second output argument to `fitfun2`. The minimization algorithm `fminsearch` ignores this argument, so it does not influence the search process. However, after the algorithm terminates, calling the `fitfun2` again with two output arguments returns the values of the linear parameters at the solution point. Global variables should not be used to obtain `p`, since there is no way of knowing if `fminsearch` evaluates `fitfun2` at its solution on its last iteration. Calling `fitfun2` after `fminsearch` finishes execution guarantees that the parameter vector `p` is evaluated at the solution returned by `fminsearch`.

38.11 PICTURE-IN-A-PICTURE ZOOM

The final example in this chapter demonstrates use of the Handle Graphics features in MATLAB. As illustrated in the next figure, this example implements a picture-in-a-picture zoom. That is, the user calls the function, then goes to the current axes and, by using the mouse, drags a selection rectangle. Once created, a dotted outline of the selection rectangle remains, and a new, but smaller, axis is created showing the graphical contents inside of the drawn selection rectangle. This function allows the user to zoom into a portion of an axis without hiding the original plot. Although not shown, the smaller axis can be selected, dragged, and resized.

Figure 38.6: P cture in a Picture Zoom

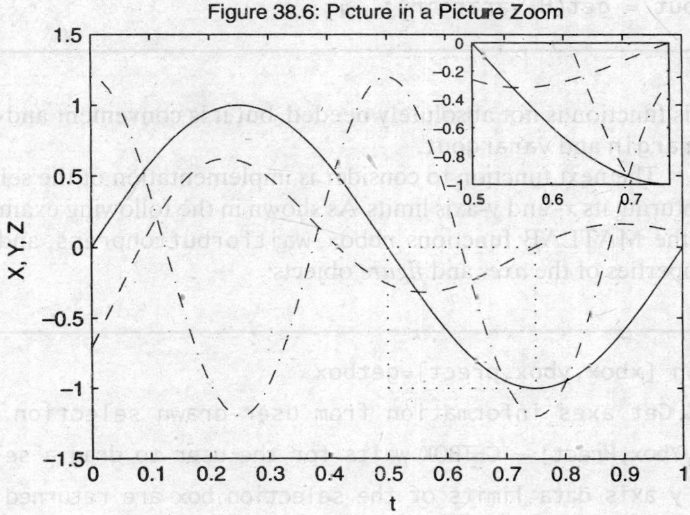

There are a number of steps involved in the creation of this function. Rather than implement the function as one large function, it is convenient to create supporting functions first that could be subfunctions of the primary functions or simply functions on the MATLAB search path. The first function getn simplifies the assignment of the output of the get function into individual variables:

```
function varargout=getn(H,varargin)
%GETN Get Multiple Object Properties.
% [Prop1,Prop2,...] = GETN(H,PName1,PName2,...) returns the requested
% properties of the scalar handle H in the corresponding output arguments.
%
% For example, [Xlim,Ylim,Xlabel] = GETN(gca,'Xlim','Ylim','Xlabel')
% returns the requested axes properties in like-named output variables.
%
% This simplifies the construct
% [Xlim,Ylim,Xlabel] = deal(get(gca,{'Xlim','Ylim','Xlabel'}))
if max(size(H))~=1 || ~ishandle(H)
    error('Scalar Object Handle Required.')
end
varargout = get(H,varargin);
```

This function is not absolutely needed, but it is convenient and demonstrates use of varargin and varargout.

The next function to consider is implementation of the selection rectangle and capturing its *x*- and *y*-axis limits. As shown in the following example, this requires use of the MATLAB functions rbbox, waitforbuttonpress, and the CurrentPoint properties of the *axes* and *figure* objects:

```
function [xbox,ybox,prect]=getbox
%GETBOX Get axes information from user-drawn selection rectangle.
% [Xbox,Ybox,Prect] = GETBOX waits for the user to drag a selection box The
% x and y axis data limits of the selection box are returned in Xbox, Ybox,
% and Prect.
% Xbox is a two element vector containing the minimum and maximum limits
% along the x axis, i.e., Xbox = [min(x) max(x)]
% Ybox is a two element vector containing the minimum and maximum limits
% along the y axis, i.e., Ybox = [min(y) max(y)]
```

```
% Prect is a four element vector containing the selection box position
% in standard position vector format, Prect = [left bottom width height]
% Data returned is in the axis data units.
%
% The selection box is limited to the x and y axis limits of the axes where
% the selection rectangle was drawn.

% waitforbuttonpress waits until user presses a mouse button over a figure
% waitforbuttonpress return False if that happens. Alternatively, it
% returns True if the user presses a key on the keyboard.

if waitforbuttonpress % Returns True if a key is pressed, abort
   xlim = [];
   ylim = [];
   prect = [];
   return
end
% Function only gets here if user presses a mouse button in a figure

Hf = gcf;      % get current figure where button was pressed
Ha = gca(Hf);  % get current axes where button was pressed

AxesPt = get(Ha,'CurrentPoint'); % get first axes data point clicked
FigPt = get(Hf,'CurrentPoint');  % get first figure point clicked

% call the function rbbox, i.e., rubberband box, to create the selection
% rectangle. This function needs to know where to start from. It does not
% automatically start at the mouse click unless told to do so.

% drag selection rectangle starting at first figure point
rbbox([FigPt 0 0],FigPt) % function returns as soon as mouse button is up

% get point on opposite corner of selection rectangle; add to first point
AxesPt = [AxesPt; get(Ha,'CurrentPoint')];
```

```
% get axis limits of axes where selection rectangle was drawn
[Xlim,Ylim] = getn(Ha,'Xlim','Ylim');

% convert AxesPt data into usable output vectors.
xbox = [min(AxesPt(:,1)) max(AxesPt(:,1))]; % x axis limits of selection
xbox = [max(xbox(1),Xlim(1)) min(xbox(2),Xlim(2))]; % limit to axes size

ybox = [min(AxesPt(:,2)) max(AxesPt(:,2))];
ybox = [max(ybox(1),Ylim(1)) min(ybox(2),Ylim(2))]; % limit to axes size

prect = [xbox(1) ybox(1) diff(xbox) diff(ybox)]; % position rectangle
```

The comments contained in getbox describe its operation. The CurrentPoint property of an *axes* object returns a two-by-three matrix containing the *x*, *y*, and *z* data points of the back and front of the current point in 3-D space. Since this is a 2-D axes, only the *x* and *y* data points in the first two columns are relevant. Manipulation of this data produces the desired output variables.

Using getn and getbox, the function mmzoom implements the picture-in-a-picture zoom:

```
function [Hza,Hzr]=mmzoom(arg)
%MMZOOM Picture in a Picture Zoom.
% MMZOOM creates a new axes containing the data inside a box formed by a
% click and drag with the mouse in the current axes. The new zoomed axes
% is placed in the upper right of the current axes, but can be moved with
% the mouse. Clicking in the figure border disables dragging.
%
% Previous axes created by MMZOOM are deleted if MMZOOM is called again.
%
% [Hza,Hzr] = MMZOOM returns handles to the created axes and rectangle
% marking the zoomed area respectively.
%
% MMZOOM DRAG enables dragging of a zoomed axes.
```

```
% MMZOOM RESET disables dragging of a zoomed axes.
% MMZOOM OFF removes the zoomed axes and rectangle marking the zoomed area.

if nargin == 0
   arg = [];
end
if isempty(arg) % zoom zoom zoom zoom zoom zoom zoom zoom zoom zoom zoom


   Hzoom = findobj(0,'Tag','MMZOOM'); % find previous zoomed axes
   if ~isempty(Hzoom)   % delete prior zoomed axes if it exists
      delete(Hzoom)
   end

   [xlim,ylim,prect] = getbox;  % get selection box for zoom

   if ~isempty(prect) % act only if rectangle exists
      Haxes = gca; % handle of axes where selection box was drawn
      Hzr = rectangle('Position',prect,... % place rectangle object
         'Linestyle',':',...               % to mark selection box
         'Tag','MMZOOM');

      Hfig = gcf; % handle of Figure where selection box was drawn
      Hzoom = copyobj(Haxes,Hfig); % copy original axes and its children


      OldUnits = get(Haxes,'Units');  % get position vector of original
      set(Haxes,'Units','normalized') % axes in normalized units
      Pvect = get(Haxes,'Position');
      set(Haxes,'Units',OldUnits)


      % scale and shift zoomed axes relative to original axes
      alpha = 1/3;   % position scaling for zoomed axes
      beta = 98/100; % position shift for zoomed axes
```

```
% compute position vector for zoomed axes
Zwidth = alpha*Pvect(3);                       % zoomed axes width
Zheight = alpha*Pvect(4);                      % zoomed axes height
Zleft = Pvect(1)+beta*Pvect(3)-Zwidth;         % zoomed axes left
Zbottom = Pvect(2)+beta*Pvect(4)-Zheight;      % zoomed axes bottom

% modify zoomed axes as required
set(Hzoom,'units','Normalized',...                     % make units normalized
   'Position',[Zleft Zbottom Zwidth Zheight],...% axes position
   'Xlim',xlim,'Ylim',ylim,...                         % axis data limits
   'Box','on',...                                      % axis box on
   'Xgrid','off','Ygrid','off',...                     % grid lines off
   'FontUnits','points',...
   'FontSize',8,...                                    % shrink font size
   'ButtonDownFcn',@selectmoveresize,...               % enable drag
   'Tag','MMZOOM',...                                  % tag zoomed axes
   'UserData',Haxes)                                   % store original axes

[Htx,Hty,Htt] = getn(Hzoom,'Xlabel','Ylabel','Title');
set([Htx,Hty,Htt],'String','')      % delete labels on zoomed axes

set(Haxes,'DeleteFcn',...           % delete both axes together
   'delete(findobj(0,''Type'',''axes'',''Tag'',''MMZOOM''))')

% place zoomed axes at top of object stack
Hchild = findobj(Hfig,'type','axes'); % get all axes in figure
Hchild(Hchild==Hzoom) = [];           % remove zoomed axes from list
```

```
    set(Hfig,'Children',[Hzoom;Hchild],... % put zoom axes at top of stack
        'CurrentAxes',Haxes,...            % make original axes current
        'ButtonDownFcn','mmzoom reset')    % enable reset

    if nargout>=1  % provide output only if requested
        Hza = Hzoom;
    end
 end

 elseif strncmpi(arg,'d',1) % drag zoom axes drag zoom axes drag zoom axes

    Hzoom = findobj(0,'Type','axes','Tag','MMZOOM');
    if ~isempty(Hzoom)
       set(Hzoom,'ButtonDownFcn',@selectmoveresize)
    end


 elseif strncmpi(arg,'r',1) % reset reset reset reset reset reset reset

    Hzoom = findobj(0,'Type','axes','Tag','MMZOOM');
    if ~isempty(Hzoom)
       [Hfig,Haxes] = getn(Hzoom,'Parent','UserData');
       set(Hzoom,'ButtonDownFcn','','Selected','off')% turn off selection
       set(Hfig,'CurrentAxes',Haxes)                 % make Haxes current
    end

 elseif strncmpi(arg,'o',1)  % off off off off off off off off off off off

    Hzoom = findobj(0,'Tag','MMZOOM');
    if ~isempty(Hzoom)
       delete(Hzoom)
```

```
    end
else
    error('Unknown Input Argument.')
end
```

The structure of mmzoom uses a *switchyard* approach that evaluates code on the basis of the input argument. When no input argument is used, mmzoom creates the zoomed *axes*. The function copyobj is used to make a copy of the original *axes* and all of its children. This new *axes* is then modified to create the zoomed *axes*. Finally, the zoomed *axes* is placed on top of the original axes, which is made the current *axes*. The ButtonDownFcn callback of the zoomed axes executes the function selectmoveresize, which performs exactly what its name implies. The ButtonDownFcn callback of the *figure* calls mmzoom('reset'), which deselects the zoomed axes and deletes its callback. Since this function is fairly simple, the function findobj is used to find the zoomed *axes* and the *rectangle* marking the selection box. Using findobj makes it difficult to allow multiple simultaneous instances of this function to exist. As a result, only one is permitted. If multiple simultaneous instances were desired, function handle callbacks with added arguments as described in Chapter 32 would be required.

Appendix

MATLAB Release Information

This appendix documents the new and revised functionality and functions available in individual releases of MATLAB, starting with MATLAB 5. This material makes it possible to identify what functionality and functions appeared in which version of MATLAB. With worldwide MATLAB users running a variety of MATLAB releases, and with the proliferation and ease of file sharing, it is important to be able to identify the backward and forward compatibility of MATLAB M-files. The information contained in this appendix facilitates this process by documenting MATLAB release information that is otherwise not centrally available.

Each MATLAB release cited here identifies the public release date, the functionality and functions introduced in the release, as well as the revised functionality and functions that became effective with the release. Obsolete functions are also identified. Changed functionality and functions have (Change) in their description. When appropriate, a reference to the *Mastering MATLAB 7* chapter covering the cited functionality is included.

The material presented is limited to the base MATLAB product only and is based on information contained in the release notes for each release. Because the release notes are not always comprehensive, some information may be missing. Furthermore, because they constitute too much information, Handle Graphics objects and their properties are not included here.

MATLAB 5.0 (December 1996)

Functionality	Description	Chapter
Multidimensional arrays	Arrays can have any number of dimensions (e.g., `A(i,j,k,...)`.	6
Structures	A container variable class identified by a variable name and fields, with fields denoted by a preceding period (e.g., `varname.field1`)	8
Cell arrays	A container variable class identified by a name, with contents enclosed with `{` and `}`	8
Object-oriented programming	User-defined variable classes with function and operator overloading, data encapsulation, methods, inheritance, etc.	33
Subfunctions	Function M-files can contain multiple functions, with those appearing after the first or primary function being subfunctions.	12
Private functions	Function M-files in `private` subdirectories just off of the MATLAB path	12
Switch/case statements	Alternative control flow construction	11
Variable length function input and output argument lists	Cell arrays `varargin` and `varargout` supported in function input and output argument lists	12
Pseudocode creation	Ability to precompile M-files into an encrypted format	12
Single byte data type for images	Image object supports 8-bit integer data, using the `uint8` data type.	7, 29
Truecolor	Images in Truecolor are supported.	28
`end` as last array element	Last element along a dimension can be addressed by using the keyword `end` (e.g., `A(1:2:end)`)	5
Scalar expansion assignment	(Change) `A(...) = x`, performs scalar expansion to fill all addressed elements of `A` with the scalar `x`.	5
Character string storage	(Change) Each character occupies 2 bytes of storage rather than 8.	9
Dimension specification in data analysis functions	(Change) Data analysis functions `sum`, `prod`, `cumprod`, and `cumsum` now accept a last input argument that specifies the dimension along which the function operates.	18

Empty arrays	(Change) Empty arrays may have some nonzero dimensions.	5
Marker Style Enhancements	(Change) New line markers are available, and markers can be specified independently from line styles.	26
Camera viewing model	Axes now have camera properties to set viewing properties.	27
TeX support	(Change)Text objects can contain TeX commands.	31
Z-buffering	Z-buffer graphics rendering supported	28
Light object	New graphics object	31

Math Function	**Description**
`airy`	Airy functions
`besselh`	Bessel functions of the third kind (Hankel)
`condeig`	Condition number with respect to eigenvalues
`condest`	1-norm matrix condition number estimate
`dblquad`	Numerical 2-D integration
`mod`	Modulus
`normest`	2-norm estimate

***n*-D Function**	**Description**
`cat`	Concatenate arrays
`flipdim`	Flip array along specified dimension
`ndgrid`	Generate arrays for *n*-D functions
`ndims`	Number of array dimensions
`permute, ipermute`	Permute and inverse permute dimensions of *n*-D array
`reshape`	Change shape of an array
`shiftdim`	Shift dimensions
`squeeze`	Eliminate singleton dimensions
`sub2ind, ind2sub`	Single index from subscripts and subscripts from single linear index

Cell Array and Structure Function	Description
`cell`	Create cell array
`cell2struct`	Convert cell to structure
`celldisp`	Display cell structure
`cellplot`	Graphically display cell structure
`num2cell`	Convert matrix to cell array
`fieldnames`	Field names of structure
`getfield`	Get field from structure
`rmfield`	Remove field from structure
`setfield`	Set field in structure
`struct`	Create structure array
`struct2cell`	Convert structure to cell array

Character Function	Description
`char`	Convert to string array
`mat2str`	Convert matrix to string
`strcat`	String concatenation
`strmatch`	Find matches for a string
`strncmp`	Compare first n characters
`strvcat`	Vertical string concatenation

Logical Function	Description
`iscell`	True for cell array
`isequal`	True if arrays are equal
`isfinite`	True for finite elements
`islogical`	True for logical arrays
`isnumeric`	True for numeric array
`isstruct`	True for structure
`logical`	Convert to logical array

M-file Function	Description
`assignin`	Assign variable in workspace
`evalin`	Evaluate expression in workspace
`inmem`	Functions in memory
`inputname`	Input argument name
`mfilename`	Name of currently running M-file
`mexext`	MEX-file extension
`pcode`	Create pseudocode
`profile`	Profile M-file execution
`varargin, varargout`	Pass or return a variable number of function arguments
`warning`	Display warning message

File and Directory Function	Description
`addpath`	Append directory to MATLAB search path
`edit`	Edit M-file
`editpath`	Modify MATLAB search path
`fullfile`	Build full filename from parts

Set, Bit, and Base Function	Description
`intersect`	Set intersection
`ismember`	Detect members of a set
`setdiff`	Set difference
`setxor`	Set exclusive OR
`union`	Union of two sets
`unique`	Unique elements of a vector
`bitand`	Bitwise AND
`bitcmp`	Compare bits
`bitget`	Get bit
`bitmax`	Maximum floating-point integer
`bitor`	Bitwise OR

Set, Bit, and Base Function	Description
bitset	Set bit
bitshift	Bitwise shift
bitxor	Bitwise XOR
base2dec	Convert base to decimal
bin2dec	Convert binary to decimal
dec2base	Convert decimal to base
dec2bin	Convert decimal to binary

Time and Date Function	Description
calendar	Produce monthly calendar
datenum	Serial date number
datestr	Create date string
datetick	Create date-formatted tick labels
datevec	Date components
eomday	End of month
now	Current date and time
weekday	Day of week

Matrix Function	Description
cholinc	Incomplete Cholesky factorization
gallery	More than 50 text matrices
luinc	Incomplete LU factorization
repmat	Replicate and tile an array
sprand	Random uniformly distributed sparse arrays

Sparse Matrix Function	Description
bicg	Biconjugate gradients method
bicgstab	Biconjugate gradients stabilized method
cgs	Conjugate gradients squared method
eigs	Find several eigenvalues and eigenvectors

gmres	Generalized minimal residual method
pcg	Preconditioned conjugate gradients method
qmr	Quasi-minimal residual method
svds	A few singular values

Data Analysis Function	Description
convhull	Convex hull
cumtrapz	Cumulative trapezoidal numerical integration
delaunay	Delaunay triangularization
dsearch	Search for nearest point
factor	Primer factors
inpolygon	Detect points inside a polygonal region
isprime	True for prime numbers
nchoosek	All possible combinations of n elements taken k at a time
perms	All possible permutations
polyarea	Area of a polygon
primes	Generate a list of prime numbers
sortrows	Sort rows in ascending order
tsearch	Search for enclosing Delaunay triangle
voronoi	Voronoi diagram
sum([]) = 0, prod([]) = 1, max([]) = [], min([]) =[]	(Change) Defined output for empty inputs

Interpolation Function	Description
interp3	3-D data interpolation
interpn	*n*-D data interpolation
ndgrid	Generate arrays for *n*-D functions and interpolation
griddata	(Change) Uses triangle-based interpolation

ODE Function	Description
ode45, ode23, ode113, ode23s, ode15s	Solve differential equations by using various methods
odefile	Problem definition file for ODE solvers
odeget	Extract options from ODE options structure
odeset	Create or edit options structure for ODE solvers

Plot Function	Description
area	Filled area plot
bar3	3-D bar chart
bar3h	3-D horizontal bar chart
barh	2-D horizontal bar chart
box	Turn On or Off axes box
countourf	Filled contour plot
pie	Pie chart
pie3	3-D pie chart
plotyy	Plot with *y*-axis labels on both the left and right
quiver3	3-D quiver plot
ribbon	Draw lines as 3-D strips
stem	(Change) stem tips can be filled or unfilled
stem3	3-D stem plot
trimesh	Triangular mesh plot
trisurf	Triangular surface plot

Color and Light Function	Description
autumn	Colormap of red and yellow
colorcube	Colormap of regularly spaced colors
colordef	Select figure color scheme
lines	Colormap that follows axes colororder property
spring	Colormap of magenta and yellow
summer	Colormap of green and yellow
winter	Colormap of blue and green

Image Function	Description
imread	Read image data
imwrite	Write image data

Handle Graphics and GUI Function	Description
dragrect	Drag rectangle
inputdlg	Display input dialog
msgbox	Display message dialog
questdlg	Display question dialog
rbbox	Rubberband box
selectmoveresize	Interactively select, move, or resize objects
uiresume	Resume suspended M-file execution
uiwait	Block M-file execution
waitfor	Block execution until condition is satisfied

MATLAB 5.1 (June 1997)

Functionality	Description	Chapter
find function returns empty	(Change) find(...) returns [] if no indices where argument is True are found.	5
Multibyte characters	(Change) Two byte characters are supported.	9

Function	Description
ismember	Now calls the MEX function ismemc to maximize speed
pagedlg	Open Page Layout dialog
printdlg	Open Print dialog
scatter	2-D scatter plot
scatter3	3-D scatter plot

MATLAB 5.2, Release 10 (March 1998)

Functionality	Description	Chapter
`try/catch` blocks	Error handling using `try/catch` blocks	11
M-file locking	M-files can now be locked so that `clear` does not purge that M-file from memory.	12
Persistent variables	Variables can be declared persistent so that they persist from one call to a function to the next.	12
`S = load(...)`	(Change) Load file contents to structure	14
HDF file support	Files in HDF format can be read and written to.	14
OpenGL support	OpenGL graphics rendering supported	28
Tooltips	UI controls have a `tooltip` string property.	32
Toggle Buttons	New *Uicontrol* object	32
Uicontextmenu	New *Uimenu* object	32
Support for cell arrays of strings	The functions `intersect`, `ismember`, `lower`, `setdiff`, `setxor`, `sort`, `union`, `unique`, and `upper` now handle inputs that are cell arrays of strings.	9

Function	Description
`camdolly`	Translate camera position and target
`camlight`	Create or move light object in camera coordinate system
`camorbit`	Rotate camera position around camera target
`campan`	Rotate camera target around camera position
`camroll`	Rotate camera about camera viewing axis
`camzoom`	Zoom camera in or out
`campos`	Set or get camera position and position mode
`camproj`	Set or get camera projection type
`camtarget`	Set or get camera target and camera target mode
`camup`	Set or get camera up vector and up vector mode
`camva`	Set or get camera view angle and view angle mode

`cholinc`	Sparse incomplete Cholesky and Cholesky-infinity factorization
`cholupdate`	Rank 1 update to Cholesky factorization
`daspect`	Set or get data aspect ratio and aspect ratio mode
`ifftshift`	Inverse FFT shift
`lastwarn`	Return last warning string
`lightangle`	Create or move light object in spherical coordinates
`mislocked`	True if M-file cannot be cleared
`mlock`	Prevent M-file clearing
`munlock`	Permit M-file clearing
`ode23t`	Solve moderately stiff differential equations
`ode23tb`	Solve stiff differential equations by using crude error tolerances
`pbaspect`	Set or get plot box aspect ratio and plot box aspect mode
`persistent`	Declare variable persistent
`strcmpi`	Compare strings, ignoring case
`strncmpi`	Compare first `n` characters in strings, ignoring case
`strjust`	(Change) Now does right, left, and center justification
`xlim`	Set or get *x*-axis limits and limit mode
`ylim`	Set or get *y*-axis limits and limit mode
`zlim`	Set or get *z*-axis limits and limit mode

MATLAB 5.3, Release 11 (March 1999)

Functionality	Description	Chapter
Integer data types	Support for `int8`, `int16`, `unint16`, `int32`, and `uint32` added	7
Single precision data	Storage support for `single` added.	7
Execute function when quitting	When MATLAB is quit, MATLAB executes the function `finish`.	4
Mass matrix support	All functions in the ODE suite support the use of a mass matrix.	25
Optimization parameters	Options for optimization functions `fminbnd`, `fminsearch`, and `lsqnonneg` are set, using an options structure variable rather than an options vector.	23

Functionality	Description	Chapter
Rectangle object	New handle graphics object for drawing rectangle, ovals, and circle	31
Double buffering	*Figure* windows now support double buffering to reduce flickering.	31
Portable Network Graphics	Support for images in PNG format	29

Function	Description
`blkdiag`	Create block diagonal matrix
`cellfun`	Perform common operations on cell arrays
`complex`	Create complex array from real and imaginary parts
`coneplot`	Velocity vector cone plot in a 3-D vector field
`contourslice`	Draw contours in volume slices
`datenum`, `datestr`, `datevec`	(Change) Now accept `pivotyear` argument
`evalc`	String evaluation with output converted to a string
`ezcontour`	Easy contour plotter
`ezcontourf`	Easy filled contour plotter
`ezmesh`	Easy mesh plotter
`ezmeshc`	Easy mesh with contour plotter
`ezplot`	Easy 2-D line plotter
`ezplot3`	Easy 3-D line plotter
`ezpolar`	Easy polar plotter
`ezsurf`	Easy surface plotter
`ezsurfc`	Easy surface with contour plotter
`findfigs`	Find all visible *Figure* windows
`fminbnd`	(Change) New name and calling sequence for function `fmin`
`fminsearch`	(Change) New name and calling sequence for function `fmins`
`hist`	(Change) Now calls MEX function `histc`
`histc`	Histogram binning given bin edges

`int8, int16, uint16, int32, unit32`	Conversion to integer data types
`isocaps`	Compute isosurface end-cap geometry
`isonormals`	Compute normals at isosurface vertices
`isosurface`	Extract isosurface data from volume data
`lsqnonneg`	(Change) New name and calling sequence for function `nnls`
`optimget, optimset`	Get, set, and modify optimization options
`pause`	(Change) Fractional second accepted
`reducepatch`	Reduce number of patch faces
`reducevolume`	Reduce number of volume data elements
`shrinkfaces`	Reduce size of patch faces
`single`	Conversion to single-precision data type
`smooth3`	Smooth 3-D data
`str2double`	Convert character string to double-precision value
`stream2`	Compute 2-D stream lines
`stream3`	Compute 3-D stream lines
`streamline`	Draw stream lines
`subvolume`	Extract subset of volume data set
`sum`	(Change) Can now be used with all integer data types
`surf2patch`	Convert surface data to patch data
`texlabel`	Create the TeX format from a character string

MATLAB 6.0, Release 12 (November, 2000)

Functionality	Description	Chapter
MATLAB Desktop	User interface organized and named the MATLAB desktop, which is implemented in the Java language	3
Java	MATLAB now supports an interface with the Java language	
Matrix math	(Change) MATLAB now uses LAPACK with BLAS for matrix computations	17

Functionality	Description	Chapter
Fast Fourier Transform	(Change) MATLAB now uses the MIT FFTW library for computing Fast Fourier Transforms	22
Function handles	New data type for capturing function information for evaluation	12
Transparency	(Change) Surfaces, patches, and images now support transparency	29
Operator precedence	(Change) Logical AND now has higher precedence than logical OR	10

Function	Description
`beep`	Make computer beep
`numel`	Number of elements in an array
`continue`	Skip rest of For Loop or While Loop
`genpath`	Generate path string that includes all directories below a specified directory
`sort`	(Change) Now works on data types other than double precision
`std`	(Change) `std([])` now returns `NaN` rather than empty.
`polyfit, polyval`	(Change) Now support centering and scaling of data

Logical Function	Description
`iskeyword`	Generate or test if argument is a MATLAB keyword
`isvarname`	True if input string is a valid variable name

M-file Function	Description
`check_syntactic_warnings`	Run syntax check on M-files
`func2str`	Construct function name string from function handle
`functions`	Display information about a function handle
`nargoutchk`	Validate number of output arguments
`rehash`	Refresh function and file system caches
`str2func`	Construct function handle from function name string

Sparse Matrix Function	Description
`colamd`	Compute approximate column minimum degree permutation
`lsqr`	LSQR implementation of Conjugate Gradients on Normal Equations
`minres`	Solve system of equations by using Minimal Residual Method
`symamd`	Symmetric approximate minimum degree permutation
`symmlq`	Solve system of equations by using symmetric LQ method

Interpolation Function	Description
`convhulln`	*n*-D convex hull
`delaunay3`	3-D Delaunay tessellation
`delaunayn`	*n*-D Delaunay tessellation
`desearchn`	n-D nearest point search
`griddata3`	3-D data gridding
`griddatan`	*n*-D data gridding
`interp1`	(Change) `'cubic'` option now calls `pchip`
`pchip`	Piecewise cubic Hermite interpolating polynomial interpolation
`voronoin`	*n*-D Voronoi diagram

Optimization or Integration Function	Description
`quadl`	Numerically compute integral by using Lobatto quadrature; replaces `quad8`
`dblquad`	(Change) Can now pass extra arguments to integrand function
`fzero`	(Change) Calling sequence changed

Differential Equation Function	Description
bvp4c	Solve two-point boundary value problem by collocation
bvpget	Get BVP option from option structure
bvpinit	Form initial guess for bvp4c
bvpset	Create or change BVP option structure
bvpval	Evaluate solution from bvp4c
ode*	(Change) ODE solvers can now solve problems without using an ODE file
pdepe	Solve partial differential equations in one dimension
pdeval	Evaluate solution computed by pdepe

3-D Visualization Function	Description
coneplot	Create 3-D coneplot
curl	Compute curl and angular velocity perpendicular to flow
divergence	Compute divergence of vector field
interpstreamspeed	Interpolate streamline vertices from speed
isocolors	Compute colors of isosurface vertices
isosurface	Extract isosurface
streamparticles	Draw stream particles
streamribbon	Draw stream ribbons
streamslice	Draw stream lines
streamtube	Draw stream tubes
volumebounds	Get coordinate and color limits for volume data

Handle Graphics and GUI Function	Description
alpha	Set or get transparency properties
alphamap	Specify figure alphamap
alim	Set or get axes alpha limits

Java Function	Description
import	Add to the current Java packages import list
isjava	True for Java Object
javaArray	Create Java array
javaMethod	Invoke Java method
javaObject	Construct Java object
methodsview	Display information on all methods implemented by Java or MATLAB class

Obsolete Function	Description
errortrap	Replaced by try-catch block
flops	Floating-point operation count
fmin	Replaced by fminbnd
fmins	Replaced by fminsearch
foptions	Replaced by optimget and optimset
interp4, interp5, interp6,	Replaced by interp2
isdir	Replaced with exist
isiee	All MATLAB platforms use IEEE arithmetic
isstr	Replaced by ischar
meshdom	Replaced by meshgrid
nnls	Replaced by lsnonneg
quad8	Replaced by quadl
saxis	No longer used
setstr	Replaced by char
str2mat	Replaced by char
table1	Replaced by interp1
table2	Replaced by interp2

MATLAB 6.1, Release 12.1 (June 2001)

Functionality	Description	Chapter
Transparent legend	Can now make axes legend box transparent	26

Function	Description
`audioplayer`	Create audio object to play audio data on Windows platforms
`audiorecorder`	Create audio object to record audio data on Windows platforms
`bvpval`	(Obsolete) Replaced by `deval`
`convhull`, `delaunay`, `griddata`, `voronoi`	(Change) Now makes use of Qhull
`cdfinfo`	Get information about a CDF file
`cdfread`	Read CDF file
`convhull`	(Change) `[K,a]=convhull(x,y)` now returns the area a of the convex hull; in addition, it now ignores the third input argument
`convhulln`	(Change) `[K,v]=convhulln(x,y)` now returns the volume v of the convex hull
`datenum`, `datestr`	(Change) Now accept date vector as an input argument
`delaunay`	(Change) Now ignores third input argument
`deval`	Evaluate ODE solution; also replaces obsolete `bvpval` function
`erfcinv`	Inverse complementary error function
`fitsinfo`	Get information about a FITS file
`fitsread`	Read FITS file
`hdfinfo`	Get information about a HDF file
`hdfread`	Read HDF file
`histc`	(Change) Bug fixed
`interp1`	(Change) Now enables data extrapolation
`numel`	(Change) `numel(A,varargin)` returns the number of subscripted elements in `A(varargin{:})`

ode*	(Change) Now optionally return solution structure for use by deval
polyeig	(Change) Can now return only the eigenvalues
ppval	(Change) Now supports ppval(xx,pp) to permit use of ppval with function functions
quad	(Change) Function sampling bug fixed
reshape	(Change) reshape(A,..., [],...) now calculates the size required for the empty dimension
sortrows	(Change) Now calls MEX function sortrowsc to maximize speed. With cell array of strings input, now calls MEX function sortcellchar to maximize speed
strfind	Search for occurrence of second string argument in first string argument
svd	(Change) Can now return only the first two outputs, U and S
tetramesh	Tetrahedron mesh plot for use with delaunayn
triplot	2-D triangular plot for use with delaunay

MATLAB 6.5, Release 13 (August 2002)

Functionality	Description	Chapter
JIT-Acceleration	For Loops with specific properties now execute at maximum speed, thereby avoiding the need to vectorize code under some circumstances.	11
Dynamic structure field names	Need for getfield and setfield eliminated; var.(fstr), where fstr is a character string, addresses the field identified by fstr in the variable var	8
Maximum name length for variables and functions	Variable names and function names can now have up to 63 characters.	2
Integer array subscripts	Array subscripts must be real positive integer values or logical values (e.g., x(1.3) reports an error).	5
Relational operators and 64 bit integer arrays	(MATLAB 6.5.1) All relational operators now support int64 and unit64 data types.	7
Delay differential equations	Support for solving delay differential equations provided	25

Functionality	Description	Chapter
BLAS for Pentium 4	Specific BLAS provided for the Pentium 4 processor	
UMFPACK support	When appropriate, sparse matrix solutions now use UMFPACK library functions.	17
Regular Expressions	MATLAB now supports regular expressions.	9
Logical class	Logical arrays are now a separate MATLAB class that use one byte of storage per array element.	10
Logical True and False	MATLAB now supports direct creation of arrays containing logical True and logical False by using the functions `true` and `false`.	10
Empty comparisons	`[]==[]` and `[]==scalar` now return empty (`[]`) result to coincide with other operators.	10
Sparse class	Sparse is now an attribute of the underlying variable class, as opposed to a distinct or separate variable class. In MATLAB 6.5, logical and double data types can be sparse.	17
Formatted error and warning strings	Functions `error` and `warning` now accept data formatting inputs similar to `sprintf`.	12
Message identifiers	Error and warning messages can now contain identifier tags to make the message uniquely identifiable.	12
Warning control	Individual warnings can be suppressed.	12
Logical operators for short-circuiting	New operators && and `||` short circuit comparisons when an early exit is possible.	10
Scheduled execution	New timer object permits scheduled execution of MATLAB code.	4
Text object properties	Text objects now have properties for their background box.	31

Function	Description
`audiodevinfo`	Get information about installed audio devices on Windows platforms
`cdfepoch`	Convert MATLAB date number or string to CDF format
`cdfwrite`	Write data to CDF file

cell2mat	Combine cell array of matrices into one matrix; previously part of the *Neural Networks Toolbox*
colormapeditor	Interactive colormap editor
copyfile	(Change) Now also copies directories
corrcoef	(Change) Three new syntaxes
dde23	Solve delay differential equations with constant delays
ddeget	Get properties from DDE options structure
ddeget	Create or modify properties in DDE options structure
deval	(Change) Now accepts output from dde23
false	Create array of logical False
fileattrib	Set or get file attributes
gallery	(Change) New test matrices available
imformats	Eases the task of adding read and write support for new file formats
int64, unit64	Create signed or unsigned 64-bit integer array
isequal	(Change) When used to compare structures, input argument field creation order no longer has an impact on equality
isequalwithequalnans	True if arrays are equal with NaNs considered equal
ismember	(Change) [tf, idx]=ismember(...) now returns indices idx of located members; in this case, MEX function ismemc2 is called to maximize speed
issorted	True if array is sorted
lasterror	Return last error message and related information
lu	(Change) Now uses UMFPACK for sparse matrices
mat2cell	Break matrix up into a cell array of matrices (previously part of the *Neural Networks Toolbox*)
movefile	(Change) Now also rename a file or directory
multibandread	Supports reading data from raw files
multibandwrite	Supports writing data to raw files
namelengthmax	Return maximum variable and function name lengths
orderfields	Order fields of a structure
perl	Call Perl script using platform executable
profview	Produce graphical profile report

Function	Description
psi	Evaluate Digamma function
qrdelete, qrinsert	(Change) Can now insert or delete rows as well as columns
regexp	Match regular expression
regexpi	Match regular expression, ignoring case
regexprep	Replace string, using regular expression
rethrow	Reissue error
rmdir	Remove directory and, optionally, contents as well
sendmail	Send e-mail
timer	Create and control timer objects to schedule execution of MATLAB code
triplequad	Evaluate triple integral
true	Create array of logical True
urlread, urlwrite	Read and write content, using URL
ver	(Change) Now returns more detailed information, and hostid information is no longer provided
winopen	On Windows platforms, opens a file in its appropriate application
xmlread, xmlwrite	Read or write XML document
xslt	Transform XML document, using XSLT engine
zip, unzip	Compress and uncompress files and directories

MATLAB 7.0, Release 14 (June 2004)

Functionality	Description	Chapter
Case sensitivity	Function and directory names are now case-sensitive; in prior versions, they were case-sensitive only on UNIX platforms.	4,12,14
Function precedence	Built-in and M-file functions now share the same calling precedence; in prior versions, built-in functions had higher precedence.	12
Nondouble arithmetic	Mathematical operations on integer and single-precision data are now supported; many built-in functions support these data types as well.	8

Anonymous functions	Single line function specification as a replacement for in-line functions	12
Nested functions	M-file functions can be nested, allowing shared workspaces among the primary and all nested functions.	12
Unicode character storage	MATLAB now encodes character strings in Unicode format.	9
Java 1.4	MATLAB now uses Java version 1.4.	
Block comments	Now supports block comments using %{ and %} syntax	4
Code cells	Editor permits creation, execution, etc., on sections of code called code cells.	4
Results publishing	M-files and figures can be published to HTML, XML, LaTeX, Word, and Powerpoint.	
Regular expressions	Expanded regular expression capabilities	9
Freeform date and time	Date and time functions now support user-specified date and time specifications.	16
File ftp support	Access files using ftp commands in MATLAB	14
Annotation layer	*Figure* windows now have an annotation layer where annotations appear. Annotations include rectangles, ellipses, arrows, double arrows, text arrows, text boxes, lines, colorbars, and legends.	31
Plot objects	High-level and specialized plotting functions now create plot objects that have properties specific to the type of plot created. In the past, these functions returned handles to the core graphics objects used to create the graphics.	31
Group objects.	Graphics objects can now be grouped or linked to each other.	31
Toolbars	New user interface object	32
Panels and button groups	New user interface container objects	32
Generic dynamic linked libraries	MATLAB supports interaction with Generic DLLs on the Windows platform.	36
TEX support	Text objects now optionally support complete TEX capabilities.	31
Code checking	M-file code can be assessed for potential problems and improvement by using the functions `mlint` or `mlintrpt`.	13

Mathematical Function	Description
`acosd, acotd, acscd, asecd, asind, atand`	Inverse trigonometric functions returning angles in degrees
`balance`	(Change) Now returns different outputs and offers balancing without permuting rows and columns
`bvp4c`	(Change) Can now solve multipoint boundary value problems
`convhulln, delaunayn, voronoin`	(Change) Now supports user-settable options
`cosd, cotd, cscd, secd, sind, tand`	Trigonometric functions with arguments in degrees
`decic`	Compute consistent initial conditions for `ODE15I`
`deval`	(Change) Now optionally returns derivative at points as well
`eps`	(Change) Now accepts arguments to specify single- or double-precision values and to return eps relative to any value, not just 1
`expm1`	Compute exp(x)-1 accurately
`eye, ones, zeros`	(Change) Now accepts a final argument specifying numeric data type of result
`fftw`	Tune or set options in FFTW library for FFT computations
`fminbnd, fminsearch, fzero`	(Change) Now support calling an output function at each iteration
`interp1, ppval, spline`	(Change) Now support multidimensional arrays for `Y`
`interp1`	(Change) Now optionally returns a pp-form for evaluation with `ppval`
`linsolve`	Solve $Ax = y$, given specific structure of A
`ltitr`	(Change, previously undocumented) Linear time-invariant time response kernel
`log1p`	Compute log$(1+x)$ accurately
`mimofr`	(Change, previously undocumented) Linear time-invariant frequency response
`nthroot`	n^{th} real root
`ode15i`	Ordinary differential equation solver for implicit equations

odextend	Extend solution of ordinary differential equations
ordqz	Reorder QZ factorization
ordschur	Reorder Shur factorization
pwch	Piecewise cubic Hermite interpolation
quadv	Vectorized quad function
sort	(Change) Now supports an optional last argument that specifies the sort direction

Logical Function	**Description**
iscom	True for COM/ActiveX objects
isevent	True if event of object
isfloat	True for floating point data
ishghandle	True for Handle Graphics Object handle
isinteger	True for integer data
isinterface	True for COM interface
ispuma	True for computers running Mac OS X 10.1.x
isscalar	True if argument is a scalar
isstrprop	True for string elements matching a variety of specifications
isvector	True if argument is a row or column vector

M-file Function	**Description**
auditcontents	Audit Contents.m file for a given directory
deleteconfirm	Confirm the deletion of a file with a dialog box
deprpt	Scan a file or directory for dependencies
diff2asv	Compare file to autosaved version, if one exists
diffrpt	Visual directory browser
dofixrpt	Scan a file or directory for all TODO, FIXME, or NOTE messages
helprpt	Scan a file or directory for help
makemcode	Make M-file for regenerating object and its children

M-file Function	Description
makecontentsfile	Make a new Contents.m file
mlint, mlintrpt	Examine M-file or a directory of M-files for potential problems and make suggestions for possible improvements
path2rc	(Obsolete) Replaced by savepath
publish	Run a script M-file and save the results
recycle	Determine if deleted files go to Recycle Bin
restoredefaultpath	Restore default MATLAB path
savepath	Save current MATLAB path; replaces path2rc function

Graphics and GUI Function	Description
addsubplot	Add subplot to figure in given location
ancestor	Get ancestor of graphics object
annotation	Add *annotation* object
axes	(Change) ActivePositionProperty, OuterPosition, TightInset properties added
axescheck	Process leading *axes* object from input list
axis	(Change) Now accepts *axes* handle as first argument
commandhistory	Open *Command History* window or select it
commandwindow	Open *Command* window or select it
datacursormode	Interactively create data cursors on plot
exportsetupdlg	Show figure export style dialog
figure	(Change) DockControls property added, KeyPressFcn property modified
figureheaderdlg	Show figure header dialog
figurepalette	Show or hide the palette for a figure
getpixelposition	Get position of object in pixels
hasbehavior	Sets or gets behaviors of Handle Graphics objects
hgexport	Export a figure
hggroup	Create a Handle Graphics group object
hgtransform	Create graphics transformation object

hold	(Change) Now supports all option, which holds the plot so that subsequent plots do not reset the color and linestyle order
linkaxes	Synchronize limits of specified *axes* objects
linkprop	Maintain same value for corresponding Handle Graphics properties
makehgtransform	Create graphical transformation matrix
pan	Interactively pan the plot view
plottools	Show or hide the plot-editing tools for a figure
printdlg	Print dialog box
printpreview	Display preview of figure to be printed
propertyeditor	Show or hide the property editor for a figure
refreshdata	Refresh data in plot
setpixelposition	Set position of object in pixels
showplottool	Show or hide one of the plot-editing components for a figure
title	(Change) Now accepts *axes* handle as first argument
uibuttongroup	Create *buttongroup* object
uicontainer	Create *container* object
uicontrol	(Change) uicontrol(h) now transfers focus to the *uicontrol* having handle h. Multiline 'edit' style *uicontrol* objects now have a vertical scroll bar. *uicontrol* objects now have a 'KeyPressFcn' callback
uigetfile	(Change) Now permits selection of multiple files
uipanel	Create *uipanel* container object
uipushtool	Create pushbutton in *uitoolbar* object
uitable	Create a *uitable* object
uitoggletool	Create togglebutton in *uitoolbar* object
uitoolbar	Create *uitoolbar* object
uitree	Create *uitree* object
uitreenode	Creates a *node* object in a *uitree* component
uiwait	(Change) uiwait(handle,t) now times out after time t has elapsed
xlabel, ylabel, zlabel	(Change) Now accepts *axes* handle as first argument

External Inteface Function	Description
calllib, libfunctions, libfunctionsview, libisloaded, libpointer, libstruct, loadlibrary unloadlibrary	Generic DLL Interface functions
callsoapservice	Send a SOAP message off to an endpoint
eventlisteners	Lists all events that are registered
ftp	Create *ftp* object
instrfindall	Find all serial port objects with specified property values
javaaddpath	Add directories to the dynamic Java path
javaclasspath	Get and set Java path
javacomponent	Create a Java AWT Component and put in a figure
javarmpath	Remove directory from dynamic Java path
registerevent	Registers events for a specified control at runtime
unregisterallevents	Unregister all events for a specified control at runtime
unregisterevent	Unregister events for a specified control at runtime

Other Function	Description
accumarray	Construct array with accumulation; that is, if any element is specified more than once, later elements add to the current value rather than overwrite it
addtodate	Modify a particular field of a date number
audiorecorder, audioplayer	(Change) Now supported on both UNIX and Windows platforms
cast	Cast a variable to a different data type
docsearch	Search HTML documentation in the Help browser
find	(Change) Now supports optional arguments specifying an upper limit on the number of indices returned, and whether the search begins at the start or end of the array

`fixquote`	Double up single quotes in a string
`genvarname`	Generate variable name from candidate name
`hd5info`, `hd5read`, `hdf5write`	HDF5 file information, read, and write
`hex2num`, `num2hex`	Convert number to and from IEEE hexadecimal format
`intmax, intmin`	Maximum and minimum integer values given integer data type
`intwarning`	Controls state of the integer data type warnings
`mmcompinfo`	Multimedia compressor information
`mmfileinfo`	Get information about a multimedia file
`save`	(Change) Now supports compressing MAT-files
`strfind, strtok`	(Change) Now support cell array of strings as input
`strtrim`	Remove leading and trailing white space from a string
`textscan`	Read text file into a cell array; has more features than `textread`
`timerfindall`	Find all timer objects with specified property values
`xlswrite`	Write Matrix to Excel spreadsheet

Index